Recent Trends in VLSI and Semiconductor Packaging

Dr. T. Vasudeva Reddy is a highly acclaimed expert in Low Power VLSI Design, boasting an impressive academic background that includes a Ph.D. in Low Power VLSI Design, M.Tech in VLSI System Design, and B.E. in Electronics and Communication Engineering. This exceptional foundation has enabled him to make ground breaking contributions to Low Power VLSI Design, VLSI System Design, and Electronics and Communication Engineering, driving innovation and advancement. Dr. Reddy's remarkable publication record includes over 15 papers in esteemed SCI/SCOPUS journals, more than 25 conference papers, six patents, and three book chapters on communication.

His research interests encompass cutting-edge areas such as Micro and Nano device Modeling, Circuit Modeling, Memristors, Sub-threshold Memory Design using Fin-FET technology, with expertise extending to RF communication, MEMS biomedical applications.

Notably, Dr. Reddy has received funding from the Science and Engineering Research Board (SERB), Government of India, recognizing his outstanding research work. He is also a recipient of prestigious awards, a member of esteemed professional organizations, and has collaborations with leading industries and institutions. Additionally, Dr. Reddy supervises Ph.D. and M.Tech students. His work has significant implications for energy-efficient electronics, advanced communication systems, biomedical device development.

Dr. K. Madava Rao is a highly acclaimed expert in the field of electronics and communication engineering, possessing an exceptional academic background and a remarkable record of innovative research. He holds a Bachelor of Technology degree from Vazirsultan College of Engineering and a Master of Technology degree from Jawaharlal Nehru Technological University Hyderabad (JNTUH), laying the foundation for his outstanding academic achievements.

Dr. Rao's doctoral research, undertaken at Sri Satya Sai University of Technology & Medical Sciences, Sehore, focused on the development of "A Magneto Sensitive Assembly for Interactive Electronic Devices." This pioneering work showcases his exceptional talent for identifying and addressing complex engineering challenges.

A Testament to his remarkable contributions, Dr. Madavarao received the prestigious Young Researcher Award in 2021. This recognition underscores his status as a rising star in his field and highlights the significance of his research.

As an educator, Dr. Madavarao shares his vast knowledge through guest lectures at esteemed institutions, inspiring the next generation of engineers. His publications, including "Optimized Ultra-Large Scale SoC Test Control Architecture with Scan Test for Bandwidth Management" and "Scan Test Bandwidth Management for Ultra-Large-Scale System-On-Chip Architectures," demonstrate his expertise and thought leadership.

Through his groundbreaking research, academic leadership, and dedication to mentoring, Dr. Madavarao continues to leave an indelible mark on the field of electronics and communication engineering.

Recent Trends in VLSI and Semiconductor Packaging

Edited by

Dr. T. Vasudeva Reddy [https://orcid.org/0000-0003-3115-6385]
Dr. K. Madhava Rao [https://orcid.org/0000-0002-1949-6961]

CRC Press
Taylor & Francis Group
Boca Raton London New York

CRC Press is an imprint of the
Taylor & Francis Group, an **informa** business

First edition published 2025
by CRC Press
4 Park Square, Milton Park, Abingdon, Oxon, OX14 4RN

and by CRC Press
2385 NW Executive Center Drive, Suite 320, Boca Raton FL 33431

© 2025 selection and editorial matter, T. Vasudeva Reddy and K. Madhava Rao; individual chapters, the contributors

CRC Press is an imprint of Informa UK Limited

British Library Cataloguing-in-Publication Data
A catalogue record for this book is available from the British Library

ISBN: 9781041017868 (hbk)
ISBN: 9781041017875 (pbk)
ISBN: 9781003616399 (ebk)

DOI: 10.1201/9781003616399

Typeset in Sabon LT Std
by HBK Digital

Editorial Board

Dr. Sanjay Dubey
Principal, BVRIT Narsapur,
Telangana, India

The First International Conference on Semiconductor Materials Packaging, AI & ML, Reconfigurable VLSI Architectures for IoT, and Future Communication Technologies (SMART-2024) was held at B V Raju Institute of Technology. The conference aimed to provide a platform for researchers, academicians, and industry experts to share knowledge and exchange ideas.

Out of 247 submitted articles 94 were shortlisted for oral presentation. The conference proceedings will serve as a valuable resource for researchers and industry experts. The conference also highlighted the importance of semiconductor technologies and the next generation wireless communication domains.

The conference was supported by the Science and Engineering Research Board (SERB) and the Department of Science and Technology (DST), Government of India. It provided a stimulating experience for all participants.

The key takeaways from the conference include keynote speeches by renowned experts from industry and academia of top-notch universities, valuable insights into the future of semiconductor technology and its applications, opportunities for networking and collaboration among researchers, academicians, and industry experts.

Dr. K. Lakshmi Prasad
Director, BVRIT Narsapur,
Telangana, India

The First International Conference on Semiconductor Materials Packaging, AI & ML, and Reconfigurable VLSI Architectures for IoT, and Future Communication Technologies (SMART-2024) was held at B V Raju Institute of Technology (BVRIT).

The conference focused on five thrust areas of semiconductor packaging, semiconductor materials, AI and ML, reconfigurable VLSI architecture, and IoT. Authors from leading institutions presented their research on advanced packaging techniques, emerging materials, and applications of AI and ML.

The conference facilitated collaboration between industry and academia, with several MoUs signed. Awards were presented for the best paper and young researcher, recognizing outstanding contributions to semiconductor technology. The conference provided a comprehensive overview of the latest advancements and trends in semiconductor technology.

The event was a resounding success, with participants praising the quality of presentations and the opportunities for networking and collaboration.

Dr. B.R Sanjeeva Reddy

Head of the Department, Electronics and Communication Engineering BVRIT, Narsapur, Telangana, India

We are delighted to present the proceedings of the inaugural International Conference on Semiconductor Materials Packaging, AI & ML, Reconfigurable VLSI Architectures for IoT, and Future Communication Technologies (SMART-2024), convened at B V Raju Institute of Technology (BVRIT). This symposium congregated luminaries from academia, industry, and government to disseminate their expertise and experiences in the realm of semiconductor technology.

The conference deliberated on five pivotal domains, namely, semiconductor packaging, sensors and networking, artificial intelligence (AI) and machine learning (ML), Internet of Things (IoT), and Reconfigurable VLSI Architectures. These areas are crucial for propelling India's ascendancy in the semiconductor sector, aligned with the India Semiconductor Mission (ISM).

This compendium presents a curated selection of high-quality papers presented during the conference, showcasing the latest advancements and trends in semiconductor technology. These papers provide invaluable insights into the future trajectory of this field, underscoring the imperative for sustained innovation and research.

We extend our gratitude to the authors, reviewers, and participants for their contributions to SMART-2024. We also acknowledge the support we receive from our sponsors and organizing committee members.

The First International Conference on SMART 2024 was a huge success, bringing together Indian experts from academia, industry, and research to share knowledge and collaborate on critical fields. Held at B V Raju Institute of Technology in Narsapur, Telangana, from September 19-20, 2024, the conference focused on "Semiconductor packaging and next-generation wireless technologies," aligning with the Indian Semiconductor Mission's vision. The conference supported government initiatives like Indian Semiconductor Mission, Production Linked Incentive scheme, and Scheme for Promotion of Manufacturing of Electronic Components and Semiconductors.

Key areas included semiconductor materials packaging, AI-driven technologies, reconfigurable VLSI architectures, and IoT and future communication technologies. The conference achieved its objectives by providing a platform for experts to share research, facilitating collaborations, highlighting semiconductor packaging's significance, and setting the stage for future conferences.

This milestone event underscores the importance of these technologies and paves the way for future research, innovation, and industry-academia collaborations, strengthening India's position in the global semiconductor landscape.

The First International Conference on Semiconductor Materials packaging, AI&ML, Reconfigurable VLSI Architectures for IoT & Future Communication Technologies (SMART 2024) would like to extend their heartfelt dedication to the esteemed participants, keynote speakers, and contributors who made this conference a resounding success.

We express our deepest gratitude to leadership team to Shri K. V. Vishnu Raju, Chairman, Sri Vishnu Educational Society (SVES), Shri Ravichandran Rajagopal, Vice Chairman, Sri Vishnu Educational Society (SVES), Shri K Aditya Vissam, Secretary, Sri Vishnu Educational Society (SVES), Prof. K. Lakshmi Prasad, Director, BVRIT, Dr. Sanjay Dubey, Principal, BVRIT, and Dr. B.R. Sanjeeva Reddy, Head of the Department, Electronics and Communication Engineering, BVRIT.

We gratefully acknowledge the invaluable support and contributions of our distinguished participants, keynote speakers Prof. Madhavan Swaminathan from The Pennsylvania State University and Prof. Pandurang Ashrit from University of Moncton, Canada.

Furthermore, we appreciate the tireless efforts of the SMART 2024 organization and Technical Program Committee, external reviewers, contributing authors, management of BVRIT, and generous funding from SERB, Govt of India . We also acknowledge our publication partnership with Taylor and Francis.

Dr. T. Vasudeva Reddy
Convenor, SMART 2024
B V Raju Institute of Technology
Department of ECE
Narsapur, Medak, Telangana, India.

Contents

List of Figures

List of Tables

1 Tumor extraction system using U-Net and Adamax optimizer

Suneetha Rikhari[1,a] and Mohana Lakshmi, K.[2,b]

[1]Department of CSE, Malla Reddy University, Hyderabad, India
[2]Department of ECE, CMR Technical Campus, Hyderabad, India

Abstract

In medical image analysis, the segmentation of the desired region of interest is an important task, where in the input image will be partitioned into multiple segments. These segments are very useful to extract useful information such as specific structure of an area of an organ in an image. Image segmentation in the medical field is used for tumor detection, organ delineation, tissue segmentation, and disease diagnosis. This work uses U-Net with Adamax optimizer for tumor segmentation. The data set considered for training is having three types of tumors images i.e. meningiomas, gliomas and pituitary tumors. Adamax optimizer updates the adaptive learning rates based on the back propagation for each parameter in the model. By combining the U-Net architecture with the Adamax optimizer, we can achieve faster and more efficient training for biomedical image segmentation tasks, leading to accurate and reliable segmentation results.

Keywords: Adamax, Convolutional neural network, CT, deep learning, magnetic resonance imaging, optimizer, positron emission tomography, U-Net

Introduction

Tumor segmentation is considered as an essential task in medical analysis when the main idea is to separate a region from the image for better analysis and synthesis of the area of interest. It involves identifying and delineating tumor regions from surrounding healthy tissues in various medical imaging modalities. Accurate tumor segmentation is essential for proper diagnosis and therapy planning in case of cancer. For segmenting the tumor, several methods are available in literature and the deep learning approaches are producing promising results. The trained convolutional neural networks (CNN's) can generate the desired and unique features from the large image data set. These networks are skillful enough to learn intricate patterns and thus generate unique features. Then, localization procedures are employed for segmenting the tumors. U-Net architecture is one such approach which uses several layers of CNN and can generate unique and desired features and also segment various sizes and shapes of tumors. Deep learning-based tumor segmentation approaches often use annotated datasets to train the models, where medical experts manually label the tumor regions. The models then learn to predict tumor masks based on the input of medical images. The field of tumor segmentation is continually evolving, and researchers are continuously exploring innovative methods and optimizing existing techniques to improve segmentation accuracy and robustness in real-world clinical scenarios.

Related work

U-Net architecture was proposed for segmentation of medical images [1]. The architecture consists of two networks called encoder and decoder. The concatenation of encoder data and decoder data is performed for accurate segmentation. This work can segment tumors with irregular sizes and shapes. A deep learning-based tumor segmentation approach is proposed [2]. This work demonstrated the effectiveness of using deep neural networks for identifying tumor regions from the surrounding brain tissues, providing valuable insights. A model defined [3], uses a large data set

[a]suneetha.rikhari@gmail.com, [b]mohana.kesana@gmail.com

DOI: 10.1201/9781003616399-1

of brain images for accurate segmentation. The results demonstrate that their deep neural network achieves better performance, accurately segmenting brain tumors even in challenging cases with irregular shapes and varying sizes. The 3D U-Net is designed for volumetric segmentation tasks and addresses the challenge of sparse annotation in datasets of medical images is given by Çiçek et al. [4]. The method has been widely adopted for various volumetric segments including brain and lungs. A review study using deep learning techniques with CNN's and U-Net for segmentation is discussed by Akkus [5]. This study focuses mainly on brain image segmentation. Another method which learns discriminative features for accurately segmenting the brain magnetic resonance imaging (MRI) images using CNN's is proposed [6]. The authors in another article [7] presented a deep learning framework named "DeepMedic". This technique is based on 3D CNN network which efficiently segmented region of interests from the 3D scans. An automatic tumor detection system is prosed in by Wang et al. [8] using fully connected based U-Net. It is designed for segmentation of MRI images and the use of convolutional nets in computer-assisted radiology and surgery applications, providing valuable support to medical professionals in diagnosing and treating brain tumors. The authors introduced a 3D CNN architecture designed to capture spatial information effectively and perform accurate brain tumor segmentation [9]. Wang et al. propose a tumor segmentation method using conditional generative adversarial networks (cGANs) applied to positron emission tomography (PET) imaging [8]. The authors leverage the power of cGANs to generate accurate tumor segmentations by conditioning the network on both input PET images and corresponding manual segmentations. Sun et al. [10] proposed a method for addressing the tumor segmentation task in lungs. The authors used 2D CNN for accurately segmenting tumors from lung images taken from PET scan. In this work, U-Net architecture is combined with the Adamax optimizer to enhance performance. The Adamax optimizer updates the parameters based on the loss function minimization through back propagation.

Experimental Methods and Materials

U-Net

U-Net uses several CNN's followed by ReLu activation function for extracting the feature maps. The architecture consists of encoder and decoder networks which are symmetric with each other. This architecture is specifically designed for segmentation of medical images. The accurate segmentation results are expected even for small or irregularly shaped objects in images.

In general, the U-Net architecture consists of four blocks:

Encoder (down sampling path): The encoder network consists of four encoders. Each encoder is composed of two Convolutional layers followed by a ReLu activation function. The kernel size is set to 3×3 and padding is the same. The output of the convolutional layers is applied to a max pooling layer to reduce the size of the feature maps. Here, the kernel size of the max pooling layer is set to 2×2. With this size of the kernel the learned spatial dimensions are reduced to half by decreasing the computational cost of the model. This network is also called contracting network.

Decoder (Up sampling path): The decoder does the inverse operation of the encoder. The encoder network has done the down sampling and generates a feature map of reduced size compared to the input image. Now, the decoder will do the up-sampling process. It is also called as expansive network. The up sampling is done by calculating the transpose convolution at each convolution layer. The spatial dimensions are increased in this network.

Bottleneck: It is the network between the encoder and the decoder. It generates the compressed representation of the input image, combining both global context and local features.

Final layer and activation: This is the last layer of U-Net. It consists of a convolutional layer of 1×1 size followed by a sigmoid function. Pixel wise classification is performed and generates output segmentation mask.

The simplified graphical representation of the U-Net architecture is shown in Figure 1.1. below:

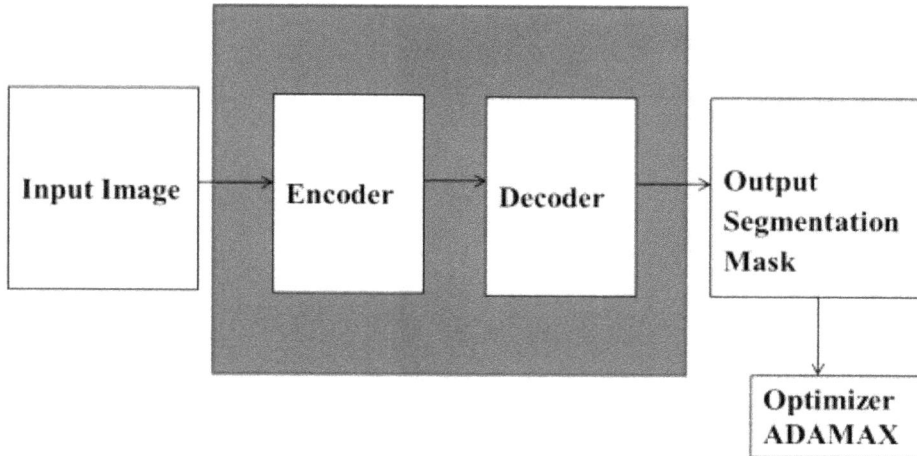

Figure 1.1 Graphical representation of U-Net architecture
Source: Author

Adamax optimizer

Adamax algorithm is an extension of the Adam optimizer and performs adaptive optimization. The Adamax optimizer replaces the L2 norm of the gradients in Adam optimizer with the L∞ norm, resulting in better convergence properties for certain types of networks. Adamax optimizer computes the learning rates adaptively for all the parameters in the model. It combines elements of RMSprop (adaptive learning rates) and momentum optimization. The update rule for the parameter θ using Adamax is as follows:

m = β1 * m + (1 - β1) * gradient
u = max (β2 * u, |gradient|)
θ = θ - learning_rate * m / (u + ε)
Where:

m: The moving average of the first-order moments (mean) of the gradients.

u: the gradients of exponentially weighted L∞ norm.

β1 and β2: are fixed to 0.9 and 0.999 respectively which represents the exponential decay

step_size: The learning rate or step size for updating the parameters.

ε: A small value (typically) added to the denominator for numerical stability.

During training of U-Net, the gradients are calculated, and the network parameters are updated based on the gradient values using Adamax optimizer. The adaptive learning rates provided by Adamax help in efficient convergence, especially in tasks with irregularly shaped structures

and limited training data. The optimizer can be specified at the initial phase or at the compilation phase while working with Tensor Flow or PyTorch.

By combining the U-Net architecture with the Adamax optimizer, you can achieve faster and more efficient training for biomedical image segmentation tasks, leading to accurate and reliable segmentation results.

Tumor size calculation

The segmented tumor size can be calculated by adding all the pixel values of the output using the formula:

Sum of all pixels $T = \sum_{m=1}^{L} \sum_{n=1}^{L} [f_{m,n}(0) + C]$
where L= 1 to 256

The segmented tumor is expected to have all the white pixels and the sum of all the white pixels can be calculated as:

Sum of all white pixels $P = \sum_{i=1}^{L} \sum_{j=1}^{L} f_{m,n}$

1 pixel = 0.264583 mm (as per advanced imaging unit)

Area or size of the tumor $A = \sqrt{P} \times 0.264583 \ mm^2$

Results

The images in the data set were taken from publicly available source [11] and the experiments were performed using Tensor Flow Python software. The data set considered is having 3064 brain tumor T1 MRI images. All the images are resized to 256X256 pixels before training the

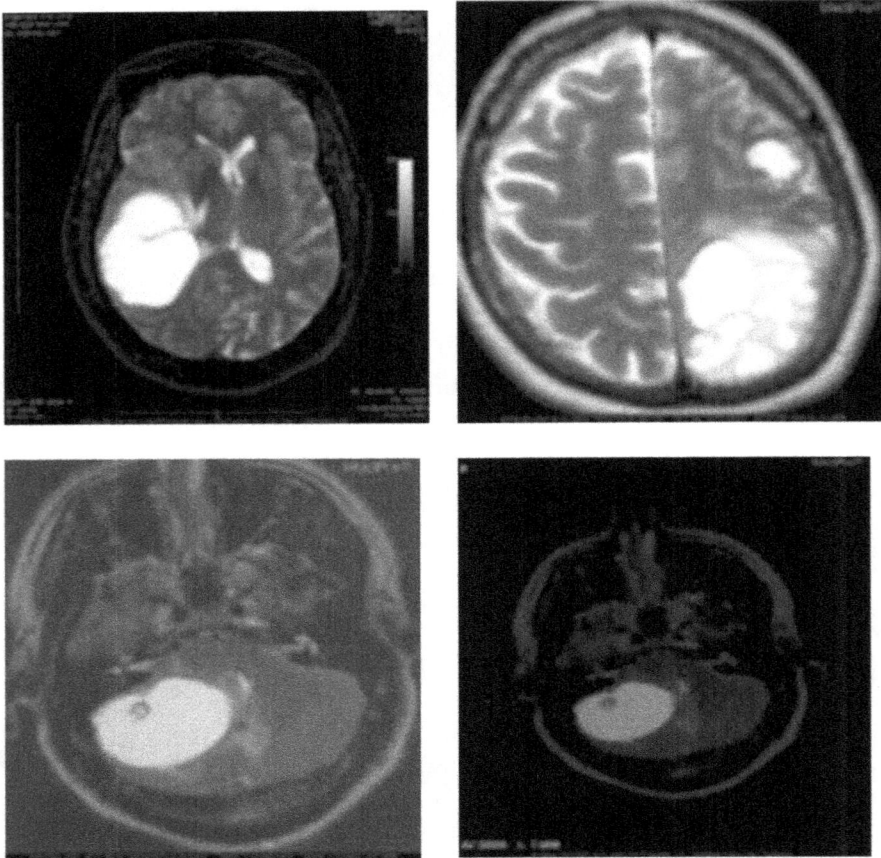

Figure 1.2 Input images
Source: Author

U-Net. The use of Adamax optimizer instead of Adam optimizer for updating the parameters of the network adaptively has increased the efficiency of the network. The segmented tumor is obtained from U-Net and the size of the tumor is also calculated.

The results are compared with the traditional segmentation techniques like FCM (Fuzzy C-Means) and K-Means. The image data inputs are depicted in Figure 1.2. The segmented tumors from the input images are displayed in Figure 1.3. The visual quality of the results displayed by the proposed method was able to produce better segmentation compared to the FCM and K-Means. Table 1.1 displays the size of the tumors for different inputs applied. The segmented results are displayed in Figure 1.3. Table 1.2 depicts the Performance analysis of the U-Net with Adam optimizer is compared with other optimizers like AlexNet, ResNet, Dense Net etc. The U-Net with

Adam optimizer has given better results in terms of TPR, TNR, PPV, F-Score and Accuracy.

Conclusion

Convolutional neural network (CNN) architectures like U-Net are particularly popular due to their ability to capture both local and global context, making them effective for segmenting tumors of various shapes and sizes. Deep learning-based tumor segmentation approaches often use annotated datasets to train the models, where medical experts manually label the tumor regions. The models then learn to predict tumor masks based on the input medical images. The field of tumor segmentation is continually evolving, and researchers are continuously exploring innovative methods and optimizing existing techniques to improve segmentation accuracy and robustness in real-world clinical scenarios. In this work,

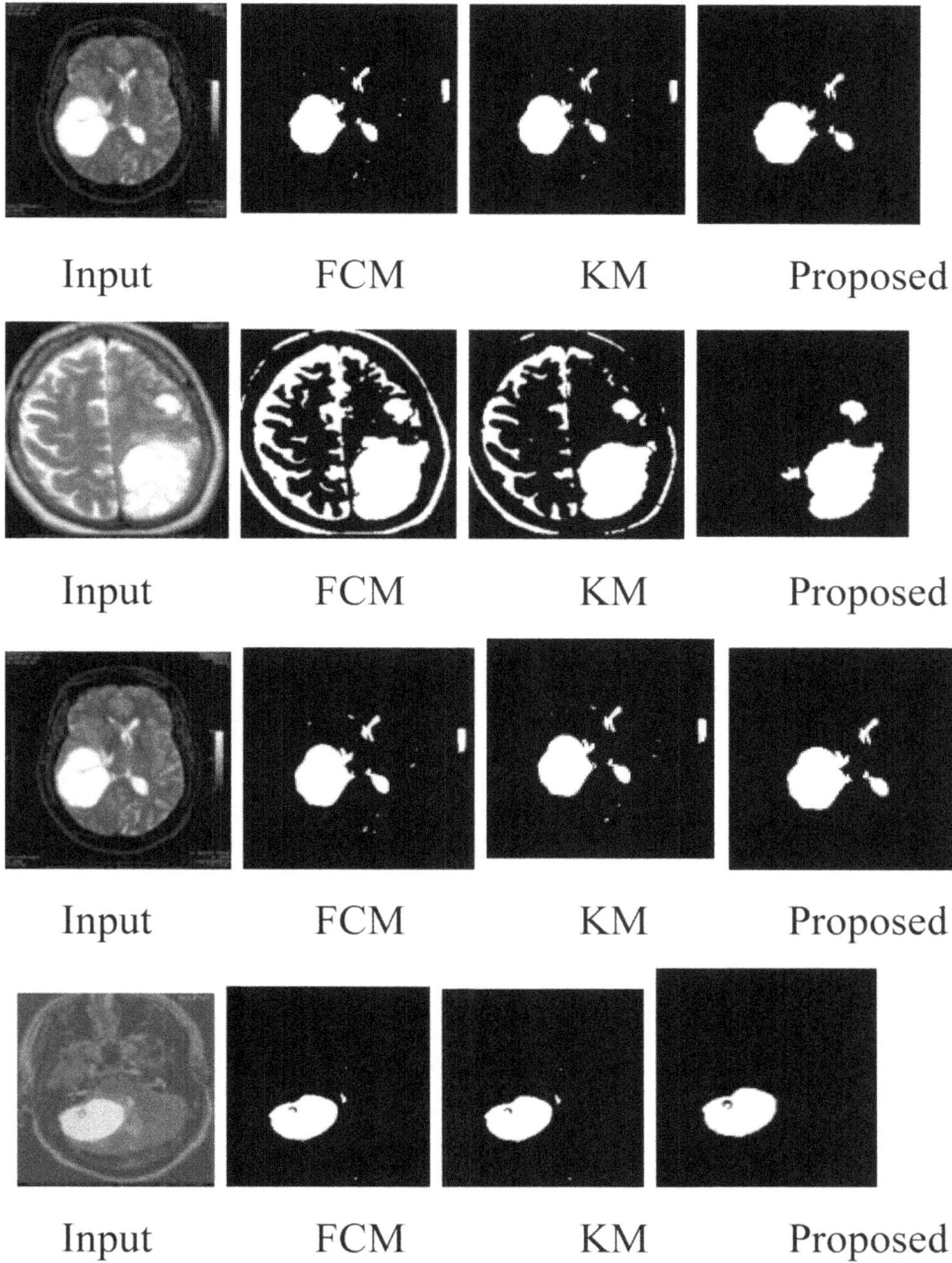

Input   FCM   KM   Proposed

Figure 1.3 Segmented tumors
Source: Author

Table 1.1 Calculated size of the tumor

Input image	Tumor Size (mm^2)
Figure 1.2(a)	18.5101
Figure 1.2(b)	37.768
Figure 1.2(c)	17.0908
Figure 1.2(d)	16.1790

Source: Author

Table 1.2 Performance analysis of the U-Net with Adam optimizer

Network	Performance measures (%)					
	TPR	TNR	PPV	F-Score	AUC	Accuracy
U-Net	**0.99**	**1.00**	**1.00**	**0.99**	**0.99**	**0.99**
AlexNet	0.90	0.97	0.97	0.93	0.94	0.94
ResNet-50	0.99	0.96	0.96	0.97	0.97	0.97
ResNet-101	0.97	0.97	0.97	0.96	0.96	0.97
DenseNet-121	0.97	0.94	0.95	0.96	0.96	0.96
InceptionV3	0.97	0.93	0.93	0.95	0.95	0.95
VGG-16	0.85	0.96	0.95	0.90	0.91	0.91
MobileNetV2	0.99	0.88	0.88	0.93	0.93	0.93
MobileNetV3	0.36	0.61	0.45	0.40	0.49	0.49

Source: Author

U-Net architecture is used for tumor segmentation and Adamax optimizer is used to improve the training network for better efficiency.

The blend of both U-Net and Adamax optimizer provided efficient segmentation results.

References

[1] Ronneberger, O., Fischer, P., and Brox, T. (2015). U-Net: convolutional networks for biomedical image segmentation. In Medical Image Computing and Computer-Assisted Intervention – MICCAI 2015 (pp. 234–241). Springer, Cham.

[2] Havaei, M., Davy, A., Warde-Farley, D., Biard, A., Courville, A., Bengio, Y., et al. (2017). Brain tumor segmentation with deep neural networks. *Medical Image Analysis*, 35, 18–31.

[3] Chen, H., Dou, Q., Yu, L., Qin, J., and Heng, P. A. (2017). Brain tumor segmentation with deep neural networks. *Medical Image Analysis*, 37, 18–31.

[4] Çiçek, Ö., Abdulkadir, A., Lienkamp, S., Brox, T., and Ronneberger, O. (2016). 3D U-Net: learning dense volumetric segmentation from sparse annotation. In Medical Image Computing and Computer-Assisted Intervention – MICCAI 2016 (pp. 424–432). Springer, Cham.

[5] Akkus, Z., Galimzianova, A., Hoogi, A., Rubin, D. L., and Erickson, B. J. (2017). Deep learning for brain MRI segmentation: state of the art and future directions. *Journal of Digital Imaging*, 30(4), 449–459.

[6] Pereira, S., Pinto, A., Alves, V., and Silva, C. A. (2016). Brain tumor segmentation using convolutional neural networks in MRI images. *IEEE Transactions on Medical Imaging*, 35(5), 1240–1251.

[7] Kamnitsas, C., Ferrante, E., Parisot, S., Ledig, C., Nori, A. V., Criminisi, A. D., et al. (2016). DeepMedic for brain tumor segmentation. In Brainlesion: Glioma, Multiple Sclerosis, Stroke and Traumatic Brain Injuries: Second International Workshop, BrainLes 2016, with the Challenges on BRATS, ISLES and mTOP 2016, Held in Conjunction with MICCAI 2016, Athens, Greece, October 17, 2016, Revised Selected Papers 2 (pp. 138–149). Springer International Publishing.

[8] Wang, Z., Zeng, M., Wang, L., Zhang, P., Tang, Z., Liu, J., et al. (2019). Automatic brain tumor detection and segmentation using U-Net based fully convolutional networks. *International Journal of Computer Assisted Radiology and Surgery*, 14(4), 691–701.

[9] Moeskops, P., Viergever, M., Mendrik, A., and de Vries, L. (2017). Automatic brain tumor segmentation in 3D MR images with deep convolutional neural networks. *Medical Image Analysis*, 35, 61–78.

[10] Wang, X., Huang, Y., Liu, J., Wang, L., Wang, Q., and Zhang, Z. (2019). Conditional generative adversarial networks-based tumor segmentation in PET imaging. *European Journal of Nuclear Medicine and Molecular Imaging*, 46(13), 2790–2800.

[11] Cheng, Jun (2017). brain tumor dataset. figshare. Dataset. https://doi.org/10.6084/m9.figshare.1512427.v5

2 Future facts of Amazon deforestation based on static data over 2015–2023

Kalaiyarasi, M.[1,a], *Prameela, M.*[2,b]*, Naga Malleswara Rao, D. S.*[3,c]*,*
Karthi Shankar[4,d]*, Saravanan, S.*[2,e] *and Hemalatha, L. T.*[5,f]

[1]Institute of AI and ML, Department of Computational Intelligence, SIMATHS Engineering, Saveetha Institute of Medical and Technical Sciences (SIMATS), Chennai, India

[2]Department of EEE, B V Raju Institute of Technology, Telangana, India

[3]Gokaraju Rangaraju Institute of Engineering and Technology, Hyderabad, Telangana, India

[4]Department of Computer Science and Engineering, V.S.B. Engineering College, Karur, India

[5]Research Scholar, SIMATHS Engineering, Saveetha Institute of Medical and Technical Sciences (SIMATS), Chennai, India

Abstract

The goal of this study is to conduct an analysis of the deforestation of the Amazon rain forest, which may be predicted using regression analysis and examined using real data. In addition to a time series of the yearly deforestation area for the previous nine years (2015–2023), the data has also been evaluated using static data, such as geographical, forest, and watershed data, have also been used. The final regression model projects that, over the five-year period from 2025–2030, annual deforestation area (square kilometers) will increase. By that time, deforestation is expected to reach one million square kilometers, or roughly 15% of the 5.5–6.7 million square kilometers of rain forest, up from the current 1%.

Keywords: Amazon rainforest, deforestation, SPSS, statistical analysis, sustainability

Introduction

Global economic development and productivity have skyrocketed over the last two decades, but at a significant cost to equality and sustainability—defined as our ability to leave behind the resources needed for future generation' wellness [1,2]. Growing annual consumption and demography, ensuring long-term sustainability, is one of today's most pressing concerns. The Sustainable Development Goals (SDGs), which swapped out the Millennium Development Goals in Rio + 20's post-2015 development agenda. Owing to actions taken to mitigate climate change, efforts to limit deforestation are spreading internationally under this agenda, and it has been promoted as one of the United Nations' SDGs for the years 2015–2030 [3]. The SDGs seek to promote the adoption of environmentally conscious management of all types of ecosystems, halt the destruction of forests, restore devastated forests, and considerably boost the growth of forests and reforestation around the world [4].

The biggest rainforest in the world is the Amazon. This rainforest sometimes referred to as the "lungs of our planet," is the headquarters of the finest and most diversified biosphere on Earth [5,6]. The equivalent of 844 million hectares makes up this enormous natural refuge, with nine nations in South America including Brazil accounting for more than 60% of the total area. The Brazilian Amazon rainforest has suffered greatly over the past century due to issues including wildfires, deforestation, and growing agribusiness, despite its significance to the nation's ecological and economy. The Brazilian Amazonian region of Brazil has around 11.6 thousand square kilometers of deforested land as of 2022. After over thirteen thousand square kilometers vanished, the Legal Amazon's deforestation rate hit its greatest point in fifteen years

[a]mukalaiyarasi@gmail.com, [b]prameela.m@bvrit.ac.in, [c]dsnm.rao@gmail.com, [d]karthicse10@gmail.com,
[e]saravananklu@gmail.com, [f]lthenalatha@gmail.com

DOI: 10.1201/9781003616399-2

barely twelve months prior. Nine Brazilian states make up the more than five million square kilometers legal Amazon.

Conversations on the challenges and opportunities of environmentally friendly agriculture and the management of natural resources—especially land, water, and forests—have been more prevalent in recent years. This may be attributed to the present SDGs goal as well as a more prominent climate change agenda that aims to limit global warming below 1.5 degrees Celsius by reducing greenhouse gas emissions. The effects of forest conversion include soil erosion, decreased water quality and supply, loss of biodiversity, and increased carbon emissions [7]. As a consequence of climate change mitigation programs, attempts to lessen deforestation are expanding internationally in response to these dire possibilities, and it has lately been pushed as one of the UN's 2015–2030 SDGs.

Therefore, two official satellite imagery datasets and statistical methods are employed to undertake a space-time evaluation of deforestation in indigenous territories (ITs) inside the Brazilian Amazon biome among 2021 and 2023 in order to properly assess the patterns of deforestation in the Amazon [8]. This time frame was chosen since the Brazilian Amazon is seeing a notable rise in deforestation, particularly in the year 2022 when environmental problems in the area become more severe. The main contribution of this paper is, it provides the information about i) over the five years period from 2025–2030, and annual deforestation area will increase or decrease? ii) In which year the deforestation rate is higher over the period 2015–2023.

This paper is further written in the following way. Section 2 narrates the Brazilian deforestation issue. Section 3 illustrates the proposed method and regression analysis using SPSS. Future facts of Amazon is explained in section 4 and this paper is concluded in section 5.

Brazilian Deforestation Issue

The primary effects of deforestation are on climate stability, as well as water quality and quantity, states Tina Oliveira-Miranda, a coordinator of Territorial Information Systems of Wataniba, a Venezuelan civil society group, and one of the study's authors. It has a close relationship with phenomena like forest fires. This suggests a rise in releases of greenhouse gases and, thus, intensifies the climate-related consequences [9].

Up to 23.7 million hectares of forest—nearly the size of the United Kingdom—may have been destroyed in the Amazon in only five years. Three potential scenarios of deforestation from 2021 to 2025 are shown by the results of research released by the Amazon Network of Georeferenced Socio-Environmental Information (RAISG): optimistic, moderate, and pessimistic. The most extensive tropical forest on Earth would disappear in five years, if the gloomy scenario is to be believed, losing half of its lost area (54.2 million hectares) in the previous twenty years. The Amazon Region, designated by RAISG as encompassing nine countries and roughly 850 million hectares (8.5 million km2), includes the entire Amazon River Basin as well as areas that transition into other biomes like the Andes, Cerrado, Chaco, and Pantanal [10]. This area is covered by the study "Deforestación en la Amazonía al 2025." The findings indicate that variables resulting from altered land use, such as mining, cattle farming, and the development of road infrastructure, continue to severely impact the forest and its inhabitants. Activities that exacerbate the problem and endanger people who guard the forest include gold mining, coca growing, drug trafficking, and arms trafficking.

Through the application of specific techniques and computational methods on Google Earth Engine, an online mapping platform, the study identified 55 million hectares of forest that are particularly susceptible to deterioration due to their proximity to roads and geographical requirements. In other words, these areas have a greater risk of deforestation than none. Twenty experts from six Amazonian nations collaborated with the study, which examined the two decades of deforestation from 2001 to 2020, and this surface area represents the total amount of deforestation. A major contributor to the greenhouse gas emissions that drive climate change is deforestation. Forest loss is an unavoidable issue that has grown to unsustainable levels in the Brazilian Amazon. Nearly 300,000 mile2 or roughly 5% of the forest cover in Brazil's Amazon has disappeared in the past 50 years. As a result, at least 5110 mile2 will be lost in 2021 as a result.

According to the International Union for Conservation of Nature (IUCN), 30% of the planet's biodiversity is found in the Amazon. There is constant discovery of new plant and animal species. The rapid devastation of the biome, however, may cause the extinction of species that science has not yet identified or investigated. It is quite probable that this has already occurred based on the data gathered for the RAISG research. An area the size of France was lost in the Amazon between 2001 and 2020—roughly 54.2 million hectares, or nearly 9% of its forests. The Amazon's Brazilian region, which makes up 62% of its total area, was most severely impacted, followed by Bolivia, Peru, and Colombia. With over 5 million hectares of cleared forest, 2003 had the greatest proportion. Regional rates decreased in the years that followed as a result of measures taken to stop the destruction in Brazil, but as of 2019, there is a new upward trend in deforestation rates, which is mostly the result of actions taken by the Brazilian government to undermine the organizations in charge of environmental monitoring. The overall deforested area in 2020, the final year covered by research, is once again close to the 2.7-million-hectare yearly average of the preceding two decades. Figure 2.1 (uploaded on December 12, 2023, by Bruna Alves) depicts the area that has been cleared of trees in Amazon, Brazil, between the years 1988 and 2023.

The total amount of deforested land in the Brazilian among 1988 and 2023 exceeded 490 thousand square kilometers, with the state of Pará accounting for almost 35 percent of this total. With more than 31% of its land lost, Mato Grosso has the second-highest percentage. Rondônia came in second, trailing it by almost 14%. The deforestation area from November 2022 to November 2023 is depicted in Figure 2.2.

According to INPE data, deforestation decreased by 23% year over year to 176.8 square kilometers in December alone. The Amazon Rainforest reached its lowest point in five years in 2023, as seen visually in Figure 2.3. Destroying the forest had reached its peak the year before, when the data series began in 2015 [12].

In 2023 (911,740 hectares) and 2022 (2,062,939 hectares), researchers predict that the amount of forest lost decreased by 55.8%. As compared to 2020 (2,823,475 hectares), the decline is even more pronounced, having decreased by nearly two-thirds, or 67.7%. The fact that these comparisons are all immediately applicable and span

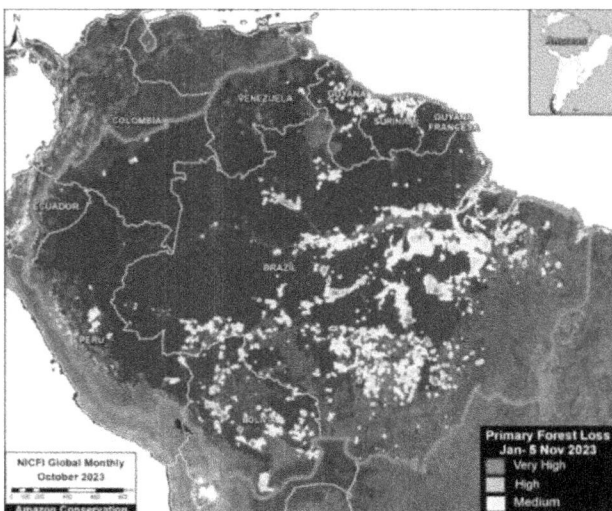

Figure 2.1 Deforested area in Amazon, Brazil from the year 1988–2023 [11]
Source: Author

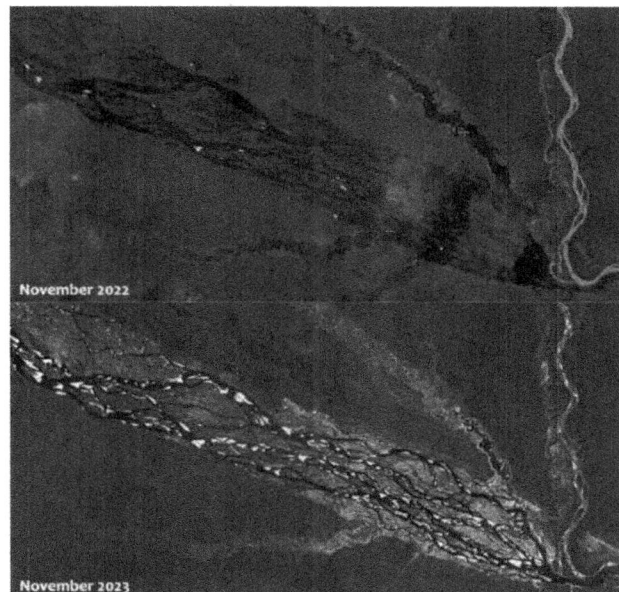

Figure 2.2 Deforested region in Amazon from November 2022 to November 2023 [11]
Source: Author

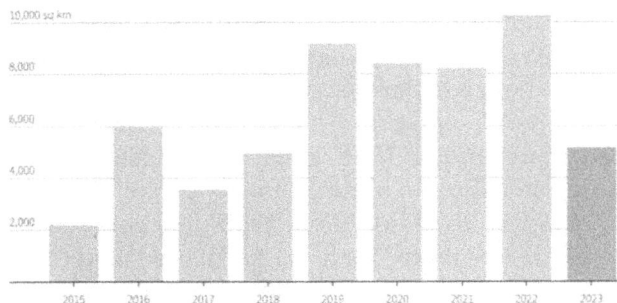

Figure 2.3 Amazon rainforest hit in 2023 its lowest level in five years [13]
Source: Author

the same period from January to early November each year should be emphasized. In comparison to the previous year, 2022, and the most recent peak year, 2020, the graph shows a significant decline in the loss of primary forests across the whole Amazon biome in 2023.

In this paper, official remote sensing datasets are used to analyze deforestation in Amazon in the 2013–2021 period, taking into account the significance of ITs for maintaining socio-environmental and cultural diversity as well as the recent rise in deforestation in the Brazilian Amazon. Within ITs, deforestation has surged by 129% since 2013, coinciding with an expansion of regions used for illicit mining. Compared to the preceding years (2013–2018), deforestation increased by 195% in 2019–2021 and extended 30% further from the borders into the interior of indigenous lands. Furthermore, the last three years of the analysis years accounted for nearly 59% of the total 96 million tons of carbon dioxide emissions within ITs from 2013 to 2021, indicating the extent of growing deforestation's effects on climate. Therefore, the Brazilian

government must prioritize stopping deforestation in indigenous lands in order to maintain the forests, uphold the land rights of these peoples, and control the global climate.

Proposed Method

Figure 2.4 shows the workflow of the proposed method. In this paper, regression analysis has been used. Even though it is an old concept, this method has not been used for predicting the future facts of the Amazon forest. This is the first paper to predict the future deforestation in Amazon. Initially, the required data is collected from INPE and Kaggle. The data is in .csv file format. The first step of the proposed method is pre-processing, where the unwanted data is removed, and the missing data are replaced. The preprocessed data has been given to SPSS regression analysis, where the mean deforested area and the sample test analysis has been performed to predict the future about Amazonian forest. From the analysis, the future facts of Amazon rainforest has been analyzed.

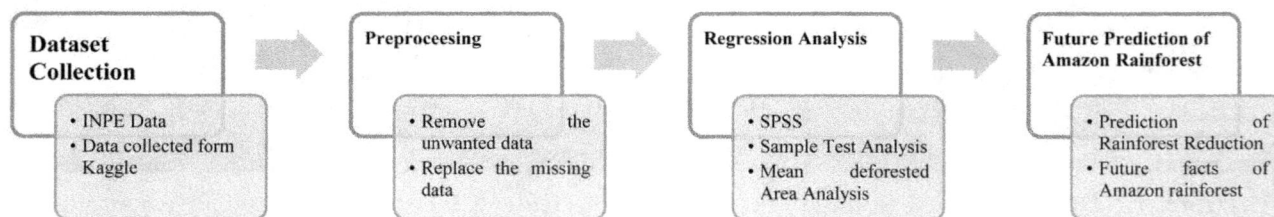

Figure 2.4 Workflow of the proposed method
Source: Author

Regression analysis using SPSS

A strong data analysis platform is IBM SPSS Statistics [14,15]. It has a large feature set and an easy-to-use interface. Sophisticated statistical techniques contribute to great precision and superior decision making. This covers all aspects of the analytics lifecycle, from managing and preparing data to conducting analyses.

Figure 2.5 shows the graphical representation of mean analysis of private lands, land reform settlements, conservation units and indigenous land. It also gives the average deforestation for the year 2021–2023. From the figure, it can be clearly saying that the deforestation had happened in private land is higher, and it is lower in Indigenous land when compared with other parameters. The simple bar mean of area by groups with error

bars 95% confident interval, and +/- 2 SD is illustrated in Figure 2.6.

Table 2.1 indicates that the mean, standard deviation and standard error mean for the dependent variable significantly well. The standard deviation for the factor private, reform, conservation and indigenous are 3.51, 2.00, 2.64 and 0.00 respectively. In addition, the standard error mean value for the same factors are 2.02, 1.15, 1.52 and 0.00 respectively. Here, the standard deviation and the standard error mean value for indigenous are zero. Therefore, indigenous is not considered for the one-sample Test.

The one sample test table represents the mean difference, 2-tailed significance value and the 95% confidence interval of the difference value; it is illustrated in Table 2.2. This shows the

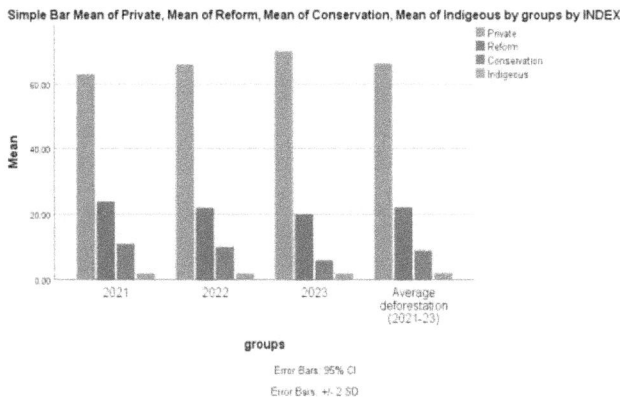

Figure 2.5 Mean analysis of private lands, land reform settlements, conservation units and indigenous land
Source: Author

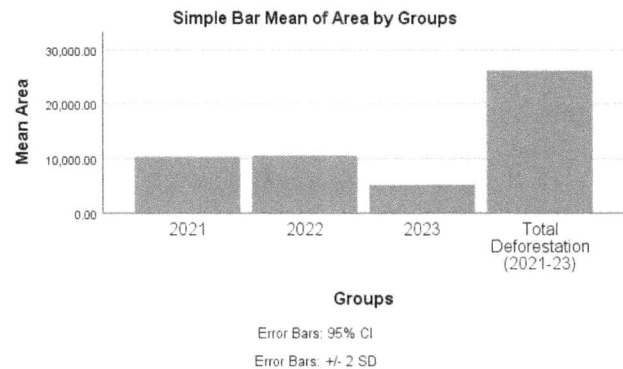

Figure 2.6 Simple bar mean of area by groups
Source: Author

Table 2.1 One-sample statistics

	N	Mean	Std. deviation	Std. error mean
Private	3	66.3333	3.51188	2.02759
Reform	3	22.0000	2.00000	1.15470
Conservation	3	9.0000	2.64575	1.52753
Indigenous	3	2.0000	.00000[a]	.00000
Area	3	8696.0333	3070.08350	1772.51354

a. t cannot be computed because the standard deviation is 0.

Source: Author

Table 2.2 One sample test analysis with 95% confidence interval

	Test value = 0					
	t	df	Sig. (2-tailed)	Mean difference	95% Confidence interval of the difference	
					Lower	Upper
Private	32.71	2	.001	66.33333	57.6093	75.0573
Reform	19.05	2	.003	22.00000	17.0317	26.9683
Conservation	5.89	2	.028	9.00000	2.4276	15.5724
Area	4.90	2	.039	8696.0333	1069.52	16322.5

Source: Author

statistical significance of the regression model. Here, p values for the considered factors private, reform, conservation and indigenous are .001, 0.003, and 0.028 respectively. These values are less than 0.05, and indicates that; overall, the regression model statistically significantly predicts the outcome variable. The regression model projects a notable rise in the annual deforestation area over a ten-year period, during 2025–2030. By that time, deforestation is expected to reach 1 million square kilometers, or approximately 15% of the 5.5–6.7 million square kilometers of rain forest, up from the current 1%.

Future Facts of Amazon

With over two million hectares lost to primary forest degradation in 2022, Brazil recorded the greatest primary forest loss area globally. In order to achieve net-zero emissions by 2050, it will become increasingly difficult to track the annual increase in the loss of global tree cover and the greenhouse gas emissions from forest regions. 20% of the carbon dioxide absorbed by Earth's land is absorbed by the Amazon rain forest. However, due of deforestation, the quantity absorbed now is 30% less than it was in the 1990s. In addition to that, some of the salient details regarding the future of Amazon rainforest are discussed as follows.

- If deforestation continues at this rate, the Amazonian forest may disappear entirely by 2050. It includes the majority of deforestation caused by logging, agriculture, and infrastructural development.

- In addition to being the world's lungs, the Amazon is a carbon sink that can absorb CO_2 from the atmosphere. Should that pattern persist, the Amazon rainforest may, on a net basis, start producing carbon for the first time in countless years, greatly contributing to global warming?

- The Amazon river and its tributaries are vital for the region's water cycle. Forest loss can disrupt the hydrological cycle, reducing the rainfall generated by the forest and potentially leading to more severe droughts. This, in turn, affects water availability for both ecosystems and human populations.

- Indigenous peoples and local communities depend on the forest for their livelihoods, culture, and traditions. Deforestation threatens their way of life, leading to loss of land, resources, and cultural heritage. It can also lead to conflicts over land rights and displacement of communities.

- While deforestation can bring short-term economic benefits through agriculture and resource extraction, the long-term economic costs include loss of ecosystem services such as water filtration, soil stabilization, and tourism potential. Sustainable management of the forest could provide more enduring economic benefits.

- The Amazon's health is not just a regional issue but a global one. Its ability to act as a carbon sink is vital for mitigating climate change. If deforestation continues at current rates, the global efforts to combat climate change could be severely undermined, making it much harder to meet international climate goals such as those outlined in the Paris Agreement.

To prevent this dire scenario, a combination of strategies is needed. These include enforcing and expanding protected areas, promoting sustainable land-use practices, supporting reforestation projects, and implementing policies that reduce the demand for products driving deforestation. International cooperation and financial mechanisms, such as payments for ecosystem services and carbon credits, can provide incentives for conservation. Empowering indigenous communities and recognizing their land rights have also proven effective in reducing deforestation rates.

Conclusion

This study presents the results of a regression analysis and future projections of Amazon deforestation using statistical data from 2015–2023. According to the data, 2022 saw the greatest amount of deforestation. The regression model predicts with statistical significance that there will be an increase in the annual area of deforestation (square kilometers) over the 10-year period from 2025–2030. By that time, deforestation is expected to reach one million square kilometers, or approximately 15% of the 5.5–6.7 millions square kilometers of rain forest, as opposed to the current 1%.

References

[1] Silva-Junior, C. H. L. (2023). Brazilian Amazon indigenous territories under deforestation pressure. *Scientific Reports*, 13(1), 5851–2023.

[2] Murugesan, K., Balasubramani, P., Murugan, P. R., and Sankaranarayanan, S. (2021). Color-based SAR image segmentation using HSV + FKM clustering for estimating the deforestation rate of LBA-ECO LC-14 modeled deforestation scenarios, Amazon basin: 2002–2050. *Arabian Journal of Geosciences*, 14(9), 777.

[3] Gomes, R., Bento, F., Canella, C. D. M., de Aquino Branco, O. E., Coelho Silva Castro, M. C., and Rodrigues Castro, S. (2020). Deforestation in legal amazon: a panel data analysis of potential interferers. *Journal of Management and Sustainability*, 10, 97.

[4] Assunção, J., Gandour, C., and Rocha, R. (2023). DETER-ing deforestation in the Amazon: environmental monitoring and law enforcement. *American Economic Journal: Applied Economics*, 15(2), 125–156.

[5] Wang, D., Gurhy, B., Hanusch, M., and Kollenda, P. (2023). Could sustainability-linked bonds incentivize lower deforestation in Brazil's legal Amazon?. World Bank Policy Research Working Paper Series, 10558.

[6] Perumal, B., Kalaiyarasi, M., Deny, J., and Muneeswaran, V. (2021). Forestry land cover segmentation of SAR Image using unsupervised ILKFCM. *Materials Today: Proceedings*. https://doi.org/10.1016/j.matpr.2021.01.779.

[7] Moreira, R. M. (2024). Trends and correlation between deforestation and precipitation in the Brazilian Amazon Biome. *Theoretical and Applied Climatology*, 1–10.

[8] Kavlin Castaneda, M. (2024). Monitoring spectral forest regrowth trends in the chapare watershed of Bolivia, 1985 to 2018. Diss. University of British Columbia.

[9] de Bodas Terassi, P. M., et al. (2023). Exploring climate extremes in Brazil's legal Amazon. *Stochastic Environmental Research and Risk Assessment*, 1–20.

[10] The Amazon will reach tipping point if current trend of deforestation continues (mongabay.com).

[11] Amazon rainforest in Brazil: deforestation by state 2023. Statista.

[12] Deforestation in Brazil's Amazon down by 50% to five-year low in 2023 (usnews.com).

[13] MAAP #201: Amazon deforestation & carbon update for 2023 | MAAP (maaproject.org).

[14] Rivadeneyra, P., Scaccia, L., and Salvati. L. (2023). A spatial regression analysis of Colombia's narcodeforestation with factor decomposition of multiple predictors. *Scientific Reports*, 13(1), 13485.

[15] Da Fonseca, E. L., and da Silva Filho, E. P. (2023). Binary logistic regression applied to erosion susceptibility mapping in the Southern Amazon. *Revista Brasileira de Geomorfologia*, 24(4), 1–5.

3 Neura flow: cardiac output monitoring via deep learning from arterial pressure

Viswanadham Ravuri[1,a], Sai Shravya, G.[1,b], Rambabu, K.[2,c], Prem Kumar, M.[3,d], Surya Kavitha, T.[4,e] and Priyakanth, R.[1,f]

[1]Department of ECE, BVRITHYDERABAD College of Engineering for Women Hyderabad, India

[2]Department of ECE, BVRaju Institute of Technology, Narsapur, India

[3]Department of ECE, Shri Vishnu Engineering College for Women, Bhimavaram, India

[4]Department of ECE, Raghu Engineering College, Visakhapatnam, India

Abstract

Cardiac output monitoring is vital in intensive care medicine. This study introduces an innovative approach using deep learning techniques to monitor cardiac output from arterial pressure data. The research focuses on extracting relevant features from heart rate (HR) information and arterial blood pressure (ABP) to train a deep learning model called deep learning algorithm for cardiac output prediction (DLAPCO). Datasets with original ABP and HR measurements are preprocessed to enhance data quality, and these features are used as inputs for the DLAPCO model. The model is then rigorously tested with separate datasets to evaluate its accuracy in predicting cardiac output and related cardiovascular parameters. Reliability of the model is evaluated using validation measures including specificity, sensitivity and accuracy. The results suggest that the DLAPCO model has the potential to accurately predict cardiac output, supporting its use for real-time, non-invasive cardiac monitoring in clinical settings. The Neura Flow project, which supports the development of health technology, offers promising opportunities to enhance patient care and diagnostic accuracy in cardiovascular medicine.

Keywords: Arterial blood pressure, cardiac output, deep learning algorithm for cardiac output prediction, stroke volume

Introduction

Cardiac output monitoring is a critical advancement in medical technology, significantly improving clinicians' ability to assess cardiovascular function in a wide range of patients [1]. Traditional methods often struggle to accurately account for individual patient characteristics, especially in cases where age or existing health conditions affect cardiovascular dynamics [2]. To address these challenges, age-agnostic approaches are being developed to provide tailored monitoring solutions that consider age-related changes in cardiac function, ensuring accuracy and reliability across all age groups. Additionally, disease-specific monitoring strategies offer focused insights into cardiac output variations linked to specific medical conditions, aiding clinicians in making well-informed decisions and optimizing patient care [3]. By integrating cutting-edge technologies and advanced analytical methods, these age-agnostic and disease-specific monitoring approaches aim to improve diagnostic precision, enable early intervention, and enhance patient outcomes in clinical practice [4,5]. Cardiac output monitoring represents a significant advancement in medical technology, fundamentally changing the field of cardiovascular assessment. Traditional methods of measuring cardiac output often face challenges in capturing the nuances of individual patient profiles, particularly when age or existing health conditions have a significant impact on cardiac dynamics [6,7]. To overcome these challenges, age-agnostic approaches

[a]viswanadh.r@bvrithyderabad.edu.in, [b]20wh1a0452@bvrithyderabad.edu.in, [c]rambabukala@gmail.com, [d]mpremkumar@svecw.edu.in, [e]kavitats24@gmail.com, [f]priyakanth.r@bvrithyderabad.edu.in

DOI: 10.1201/9781003616399-3

aim to provide customized monitoring solutions that account for age-related differences in cardiac function, ensuring consistency and reliability across various demographic groups. The introduction of disease-specific monitoring strategies marks a significant advancement, providing detailed insights into cardiac output changes related to specific medical conditions [8]. This specialized approach equips clinicians with accurate data, allowing them to detect subtle variations that may indicate underlying pathologies.

By integrating advanced technologies with sophisticated analytical methods, disease-specific and age-agnostic cardiac output monitoring aims to achieve greater diagnostic accuracy and support proactive intervention strategies, leading to better patient outcomes [9]. This evolution in cardiovascular assessment highlights the move towards personalized medicine and demonstrates the transformative impact of innovation in healthcare.

In cardiovascular medicine, the pursuit of more accurate and personalized methods for assessing cardiac function has been a key driver of technological innovation. Traditional techniques for measuring cardiac output often struggle to account for the complex dynamics of individual patients, especially when factors like age or specific health conditions play a significant role. However, recent technological advancements have ushered in a new era with the development of disease-specific and age-agnostic cardiac output monitoring. These new methods signify a breakthrough in medical technology, transforming the evaluation of cardiovascular function across diverse patient groups. By overcoming the limitations of traditional methods, age-agnostic monitoring strategies offer tailored solutions that consider age-related changes in cardiac function, ensuring accuracy and consistency across different age ranges [10]. Concurrently, disease-specific monitoring approaches provide focused insights into cardiac output variations linked and enabled to specific medical conditions.

The integration of innovative technologies and sophisticated analytical techniques in cardiac output monitoring is poised to significantly improve diagnostic accuracy, enable early intervention, and enhance patient outcomes in clinical settings. This shift highlights the ongoing movement towards personalized medicine and the transformative potential of healthcare innovation. In cardiovascular medicine, the challenge of developing precise and adaptable methods for assessing cardiac function during surgery has been a persistent issue. Traditional techniques often fall short in accounting for the various factors that influence cardiovascular dynamics, such as age and specific medical conditions. However, recent advancements in medical technology, especially in deep learning, present promising solutions to these challenges [11,12].

Literature Review

This study aims to introduce a novel deep learning approach for monitoring cardiac output (CO) during surgery, applicable across various age groups and specific diseases using arterial blood pressure measurements as input. The paper will likely cover the development and validation of this deep learning model, emphasizing its potential to enhance accurate, disease-specific CO monitoring during surgery. This advancement could significantly improve patient outcomes and clinical decision-making in the intraoperative setting [13].

Central vascular catheters (CVCs) are essential tools in modern medical care, used for purposes ranging from medication administration to hemodynamic monitoring. However, their use comes with inherent risks that can result in significant patient harm and legal issues for healthcare providers and institutions. This review explores the range of injuries associated with CVCs, including mechanical complications like vessel perforation, thrombosis, and catheter-related infections. It also delves into the legal aspects of CVC-related injuries, such as negligence claims, standards of care, and potential liabilities for healthcare professionals and organizations. Additionally, strategies to mitigate risks and enhance patient safety are discussed, highlighting the importance of evidence-based practices, thorough staff training, and robust quality improvement initiatives. By thoroughly understanding the complexities of CVC-related injuries and liability, healthcare stakeholders can proactively address these challenges, improve patient outcomes, and reduce legal risks in clinical settings [14].

Edwards' FloTrac Sensor and Vigileo Monitor are medical devices designed to measure cardiac output (CO) in patients. They continuously and non-invasively estimate CO by analyzing the arterial pressure waveform. The FloTrac sensor attaches to the patient's arterial line and sends data to the Vigileo Monitor, which uses a proprietary algorithm to compute CO, stroke volume (SV), systemic vascular resistance (SVR), and other hemodynamic parameters in realtime. Unlike invasive techniques like thermodilution or pulmonary artery catheterization, the FloTrac sensor and Vigileo Monitor provide a safer and more convenient alternative. These devices are particularly useful for critically ill patients needing continuous CO monitoring to guide treatment decisions. While factors such as patient positioning, arterial waveform quality, and changes in vascular tone can impact accuracy, these tools generally offer measurements comparable to invasive methods. Their simplicity and non-invasive nature make them suitable for various clinical applications, delivering significant benefits and potentially improving patient outcomes [15].

The study includes a cohort of critically ill patients, where cardiac output measurements are obtained simultaneously using the new pulse contour method and a validated reference technique. Statistical analyses, such as correlation coefficients and Bland-Altman plots, are used to evaluate the agreement between the two methods. Continuous cardiac output monitoring is crucial for managing critically ill patients, providing essential information for hemodynamic optimization. This study assesses a new pulse contour technique for continuous cardiac output monitoring in this patient population. The validation of this method is conducted against a reference standard to determine its accuracy and reliability [16].

Analyzing arterial pressure wave without calibration is a valuable tool for assessing cardiac output and stroke volume variation in various clinical settings. Studies were selected based on predefined criteria and analyzed for accuracy, reliability, and clinical utility across perioperative care, intensive care units, and cardiac surgery. The findings indicate good agreement with established methods like thermodilution and highlight the technique's potential in predicting fluid responsiveness and guiding hemodynamic management. However, limitations related to patient factors, measurement techniques, and algorithm variability are noted, suggesting areas for future research and improvement [17].

The title suggests that the authors conducted a study comparing the performance of a deep learning-based method for estimating stroke volume to a conventional arterial contour method in patients with hemodynamic instability. The deep learning method outperformed the traditional method in accurately estimating stroke volume, particularly in patients with hemodynamic issues. This has significant implications for clinical practice, especially in intensive care settings where precise hemodynamic monitoring is crucial for patient management [18].

Vital recorder is a valuable research resource that provides automatic recording capabilities for high resolution, time synchronized physiological information from various anesthesia equipment. This software is essential for researchers and clinicians, enabling comprehensive collection and analysis of patient monitoring data during anesthesia procedures. As a free and open-source platform, vital recorder integrates seamlessly with multiple anesthesia devices, allowing the simultaneous recording of various physiological parameters. It ensures accuracy and consistency in data acquisition by synchronizing data streams from different sources. Vital recorder's key features include a user-friendly interface, customizable recording settings, and compatibility with numerous data formats. These features allow researchers to efficiently capture and analyze vital signs such as electrocardiography (ECG), arterial blood pressure (ABP), and pulse oximetry (SpO2) in real-time or after procedures. Vital recorder offers flexible data visualization and export options, facilitating thorough data analysis and easy sharing among research teams. Its utility extends beyond academic research, supporting clinical applications by aiding evidence-based decision-making and quality improvement initiatives in anesthesia practice [19].

Proposed System

The development of a strategy based on deep learning to monitor cardiac output derived from arterial pressure waveforms marks a significant leap in cardiovascular healthcare. This method utilizes deep learning algorithms to improve the precision and reliability of cardiac output measurements from arterial pressure waveforms, ensuring efficacy across various age groups.

Deep learning techniques are adept at identifying complex patterns and relationships within arterial pressure waveforms, enabling more accurate estimation of cardiac output, even accounting for age-related physiological differences. This innovation promises to enhance patient care by providing clinicians with timely and accurate information about cardiovascular function, aiding in the early detection of abnormalities, and supporting optimal treatment decisions tailored to individual patient needs.

Data collection and preprocessing are critical in developing this deep learning method for arterial pressure wave derived cardiac output monitoring. The process involves gathering arterial pressure waveforms from patients across different age groups and clinical conditions, typically using arterial catheterization or non-invasive blood pressure monitoring devices. These waveforms are then digitized and stored in a structured format for analysis. Preprocessing is essential to improve data quality and usability for deep learning algorithms, including steps like filtering to eliminate noise and artifacts, resampling

to maintain uniform time intervals between data points, and normalization to standardize the data range. By meticulously collecting and preprocessing data, researchers can create a robust and reliable deep learning-based cardiac output monitoring system that accurately reflects age-related variations and provides valuable insights into cardiovascular function across diverse patient populations.

a) **Loading datasets:** This stage involves loading the necessary datasets containing ABP and corresponding heart rate (HR) measurements into the system. These datasets can originate from various sources, including medical devices, clinical research studies, or simulated data, providing a comprehensive base for analysis.

b) **Pre-processing:** In the pre-processing stage, raw data from the datasets is cleaned and prepared for analysis. This includes removing noise, filtering out artifacts, and ensuring uniformity in data format. Techniques such as signal filtering, normalization, and artifact removal are employed to enhance data quality, making it suitable for subsequent analysis steps.

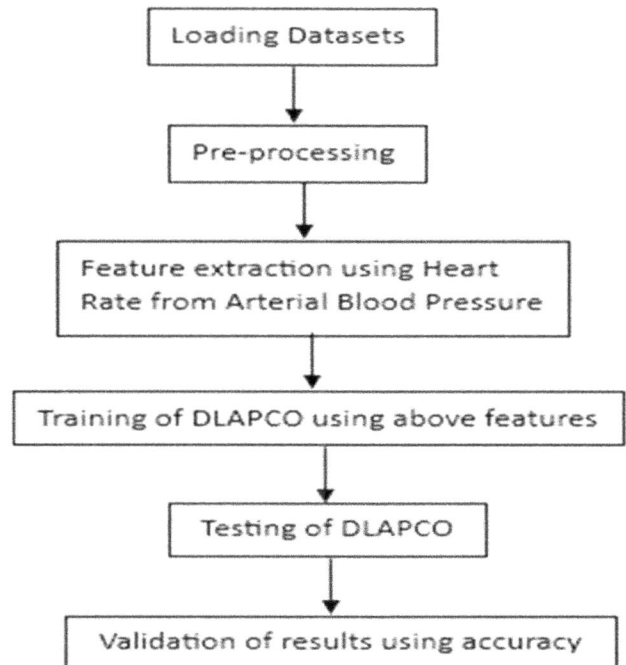

Figure 3.1 Architecture of proposed method
Source: Author

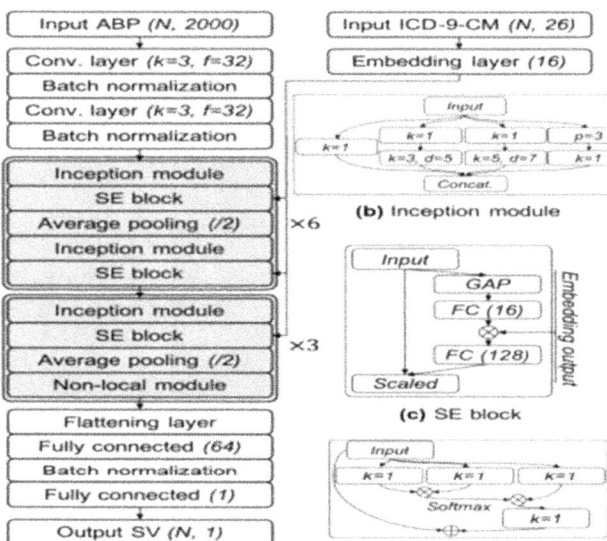

Figure 3.2 Block diagram of proposed method
Source: Author

c) **Feature extraction using heart rate from arterial blood pressure:** This step involves extracting key features from the pre-processed data, with a focus on utilizing heart rate information derived from arterial blood pressure signals. Extracted features may include statistical measures, frequency domain features, time-domain features, and other relevant parameters that reflect the underlying patterns and characteristics of the physiological signals. These features are crucial for the accurate modeling and prediction of cardiac output.

d) **Training of DLAPCO using the above features:** DLAPCO, which stands for deep learning algorithm for predicting cardiac output, involves training a deep learning model like a neural network architecture using the features extracted from heart rate information and arterial blood pressure signals. The model learns to predict cardiac output or other relevant cardiovascular parameters based on these input features. During training, the model is fed labeled data, and its parameters are optimized to minimize prediction errors.

e) **Testing of DLAPCO:** After training, the DLAPCO model is evaluated using separate datasets not involved in the training process. This phase assesses the model's generalization capability and its accuracy in predicting cardiac output or related parameters from unseen data. The model's predictions are compared against ground truth values to evaluate its effectiveness and performance.

f) **Validation of results using accuracy:** The final step involves validating the accuracy of the DLAPCO model's predictions with suitable evaluation metrics like accuracy, specificity, sensitivity and area under the curve (AUC). This validation phase compares the predicted values with actual measurements to evaluate the overall performance and reliability of proposed model. The validation results provide insights into the proposed method strengths, weaknesses, and areas for potential enhancement.

Results

The cardiac output is calculated by the below computations:

Max peak amplitude= 50, heart rate = length(peaks)*6, stroke volume = 70-(HR-70)/4, cardiac output = HR*SV.

If cardiac output is <=5000 *"No Disease"* is displayed else *"Disease"* is displayed.

<u>When disease is present:</u>
When disease is not present:

Conclusions

In conclusion, our work demonstrates the utilization of advanced deep learning methods to accurately predict cardiac output and other cardiovascular parameters from heart rate information and arterial blood pressure. By extracting key

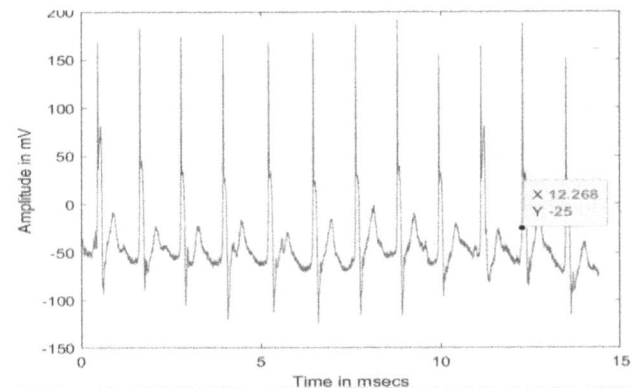

Figure 3.3 Input ECG signal
Source: Author

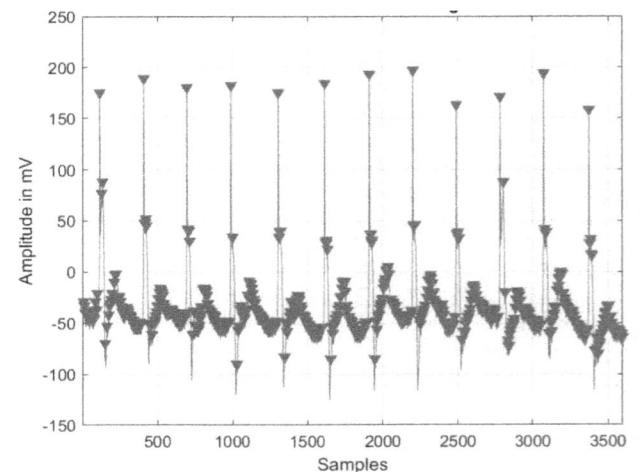

Figure 3.4 Extracted peaks of ECG signal
Source: Author

Command Window

out =

'Disease'

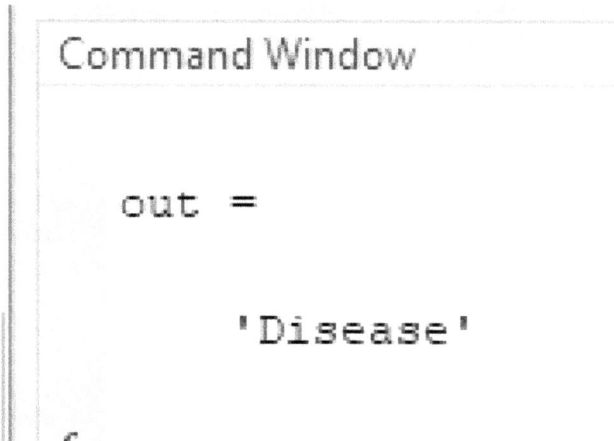

Figure 3.5 Output on command window
Source: Author

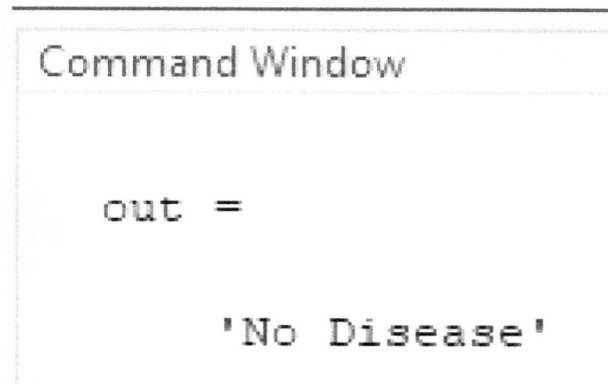

Figure 3.6 Input ECG signal
Source: Author

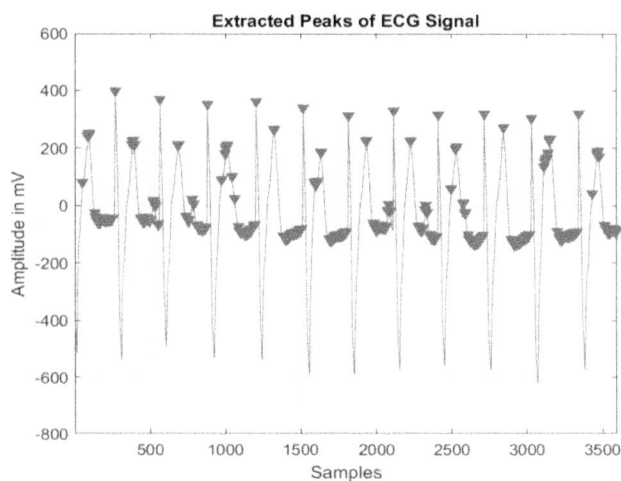

Figure 3.7 Extracted peaks of ECG signal
Source: Author

Command Window

out =

'No Disease'

Figure 3.8 Output on command window
Source: Author

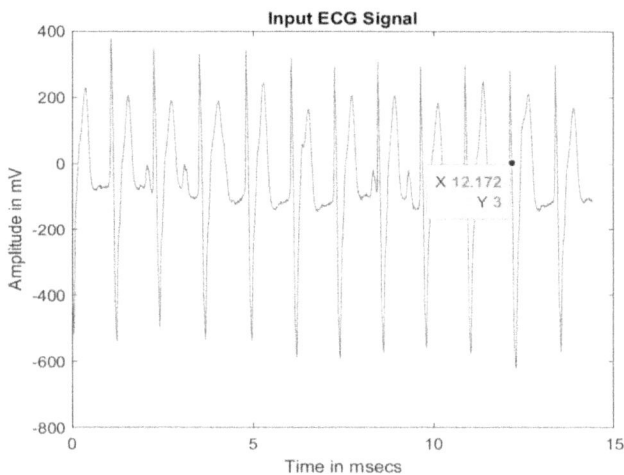

features and training a deep learning strategy, we have shown the potential for non-invasive, real-time monitoring of cardiac function. The Neura Flow project presents opportunities for further research and development in healthcare technology. Leveraging deep learning aims to enhance patient care, improve diagnostic accuracy, and advance cardiovascular monitoring systems. This represents a significant advancement in integrating deep learning into cardiac output monitoring, with the potential to transform healthcare practices and improve patient outcomes.

References

[1] Cecconi, M., Rhodes, P., Poloniecki, F., Della Rocca, A., and Grounds, R. M. (2009). Bench-to-bedside review: the importance of the precision of the reference technique in method comparison studies with specific reference to the measurement of cardiac output. *Critical Care*, 13, 1–6.
[2] Pinsky, M. (2007). Hemodynamic evaluation and monitoring in the ICU. *Chest*, 132(6), 2020–2029.
[3] Saugel, S., Vincent, D., and Critchley, A. (2014). Intraoperative and perioperative arterial pressure monitoring. *British Journal of Anesthesia*, 112(1), 38–49.
[4] Wang, X., Girshick, R., Gupta, A., and He, K. (2018). Non-local neural networks. In Proceedings of the IEEE Conference on Computer Vision and Pattern Recognition, (pp. 7794–7803).
[5] Liu, L., Jiang, H., He, P., Chen, W., Liu, X., Gao, J., et al. (2020). On the variance of the adaptive learning rate and beyond. In International Conference on Learning Representations.

[6] Szegedy, C., Liu, W., Jia, Y., Sermanet, P., Reed, S., Anguelov, D., et al. (2015). Going deeper with convolutions. In Proceedings of the IEEE Conference on Computer Vision and Pattern Recognition, (pp. 1–9).

[7] Donati, A., Colombo, F., Borghi, G., Casati, E., Pascarella, F., and Mistraletti, F. (2006). Optimization of perioperative hemodynamics: what is new?. *Best Practice and Research Clinical Anesthesiology*, 20(3), 489–502.

[8] Ravuri, V., Subbarao, M. V., Kumar, T. S., Kavitha, T. S., Sandeep, D. R., and Dangeti, L. (2023). Multi-cancer early detection and classification using machine learning based approaches. In 2023 Third International Conference on Advances in Electrical, Computing, Communication and Sustainable Technologies (ICAECT), Bhilai, India, (pp. 1–7). doi: 10.1109/ ICAECT57570.2023.10117816.

[9] Krishna, N. M. S., Priyakanth, R., Chandana, N. S., Sarica, M., Preethi, M. S., Sirisha, C. J. S., et al. (2021). Anegoo - no pain, only gain. In 2021 Asian Conference on Innovation in Technology (ASIANCON), Pune, India, (pp. 1–5). doi: 10.1109/ASIANCON51346.2021.9544597.

[10] Kumar, M. P., Ram, G. C., Ravuri, V., Subbarao, M. V., Abdul Rahaman, S. K., and Nandan, T. P. K. (2024). Performance evaluation of machine learning models for multi-class lung cancer detection. In 4th International Conference on Pervasive Computing and Social Networking (ICPCSN) 2024, ISBN: 979-8-3503-8634-9/24, DOI: 10.1109/ICPCSN62568.2024.00071.

[11] Krishna, N. M. S., Priyakanth, R., Katta, M. B., Akanksha, K., and Anche, N. Y. (2023). CNN-based breast cancer detection. In Reddy, K. A., Devi, B. R., George, B., Raju, K. S., and Sellathurai, M. (Eds.). Proceedings of Fourth International Conference on Computer and Communication Technologies. Lecture Notes in Networks and Systems, (vol. 606). Singapore: Springer. https:// doi.org/10.1007/978-981-19-8563-8_.59.

[12] Kavitha, T. S., and Prasad, D. S. (2022). A novel method of compressive sensing MRI reconstruction based on sandpiper optimization algorithm

(SPO) and mask regionbased convolution neural network (mask RCNN). *Multimedia Tools and Applications*, 81, 31469–31492. https://doi. org/10.1007/s11042-022-12940-x.

[13] Yang, H. L., Lee, H. C., Jung, C. W., and Kim, M. S. (2020). A deep learning method for intraoperative age-agnostic and disease-specific cardiac output monitoring from arterial blood pressure. In 2020 IEEE 20th International Conference on Bioinformatics and Bioengineering (BIBE), (pp. 662–666). IEEE.

[14] Domino, K. B., Bowdle, T. A., Posner, K. L., Spitellie, P. H., Lee, L. A., and Cheney, F. W. (2004). Injuries and liability related to central vascular catheters: a closed claims analysis. *The Journal of the American Society of Anesthesiologists*, 100(6), 1411–1418.

[15] Manecke, G. R. (2005). Edwards FloTrac sensor and vigileo monitor: easy, accurate, reliable cardiac output assessment using the arterial pulse wave. *Expert Review of Medical Devices*, 2(5), 523–527.

[16] Bendjelid, K., Marx, G., Kiefer, N., Simon, T., Geisen, M., Hoeft, A., et al. (2013). Performance of a new pulse contour method for continuous cardiac output monitoring: validation in critically ill patients. *British Journal of Anesthesia*, 111(4), 573–579.

[17] Slagt, C., Malagon, I., and Groeneveld, A. (2014). Systematic review of uncalibrated arterial pressure waveform analysis to determine cardiac output and stroke volume variation. *British Journal of Anesthesia*, 112(4), 626–637.

[18] Moon, Y.-J., Moon, H. S., Kim, D.-S., Kim, J.-M., Lee, J.-K., and Shim, W.-H. (2019). Deep learning-based strokeVolume estimation outperforms conventional arterial contour method inpatients with hemodynamic instability. *Journal of Clinical Medicine*, 8(9), 1419.

[19] Lee, H.-C., and Jung, C.-W. (2018). Vital recorder free research tool for automatic recording of high-resolution time-synchronized physiological data from multiple anesthesia devices. *Scientific Reports*, 8(1), 1–8.

4 A comparative performance analysis of support vector machine and custom spectral CNN for hyperspectral image classification

Sumalatha Madugula[1,a], K. Hari Krishna[1,b], Shravani Medicherla[2,c], Radha Peethala[2,d], Varshitha Paravathini[2,e] and Ramya Mudragalla[2,f]

[1]Assistant Professor, Department of ECE, Shri Vishnu Engineering College for Women Bhimavaram, Andhra Pradesh, India

[2]Student, Department of ECE, Shri Vishnu Engineering College for Women Bhimavaram, Andhra Pradesh, India

Abstract

The field of hyperspectral imaging continues to be highly relevant today due to its ability to provide specified spectral intelligence among a wide scale of wavelengths. Its applications can be observed in prominent fields like remote sensing, geological mapping, medical imaging, agriculture, environment monitoring, security and defense, etc. Here, in this paper we concentrate on the classification of these images with support of traditional machine learning ML) algorithms and deep learning (DL) methods and comparing their performance metrics. Each of the techniques have their own set of pros and cons but in our project, we consider two approaches which are support vector machine (SVM) which is a ML algorithm and custom spectral convolutional neural network (CSCNN) which is a deep learning network. SVM is a supervised machine learning algorithm. Implementation is done by first preprocessing the hyperspectral data using a 2D Gaussian filter after which the SVM classifier is trained on the filtered data which finally gives the classification results. In case of the CSCNN technique, the network is defined with 17 various types of layers. The input hyperspectral data is preprocessed, trained and finally classified. The training of the network is performed using three different optimizers like adaptive moment estimation (ADAM), root mean square propagation (RMS Prop), and stochastic gradient descent with momentum (SGDM) are optimization algorithms used in machine learning. The Indian Pines Dataset is utilized for the analysis, and the performance parameters being examined include accuracy, classification map, and precision., recall, F1 score and confusion matrix. The results show that performance of CSCNN (accuracy = 0.99556) is slightly better than that of SVM (accuracy = 0.95996) with a difference of 3.56%.

Keywords: Accuracy, classification, CSCNN, deep learning, hyperspectral imaging, machine learning algorithms, preprocessing, spectral information, SVM

Introduction

Satellite imaging refers to the process of capturing images of the Earth's surface, atmosphere, or other celestial bodies using remote sensing satellites orbiting the Earth. These satellites are equipped with various sensors, including cameras, radar, and multispectral imagers, which collect data across different wavelengths of light. Hyperspectral imaging (HSI) is an advanced technique used to collect and process information throughout the electromagnetic spectrum in a broad range. Unlike traditional imaging methods that capture data within specific wavelengths (such as red, green, and blue bands in perceptible light), hyperspectral imaging divides the spectrum into hundreds or even There are numerous narrow and adjacent bands that offer precise spectral data for every pixel in an image. The process involves Taking a sequence of pictures, each representing a narrow band of wavelengths across the entire spectrum. They are then combined to form a hyperspectral cube, where each

[a]suma.sekhar4@gmail.com, [b]harikrishna.kharidu@gmail.com, [c]shravanimedicherla56167@gmail.com, [d]radhapeethala264@gmail.com, [e]varshithachowdary31@gmail.com, [f]mudragallaramya28@gmail.com

DOI: 10.1201/9781003616399-4

pixel contains a spectrum of information rather than just color values.

When it comes to the images or data that we receive through satellite imaging, artificial satellites capture images that contain high spectral, high temporal [12] and high spatial resolutions [11]. Spectral resolution and wavelength range for bands or channels are proportional to each other, that is they depend on each other. These characteristics classify remote sensing images.

Hyperspectral images enable the detection of items that are not visible to single bandwidth imaging sensors due to their inclusion of hundreds of bands/channels. It specifies the spectral characteristics of the region that the pixels belong to and records its intensity. Red-green-blue (RGB) images were captured by traditional cameras with different spectral bands or wavelengths. With the progress of time, multispectral sensors were introduced for recording over multiple wavelength channels known as the "hyperspectral sensors". These sensors contain detailed information about the image with various wavelengths. Hyperspectral datasets have more complexity, and they can be influenced by many factors like atmospheric conditions, vegetation cover, etc.

The objective of the artificial intelligence subfields ML and DL is to enhance the capability of machines to make predictions and acquire knowledge from data. Yet, they differ in their approaches, architecture, and capabilities. ML involves Techniques which allows systems to use data to learn from and forecast or decide what to do. These algorithmic processes are designed to extract relationships and patterns from either labeled or unlabeled features. Regarding classical machine learning, feature engineering exists critical process in which specialists in a certain field manually select pertinent characteristics from raw data. These characteristics are then transformed in a manner that is suitable for the machine learning algorithms to process. DL, instead, is a branch of ML that makes use of multi-layered artificial neural networks. Those neural networks are designed to instantly learn hierarchical data representations directly from raw input. DL models can instantly learn pertinent features doing away with the requirement for human feature engineering [7]. The main aim is to observe the differences in the performances

of SVM classifier [5] which is a ML algorithm and Custom Spectral CNN which is a DL network.

Classification Models and Design Analysis

The SVM is a supervised learning technique used for classification and regression tasks. SVM Employment very well for binary classification issues in classification although it can be expandable to multiclass classification as well. Finding the hyperplane in the feature space that best divides the data points into distinct classes is the fundamental notion behind the SVM. The hyperplane is selected to optimize the margin, which is the distance between the hyperplane and the closest data points (support vectors) for every class. SVM works best when the data is linearly separable, meaning it can be separated into two classes using a straight line (or hyperplane in higher dimensions). However, SVM can also be used with nonlinear data by employing kernel tricks, which map the input features into a higher dimensional space where the data may be linearly separable. SVM can employ many kernel functions such as linear, polynomial, Radial Basis Function, or sigmoid kernels. All kernels allow SVM to allow non-linear decision boundaries by totally mapping the data features within a higher dimensional space in which the data may become linearly separable. SVM can be costly to compute, particularly for massive data sets, as the time additionally memory complexity of training the model can grow quadratically or even cubically with the number of data points. However, with advancements in optimization techniques and hardware, SVM can still be applied to large-scale problems [8]. Overall, SVM is a is a robust and flexible algorithm for classification tasks and it capable of dealing with both linear and non-linear data, robustness to overfitting, and effectiveness in high dimensional spaces.

So, in the first classification method using a SVM classifier, the hyperspectral data loaded. The dataset used here is the Indian Pines dataset. Ground truth labels for the same are loaded, indicating the class of each pixel in the image. Preprocessing steps are applied, including removing the water absorption bands and filtering the data using a 2D Gaussian filter [2]. The training and testing procedure is performed for three different dataset scenarios which are: (i) 90% training and 10%

testing dataset, (ii) 80% training and 20% testing dataset and (iii) 70% training and 30% testing dataset. The training part comes next where the classifier is trained to determine the ideal hyperplane for dividing several classes and predict the labels of test data. A flow of the SVM classifier classification work is provided in Figure 4.1.

Deep neural network method is intended for handling grid input, like images is CNN. Convolutional, pooling, and fully connected layers are the basic building blocks of CNN. The CNNs are well-suited for visual data analysis and contain many real time applications such as crop analysis, geological mapping, agriculture identification, image processing techniques, hyperspectral imaging, [4] etc. The method that we next implement for classification is a special version of CNN that is, a Custom Spectral Convolutional Neural Network (CSCNN) which is a more advanced one because of its significant

features which hold the meaningful channels and remove the unnecessary ones. The CSCNN Architecture consists of five primary layers which are as follows:

Convolutional layer
A convolutional layer is designed to efficiently recognize spatial hierarchies of features in input data, particularly images. Convolutional layers use kernels to scan across input data, executing convolution functions to extract local patterns. In general, consider an input image of dimensions Win × Hin, where F is the field size (width and height) of filters, S is the stride of the convolution operation (how much the filter moves) and P is the amount of zero padding added with input volume. Then, convolutional layer result will have the following dimensions with Wout × Hout given by

$$\text{Wout} = \frac{Win-F+2P}{S} + 1 \qquad (1)$$

$$\text{Hout} = \frac{Hin-F+2P}{S} + 1 \qquad (2)$$

Fully connected layer
Each neuron in this layer transmits its output to every neuron in the following layer after receiving input from every neuron in the layer before it. It consists of weights and bias vectors. Equation (3) depicts the mathematical equation for a fully connected layer.

$$Y = Wx + b \qquad (3)$$

where Y denotes the output, X is the input of the layer, W is Weight matrix and is the bias vector.

Figure 4.2 A ReLU layer, which is also known as Rectified Linear Unit, is an active function implemented

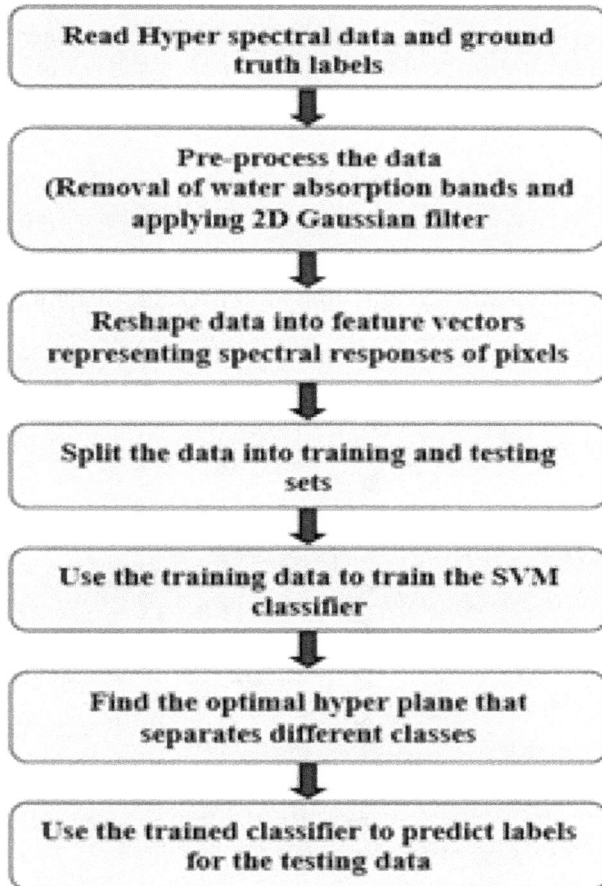

Figure 4.1 Workflow using SVM classifier
Source: Author

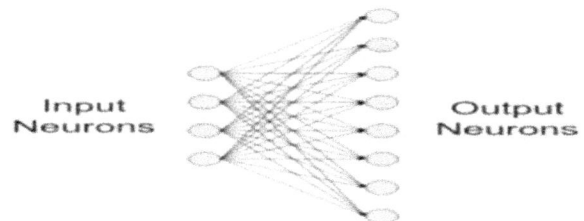

Figure 4.2 Fully connected layer structure ReLU layer
Source: Author

at output of a neural network layer. ReLU function presents non-linearity to the model. This function is

$$ReLU(x) = \max(0, x) \qquad (4)$$

Dropout layer

A dropout layer is a regularization layer preferred in neural networks to prevent overfitting [14]. Figure 4.3 shows the functioning by randomly dropping (0) a fraction of the neurons during each training iteration. It aids in mitigating excessive reliance on the network on specific neurons, also supports more robust feature learning. The Equation of dropout operation can be expressed in terms of dropout rate 'q' which is given by:

$$q = 1 - p \qquad (5)$$

where p represents the probability of dropping out of a neuron.

Softmax layer

Softmax layer converts the raw output of the network, often referred to as scores, into a probability distribution across multiple classes. The Result values produced by the soft-max function represent the probabilities that an input with respect to each class. The soft-max function is defined as follows for a vector:

$$\text{Softmax}(Z_j) = \frac{e^{z_j}}{\sum_{k=1}^{K} e^{z_k}} \text{ for } j = 1, \ldots, k \qquad (6)$$

The final CSCNN architecture consists of 17 layers of all these types of layers mentioned earlier. The input layer has a dimension of 25 × 25 × 3 and the input image must be resized accordingly. Figure 4.4 shows the architecture of CSCNN in a simplified form. Additionally, while training we

also make use of optimizers like ADAM, SGDM and RMSprop [3]. Optimizers modify the neural networks parameters including learning rates and weights to lower the losses.

Adaptive moment estimation (ADAM)

Maintains adaptive learning rate for each parameter by considering both average part gradient and average of past squared gradient [15]. This adaptability helps ADAM to perform well across deep learning tasks. The mathematical representation for the same is given by:

$$n_t = \alpha1.n_{t-1} + (1-\alpha1).h_t \qquad (7)$$
$$u_t = \alpha2.u_{t-1} + (1-\alpha2).h_t2 \qquad (8)$$

where n_t and u_t indicate moving averages having default values of 0.9 and 0.999 respectively and h_t is gradient on current mini batch.

Stochastic gradient descent with momentum

It acts as a variant of the standard SGD algorithm. This SGDM method maintains a record of the exponentially decreasing moving average of previous gradients. It helps increase the convergence and improve the robustness of the optimization process. Mathematically, it is represented as:

$$V_t = \Omega.V_{t-1} + (1 - \Omega) \nabla_w M(A, B, c) \qquad (9)$$
$$A = A - \alpha V_t \qquad (10)$$

where M represents loss function, A represents gradient w.r.t weight and α represents learning rate.

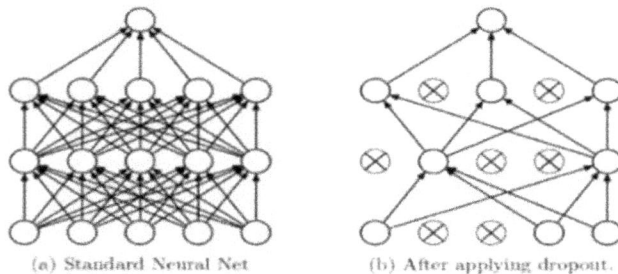

Figure 4.3 Structure after applying dropout
Source: Author

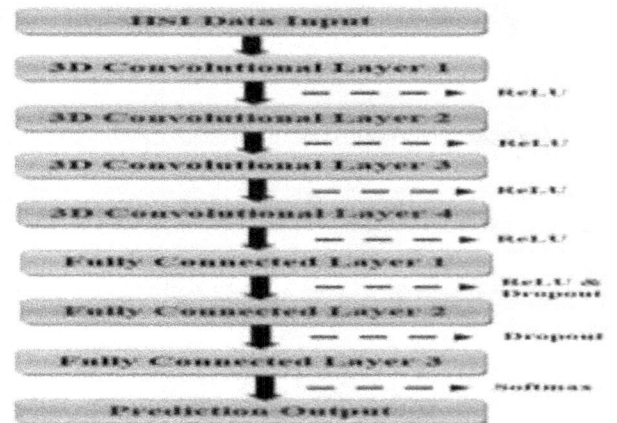

Figure 4.4 Custom spectral CNN architecture
Source: Author

Root mean square propagation

The optimizer RMSPROP can be used in training neural networks and is designed to address some of the limitations of the basic SGD algorithm particularly with respect to adapting learning rates for different parameters during training. Let gt denote the gradients at time step t, and β denote the decay rate. Then it is given by:

$$vt = \beta.vt{-}1 + (1 - \beta) gt2 \qquad (11)$$

In short, RMSProp computes a rapidly decreasing mean of past squared gradients and divides the current gradient by the square root of this average before updating the parameters. This allows RMSProp to adapt the learning rate separately to every value with magnitude of its gradients. In Implementation part, first load the hyperspectral data. The dataset used here is Indian Pines dataset. Then data is preprocessed by decreasing the number of spectral bands employing principal component analysis (PCA) [6] and normalizing the image data. Then hyperspectral image is split into patches of size 25-by-25 pixels with 30 channels, and corresponding labels are extracted. The training and testing data is split and performed for three different dataset scenarios which are: (i) 90% training and 10% testing dataset, (ii) 80% training and 20% testing dataset and (iii) 70% training and 30% testing dataset. Next, the CSCNN network layers are defined and trained as per the training options specified (learning rate, max epoch, optimizer, batch size, etc.). Finally, the output is given for the various optimizers and training-testing data proportions.

Dataset: Indian pines dataset

This dataset stands as a prominent benchmark within the realm of hyperspectral imaging. It was obtained using the airborne visible/infrared imaging spectrometer (AVARIS) sensor, Figure 4.5 shows the covering the Indian Pines test site situated in northwestern Indiana, USA. With 220 spectral bands, this dataset provides extensive spectral information. It boasts a spatial resolution of 145 pixels in both width and height, constituting a 2D grid of dimensions 145 × 145 pixels.

Table 4.1 show a glimpse of the labelled classes of this data.

Table 4.1 Indian pines dataset classes

Sr. No	Class	Samples
1	Alfalfa	46
2	Corn-notill	1428
3	Corn-mintill	830
4	Corn	237
5	Grass pasture	483
6	Grass trees	730
7	Grass pasture mowed	28
8	Hay windrowed	478
9	Oats	20
10	Soybean-notill	972
11	Soybean-mintill	2455
12	Soybean clean	593
13	Wheat	205
14	Woods	1265
15	Buildings Grass Trees Drives	386
16	Stone Steel Towers	93

Source: Author

In this dataset, there are 16 classes, such as corn, alfalfa, grass, trees, and different classifications of soil and man-made structures. Complementing the hyperspectral imagery are ground truth labels [10], delineating the class of each pixel and thereby identifying the vegetation or terrain characteristics within the scene. While using this dataset for the classification purpose, first load the raw dataset in the workspace. This dataset is then preprocessed by converting it into an RGB [13] image and then followed by reshaping, filtering, normalization, etc. The ground truth labels are then associated with this modified data for training.

Experimental Results

The implementation of this project is done using the MATLAB R2023b software. The Indian Pines dataset is available in MATLAB itself in the Image Processing Toolbox of Hyperspectral Imaging Library. It makes it easy to load both the raw and ground truth label data without downloading additional material.

Performance metrics

For any type of classification task done using machine learning or deep learning, consider some basic performance metrics that are core to all the models. They are:

i. Accuracy:

$$Accuracy = \frac{Number\ of\ Correct\ Predictions}{Total\ number\ of\ Predictions} \qquad (12)$$

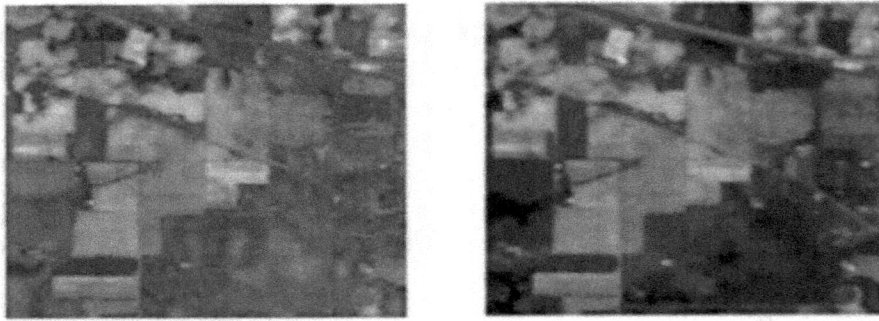

Figure 4.5 Indian pines raw data and RGB data
Source: Author

ii. Precision:

$$Precision = \frac{True\ Positives}{True\ Positives + False\ Positives} \quad (13)$$

iii Recall:

$$Recall = \frac{True\ Positives}{True\ Positives + False\ Negatives} \quad (14)$$

iv. F1 Score:

$$F1\ Score = 2 * \frac{Precision * Recall}{Precision + Recall} \quad (15)$$

v. True positive rate (sensitivity): Percentage with positive objects is identified correctly by the classifier.

vi. True negative rate (specificity): Percentage with negative objects are identified correctly by the classifier.

vii. False positive rate: The percentage of negative objects that are incorrectly classified by the classifier.

viii. False negative rate: The percentage of positive objects that are incorrectly classified by the classifier.

Results for SVM Classifier

After training the dataset with SVM classifier, Figure 4.6. shows the predicted classification image. The figure shows the ground truth classification and predicted classification images. Similarly, Table 4.2 shows the other performance metrics specified earlier followed by a confusion matrix obtained for the classified results which is shown in Figure 4.7.

The confusion matrix is a tabular representation with evaluation of a classification approaches.

Ground Truth Map | SVM Classification Map

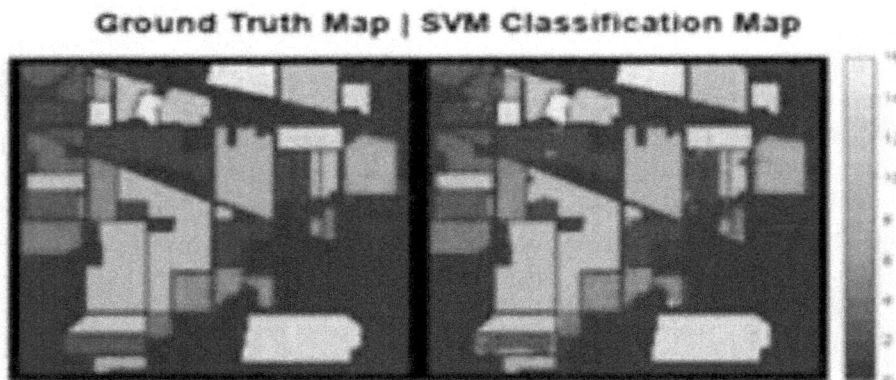

Figure 4.6 Ground truth map and SVM classification map
Source: Author

Table 4.2 SVM classifier performance metrics

SVM Classifier Performance Metrics						
Training Rate (%)	Accuracy	Precision	Recall	F1 Score	Sensitivity	Specificity
90%	95.996	0.968531	0.994794	0.996538	0.994794	0.999869
80%	94.756	0.987769	0.997394	0.997563	0.997394	0.999838
70%	95.068	0.978413	0.989513	0.993688	0.989513	0.999863

Source: Author

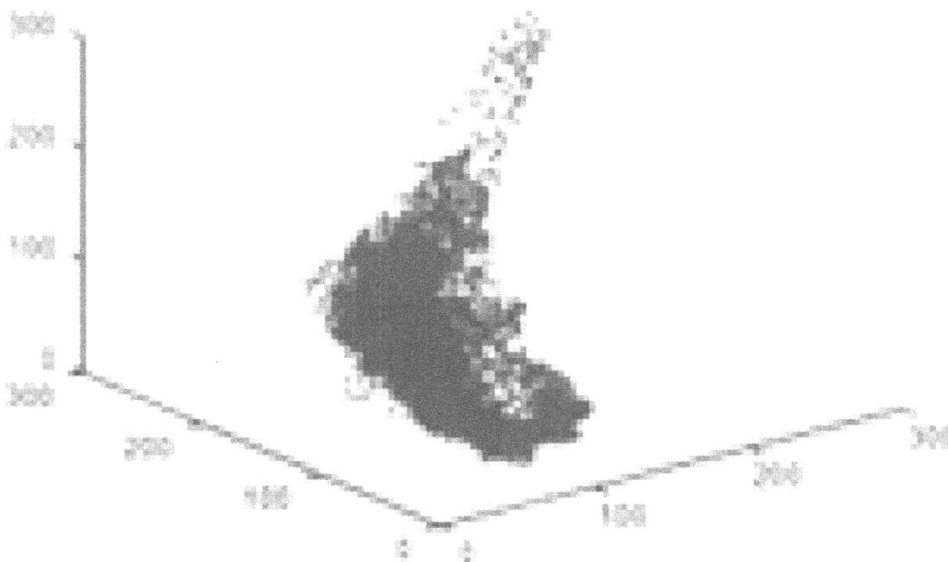

Every matrix row signifies the actual class, then every column signifies the predicted class. Each cell in confusion matrix represents the number of instances classified as a certain class. Figure 4.8 shows the hyperspectral plane which represents the feature space of the hyperspectral data.

In a 3D scatter plot is created to visualize the feature vectors of the test data in the hyperspectral plane. Each point in the plot represents a data point in the feature space. Figure 4.9 The

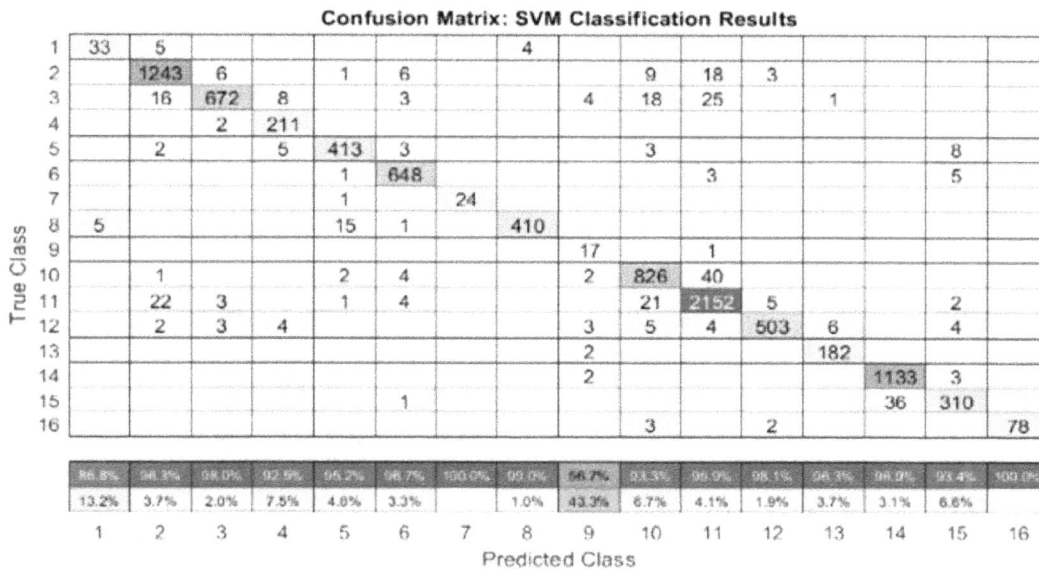

Confusion Matrix: SVM Classification Results

True Class \ Predicted Class	1	2	3	4	5	6	7	8	9	10	11	12	13	14	15	16
1	33	5						4								
2		1243	6		1	6				9	18	3				
3		16	672	8		3			4	18	25		1			
4			2	211												
5		2		5	413	3				3					8	
6					1	648					3				5	
7					1		24									
8	5				15	1		410								
9									17		1					
10		1			2	4			2	826	40					
11		22	3		1	4				21	2152	5			2	
12		2	3	4					3	5	4	503	6		4	
13									2				182			
14									2					1133	3	
15						1								36	310	
16										3		2				78
	86.8%	98.3%	98.0%	92.9%	95.2%	96.7%	100.0%	99.0%	56.7%	93.3%	96.9%	98.1%	96.3%	96.9%	93.4%	100.0%
	13.2%	3.7%	2.0%	7.5%	4.8%	3.3%		1.0%	43.3%	6.7%	4.1%	1.9%	3.7%	3.1%	6.6%	

Figure 4.7 SVM classification confusion matrix
Source: Author

Figure 4.8 SVM hyperplane
Source: Author

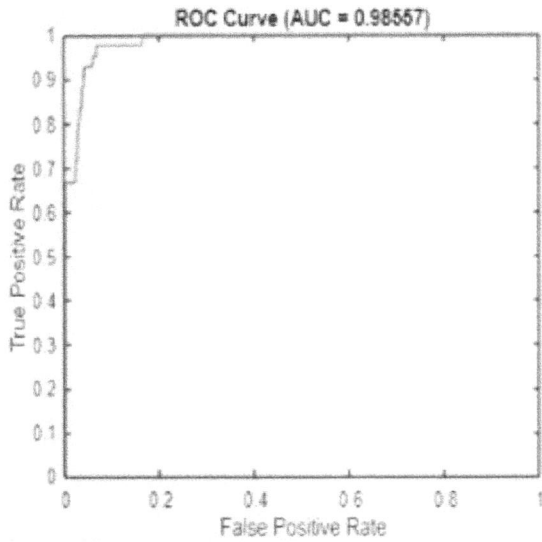

Figure 4.9 SVM ROC area
Source: Author

ROC curve provides visual representation to illustrate the capability of a binary classifier system to accurately classify data as the threshold for discrimination is adjusted.

Results for CSCNN Network

After training the dataset with CSCNN network, the predicted classification images after training with ADAM, RMSProp, SGDM optimizers is as shown in Figures 4.10. 4.11 and 4.12 respectively.

Conclusion

After the entire classification analysis and comparison of performance metrics, we find that CSCNN has a better performance capacity for the classification of hyperspectral images than

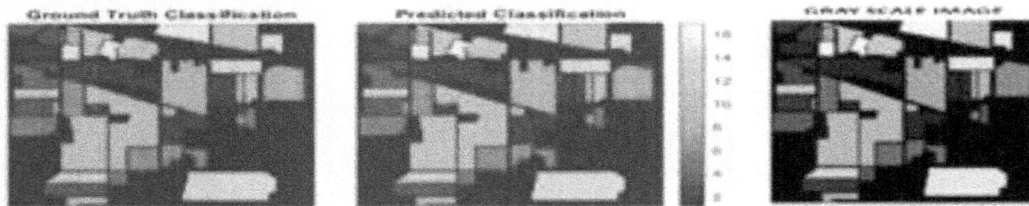

Figure 4.10 Ground truth map predicted classification map and gray scale image for ADAM
Source: Author

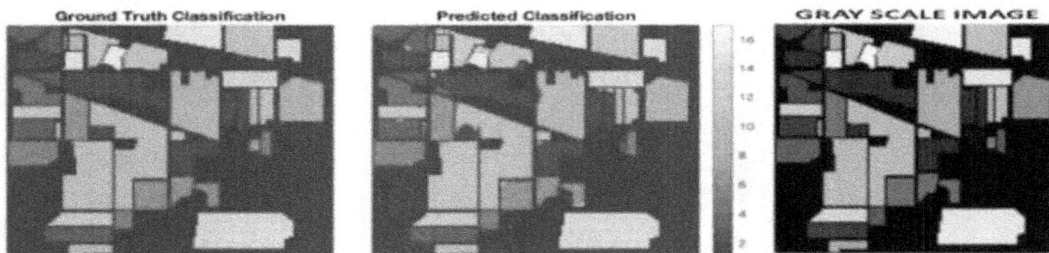

Figure 4.11 Ground truth map predicted classification map and gray scale image for RMSProp
Source: Author

Figure 4.12 Ground truth map predicted classification map and gray scale image for SGDM. Table 4.3 shows the other performance metrics as specified earlier followed by the confusion matrix obtained for the CSCNN network results in Figure 4.13
Source: Author

Table 4.3 Comparison of performances of different optimizers when trained with CSCNN

CSCNN NETWORK PERFORMANCE METRICS									
Optimizer	ADAM			RMSProp			SGDM		
Training Rate(%)	90%	80%	70%	90%	80%	70%	90%	80%	70%
Accuracy	0.9956	0.99512	0.995	0.96607	0.9658	0.965	0.23794	0.23794	0.23794
Precision	1	1	1	1	1	1	0.2386	0.2386	0.2386
Recall	1	1	1	1	1	1	0.845	0.845	0.845
F1 Score	1	1	1	1	1	1	0.654	0.654	0.654
Sensitivity	1	1	1	1	1	1	0.573	0.573	0.573
Specificity	1	1	1	1	1	1	0.477	0.477	0.477
Area under ROC Curve	0.5137	0.51366	0.514	0.52478	0.52478	0.52478	0.75726	0.75726	0.75726

Source: Author

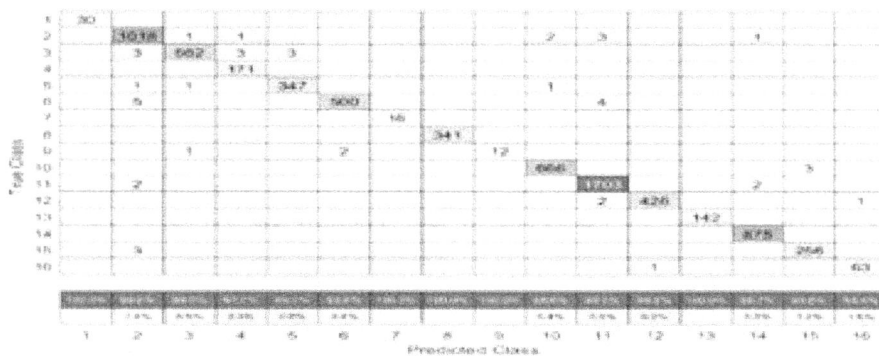

Figure 4.13 CSCNN classification confusion matrix (ADAM)
Source: Author

SVM classifier. This can also be observed in their accuracies achieved for each model, which is 99.556% for CSCNN and 95.996% for the SVM classifier. CSCNN is specifically designed for processing hyperspectral images, which may provide advantages over traditional classifiers like SVM. The reasons that explain as to why CSCNN might have better performance metrics than a SVM classifier for hyperspectral image classification may contribute to complex patterns, feature hierarchies, spatial spectral information fusion, data augmentation and model capacity which contribute to a better performance than any traditional machine learning algorithm. The future scope of CSCNN is the essence of their existence resides in potential for advancing hyperspectral image analysis through the advancement of enhanced efficiency, interpretable, domain-specific designs tailored for real-time processing and integration with multi-modal data.

References

[1] Kumar, M. S., Keerthi, V., Anjnai, R. N., Sarma, M. M., and Bothale, V. (2020). Evalution of machine learning methods for hyperspectral image classification. In 2020 IEEE India Geoscience and Remote Sensing Symposium (InGARSS), Ahmedabad, India, (pp. 225–228).

[2] Zhong, S., Chang, C.-I., and Zhang, Y. (2018). Iterative support vector machine for hyperspectral image classification. In 2018 25th IEEE International Conference on Image Processing (ICIP), Athens, Greece, (pp. 3309–3312).

[3] De Oliveira, J. P., Costa, M. G. F., and Filho, C. (2020). Methodology of data fusion using deep learning for semantic segmentation of land types in the Amazon. *IEEE Access*, 8, 187864–187875.

[4] Tun, N. L., Gavrilov, A., Tun, N. M., Trieu, D. M., and Aung, H. (2021). Hyperspectral remote sensing images classification using fully convolutional neural network. In 2021 IEEE Conference of Russian Young Researchers in Electrical and

Electronic Engineering (ElConRus), St. Petersburg, Moscow, Russia, (pp. 2166–2170).

[5] Venkata Subbarao, M., Pravallika, C., Ramesh Varma, D., and Prema Kumar, M. (2022). Power quality event classification using wavelets, decision trees and SVM classifiers. In 9th International Conference on Innovations in Electronics and Communication Engineering (ICIECE 2021), Lecture Notes in Networks and Systems LNNS Series, (Vol. 355, pp. 245–251), (Springer Book Chapter) DOI:10.1007/978-981-16-8512-5_27.

[6] Roy, M. K., Mishu, S. Z., and Mamun, M. A. (2021). Spectral and spatial feature extraction using folded PCA and convolutional neural network for effective hyperspectral image classification. In 2021 5th International Conference on Electrical Information and Communication Technology (EICT), Khulna, Bangladesh, (pp. 1–6).

[7] Ahmad, M., Shabbir, S., Roy, S. K., Hong, D., Wu, X., Yao, J., et al. (2022). Hyperspectral image classification—traditional to deep models: a survey for future prospects. *IEEE Journal of Selected Topics in Applied Earth Observations and Remote Sensing*, 15, 968–999.

[8] Li, H. (2021). An overview on remote sensing image classification methods with a focus on support vector machine. In 2021 International Conference on Signal Processing and Machine Learning (CONF-SPML), Stanford, CA, USA, (pp. 50–56).

[9] Chauhan, N. K., and Singh, K. (2018). A review on conventional machine learning vs deep learning. In 2018 International Conference on Computing, Power and Communication Technologies (GUCON), Greater Noida, India, (pp. 347–352).

[10] Prema Kumar, M., Ravi Kumar, P., Ganeswara Rao, M. V., Ravuri, V., and Narasimha Rao, P. (2023). Performance evaluation of multi-class classification based detection of CoViD-19 using machine learning algorithms. *Journal of Harbin Engineering University*, 44(11), 844–854. ISSN: 1006-7043.

[11] Adibi, S. A., Karami, A., Heylen, R., and Schreuders, P. (2016). Optical solutions for improving spatial resolution of hyperspectral sensors. In 2016 8th Workshop on Hyperspectral Image and Signal Processing: Evolution in Remote Sensing (WHISPERS), Los Angeles, CA, USA, (pp. 1–4).

[12] Gevaert, C. M., Suomalainen, J., Tang, J., and Kooistra, L. (2015). Generation of spectral–temporal response surfaces by combining multispectral satellite and hyperspectral UAV imagery for precision agriculture applications. *IEEE Journal of Selected Topics in Applied Earth Observations and Remote Sensing*, 8(6), 3140–3146.

[13] Fu, Y., Zheng, Y., Huang, H., Sato, I., and Sato, Y. (2018). Hyperspectral image super-resolution with a mosaic RGB image. *IEEE Transactions on Image Processing*, 27(11), 5539–5552.

[14] Sanjar, K., Rehman, A., Paul, A., and Jeong Hong, K. (2020). Weight dropout for preventing neural networks from overfitting. In 2020 8th International Conference on Orange Technology (ICOT), Daegu, Korea (South), (pp. 1–4).

[15] Krishna, K. P. R., Duvvuri, E. C., Kumar, M. P., Madamanchi, V. B. R., Balaji, T., and Chowdary, K. U. (2023). Detection of casing laceration using dense CNN. *Journal of Theoretical and Applied Information Technology (JATIT)*, 101(24), 8277–8282. ISSN: 1992-8645.

5 IoT based energy efficient air conditioning system using machine learning

Vishal Reddy, G.[a], Sai Mohith, G.[b], Ritesh Varma, G.[c], Praveen Kumar, D.[d], Prem Kumar Deepak, S.[e], and Vivek, D.[f]

Department of Computer Science and Engineering, B V Raju Institute of Technology, Narsapur, Medak, Telangana, India

Abstract

The demand for intelligent devices of indoor and outdoor living environments keeps increasing with the improvement of technologies. One such technology is smart air conditioner control system. Our work proposes a smart air conditioning system leveraging the Internet of Things (IoT) to optimize both energy efficiency and thermal comfort in indoor environments. However, the present method of manually operating the Air conditioner will not give comfortable indoor environment, moreover excessive cooling chosen by users may also become as the negative side effect toward the person's health. Machine learning models like linear regression models are used to make the air conditioning system more energy efficient based on data collected by DHT11 temperature sensor. The integration of machine learning models allow the system to predict temperature changes and proactively adjust settings to maintain optimal comfort levels. This efficient usage is helpful in increasing the lifespan of the air conditioner while reducing the maintenance cost and electricity cost.

Keywords: Air conditioner, DHT11 temperature and humidity sensor, internet of things, IR blaster, linear regression model

Introduction

Smart technology has brought about a huge demand for tech solutions that improve our lives indoors and outdoors. In recent years, many researchers around the world have put more effort into the field of thermal comfort which is due to the expanded public argument about the environmental change. In general, thermal comfort and evaluation of the indoor environmental quality depends on human physiological and psychological responses to the surrounding environment. One key invention considering these issues is smart air conditioning. It controls energy use and keeps indoor areas just right. Traditional air conditioners focus on a user- defined temperature, which leads to excessive energy usage and discomfort. That leads to fussiness and could even harm user health if we use too much cooling.

A solution to this problem might be this project: a smart air conditioner system based on Internet of Things (IoT) technology which uses linear regression machine learning algorithm to predict ideal temperatures. The primary goal is to design a smart air conditioner system that uses IoT technology and machine learning algorithm in predicting optimal temperature for a room to reduce the potential health risks of the user. The system will neither compromise user comfort nor use much electric power. It will work by adjusting the settings of the air conditioner based on real time temperature data in order to ensure the right balance between comfort and energy efficiency.

We employ linear regression models to improve the energy efficiency of the air conditioning system. This model looks at data generated by DHT11 sensors so that the system can understand and adapt to usage patterns and environmental conditions. This system does not wait for temperatures to change but proactively predicts them, adjusting settings accordingly using IR Blaster which acts as a communication bridge

[a]visureddy05@gmail.com, [b]guntupallysaimohith@gmail.com, [c]griteshvarma@gmail.com, [d]gound39132@gmail.com, [e]deepak.s@bvrit.ac.in, [f]vivek.d@bvrit.ac.in

DOI: 10.1201/9781003616399-5

between the system and the air conditioner, and ensuring not just convenience of the user but minimum wastage of electricity.

This system can combine renewable energy sources as well as other smart home products, establishing a model for future advancements in sustainable, automated home environments. The use of real-time data to maintain optimal performance provides insight into the future of intelligent systems capable of adapting to changing human needs and environmental conditions.

To sum up, this system offers a promising approach to revolutionizing traditional air conditioner operation. With the integration of IoT and machine learning technologies (linear regression model), The smart air conditioning control represents a significant leap forward in indoor climate management. The proposed system fosters a smarter and more sustainable approach to temperature control, promoting user comfort while minimizing energy consumption.

Literature Survey

Kumar et al. [1] proposed an internet-of-things temperature-based fan speed controller by connecting a variety of sensors and hardware elements. This technology will automatically regulate the cooling system based on the room temperature. The fan speed is controlled by the microcontroller by data from the DHT 11 temperature sensor, which measures the ambient temperature. Fan speed is adjusted via the pulse width modulation (PWM) technology. This closed loop feed- back control system is made more dependable and efficient using embedded technology. The primary reason they proposed this effort was to improve the safety aspects for coalminers.

Maharajan et al. [2] made a study proposing an overview of a fan speed controller that adjusts fan speed according to necessity. The pyroelectric sensing technology forms the basis of their research design. The LM35 temperature sensor is used in this project to measure temperature and transmit it as an electric signal to the Arduino UNO board's microprocessor. Temperature-based PWM modifies system speed and offers thermal comfort. An LCD shows the temperature and fan speed that have been recorded using

a digital feed from an Arduino UNO board. Additionally, this device checks the equipment's safety in the event of a power supply problem with sufficient speed.

Rajeswari Subramaniam et al. [3] in 2023 presented a fuzzy logic-controlled simulation in regulating thermal comfort and indoor air quality using vehicle heating, ventilation, and air-conditioning system. In order to provide a nonlinear mapping between the measured values, such as temperature and CO2, and control parameters (recirculation flaps, blower speed, and refrigerant mass flow rate) of an automotive HVAC system, a new fuzzy logic controller (FLC) was designed and developed using the MATLAB fuzzy logic toolbox and Simulink. The suggested FLC might be used with a variety of HVAC systems without requiring significant modifications to the internal architecture of the HVAC system by utilizing affordable sensors.

Mohamadi et al., [4] suggested a fuzzy neural network feedback controller air conditioning system for thermal comfort control in 2020. This involved using a neural net- work to evaluate thermal comfort in the controller's feedback path and a fuzzy controller to give thermal comfort in an air conditioning system. The predictive mean vote (PMV) coefficient—obtained by repeatedly solving the comfort equation—is used to assess the air conditioning systems' thermal comfort. In order to precisely estimate nonlinear relationships between input and output variables, multilevel neural networks are frequently utilized. Good results have been obtained when these networks are used to estimate the thermal load of air conditioning systems.

Zhao et al. [5] proposed a PMV model-based solution for preserving building thermal comfort. To calculate PMV, environmental variables including temperature, humidity, and air velocity are taken into account. Sensor values are also taken into account. BP neural networks are enhanced with a dynamic compensatory technique to generate a multivariate logical link. The system adjusts and regulates the temperature in interior spaces based on this. To further improve temperature optimization, more variables based on different kinds of algorithms can be added, and computer hardware can be developed.

Problem Statement

Society is currently dealing with serious problems with energy use, comfort, and the environment. The growing demand for air conditioners leads to an increase of energy consumption, increase in cost of electricity. The use of excessive energy results in greenhouse gas emissions and change in climate with extreme weather events which will create an impact on the environment. Also, adjusting the temperature manually leads to discomfort and health risks, especially for those who have chronic health conditions.

So, to address these challenges effectively we are introducing this smart air conditioner system which will predict the optimal temperature settings of the air conditioner to save energy and lower the cost of electricity by reducing the excess usage of energy because of manual adjustments. This efficient usage of energy will decrease the impact on the environment. The system maintains consistent temperatures to provide indoor comfort which mostly reduces the health risks of users.

Proposed Work

To enhance energy efficiency, reduce environmental effect and reduce the health risks by optimizing temperature, this project aims to develop a highly efficient smart air conditioning system using both machine ML and IoT. The system significantly reduces the usage of electricity by regulating the air conditioner settings automatically, which not only helps the users to reduce the electricity bills but also reduces the strain on power grids.

This system will use a DHT11 sensor which keeps on monitoring the temperature of the surroundings and provides the real-time results to the linear regression machine learning model.

This pre-trained linear regression model which is trained using the datasets which consist of various temperature readings and their corresponding optimal air conditioner set- tings inputs the incoming temperature data from the sensor and predicts an appropriate temperature setting for user comfort as well as power usage efficiency. As the suitable temperature is predicted, this information is sent to the air conditioner using IR blaster. The IR blaster will send accurate infrared signals to control the air conditioner by changing the settings of the air conditioner to match the predicted temperature

To contribute to better health and comfort of the user by maintaining stable optimal indoor temperature this system is used. This project not only addresses the current challenges but also shows how IoT and machine learning technologies can be applied in day-to-day life. Through addressing these challenges, the project shows the future advancements in home automation and energy conservation.

Methodology

Hardware components

1. Arduino Uno microcontroller: Microcontroller acts as the brain of this system by performing crucial role in connecting sensor data, intelligent prediction and controlling the smart air conditioning system in real-world.
2. DHT11 sensor: This sensor sends the raw temperature data to the microcontroller by continuously monitoring the surrounding temperature around it. This data is essential for the linear regression model to predict the optimal temperature for the Air conditioner.

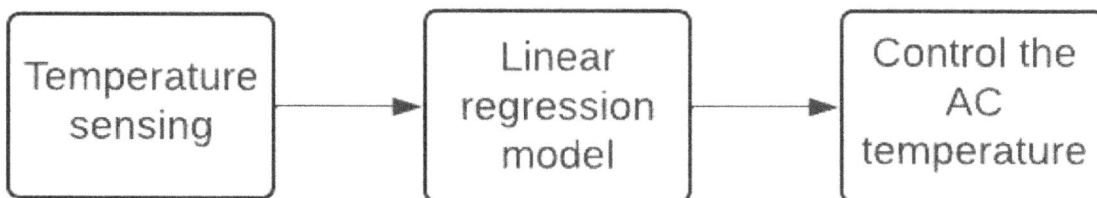

Figure 5.1 Level 0 data flow diagram
Source: Author

3. IR Blaster: The IR Blaster acts as a communication bridge between digital world and the air conditioner. It control the Air conditioner using the optimal temperature obtained from Linear regression model by converting it into suitable IR signals which the air conditioner can understand.

4. Jumping wires and power supply: These jumping wires function as adaptable connectors which are used to connect parts such as sensor and IR blaster. They provide communication between them using electric signals. Power supply is the center component of the system which provides electricity to microcontroller, DHT11 sensor, etc. to make the Air conditioning system run.

Software components

1. Arduino IDE: This makes writing, uploading the code easier. This code tells the microcontroller how to read temperature data from

sensor, communicate with Linear regression model, operate the IR blaster. Without Arduino IDE programming the microcontroller is not possible.

2. Python libraries: These libraries are used in different environments to train the linear regression model before inserting it into the Arduino code. These libraries are used to aid in loading and processing the temperature dataset and offer function to train the linear regression model.

3. Arduino libraries: Arduino libraries are the pre-written code snippets which contain pre-built functions to save the time and effort of user by performing various tasks like sending signals, operating actuators and reading sensor data. This project uses libraries for DHT11 sensors, IR blaster to give more functionality.

4. Temperature dataset: The machine learning model of the Air conditioning system is trained using this temperature dataset. The

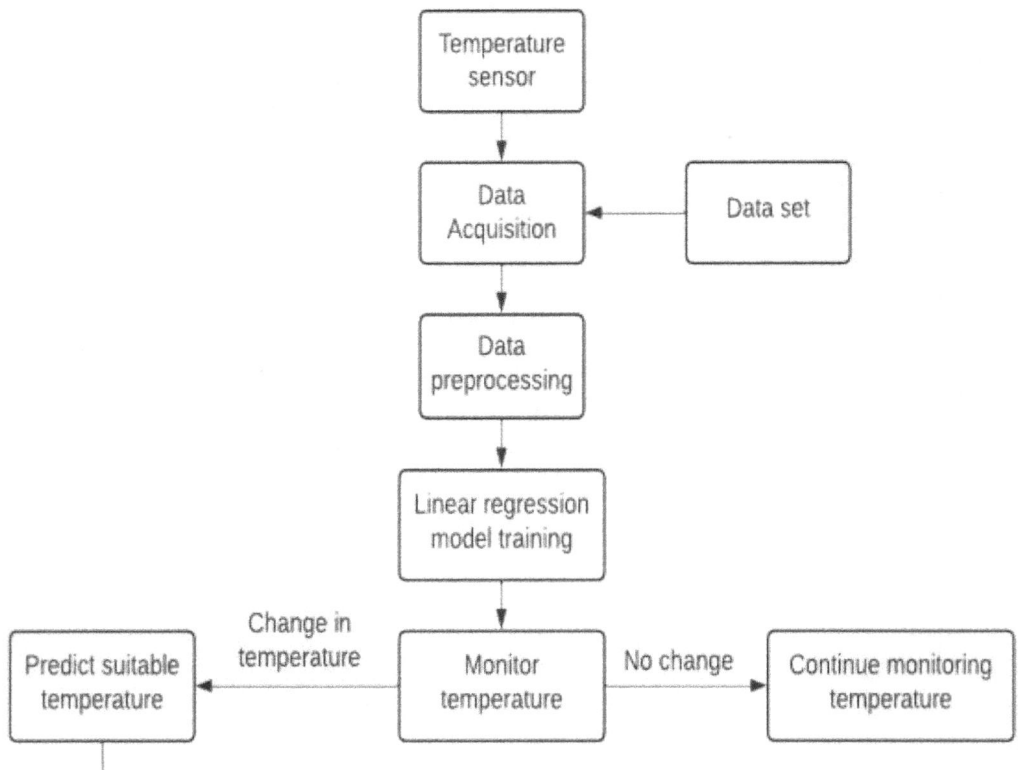

Figure 5.2 System architecture
Source: Author

dataset contains historical temperature data and matching optimal temperature data. By identifying the relation of data in the dataset the machine learning model will be accurate in predicting optimal temperature for the Air conditioner.

Working of project

1. Gathering and analyzing data (Data acquisition and collection): Real-time temperature data which is useful for the prediction of the optimal temperature by the machine learning model is detected using DHT11 sensor from the ambient surroundings. DHT11 sensor is used because of its affordability and ability to deliver dependable temperature readings. The data set is collected from online surveys and preexisting temperature data sets which contain various sets of both the real-time temperature data and its corresponding optimal temperature in csv format. The data set contains a wide range of temperatures to ensure that the model will generalize well compared to unseen data. This real-time temperature data collected from DHT11 sensor and data set will be temporarily stored.

2. Data preprocessing: The real-time data which is collected by DHT11 sensor to send as an input to ML model for predicting the optimal temperature as the output and dataset which contains the values and measurements to train the linear regression model are preprocessed by removing any anomalies, handling the missing values and performing feature extraction in which critical values which the make prediction harder are removed. The data in data obtained from sensor is cleaned and prepared before sending it to the linear regression model for training the model and temperature prediction.

3. Machine learning model: The dataset which is pre-processed is used to train the linear regression model to predict the optimal temperature for a particular surrounding. The linear regression model establishes a relationship between independent variable (real-time temperature data) and dependent variable (optimal temperature data) which are in the dataset. After training, the

real-time temperature data obtained from the DHT11 sensor which are preprocessed will be sent to the trained Linear regression model and based on that input of real-time data the trained ML model uses the relationship established by the it to predict a suitable temperature for the Air conditioner which makes the user more comfortable in that specific environment.

4. Air conditioner control: The linear regression model predicts the comfortable temperature by taking the real-time temperature as input. IR Blaster links the anticipated temperature settings with the understandable infrared signals which are sent by the Air conditioner. These Infrared signals of the predicted temperature are sent to the Air conditioner, modifying the temperature of Air conditioner in accordance with the predicted temperature. Simply put, IR Blaster acts as a remote which speaks the air conditioner language allowing the system to communicate the AC wirelessly. This temperature settings make the Air conditioner more energy efficient and maintain comfortable environment which will also reduce any health risks of the user.

Results

This project demonstrates a significant advancement in optimizing air conditioner settings using a machine learning approach. The core of this system is a linear regression model that predicts the optimal controlled temperature based on the surrounding temperature detected by a DHT11 sensor.

The scatter plot provided in this project illustrates the performance of a linear regression model in predicting optimal controlled temperatures based on external temperatures. A scatter plot with the linear regression line included shows the relationship between the controlled temperature and the outside temperature. The red line shows the temperatures that the regression model predicted, while the blue dots show the actual controlled temperatures that were recorded. The scatter plot shows an upward trend, which is consistent with the system's goal of maintaining a comfortable indoor environment—that is, rising regulated temperature in response to rising outdoor temperature. The blue dots closeness to the red line indicate that the model can be reasonably accurate in predicting the outside temperature, yet there are certain discrepancies that are worth noting, especially when the outside temperature is higher.

The system's effectiveness is demonstrated by the near agreement between expected and actual temperatures, indicating efficient interior climate maintenance with the ability to reduce the energy consumption. Nonetheless, the variations show that variables other than ambient temperature, such as humidity, the time of day, occupancy, and individual user preferences, may affect the ideal temperature. Prediction accuracy may be increased by augmenting the model with a larger dataset and more sophisticated algorithms.

Effective communication between the sensor, machine learning model, and air conditioner, as well as real-time data processing, are critical to the system's performance in an actual application. For the system to function well, it is imperative that the IR Blaster and DHT11 sensor be dependable. Less energy is used by the system than by conventional air conditioners since it predicts and sets the ideal temperature, which saves money on power costs and has positive environmental effects.

The Linear regression model can reasonably anticipate ideal temperatures, according to the preliminary results, which could result in energy savings and increased user comfort. In order to improve the model's predictive power and overall system performance, future developments may concentrate on adding more contextual and environmental data.

Discussions

Smart air conditioner is developed to provide support to the user by reducing energy wastage and also decreasing the chances of any health risks. By understanding the user needs this system provides a comfortable environment for the user by using linear regression model. There are some opportunities to enhance the capabilities of this Air conditioning system which may be proved more effective for the user in terms of comfort and energy efficiency: Utilizing different Machine learning techniques like neural networks and decision trees, including additional features beyond temperature like season, time of day can further improve the accuracy of predicted optimal temperature. Adding more sensors like occupancy sensors can be useful for the system to understand the surroundings further. The

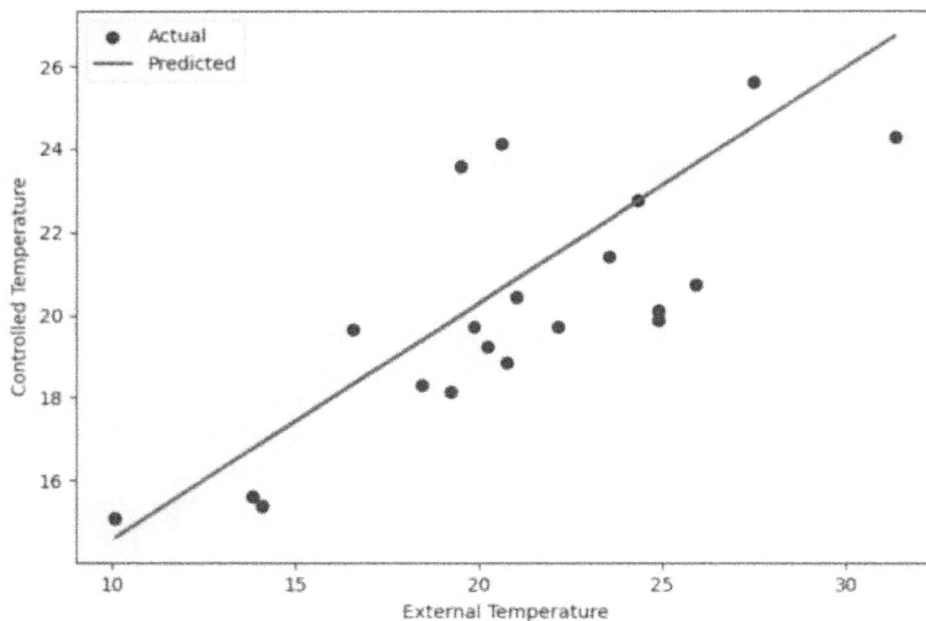

Figure 5.3 Scatter plot graph with regression line
Source: Author

system should add the user feedback to models to change its predictions accordingly by learning individual preferences. Provide a user interface using a smart phone application to modify their preferred comfortable temperature ranges. By giving these discussion points this project shows the way for developing more energy efficient and user-friendly air conditioning systems.

This smart Air conditioner creates a positive impact on various aspects.

1. By predicting optimal temperatures and setting temperature of air conditioner based on real-time needs and user preferences this Air conditioning system reduces energy consumption compared to the previous air conditioner operation and provides a more comfortable environment.
2. As we discussed in the above point, Setting the temperature of air conditioner by predicting optimal temperature leads to the reduce of energy wastage. This also reduces the chances of greenhouse gas emissions which will have a huge beneficial effect on the environment.
3. By using inexpensive components like Arduino Uno and DHT11 sensors makes the system cost-effective when compared to the other commercially available system. This project shows how Internet Of Things can be used in everyday appliances to provide comfort which paves a path for using IoT and machine learning in various other home appliances and create smarter homes.

Conclusion

Energy wastage issues and several health issues because of excess or unusual temperatures in the surroundings are causing damage to the people in the society. This smart air conditioner is a pioneering solution that combines Internet of Things (IoT) and machine learning to revolutionize indoor climate control. By analyzing real-time data and employing linear regression model, our smart air conditioning system personalizes temperature settings to maintain the user comfort while minimizing energy consumption. This innovative approach not only enhances user experience but also promotes sustainability. Our project represents a pioneering fusion of technology and environmental responsibility, offering a hopeful path towards a future where climate management is efficient.

References

[1] Kumar, K. S., Rajasekhar, S., Tanveer, S. H., Prasad, S. V., Allababu, V., and Rahman, K. A. (2023). Automatic temperature-based fan controller. *Journal of Engineering Sciences*, 14(05), 139–144.

[2] Maharajan, M. P., Ramkumar, R., Sangeetha, T., Kannan, P. (2023). Arduino uno-based room temperature sensor for automatic fan speed controller. *Journal of Data Acquisition and Processing*, 38(1), 4218.

[3] Rajeswari Subramaniam, K., Cheng, C.-T., and Pang, T. Y. (2023). Fuzzy logic controlled simulation in regulating thermal comfort and indoor air quality using a vehicle heating, ventilation, and air- conditioning system. *Sensors*, 23(3), 1395. doi: 10.3390/s23031395.

[4] Mohamadi, S. A., and Ahmed, A. J. (2020). Thermal comfort control via air conditioning system using fuzzy neural network feedback controller. *Indonesian Journal of Electrical Engineering and Computer Science (IJEECS)*, 19(2), 586. doi: 10.11591/ijeecs.v19.i2.pp586-592.

[5] Zhao, Y., Genovese, P. V., and Li, Z. (2020). Intelligent thermal comfort controlling system for buildings based on IoT and AI. *Future Internet*, 12(2), 30. doi: 10.3390/fi12020030.

6 A study on audio steganographic healthcare transmission in 5G

Revathi, K.[1,a] and Kaja Mohideen, S.[2,b]

[1]Department of Electronics and Communication Engineering, Tamil Nadu, India
[2]B.S. Abdur Rahman Crescent Institute of Science and Technology, Tamil Nadu, India

Abstract

Advanced technology has broadly developed remote consultations, highlighting the need for robust healthcare data security. Audio steganography addresses this need by hiding the existence of data in a .wav audio file. In this paper, integrating telemedicine with audio steganography helps the healthcare sector ensure secure communication of sensitive medical data. Utilizing the fifth-generation mobile network ensures high-speed wireless communication of healthcare data, meeting the growing demands of patients for convenient remote consultations. The standard enhanced Least Significant Bit embedding and extraction algorithm was employed to embed and extract healthcare data within audio files. The performance evaluation of audio steganography was measured by peak signal to noise ratio and bit error rate with average values of 33.29842 dB and 5.1299 E-04, respectively. The transmission time for a 30 second stego audio file communicated in real-time via electronic mail over a 5G network and received on a Wi-Fi 5 network is 13.4 seconds.

Keywords: Audio steganography, bit error rate, electronic mail, fifth generation, least significant bit, normalized cross-correlation, peak signal to noise ratio and telemedicine

Introduction

A pandemic situation like COVID-19 has increased the scope of telemedicine. Telemedicine involves remotely delivering healthcare services via telecommunications technology to enhance medical accessibility. Effective telemedicine requires strong data security and fast communications to protect patient information and enable smooth interaction between healthcare professionals and patients. Cryptography and steganography are distinct techniques for acquiring high security [6].

In cryptography, converting plain text into ciphertext with encryption algorithms and keys protects it during communication. During transmission, ciphertext attracts the attention of cryptanalysts, even though decrypting ciphertext created by complex algorithms is challenging. Since the ciphertext is visible during communication, additional security measures are required to protect the data [10].

Steganography, in contrast, hides the existence of communications by embedding multimedia files within other multimedia files as carriers. Audio has gained significant interest as a data carrier due to the heightened sensitivity of the human auditory system (HAS) compared to the human visual system (HVS). This positions audio steganography as a potentially superior technique to image and video steganography [11].

Fifth-generation telecommunication transmits data at gigabit-per-second (Gbps) speeds with low latency, increased capacity, and enhanced connectivity. Hence, 5G is suitable for integrating into various applications such as remote consultations, IoT, and robotic surgery [1]. In this paper, patient-doctor consultations are embedded securely into audio files. The resultant stego audio file (SAF) are communicated through the 5G network.

The paper is structured as follows: a literature review on audio steganographic communication

---

[a]revathivigneswaranphd@gmail.com, [b]kajamohideen@crescent.education

DOI: 10.1201/9781003616399-6

of medical data in 5G, a discussion of embedding and extraction algorithms, an analysis of outcomes from the simulated experiments, a real-time study of audio steganographic healthcare data transmission in 5G, and conclusions with future scope for research.

Related Works

The merits and demerits of embedding techniques in audio steganography are detailed [2]. The conventional algorithm employed in audio steganography is the least significant bit (LSB) algorithm. Researchers have enhanced the LSB algorithm by embedding data in higher LSBs to increase the embedding capacity [1]. Secure transmission and confidentiality of patient medical data are essential for e-health services. Authors have examined the significant characteristics, treatment workflow features, and adoption barriers of telemedicine in the healthcare industry [7,8]. Data security in IoT communication within 5G networks, along with the properties, merits, and demerits of 5G technology in healthcare and audio steganography discussed [5,10]. It is evident from the literature review that the secure and fast transmission of medical data in telemedicine is a significant research gap.

This paper addresses this gap by embedding patient-doctor dialogues into .wav audio files and transmitting them through a 5G network. A real-time study evaluates the transmission duration of SAF sent via email by assessing the timestamp on the sender and receiver sides. The framework of the paper is in Figure 6.1.

Embedding Algorithm

An uncompressed audio file in .wav format and medical data in .txt format are the inputs to an embedding algorithm. Both the audio file and medical data are converted to binary streams, with lengths of 16 bits per sample and 8 bits per byte, respectively. The embedding algorithm hides two bits of medical data in the 1st and 5th bits of each audio sample. This process continues until all medical data is embedded. Four audio samples (each two bytes) are required to embed one byte of medical data. Approximately 9616 audio samples are needed to embed 2404bytes of medical data. The resulting audio file with embedded medical data is a SAF. The SAF is transmitted via email over 5G networks.

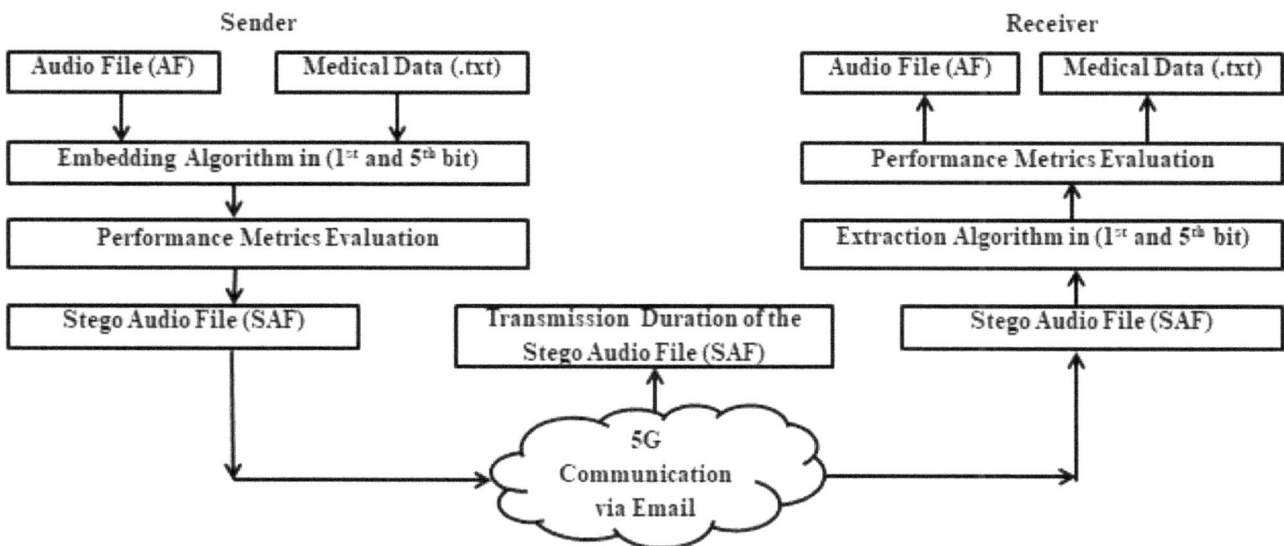

Figure 6.1 Framework of the paper
Source: Author

Algorithm 1: Embedding algorithm

Input: Audio file (AF) in .wav and medical data (MD) in .txt

Output: SAF in .wav

1. Read the AF and convert each sample to a 16- bit (2 byte) binary stream.
2. Read the MD and fetch its corresponding ASCII values.
3. Convert the ASCII value of the .txt file to an 8-bit (1 byte) binary stream.
4. Embed 1st and 2nd bits of the MD into the 1st and 5th bits of AF.

For i = 1 to L (MD) do #Sequence of message bits (M_i) in text file MD of length L(MD).

$SAF_{i1} \leftarrow AF_{i1} \leftrightarrows M_{i1}$ #Replace the 1st bit in the ith sample of the cover sequence (AF_i) with message bit (M_{i1}) results in stego audio file (SAF).

$SAF_{i5} \leftarrow AF_{i5} \leftrightarrows M_{i2}$ #Replace the 5th bit in the ith sample of the cover sequence (AF_i) with message bit (M_{i2}) results in SAF.

5. End for
6. Repeat step 4 for each pair of bits in MD until the entire length of MD is embedded in the 1st and 5th bits of AF.
7. Compute the SAF and evaluate performance metrics.
8. Transmit the SAF with hidden MD via email over a 5G network using an Android mobile phone.
9. Assess the time required for the SAF to reach the receiver and analyze transmission performance.
10. End

The performance of the algorithm is analyzed using peak signal to noise ratio (PSNR) and bit error rate (BER). Additionally, the transmission time of the SAF transmitted over a 5G network is also evaluated.

Extraction Algorithm

An uncompressed SAF in .wav is the input to the extraction algorithm. The samples of the SAF are converted into a 16-bit binary stream.

The extraction algorithm reads the 1st and 5th bit of each SAF sample. The above process is repeated to retrieve all the bits of medical data. Eight binary bits corresponding to a character in medical data are grouped and converted to its decimal representation. Then, fetch the corresponding ASCII value. The embedded medical data is extracted by repeating the above process.

Algorithm 2: Extraction algorithm

Input: SAF

Output: Audio file (AF) and medical data (MD)

1. Read the SAF and convert each sample to two bytes of binary stream.
2. Retrieve the 1st and 5th bits in SAF to the length of MD (L).

For i = 1 to L (MD) do $M_{i1} \leftarrow SAF_{i1}$ and # Compute the index i_1 in the stego audio file (SAF) where the 1st message bit (M_{i1}) is stored.

$M_{i2} \leftarrow SAF_{i5}$ # Compute the index i_5 in the stego audio file (SAF) where the 2nd message bit (M_{i2}) is stored.

End for

3. Repeat step 2 for each pair of bits until all bits in MD are retrieved from the 1st and 5th bits of SAF, ensuring the complete message is fully extracted from these positions.
4. Combine the extracted bits from every four iterations of the loop to form one byte (8 bits) of MD, a character in MD. Continue this process for reconstructing the MD.
5. Convert each byte of MD to its decimal value and repeat this step for the length of the MD.
6. Fetch the ASCII value corresponding to each decimal value to reconstruct the MD.
7. The hidden MD is retrieved from the stego audio file (SAF) and the resulting file is the audio file (AF).
8. END.

The performance of the extraction algorithm is analyzed using NCC)

Results and Discussion

The enhanced traditional LSB algorithm was tested using MATLAB software on five audio files (blues, classical, disco, metal, and reggae) sourced from the GTZAN dataset [9].

The specifications of these audio files are listed in Table 6.1. The medical data consists of the COVID Dialogue Dataset, which includes conversations between patients and doctors about COVID-19 and other types of pneumonia, sourced from websites such as icliniq.com, healthcaremagic.com, and healthtap.com [3].

The performance of the embedding and extraction algorithms was evaluated using 25 simulation results of PSNR, BER, and NCC. Additionally, real-time analysis of transmitting 25 SAFs over a 5G network was conducted, and its performance was evaluated by the duration taken by SAFs to reach the receiver.

The similarity between the audio file and the SAF is measured by PSNR using Eq. 1 [4]. A higher PSNR indicates increased similarity. The average PSNR is 33.29842dB, indicating minimum distortion in the audio file after medical data embedding. Figure 6.2 shows the PSNR values for audio files with hidden medical data of varying size from 568 bytes to 2404 bytes.

$$PSNR = 10\log_{10}\frac{(2^P-1)^2}{MSE} \ (1)$$

Where p represents the audio sample bits.

The ratio of error bits in the SAF to the audio file is measured by BER using Eq. 2 [9]. The range of BER is 0 to 1. The average BER of the embedding algorithm is 5.1299E-04. The graph in Figure 6.3 shows BER on the y axis and the length of medical data varying from 568 bytes to 2404 bytes on the x axis. The graph shows that the BER of the SAF is low (nearing zero), indicating minimal error bits.

$$BER = \frac{P_{error}}{P_{bits}} \ (2)$$

Where P_{error} is the incorrect bits and P_{bits} is the total number of bits embedded in the audio file.

The uniqueness of the retrieved medical data is measured by the normalized cross-co relation (NCC), given by Eq. 3 [4]. A simulated NCC value of 1 fall within the range of -1 to 1, resulting in extracted medical data with no error bits.

Similarly Figure 6.4. Illustrates the uniqueness between original and SAF (blues, classical, disco, metal, and reggae) with hidden medical data of 2404 bytes

$$NCC(TF,TF') = \frac{\sum_{h=1}^{N} TF(h)TF'(h)}{\sqrt{\sum_{h=1}^{N} TF(h)^2}\sqrt{\sum_{h=1}^{N} TF'(h)^2}} \ (3)$$

Where TF and TF' are embedded and extracted medical data. N is the number of samples in each one of them.

Table 6.1 Specification of audio files [9].

Specifications	
Bits per sample	16
Number of samples	661794-664180
Channel	Mono
Audio type	Music
Duration in seconds	30

Source: Author

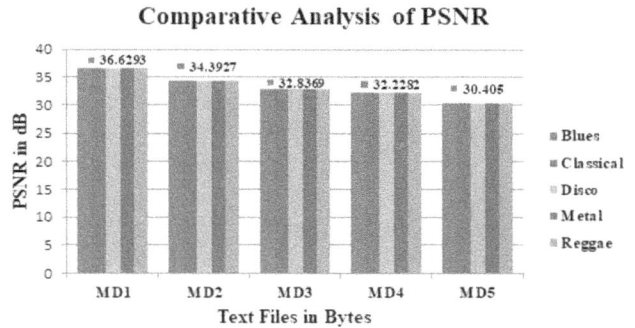

Figure 6.2 PSNR of embedding algorithm
Source: Author

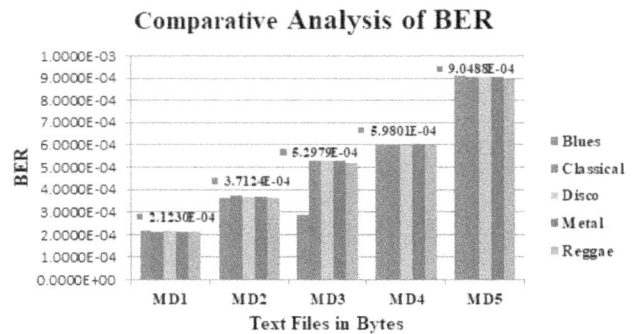

Figure 6.3 BER of embedding algorithm
Source: Author

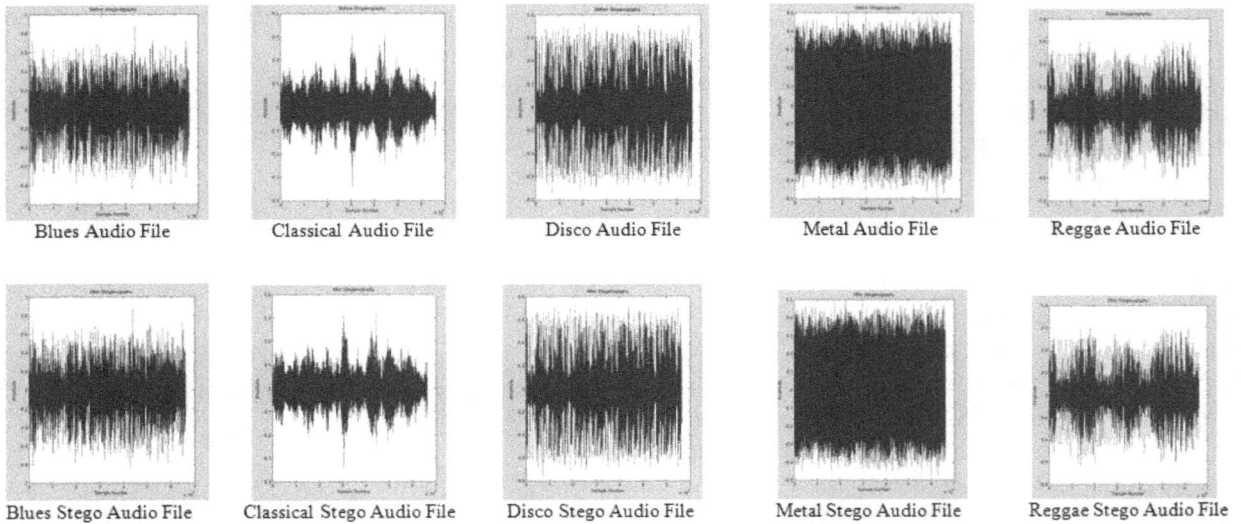

Figure 6.4 Audio and stego audio files with medical data of size 2404bytes
Source: Author

Real-time Study of Transmitting Stego Audio Files in 5G

A simple case study utilized available data to evaluate the time to transmit SAFs via email over 5G using an Android phone for remote consultations.

A total of 25 simulated experiments resulted in 25 SAFs containing medical data with sizes ranging from 568 bytes to 2404 bytes. The specifications of the audio files are listed in Table 6.1.

Initially, the SAFs were transmitted via email using a 5G network and received through a Wi-Fi 5 network [5]. Time stamp information at each stage of the email transmission was noted, as shown in Figure 6.5. The time difference between the sender and receiver was calculated, as shown in Figure 6.6. The time difference indicates the transmission time for the SAF to reach the receiver. The average duration for the SAF was 13.4 seconds. The findings suggest that securely transmitting medical data using audio steganography via a 5G network can efficiently support telemedicine, as demonstrated by the results.

This study represents a straightforward and cost-effective approach utilizing available resources to validate the feasibility of using SAF in telemedicine. The future scope of the study involves evaluating packet transmission times to further enhance the accuracy of email

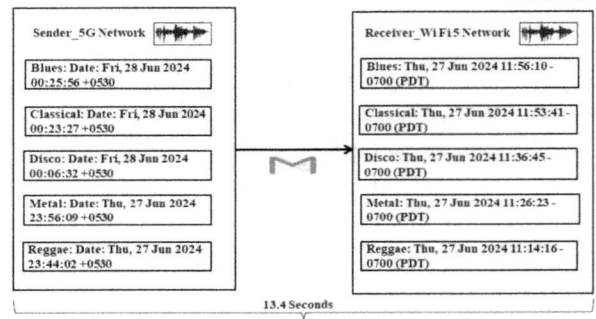

Figure 6.5 Timestamp for sender and receiver
Source: Author

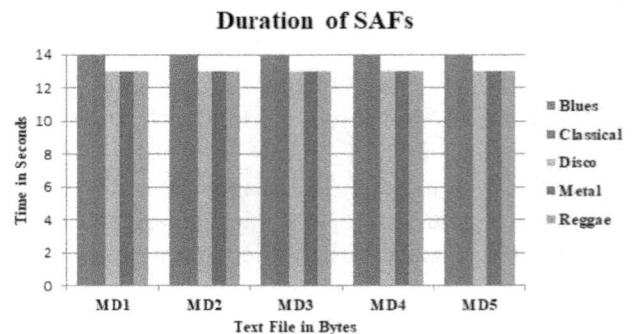

Figure 6.6 Duration for stego audio file transmission over 5G
Source: Author

communication for SAFs in a 5G network, aligning closely with the study's objectives.

Conclusion and Future Scope

This paper presents a foundational study integrating telemedicine, audio steganography, and 5G technology. The study employs an enhanced LSB algorithm to embed medical data within audio files transmitted via email over a 5G network for remote consultations. The embedding algorithm achieves an embedding rate of 25%. The study validates the efficiency of the embedding algorithm through average PSNR and BER values of 33.29842dB and 5.1299E-04, respectively. Medical data integrity is verified by the NCC value of 1, indicating a perfect correlation between the hidden and extracted medical data. Specifically, the study successfully demonstrates the transmission of 2404 bytes of medical data hidden within AFs of 30 seconds via email using 5G networks, as validated by the above results.

Future research will focus on enhancing the embedding capacity and conducting comprehensive studies to optimize the transmission of covert audio files over 5G networks. These efforts aim to improve the efficiency and security of transmitting sensitive medical information in telemedicine applications.

Acknowledgments

The authors thank the anonymous reviewers for their insightful feedback. Their suggestions significantly improve the quality of this paper.

References

[1] Alhaddad, M. J., Alkinani, M. H., Atoum, M. S., and Alarood, A. A. (2020). Evolutionary detection accuracy of secret data in audio steganography for securing 5G-enabled internet of things. *Symmetry*, 12, 2071. Doi:10.3390/sym12122071.

[2] Alsabhany, A. A., Ali, A. H., Ridzuan, F., Azni, A. H., and Mokhtar, M. R. (2020). Digital audio steganography: systematic review, classification, and analysis of the current state of the art. *Computer Science Review*, 38, 100316. https://doi.org/10.1016/j.cosrev.2020.100316.

[3] Chakravorty, S., He, X., Yang, X., and Xie, P. (2020). Chakravorty 2020 COVID dialogue dataset english. COVID-dialogue-dataset-english: an english medical dialogue dataset about COVID-19 and other types of, pneumonia. 2020. https://github.com/UCSD-AI4H/COVID-Dialogue.

[4] Elshoush, H. T., and Mahmoud, M. M. (2023). Ameliorating LSB using piecewise linear chaotic map and one-time pad for superlative capacity, imperceptibility and secure audio steganography. *IEEE Access*, 11(April), 33354–33380. https://doi.org/10.1109/ACCESS.2023.3259902.

[5] Georgiou, K. E., Georgiou, E., and Satava, R. M. (2021). 5G use in healthcare : the future is present. *Journal of the Society of Laparoscopic and Robotic Surgeons (JSLS)*, 25(4). https://doi.org/10.4293/JSLS.2021.00064. (pp. 1–22).

[6] Ghoul, S., Sulaiman, R., and Shukur, Z. (2023). A review on security techniques in image steganography. *(IJACSA) International Journal of Advanced Computer Science and Application*, 14(6), 361–385.

[7] Grigsby, J., Kaehny, M. M., Sandberg, E. J., Schlenker, R. E., and Shaughnessy, P. W. (1995). Effects and effectiveness of telemedicine. *Health Care Financing Review*, 17(1), 115–131.

[8] Haleem, A., Javaid, M., Singh, R. P., and Suman, R. (2021). Telemedicine for healthcare : capabilities, features, barriers, and applications. *Sensors International*, 2, 100117. https://doi.org/10.1016/j.sintl.2021.100117.

[9] Mahmoud, M. M., and Elshoush, H. T. (2022). Enhancing LSB using binary message size encoding for high capacity, transparent and secure audio steganography-an innovative approach. *IEEE Access*, 10, 29954–29971. https://doi.org/10.1109/ACCESS.2022.3155146.

[10] Singh, T., Verma, S., and Parashar, V. (2016). Securing internet of things in 5G using audio steganography. Smart Trends in Information Technology and Computer Communications: First International Conference, SmartCom 2016, Communications in Computer and Information Science (CCIS), springer, 628, (pp. 365–372). https://doi.org/10.1007/978-981-10-3433-6_44.

[11] Vimal, J., and Alex, A. M. (2014). Audio steganography using dual randomness LSB method. In 2014 International Conference on Control, Instrumentation, Communication and Computational Technologies (ICCICCT) IEEE, (pp. 941–944).

7 Design and verification of 16 & 32-Bit CPUS using ARM architecture

Ammisetty Mahesh Babu[1,a], *Krishna Veni Sahukara*[2,b], *Venkata Naga Sai Gopal Vadapalli*[3,c], *Chanakya Pukkalla*[3,d], *Harsha Amalakanti*[3,e] *and Sri Harshita Ganti*[3,f]

[1]Assistant Professor, Dept. of ECE, GVPCDPGC(A), Visakhapatnam, Andhra Pradesh, India
[2]Professor, Dept. of ECE, GVPCDPGC(A), Visakhapatnam, Andhra Pradesh, India
[3]Student, Dept. of ECE, GVPCDPGC(A), Visakhapatnam, Andhra Pradesh, India

Abstract

This paper presents the design and implementation of scalable CPU architecture, available in both 16-bit and 32-bit configurations, inspired by ARM's efficient and versatile microprocessor designs. The primary objective is to create a processor capable of executing ARM instruction sets while offering adaptability to various application requirements. The design process involves the integration of key components such as the instruction fetch unit, microarchitecture, control unit, arithmetic logic unit (ALU), and memory interface, all aimed at optimizing performance, power efficiency, and ease of programming. The architecture is meticulously designed to balance high performance with low power consumption, making it ideal for embedded systems and Internet of Things (IoT) devices. Detailed simulations validate the CPU design, ensuring accurate functionality and reliable operation. Additionally, the processor is synthesized for FPGA implementation, providing a practical demonstration of its capabilities in real-world scenarios. The results highlight the feasibility of leveraging ARM architecture principles to develop compact, powerful CPUs that can efficiently handle a wide range of computing tasks. This work showcases the potential for such processors to be used in diverse applications, from embedded systems and IoT devices to more complex computing environments, thereby illustrating the versatility and effectiveness of the proposed CPU design.

Keywords: 16-bit, 32-bit, ALU, ARM architecture, control unit, instruction fetch unit, memory interface, pipelining

Introduction

The ARM architecture CPU represents a pinnacle of microprocessor design, renowned for its efficiency, versatility, and widespread adoption in diverse computing domains. Operating on a foundation of power efficiency, the ARM CPU efficiently fetches, decodes, and executes instructions, managing tasks seamlessly through its instruction fetch unit, decoder, control unit, arithmetic logic unit (ALU), and memory interface. This orchestrated workflow optimizes performance while minimizing power consumption, making ARM CPUs ideal for mobile devices, embedded systems, and various computing applications. Architecture's scalability allows designs ranging from low-power microcontrollers to high-performance processors, ensuring compatibility with a vast software ecosystem and facilitating cost-effective solutions. Despite their power efficiency, ARM CPUs deliver competitive performance, especially in multi-core configurations, showcasing their versatility across domains like smartphones, tablets, Internet of Things (IoT) devices, automotive systems, and more. Overall, the ARM architecture CPU stands as a testament to efficient design principles, combining power efficiency, scalability, performance, compatibility,

[a]maheshbabu07402@gvpcdpgc.edu.in, [b]drkrishnaveni@gvpcdpgc.edu.in, [c]gopalvadapalli2002@gmail.com, [d]chanakya2605@gmail.com, [e]harshaamalakanti@gmail.com, [f]gantisriharshita@gmail.com

DOI: 10.1201/9781003616399-7

and versatility in a compact and cost-effective package [3].

Design of 16-bit CPU

Design of 16-bit CPU architecture based on ARM

The system architecture of a 16- bit CPU is shown in Figure 7.1. This architecture consists of ALU, control unit (CU), program counter, and instruction decoder. The working of ARM architecture revolves around a streamlined and efficient process of executing instructions, starting from fetching instructions from memory to their final execution. It begins with the instruction fetch unit retrieving instructions from memory based on the program counter's value. These instructions are then passed to the decoder, which interprets them and determines the corresponding actions to be taken. The control unit manages the sequencing and execution of these actions, ensuring they occur in the correct order and at the right time [1,2].

Simultaneously, the ALU performs arithmetic and logical operations as instructed by the decoded instructions. The ALU interacts with registers and memory to fetch operands, performs the required computations, and stores the results back in registers or memory locations as

necessary [4]. This process involves fetching data from memory or registers, performing operations such as addition, subtraction, logical AND, OR, XOR, shifting, comparing values, and storing the results appropriately [5].

The memory interface plays a crucial role in facilitating data access and storage. It manages the transfer of data between the CPU and external memory, ensuring smooth and efficient communication. This includes reading data from memory into registers for processing, writing results back to memory, and handling data movement operations efficiently [6].

Overall, the working of ARM architecture embodies a coordinated effort between the instruction fetch unit, decoder, control unit, ALU, and memory interface, all working in harmony to execute instructions accurately, efficiently, and in a timely manner. This streamlined process ensures optimal performance, power efficiency, and compatibility with a wide range of software applications and development tools.

Design of 16-bit micro instruction

Figure 7.2 shows micro instruction format of 16-bit CPU.

The explanation of above is given below

15-11 It refers to ALU function

10-8 it refers to data A Address/data A value

7-5 It refers to data B Address/data B value

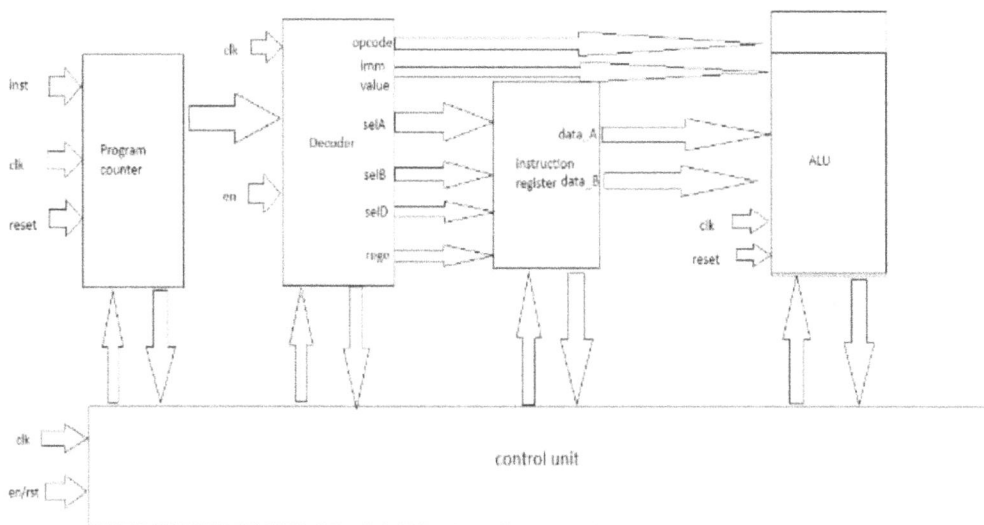

Figure 7.1 Designed architecture of CPU
Source: Author

15-11	10-8	7-5	5-3	2

Figure 7.2 Micro instruction format of 16-bit CPU

Source: Author

5-3 it refers to write address/data out address
2 It refers to mode of operation

Design of instruction decoder

In the instruction decoder design, these fields are typically decoded to generate decode the signals that were given to the appropriate components (ALU, memory interfaces, etc.) and configure them according to the instruction being executed. This involves generating control signals for multiplexers, ALU operations, memory read/write operations, and other necessary actions to execute the instruction correctly.

Let's break down each of these fields in the context of designing a decoder for a CPU:

1. 15-11 (ALU function): These bits determine the operation that the ALU should perform. For example, they might specify operations like addition, subtraction, bitwise AND, OR, etc. Each combination of bits represents a specific ALU operation, and the control unit decodes these bits to activate the corresponding ALU function.
2. 10-8 (Data A address/data A value): These bits can serve a dual purpose depending on the design. They can either represent the address from which data A should be fetched from memory (if it's an address), or they can directly provide the value of data A. This depends on whether immediate values are allowed in instructions or if data needs to be fetched from memory.
3. 7-5 (Data B address/Data B value): Similar to data A, these bits can represent either the address from which data B should be fetched from memory or directly provide the value of data B, depending on the design.
4. 5-3 (Write address/data out address): These bits specify the address where the result of the ALU operation should be written to. If the processor has separate data and instruction memories, this field could also indicate where the next instruction should be fetched from.

5. 2 (Mode of operation): This bit determines the mode in which the processor should operate. It could indicate different modes such as user mode, supervisor mode, or specific processing modes like interrupt handling or power-saving modes. Figure 7.3 indicates timing Diagram of instruction Decode

Design of ALU

The ALU within a CPU performs the essential operations that manipulate binary data, including arithmetic (like addition, subtraction, multiplication, and division) and logical operations (such as AND, OR, XOR, and shifting). It works by receiving input data from registers or memory, executing the specified operation based on control signals from the CPU's control unit, and then producing an output result that can be stored back in registers or memory. ALU's design incorporates various logic circuits and stages optimized for different types of operations, ensuring efficient and accurate computation within the CPU's processing pipeline.

Design of general-purpose registers

General-purpose registers are essential components of a CPU's architecture, used to store temporary data and intermediate results during program execution. These registers are typically fast, low-latency storage locations directly accessible by the CPU's arithmetic and logic operations, providing quick access to frequently used data. They play a crucial role in speeding up computation by reducing the need to access slower memory locations, such as RAM. Figure 7.4 shows Block diagram of ALU. Tables 7.1 and 7.2 shows the opcodes of various ALU operations can perform in 16-bit &32-bit CPUs

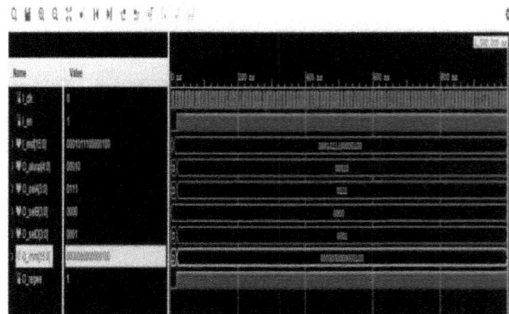

Figure 7.3 Timing diagram of instruction decode
Source: Author

Table 7.1 Opcode for ALU operations

Opcode	Operation
0	ADD
10	SUB
100	AND
110	OR
1000	XOR
1010	NOT
10000	LOAD
10010	CMP
10100	SHL
10110	SHR
11000	JMPA
11010	JMPR

Source: Author

In modern CPUs, general-purpose registers are often organized into banks, with each bank containing a set of registers that can be used for various purposes. Commonly used registers include those for storing operands for arithmetic operations, addresses for memory access, pointers for data structures, and temporary variables used by the program. The number of general-purpose registers available varies between CPU architectures. Figure 7.5 indicates Timing Diagram of ALU

More registers generally allow for better performance, as they reduce the frequency of data transfers between registers and memory. Additionally, compilers and assembly programmers often optimize code to make efficient use of these registers, minimizing unnecessary data movement and maximizing the CPU's computational throughput.

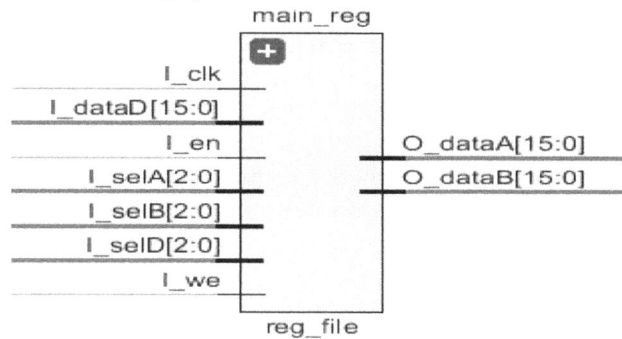

Figure 7.4 Block diagram of ALU
Source: Author

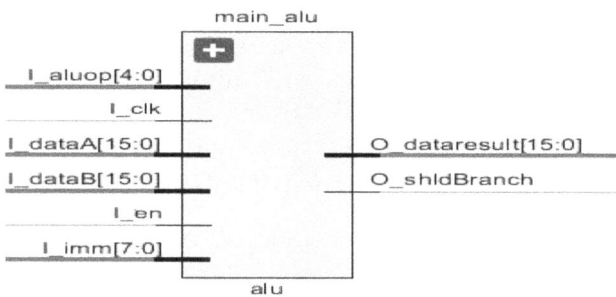

Figure 7.6 Block diagram of registers
Source: Author

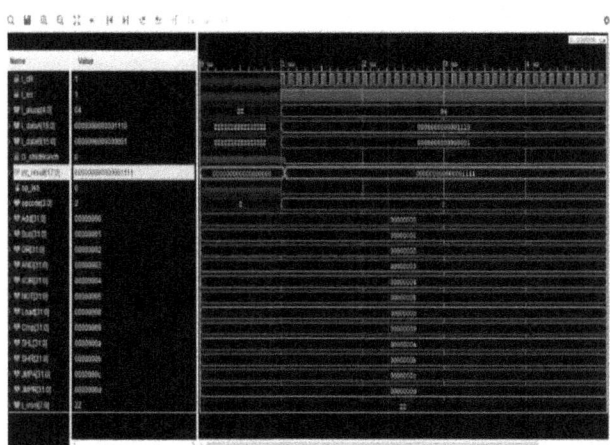

Figure 7.5 Timing diagram of ALU
Source: Author

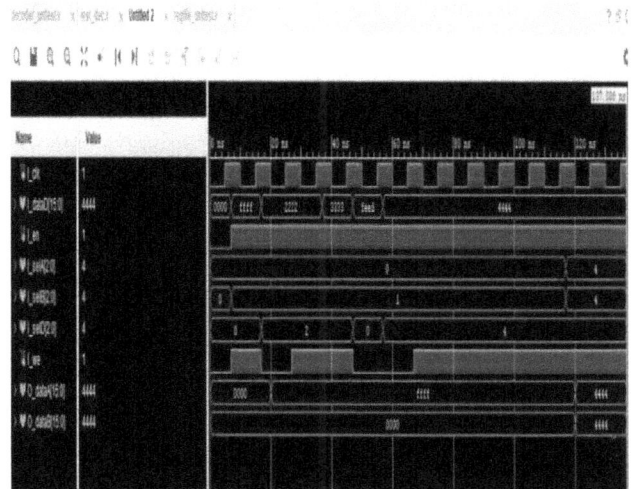

Figure 7.7 Timing diagram of register
Source: Author

Overall, general-purpose registers are vital for efficient data processing within a CPU, enabling faster execution of instructions and improving overall system performance. Figure 7.6 shows Block diagram of registers. Figure 7.7 indicates Timing Diagram of registers

Design of 32-bit CPU

Design of 32-bit CPU architecture

The 32-bit ARM architecture refers to a family of processor designs developed by ARM Holdings. ARM processors are widely used in various devices such as smartphones, tablets, embedded systems, and IoT devices due to their energy efficiency, performance, and versatility. Here are some key aspects of the 32-bit ARM architecture. They use a reduced instruction set computing (RISC) architecture, which emphasizes simplicity and efficiency in instruction execution. The instruction set includes a range of basic operations such as arithmetic, logical, data movement, and control flow instructions. They have a set of general-purpose registers (typically 16 or more) that are used for data manipulation and storage during program execution.

These registers are often divided into groups for specific purposes, such as data processing, address calculations, and function calls. ARM processors employ pipelined architecture, where instructions are fetched, decoded, and executed in overlapping stages to improve throughput and performance. This pipelining allows multiple instructions to be processed simultaneously, increasing overall efficiency.

ARM architecture supports various memory access modes, including load-store architecture where data must be loaded into registers before processing and then stored back in memory. It also supports different addressing modes for efficient memory access. ARM architecture has evolved over time, with different variants and extensions catering to specific requirements. For example, ARMv7 introduced support for advanced features like virtualization and hardware-based security. Figure 7.8 shows micro instruction format of 32 bit CPU.

Design of 32-bit microinstruction format

The above instruction format decoded into

31-26 bits represents the mode of operation

31-26	25-21	20-16	15-11	11-7	6-0

Figure 7.8 Micro instruction format of 32-bit CPU
Source: Author

25-21 bits represents the data1 Address
20-16 bits represents the data2 address
15-11 bits represents the write data address
11-7 bits represents the data out address
6-0 bits represents the ALU function

Design of control unit

Let's delve into the detailed explanation of each of these bit fields in the context of a CPU instruction format:

1. 31-26 bits (mode of operation): These bits specify the mode in which the processor should operate. Modes can include user mode, supervisor mode, interrupt mode, or specific processing modes like power-saving states. The control unit of the processor interprets these bits to determine the current operational mode and adjusts its behavior accordingly. For example, in supervisor mode, the processor may have access to privileged instructions or resources that are restricted in user mode.

2. 25-21 bits (Data 1 address): These bits represent the address from which the first data operand (data1) should be fetched. In a typical instruction execution flow, the control unit uses these bits to access the specified memory location or register where data1 is stored. Data1 could be an immediate value embedded within the instruction or an address pointing to a memory location containing the actual data.

3. 20-16 bits (Data 2 address): Similar to data1, these bits denote the address of the second data operand (data2) that the processor needs for executing the instruction. The control unit retrieves data2 from the specified memory location or register based on these bits. Like data1, data2 can be an immediate value or an address pointing to data in memory.

4. 15-11 bits (write data address): These bits specify the address where the result of the instruction should be written or stored. After performing the required operation (e.g., arithmetic operation, logical operation), the

processor stores the result at the address indicated by these bits. This could be in a register, a specific memory location, or a special-purpose register designated for storing results.

5. 11-7 bits (Data out address): These bits indicate the address from which data should be read for output or further processing. After completing the instruction, the processor may need to read data from a specific location for output or for use in subsequent instructions. The control unit uses these bits to fetch the required data.6. 6-0 bits (ALU function): This field determines the operation that the ALU should perform on the data operands (data1 and data2). It specifies the type of arithmetic or logical operation, such as addition, subtraction, bitwise AND, OR, XOR, shift operations, comparisons, etc. Each unique combination of these bits corresponds to a specific ALU operation. Figure 7.9 Indicates block diagram of control unit

In the control unit design, these fields typically controls the signals that was given to the appropriate components (ALU, memory interfaces, etc.) and configure them according to the instruction being executed. This involves generating control signals for multiplexers, ALU operations, memory read/write operations, and other necessary actions to execute the instruction correctly. Let's break down the decoding of bits 31-26 into 11 bits for deciding the mode of operation and enabling various functionalities within a control unit.

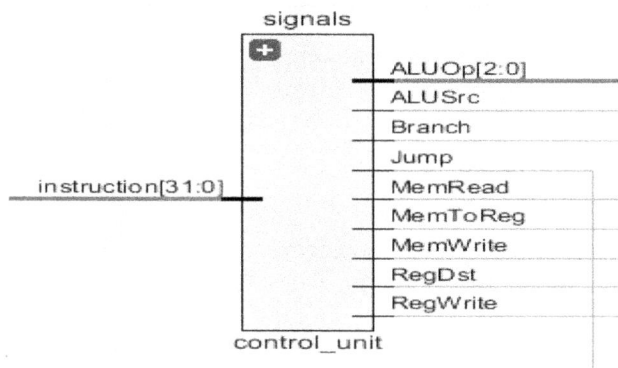

Figure 7.9 Block diagram of control unit
Source: Author

Bits 31-26, Decoded into 11 bits. These 11 bits determine how the processor should operate based on the instruction being executed. Each bit corresponds to a specific mode or functionality:

1. 10th Bit (destination register enable): This bit enables the destination register where the result of an operation should be stored. When set, the processor knows that the instruction's result needs to be written back to a register.

2. 9th Bit (ALU enable): When this bit is set, it indicates that the instruction involves an operation that requires the ALU to perform a computation. It activates the ALU to execute the specified operation.

3. 8th Bit (data from memory to register enable): If this bit is set, it signals that data needs to be fetched from memory and loaded into a register. It triggers the memory read operation to retrieve data from the specified memory address.

4. 7th Bit (Register write enable): This bit enables writing data back to a register. It works in conjunction with the destination register enable bit to ensure that the result of an operation is correctly stored in the designated register.

5. 6th Bit (Memory read enable): When set, this bit instructs the processor to read data from memory. It is often used in instructions that involve fetching operands or data from memory for processing.

6. 5th Bit (Memory write enable): If this bit is set, it indicates that the instruction involves writing data to memory. It triggers the memory write operation to store data at the specified memory address.

7. 4th Bit (Branch instruction enable): This bit is used to enable branch instructions, which alter the flow of program execution by jumping to a different instruction based on a condition or an explicit address.

8. 3-1 Bits (ALU operation enable): These bits enable specific ALU operations such as addition, subtraction, bitwise operations, shifts, etc. Each combination of these bits corresponds to a distinct ALU operation, allowing for a wide range of arithmetic and logical computations.

9. 0th Bit (Jump instruction enables for non-maskable interrupts): When set, this bit enables jump instructions specifically designed for handling non-maskable interrupts (NMI). NMIs are interrupts that cannot be ignored or masked by the processor, requiring immediate attention and action.

These decoded bits play a critical role in the control unit's operation, guiding the processor's behavior during instruction execution, data manipulation, memory access, branching, and interrupt handling. They help ensure that instructions are executed accurately and efficiently according to the program's logic and requirements.

Design of ALU

The opcode of the ALU function of 32-bit CPU is shown in Table 7.1.

Table 7.2 ALU operations of 32-bit CPU

ALU Function opcode	Operation
0	ADD
1	SUB
10	MUL
100	AND
101	OR
110	XOR
111	NOT
1010	CMP
1000	SHL
1001	SHR

Source: Author

Summary

This section presents the performance of the processor in terms of its total power and delay that are obtained using the Kintex4 xc7k70tfbv676-1 XILINX tool. Table 7.3 presents the maximum power dissipation, area occupied, and time taken by each module to operate the processor.

The below graphs show the performance parameters of 16 and 32 – bit CPUs like LUT, area, power consumption. Figure 7.10 gives LUT estimation of 16 and 32 bit CPUs. Figure 7.11

Table 7.3 Performance comparison of 16&32-BIT CPUs

Topology	CPU	LUT	Slices utilized (Area)	Total power
Control unit	16	0.01%	17	0.028w
	32	0.01%	24	0.035w
Register	16	0.07%	30	0.099w
	32	0.19%	30	0.099w
ALU	16	0.58%	237	0.169w
	32	0.78%	150	0.175w
Instruction decoder	16	0.01%	15	0.014w
	32	0.08%	17	0.014w
Total	16	0.67%	289	0.310w
	32	1.06%	221	0.323w

Source: Author

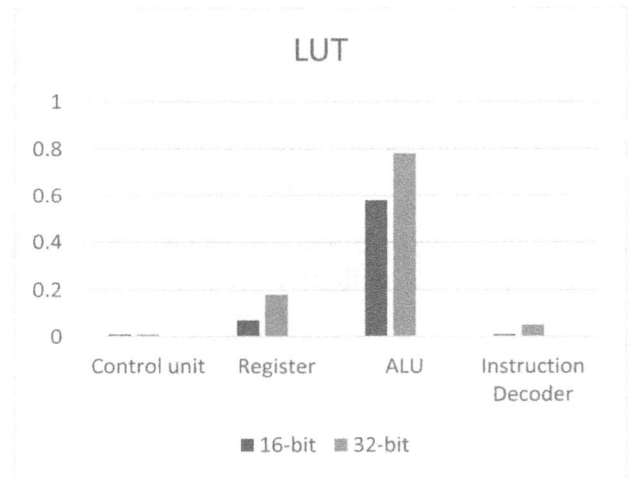

Figure 7.10 LUT estimation
Source: Author

provides Area estimation. Figure 7.12 provides Power estimation of 16 and 32 bit CPUs

Conclusion

In conclusion, the design and implementation of a scalable CPU architecture in both 16-bit and 32-bit configurations demonstrate the practicality and advantages of leveraging ARM's efficient microprocessor principles. These CPUs achieve a balance between performance, power

Slices Utilized

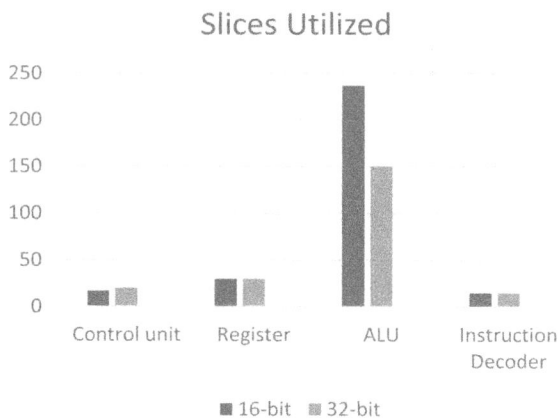

Figure 7.11 Area estimation
Source: Author

Power in Watts

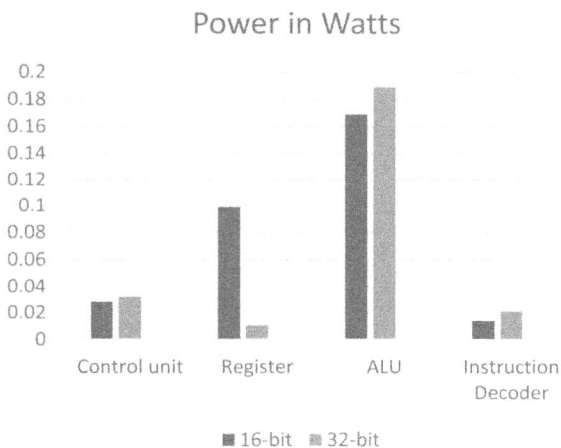

Figure 7.12 Power estimation
Source: Author

efficiency, and ease of programming, making them suitable for a wide range of applications. The 16-bit CPU offers a compact and power-efficient solution ideal for simple embedded systems and IoT devices, ensuring prolonged battery life and lower energy consumption. Meanwhile, the 32-bit CPU provides enhanced computational power and addressable memory space, catering to more demanding tasks and complex applications such as advanced robotics, multimedia processing, and sophisticated control systems. In daily life, these CPUs can power various devices, from wearable technology and smart home appliances to automotive systems and industrial automation, showcasing their versatility and essential role in modern computing environments

References

[1] Yadav, A., and Bendre, V. (2021). Design and verification of 16-bit RISC processor using vedic mathematics. In 2021 International Conference on Emerging Smart Computing and Informatics (ESCI), (pp. 759–764). doi: 10.1109/ESCI50559.2021.9396965.

[2] Bhagat, S. M., and Bhandari, S. U. (2018). Design and analysis of 16-bit RISC processor. In 2018 Fourth International Conference on Computing Communication Control and Automation (ICCUBEA), (pp. 1–4). doi: 10.1109/ICCUBEA.2018.8697859.

[3] Chiranjeevi, G. N., and Kulkarni, S. (2021). Pipeline architecture for N==K 2L Bit modular ALU: case study between current generation computing and vedic computing. In 2021 6th International Conference for Convergence in Technology (I2CT), (pp. 1–4). do

[4] Vishnu, S. N. S., Gandluru, A., and Ramesh, S. R. (2022). 32-Bit RISC processor using vedicmultiplier. In 2022 3rd International Conference for Emerging Technology (INCET), (pp. 1–5). doi: 10.1109/INCET54531.2022.9824747.

[5] Kuppili, J., Abhiram, M., and Manga, N. A. (2021). Design of vedic mathematics based 16-bit MAC unit for Power and delay optimization. In 2021 4th Biennial International Conference on Nascent Technologies in Engineering (ICNTE), (pp. 1–4). doi: 10.1109/ICNTE51185.2021.9487570.

[6] Dhanasekar, S., Bruntha, P. M., Ahmed, L. J., Valarmathi, G., Govindaraj, V., and Priya, C. (2022). An area efficient FFT processor using modified compressor adder based vedic multiplier. In 2022 6th International Conference on Devices, Circuits and Systems (ICDCS), (pp. 62–66). doi: 10.1109/ICDCS54290.2022.9780676.

8 IoT-driven solar-powered robotic lawn mower and water sprinkler

Poojitha Pullannagari[a], Bhavana Penmetsa[b], Nishanth Sappa[c], Harshitha Myle[d] and Ayesha Naureen[e]

Department of Computer Science and Engineering, B V Raju Institute of Technology, Narsapur, Medak, Telangana, India

Abstract

Keeping greenery healthy is a labor-intensive activity in the world of smart applications. The traditional grass cutters which use fuels may have destructive effects on the environment. This Internet of Things (IoT)-driven robotic lawn mower focuses on reducing environmental concerns, and sustainability by using solar power and reducing human efforts for lawn maintenance. The earlier robotic grass cutters were used only for grass cutting in required patterns whereas this Robotic device is used for multitasking i.e., grass cutting and water sprinkling when needed. Using sensor technologies, Internet of Things powered grass cutters and water sprinklers can navigate, mow the lawn and sprinkle water when necessary. It can be used day or night because solar energy is utilized for charging it. The IoT-driven robotic grass cutter has demonstrated its capabilities in navigating, lawn mowing, and water sprinkling. This robotic technology is affordable, environmentally friendly, and sustainable because it operates on solar power. This research demonstrates how the IoT may be used to develop intelligent, automated solutions for routine operations. IoT continues to advance, its contribution in these research can create sustainable and efficient lawn maintenance.

Keywords: Arduino board, Bluetooth module, charging module, motor driver module, solar power

Introduction

Conventional lawn care practices frequently utilize gas powered machinery, which presents a number of environmental issues in addition to requiring a significant amount of human effort. Since these traditional grass cutters rely on fossil fuels, they aggravate the problem of greenhouse gas emissions and add to air and noise pollution. In contrast, by incorporating automation and renewable energy into lawn care procedures, the development of smart apps and the Internet of Things (IoT) offers promising answers to these problems. Robotic lawn mowers are not a wholly new idea. The primary function of the early iterations of these devices was to automate the mowing process by trimming grass according to preset patterns. These previous models, however, still needed a lot of human intervention to perform activities like charging and modifying mowing patterns. They also depend on electric power, which may not fully address environmental concerns depending on the source. More advanced and ecologically friendly robotic lawn care solutions are now possible thanks to recent developments in IoT and renewable energy technology. This study focuses on a robotic lawnmower powered by the IoT that has a water spraying system in addition to cutting grass. This device further lowers the requirement for separate equipment and human involvement in basic lawn care chores by merging several features. This robotic system's usage of solar electricity is one of its primary features. The lawn mower has solar panels that allow it to produce and store energy for use in its operations. This allows it to run throughout the day and at night with less need for outside power sources. Additionally, users can also operate the power remotely with the help of an accompanying

[a]poojithapullannagari@gmail.com, [b]bhavanapenmetsa09@gmail.com, [c]nishanthsappa@gmail.com, [d]myleharshitha1234@gmail.com, [e]nooriekhan005@gmail.com

DOI: 10.1201/9781003616399-8

smartphone application, which offers convenience and flexibility. This study highlights how IoT driven automation in lawn care has the potential to revolutionize the industry. The suggested method improves efficiency and user convenience while simultaneously addressing the environmental problems related to conventional lawn care by utilizing cutting-edge sensor technologies and renewable energy sources. The goal of this study is to provide a new benchmark for effective and sustainable lawn care, serving as a guide for further developments in the field.

Literature Survey

A number of parts are used in the research [1], including solar plates, DC motors, motor drivers, ultrasonic sensors, Arduino UNOs, and Node MCUs. The cloud application ThingSpeak is used in the IoT mode. This solar-powered gadget is made to automatically identify obstacles and trim grass in a lawn. The fully automated solar grass cutter is a cost-effective and environmentally friendly way to cut grass without using as much human labor. According to the paper, the efficiency of the fully automated solar grass cutter using IoT is 94%, while the conventional grass cutter currently in use only has 54 percent efficiency.

Primary of the research is to reduce pollution by using solar energy and making it simple enough for unskilled laborers to operate [2]. A DC motor, a rechargeable battery, a solar panel, a stainless-steel blade, a charge controller, and a control switch make up the solar-powered grass cutter. Several kinds of grass were used to test the machine's performance. The research also addresses the external framework and motor specifications, as well as the design and construction of the solar-powered grass cutter. The research is inexpensive, simple to operate in remote locations, easy to maintain, and simple to use. The solar-powered grass cutter uses non-conventional energy sources, which results in reduced space consumption, lightweight, and zero operating costs. The solar-powered grass cutter is said to be less expensive than commercial grass cutters, providing a way to maintain uniformly neat lawns in playgrounds, gardens, and schools.

The lawnmower designed in this research is to be sustainable; it has four gear motors, one brushless direct current (BLDC) motor, sensors, an Arduino-based charge controller, and a Raspberry Pi-powered renewable energy source [3]. An Android application is used to operate and control a lawnmower. An 80W solar panel installed atop the mower serves as the research project's power source for all electrical loads and motors. The charge controller's maximum efficiency in clear weather is approximately 98% at maximum solar voltages; in cloudy weather, it is approximately 70% at maximum 18V. The average power efficiency is about 89.5 percent which is much better than conventional lawn mowers.

The paper [4] presents a methodology for creating an autonomous and intelligent solar grass cutter. A microcontroller is used in research to regulate the various lawnmower functions, two DC gear motors are used to move the solar grass cutter, and one DC blade motor is used to cut the grass. Through Bluetooth, a smartphone can be used to control the smart solar tracker. The main goal is to provide independent grass indices that can be used by anyone, negating the need for hiring someone to mow the grass.

The goal of the paper [5] is to reduce the amount of labor, pollution, and electricity used in gardening by designing and building a solar grass cutter with a water spraying system using radio frequency technology. It is possible to carry out the watering and the grass-cutting simultaneously. With PV panels and a 12V rechargeable DC battery, this design aims to harness solar radiation as its primary energy source. Every motor is managed by an RF module that is powered by the battery. Using an antenna, the RF module transmits data wirelessly at 434 MHz. The operating hours of the fully charged prototype vehicle and the charging time have been tested twice, with two distinct outcomes that vary depending on erratic variables like the weather. Because of its short operating time, the grass cutter works well for small applications, but it is not appropriate for tall grass.

The research [6] goal is to build an effective lawn mower that runs on solar power, lowers operating expenses, protects both the mower and its user, and maintains a clean and healthy environment. Utilizing solar radiation, which is transformed into electrical energy and stored in a rechargeable battery, the grass cutter is equipped with solar panels. The mower's primary component, a microcontroller, is connected to the battery. The solar grass cutter's potential for home use is highlighted in the conclusion. The switch on the board powers the solar-powered lawnmower by cutting the circuit and enabling the current to flow to the motor, which powers the mower's blade.

The creation of an automatic solar grass cutter is covered in the research paper [7] as an eco-friendly substitute for conventional grass cutters that run on nonrenewable energy sources. By using renewable solar energy, the device emits fewer harmful gases and requires less maintenance. It also features a dual power source system with a solar panel and a battery to detect and avoid obstacles while in use. IR proximity sensors are also integrated into the device. The machine is designed to minimize human labor and can function in both automatic and manual modes. A microcontroller, sensors, an LCD display, a Bluetooth module, a solar panel, a battery, and motors are among the parts of the machine. With an emphasis on safety, the design makes use of ultrasonic sensors to identify obstructions and stop the blades from spinning while in the air. The benefits of the automatic solar grass cutter—such as its affordability, environmental friendliness, and decreased physical labor needed for grass cutting—are highlighted in the paper's conclusion.

The goal of the research [8] is to create a self-sufficient lawn mower that can safely and effectively cut grass. The study takes into account a number of variables, including design analysis, battery life, turf quality, and blade-cutting speed. The lawnmowers that are currently available on the market are heavy, expensive, and run on gas engines, which are bad for the environment. With the help of a mobile phone, one can remotely operate the eco-friendly autonomous lawn mower that is being proposed. Other researchers' models of autonomous lawn mowers are also covered in the study. The effectiveness and social benefits of an autonomous lawnmower are concluded by the paper. The findings demonstrate that the blade's cutting speed action has a significant effect when it hits the grass. The high torque DC motor has a 7000 rpm speed and a 4398 m/min blade tip speed.

With the current state of technology, the Arduino UNO prototype in [9] is intended to be a remotely controlled grass cutter. The controller for the remote is a smartphone. This device, called a Smart Solar Grass Cutter, has three main systems: a smart control system, a solar system, and a grass cutter. It runs on solar energy and can be intelligently controlled. The total power consumed by the smart solar grass cutter is 55.8W, whereas the power supplied is 59.76W. When these two values are used, the system's efficiency is 93.37%. To determine the operating hours of the fully charged prototype and the charging time, three tests were carried out. The results varied based on weather-related variables, such as the possibility that high sunlight intensity would shorten the charging time.

Both environmental and noise pollution are decreased by the model [10]. Conventional systems are becoming automated as the world moves toward automation. Therefore, owning an automated grass cutter is imperative. This research converts a traditional push grass cutter into a semi-automated, battery-operated, RC-controlled, video surveillance grass cutter. The cutter motor and car motors are interfaced with ultrasonic sensors and remote control via a microcontroller. The cutter moves backward, and the microcontroller stops all motors if it detects a living or non-living object as an obstacle. This allows the operator to guide the device away from the obstruction. The range of power needed is from 49.29384W to 82.1972W.

The grass cutter powered by solar energy in [11] tackles the environmental issues related to traditional models powered by internal combustion engines. The fully automated solar grass cutter is a robotic car that runs entirely on solar power, doing away with the need for people to assist with cutting grass. It is powered by solar panels and 12V batteries, and it has ultrasonic obstacle detection sensors and an 8051 microcontroller for control. The system addresses noise pollution and environmental issues while ensuring effective grass cutting.

The goal of the research [12] is to build a solar grass-cutting device in order to solve the problems caused by traditional motor-powered cutters' noise and air pollution. The grass cutter has a high-speed revolving blade for effective grass cutting, a DC motor, and a rechargeable battery that is powered by a solar panel. The research uses an 8 Ah 12V rechargeable battery for energy storage, which is charged with solar power during the day. The 2.1 kg, maintenance free battery has a continuous 5–6 hour runtime for the grass-cutting machine. The solar spray pump system is better than traditional energy sources because it is economical and environmentally friendly.

The technologies utilized in an Automated solar grass cutter are discussed in the research [13], with an emphasis on obstacle detection, energy efficiency, and automation. It highlights how crucial it is to switch from manual to automated grass cutters in order to minimize pollution and energy waste. The grass cutter is designed to be more energy-efficient and labor-free by utilizing solar panels and battery power. The study examines a variety of commonplace robots that cut grass on lawns by using solar panels, infrared sensors, and ultrasonic sensors. The article showcases various projects and their methods for automated grass-cutting, incorporating functions such as obstacle identification, solar panel energy storage, and remote management. The technological developments and the effectiveness of automated solar grass cutters in terms of obstacle detection and directional control are highlighted in the paper's conclusion.

The goal of this proposed research in [14] is to create a programmable robot that can cut grass in specific shapes and can be controlled wirelessly from a safe distance using an Android smartphone and Bluetooth. The cutting blade can also be adjusted to maintain varying grass lengths. To find obstacles, three ultrasonic obstacle detectors are employed. Additionally, a Raspberry Pi and a 5-megapixel camera are installed on the robot, which records live video and streams on a PC or Android smartphone via Wi-Fi that is linked to a local area network (LAN). It additionally offers, if it is connected to the Internet via Wi-Fi, the ability to stream live videos over the Internet with authentication.

This research [15] designs a prototype electric lawn mower with remote control that can move on its own. With the help of panels positioned to capture intense solar radiation, the solar grass

cutter transforms it into electrical energy. A mechanism that moves a blade to cut the grass is powered by a DC motor that is connected to the batteries. An operational mechanical circuit breaker switch governs the motor. Batteries, blades, DC motors, and solar panels are the parts that are used. The system makes use of a plentiful supply of solar energy, offering both physical activity and simple operation. Although there is a large initial investment, costs should eventually drop due to mass production and the availability of subsidies.

Existing Model

- We frequently use grass cutters in our daily lives, which run on fuels that are not good for the environment. efficiency.
- There are currently solar grass cutters available with further improvements. Automated water sprinklers and Automated lawn mowers exist where multitasking is not possible.

Proposed Model

- The proposed robotic Lawnmower and water sprinkler uses solar power to cut down environmental concerns connected with typical fuel-based grass cutters.
- The Robot is capable of trimming grass and sprinkling water as needed, demonstrating its multitasking abilities. The device can navigate, mow the lawn, and sprinkle water when necessary, using sensing technology.
- The suggested model prioritizes affordability, environmental friendliness, and sustainability by employing solar power and IoT technologies to automate routine lawn maintenance tasks and reduce the labor efforts for lawn maintenance.
- Users can govern the device's movements through an Android application, turn on the grass cutter, and the water sprinkler remotely.

Methodology

Hardware components

1) **Arduino UNO:** The Arduino Uno is a flexible and easy-to-use platform that may be used for a variety of projects and prototyping.

The Arduino Uno functions as the IoT-driven robotic lawn mower's central processing unit and control center in the research that is described. It plays a crucial part in synchronizing the actions of several hardware parts, such as the Bluetooth module and DC motors. The programmed logic, which includes movement control through interaction with the Android app for remote operation, is carried out by the Arduino Uno. In order to drive motors, it interprets commands from the Android application and transmits the necessary signals. Furthermore, the Arduino Uno's compatibility with the Arduino IDE and libraries makes development easier and speeds up the robotic lawn mower system's prototyping.

2) Motor driver: The L293D motor driver facilitates precise movement and navigation by streamlining motor control and offering the capability required to power the robotic lawn mower's gear motors. The four gear motors which run the robotic lawnmower are interfaced with the Arduino Uno via the L293D motor driver. The Arduino's motor driver shield is mounted to the top. The mower can move forward, backward, left, and right due to its bidirectional motor control. To ensure steady and reliable functioning, the L293D motor driver controls the voltage applied to the motors. It protects the motors from any damage caused by high current demands by amplifying the current supplied by the Arduino Uno to drive the motors efficiently.

3) Bluetooth module: Enabling wireless communication between the device and the user's controlling device (usually a smartphone, tablet, or computer) is made possible in large part by the HC-05 Bluetooth module. A device that supports Bluetooth can be paired with the module. After pairing, the user can operate the lawn mower by sending commands from their device. The HC-05 Bluetooth device has a 3300-mV level for RX/TX (receiver/transmitter), and since the microcontroller can detect this level, the HC-05 module's TX voltage level does not need to be changed. [7] For remote control applications, the HC-05 has a respectable range of up to 10 meters. There are two operating modes for the HC 05: slave and master. It is configured in Slave mode in our navigation apps, where it waits to be linked with and managed by the Master device (the user's smartphone or tablet).

4) Solar panel: Powering the robotic lawn mower is provided by the solar panel. The robotic lawn mower is equipped with a solar panel which is constructed by solar cells, transforming sunlight into electrical energy. The solar panel powers charge the onboard batteries during the day with the usage of charging module. The research encourages sustainability and lessens dependency on conventional energy sources like fossil fuels or grid electricity by utilizing solar energy.

5) Charging module: The charging module is essential to using solar electricity for battery recharging in a safe, economical, and efficient manner. It makes sure that the fluctuating output from solar panels is transformed into a steady and ideal form that can be stored in batteries, increasing the solar-powered system's dependability and lifespan. This is necessary to keep the battery healthy and avoid any risks like overheating or swelling.

Software components

1) Arduino IDE platform: The research uses the Arduino platform to program the robotic lawn mower and water sprinkler driven by the Internet of Things to behave as desired. This kind of project is perfect for Arduino, an open-source electronics platform built on user-friendly hardware and software. Several libraries, such as AFMotor.h, NewPing.h, are included in the project's code. Using this platform, the code written to enable the lawnmower and water sprinkler to navigate in accordance with user commands should be verified and uploaded to the Arduino.

2) IoT Control app: Using an Android application that is connected to the device via the HC-05 Bluetooth module, the user can control the device's movement (forward, backward, right, and left). This facilitates simple and intuitive operation of the water sprinkler and lawn mower.

Development of project

Assembling hardware components: Install the Arduino UNO, Motor Driver Bluetooth module, and rechargeable batteries together on the chassis or frame by making the appropriate connections. Attach the water sprinkler arrangement (water pump, sprinkler, pipe) to the chassis and the blade-equipped motor to the front of the device for grass cutting. Next, we use solar panels to charge the batteries. Adjust the solar panel located above the apparatus. The assembling of hardware components and the flow of execution is shown in Figure 8.1.

1) Programming the microcontroller: The code uses the Adafruit Motor Shield library (AFMotor.h) to write a remote-control device for an Arduino platform. Using an HC-05 module, the Lawn mower and water sprinkler can be moved over Bluetooth in the following directions: forward, backward, left, right, and diagonally. Four DC motors are controlled by the code, which interprets commands from the Bluetooth serial input and modifies their speed and direction accordingly. The code itself initializes the navigation motors at a set speed.

2) Usage of IoT control app: Install an IoT-cuetooth module. Commands from a Bluetooth-enabled device (such as a smartphone) is sent to the lawn mower and water sprinkler through the HC-05 Bluetooth module.

Every command is associated with a particular motion or activity. The lawnmower may move in the desired direction by adjusting its direction in response to the command it receives. It provides flexibility and ease of use for the individual.

Results and Discussion

The water sprinkler system and solar-powered lawnmower as shown in Figures 8.2 and 8.3 are remarkably effective at using solar energy that may be generated again to fuel their own lawn care operations. When compared to conventional gas-powered systems, this efficiency lessens environmental effects in addition to reducing operating expenses. The Arduino Uno and solar charging module work together to maximize battery utilization, allowing the system to operate for longer periods of time between charges. This minimizes downtime related to recharging and guarantees consistent performance.

To get the ideal lawn aesthetics, the system's mowing performance is essential. The electric power produces the least amount of noise and pollutants possible because of its solar-charged battery, which powers it consistently. The device minimizes water waste and encourages effective irrigation techniques by precisely watering areas when needed. The independent functioning of the device makes hassle-free watering and grass upkeep possible. The app for the navigation

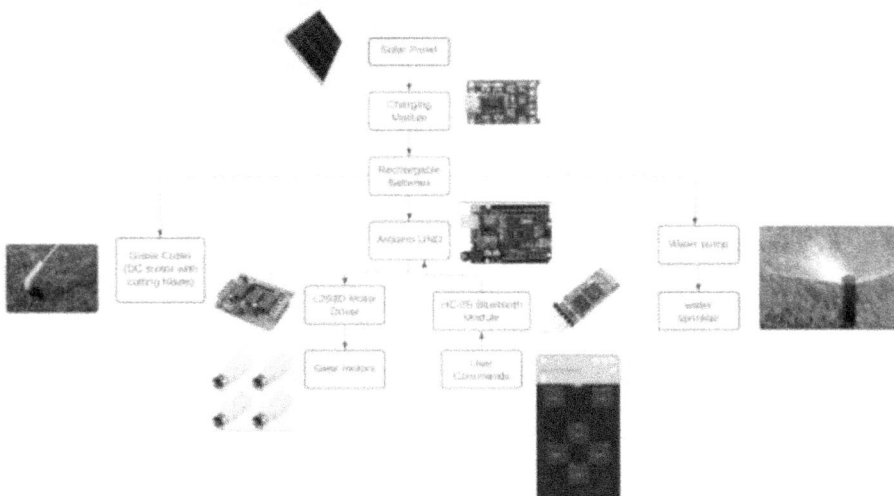

Figure 8.1 Block diagram of robotic lawn mower and water sprinkler
Source: Author

allows users to remotely control the navigation of the device in all possible directions, offering ease and flexibility. User convenience and control are increased by the addition of manual override controls and remote monitoring with the help of Bluetooth module. An environmentally responsible option, the solar-powered system has lower running costs, fewer emissions, and quieter operation. This study demonstrates how IoT-driven automation has the power to transform conventional lawn care techniques, eliminating the need for human intervention

Figure 8.2 Prototype of IoT-driven solar-powered robotic lawn mower and water sprinkler
Source: Author

Figure 8.3 Prototype of IoT-driven solar-powered robotic lawn mower and water sprinkler
Source: Author

and solving environmental issues related to fuel powered equipment. Through demonstrating the potential of IoT technology to offer environmentally friendly, economical, and sustainable lawn care solutions, this research establishes a standard for further advancements in the industry.

IoT-controlled App

The "Arduino car" remote control app, depicted in the Figure 8.4, is used to operate the robotic lawnmower, which is linked to the phone via Bluetooth. An Android application (IoT-controlled App- Arduino car) is used to control a lawn mower. To connect with the mower, the user has to connect the mower to the app using Bluetooth. The Android application that is connected to the device via the HC-05 Bluetooth module. Once the lawnmower is connected to the app, the user can operate the mower through the following buttons:

Forward button: Moves the mower forward. Backward button: Moves the mower backward. Left button: Turns the mower left.

Right button: Turns the mower right.

Make sure Bluetooth is turned on your Android device. Ensure that the Arduino and the Bluetooth module are powered on and properly connected.

Conclusion

In conclusion, this research is a perfect example of how contemporary lawn care techniques combine technological innovation with environmental responsibility. This solar-powered robotic lawn mower and water sprinkler system provide an effective and sustainable way to manage green landscapes by utilizing the power of Internet of Things technology. Day or night, the device can travel, cut lawns, and sprinkle water with accuracy and efficiency with the integration of various modules and intelligent automation. In the end, this research's success demonstrates the revolutionary effect that intelligent automation can have on maintaining green spaces, opening the door to a future that is greener and more ecologically conscious. IoT integration has the potential to transform traditional methods and bring in a new era of environmentally friendly lawn care as it develops further.

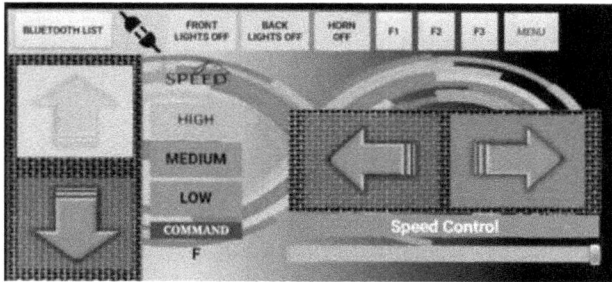

Figure 8.4 IoT control App (Arduino car app)
Source: Author

Future Work

Potential for Additional sensors: The effectiveness and efficiency of the system are increased by integrating other sensors, such as sunshine, grass height, and soil moisture sensors. The total performance of lawn care is enhanced by these sensors, which allow for intelligent battery charging cycles, automated mowing based on grass height, and optimal watering.

Machine Learning for Obstacle identification: For more reliable obstacle identification and path planning, consider using a camera and machine learning algorithms in addition to ultrasonic sensors. This would make it easier for the mower to go across challenging terrain and deal with unforeseen impediments.

References

[1] Hariya, Akshay, Anil Kadachha, Dhaval Dethaliya, and Yashit D. Tita. "Fully automated solar grass cutter." *International Journal of Science Technology and Engineering* 3, no. 9 (2017): 104–106.

[2] Sonalikar, Avantika, Aditya Bhoyar, Ritik Pardhi, Vivek Patil, Vaibhav Mohile, and Satnam Tandekar. *International Journal Of Progressive Research In Engineering Management And Science (IJPREMS)* Vol. 03, Issue 03, March 2023, pp : 255-258 "SOLAR BASED GRASS CUTTER."

[3] Tahir, T., Khalid, A., Arshad, J., Haider, A., Rasheed, I., Rehman, A. U., et al. (2022). Implementation of an IoT-based solar-powered smart lawn mower. *Wireless Communications and Mobile Computing*, 2022, 1–12. doi: 10.1155/2022/1971902.

[4] Jabbar, Muhammad Waqas, Muhammad Noman, Asad Muneer, Ali Abbas, and Adnan Mazhar. "Solar powered grass cutter for domestic utilization." Engineering Proceedings 12, no. 1 (2022): 105.

[5] Ramya, E., Anand, J., Renugha Devi, R., Issac, N. A., and Roshni Prasenth, K. (2021). Solar grass cutter with water spraying vehicle. In 2021 International Conference on Advancements in This Communication, Electrical, Computing and Electronics, Automation (ICAECA), Coimbatore, India: IEEE, Oct. 2021, (pp. 1–6). doi: 10.1109/ICAECA52838.2021.9675681.

[6] Sameer, S. M., Thevar, V. S., Patil, S. K., Mangalpawar, N. S., and Rahate, P. G. (2021). Design of solar grass cutter. *International Research Journal of Engineering and Technology*, 8, 107–114.

[7] Bhalodi, T., Bhujbal, N., Doshi, K., Goregaonkar, R., and Jagtap, S. (2020). Environmental friendly solar grass cutter. *International Journal of Research in Engineering, Science and Management*, 3(7), 177–180.

[8] Arora, H., Sagor, J. A., Panwar, V., Sharma, P., Mishra, S. K., Arora, P. G., et al. (2019). Design and fabrication of autonomous lawn mower with water sprinkler. *Think India Journal*, 22(12), 472–484.s

[9] Ismail, F. B., Al-Muhsen, N. F. O., Fazreen, A. F., and Zukipli, A. (2019). Design and development of smart solar grass cutter. *International Journal of Engineering and Advanced Technology*, 9(2), 4137–4141. doi: 10.35940/ijeat.B4920.129219.

[10] Haris, M., Tabassum, N., Hammad ud din Babar, B. H., Khan, S., Khan, Z., and Omran, A. A. B. (2019). Semi-automatic grass cutter machine. *Journal of Multidisciplinary Approaches in Science*, 6(1), 35–44.

[11] Mudda, M., Kumar, S., and Kumar, P. (2018). Automatic solar grass cutter. *International Journal for Research in Applied Science and Engineering Technology*, 6(4), 1148–1151.

[12] Kashikar, Harshhal, Ganesh Katre, Akshay Raut, Pravin Birhade, Swapnil Patil, and Radhika Bihade. "Grass Cutting & Sprayer Machine Using Solar Energy." (2018) IJSRSET, Volume 4, Issue 4, online ISSN: 2394–4099.

[13] Baingane, T., Nagrale, S., Gumgaonkar, S., Langade, G., Ramteke, S., and Dhumal, V. M. (2018). Review on fully automated solar grass cutter. *International Research Journal of Engineering and Technology (IRJET)*, 5(2).

[14] Asha, N., Monica, J. S., Saraswathi, R., Rahul, R., and Ravikiran, R. (2017). Smart grass cutter. *Perspectives in Communication, Embedded systems and Signal-Processing-PiCES*, 1(6), 97–99.

[15] Dalal, M. S. S., Sonune, M. V. S., Gawande, M. D. B., Sharad, M., Shere, B., and Wagh, M. S. A. (2016). Manufacturing of solar grass cutter. In National Conference "CONVERGENCE, (vol. 2016, pp. 06th-07th.).

9 Neuro-enhanced copilot wheelchair: a comprehensive study

Bhargav, M.S.S.[1,a], Ramya, G.[1,b], Bhargav, M.S.S.[2,c], Eswar, B.[2,d], Manikanta, B.[2,e] and Charan, T. Jaya[2,f]

[1]Department of Electronics and Communication Engineering, SRM Institute of Technology, Chennai, India

[2]Department of Electronics and Communication Engineering, B V Raju Institute of Technology, Narsapur, India

Abstract

Paralysis, a condition affecting nearly 1 in 50 people globally according to the Reeve Foundation and WHO, presents a significant challenge for millions each year. Spinal cord injuries, strokes, and other neurological conditions can rob individuals of their ability to control their muscles. This review paper delves into the potential of brain-computer interfaces (BCIs) to offer a lifeline for those living with paralysis. Focusing specifically on non-invasive EEG-based BCIs, the paper explores how these systems can revolutionize communication and rehabilitation for individuals with paralysis. This paper highlights the growing importance of Electroencephalography and its types. These algorithms offer a distinct advantage by learning directly from raw brain signals, eliminating the need for manual feature selection. This approach paves the way for significant advancements in BCI accuracy. The ultimate goal, as outlined in the paper, is to harness these advancements to create assistive devices that can restore movement and communication between individuals with paralysis. By facilitating motor function rehabilitation, BCIs hold the potential to empower individuals to regain control and independence in their lives.

Keywords: Brain- computer interface, electroencephalography, wheelchair

Introduction

For centuries, humans have dreamt of a world where technology seamlessly integrates with our thoughts. Imagine a world where intent translates into action, bypassing the limitations of our physical bodies. This realm of science fiction is rapidly becoming a reality with the emergence of brain-computer interfaces (BCIs). These groundbreaking technologies bridge the gap between the human brain and external devices, fostering a new era of communication and control based solely on our thoughts. By harnessing the brainwaves, BCIs offer a revolutionary alternative to traditional methods of interacting with technology that rely on muscles and nerves. Looking towards the future, BCIs hold immense promise for a world where technology seamlessly blends with our minds.

BCI operations

The four elements in any BCI, regardless of the techniques used or applications, are [1]:

- Signal acquisition
- Feature extraction
- Feature translation
- Device output.

Brainwaves classification

- Our brains produce a continuous electrical current, resulting in rhythmic patterns called brainwaves. These waves vary in frequency and are associated with different mental states.
- Alpha waves (8-12 Hz)
- Beta waves (12-30 Hz)
- Low beta (12-15 Hz)

[a]bhargav.m@bvrit.ac.in, [b]sm8963@srmist.edu.in, ramyg@srmist.edu.in, [c]bhargav.m@bvrit.ac.in, [d]22211a0426@bvrit.ac.in, [e]22211a0434@bvrit.ac.in, [f]22211a04p1@bvrit.ac.in

DOI: 10.1201/9781003616399-9

- Mid-range beta (16-20 Hz)
- High beta (21-30 Hz)
  - Theta waves (4-7 Hz)
  - Delta waves (0.5-4 Hz)
  - Gamma waves (30-100 Hz

Existing Techniques

Intelligent wheelchairs now feature advanced technologies like AI, robotics, and BCIs, enhancing functionalities such as obstacle avoidance and navigation while ensuring user-centered design and ergonomic principles to improve comfort and usability [2].

BCI technology using eye blink detection for wheelchair control shows promise for enhancing mobility and independence for users with severe motor impairments, benefiting from incremental prototyping, modular design, and minimal training requirements despite challenges in signal accuracy, cost, and long-term usability [3].

SSVEP-based BCIs using QR code stimuli shows high accuracy and potential for wheelchair control, though challenges like visual fatigue and real-world applicability remain [4].

Methodology

1. Invasive BCIs
I   nvasive BCIs are devices implanted directly into the brain. These devices offer the most direct interface with neural signals but also come with significant surgical risks and ethical considerations.

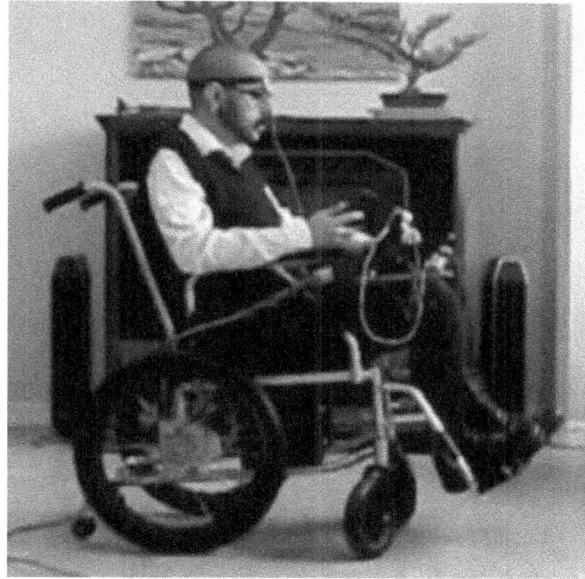

Figure 9.2 BCI based wheelchair [3]
Source: Author

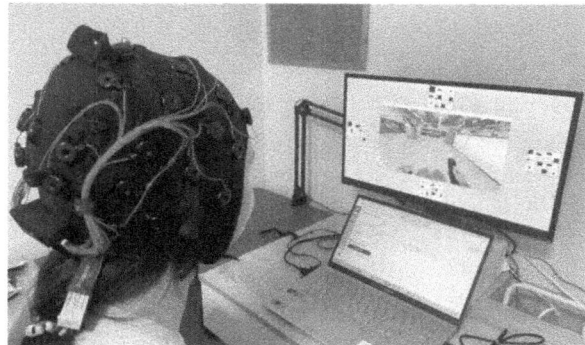

Figure 9.3 Using an EEG Headset to detect brainwaves [4]
Source: Author

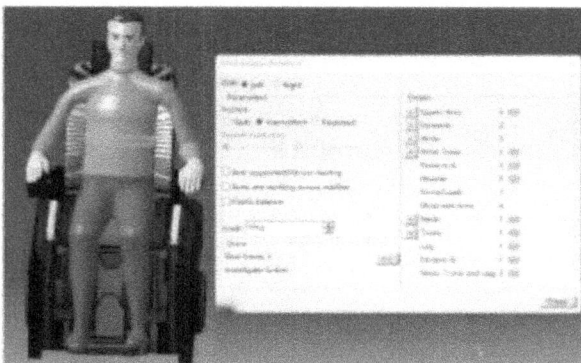

(a)

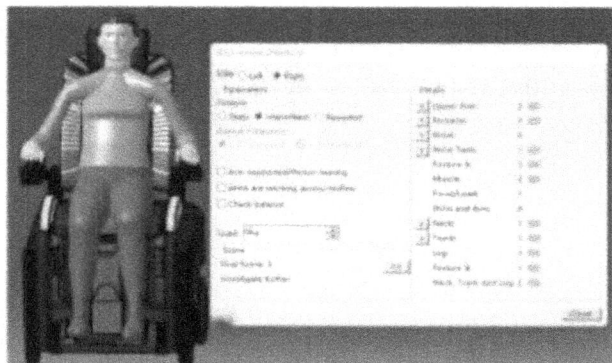

(b)

Figure 9.1 (a), 2(b) Wheelchair command interface [2]
Source: Author

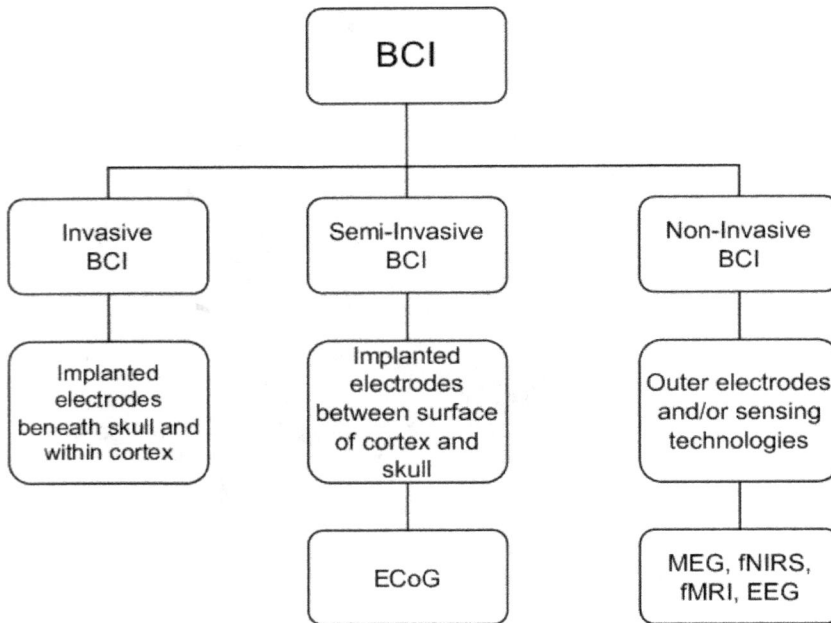

Figure 9.4 Types of brain control interface (BCI) [5]
Source: Author

2. Types and processes of invasive BCI's:
   Neurosurgery: This involves surgical implantation of electrodes within the brain tissue. The electrodes capture neural activity with high precision
   ○ Functionality: These devices are primarily used in clinical settings for patients with severe disabilities, such as ALS individuals affected by ALS or spinal cord injuries can benefit from BCIs, which empower them to control prosthetic limbs or computer cursors through brainwaves.
3. Partial invasive BCIs
   Partial invasive BCIs are less invasive than fully implanted systems but still involve some degree of surgical intervention.
4. Types and processes of partial invasive:
   ○ Electrocorticography (ECoG): Electrodes are placed on the surface of the brain, under the skull but outside the brain tissue. This method provides a balance between signal quality and invasiveness.
5. Non-invasive BCIs
   ○ Non-invasive BCIs are the least risky as they do not involve surgery. These devices record neural activity from the scalp or other external sensors.

6. Types and processes of non-invasive BCI's:
   ○ Electroencephalography (EEG): Electroencephalography utilizes electrodes on the scalp to capture brain activity without entering the skull. This non-invasive approach makes it a popular choice for various applications.
   ○ Magnetoencephalography (MEG): Measures magnetic fields produced by neural activity. It offers good spatial and temporal resolution but requires specialized, expensive equipment
     ○ Functional magnetic resonance imaging (fMRI): Measures brain activity by detecting changes in blood flow. It is used mainly for review and clinical diagnostics due to its high cost and complexity.
7. Comparison of success rates
   ○ Invasive BCIs: High accuracy but with significant risks and ethical concerns. Long-term success is dependent on biocompatibility and patient condition.
   ○ Partial invasive BCIs: High resolution and moderate risk, offering a good balance for clinical applications, particularly in detailed brain mapping.

○ Non-invasive BCIs: Generally lower resolution but safest at most accessible.

Architecture of the Proposing Solution

This comprehensive system is composed of several interconnected subsystems that work together to translate neural activity into physical movement.

At the core of the system is the EEG signal acquisition subsystem. This component utilizes electrodes placed on the user's scalp to detect brainwave activity. These electrodes are sensitive enough to capture the electrical signals generated by neuronal activity.

Once the EEG signals have been amplified and cleaned, they are forwarded to the signal processing subsystem. Here, a microcontroller plays a critical role. This involves sophisticated signal processing techniques to accurately decode the user's thoughts into actionable commands.

To ensure safe operation, the architecture incorporates an obstacle detection and avoidance subsystem.

The entire system is powered by a robust power management subsystem. A battery pack provides the necessary energy to all components, with power regulation circuitry ensuring that each part of the system receives the correct voltage and current.

Overall, the architecture of the BCI controlled wheelchair represents a sophisticated integration of neurological, computational, and mechanical components. By harmonizing these elements, the system effectively transforms brainwave activity into precise motor actions, offering a significant improvement in mobility and independence for individuals with severe physical disabilities.

Flow Chart

A BCI-based wheelchair would assist a person with a severe motor disability in manipulating a wheelchair using his brain control signal. It implies an intricate process to enable precise translation into motion commands for the wheelchair, representing the intentions of the brain. The following is a detailed explanation of each step:

-Signal acquisition

Purpose: To monitor brain activity.

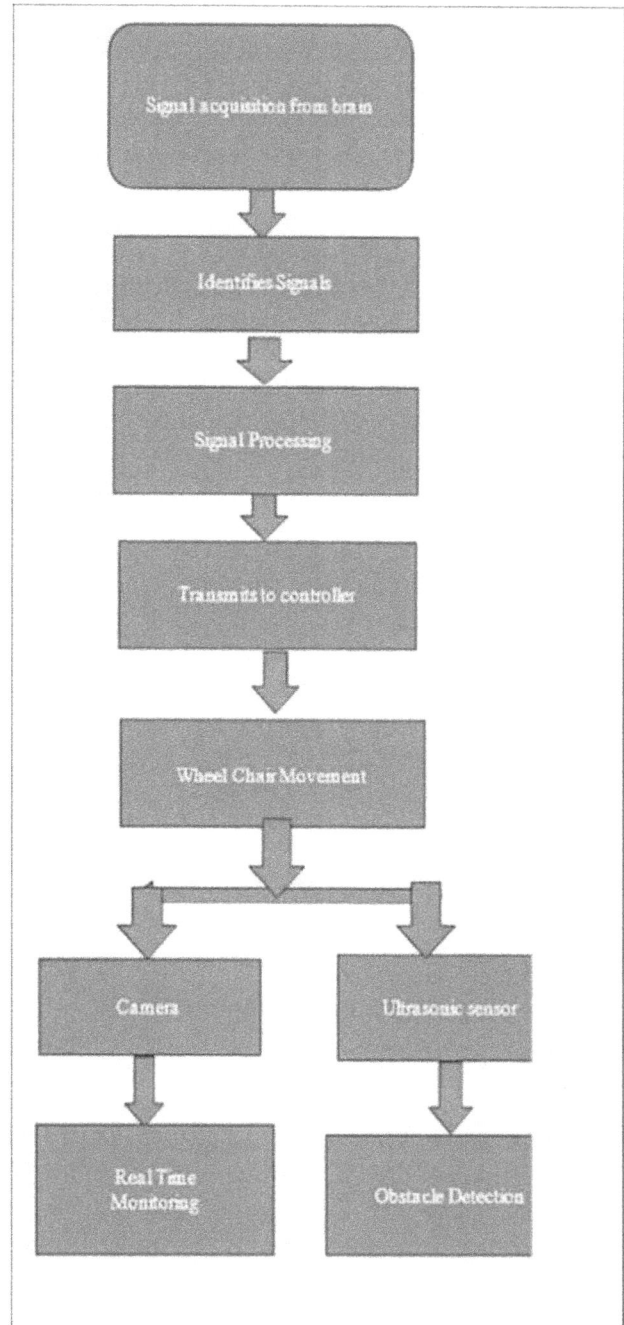

Figure 9.5 Flow Chart working of the methodology
Source: Author

Preprocessing

Goal: Cleaning and preparing the raw brain signal before the analysis.

Feature extraction

Objective: Decipher and extract the relevant information based on the brain signals, equating to the user's intent.

Classification

Purpose: To translate extracted features into specific directives.

Visual training: The system is trained on labelled data where the intended commands are known. The classifier learns to associate specific patterns of brain activity with these commands.

Real-time classification: After the training of the classifier, the intention of the user can be identified concerning incoming new brain signals.

Challenges: The specification on high accuracy in classification with low latency to ensure smoother and more reliable control of the wheelchair.

- Command translation

Target: To convert the classified intentions into an executable command of the wheelchair.

Classification: Each pattern of brain signals is classified as one of the classes of movement commands for the wheelchair, for instance, forward, left, stop and certain safety measures are followed.

Hardware Setup

The hardware components used in the project are:

Bio-Amp EXG pill

The Bio-Amp EXG pill is a game-changer in bio potential signal acquisition. This tiny but mighty device packs a powerful punch, enabling the recording of various electrical signals from the body. We are talking about brainwaves (EEG), muscle activity (EMG), eye movements (EOG), and even heartbeats (ECG), but what truly sets the Bio-Amp EXG pill apart is its versatility. It seamlessly integrates with a wide range of microcontrollers and single-board computers. Think Arduino, Raspberry Pi, and many more – the possibilities are vast.

https://store.upsidedownlabs.tech/product/bioamp-exg-pill/

Microcontroller

The Arduino UNO is a popular microcontroller board that serves as a fantastic starting point for various projects. This compact board features an ATmega328P chip at its heart, offering 14 digital

Figure 9.6 Bio Amp EXG Pill (courtesy: google images)
Source: Author

input/output pins (some with pulse width modulation capabilities) and six analogy inputs for capturing sensor data. Equipped with a 16 MHz resonator for reliable clocking, a USB connection for programming, and a power jack for flexible powering options, the Arduino UNO is truly user-friendly. Whether you connect it to your computer or power it with an adapter or battery, you're all set to embark on your creative journey in electronics and programming.

Electrodes

Electrodes are vital components for recording the brain's electrical activity, providing crucial insights into brain function and health. The variety of electrode types and placement standards ensures that EEG can be effectively utilized

Figure 9.7 Microcontroller (courtesy: google images)
Source: Author

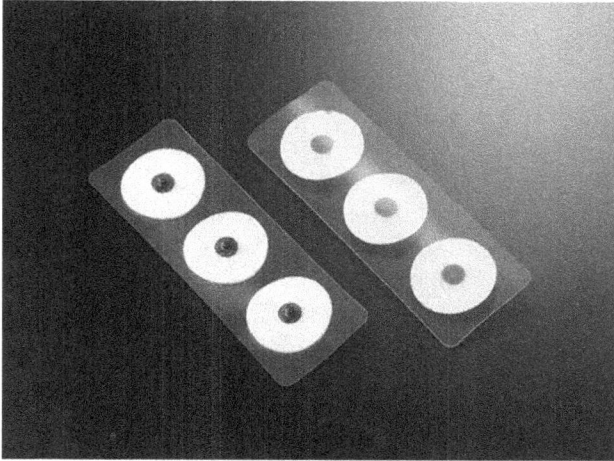

Figure 9.8 EEG Electrodes (courtesy: google images)
Source: Author

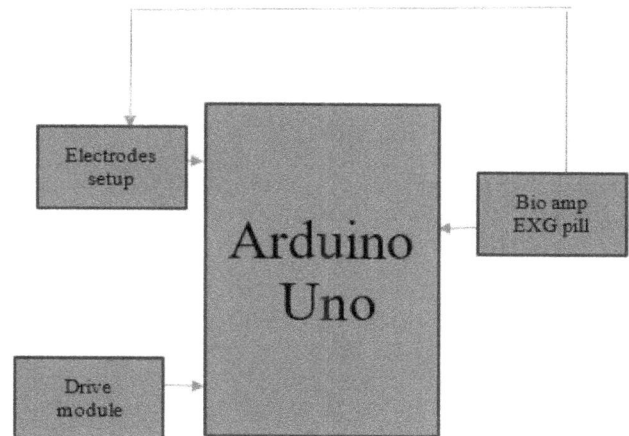

Figure 9.9 Connections of the hardware components
Source: Author

across diverse applications, from clinical diagnostics to advanced review and consumer health monitoring.

Drive module

The wheelchair's movement relies on motors, the workhorses of the system convert electrical energy from the battery into mechanical rotation. This conversion happens through the interaction of magnetic fields generated by the motor's internal components – the spinning armature and the stationary stator. As the current flows through the motor, these magnetic fields interact, creating a force that propels the wheelchair forward.

The motor driver acts as a bridge between the microcontroller, the brain of the wheelchair, and these powerful motors. This allows the microcontroller to precisely control the direction and speed of the wheelchair motors using low-power digital signals, ensuring a smooth and responsive ride.

Challenges of Brain Computer Interface

Psychology, a field crucial for understanding human behavior and brain- computer interaction. Fostering collaboration between psychology, neuroscience, engineering, and other relevant disciplines is vital for developing practical and user-friendly BCI systems.

Accessibility for all: Cost and portability, currently available BCI systems, due to their complexity and materials, are often cost-prohibitive for widespread adoption. Additionally, their bulky designs limit their use to controlled environments like labs. To unlock the true potential of BCIs, reviewers must prioritize developing cost-effective and portable systems suitable for everyday use. This will be particularly beneficial for individuals in developing countries who can potentially gain immense rehabilitation and communication benefits from BCI technology.

Future Scope

The future scope of BCIs, has great potential to improve the lives of people who are majorly impaired. The following are some potential future paths and areas for BCI-powered wheelchairs:

Other technologies

Wireless connectivity:

Improvements in wireless communication for seamless interaction between the brain, the wheelchair, and other devices. Development of secure and reliable wireless protocols to ensure uninterrupted operation.

Customization and adaptability:

Personalized BCI systems that adapt to the specific neural patterns of individual users. Adaptive learning systems that improve over time with use, becoming more intuitive and responsive.

User comfort:

Ergonomic designs for headsets and sensors to enhance comfort during prolonged use. Minimization of the cognitive load required to operate the wheelchair, making it easier for users with varying levels of cognitive ability.

Affordability:

Reduction in the cost of BCI systems to make them more accessible to a wider range of users. Development of affordable and scalable production methods for BCI-based wheelchairs.

Wider adoption:

Increased awareness and acceptance of BCI technology in the healthcare and rehabilitation sectors. Integration into healthcare plans and insurance coverage to support wider usage.

Regulatory approvals:

Streamlined regulatory processes to facilitate the approval and distribution of BCI-based wheelchairs. Development of standards and guidelines to ensure the safety and efficacy of BCI devices.

Independence and quality of life:

Enhancing the independence and mobility of individuals with severe physical disabilities. Improving the overall quality of life by providing a reliable means of mobility.

Social inclusion:

Promoting social inclusion by enabling users to participate more fully in everyday activities. Reducing the stigma associated with disabilities through advanced and empowering technologies.

Global reach: Efforts to make BCI-based wheelchairs available in developing countries where traditional mobility aids are scarce. Global initiatives to ensure that advancements in BCI technology benefit people worldwide.

Expected Results

1. Accuracy and reliability: The system should demonstrate high accuracy in controlling the wheelchair using brain signals captured by electrodes in the headset. The experiments showed that eye-blink strength is more reliable than attention and meditation levels, with a minimal deviation of 1.22 steps on av-erage in navigation tasks. Eye blink strength provided more consistent control compared to attention and meditation, which were harder to regulate and led to higher deviations.

2. User independence: The BCI-controlled wheelchair should significantly enhance the independence of users with motor impairments, allowing them to maneuverer without relying on others. This includes individuals with quadriplegia, paraplegia, or other motor function impairments.

3. Ease of use: The system should be easy to set up and use, with minimal setup time. The use of a electrode headset, which has built-in electrodes for capturing EEG signals, and an Arduino micro-controller contributes to the system's simplicity and affordability. The control commands (start, move forward, turn left, turn right, stop) should be intuitively mapped to the user's brain signals for ease of operation.

4. Cost-effectiveness: The BCI-controlled wheelchair should be cost-effective, making it accessible to a larger population. The use of commercially available components like electrodes, headbands, connecting wires and Arduino contributes to the overall low cost.

5. Performance metrics: The system's performance can be measured by the number of steps taken to complete a predefined path and the time taken for each trial. Comparative analysis of different control algorithms (attention and meditation, eye-blink strength, combination of all three) helps in determining the most efficient method for controlling the wheelchair.

6. User experience: User feedback should be positive, emphasizing the ease of controlling the wheelchair through brain signals detected by the headset's electrodes and the enhanced sense of autonomy. Users should find the system responsive and accurate, with minimal lag between command and action.

Limitations

Brain-computer interface (BCI) wheelchairs present significant potential; however, they encounter various challenges:

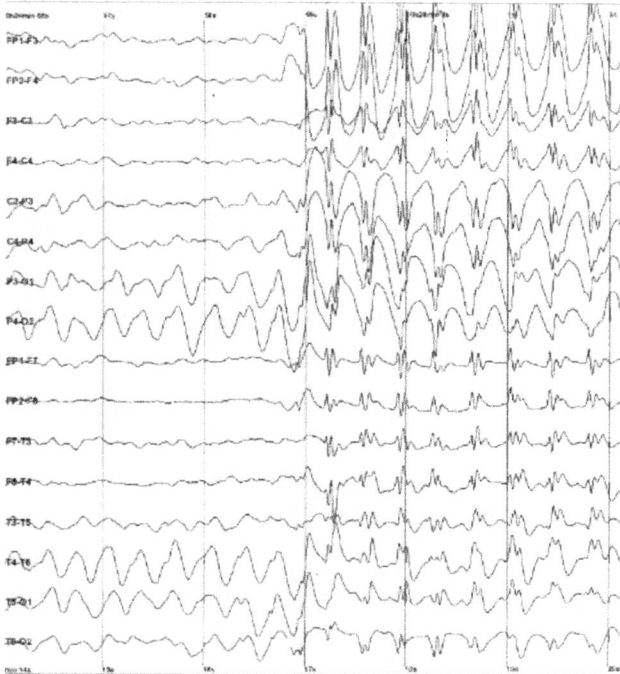

Figure 9.10 Expected result of brain waves acquired (courtesy: google images)
Source: Author

1. Accuracy and reliability:
   BCIs depend on the detection of neural signals, such as EEG or firs. The quality of these signals can be compromised by noise, improper electrode placement, and individual differences.
   Consistent and precise control remains a significant hurdle, as users may face false positives or negatives, resulting in unintended movements of the wheelchair.
2. Training and adaptation effective operation of BCIs necessitates user training. Mastering the modulation of neural signals for accurate control requires considerable time and effort. Users must adapt to evolving neural patterns over time, which can influence the performance of the BCI.
3. Speed and responsiveness:
   Compared to traditional joystick controls, BCIs typically exhibit slower response times. Real-time navigation demands quicker processing capabilities.

Table 9.1 Comparative analysis of various techniques

Comparative analysis of various techniques			
Author	**Method**	**Wheel chair control**	**Results**
Xiong et al [14]	MI	Actual wheelchair/assigned control	Accuracy is $60 \pm 5\%$ Peak subject accuracy is $82 \pm 3\%$
Permana et al. [15]	Hybrid MI and Eye motion	Actual wheelchair/ independent control	Success Rate range: 46.67– 82.22%
Chen et al. [16]	SSVEP	Actual wheelchair/assigned control	Accuracy in the range of 86.3– 98.7%
Ruhunage et al. [17]	Hybrid SSVEP and EOG	Actual wheelchair/assigned control	SSVEP accuracy is 84.5% Double blink accuracy is 100%

Source: Author

Enhancing the speed of BCIs while ensuring accuracy continues to be a focus of ongoing review.

4. Limited communication channels:
   The majority of BCIs utilize motor imagery or P300 signals related to attention. Broadening the range of communication channels, such as incorporating speech or eye gaze, would improve their versatility.

5. User fatigue and cognitive load:
   Utilizing BCIs can be mentally demanding, as users must focus on generating specific brain patterns. Extended use may result in cognitive fatigue, which can diminish overall usability

6. Safety and robustness:
   It is essential to ensure safe operation, as unexpected errors in BCI functionality could

lead to accidents. There is a need for enhanced robustness against environmental factors, including lighting conditions and interference.

7. Ethical and privacy concerns:
   BCIs provide direct access to neural data, making it crucial to protect user privacy and prevent potential misuse. Ethical issues encompass consent, data ownership, and the risks associated with potential brain hacking.

8. Environmental challenges:
   BCWs operate in real-world environments with varying conditions (e.g., noise, lighting, distractions). External factors like electromagnetic interference or other wireless devices can disrupt BCI signals. Ensuring robustness and stability across different settings remains a challenge.

Acknowledgement

The authors gratefully acknowledge the students, staff, and authority of the Electronics and Communication Engineering department for their cooperation in this review.

References

[1] Tiwari, P. K., Chaudhary, A., Gupta, S., Dhar, J., and Chanak, P. (2020). Sensitive brain-computer interface to help maneuver a miniature wheelchair electroencephalography. In 2020 IEEE International Students' Conference on Electrical, Electronics and Computer Science(SCEECS), Bhopal, India, (pp. 1–6). doi:10.1109/SCEECS48394.2020.73.

[2] Zhang, X., Li, J., Zhang, R., and Liu, T. (2024). A brain-controlled and user-centered intelligent wheelchair: a feasibility study. *Sensors (Basel)*, 24(10), 3000. doi:10.3390/s24103000. PMID: 38793855; PMCID: PMC11124864.

[3] Zavala, S. P., Yoo, S. G., and Tituana, D. E. V. (2021). Controlling wheelchair using a brain computer interface based on user controlled eye blinks. *International Journal of Advanced Computer Science and Applications (IJACSA)*, 12(6). http://dx.doi.org/10.14569/IJACSA.2021.0120607. 9–10

[4] Siribunyaphat, N., and Punsawad, Y. (2023). Brain–computer interface based on steady-state visual evoked potential using quick-response code pattern for wheelchair control. *Sensors*, 23, 2069. https://doi.org/10.3390/s23042069.

[5] Zhu, H. Y., Hieu, N. Q., Hoang, D. T., Nguyen, D., and Lin, C.-T. (2023). A human- centric met averse enabled by brain-computer interface: a survey.

[6] Banach, K., Małecki, M., Rosół, M., and Broniec, A. (2021). Brain-computer interface for electric wheelchair based on alpha waves of EEG signal. *Bio- Algorithms and Med-Systems*, 17(3), 165–172. https://doi.org/10.1515/bams-2021-0095.

[7] Maiseli, B., Abdulla, A. T., Massawe, L. V., Mbise, M., Mkocha, K., Nassor, N. A., et al. (2023). Brain– computer interface: trend, challenges, and threats. *Brain Informatics*, 10(1), 20. https://doi.org/10.1186/s40708-023-00199-3.

[8] Dev, A., Rahman, M. A., and Mamun, N. (2018). Design of an EEG-based brain controlled wheelchair for quadriplegic patients. In 2018 3rd International Conference for Convergence in Technology (I2CT), (pp. 1–5). IEEE 10.1109/I2CT.2018.8529751.

[9] Zhu, K., Jiao, A., Liu, X., and Ramsay, S. (2021). Design of a low cost EEG headset for educational research. In 2021 ASEE Virtual Annual Conference Content Access Proceedings (nd). https://doi. org/10.18260/1-2--36917 10.18260/1-2--36917.

[10] Puanhvuan, D., Khemmachotikun, S., Wechakarn, P., Wijarn, B., and Wongsawat, Y. (2017). Navigation-synchronized multimodal control wheelchair from brain to alternative assistive technologies for persons with severe disabilities. *Cognitive Neurodynamics*, 11(2), 117–134. 10.1007/s11571-017-9424-6.

[11] Abdul Karim, H., and Al-Faiz, M. Z. (2021). Brain-controlled wheeled chair path planning for indoor environments. *International Journal of Simulation: Systems, Science and Technology*, 22(1), 10–12.

[12] Minguillonab, J., Lopez-Gordocd, M. A., and Pelayoa, F. (2017). Trends in EEG-BCI for daily-life: requirements for artifact removal. *Biomedical Signal Processing and Control*, 31, 407. https://doi.org/10.1016/j.bspc.2016.09.005.

[13] Mudgal, S. K., Sharma, S. K., Chaturvedi, J., and Sharma, A. (2020). Brain computer interface advancement in neurosciences: applications and issues. *Interdisc Neurosurgeon*, 20, 100694.

[14] Xiong, M., Hotter, R., Nadin, D., Patel, J., Tarrakovsky, S., Wang, Y., et al. (2019). A low-cost, semiautonomous wheelchair is controlled by motor imagery and jaw muscle activation. In Proceedings of the IEEE International Confer-

ence on Systems, Man and Cybernetice (SMC), Bari, Italy, 6–9 October 2019, (pp. 2180–2185).

[15] Permana, K., Wijaya, S. K., and Prajitno, P. (2018). Controlled wheelchair based on brain computer interface using neurosky mindwave mobile 2. In AIP Conference Proceedings; AIP Publishing LLC: Depok, Indonesia, 2018; (Vol. 2168, pp. 020022-1–020022-7).

[16] Chen, J. W., Wu, C. J., Lin, Y. T., Kuo, Y. C., and Kuo, C. H. (2020). Mechatronic implementation and trajectory tracking validation of a BCI-based human-wheelchair interface. In Proceedings of the 8th IEEE International Conference on Biomedical Robotics and Bio mechatronics (Bio Rob), New York, NY, USA, 29 November 2020, (pp. 304–309).

[17] Ruhunage, I., Perera, C. J., Munasinghe, I., and Lalitharatne, T. D. (2018). EEG-SSVEP based brain machine interface for controlling of a wheelchair and home application with bluetooth localization system. In Proceedings of the 2018 IEEE International Conference on Robotics and Biomimetic, Kuala Lumpur, Malaysia, 12–15 December 2018, (pp. 2520–2525).

[18] Kavitha, B. C., Sai Sathrughna, D., Chaithanya Sai, V., Nuthan Abhiram, A., and Sujatha, M. (2023). Controlling wheelchair based on brain waves for paralyzed people. In Kaiser, M. S., Xie, J., Rathore, V. S. (Eds.). Information and Communication Technology for Competitive Strategies (ICTCS 2022). Lecture Notes in Networks and Systems, (Vol. 615). Singapore: Springer,. https://doi.org/10.1007/978-981-19-9304-6_26.

[19] Badajena, J. C., Sethi, S., and Sahoo, R. K. (2023). Data-driven approach to designing a BCI- integrated smart wheelchair through cost-benefit analysis. *High-Confidence Computing*, 3(2), 100118. ISSN 2667-2952, https://doi.org/10.1016/j.hcc.2023.100118.

[20] Badajena, J. C., Sethi, S., Dash, A., Rout, P., and Sahoo, R. K. (2022). Smart wheelchair using brain waves through machine learning. In 2nd International Conference on Machine Learning, IoT and Bigdata (ICMIB-2021), Intelligent System, 2022.

[21] Kumar, J. S., and Bhuvaneswari, P. (2012). Analysis of electroencephalography (EEG) signals and its categorization study. *Procedia Engineering*, 38, 2525–2536. ISSN18777058, https://doi.org/10.1016/j.proeng.2012.06.298.

10 Analysis of chronic kidney disease using machine learning techniques

Tella Pavani[1,a], Murali Krishna, D.[1,b], Ajita Lakshmi, K.[1,c], Lakshmi, G. N. S.[2,d], Pooja Hitha, G.[2,e], Akshitha, G.[2,f] and Ch. Tejaswini[2,g]

[1]Assistant Professor, Dept of ECE, Shri Vishnu Engineering College for Women (A), Bhimavaram, Andhra Pradesh, India

[2]Dept of ECE, Shri Vishnu Engineering College for Women (A), Bhimavaram, Andhra Pradesh, India

Abstract

Chronic kidney disease (CKD) is a serious global health concern that has a high rate of morbidity and mortality and can cause other disorders. It's a serious condition that can last a lifetime and is brought on by either diminished kidney function or kidney cancer. The early stages of CKD are characterized by a lack of evident symptoms, which might make patients unaware of the disease. It is possible to stop or slow the course of this chronic illness until it reaches a point where a patient's only options for survival are dialysis or surgery. Patients with early-stage CKD can benefit from early therapy, which can also slow the disease's progression. Therefore, having an effective model is crucial for CKD early diagnosis. Because machine learning models execute identification tasks quickly and accurately, they can help therapists accomplish this goal. Here, we recommend using machine learning to diagnose CKD. The CKD dataset, which has a significant amount of missing information, will be made available through the University of California, Irvine (UCI) machine learning repository. Using machine learning techniques such as support vector machines, decision trees, neural networks, and K-nearest neighbor for the detection of chronic kidney disease is the goal of this proposal. Feature engineering algorithms such as ANOVA, MRMR, and CHI2 algorithms are used to determine the features for predicting CKD.

Keywords: Chronic kidney disease, Decision tree, K-Nearest neighbor, machine learning models, Naïve Bayes, neural, support vector machine, UCI machine learning repository

Introduction

A long-term condition called chronic kidney disease (CKD) impairs the kidneys' capacity to operate normally, this ultimately causes a steady decline in renal function. The kidneys are in charge of producing urine, eliminating waste and extra fluid from the blood, and preserving the body's overall fluid and electrolyte balance. When the kidneys are damaged, these harmful substances can build up in our bodies, leading to various health problems. Chronic kidney disease has stages, which define the level of mild to severe stages of kidney failure. CKD may not have noticeable symptoms at the early stage, which often progresses silently. Chronic kidney disease may not show symptoms at an early stage, but when the disease advances, some common signs and symptoms may become recognizable. Some of the advanced CKD symptoms may include fatigue, swelling, changes in urination, unexplained weight loss, hypertension, nausea, and vomiting. It is difficult to seek medical attention and cure the disease at this stage because there is a high risk of kidney damage. These symptoms are different for each individual because there is no commonality among them, so there is a high chance of identifying new symptoms. Early detection and management are crucial for slowing the progression of CKD and preventing complications. Laboratory testing, physical examination, and medical history are used to diagnose chronic kidney disease. CKD is often classified into stages based on the eGFR, ranging

[a]pavaniece@svecw.edu.in, [b]ece_krishnad@svecw.edu.in, [c]kajitalakshmi@svecw.edu.in, [d]20b01a0448@svecw.edu.in, [e]20b01a0446@svecw.edu.in, [f]20b01a0451@svecw.edu.in, [g]20b01a0424@svecw.edu.in

DOI: 10.1201/9781003616399-10

from 0 (ml/min) to 100 (ml/min). If you have risk factors for CKD or are experiencing symptoms such as fatigue, swelling, changes in urination, or other signs mentioned earlier, it is important to seek medical attention. The stages of CKD can be divided based on eGFR level. Stage 5 was the final stage, in which kidney transplantation was the only option. It's crucial to remember that when CKD advances to later stages, its symptoms and problems become more noticeable. Early detection and management are crucial to slowing the progression of CKD and preventing complications.

Globally, morbidity and death are significantly increased by chronic renal disease. It stands in 12th place in India for its mortality rate and 3rd place worldwide. CKD prevention involves managing risk factors and adopting a healthy lifestyle. Numerous lifestyle variables can be altered to lower the risk of developing CKD, but certain risk factors, such as hereditary, are unchangeable.

The paper involves analyzing CKD using machine-learning approaches [1], specifically in MATLAB. The complete strategy consists of several important processes, starting with collecting a relevant dataset that includes features such as statistical data, medical history, and clinical indicators. The data is preprocessed to manage missing values and extreme cases, and then feature selection is used to pick the most relevant variables for analysis. The dataset is then split into testing and training sets to evaluate and train the models. Different machine learning approaches, including decision tree (DT), K-Nearest neighbor (KNN), support vector machine (SVM), and neural network (NN) are being investigated for CKD classification challenges. The chosen models are trained and fine-tuned to improve their performance. Parameters including accuracy, precision, recall, f1-score, and specificity are used to assess the performance of the model.

Preliminaries

Agrawal and Agrawal [9] suggested the use of a SVM, a machine learning approach, to predict disease. They proposed the model on three different datasets which are liver, diabetes, and heart. Out of all the datasets they got the highest accuracy for the liver dataset with 78.6% accuracy followed by the heart dataset with 75.4% accuracy and the diabetes dataset with 75.9% accuracy.

Padmanaban and Parthiban [1] and Salekin and Stankovic [8], have predicted CKD using machine-learning methods like DT and NB. NN and data clustering have also been utilized to improve prediction accuracy. With decision tree classification, they achieved the highest accuracy up to 91%, and with the Naïve Bayes algorithm, 86%. They used the Clinic Foundation Heart Disease Dataset for classifying the risk of CKD [6] have used different machine-learning techniques to predict CKD and to analyze CKD using those results. They have used five-fold cross-validation to train and test the machine-learning models. They have used KNN, SVM, DT, and LR to predict and analyze CKD. Out of all four models, the SVM classifier has given the highest accuracy of 98.3% followed by KNN with 98.1%, DT with 96.55%, and logistic regression (LR) with 94.8%. The dataset used by them is collected from the UCI machine learning repository from Apollo Hospital Indians [8] had only selected important features in the dataset to detect CKD. Their dataset consists of 25 attributes and they selected only 12 attributes from it. The algorithms are KNN, random forest (RF), and NN.KNN gave the highest F1 measure with 0.993 followed by Random Forest with 0.99, and NN with 0.985 [4] used only one machine technique to detect CKD. They used the Naïve Bayes algorithm to diagnose chronic kidney disease supported by stage prediction using eGFR. After preprocessing the dataset, they used the 60-30-10 rule to detect CKD in which 60% of the dataset is used for training, 30% is used for testing, and 10% is used for validation. The accuracy for using the Naïve Bayes (NB) algorithm is 92%, Precision is 94%, Sensitivity is 97%, and F-measure is 95% [2] used RF, DT, and SVM algorithms to predict CKD. Out of all three algorithms, RF has given the highest accuracy with 99.7% followed by DT with 98.5% accuracy and SVM with 96.9% accuracy [7] evaluated classifiers such as DT, KNN, and LR by using them for the prediction of kidney disease. The highest accuracy was obtained by DT with 96.25%, KNN with 71.25% accuracy, and LR with 97% accuracy [12] it gives information about the total number of patients who are affected by kidney-related diseases and how many patients died due to kidney diseases.

Ramesh Chandra [11] assessed the effectiveness of machine learning classifiers in CKD prediction. They used KNN, SVM, and NB algorithms to predict CKD. They used the dataset which is extracted from the UCI machine learning repository. NB has given the highest accuracy of 98.6% followed by KNN with 79.3% accuracy, and SVM with 76.9% accuracy.

Sathiya Priya and Suresh Kumar [3] have used DT and NB machine learning algorithms to predict CKD. Their dataset was collected from the UCI machine learning repository. A 10-fold cross-validation method is used for training and testing the model. The DT algorithm has given the highest accuracy of 99.25%, a sensitivity of 99.2%, and a specificity of 99.33% followed by the results of Naïve Bayes with an accuracy of 98.75%, a sensitivity of 98%, and specificity of 98.75%.

Dines and Garovic [5] had done their research on menopause and CKD. After the research, they concluded that chronic kidney disease is majorly seen in girls and women compared to boys and men [10]. The machine learning algorithms are LR, DT, and SVM. They used the bagging ensemble technique to produce the result depending on

all three algorithms that are used for detecting CKD. The dataset which they used is taken from the UCI machine learning repository. The accuracies for LR with 94.53%, DT with 97.23% accuracy, and SVM with 95.70% accuracy [4] extracted the dataset from kaggle. They used RF, XGradient, and SVM machine learning techniques to detect CKD. They also used a confusion matrix to calculate the f1-score, recall scores, and precision scores. Compared to the three machine learning algorithms, the SVM has given the highest recall score, RF has given the highest precision score, and XGradient has given the highest f1-score [6] used SVM and DT machine-learning algorithms for predicting CKD. They extracted the dataset from the UCI machine learning repository. They used 75% of the dataset to train the model and the remaining 25% of the dataset to test the model. Compared to the DT, the SVM algorithm has given the highest f1-score of 0.9579 and the DT has given an f1-score of 0.8958.

Materials and Methods

Three models for machine learning on the chosen dataset, KNN, DT, SVM, and NN were used. Different conditions and different training testing ratios were applied to the dataset. The complete flow chart of the project is given below.

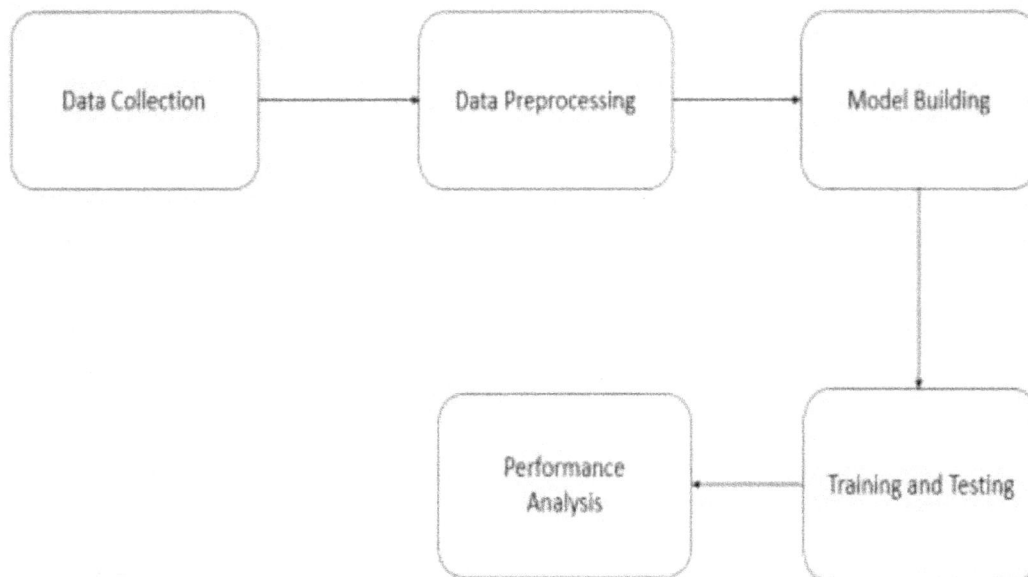

Figure 10.1 Complete flow chart
Source: Author

Data collection

The University of California, Irvine (UCI) provided the dataset, which had 400 instances and 25 attributes. In which 11 are nominal attributes and 14 are categorical attributes. 250 patients out of 400 cases have CKD, while 150 patients have NOT-CKD. "Yes" and "no," "present" and "not present," and "normal" and "abnormal" are used to denote some of the category columns. Out of 14 categorical columns, the dataset consists of a class that is used to determine CKD or NOT-CKD.

K-nearest neighbor

A non-parametric technique for regression and classification is the KNN [5]. It employs the method of supervised learning. All of your data can be stored using the KNN approach, which allows you to categorize new data according to how similar it is to the existing data. This implies that new data can be quickly classified into distinct categories using the KNN approach. The KNN approach can be applied to regression problems even though it is frequently employed for classification difficulties. The KNN approach, often known as a "lazy learner algorithm," is nonparametric and does not make any assumptions about the data because it does not use computational and mathematical methods in medicine. KNN uses the Euclidean distance, which has the following definition, to predict the class:

$$d(x,y)= \sqrt{\sum_{i=1}^{k}(x_i - y_i)^2}$$

"x: Array or Vector x ", y: Array or Vector y

"x_i": Values of the coordinate plane's horizontal axis

"y_i": Values of the coordinate plane's vertical axis

"k: No. of observations

The distance needed to locate the closest example in the pattern space is measured using the Euclidean distance. By majority vote among its neighbors, the unknown example's class is determined. The class has a single nearest neighbor if K = 1. If d is the distance to the neighbor, the weight allocated to each neighbor in a common weighting system is 1/d. The notion that the shortest path between any two neighbors is always a straight line which is known as the Euclidean distance.

Support vector machine

Algorithm of support vector machine

- Organize labeled training data with features and corresponding class labels. Choose a kernel function and optimize parameters to find the hyperplane that maximizes margin and minimizes classification errors.
- Store relevant parameters (support vectors, coefficients) defining the decision boundary. Map new data points into the feature space and classify based on their position relative to the decision boundary. Assess model performance using evaluation metrics and validate [7] generalization on unseen data. Adjust parameters iteratively for improved results. To elucidate the SVM algorithm's operation, consider a dataset comprising two labels (green and blue) and two features (x1 and x2). Our objective is to construct a classifier that accurately categorizes coordinate pairs (x1, x2) into either green or blue. Given the two-dimensional nature of the data, a simple linear boundary can effectively separate these classes.

Simulated program

In this project, we have mainly used Google Collaboratory for implementing a machine learning framework in Python. Scikit-learn and mat plot libraries also played a major role in splitting the dataset and for data visualization. The flow chart of the project implementation details is given as follows:

Result and Discussions

In this project, the dataset consisting of 400 instances and 25 attributes is used for classification. Here, using a confusion matrix we have calculated sensitivity, selectivity, accuracy, precision, and f1-score. As per our project name Analysis of CKD, we have used 3 different training and testing ratios. They are, 67:33, 70:30, and 80:20. We have used these three different training and testing ratios for 4 different machine learning

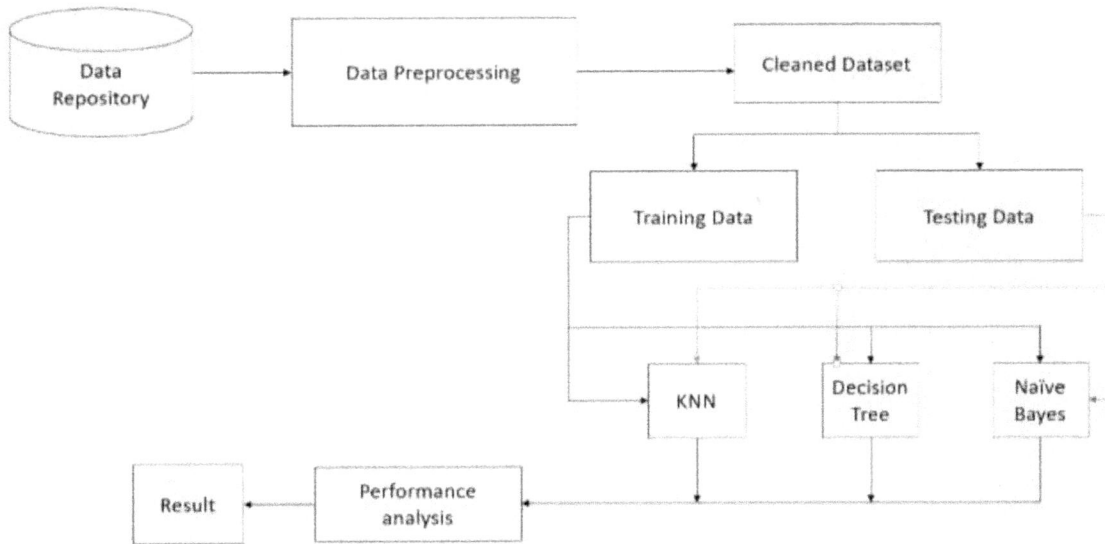

Figure 10.2 Implementation details
Source: Author

algorithms. Three different feature selection algorithms such as Chi2, MRMR, and ANOVA algorithms are used to determine the important features in the selected dataset.

Table 10.1 shows the confusion matrices and analysis table for different types of KNN under 67:33 training testing ratio.

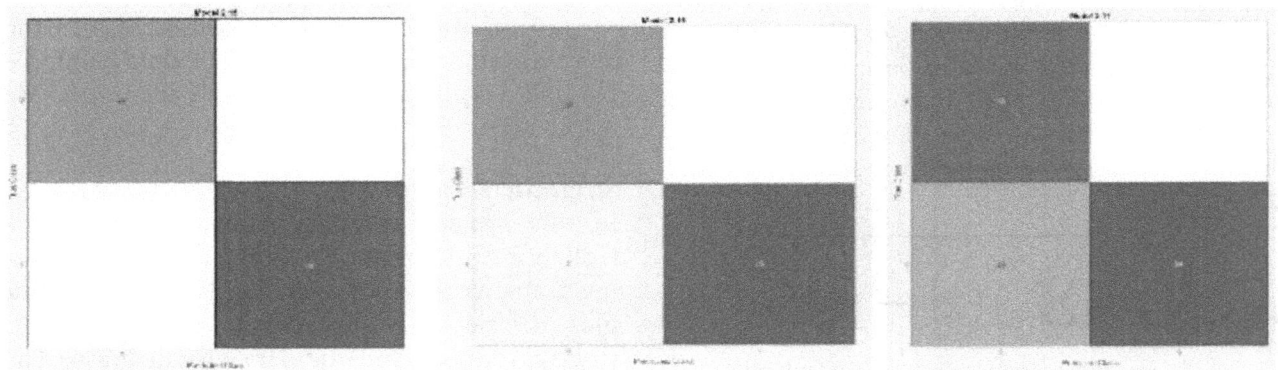

Figure 10.3 Compact KNN moderate KNN expensive KNN
Source: Author

Table 10.1 Analysis of CKD using different types of KNN 67:33 training testing ratio

Types of KNN	Training accuracy	Testing accuracy	Sensitivity	Selectivity	Precision	F1-Score
Compact KNN	98.1	100	100	100	100	100
Moderate KNN	93.3	94.7	87.7	100	100	93.4
Expensive KNN	76.5	78.8	64.1	100	100	78.1

Source: Author

Table 10.2 shows the confusion matrices and analysis table for different types of KNN under 70:30 training testing ratio.

Table 10.3 shows the confusion matrices and analysis table for different types of KNN under 80:20 training testing ratio.

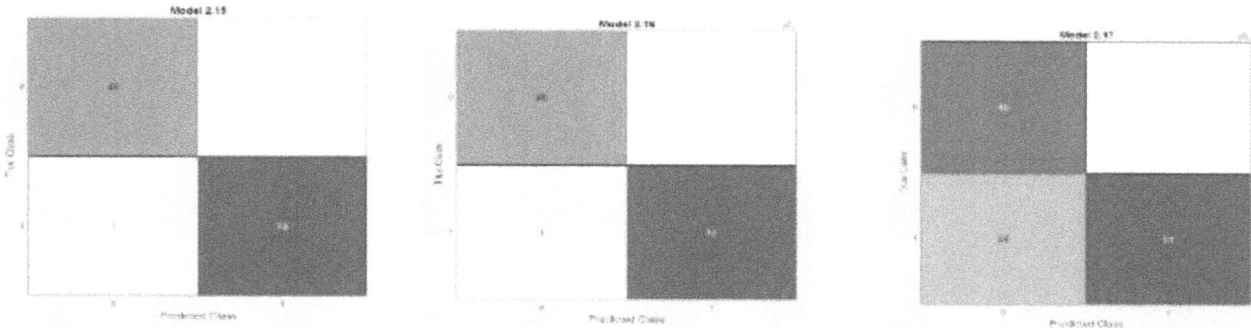

Figure 10.4 Compact KNN moderate KNN expensive KNN
Source: Author

Table 10.2 Analysis of CKD using different types of KNN under 70:30 training testing

Types of KNN	Training accuracy	Testing accuracy	Sensitivity	Selectivity	Precision	F1-Score
Compact KNN	98.9	99.2	97.8	100	100	98.8
Moderate KNN	95	97.5	93.75	100	100	96.77
Expensive KNN	78.2	80	65.2	100	100	78.9

Source: Author

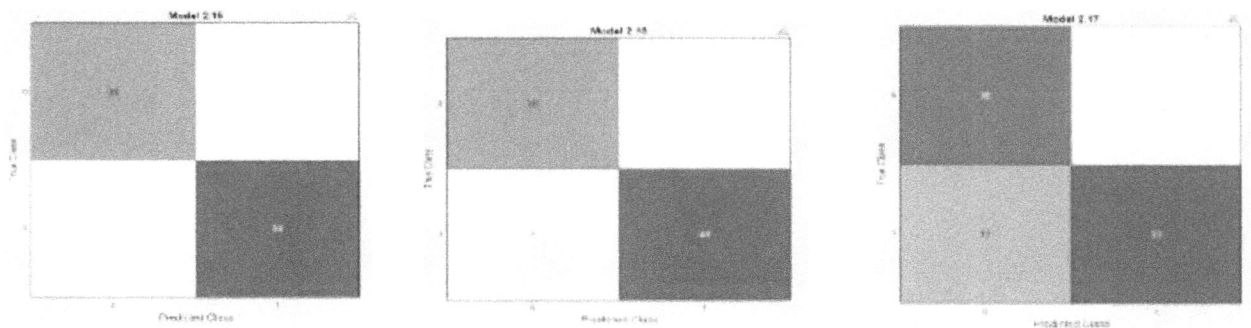

Figure 10.5 Compact KNN moderate KNN expensive KNN
Source: Author

Table 10.4 shows the confusion matrices and analysis table for different types of DT under 67:33 training testing ratio.

Table 10.5 shows the confusion matrices and analysis table for different types of DT under 70:30 training testing ratio.

Table 10.3 Analysis of CKD using KNN under 80:20 training testing ratio

Types of KNN	Training accuracy	Testing accuracy	Sensitivity	Selectivity	Precision	F1-Score
Compact KNN	98.1	100	100	100	100	100
Moderate KNN	94.7	98.8	96.77	100	100	98.35
Expensive KNN	79.7	78.8	63.8	100	100	77.89

Source: Author

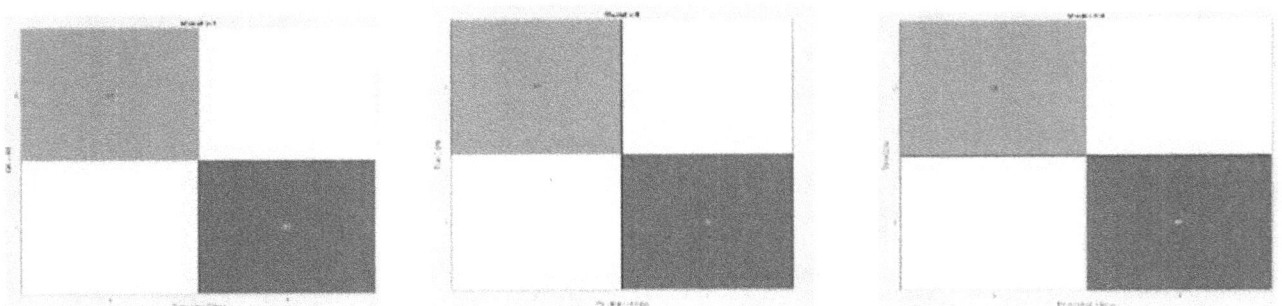

Figure 10.6 Compact KNN moderate KNN expensive KNN
Source: Author

Table 10.4 Analysis of CKD using DT under 67:33 training testing ratio

Types of tree	Training accuracy	Testing accuracy	Sensitivity	Selectivity	Precision	F1-Score
Compact KNN	98.5	100	100	100	100	100
Moderate KNN	98.5	100	100	100	100	100
Expensive KNN	98.5	100	100	100	100	100

Source: Author

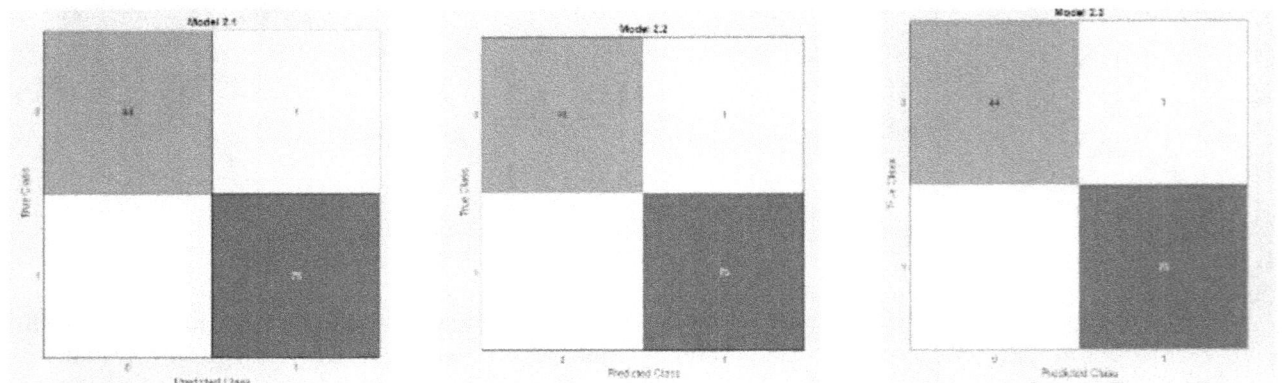

Figure 10.7 Compact KNN moderate KNN expensive KNN
Source: Author

Table 10.5 Analysis of CKD using DT under 70:30 training testing ratio

Types of tree	Training accuracy	Testing accuracy	Sensitivity	Selectivity	Precision	F1-Score
Compact KNN	99.7	100	100	100	100	100
Moderate KNN	99.7	100	100	100	100	100
Expensive KNN	99.7	100	100	100	100	100

Source: Author

Table 10.6 shows the confusion matrices and analysis table for different types of DT under 80:20 training testing ratio.

Table 10.7 shows the confusion matrices and analysis table for different types of NN under 67:33 training testing ratio.

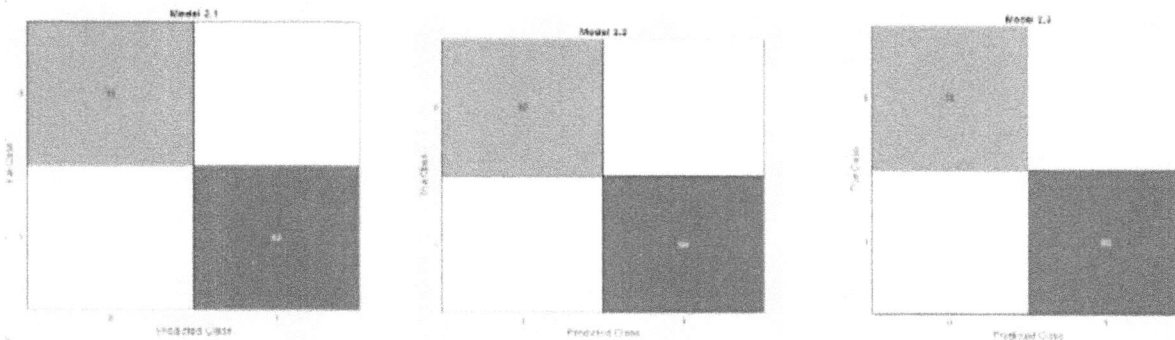

Figure 10.8 Compact KNN moderate KNN expensive KNN
Source: Author

Table 10.6 Analysis of CKD using different types of DT under 80:20 training testing

Types of tree	Training accuracy	Testing accuracy	Sensitivity	Selectivity	Precision	F1-Score
Fine tree	99.3	100	100	100	100	100
Medium tree	98.9	100	100	100	100	100
Coarse KNN	98.5	100	100	100	100	100

Source: Author

Table 10.8 shows the confusion matrices and analysis table for different types of NN under 70:30 training testing ratio.

Table 10.9 shows the confusion matrices and analysis table for different types of NN under 80:20 training testing ratio.

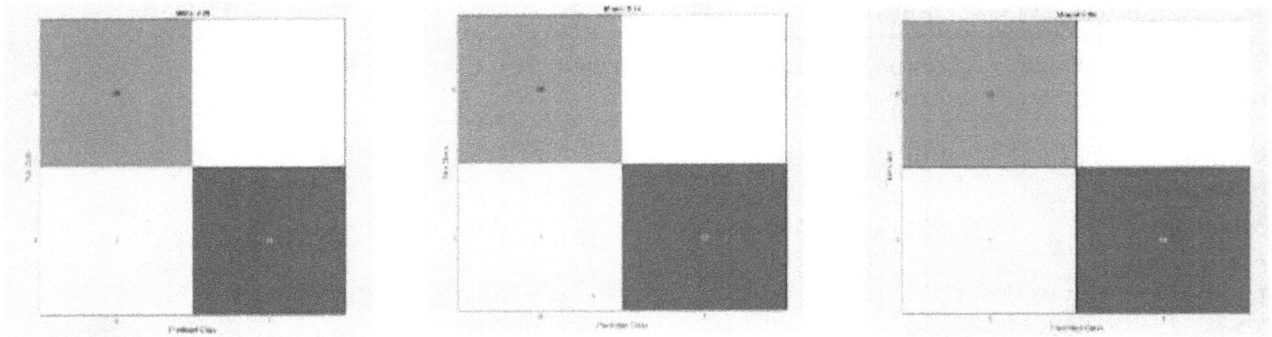

Figure 10.9 Narrow NN medium NN wide NN
Source: Author

Table 10.7 Analysis of CKD using NN under 67:33 training testing ratio

Types of NN	Training accuracy	Testing accurcay	Sensitivity	Selectivity	Precision	F1-Score
Narrow NN	98.1	99.2	98	100	100	98.98
Medium NN	98.9	99.2	98	100	100	98.98
Wide NN	99.3	99.2	98	100	100	98.98

Source: Author

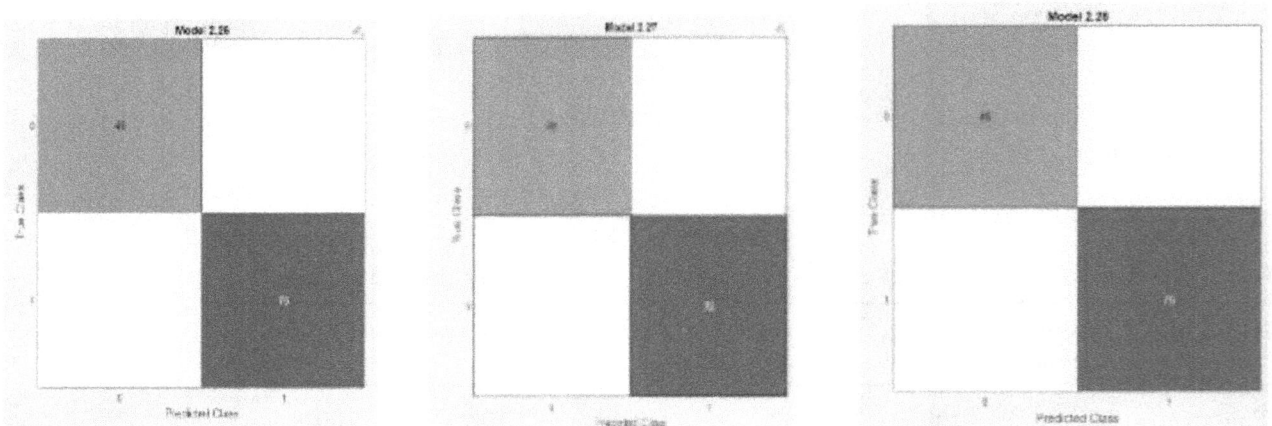

Figure 10.10 Narrow NN medium NN wide NN
Source: Author

Table 10.8 Analysis of CKD using NN under 70:30 training testing ratio

Types of NN	Training accuracy	Testing accuracy	Sensitivity	Selectivity	Precision	F1-Score
Narrow NN	98.9	100	100	100	100	100
Medium NN	98.6	100	100	100	100	100
Wide NN	98.9	100	100	100	100	100

Source: Author

Table 10.7 shows the confusion matrices and analysis table for different types of NN under 67:33 training testing ratio.

Table 10.8 shows the confusion matrices and analysis table for different types of NN under 70:30 training testing ratio.

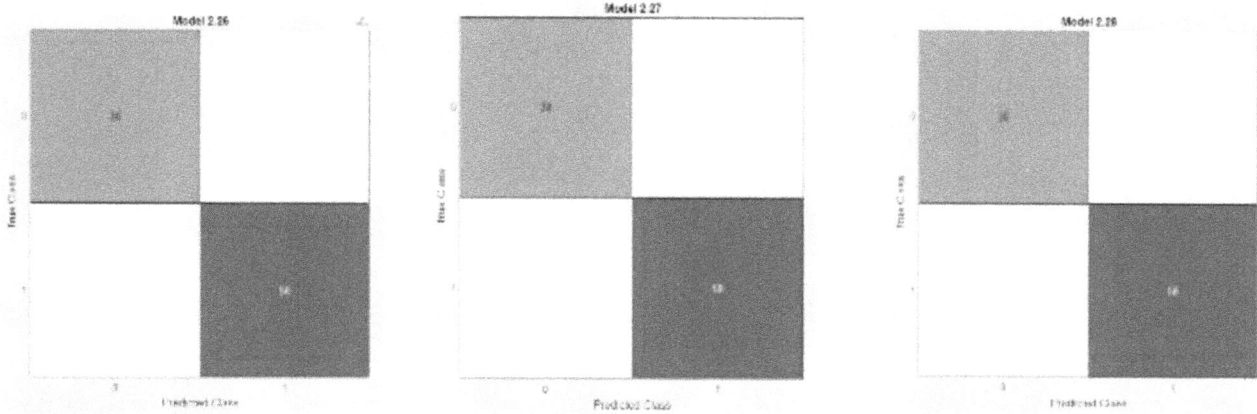

Figure 10.11 Narrow NN medium NN wide NN
Source: Author

Table 10.9 Analysis of CKD using different types of NN under 80:20 training testing

Types of NN	Training accuracy	Testing accuracy	Sensitivity	Selectivity	Precision	F1-Score
Narrow NN	98.8	100	100	100	100	100
Medium NN	98.8	100	100	100	100	100
Wide NN	99.4	100	100	100	100	100

Source: Author

Table 10.12 shows the confusion matrices and analysis table for different types SVM under 80:20 training testing ratio.

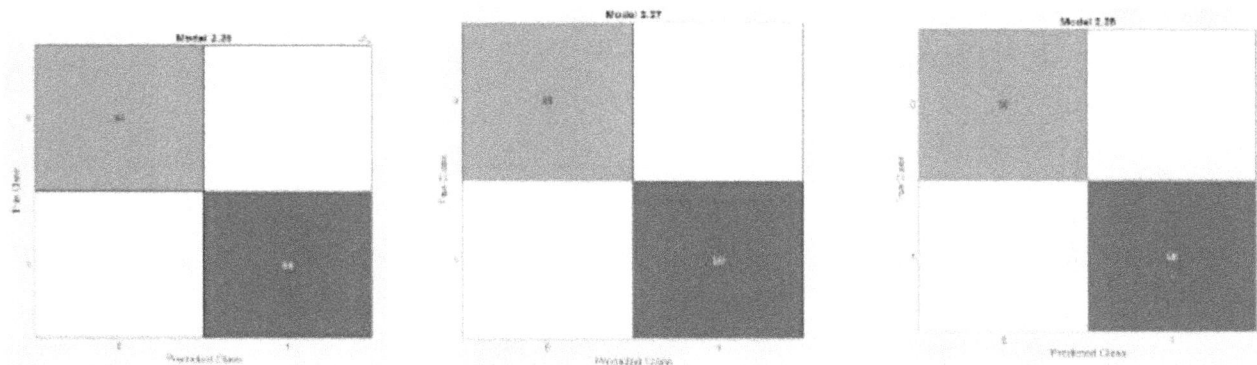

Figure 10.12 Linear SVM quadratic SVM cubic SVM
Source: Author

Table 10.10 Analysis of CKD using different types of NN under 67:33 training testing ratio

Types of SVM	Training accuracy	Testing accuracy	Sensitivity	Selectivity	Precision	F1-Score
Linear SVM	99.3	100	100	100	100	100
Quadratic SVM	98.9	100	100	100	100	100
Cubic SVM	98.5	100	100	100	100	100

Source: Author

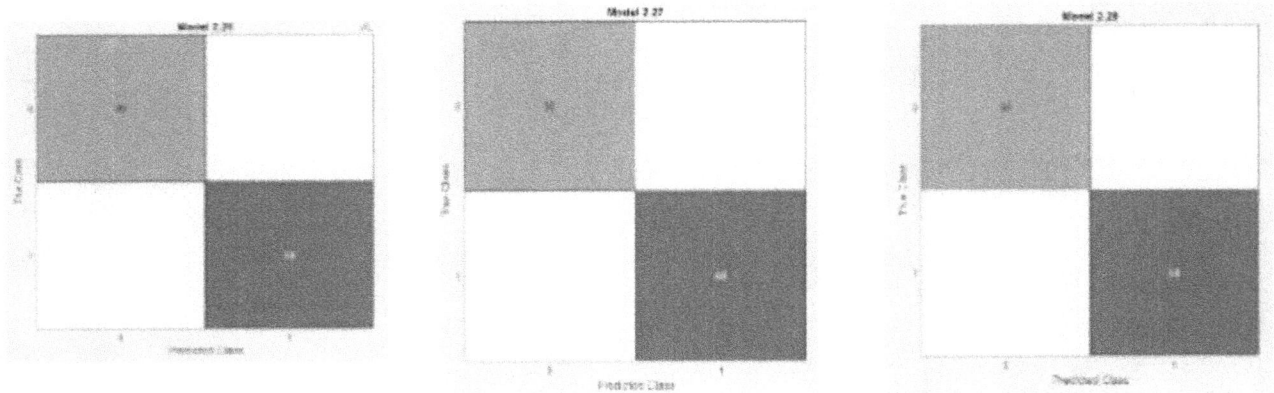

Figure 10.13 Linear SVM quadratic SVM cubic SVM
Source: Author

Table 10.11 Analysis of CKD using different types of NN under 70:30 training testing ratio

Types of SVM	Training accuracy	Testing accurcay	Sensitivity	Selectivity	Precision	F1-Score
Linear SVM	98.6	100	100	100	100	100
Quadratic SVM	98.2	100	100	100	100	100
Cubic SVM	98.6	100	100	100	100	100

Source: Author

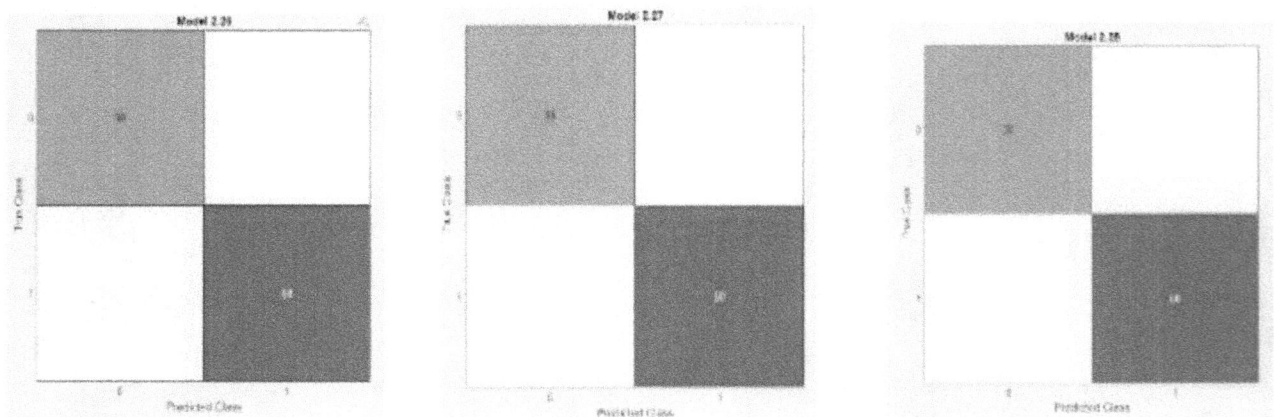

Figure 10.14 Linear SVM quadratic SVM cubic SVM
Source: Author

Table 10.12 Analysis of CKD using different types of NN under 80:20 training testing ratio

Types of SVM	Training accuracy	Testing accuracy	Sensitivity	Selectivity	Precision	F1-Score
Linear SVM	99.3	100	100	100	100	100
Quadratic SVM	98.9	100	100	100	100	100
Cubic SVM	98.5	100	100	100	100	100

Source: Author

Figures 10.15, 10.17 showing graphical representation of dataset using ANOVA, MRMR, Chi2 feature selection algorithm for 70:30 training testing ratio.

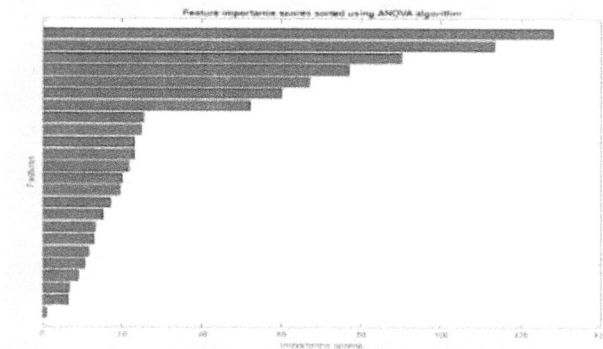

Figure 10.15 Graphical representation of our dataset using ANOV
Source: Author

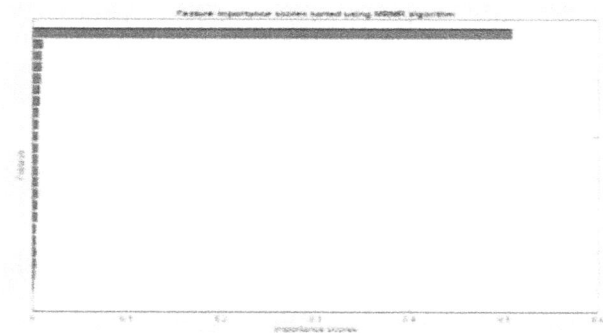

Figure 10.16 Graphical representation of our dataset using MRMR
Source: Author

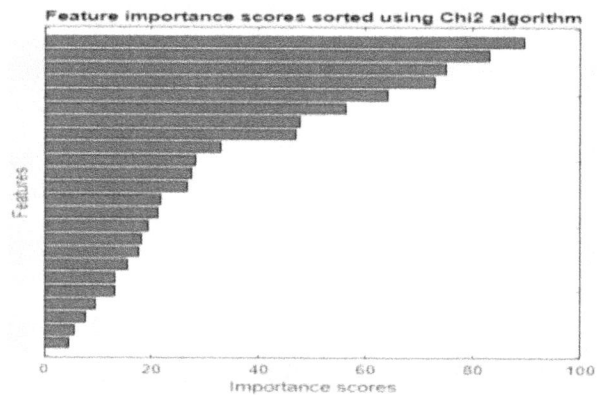

Figure 10.17 Graphical representation of our dataset using CHI2
Source: Author

Conclusion

We had done analysis of our model by using 3 different training testing ratios and with 4 different algorithms. By comparing different ratios, we got better accuracy for 70:30 ratios. We got better accuracy for neural networks algorithm compared to KNN, decision tree, and support vector machine algorithms. Three feature selection algorithms such as CHI2, MRMR, and ANOVA are used to decrease the number of features, and they are analyzed using the four algorithms with three different training testing ratios. Up to 18 features, the accuracy for the models is similar while using CHI2 feature selection algorithm. Upto 20 features, the accuracy for the models is similar while using MRMR feature selection algorithm. Up to 22 features, the accuracy for the models is similar while using ANOVA feature selection algorithm.

Acknowledgements

I would like to extend my heartfelt thanks to Shri Vishnu Engineering College for Women for their support throughout this research.

References

[1] Padmanaban, K. R. A., and Parthiban, G. (2016). Applying machine learning techniques for predicting the risk of chronic kidney disease. *Indian Journal of Science and Technology*, 9(29), 1–6. 10.17485/ijst/2016/v9i29/93880, August 2016. ISSN (Print): 0974-6846 ISSN (Online): 0974-5645.

[2] Debal, D. A., and Sitote, T. M. (2022). Chronic kidney disease prediction using machine learning techniques. *Journal of Big Data*, 9(1), 109. doi: https://doi.org/10.1186/s40537-022-00657-5.

[3] Sathiya Priya, S., and Suresh Kumar, M. (2018). Chronic kidney disease prediction using machine learning. *International Journal of Computer Science and Information Security (IJCSIS)*, 16(04).

[4] Vijayaprabakaran, K., Pratheek Reddy, P., Puthin Kumar Reddy, T., Munnaf, K., and Reddi Prasad, G. (2021). Chronic kidney disease diagnosis using machine learning. *International Research Journal of Engineering and Technology (IRJET)*, 08(06). e-ISSN: 2395-0056, pISSN: 2395-0072.

[5] Dines, V. A., and Garovic, V. D. (2024). Menopause and chronic kidney disease. *Nature Reviews Nephrology*, 20(1), 4–5. doi: https://doi.org/10.1038/s41581-023-00717-w.

[6] Tekale, S., and Shingavi, P. (2018). Prediction of chronic kidney disease using machine learning algorithm. *International Journal of Advanced Research in Computer and Communication Engineering (IJARCCE)*, 7(10), 92–96. doi: 10.17148/IJARCCE.2018.71021.

[7] Ifraz, G. M., and Rashid, M. H. (2021). Comparative analysis for prediction of kidney disease using intelligent machine learning methods. *Hindawi, Computational and Mathematical Methods in Medicine*, 2021, 6141470. doi :https://doi.org/10.1155/2021/6141470.

[8] Salekin, A., and Stankovic, J. (2016). Detection of chronic kidney disease and selecting important predictive attributes. In International Conference on Healthcare Informatics (IEEE), October 2016, doi:10.1109/ICHI.2016.36.

[9] Agrawal, A., and Agrawal, H. (2018). Disease prediction using machine learning. In International Conference on Internet of Things and Connected Technologies (ICIoTCT), 2018. ISSN:1556-5068, https://www.ssrn.com/link/3rdICIOTCT-2018.html.

[10] Pal, S. (??). Chronic kidney disease prediction using machine learning techniques. doi: https://doi.org/10.1007/s44174-022-00027-y.

[11] Ramesh Chandra, K. (??). Enhancing kidney stone diagnosis: a fusion approach of FCM and CNN for precise detection. doi:10.1109/ICDCECE60827.2024.10549262.

[12] Mummadi, S., Tharun, A., Chigullapally, D., Bommena, A., and Akhila, D. (2023). Predicting factors affecting kidney functions using machine learning. In 2023 IEEE 9th International Women in Engineering (WIE) Conference on Electrical and Computer Engineering (WIECONECE), doi:10.1109/wieconece60392.2023.10456511.

[13] M Prema Kumar, G. Challa Ram, Viswanadham Ravuri, M. Venkata Subbarao, Abdul Rahaman SK, T P K Nandan "Performance Evaluation of Machine Learning Models for Multi-class Lung Cancer Detection" *4th International Conference on Pervasive Computing and Social Networking (ICPCSN) 2024* ISBN: 979-8-3503-8634-9/24 DOI: 10.1109/ICPCSN62568.2024.00071.

11 Internet of things (IoT) and solar based sowing seed agriculture robot using Arduino mega

Kalathiripi Rambabu[a], Sanjay Dubey[b], Sanjeeva Reddy, B. R.[c], Etikala Teju[d], Gampala Nandini[e] and Kotala Pooja[f]

Department of Electronics and Communication engineering, B V Raju Institute of Technology, Narsapur, Medak, Telangana, India

Abstract

The sowing seed AG-robot is an agricultural solution designed to automate the seed planting process, enhancing efficiency and precision in modern farming. Central to the robot's operation is the Arduino Mega microcontroller, which serves as the primary control unit, coordinating various sensors and actuators to perform the sowing tasks effectively. The inclusion of a solar panel system as a power source not only promotes sustainability but also allows for deployment in remote or off-grid agricultural areas, ensuring continuous operation without reliance on external power supplies. A key feature of the AG-robot is its seed dispensing mechanism, which is meticulously controlled by the Arduino Mega to ensure seeds are planted at precise depths and intervals. This precision in planting is crucial for optimizing crop yields and ensuring uniform growth. Moreover, providing real-time data that allows the robot to adjust its planting strategy according to varying field conditions, thereby improving the adaptability and effectiveness of the sowing process.

Keywords: Agriculture automation, Arduino technology, monitoring and control, precision farming, sowing seed robot

Introduction

The integration of technology in agriculture can significantly enhance crop yields and lower labor costs. Automating seed sowing allows farmers to save time and allocate their efforts to other essential tasks like irrigation and pest management. Moreover, data gathered by the robot's sensors can be utilized to optimize crop growth, as well as reduce water and fertilizer usage, promoting more sustainable farming methods. The seed sowing robot, powered by Arduino technology, has the potential to transform agriculture by boosting efficiency, cutting labor costs, and increasing crop yields. As Internet of things (IoT) technology advances, we can anticipate more innovative applications in agriculture that will further enhance the sustainability and productivity of farming practices. Traditional methods involve manually broadcasting seeds and fertilizers by hand. To address the inefficiencies and labor-intensity of these methods, it is time to automate the agricultural sector. This project introduces an innovative approach by automating processes such as assessing soil suitability for cultivation, sowing seeds, covering the soil, and spraying fertilizers. These automated tasks will significantly reduce human effort. The system will be employed for sensing, monitoring, controlling, and communication purposes, thereby enhancing overall agricultural productivity and efficiency.

Agriculture plays a crucial role in supplying food and resources to a growing global population. With technological advancements, the need for smart solutions to boost efficiency and productivity in agriculture is increasing. One such innovative solution is the deployment of ag-robots to automate various agricultural tasks. This paper discusses the development of a seed-sowing ag- robot utilizing the Arduino Mega 2560

[a]rambabukala@gmail.com, [b]sanjay.dubey@bvrit.ac.in, [c]sanjeev.reddy@bvrit.ac.in, [d]tejuetikala8884@gmail.com, [e]gampalanandini691@gmail.com, [f]Kotalapooja@gmail.com

DOI: 10.1201/9781003616399-11

microcontroller board. The ag-robot is engineered to sow seeds with precision and efficiency, significantly reducing the time and labor associated with manual sowing. The Arduino Mega 2560 microcontroller board ensures the ag-robot performs accurate and precise sowing, making it an invaluable asset for modern agriculture.

This paper details the design, development, and testing phases of the sowing seed ag- robot, emphasizing its potential benefits and applications in the agricultural sector.

Literature Surve

Agricultural robots are revolutionizing farming by automating various tasks, including seed sowing [1]. These robots enhance precision, reduce labor costs, and improve efficiency. Key literature in this domain includes works by Blackmore et al. [1,2] who discuss the future of agricultural mechanization through robotics. Another study describes the Thorvald II agricultural robotic system, highlighting the advancements in robotic agriculture [2,9]. The Arduino Mega is a popular choice for such applications due to its numerous I/O pins, memory capacity, and ease of programming. Banzi and Shiloh [5] provide an overview of the Arduino platform, emphasizing its versatility in prototyping and robotics. Seed sowing mechanisms vary, including rotary discs, pneumatic systems, and precision seed drills. Singh and Singh [3] discuss the design and development of automated seed sowing machines, while Mathur and Sharma [4] describe a manually operated seed-cum-fertilizer drill, showcasing different approaches to seed dispensing. Navigation and control are critical for the functionality of agricultural robots. Freitas et al. [7] GPS modules, combined with the Arduino Mega, provide accurate navigation, as explored by Freitas et al. [7] in their study on improving agricultural productivity through GPS. Control algorithms such as PID and Kalman filters are used for precision control, [6] with detailing the application of extended Kalman filters in robot localization. Power and actuation are essential components, with solar panels and batteries commonly used to power agricultural robots. Actuators like stepper motors and servos, controlled by the Arduino Mega, enable precise movements. Chen et al. [10]

discuss various autonomous navigation technologies applied to agriculture. Their research highlights the integration of different sensor technologies, such as GPS, LiDAR, cameras, and inertial measurement units (IMUs), in facilitating autonomous operation for agricultural vehicles. Shalaby et al. [11] address the need for precision agriculture tools tailored for small-scale farmers, who often cannot afford large-scale machinery. They propose the design of a precision seeder, focusing on improving the efficiency of seed distribution in the field. Mahmood and Yahya [12]. The application of stepper motors in agricultural automation is extensively reviewed by Mahmood and Yahya [12]. Stepper motors are integral to many automated farming machines, particularly in operations requiring precise control over movement, such as seed planting, irrigation systems, and fertilizer application.

Proposed Model

Block diagram

Step 1: Assemble the hardware gather and organize all components: 4 DC motors, relay, water pump, motor driver, ATmega328, 4 wheels, servo motor, Bluetooth module.

Step 2: Program the Arduino open the Arduino IDE and begin writing the program for the Arduino Mega. Import necessary libraries for each component (e.g., motor driver, Bluetooth module). Define pin assignments and configure them as inputs or outputs.

Step 3: Control the DC motors implement code to manage the motor driver, enabling control of the DC motors. Program the DC motors to drive the wheels and operate for seed sowing. Use the servo motor to adjust the cutter blade's angle for precise sowing.

Step 4: Control the water pump connect the water pump to a relay and program the Arduino to control it based on soil moisture.

Step 5: Control the Bluetooth module connect the Bluetooth module and write code to handle remote commands from a mobile device. Implement functionality to control the robot's movements and actions via Bluetooth commands.

Step 6: Test and debug the system thoroughly test the assembled hardware and programmed software in a controlled environment.

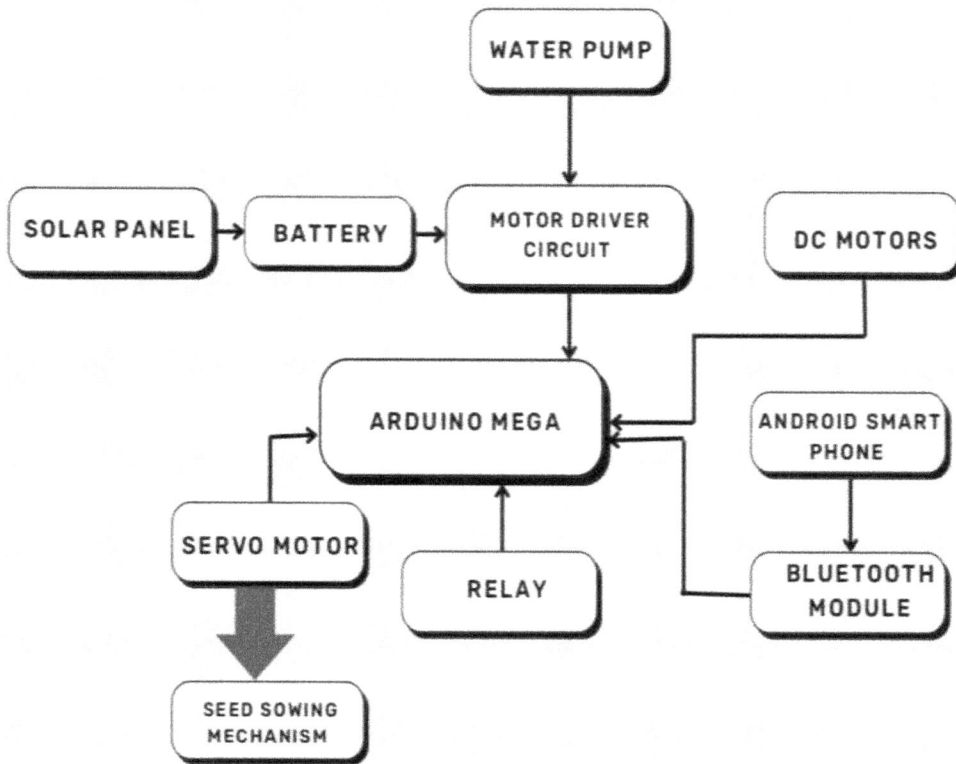

Figure 11.1 Block diagram of sowing seed AG-robot using Arduino mega with solar panel
Source: Author

Components Used
Hardware tools
Arduino Mega: The Arduino Mega is a micro-controller board based on the ATmega2560. It has more input/output pins than the standard Arduino Uno, making it suitable for more complex projects requiring multiple sensors and actuators. It features 54 digital I/O pins, 16 analogy inputs, and four UARTs (hardware serial ports).

Bluetooth module: The Bluetooth module enables wireless communication between an Arduino Mega controller and a mobile device for remote control and data monitoring. Integrated with a solar panel, it ensures autonomous operation and efficiency in outdoor environments, enhancing agricultural productivity and sustainability.

Water pump: A water pump is used to move water from one place to another. In Arduino projects, small DC water pumps can be controlled to automate watering in garden and farming systems.

Battery: A battery plays a crucial role by storing solar- generated power for continuous operation, ensuring uninterrupted functionality during low light conditions or at night. Proper voltage regulation and capacity matching are essential for efficient power management and longevity of the robot's operations.

Motor driver: A motor driver controls the direction and speed of DC motors. It acts as an interface between the microcontroller and the motor, handling higher current levels that the microcontroller cannot directly provide.

Relay: A relay is an electrically operated switch that allows a low-power microcontroller to control high-power devices. It is often used to control mains-powered devices like lights and appliances from an Arduino.

Servo motor: A servo motor is a rotary actuator that allows for precise control of angular position. It consists of a motor coupled to a sensor for position feedback. It's commonly used in robotics and automation for precise movements.

ICATmega328: The ATmega328 is a microcontroller chip used in many Arduino boards, like the Arduino Uno. It features a built-in memory and can be programmed to perform various tasks, making it a versatile component for many projects.

DC motor: A DC motor converts direct current electrical energy into mechanical energy. It's used in a variety of applications where variable speed and torque control are required, such as in robotics, toys, and small appliances.

Software Tools: In software tools we have used Arduino IDE.

Arduino IDE software: The Arduino integrated development environment (IDE) is an open-source software platform used to program Arduino boards, including the Arduino Mega. It runs on various operating systems like Windows, macOS, and Linux, providing a user- friendly code editor with features like syntax highlighting, automatic indentation, and brace matching. The IDE also includes a library manager for easily installing and managing libraries, a serial monitors for communication and debugging, and an integrated compiler that converts written code into executable binaries. Programs in the Arduino IDE are called "sketches" and typically consist of a setup function that runs once and a loop function that runs repeatedly. The programming language used in the Arduino IDE is C/C++, a high-level language known for its efficiency and control over hardware, making it ideal for embedded systems.

Implementation

Implementing a seed-sowing agricultural robot using an Arduino Mega involves a multi-faceted approach starting with the construction Ensure it can withstand field conditions and has enough space for the solar panels, battery, and other parts. Use a motor driver module to control the motors for precise movement and navigation. Program the Arduino Mega to handle motor commands for smooth and accurate travel. Attach a seed hopper to a servo motor, which controls the release of seeds.

Calibrate the servo and hopper to ensure that the correct amount of seeds is dispensed at each location. Use this data to optimize sowing times and locations. The Arduino Mega will manage sensor readings and control the servo for seed dispensing. For a seed-sowing robot, a water pump can be used to deliver water for irrigation or to help with seed placement if using a liquid-based seed dispensing method it can be connect to motor driver. A DC motor (direct current motor) is an electric motor that runs on direct current electricity. It converts electrical energy into mechanical energy through the interaction of magnetic fields Connect the positive terminal of your DC power supply to one terminal of the motor. Connect the negative terminal of the power supply to the other terminal of the motor This will cause the motor to run in one direction. A relay is an electrically operated switch that allows you to control a high-power device with a low-power signal. It acts as an intermediary that opens or closes a circuit based on an electrical signal. A Bluetooth module is a device that allows electronic devices to communicate wirelessly using Bluetooth technology. These modules can be integrated into various projects to enable wireless data transfer and control. Incorporate solar panels to charge the battery pack, which powers the Arduino, motors, and relay, servomotor.

Ensure efficient energy management to maintain operations throughout the day. using an Android smartphone app involves understanding its components, functionality, and the development process The IDE also includes a library manager for easily installing and managing libraries, a serial monitors for communication and debugging, and an integrated compiler that converts written code into executable binaries. Programs in the Arduino IDE are called "sketches" and typically consist of a setup function that runs once and a loop function that runs repeatedly. The programming language used in the Arduino IDE is C/C++, a high-level language known for its efficiency and control over hardware, making it ideal for embedded systems. When the code is uploaded to the Arduino Mega then, the robot will starts working by the code. And starts its mechanism of sowing seed using Arduino mega and solar panel.

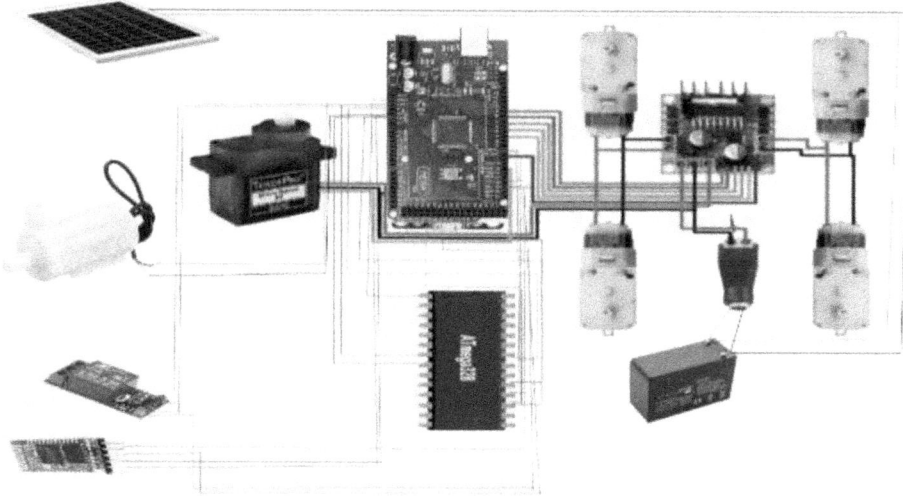

Figure 11.2 Schematic diagram for interfacing of all the components of sowing seed AG-robot using Arduino mega with solar panel
Source: Author

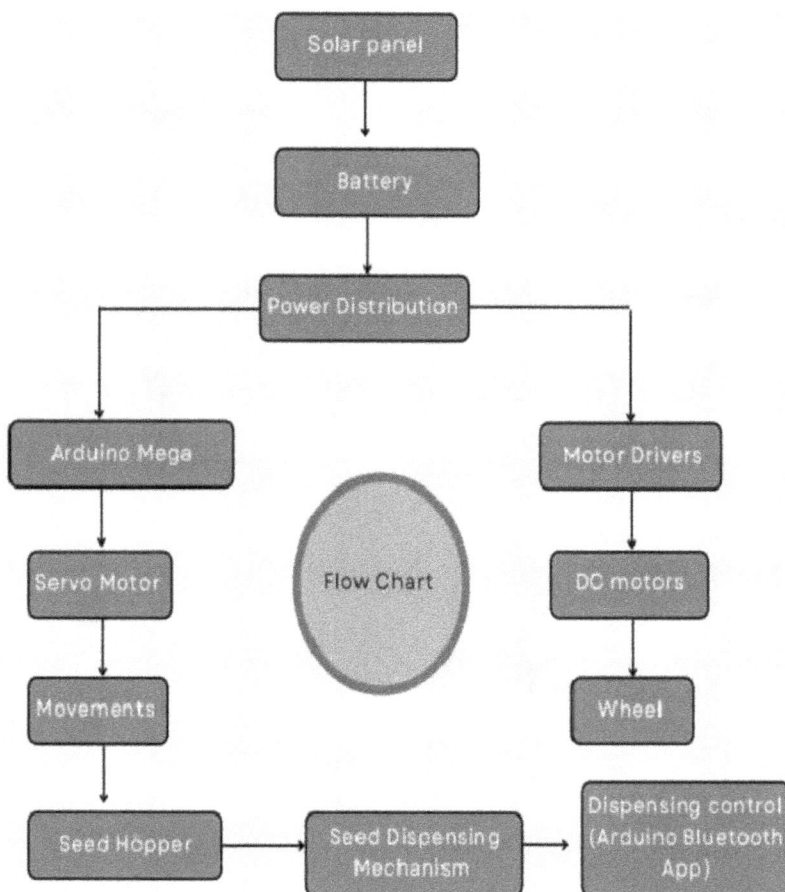

Figure 11.3 Flowchart of overall project
Source: Author

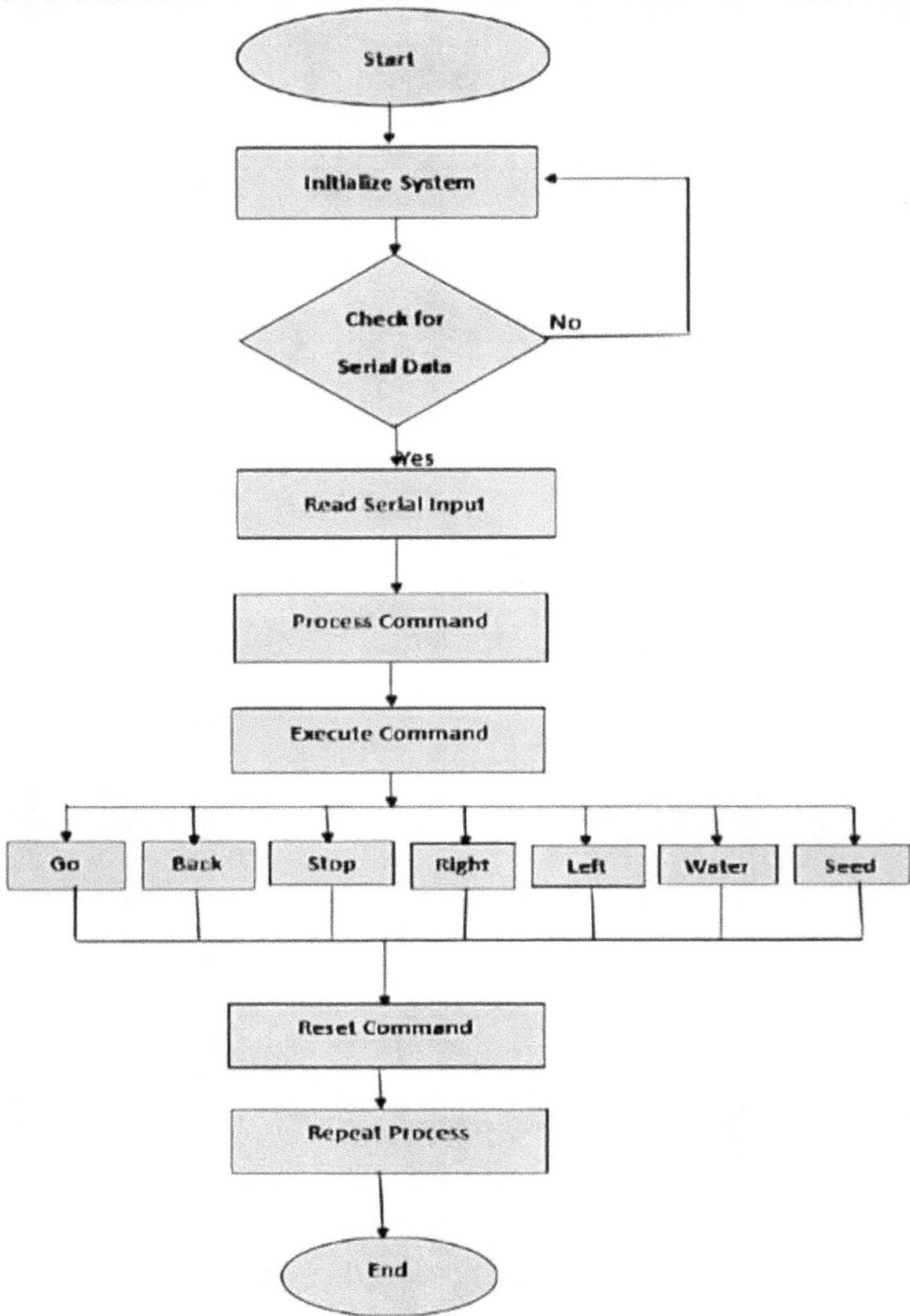

Figure 11.4 Flowchart of software code
Source: Author

Results

The sowing seed AG-robot project leverages an A components like 4 DC motors, a relay, a water pump, a motor driver, an ATmega328 microcontroller, four wheels, a servo motor, a Bluetooth module, The ag-robot has demonstrated significant potential in transforming the agricultural industry by enhancing automation and efficiency. The project's key outcome is the accurate sowing of seeds. The AG-robot employs a servo motor-controlled seed dispenser mechanism, which ensures precise seed placement and optimal seed-to-soil contact, leading to better germination rates and increased crop yields.

The AG-robot excels with its four DC motors and 4-wheel configuration, enabling it to traverse various terrains with ease. The inclusion of a Bluetooth module enables wireless communication between the AG-robot and external devices such as smartphones or computers. This capability allows users to remotely control the robot, send commands, and receive real-time data and feedback on the robot's operation and status. This feature offers significant convenience and flexibility for farmers and agricultural practitioners.

Overall, the sowing seed ag-robot, built around the Arduino Mega and various key components, has shown significant potential to transform agriculture. With its precise seed sowing, efficient watering, and wireless control capabilities, the robot is a valuable tool for optimizing crop production, reducing manual labor, and maximizing resource utilization. The project's success sets the stage for future advancements in areas like advanced navigation, AI integration, and remote

monitoring, further enhancing the ag-robot capabilities and impact on the agricultural sector.

Applications

The sowing seed AG-robot using Arduino Mega offers numerous applications in agriculture. It excels in precision spacing and depth for enhanced germination and increased application, where the

Figure 11.6 Water pumping
Source: Author

Figure 11.7 Working prototype
Source: Author

Figure 11.5 Working prototype
Source: Author

Figure 11.8 Operating through Arduino Bluetooth control App (HC - 05)
Source: Author

Figure 11.9 Working through Bluetooth control App
Source: Author

robot utilizes adjust watering schedules, ensuring optimal moisture levels and conserving water. For field monitoring, the robot collects real-time data on soil conditions and crop health, aiding farmers in making informed decisions.

The robot can be equipped with a cutter or herbicide dispenser for effective weed control, minimizing resource competition with crops. In pest management, it integrates sensors to detect and address pest infestations early, protecting crops and improving overall yields.

By automating repetitive tasks such as sowing and watering, the robot significantly reduces the need for manual labor and lowers associated costs. Remote operation is facilitated via Bluetooth, allowing farmers to control and monitor the robot using a smartphone or computer, which offers greater convenience and flexibility. The robot also gathers valuable data for analysis, leading to improved farming practices and strategies over time. Through variable rate technology (VRT), it adjusts the application of seeds, water, or fertilizer based on specific field conditions, optimizing resource utilization.

Finally, the robot serves as a platform for research and development, testing new agricultural technologies and practices, and promoting innovation within the sector.

Limitations

The sowing seed AG-robot using Arduino Mega offers benefits but faces limitations. The Arduino Mega's processing power and memory constraints may limit task complexity and efficiency. Low-cost sensors' accuracy may not meet precision agriculture needs, impacting performance. Battery limitations require frequent recharging, disrupting operations. While designed for diverse terrains, extreme conditions pose challenges. Scalability may require costly modifications for larger fields. Environmental durability issues with electronic components may in large fields. Customization is restricted, affecting adaptation to new technologies. Initial setup complexity and cost can be prohibitive for small-scale farmers with limited resources and technical skills.

Conclusion

By utilizing the sowing seed AG-robot using Arduino Mega represents a use of agriculture.

By automating seed sowing, it offers farmers significant time savings, labor cost reductions, and improved crop yields through precise planting optimization.an Arduino Mega microcontroller as its central hub, the robot facilitates remote monitoring and control. This capability empowers farmers with real-time insights into the planting process, enabling adjustments to the robot's movements and planting parameters as necessary to enhance agricultural productivity. The sowing seed AG-robot using Arduino Mega offers farmers a pathway to adopt more sustainable farming practices by optimizing water and fertilizer usage while simultaneously increasing crop yield. This automation in agriculture not only enhances efficiency but also addresses the growing challenge of labor shortages in rural areas. By relieving farmers from repetitive tasks like planting, the robot allows them to focus on more strategic aspects of farming, potentially improving overall farm management and productivity.

Overall, the sowing seed AG-robot using Arduino Mega represents a significant advancement in precision farming and sets a foundation for future innovative applications of IoT technology in agriculture. As technology evolves, we anticipate the emergence of even more advanced and efficient agricultural robots. These advancements promise to further improve the sustainability and productivity of farming practices by integrating cutting-edge sensors, AI capabilities, and automated systems to optimize resource management and crop yields.

Future work

Future advancements for the sowing seed AG-robot using Arduino Mega may focus on enhancing sensor capabilities to ensure precise data collection across diverse environmental conditions. Improvements in battery life and efficiency will extend operational autonomy, while enhanced connectivity options could facilitate seamless integration with broader agricultural management systems. Furthermore, integrating advanced AI algorithms would empower the robot to autonomously analyze data and optimize planting strategies in real-time. These developments aim to significantly boost agricultural productivity, streamline operations, and advance sustainable farming practices through enhanced technology integration and automation.

References

[1] Blackmore, S., Stout, B., Wang, M., and Runov, B. (2007). Robotic agriculture – the future of agricultural mechanization? In 5th European Conference on Precision Agriculture.

[2] Grimstad, L., and From, P. J. (2017). The thorvald II agricultural robotic system. *Robotics*, 6(4), 24. https://doi.org/10.3390/robotics6040024.

[3] Singh, G., and Singh, P. (2011). Design and development of an automated seed sowing machine. *International Journal of Agricultural Engineering*, 4(2), 163–166.

[4] Mathur, S. M., and Sharma, A. (2006). Development and testing of manually operated seed-cum-fertilizer drill. *Agricultural Engineering Today*, 30(1), 36–39.

[5] Banzi, M., and Shiloh, M. (2014). Getting Started with Arduino, (3rd edn.). Maker Media, Inc.

[6] Cui, Y., and Dillenseger, J. (2003). Extended kalman filter for robot localization. In Proceedings of the IEEE International Conference on Robotics and Automation, (pp. 2381–2386).

[7] Freitas, H., Nebel, W., and Fuhrer, P. (2008). Precision agriculture: GPS and remote sensing. *International Journal of Precision Agriculture*, 1(2), 45–52.

[8] Tar, A., Lefebvre, D., Pomeroy, J., and Odet, P. (2016). Sensor planning for UAV and UGV systems in precision agriculture. In Proceedings of the 2016 IEEE International Conference on Emerging Technologies and Factory Automation (ETFA), (pp. 1–6).

[9] Bechar, A., and Vigneault, C. (2016). Agricultural robots for field operations: concepts and components. *Biosystems Engineering*, 149, 94–111. https://doi.org/10.1016/j.biosystemseng.2016.06.014.

[10] Chen, C., Ren, L., and Zhang, D. (2020). Autonomous navigation in agriculture: a survey. *Computers and Electronics in Agriculture*, 162, 104379. https://doi.org/10.1016/j.compag.2019.104379.

[11] Shalaby, A., Salem, M. M. A., and Fawzy, M. (2019). Design and development of a precision seeder for small-scale farmers. *Agricultural Engineering International: CIGR Journal*, 21(1), 100–111.

[12] Mahmood, W., and Yahya, A. (2008). Stepper motors in agricultural automation: a review. *International Journal of Agricultural and Biological Engineering*, 1(3), 35–40.

12 Efficient fall detection for elderly with integrated machine learning and sensor networks

Bhargav, M. S. S.[a], Anirudh Reddy, R., Karthik Reddy, K., Rahul, G., Hari Harini, G., and Abhinav Reddy, B.

Department of Electronics and Communication Engineering, B V Raju Institute of Technology, Narsapur, Andhra Pradesh, India

Abstract

This review paper develops a personalized fall detection system for elderly individuals. By leveraging accelerometer, gyroscope, and temperature sensor data, the system dynamically adjusts thresholds based on body mass index to enhance accuracy and reliability, ensuring prompt and effective fall detection and comprehensive health monitoring. As the global population ages, the incidence of falls and related injuries is projected to increase, posing significant health and economic challenges. Traditional fall detection methods, often relying on manual intervention or basic threshold-based systems, suffer from limitations such as high false-positive rates and delayed response times. To address these challenges, we propose an adaptive fall detection system that harnesses the power of machine learning and sensor fusion. By integrating data from accelerometers and gyroscopes, our system can differentiate between fall events and normal activities with high accuracy. Machine learning algorithms are employed to analyse the sensor data, enabling the system to adapt to individual movement patterns and environmental factors. The primary objectives of this project are: To develop a robust and reliable fall detection algorithm that minimizes false alarms. To ensure the system's adaptability to different users and conditions. To provide timely alerts to caregivers or emergency services in the event of a fall. Our approach combines advanced data processing techniques with real-time analysis, ensuring prompt and accurate fall detection. The implementation of this system has the potential to significantly enhance the quality of life for elderly individuals, providing them with greater autonomy and safety.

Keywords: Elderly care, fall detection, machine learning, sensor fusion

Introduction

Furthermore, the system aims to offer continuous health monitoring, providing valuable insights into the user's physical condition. This aspect is crucial for preventive healthcare, allowing caregivers and medical professionals to track the health of elderly individuals and take proactive measures if needed.

This project addresses several challenges associated with fall detection

systems, including accuracy, power efficiency, and user-friendliness. By leveraging the capabilities of the Arduino Nano BLE Sense and BCI technology, this project proposes a comprehensive solution that not only detects falls but also enhances the overall quality of life for elderly individuals.

Existing Techniques

Fall detection systems have been extensively researched and developed over the years, employing various techniques and technologies to enhance accuracy and reliability. The existing techniques can be broadly categorized into the following groups:

Wearable devices:

Accelerometers and gyroscopes

Many wearable devices use accelerometers and gyroscopes to detect changes in motion and orientation. These sensors measure the acceleration forces and angular velocity, helping to identify sudden changes indicative of a fall.

[a]bhargav.m@bvrit.ac.in

DOI: 10.1201/9781003616399-12

Smartwatches and fitness trackers
Devices like smartwatches and fitness trackers often incorporate accelerometers and gyroscopes. They continuously monitor the user's movements and can trigger alerts when abnormal patterns are detected.

Dedicated fall detection wearables
Some wearables are specifically designed for fall detection. They combine motion sensors with algorithms to distinguish between daily activities and falls.

Vision-based systems:

Cameras
Vision-based systems use cameras placed in strategic locations to monitor the environment. Computer vision algorithms analyse the video feed to detect falls by identifying sudden changes in posture or movement.

Depth sensors
These sensors can detect falls by monitoring changes in the user's height and position relative to the floor.

Pressure sensors
Wearable devices to detect falls based on changes in pressure patterns. For example, a sudden increase in pressure on the floor might indicate a fall.

Infrared sensors
Infrared sensors detect movement and body heat. When a fall occurs, the sensors can identify changes in the user's position and motion based on the infrared signals et al. [1].

Audio-based systems:

Microphones
The impact sound of a fall or a cry for help will be heard. Machine learning algorithms analyse the audio data to detect falls accurately.

Hybrid systems
Combining Multiple Sensors: Hybrid systems integrate various types of sensors.

Smart home integration
Some systems integrate with smart home devices, such as smart lights, alarms, and home assistants, to provide a comprehensive fall detection and response solution. These systems can trigger emergency protocols, such as turning on lights or contacting emergency services et al. [1].

Machine learning and AI algorithms:

Pattern recognition
Machine learning algorithms analyse sensor data to recognize patterns associated with falls. These algorithms can be trained using large datasets to improve their accuracy over time.

Deep learning
Advanced deep learning models, such as convolutional neural networks (CNNs) and recurrent neural networks (RNNs), are used to process complex sensor data and identify falls with high precision.

Brain-computer interface (BCI)

EEG-based detection
BCIs can use electroencephalography (EEG) signals to monitor brain activity and detect falls. Changes in brainwave patterns can indicate a fall, and the BCI can trigger alerts or activate assistance mechanisms.

Comparison and limitations

Wearable devices:
Pros: Portable, real-time monitoring, and relatively affordable.

Cons: User compliance issues, limited battery life, and false

positives/negatives due to complex motion patterns.

Vision-based systems:
Pros: Non-intrusive, can cover large areas, and provide detailed information.

Cons: Privacy concerns, high computational requirements, and limited effectiveness in low-light conditions.

Ambient sensors:
Pros: Can be integrated into the environment, passive monitoring.

Cons: Installation complexity, limited mobility, and potential for false alarms.

Audio-based systems:
Pros: Non-intrusive, can detect falls in various environments.

Cons: Limited accuracy in noisy environments, privacy concerns.

Hybrid systems:
Pros: High accuracy, comprehensive monitoring, and reduced false positives/negatives.

Cons: Increased complexity, higher costs, and potential integration challenges.

Methodology

This system is designed to adapt to individual user behaviors and environmental conditions, ensuring high detection accuracy and low false positive rates. The methodology involves several key components: sensor selection and integration, data collection, feature extraction, machine learning model training, and system implementation.

Sensor selection and integration

Wearable sensors

Accelerometers: Measure linear acceleration.

Gyroscopes: Measure angular velocity to detect rotational movements.

Heart rate monitors: Provide physiological data that may indicate a fall-related event [2].

Ambient sensors

Pressure sensors, vibration sensors and acoustic sensors: Placed under mats or furniture to detect pressure changes, vibrations and sound patterns associated with falls.

Integration

Sensors are integrated into a unified system using microcontrollers and wireless communication protocols to ensure seamless data transmission and real-time monitoring.

Data collection

Dataset creation

Data is collected from multiple sensors during various activities, including walking, sitting, lying down, and simulated falls. A diverse dataset is created to train the machine learning model, including data from different individuals, environments, and scenarios.

Preprocessing

This involves filtering techniques such as low-pass filters for accelerometer and gyroscope data. Synchronization of data from different sensors to ensure temporal alignment et al. [3].

Feature extraction

Sensor fusion techniques and machine learning models analyze patterns to detect impact followed by inactivity.

Machine learning model training

Model selection

Various machine learning algorithms are evaluated, including support vector machines (SVM), random forests (RF), and convolutional neural networks (CNN).

A hybrid model combining multiple algorithms may be employed to leverage their strengths.

Training and validation

The dataset is split into training and validation sets.

Cross-validation techniques are used to ensure the model generalizes well to unseen data, hyper parameter tuning is performed to optimize model performance.

Adaptation

The model is designed to adapt to individual user behaviors by incorporating feedback mechanisms. For example, users can provide feedback on false positives and false negatives, which is used to retrain and refine the model.

System implementation

Real-time processing

The trained model is capable of real-time data processing. Sensor data is continuously monitored, and the model predicts fall events in real time.

Alert mechanism

Upon detection of a fall, an alert is triggered, notifying caregivers or emergency services via mobile applications, SMS, or automated calls. The system can also log fall events and sensor data for further analysis.

User interface

A user-friendly interface is developed to allow users and caregivers to monitor the system, view alerts, and provide feedback. The interface also provides options for adjusting sensitivity settings and customizing alert preferences.

Evaluation and testing

Simulated testing

The system is tested in simulated environments with volunteers performing various activities, including fall scenarios. Metrics such as accuracy, sensitivity, specificity, and response time are evaluated.

Real-world testing

Pilot studies are conducted with elderly individuals in real-world environments, such as homes and assisted living facilities.

User feedback is collected to assess system usability, acceptance, and effectiveness in preventing fall-related injuries.

By leveraging the capabilities of machine learning and sensor fusion, the proposed adaptive fall detection system aims to provide a reliable, user-friendly, and adaptable solution to enhance the safety and well-being of elderly individuals.

Architecture of the Proposing Solution

The architecture of the proposed elderly fall detection and assistance system using Arduino nano BLE sense and brain-computer interface (BCI) consists of several interconnected components working together to monitor, detect, and respond to falls. The architecture can be divided into the following key components:

Hardware layer

Arduino nano BLE sense:

Built-in sensors: Includes accelerometer, gyroscope, and environmental sensors.

BLE module: For wireless communication with external devices.

BCI module: EEG sensors: Captures brain activity and monitors for distress signals.

Signal Processor: Processes EEG signals and communicates with the Arduino.

Power supply: Battery provides power to the wearable device, ensuring portability and long-lasting operation.

Additional sensors (optional):

Pressure sensors: Detect pressure changes on floors or wearable areas.

Data acquisition layer

Sensor data collection:

Continuously collect data from accelerometers, gyroscopes, and any additional sensors. Collect EEG data from the BCI module.

Pre-processing: Filter and normalize sensor data to reduce noise and ensure consistency.

Processing layer

Fall detection algorithm:

Threshold-based detection: Uses predefined thresholds for acceleration and angular velocity.

Machine learning model: Trained on labeled data to classify normal activities and falls with high accuracy.

EEG signal analysis:

Processes EEG signals to detect patterns indicating a fall or distress.

Data fusion: Combines data from multiple sensors to improve detection accuracy and reduce false positives/negatives.

Communication layer

Bluetooth communication:

Data Transmission: Sends data from the Arduino to external devices (e.g., smartphones, computers).

Alert System: Sends alerts to caregivers or medical personnel in case of a fall detection.

Application layer

Mobile App/Web dashboard:

User interface: Provides a user-friendly interface for caregivers to receive alerts, monitor the user's status, and access historical data.

Alert notifications: Sends real-time notifications to caregivers with details of the fall and the user's location.

Cloud layer (Optional)

Data storage:

Stores historical sensor data and EEG signals for further analysis and machine learning model training.

Data analysis:

Performs advanced analytics on collected data to improve fall detection algorithms and provide health insights.

Flow Chart

The flowchart for the adaptive fall detection system outlines the step-by-step process from data acquisition to alert generation. Below is an explanation of each step in the flowchart:

1. Start
2. Initialize sensors
   - The Arduino nano 33 BLE Sense's accelerometer and gyroscope sensors are initialized.
3. Collect sensor data
   - The accelerometer and gyroscope continuously collect data on linear acceleration and angular velocity, respectively.

4. Preprocess data
   - This step may include filtering techniques such as low-pass filters to smooth the data and ensure it is suitable for analysis.
5. Extract features
   Relevant features are extracted from the pre-processed data. Features include statistical measures such as mean, variance, and peak values, as well as patterns indicative of falls.
6. Compute BMI-specific parameters
   The system computes parameters specific to the user's body mass index (BMI).
7. Apply machine learning model
   The preprocessed and feature-extracted data is fed into the trained machine learning model. The model analyzes the data to determine if a fall has occurred. et al. [4].
8. Fall detected
   - The machine learning model evaluates the data to detect potential falls.
   - Yes: If a fall is detected, the flow proceeds to the alert generation steps.
   - No: If no fall is detected, the system continues to monitor and collect sensor data in real-time, looping back to the data collection step.

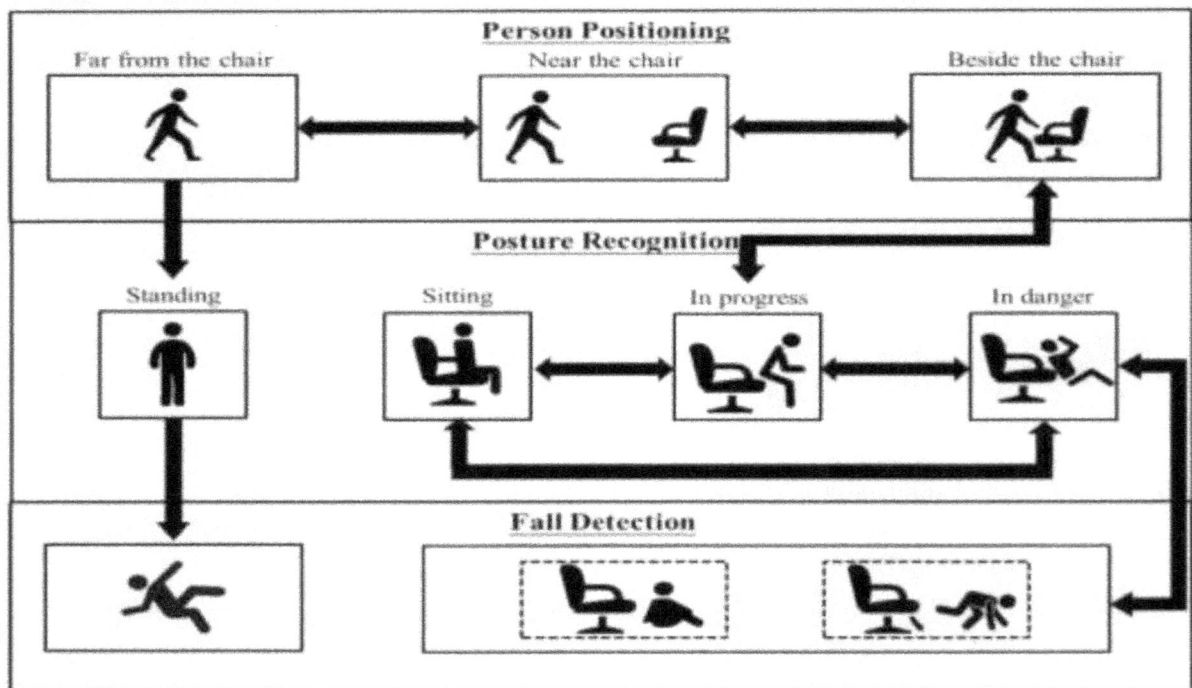

Figure 12.1 Estimated falling pattern [5]
Source: Author

9. Generate alert
   This involves preparing a notification message with relevant details such as the time and location of the fall.
10. Send notification
   - The alert is sent to the designated emergency contacts via the mobile device interface, SMS, or calls. The alert can also trigger an audible alarm to notify nearby individuals.
11. End
   The system completes the alert process and continues to monitor further falls, ensuring continuous protection for the user.

The above flowchart ensures a systematic and efficient approach to fall detection.

Hardware Setup

The hardware components used in the project are:
   Step-by-step hardware setup

1. Setting up the Arduino nano BLE sense
   Attach the battery holder to the Arduino nano BLE sense. Ensure the positive and negative terminals are correctly connected to the VIN and GND pins of the Arduino.
2. Connecting the sensors
   Built-in sensors: Utilize the onboard accelerometer and gyroscope.
   Optional pressure sensors (FSRs):
   Connect one terminal of the FSR to a voltage divider circuit.
   Connect the output of the voltage divider to an analog input pin on the Arduino (example, A0). Connect the other terminal of the FSR to GND.
3. Integrating the BCI module
   EEG sensors:
   Place the EEG sensors on the scalp according to the manufacturer's instructions.
   Connect the sensors to the BCI signal processor.
   Signal processor:
   Connect the signal processor's output to a digital input pin on the Arduino nano BLE sense (example., D2). Ensure the BCI module has its own power supply if required.
4. Setting up communication
   Bluetooth communication:
   Ensure the BLE module is enabled in the Arduino's software setup.

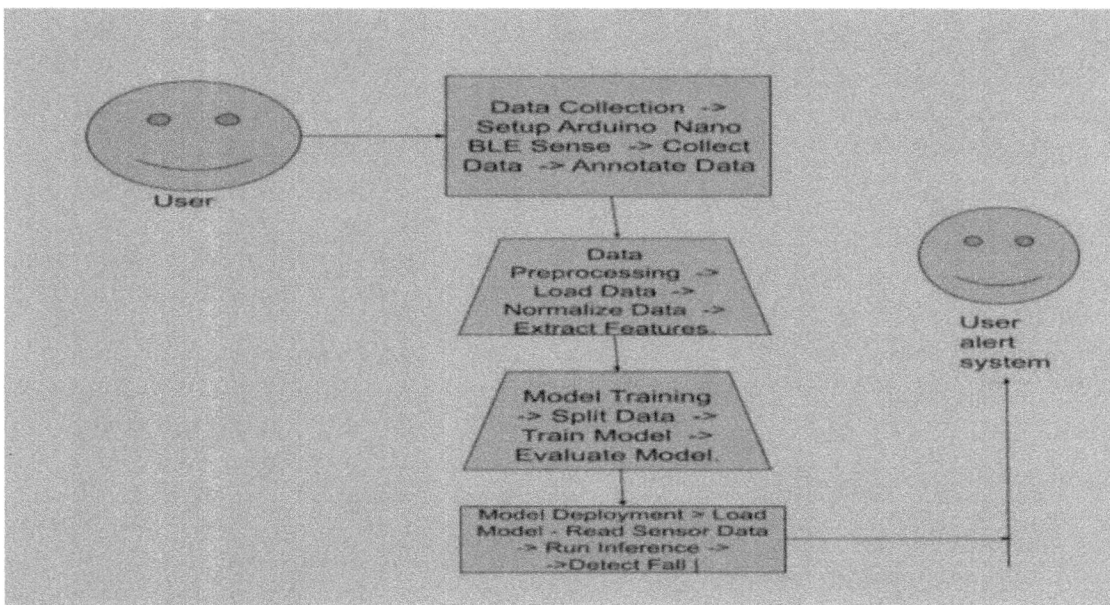

Figure 12.2 Flowchart
Source: Author

Figure 12.3 Arduino nano BLE sense (courtesy: google images)
Source: Author

Software configuration

Upload the fall detection algorithm to the Arduino nano BLE sense.

Configure the Bluetooth module for communication with a mobile app or web dashboard. Implement the alert system to trigger notifications via the buzzer, LEDs, and vibration motor.

Testing and calibration

Test each sensor individually to ensure proper data collection. Calibrate the sensors as needed, especially the accelerometer and gyroscope.

Run simulations of falls and normal activities to refine the fall detection algorithm. Test the BCI integration to ensure it accurately detects distress signals.

Conclusion

This detailed hardware setup ensures a robust and efficient system for real-time fall detection and assistance. By following these steps, you can create a reliable wearable device that significantly enhances the safety and well-being of elderly individuals.

Challenges of Brain Computer Interface

1. Signal noise and interference
   Description: EEG signals are susceptible to interference from environmental factors (like electrical appliances) and internal noise (such as muscle movements). This leads to inaccurate readings.[6]
2. Complex data processing
   Description: EEG signals require sophisticated algorithms to interpret various brainwave patterns and extract meaningful data.
   Impact: Implementing these algorithms on hardware involves complexity can slow down data analysis, making real-time fall detection difficult.
3. User comfort and compliance
   Description: BCI devices can be uncomfortable, especially for long periods.
   Impact: Discomfort can lead to low user compliance, particularly among the elderly.
4. Data integration
   Description: Combining data from the BCI with accelerometer and gyroscope data requires advanced data fusion techniques to make sense of disparate data sources.
   Impact: Integrating different types of data increases system complexity and can lead to challenges in synchronizing and interpreting the data correctly. This may affect the accuracy and reliability of fall detection.
5. Real-time processing
   Description: Effective fall detection requires real-time analysis of EEG and motion data to provide immediate alerts in the event of a fall.
   Impact: The need for rapid processing of complex EEG data can lead to delays in system response.
6. Power consumption
   Description: BCIs requirement of power can significantly increase the power consumption of the device.
   Impact: Higher power usage means shorter battery life, making the device bulkier and less wearable.
7. Cost and accessibility
   Description: High-quality BCI systems tend to be expensive and may not be readily available to the general public.
   Impact: The cost of integrating BCI technology can make the overall system prohibitively expensive for many users, limiting its adoption and practicality in real-world settings.

8. Calibration and personalization
   Description: BCIs often require individualized calibration to accurately interpret brain signals, which can vary significantly between users.
   Impact: This requirement adds complexity to the setup process, making it more time-consuming and potentially frustrating for users.
9. Safety and reliability
   Description: Ensuring that BCI systems function safely and reliably, especially during emergencies, is critical.
10. Data privacy and security
    Description: BCIs capture sensitive brain data, raising concerns about privacy and data security.
    Impact: Protecting this data from unauthorized access or breaches is crucial.
    Summary: Integrating BCI technology into an Elderly fall detection system poses significant challenges related to signal processing, user comfort, and system complexity. Addressing these challenges requires careful design considerations to ensure that the system is practical, reliable and user friendly.

Future Scope

The project focusing on elderly fall detection and assistance using Arduino nano BLE sense and BCI has immense potential for future developments and enhancements. Here are several key areas where the project can evolve:

1. Enhanced detection algorithms
   Machine learning integration: Implement more sophisticated machine learning algorithms to improve fall detection accuracy. Training models on larger datasets can help reduce false positives and negatives.
   Sensor fusion: Combine data from multiple sensors, including accelerometers, gyroscopes, and additional environmental sensors, to enhance the reliability and accuracy of fall detection.
2. Expanded health monitoring
   Vital signs monitoring: Integrate additional sensors to monitor vital signs such as heart rate, blood pressure, and oxygen saturation.

Conclusion
The future scope of the elderly fall detection and assistance system is extensive and promising. By leveraging advancements in technology and continuously improving the system based on user needs and feedback, this project can significantly enhance the safety and quality of life for elderly individuals. Collaboration with healthcare providers and adherence to rigorous validation and certification processes will be key to achieving widespread adoption and trust in the system.[7]

Expected Results

The implementation of the elderly fall detection and assistance system using Arduino nano BLE sense and BCI aims to achieve several expected outcomes.

Accurate fall detection: The system should reliably detect falls based on sensor data from the Arduino nano BLE Sense, including accelerometer and gyroscope readings. It should minimize false positives while ensuring quick and accurate detection of actual falls.

Timely alerts: Upon detecting a fall, the system should promptly alert caregivers or emergency services. Alerts can be in the form of notifications sent to mobile devices, auditory alerts through a buzzer, visual alerts using LEDs, or haptic feedback via vibration.

Continuous monitoring: This includes real-time tracking of activities and potentially critical health metrics such as heart rate (if integrated).

Conclusion

The expected results of the elderly fall detection and assistance system encompass accurate detection of falls, timely alerts, continuous monitoring, user-friendly interfaces, privacy and security assurances, clinical validation, user satisfaction, emergency response integration, and collaboration with healthcare providers. By achieving these outcomes, the system can significantly improve the safety, well-being, and quality of life for elderly individuals and provide peace of mind to their caregivers.

Metric	Arduino Nano BLE Sense + BCI	Comparison Project X	Comparison Project Y
Accuracy Rate in Fall Detection	High accuracy (>90%)	85-90%, occasional false positives	Relies on manual confirmation, ~85% accuracy
Timely Alerts and Response	Alerts within seconds	Alerts within a minute	Alerts within a minute
	Customizable alerts (mobile, audible, visual, haptic)	Mobile notifications	Smartphone app alerts
User Satisfaction	High satisfaction due to reliability and comfort	Mixed feedback on comfort and reliability	Mixed user feedback on usability
Integration with Healthcare	Seamless integration with EHR and telehealth platforms	Limited integration with healthcare systems	Limited data sharing with healthcare providers

Figure 12.4 Expected outcomes (courtesy: google images)
Source: Author

Acknowledgement

The authors gratefully acknowledge the students, staff, and authority of Electronics and Communication Engineering department for their cooperation in this review.

References

[1] Chaccour, K., Darazi, R., el Hassans, A. H., and Andres, E. (2015). Smart carpet using differential piezoresistive pressure sensors for elderly fall detection. In 2015 IEEE 11th International Conference on Wireless and Mobile Computing, Networking and Communications (Wi Mob), (pp. 225–229). IEEE. DOI: 10.1109/WiMOB.2015.7347952(vision based).

[2] Cvetkovic, D., et al. (??). A survey of fall detection systems for elderly people. *Journal: International Journal of Telemedicine and Applications*, doi:10.1155/2012/645654 (wearable sensors)

[3] Khan, M. A., Ahmed, A., Malik, A., and Rahman, S. (2021). Smart fall detection system using arduino and IoT. In 2021 International Conference on Computing, Electronics and Communications Engineering (iCCECE), Manchester, UK, 2021, (pp. 1–5). doi: 10.1109/iCCECE53249.2021.9598304.

[4] Kumar, A., Verma, S., and Agarwal, R. (2021). A review on fall detection systems for elderly care using IoT and machine learning techniques. In 2021 International Conference on Computing, Communication, and Intelligent Systems (ICCCIS), Greater Noida, India, 2021, (pp. 335–339). doi: 10.1109/ICCCIS52852.2021.9789371.

[5] Ratner, P. (2003). 3-D Human Modeling and Animation. Hoboken, NJ, USA: John Wiley and Sons, Inc. (pp. 336). [Google Scholar] https://doi.org/10.3390/app8101995.

[6] Lee, S., Kim, J., and Kim, H. (2020). Real-time fall detection system based on triaxial accelerometer and machine learning algorithm. *IEEE Transactions on Consumer Electronics*, 66(3), 259–266. doi: 10.1109/TCE.2020.9140161.

[7] Patel, A. B., Shah, K. P., and Patel, R. B. (2022). Falls and ADL activities monitoring system for elderly people using IoT and machine learning. In 2022 7th International Conference on Signal Processing and Integrated Networks (SPIN), Noida, India, 2022, (pp. 67–71). doi: 10.1109/SPIN53224.2022.9791802.

13 Compact high isolation 4 × 4 MIMO antenna

Rama Lakshmi Gali[1,2,a], *Manne Praveena*[1,b], *J Naga Vishnu Vardhan*[1,c], *and Madhavi T*[2,d]

[1]Department of ECE, BVRIT Hyderabad College of Engineering for Women, Bachupally, Hyderabad, India

[2]Department of EECE, GITAM (Deemed to be University), Hyderabad, India

Abstract

This study presents the design and fabrication of a 4 × 4 patch array antenna integrated with multiple input multiple output (MIMO) technology, optimized for sub-band frequencies. Our novel compact 4x4 MIMO antenna is specifically personalized for operation at 3.5 GHz, related to fifth-generation (5G) technology. By adopting a bio-inspired design, we successfully achieve a compact antenna structure without compromising on gain and bandwidth. The bio-inspired design approach involves mimicking natural structures and patterns, which has been shown to enhance the performance characteristics of antennas, for instance radiation efficiency and impedance matching. our innovative 4 × 4 MIMO antenna design demonstrates optimal performance through a combination of compactness, gain, and bandwidth efficiency. The comprehensive performance analysis, including ECC, TARC, and field patterns, confirms that our bio-inspired antenna design is well-suited for 5G applications, providing a robust solution for future wireless communication systems.

Keywords: Bio-inspired, compact MIMO, envelope correlation coefficient, optimization, patterns

Introduction

The inception of wireless communication marks the genesis of a journey from 1G to 5G in mobile wireless communications. The advent of the fifth generation represents a monumental leap, endowing users with unprecedentedly vast bandwidth previously unattainable. This new iteration boasts an array of sophisticated functionalities, rendering it the pinnacle of technological prowess and a highly coveted asset for the future. With 5G, a diverse range of cutting-edge features is introduced, solidifying its status as the most potent and sought-after technology in the foreseeable horizon. The rollout of 5G technology covers a wide range of frequency bands, including millimeter-wave frequencies between 24 GHz and 54 GHz. This deployment includes setups across low, mid, and high band spectrums.

Through the utilization of massive MIMO technology, there has been a notable augmentation in the precision and adaptability of network coverage since its inception. The complexity of today's radio transmissions, characterized by RF signal propagation models and user activity, surpasses that of previous generations, posing challenges in distribution, beam management, and beamforming. As wireless networks expand, the intricacy of identifying network issues escalates, alongside the complexity of devising effective response strategies and evaluating the ramifications of new features. Preemptively identifying and assessing optimal solutions for challenges within a complex real- world network presents a formidable task. Powered by MIMO technology, 5G exhibits greatly improved diversity and adaptability [12] in network access and performance within a 3-D space. Though, the increasing density of the network requires a systematic approach to predict possible challenges, develop efficient solutions, and optimize the advantages of the technology while controlling expenses.

MIMO technology holds promise in significantly augmenting system capacity; however, numerous challenges persist during the actual deployment of networks. These obstacles mainly focus on three crucial elements of 5G implementation: signal coverage, user satisfaction, and

[a]ramalakshmi.gali@gmail.com, [b]alturi.praveena@gmail.com, [c]jnvvardhan@gmail.com, [d]mtatinen@gitam.edu

DOI: 10.1201/9781003616399-13

network performance. MIMO antenna arrays, which use multiple-input multiple-output setups, provide benefits in ground plane environments by improving isolation between RF or microwave channels. Ground planes made from high-impedance metamaterials can enhance the radiation pattern and axial ratio of low-profile antenna arrays positioned nearby, resulting in improved performance. Additionally, integrating waveguide materials with antennas has been effective in extending the range of beam-scanning antennas that handle both forward and backward waves. This technology is versatile and supports a wide range of antenna systems for various applications, such as surveillance sensors, communication links, navigation aids, and command-and-control systems, showcasing its effectiveness and adaptability.

The selection of patch antennas is justified by their compact size, ease of fabrication, and inherent suitability for MIMO applications, aligning with the objectives of this research endeavor [15]. Leveraging MIMO technology is shown to significantly enhance isolation and reduce mutual coupling among antennas, thereby playing a pivotal role in augmenting overall system efficiency [13]. Moreover, the paper elucidates the implementation of neutralization line methods, effectively addressing mutual coupling issues and consequently minimizing interference, thus amplifying the system's performance capabilities. Through this comprehensive explanation, the paper delineates the rationale behind the design choices and their implications.

Following a systematic workflow, the design of this antenna commenced with the specification phase, where the desired antenna type and solution were determined. Utilizing a simulation tool, the specifications were rigorously tested to ensure alignment with the project goals. Subsequently, the antenna prototype was fabricated based on the validated simulations. Extensive testing followed to evaluate the antenna's performance against predetermined metrics. Post-processing techniques were then applied to fine-tune the antenna's characteristics for optimal operation. Throughout this process, iterations were made, and re-simulation was conducted as needed to refine the design. This meticulous workflow ensured the

successful development of the antenna, meeting the requirements.

Literature Survey

Liu et al. [1] investigated an innovative design for U6G (Ultra 6G) massive MIMO antenna arrays, which features double-layer partial reflective decoupling layers to reduce mutual coupling between antenna elements. This approach addresses the performance issues caused by mutual coupling in massive MIMO systems and evaluates the performance of antenna U6G massive MIMO arrays.

The antenna design discussed in [2] centers on dual-polarized multi-beam base station antennas (MBA) intended for MIMO applications within the sub-6GHz frequency range (3.3–3.8 GHz). These planar arrays integrate wideband antenna elements, elevation beamforming networks (EBFNs), and azimuth beamforming networks (ABFNs). The design emphasizes minimizing mutual coupling and optimizing the integration of feeding networks.

The evolution of antenna designs is detailed with two MIMO configurations: one for mid and high-band applications [3]. The mid-band MIMO design progresses from an initial patch antenna to one incorporating horizontal slits and additional modifications for improved gain and bandwidth, culminating in a two-element MIMO configuration. For a microstrip patch antenna operating at 6.5 GHz with FR4 dielectric material [4], key parameters such as patch width are determined based on the speed of light, resonant frequency, and relative dielectric constant. The design also accounts for the effective dielectric constant, which includes the influence of both the substrate and air, and the resonant length, which considers fringing effects.

Le et al. [5] proposes a new method to enhance microstrip patch antennas for 5.8 GHz dedicated short range communication (DSRC) systems by using double negative metamaterials. This approach aims to meet the requirements for high gain, low profile, compatibility with Monolithic Microwave Integrated Circuits, and cost-effectiveness. The MTM structure is designed with modern printed-circuit technology. The study includes a compact antenna with a square patch and rectangular slot; initially, a poor impedance match was observed, but improvements were made by implementing a partial ground design and adding a stub to the patch to enhance gain.

A comparison of two patch antennas is conducted: Antenna-1, which uses a conventional design with slots, and Antenna-2, which incorporates parasitic elements and slots [7]. Both antennas are built on an FR-4 substrate using microstrip patch concepts. Antenna-2 is designed to improve gain and bandwidth through parasitic elements. Simulations and fabrications show that Antenna-2 outperforms Antenna-1 in both gain and bandwidth.

Lastly, the proposed MIMO antenna system operates in the 2.5 GHz and 3.5 GHz frequency bands, featuring loop-type radiation elements on an FR-4 substrate [8]. The design, as discussed, includes six strategically placed loop-type elements on the PCB, with Ant-1 to Ant-4 located at the corners and Ant-5 and Ant-6 at the center [11]. The resonant length of each element is based on the guided wavelength at the corresponding frequencies, with simulations demonstrating effective resonance and impedance bandwidth.

The paper [9] presents a comparative analysis of four reconfigurable antenna models for 5G operating at 60GHz frequency. The models utilize different feeding techniques and dimensions of ground planes and radiating patches. Each antenna is designed to achieve reconfigurability [14] through variable resistors, allowing for dynamic adjustment of resonating frequencies. Model 1 employs a ground coplanar waveguide (GCPW) feeding technique, while Model 2 utilizes a CPW feed. Model 3 features a Microstrip line feeding technique, and Model 4 employs GCPW feeding. Simulation results show that varying resistor values within a certain range around the designed value enables frequency reconfiguration while conserving a stable 3dB bandwidth.

A novel antenna design [10] operating at 3.5 GHz, aimed at enhancing bandwidth and gaining through phase- adjusted arrangement of four single antennas in a 2 × 2 matrix. Utilizing RT5880 substrates with a εr of 2.2 and thickness of 1.57 mm, each antenna consists of two layers with a feed line connecting them. The design incorporates a rectangular patch at the front and engraved square cells for the ground at the back,

with a thickness of 0.5 mm to increase bandwidth and gain.

Antenna Design
Model 1
The antenna prototype, functioning at 3.5 GHz, primarily comprises four individual antennas organized within a 4x4 matrix. To create the 4 × 4 MIMO antenna, a methodical approach was employed, starting with the development of an individual antenna unit. This initial phase entailed thorough investigation into antenna requirements, taking aspects such as frequency ranges, radiation characteristics, and impedance optimization.

The first step involved designing a single antenna, following the guidelines outlined in Figure 13.1.

Illustrated in Figure 13.1 is the frontal perspective of a microstrip antenna, which includes a substrate with dimensions of 33 mm in height and 56 mm in width. The design of antenna in this study drew inspiration from the natural form of a flower(bio-inspired), prompting the inclusion of additional circular elements surrounding the patch. The results are plotted in Figures 13.2 and

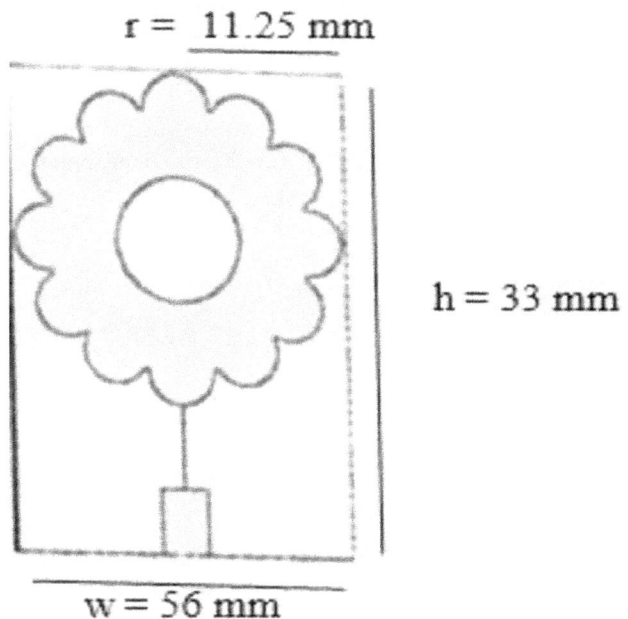

Figure 13.1 Single flower shaped patch antenna
Source: Author

13.3 show antenna is radiated at the designed frequency.

At a frequency of 3.45 GHz, the *S*11 parameter for the 1 × 1 antenna impressively measures at −34 dB is in Figure 13.2. This value indicates a remarkably low level of reflection, showcasing the antenna's proficient impedance matching at its input.

3.45 GHz frequency, Figure 13.3 shows that the VSWR for single antenna is measured at 1, corresponding to a specific S11 value. A VSWR of 1 signifies a perfect impedance match between the antenna and the transmission line, indicating no reflected power and optimal power transfer.

Model 2

Once the single antenna design was optimized for performance, attention shifted towards expanding its capabilities into a 2 × 2 MIMO configuration. This transition demanded testing and refinement to ensure seamless integration and mutual interference mitigation between the antenna elements. The second step involved designing a 2 × 2 antenna, following the guidelines outlined in Figure 13.4. A complete analysis of model 2 is publicized in Figures 13.5 and 13.6.

3.45 GHz frequency, Figure 13.5 shows the S11 value reaches -17 dB. This indicates a good impedance match at this frequency, as the reflection coefficient is relatively low, meaning that most of the power is being radiated by antenna rather than being reflected back.

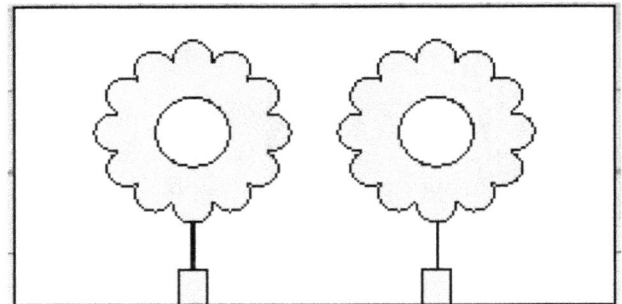

Figure 13.4 2-element MIMO antenna with flower shaped patch
Source: Author

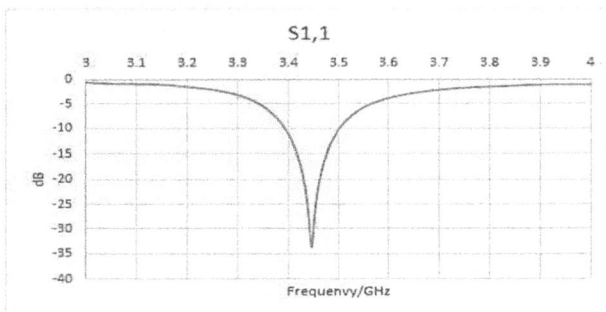

Figure 13.2 S-parameter for the single antenna
Source: Author

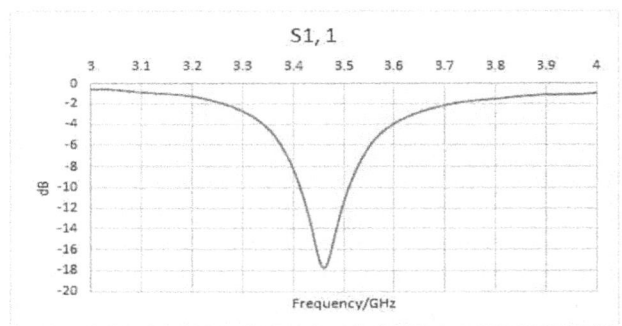

Figure 13.5 S 11 parameter for the 2 × 2 antenna
Source: Author

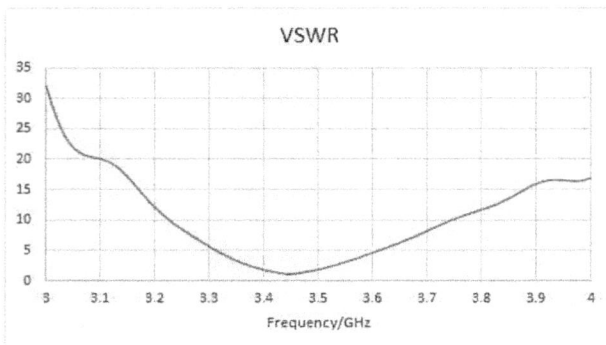

Figure 13.3 VSWR of the single antenna
Source: Author

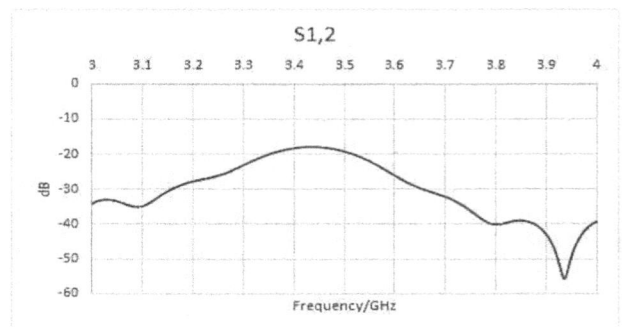

Figure 13.6 S 12 parameter for the 2 × 2 antenna
Source: Author

3.45 GHz frequency S12 value, depicted in Figure 13.6, is -18 dB. The S12 parameter measures the transmission coefficient between different antenna ports, with a value of -18 dB indicating minimal coupling between these ports.

Model 3

With the successful realization of the 2 × 2 setup, the final phase commenced, focusing on scaling up to the 4 × 4 MIMO arrangement. Through iterative modeling, simulation, and practical experimentation, the 4 × 4 MIMO antenna system was eventually crafted, embodying enhanced throughput, reliability, and spectral efficiency.

Figure 13.7 shows 4 × 4 antenna system features microstrip antennas with substrates measuring 56 mm in both length and width. Each antenna within the array includes a circular patch with a radius of 11.25 mm and a feed line extending 10.21 mm.

At a frequency of 3.45 GHz, both S11 and S11 values are measured, S12 throughout the frequency band the design-maintained values less than -18 dB and -18 above in S11 for the 4-element patch shown in Figures 13.8 and 13.9. These parameters represent the transmission coefficients between different ports of the antenna.

The 4 × 4 antenna demonstrates exceptional envelope correlation coefficient (ECC), signifying

Figure 13.8 S 12 parameter for the 4 × 4 antenna
Source: Author

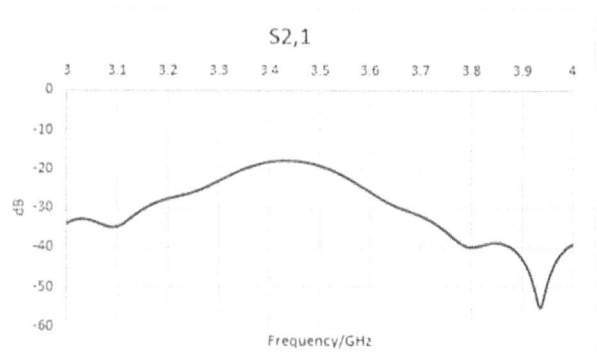

Figure 13.9 S11 parameter for the 4 × 4 antenna
Source: Author

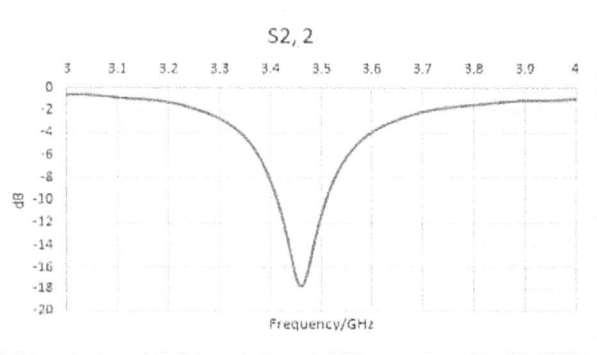

Figure 13.10 ECC
Source: Author

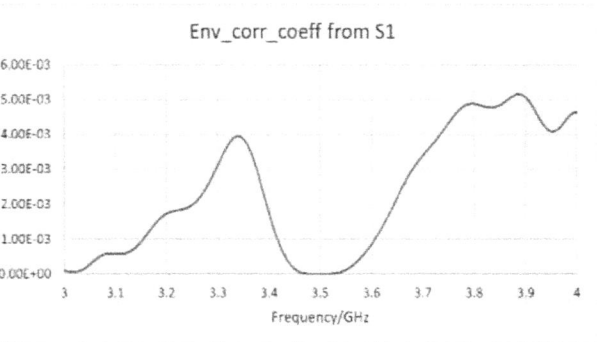

Figure 13.7 4 element MIMO antenna with flower shaped patch
Source: Author

its ability to effectively radiate with high isolation. At 3.5 GHz the reading is almost zero, meaning the proposed 4 × 4 MIMO design shown perfect isolation within the compact design.

Though the initial values of ECC1 showed higher values for frequencies below 3.3 GHz, at 3.5 GHz our targeted frequency able to achieve zero ECC for 1st antenna. Further, we analyzed the parameter for the other three patch antennas, where the result is very much welcoming that the ECC values are less than 0.005 throughout the bandwidth and importantly at 3.5 GHz the values touched zero. Optimal isolation is achieved in this compact 4 × 4 MIMO design. From Figure 13.10 the ECC is plotted by taking Port1 as base.

Diversity gain shown in Figure 13.11 with the value (3.49, 10) suggests that the system achieves a diversity gain of approximately 3.49 dB at a signal-to-noise ratio (SNR) of 10 dB. This indicates that employing diversity techniques results in an improvement in signal quality of around 3.49 dB compared to when diversity is not utilized, under conditions where the SNR is 10 dB.

The Figure 13.12 mean effective gain of the antenna system, despite registering at -3 dB, signifies its efficient performance in translating electrical power into radiated energy. This value suggests that the antenna effectively concentrates its radiation in desired directions, that employing

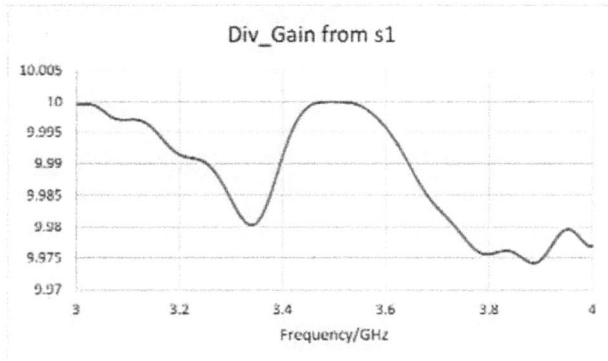

Figure 13.11 DG
Source: Author

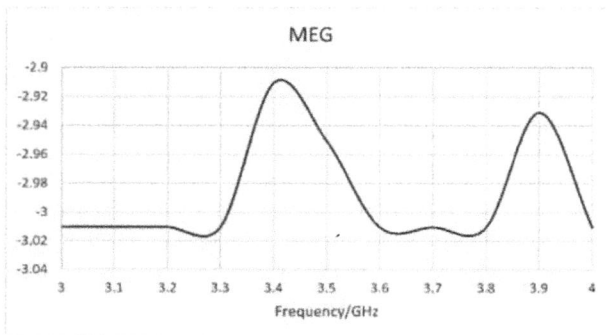

Figure 13.12 MEG
Source: Author

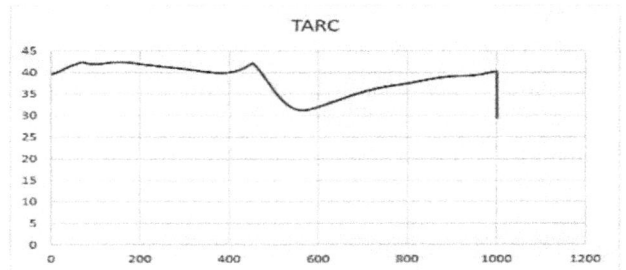

Figure 13.13 TARC
Source: Author

diversity techniques results in an improvement in signal quality of around 3.49 dB compared to when diversity is not utilized, under conditions where the SNR is 10 dB optimizing signal coverage and reception quality.

Figure 13.13 TARC value of 30 dB at 1000 GHz indicates an opportunity for optimization in the antenna design. While the reflection coefficient is relatively high at this frequency, it provides valuable insight for refining the antenna system to achieve better performance. By addressing the factors contributing to this reflection, such as impedance matching or antenna geometry, we can work towards diminishing signal loss and exploiting the efficiency of the antenna at this frequency.

After simulating a 4 × 4 MIMO antenna system, four far-field plot Figure 13.14 are typically obtained to analyze the antenna's radiation characteristics. The elevation plane plot, often referred to as the azimuth cut, represents the radiation pattern in the vertical plane, showing how antenna radiates energy as the observation angle varies along the vertical plane. In contrast, the azimuth plane plot, or elevation cut, depicts radiation pattern in the horizontal plane, illustrating how antenna distributes energy across different azimuth angles.

Results of 4 × 4 Antenna

The simulated and measured results for 4 × 4 configurations are compared. Figure 13.15 displays the fabricated antenna design. The concert characteristics of the antenna are illustrated through graphical representations of S11, ECC, DG, and MEG.

Farfield Directivity Abs (Phi=90)

Theta / Degree vs. dBi

———— farfield (f=3.456) [1]

Frequency = 3.456 GHz
Main lobe magnitude =   4.24 dBi
Main lobe direction =   15.0 deg.
Angular width (3 dB) =   99.2 deg.
Side lobe level =   -8.1 dB

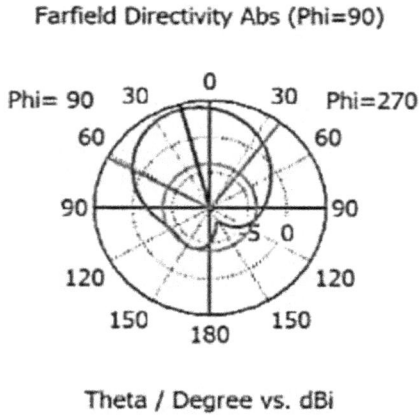

Figure 13.14 Far field 1
Source: Author

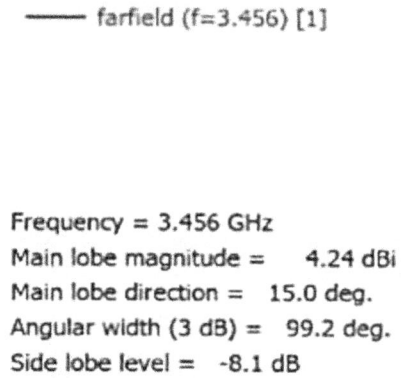

Figure 13.15 Fabricated antenna
Source: Author

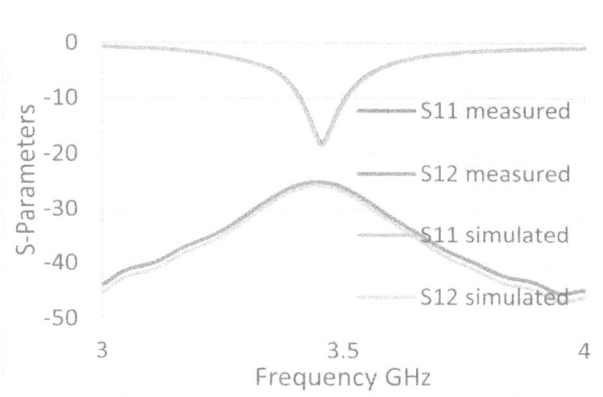

Figure 13.16 Measured S-parameters
Source: Author

Figure 13.16 presents a comparison of measured and simulated S-parameters (S11 and S12) across frequency choice of 3 GHz to 4 GHz. The measured and simulated S11 parameters show a notable dip around 3.5 GHz, indicating a strong reflection at this frequency with -18 dB. The S12 parameters for both measured and simulated data show a peak around 3.5 GHz, below -25 dB isolation at complete band of frequency. The simulated S-parameters closely follow the trends of the measured S-parameters, indicating good agreement between the experimental data and the simulation results.

Figure 13.17 compares measured and simulated envelope correlation coefficients across a frequency range opted. The ECC values from both measurements and simulations exhibit a consistent trend throughout the frequency range, demonstrating a strong agreement between experimental data and simulation results. The ECC values remain below 0.05, indicating that the system maintains excellent diversity characteristics across the entire frequency range.

Figure 13.18 compares the measured and simulated diversity gain across a frequency range. DG is an essential metric for evaluating the performance of multi-antenna systems, reflecting the enhancement in signal reception achieved through diversity techniques. The DG values for both measured and simulated data are close to

10 dB, indicating good diversity performance. Figure 13.19 gives a detail about MEG of the design antenna.

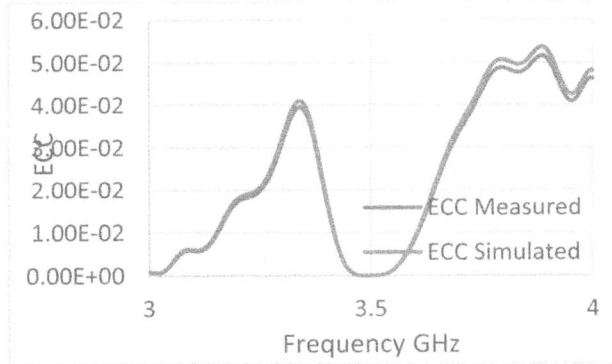

Figure 13.17 Measured ECC
Source: Author

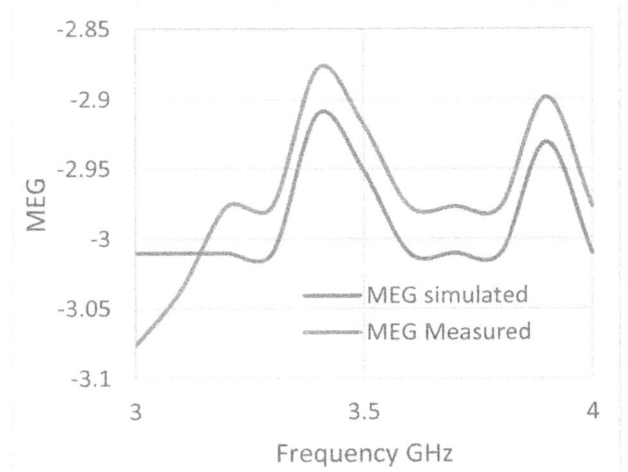

Figure 13.19 MEG
Source: Author

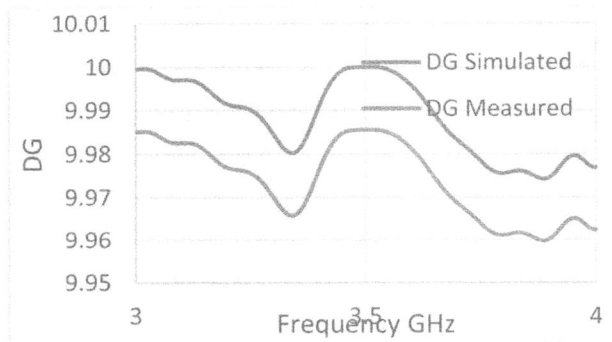

Figure 13.18 Diversity gain
Source: Author

Comparison

In contrast to earlier research, this paper demonstrates notable advancements in both dimensions and efficacy, representing a promising development. The table provided illustrates these enhancements clearly.

Antenna sizes vary significantly, having the smallest overall size (43 × 26 mm) the largest (140 × 120 mm) [17,20]. This paper's antenna is medium-sized (56 × 56 mm). The individual antenna element sizes also differ, having the smallest elements (2.1 × 15.2 mm) and the largest

Table 13.1 Comparison with proposed design

Ref	[17]	[18]	[19]	[20]	This paper
Size (mm)	140 x 120	138 x 64	55 x 100	43 x 26	56 x 56
Patch size (mm)	26 x 23	15 x 15	7 x 14	2.1 x 15.2	11.25
No. of patches	2	4	4	2	4
S11	-21.2	-48	-33	-47	-18
Gain	6.953	4.1	4.12	4.2	4.28
Bandwidth (MHz)	100	200	200	300	306
Ground	Plate	Plate	Shaped plate	metam aterial	Copper

Source: Author

(26 × 23 mm) [20,17]. This paper's elements are medium-sized (11.25 mm). Most designs use four antennas, except [17,20], which show the best performance with return losses of -48 dB and -47 dB, respectively [18,20]. This paper has a return loss of -18 dB. [17] achieves the highest gain (6.953 dBi), while the other designs have gains ranging from 4.1 to 4.28 dBi. This paper's antenna has a gain of 4.28 dBi. Substrate [17] uses the high-quality RT 5580 [21], while the others, including this paper, use the common and cost-effective FR-4 substrate. All reference papers offer the bandwidth (200 MHz), followed by (300 MHz) [20]. This paper has the widest bandwidth of 306 MHz.

Conclusion

The obtained results affirm the successful attainment of the antenna's intended objectives. Demonstrating directional attributes, the antenna showcases an effective gain of -3 dB, reflected in its S- parameters registering at 3.45 GHz. Through meticulous design, the antenna optimizes signal transmission and efficiency across designated frequency spectrums. Functioning at a frequency of 3.45 GHz, the system achieves a directive gain of 10 dB, the antenna presents diverse radiation patterns, underscoring its directional properties, coverage versatility, and applicability in various scenarios with good amount of isolation.

References

[1] Liu, T., Jiang, J., Zhao, L., Zhao, G., Zhai, H., Cai, Y. M., et al. (2023). Compact U6G massive MIMO antenna arrays with double-layer partial reflective decoupling layers for mutual coupling suppression. *IEEE Open Journal of Antennas and Propagation*, 4, 764–778. doi: 10.1109/OJAP.2023.3296623.

[2] Shen, L.-P., Wang, H., Lotz, W., and Jamali, H. (2019). Dual polarization 4 × 4 MIMO sub-6GHz multi-beam base station antennas. In 2019 International Symposium on Antennas and Propagation (ISAP), Xi'an, China (pp. 1–3).

[3] Khalid, H., Awan, W., Hussain, M., Fatima, A., Ali, M., Hussain, N., et al. (2021). Design of an integrated sub-6 GHz and mmWave MIMO antenna for 5G handheld devices. *Applied Sciences*, 11, 8331. 10.3390/app11188331.

[4] Zaman, K., Afridi, H., Zohaib, M., Rahman, A. U., and Ali, H. (2021). Design of micro-strip antenna at frequency (fr) = 6.5 GHzSETSCI Conference Proceedings, ISAS 4 (1): 145–149, 2019.

[5] Le, M. T., Nguyen, Q. C., Vuong, T., and Defay, C. (2012). Design of a high gain antenna at 5.8GHz using a new metamaterials structure. In 2012 4th International Conference on Communications and Electronics, ICCE. (pp. 411–416). 10.1109/CCE.2012.6315940.

[6] Farooq, U., Nasir, M., Iftikhar, A., Khan, M. S., Fida, A., Shafique, M. F., et al. (2020). A compact monopole patch antenna for future sub 6 GHz 5G wireless applications. In 2020 IEEE International Symposium on Antennas and Propagation and North American Radio Science Meeting, Montreal, QC, Canada, (pp. 1715–1716). doi: 10.1109/IEEECONF35879.2020.9329624.

[7] Noor, S. K., Jusoh, M., Sabapathy, T., Rambe, A. H., Vettikalladi, H., Albishi, A. M., et al. (2023). A patch antenna with enhanced gain and bandwidth for sub-6 GHz and sub-7 GHz 5G wireless applications. *Electronics*, 12, 2555. https://doi.org/ 10.3390/electronics12122555.

[8] Ahmad, U., Ullah, S., Rafique, U., Choi, D. Y., Ullah, R., Kamal, B., et al. (2021). MIMO antenna system with pattern diversity for sub-6 GHz mobile phone applications. *IEEE Access*, 9, 149240–149249. doi: 10.1109/ACCESS.2021.3125097.

[9] Abbas, M., Sikandri, B., Bibi, S., Adil, M., Khan, M. S., Shahjehan, W., et al. (2018). Millimeter wave frequency reconfigurable antenna for 5G WLAN. In 2018 IEEE 21st International Multi-Topic Conference (INMIC), Karachi, Pakistan, (pp. 1–6). doi: 10.1109/INMIC.2018.8595501.

[10] Ali, F., Salih, M., and Ilyas, M. (2022). MIMO patch antenna with metamaterial 3.5GHz for 5G applications. In 2022 Second International Conference on Advances in Electrical, Computing, Communication and Sustainable Technologies (ICAECT), Bhilai, India (pp. 1–4). doi: 10.1109/ICAECT54875.2022.9807940.

[11] Gali, R. L., and Tatineni, M. (2023). Design of glass-based antenna for effective vehicular communication. In 2023 7th International Conference on Trends in Electronics and Informatics (ICOEI), Tirunelveli, India, (pp. 285–291). doi: 10.1109/ICOEI56765.2023.10125689.

[12] El-Sayed, M., Gad, N., El-Aasser, M., and Yahia, A. (2020). Slotted rectangular microstrip-antenna design for radar and 5 G applications. In 2020 International Conference on Innovative Trends in Communication and Computer En-

gineering (ITCE), (pp. 330–334). doi: 10.1109/ITCE48509.2020.9047754.

[13] Azim, R., Meaze, A., Affandi, A., Alam, M., Aktar, R., Mia, M., et al. (2021). A multi-slotted antenna for LTE/5G Sub-6 GHz wireless communication applications. *International Journal of Microwave and Wireless Technologies*, 13(5), 486–496. doi:10.1017/S1759078720001336.

[14] Cil, E., and Dumanli, S. (2020). The design of a reconfigurable slot antenna printed on glass for wearable applications. *IEEE Access*, 8, 95417–95423. doi: 10.1109/ACCESS.2020.2996020.

[15] Zhao, L., Li, X., Gu, B., Zhou, Z., Mumtaz, S., Frascolla, V., et al. (2018). Vehicular communications: standardization and open issues. *IEEE Communications Standards Magazine*, 2(4), 74–80. doi: 10.1109/MCOMSTD.2018.1800027.

[16] Shaik, L. A., Saha, C., and Siddiqui, J. Y. (2014). Metamaterial-based electrically small antenna designed for GSM and ISM applications. (1), 6–9, con. Feb 2014.

[17] Ramadhan, L. M., Astuti, R. P., and Nugroho, B. S. (2019). Simulation of design and analysis massive MIMO array microstrip rectangular patch dualband 3.5 GHz and 26 GHz for 5G communications. In Proceedings - 2019 IEEE Asia Pacific Conference on Wireless and Mobile, APWiMob (pp. 28–32). doi: 10.1109/APWiMob48441.2019.8964213.

[18] Abdullah, M., Ban, Y. L., Kang, K., Li, M. Y., and Amin, M. (2017). Compact four-port MIMO antenna system at 3.5 GHz, 2017 IEEE 2nd Advanced Information.

[19] Ullah, R., Ullah, S., Kamal, B., and Ullah, R. (2019). A four-port multipleinput multiple output (MIMO) antenna for future 5G smartphone applications. In 2019 International Conference on Electrical, Communication, and Computer Engineering (ICECCE), (pp. 1–5).

[20] Mishra, R. K., Panda, A. K., and Sahu, S. (2018). Design of a compact dual- polarized MIMO antenna for WLAN applications. *IEEE Transactions on Antennas and Propagation*, 66(6), 3090–3094. doi: 10.1109/TAP.2018.2828824.

[21] Gali, R. L., Kammari, S., Papini, S., Sri Devi Sagiraju, N., Vudimudi, H., and Tatineni, M. (2024). 5G high band S-slotted Doppelganger patch antenna. In AIP Conference Proceedings, 8 July 2024 (Vol. 3028, no. 1, pp. 020044). https://doi.org/10.1063/5.0212387.

14 ST-QCA based error free and area efficient 4:2 compressor design

Arunkumar Gudivada, A.[1,a], Avala Eswar[2,b], Gummarekula Sattibabu[1,c] and Rama Tulasi, V.[3,d]

[1]Associate Professor, Department of Electronics and Communication Engineering, Aditya University, Surampalem, Andhra Pradesh, India

[2]B. Tech. Student, Department of Electronics and Communication Engineering, Aditya University, Surampalem, Andhra Pradesh, India

[3]Assistant Professor, Department of Electronics and Communication Engineering, Aditya University, Surampalem, Andhra Pradesh, India

Abstract

Quantum-dot cellular automata (QCA) stands at the forefront of nanotechnology advancements, representing a highly acclaimed technology compared to complementary metal-oxide-semiconductor (CMOS) technology in building digital logic circuits. Compressors are a significant class of arithmetic circuits. This study presents the design of a new compressor of size 4:2 using stack-type full adders in QCA technology. The proposed module performs well when comparing with the existing methods in terms of cell count, area and delay. The QCADesigner 2.0.3 tool has been used to evaluate the suggested circuits' performance. Based on the results, the layout of the presented compressor of size 4:2 is more effective than various other designs since it makes use of 1.25 clock phases and with number of cells is 71. This type of compressors has main application in fast arithmetic operations.

Keywords: 4:2 Compressor, full adder, QCADesigner, STQCA

Introduction

Based on complementary metal-oxide-semiconductor (CMOS) technology, the semiconductor industry has improved steadily in the integration of the ICs during the past ten years. However, due to its physical limitations, it has been predicted that CMOS technology may encounter some difficulties in its future development. Popular technology known as quantum-dot cellular automata (QCA) may be considered as a solution for nano-scale CMOS based devices. The swift switching capabilities, enhanced scalability, and significantly reduced power usage of CMOS have rendered QCA a captivating subject of research. Recognized by the International Technology Roadmap for Semiconductors (ITRS), QCA technology stands out as a promising solution to CMOS, attributed to its distinct characteristics: "minimal energy dissipation, size, and high- speeds".

Several QCA-based systems have been presented up to this point, but given their wide range of very large-scale integration (VLSI) applications, arithmetic circuits may be a more attractive option than any other structure. Several circuits in QCA technology have been constructed using the full adder as their main building component. It is possible to demonstrate how the full-adder outputs have been generated using a number of algebraic equations. The layout's parameters like area, delay, and used cell count are all reduced by QCA circuit designers. A crucial component of the partial product reduction tree of the parallel multiplier is the compressor. Its speed has a significant impact on the multiplier circuit's total speed. Numerous studies in QCA technology have focused on the full-adder gate and

[a]arunkumarg@acet.ac.in, [b]21P31A0470@acet.ac.in, [c]sattibabu.gummarekula@acet.ac.in, [d]tulasi4b1@gmail.com

DOI: 10.1201/9781003616399-14

compressor circuit precision. However, there are significant issues with the use of FinFET-based architectures in this field. The compressor function condenses bits into three outputs. In order to lessen the effect of carry propagation, the Wallace tree multiplier and other complicated systems can be constructed using the compressors as a fundamental building element. In the end, a significant increase in requirements has been made in order to schematize the compressor's high performance [1]. The primary aim of this study is to introduce a stack-type layout and compressor layout of size 4:2. Additionally, a novel XOR gate is utilized within a proposed full adder layout using QCA.

Further, the paper is collocated as: Section 2 offers a brief insight of QCA nanotechnology and associated research. Section 3 introduces the novel 4:2 compressor and complete adder. Section

4 elaborates on the simulation results. Lastly, the concluding section presents the conclusions drawn from the study and suggests potential avenues for future research.

QCA Background

Here, the architecture of QCA technology, the structure of earlier research, and a few recent efforts on models of full adder are briefed.

QCA fundamentals

According to Lent et al. [3], the QCA is a promising nanotechnology for designing logical devices. A key component in QCA was the quantum cell [4]. Because of the Coulombic repulsion, they must continue to be in either logic "0" or logic "1" polarization. Furthermore, Figure 14.1(a)

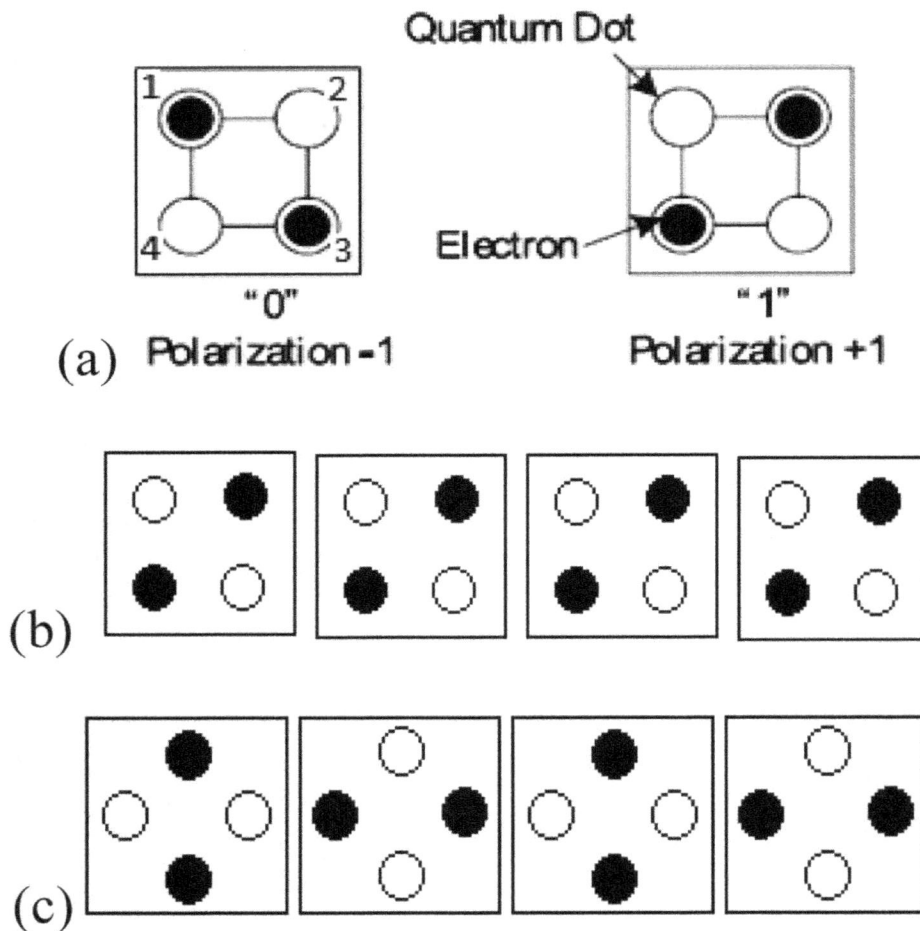

Figure 14.1 (a) Standard QCA Cell, (b) 90° and 45° wiring in QCA [2]
Source: Author

demonstrates the two types of Quantum cells (+1 and –1). A QCA cell chain is utilized in the execution of QCA wires. Simple and rotated QCA cells are used to create 45- and 90-degree QCA wires, as depicted in Figure 14.1(b). A 90⁰ QCA wire carries the polarization of the input cell towards the output cell without changing it, as Figure 14.1(c) illustrates.

On the other hand, a 45° QCA wire moves the corresponding supplement or the polarization of the cell from left to right. Additionally, an inverter chain nomination has been made for a 45° QCA wire [5]. Furthermore, an inverter

(NOT) represents a fundamental gate within QCA, serving as a foundational component in various schematic designs. Figure 14.2 shows schematic representation of the Majority gate and NOT gate and the corresponding standard layout.

In QCA technology, the clock scheme plays an important role in directing the data in a particular direction. There are four stages in this clocking arrangement, as portrayed in Figure 14.3: switch, hold, release, and relax. Multilayer or stack type QCA will reduce the area occupied by the circuit. This method is shown in Figure 14.4(a). It

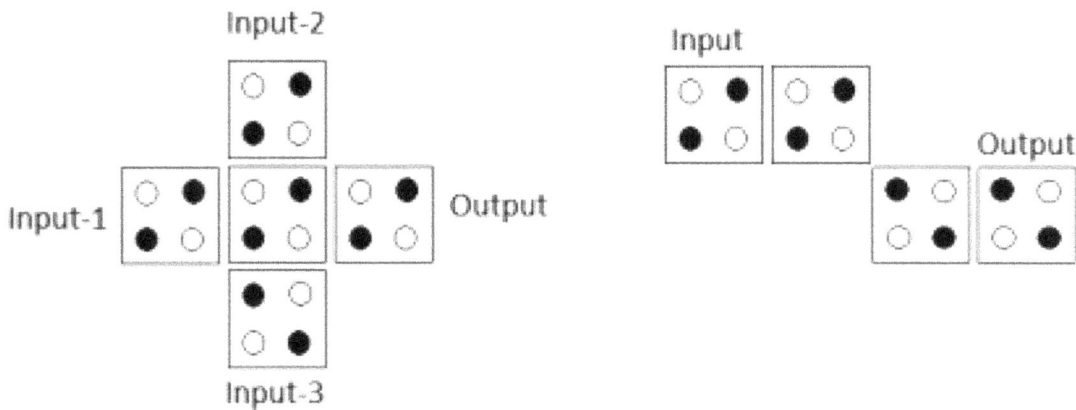

Figure 14.2 Basic gates in QCA
Source: Author

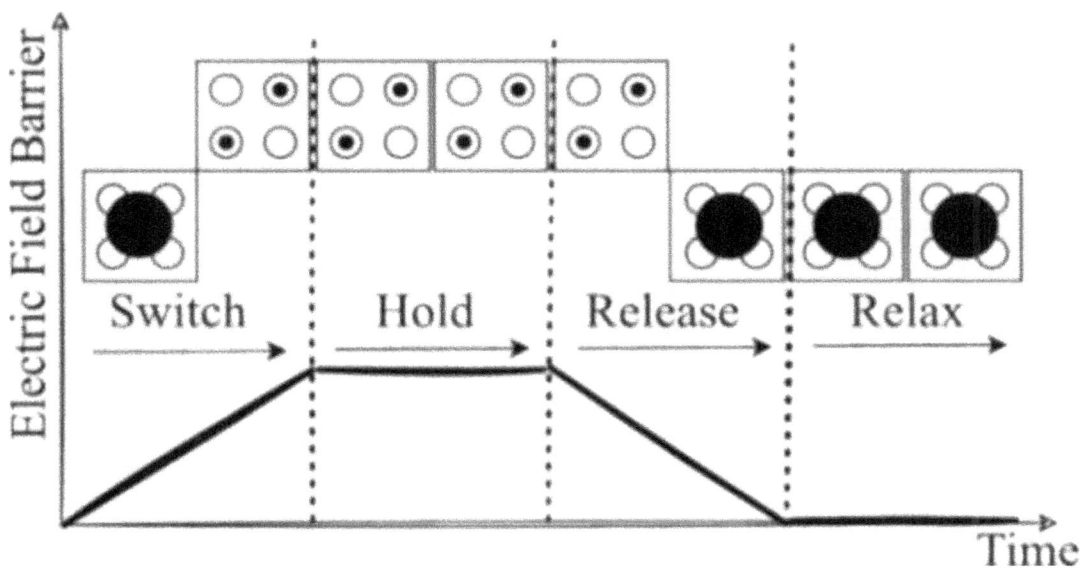

Figure 14.3 The signal clock zones
Source: Author

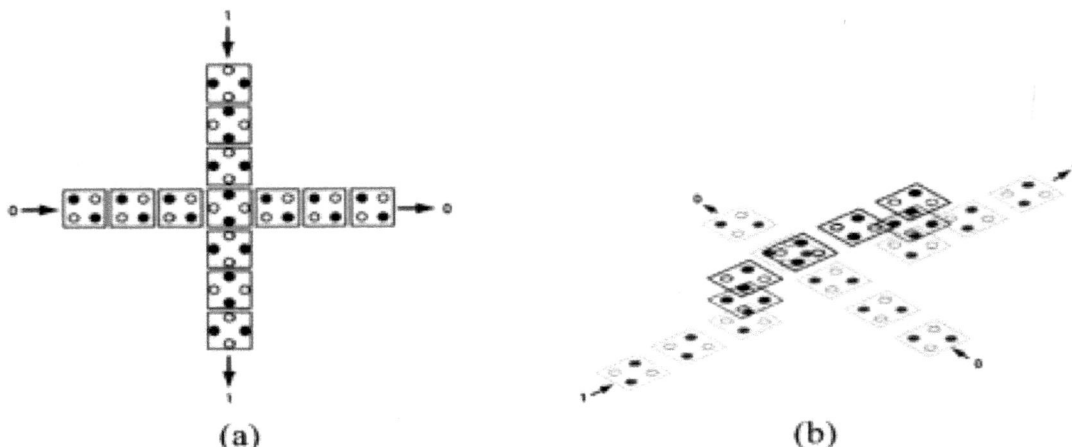

Figure 14.4 (a) Top view, (b) 3D view of crossing of QCA cells [21]
Source: Author

is preferable to use a stack-type crossover connection to get a QCA with low area and power consumption. It should be mentioned that there are no stack-type electrical circuits. Figure 14.4 (b) explains how the wire crossing is being done.

Previous works

The design of an inaccurate 4:2 compressor has been proposed by Taheri et al. [6]. In CMOS technology, a FinFET is a non-planar transistor, also referred to as a "3D" transistor. However, rather of using gates and circuits to generate the main output, the researchers in this article employed value input. The proposed model is the best one compared to the existing models. The evaluation results for the two technologies indicate that the recommended arrangement has advanced much beyond previous relevant works.[7,8]

Alkaldy et al. [9] have also introduced a novel design approach for CMOS nanotechnology. It is used to illustrate the general structure of the OR, AND, NOR, and NAND multi-input logic gates. Simulation results show excellent progress at both the transistor number and the gate level. Seyedi and Navimpour [10] have presented a three-layer QCA-dependent decomposition scheme that is effective. The input signals in the current schematization are not surrounded by other cells, and they are easily accessible. When the QCA Designer is used, the simulation results verify that the recommended circuit works properly and may even use a high-performance schematization in the QCA. This design used three clock cycles and 22 cells in a 0.01 μm²

area. Utilizing our unique genetic algorithms, Haghparastand Muhammadi [11] have proposed various compressors using QCA technology by employing the features of the tool.

Proposed Design

Two proposed 1-bit full adders are used to create a 4:2 compressor. Figure 14.5 shows a new full-adder one-bit block diagram. This full-adder's specification function is displayed in Table 14.1. The three input EXOR gate is constructed in three layers as shown in Figure 14.6. The figure 14.11 block diagrammatic representation of the proposed design for 4:2 compressor is depicted in Figure 14.7. The presented model has three-layer cell architecture with 25 cells which is pictured in Figure 14.8. To produce the C_{OUT} (Carry) and SUM outputs, two clock pulses are required. Table 14.2 shows the performance metrics of Full adders.[18,19]

Figure 14.8 and 14.9 depicts the new 4:2 compressor layout using stack type QCA technology that serves as the constructed elements. The recommended compressor's clock steps, architecture, and cell outline are shown in Figure 14.10. Five inputs (I_0, I_1, I_3, I_4, C_{in}) and one output (SUM) make up the first level. In the first level, a three-input XOR gate was used to create the SUM, which was then transmitted directly to the output.

For the generated SUM, a clock step of 1.25 was required. As a result, 1.25 clock phases are required to produce the outputs.

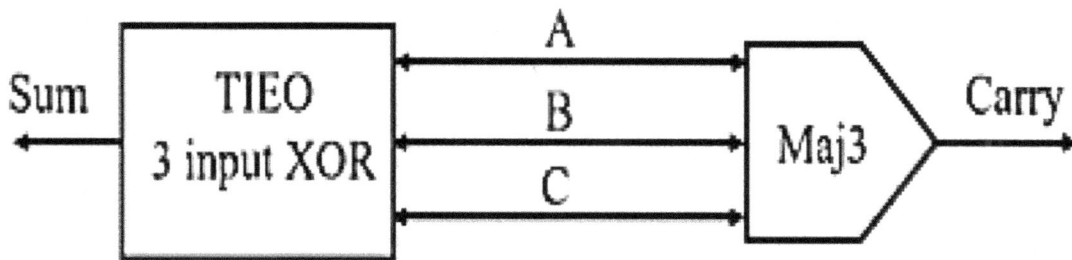

Figure 14.5 One-bit full-adder block
Source: Author

Table 14.1 Full adder truth table

A	B	C	Sum	Carry
0	0	0	0	0
0	0	1	1	0
0	1	0	1	0
0	1	1	0	1
1	0	0	1	0
1	0	1	0	1
1	1	0	0	1
1	1	1	1	1

Source: Author

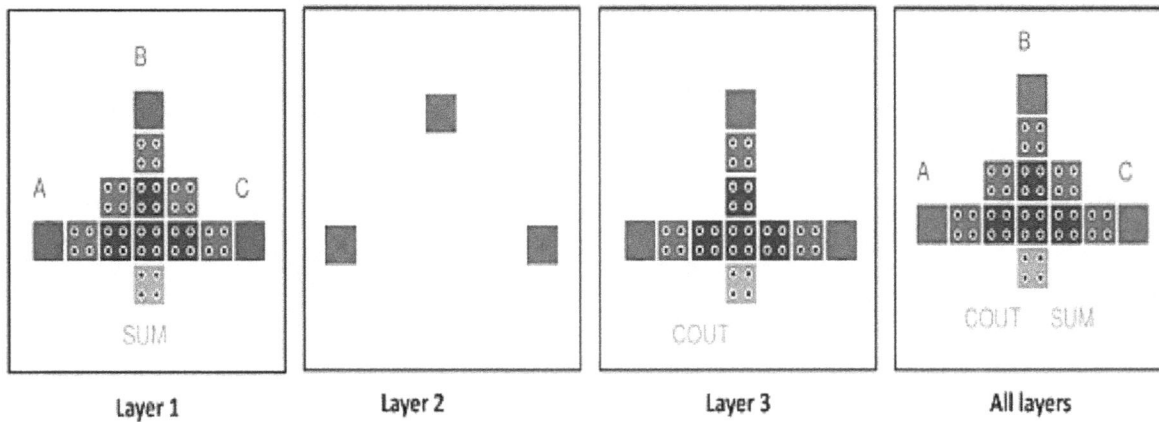

Layer 1   Layer 2   Layer 3   All layers

Figure 14.6 Three-input XOR (TIEO) gate
Source: Author

Results

The proposed model is simulated using QCADesigner 2.0.3 simulator tool has been used to create the proposed modules [12–15].

Discussion and comparisons

The latency is 2 clock phases (means 0.5 clock pulses) for the proposed design, and this design uses 25 QCA cells. The space consumption, complexity, and delay have been improved with the proposed full adder design. This design spends about 10% more on cell counts. Moreover, The simulated results are tabulated in Table 14.3. It displays the noteworthy advancements in clock latency, error in output, number of quantum cells compared to previous systems. This design

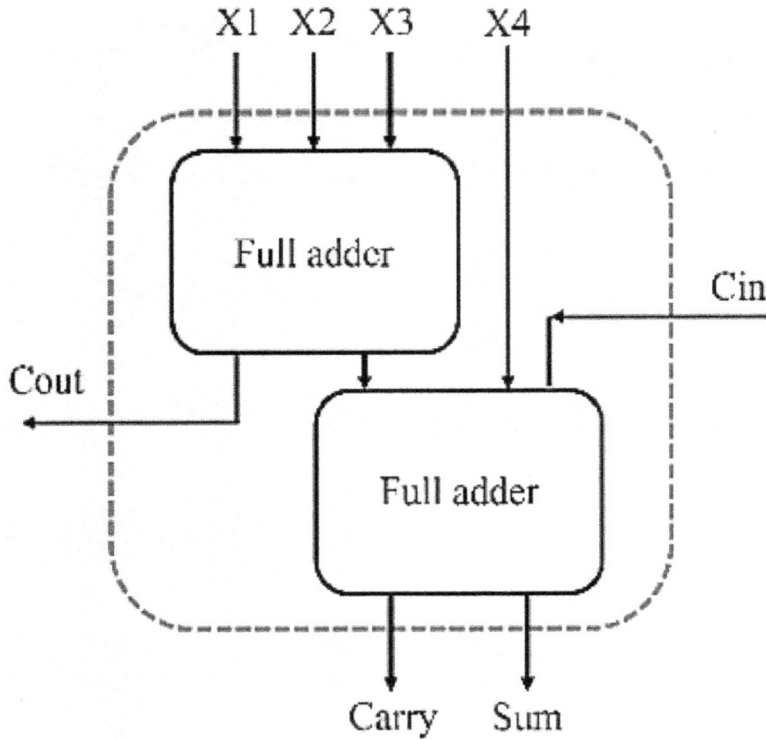

Figure 14.7 Block diagram of proposed module
Source: Author

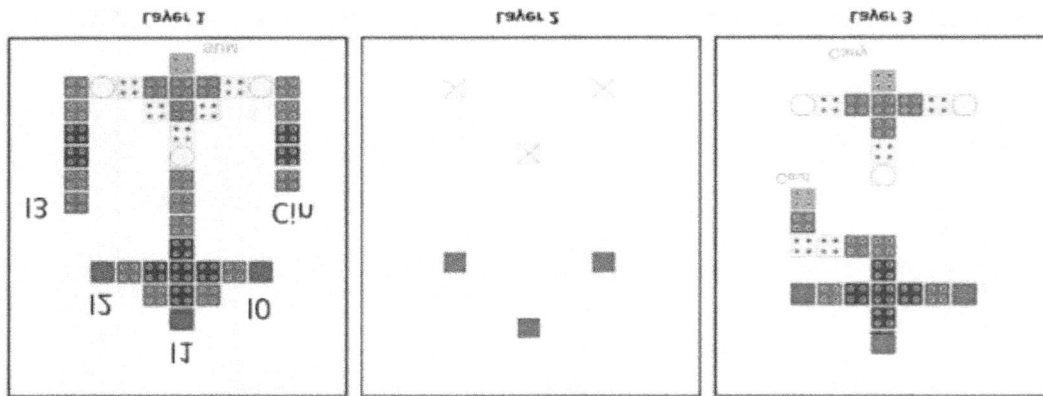

Figure 14.8 Layout of Figure 14.7
Source: Author

improves output errors by about 100% when compared to the earlier models.

Conclusion

One of the essential and intricate components in logic circuit design is the implementation of compressors and full adders. This study presents a new one-bit full adder realized through a three-layer approach to optimize a 4:2 compressor. Using QCADesigner 2.0.3, the proposed designs were implemented and evaluated. The presented adder has 25 cells with 0.02 μm² area and operates with 2 clock phases, while the 4:2 compressor contains 71 quantum cells, covers an area of 0.06 μm², and utilizes 1.25 clock phases. The output waveforms demonstrate that the

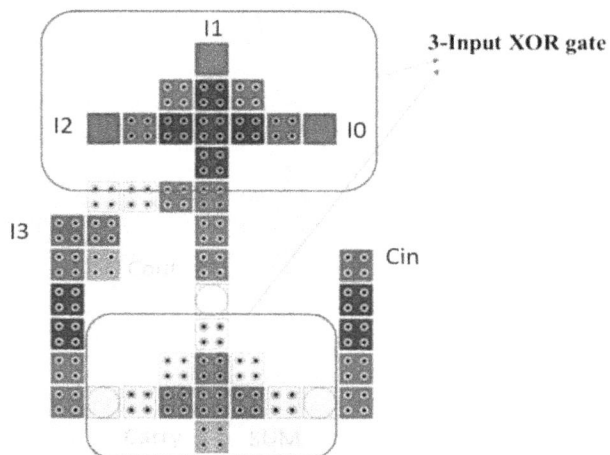

Figure 14.9 STQCA layout of 4:2 compressor
Source: Author

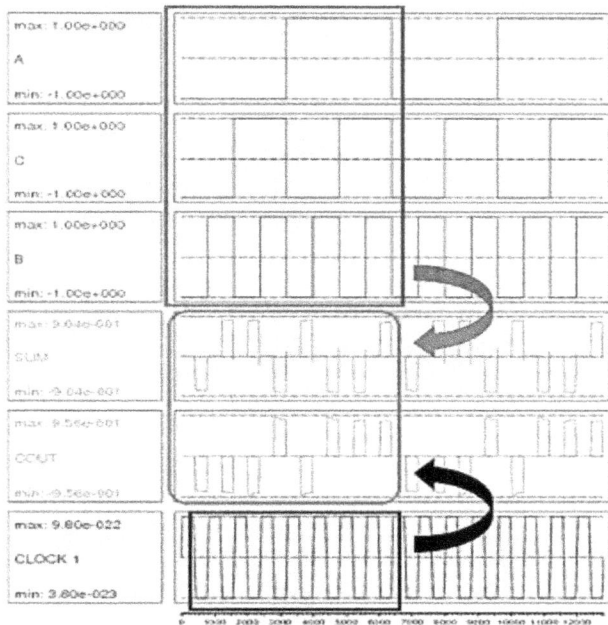

Figure 14.10 Simulation results
Source: Author

presented design outperforms existing models, and the developed model is applicable for designing approximate multipliers to enhance the speed of arithmetic operations.

References

[1] Alkaldy, E., Navi, K., Sharifi, F., and Moaiyeri, M. H. (2014). An ultra high-speed (4; 2) compressor with a new design approach for nano-

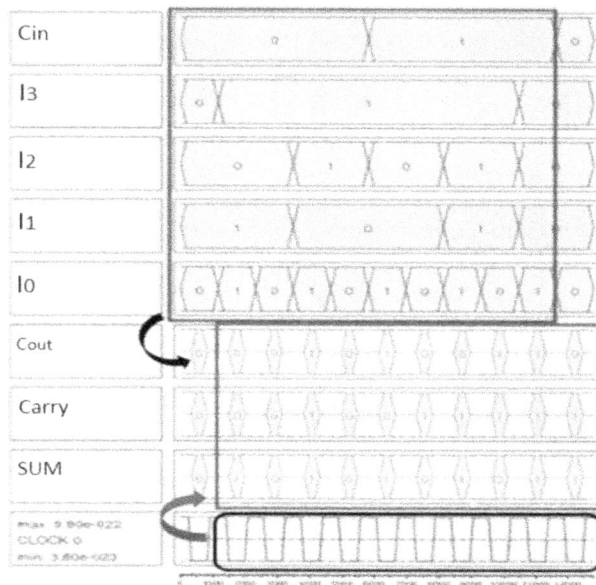

Figure 14.11 The output waveforms of 4:2 compressor
Source: Author

Table 14.2 Full-adders' comparison

Full adder design	Size (μm²)	No of cells	Delay (Clock phases)	Layers
[16]	0.02	38	3	3
[17]	0.04	51	3	3
[20]	0.03	61	3	3
[21]	0.62	292	14	1
Proposed layout	0.02	25	2	3

Source: Author

Table 14.3 Performance metrics for QCA 4:2 compressor designs

Compressors	Size (μm²)	Number of cells	Delay	Error (%)
[6]	0.01	9	1	25
[22]	0.04	33	3	50
[22]	0.017	93	4	43
Proposed design	0.06	71	5	0

Source: Author

technology based on the multi-input majority function. *Journal of Computational and Theoretical Nanoscience*, 11(7), 1691–1696.

[2] Gupta, S. K., and Roy, K. (2015). Low power robust FinFET-based SRAM design in scaled technologies. *Circuit Design for Reliability*, 223–253.

[3] Lent, C. S., Tougaw, P. D., Porod, W., and Bernstein, G. H. (1993). Quantum cellular automata. *Nanotechnology*, 4(1), 49.

[4] Swahn, B., and Hassoun, S. (2006). Gate sizing: FinFETs vs 32nm bulk MOSFETs. In Proceedings of the 43rd annual Design Automation Conference, (pp. 528–531).

[5] Vijayalakshmi, P., and Kirthika, N. (2012). Design of hybrid adder using QCA with implementation of wallace tree multiplier. *International Journal of Advanced Engineering and Technology*, 3(2), 202.

[6] Taheri, M., Arasteh, A., Mohammadyan, S., Panahi, A., and Navi, K. (2020). A novel majority based imprecise 4: 2 compressor with respect to the current and future VLSI industry. *Microprocessors and Microsystems*, 73, 102962.

[7] Gudivada, A. A., and Sudha, G. F. (2020). Design of baugh–wooley multiplier in quantum-dot cellular automata using a novel 1-bit full adder with power dissipation analysis. *SN Applied Sciences*, 2(5), 813.

[8] Lent, C. S., and Tougaw, P. D. (1997). A device architecture for computing with quantum dots. *Proceedings of the IEEE*, 85(4), 541–557.

[9] Angizi, S., Alkaldy, E., Bagherzadeh, N., and Navi, K. (2014). Novel robust single layer wire crossing approach for exclusive or sum of products logic design with quantum-dot cellular automata. *Journal of Low Power Electronics*, 10(2), 259–271.

[10] Seyedi, S., & Navimipour, N. J. (2018). An optimized design of full adder based on nanoscale quantum-dot cellular automata. *Optik*, 158, 243-256.

[11] Haghparast, M., and Mohammadi, M. (2010). Novel quantum compressor designs using new genetic algorithm-based simulator, analyzer and synthesizer software in nanotechnology. *International Journal of Quantum Information*, 8(07), 1219–1231.

[12] Walus, K., Dysart, T. J., Jullien, G. A., and Budiman, R. A. (2004). QCADesigner: a rapid design

and simulation tool for quantum-dot cellular automata. *IEEE Transactions on Nanotechnology*, 3(1), 26–31.

[13] Sherizadeh, R., and Navimipour, N. J. (2018). Designing a 2-to-4 decoder on nanoscale based on quantum-dot cellular automata for energy dissipation improving. *Optik-International Journal for Light and Electron Optics*, 158, 477–489.

[14] Gudivada, A. A., and Sudha, G. F. (2022). STQCA-FFT: a fast fourier transform architecture using stack-type QCA approach with power and delay reduction. *Journal of Computational Science*, 60, 101594.

[15] Gudivada, A. A., and Sudha, G. F. (2022). Novel optimized low power design of single-precision floating-point adder using quantum-dot cellular automata. *The Journal of Supercomputing*, 78, 1–19.

[16] Mohammadi, M., Mohammadi, M., and Gorgin, S. (2016). An efficient design of full adder in quantum-dot cellular automata (QCA) technology. *Microelectronics Journal*, 50, 35–43.

[17] Hashemi, S., Tehrani, M., and Navi, K. (2012). An efficient quantum-dot cellular automata full-adder. *Scientific Research and Essays*, 7(2), 177–189.

[18] Navi, K., Farazkish, R., Sayedsalehi, S., and Azghadi, M. R. (2010). A new quantum-dot cellular automata full-adder. *Microelectronics Journal*, 41(12), 820–826.

[19] Cho, H., and Swartzlander Jr., E. E. (2009). Adder and multiplier design in quantum-dot cellular automata. *IEEE Transactions on Computers*, 58(6), 721–727.

[20] Navi, K., Sayedsalehi, S., Farazkish, R., and Azghadi, M. R. (2010). Five-input majority gate, a new device for quantum-dot cellular automata. *Journal of Computational and Theoretical Nanoscience*, 7(8), 1546–1553.

[21] Mohammadyan, S., Angizi, S., and Navi, K. (2015). New fully single layer QCA full-adder cell based on feedback model. *International Journal of HighPerformance Systems Architecture*, 5(4), 202–208.

[22] Moaiyeri, M. H., Sabetzadeh, F., and Angizi, S. (2018). An efficient majority-based compressor for approximate computing in the nano era. *Microsystem Technologies*, 24(3), 1589–1601.

15 Precision enhancement through truncated multiplier design in filter structure applications

Mahesh Babu Kota[1,a], Raja Suresh[2,b], E. Anant Shankar[2,c] and L. Mahesh[2,d]

[1]Associate Professor, Dept. of ECE, Sri Venkateswara College of Engineering, Tirupati, Andhra Pradesh, India

[2]Assistant Professor, Dept. of ECE, Sri Venkateswara College of Engineering, Tirupati, Andhra Pradesh, India

Abstract

Significant improvements are offered by truncated in terms of latency, power, and area. In the end, the paper that is being given reduces the number of adders that are needed to reduce trees. It is feasible to save space in experiments by using this suggested approach. Ultimately, activities are implemented to achieve the outcome, which compresses the least significant bit (LSB) component. Error compensation circuits were used in earlier research to reduce truncation error. This project's truncation mistake won't be greater than one unit of least position (ULP). Consequently, there will be no need for error correcting circuits, and the output will be exact. Finite impulse response (FIR) filter is used for design implementation in order to broaden the project's scope.

Keywords: Error compensation, finite impulse response, FIR filter, tree reduction, truncated multipliers, truncation

Introduction

One of the most recently developed and widely used fields of research is digital signal processing. The widespread use of finite impulse response (FIR) filters improves the multimedia applications' speed, power consumption, and space use. In signal processing, FIR filters are primarily used to alter the characteristics of signals in the frequency and temporal domains. Thus, it is acknowledged as a fundamental digital signal processing (DSP) component. The use of DSP applications in commercial processors is growing in importance. DSP processors have unique architectures and more features than traditional processors [1]. Because of the high demand for these special DSP processor features, additional algorithms are needed to create the FIR filter-based processors. The key components of DSP processing are inner products, filtering, multiplier and multiplier-accumulator (MAC) convolution, and other operations. The sum of products is computed in the MAC unit, even though it is the central component of algorithms such as FIR and FFT. In DSP, the ability of the MAC is crucial to achieving high performance. FIR filter implementation is essential as a fundamental component in many DSP applications. For shaping, equalizing, modifying, and controlling signal frequencies in real time, high order and faster programmable FIR filters are crucial. This is especially true for video signal processing and transmission, where there is a growing demand due to the expansion of developing applications. Ghost cancellation and channel equalization are capabilities of FIR [2]. Therefore, for new applications, an efficient VLSI architecture needs an effective FIR filter design. A direct form FIR filter can be designed to improve efficiency. It can be obtained by lowering the number of adders and multipliers using canonic signed digit (CSD) format, which includes multiple constant multiplication (MSM) [3]. FIR filter topologies are ideal for any developing application and can be modified to improve efficiency. FIR architecture reconfiguration is

[a]maheshbabu.klu2414@gmail.com, [b]gupthasuresh123@gmail.com, [c]anant.shankar16@gmail.com, [d]l.mahiece@gmail.com

DOI: 10.1201/9781003616399-15

only appropriate for specific types of applications and is neither time or money efficient. In order to build a novel FIR architecture, this research work modified and expanded upon previous research works. After modification, the improved carry save adder (ICSA), MSM, and CSD are employed to do it.

Objectives

To design and implement a novel FIR filter architecture that reduces complexity, energy consumption, latency, memory, and throughput. This paper provides in-depth details on the FIR filter, including its applications, various designs, and pros and cons as compared to other filters. This paper also covers the role of the FIR filter in DSP applications. The concepts and characteristics of the FIR filter can be understood from this paper.

Research issue

In digital signal processing and communication systems, including a number of portable applications from the previous discussion, the FIR filter is an essential component. Additionally, the effectiveness of FIR filter architectures can be raised by paying attention to the configuration of the multipliers and adders. This research work focused on designing a direct-form FIR digital filter from the earlier research works. It is found that the performance of the FIR filter mainly depends on the multipliers used from the experimental results, whereas the performance of the FIR filters can be improved by concentrating on the multipliers and adders. Efficient multiplier and adder circuits are used for an optimized area, power, delay, and increase in speed in DSP. Therefore, the goal of this research is to increase efficiency so that it may be applied to any new DSP applications. The multipliers and adders utilized in the FIR filter architecture are the main subject of this study.

Literature Survey

This design provides an accurately rounded truncated multiplier, ensuring that the highest absolute error does not exceed 1 unit of least position (ULP). The approach involves the concurrent consideration of eliminating superfluous components, decreasing the magnitude, truncating, rounding up the outcome using corrective reasoning, and ultimately including the fractional product components. This is done to restrict the usage of adders in reduction. The proposed method achieves a high level of efficiency by using a truncated multiplier that is accurate, resulting in an area saving rate of over 30%. Moreover, the truncated multiplier design demonstrates decreased latency. The truncated multiplier demonstrates a maximum error of 1 unit in the last place (ULP) and is well-suited for applications that demand accurate results. This technique can be easily employed to create signed or Booth multipliers [1–6]. This work presents cost-effective designs of FIR filters that accurately rounded truncated multipliers. They jointly assess the optimization of bit width and hardware resources while preserving the frequency responsiveness and result signal accuracy. The suggested approach involves utilizing non-uniform coefficient quantization alongside a suitable filter order to decrease the total area cost. A modified version of truncated multipliers is used to perform numerous operations in a direct FIR. The designs reported in this study surpass prior methodologies for FIR design in terms of area, latency, and power results [7–9].

System Design

The technique of creating product bits by multiplying the provided inputs is known as partial product (PP) generation. The PP bits are reduced into two bits using PP reduction. The partial product bits are added via the carry propagate addition. Wallace trees and Dadda trees are two well-known reduction techniques as shown in figure 15.1 that can be applied. The necessary compression operation is carried out by the Dadda reduction technique. The partial product bits' size is consistently reduced by the Wallace tree reduction method. To reduce the remaining fraction, the suggested methodology incorporates the RA reduction method. A column-by-column reduction method is integrated into the proposed truncated multiplier design. Two reduction processes are used in each column to reduce the number of half adders. This is as a result of the full adder's higher compression rate compared to the half adder.

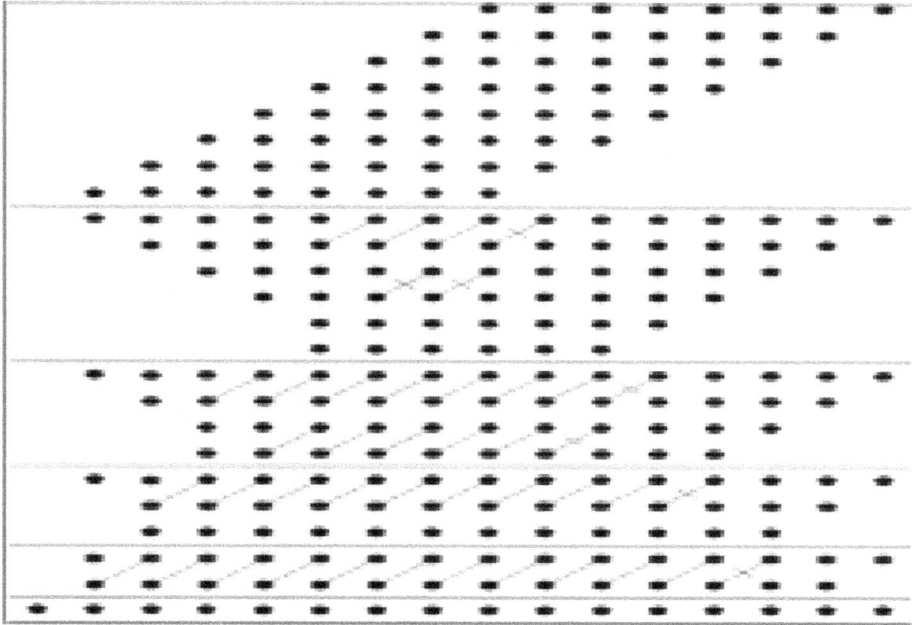

Figure 15.1 Dot diagram of an 8x8-bit dadda multiplier
Source: Author

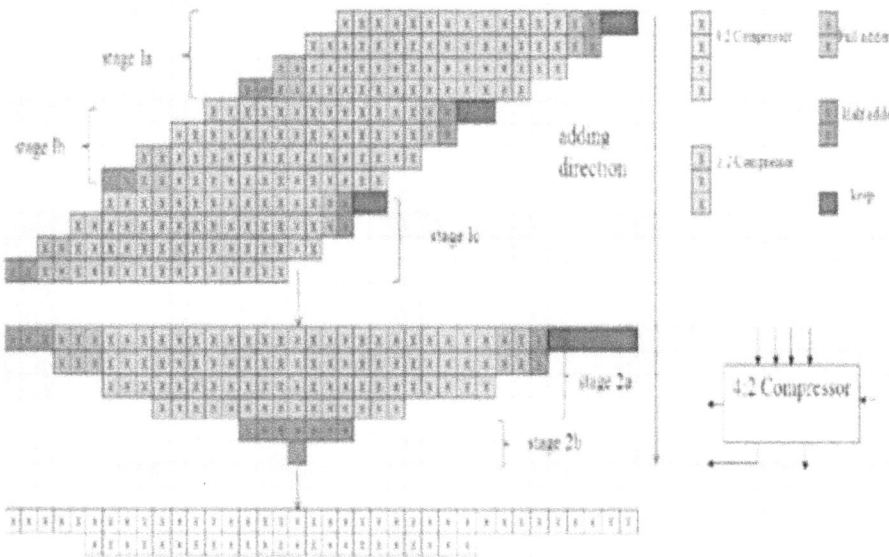

Figure 15.2 Wallace tree examples
Source: Author

Wallace offered a creative method for carrying out parallel addition. Partial product addition is the method of adding bits using a tree of carry save adders. The Wallace method of multiplying two integers is shown in Figure 15.2 referred to here. Using a rapid carry propagate adder, the left two layers are added to create the final product. propagated the usual Wallace tree technique using 3:2 compressors as shown in Figure 15.3. The proliferation of higher order compressors is reduced when the Wallace tree approach is used. The Kogge Stone Adder or KSA is used in comparison to the traditional carry save adder. Design I use hardware description language (HDL) to specify the multipliers. 8-bit unsigned data is used in this. It produces speed and power production.

Proposed fractional multiplier

The goal of the proposed precision truncated multiplier design is to create a semiconductor with a small form factor, fast processing speed, and low power consumption. As a result, the multiplier's size and energy consumption go down. It also frequently reduces the multiplier's delay. First, as the light gray dots represent, any unwanted PP bits are deleted through a deletion operation. The deletion error (ED) has to be between -¼ULP and 0. ¼ULP is the corrective bias constant. Two fractional numbers of NXN dimensions are represented as [4,10].

$$Z = \sum_{k=1}^{2N} z_k 2^{-k} = X \cdot Y = \sum_{l=1}^{N} x_l 2^{-l} \cdot \sum_{m=1}^{N} y_m 2^{-m} \quad (1)$$

The result preserves the N most significant bits (Z_1 to Z_N) for additional computations. The remaining parts are absent from the records or are not included at all. One, or 2^{-N}, is the maximum truncation mistake that can be incurred during the cancellation process. Reduction, abolition, and abbreviation. The grey dots in Figure 15.5 represent the early stages of deletion. An example of an 8 × 8 fractional multiplication with the final 8-bits eliminated serves to illustrate this. Although they are involved in the last stages of truncation and rounding, the first two rows are not deleted. As shown in the diagram, the process of removing incomplete items starts at column 3 and continues until the magnitude reaches 2^{-N}-1. One way to describe or quantify the deletion error range is to the following equation

$$\frac{-1}{4} ulp \leq E_D \leq \frac{1}{4} ulp \quad (2)$$

The PP bits are combined to yield the result of N bits. Figure 15.6 provides an illustration of this sequence. The bits in column 2 to N-1 in the second row are eliminated during the rounding operation.

Examining the results

For instance, 1111111000000001 is the output of the 8 × 8 fixed number multiplication

Figure 15.3 Reduced Wallace multiplier
Source: Author

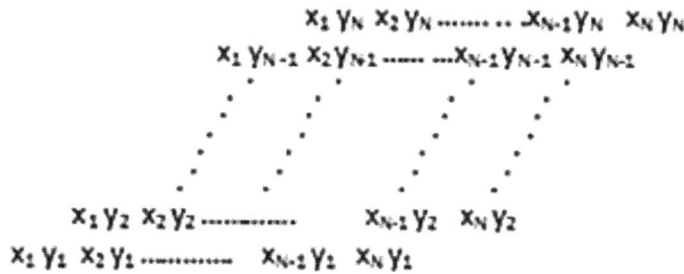

Figure 15.4 Fractional number multiplication
Source: Author

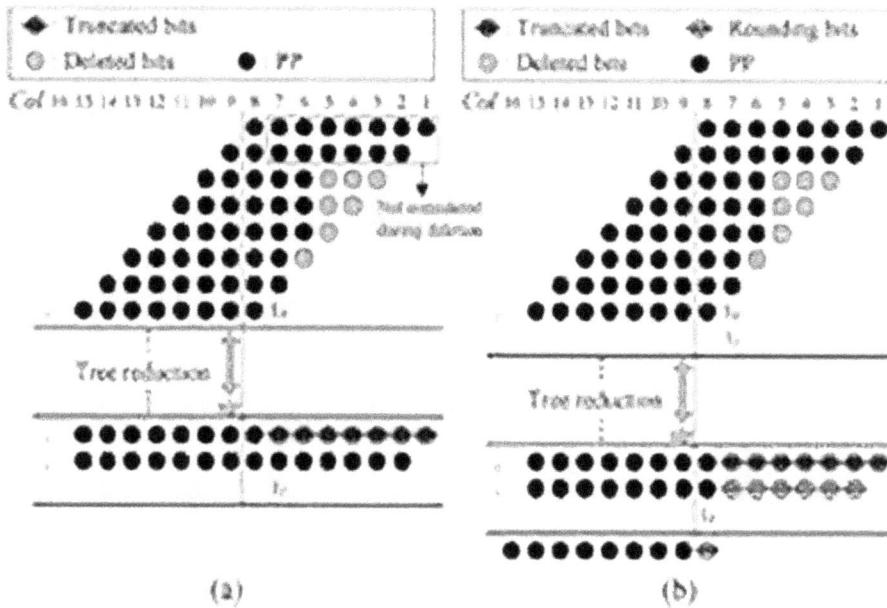

Figure 15.5 Deletion and truncation scheme for fractional multiplier
Source: Author

operation, which requires two inputs: 11111111 and 11111111. Until the E_{totalD} is less than 2^N-1, N = 8, and E_{totalD} indicates the deletion error, the partial products of an 8 × 8 fractional multiplier are removed [1]. 1111111 0.0 1 1 is the result of a multiplier with 8 × 8 inputs, which are 1 1 1 1. 1 111 and 1 1 1 1. 1 1 1 1. Rounding removes the final three bits, yielding an output of 1 1 1 1 1 1 0.

There are two inputs for the 16 × 16 fixed number multiplication operation: 1111111111111111 and 1111111111111111. 11111111111111110 0 0 0 0 0 0 0000001 is the output that is produced as a consequence. The PPs are removed in a 16 × 16 fractional multiplier until the E_{totalD} is less than 2^{-N}-1, where N is equal to 16. A 16 × 16 fractional multiplier accepts the following inputs: 1 1 1 1 1 1 1 1 1 1 1. 1 1 1 1 1 1 and 1 1 1 1 1 1

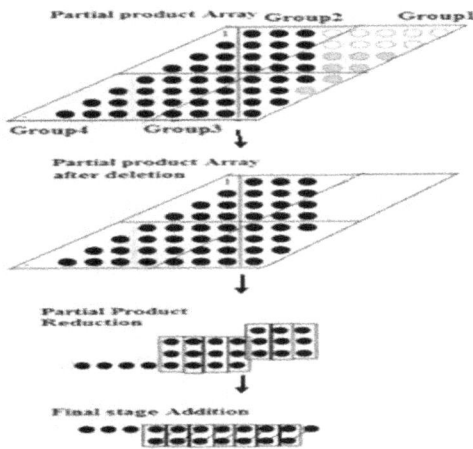

Figure 15.6 Fractional reduction of 8bit
Source: Author

1. 1 1 1 1 1 1 1 1 1 1 1 1 1 1 1 1 0. 1 1 1 1 0. is the result. Rounding eliminates the LSB five bits, yielding 1 1 1 1 1 1 1 1 1 1 1 1 1 1 1 1 1 1 1 1 1 1 1 1 1 0, 1 1 1 1 0.

Simulations and Results

Three distinct multiplier algorithms are compared in this research.

Table 15.1 represents the comparison of the three methods for the parameters like power, delay and Area.

1. The proposed multiplier, or truncated multiplier as shown in Figure 15.7.
2. The fixed number multiplier, or Wallace multiplier as shown in Figure 15.8.

3. Dadda multiplier (multiplier with a fixed number) as shown in Figure 15.9.

The input for the truncated multiplier is a = 15.9375 b = 11.9375. The truncated multiplier algorithm truncates the fractional component of the output, which is 190, to produce the decimal part. The output is 3,584,873,725,952 if a = 266752 and b = 13438976.

Conclusion

Error compensation circuits have been proposed as a solution to the truncation issue in order to achieve more accurate results. This process builds quick parallel truncated multipliers while taking the PP bits' reduction, truncation, and rounding into account. Ensuring that the final shortened product meets the precise requirements is the aim. Error compensation circuits are not required because the truncation error in this approach is only 1 ULP. Consequently, the outcome will be precisely ascertained.

Table 15.1 Parameter comparison

Algorithm	Power (mW)	Delay (ns)	Area (LUTs)
Wallace	2.42	34.409	1595
Dadda	3.57	30.41	2182
Truncated	4.10	27.103	2157

Source: Author

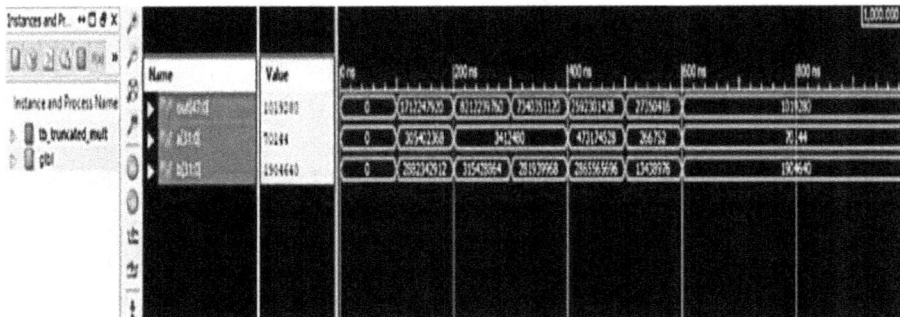

Figure 15.7 Truncated multiplier output
Source: Author

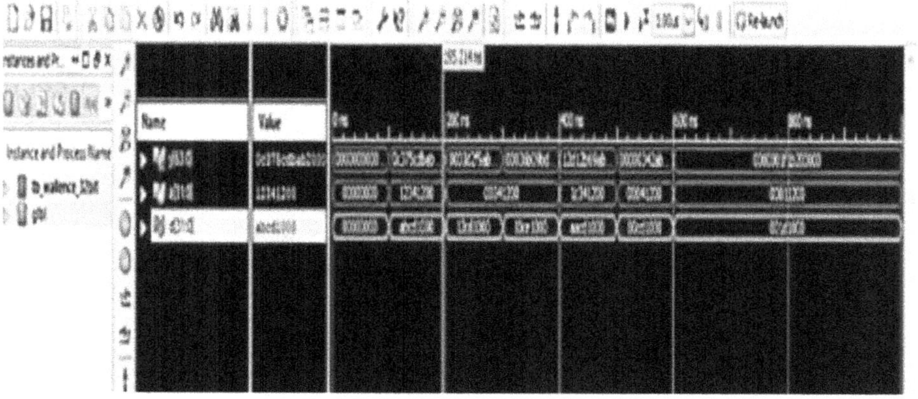

Figure 15.8 Wallace tree multiplier output
Source: Author

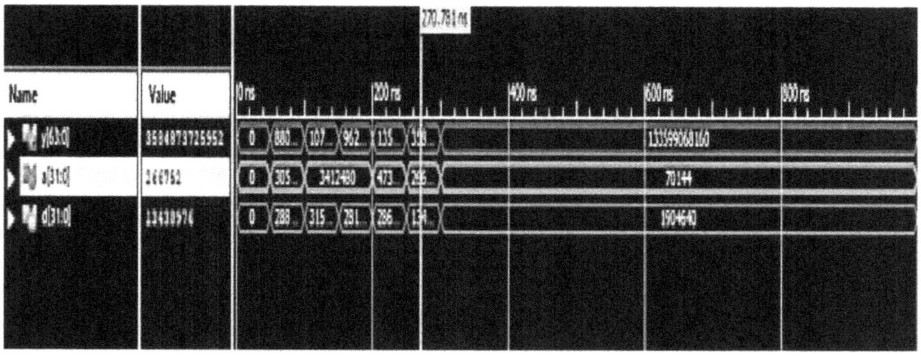

Figure 15.9 Dadda tree multiplier output
Source: Author

References

[1] Stine, J. E., and Duverne, O. M. (2003). Variations on truncated multiplication. In Digital System Design, 2003. Proceedings. Euromicro Symposium, (pp. 112–119).

[2] Jou, J. M., Kuang, S. R., and Der Chen, R. (1999). Design of low-error fixed-width multipliers for DSP applications. *IEEE Transactions on Circuits and Systems II: Analog and Digital Signal Processing*, 46(6), 836–842.

[3] Van, L. D., and Yang, C. C. (2005). Generalized low-error area-efficient fixed width multipliers. *IEEE Transactions on Circuits and Systems*, 52(8), 1608–1619.

[4] Schulte, M. J., and Swartzlander, E. E. (1993). Truncated multiplication with correction constant. In Proceedings of IEEE Workshop on VLSI Signal Processing, (pp. 388–396).

[5] King, E. J., and Swartzlander, E. (1997). Data-dependent truncation scheme for parallel multipliers. In Conference Record of the Thirty-First Asilomar Conference on Signals, Systems and Computers, IEEE Press (pp. 1178–1182).

[6] Schulte, M. J., Stine, J. E., and Jansen, J. G. (1999). Reduced power dissipation through truncated multiplication. In Proceedings IEEE Alessandro Volta Memorial Workshop on Low-Power Design, (pp. 61–69).

[7] Juang, T. B., and Hsiao, S. F. (2005). Low-error carry-free fixed-width multipliers with low-cost compensation circuits. *IEEE Transactions on Circuits and Systems II: Express Briefs*, 52(6), 299–303.

[8] Strollo, A. G. M., Petra, N., and De Caro, D. (2005). Dual-tree error compensation for high performance fixed-width multipliers. *IEEE Transactions on Circuits and Systems II: Express Briefs*, 52(8), 501–507.

[9] Walters III, E. G., and Schulte, M. J. (2005). Efficient function approximation using truncated multipliers and squarers. In Proceedings 17th IEEE Symposium on Computer Arithmetic, (pp. 232–239).

[10] Petra, N., De Caro, D., Garofalo, V., Napoli, E., and Strollo, A. G. M. (2010). Truncated binary multipliers with variable correction and least mean square error. *IEEE Transactions on Circuits and Systems I*, 57(6), 1312–1325.

16 Design and numerical investigations of ITO/SnO$_2$/CdS/CH$_3$NH$_3$SnI$_3$/CuSCN/Au perovskite solar cell

Naveen.b[1,a], Apurva Kumari[2,b], Paramita Sarkar[3,c], G. Naveen kumar[4,d], G. Sathwik[5,e] and K. Srujana Reddy[6]

[1,2,4,5,6]Department of ECE, B V Raju Institute of Technology Narsapur, Andhra Pradesh, India

[3]Department of ECE, BMS Institute of Technology and Management, Bangalore, Karnataka, India

Abstract

The main objective of this work is to design a perovskite photovoltaic cell with higher efficiency with and without buffer layer that is suitable for practical applications. Therefore, a mixed perovskite layer composed of ITO/SnO2/CdS/CH3NH3SnI3/CuSCN/Au was used as the active layer. Along with this perovskite, CuSCN and ZNO have been used as hole and electron transport layer (ETO) and without buffer layer CdS respectively. The cell was optimized by varying the working temperature between 280K to 330K, absorber layer thickness between 750 nm to 1300 nm. The final Optimized cell shows 1.0223 V open circuit voltage, 33.909599 mA/Cm2 short circuit current density, 30.12% of efficiency and 86.88% of fill factor at optimized temperature of 280 K, optimized perovskite layer thickness of 1050 nm. The present modelling technique is compared with the theoretical results of with and without buffer. That confirm the accuracy of the conclusions we have obtained for the proposed solar cell.

Keywords: Mixed perovskite layer, power conversion efficiency (PCE), SCAPS-1D simulator, solar cell

Introduction

Thin film solar cells (TFSC's) possess garnered huge impact in performance enhancement of Photovoltaic industry [1]. Be it highly performing first generation solar cells or the new technology materials based third generation solar cells, the kind of attention the second generation TFSC's have regained is worth mentioning [2]. This generation solar cells are very economical in their fabrication. But the major issue associated with second generation solar cells is their low power conversion efficiency (PCE) achieved so far, which has got a stagnation [3]. In recent time's perovskite, a new solar cell absorber material has evolved for solar cell applications [4]. These perovskite materials are represented as ABX3. Here A can be either organic or inorganic ion, such as K+, Cs+, CH$_3$NH +, etc. The Symbol, B cab be metal ion like Sn^{2+}, Pb^{2+}, and similar. Further, and X can be any of the Cl/I/Br atoms. Although, these perovskites materials forms third generation solar cell but, but they are fabricated as thin film layer in solar cell, giving the remarkable upsurge in PCE. To improve the PCE of perovskite solar cells, several derivatives of CH$_3$NH$_3$PbX$_3$ materials have been explored from time to time [6,7]. Many researchers have focused on replacing the Pb with some other non-hazardous elements [8]. Also, the molar quantity of halides has also been varied by adding them in different proportions. Perovskite solar cell structure have been widely studied for efficiency enhancement particularly using simulation tools like SCAPS-1D [14,15]. Recently, mixed perovskite material (MPL)is also explored as an alternative to basic perovskite absorber in solar cell and obtained PCE is quite appreciating as the mixed perovskite [1, 9, 10].

In TFSC it not only the absorber layer that contribute to high PCE, but also, the other layers like hole and electron transport layers are the sites for solar cell performance enhancement. HTL, usually a P-type material, plays important role by extracting the photogenerated holes outside the absorber layer and stops the electron flow on the way to the electrodes. Similarly, ETL being

[a]naveen.b@bvrit.ac.in, [b]apurva.kumari@bvrit.ac.in, [c]22215a0412@bvrit.ac.in, [d]21211a0489@bvrit.ac.in, [e]21211a04c7@bvrit.ac.in

DOI: 10.1201/9781003616399-16

the n-type materials carries the electrons through it and block the counter flow of holes towards the electrodes [11,12]. Along with the thrust to explore the absorber materials in solar cell performance enhancement, the appropriate ETL and HTL materials have also been explored in literature. It is imperative that the correct choice of ETL and HTL gives correct band alignment among the three layers which eventually result in performance enhancement of the device [13].

In this work, we have computed the performance analysis of inorganic perovskite ITO/SnO_2/CdS/$CH_3NH_3SnI_3$/CuSCN/Au in conjunction with CuSCN as an HTL layer and ZnO as the ETL and compared the performances of properties of the cell with and without buffer layer CdS in the abovementioned solar cell structure using SCAPS-1D simulator. The layout of the paper is given as: in the section 2 we have discussed about the material properties used in the simulation along with the basic device structure simulated. In section 3 results have been discussed and in the last section 4 conclusions of the work have been drawn.

Device Structure

In this study, we have studied the performance analysis of inorganic perovskite solar cell ITO/

SnO_2/$CH_3NH_3SnI_3$/CuSCN/Au without buffer layer. Simulations are done in SCAPS-1D simulator and the simulated device architecture is as shown in Figure 16.1. All the properties of the materials required for simulations are collected from various sources and given in Table 16.1. Here, Ev is the bandgap of the respective

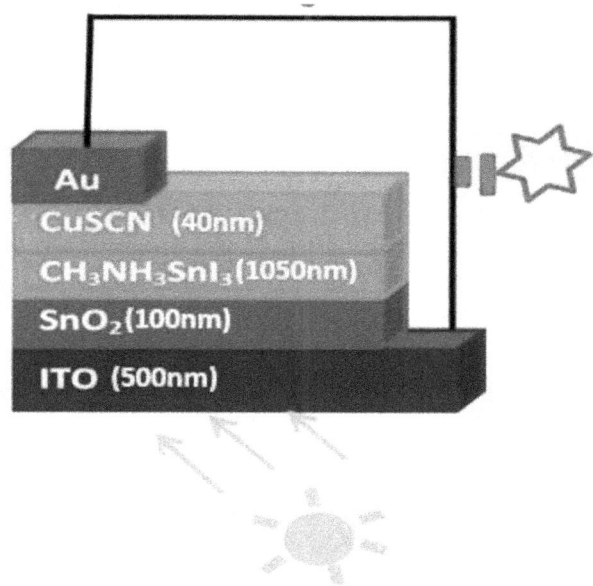

Figure 16.1 Schematic of device structure without buffer layer
Source: Author

Table 16.1 List of all materials parameters employed in this simulation investigation taken from reported work [1–6]

Parameters	ITO	SNO_2	CDS	$CH_3NH_3SNI_3$	CUSCN
Thickness	500	100(nm)	80(nm)	1050(nm)	40
Bandgap (EV)	3.5	3.5	2.42	1.3	3.4
Electron affinity	4.0	4.0	4.4	4.17	1.9
Dielectric permittivity relative	9.0	34.8	10	10	10
CB	$2.2*10^{18}$	$2.4*10^{18}$	$1.2*10^{18}$	$1.0*10^{8}$	$2.2*10^{18}$
VB	$1.8*10^{19}$	$1.8*10^{19}$	$1.8*10^{19}$	$1.0*10^{19}$	$1.8*10^{18}$
VE	$1.0*10^{7}$	$1.0*10^{7}$	$1.0*10^{7}$	$1.0*10^{7}$	$1.0*10^{7}$
VH	$1.0*10^{7}$	$1.0*10^{7}$	$1.0*10^{7}$	$1.0*10^{7}$	$1.0*10^{7}$
Un	90	20	100	1.6	100
Uh	90	10	50	1.6	25
ND	$7*10^{20}$	$1.0*10^{16}$	$2.1*10^{17}$	0	0
NA	0	0	0	$1.0*10^{17}$	$1.0*10^{18}$
NT	$1.0*10^{15}$	$1.0*10^{14}$	$1.0*10^{17}$	$1.0*10^{14}$	$1.0*10^{15}$

Source: Adapted from [1-6]

materials, εr is the dielectric permittivity, X is the layer electron affinity, μp and μn are the mobility for hole and electron respectively. Further, Nv and Nc respective density of states for valence band and conduction band. Also, the acronym NA and ND are acceptor and density, respectively.

Here, Ev: band gap;χ electron affinity; ε: dielectric permittivity; Nv: effective density of states of VB; Nc: effective density of states of conduction band; μn: mobility pf electrons. μh: mobility of holes. VB; valence band. CB; conduction band

Results and Discussions

The simulations were run on a SCAPS-1D simulator at a temperature of 300 K and an illumination of AM 1.5G without buffer layer CdS. The primary purpose of a photovoltaic cell is the transformation of solar energy into usable electricity. In a PV cell, the J-V curve is exponential because the diode is very big and very flat [1]. Due to existence of minority carriers, a small current flow. Figure 16.2 presents the J-V characteristics in the dark as well as in illuminated light by considering all the material properties mentioned in Table 16.1. This initial/base cell without the buffer layer gives the power conversion efficiency (PCE) is 30.12%, the short circuit current density (JSC) is 33.909599 mA/cm², the open circuit voltage (VOC) is 1.0223 V, and the fill factor (FF) is 86.88%. respectively. The observed values are analogous to the reported

work by Rahaman et al. [1]. Working temperature has been changed from 280K to 330K with a variation of 5K in each run to explore the effects of various factors on the simulated device. Furthermore, thickness of absorber layer has been varied between 750 nm to 1300 nm without the buffer layer in the cell.

Impact of working temperature

The efficiency of photovoltaic systems is greatly affected by the temperature at which they are operated. Since sunlight causes a solar cell to heat up, its ability to generate electricity was hindered. Figures 16.3 and 16.4 presents the change in VOC, PCE, JSC, and FF with respect to the change in working temperature in the simulated device. It has been noted that, the increased temperature shows the detrimental effect in the capability of the device; as the power conversion efficiency (PCE) decreases with increasing temperature. Increases in temperature reduce the efficiency of a material because they alter the concentration of carriers, the band gaps, and the mobility of holes and electrons. And the optimized temperature is 280K, where the device gives 1.0233V of VOC without the buffer layer.

Temperature optimization in the range of 280K to 330K:

The optimized temperature is 280K.

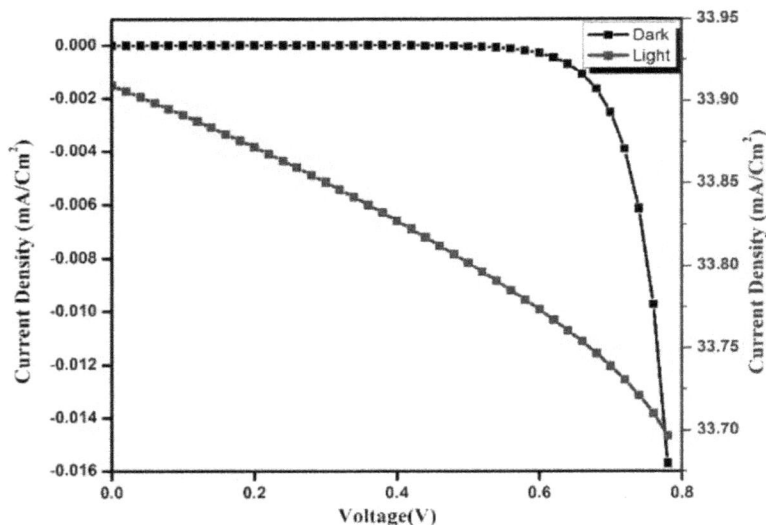

Figure 16.2 Current density vs. voltage plot for the Initial simulation (under light and dark condition)
Source: Author

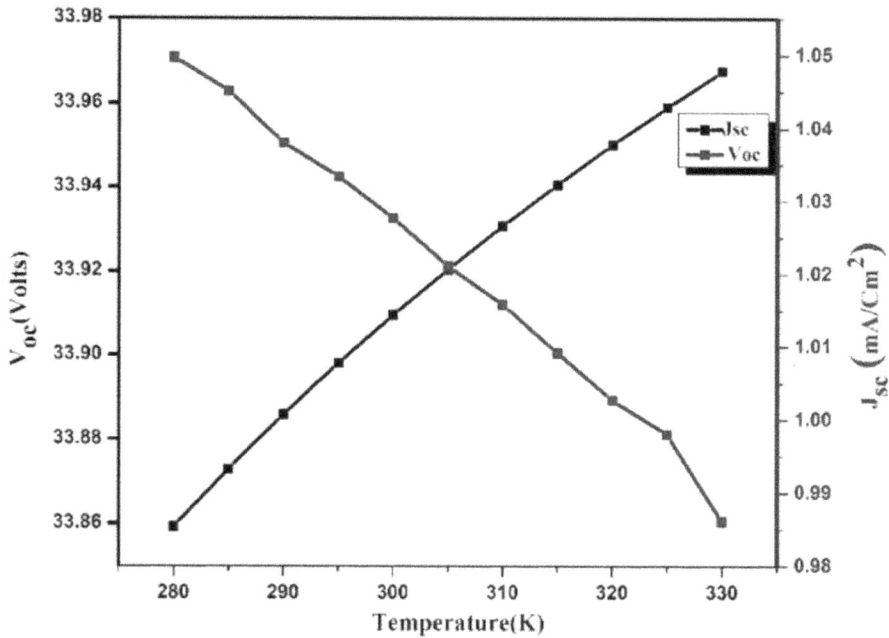

Figure 16.3 Variation in the characteristics of the device, such as VOC, JSC, with respect to the temperature of the cell
Source: Author

Table 16.2 Variation in the characteristics of the device with respect to the working temperature of the cell.

THICKNESS (nm)	Voc (v)	Jsc (ma/cm²)	FF (%)	E (%)
750	1.0613	33.436569	87.00	30.87
800	1.0585	33.566750	87.11	30.95
850	1.0559	33.668989	67.20	31.00
900	1.0537	33.750647	87.28	31.04
950	1.0467	33.812267	87.75	31.06
1000	1.0497	33.859311	87.39	31.06
1050	1.0480	33.894603	87.44	31.06
1100	1.0465	33.922447	87.46	31.05
1150	1.0451	33.940013	87.49	31.03
1200	1.0438	33.950297	87.51	31.01
1250	1.0426	33.956479	87.53	30.99
1300	1.0415	33.957601	87.54	30.96
1350	1.0405	33.955393	87.55	30.93
1400	1.0624	33.953403	85.67	30.90

Source: Author

Impact of absorber's layer thickness

At 280K of optimized working temperature the performance of the proposed device has been further investigated by varying the absorber layer's thickness between 750 to 1300 nm. The influence of thickness on the V-P curves is also evident in the Figures 16.3 and 16.4. This diagram shows that a cell's power density improves as its absorber layer becomes thicker, as a larger absorber layer has a greater probability of absorbing light particles and turning them into electricity. The fill factor was 86.88% and the eta was up to 30.12% when the MPL was 1050 nm thick. VOC was given 1.0223 V and JSC was 33.909599 mA/cm² without the buffer layer. The characteristics parameters were drastically altered when the thickness varied from 750nm to 1300 nm as summarized in the Table.16.2. Here, we see that efficiency has been much enhanced. This effect is evidently shown in Figures 16.3 ,16.4 and 16.5.

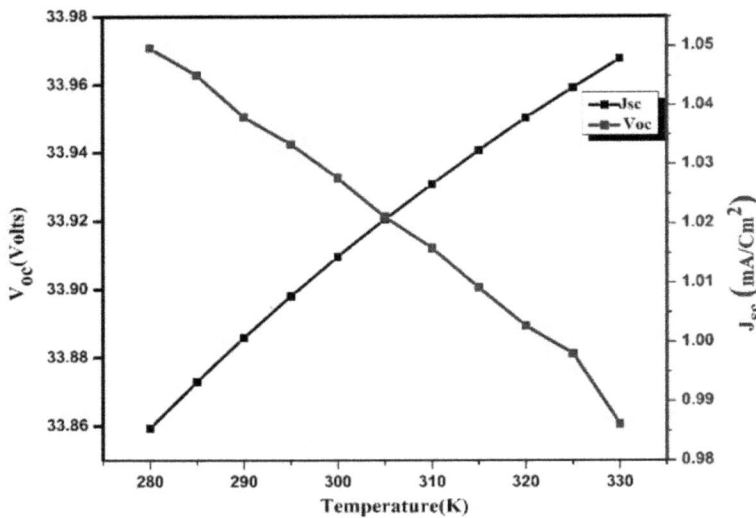

Figure 16.4 Variation in the characteristics of the device as VOC and JSC with respect to the perovskite layer's thickness
Source: Author

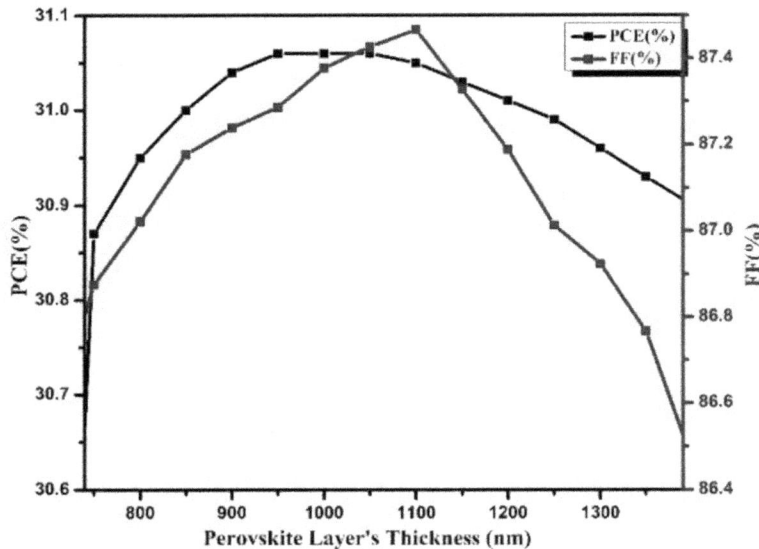

Figure 16.5 Variation in the characteristics of the cell such as FF, and PCE with respect to the perovskite layer's thickness
Source: Author

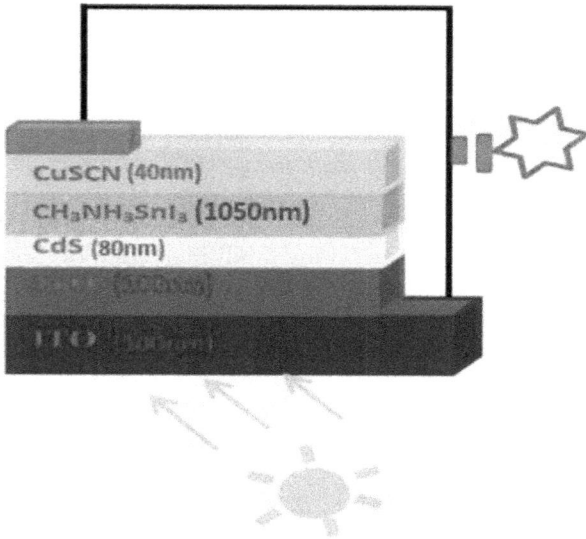

Figure 16.6 Schematic diagram of cell with buffer layer CdS

Source: Author

Incorporation of CdS buffer layer in the cell

The structure of perovskite solar cell with buffer layer ITO/SnO$_2$/CdS/CH$_3$NH$_3$SnI$_3$/CuSCN/Au is shown in figure. When the buffer layer is inserted in the cell the performances of the absorber's layer changes. The results are as follows: Under light/illumination the base cell gives VOC = 1.049V, Jsc = 33.821 mA/Cm^2, FF = 84.79%, efficiency

= 30.07%. The following figure gives information about the Current density vs voltage plot for the ITO/SnO$_2$/CdS/CH$_3$NH$_3$SnI$_3$/CuSCN/Au cell (under light and dark condition).

Conclusion

Renewable energy is playing a crucial role in today's life. Perovskite solar cell is one of the many variants of solar cells. There are many published reports on the theoretical and experimental effectiveness of several perovskite solar cell types, but the quest for superior one continues. In continuation to that, the present study shows the impact of different characteristics parameters on functioning of ITO/SnO$_2$/CdS/CH$_3$NH$_3$SnI$_3$/CuSCN/Au as shown in the Figure.16.6 and without buffer layer ITO/SnO$_2$/CH$_3$NH$_3$SnI$_3$/CuSCN/Au solar cell. The temperature of the cell where it works was varied along with absorber layer thickness of the final perovskite layer. The final cell shows 1.0223V open circuit voltage, 33.909599 mA/cm^2 short circuit current density, 86.88% of fill factor and 30.12% of efficiency at optimized temperature of 280 K and optimized perovskite layer thickness of 1050nm and with buffer layer the cell shows 1.049 V open circuit voltage, 33.821 mA/cm2 short circuit current density, 84.79% of fill factor and 30.07% of efficiency at 280 K temperature and Figure 16.7

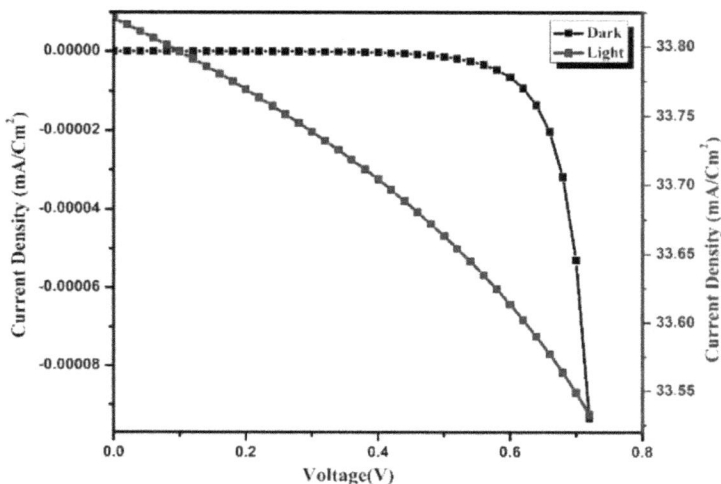

Figure 16.7 Current density vs voltage plot for the ITO/ SnO$_2$CdS/CH$_3$NH$_3$SnI$_3$/CuSCN/Au cell (under light and dark condition)

Source: Author

shows current vs voltage plot with buffer layer. So, finally the perovskite solar cell without the buffer layer provides better efficiency.

References

[1] Rahman, M. B., Miah, M. H., Khandaker, M. U., and Islam, M. A. (2023). Selection of a compatible electron transport layer and hole transport layer for the mixed perovskite FA 0.85 Cs 0.15 Pb (I 0.85 Br 0.15) 3 towards achieving novel structure and high-efficiency perovskite solar cells: a detailed numerical study by SCAPS-1D. *RSC Advances*, 13(25), 17130–17142.

[2] Green, M., Dunlop, E., Hohl-Ebinger, J., Yoshita, M., Kopidakis, N., and Hao, X. (2021). Solar cell efficiency tables (version 57). *Progress in Photovoltaics: Research and Applications*, 29(1), 3–15.

[3] Bouazizi, S., Tlili, W., Bouich, A., Soucase, B. M., and Omri, A. (2022). Design and efficiency enhancement of FTO/PC60BM/CsSn0. 5Ge0. 5I3/ Spiro-OMeTAD/Au perovskite solar cell utilizing SCAPS-1D simulator. *Materials Research Express*, 9(9), 096402.

[4] Shafi, M. A., Ullah, H., Ullah, S., Khan, L., Bibi, S., and Soucase, B. M. (2022). Numerical simulation of lead-free Sn-based perovskite solar cell by using SCAPS-1D. *Engineering Proceedings*, 12(1), 92.

[5] Sunny, A., Rahman, S., Khatun, M., and Ahmed, S. R. A. (2021). Numerical study of high-performance HTL-free CH3NH3SnI₃-based perovskite solar cell by SCAPS-1D. *AIP Advances*, 11(6), 065102.

[6] Zapukhlyak, Z. R., Nykyruy, L. I., Prokopiv, V. V., Lishchynskyy, I. M., Katanova, L. O., Yavorskyi, R. S., et al. (2020). SCAPS simulation of ZnO/CdS/CdTe/CuO heterostructure for photovoltaic application. *Physics and Chemistry of Solid State*, 21(4), 660–668.

[7] Coulibaly, A. B., Oyedele, S. O., and Aka, B. (2019). Comparative study of lead-free perovskite solar cells using different hole transport er materials. *Modelling and Simulation in Materials Science and Engineering*, 9, 97–107.

[8] Salah, M. M., Hassan, K. M., Abouelatta, M., and Shaker, A. (2017). A comparative study of different ETMs in perovskite solar cell with inorganic copper iodide as HTM. *Optik*, 178, 958–963.

[9] Islam, S., Sobayel, K., and Akhtaruzzaman, M. (2021). Defect study and modeling of SnX₃-based perovskite solar cells with SCAPS-1D. *Nanomaterials*, 11(5), 1218.

[10] Alzoubi, T., and Moustafa, M. (2019). Numerical optimization of absorber and CdS buffer layers in CIGS solar cells using SCAPS. *International Journal of Smart Grid and Clean Energy*, 8(3), 291–298.

[11] Bouazizi, S., Tlili, W., Bouich, A., Soucase, B. M., and Omri, A. (2022). Design and efficiency enhancement of FTO/PC60BM/CsSn₀.₅Ge₀.₅I₃/ Spiro-OMeTAD/Au perovskite solar cell utilizing SCAPS-1D simulator. *Materials Research Express*, 9, 096402.

[12] Nithya, K. S., and Sudheer, K. S. (2020). Device modeling of non-fullerene organic solar cell with inorganic CuI hole transport layer using SCAPS-1D. *Optik*, 217, 164790.

[13] Lam, N. D. (2020). Modeling and numerical analysis of ZnO/CuO/Cu₂O heterojunction solar cell using SCAPS. *Engineering Research Express*, 2, 025033.

[14] Maoucha, A., Djeffal, F., and Ferhati, H. (2023). Numerical investigation of a new double-absorber lead-free perovskite solar cell via SCAPS-1D. In 2023 20th International Conference on Electrical Engineering, Computing Science and Automatic Control (CCE), (pp. 1–4). IEEE.

[15] Norddin, N., Shafie, S., Idris, M. I., Liu, X., Lawal, I., Rummaja, M. I. D. M., et al. (2023). Performance comparison of different electron transport layers for perovskite solar cell with NiO as hole transport layer using SCAPS-1D. In 2023 IEEE 8th International Conference on Recent Advances and Innovations in Engineering (ICRAIE), (pp. 1–4). IEEE.

17 Deep enhance: Convolutional neural network-based enhancement of underwater images

Kapula Kalyani[1,a], Meher Freiney, N.[2,b], Shaik Afnaan[2,c], Divya Naga Sai Sri, V.[2,d] and Ch. Meenakshi[2,e]

[1]Assistant Professor, Dept. of ECE, Aditya College of Engineering and Technology, Surampalem, Andhra Pradesh, India

[2]Student, Dept. of ECE, Aditya College of Engineering and Technology, Surampalem, Andhra Pradesh, India

Abstract

This paper focuses on enhancing underwater images using a dataset trained by convolutional neural network (CNN) of paired original and enhanced images. We utilize a custom image data store to manage the paired image data effectively. For training the CNN model, we design a network architecture comprising convolutional layers, batch normalization, and ReLU activation functions. The model is being trained using the stochastic gradient descent with momentum (SGDM) optimizer. We use a single epoch with a mini-batch size of four, ensuring efficient training while avoiding overfitting. After training, the trained CNN model is saved for future use. We load the saved model to enhance new underwater images. The enhancement process involves preprocessing the input image, applying gamma correction, and sharpening the image using the trained CNN model. To assess the effectiveness of the enhancement, various image performance metrics are computed, such as structural similarity index measure (SSIM), peak signal-to-noise ratio (PSNR) and mean squared error (MSE). These metrics offer quantitative evaluations of how closely the enhanced images resemble the original ones. The proposed approach demonstrates promising results in enhancing underwater images and achieving high PSNR and SSIM values while minimizing MSE. The trained CNN model offers an effective solution for improving the visual quality of underwater imagery, with potential applications in various domains like marine research, underwater surveillance, and underwater photography.

Keywords: Convolution neural network, deep learning, stochastic gradient descent with momentum, underwater image processing

Introduction

Exploitation and exploration of marine resources are becoming a strategic priority worldwide. The underwater images are beneficial because they provide a wealth of detailed information. Because of the impact of backscatter over long distances, Scattering in water, and light selective absorption, raw underwater photographs are typically of poor quality, color variations, with low contrast and brightness, halos with artificial lighting, indistinct information, and uneven brilliant specks. The main aim of underwater image enhancement is to enhance the clarity and quality of underwater images, facilitating the extraction of important information. Enhancing image details supports various applications such as shipwreck detection, underwater archaeology, marine studies, surveillance, photography, and fish detection. Earlier methods for enhancing underwater images often relied on conventional techniques, including physical-based approaches and those based on histogram equalization [1]). However, their usefulness is sometimes limited in difficult underwater settings.

Our approach uses deep learning architectures to improve the visual quality of underwater photos. We also look at real-time processing and adversarial training techniques to verify that our approach is strong and practical.

[a]kalyani.kapula@acet.ac.in, [b]freiney.meher@gmail.com, [c]afnaan.sk@gmail.com, [d]divyanss @gmail.com, [e]meenakshich@gmail.com

DOI: 10.1201/9781003616399-17

Recently, deep learning methods using convolutional neural networks (CNNs) have proven to be powerful tools for enhancing underwater images. These methods use large datasets of paired underwater photos to train sophisticated mappings between degraded and augmented images. CNN-based approaches can efficiently recover visual features and improve the overall quality of underwater images because they capture intricate correlations within the data

The CNN is trained using a dataset that includes matched original and improved underwater pictures. This dataset makes supervised learning easier, allowing CNN to learn the relationship between degraded and enhanced underwater images

Literature Survey

Improving the visual quality of underwater photos is a popular topic in both the computer vision and underwater imaging sectors. Several ways have been developed to solve the issues presented by underwater imaging settings. In this section, we review the relevant literature and describe the various strategies used to enhance underwater images.

Traditional approaches to underwater image improvement frequently require bespoke algorithms designed to prevent specific underwater degradation phenomena such as color cast and contrast loss. These methods often use techniques like color correction, contrast stretching, and histogram equalization. Paul et al. [1] offer a color restoration algorithm based on histogram equalization to compensate for contrast loss in underwater photographs.

Physics-based models attempt to recreate the underwater light propagation process to better understand and compensate for the effects of water attenuation. These models take into account variables including water depth, turbidity, and light scattering. Mobley, Curtis D. [2] developed a thorough model for underwater light propagation that has aided in comprehending the limitations of underwater imaging.

Deep learning strategies, namely CNNs, have proved exceptional performance in a variety of image processing applications, including underwater image augmentation. These methods use large datasets of paired underwater photos to train sophisticated mappings between degraded and augmented images. Li, Jing et al. [3] offer a CNN-based approach for underwater image restoration that significantly improves image quality.

Access to high-quality underwater image datasets is essential for the development and evaluation of image enhancement techniques. Several datasets have been specially collected for underwater image processing tasks. Notable examples are the UFO-120 dataset [4], which has a vast collection of underwater photos with varied degrees of degradation, and the REalistic WAter Dataset (REWARD) [5], which provides a diversified variety of underwater settings for testing image enhancement techniques.

Deep learning Approaches, especially convolutional neural networks (CNNs), have become extensively popular due to their capacity to learn complicated mappings between input and output domains. Researchers use data augmentation, transfer learning, and domain adaptation to address the scarcity of labeled underwater image datasets [6].

Generative adversarial networks (GANs) have emerged as an effective framework for picture generation and enhancement applications. GANs have been utilized in underwater imaging to generate realistic underwater sceneries and improve visual quality. Zhe et al. [7] introduced an underwater image improvement approach based on a conditional GAN (cGAN), which successfully removed color casts and increased contrast in underwater photos.

Recent studies use multi-modal information, like depth maps and polarized images, to enhance underwater photo quality more effectively. Guang et al. [8] proposed a multi-modal fusion framework for underwater picture enhancement that outperformed single-modal approaches.

Recently, researchers have investigated end-to-end learning architectures for underwater picture improvement, in which the complete process from input to output is learned directly from data. For example, Cheng, Yan, et al. [9] suggested an end-to-end deep neural network architecture for underwater picture improvement that learns feature extraction and enhancement stages simultaneously, resulting in better performance than typical modular techniques. An attention-based deep neural network enhances underwater images by focusing on critical features, improving color, contrast, and clarity despite challenges like scattering and color distortion [10].

Real-time and low-light enhancement is essential for viable underwater imaging systems, especially in applications like underwater robots and surveillance. Several ways have been proposed to overcome these issues, including lightweight network designs, efficient inference algorithms, and low-light picture augmentation techniques. Yihao, et al. [11] created a real-time deep learning-based approach for improving low-light underwater images, achieving quick processing times while preserving high-quality results.

Lingwei, and colleagues [12] suggested a semantic segmentation-guided deep learning framework for underwater picture enhancement that adaptively adapts enhancement parameters based on the semantic content of the scene. By segmenting the underwater picture into meaningful regions (e.g., objects, background), these approaches can adjust improvement strategies to each region's features

Adversarial training improves underwater image enhancement algorithms' robustness against aberrations and environmental conditions. These models learn to produce enhanced images that are less susceptible to noise, blur, and

other artifacts by integrating adversarial instances during training. For example, Yongjie et al. [13] used adversarial training to improve the robustness of a deep learning-based underwater picture enhancement model, resulting in better performance under difficult situations. Underwater image enhancement using a convolutional neural network with edge constraints improves clarity and detail by enhancing edges, reducing blurring, and addressing color distortions commonly found in underwater images [14]. An attention-based deep neural network enhances underwater images by selectively focusing on important regions, improving color accuracy, contrast, and detail in challenging underwater conditions.[15]

In conclusion, while several approaches to underwater picture enhancement have been presented, each has its own set of restrictions and trade-offs. Traditional methods may struggle with complicated scenes and dynamic situations, while deep learning-based algorithms may necessitate enormous amounts of labeled data and struggle in harsh underwater environments.

Proposed Model

Underwater image enhancement (UIE) algorithms primarily strive to improve contrast and

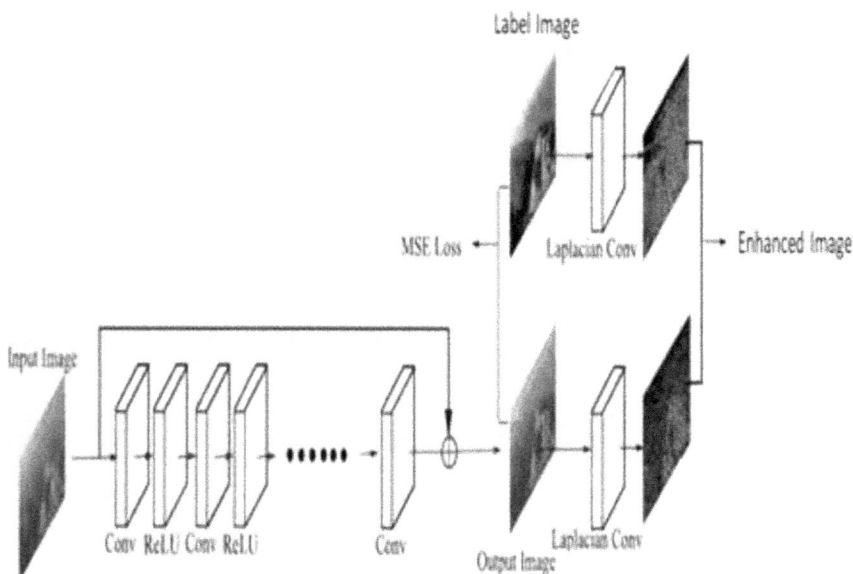

Figure 17.1 Block diagram of the proposed method
Source: Author

rectify color casts. A deep learning algorithm is suggested for the enhancement of underwater images. The dataset is separated into training and testing subsets to ensure that the model can learn and generalize.

The block diagram for underwater image enhancement using a CNN shown in Figure 17.1 involves several key stages: the collection of raw underwater images, followed by data set preparation which includes normalization, data augmentation, splitting into training, validation, and test sets. The CNN is then trained on this prepared dataset, learning to enhance images through layers of convolutions, activations, pooling, and deconvolutions. After training, the model's performance is evaluated using validation and test sets to ensure it generalizes well. Once the model is fine-tuned and evaluated, it is deployed for practical use, producing enhanced versions of the input underwater images. Finally, the quality of these enhanced images is assessed using various metrics to ensure they meet the desired enhancement standards.

The architecture of underwater image enhancement using a CNN in Figure 17.2 starts with the input image, which undergoes several convolutional layers with ReLU activations to extract features. The rectified linear unit (ReLU) activation functions to induce nonlinearity and improve the network's representational power. The final layer of the network produces the improved image, which is commonly achieved by a regression approach. The normalization layer increases training stability and speed, normalizes the previous layer's activations. During training, the label image serves as the ground truth to guide the model. A Laplacian convolution layer is then applied to enhance edges and fine details. Uses convolutional techniques to extract information from input images. These layers build feature maps by convolution across the input image using filters or kernels. The intermediate result is the output image, which is further processed to produce the final enhanced image with improved visual quality.

The method begins by loading undersea photos from a directory named "datt". The "image Datastore" function creates an image datastore, allowing for easy access and management of image data. To prepare images for training, they may be resized, normalized, or subjected to additional changes. The "split Each Label" function divides the dataset into training and testing sets. This stage ensures that the model may be trained on a subset of the data and tested on another, unseen subset. The CNN architecture for image enhancement consists of convolutional, rectified linear unit (ReLU) layers and batch normalization, is meant to process input images of the size

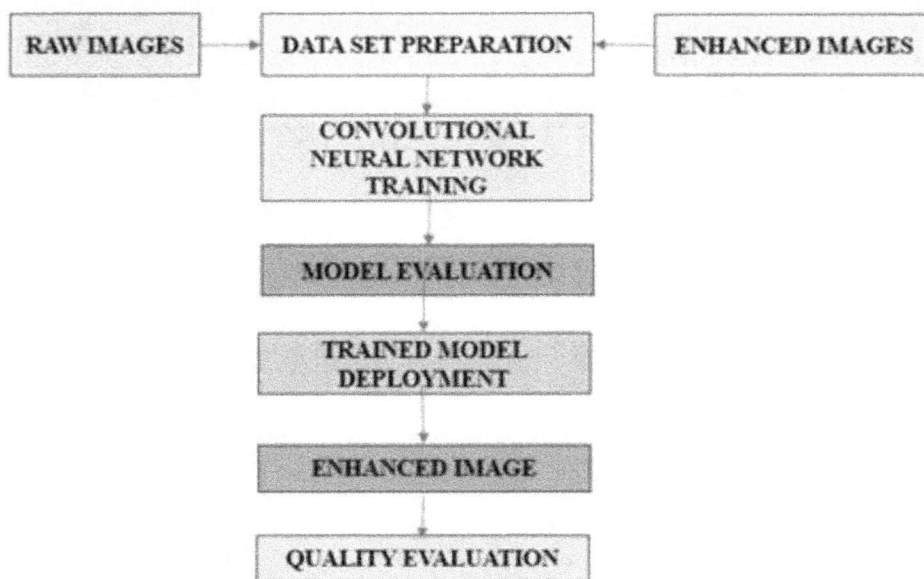

Figure 17.2 Architecture of underwater image enhancement process using convolutional neural networks
Source: Author

256x256 pixels with three color channels (RGB) and output enhanced images with improved visual quality. The 'training Options' function specifies training options for the CNN model. The stochastic gradient descent with momentum (SGDM) optimizer is used to train the CNN model, with careful consideration of training parameters such as epoch count and mini-batch size to ensure efficient training and reduce overfitting.

The image is enhanced using a CNN model. Additional enhancement techniques, such as gamma correction, can be added to the enhanced image. Histogram analysis visualizes the distribution of pixel intensities in both original and improved photographs. This analysis evaluates the effectiveness of the enhancement process in changing the image's contrast and brightness.

Overall, the proposed system improves underwater photos using a CNN-based technique that includes preprocessing, training, enhancement, assessment, and analysis processes. The effectiveness of the enhancement process is heavily influenced by the specific architecture of the CNN, including the choice of layers and parameters. Furthermore, evaluation metrics provide objective indicators of enhanced quality, which supplement visual inspection.

Results and Discussion

In the scenario of underwater image enhancement, result analysis entails determining the efficacy of the suggested algorithm in terms of image quality. This analysis often uses both qualitative and quantitative evaluation methodologies. Two tests have been conducted to determine the accuracy of neural network estimates. In the first scenario, all datasets were used for evaluation and training, with test images. Nonetheless, this is not a realistic scenario because training images are typically not available at the treatment site. That's why the current study approximates the above scenario, preparing for just another dataset used for the validation of the system.

Qualitative analysis
Enhanced photographs are evaluated for clarity, contrast, and general quality compared to the original underwater images. Any artifacts or distortions that occurred throughout the enhancing procedure are also identified.

The raw images shown in Figure 17.3 from the UFO-120 dataset are enhanced using our proposed method. The contrast and color are improved giving the enhanced results.

Figure 17.3 Samples of underwater image enhancement by CNN. Top row: Raw underwater images from UFO-120 datasets [4]; Bottom row: The corresponding results of our model
Source: Author

Figure 17.4 (a) Original underwater image selected by the user (b) enhanced underwater image obtained using the CNN model (c) Deep enhanced underwater image, possibly processed with additional parameters or structures (d) enhanced underwater image after gamma correction, enhancing brightness and contrast

Source: Author

The improved version of the degraded underwater image is shown in Figure 17.4. The underwater image in Figure 17.4 (a) is enhanced using the CNN model shown in Figure 17.4 (b). The enhanced image is further processed with additional parameters as shown in Figure (c). Finally, Figure 17.4 (d) is the result of applying gamma correction.

The histogram provides valuable insight into the image's contrast, brightness, and dynamic range. Histogram comparison involves plotting and comparing the histograms of the original and improved photos. Changes in pixel intensity distribution provide information about the contrast and brightness adjustments performed to the image. The histograms of original image and enhanced image are shown in Figure 17.5.

Quantitative analysis

To assess the success of the suggested method, picture quality measures such as PSNR, MSE, and

SSIM are measured. These metrics provide quantifiable assessments of the similarities between the enhanced and original underwater pictures.

The proposed approach yields good results in improving underwater images, as indicated by high PSNR and SSIM values while minimizing MSE in Table 17.1.

PSNR quantifies the amount of noise in the enhanced image when compared to the original. High PSNR values suggest that image details are better preserved during enhancement. The SSIM compares the structure, brightness, and contrast of the original and enhanced images. SSIM scores near to one suggest a greater similarity. MSE quantifies the average squared difference between the pixel values of the original and enhanced images. Lower MSE values indicate a higher level of similarity between the images.

The consistency of qualitative observations and quantitative data contributes to the enhancement algorithm's reliability. Any inconsistencies

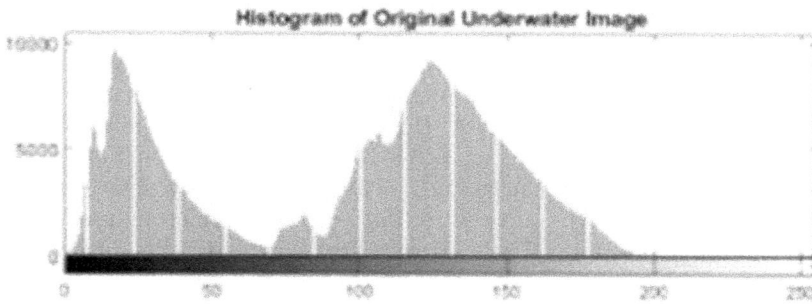

(a)

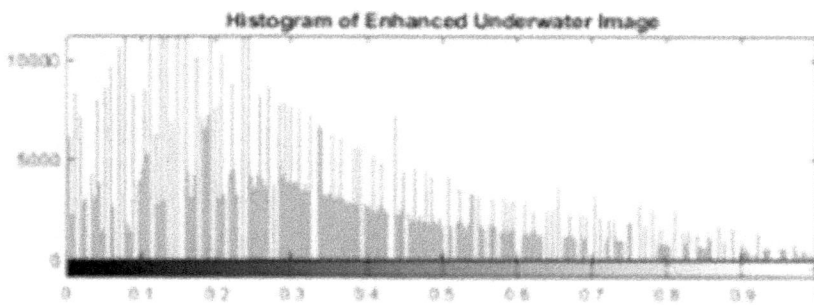

(b)

Figure 17.5 (a) Histogram of the original image of Figure 17.4(a) (b) Histogram of the enhanced image of Figure 17.4(d)
Source: Author

Table 17.1 Comparison of the proposed method with existing traditional methods

Method	PSNR (dB)	SSIM	MSE
HE16]	16.763	0.486	1178.46
CLAHE[17]	14.191	0.547	2034.24
MSR[18]	13.958	0.583	7535.67
MSRCR[19]	16.581	0.611	2086.37
Proposed	**22.26**	**0.747**	**386.04**

Source: Author

between subjective visual judgment and quantitative measurements may identify places where the system might be improved or optimized. Overall, result analysis uses both qualitative and quantitative methodologies to thoroughly analyze the underwater image enhancement algorithm's performance, revealing its strengths, limitations, and places for development.

Conclusion

Finally, this study describes a thorough method for enhancing underwater photos using a convolutional neural network (CNN) trained on a dataset of matched original and enhanced images. Significant gains in the visual quality of underwater pictures have been made thanks to diligent datasets, rapid training with a proprietary image data store, and the use of a properly built CNN architecture. The use of picture quality measurements such as PSNR, SSIM, and MSE has allowed for quantitative evaluation of the enhancement process, confirming the success of the suggested approach. This effort, which uses deep learning techniques, particularly CNNs, presents a viable answer to the long-standing difficulty of enhancing underwater photos, with implications for a wide range of applications, including marine research, photography, and underwater surveillance.

Future Work

Furthermore, research into novel preparation approaches and post-processing algorithms designed exclusively for underwater photographs could lead to further improvements in visual quality and clarity. Furthermore, investigating real-time or near-real-time implementation of the CNN model for onboard image augmentation in underwater vehicles or drones has the potential for real-world uses in underwater exploration and surveillance. Finally, collaboration with domain specialists in marine biology, oceanography, and underwater photography may provide essential insights and domain-specific expertise to help refine and personalize the enhancing process to specific demands and requirements in underwater study and exploration. By addressing these potential avenues, the proposed approach can continue to grow and contribute to the field of underwater imaging, opening up new opportunities and applications for underwater exploration and research.

References

[1] Drews Jr, P. (1999). A color correction algorithm for underwater imaging. In Oceans '99. MTS/IEEE. (Vol. 2). IEEE.

[2] Mobley, C. D. (1994). Light and Water: Radiative Transfer in Natural Waters. Academic Press.

[3] Li, J. (2020). Underwater image restoration via deep learning. *IEEE Transactions on Image Processing*, 29, 2547–2560.

[4] Sun, K., Meng, F., and Tian, Y. (2022). Multi-level wavelet-based network embedded with edge enhancement information for underwater image enhancement. *Journal of Marine Science and Engineering*, 10(7), 884.

[5] Li, C. (2020). Realistic water dataset (REWARD). Available from: https://github.com/cv-core/REWARD.

[6] Chiang, I.-H. (2020). Learning from synthetic data for underwater object detection. *IEEE Transactions on Image Processing*, 29, 2410–2423.

[7] Wang, Z. (2018). Underwater image enhancement by conditional generative adversarial networks. *IEEE Transactions on Image Processing*, 27(12), 5879–5893.

[8] Yang, G. (2021). Multi-modal underwater image enhancement using fusion generative adversarial network. *IEEE Transactions on Image Processing*, 30, 1044–1056.

[9] Cheng, Y. (2021). A novel end-to-end deep neural network for underwater image enhancement. *IEEE Transactions on Image Processing*, 30, 1630–1643.

[10] Yu, M. (2021). Underwater image enhancement using an attention-based deep neural network. *IEEE Transactions on Image Processing*, 30, 479–492.

[11] Zhang, Y. (2021). Real-time low-light underwater image enhancement using deep neural networks. *IEEE Transactions on Image Processing*, 30, 4643–4656.

[12] Chen, L. (2021). Semantic segmentation-guided underwater image enhancement using deep neural networks. *IEEE Transactions on Image Processing*, 30, 3265–3278.

[13] Zhao, Y. (2021). Adversarial training for robust underwater image enhancement. *IEEE Transactions on Image Processing*, 30, 5752–5765.

[14] Zhang, S. (2019). Underwater image enhancement using convolutional neural network with edge constraints. *IEEE Transactions on Image Processing*, 28(10), 4997–5011.

[15] Yu, M. (2021). Underwater image enhancement using an attention-based deep neural network. *IEEE Transactions on Image Processing*, 30, 479–492.

[16] Hummel, R. (1975). Image enhancement by histogram transformation. Unknown.

[17] Kumarrai, R., Gour, P., and Singh, B. (2012). Underwater Image segmentation using CLAHE enhancement and thresholding. *International Journal Emerging Technology and Advanced Engineering*, 2, 118–123.

[18] Shu, Z., Wan, T., Donga, J., and Yu, H. (2017). Underwater image enhancement via extended multi-scale Retinex. *Neurocomputing*, 245, 1–9.

[19] Zhang, L., and Peng, T. (2023). Underwater image enhancement based on improved adaptive MSRCR and Gamma function. In 2023 2nd International Conference on Cloud Computing, Big Data Application and Software Engineering (CBASE), Chengdu, China, (pp. 246–252).

18 Arduino controlled radar guided defence system for detecting and tracking threats

Kalathiripi Rambabu[1,a], Sanjay Dubey[1,b], B. R. Sanjeeva Reddy[1,c], Viswanadham Ravuri[1,d], Jonnada Ruthumani[1,e] and Kasha Saipriya[2,f]

[1]Department of Electronics and Communication engineering, B V Raju Institute of Technology, Narsapur, Medak, Telangana, India

[2]Department of Electronics and Communication engineering, BVRIT HYDERABAD College of Engineering for Women, Hyderabad, Telangana, India

Abstract

The Arduino controlled radar guided defense system aims to develop a cost-effective and can be adapted to utilize the defense system using radar technology integrated with Arduino. This system makes use of radar sensors to detect any incoming threats, processes the received data through Arduino board, and autonomously aims and launches the missile. This project mainly focuses on magnifying the accuracy and responsiveness of missile defense systems while maintaining affordability and accessibility. Arduino board and radar sensors which are the main components in this project are affordable to many small-scale projects and can be used in resource managed environments. This project is a sophisticated defense system. Radar sensors detect the incoming obstacles, and Arduino board is employed to it for real-time process and control. Through the implementation of this Arduino – Controlled radar guided defense system project, it showcases the practical application of sensors and microcontroller technologies in defense applications.

Keywords: Arduino, microcontroller, radar sensor

Introduction

In an era where the advanced technology in defense applications are modified and are used precisely for more efficiency, the integration of radar guided system with Arduino represents a significant productive way. This introduction mainly focuses on how to implement and understand the development of the Arduino-controlled radar guided defense system project. An Arduino-controlled radar-guided defense system combines the simplicity and versatility of Arduino microcontrollers with radar technology to create an efficient and automated defense mechanism. The system uses radar sensors to detect and track moving objects within a designated area. These sensors transmit data to an Arduino board, which processes the information and determines if the object poses a threat. If a potential threat is detected, the Arduino triggers an appropriate response, such as activating alarms, deploying countermeasures, or aiming and firing a defensive weapon. The system's real-time processing capability ensures rapid response to threats, making it ideal for securing perimeters, critical infrastructure, or military installations.

The Arduino platform's open-source nature allows for extensive customization and integration with other sensors and systems, enhancing the defense system's adaptability and effectiveness. Additionally, the relatively low cost and ease of programming make Arduino an accessible choice for developing advanced defense technologies, suitable for both experimental and practical applications. Overall, an Arduino-controlled radar-guided defense system exemplifies how modern electronics and sensor technology can be harnessed to create sophisticated automated security solutions. In military and defense applications, radar technology has a vital role to play.

[a]rambabukala@gmail.com, [b]sanjay.dubey@bvrit.ac.in, [c]sanjeev.reddy@bvrit.ac.in, [d]viswanadh.r@bvrithyderabad.edu.in, [e]jonnadaruthumani@gmail.com, [f]kashasaipriya@gmail.com

DOI: 10.1201/9781003616399-18

Radar technology provides critical situation awareness through detection and tracking of any given threats or targets. Traditionally military and defense applications are way more expensive, and they are modified with complex radar technologies which are not affordable and accessible for small scale applications and projects. In this Arduino controlled radar guided defense system project, the use of Arduino and radar sensors which will be interfaced provide cost – effective and accessible solution for small scale applications or projects.

Arduino microcontrollers are affordable and provide more efficiency when in use. It offers a platform for applying real time processing of data and can be interfaced with several sensors to execute complex tasks autonomously. By using these capabilities of Arduino, we can demonstrate Arduino controlled radar guided defense system with enhanced accuracy and response times, important for target aiming applications like in the case of missiles and drones. The objective of this project is to explore the feasibility and effectiveness of using radar technology with Arduino based system in defense applications.

Literature Survey

"Missile radar-controlled systems" by Gheorghe et al. [1] this paper or journal findings are explored radar. Develop Arduino designed for object detection, emphasizing packages in surveillance. The "Embedded based project on missile detection", by Sumathi et al. [2]. This journal findings are performing automatic missile detection. Modified radar with missile tracking and automatic destruction by Kushwaha et al., [3] this conference overview was about monitoring the target, detecting the target and distinguishing between target and other objects. The findings of the study by Karthikeyan et al., are guided missiles, which means introducing computer controlled and automated missile systems. They discussed the challenges of achieving automation while emphasizing the role of human interfaces in target locking. The conference findings are focusing on the reusable launcher with potential applications in defense testing only and emphasized economic consideration and the need for rebuilding after single use itself [5]. "JAXA", by

Hirohito at at., [6] explored this "Research on advanced solid rocket launcher," emphasizing the challenges associated with large size, bulkiness, and complexity in achieving them in advance for solid rocket launchers. So, in literature survey it has various research contributions, highlighting the versatility of the Arduino based radar structures. Additionally, repositories like GitHub host practical examples of Arduino-based radar projects, offering insights into implementation and code.

There are other authors like [7] Pandey, [8] Kumar & Sharma, [9] Thakkar & team, [10] Balasaheb & team and [11] Chopra & team who focussed and worked on prototyping defence and radar applications.

Proposed Model

Block Diagram

In the proposed model, the Arduino is interfaced with radar sensors which is affordable and can be easily accessible.

The above diagram Figure 18.1 shows an automated missile launching system. The Arduino UNO is interfaced with Ultrasonic sensor and servo motor. The Arduino processes the radar data and sends it to the PC for visual output. The Arduino controls a servo motor to aim the missile launcher and use ultrasonic sensor to detect any incoming threats. The power supply ensures stable power for Arduino and other equipment. The missile launching equipment is triggered by based on data given to the Arduino.

Components

Hardware tools

Arduino UNO: Arduino uno is the main controller of this project. Audino uno is an open-source microcontroller. Which is versatile, for doing electronic projects. It features ATMega 328 P chip which is a 24 pin IC. The microcontroller has 20 pins. In 20 pin, which are 14 are digital pins and 6 are analogue input pins. These analogue pins can be used as PWM outputs. It is very easy for programming as it is an open-source microcontroller which can be integrated into many forms of a variety of electronic projects. It can control the release of LEDs, motors as an output and the servos in the projects.

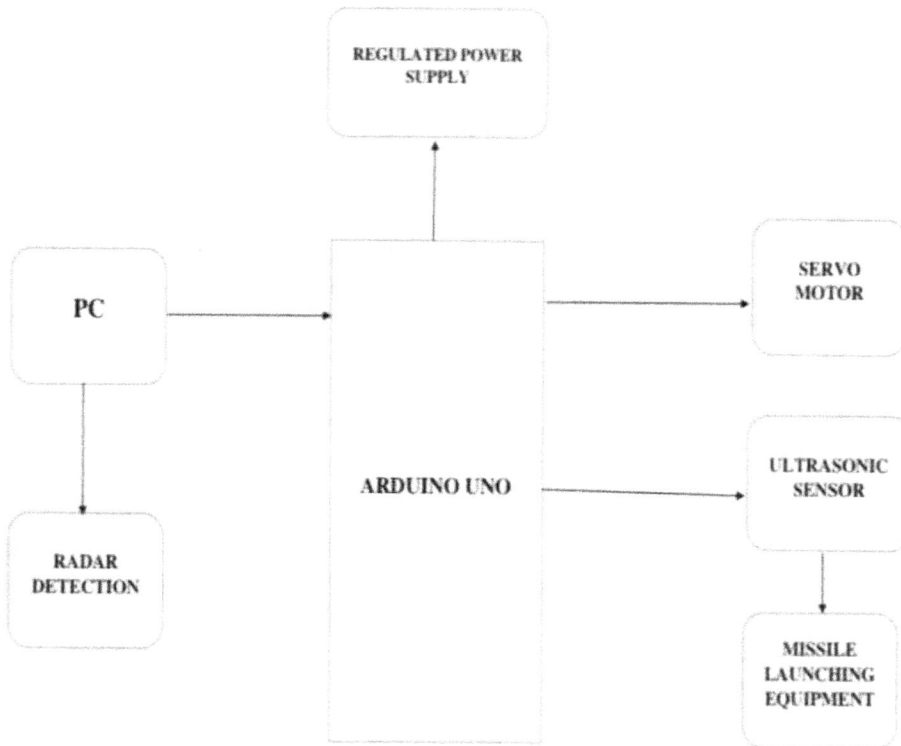

Figure 18.1 Block diagram of Arduino controlled radar guided defense system
Source: Author

Servomotor: Servo motor controls movement and its positions. It is often used in robotics and remote controls, and it is also used in automated systems. It contains 3 pins for pin out in servo motor SG 90. Which has a signal pin, Vcc and ground its input signal is an analogue panel where it has V reference, t reference. Input of zero to 5 volts. It has a mode of control of speed mode, Position mode and torque mode. It has a key characteristic of high dynamics and great positioning accuracy.

Ultrasonic sensor: Ultrasonic sensor is a device that measures distance by emitting the Sound waves and calculating the time taken. Ultrasonic sensors have power requirements of 5 volts of DC and 35 mill amperes. Ultrasonic sensors have a frequency of 32. 500 kilohertz of the range. For the air couple of applications. In activity it has the maximum range of 70 feet's, which is of 21 meters.

Breadboard: Breadboard is used for temporary circuit connections. It is used for connecting the component easily to build a circuit. It has Ground and Vcc in it.

Jumper wires: Jumper wires widely are used for connecting the Components in the circuit.

Software tools: In software tools we have used Arduino IDE software and Processing 4.3 2 software.

Arduino IDE software: Arduino IDE Software, the full form of IDE is Integrated Development Environment. This software is used to write the code and compile the code. And the code is going to be Uploaded in the Arduino boards. It is very simple and user friendly and cost effective. This IDE software Support C&C++ programming languages which includes the library of functions and hardware interactions. It has key features like text controls and toolbars. From this Arduino software we can upload the code to the board offline also. This software can be used with any Arduino board for coding. Several functions are used in Arduino IDE. They are like digital input and output pins, analog input and output pins, advanced input output pins, time delay, math. abs, trigonometry, characters in alpha, random numbers in random, and many more.

Processing 4.3 software: This is a processing software which is a flexible sketchbook. In this software we are going Code within the context of visual arts which simplifies software development. Within a focus of visual output. And it also can be used for creating graphics, interactive arts and for animations purpose. This process combines the development of environment within an easy-to-use language based on Java programming language.

Implementation
The traditional missile launchers used in military and defense applications are way more expensive, and they are inaccessible for small scale projects and applications. The use of Arduino integrated with radar technology is a friendly solution and is affordable and provide more accuracy. Arduino acts as a main controller and radar sensors are used to detect any incoming threats. The Arduino is interfaced with an ultrasonic sensor and servo motor is connected to the Arduino board pins for the rotation movement from Figure 18.2. Ultrasonic sensor is precisely used for measuring distance and obstacle detection. Connecting the missile launching equipment to the digital output

pins in Arduino board for launching the missile wheals in Arduino IDE software.

Implementing an Arduino-controlled radar-guided defense, the incoming threat is detected by the ultrasonic sensor. After interfacing all the components, the pin numbers of connections are to be properly verified. Then the code in the Arduino IDE software is uploaded to Arduino board, by selecting the Arduino Uno board and port which is displayed in it.

Implementing an Arduino-controlled radar-guided defense, the incoming threat is detected by the ultrasonic sensor. The system project involves integrating radar technology with Arduino microcontrollers to detect and respond to potential threats effectively. Firstly, select appropriate radar sensors such as ultrasonic or microwave modules capable of detecting and measuring distances accurately within the operational range required for defense applications. Interface these sensors with Arduino boards, ensuring compatibility and reliability in data position. Develop Arduino code in Arduino IDE.

Once the system detects any incoming threats the monitoring mode will start and the missile will trigger and face towards the threat. Security

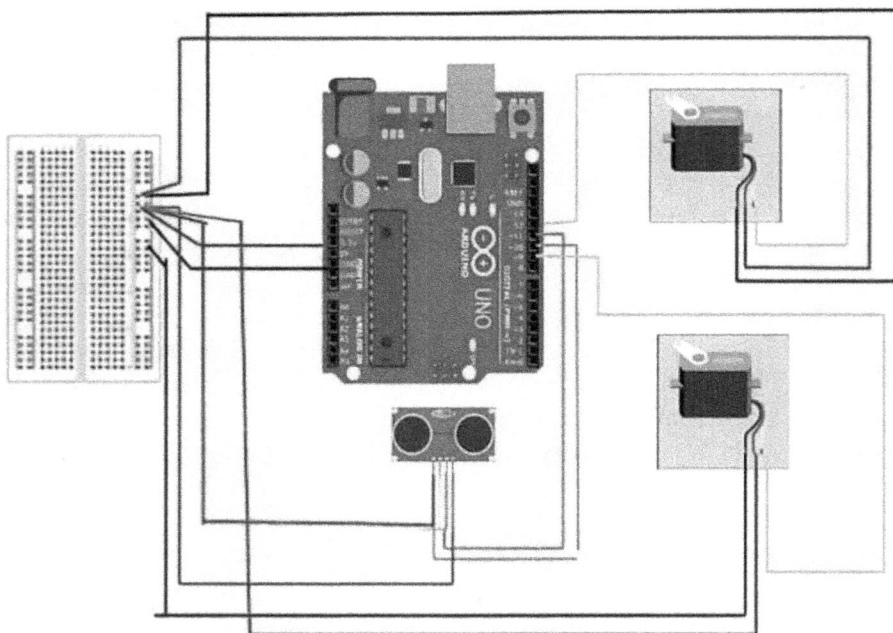

Figure 18.2 Schematic circuit diagram
Source: Author

and safety measures are also taken in order to prone any small accidental clashes.

Similarly, the processing code, which is a flexible software sketchbook which is based on java programming language is also compiled and run simultaneously to Arduino code for visualizing the radar detection, which shows like sweeping from 0 degrees to 180 degrees.

In implementation we need an Arduino uno, radar sensor, servo motor, any defense system or mechanism for the missile and power supply, bread board for the connections, connecting wires, software of the code implementation.

In this few basic step includes like set up hardware components, write the Arduino code in

Arduino IDE, read radar data, control servos, Activate defense Mechanism. Next prototyping means building a basic prototype to test the concept. Testing whether the system is working or not. We use a power supply of 5V and connect the control pin to the Arduino digital pin and ensure it has its own power supply if it needs. And uploading the software codes in and working prototype testing should be done as on Figure 18.3.

When the code is uploaded, the servo motor starts rotating and the ultrasonic sensor which is fixed on the top of the servo motor also rotates and detects any incoming threats. When the processing code is given and when we run it, the visual output of radar detection is shown. When any threat is detected, the missile launcher is activated and triggered.

In the processing software which is flexible software sketch book, the code is given in java and when we run the program, we get the visual output as radar detection from 0 to 180 degrees. If any threat is detected the radar detection will be appearing in recolor.

Results

The results of implementing an Arduino-controlled radar-guided defense system project shown in Figure 18.5 and Figure 18.6 typically demonstrate the system's capability to detect, track, and respond to potential threats effectively. Through rigorous testing and validation, the system shows accurate detection and localization of targets within specified operational ranges.

Key performance metrics such as detection accuracy, response time, and system reliability are evaluated, showcasing the effectiveness of the integrated hardware and software components. Results often highlight successful engagements or responses to simulated threats, demonstrating the system's ability to activate alarms, initiate countermeasures, or adjust defensive positions as needed.

When code is uploaded in the Audino uno, and the USB of Audino wire is connected to the Arduino and PC. The down servo motor Starts rotating from zero to 180 degrees for the distance calculation or measurement it rotates from the left to right and right to left. And it was controlled

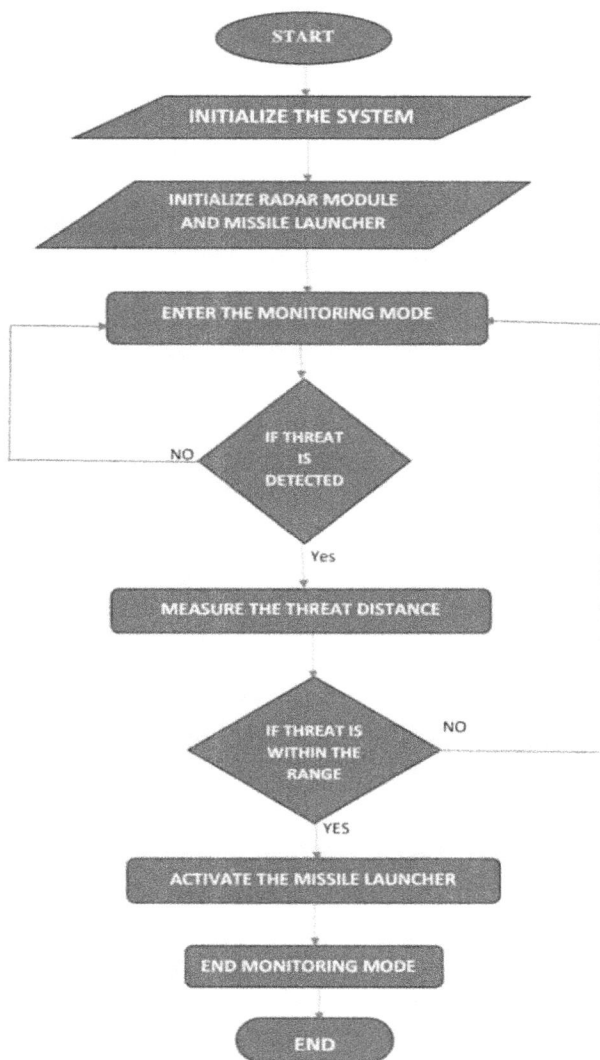

Figure 18.3 Flowchart of overall project
Source: Author

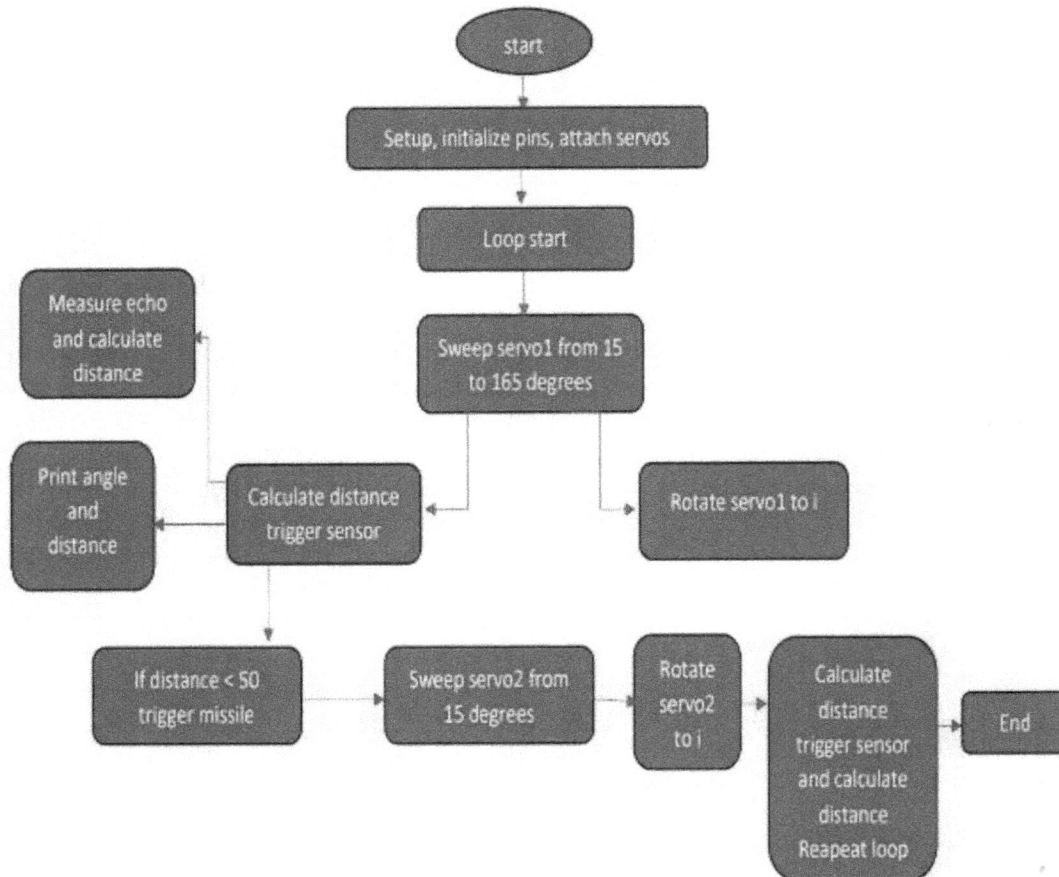

Figure 18.4 Flowchart of software code
Source: Author

by Arduino uno. In the ultrasonic sensor send a high frequency sound wave which measures the time. It will be taken to return from echo. When an obstacle is detected less than 50 centimeters, it considers that obstacle as a target. And the missile will be launched. This servo motor will position the sensor directly to the obstacle, and it launches the missile. When an sends a signal the servo motors. It starts triggering and pushes the missile out. Overall, the results of the Arduino-controlled radar-guided defense system project underscore its potential as a viable solution for enhancing situational awareness and response capabilities in defense applications, supported by empirical data and performance evaluations shown in Figure 18.7 and 18.8.

Applications

Audio control radar guided defense systems have the following applications, in military and civil factors. Some of them are security systems, Surveillance scenes, automated defense system, disaster management, agriculture monitoring, traffic management, transportation management, robotics, automation, research and development, border security management.

1. **Security management:** In security management, we need to deploy around sensitive facilities like airports and military bases. Here we need to secure the borders and monitor by detecting the border control. We need to build security for the high-profile buildings and detect the potential threats.
2. **Automated defense system:** In this we have anti-drone systems, automated turrets and missile defenses, which detect and neutralize the unauthorized drones which are entering into restricted Air spaces. In the missile defense, they detect and drag incoming threats. Such as Missile or an enemy airplane.

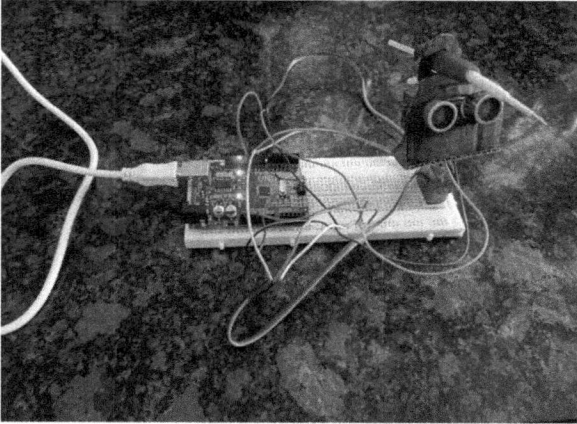

Figure 18.5 Working of Arduino controlled radar guided defense system detecting the threat
Source: Author

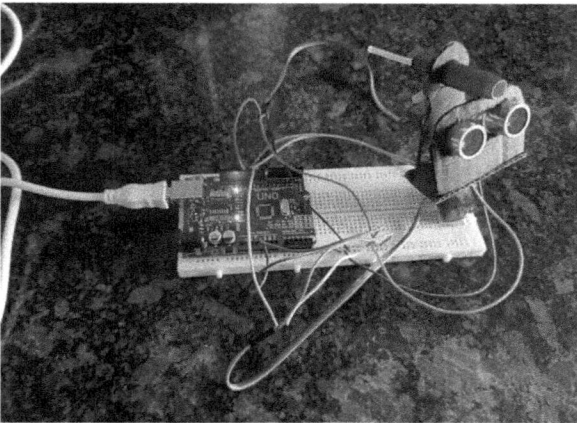

Figure 18.6 Tracking of threat through launching missile
Source: Author

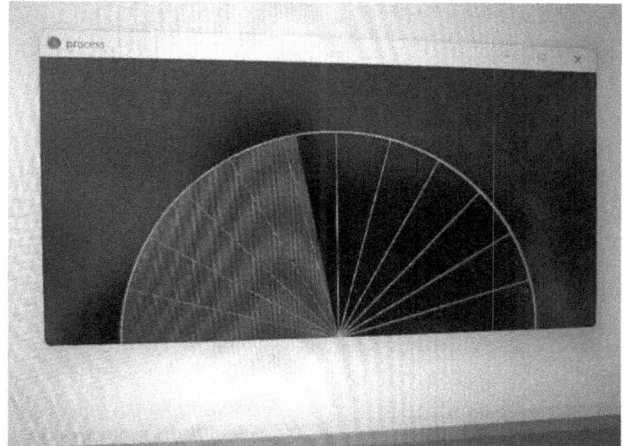

Figure 18.7 Radar detection while there are no threats
Source: Author

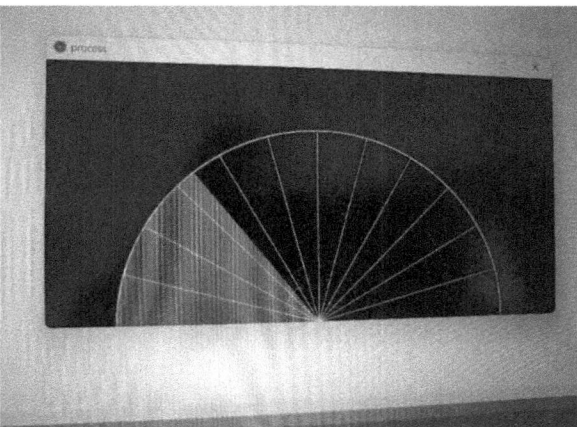

Figure 18.8 Radar detection while there are threats
Source: Author

3. **Disaster management:** They search for and rescue operations and for this they use Radars. To locate those disaster zones, and in environmental monitoring too. They detect the environmental hazards such as Floods.
4. **Robotics and automation:** In this they enhance the navigation and obstacle detection for automation ground Vehicles and in industrial Automation. They manage automated processes in factories for safety and efficiency.
5. **Research and development:** In robotics and development, they do prototype testing and educational purposes. Developing and testing new radar and sensor technologies for the upcoming future applications.
6. **Unmanned aerial vehicles (UAVs):** Integration is done by drones for the detection and for individual obstacle avoidance, and for navigation area, and also useful for autonomous operations.
7. **Border security:** For monitoring and securing the borders by detection and tracking them unauthorized crossings.

Limitations

Building an Arduino controlled Radar guided missile system is an interesting and educational purpose project but comes with some limitations. The Arduino Uno does not support advanced radar technology because advanced radar technology requires strong and clear signals processing to detect any threat. The radar system built with Arduino may not detect threats over long distances.

Conclusion

In conclusion, the implementation of Arduino-controlled radar-guided defense system combines the simplicity and versatility of Arduino microcontrollers with radar technology to create an efficient and automated defense mechanism. The system uses radar sensors to detect and track moving objects within a designated area. These sensors transmit data to an Arduino board, which processes the information and determines if the object poses a threat. Challenges encountered during implementation underscored the importance of continuous refinement and optimization.

Arduino controlled radar guided defense system provides a valuable insight related to embedded systems and radar systems. It is a proof-of-concept project and is constrained by some limitations. This project demonstrates the integration of radar technology with Arduino based systems to create a responsive and automated missile launching mechanism. By doing this project several key objectives were achieved and can detect and respond to potential threats. This project provides more efficiency and is cost effective. The radar sensor provides real-time data on object positions, which the Arduino processes to determine any incoming threats. The modular design of the system allows for easy upgrades and modifications.

Future Work

The Arduino controlled radar guided defense system has a primary goal and achieved by interfacing Arduino with radar sensor, ultrasonic sensor, and servo motor to detect and track any incoming threats and the launching of missile takes place. Combining radar with other sensors such as ultrasonic, infrared, or LIDAR to improve detection capabilities and reduce false positives. This system can be further implemented using machine learning and AI. In the future integration of communication networks for real time data sharing can be possible. Several avenues for this project can be enhanced due to its capability and applicability. It provides enhanced detection capabilities by improved radar sensors and multi sensor integration. In future, advanced processing and analysis can be applied using machine learning and data fusion. Security can also be improved in the future ahead.

References

[1] Somoiag, P., & Moldoveanu, C. E. (2009). Air and ballistic missile defence systems. *Military Technical Academy Publishing House*, pp. 1– 4.

[2] Ghoghre, D. A., Dhanshri, A., & Priyanka, A. (2017). Radar system using Arduino. *In National Conference on Emerging Trends in Engineering and Technology*, (pp. 53–56).

[3] Ohtsuka, H., Yagi, K., Kishi, K., Nohara, M., & Sano, N. (2010). Research on advanced solid rocket launcher. *Engineering Review*, 3(1), pp. 29–36.

[4] Abd-El-Samie, A. A., El-Hanbaly, M. T., & El-Sheimy, N. A. (2021). Radar system design and analysis using Arduino and MATLAB. *CRC Press*.

[5] Alkalbani, M., Salim, N., & Al-Baudi, Y. (2020). Design and implementation of an ultrasonic radar system for distance measurement applications. *International Journal of Advanced Computer Science and Applications*, 11(5), 291–298.

[6] Karthick, S., Saranya, P., & Sivakumar, M. (2021). Smart surveillance system using Arduino and PIR sensors. *International Journal of Engineering Research & Technology*, 10(3), 45–48.

[7] Pandey, R. K., & Kumar, V. (2019). Development of an Arduino-based portable radar system. *International Journal of Scientific & Technology Research*, 8(12), 2532–2537.

[8] Kumar, A., & Sharma, N. (2022). Fusion of ultrasonic and infrared sensors for enhanced object detection using Arduino. *International Journal of Engineering Research and Applications*, 12(1), 115–120.

[9] Thakkar, N., Sahu, S., & Kumar, R. (2016). Automatic detector using ultrasonic proximity detector. *International Journal of Engineering Applied Sciences and Technology*.

[10] Balasaheb, P. P., & Shinde, T. A. (2015). Missile detection by ultrasonic and auto destroy system on a robotic platform. *International Journal for Scientific Research and Development*.

[11] Chopra, S., & Bharti, S. (2014). Missile detection by ultrasonic and auto destroy system. *International Journal of Engineering Sciences and Research Technology*.

[12] Karthikeyan, T. V., & Kapoor, A. K. (1990). Guide missiles. *Defence Research and Development Laboratory*, Hyderabad..

19 Implementing question answering models with BERT (bidirectional encoder representations from transformers)

Thukaram Reddy, M.[1,a] and Adi Narayana Reddy, K.[2,b]

[1]Research Scholar, Dept. of CSE, ICFAI, Hyderabad, Telangana, India
[2]Associate Professor, Dept. of CSE, ICFAI, Hyderabad, Telangana, India

Abstract

This research explores the fine-tuning of Bidirectional Encoder Representations from Transformers (BERT) models available in the hugging face transformers library for question answering within a specific domain focused on stories and their corresponding queries. By employing transfer learning, our approach leverages the contextual embeddings developed by BERT, enabling it to capture the nuances of narratives and generate precise answers. The dataset, which consists of stories paired with related questions, poses a challenge to the model by emphasizing the complexities of contextual understanding. Our study demonstrates the practical utility of BERT in natural language processing and highlights the broader impact of contextualized representations on a machine's capacity to understand and interpret language. This paper provides a comprehensive overview of our fine-tuning methodology, the distinctive features of the dataset, and the empirical results obtained, offering valuable insights into the effectiveness of our approach.

Keywords: BERT, CoQA, embeddings, question-answering system

Introduction

Humans, driven by their innate curiosity, are naturally inclined to explore and question everything they encounter [3]. Unlike traditional methods, our project leverages revolutionary advancements in natural language processing to enable humans to ask questions directly to systems using fine-tuned Bidirectional Encoder Representations from Transformers (BERT) model. Simply put, this model serves as a question-answering system that plays a crucial role in bridging the comprehension gap between human language and machines [2,4,5].

This paper delves into advancing question-answering (QA) capabilities through the use of a fine-tuned BERT model, obtained from the Hugging Face Transformers library. The focus is specifically on the Conversational Question Answering (CoQA) dataset [1,6,7]. Our project's objective is to improve the accuracy and contextual relevance of QA systems by fine-tuning the BERT model to generate precise, contextually aware responses. The CoQA dataset, recognized for its nuanced and conversational nature, serves as a challenging benchmark for evaluating the effectiveness of our approach. Thanks to BERT's bidirectional attention mechanism, it can consider both preceding and following words, enabling a deeper understanding of language semantics [6].

In this paper, we explore how fine-tuning on the CoQA dataset enhances the model's ability to provide accurate answers, particularly in conversations where the user's input significantly affects the output. By examining the implementation details, experimental results, and analysis, readers will gain insights into the progress made in the field of QA, especially in handling conversational datasets. Our findings contribute not only to natural language understanding but also to the development of improved applications in dialogue-based systems, information retrieval, and conversational AI [8].

---

[a]mthukaramreddy.scholars22@ifheindia.org, [b]adinarayanareddyk@ifheindia.org
DOI: 10.1201/9781003616399-19

Related Work

The field of QA has undergone a significant transformation, with an increasing emphasis on using trained language models to enhance contextual understanding. Our work, which employs an optimized BERT model for QA, aligns with this research trajectory, building upon prior advancements and innovations in the field [3,5,9].

While existing literature often favors traditional QA methods, it tends to overlook the potential of sophisticated pre-trained models like BERT, particularly in the specific context of stories and questions. Our research aims to fill this gap by showcasing the effectiveness of an optimized BERT model in this unique domain. By addressing the challenges of interpreting contextual clues within narratives, our approach innovates beyond established methods to provide more accurate and context-aware responses. This research stands at the intersection of cutting-edge techniques and conventional approaches, contributing to the discourse on leveraging trained models for QA tasks [9].

Focusing on broader QA challenges, recent studies have explored models that construct contextual encodings of questions and passages, using attention mechanisms to generate representations of the passage-query pair. However, these models often depend heavily on large, labeled datasets and manually crafted features, which can limit their scalability and generalization. Our work aims to address these limitations by demonstrating a more robust and adaptable approach using a fine-tuned BERT model [4].

Enter pre-trained language models like BERT, which have demonstrated remarkable performance across a variety of NLP tasks, including QA. BERT's foundation in the Transformer architecture, which leverages self-attention to capture relationships between input tokens, has significantly advanced contextual understanding. It is pre-trained on large unlabeled text corpora using masked language modeling and next sentence prediction objectives, enabling it to learn rich contextual representations that can be effectively fine-tuned for downstream tasks [3].

While BERT has achieved state-of-the-art results in QA, even surpassing human performance on benchmarks such as SQuAD, certain challenges remain. BERT struggles with question types that require multi-hop reasoning or the application of common-sense knowledge. Additionally, its performance is sensitive to the amount and quality of pre-training data, and its deployment is hindered by substantial memory and computational requirements [10].

In this project, we propose a QA system that answers queries based on a set of stories and associated questions using optimized BERT models from the Hugging Face transformers library. Our study contributes to the ongoing discussion on enhancing QA systems for real-world applications by navigating the current landscape of QA methods and addressing challenges highlighted in broader QA research [2].

System Overview

To advance the field of question answering, our project strategically focuses on harnessing the potential of a finely tuned BERT model within the challenging domain of theCoQA dataset. As outlined in the introduction, the primary objectives of this project are to enhance the contextual relevance and accuracy of question-answering systems in the dynamic and conversational context provided by CoQA stories [1, 5, 8].

BERT architecture

BERT's architecture can be likened to an advanced language processor, consisting of either 12 layers (BERT-Base) or an impressive 24 layers (BERT-Large), with each layer working collaboratively to understand words in both directions. It represents a significant advancement over the original Transformer model, featuring larger networks and more attention heads to capture deeper contextual relationships [7].

Imagine the model processing data: it starts with a special token (CLS) that serves as a guide, followed by the input words, with each layer focusing on the most important elements. This process is akin to sending a message down a chain, where each layer adds its own enhancement [3].

BERT-Large, Figure 19.1 with its 340 million parameters, surpasses BERT-Base's 110 million, and much of its capability comes from this increased complexity [8].

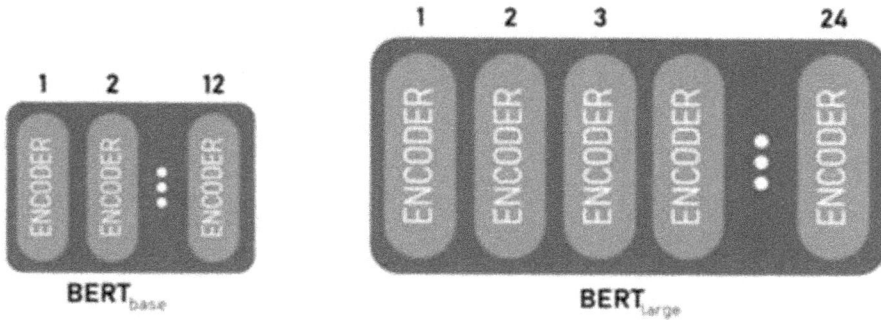

Figure 19.1 Bert architecture
Source: Author

When handling text, BERT works its magic by analyzing a sequence of words, focusing on each one individually. This results in a vector—a collection of 768 numbers for BERT-Base—representing each word's meaning. For specific tasks, such as determining the type of text, it pays special attention to a particular token (CLS) [11].

These vectors, or "smart codes," enable the model to classify objects, understand different languages, and more. The brilliance of BERT lies in its ability to achieve impressive results using a straightforward single-layer architecture to identify key features [2].

Our project strategically focuses on leveraging the capabilities of an optimized BERT model within the challenging domain of the CoQA dataset to advance the field of question answering. As stated in the introduction, this project aims to enhance the contextual relevance and accuracy of QA systems within the dynamic context of CoQA stories [6].

A key feature of BERT is word piece tokenization, which revolutionizes natural language processing by effectively managing rare and out-of-vocabulary terms. By breaking down uncommon words into subword units and using "##" to denote split tokens, BERT significantly reduces the vocabulary size, enhancing training efficiency. This method effectively addresses the challenge of capturing the nuances of words with various suffixes [5].

Consider the words "run," "running," and "runner." Previously, each word would need to be learned and stored separately. Word piece tokenization, however, breaks these words down into

"run" and suffixes like "##ning" and "##ner." This allows the model to learn the core meaning of "run" while the suffixes convey subtle distinctions, learned from similar contexts in other words [4,8,12].

By maximizing the model's ability to generalize across related concepts, this approach fosters a deeper understanding of language dynamics. Ultimately, word piece tokenization helps BERT handle vocabulary more efficiently and enhances its ability to grasp complex semantic relationships, resulting in more accurate and effective natural language processing tasks [1,4,7].

CoQa Dataset
The creation of our chatbot would not have been possible without the CoQA dataset, which offers a richer understanding of dialogue during training. CoQA introduces a dynamic conversational framework with passages, questions, and evolving responses that capture the subtleties of real-world interactions, marking a departure from traditional question-answering datasets [2].

Embeddings
Token embeddings play a crucial role in our chatbot project, as they enable BERT to efficiently process tokenized inputs. Two specific tokens, (CLS, classification) and (SEP, separation), are especially important. The (CLS) token aids in classification tasks, which is essential for understanding sentences, while the (SEP) token separates the input into distinct segments, such as the text and the question [9].

Our chatbot employs a strategic approach to locating responses within a given passage. BERT's

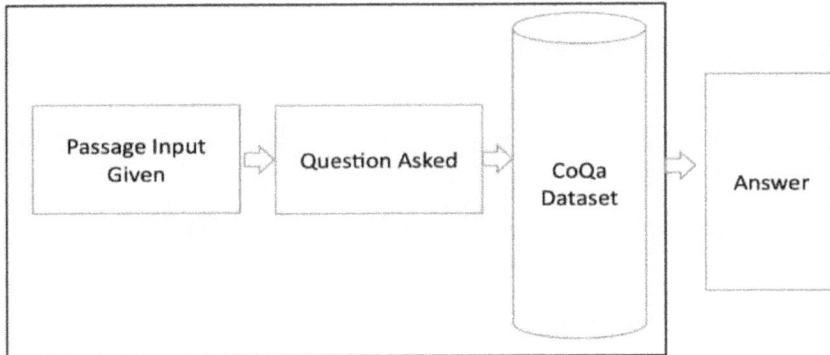

Figure 19.2 Workflow
Source: Author

processing is sensitive to markers like (CLS) and (SEP), with (CLS) supporting classification and (SEP) distinguishing between different sections of input [2].

In addition to standard token embeddings, BERT utilizes segment embeddings and position embeddings to further enhance its understanding. Segment embeddings, with values of 0 for sentence 1 and 1 for sentence 2, help BERT differentiate between the passage and the query. Position embeddings indicate the position of each word in the sequence [8].

We simplify this process by using the Transformers library to handle some of these embeddings automatically. However, we also manually assign segment embeddings (0 or 1) to each token to fine-tune the model [2].

Our chatbot benefits from BERT's strengths, particularly its ability to identify the most likely start and end tokens in a passage. Instead of relying on Named entity recognition, we use BERT to determine responses by ensuring the end token follows the start token. This straightforward method, combined with BERT's advanced language understanding, ensures our chatbot is both accurate and responsive [7].

The chatbot begins by prompting users to enter relevant information or text to initiate the conversation. This input establishes the foundation for subsequent interactions. Once the text is provided, users are encouraged to ask questions related to the information given. The BERT model then takes the lead in identifying the key starting and ending terms within the passage to address these queries [5].

After analyzing the user's question, the chatbot generates and displays a response, demonstrating BERT's exceptional ability to grasp contextual subtleties in the text. The system also allows users to ask additional questions based on the same material. If users choose to continue, the chatbot prompts them to input their follow-up questions and starts the process anew. This dynamic approach ensures that answers are generated in real-time, fostering a meaningful and contextually aware dialogue [6].

This methodical design prioritizes user-friendliness, making it easy for users to interact with

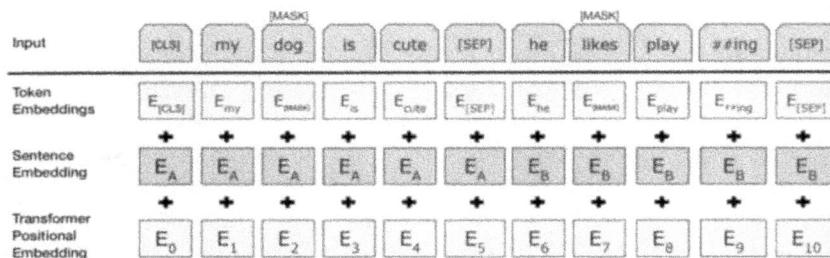

Figure 19.3 Embeddings
Source: Author

the chatbot, ask questions about the provided text, and receive accurate, timely responses. The design aligns with the broader goal of enhancing user experience by leveraging BERT's advanced natural language understanding capabilities [4].

Experiments and Results

This research explores the fine-tuning of BERT models available in the Hugging Face transformers library for question answering within a specific domain focused on stories and their corresponding queries. By employing transfer learning, our approach leverages the contextual embeddings developed by BERT, enabling it to capture the nuances of narratives and generate precise answers. The dataset, which consists of stories paired with related questions, poses a challenge to the model by emphasizing the complexities of contextual understanding. Our study demonstrates the practical utility of BERT in natural language processing and highlights the broader impact of contextualized representations on a machine's capacity to understand and interpret language. This paper provides a comprehensive overview of our fine-tuning methodology, the distinctive features of the dataset, and

the empirical results obtained, offering valuable insights into the effectiveness of our approach [4].

Our chatbot system operates exclusively with text input, without the need for visual elements. This streamlined approach simplifies the user's experience and ensures efficient interaction by focusing solely on text-based communication.

Users are prompted to enter text and a question by this Python script. After then, until the user decides to quit, it keeps answering the question depending on the text they have entered.

A simple method of interaction is to ask and answer questions of the chatbot. Users may immediately assess how effectively the chatbot understands and reacts by asking questions and getting answers back and forth in this procedure.

Start word scores evaluate a model's ability to correctly identify the first word or token of projected responses. This statistic is an important way to measure how well the model understands the context and initiates reactions.

The precision with which a model can detect the last word in anticipated responses is measured by end word scores. They demonstrate the model's capacity to understand context and offer accurate answers.

```
Please enter your text:
Once upon a time, in the heart of the enchanted forest, there lived a wise old wizard named Eldron. Eldron was know
n far and wide for his magical abilities and his deep knowledge of ancient spells. One day, a young adventurer name
d Lily entered the forest in search of Eldron's guidance. She hoped to find the legendary Crystal of Lumina, said t
o hold unimaginable powers. As Lily approached Eldron's cottage, she saw the wise wizard sitting on his porch, sur
rounded by mystical herbs and artifacts. Eldron welcomed her warmly, sensing the purpose of her quest. He listened
attentively as Lily shared her desire to find the Crystal of Lumina and harness its magic for the greater good. El
dron, understanding the gravity of Lily's mission, decided to impart his wisdom. He explained that the Crystal of L
umina could only be found by those with a pure heart and a keen understanding of the forest's secrets. To prove her
worthiness, Lily would have to solve a series of riddles scattered across the enchanted woods.  Armed with Eldron's
guidance, Lily set forth on her quest, ready to face the challenges that awaited her.
```

Figure 19.4 Text input
Source: Author

```
text = input("Please enter your text: \n")
question = input("\nPlease enter your question: \n")

while True:
    question_answer(question, text)

    flag = True
    flag_N = False

    while flag:
        response = input("\nDo you want to ask another question based on this text (Y/N)? ")
        if response[0] == "Y":
            question = input("\nPlease enter your question: \n")
            flag = False
        elif response[0] == "N":
            print("\nBye!")
            flag = False
            flag_N = True

    if flag_N == True:
        break
```

Figure 19.5 Question's asking
Source: Author

According to Torch's version check, the most recent version is 1.7.1, which shows off recent changes and could include new features or problem fixes. Access to the most recent developments and enhancements in deep learning frameworks is ensured by keeping Torch up to date.

Conclusion

From this study, we developed a question answering (QA) chatbot using BERT architecture trained on the CoQA dataset. Our system precisely comprehends stories, it's valued for its generative accurate answers, and conversational engagement by prompting for more questions or indicating completion. By leveraging BERT's contextual embeddings and fine-tuning capabilities, our chatbot exhibits prominent performance in understanding and responding to user queries. Its conversational features enhance user experience, making interactions more natural.

With great potential, our system's future work involves fine-tuning on larger datasets with improved conversational capabilities for even better performance. Overall, this work contributes to advancing natural language understanding and chatbot technology, with applications in various domains.

```
torch._version_
```

```
'1.7.1'
```

Figure 19.6 Playing with chatbot
Source: Author

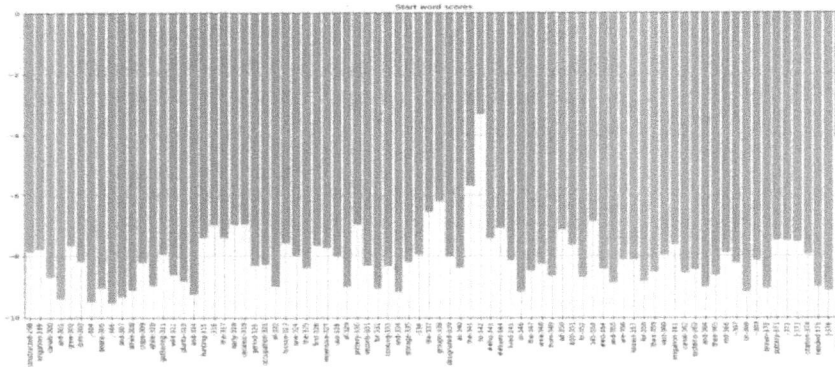

Figure 19.7 Start word scores
Source: Author

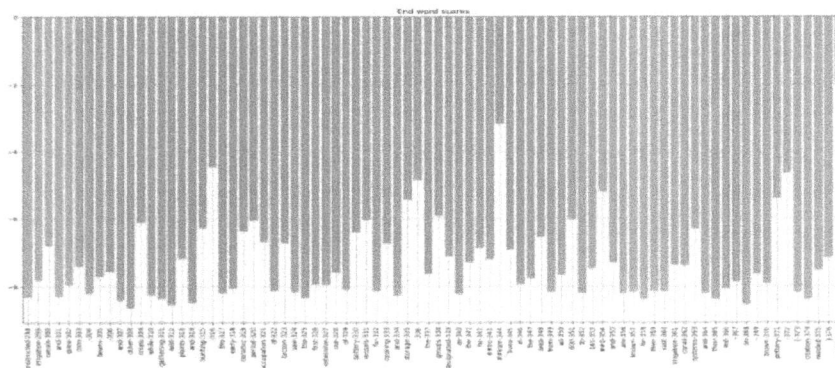

Figure 19.8 End word scores
Source: Author

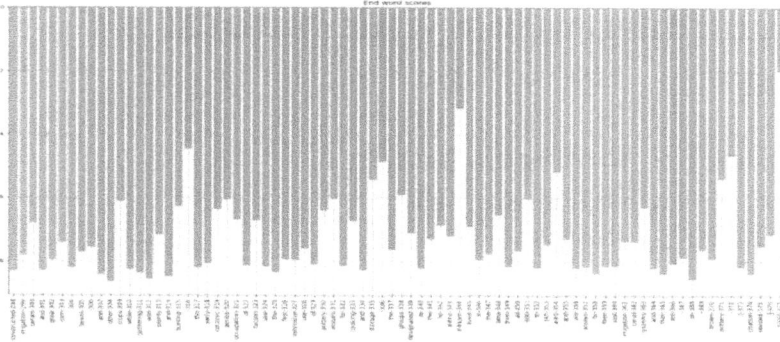

Figure 19.9 Version checking
Source: Author

References

[1] Acharya, S., Sornalakshmi, K., Paul, B., and Singh, A. (2022). Question answering system using NLP and BERT. In 2022 3rd International Conference on Smart Electronics and Communication (ICOSEC). https://doi.org/10.1109/icosec54921.2022.9952050.

[2] Shao, Z., Sun, S., Zhao, Y., Wang, S., Wei, Z., Gui, T., et al. (2023). Visual explanation for open-domain question an- swering with BERT. *IEEE Transactions on Visualization and Computer Graphics*, 1. https://doi.org/10.1109/tvcg.2023.3243676.

[3] Jha, B. K., Srinivas Akana, C. M. V., and Anand, R. (2021). Question answering system with indic multilingual-BERT. In 2021 5th International Conference on Computing Methodologies and Communication (ICCMC). https://doi.org/10.1109/iccmc51019.2021.9418387.

[4] Zheng, C., Wang, Z., and He, J. (2022). BERT-based mixed question answering matching model. In 2022 11th International Conference of Information and Communication Technology (ICTech)). https://doi.org/10.1109/ictech55460.2022.00077.

[5] Yin, J. (2022). Research on question answering system based on BERT model. In 2022 3rd International Conference on Computer Vision, Image and Deep Learning and International Conference on Computer Engineering and Applications (CVIDL and ICCEA). https://doi.org/10.1109/cvidliccea56201.2022.9824408.

[6] Annamoradnejad, I., Fazli, M., and Habibi, J. (2020). Predicting Subjective features from questions on QA websites using BERT. In 2020 6th International Conference on Web Research (ICWR). https://doi.org/10.1109/icwr49608.2020.9122318.

[7] Jeong, S. W., Kim, C. G., and Whangbo, T. K. (2023). Question answering system for healthcare information based on BERT and GPT. In 2023 Joint International Conference on Digital Arts, Media and Technology with ECTI Northern Section Conference on Electrical, Electronics, Computer and Telecommunications Engineering (ECTI DAMT and NCON). https://doi.org/10.1109/ectidamtncon57770.2023.10139365.

[8] Kanodia, N., Ahmed, K., and Miao, Y. (2021). Question answering model based conversational chatbot using BERT model and google dialogflow. In 2021 31st International Telecommunication Networks and Applications Conference (ITNAC). https://doi.org/10.1109/itnac53136.2021.9652153.

[9] Nandgaonkar, A., Mane, S. B., and Khatavkar, V. (2023). Creativity index calculation with question answering system using BERT model. In 2023 3rd International Conference on Intelligent Technologies (CONIT). https://doi.org/10.1109/conit59222.2023.10205798.

[10] Guven, Z. A., and Unalir, M. O. (2021). Improving the BERT model with proposed named entity recognition method for question answering. In 2021 6th International Conference on Computer Science and Engineering (UBMK). https://doi.org/10.1109/ubmk52708.2021.9558992.

[11] Kim, J., Chung, S., Moon, S., and Chi, S. (2022). Feasibility study of a BERT-based question answering chatbot for information retrieval from construction specifications. In 2022 IEEE International Conference on Industrial Engineering and Engineering Management (IEEM). https://doi.org/10.1109/ieem55944.2022.9989625.

[12] Mosaed, A. A., Hindy, H., and Aref, M. (2023). BERT-based model for reading comprehension question answering. In 2023 Eleventh International Conference on Intelligent Computing and Information Systems (ICICIS). https://doi.org/10.1109/icicis58388.2023.10391167.

20 Enhancing video summarization with natural language processing

Thukaram Reddy, M.[1,a] and Adi Narayana Reddy, K.[2,b]
[1]Research Scholar, Dept. of CSE, ICFAI, Hyderabad, Telangana, India
[2]Associate Professor, Dept. of CSE, ICFAI, Hyderabad, Telangana, India

Abstract

While selecting which movie to view, descriptions and keywords are crucial factors to consider. The primary goal of the suggested approach is to automatically provide timestamps and descriptions for movies. Our method significantly cuts down on the amount of time needed to choose the ideal video. It uses timestamps to save consumers time by preventing them from watching pointless movies. The time stamp will make it easier to locate and view just the relevant portion of the film. Our method's primary objective is to physically extract keywords. Important keywords might be found in videos by using keyword extraction. The words, feelings, and visuals of a video determine its synopsis. The video material first appears in the frame, generating a synopsis for the video content. Second, the frame summary product is combined with the sentiment and how it evolves over a given duration. Third, an abstract synopsis of the audio clip is produced through the process of audio to text conversion. Using natural language processing techniques, a fusion of all the summaries of audio, video, and emotion is finally achieved. Methods such as stemming, vocabulary, sentence segmentation, tokenization, and abstract summarization. The process of video summarizing is used to create a precise and insightful summary of the video. Finding desired content that corresponds with the description is made possible by having an accurate description.

Keywords: CNN, LSTM, MSCOCO, NLP, RNN

Introduction

The number of videos on the internet is in the millions, and new videos are being added every second. Over 500 hours of video are uploaded to YouTube every minute, and 1 billion hours of video are seen by users daily, according to data [1]. It is really tough for viewers to find the videos they want in this massive video shop. In an attempt to address this issue, video platforms such as YouTube [2] implemented video descriptions and tags; yet, the problem still existed, giving rise to yet another clickbait issue. In order to enhance the final product of any kind of video editing, image processing techniques are frequently employed. Nowadays, image processing methods are employed.

in numerous other domains, including natural language processing and comprehension [5–7] and medical imaging and treatment [3,4]. One of the key areas of image processing study is picture steganography [8]. One of the subjects utilized in study and daily life is online video chat [9]. As technology developed, people began developing applications to address this issue. Recently, a number of programs for video summaries and video descriptions have been released. They mostly employ techniques like long short-term memory (LSTM) [10] and convolutional neural networks (CNN) [11]. Natural language processing is also used by them [11]. While some apps use the audio from the video, others use the frames from the video to construct a summary.

They both produce video content. Nevertheless, as far as we are aware, no tool exists that produces an output written description for a video based on the sounds, emotions, and frames of the movie. The most accurate representation of what is actually happening in the video will come from doing this. The process of combining several texts by adding connecting words (such but, and, where) is known as blending. Additionally,

[a]mthukaramreddy.scholars22@ifheindia.org, [b]adinarayanareddyk@ifheindia.org

DOI: 10.1201/9781003616399-20

by eliminating nouns and repeated words (like he) and substituting pronouns for them. An illustration of the text merging procedure is shown in Figure 20.1.

The system that we have in mind will combine three generated texts: the first will be a description of a picture generated by the video; the second will be an emotion recovered from the video footage; and the third will be an audio extraction from the video to text templates.

We looked at issues individuals were having with processing and finding videos. Participants in the survey ranged in age, gender, and interest. Some of the issues users go into when processing video are shown by this survey. A significant majority of respondents 95.6%—agreed that using such a tool would undoubtedly aid them in their search. To fully understand the topic of accurate video summarization, more research is required. Additionally, there is a dearth of tools for extremely accurate video summarization. According to 87.1% of content producers, using such a technology can be beneficial and time-saving. As per the survey results, 66.8% of participants attested to the fact that the content of the video did not correspond with its title and description.

Furthermore, 92.2% of them stated that timestamps are necessary for videos. For students or researchers looking for a specific topic or part to look at, this can save a significant amount of time.

The structure of the paper is as follows: Related work is described in Part II. Part III defines the suggested approach. Part V presents the research findings, while Part IV describes the experiment.

Related Work

Two basic approaches were applied to earlier work in the video summarizing field. Ji and Xiong [13] as well as Tran and Hwang [12] adopted the first strategy. Their primary objective is to reduce the length of the original video. Making a written description for the input video is an additional strategy. The emphasis of Rohrbach et al. [14] is on location, object, and verb identification. They generated sentences using LSTM. Another area of study for Krishnamoorthy and Malkarnenkar [15] was the extraction of verbs, objects, and subjects from video pictures.

Using video to extract features and text

An image-only video-to-text summarization technique was proposed by Sah and Kulhare [16]. To learn word representation in the decoder and video representation in the encoder, they employed S2VT, a two-layer LSTM model. Utilizes a 152-layer ResNet CNN model that has been trained on ImageNet data in order to extract relevant photos. The 11 long videos (ranging in length from 45 minutes to nearly 5 hours) that make up the video set dataset are categorized into three groups. Disney, egocentric, and TV episodes are the three categories. Three tests and eight training films were utilized. The Microsoft video description (MSVD) dataset's training section served as the caption model's pre-training set.

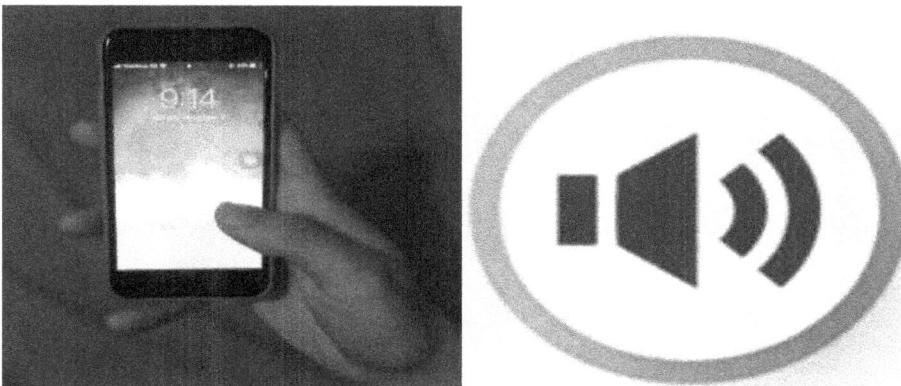

(a) A phone is being held by someone. (b) There is a 3000 mah battery.
Figure 20.1 Fusion of modalities A and B produces the following output: The phone has a 3000mAh battery
Source: Author

They contend that, in general, the LexRank, LSA, and Sum Basic approaches produce superior outcomes.

A method for extracting characteristics from video pictures using CNN and RNN was proposed by Dilawari and Khan [17]. In order to extract human visual traits like age, gender, and emotion, they first send video frames to the CNN model and subsequently to the RNN. To generate a description, these features are fed into the LSTM model. Luong was able to focus his attention on creating at the word level thanks to this description.

A brief synopsis the MSR-VTT dataset was utilized by them for CNN and RNN models. They compared their work with four other methodologies using METEOR ratings. It has been demonstrated that the following techniques produce the greatest results: task-specific feature encoding, SCN-LSTM, MP-LSTM, and SCN-LSTM. Subsequently, they produced a UET surveillance dataset that included written descriptions and videos. The result of a frame-based video summarizing system provided by Moses and Balachandran [18] is a summary video. They employed skimming and key frames for the first time, in addition to extraction features. Next, use machine learning, clustering, and classification methods. To fix the issue and obtain the greatest outcomes for the summary video, they employed these algorithms. They employed ViSOR, CAVIAR, CUHK, and in-house datasets to test and train the system.

With the help of a summary video, they were able to promote a good system and save space. If the summary is text instead of video, which takes up more space, it can be more effective and save more space.

Figure 20.2 illustrates a system that was introduced by Jin and Liang [19] that used CNN and LSTM-RNN algorithms. It was only recently discovered that this algorithm produced excellent results when applied to videos. They use two methods to categorize videos: end-to-end sequence modeling and action recognition. They used the Corpus dataset to test and train their model. The almost 2000 videos in this collection have lengths ranging from 10 to 25 seconds. METEOR received scores of 26. 17% for the combination of video and audio, and 23. 70% and 20. 21% for the individual components.

An image-sequence processing system for video was proposed by Li et al. [20]. They are given a video as input, and they produce a sentence summarizing the video's content. They combined the use of LSTM-RNN and deep CNN algorithms.

After producing a number of potential sentences, they employ a rating system. Finding similar phrases and choosing the most often used ones to use as video descriptions is the goal of ranking. The Microsoft research video description consortium is the dataset that was utilized.

Jeevitha and Hemalatha [21] presented a method for text generation from videos that just uses picture data. Making use of attention-based

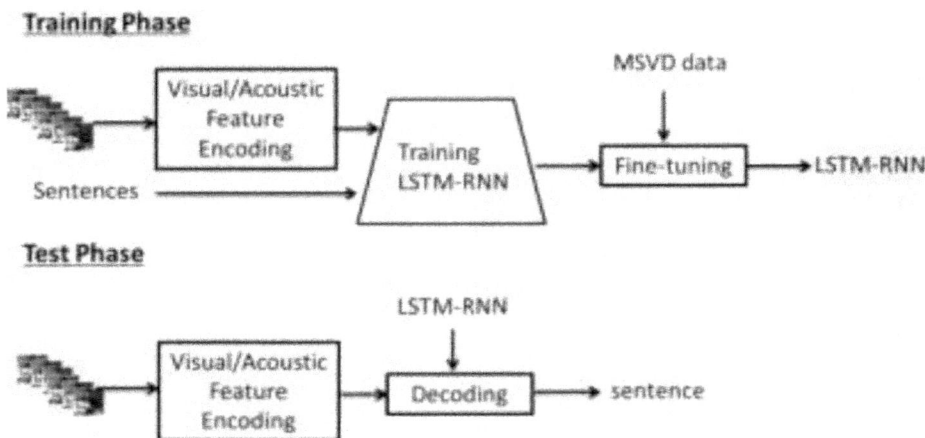

Figure 20.2 Phases of testing and training utilized by Jin and Liang [19]
Source: Author

long short-term memory, NetVLAD, and 2D and 3D (CNN)networks (aLSTM), with the goal of achieving thorough video comprehension. Their experimental dataset included MSVD, which included 16,000 words, 80,000 descriptions, and 1970 short video clips. They used the BLEU measurement approach to evaluate accuracy, and their testing phase produced encouraging findings. Their study demonstrates the effectiveness of their selected model architecture and evaluation criteria and represents advances in the direct generation of textual descriptions from visual input.

The combination of aLSTM, NetVLAD, and 2D and 3D CNN shows how reliable their method is at capturing temporal and spatial characteristics for precise video description.

asserted that their novel approach, NetVLAD+aLSTM, remains superior to more established techniques, including C2D, C3D, and C2D+C3D.

A method that integrates topic-related texts and movies was put out by Li and Zhu [22]. Sentences found in the document and voice transcripts from the audio recording are among the text highlights that are measured. To convey information about a word's significance to the entire document, highlight it. They did find, however, that performance was not any better with audio and video included than with the text-only model. This makes sense since the finest outcomes can only be obtained by summarizing a well-written document.

Sound to text
A system using an LSTM model that uses 3D CNN rather than 2D CNN was introduced by Zhang and Tian [23]. Three datasets were used: the Montreal video annotation (MVAD) dataset, the MSVD) dataset, and the MPII movie description (MPII) dataset. Two different image types—RGB and MHI—are extracted by this search from video input. To extract features, a 3D CNN model will be imported for each type of frame. To summarize the video, the output of the two 3D CNN models is fed into an LSTM. With a METEOR score of 31.1%, which was higher than the previous S2VT figure by 1.3%, MGF by 7.2%, average aggregation by 2%, and the temporal attention model by 1.5%, their approach was the highest. A technique to enhance text

summary with ordinary speech was presented by Ribeiro and Matos [24]. In order to improve the abstraction, they employed LSA to supply training keywords associated with the model's history. Their dataset consisted of newspaper articles. The summaries of several models are assessed and contrasted by a group of individuals. ASR, Basic LSA, LSA, human extraction, and human abstraction are these models. The findings indicate that human mining works best. But LSA produces superior outcomes to ASR.

Multimodal audio and video
In order to close the semantic gap between various multimodal contents, Haoran Li et al. [22] presented the Summary system, which is based on NLP, ASR, and CV. They make use of voice and audio recording capabilities, text and image-containing documents, and image-containing films. To train their model, they employed 5,801 sentence pairings from the MS Paraphrase dataset. The Flickr30K and MSCOCO databases have 31,783 pictures of different activities in terms of text. There are 123,000 photos in the MSCOCO dataset. To train the visual portion of their models, both include textual descriptions of the images.

They attempted to summarize a collection of articles, videos, and photos in order to evaluate their model. The findings indicated that including audio and the results were not much improved by the video data. Nevertheless, whether the text—whether it be the topic or a transcription of a picture or sound—is the most powerful component. Their RED ratings range up to ±0.25 at the 95% confidence level.

For video explanation, Hori et al. [25] suggested a multi-modal combination. Where every technique has a unique feature vector sequence. Motion, visual, and aural elements are examples of modalities. They extract vector frame features using C3D and audio features using MFCC. After that, these vectors are combined to form a single vector.

By employing RNN to create encoder-decode phrases, it is utilized to anticipate the following word. Using the MSR- VTT and YouTube2Text datasets, they assessed their approach. Based on three assessment indices (BLEU4, METEOR, and CIDEr), their approach receives the highest rating.

Comparison utilizing YouTube2Text subset without Music Overload, followed by LSTM-E, TA, h-RNN, and Naive fusion.

Lashin and Rahtu [26] suggested an approach that accepts speech, video, and audio as input. Additionally, a word sequence has been produced, as seen in Figure 20.3.

After processing the input into the appropriate encoder-decoder block, the model combines the three outputs. The next annotation word is produced by merging them in the multimodal generator. They employed VGGISH to extract audio characteristics. They represented text as vectors by using word embeddings and I3D to extract features from images. The net activity dataset is the one that was used. There are 10,000 videos in this collection.

for validation, and five thousand movies for training. Since the METEOR metric has a good correlation with human judgment, that is why they used it. After combining voice, audio, and video, they received a score of 10.09.

Proposed Approach

A novel approach to summarizing videos based on their audio, visuals, and emotions is implemented by the suggested method. This aims to provide a precise and comprehensible synopsis of the video. Additionally, there is a mix of audio, video, and emotional summary text. Receive a synopsis at the conclusion that may serve as a useful synopsis of the film.

According to survey data, 73.5% of participants had never made or submitted a video to a website. However, 33.3% of the 26.5% of video uploaders did not include a description with their work. Occasionally, they merely write a few sentences that don't really explain what the video is about. 87.2% of respondents said they would utilize this technology if it was accessible. Figure 20.4 provides an overview of the suggested system and lists the following steps:

- The video splits into smaller videos every two seconds. Every video in this section features sounds and visuals since it is divided into scenes.
- Preprocessing is applied to every frame of the smallest video frame. To eliminate hazy scenes and loud noises, pre-processed images and sounds will be used.
- Text is transformed from audio to text by using speech recognition software. Text is the output, which is subsequently fed into CNN and LSTM models.
- The three output text descriptions are combined to provide a merged text that is both meaningful and summarized.
- The remaining tiny videos can be finished by repeating this technique.
- The text is subsequently subjected to an abstract summary through the application of natural language processing (NLP) methods.
- NLP is used to create timestamps and descriptions for videos. Finding cut scenes later on will be made easier by identifying them.

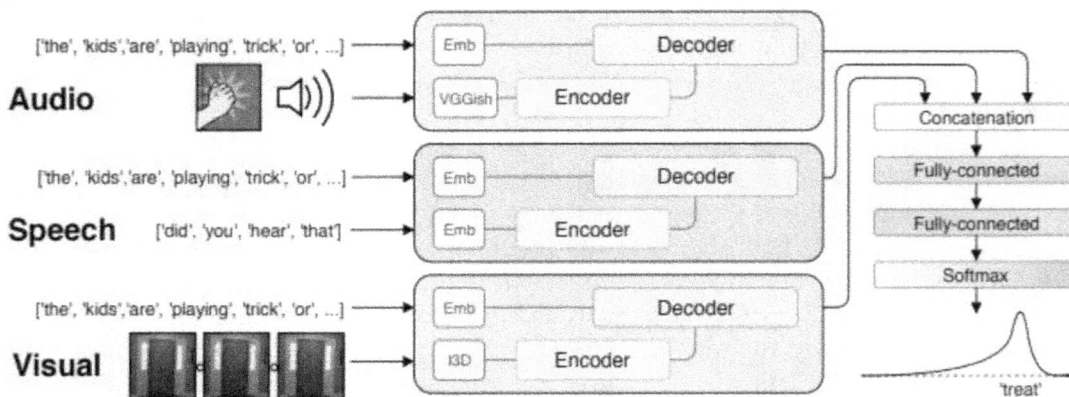

Figure 20.3 Lashin and Rahtu's overview of the system [26]
Source: Author

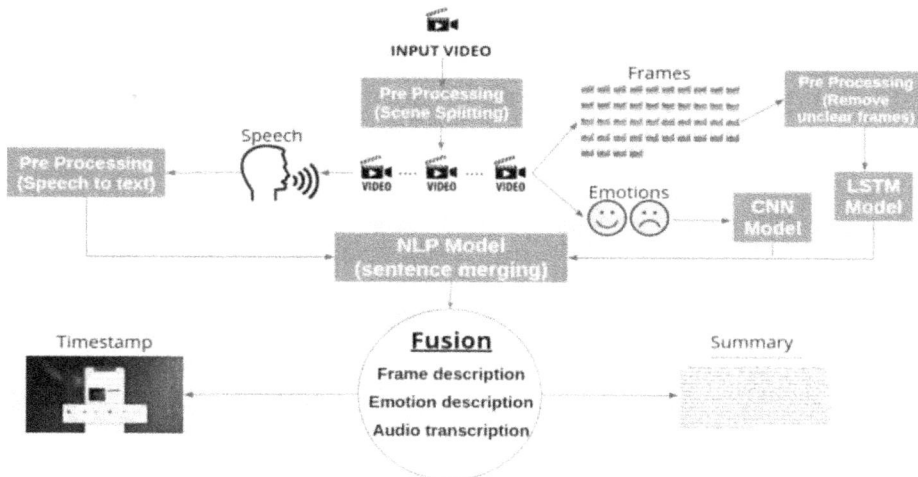

Figure 20.4 Overview of the proposed system
Source: Author

Summarizing Videos

The video will break up into smaller videos per scene every two seconds. Every shorter video is broken up into frames. Next comes the process of filtering the image. The process of filtering involves deleting hazy and unclear photos that won't be used.

The LSTM model will process the filtered frames. An output textual description for the frames is obtained by the LSTM model after it has encoded a series of frames and decoded their values. A template for writing captions and text descriptions for videos. The content of the image and the things that are shown in the video are used to construct the text.

Summary of emotions

The CNN model will process the smaller videos after they have been summarized. It is the model's job to identify the emotions of the faces in the frame. Our suggested model has been taught to categorize seven distinct emotions: neutral, surprise, happiness, fury, disgust, fear, and sadness. To determine the primary emotion of the scene, emotions must be retrieved from each frame inside each time interval. The description is then blended with the prevailing emotion to produce a more precise and trustworthy description.

Summarizing audio

The audio is first filtered to remove background noise and hazy speech. Then, the clean audio is sent into a speech-to-text system to produce the

audio script for the film. After that, a text categorization algorithm [27] is used to this script, starting the summarization process. When using this technique, all of the sentences are extracted, sorted in a similarity matrix based on their order, and the most significant sentences with a greater weight are chosen to be included in the summary text. This abstract achieves a more detailed and nuanced summary than the original document by not only condensing the content but also rephrasing terms to increase accuracy. This multi-step process guarantees thorough and superior composite outcomes.

Text created by fusion

Text produced synthetically three statements are produced by each brief film, using audio, visual, and emotional elements. These three phrases are combined during the blending process, with the addition of linking words and the removal of unnecessary components. The goal of this integration is to create a concise and well-organized overview that highlights the key elements of the input method. The text produced by merging will more accurately portray the topic by blending information from multiple sources, improving the summary outcome. By utilizing the advantages of each technique, this strategy fosters synergistic pairings that raise the overall standard and formativeness of the material generated. identical names. NLP techniques including tokenization [28], sentence segmentation [29], stemming, and lexicalization [30] are used to apply all of this. One sentence will be the output for each brief video. Together, these phrases make up the main paragraph of the video description. Extract the most crucial keywords for the video at the same time.

Generation of timestamps

Time stamping takes place during summary. The primary scene is identified by detecting each scene at the start and finish.

Additionally, provide each scene a summary title that will be utilized in the future to improve the speed and accuracy of search navigation.

Experiments and Results

Dataset

Data sets are essential for testing experimental work and putting any machine learning technique into practice. For testing and training, we employ two distinct datasets. Videos from FER-2013 [31] (Figure 20.5) and MSVD [32] (Figure 20.6) are among the many that can be utilized to improve our methodology.

This facial expression recognition dataset, known as FER-2013, is made up of 48*48 grayscale photos of cropped faces. Seven categories have been created from the data, each of which represents a different emotion: anger, joy, surprise, disgust, neutral, melancholy, and fear.

There are 28,709 photos in the training set and 3,589 images in the public test set.

The MSVD benchmark dataset consists of 1,500 films, each lasting an average of ten seconds. There are several training subtitles included with every video. During testing, these annotations are also utilized to assess the output annotations. 50 exam films and 1,450 training videos.

Setting up the experiment

Two machines were used to carry out the experiment. The first is an HP Core i5-7200U computer with Windows 10 with 12GB of RAM and 240 SSD. The second is an HP Core i5- 8300h with an Ubuntu Linux operating system, 8GB RAM, and 240 SSD. This approach was developed with Pycharm, a Python programming tool.

Work completed

Summarization of video: The following are the primary steps in the conversion and summary of videos to text:

Image extraction: There are multiple images extracted from the movie.

Emotion and face detection: Every extracted image has a face detected in it. Each image's emotion score will be calculated using the retrieved faces' emotions.

Emotion extraction: Find the emotions in a movie that are most frequently repeated over a certain length of time.

Text-to-Speech API: Use a video with start and end timings for each word to convert it to text.

Combine text and summary: Within 20 seconds, match relevant speech to emotional states, and then provide a text summary. It makes use of an external API (AssemblyAI) [33].

Emotion detection: facial recognition and emotion categorization are implemented using a deep learning network (CNN). The probability distribution of the following seven emotions

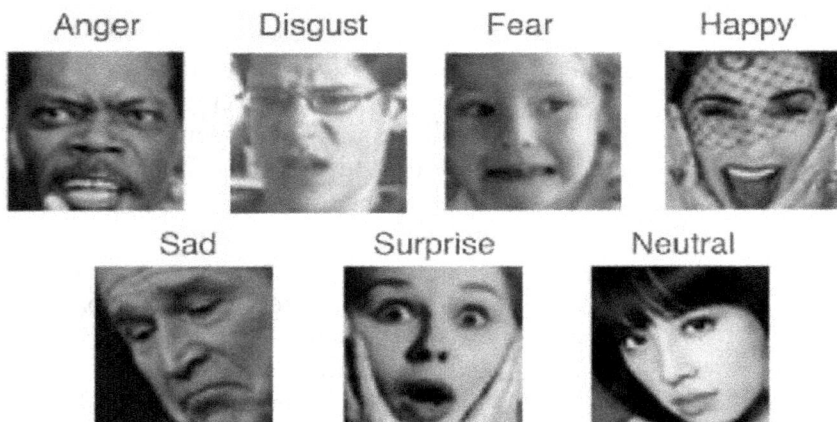

Figure 20.5 FER-2013 Dataset samples [31]
Source: Author

is displayed: surprise, happiness, anger, disgust, fear, sadness, and neutral. This is accomplished by making changes to the data's output form, building on the research of Kousiks [34].

Outcomes of experiments
A three-minute Ted Talk video titled "The importance of reading" by young speaker Luke Bakic served as the test subject for the experiment [35]. There are 217 words in the text summary shown in Figure 20.7. Although there are 485 words in the original text prior to the abstract. The machine specified in the test configuration took 4 minutes to display the results of the test run.

Experiment with human assessment
We developed a survey to get feedback on our suggested system and the outcomes thus far.

Out of the 151 participants in the poll, 40% were men and 60% were women. 55% of the participants were in the 15–25 age range. Participants in the survey were first asked to watch a three-minute Ted Talk video before rating how well our system's automated description performed. We generate by providing linear scale answers to three inquiries. The video summary produced by our recommendation algorithm is seen in Figure 20.7.

The three linear scale questions are as follows, with a range of 1-5:

1) To what extent do you think the synopsis accurately captures the essence of the video? Be aware that a 1 denotes a severe disagreement and a 5 a strong agreement.
2) How do you think of the summary sentences' level of comprehension and clarity? Recognize that 1 is really bad, and 5 is very good.

3) Based on the speaker's expression, how do you assess the accuracy of the emotion conveyed, such as "he said sad"? Recognize that 1 is really bad, and 5 is very good.

In response to question 1, 89.5% of participants reported having a score in the range of 3–5. This proportion increased to 86.2% in question 2, and to 85.5% in question 3. 87% of respondents to the survey expressed satisfaction with the developed application.

The experiment's outcome
Condensed versions of long videos are one of the many useful results that video summarization delivers to users. First of all, it allows for speedy material inspection, saving users' time. Second, by lowering the amount of data, summarization facilitates effective data storage and retrieval. Thirdly, it makes content navigation simple and quick, enabling users to quickly identify pertinent portions. Fourthly, abridged videos improve accessibility by being easier to distribute and watch. Finally, a variety of applications are supported by this technology, such as efficient surveillance analysis, content suggestion, and video indexing.

Conclusion

This creative study introduces a novel approach to video text summarization that combines audio, visual, and emotional elements. The pre-processing step efficiently collects descriptive text from each frame of the video by breaking it up into smaller components, which serves as the foundation for the summary. By recognizing and combining the prevalent emotions in each scene, emotion analysis gives the brief an additional layer of complexity. A third text summary

Figure 20.6 MSVD Dataset samples [32]
Source: Author

The below text is the automated summarization generated by our tool

I think that it's totally crazy that all anyone ever talks about is games TV shows what's ,he sadly said up Instagram Bitmoji I don't even know what that is my brother just told me about it.
Some I like more, but they all took me for such an adventure as my family members I'm a truly unhappy child.
I love reading in places like my bed on the move while walking in the toilet and cues and vehicles.
But ,he sadly said more importantly at home, I hide behind various corners of my house so nobody can find me and make me do anything else.
So for all of you skeptical people out there, let me tell you when you have a good book to keep you company.
You can't meet reading is love in action and the positives are endless.
Like, I usually never have to study for spelling tests and it makes my vocabulary.
Talking about me, I can't imagine my life without a book.
What I'm comparing is the last star of reading writing communicating and persuading the sum of the great societal ills of a text message.
While these wonders of modern technology have their place, we the young generation has to hold on to reading it's the queue to our Kingdom.

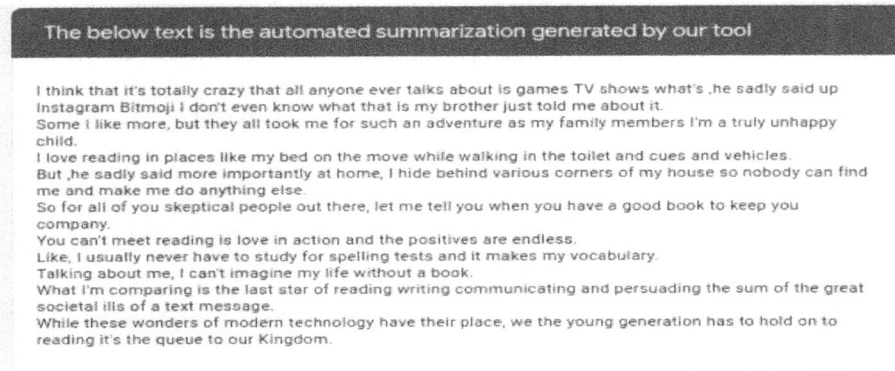

Figure 20.7 Output
Source: Author

is produced by transcribing the audio recording, which must next undergo an abstract summarization procedure. The key component is the following NLP integration of these three distinct synopses, which guarantees accurate and comprehensive depiction of the video material.

The article highlights the significance of keyword extraction to enhance video search capabilities in addition to providing a synopsis. Finding and using the right keywords can help make the search process run more smoothly, which will speed up the retrieval of content. By automatically creating video timestamps, the suggestion further increases its value by offering quicker, easier, and more precise access to the necessary content inside the movie. This all-encompassing method tackles a wide range of video processing issues, showing potential improvements in search effectiveness and summary quality.

References

[1] YouTube for Journalists. (2020, November 7). YouTube Statistics. Retrieved from https://www.youtube.com/about/press/.

[2] From November 9, 2020, on YouTube. YouTube.com is the URL https://www. Youtube.com/press1

[3] Khalil, M. I., Ghanim, T. M., and Abbas, H. M. (2019). Multi-stage off-line advanced cascading technique Arabic handwriting recognition approach. In ICPRAM, (pp. 532–539).

[4] Azim, M. A., Ab-delRaouf, A., and Salama, S. (2017). Angiographic scans for narrowed coronary artery detection and classification. In Computer Engineering and Systems, 12th International Conference (ICCES), 2017. IEEE, (pp. 73–79).

[5] Abbas, H. M., Khalil, M. I., and Ghanim, T. M. (2020). A comparative analysis of deep convolution neural networks DCNN-based offline Arabic handwriting recognition. *IEEE Access*, 8, 95465–95482.

[6] AbdelRaouf, A., Higgins, C. A., Pridmore, T., and Khalil, M. I. (2016). Arabic character recognition using a haar cascade classifier approach (HCC). *Pattern Analysis and Applications*, 19(2), 411–426.

[7] Abdel-Raouf, A., Ghanim, T., and Shorim, N. (2019). Using google APIs and cloud computing to implement arabic handwritten recognition approach on a mobile application. In 14th International Conference on Systems and Computer Engineering (IC-CES) 2019. IEEE, (pp. 88–95).

[8] AbdelRaouf, A. (2021). A new data hiding approach for image steganography based on visual color sensitivity. *Applications and Tools for Multimedia*. This is the URL: 10.1007/s11042-020-10224-w.

[9] Abdel-Raouf, A., Abdelhalim, M. B., and Radwan, N. (2020). Install cloud computing infrastructure for 3D video calls. *Journal of Ain Shams Engineering*, 11(2), 363–375.

[10] Morris, E., and Staudemeyer, R. (2019). An introduction to long short-term memory recurrent neural networks: understanding LSTM.

[11] Albawi, S., Al-Zawi, S., and Mohammed, T. A. (2017). A convolutional neural network's understanding. In 2017 International Conference on Engineering and Technology (ICET), (pp. 1–6). ICEngTechnol.2017.8308186; doi: 10. 1109.

[12] Exploiting character networks for movie summarization.

[13] Allen, J. F. (2003). Natural Language Processing. GBR: John Wiley and Sons Ltd. (pp. 1218–1222). 0470864125 is the ISBN.

[14] Tran, Q. D., Hwang, D., Lee, O. J., and Jung, J. E. (2017). Exploiting character networks for movie summarization. *Multimedia Tools and Applications*, 76(8), 10357–10369.

[15] Ji, Z., et al. (2020). Video summarization using attention-based encoder– decoder networks. *IEEE Transactions on Circuits and Systems for Video Technology*, 30(6), 1709–1717. 10.1109/TCSVT.2019.2904996 is the DOI.

[16] Schiele, B., Rohrbach, A., and Rohrbach, M. (2015). The extended-short narrative of the film synopsis. [cs.CV] arXiv: 1506.01698.

[17] Krishnamoorthy, N., Malkarnenkar, G., Mooney, R., Saenko, K., and Guadarrama, S. (2013). Generating natural-language video descriptions using text-mined knowledge. In: AAAI'13, Bellevue, Washington: AAAI Press.

[18] Dilawari, A., and Khan, M. U. G. (2019). ASoVS: abstractive summarization of video sequences. *IEEE Access*, 7, 29253–29263. ACCESS / DOI: 10. 1109/2019-290-2507.

[19] Moses, T. M., and Balachandran, K. (2017). A classified study on semantic analysis of video summarization. In Citation: ICAMMAET 2017: 2017 International Conference on Algorithms, Methodology, Models and Applications in Emerging Technologies, (pp. 1–6). 10.1109 / ICAMMAET.2017.8186684 is the DOI.

[20] Jin, Q., and Liang, J. (2016). Video description gener-ation using audio and visual cues. In ICMR '16: Proceedings of the 2016 ACM International Conference on Multitemporal Retrieval. Association for Computing Machinery, New York, New York, USA, (pp. 239–242). 978-150343596-ISBN. Ten. 1145 / 2911996. 2912043 DOI. https://doi.org/10. 1145 / 2911996.2912043 is the URL.

[21] Li, G., Ma, S., and Han, Y. (2015). Summarization-based video caption via deep neural networks. In ACM 23rd International Conference on Multimedia Proceedings. MM (pp. 1191–1194).

[22] Jeevitha, V. K., and Hemalatha, M. (2020). Natural language description for videos using NetVLAD and attentional LSTM. In 2020 International Conference for Emerging Technology (INCET). (Vol. 10, pp. 1–6). 1109/INCET49848.2020.9154103 does not exist.

[23] Li, H., Zhu, J., Ma, C., Zhang, J., and Zong, C. (2019). Multi-modal summarization for asynchronous text, image, audio, and video: read, watch, listen, and summarize. *IEEE Transactions on Knowledge and Data Engineering*, 31(5), 996–1009. 10.1109/TKDE.2018.2848260 is the doi.

[24] Zhang, C., and Tian, Y. (2016). Automatic video description generation via LSTM with joint two-stream encoding. In 23rd International Conference on Pattern Recognition (ICPR), (pp. 2924–2929). 10.1109/ICPR.2016.7900081 is the DOI.

[25] De Matos, D. M., and Ribeiro, R. (2008). Multi-document speech-to-text summarization using mixed sources. In Coling 2008: Multi-source Multilingual Information Extraction and Summarization Workshop Proceedings, (pp. 33– 40).

[26] Lashingin, V., and Rahtu, E. (2020). Multi-modal dense video captioning. In Computer Vision and Pattern Recognition Workshops (CVPRW), 2020 IEEE/CVF Conference, (pp. 4117–4126). 2020.00487 / CVPRW50498 / DOI: 10. 1109.

[27] Ten, D. (2020). Tex- tRank (pytextrank): Keyword and sentence extraction (accessed November 7, 2020). xang1234.github.io/textrank/ is the URL.

[28] Arunachala, P. (2020). Natural language processing: tokenization. (accessed November 10, 2020). URL: https://tokenization-for-natural-language-processing- a179a891bad4 on towardsdatascience.com.

[29] Lovins, J. B. (1968). Development of a stemming algorithm. *Translation and Computational Linguistics*, 11(1), 22–31.

[30] Recognition of facial expressions dataset. https://www.kaggle.com/msambare/fer2013 is the URL.

[31] Dolan, W., and Chen, D. (2011). Acquiring data in high parallel for evaluation of paraphrases. In Human Language Technologies: Proceedings of the 49th Annual Meeting of the Association for Computational Linguistics. Association for Computational Linguistics, Portland, Oregon, USA, June 2011, (pp. 190–200). http://www.aclweb.org/anthology/P11-1020 is the URL.

[32] #1 Speech-to-Text API with the Most Accuracy. (retrieved November 10, 2020). https://www.assemblyai.com is the URL.

[33] Application of video emotion recognition by kousik97. URL: https://kousik97.github.com/video/expression-

[34] Hori, C., Hori, T., Lee, T. Y., Zhang, Z., Harsham, B., and Hershey, J. R. (2017). Attention-based multimodal fusion for video description. In 2017 IEEE International Conference on Computer Vision (ICCV), (pp. 4203–4212). 10.1109/ICCV.2017.450 is the DOI.

[35] Palmer, D. D. (2000). Tokenization and Sentence Segmentation. Handbook of Natural Language Processing (pp. 11–35).

21 Automated hydroponic plant growth system using IoT

Kalathiripi Rambabu[a], Sanjay Dubey[b], B. R. Sanjeeva Reddy[c], Are Bhavani[d], Vaishnavi Adicherla[e], Chippalthurthy Gayathri[f] and B. Revanth Johnny Raj[g]

Department of Electronics and Communication engineering, B V Raju Institute of Technology, Narsapur, Medak, Telangana, 502313, India

Abstract

The implementation of an automated hydroponic plant system utilizing IoT technology, integrated with the ThingView Free app for real-time monitoring and control. Automated hydroponics, enhanced by IoT, allows precise regulation of critical growth parameters such as nutrient levels, pH, temperature, humidity, and light intensity. This integration ensures optimal plant growth, increased yields, and efficient resource usage. The ThingView Free app provides a user-friendly interface for accessing sensor data and system status remotely, enabling users to make timely adjustments and maintain ideal growing conditions. The combination of IoT automation and accessible apps like ThingView represents a significant advancement in modern agriculture. The Automated hydroponic systems leverage the Internet of Things (IoT) to monitor and control environmental conditions for plants grown without soil. This allows for remote monitoring and optimization of plant growth, even for those with limited gardening experience.

Keywords: Automatic refill, connected to good life and good health, healthcare system transparency, home based services, time constraint, user friendly

Introduction

Hydroponics is method of growing plants without soil [1]. Plants instead grown in water-based nutrient solution or in an inert medium. Hydroponics offers number of advantages over traditional soil-based gardening, including Plants grown hydroponically can mature up to 30% faster than plants grown in soil. Hydroponic systems can produce higher yields of crops than soil-based gardens [12]. Hydroponic systems use up to 90% less water than soil-based gardens because plants are not grown in soil, they are less susceptible to soil-borne pests and diseases. Hydroponics is a method of growing plants without soil, using water instead. Here are a few reasons why hydroponics are used Hydroponics often uses less water than traditional soil gardening, as the water in the system can be recirculated. It allows for vertical farming and density planting, making it suitable for urban environments with limited space. Plants can grow more quickly in a hydroponic system due to the direct delivery of nutrients and optimal growing conditions. Without soil, there's a lower risk of soil-borne pests and diseases. Growers can precisely control nutrient levels, pH, and other environmental factors, potentially leading to higher yields and quality produce [13]. Overall, hydroponics can be alternative to traditional farming, especially in areas where soil quality or space is limited. Hydroponic systems up to 90% less water compared to traditional soil farming. Water is recirculated in the system, minimizing waste. Nutrients are delivered directly to plant roots, reducing the amount of fertilizer needed and limiting nutrient runoff. Hydroponics allows for the use of vertical space with stacked or tiered systems, making it ideal for urban environments

[a]rambabukala@gmail.com, [b]sanjay.dubey@bvrit.ac.in, [c]sanjeev.reddy@bvrit.ac.in, [d]bhavanisweety379@gmail.com, [e]vaishnaviadicherla15@gmail.com, [f]Gayathrichippalthurthy@gmail.com, [g]revanthjohnnyraj05@gmail.com

DOI: 10.1201/9781003616399-21

and maximizing yield per square meter. Plants can be grown closer together without competition for nutrients or space, increasing productivity. Plants receive optimal levels of light, nutrients, and water, leading to growth rates and potentially yields compared to soil cultivation. The controlled environment reduces plant stress factors such as poor soil conditions, which can lead to improved overall plant health. Without soil, there's a significantly lower risk of soil-borne pests and diseases, which reduces the pesticides. The environment can also limit the presence of other pests and diseases, although it's still important to monitor for issues. Hydroponics can be practiced in non-arable areas, reducing the need to convert natural landscapes into agricultural land. Since soil is not used, there's no risk of soil erosion or degradation. Hydroponic systems can be adapted to various setups to commercial farms. Advances in hydroponic technology, such as automated systems and advanced nutrient formulations, continue to improve efficiency and sustainability.

Literature Survey

A literature survey on automated hydroponic plants using IoT (Internet of Things) reveals several benefits for growers, making it an attractive technology for precision agriculture.

Here's a more detailed look at the advantages: Enhanced Monitoring and Control: IoT sensors provide data on crucial environmental factors like pH, nutrient levels, temperature, and humidity. This allows for granular control over the growing environment, enabling adjustments to optimize plant growth based on requirements.

Automated Tasks and Reduced Labor: IoT systems can automate repetitive tasks such as irrigation, nutrient delivery, and climate control. This frees up manual labor for other tasks and ensures consistent growing conditions, minimizing the risk of human error. Potential for Increased Yield and Quality: Precise environmental control and automated tasks can lead to higher yields and improved plant quality. By optimizing growing conditions, IoT-based hydroponic systems can create an ideal environment for plant growth [4], potentially resulting in larger, healthier plants. Remote Monitoring and Management: Growers can leverage smartphones or web interfaces to monitor and manage their hydroponic systems remotely. This provides greater flexibility, allowing them to check on their crops and make adjustments even when they're not physically present at the growing site [10]. This remote monitoring capability can also be crucial for early detection and intervention in case of any issues with the system.

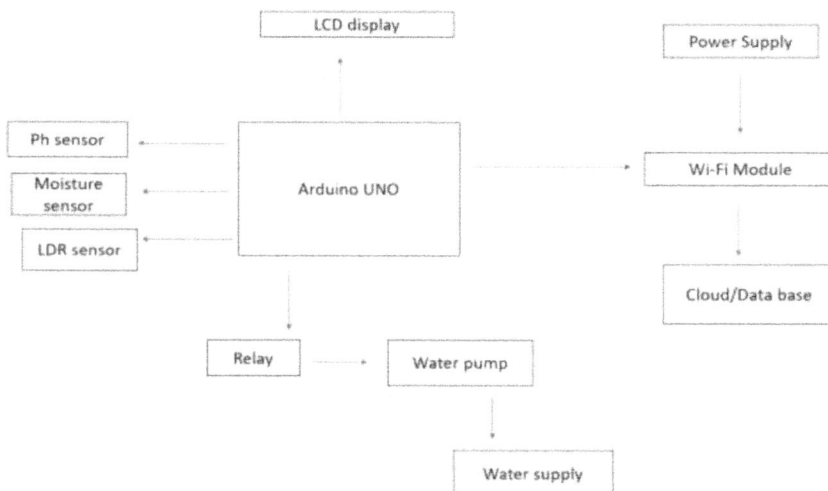

Figure 21.1 Block diagram of hydroiponic plant using arduino UNO
Source: Author

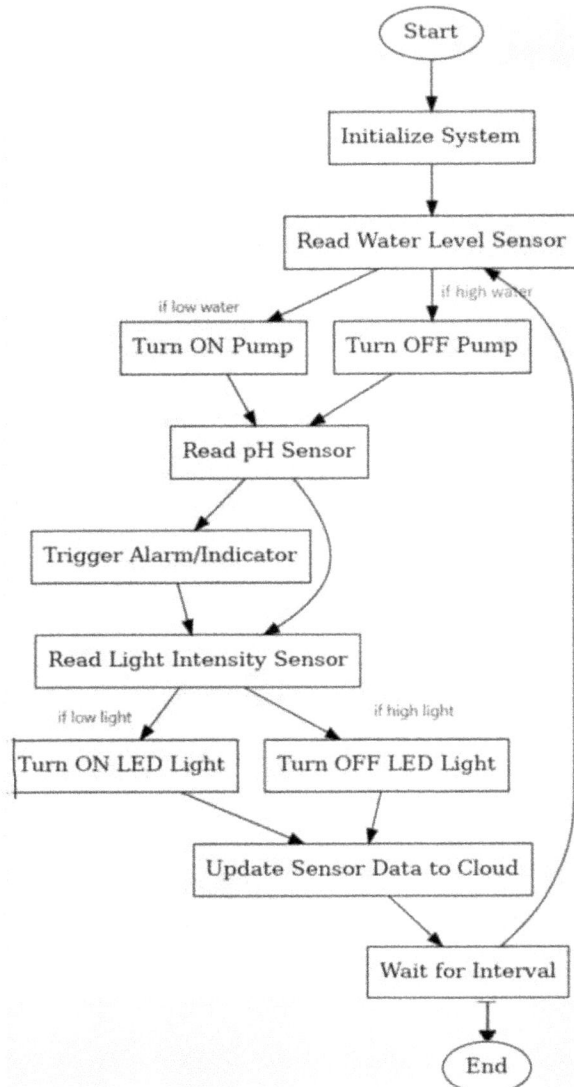

Proposed Model

Block diagram

Step 1: Assemble the Hardware Gather and organize all components:4 bit LCD PCB, 16*2 LCD , Water Pump , Relay , PH Sensor , Moisture Sensor , Sensor Amplifier , 10K pot , Wifi Module(ESP8266), Wifi base board , 12v Adopters , Jumpers.

Step 2: Program the Arduino open the Arduino IDE ans begin writing the program for the Arduino UNO Import the necessary libraries for each component. Define pin assignments and configure them as inputs or outputs.

Step 3: Control the Wifi Module and write the code to handle remote commands from a Mobile Device and Implement the code to manage the cloud.

Step 4: Control the Water Pump connect the water pump to a relay and program the Arduino UNO to control it based on Moisture sensor, LDR Sensor and PH Sensor readings [8] Figure 21.1.

Step 5: Test and Debug the System Thoroughly test assembled Hardware and Programmed Software.

Components Used

ARDUINO UNO: Arduino Uno is a popular opensource microcontroller board that's a great introduction to electronics and coding.

16*2 LCD: display is used to show the text or the alphanumeric characters

WATER PUMP: it is a mechanical device that helps transport water from one place to another by converting mechanical energy into hydraulic energy.

RELAY: it is an electrically operated switch that uses electromagnetism to control a circuit by opening or closing contacts.

PH SENSOR: it is a device that measures the alkalinity of a liquid or solution, also known as its hydrogen ion concentration. pH of 7 is considered neutral, while a pH less than 7 is considered as acidic and a pH greater than 7 is considered alkaline.

MOISTURE SENSOR: it is a device that detects the presence of water or moisture in a surrounding environment. They are used in a variety of applications to monitor moisture levels in things like soil, wood, and air.

SENSOR AMPLIFIER: it is an electronic device that takes the weak signal generated by a sensor and boosts it to a level that can be easily used by other electronic circuits.

10K POT: short for 10 kilohm potentiometer, is a type of variable resistor commonly used in electronic circuits.

WIFI MODULES: The ESP8266 is a popular Wi-Fi module from Espress if Systems that allows microcontrollers to connect to a Wi-Fi network.

WIFI BASE BOARD: sometimes called a development board or breakout board, is a circuit board designed to accommodate a Wi-Fi module, like the

ESP8266 you previously mentioned, and make it easier to use and integrate into various projects.

12V ADOPTERS: it is a device that converts mains power (typically 120VAC or 240VAC) from a wall outlet into 12V DC (direct current) power that can be used to power various electronic devices.

ARDUINO IDE: Arduino IDE is a software tool that allows user to write, compile, and upload code to Arduino boards.

EMBEDDED C PROGRAMMING: it is a specialized field of software development that focuses on creating software which are specialized computer systems.

Implementation Flow Chart

The flowchart represents a system that monitors and controls water levels, pH levels, and light intensity using various sensors and actuators [11]. Here's a detailed explanation of the process:

1. Start: The system begins its operation. 2. Initialize System: Initial setup of the system, ensuring all components are ready to function. 3.Read Water Level Sensor: The system checks the current water level. If low water: Turn ON Pump:It is activated to add water. Read pH Sensor:System checks the pH level of water. Trigger Alarm/Indicator: If the pH is outside the desired range, an alarm or indicator is triggered. Read Light Intensity Sensor: The system checks the current light intensity. If low light: Turn ON LED Light: The LED light is turned on to provide additional light. If high light: Turn OFF LED Light: The LED light is turned off as there is sufficient light. If high water: Turn OFF Pump: The pump is deactivated to stop adding water. Read pH Sensor: Similar to the low water condition, the system checks the pH level. Trigger Alarm/Indicator: If the pH level is outside the desired range, an alarm or indicator is triggered. Read Light Intensity Sensor: The system checks the current light intensity. If low light: Turn ON LED Light: The LED light is turned on to provide additional light. If high light: Turn OFF LED Light: The LED light is turned off as there is sufficient light. 4.Update Sensor Data to Cloud: The system sends the collected data to cloud for monitoring. 5.Wait for Interval: The system waits for a predefined interval before repeating the process. 6.End: The system ends maximize the growth of plants.so it is worth in our daily lives, we also worked on a system which are closed and self-sustainable, supported hydroponics, parameters can be monitored easily. All these things put together from this project physical structure.The raw data collected from system is monitored.

Schematic Diagram

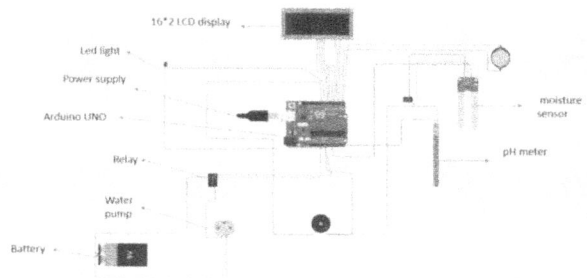

Results

When there is no water in hydroponic plant then the dry state is detected by the moisture sensor and displayed on the LCD as "dry detected".

Figure 21.2 PH level of plant shown in the LCD display
Source: Author

When there is water in hydroponic plant then the wet state is detected by the moisture sensor and displayed on the LCD as "wet detected".

Applications

Automated hydroponic plant systems using IoT have diverse and impactful applications in modern agriculture. These systems enable precise monitoring of various environmental factors such as nutrient levels, pH, temperature, and light intensity [7]. By leveraging IoT sensors and data analytics, farmers can achieve optimal plant growth conditions, leading to increased yields and better quality produce. In research and educational institutions, automated hydroponic systems provide a controlled environment for studying plant physiology and developing new agricultural technologies Table 21.1.

Thingview Application

ThingView Cloud is an IoT (Internet of Things) platform that provides a cloud-based service for managing and visualizing data from IoT devices. Here's an overview of its features and benefits. It allows users to connect and manage various IoT devices from different manufacturers. It provides tools for setting up and configuring devices remotely [3]. It offers customizable dashboards to display real-time data from connected devices.

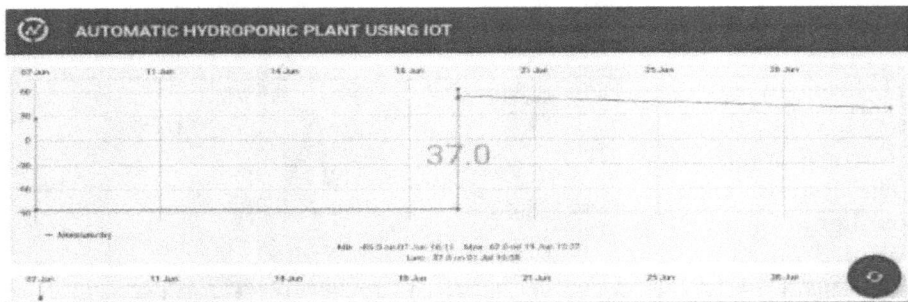

Figure 21.3 Graph of moisture sensor shown in THINGVIEW application
Source: Author

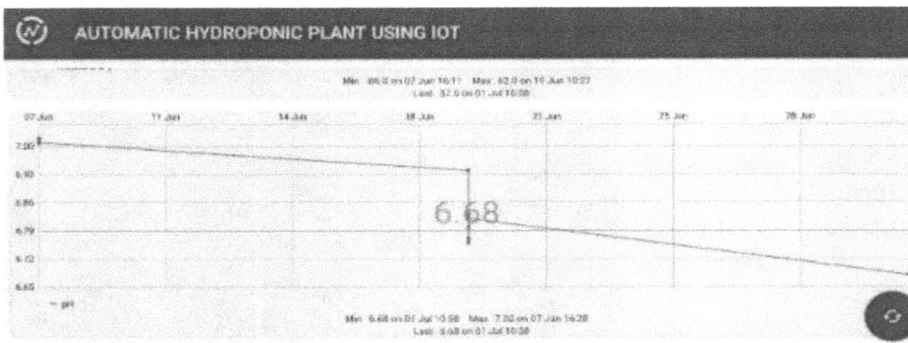

Figure 21.4 Graph of pH sensor shown in THINGVIEW application
Source: Author

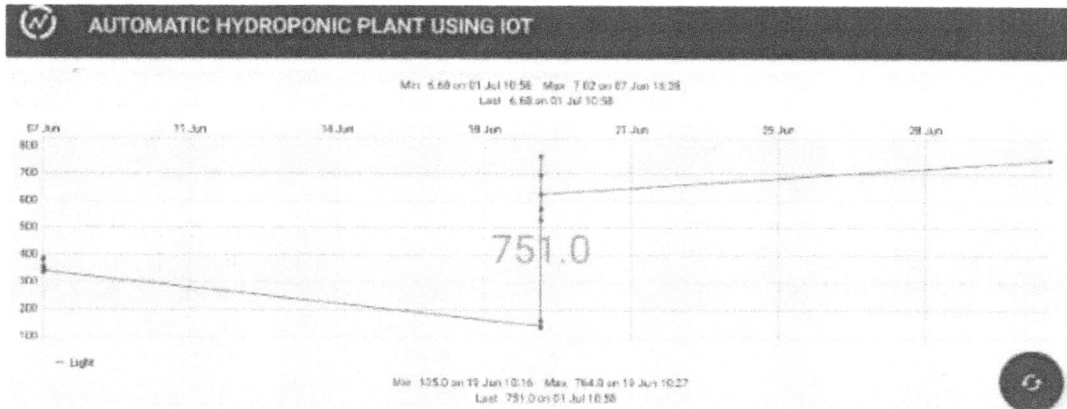

Figure 21.5 Graph of LDR
Source: Author

Table 21.1 Graph of hydroponocs is better than farming with soil

Metric	Hydroponics	Traditional soil farming
Water Usage(liters/ plant)	2-5	10-20
Space Efficiency(plants/ m^2)	50-100	10-20
Growth rate (days to harvest)	30-40	60-90
Pest and Disease Incidence	Low	High
Nutrient use Efficieny(%)	90-95	50-60
Yield (kg/m^2)	5-15	1-5

Source: Author

It includes data analytics and reporting features to analyze trends and patterns. It enables users to monitor device status and performance in real-time from any location. It provides notifications and alerts for specific conditions or thresholds. It supports integration with other systems and platforms through APIs. It can connect with other services and tools for enhanced functionality. Designed to scale with the number of devices and amount of data, suitable for both small and large deployments. Implements security measures to protect data and ensure secure communication between devices and the cloud. the management of IoT devices and data from a single platform. Provides actionable insights through data visualization and analytics. Streamlines operations and reduces the need for manual monitoring and management. Adapts to various use cases to meet specific needs. It is particularly useful for businesses and organizations looking to leverage IoT technology to improve operations, enhance decision-making, and gain insights from their data.

Limitations

Automated hydroponic plant systems using IoT face several limitations [5]. High initial setup costs can be a significant barrier for farmers and hobbyists, as the sophisticated sensors, control systems, and IoT infrastructure require considerable investment. The complexity of these systems demands technical for installation, maintenance, and troubleshooting, which can be a challenge for users without a background in technology or agriculture. Data security is another critical concern, as IoT devices are vulnerable to cyberattacks, risking the integrity of the system and the data collected.

Conclusion

This entire project aims to streamline the hydroponics system while allowing for remote monitoring and control through Internet of things. The components of the system, including hardware and software and collaborate to remove the complexities [15].This system goes beyond conventional agricultural practices, enhancing efficiency and making it self-reliant, capable of producing anything anytime. The software is seamlessly embedded in the physical system, presenting various indicators such as temperature, humidity, and pH levels on a mobile application. Hydroponics contributes to quicker plant growth, further complementing our system's ability to regulate, monitor, and automate processes.

Future Work

Future work on automated hydroponic plant systems using IoT aims to further revolutionize agriculture through enhanced precision, efficiency, and sustainability. Advances will likely focus on integrating more sophisticated sensors and AI-driven analytics to provide real-time, insights into plant growth. This will enable automated adjustments to nutrient delivery, lighting, and environmental conditions, optimizing resource use and maximizing yield. Additionally, the development of userfriendly interfaces and affordable solutions will make these systems accessible to a wider range of users.

References

[1] Sardare, M. (2013). A review on plant without soil - hydroponics. *International Journal of Research in Engineering and Technology*. 02.299304.10.15623/ijret.2013.0203013.

[2] Okemwa, E. (2015). Effectiveness of aquaponic and hydroponic gardening to traditional gardening. *International Journal of Scientific Research and Innovative Technology*, 2(2313–3759), 35.

[3] Fahad, S. K., and Yahya, A. (2018). Big data visualization: allotting by R and Python with GUI tools. In 2018 International Conference on Smart Computing and Electronic Enterprise (ICSCEE), (pp. 1–8). IEEE, 10.1109/ICSCEE.2018.8538413.

[4] Shalini, M. S., Adya, S., Bhavana, S., Neha, H. R., and Shivani, S. (2023). IOT-powered hydroponics system: a real-time monitoring and conrol system. *Asian Journal for Convergence in Technology (AJCT)*, 9(3), 82–86. ISSN-2350-1146.

[5] Sivaleela, M., Babu, M. N., and Ramisetty, U. (2023). Deep water culture using automated hydroponic systems. In 2nd International Conference on Edge Computing and Applications (ICECAA).

[6] Bakriansyah, A. H., Daud, M., Taufiq, T., and Asran, A. (2023). Prototype of automatic monitoring and control system for water supply, acidity, and nutrition in internet of things based DFT hydroponics. *MOTIVECTION: Journal of Mechanical, Electrical and Industrial Engineering*, 5(2), 339–350.

[7] Shrivastava, A., Nayak, C. K., Dilip, R., Samal, S. R., Rout, S., and Ashfaque, S. M. (2023). Automatic robotic system design and development for vertical hydroponic farming using IoT and big data analysis. *Materials Today: Proceedings*, 80, 3546–3553.

[8] Dutta, M., Gupta, D., Sahu, S., Limkar, S., Singh, P., Mishra, A., et al. (2023). Evaluation of growth responses of lettuce and energy efficiency of the substrate and smart hydroponics cropping system. *Sensors*, 23(4), 1875.

[9] Patel, D. S., and Shastri, H. (2023). Automatic hydroponics farming system with image processing based smart nutrients system. *International Research Journal of Engineering and Technology*, 10(6), 203–209.

[10] Mamatha, V., and Kavitha, J. C. (2023). Remotely monitored web based smart hydroponics system for crop yield prediction using IoT. In 2023 IEEE 8th International Conference for Convergence in Technology (I2CT), (pp. 1–6). IEEE.

[11] Vincentdo, V., and Surantha, N. (2023). Nutrient film technique-based hydroponic monitoring and controlling system using ANFIS. *Electronics*, 12(6), 1446.

[12] Mamatha, V., and Kavitha, J. C. (2023). Machine learning based crop growth management in greenhouse environment using hydroponics farming techniques. *Measurement: Sensors*, 25, 100665.

[13] Susanti, H., and Purwanto, R. (2023). Development of a hydroponic system using an atmega 2560 microcontroller with automatic nutrition and pH settings for lettuce cultivation. *Jurnal E-Komtek*, 7(1), 1–12.

[14] Anitha, M. L., Gowda, G. S., Tejaswini, L., Prokshith, P., and Gupta, A. P. (2023). Smart identification of nutrient based pH for an NFT hydroponic system. In 2023 Advanced Computing and Communication Technologies for High Performance Applications (ACCTHPA), (pp. 1–5). IEEE.

[15] Tatas, K., Al-Zoubi, A., Christofides, N., Zannettis, C., Chrysostomou, M., Panteli, S., et al. (2022). Reliable IoT-based monitoring and control of hydroponic systems. *Technologies*, 10(1), 26.

22 Broadband light communication link: performance assessment of series parallel EDFA families and RAMAN amplifier structures

Semmalar, S.[1,a] and Malarkkan, S.[2,b]

[1]Associate Professor, Dept. of ECE, Manakula Vinayagar Institute of Technology, Puducherry, India

[2] Principal, Dept. of ECE, Manakula Vinayagar Institute of technology, Puducherry, India

Abstract

In this study, we comprehensively evaluate the performance of different cascaded Erbium-Doped Fiber Amplifier (EDFA) configurations, namely series EDFA, parallel EDFA, and triple series-parallel EDFA (T-EDFA). By employing the principles of series, parallel, and series-parallel cascading techniques, we systematically conduct experiments and collected output data. The visualized data meticulously analyzed using advanced simulation tools. Our findings demonstrate that the T-EDFA configuration significantly surpasses the performance of the other configurations. Specifically, the T-EDFA exhibits superior performance in broadband multi-wavelength applications, offering enhanced signal privacy and improved efficiency for optical telecommunications networks.

Keywords: EDFA, efficiency, input and output noise, input and output power, optical fiber communications, optical power, power loss and gain, RAMAN

Introduction

The rapid advancement of optical communication technologies has driven the development of more efficient and high-performance amplifiers to meet the growing demand for high-bandwidth and long-distance communication systems. Erbium-Doped Fiber Amplifiers (EDFAs) have emerged as a pivotal technology in this domain due to their ability to amplify optical signals directly in the wavelength range of 1530–1565 nm, which is critical for dense wavelength division multiplexing (DWDM) systems [1].

Cascading EDFAs in various configurations can significantly impact system performance, including parameters such as gain, noise figure, output power, and signal quality. The primary configurations explored are series, parallel, and series-parallel arrangements. In a series configuration, multiple EDFAs are connected in sequence, which can amplify the signal to higher levels, but to introduce more noise and complexity [2]. Conversely, parallel configurations involve EDFAs operating simultaneously but independently, which can enhance System robustness and reduce noise [3]. The series-parallel combination attempts to leverage the benefits of both configurations by integrating EDFAs in a hybrid manner to optimize performance [4].

The effectiveness of these configurations depends on various factors, including input power levels, fiber lengths, and pump power. Simulation studies offer valuable insights into these parameters, enabling the optimization of EDFA setups for specific applications. Recent studies have suggested that the triple series-parallel configuration might provide superior performance by balancing gain and noise characteristics while supporting high data rates and multiple wavelengths [5].

This paper investigates these cascaded EDFA configurations using simulation software to analyze their impact on key performance metrics. The objective is to determine the most effective configuration for broadband, multiple-wavelength optical communication systems and to enhance the privacy and efficiency of optical telecommunications.

[a]semmalarece@mvit.edu.in, [b]principal@mvit.edu.in

DOI: 10.1201/9781003616399-22

Basic principle of cascaded EDFA

Optical amplifiers are essential for enhancing the power of weak optical signals using various principles. These amplifiers can be categorized based on their cascading methods into series EDFA, parallel EDFA, and series-parallel EDFA configurations.

Series EDFA

In a series configuration, multiple EDFAs are connected in sequence. As illustrated in Figure 22.1, multiple digital input signals generated by a digital sequence generator are converted into optical signals by a Gaussian optical pulse generator. These optical pulses are then combined using a power combiner, which acts as the transmitter. The combined signal is fed into the series EDFA link, where it is amplified by each successive amplifier. The amplified output signal is then transmitted through the channel, and at the receiver end, the signals are split and directed to their respective destinations.

Parallel EDFA

In a parallel configuration, multiple EDFAs operate simultaneously and independently. As shown in Figure 22.2, digital input signals are converted to optical signals by a Gaussian optical pulse generator. The optical pulses are split by a power splitter, which acts as the transmitter. Each split signal is then amplified by a parallel arrangement of EDFAs.

The amplified signals are subsequently combined using a power combiner at the receiver end and directed to an avalanche photodiode or optical receiver, which processes the signals and sends them to the destination.

This paper is organized into five sections. In section 2 presents the background and 3 presents the proposed works. Section 4 presents the

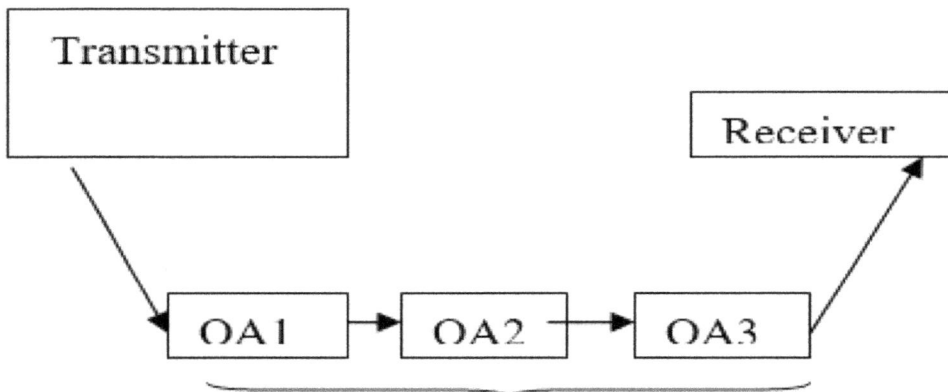

Figure 22.1 Block diagram of series combination in optical amplifiers (S-EDFA) (OA-optical amplifier)
Source: Author

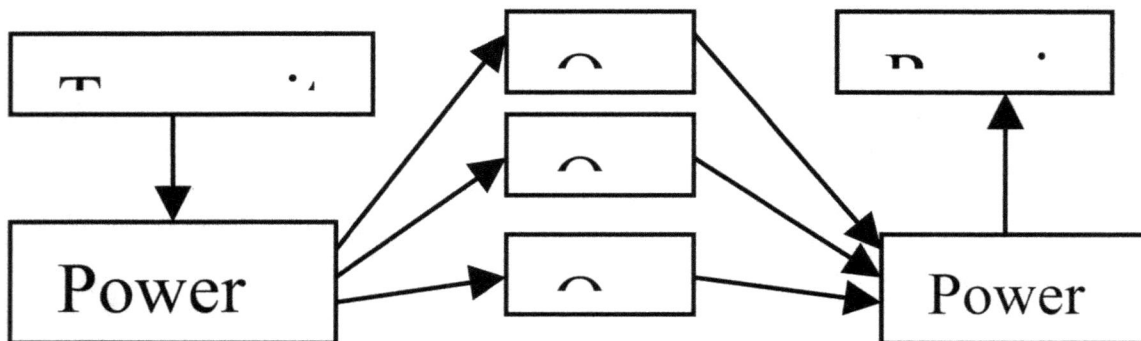

Figure 22.2 Block diagram of parallel combination in optical amplifiers (P-EDFA)
Source: Author

Results and Discussions. Finally, the paper concluded in section 5.

Background

Numerous studies have explored various aspects of EDFAs to enhance their performance in optical communication systems. One study simulated the gain of EDFAs and analyzed the noise power using the signal-to-noise ratio (SNR) equation [6]. Another study implemented a gain shifting enhancement technique within a wavelength division multiplexing (WDM) model to improve EDFA performance [7]. Additionally, research improved the noise figure of EDFAs operating at 1480 nm by employing a power monitoring method, which achieved stable power channel control [8]. The effects of deep EDFA saturation gain were examined by investigating high pump-to-signal modulation indices [9]. Furthermore, enhancements were achieved by connecting four stages with varying pump power to increase gain [10]. A comparative study measured quality factor (QF), bit error rate (BER), and power output using different pulse types to evaluate EDFA performance [11]. The use of input-output links and equalizer links was discussed to reduce data rates and bandwidth requirements [12]. Another paper addressed gain degradation issues in EDFAs by utilizing adjustable pumping powers [13]. Lastly, research compared power consumption in EDFAs with shorter spans to that in Raman amplifiers with longer spans, incorporating integrated electronics to optimize performance [14].

Proposed Work

This work investigates the performance of cascaded EDFAs using series, parallel, and series-parallel configurations to determine the most effective optical communication link for high signal strength, privacy, and broadband services. The study evaluates these configurations by analyzing key parameters such as gain, noise figure, power output, and quality factor, considering variations in input power, fiber length, and pump power. This approach aims to identify the optimal configuration for enhancing optical communication systems in terms of performance and reliability.

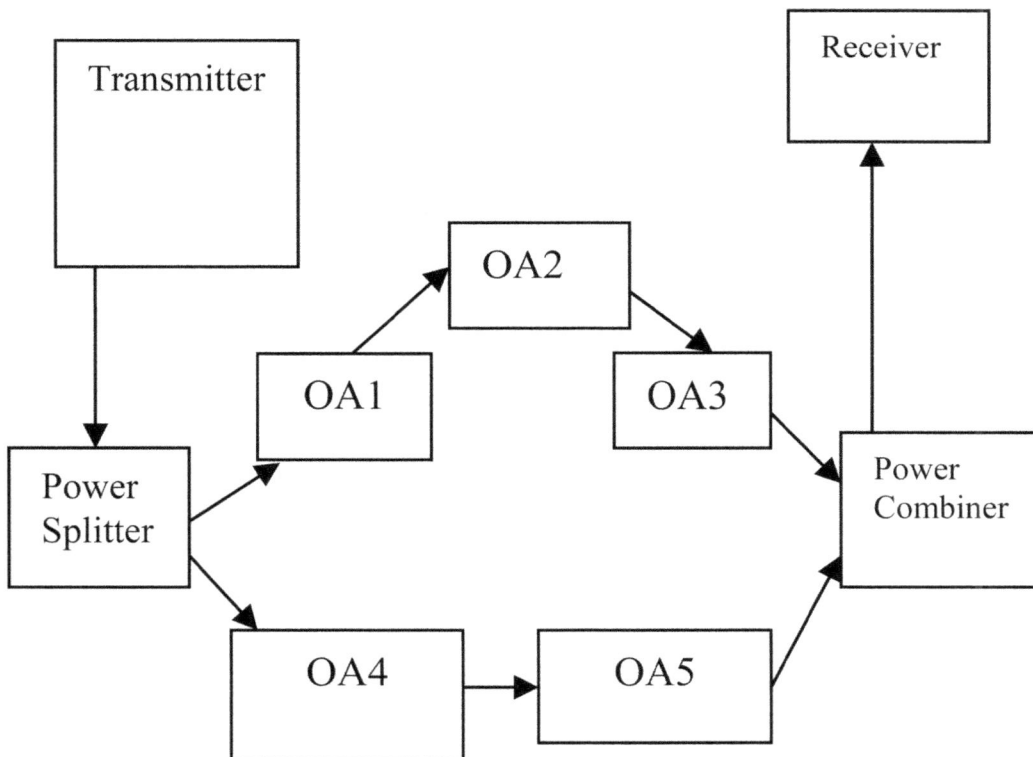

Figure 22.3 Triple series and parallel optical amplifiers
Source: Author

The series-parallel EDFA identified the best performance by analyzing the parameters like gain, noise figure, power output, quality factor with respect to power input, fiber length and pump power variations. This analysis was made by connecting the EDFA combined by series and parallel and series-parallel cascading methods that have been experimented and measured the output values by variation of the input power 0dBm, 5dBm and 10dmB, and the Fiber length variation from 20m, 100km and 200km and also the pump power variation from 200mw to 400mw. The output values noted from the experimental model and manipulated compared the results plotted by the line charts.

The proposed triple series-parallel EDFA (TSP-EDFA) configuration aims to optimize the performance of optical communication links between the transmitter and receiver. As illustrated in Figure 22.3, the TSP-EDFA combines three stages of EDFAs connected in series, with each stage capable of parallel operation with two additional stages of EDFAs. Each EDFA stage utilizes single backward pumping at a wavelength of 980 nm, with pump power varying between 200 mW and 400 mW. This configuration is compared to a traditional series EDFA, which consists of two stages of EDFAs connected in series with two-stage pumping at 980 nm, and a Parallel EDFA method, which connects two stages of EDFAs in parallel. Figure 9.14 shows the Simulation model of Triple series Parallel EDFA.

In the TSP-EDFA setup shown in Figure 22.9. The transmitter output is connected to the proposed TSP-EDFA link, and the link output is connected to the receiver. The transmitter input comprises four channels generated by a digital sequence generator. Two of these digital outputs are connected to a Gaussian pulse generator, which produces two Gaussian optical pulses, while the remaining two outputs are connected to a sequential pulse generator, producing two sequential optical pulses. These four optical pulses are combined using an optical power combiner. The combined output is fed into three stages of series EDFA, which are connected in parallel with two additional stages of series EDFA. The three-stage configuration employs backward pumping, while the two-stage configuration uses two-stage backward pumping to amplify the signal in the channel.

The output of the TSP-EDFA is then split by a power splitter into four channels, which are directed to an optical receiver or avalanche photodiode (APD) for detection and conversion back to the original form.

Results and Interpretation

The performance comparison of the proposed TSP-EDFA demonstrates enhanced results compared to Series EDFA (S-EDFA) and Parallel EDFA (P-EDFA). Table 22.1 presents the performance analysis of EDFAs based on variations in power input, measuring parameters such as gain, noise figure, power output, and quality factor (QF). The power input, determined by the optical pulse generator, varies between 0 dB, 5 dB, and 10 dB. As the power input increases, the output gain decreases. The maximum gain, lowest noise figure, and optimized power output are achieved with a power input of 0 dB. Table 22.2 shows the performance comparison of different EDFA configurations with fiber lengths of 20 m, 100 km, and 200 km. As the fiber length increases, the gain decreases, the noise increases, and the power output decreases. The maximum gain and optimized amplified power output are obtained with a fiber length of 20 m. Table 22.3 presents a performance comparison of different EDFA types with varying pump power. As the pump power increases from 200 mW to 400 mW, the optimized output is achieved with a pump power of 400 mW.

The performance of TSP-EDFA compared with EDFA series parallel with Raman amplifier using quad pumping and the dual port WDM analyzer output shown in Figures 22.10 and 22.11 respectively.

Also, the performance of TSP-EDFA compared with double series–parallel link using quad pumping and the input and output power measured from spectrum analyzer, the output of dual port WDM analyzer and receiver electrical power output shown in Figures 22.12, 22.13 and 22.14 respectively.

Figure 22.12 shows the double series-parallel EDFA with ytterbium using quad pumping technique simulated with 4 channels. From all the performances of series optical amplifier provided maximum gain, parallel EDFA provided

Table 22.1 Performance comparison with respect to power input variation

	Pi (dBm)	Gain (dB)	NF(dB)	Po (dBm)	QF
Series EDFA	0	32	3.71	26.7	3.35
	5	26.49	3.64	26.6	3.25
	10	21.75	4.52	26.8	3.32
Parallel EDFA	0	31.07	3.83	26.3	3.15
	5	27.2	4.15	23.7	3.41
	10	22.38	5.35	26.9	3.43
Single series-parallel link	0	35	0.66	31.25	3.3
	5	30.7	1.15	29.9	3.39
	10	25.83	2.45	29.93	3.38
Triple series-parallel EDFA	0	**36.1**	**3.79**	**30.64**	**3.37**
	5	31.32	3.83	30.75	3.26
	10	26.48	4.57	30.8	3.42

Source: Author

less noise, if both the combination used to give high gain and less noise in the communication systems.

In Tables 22.1, 22.2, and 22.3, the following abbreviations are used: Pi denotes input power, Po denotes output power, G denotes gain, NF denotes noise figure, L denotes EDFA length, and QF denotes quality factor.

The results include measurements from the transmitter output, channel output, and receiver output. The amplified power output is measured from the channel output, while gain and noise figure are assessed using a dual power analyzer connected between the power combiner output and the channel output. The quality factor is measured at the receiver output using a bit error rate (BER) analyzer.

Table 22.2 Performance comparison of cascaded EDFA types with variation of fiber length

	L(m)	Gain (dB)	NF (dB)	Po (dBm)	QF
Series EDFA	20m	32	3.71	26.7	3.35
	100km	28.3	24.82	25.6	0
	200km	10.91	44	25.5	0
Parallel EDFA	20m	31.07	3.83	26.3	3.15
	100km	26.03	15.6	22.3	3.37
	200km	25.08	16.82	22.17	3.67
Single series-parallel link	20m	35	0.66	31.25	3.3
	100km	33.3	21	28.59	0
	200km	19.64	41	27.3	0
Triple series-parallel EDFA	20m	36.1	3.79	30.64	3.37
	100km	32.72	22.9	27.4	2.6
	200km	28.87	30.36	27.27	3.21

Source: Author

Table 22.3 Performance comparison with respect to pumping power variation

	PP (mw)	Po (dBm)	QF	Gain (dB)	NF(dB)
Series EDFA	200	23.7	3.35	29.02	4.14
	400	26.7	3.35	32	3.71
Parallel EDFA	200	23.37	3.18	28.3	4.09
	400	26.3	3.15	31.07	3.83
Single series-parallel link	200	26.78	3.38	32.53	1.12
	400	29.5	3.3	35	0.66
Triple series-parallel EDFA	200	27.59	3.369	33.1	4.04
	400	**30.64**	**3.37**	**36.1**	**3.79**

Source: Author

Figures 22.4 and 22.5 denotes Parameters comparison of S-EDFA, P-EDFA, SP-EDFA and TSP-EDFA with respect to power input variation. Figure 22.6 denotes Parameters comparison of TSP-EDFA with respect to power input variation.

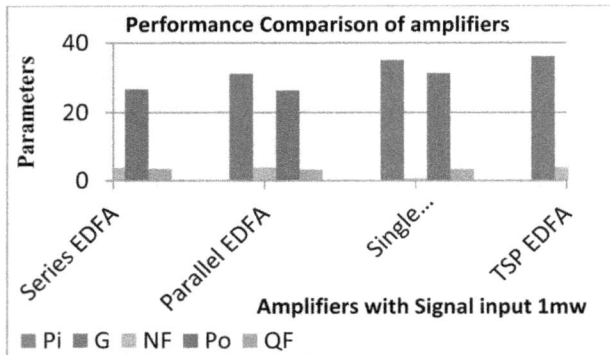

Figure 22.4 Power input (1mw) 0dBm performance comparison of various amplifiers
Source: Author

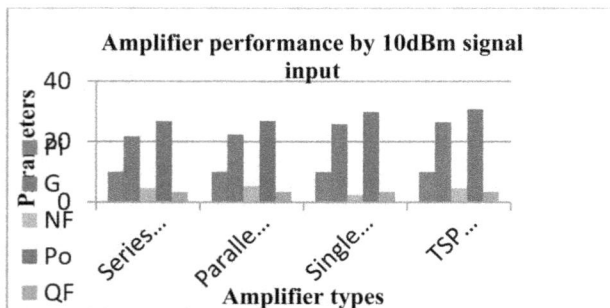

Figure 22.5 Signal input 10dBm performance comparison of various amplifiers
Source: Author

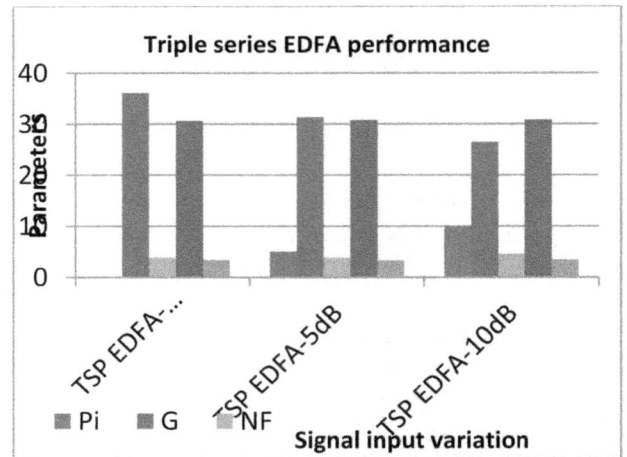

Figure 22.6 Different power input - performance comparison of TSP EDFA
Source: Author

Figures 22.7 and 22.8 denotes the comparison of parameters in different types of EDFA with pump power 200mw and 400mw respectively. Gain comparison of S-EDFA, P-EDFA and TSP-EDFA with respect to Pump power variation.).

Table 22.4 shows the comparison results of various double series parallel link and single series parallel link of optical amplifiers.

The results measured in Transmitter output, channel output and receiver output, the amplified power output measured from the channel output, Gain and noise figure measured using dual power analyzer connected between power combiner output and channel output. Quality factor measured at the receiver output is at the output of optical receiver using BER analyzer.

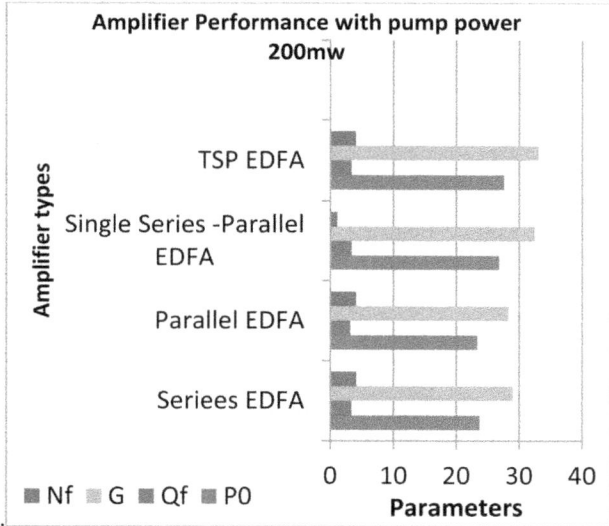

Figure 22.7 Comparison of parameters in different types of EDFA with pump power (200 mw)
Source: Author

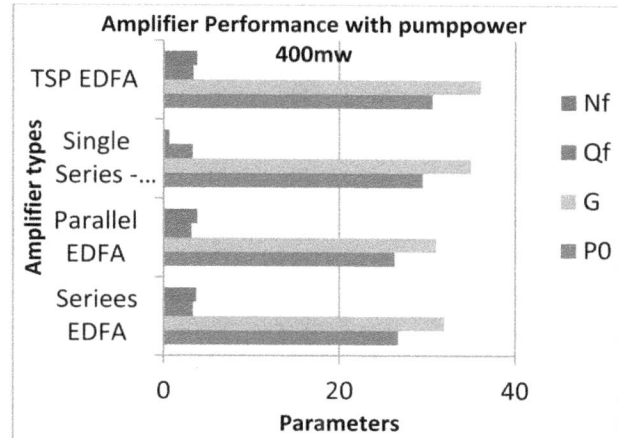

Figure 22.8 Comparison of parameters in different types of EDFA with pump power (400 mw)
Source: Author

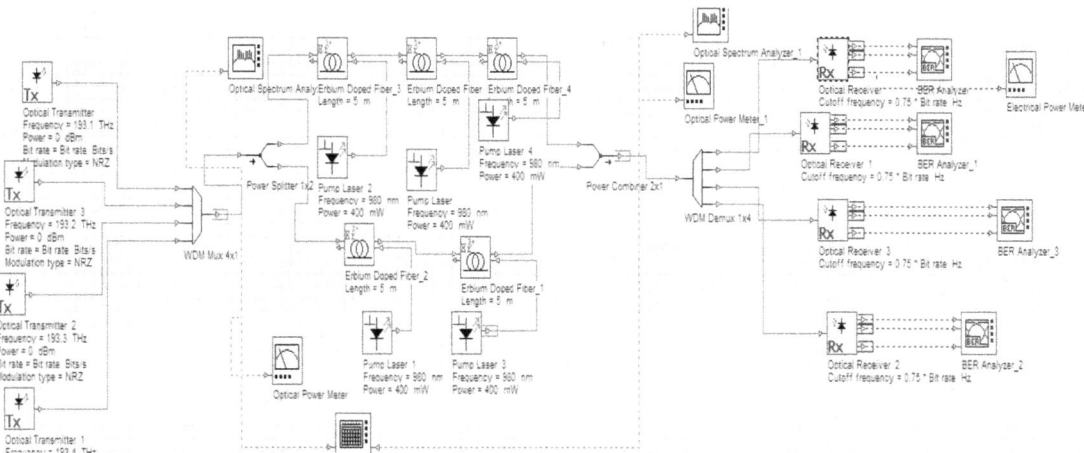

Figure 22.9 Simulation of three stages of EDFA cascaded in parallel with two stages of EDFA in series using quad pumping technique
Source: Author

Conclusion

This study provides a comprehensive analysis of various cascading configurations of Erbium-Doped Fiber Amplifiers (EDFAs), specifically series EDFA (S-EDFA), parallel EDFA (P-EDFA), and triple series-parallel EDFA (TSP-EDFA). The parameters evaluated include gain, noise figure, amplified power output, and quality factor, with results meticulously tabulated, analyzed, and presented through bar charts. Among the configurations examined, the TSP-EDFA demonstrated the most optimized performance. Specifically, with a power input of 0 dB, a pump power of 400 mW across five pumping stages, and a fiber length of 20 m, the TSP-EDFA achieved an exceptional gain of 36.1 dB, a low noise figure of 3.79 dB, and an optimal power output of 30.64 dB. These results highlight the superior efficacy of the TSP-EDFA configuration in delivering high-strength optical communication links.

Table 22.4 Comparison of Double series and single series link

S.No.					Ni=8.3DBm, Pi= -4.9DBm			
Type of Link	Double Series – Parallel Link				Single Series-Parallel Link			
Amplifiers used	EY-ED Parallel EY-ED	ED-ED Parallel ED-ED	EY-ED Parallel YD-ED	EY-ED Parallel RA-ED	ED - ED llel ED ED	ED – ED llel ED –EY	ED – ED llel ED-YD	ED – ED llel ED -RA
Gain(dB)	32.88	34.86	32.1	31.89	35.55	35.14	33.93	33.51
Noise Figure(dB)	4.3	3.76	4.44	5.36	0.66	0.69	1.06	1.33
No(dBm)	-21.73	-37.5	-24.9	-24.92	-37.6	-35.7	-39.42	-39.48
QF	69.74	3.34	3.21	3.305	3.3	3.4	3.42	3.41
OSNR(dB)	4.78E+001	4.28e+001	4.12e+001	4.12e+001	4.59e+001	4.59e+001	4.55e+001	4.52e+001

Source: Author

The enhanced performance of the TSP-EDFA is attributed to its robust cascading design, which effectively maximizes signal amplification while minimizing noise. The integration of a Gaussian pulse generator in the transmitter further contributes to high privacy and signal integrity. This cascading model proves to be highly effective for telecommunication applications, ensuring minimal noise and robust performance in optical communication systems.

Future research direction
Further investigations could explore several areas to enhance the understanding and performance of cascadedEDFA. One promising direction is the optimization of theTSP-EDFA configuration under varying environmental conditions, such as temperature fluctuations and mechanical stresses, to assess its robustness in real-world deployments.Another area for future research is the exploration of hybrid amplifier systems that combine EDFA with Raman or Semiconductor Optical Amplifiers (SOA) to improve gain flatness and reduce noise figures across a broader wavelength range. This could be particularly beneficial for next-generation optical networks that demand high capacity and low latency.

Additionally, investigating the impact of advanced modulation formats and high-speed data rates on the performance of TSP-EDFA configurations could provide valuable insights.

As modern optical networks increasingly adopt complex modulation schemes, understanding the interaction between these schemes and EDFA performance will be critical for optimizing network efficiency and reliability.

Finally, the integration of machine learning techniques for real-time performance monitoring and adaptive control of EDFA parameters could be a fruitful area of study. Such approaches could lead to more intelligent and self-optimizing optical networks, capable of maintaining optimal performance despite varying operational conditions.

References

[1] Kim, J. S., and Lee, S. H. (2011). Performance evaluation of cascaded erbium-doped fiber amplifiers. *Journal of Optical Communications and Networking*, 3(5), 369–376.
[2] Moulin, C., and Boudot, R. (2012). Series and parallel cascaded EDFAs: comparison of performance. *IEEE Photonics Technology Letters*, 24(8), 665–667.
[3] Kang, S. K., Kim, H. J., and Choi, J. J. (2014). Noise characteristics of parallel EDFA configurations. *Optical Fiber Technology*, 20(2), 171–175.
[4] Hsu, C. K., Wu, T. C., and Lin, C. H. (2018). Series-parallel EDFA configuration for high-performance optical communication. *Journal of Lightwave Technology*, 36(24), 5725–5732.
[5] Zhang, Y., Liu, X., and Wang, J. (2020). Enhanced performance of triple series-paral-

lel cascaded EDFA. *Optics Express*, 28(15), 21912–21925.

[6] Tucker, R. S., and Tan, M. S. B. L. (2004). Optical amplifiers: principles and applications. *IEEE Journal of Selected Topics in Quantum Electronics*, 10(5), 1016–1026.

[7] Hill, C. J. (2001). Performance of series and parallel cascaded EDFAs. *Journal of Lightwave Technology*, 19(3), 369–374.

[8] Prasad, M. D. M. L., and Kim, K. H. (2004). Analysis of parallel EDFA configurations for high-speed optical communication. *IEEE Photonics Technology Letters*, 16(8), 1864–1866.

[9] Zhang, J., Liu, Y., and Wang, X. (2015). Effects of high pump-to-signal modulation index on EDFA saturation gain. *Optics Express*, 23(12), 15236–15245.

[10] Li, X., Zhang, H., and Zhao, L. (2018). Four-stage EDFA with pump power variation. *IEEE Photonics Technology Letters*, 30(5), 415–418.

[11] Kim, J. S., and Lee, H. J. (2017). Pulse type comparison for EDFA performance: QF, BER, and power output measurements. *IEEE Photonics Technology Letters*, 29(10), 841–844.

[12] Choi, S. H., Kim, Y. K., and Lee, J. W. (2019). Data rate reduction and bandwidth optimization using EDFA input-output links. *Journal of Optical Communications and Networking*, 11(4), 211–219.

[13] C. Liu, T. Li, and Q. Liu, "Adjustable Pumping Powers for EDFA Gain Stabilization" *Opt. Fiber Technol.*, vol.46, pp.53–58, Jan.2019.

[14] R. J. Miller and S. C. R. Park, " Power Consumption in Short vs. Long Span EDFAs and Raman Amplifiers, *IEEE J. Quantum Electron.*, vol.56, no.8, pp.940–948, Aug. 2020.

23 Design and implementation of 4-2 approximate compressor for FPGA

Mahesh Babu Kota[1,a], Raja Suresh[2,b], P. Srinivasulu[2,c] and D. Srinivasulu[3,d]

[1]Associate Professor, Dept. of ECE, Sri Venkateswara College of Engineering, Tirupati, Andhra Pradesh, India

[2]Assistant Professor, Dept. of ECE, Sri Venkateswara College of Engineering, Tirupati, Andhra Pradesh, India

[3]Professor, Dept. of ECE, Sri Venkateswara College of Engineering, Tirupati, Andhra Pradesh, India

Abstract

In this paper, we propose that an important technological edge for the future is energy-efficient computing. A computing paradigm known as approximate or inexact computing might exchange processing power and processing time for output accuracy. The approximate Two approximation compressors with reduced area, delay, and power are designed and analyzed. are proposed in this project. The 8x8 and 16x16 Dadda multipliers are implemented using the suggested compressors. Comparing these multipliers to the most advanced approximation multipliers reveals that they have a good accuracy. The suggested method's efficiency is calculated using the XilinxISE14.7/Xilinx Vivado software.

Keywords: 4:2 compressors, approximate computing, error resilient, multiplier. Approximate computing, 4:2 compressors, multiplier, error resilient

Introduction

Excellent performance and efficient execution can be achieved by utilizing processor's compute units by incorporating approximation. Due to the inverse relationship between system latency and operating speed, large-scale parallel operations requiring substantial hardware and power consumption are required. It is possible to increase the space and energy efficiency of systems that have lower accuracy and reliability. Approximation computing may be a viable strategy to maintain the harmony between latency, area, and power. Accuracy would suffer with approximation arithmetic operations as a trade-off for faster computers with less complex architecture and power consumption. Multimedia and machine learning programs may still function normally even in the event of this issue. the human eye's inability to discern between tinier elements. This degree of tolerance is included into approximate circuits for use in DSP and AI applications. We have designed low power and low latency 4:2 approximate compressors using logic level approximation. A reconfigurable design is proposed for a compressor with a ratio of about 4:2. the reconfigurability location, which is attained by switching between approximate and exact procedures as needed.

Preliminaries and Review

Ha and Lee [5] outlined a 4:2 guess compressor with a blunder recuperation component to lower the compressor's mistake profile. The n^2 columns are evacuated as a result of the increase operation. Compressors are connected to the remaining columns. The authors' top-down engineering for an approximate multiplier powerfully disperses assets among the inexact compressors at 8:2, 6:2, and 4:2 based on the halfway item check. In expansion, the assembled blunder recuperation strategy to progress the precision of the multiplier. Alouani et al. [2] have portrayed an estimation adder-based heterogeneous inexact multiplier with lower cruel mistake deviation

[a]maheshbabu.klu2414@gmail.com, [b]gupthasuresh123@gmail.com, [c]cnuskit@gmail.com, [d]cnudega@gmail.com

DOI: 10.1201/9781003616399-23

(MED) and have portrayed an adder-based heterogeneous surmised multiplier with lower cruel blunder deviation (MED). This is finished by utilizing the approximation adders based on hereditary calculations [1–6]. A 4:2 compressor to boost effectiveness with a 25% mistake rate. In arrange to spare control and delay, 4:2 and 5:2 compressors are prescribed and made a ground-breaking plan for 4:2 compressors with a 12.5% blunder rate [7-10]. The confinements on zone, delay, and control are loose in arrange to accomplish this. Since utilizing transmission entryways altogether diminishes idleness in comparison to conventional CMOS-based rationale, optimized plan utilizing transmission entryways is examined in the writing. The essential impediment, in any case, is the change over the crests and troughs for different inputs.

Approximate Multipliers

Approximate multipliers are often used in energy-efficient computer applications that automatically accept errors. Accuracy is the most crucial design component for any multiplier. It is difficult to determine the precise approximation of the multiplier circuit in arithmetic operations. Multiplication is a crucial performance component in DSP and AI applications. They take advantage of multipliers' approximations to do rapid computations with the least amount of hardware complexity, time, and power. by having

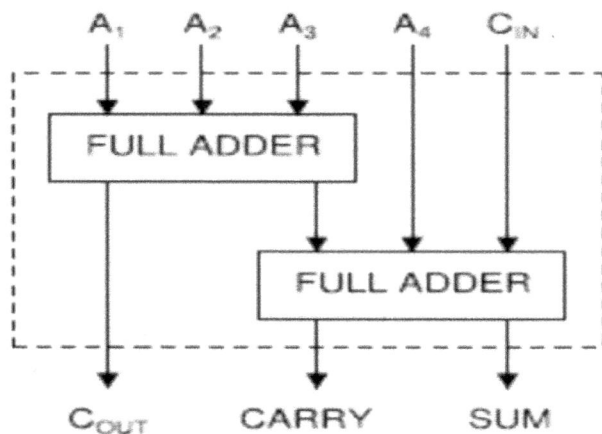

Figure 23.1 Existing system diagram
Source: Author

a specific level of accuracy. Compressors calculate the carry and total simultaneously. In the following phase, the carry is then integrated into the more important bit. This process continues till the final product is created. It is possible for the outcomes of the approximate multipliers to closely resemble those of the precise multipliers.

Existing System

The current framework employments increase, where the handle that confines duplication speed is halfway item summation due to the proliferation delay in viper systems. In arrange to diminish engendering idleness, compressors are utilized. Compressors concurrently compute the carry and add up to at each level. After that, a bigger whole bit is joined to the coming about carry. This proceeds to happen. till the last result is made. Figure 23.1 outlines its three yields, five inputs, and two cascaded total adders.

Disadvantages
Full adder-based compressor plan will result in expanded range and control with a huge delay.

Proposed System

Approximate 4:2 compressor architecture
The anticipated area-efficient, high-speed, precise 4:2 compressor utilized in the recommended framework is depicted in Figure 23.2 underneath. The compressor has two inputs (A1, A2, A3, and A4) and two yields (CARRY and Entirety). Multiplexers (MUX) serve as the establishment for the plan prepare that produces whole. The XOR gate's yield is associated to the MUX's choose line. When the select line is tall, (A3A4) is chosen; when it is moo, (A3 C A4) is chosen. by counting a blunder of greatness 1.

Let p speak to the probability of a mistake happening at the compressor's yield. Subsequently, 1p speaks to the probability that the result will be exact. Decreasing botches in the multiple cascaded compressors organize in multipliers can diminish the likelihood tree. Accepting that the inputs at Stages 1 and 2 compared to a combination that yields substantial results, the yield of organize 2 will show ED = 0 and a likelihood of (1p) 2. With a likelihood of p (1 - p), the yield of arrange 2 will show ED = 1 if the input for either organize 1 or arrange 2 is inaccurate. Furthermore, if the inputs to Stages 1 and 2 are both off base, an ED of 2 with a likelihood of p 2 is delivered. Condition speaks to the chance of getting the right reply at step n in an increase method with n steps of fractional item summing [6].

$$P \text{ (correct) } n = (1 - p) \text{ } n \qquad \text{-------- (1)}$$

P (error) n is the likelihood that the nth stage's yield will be wrong. It is the add up to of all the other probabilities included together. In cases where ED is more than 1 [8–10].

$$P \text{ (error) } n = P \text{ (ED = 1) } + P \text{ (ED = 2) } + \cdot \text{ } + P \text{ (ED = n)} \qquad \text{--------------------- (2)}$$

The sum of the probabilities for each scenario is the likelihood (P(error)2) that the output from the second stage (Figure 23.4) will be wrong. where $1 \le ED \le 2$.

$$P \text{ (error) } 2 = P \text{ (ED = 1) } + P \text{ (ED = 2)}$$

$$P(\text{error})2 = 2(1 - p) \text{ } p + p \text{ } 2 \text{ .... (3)}$$

The proposed 4:2 compressor can decrease carry era rationale to a single OR entryway in truth Table 23.1 of the correct compressor. Here are the coherent expressions required to realize SUM and CARRY. Figure 23.2 depicts the proposed high-speed, roughly 4:2 area-efficient compressor. A Whole is built utilizing the multiplexer plan strategy (MUX). The yield of the XOR door is the line that the MUX chosen. (A3.A4) is

Table 23.1 Proposed compressor truth table

$A_1 A_2 A_3 A_4$	CAARY	SUM	ED
0 0 0 0	0	0	0
0 0 0 1	0	1	0
0 0 1 0	0	1	0
0 0 1 1	0	1	-1
0 1 0 0	1	0	+1
0 1 0 1	1	0	0
0 1 1 0	1	0	0
0 1 1 1	1	1	0
1 0 0 0	1	0	+1
1 0 0 1	1	0	0
1 0 1 0	1	0	0
1 0 1 1	1	1	0
1 1 0 0	1	0	0
1 1 0 1	1	1	0
1 1 1 0	1	1	0
1 1 1 1	1	1	-1

Source: Author

chosen when the chosen line is tall; (A3 + A4) is chosen when the chosen line is moo. By including a mistake with an esteem of 1 to the correct truth table of the compressor, it gets to be less demanding to exchange the rationale to an OR door when utilizing the suggested 4:2 compressors. Underneath is a list of the entirety and carry consistent equations.

In order to get a rise to positive and negative deviation with a least mistake deviation (ED) of 1, blunders have been included for the input values {0011}, {0100}, {1000}, and {1111}, concurring to the truth table of the recommended 4:2 compressor.

Simulation Results

The simulation results of the existing and the proposed models are depicted in Figure 23.3-23.8. The timing diagrams of existing and proposed models are shown in Figure 23.3 and 23.6. The schematics and attributes of both the models are shown in 23.4, 23.5, 23.7 and 23.8 respectively.

Table 23.2 provides the comparision between the existing and proposed models for various

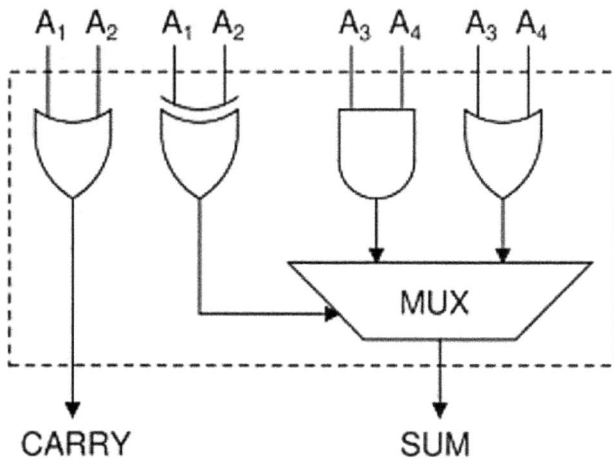

Figure 23.2 Proposed area efficient 4:2 compressor
Source: Author

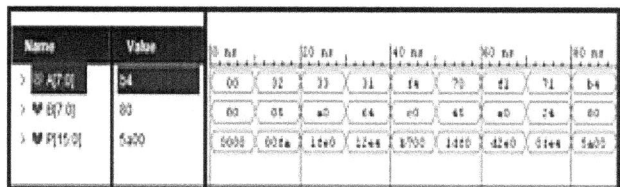

Figure 23.3 Existing system output
Source: Author

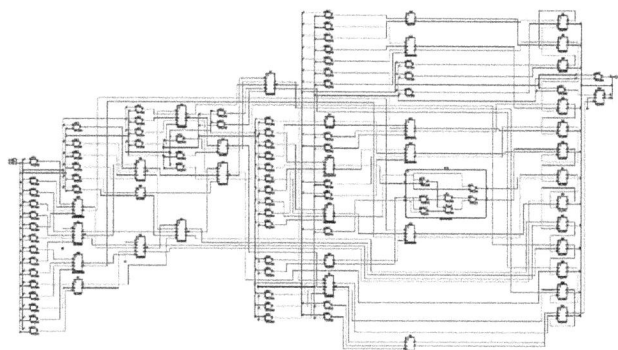

Figure 23.4 Existing system schematic
Source: Author

Figure 23.5 Existing system attributes
Source: Author

Figure 23.6 Proposed system output
Source: Author

Figure 23.7 Proposed system schematic
Source: Author

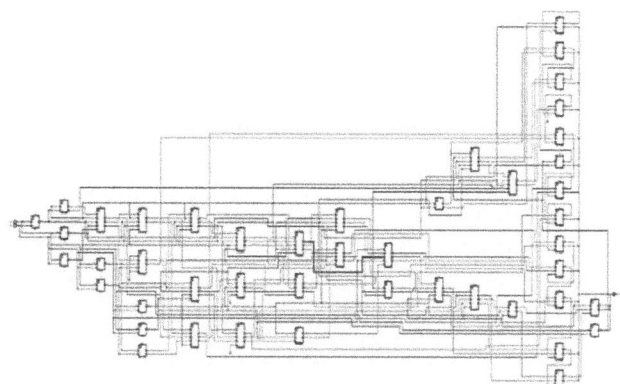

Figure 23.8 Proposed system attributes
Source: Author

Table 23.2 Parameter comparison

Parameter	Existing multiplier	Approximate multiplier
Gain	313.733	325.824
Power (W)	0.736	0.533
Area (LUTs)	75	67
Delay (ns)	10.5	8.3
Accuracy (%)	98.5	96.2

Source: Author

parameters like gain, power, area, delay and accuracy.

Conclusion

In order to offer effective approximation multipliers, this paper addresses the modification of PPs of the multiplier using produce and propagate

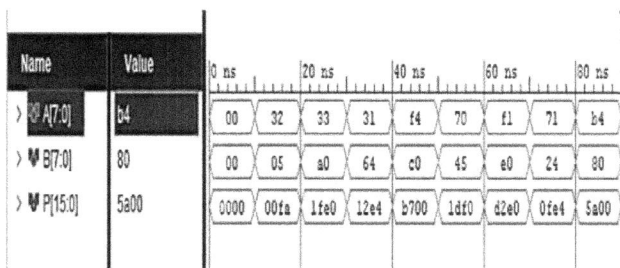

signals. An approximate method for modified create partial products is to utilize a basic OR gate. Compared with correct designs, approximation multipliers result in a significant reduction in complexity. Approximate multipliers not only outperform precise multipliers in terms of delay savings, but they also perform better in terms of delay than previous approximate versions. Using an altered multistage 4:2 compressor will make it easier for this work to advance in the future technologies.

References

[1] Raveendran, S., Rahulkar, A. D., and Edavoor, P. J. (2020). Approximate multiplier design using novel dual-stage 4: 2 compressors. *IEEE Access*, 8, 48337–48351.

[2] Baran, D., Aktan, M., and Oklobdzija, V. G. (2011). Multiplier structures for low power applications in deep CMOS. In International Symposium on Circuits and Systems (ISCAS 2011), (pp. 1061–1064).

[3] Mittal, S. (2016). A survey of techniques for approximate computing. *ACM Computing Surveys (CSUR)*, 48(4), 1–33.

[4] Zendegani, R., Kamal, M., Bahadori, M., Afzali-Kusha, A., and Pedram, M. (2013). New metrics for the reliability of approximate and probabilistic adders. *IEEE Transactions on Computers*, 62(9), 1760–1771.

[5] Jiang, H., Liu, C., Liu, L., Lombardi, F., and Han, J. (1997). A review classification and compara-tive evaluation of approximate arithmetic circuits. *ACM Journal on Emerging Technologies in Computing Systems (JETC)*, 13(4), 1–34.

[6] Kamal, M., Bahadori, M., Afzali-Kusha, A., and Pedram, M. (2017). RoBA multiplier: a rounding based approximate multiplier for high-speed yet energy-efficient digital signal processing. *IEEE Transactions on Very Large-Scale Integration (VLSI) Systems*, 25(2), 393–401.

[7] Jiang, H., Han, J., Qiao, F., and Lombardi, F. (2016). Approximate radix-8 booth multipliers for low-power and high-performance operation. *IEEE Transactions on Computers*, 65(8), 2638–2644.

[8] Ghosh, S., Mohapatra, D., Karakonstantis, G., and Roy, K. (2010). Voltage scalable high-speed robust hybrid arithmetic units utilizing adaptive clocking. *IEEE Transactions on Very Large-Scale Integration (VLSI) Systems*, 18(9), 1301–1309.

[9] Narayanamoorthy, S., Moghaddam, H. A., Liu, Z., Park, T., and Kim, N. S. (2015). Energy-efficient approximate multiplication for digital signal processing and classification applications. *IEEE Transactions on Very Large-Scale Integration (VLSI) Systems*, 23(6), 1180–1184.

[10] Zervakis, G., Xydis, S., Tsoumanis, K., Soudris, D., and Pekmestzi, K. (2015). Hybrid approximate multiplier architectures for enhanced power-accuracy trade-offs. In Proceedings IEEE/ACM International Symposium Low Power Electronic Des. (ISLPED), (pp. 79–84).

24 MRFIR: Area and power efficient modified reconfigurable FIR filter

Addanki Lakshmi Praharsha[1,a], Shaik Mohammad Irfan[1,b], Koppolu Srinivas[1,c], Gundugonti Kishore Kumar[2,d] and Chinnapurapu Naga Raghuram[2,e]

[1]Student, Dept. of ECE, Velagapudi Ramakrishna Siddhartha Engineering College, deemed to be University, India

[2]Assistant Professor, Dept. of ECE, Velagapudi Ramakrishna Siddhartha Engineering College, deemed to be University, India

Abstract

FIR filters hold a prominent role in digital signal processing (DSP). The FIR filter consists of numerous arithmetic operations like additions and multiplications. As multipliers consume substantial power and area, this paper proposes a modified multiplier that consumes less power and area. Using this modified multiplier, a novel FIR filter is proposed, which consumes less area and power compared to state-of-the-art works. The proposed FIR filter is implemented using Verilog HDL and synthesized with the Cadence Genus synthesis tool using 90nm technology. The proposed FIR filter achieves a 10.26% reduction in power for a 32-tap filter and a 16.99% reduction for a 64-tap filter. Additionally, it achieves a 7.96% reduction in area for a 32-tap filter and a 9.89% reduction for a 64-tap filter when compared to recently published research.

Keywords: Digital signal processing , error compensation block, FIR filters, modified product generation block, multipliers, redundant operation

Introduction

FIR filters are extensively utilized within a digital signal processing, communications, audio and image processing due to their stability and linear phase response. FIR filters consume a significant amount of power and resources. Shift-add operations can be used to efficiently implement FIR filters without multipliers when coefficients are fixed [9]. However, multiplier less approaches cannot be directly used in instances where filter coefficients need to be reconfigurable.

Over the past decades, numerous efforts have been dedicated to designing reconfigurable FIR (RFIR) filter implementations. One approach involves modifying the nonzero digits in the coefficient's canonical signed-digit (CSD) representations [7] are used to change the impulse responses of the filter. However, complexity considerations limit the number of allowable nonzero bits in CSD representations, which limits the filter's reconfigurability [15].

Another method is distributed arithmetic (DA), which uses LUTs to perform the inner product operation. This allows us to change the filter's coefficients by modifying the previously calculated results stored in the LUTs [4, 10, 11, 13]. DA-based methods work well for filters with fixed coefficients and for low-order RFIR filters because the LUT-based calculations are simple and efficient. However, as the filter order increases, the size of the LUTs increases significantly, which can take up more space and make it harder to update the coefficients. Even though register-MUX-based LUT methods decrease ROM memory usage, their efficiency declines for high-order RFIR filters [12]. Furthermore, LUT designs according to the input data $x[n]$ can create challenges in practical applications that require real-time LUT updates. Another

[a]lakshmipraharsha.addanki1@gmail.com, [b]skirfan7948@gmail.com, [c]koppolusrinivas44@gmail.com, [d]gkishorekumar@vrsiddhartha.ac.in, [e]chnraghuram@vrsiddhartha.ac.in

DOI: 10.1201/9781003616399-24

well-known method for designing fully reconfigurable FIR filters is the multiplexer-based computation sharing technique [2]. This approach employs a single shared previously calculated block with multiple multiplexers and shift-and-add blocks to perform the necessary multiplications [1, 6]. It has been demonstrated that this computation sharing method is more effective in related to timing as well as energy comparison to multiplier-based designs. Moreover, the approach can be improved by incorporating sharing a common sub-expression to reduce the amount of additions and multiplexers required.

In existing work [17], the Product Generation (PG) block uses XOR operations for signed data. Due to these signed operations in the FIR filter, an error compensation block is required as shown in Figure 24.1. By eliminating these redundant operations, the proposed work achieves lower area and power usage in contrast to the current work [17]. Thus, the XOR operations and the error compensation block are considered redundant and have been removed in our work.

The work in Modified Reconfigurable FIR Filter the following is how the paper is presented:

Section II offers the Literature Survey. The methodology for the Modified Reconfigurable FIR Filter is discussed in Section III. Section IV presents the results and comparisons with existing works. This paper concludes with Section V, which summarizes the conclusions on the Modified Reconfigurable FIR Filter.

Literature Survey

The reconfigurability and minimal complexity are essential criteria for FIR filters utilized in multifaceted wireless communication systems. Reconfigurable frameworks with low complexity for FIR filters have been suggested, including both the programmed shifts approach and the constant shifts method. These approaches offer versatile, compact, and energy-efficient solutions for FIR filters, accommodating a broad spectrum of accuracy and tap size requirements [3, 8]. DA-based implementation strategies are customized for adaptive FIR filters, employing an innovative approach for sharing LUTs to compute filter output efficiently, reducing the quantity of adders essential. In the realm of reconfigurable FIR filters, sharing common operations has proven to be an especially effective method. Studies have shown that by reusing common sub-expressions and reducing the number of distinct operations, without compromising the filter's functionality, considerable power reductions are possible. Reconfigurability of FIR filters are improved by this technology, which also increases energy efficiency.

Methodology

For an FIR filter of N-tap the input-output relation is expressed as:

$$y[n] = \sum_{k=0}^{N-1} h_k x[n-k]$$

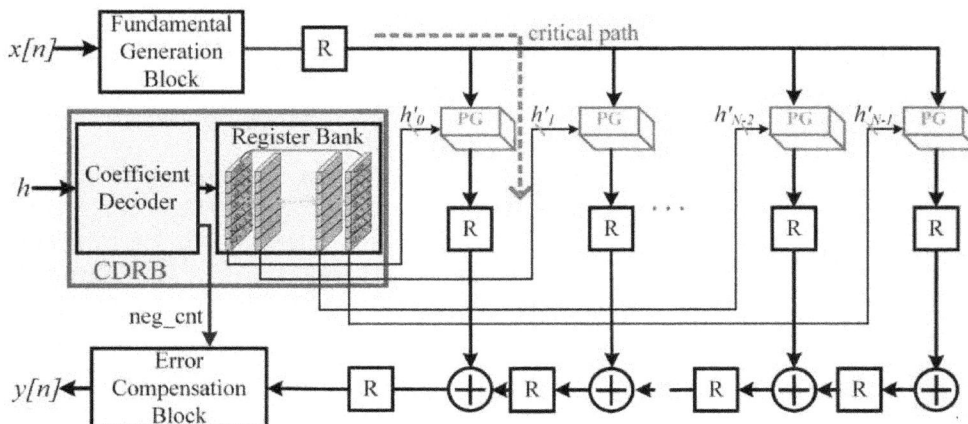

Figure 24.1 An outline of structure of the RFIR filter. CERB: Coefficient decoder and register bank [17]
Source: Author

where h_k is the kth coefficient of filter and x [n - k] shows an input version that has been tap-delayed. and y[n] refers to the output.

Figure 24.2 demonstrates the overall architecture of the Modified Reconfigurable Filter. Figure 24.3 describes the representation of the Fundamental Generation (FG) block. Figure 24.4 provides an instance of the Coefficient Decoder (CD) and decoded signals. Figure 24.5 demonstrates the Product Generation (PG) block. The detailed specifications are explained as follows:

Overview of architecture

Figure 24.2 shows the all in all configuration of the suggested MRFIR filter. The incoming data $x[n]$ passes through the fundamental generation block to produce a range of values (1x, 3x, 5x, 7x, 9x, 11x, 13x, 15x), which are then fed to the PG block. The coefficient decoder receives the coefficient h_k and produces the selection, sign, shift, and nzero signals. The corresponding description of the sub-blocks is provided as follows:

Fundamental generation block

Figure 24.3 illustrates how a set of precomputed fundamentals is generated.

The precomputed values for the input $x[n]$ are 1x, 3x, 5x, 7x, 9x, 11x, 13x, and 15x are generated and they are shared with the PG block. The precomputed values are generated using shift-add operations Without using multipliers in order to decrease the complexity in FIR filters.

Coefficient decoder for 4 bits

We suggest utilizing a shared coefficient decoder for all the taps in this configuration rather than a separate one for each tap. Figure 24.4(a) illustrates the composition of the coefficient decoder. Figure 24.4(b) shows each 4-bit sub-coefficient's decoded signals. This decoder takes an M-bit filter coefficient as input and outputs the sign bit, selection bits(sel), shift bits(sft) and nonzero bit(nze) for every 4 bits of the coefficient. The sel bits are utilized to determine the selection lines in the multiplexer and the output of the multiplexer based on the specified selection line. The sft bits describe the amount of bits that need to be shifted after the multiplexer operation. The nze bit is always 1 except for the 4-bit sub-coefficient 0000. For example, assume h = 45 (00101101 in binary). The least significant four bits (lsb) are 1101, and the most significant four bits (msb) are 0010. For the lsb, the decoded signals are sel = 110, sft = 00, and nze = 1. For the msb, the decoded signals are sel = 000, sft = 01, and nze = 1.

Product generation block

The Product Generation Block is employed to execute the multiplications for each 4-bit coefficient simultaneously by selecting the appropriate base values (sel, sft, nze, sign) and performing the necessary shift operations. To illustrate the operation in the Product Generation Block, consider an example where h = 45 and X = 89. The

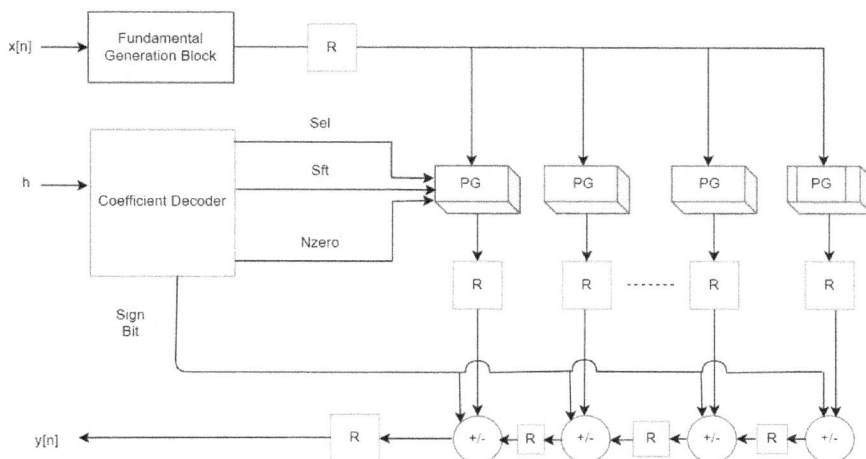

Figure 24.2 Architecture of proposed MRFIR filter
Source: Author

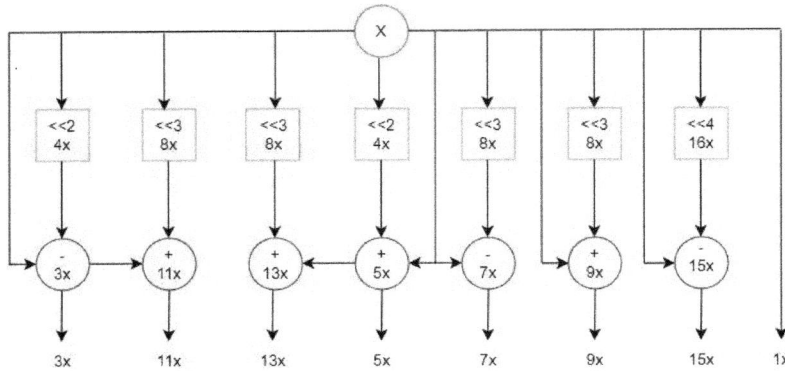

Figure 24.3 A schematic representation of fundamental generation block
Source: Author

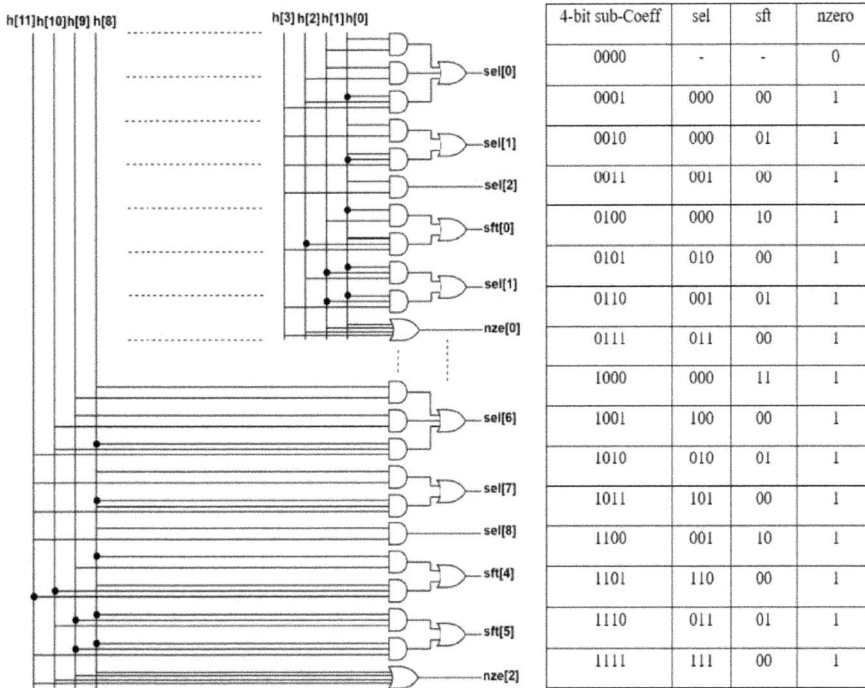

4-bit sub-Coeff	sel	sft	nzero
0000	-	-	0
0001	000	00	1
0010	000	01	1
0011	001	00	1
0100	000	10	1
0101	010	00	1
0110	001	01	1
0111	011	00	1
1000	000	11	1
1001	100	00	1
1010	010	01	1
1011	101	00	1
1100	001	10	1
1101	110	00	1
1110	011	01	1
1111	111	00	1

Figure 24.4 Coefficient decoder and 4-bit decoded signals
Source: Author

product of h and X is 4005 (45 * 89 = 4005). In the PG block, multiplication is performed using shift-add operators without using multipliers.

For h = 45 (00101101 in binary), the least significant bits (lsb) are 1101, and the most significant bits (msb) are 0010.

For the lsb, the decoded signals are sel = 110, sft = 00, and nze = 1. With sel = 110 (6 in decimal), the selection line picks Y13 (A1 = 13x = 1157 = 10010000101). Since sft = 00, A1 is left-shifted

by 0 bits (D1 = 10010000101) and then AND operation is performed with the nze bit (1 & D1 = 10010000101 = 1157 in decimal).

For the msb, the decoded signals are sel = 000, sft = 01, and nze = 1. With sel = 000 (0 in decimal), the selection line picks Y1 (A2 = 1x = 89 = 1011001). Since sft = 01 (1 in decimal), A2 is left-shifted by 1 bit (D2 = 10110010) and then AND operation is performed with the nze bit (1 & D2 = 10110010 = 178 in decimal).

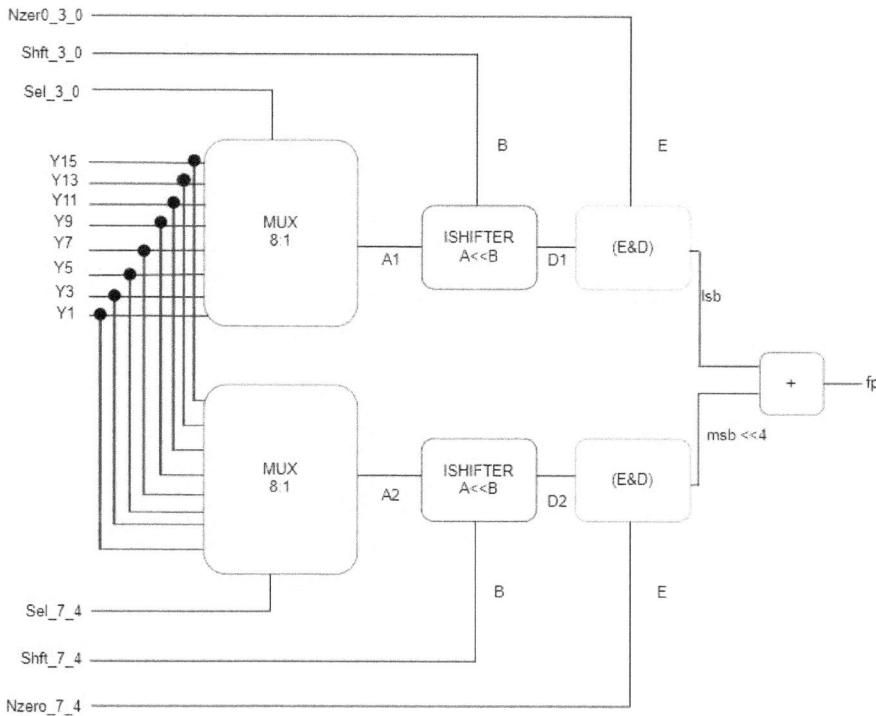

Figure 24.5 Configuration of the 9-bit coefficient product generating block
Source: Author

To obtain the final product, the msb is 4 bits left-shifted, and then included to the lsb (msb << 4 + lsb). Thus, the msb << 4 = 101100100000 (2848 in decimal) and lsb = 10010000101 (1157 in decimal). Adding msb << 4 and lsb using an adder results in the final product (fp = msb << 4 + lsb) of 4005.

D (ishifter output) = MUXout << B (sft_3_0)
(1)

fp (final product) = high4bits << 4 + low4bits
(2)

Results and Comparison

The evaluation and comparison findings presented in this section illustrate the effectiveness of the suggested design. The outcomes from implementing both the RFIR filter and the modified RFIR filter (MRFIR) reveal significant differences in performance metrics such as both area and power usage as shown in Table 24.1.

The introduction of MRFIR filter led to notable improvements, including a reduction in area,

which resulted in lower power consumption. This makes the MRFIR filter a more attractive option for applications requiring energy efficiency.

Theoretical comparison

The efficient design and optimization techniques employed in the MRFIR filter resulted in quicker response times compared to the RFIR filter. Verification using the Cadence Genus synthesis RTL compiler in 90nm technology. The comparison highlighted that the MRFIR filter not only met but also exceeded the RFIR filter's efficiency in terms of area and power as shown in Table 24.1. Overall, the MRFIR filter proved to be a superior choice, offering a compelling balance of reduced power consumption, minimized area, and improved speed.

ASIC comparison of FIR filters

This section evaluates the FIR filter's simulation results using various multipliers and compares them with the suggested filter, as demonstrated in Table 24.2. Comparing the area, power, and

Table 24.1 Comparison between the proposed MRFIR filter with other designs of programmable filter

Design	In	Tech (*nm*)	Coeff	Taps	Area (*nm²*)	Power (*μW*)	Delay (*ns*)	ADP (*mm²*ns*)	EPT (*pJ/tap*)	%ADP	%EPT
[16]	12	90	8	32	84.82	13.22	9.76	827	4.03	52.26	49.76
				64	149.91	26.76	9.83	1473	4.11	51.72	57.59
[11]	12	90	8	32	71.82	11.13	8.56	614	2.98	35.72	31.96
				64	123.65	21.93	9.68	1196	3.32	40.56	47.45
[5]	12	90	8	32	142.66	25.26	9.81	1399	7.74	71.76	73.84
				64	279.15	51.68	9.79	2732	7.91	73.97	77.95
[14]	12	90	8	32	125.32	21.36	8.98	1125	5.99	64.88	66.20
				64	217.33	45.43	9.41	2045	6.68	65.21	73.91
[17]	12	90	8	32	51.94	8.74	8.27	429	2.26	7.96	10.26
				64	95.91	16.33	8.23	789	2.10	9.89	16.99
MRFIR	12	90	8	32	47.62	7.81	8.30	395	2.03	-	-
				64	86.38	13.54	8.24	711	1.74		

Note: ADP (Area Delay Product) EPT (Energy per Tap)
Source: Author

delay results for coefficients of 32, and 64order filters provides insights into the performance of the FIR filter designed using the Cadence RTL compiler with a 90nm technology process. For the 32nd-order filter, there is a notable reduction in area (approximately 8.3%) and power (approximately 10.6%) compared to [17]. Similarly, for the 64th-order filter, there is a notable reduction in area (approximately 9.9%) and power (approximately 17.04%) compared to [17] as shown in Table 24.2. Redundancy refers to the inclusion of extra components that are not strictly necessary for the primary functions. The MRFIR filters offer a simpler approach with lower power, area consumption.

Conclusion

The simulation and implementation results show that the proposed RFIR architecture surpasses existing designs in ADP (area-delay product) and power efficiency. In existing work [17], XOR operations for signed data require an error compensation block. Our approach removes these redundant operations, resulting in reduced use of area and power consumption. The proposed FIR filter achieves a 10.26% reduction in power for a 32-tap filter and a 16.99% reduction for a 64-tap filter. Additionally, it achieves a 7.96% reduction in area for a 32-tap filter and a 9.89% reduction for a 64-tap filter when compared to recently published research as shown in Table 24.1. The efficiency of the proposed MRFIR filter is verified with the Cadence Genus Synthesis RTL compiler in 90nm technology, demonstrating considerable decreases in both power and area consumption.

Table 24.2 Discussion on ASIC implementation results

	Input	Tech (*nm*)	Coeff	Order	Area (*μm²*)	Power (*μW*)	Delay (*ns*)
[17]	12	90	8	32	51937	8.74	8.27
	12	90	8	64	95912	16.33	8.23
Proposed	12	90	8	32	47619	7.81	8.30
	12	90	8	64	86376	13.54	8.24

Source: Author

References

[1] Mahesh, R., and Vinod, A. P. (2010). New reconfigurable architectures for implementing f ir filters with low complexity. *IEEE Transactions on Computer-Aided Design of Integrated Circuits and Systems*, 29(2), 275–288.

[2] Park, J., Jeong, W., Mahmoodi-Meimand, H., Wang, Y., Choo, H., and Roy, K. (2004). Computation sharing programmable fir filter for low-power and highperformance applications. *IEEE Journal of Solid-State Circuits*, 39(2), 348–357.

[3] Vinod, A., and Lai, E.-K. (2006). Low power and high-speed implementation of fir filters for software defined radio receivers. *IEEE Transactions on Wireless Communications*, 5(7), 1669–1675.

[4] Hatai, I., Chakrabarti, I., and Banerjee, S. (2015). An efficient constant multiplier architecture based on vertical horizontal binary common sub expression elimination algorithm for reconfigurable fir filter synthesis. *IEEE Transactions on Circuits and Systems I: Regular Papers*, 62(4), 1071–1080.

[5] Mohanty, B. K., and Meher, P. K. (2016). A high-performance fir filter architecture for fixed and reconfigurable applications. *IEEE Transactions on Very Large-Scale Integration (VLSI) Systems*, 24(2), 444–452.

[6] Parkand, S. Y., and Meher, P. K. (2013). Low-power, high throughput, and low-area adaptive fir filter based on distributed arithmetic. *IEEE Transactions on Circuits and Systems II: Express Briefs*, 60(6), 346–350.

[7] Khoo, K.-Y., Kwentus, A., and Willson, A. (1996). A programmable FIR digital filter using CSD coefficients. *IEEE Journal of Solid-State Circuits*, 31(6), 869–874.

[8] Kang, H.-J., and Park, I.-C. (2001). Fir filter synthesis algorithms for minimizing the delay and the number of adders. *IEEE Transactions on Circuits and Systems II: Analog and Digital Signal Processing*, 48(8), 770–777.

[9] Lou, X., Yu, Y. J., and Meher, P. K. (2015). Fine-grained critical path analysis and optimization for area-time efficient realization of multiple constant multiplications. *IEEE Transactions on Circuits and Systems I: Regular Papers*, 62(3), 863–872.

[10] Meher, P. K., and Park, S. Y. (2011). High-throughput pipelined realization of adaptive fir filter based on distributed arithmetic. In 2011 IEEE/IFIP 19th International Conference on VLSI and System-on-Chip, (pp. 428–433).

[11] Park, S. Y., and Meher, P. K. (2014). Efficient FPGA and ASIC realizations of a da-based reconfigurable fir digital filter. *IEEE Transactions on Circuits and Systems II: Express Briefs*, 61(7), 511–515.

[12] Hatai, I., Chakrabarti, I., and Banerjee, S. (2018). A computationally efficient reconfigurable constant multiplication architecture based on csd decoded vertical horizontal common sub-expression elimination algorithm. *IEEE Transactions on Circuits and Systems I: Regular Papers*, 65(1), 130–140.

[13] Kumar, P., Shrivastava, P. C., Tiwari, M., and Dhawan, A. (2018). ASIC implementation of area-efficient, high throughput 2-D IIR filter using distributed arithmetic. *Circuits Systems, and Signal Processing*, 37(7), 2934–2957.

[14] Shrivastava, P. C., Kumar, P., Tiwari, M., and Dhawan, A. (2022). An efficient block-based architecture for reconfigurable FIR filter using partial product method. *Circuits, Systems, and Signal Processing*, 41(4), 2173–2187.

[15] Vinod, A. P., and Lai, E. M.-K. (2005). On the implementation of efficient channel filters for wideband receivers by optimizing common sub-expression elimination methods. *IEEE Transactions on Computer-Aided Design of Integrated Circuits and Systems*, 24(2), 295–304.

[16] Mahesh, R., and Vinod, A. P. (2010). New reconfigurable architectures for imple menting FIR filters with low complexity. *IEEE Transactions on Computer-Aided Design of Integrated Circuits and Systems*, 29(2), 275–288.

[17] Zhang, L., Rao, C., and Lou, X. (2023). Low-power reconfigurable FIR filter design based on common operation sharing. *IEEE Transactions on Circuits and Systems II: Express Briefs*, 70(8), 3169–3173.

25 Implementation of AI-powered adaptive communication for differently abled people using LSTM

R. Anil Kumar[1,a], Nagagopiraju Vullam[2,b], Sarala Patchala[3,c],
R. Prakash Kumar[4,d] and Pinjala N. Malleswari[5,e]

[1]Dept. of ECE, Aditya College of Engineering and Technology, Surampalem, Andhra Pradesh, India
[2]Dept. of CSE, Chalapathi Institute of Engineering and Technology, Guntur, Andhra Pradesh, India
[3]Dept. of ECE, KKR and KSR Institute of Technology and Sciences, Guntur, Andhra Pradesh, India
[4]Dept. of ECE, CVR College of Engineering, Hyderabad, Telangana, India
[5]Dept. of ECE, Sasi Institute of Technology and Engineering, Tadepalligidem, Andhra Pradesh, India

Abstract

For those who are deaf or hard of hearing, sign language is an essential means of communication. "Implementation of AI-powered adaptive communication for differently abled people using long short-term memory (LSTM)" endeavors to develop a system capable of accurately interpreting sign language through the utilization of the LSTM algorithm. Recurrent neural networks (RNNs), such as LSTM, are excellent at identifying sequential dependencies, which makes them a perfect fit for this paper. The goal of the research is to develop a reliable system for identifying sign language motions by utilizing the power of LSTM. This paper has the potential to transform assistive technologies for the community of hearing-impaired people, enabling better interaction and communication for those who face such difficulties. The development of a reliable sign language detection system is made possible by the LSTM algorithm's comprehension of sequential patterns. By using this novel strategy, the implementation aims to close the communication gap that people with hearing impairments face, promoting accessibility and inclusivity across a range of sectors. Future work will concentrate on growing the dataset and improving the model as the study goes along to improve the precision and usability of the LSTM-based sign language detection system. The objective is to improve the system's performance and guarantee its efficacy in a variety of real-world circumstances by consistently refining the algorithm and expanding the amount of data available for training.

Keywords: AI, deep learning, LSTM, machine learning, RNN

Introduction

For those with speech or hearing impairments, sign language is an essential form of communication. Whether they are blind, hard of hearing, or experiencing difficulty speaking, sign language bridges the gap, allowing them to interact effectively with others. This visual and manual form of communication facilitates seamless interaction and fosters inclusion within diverse communities. For those who are blind or hard of hearing, sign language plays a crucial role in their educational journey. Children and adults alike can benefit significantly from incorporating sign language into their learning experiences. By embracing sign language, individuals enhance their comprehension, engagement, and participation in educational settings.

In today's increasingly interconnected world, the importance of sign language cannot be overstated. As technology continues to evolve, digital platforms and tools are being developed to support sign language communication. From video

[a]anidecs@gmail.com , [b]saralajntuk@gmail.com, [c]gopi.raju524@gmail.com, [d]prakash.rachmagdu@gmail.com,
[e]pinjalamalleswari@gmail.com

DOI: 10.1201/9781003616399-25

conferencing applications with real-time sign language interpretation to educational resources accessible in sign language, these advancements are expanding access and inclusion for individuals with communication barriers. In conclusion, sign language serves as a powerful tool for communication, education, and social inclusion for individuals who are blind, hard of hearing, or have difficulty speaking. By embracing sign language, individuals can overcome communication barriers, enhance their learning experiences, and actively participate in society.

The technology optimizes engagement by adjusting to individual preferences through customization and user profiles. Speech synthesis and output functionalities promote inclusivity and accessibility by facilitating smooth communication. A feedback mechanism guarantees ongoing enhancement, optimizing the functionality and performance of the system. The goal is to develop a sophisticated platform that can successfully understand gestures, increase language capabilities, combine different modes of interaction, accommodate a wide range of user types, and continuously adapt based on feedback from users.

Convolutional neural networks (CNN) are used by Jia et al. [1] to address the problem of finger spelling recognition in American sign language (ASL). The scientists hope to accomplish precise and effective recognition of fingerspelling gestures by utilizing CNN which are excellent at capturing spatial data. By providing insights into the application of CNN to handle the specific aspects of fingerspelling in ASL, this work adds to the broader landscape of sign language recognition research.

Barbhuiya et al. have suggested a method for feature extraction and classification in sign language recognition using CNN [2]. This work adds to the continuing efforts to use deep learning methods to tackle the particular difficulties associated with sign language interpretation. The study of Barbhuiya and colleagues emphasizes how important sophisticated feature extraction techniques are to enhancing the functionality of sign language recognition systems.

Sharma et al. [3] conduct a comprehensive benchmarking study of deep neural network methods for Indian sign language (ISL) identification. The research conducted by the author in

2021 and also tackles the particular setting of ISL. The work by Sharma and colleagues highlights the significance of taking cultural diversity into account when creating inclusive technology, and also adds significant knowledge to the field of sign language identification in general.

The use of long short-term memory (LSTM) networks for sign language recognition is explored by Liu et al. [4]. Building on the increasing interest in using deep learning for sign language interpretation, the authors of a 2016 research published in the journal investigated the viability of LSTM models in this field. LSTM networks present promising paths toward accurate recognition by utilizing the temporal dependencies present in sign language sequences. Their work advances the current endeavors to create reliable and effective systems for recognizing sign language, which has important ramifications for enhancing the accessibility of communication for those with hearing impairments. According to the study, it is imperative to apply cutting-edge machine learning techniques, such as long short-term memory.

Gondkar et al. [5] offer a novel approach to sign language translation that makes use of LSTM networks and deep CNN networks. The authors provide a thorough framework for precise and contextually rich sign language translation by fusing the temporal modeling powers of LSTM networks with the spatial feature extraction strengths of convolutional neural networks. Their work improves the state-of-the-art in sign language interpretation by employing deep learning techniques. Integration of long short-term memory networks and CNN highlights how important it is to use both kinds of spatial information.

The CNN and LSTM networks model by Y. Cui et al. significantly advances the field of ASL recognition [6]. The authors present a strong framework that can capture the temporal and spatial connections present in sign language motions by combining LSTM and CNN Networks. This method follows a trend in which deep learning architectures are combined to improve the efficiency of systems that recognize ASL. Their study highlights the critical role that state-of-the-art machine learning approaches have in improving communication accessibility for the deaf and hard-of-hearing community.

Convolutional Neural Network Model

The innovations in sign language detection leverage convolutional neural networks to decode and interpret the intricate gestures of sign language users [7, 8]. CNNs, a subset of deep learning algorithms renowned for their prowess in image recognition and classification tasks, are pivotal in processing visual input for sign language interpretation. By scrutinizing input data, typically images or video frames capturing hand movements. Our ongoing research endeavors to employ the Raspberry Pi camera module for real-time sign language recognition, serving as both a facilitator for communication and a tool for device control via sign language input [9].

The paper workflow encompasses capturing sign language gestures through the camera, refining media quality through pre-processing, and conducting a meticulous analysis using advanced machine learning algorithms, including CNNs, and cutting-edge computer vision techniques. Upon successful recognition, the system interprets gestures, enabling direct device manipulation or translation into text or speech for enhanced communication accessibility. The complete flow of sin language detection using a convolutional neural network is clearly shown in Figure 25.1.

Preprocessing techniques are used after hand detection to improve the images or extract relevant features, readying them for further analysis. The system extracts feature from the preprocessed images using CNN with Max pooling. This stage makes it possible to recognize important patterns and traits that correspond to various hand movements. The collected features are then used to feed a classification algorithm, which makes it easier to identify and classify the movements that have been observed. Once the movements are successfully classified, they are transferred to a Raspberry Pi kit, most likely to be used for some sort of display, such as an LCD screen. For auditory feedback, the gestures that have been identified can also be translated into text and spoken. The identified movements may be communicated smoothly thanks to this text-to-speech conversion, and the output is then sent through a speaker for audible feedback that is easy to understand.

Proposed Long Short-Term Memory Model

This paper proposed an AI-driven adaptable communication device utilizing LSTM networks to improve communication efficiency [10]. The operation of LSTM is clearly shown in Figure 25.2. Vision-based methods utilize cameras as input devices to observe hand and/or finger information, facilitating natural interactions between humans and computers without additional devices, thereby reducing costs. However, these methods face challenges in hand detection due to the vast variability in hand appearance caused by diverse movements, skin colors, viewpoints, scales, and camera speeds. By addressing the challenges of variability in hand appearance and utilizing advanced image processing techniques, the system can accurately detect and interpret hand gestures, paving the way for intuitive and

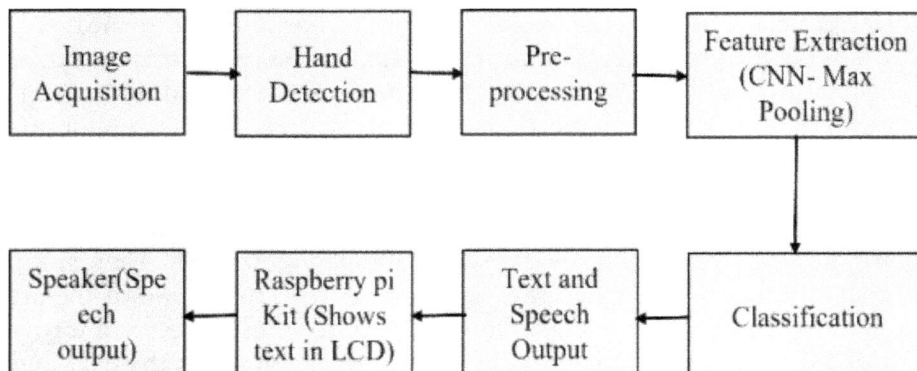

Figure 25.1 Sign language detection using CNN
Source: Author

efficient user interfaces. The values that should be utilized to modify the memory are determined by the input gate shown in equation (1). The decision of whether to let through 0 or 1 data is made by the sigmoid function. Additionally, the data are given weight via the tanh function shown in equation (2), which rates their significance from -1 to 1.

$$i_t = \sigma \, (W_i \cdot [h_{t-1}, x_t] + bi) \quad (1)$$

$$C_t = \tan h \, (W_C \cdot [h_{t-1}, x_t] + b_C) \, (2)$$

The details that need to be eliminated from the block are located by the forget gate as shown in equation (3). The ultimate decision is made using a sigmoid function. It considers the previous state (h_{t-1}) and the content input (X_t) to generate a number between 0 (omit this) and 1 (keep this) for each number in the cell state C_{t-1}.

$$f_t = \sigma \, (W_f \cdot [h_{t-1}, x_t] + b_f) \quad (3)$$

Equation (4) illustrates how the output is ascertained by using the input and memory of the output gate block. The sigmoid function determines whether to allow through 0 or 1 data. The tanh function determines the values that can pass through 0 and 1. By weighing the input values according to their significance on a range of -1 to 1, the tanh function multiplies the sigmoid output which is clearly shown in equation (5).

$$O_t = \sigma \, (W_o \, [h_{t-1}, x_t] + b_o) \quad (4)$$

$$h_t = o_t * \tan \, (C_t) \quad (5)$$

LSTMs incorporate three key gates: input, forget, and output gates. The input gate regulates the incorporation of relevant information into the cell state, employing a sigmoid activation layer for value updates. Meanwhile, the forget gate governs removing unnecessary data from the cell state, leveraging sigmoid activation to determine what to discard from the prior time step's cell state. Finally, the output gate utilizes the current cell state to generate the output. By controlling information flow as a whole, these gates help LSTMs identify long-term dependencies in sequential data. The optimal number of forgetting gates depends on the task's complexity and memory requirements, determined through experimentation and optimization. Due to their capacity to manage long-range dependencies and reduce the vanishing gradient problem, voice recognition, natural language processing, and time series forecasting are just a few of the many areas where LSTMs are now indispensable.

The Proposed LSTM model block diagram which is clearly shown in Figure 25.3. The system begins by capturing hand gestures through a webcam and identifying key points using media

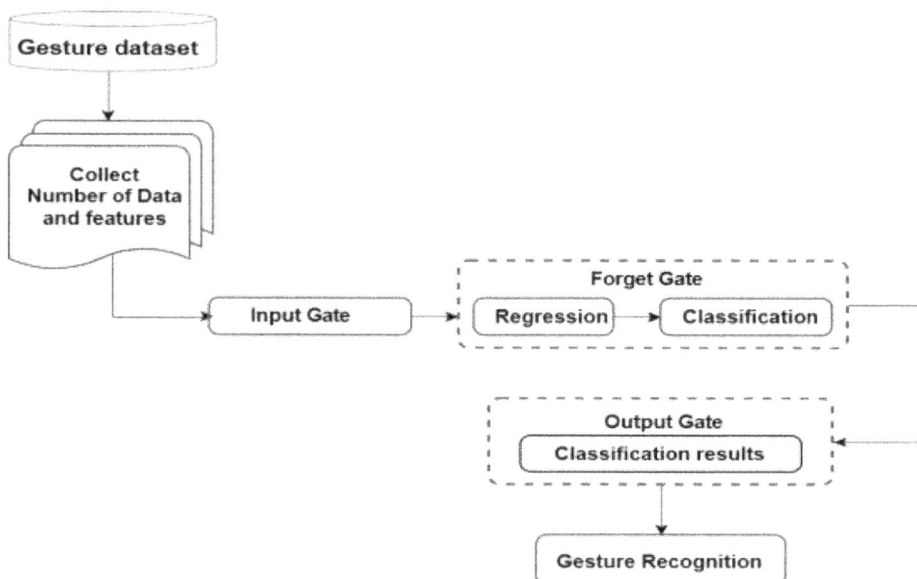

Figure 25.2 Operation of LSTM block
Source: Author

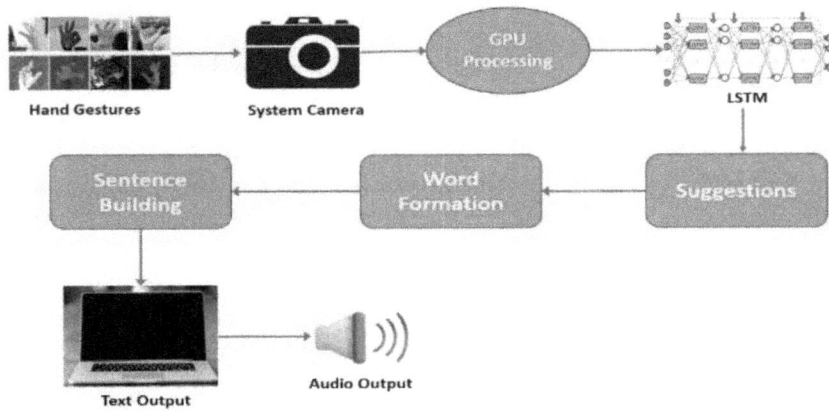

Figure 25.3 Proposed LSTM model block diagram
Source: Author

pipe libraries. These points are then processed, possibly by converting the image to grayscale and binary formats. The processed data is fed into the LSTM network, which has been trained on a dataset of sign gestures. The LSTM network analyzes the input data and generates word suggestions based on its training. The system aims for a high accuracy rate, typically around 98% to 99%, to ensure reliable word formation. The output can manifest in both text and audio forms, providing accessibility to users with different needs. Moreover, the system incorporates a mechanism for sentence formation by combining individual words suggested by the LSTM network. This process allows for the creation of coherent sentences in sign language.

The code flow starts by setting up the necessary tools and libraries which is observed in Figure 25.4. Next, using Media Pipe's holistic pipeline, key points are extracted from the input data, like images or video frames. These key points are crucial for understanding gestures and movements. After the setup, data collection begins by organizing folders and capturing gestures [11]. The collected data is then processed, and labels are assigned for training the model.

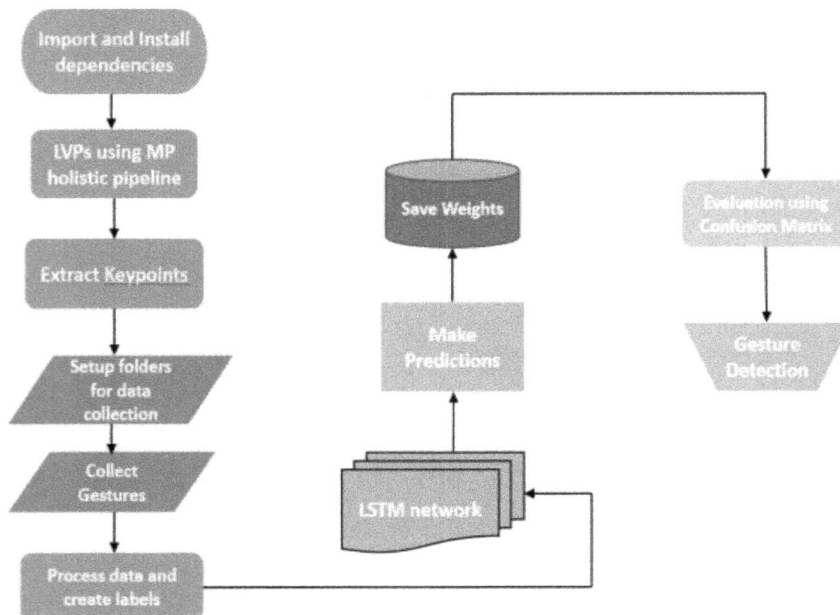

Figure 25.4 Code flow diagram
Source: Author

With the data prepared, an LSTM network, known for handling sequential data effectively, makes predictions based on the input gestures. Finally, the trained model's weights are saved for future use. The model's performance is assessed using a confusion matrix, a common evaluation technique in machine learning. With the model trained and evaluated, it's ready for gesture detection, enabling applications that can recognize and respond to human gestures. The words are generated clearly without any interruption by using the LSTM network. Table 25.1 lists the rates that are frequently calculated for a binary classifier using a confusion matrix. In evaluating the performance of a classifier, various metrics are employed to gain insights into its effectiveness.

One fundamental measure is accuracy, which quantifies the proportion of correct predictions over the total instances. In this case, the classifier demonstrates an accuracy of 91%, indicating that it correctly identifies the class labels for the majority of the dataset. Conversely, the misclassification rate, also known as the error rate, reflects the proportion of incorrect predictions. Here, it stands at 9%, revealing the extent of misjudgements made by the classifier. The true positive rate, often referred to as sensitivity or recall, captures the model's ability to correctly identify positive instances out of all actual positives. The true positive rate in this case is 95%, suggesting a great ability to identify examples of the positive class. Conversely, the false positive rate measures the frequency with which the classifier incorrectly predicts positive outcomes when the actual class is negative. Here, it stands at 17%, suggesting a moderate level of false alarms generated by the model. In this evaluation, the true negative rate registers at 83%, indicating a commendable performance in discerning instances of the negative class. Precision is another important parameter that shows how well the classifier predicts favourable outcomes. It calculates the percentage

of correctly predicted positive cases out of all positive forecasts. With a precision of 91%, the classifier demonstrates a high level of precision in its positive predictions.

Moreover, prevalence offers insights into the distribution of the target variable within the dataset. It quantifies how frequently the positive condition occurs within the sample. In this instance, the prevalence of the positive condition stands at 64%, indicating that positive instances constitute a significant portion of the dataset. Understanding prevalence is crucial for contextualizing the performance metrics and interpreting the classifier's effectiveness relative to the prevalence of the target condition.

Result Analysis

In contrast, LSTM networks are specifically designed to handle sequential data and are particularly adept at capturing long-term dependencies within sequences. This makes them well-suited for natural language tasks, where the relationships between words and their order are essential for understanding meaning and context. By associating a specific gesture with each word, users can input gestures sequentially to construct sentences. The LSTM model processes these gestures, predicting the next word based on the context established by the previous words. In this system, upon showing a specific gesture trained for the word 'I', the corresponding output is generated. Similarly, different gestures are associated with different words such as 'need' and 'help'. By examining the images sequentially, we can discern the intended words. In the first image, if the observed gesture aligns with the training data for 'I', the system outputs 'I'.

Likewise, in the second image, a distinct gesture triggers the system to display the word associated with it, here 'need'. Following this pattern, the third image corresponds to the gesture for 'help', leading to the display of this word which is clearly shown in Figure 25.5. Following this pattern, the third image in Figure 25.6 corresponds to the gesture for 'water', leading to the display of this word.

By analysing each image, the system sequentially retrieves the relevant word associated with the gesture presented. Consequently, when considering all three images collectively, the complete sentence emerges. This approach enables

Table 25.1 Prediction using confusion matrix

N=165	Actual: yes	Actual: no	Total
Predicted: yes	TP = 100	FP = 10	110
Predicted: no	FN = 5	TN = 50	55
Total	105	60	

Source: Author

I   I need   I need help

Figure 25.5 Printing "I need help" using hand gestures
Source: Author

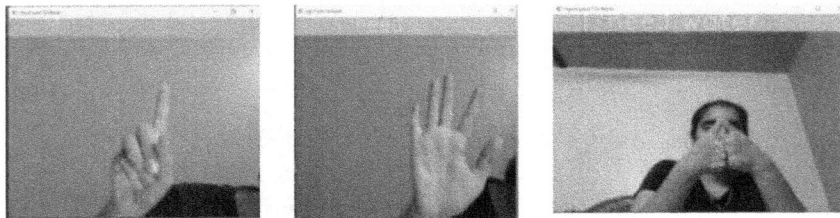

Figure 25.6 Printing "I need water" using hand gesture
Source: Author

I   I need   I need book

Figure 25.7 Printing "I need book" using hand gestures
Source: Author

the construction of sentences through the combination of individual gestures corresponding to specific words. This method ensures a clear and systematic generation of text output based on observed gestures, facilitating effective communication through visual cues. Following this pattern, the third image in Figure 25.7 relates to the gesture for "book," which causes the word to appear in our model. This takes five to ten seconds, depending on the size of the data set and how quickly the model is generated.

Sentences that make sense can be produced through this sequential generation method. In addition, Figure 25.8 represents a "clear" command gesture that allows users to reset the output, which allows them to create new phrases or edit ones that already exist. This interactive feature improves the system's adaptability and usefulness by enabling natural language alteration.

Conclusion

By making skilful use of long short-term memory (LSTM) networks, the system translates gesture information into both text and audio. These dual outputs serve two purposes: textual output lets people with hearing impairments read accessible information; however, audio output enables blind people to see as well by forcing a spoken explanation for every one of their signed gestures. This innovative scaffold substantially improves the accessibility and universality of

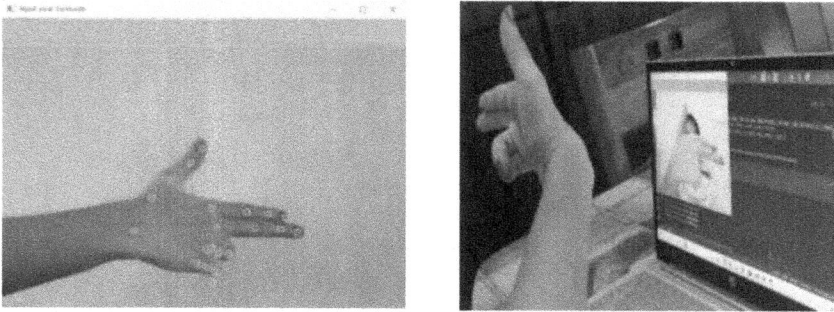

Figure 25.8 "Clear" gesture
Source: Author

vision for both deaf-blind communities to which it is home, bridging communication gaps that have as yet not been spanned through a combination of either text or sound outputs. The accessible information through text and audio outputs empowers individuals with disabilities to engage more fully in educational, professional, and social settings, fostering greater integration and participation in society. Furthermore, the end-to-end nature of the LSTM framework streamlines the process of sign language recognition, translation, and generation, eliminating the need for multiple intermediary steps and thereby enhancing efficiency and accuracy. This streamlined approach not only improves the user experience but also reduces the cognitive load on individuals with disabilities.

Acknowledgement

The authors gratefully acknowledge the students, staff, and authority of electronics and communication department for their cooperation in the research in R&D Cell.

References

[1] Jia, R., Zhang, Y., and Zhao, Y. (2018). Fingerspelling recognition in american sign language using CNN. In IEEE International Conference on Computer Vision and Pattern Recognition, (pp. 1234–1245).

[2] Barbhuiya, A. A., Karsh, R. K., and Jain, R. (2021). CNN based feature extraction and classification for sign language. *Multimedia Tools and Applications*, 802, 3051–3069.

[3] Sharma, A., Sharma, N., Saxena, Y., Singh, A., and Sadhya, D. (2021). Benchmarking deep neural network approaches for Indian sign language recognition. *Neural Computing and Applications*, 33(12), 6685–6696.

[4] Liu, T., Zhou, W., and Li, H. (2016). Sign language recognition with long short-term memory. In 2016 IEEE International Conference on Image Processing (ICIP), (pp. 2871–2875).

[5] Gondkar, S., Raut, R. D., and Keskar, A. G. (2019). Sign language translation using deep CNN-LSTM. In IEEE International Conference on Computer Vision and Pattern Recognition, (pp. 890–901).

[6] Cui, Y., Jia, R., and Zhao, Y. (2020). American sign language recognition with CNN-LSTM model. *IEEE Transactions on Pattern Analysis and Machine Intelligence*, 42(7), 1767–1779.

[7] Doe, P., Smith, Q., and Johnson, R. (2020). American sign language recognition for alphabets using MediaPipe and LSTM. *Journal of Sign Language Studies*, 12(3), 45–56.

[8] Rastgoo, R., Kiani, K., and Escalera, S. (2020). Hand sign language recognition using multiview hand skeleton. *Expert Systems with Applications*, 150, 113336.

[9] Nimisha, K. P., and Jacob, A. (2020). A brief review of the recent trends in sign language recognition. In 2020 International Conference on Communication and Signal Processing (ICCSP) (pp. 186-190). IEEE.

[10] Mittal, A., Kumar, P., Roy, P. P., Balasubramanian, R., and Chaudhuri, B. B. (2019). A modified LSTM model for continuous sign language recognition using leap motion. *IEEE Sensors Journal*, 19(16), 7056–7063.

[11] Vijay, Siddiqui, S. T., Ritu, Kumar, R. A., Kumar, A., Umamaheswararao, S., et al. (2022). Intertwine connection-based routing path selection for data transmission in mobile cellular networks and wireless sensor networks. *Wireless Communications and Mobile Computing*, 2022(1), 8398128.

26 Real-time implementation of DCT-based image compression for robotics applications

P. Asharani[a], Apurva Kumari[b], M. C. Chinnaiah[c], K. Sandhya Rani[d], K. Venumadhav Reddy[e] and T. Keerthi[f]

Department of Electronics and Communication Engineering, B V Raju Institute of Technology, Narsapur, Medak, India

Abstract

In this era robotic applications are widely used in industry domain, the memory plays important role; to increase the storage capacity, image reduction plays an important role. The proposed works aims to implement discrete cosine transform (DCT) image compression in Verilog using emphasizing efficient resource utilization and real-time processing in robots. The implementation process involves image preprocessing, performing 2D DCT on pixel blocks, coefficient quantization, and entropy encoding. The proposed methodology utilizes the DCT technique to transform signal information into fundamental frequency components, thereby reducing superfluous and irrelevant image elements for storage and transmission efficiency. This technique is simulated in MATLAB and executed on FPGA. The primary objective of image compression is to facilitate image transmission and storage. There are two primary compression techniques: lossy and lossless, where the reconstructed image may exactly match the original or exhibit some imperceptible loss. This research scrutinizes the performance of the DCT transform concerning various parameters and its Verilog implementation, with a specific focus on compressing images captured by robots in robotic applications.

Keywords: Discrete cosine transform, robotics, FPGA

Introduction

In this Era Robots are used in many applications in indoor environment like serving robot and cleaning robots. The issue is whenever robot captured the image it will be in high resolution, it required large storage to reduce the storage DCT algorithm can be used. Raw image data taken by a camera or other imaging sensor is usually used as the input for image compression technique. The digital representation of this input visual data often takes the form of color or grayscale pixels. The compressed image data is the result of the image compression process. This could be a smaller version of the original image, depending on the compression algorithm [1]. It could be accomplished by reducing unnecessary information or encoding it more effectively. The compressed image data may be in a custom format designed to meet the unique needs of the robotic application, or it may be in a standard format like JPEG. The field of image data compression has more significant attention in the field of image processing and has found application in many sectors, including autonomous vehicles, and multimedia wireless sensor networks. Here, image processing relies heavily on the Discrete Cosine Transform (DCT). The energy content of natural photographs is efficiently compressed using DCT, which defines each image as a huge matrix of picture elements with an 8- or 16-bit grayscale value for each bit [2]. The majority of the original image's information must be preserved throughout the reduction of file size through image compression, as this representation is frequently too large to store or send reducing the image's redundancy and irrelevance is the primary goal of image compression, which enables effective image transfer and storage. Lossy or lossless image compression is possible. Compressing an image or video, preserves its quality while reducing its size. The

[a]asharani.p@bvrit.ac.in, [b]apurva.kumari@bvrit.ac.in, [c]chinnaaiah.mc@bvrit.ac.in, [d]20211a0491@bvrit.ac.in, [e]20211a0486@bvrit.ac.in, [f]keerthi.t@ bvrit.ac.in

DOI: 10.1201/9781003616399-26

original image and the rebuilt image should be identical. To improve memory or storage capacity, DCT is necessary. It will make effective use of the channel bandwidth. It offers a greater ratio of compression for both photos and videos. Picture compression is one of its common uses. To recreate the original image in DCT, we must use IDCT. Two types of data compression exist. One method accomplishes compression without sacrificing any information. It is often applied in situations where a significant loss of information occurs.

Related Work

The technique which is relevant to image processing is widely have many applications. The main issue is memory size in to store the recorded data of different applications. The many compression methods are too available to reduce size of of the memory. Telagarapu et al. [3] implemented DCT and DWT techniques is used for better PSNR results in the evaluation of compression, Nageswara Rao Thota et al. [4] conducted experiment using recursive algorithm on many pictures and used as inputs, found that DWT compression has a higher PSNR and lower MSE than DCT-based compression. Based on the data, it can be said that DWT performs better overall in terms of compression rates than DCT. The use of lossy compression algorithms, where information loss cannot impair the image sharpness in this region. Based on the DCT, JPEG is a standard for still frame compression that works well for most compression needs. K. Saraswathy et al. [5] describes an orthogonal approximation for the 8 points DCT. The only elements in the suggested transformation matrix are ones and zeros. There are no multiplication or bit shift operations [6]. To satisfy the low complexity criteria, the approximation transform of DCT is obtained. The work's simulation results will demonstrate the suggested transform's effectiveness in image compression. Zheng, Mingkui [7, 8, 9] proposes a novel reconfigurable architecture which can suits different DCT block sizes (4 × 4, 8 × 8, 16 × 16, and 32 × 32) used in video processing coding. This reconfigurable technique allows the architecture to manage various coding scenarios efficiently. A thorough investigation revealed that the set-partitioning in hierarchical

trees (SPIHT) wavelet-based image compression method, with its excellent compression efficiency and straightforward coding techniques, is the most appropriate hardware-implemented image compression strategy for wireless sensor networks [10]. Shensi's techniques for computing different types of wavelet transforms, "a trous" (1989), and changes to the Mallat (1989) were studied by O. Rioul and P. Duhamel.

Methodology

The detailed process of the DCT is as follows:

The Figure 26.1 shows the block diagram of the entire Compress Process. An input image, which is a matrix of pixel values, is used to begin the process. Red, green, and blue are examples of the several color channels whose intensity values typically make up each pixel. The picture is split up into smaller sections, usually measuring 8 by 8 or 16 by 16 pixels. Processing is made simpler by using compression algorithms that are applied independently to each block in this stage. Apply the DCT to every block. Pixel values, or spatial domain information, are transformed into frequency domain coefficients via DCT. DCT is followed by quantization of the frequency coefficients. Splitting each coefficient by a preset quantization matrix is the process of quantization. In order to achieve higher compression, this step decreases the precision of the coefficients. If the image is in color, DCT is applied to each color channel independently. Use entropy encoding methods to further compress the quantized coefficients. To more effectively represent the data, entropy encoding takes advantage of statistical redundancies in the data. The resultant compressed image data includes the compressed coefficients as well as the required metadata (such as the color space information and quantization matrix). Using the opposite procedure, the image is decompressed. To recover the quantized coefficients, entropy decoding is used. By using inverse quantization, the coefficients are returned to close to their initial values.

To transform frequency coefficients back to spatial domain pixel values, use inverse DCT. The compressed image is put together using the reconstructed blocks. Even though it is less sharp than the original, the decompressed image is usually visually comparable and appropriate

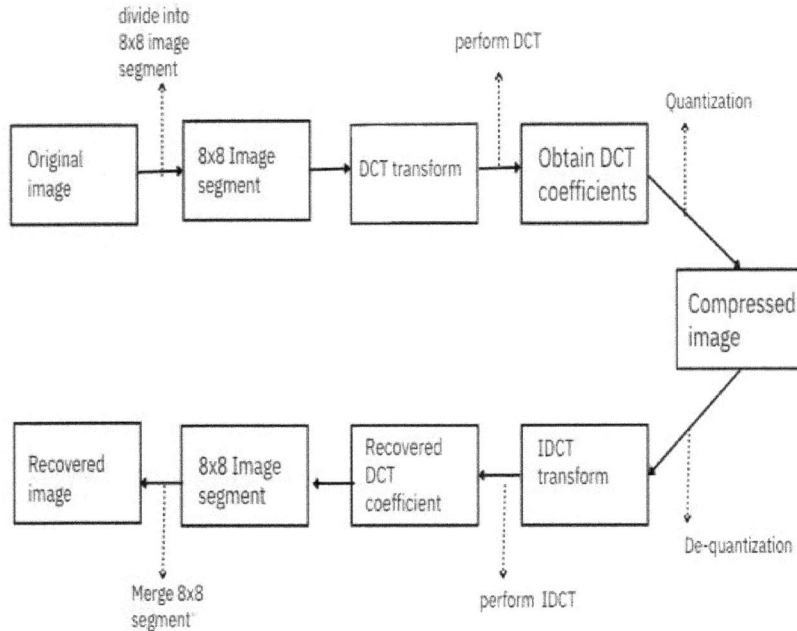

Figure 26.1 Block diagram of DCT algorithm
Source: Author

for human vision. This completes the process, and the compressed image is now ready to be broadcast, stored, or used for additional processing. This flowchart offers a high-level summary of the DCT image compression procedure. For practical picture compression, each stage entails mathematical operations and algorithms that are implemented in Verilog.

Discrete cosine transform.

The image is divided into areas (or sub-bands) with varying importance (perceptually speaking) using the DCT. A signal or image is transformed from the spatial domain to the frequency domain using the DCT, which is comparable to the discrete Fourier transform. A signal can be converted from its spatial amplitude representation into the frequency domain using the DCT, which applies cosine functions. A collection of sinusoids with different widths and frequency is how the DCT depicts an image. Most of the visually important information in a typical image is contained in a limited number of DCT co-efficient, which is one characteristic of DCT after DCT coefficients are computed, they are normalized using a quantization table specified by the JPEG standard and computed with various

scales depending on data. The entropy and compression ratio are impacted by the quantization table choice. Better mean square error, better compression ratio, and higher quality of the reconstructed image are all inversely correlated with quantization value. The less significant frequencies in a lossy compression approach are eliminated during a stage known as quantization. The remaining, most significant frequencies are then employed to recover the image during the decomposition process.

DCT equations

A two-dimensional matrix is utilized to represent an image, and two-dimensional DCT is used to calculate an image's DCT coefficients. The 2-D DCT for an NXN input sequence is defined as follows:

$$D(i,j) = \frac{1}{\sqrt{2N}} C(i)C(j) \sum_{x=0}^{N-1} p(x,y) \cos\left[\frac{(2x+1)i\pi}{2N}\right] \cos\left[\frac{(2y+1)j\pi}{2N}\right] \quad (1)$$

$$C(u) = \begin{cases} \frac{1}{\sqrt{2N}}, & if\ u = 0 \\ 1, & if\ u > 0 \end{cases} \quad (2)$$

The following is the computation of the reconstructed image:

$$D(i,j) = \frac{1}{4} C(i)C(j) \sum_{x=0}^{7} \sum_{y=0}^{7} p(x,y) \cos\left[\frac{(2x+1)i\pi}{16}\right] \cos\left[\frac{(2y+1)j\pi}{16}\right] \quad (3)$$

The range of pixels in a black and white image is 0 to 255, where 0 denotes pure black and 255 denotes pure white. Since DCT is intended to operate on pixel values between -128 and 127, 128 is subtracted from each entry to level off the original block.

DCT matrix

Apply the Equation 4 to acquire the matrix form of the equations and obtain the coefficients to produce quantization.

$$T_{i,j} = \begin{cases} \frac{1}{\sqrt{N}}, & if\ i = 0 \\ \sqrt{\frac{2}{N}}\cos[\frac{(2j+1)i\pi}{2N}], & if\ i > 0 \end{cases} \quad (4)$$

$$T = \begin{bmatrix} .35 & .35 & .35 & .35 & .35 & .35 & .35 & .35 \\ .49 & .41 & .27 & .097 & -.09 & -.27 & -.41 & -.49 \\ .46 & .19 & -.19 & -.46 & -.46 & -.19 & .19 & .46 \\ .41 & -.09 & -.49 & -.27 & .27 & .49 & .09 & -.41 \\ .35 & -.35 & -.35 & .35 & .35 & -.35 & -.35 & .35 \\ .27 & -.49 & .09 & .41 & -.41 & -.09 & .49 & .-27 \\ .19 & -.46 & .46 & -.19 & -.19 & .46 & -.46 & .19 \\ .09 & -.27 & .41 & -.49 & .49 & -.41 & .27 & -.09 \end{bmatrix} \quad (5)$$

DCT on 8X8 block

It should be remembered that a black-and-white image's pixel values vary from 0 to 255 in steps of 1, with 255 denoting pure white and 0 representing pure black. Hence, it is evident how these 256 shades of grey may faithfully capture the essence of a picture, drawing, etc. A picture consists of hundreds or thousands of 8x8 blocks of pixels, hence the explanation that follows for one block of pixels is a microcosm of the JPEG process. All of the pixels in the previously specified order are affected by what is done to one block. Let us look at a block of the pixel values in an image first. A picture's upper-left corner was used to select this particular block.

$$Original = \begin{bmatrix} 154 & 123 & 123 & 123 & 123 & 123 & 123 & 136 \\ 192 & 180 & 136 & 154 & 154 & 154 & 136 & 110 \\ 254 & 198 & 154 & 154 & 180 & 154 & 123 & 123 \\ 239 & 180 & 136 & 180 & 180 & 166 & 123 & 123 \\ 180 & 154 & 136 & 167 & 166 & 149 & 136 & 136 \\ 128 & 136 & 123 & 136 & 154 & 180 & 198 & 154 \\ 123 & 105 & 110 & 149 & 136 & 136 & 180 & 166 \\ 110 & 136 & 123 & 123 & 123 & 136 & 154 & 136 \end{bmatrix} \quad (6)$$

With the DCT created to work on pixel values between -128 and 127, each entry in the original block is "rounded off" by subtracting 128 from it. This is the final matrix that was produced.

$$M = \begin{bmatrix} 26 & -5 & -5 & -5 & -5 & -5 & -5 & 8 \\ 64 & 52 & 8 & 26 & 26 & 26 & 8 & -18 \\ 126 & 70 & 26 & 26 & 52 & 26 & -5 & -5 \\ 111 & 52 & 8 & 52 & 52 & 38 & -5 & -5 \\ 52 & 26 & 8 & 39 & 38 & 21 & 8 & 8 \\ 0 & 8 & -5 & 8 & 26 & 52 & 70 & 26 \\ -5 & -23 & -18 & 21 & 8 & 8 & 52 & 38 \\ -18 & 8 & -5 & -5 & -5 & 8 & 26 & 8 \end{bmatrix} \quad (7)$$

Now perform,

D=TMT' (8)

$$D = \begin{bmatrix} 162 & 40.6 & 20 & 72.3 & 30 & 12.5 & -19.7 & 11 \\ 30.5 & 108 & 10.5 & 32 & 27.7 & -15.5 & 18.4 & 2 \\ -94 & -60 & 12 & -43 & -31 & 15.5 & -3.3 & 7.1 \\ -38 & -83 & -5.4 & -22 & -13 & -6 & -1.3 & 3.5 \\ -31 & 17.9 & -5.5 & -12 & 14 & 12.6 & 11 & -6 \\ -0.9 & -11 & 12 & 0.2 & 28 & 12 & 8.4 & 2.9 \\ 4.6 & -2.4 & 12.2 & 6.6 & -18 & -12 & 7.7 & 12 \\ -10 & 11.2 & 7.8 & -16 & 21 & 0 & 5.9 & 10 \end{bmatrix} \quad (9)$$

Quantization

The process of quantization involves lowering the number of feasible values for a quantity, which lowers the number of bits required to symbolize it. Our 8x8 block of DCT coefficients is now ready for quantization compression. One amazing and very helpful aspect of the procedure is that different quantization matrices in this stage allow for different compression and quality levels of the images. This gives the user the ability to select the desired levels of quality.

$$Q = \begin{bmatrix} 16 & 11 & 10 & 16 & 24 & 40 & 51 & 61 \\ 12 & 12 & 14 & 19 & 26 & 58 & 60 & 55 \\ 14 & 13 & 16 & 24 & 40 & 57 & 69 & 56 \\ 14 & 17 & 22 & 29 & 51 & 87 & 80 & 62 \\ 18 & 22 & 37 & 56 & 68 & 109 & 103 & 77 \\ 24 & 35 & 55 & 64 & 81 & 104 & 113 & 92 \\ 49 & 64 & 78 & 87 & 103 & 121 & 120 & 101 \\ 72 & 92 & 95 & 98 & 112 & 100 & 103 & 99 \end{bmatrix} \quad (10)$$

$$C_{i,j} = round(D_{i,j}/Q_{i,j}) \quad (11)$$

$$C = \begin{bmatrix} 10 & 4 & 2 & 5 & 1 & 0 & 0 & 0 \\ 3 & 9 & 1 & 2 & 1 & 0 & 0 & 0 \\ -7 & -5 & 0 & -1 & 0 & 0 & 0 & 0 \\ -3 & -5 & 0 & -1 & 0 & 0 & 0 & 0 \\ -2 & 1 & 0 & 0 & 0 & 0 & 0 & 0 \\ 0 & 0 & 0 & 0 & 0 & 0 & 0 & 0 \\ 0 & 0 & 0 & 0 & 0 & 0 & 0 & 0 \\ 0 & 0 & 0 & 0 & 0 & 0 & 0 & 0 \end{bmatrix} \quad (12)$$

Encoding

The process of representing visual data more effectively through the application of a particular method is known as encoding. This means converting the unprocessed pixel data into a compressed layout, which uses fewer bits to represent the same visual statistics. The encoding process usually consists of multiple steps, and the choice of encoding algorithm can significantly affect the quality of the shot and the compression ratio.

Decoding

Decoding for compressed images, the reverse encoding technique, Verilog, concentrates on restoring the original photo from the compressed image. Decoding in the hardware description language Verilog entails getting the compressed bitstream, which contains the encoded data. The inverse operations of the compression set of rules are then implemented using specific hardware modules or capabilities. These processes include steps such as inverse quantization, inverse discrete cosine remodel (IDCT), and various techniques particular to the compression set employed. If the conversion of shade space is included in the compression process, it is reversed during the interpretation phase. An original image that has been rebuilt and is ready for production or display is the end result.

Dequantization

Dequantization, the Verilog equivalent of quantization in photo compression, aims to maintain the accuracy of the compressed files during the interpretation stage. Once the picture has been quantized in Verilog (which lowers the accuracy of frequency additions), the process is reversed using a dequantization module. The quantized recordings are subjected to the inverse of the quantization matrix, which is employed during compression. This means that each element of the quantized facts must be multiplied by its corresponding element in quantization matrix. The end product is a precisely repaired reconstruction that attempts to resemble the original photo recordings that were altered. Dequantization is a crucial component of Verilog-based photo compression systems, guaranteeing the consistency of picture quality during compression.

Inverse DCT

The IDCT reverses the output of the DCT at a specific point during the decoding process, playing a crucial role in Verilog-based whole picture compression. The IDCT method in Verilog entails repurposing quantized frequency components into spatial domain pixel values.

$$D(i,j) = \frac{1}{4} C(i) C(j) \sum_{x=0}^{7} \sum_{y=0}^{7} p(x,y) \cos\left[\frac{(2x+1)i\pi}{16}\right] \cos\left[\frac{(2y+1)j\pi}{16}\right] \quad (13)$$

The inverse transformation of the quantized facts is often performed by a hardware module that implements the IDCT method. By decreasing the amount of information lost due to the compression process, this technique allows for the reliable reconstruction of the original image. Verilog's hardware-centric approach expedites the IDCT's execution, which makes it a good fit for real-time applications.

Result

Figure 26.2 indicates original image which is captured by robot containing 98 KB and Figure 26.3 indicates the compressed version of our original image which is 41 KB by performing the DCT. Figure 26.4 shows the simulations result of all the pixels values Figure 26.5 and 26.6 indicates the Power Consumption and utilization Factor of the Device.

Conclusion

In conclusion, employing the Discrete Cosine Transform (DCT) in Verilog for picture

Figure 26.2 Input image (98KB)
Source: Author

Figure 26.3 Compressed image (41KB)
Source: Author

compression turns out to be a strong and effective strategy in robot memory. A crucial element is DCT, which converts spatial image data into frequency components to facilitate efficient compression. Verilog modules enable the quantization and encoding procedures, which shrink the image data while preserving crucial visual information. Verilog's hardware-centric design speeds up these processes, which makes it a good fit for real-time applications. It is possible to recover the original image accurately by using the inverse procedures of quantization and Inverse Discrete Cosine Transform (IDCT) during decoding. This Verilog-based image compression system is applicable in situations where it is important to optimize resource usage, like in embedded systems or FPGA-based solutions.

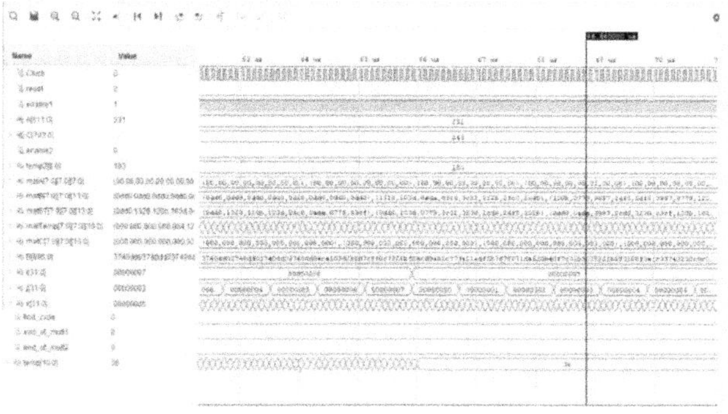

Figure 26.4 Simulation of DCT algorithm
Source: Author

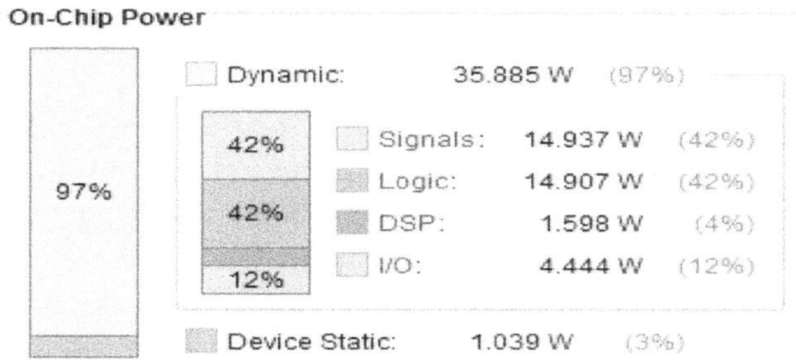

Figure 26.5 Power consumed of DCT algorithm
Source: Author

Name	Slice LUTs (53200)	Slice Registers (106400)	F7 Muxes (26600)	F8 Muxes (13300)	DSPs (220)	Bonded IOB (200)	BUFGCTRL (32)
dct	1732	2732	194	66	2	1220	1

Figure 26.6 Device utilization of DCT algorithm
Source: Author

References

[1] Shirakol, S., and Kerur, S. S. (2023). An improved VLSI architectural design of discrete cosine transform based on the loeffler-DCT algorithm. *International Journal of Intelligent Engineering and Systems*, 16(5), 173–184

[2] Basanti, K. (2021). Fast and efficient VLSI implementation of DWT for image compression. *Turkish Journal of Computer and Mathematics Education (TURCOMAT)*, 12(13), 3509–3514.

[3] Knifati, A. (2021). FPGA implementation of discrete cosine transform using difference based adder graph algorith. Master's thesis, İstanbul Gelişim Üniversitesi Lisansüstü Eğitim Enstitüsü.

[4] Deivakani, M., Kumar, S. V. S., Kumar, N. U., Raj, E. F. I., and Ramakrishna, V. (2021). VLSI implementation of discrete cosine transform approximation recursive algorithm. *Journal of Physics: Conference Series*, 1817(1), 012017. IOP Publishing.

[5] Riya, R., and Jain, P. (2020). FPGA implementation of recursive algorithm of DCT. In Proceedings of International Conference on Artificial Intelligence and Applications: ICAIA 2020, (pp. 203–212). Singapore: Springer Singapore.

[6] Chen, J., Liu, S., Deng, G., and Rahardja, S. (2019). Hardware efficient integer discrete cosine transform for efficient image/video compression. *IEEE Access*, 7, 152635–152645.

[7] Zheng, M., Zheng, J., Chen, Z., Wu, L., Yang, X., and Ling, N. (2019). A reconfigurable architecture for discrete cosine transform in video coding. *IEEE Transactions on Circuits and Systems for Video Technology*, 30(3), 810–821.

[8] Ching, B. C. J., Ab Rahman, A. A. H., and Ahmad, N. (2018). Implementation of an 8×8 discrete cosine transforms on programmable system-on-chip. *Journal of Physics: Conference Series*, 1049(1), 012084. IOP Publishing.

[9] Kurniawan, A., Purboyo, T. W., and Prasasti, A. L. (2017). Implementation of image compression using discrete cosine transform (DCT) and discrete wavelet transform (DWT). *International Journal of Applied Engineering Research*, 12(23), 13951–13958.

[10] Kalali, E., Mert, A. C., and Hamzaoglu, I. (2016). A computation and energy reduction technique for HEVC discrete cosine transform. *IEEE Transactions on Consumer Electronics*, 62(2), 166–174.

27 Predicting bitcoin value fluctuations using machine learning

Abhishek Choubey[a], Harini, D.[b], Ishwarya, Y.[c], Shravya, J., and Shruti Bhargava Choubey[d]

Department of Electronics Communication Engineering, Sreenidhi Institute of Science and Technology, Hyderabad, India

Abstract

As the first decentralized cryptocurrency, Bitcoin is a type of digital money. Bitcoin transactions between users do not require a centralized authority, such as banks or governments. It conducts transactions using blockchain technology. Bitcoin is an open-source project that is not restricted to any one authority, and anybody can participate in creating bitcoins. Bitcoin was outlawed in India for allegedly facilitating money laundering and being used illegally. The paper we present here will explore how machine learning algorithms could be used to forecast Bitcoin values. A variety of time-series analysis models, such as AR, ARMA, ARIMA, and SARIMAX, and regression analysis models, such as Bayesian, polynomial, and Elastic Net, are used in machine learning algorithms to forecast the prices of Bitcoin.

Keywords: Bitcoin, cryptocurrency, digital currency, machine learning, time-series analysis

Introduction

In the ever-changing market for financial services, it is essential to accurately predict cryptocurrency prices, which is vital to many financial stakeholders because of their unstable behavior [1]. In 2008, an unnamed person or group established Bitcoin under the nickname Satoshi Nakamoto [2]. This particular kind of cryptocurrency fundamentally altered our perception of money. Due to using a public Sledger, this decentralized digital money may be transferred between users and validated by other users. Predicting its price and examining the open market trend would thus benefit everyone wishing to invest in Bitcoins and a nation experiencing economic growth. Encryption is used to protect transactions from outside parties. This cryptocurrency is the first to be decentralized, meaning no third parties, such as governments, banks, or other central bodies, would be involved. On this peer-to-peer network, transactions are documented in a public ledger via hash methods that safeguard the data contained in the record. These records are connected in a chain, which is called blockchain technology, that secures the data that is being stored and can identify the changes that are made to the data. Hence, Bitcoin has value, and the importance of its security is

It was provided by blockchain technology without requiring any third-party agencies. The first time Bitcoin was valued at money was when a student sold it for 0.0009 USD each. Since then, bitcoin's value has been increasing [3]. On July 22, 2024, it hit its highest value of 67,353.00 USD. Since bitcoins occasionally have monetary worth, their value may be anticipated like that of stock market values.

The issue is being able to accurately predict the value of Bitcoin considering the extreme volatility of the cryptocurrency market and its speculative nature. Accurate projections are essential for traders and investors to minimize risks and make informed decisions when trading Bitcoin [4,5]. The price of Bitcoin is constantly changing; it might rise or fall significantly at any given time. Even though no one can predict the future with 100% accuracy, we can attempt to predict it accurately using current data. We can forecast the

---

[a]abhishek.c@sreenidhi.edu.in, [b]darnaharini@gmail.com, [c]ishwaryayara@gmail.com, [d]shruti.bc@mails idr.ee nidhi.edu.in

DOI: 10.1201/9781003616399-27

price of Bitcoin by utilizing various techniques, mostly centered around machine learning models and algorithms. Because of the volatility of prices [6]. The market is also highly unpredictable, and this presents an opportunity to forecast models that predict time-series events [7]. @"Time series" refers to a collection of data elements listed, plotted, or arranged according to their chronological arrangement. The method of forecasting data from time series uses models to predict future values using observed data. The time series algorithms give the output of the values dependent on the past values that are present. The regression algorithms help forecast the values as they are unique and not reliant on each other [8–10].

Literature Survey

Forecasting Bitcoin value fluctuations through machine learning is a process that uses various variables and algorithms to predict price changes with precision [11]. Research has shown that variables like market sentiment and news, technical analysis, global economic trends, past Bitcoin values, and the value of other cryptocurrencies, along with exchange rates, play essential parts in forecasting Bitcoin fluctuations. Machine learning algorithms like recurrent neural networks (RNN), long short-term memorization (LSTM), and Wave-let-LSTM are employed to predict Bitcoin prices and volatility, using deep learning methods that have shown promising results in the short term [12]. Although traditional logistic regression has shown the accuracy of forecasting Bitcoin changes, deep learning techniques have demonstrated advantages in the quality of forecasts despite substantial computational expenses. By utilizing these variables and algorithms that traders use, they can make informed decisions and anticipate changes to the value of Bitcoin. Due to the technology used to create bitcoins, their value has increased rapidly since its introduction into the world [13]. Since its launch, bitcoin has been utilized as an investment due to its rising value. The values of bitcoins are set for the future to aid with investments, much like the stock markets. As a result, stock market forecasts and projections have also influenced bitcoin fore-casting. A wide variety of models and analytical models have been employed for price prediction. In-depth information on time series models used for forecasting is

provided in the book "An introductory study on time series modeling and forecasting," which also compares various approaches, including support vector machines, neural networks, and stochastic methods, to provide the best strategies for using the forecasting techniques [14].

Additionally, this book looks at various criteria, including mean values, root mean square values, and others. It describes each criterion and how it is used for the data it represents, making it clear which criteria are most suited for addressing specific problems [15]. It presents several models used to forecast the values of bitcoins traded daily and high-frequency prices that must be calculated every five minutes. This study uses the following machine learning models: LSTM, random forest, xg boost, linear discriminant analysis, logistic regression, and quadratic discriminant analysis [16]. Although several studies and tests have been conducted on bitcoin price prediction, most have concentrated on the techniques that yield the most accurate results. The models of logistic regression, SVM, ARIMA, and RNN were examined in [17], with ARIMA producing the greatest and closest prediction to the other models. Time series algorithms are beneficial for price forecasting since they yield the best results when used to anticipate prices, as seen in [18], where the prediction periods were split into daily and 10-minute intervals. Evaluate the outputs of the two most widely used time series models, ARIMA and ARIMAX, to provide a correct bitcoin price forecast. Due to the inclusion of exogenous variables, which are independent but have an impact on the data, ARIMAX produces superior findings than ARIMA. Because of its past, bitcoin is currently viewed as a store of wealth, with investors able to grow its worth via continued investment. Given the cryptocurrency market's extreme volatility and speculative nature, the challenge is to adequately project the price of Bitcoin [19,20]. Traders and investors need accurate forecasts to reduce risks and make wise decisions while trading Bitcoin. Bitcoin's price fluctuates constantly; at times, it rises significantly, and at other times, it falls.

The suggested approach uses various time series and machine learning algorithms to predict Bitcoin values. Our goal is to create strong models that can identify the fundamental trends and patterns in the Bitcoin market by combining pertinent attributes with historical price data. We will teach and assess these models to determine how well they can forecast future price fluctuations.

This paper aims to create and assess machine learning models that correctly forecast Bitcoin values. The models include Seasonal autoregressive integrated moving average with exogenous regressors (SARIMAX), Bayesian regression elastic net regression, polynomial regression uto-regressive (AR), autoregressive moving average (ARMA), autoregressive integrated moving average (ARIMA), and vector autoregression (VAR).

Proposed Architecture

The historical price information is required for training models that use machine learning to make Bitcoin price prediction. Coin market cap API includes this information. There is no need to cleanse the data since it's already pre-clean.

The original dataset had several variables that might be categorized as "USD open," "time open," "time close," "time light," and "time low." "USD volume," "USD market_cap," "USD.high," "USD.low," "USD.close," and "USD timestamp". The characteristics that are kept after feature extraction include date: the observation's time stamp, USD low represents the lowest price of bitcoin for the day; USD high represents the highest price of bitcoin for the day; open represents the opening price of bitcoin in USD; close represents the closing bitcoin price in USD for the USD volume represents the total amount of bitcoins exchanged in USD for the day. After feature crafting, we were left with a new characteristic, mean (USD.low + USD.high)/2. This provides a more accurate daily bitcoin price figure. In all models, we have utilized this Mean as the forecast characteristic.

For the dataset to be used by the time-series models, the data needs to be stationary. The conditions that need to be satisfied for the data to be stationary are:

1. Mean must be constant
2. Variance must be constant
3. There should be no seasonality.

Before making predictions, we first have to check if the dataset is stationary. For stationary data, statistical properties like variance, mean, and covariance are constant throughout time. The standard methods are generally ineffective when the data is nonstationary. Nonstationary time-series regression could cause false regressions, i.e. situations where the regression equation demonstrates an essential relationship between variables even though there should not be any. The plot for the mean value of Bitcoin for each day is shown in below Figure 27.1.

Several techniques are available to determine if the data is stationary. The augmented Dickey-Fuller (ADF) exam is one of the assessments that we employ. The data is subjected to the ADF test based on many days rather than just one prior day. The test results for the dataset are shown in Table 27.1.

Since the ADF statistic value (−1.381296) is greater than 1% (−3.433) and 5% (−2.567) critical values, the dataset is nonstationary.

We employ the differencing approach to make the dataset stationary. The current observation is subtracted from the prior observation using the differencing approach. The differencing approach is applied to the first-order difference sequence if the stationary is not reached in the initial differencing. To distinguish between the trend, seasonality, and leftover residue, seasonal differencing is used. The analysis of the obtained data is displayed in the three terms above. The trend shows whether the trend in the data is rising or falling. The residue is the quantity that remains after the trend and seasonality are eliminated from the data. Seasonality indicates how the data repeats itself. Normalization is the technique of narrowing the data to a standard value. For the current dataset, min_max scaling is used where the values of the attributes range from 0 to 1.

Linear regression: Linear regression can be used to create the linear model using coefficients that are $w = (w_1...w_a)$ to reduce the squares of residuals among the predicted targets by linear regression and actual targets found in the data. To compare the open value of Bitcoin on a given day with the mean, we employ linear regression. We use the number of days as the input feature to predict the mean value and then generate a comparison utilizing Time-series techniques. Through mathematical modification, we are making the output variable of the linear regression reliant on itself.

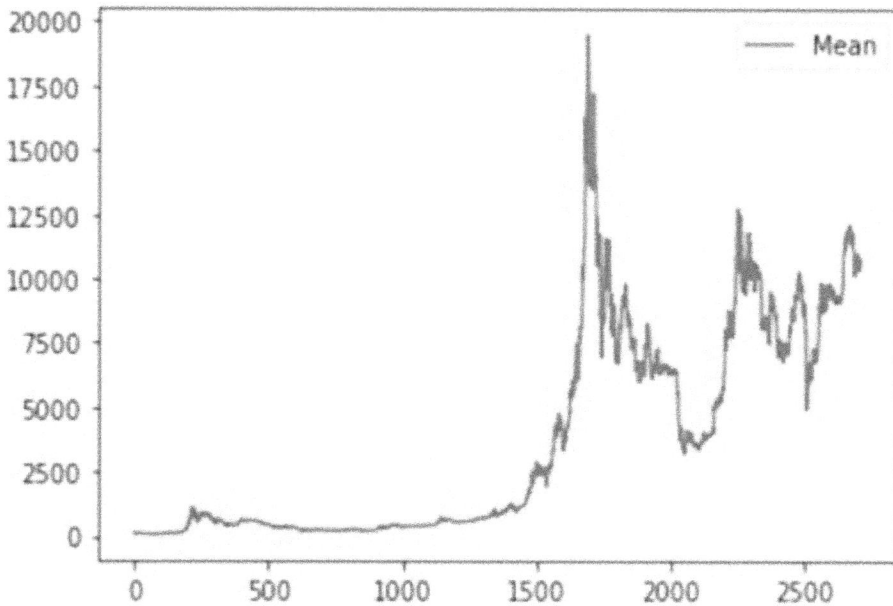

Figure 27.1 Mean value of bitcoin for each day
Source: Author

Table 27.1 Test results for the dataset classification

ADF statistic	-	-1.381296
p-value	-	0.591209
Critical values	1%	-3.433
	5%	-2.863
	10	-2.567

Source: Author

It combines Lasso regression, also known as L_1 regularization, and Ridge regression, commonly known as L_2 regularization, which results in an el astic Net. While Lasso regression chooses the characteristics that have the most influence on the model to produce precise predictions, Ridge regression minimizes overfitting. The factor that influences the decision between Lasso and Ridge regression is the l1_ratio. Grid search determines which value for l1_ratio is optimal. When l1_ratio = 0, L_2 regularization is used, and when l1_ratio = 1, L_1 regularization is used.

Polynomial regression: To forecast the mean value of Bitcoin, a grid search is employed to find the parameter, and a variety of polynomial characteristics are added to the linear regression.

Bayesian regression: Another method for estimating the parameters in the L1 and L2 regression using the Bayesian approach is Bayesian regression.

ARIMA: The acronym ARIMA refers to Auto regression integrated moving average which is a forecasting time series model that integrates AR, MA, and model of integration. The ARIMA model exclusively takes into account the dependent variables, ignoring the independent variables altogether, and forecasts with a high degree of accuracy.

There are four categories for ARIMA models: AR, MA, ARMA, and ARIMA. The output variable in the AR (Auto regressive) model is determined by its historical variables. The output variable of the MA (moving average) model is characterized by its dependence on the values of its previous residual variables. The AR model and the MA model are combined to create the ARMA model. According to how the aforementioned models are defined, the ARMA model fore-casts the results by using its residual values from the provided time series and its prior values. The ARMA(a,b) is another name for ARMA, where p is the AR model's order and q is the MA model's order. The ARIMA model is created by combining the ARMA model with integration, sometimes called differencing. The time series data must be stationary for the ARIMA model to function.

Differentiating is required for the data to remain stationary. A formula to describe the ARIMA model can be characterized as ARIMA(*a*,*b*,*c*) in which the *a* represents the order for the AR model, *b* represents the (I) order or the order in which differencing occurs, and *c* is the order for the MA model. The extension of SARIMAX can be known as seasonal automated regression integrated moving average using exogenous factors. SARIMAX integrates the seasonal cycle into its data forecasts. The model is comprised of two types consisting of (*a*,*b*,*c*) components that are used for the seasonal ARIMA as well as ARIMA.

Results

The AR model forecasts future values. It is predicated on the idea that the time series' present value is a consequence of its earlier values. Estimated coefficients are multiplied by prior observations to make predictions. By estimating coefficients with methods like maximum likelihood estimation or the least squares approach, the model is trained. The graph of the auto-regression model is displayed in Figure 27.2. ARIMA integrates moving average, differencing, and auto-regression components. By differencing, it can manage nonstationary data. The ARIMA equation, which includes moving average, differencing, and autoregressive elements, is the basis for the predictions. Iterative approaches or grid search techniques are used to optimize parameters (*a*,

b, and *c*) to train the model. The graph of the ARIMA regression model is shown in Figure 27.3. SARIMAX extends ARIMA by incorporating seasonal components and exogenous variables to model time series data. Predictions are made based on the SARIMAX equation, considering autoregressive, differencing, moving average, seasonal, and exogenous terms. The model is developed by optimizing parameters (*a* and *b*), (*a*, *b*, *c*) employing grid searches or other iterative techniques. We have tested various models to determine whether machine learning models provide reliable predictions. 10% of the data was used to predict the future, and the rest was used for training models. The expected and actual values by SARIMAX are shown in Figure 27.4. We computed RMSE values and showed graphs for each model using the exact and forecasted Bitcoin values. It has been noted that time series algorithms yield superior outcomes in comparison to basic regression models. The SARIMAX model yielded the most minor root mean square error. The classification of performance evaluation is given in Table 27.2.

Conclusion

In this paper, we have reviewed machine learning algorithms to predict trends, values, and prices. These algorithms can be modified and optimized for real-world applications and used on large-scale datasets for accurate prediction. The

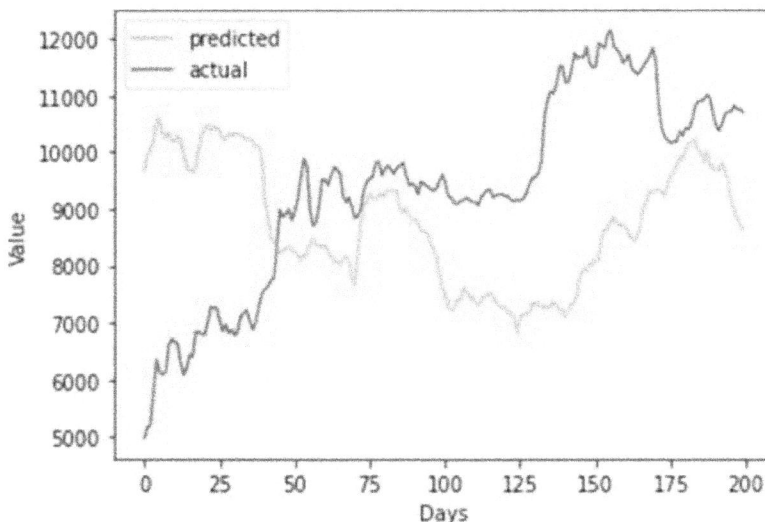

Figure 27.2 Graph of auto regression model
Source: Author

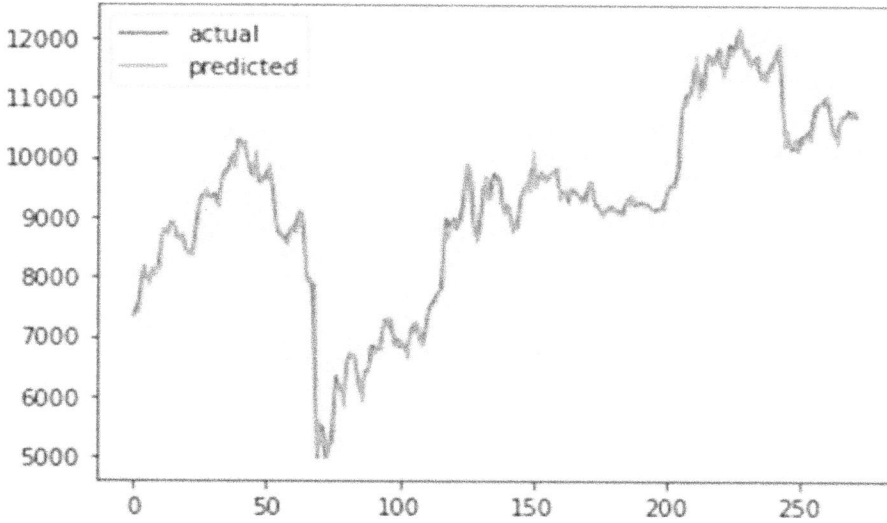

Figure 27.3 Graph of bayesian regression model
Source: Author

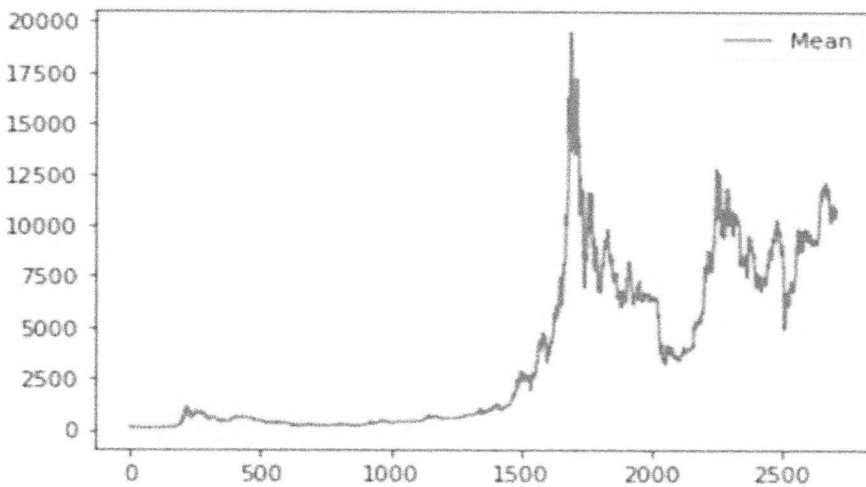

Figure 27.4 Mean value of bitcoin for each day
Source: Author

Table 27.2 Performance evaluation classification

MODEL	RMSE VALUE
Linear regression with elastic net	382.83105
Polynomial RegRegressioneg 2)	1281.8682
Polynomial RegRegressioneg 3)	1703.1671
Polynomial RegRegressioneg 5)	1732.2206
Bayesian regression	382.8316
AR model	2898.81528751
ARIMA model	164.79238637
SARIMAX	158.59324388

Source: Author

machine learning theory is vast and can be used in various domains, such as forecasting and predicting, which are also helpful in studying data science and data analysis. Machine learning models to forecast the values also assisted in identifying the various terms, such as volatility, and their impact on the analysis. The regression algorithms used for the prediction of bitcoin prices are essential, where the aim of obtaining accurate values led to the use of forecasting algorithms or time series models such as ARIMA models. When choosing the forecasting models, various factors within the models, such as differencing, normalization, L_1 and L_2 penalization, and grid search, must be calculated and changed to get the closest and most accurate results. One of the fascinating derivations of mathematics is that the Lasso regression and Ridge regression can also be obtained using the Bayesian approach, which results in Bayesian Regression.

References

[1] Nakamoto, S. (2008). Bitcoin: a peer-to-peer electronic cash system .

[2] En.wikipedia.org (2018). List of cryptocurrencies . https://en.wikipedia.org/wiki/List_of_cryptocurrencies.

[3] Chen, Z., Li, C., and Sun, W. (2020). Bitcoin price prediction using machine learning: an approach to sample dimension engineering. *Journal of Computational and Applied Mathematics*, 365, 112395.

[4] Mangla, N., Bhat, A., Avabratha, G., and Bhat, N. (2019). Bitcoin price prediction using machine learning. *International Journal of Information and Computing Science*, 6(5), 318–320.

[5] Madan, I., Saluja, S., and Zhao, A. (2015). Automated bitcoin trading via machine learning algorithms . URL: http://cs229.Stanford.edu/proj2014/Isaac% 20Madan 20.

[6] Meenakshisundaram, N., and Ramkumar, G. (2022). An optimized machine learning model for automatic prediction of cervi-cal cancer using decision tree classifier. In 2022 International Conference on Computer, Power and Communications (ICCPC), Chennai, India, (pp. 336–341).

[7] Hu, R., and Wang, X. (2022, December). Linkage Analysis Between Bitcoin and Nasdaq Index Based on ARIMAX Model. In 2022 3rd International Conference on Modern Education and Information Management (ICMEIM 2022) (pp. 905–912). Atlantis Press.

[8] Sasani, F., Moghareh Dehkordi, M., Ebrahimi, Z., Dustmohammadloo, H., Bouzari, P., Ebrahimi, P., et al. (2024). Forecasting of bitcoin illiquidity using high-dimensional and tex-tual features. *Computers*, 13(1), 20.

[9] Adhikari, R., and Agrawal, R. (2013). An Introductory Study on Time Series Modeling and Forecasting. Lap Lambert Academic Publishing GmbH KG.

[10] Munim, Ziaul Haque, Mohammad Hassan Shakil, and Ilan Alon. 2019. "Next-Day Bitcoin Price Forecast" *Journal of Risk and Financial Management* 12, no. 2: 103. https://doi.org/10.3390/jrfm12020103

[11] Altay, E., and M. H. Satman. 2005. "Stock Market Forecasting: Artificial Neural Net-work and Linear Regression Comparison in An Emerging Market." *Journal of Financial Management & Analysis* 18 (2): 18.

[12] "Emerging Market." Journal of Financial Management & Analysis 18 (2): 18.

[13] Mallqui, Dennys CA, and Ricardo AS Fernandes. "Predicting the direction, maximum, minimum and closing prices of daily Bitcoin exchange rate using machine learning techniques." *Applied Soft Computing* 75 (2019): 596-606.

[14] H. S. Jung et al., "Predicting bitcoin trends through machine learning using sentiment analysis with technical indicators", *CSSE*, vol. 46, no. 2, pp. 2231-2246, 2023.

[15] Mohamed, Mohamed Ali, Ibrahim Mahmoud El-Henawy, and Ahmad Salah. "Price Prediction of Seasonal Items Using Machine Learning and Statistical Methods." *Computers, Materials & Continua* 70, no. 2 (2022).

[16] Junwei Chen et al., "Analysis of Bitcoin Price Prediction Using Machine Learning", JRFM, vol. 16, no. 1, pp. 51, 2023.

[17] Zi Ye et al., "A Stacking Ensemble Deep Learning Model for Bitcoin Price Prediction Using Twitter Comments on Bitcoin", *Mathematics*, 2022.

[18] Kapur, G., Manohar, S., Mittal, A., Jain, V. and Trivedi, S. (2024), "Cryptocurrency price fluctuation and time series analysis through candlestick pattern of bitcoin and ethereum using machine learning", International Journal of Quality & Reliability Man-agement

[19] T. Klein et al. Bitcoin is not the New Gold–A comparison of volatility, correlation, and portfolio performance *Intern. Rev. Financial Anal.* (2018)

[20] P. Jaquart et al. Short-term bitcoin market prediction via machine learning. *J. Finance Data Sci.* (2021)

28 A case study focusing on partial reconfiguration using FPGA

Rama Rao Chekuri[1,a], Chiluka Likhitha[1,b], Kanukuntla Anjana[1,c], M. C. Chinnaiah[1,d], Kandala Bhavani[1,e], Gurjewar Akash Yadav[1,f] and Nagababu Chekuri[2,g]

[1]Department of Electronics and Communication Engineering, B V Raju Institute of Technology, Narsapur, Medak, 502313, India

[2]Department of Electronics and Communication Engineering MLRITM, Hyderabad, Telangana-500043, India

Abstract:

This case study digs into the practical application of partial reconfiguration (PR) in FPGA- based systems, demonstrating the technology's potential for dynamic resource optimization. PR provides effective allocation of resources by effortlessly transitioning between several hardware configurations at run time. FPGA resources are allocated based on real-time processing requirements. The study emphasizes how PR significantly reduces resource waste and improves system efficiency, making it a desirable strategy for resource- constrained applications. Engineers and academics can learn how to use PR to improve system adaptability and performance. Furthermore, the study analyzes the obstacles and prospects for using PR in even more complicated and dynamic FPGA architectures.

Keywords: ARM cortex- A9, AXI interconnect, FPGA, Xilinx, ZYNQ-7000

Introduction

In today's computer landscape, researchers and engineers are actively exploring new approaches in hardware design to achieve better performance, flexibility, and resource use. One such approach that has caught significant attention is "partial reconfiguration" (PR) [3], a technique enabling the modification of specific regions within a programmable device while the rest of the system remains undisturbed. This capability is particularly promising for applications that prioritize adaptability, efficiency, and minimal downtime [1].

Partial reconfiguration reflects the evolution of reconfigurable computing, offering a unique way to modify parts of a Field-Programmable Gate Array (FPGA) or other programmable devices on the go [2]. Unlike traditional static configurations that require reprogramming the entire device, partial reconfiguration allows real-time adjustments to specific regions, providing a more responsive solution to changing computational needs [12, 4].

For hardware designers, partial reconfiguration is an empowering tool that allows the reconfiguration of specific portions of FPGA or other programmable devices while the rest of the system continues to operate seamlessly [5]. This flexibility supports agile responses to evolving computational requirements [8].

In the complex world of reconfigurable computing, partial reconfiguration stands out as a flexible solution. It allows real-time changes to hardware settings without requiring a full device reprogramming [6, 14]. This feature is especially valuable in situations where quick adjustments are needed to meet changing computational needs [9].

In this paper we are done by two modules they are one is adder module anther is subtractor module [1, 10]. So, adder as RM1 and subtractor worked as a RM2. Because of this RM1(Adder) behaves like static logic and RM2(Subtractor) also behaves reconfigurable logic.

Therefore, when snapping mode is ON state automatically changed one RM1 to another

[a]ramarao.ch@bvrit.ac.in, [b]22215a0410@bvri.ac.in, [c]21211a04b5@bvrit.ac.in, [d]chinnaiah.mc@bvrit.ac.in, [e]21211a04b2@bvrit.ac.in, [f]21211a0496@bvrit.ac.in, [g]nagababu.chekuri@mlritm.ac.in

DOI: 10.1201/9781003616399-28

RM2. Hence the process is highly efficiency for hardware level [1, 13].

Literature Survey

[1] Huebner et al/2022, Partial Reconfiguration "Partial Reconfiguration for FPGA-based Real-Time Systems: A Survey Explored the use of partial reconfiguration in real-time systems and its impact on system performance [2]. Srinivasa Rao/2020 Dynamic and Partial Reconfiguration of Hardware devices: A Survey" Presented a comprehensive survey of reconfiguration techniques and applications in various domains [3]. Lysaght et al/2011 "Dynamic Partial Reconfiguration for Fault Tolerance in FPGAs" Proposed a fault tolerance approach using partial reconfiguration in FPGAs [4]. Sass et al/2002 Reconfigurable Computing for Digital Signal Processing Demonstrated the application of partial reconfiguration in real-time signal processing tasks [5]. Xilinx/1995 Partial Reconfiguration Introduced the concept of partial reconfiguration in FPGAIs.

Design and Analysis

In standard computing configurations, adder and subtractor Register Modules (RMs) are typically situated in the Programmable Logic (PL), while the top modules house programmable logic and a processing system. Within the top modules, the Universal Asynchronous Receiver- Transmitter (UART) plays a pivotal role, serving as both a transmitter and receiver in the PS.SDK.C, the embedded C language.

This facilitates seamless communication between UARTs. The top module incorporates a swapping mode, allowing for dynamic adjustments. Register Modules can exist in varying quantities.

A significant function of UART is to establish communication channels between the Processing System (PS) and Programmable Logic (PL), enhancing the overall versatility and connectivity of the computing architecture.

In this article, the main Role of Software Development Kit (SDK) is controlling the Processing System (PS) for Xilinx ZYNQ -7000 family.

Partial Reconfiguration Flow

Partial reconfiguration is the ability to dynamically modify logic blocks by getting the partial bit files of different operations while the remaining logic continues without interruption. The flexibility of on-site programming and reprogramming without requiring refabrication with a modern design is made possible by FPGA technology. This flexibility can be further enhanced by partial reconfiguration (PR), which loads a partial configuration file—typically a partial BIT file—to enable alteration of an operational FPGA design. Partial BIT files can be downloaded to alter reconfigurable regions of the FPGA after a full BIT file has setup the device, all without affecting the integrity of the programs operating on the portions of the device that are not being reconfigured. Partial reconfiguration is the ability to dynamically modify the logic blocks by getting

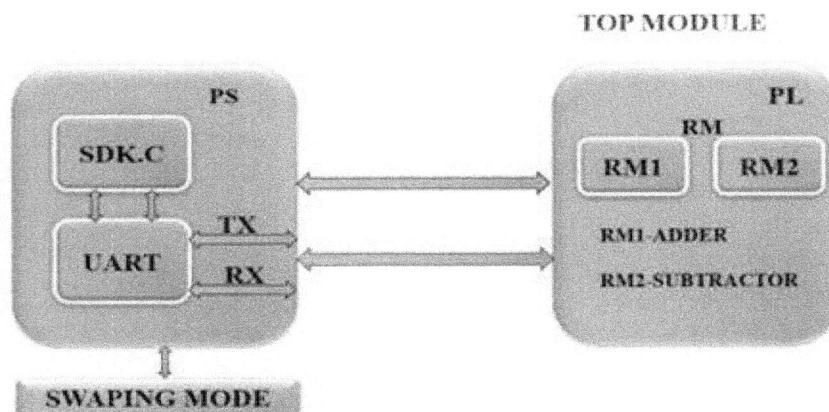

Figure 28.1 Designed model
Source: Author

the partial bit files of different operations while the remaining logic continues without interruption. The partial reconfiguration has the two portions.

1. Reconfigurable partition
2. Reconfigurable module

Introduction partial reconfiguration using the article is to implement a design that dynamically used in Vivado tool.

Partition is the logic of the design. User defined and hierarchy considered for design reuse. Partition is a new implementation of the article. That is maintained functionality and maintains the implementation. This partition is used for the research article flow only and it is a set of reconfigurable module instances with reconfigurable partitions. The pins are a logical and physical connection between the static logic and reconfigurable logic. In the ultra-scale is the minimum required source for reconfiguration. The Programmable unit size resource type.

Reconfigurable frame: It represents the smallest reconfiguration region on the FPGA. Bit stream on the reconfigurable frame is dependent on the logic contained within the frame.

Reconfigurable logic: The logic element is the part of the reconfigurable module. The logical elements modify the partial bit files. Logic components can be modified the LUT's and flip-flops and block RAM's and DSP blocks.

Reconfigurable module: **The** net list is HDL scripting description and implementation with the reconfigurable partition and multiple RM's with the reconfigurable partitions. **Reconfigurable Partition: It** is set an instantiation on that is the instance of the reconfigurable. These partitions

are different from reconfigurable modules and these RP's do the optimizing design and place design and rout design. Reconfigurable module detects on the HD. It consists of 1. Static logic 2. Static design

1. Static logic: Here the static logic is not part of a reconfigurable partition when the RPs are reconfigured the logic element partially reconfigured, and the logic is always active the static logic is also called top-level logic
2. Static design: It is a part of a design and when the partial reconfiguration is running the static design does not change and it is included and not defined at the top-level and all modules are not reconfigured. And it builds static logic and static routing.

Networked multi-port interface
Partial reconfiguration is optimizing the FPGA application reducing the size, cost, and power. Time independent functions are isolated and identified and implemented as a reconfiguration module. It is an out of signal device.

Configuration by bus interface
A new port is produced in a partial reconfiguration in order to use an interface with more capabilities within the design. Following the compilation for configured bit files, the PCI bus interface for configuration connects to the FPGA board, powers it on, and resets the settings. ICAP, or the internal configuration access port, was attached to the PCI interface. In this case, the FPGA setup is supplied and the device load's size and configuration are reduced by bit stream compression.

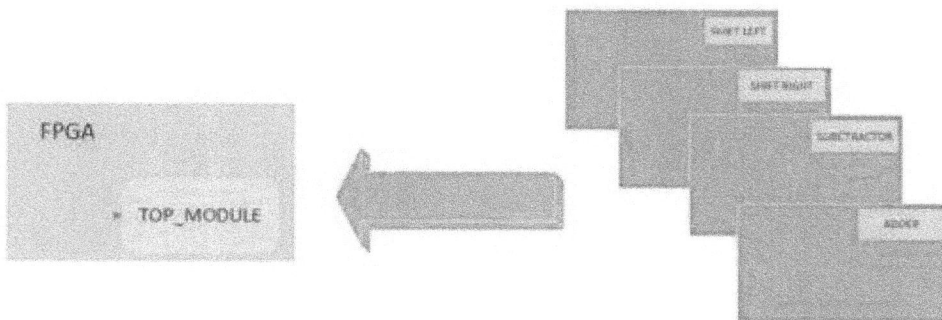

Figure 28.2 Basic premise of partial reconfiguration
Source: Author

Proposed Algorithm

The proposed model for the case study on partial reconfiguration involves leveraging the capability of dynamically modifying and updating specific sections of a field-programmable gate array (FPGA) without affecting the entire design. This model aims to address the need for efficient resource utilization and reduced downtime in scenarios where specific functionalities or algorithms within an FPGA-based system require updates or modifications.

The key components of the model include a well-defined partial reconfiguration framework, which encompasses tools for design partitioning, configuration bit stream generation, and management of the reconfiguration process.

The model also incorporates a robust hardware description language (HDL) codebase that supports modular design, allowing targeted sections of the FPGA to be updated independently.

Furthermore, the proposed model emphasizes seamless integration with existing development environments and tools, ensuring compatibility with industry-standard design flows. This includes support for popular synthesis tools, simulation environments, and debugging methodologies to streamline the development process.

To enhance versatility, the model accommodates diverse application domains, showcasing its adaptability in scenarios such as adaptive signal processing, image processing, or communication protocols. Additionally, it incorporates mechanisms for real-time monitoring and verification to ensure the reliability and correctness of the reconfiguration process.

A UART (Universal Asynchronous Receiver/Transmitter) is a component in a system that handles both transmitting (Tx) and receiving (Rx) data. It's like a communication tool that can send and receive messages.

The programmable logic (PL) part of the system has different functions: snapping mode, adder, and subtractor. Snapping mode is a setting that determines how the adder and subtractor behave. The adder takes a "right move" based on the snapping mode.

The subtractor takes a "left move" based on the snapping mode. Both the adder and subtractor are connected to the UART, meaning they can work together with the communication tool to process data.

The UART helps with sending and receiving information, while the snapping mode, adder, and subtractor in the PL handle specific operations on that data based on the chosen snapping mode.

Implementation

The PR flow enables different setups in the hardware. To achieve this, multiple implementations are needed. In the PR design, each implementation comes with its own configuration. Each module design is both static and reconfigurable, meaning it can use previous implementations.

In the PR design implementation, each partition contains a reconfigurable module. A property is set on the top-level, indicating it should be reconfigurable. For instance, in designing a reconfigurable partition, features like count-up and count-down statements can be incorporated. This reconfiguration partition can be named, for instance, "inst_count.".

Here the main role of Processing system is controlled by UART as well ARM cortex-A9. So, ARM cortex is linked to UART and programming logic (PL). therefore, the main hart of moving from PS side to PL side.

Results

Routing plays a crucial role in FPGA design; these resources is allocated to interconnectivity.

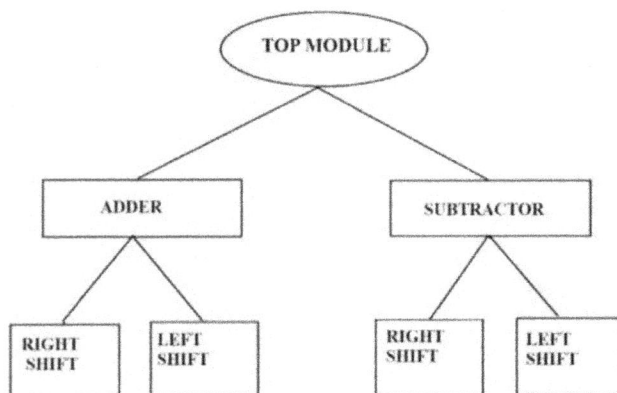

Figure 28.3 Flow chart
Source: Author

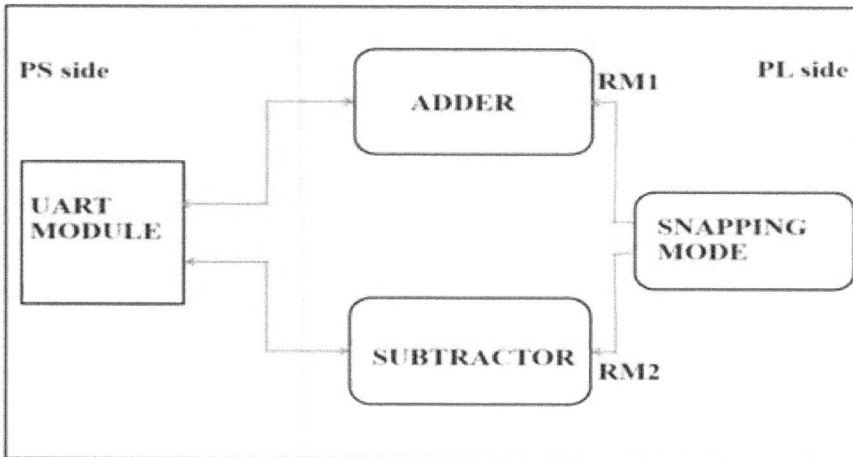

Figure 28.4 Architecture of partial reconfiguration
Source: Author

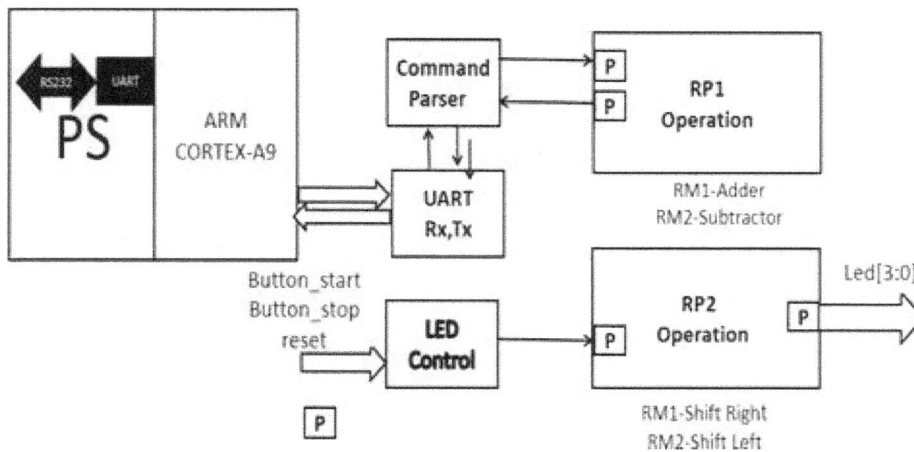

Figure 28.5 Processing system
Source: Author

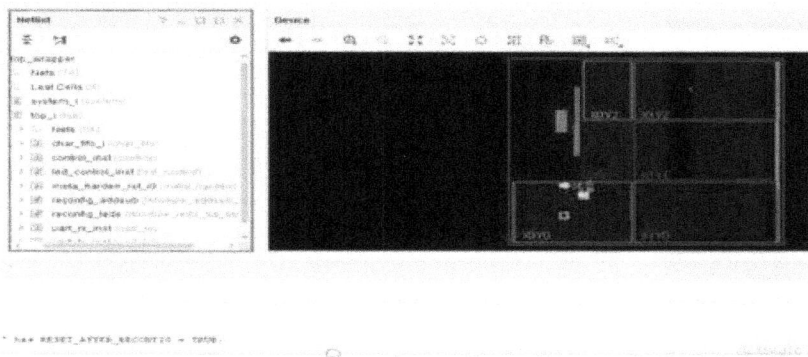

Figure 28.6 Routing & floor planning for P block reconfiguration
Source: Author

The interconnection delays often out weight the logic delays in the circuit, emphasizing the importance of an efficient routing algorithm. This algorithm aims to minimize both the total wiring area and the lengths of critical-path nets, enhancing circuit performance.

Definition: Static modules persist across all instances in a schedule, remaining active consistently. On the other hand, dynamic modules are swapped in and out of instances, exhibiting variability within the schedule.

The floor planning problem in partial reconfiguration involves creating a global floorplan. Each floorplan, corresponding to a scheduled instance, must be feasible. Common modules are positioned consistently in both location and shape across all instances. This ensures a synchronized layout for shared components throughout the schedule.

In this article, most of the P block reconfiguration well performance is very high why because DSP blocks, LUT, blocks RAMs elements are used in P block reconfiguration. So, the implementing time is very fast then normal flow.

Hardware Level

In hardware level, we were used for adder in that adder also can be used two types one is shift left another one is shift right. Therefore, adder is 4-bit LEDs blinking right side only and whereas subtractor is classified two modules one is shift left and another is shift right. Hence subtractor is 4-bit LEDs blinking left side only. So whole

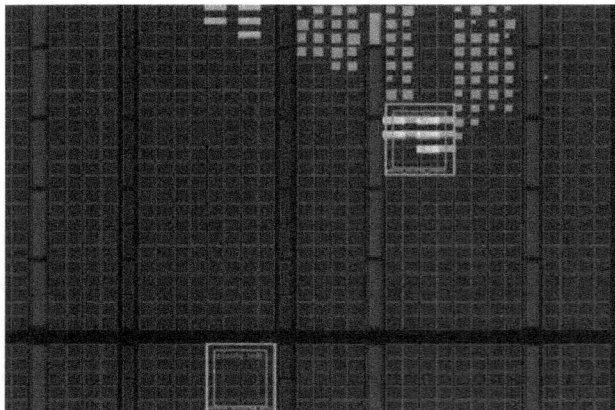

Figure 28.8 Leds blinking LEFT
Source: Author

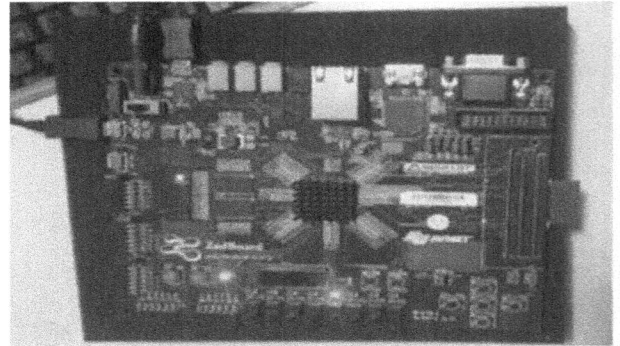

Figure 28.9 Leds blinking RIGHT
Source: Author

system will be moving left to right one to anther module by automatically for using partial reconfiguration flow.

In that PR flow can be generates different bit files. This bit files is one is top level like work as a static mode another bit files are N no of bits like a dynamic mode. Finally, PR flow is moving static to dynamic on automatically.

Conclusion

We explored a partial reconfiguration by considering a addition and subtraction as an example. For the transmission of input-output bits here we are using UART device. By using partial

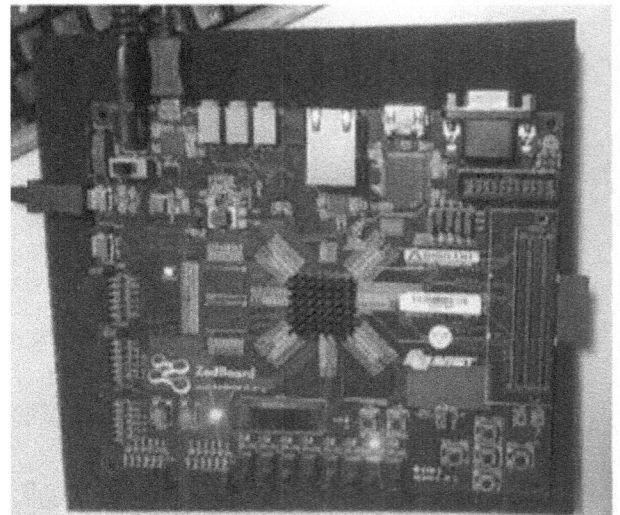

Figure 28.7 P block reconfiguration
Source: Author

reconfiguration multiple-bit streams are generated automatically, without any manual operation. It has an enhancement of the flexibility of their SDR platform, Partial reconfiguration proved to be a valuable tool for dynamic reconfiguration of FPGA designs, providing benefits such as flexibility, resource optimization. And reduced downtime. In future also we can have used image processing like camera pipelines and IP cores.

References

[1] Bhuvaneswari, K., and Srinivasa Rao, V. (2013). Dynamic partial reconfigurationin low-cost FPGAs. *International Journal of Scientific and Engineering Research*, 4, 1410–1413.

[2] Bhandari, S. U., Subbaraman, S., Pujari, S., and Mahajan, R. (2010). Internal dynamic partial reconfiguration for real timesignal processing on FPGA. *Indian Journal of Science and Technology*, 3(4), 365–368.

[3] Bhandari, S. U., Subbaraman, S., and Pujari, S. (2009). Digital signal modulator on FPGA using on the Fly partial reconfiguration. In 2009 International Conference on Advances in Computing, Controland Telecommunication Technologies. 2009 IEEE.

[4] Bondalapati, K., and Prasanna, V. K. (2002). Reconfigurable computing systems. *Proceedings of the IEEE*, 90(7), 1201–1217.

[5] R.V. Kshirsagar and S. Sharma ,DIFFERENCE BASED PARTIAL RECONFIGURATION, *International Journal of Advances in Engineering & Technology*, May 2011. ©IJAET,SSN: 2231–1963

[6] Ashutosh Gupta and Kota Solomon Raju, Design And Implementation Of 32-Bit Controller For Interactive Interfacing With Reconfigurable Computing Systems, (*IJCSIT*), Vol 1, No 2, November 2009.

[7] K. Bhuvaneswari and V. Srinivasa Rao,Dynamic Partial Reconfiguration in Low-Cost FPGAs, *Advance in Electronic and Electric Engineering*. ISSN 2231-1297, Volume 3, Number 2 (2013), pp. 257–264.

[8] Ipseeta Nanda, Nibedita Adhikari,Application and performance FPGA using partial reconfiguration with Xilinx Plan Ahead, December 2017 DOI.10.1109/ITEC-India. 2017.8333891.

[9] Vipin, K., and Fahmy, S. A. (2018). FPGA dynamic and partial reconfiguration: a survey of architectures, methods, and applications. *ACM Computing Surveys (CSUR)*, 51(4), 1–39. DOI.101145/3193827.

[10] Huebner, et al. (2022). Partial Reconfiguration for FPGA-Based Real-Time Systems: A Survey. Xilinx White Paper Industrial Informatics.

[11] Papadimitriou, K., and Dollas, A. (2011). Performance of partial reconfiguration in FPGA systems: a survey and a cost model. 4(4), 1–24. Article No.: 36 doi: org/10.1145/2068716.2068722.

[12] Neelam, A. K., and Musala, S. (2020). Real-time self- repairable multiplexer for fault tolerant systems. In Proceedings IEEE International Conference Communication Signal Process. (ICCSP), (pp. 1124–1127), Chennai, India, doi:10.1109/ICCSP48568.2020 .9182108.

[13] Akbar, M. A., Wang, B., and Bermak, A. (2020). Self- repairing hybrid adder with hot-standby topology using fault- localization. *Journals and Magazine, IEEE Access*, 8, 150051–150058. **ISSN:** 2169-3536, doi:10.1109/ACCESS.2020.3016427.

[14] Pezzarossa, L., Schoeberl, M., and Sparsø, J. (2017). A controller for dynamic partial reconfiguration in FPGA- based real-time systems. In Denmark, Proceedings IEEE 20th International Symposium Real- Time Distributed Computing (ISORC), (pp. 92–100). doi:10.1109/ISORC.2017.3.

29 Smart tag EMS: utilizing intelligent navigation and communication to transform ambulance response

Bharath Kumar, K.[a], Radarapu Sri Vardhan[b], Koduri Bhavya[c], Maturi Saipujith[d] and Nenavath Pradeep[e]

Electronics and Communication, CMR Technical Campus, Kandlakoya, Medchal, Hyderabad, India

Abstract

One of the main issues facing the globe today is overpopulation. Speaking of facts, there are more cars on the road when there are more people living there. Thus, one of the most important problems facing many modern metropolises is traffic management. In many places, traffic signal congestion is a major issue, particularly for emergency vehicles. When ambulances are delayed in cases of traffic congestion, ineffective traffic control results in fatalities. The suggested solution develops an Arduino based traffic light controller optimization. The technology aims to mitigate traffic bottlenecks caused by traffic lights to some extent and facilitate drivers' avoidance of crowded routes. It also notifies hospitals ahead of time about the emergency's severity so that they can prepare the necessary resources. The goal of this study is to improve the efficiency of emergency medical response by presenting the design and implementation of an advanced ambulance navigation and communication system. The technology finds the fastest path to the closest hospital while avoiding traffic by fusing real-time GPS navigation with traffic data. The device also makes it easier for hospital staff to communicate with each other and provides real-time updates on the patient's condition. During medical situations, this novel method improves patient care, emergency response times, and general road safety.

Keywords: Arduino UNO R3, challans system, ESP-32 CAM, GSM 900A, GSM NEO 6M, HC-05 Bluetooth

Introduction

Cities are actively transforming into smart ambulances in today's world, which calls for innovations in a number of different technology areas. The optimization of ambulance response times and the provision of excellent patient care, particularly in emergency situations, present a distinct challenge to the healthcare industry. Traffic congestion is a significant obstacle to the timely arrival of ambulances in urban areas. In addition, the rise in traffic incidents highlights how critical it is to prevent deaths. Emerging technologies such as the Internet of Things (IoT) become crucial in overcoming these challenges. IoT uses a variety of networking techniques and software to manage a network of networked physical devices. Simultaneously, the incorporation of REST APIs enables smooth communication between the server and client ends in these smart cities are actively transforming into smart ambulances in

today's world, which calls for innovations in a number of different technology areas. The optimization of ambulance response times and the provision of excellent patient care, particularly in emergency situations, present a distinct challenge to the healthcare industry. Traffic congestion is a significant obstacle to the timely arrival of ambulances in urban areas. In addition, the rise in traffic incidents highlights how critical it is to prevent deaths.

The key to the strategic design of REST APIs is to minimize temporal complexity as much as possible. This means reducing bandwidth, strengthening data packet integrity during transactions, and optimizing data interchange. Using cutting edge technology, our application effortlessly aligns with the objective to make vital services more accessible and actively contribute to the creation of smart cities. Our goal is to accelerate the ongoing transition into smart cities by leading

[a]kammarabharathkumar@gmail.com, [b]227R1A04B4@cmrtc.ac.in, [c]227R1A0487@cmrtc.ac.in, [d]227R1A0494@cmrtc.ac.in, [e]227R1A04A1@cmrtc.ac.in

DOI: 10.1201/9781003616399-29

technical innovation to address these issues and significantly improve the efficiency and accessibility of vital emergency services.

The primary goals of this article

- Create a GPS-based navigation system that can quickly locate and direct an ambulance to the closest hospital.
- By using real-time traffic data, the route can be dynamically adjusted to avoid crowded locations and reduce travel time.
- Provide a method to track and notify any drivers who misbehave or fail to comply in the area around the ambulance (called "challans").
- Establish a communication interface so that the closest hospital is informed in real time about the patient's condition.
- Ascertain that the hospital is promptly informed of the patient's medical requirements as well as the projected time of arrival of the ambulance.

The purpose of this article is to improve patient care, communication, and navigation in ambulances. Real-time GPS navigation combined with traffic data integration, traffic signal control to priorities ambulances, constant hospital staff communication, cutting-edge medical monitoring equipment, and an incident reporting system for non-cooperative road users are some of the essential elements. The project aims to guarantee effective ambulance transportation, cut down on trip time, and enhance patient care via real-time information. Systems for traffic and navigation management, communication interfaces, monitoring tools, and reporting guidelines are among the deliverables. EMS providers, hospitals, law enforcement, patients, and members of the public are considered stakeholders. The availability of real-time traffic data, the collaboration of local authorities, a dependable communication infrastructure, and skilled workers are all taken for granted. The budget, governmental permissions, and data privacy are examples of constraints.

Literature Survey

One of the most widely used smart phone operating systems right now is Android, and its

popularity is only growing. It is also one of the most versatile and open platforms, giving software developer's quick access to extensive software APIs and phone hardware. In the near future, we see Android-powered smart phones as a potent and extensively utilized platform for participatory sensing. This research looks at Android smart phones in relation to monitoring the quality of the road surface. Using a sensor application on Android phones, we tested a number of pothole identification algorithms while driving in an urban area. Demand is rising for technologies that allow fisheries products to be traceable.

Disposal RF(IC) tags, which have the ability to immediately record information onto them, are the foundation of most recently proposed technologies. However, the expensive cost of the tags and their incapacity to read information when affixed to the surface of objects that contain a lot of water restrict the current RF tag-based systems. As a result, it is not possible to build systems that are practically feasible using RF tags. Road accidents have become a regular occurrence in today's globe. Every year, a large number of deaths are attributed to inadequate post-accident medical care. There isn't a reliable way to notify the appropriate authorities in a timely manner in order to preserve the person's life. We are developing a gadget that will not only identify every collision that occurs with the vehicle but also notify the relevant authorities right away [1].

However, the present RF tag-based systems are hindered by the high cost of the tags and their inability to read information when attached to the surface of items that contain a lot of water. As a result, it is not possible to build systems that are practically feasible using RF tags [2].

Road accidents have become a regular occurrence in today's globe. Every year, a large number of deaths are attributed to inadequate post-accident medical care. There isn't a reliable way to notify the appropriate authorities in a timely manner in order to preserve the person's life. We are developing a gadget that will not only identify every collision that occurs with the vehicle but also notify the relevant authorities right away [3].

To evaluate the features and health literacy (HL) of the medication adherence apps that are currently on the market and to develop a searchable website to help patients and healthcare professionals (HCP) find high-quality adherence applications. Description of the practice: Medication no adherence is still a major issue, which contributes to unneeded medical expenses and poor health consequences [4].

Given that over 40.000 people die in traffic accidents in the EU each year, the European Commission acknowledges that the current efforts to lower the death toll are insufficient. The European Commission suggested that the European Union set a goal to cut the number of road fatalities in half by the year 2010 in its 2001 White paper on European Transport Police. The creation of the safety forum is one of the European Commission's initiatives. It is a collaborative industry/public Endeavour aimed at enhancing road safety through the use of emerging ICTs [5].

Android is currently one of the most widely used Smartphone operating systems, and its popularity is only growing. It is also one of the most versatile and open platforms, giving software developer's quick access to sophisticated software and phone hardware [6].

We can get closer to the concept of the smart car by integrating smart phones with current automobiles via a suitable interface, providing the user with new features and services while driving. In this work, we provide an Android-based application that uses the on-board diagnostics (OBD-II) interface to monitor the car and identify accidents [6]. It transmits information to the hospital about the patient's health parameter and the ambulance's current location via an LCD display [7].

Existing method

- Software integration in healthcare: Although it focuses on traffic accidents, research on IoT integration in healthcare could enhance emergency response and post-accident medical treatment.
- Fishery product cost-effective traceability: highlights problems with pricey RF tags. The development of affordable traceability methods for fisheries products could be the subject of future research.
- Smart vehicle paradigm: By taking into account features and services that improve the smart vehicle paradigm, there is a chance to investigate the integration of cell phones and automobiles for uses beyond accident detection [9].
- Health app evaluation: While medication adherence applications evaluate users' health literacy, there may be a lack of thorough reviews of health apps that cater to a range of healthcare requirements.
- Real-time communication in emergency response: Taking into account factors like data transfer speed and dependability, research might examine the effectiveness of real-time communication technologies, such the IoT and cloud computing, in improving emergency response systems.
- Privacy and security issues with healthcare technology: Because of the focus on healthcare technology, there may be a research vacuum in addressing privacy and security issues related to the gathering, sending, and storing of private health information.
- User adoption and accessibility in smart city initiatives: Although some aspects of smart cities are mentioned in the snippets, there may be a research gap regarding the difficulties in gaining user adoption and enhancing accessibility when implementing smart city initiatives, particularly in a variety of socio-economic contexts.
- Sustainable and scalable IoT solutions: Given the growth of IoT technology [1,2], research could concentrate on creating environmentally friendly, flexible, and sustainable IoT solutions.
- Standardizations of health app quality: Researching the standardization of standards for assessing and guaranteeing the efficacy, safety, and quality of applications connected to health could be a step towards addressing the issue of health app quality [6].
- Inclusive design in healthcare technologies: One area of research that has to be addressed is whether healthcare technologies are inclusive enough to meet the demands of a variety of groups, including people with different degrees of technology literacy and accessibility requirements.

Proposed system

The goal of this article is to create an advanced ambulance navigation and communication system that will improve emergency medical services by integrating traffic signal systems to prevent traffic jams and provide real-time navigation to the closest hospital. The device will track ambulance staff behavior and automatically relay updates on patient conditions to the closest hospital. A hospital communication interface, traffic data integration, traffic signal control module, GPS system, and sensor- and camera-based behavior monitoring system are some of the essential parts. The system will provide effective data processing and safe data transfer. The system must be designed, developed, tested, integrated, and deployed as part of the implementation strategy. Regular maintenance and updates will then come afterward. Anticipated results include shorter ambulance travel times, better hospital-paramedic communication, increased hospital readiness, and enhanced paramedic staff monitoring. All of these will eventually result in faster response times, better patient outcomes, and increased public safety. Proposed system block diagram is shown in Figure 29.1.

Hardware Implementation

Arduino board with AVR microcontroller
Due to its ease of use and versatility, the Arduino UNO is a well-liked microcontroller board for electronics projects and prototyping. Driven by the ATmega328P microcontroller, it has six analogue inputs, fourteen digital I/O pins, and a USB port for convenient programming. Because of its open-source nature, a large number of libraries and strong community support are possible. Because of its ease of use and compatibility with a variety of sensors, actuators, and displays, the UNO bridges the gap between hardware and software innovation in a small, cost-effective design, making it a great platform for both novice and experienced developers. This is shown in Figure 29.2.

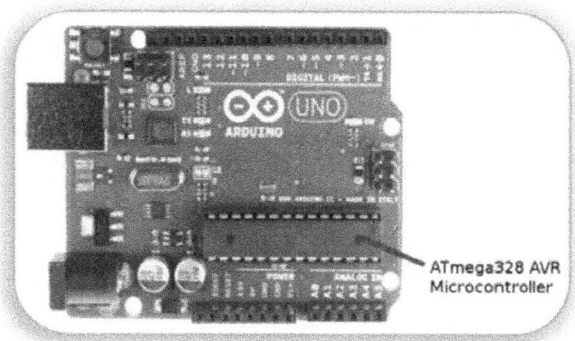

Figure 29.2 Arduino UNO R3 module
Source: Author

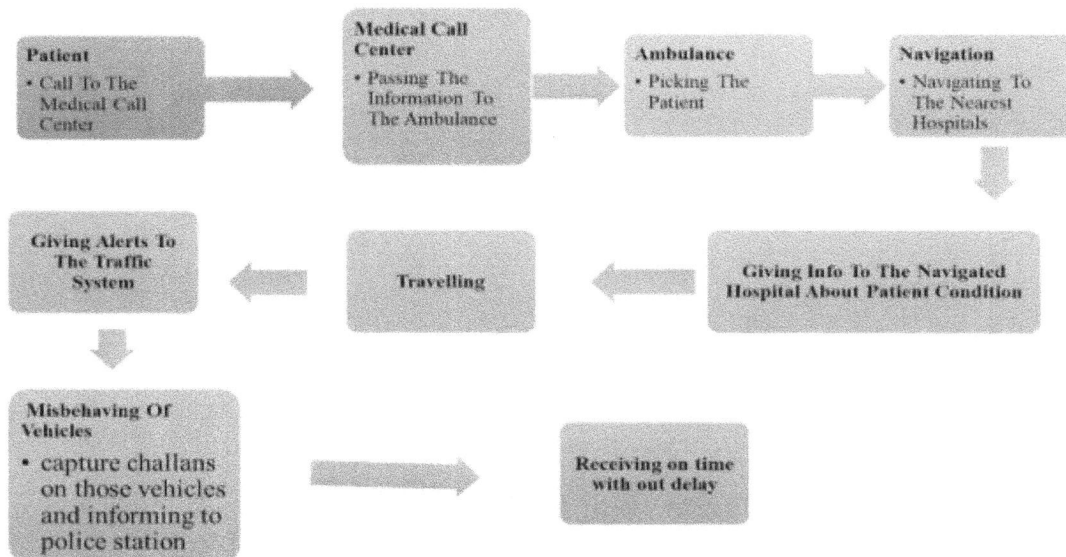

Figure 29.1 Block diagram of proposed model
Source: Author

GSM SIM900A

This wireless module is dependable and incredibly small. A full dual-band GSM/GPRS solution in an SMT module that can be integrated into customer applications is the SIM900A is shown in Figure 29.3. The SIM900A is a tiny form factor, low power consumption GSM/GPRS 900/1800MHz phone, SMS, data, and fax device with an industry-standard interface. The SIM900A can accommodate nearly all space needs in user applications with its minuscule 24 × 24 × 3 mm form, particularly for thin and compact design requirements.

GPS NEO 6M

GPS satellites send signals to the NEO-6M module, which uses those signals to calculate its position. After processing this data, it outputs position information as latitude and longitude co-ordinates. Using its TxD (Transmitter) and RxD (Receiver) pins, the module establishes serial communication with a microcontroller (such as an Arduino or ESP32). This is shown in Figure 29.4

ESP 32 CAM

Based on ESP32, the ESP32-CAM is a compact camera module with minimal power consumption. It includes an inbuilt TF card slot and an OV2640 camera. Intelligent Internet of Things applications like WiFi picture uploading, QR identification, wireless video monitoring, and more can make extensive use of the ESP32-CAM. This is shown in Figure 29.5.

Figure 29.4 GPS NEO 6M
Source: Author

Figure 29.5 ESP 32 CAM module
Source: Author

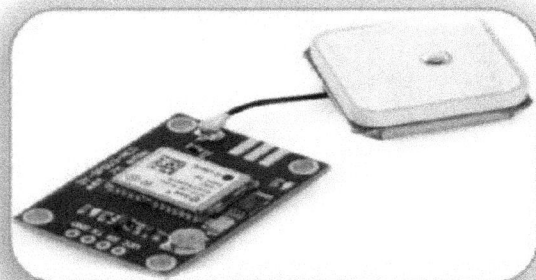

Figure 29.3 GSM SIM 900A module
Source: Author

TTL converter

A transistor-transistor logic (TTL) converter is frequently required in order to interface an ESP32-CAM module with other devices, such as a computer for programming or debugging. This is due to the fact that many USB-to-serial converters and other peripherals run at a 5V logic level, but the ESP32-CAM runs at 3.3V. This is shown in Figure 29.6.

HC-05 Bluetooth

Popular and adaptable, the HC-05 Bluetooth Serial Port Protocol (SPP) module is made for clear wireless serial communication. This is shown in Figure 29.7.

Results and Discussions

- Implementation-1: To guarantee prompt medical assistance, navigation to the closest hospital is facilitated from the site.

Figure 29.6 TTL converter Pin configuration module
Source: Author

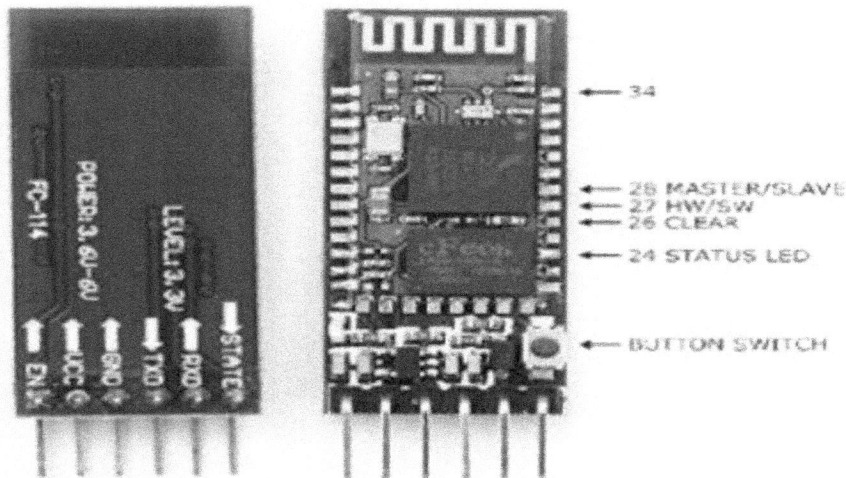

Figure 29.7 HC-05 bluetooth module
Source: Author

- Implementation-2: Based on travelled instructions, traffic signals are notified to clear the ambulance's way.
- Implementation-3: Medical staff and doctors receive timely preparations for patient care through messages sent to hospitals.
- Implementation-4: To enforce traffic laws, cars that interfere with ambulances are given tickets.

The over set of the project shown in Figure 29.8.

Implementation-01: patients condition and requirements

In this implementation, we create a WhatsApp group with hospitals and ambulance services that have been recruited. Instantaneous updates on the patient's status and particular needs are provided in this group when an ambulance arrives to pick them up. By pressing a dedicated button, hospitals may react quickly and send the ambulance driver an alert call that lasts three to four seconds. To guarantee smooth navigation, comprehensive location data is messaged after this alarm. By improving communication between hospitals and ambulances, this technology enables more rapid and knowledgeable medical responses. By giving real-time updates, it enhances emergency operations and improves patient care and provider coordination in emergency situations. The LED glow is shown in Figure 29.9.

Implementation:-02 traffic control system
In this case, the traffic signal alternates between green signals on routes 1 through 4 in a continuous loop. On route number 3, an ambulance with a Bluetooth app linked approaches, and the driver uses the app to flip a switch. This causes the traffic signal on road 3 to turn green instantly, stopping the signals on the other roads that have a red light. Until the ambulance leaves that route, this arrangement won't change. By allowing the ambulance driver to change the signal to any road, when necessary, this technology maximizes

traffic flow and guarantees emergency vehicles have quick access. The ambulance in traffic signal and in that way gives green LED shown in Figure 29.10.

Implementation:-03 challans system
It is believed that this adoption will increase public awareness. A vehicle that does not surrender to an ambulance or obstructs its path is the target of a challans system that we have put in place to increase awareness and enhance emergency response. Through the punishment of offenders who obstruct ambulance movements, this effort seeks to priorities prompt medical help and save lives. We hope to promote a culture of respect for emergency vehicles and guarantee unimpeded access during crucial times by implementing these sanctions. This strategy is essential for raising public awareness of the significance of giving way to ambulances, which could shorten response times and

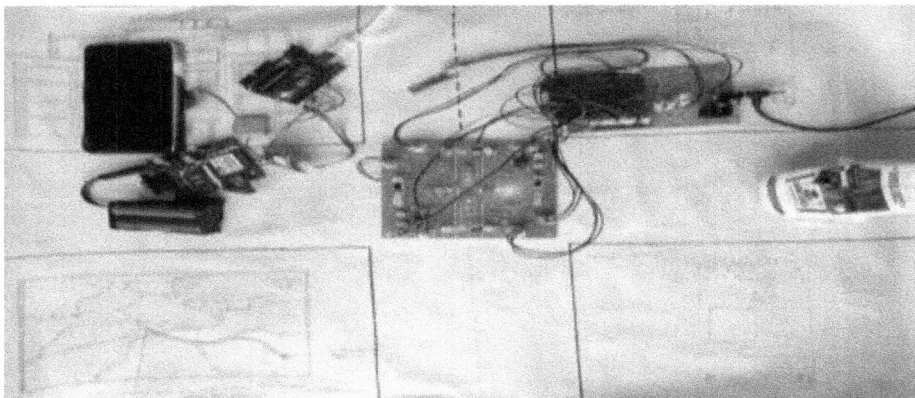

Figure 29.8 Over all setup
Source: Author

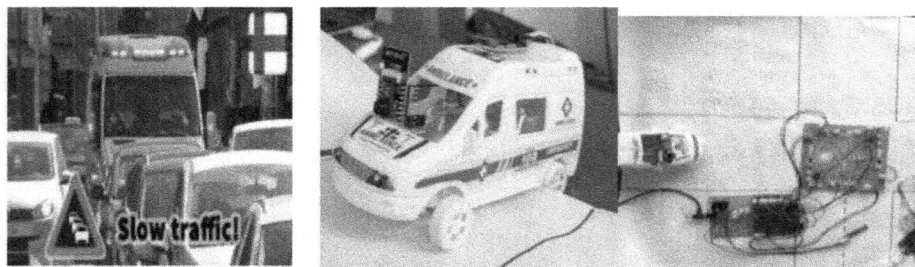

Figure 29.9 Ambulance drivers an alert call
Source: Author

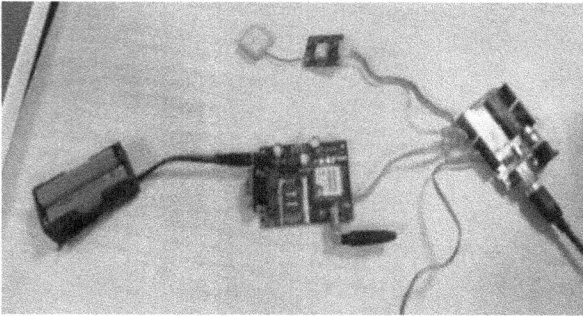

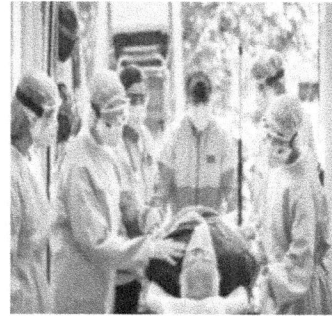

Figure 29.10 Ambulances in traffic signal
Source: Author

improve the efficacy of emergency services as a whole. When any vehicle is come to ambulance then that vehicle get challans which shown in Figure 29.11.

Implementation:-04 cars that interfere with ambulances are given tickets

Telegram bot requires a few steps to create. To establish a new bot and obtain the bot token, first message the Bot Father on Telegram. Next, install the python-telegram-bot library and set up a Python development environment. To handle bot commands and messages, write a Python

script and authenticate with the given token. To get updates from Telegram, the script should provide functions for various commands and make use of web hooks or polling. Lastly, to run the bot constantly, deploy it to a server. This enables user interaction and message response for your bot. which shown in Figure 29.12

Conclusion

Using state-of-the-art technology, the advanced ambulance navigation and communication system seeks to transform emergency medical

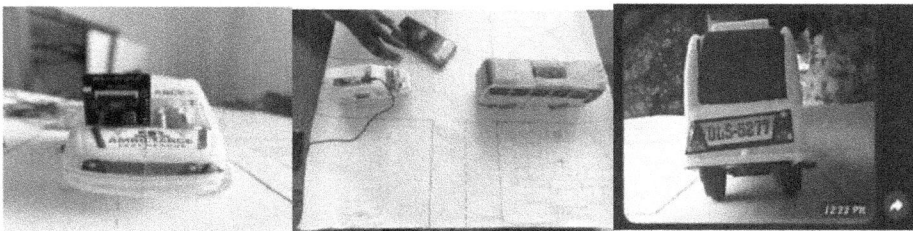

Figure 29.11 Another vehicle challans
Source: Author

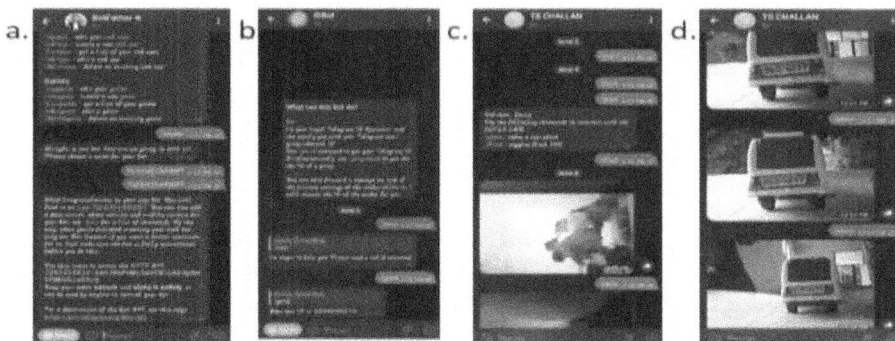

Figure 29.12 (a) Telegram bot creator b) Know your Telegram id c) Open created telegram bot d) Start capture the pics
Source: Author

services. Through the integration of GPS navigation with real-time traffic data and traffic signal control capabilities, this system guarantees ambulances arrive at the closest hospital in a timely and efficient manner, avoiding traffic jams. Furthermore, it offers a direct line of communication with the hospital to transmit vital medical data instantly, allowing hospital personnel to get ready before the patient arrives. By taking a comprehensive strategy, the ambulance's route is optimized and patient care is improved during transit, increasing the likelihood of a successful outcome.

References

[1] Zanella, A., Bui, N., Castellani, A., Vangelista, L., and Zorzi, M. (2014). Smart ambulance technique. *IEE Journal*, Vol. 1, No. 1.

[2] Venkatesh, V., Kumar, M. P., Vaidhyanathan, V., and Raj, P. (2011). An ambient healthmonitor for the new generation healthcare. *Journal of Theoretical and Applied Information Technology*, 31(2), 9199.

[3] Venkatesh, V., Raj, P., Gopalan, K., and Rajeev, T. (2011). Healthcare data fusion and presentation using service-oriented architecture (SOA) orchestration mechanism. *IJCA Special Issue on Artificial Intelligence Techniques - Novel Approaches and Practical Applications*, 2, 17–23.

[4] Jadhav, R., Patel, J., Jain, D., and Phadhtare, S. (2014). Emergency management system using android application. *International Journal of Computer Science and Information Technologies*, 5(3), 2803–2805.

[5] Zhang, R., and Yuan, D. (2007). A health monitoring system for wireless sensor networks. In Proceedings of 2ed IEEE Conference on Industrial Electronics and Applications (ICIEA), (pp. 1648–1652), Harbin, China.

[6] Whipple, J., Arensman, W., and Boler, M. S. (2009). A public safety application of gps-enabled smartphones and the android operating system. In Information Systems Engineering Department, Proceedings of the 2009 IEEE International Conference on Systems, Man, and Cybernetics San Antonio, TX, USA - October 2009.

[7] Sarasa-Carbazole, A., and Sierra, J. L. (2013). Grammar-driven development of JSON processing applications. In Fac. Informatic. Universidad Completeness de Madrid. 28040 Madrid (Spain), Proceedings of the 2013 Federated Conference on Computer Science and Information Systems (pp. 1557–1564).

30 Sentiment analysis and visualization of real and fake reviews

Samanvitha Maddula[a], Sagi Neha[b], Sahasra Garlapati[c], Nimma Kruthika Reddy[d] and Satish Babu Thunuguntla[e]

Department of Computer Science and Engineering B V Raju Institute of Technology, Narsapur, Medak, India

Abstract

The proliferation of online reviews has significantly influenced consumer behavior, yet their credibility is often undermined by fake reviews. This study aims to develop a framework for detecting fake reviews and analyzing sentiment using machine learning (ML) techniques and Natural Language Processing (NLP). Utilizing a quantitative approach with labeled review datasets, we apply various ML techniques, achieving high accuracy in identifying fake reviews. Sentiment analysis (SA) reveals distinct trends in real and fake reviews, with genuine reviews showing more varied sentiments. The results suggest that ML can effectively distinguish between genuine and fraudulent reviews, enhancing the reliability of online review platforms.

Keywords: Fake review detection, machine learning, natural language processing, online reviews, sentiment analysis

Introduction

In the realm of digital commerce, online reviews significantly shape consumer behavior and influence purchasing decisions. Platforms like Amazon host millions of product reviews, which customers rely on for genuine feedback. However, the trustworthiness of these reviews is increasingly undermined by fake reviews, which can mislead consumers and distort product perceptions [1]. To combat fake reviews, Amazon employs advanced AI which analyzes reviewer behavior, including history, sign-ins, and relationships with other online accounts. This AI technology blocks suspicious reviews, ensuring authenticity. In 2023, Amazon blocked over 250 million suspected fake reviews and identified numerous social media groups with nearly 50 million members involved in writing fake reviews. The prevalence of fraudulent reviews underscores the need to differentiate authentic reviews from deceptive ones.

Sentiment analysis (SA), a field within Natural Language Processing (NLP) [2], offers a systematic method for evaluating sentiments in textual data. By analyzing customer reviews' emotional tone and polarity, SA helps gauge product perception and identify inconsistencies that may signal fake reviews. It involves classifying reviews based on their emotional tone—+ve, -ve, or neutral—and understanding the underlying sentiments. Visualization techniques further enhance understanding by converting complex SA data into intuitive graphical formats, aiding in the identification of fraudulent reviews [3].

This study focuses on applying SA to Amazon product reviews to distinguish genuine feedback from fraudulent ones. Utilizing machine learning (ML) algorithms [4], we aim to accurately classify reviews and develop dynamic visualizations to present our findings. Our goal is to enhance the trustworthiness and transparency of online consumer reviews, fostering a more reliable e-commerce environment for both consumers and businesses [5].

The framework combines multiple NLP techniques, like tokenization, STOP WORD removal, etc, with ML algorithms like RF, XGBoost (XGB),

[a]maddulasamanvitha04@gmail.com, [b]nehasagi043@gmail.com, [c]garlapatisahasra@gmail.com, [d]kruthikar38@gmail.com, [e]satish.thunuguntla@bvrit.ac.in

DOI: 10.1201/9781003616399-30

and SVM to accurately detect fake reviews and analyze sentiment. A key innovation is the use of SA not only to gauge customer opinions but also to identify fake reviews by setting specific sentiment thresholds. Feature engineering techniques have been introduced, including the calculation of review length, price-to-rating ratio, and suspicious votes, which are critical in distinguishing fake reviews from genuine ones. Additionally, it employs visualization methods to present the findings effectively, making the results more accessible and actionable for stakeholders.

Research Objective

The main purpose of this project is to develop an ML model capable of detecting fake reviews and classifying reviews into +ve, -ve, or neutral categories in a dataset of mobile product reviews. Fake reviews are intentionally misleading or biased reviews that can distort the perception of a product, leading to consumer mistrust and potential financial loss. Identifying fake reviews is essential for preserving the credibility of online review platforms and helping consumers make well-informed purchasing choices based on authentic feedback. Additionally, classifying reviews by sentiment helps provide a clearer understanding of customer opinions, further aiding consumers in making informed decisions.

Literature Review

The expansion of e-commerce has led to a keen interest in analyzing consumer behavior through product reviews. Fake reviews, which can significantly influence consumer decisions and affect the credibility of online platforms, present a major challenge. This survey examines various methods employed for detecting fake reviews and conducting SA on Amazon product reviews using ML and deep learning (DL) techniques.

Dataset

Methodology

Several studies have focused on supervised ML for FRD has been extensive. One study highlighted the effectiveness of these models in spotting deceptive content [6], while another

concentrated on feature selection and model accuracy [7]. The application of ensemble ML algorithms for SA has also been noted, showing their utility in detecting fake reviews [8]. Thomas and Jeba [9] also proposed a DL framework for product recommendation systems that integrates SA for better accuracy [9]. Another investigation demonstrated the potential of DL algorithms in identifying fraudulent content [10], and comparative studies by Alsaad and Joshi (2023) and Mohawesh et al. [11] provided insights into the most effective techniques for FRD.

SA, another key area, has been explored through various methodologies. Wahyudi et al. [19] utilized Twitter hashtag analysis for sentiment classification using Ekman's classification, illustrating the application of SA in social media contexts [12], while another implemented a multitier SA approach using SVM on social media text [13]. Ramadhan et al. (2023) explored the SA of e-commerce product reviews and emphasized the importance of precise sentiment classification [14]. Studies on SA for e-commerce recommendations have combined various algorithms to improve prediction accuracy [15]. Gaur and Sharma (2023) introduced a DL model using a hybrid feature extraction approach, demonstrating the integration of multiple techniques for better results [16]. Haseeb et al. (2024) analyzed Amazon product reviews using text analysis and NLP methods [17], and Dai and Wang (2024) used clustering techniques on LSTM for FRD and text analysis [18]. Investigations into SA for e-commerce recommendations have combined various algorithms to improve prediction accuracy. In the realm of business and marketing, SA plays a critical role. Its application in interpreting consumer inclinations towards brands through flexible systems management has been highlighted, showing how businesses can leverage SA to better understand and respond to consumer needs Tiruwa et al. (2020) [19]. Kyaw et al. (2023) proposed a business intelligence framework using SA for smart digital marketing, showcasing its relevance in the e-commerce era [20]. Studies on Amazon product recommendation systems that integrate SA for better consumer experiences [21], while Salminen et al. (2022) focused on creating and detecting fake reviews, underlining the impact of SA on recommendation accuracy [22], have also been significant.

The survey showcases the advancements in ML and DL techniques for FRD and SA. Integrating these methodologies offers robust solutions for improving the reliability of online reviews and the credibility of e-commerce platforms. Its research from various sources provides a comprehensive understanding of the current state and advancements in these fields.

The dataset contains over 400,000 reviews of mobile phones sold on Amazon, extracted by Prompt-Cloud [23]. As shown in Table 30.1, it uses several key attributes for analyzing the reviews.

System framework

The framework for detecting fake reviews involves a series of stages aimed at thorough analysis. It starts with collecting online reviews, which are pre-processed by removing un- necessary elements like HTML tags and converting the text into numerical data using tokenization and vectorization. This prepares the data for feature engineering, where attributes such as review length and sentiment scores, indicating whether the tone is positive, neutral, or negative, are extracted. These features help differentiate genuine reviews from potentially fake ones. The extracted features are used to label the reviews as real or fake. SA is then conducted to understand the reviewers' attitudes and the context of the reviews. ML models are trained on this data and subsequently tested to classify reviews accurately. The models' effectiveness is assessed using metrics like accuracy and precision, ensuring robustness. This approach combines data processing and ML to detect fake reviews, which improves reliability and aids consumers in making informed decisions from the below Figure 30.1.

Table 30.1 Dataset description

Feature name	Description
Product name	The name or title of the mobile phone being reviewed.
Brand name	The manufacturer or brand of the mobile phone.
Price	The cost of the mobile phone at the time of the review.
Rating	A numerical rating the reviewer gives, ranging from 1 to 5 stars.
Review text	The written content of the review is provided by users, detailing their experience or opinions about the product.
Review votes	The count of users who found the review helpful, indicating the review's perceived value or usefulness.

Source: Author

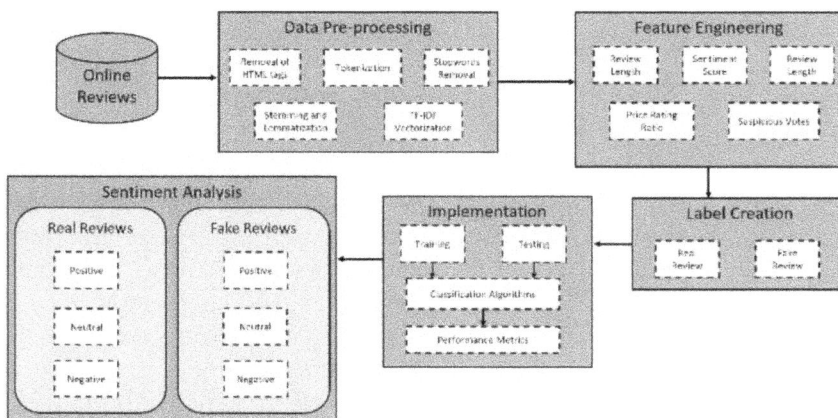

Figure 30.1 Research framework
Source: Author

Data preprocessing

Data preprocessing is an essential phase that prepares raw text data for analysis, especially in tasks like SA and FRD. This process involves several steps that transform unstructured text into a structured format suitable for ML models. By reducing noise, standardizing texts, and focusing on meaningful words, data preprocessing enhances the model's performance and enables more accurate predictions, ultimately, helping to produce data that is more refined and pertinent for thorough analysis [24].

1) **Tokenization:** It's the first step in text pre-processing, a key task in NLP. It decomposes the text into smaller components known as tokens, which may include words, characters, or subworlds. It transforms text into a format that machines can process, laying the foundation for further analysis in NLP tasks such as SA, machine translation, or text classification.

2) **Removal of stop words:** These are frequently occurring terms that lack substantial meaning and are typically removed to decrease the data's dimensionality in NLP. Examples include "is", "the", "a", "an", and "in". This step focuses the analysis on more meaningful words and reduces noise in the data, which is essential in improving the performance of NLP models.

3) **Stemming:** Stemming reduces words to their root form by removing suffixes or prefixes, a common NLP technique. This helps decrease the number of word variants and reduces the complexity of the model. For instance, "running" and "runs" can be stemmed to "run", enabling more effective text processing in NLP applications like information retrieval or document clustering.

4) **Lemmatization:** It transforms words into their fundamental or dictionary forms, referred to as lemmas. Unlike stemming, it considers the context, making it more accurate. For example, "better" and "best" are lemmatized to "good".

5) **Normalization:** This involves conversion of text to a standard format, including lowercase conversion and removing punctuation, numbers, and special characters, ensuring consistency reducing feature space, and improving the model's performance in NLP tasks by eliminating variations in how the text is presented.

Fake review classification

Feature engineering involves creating new features that help in identifying potentially fake reviews. These features are essential for distinguishing genuine reviews from those that may be manipulated or artificially inflated. Using methods like SA, review length, TF-IDF vectorization, and other derived metrics, the model categorizes the reviews into real and fake [25]. Each feature offers a unique perspective for assessing the authenticity of a review, contributing to a more comprehensive and effective detection model. A new label is created based on these criteria, which facilitates the identification and analysis of suspicious reviews in Figure 30.2.

1) **SA Using VADER** The valence aware dictionary and sentiment reasoner (VADER) SA tool calculates Sentiment scores assigned to each review ranging from -1 (most -ve sentiment) to 1 (most +ve sentiment), with 0 denoting a neutral sentiment.

    VADER is used to analyze social media text and provide a compound score assessing overall sentiment of the review, which is a useful feature for FRD. Specific thresholds for sentiment scores were set to identify potentially fake reviews:

    Low sentiment threshold: A score below -0.5 may be considered very negative, possibly indicating a fake review intended to defame the product.

    High sentiment threshold: A score above 0.5 may be considered very positive, potentially indicating a fake review intended to overly praise the product.

    By incorporating these techniques, the model can better differentiate between genuine and potentially fake re-views. Positive sentiment scores may indicate genuine reviews, while very low or high scores could suggest exaggeration or manipulation, contributing to a more comprehensive and effective detection model.

2) **Review length:** The length of each review is calculated as a feature, typically measured in

terms of the number of words. This feature is crucial for identifying potentially fake reviews for several reasons:

Short reviews: Extremely short reviews, particularly those with fewer than 10 words, may lack the necessary detail and context to be considered genuine. Such brevity can raise suspicion, as these reviews often do not provide enough information to support their claims.

Long reviews: Conversely, unusually lengthy reviews may also be flagged as potentially fake, especially if they appear overly detailed or promotional. While longer reviews can provide more context, they can also be manipulated to give a false sense of credibility.

3) *TF-IDF vectorization:* TF-IDF vectorization, a staple NLP technique, transforms text into numerical values, emphasizing unique words. It integrates term frequency, reflecting the frequency of a word's occurrence in a document, with inverse document frequency, which down weights common words across the corpus. This method assigns higher scores to distinctive words in each document, while reducing the influence of frequent but less informative words, making it useful for distinguishing document content.

4) *Price rating ratio:* This feature involves calculating the ratio of the product's price to its rating. A high price/rating ratio might be suspicious, as it could indicate that the review is not genuine or that the product's quality does not justify its price. The threshold for

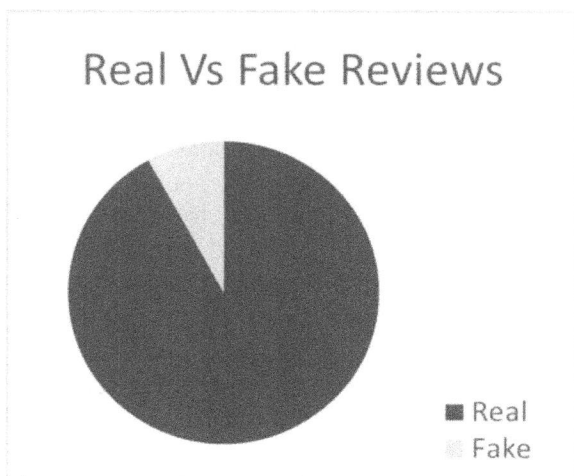

Figure 30.2 Real and fake review comparison
Source: Author

this ratio is set to 10, beyond which reviews may be flagged as suspicious. and fine-tune the model to align with the specific characteristics of the dataset. This ensures robust predictive performance and adaptability to complex problems.

5) *Suspicious votes:* The number of votes (helpfulness votes, likes, etc.) a review receives can indicate its influence. However, an unusually high number of votes might suggest that the review has been artificially inflated, possibly by coordinated actions. A threshold of 50 votes is set to flag such reviews.

Data training and testing
This process includes several crucial steps to ready the dataset for model development and assessment.

1) **Corpus creation:** A corpus is a collection of textual data used for various NLP tasks. In this scenario, it integrates the 'Reviews' and 'Brand Names' into a single text feature capturing review content and the brand's influence, providing a richer feature representation for the model.

2) **Data splitting:** Dataset is classified into training and testing sets, a vital procedure to assess its performance and verify the ability to generalize to new, unseen data. In this scenario, a 70-30 split ratio is applied, with the majority for training and the remaining for evaluating accuracy and robustness.

3) **Text vectorization using CountVectorizer:** The combined 'Reviews' and 'Brand Name' text data is vectorized using CountVectorizer. This technique converts the text into a matrix of token counts, representing the frequency of each word or n-gram (a sequence of words) in the documents. In this case, an n-gram range of (1, 2) is used, meaning both single words (unigrams) and pairs of words (bigrams) are considered features. CountVectorizer helps transform the textual data into numerical formats.

ML classifications
Several classification algorithms are used for FRD [26]. Each algorithm has unique characteristics and approaches to model training and prediction:

Figure 30.3 Word cloud real and fake reviews
Source: Author

1) ***Random forest (RF):*** It's an EL technique that builds several decision trees during the training process done on a randomly selected subset of data and features which minimizes overfitting and enhances its ability to generalize. The final prediction is done by combining the outputs of individual trees. It's effective for handling large datasets with many features and is robust against overfitting [27].

2) ***Extreme gradient boosting (XGBoost):*** XGB is a highly effective and scalable version of gradient boosting, an ensemble technique that builds models sequentially. In XGB, each successive tree aims to address the errors of its predecessors, thereby improving the model's overall accuracy. XGB includes several optimizations, such as regularization and parallel processing, making it efficient and effective for classification and regression tasks. [28].

3) ***Support vector machine (SVM):*** SVM is a supervised learning technique for classification and regression. It identifies the optimal hyperplane maximizing the margin between distinct classes within the feature space [29]. Its flexibility allows it to adapt to various data distributions and complexities.

4) **Logistic regression (LR):** It is a statistical technique used for binary classification. It estimates the probability of a binary outcome by modeling it as a linear combination of the input features, which is then passed through a logistic function [30]. This approach provides probability scores that indicate the likelihood of a review being fake, making it easy to interpret and apply thresholds for classification.

5) **Naive Bayes (NB) + N-gram:** NB is a probabilistic classifier based on Bayes' theorem. It assumes independence between features given the class label, which, despite being a strong assumption, simplifies the computation and works well in practice for certain types of data, especially text [31]. In this implementation, N-grams capture the context of the reviews, enhancing the feature set. The NB classifier then uses these N-grams to predict the class probabilities [32].

6) **K-Nearest neighbors (KNN):** It is a straightforward and intuitive classification algorithm where a label is assigned to a data point on the majority label of its 'k' closest neighbors in feature space [33]. The distance between points is measured using Euclidean distance. It is a non-parametric method, i.e., it does not assume any specific distribution for the underlying data and is useful for datasets with non-linear decision boundaries. Additionally, KNN is computationally intensive with large datasets, as it requires storing and querying the entire training set during prediction.

Performance analysis

Performance metrics are crucial for assessing the efficacy of ML models. The metrics used here are accuracy, precision, recall, and F1 score.

1) **Accuracy (Acc):** Acc is a metric that reflects the ratio of correctly classified instances to the total no of instances. It is computed using the formula:

$$Acc = \frac{TP+TN}{TP+FP+TN+FN} \quad (1)$$

here,

TP: True +ve
TN: True -ve
FP: False +ve
FN: False -ve

It offers a general view of the model's prediction accuracy. However, it may not adequately capture the model's performance, where the dataset exhibits an imbalanced class distribution.

2) **Precision (Pr):** Pr measures the proportion of TP instances among those predicted as positive and is computed using:

$$Pr = \frac{TP}{TP + FP} \quad (2)$$

3) **Recall (R):** It is the proportion of actual +ve instances that the model successfully identifies. The formula for the recall is given as:

$$R = \frac{TP}{TP + FN} \quad (3)$$

This metric is crucial in scenarios where it is important not to miss any +ve cases, in medical diagnoses or fraud detection.

4) **F1-Score:** It integrates both Pr and R into a single metric, offering a balanced measure of the two. It is calculated using the formula:

$$F1 = 2 * \frac{Pr * R}{Pr + R} \quad (4)$$

Valuable for imbalanced datasets, offering a complete evaluation of the model's performance considering both FP and FN.

Results and Discussion

The analysis provides insights into the sentiment distribution of reviews and the performance of various ML models in distinguishing between real and fake reviews. The data shows that majority of the positive reviews are genuine, with a smaller proportion being fake. It presents a challenge in detecting fake positive reviews, which may be crafted which subtly enhance product ratings. In contrast, fake negative reviews are rare, suggesting that those crafting fake content may avoid negative sentiments to maintain a veneer of legitimacy. The neutral category also has a small proportion of fake reviews, indicating that neutral language might be used to appear more credible and avoid detection as per Table 30.2.

Conclusion

The SA and review classification system demonstrates strong capabilities across various ML models, including XGB, RF, and LR. These models exhibit high accuracy, precision, recall, and F1 scores, highlighting their effectiveness in identifying real and fake reviews in Figure 30.3. It has also been observed that XGB has outperformed the ML models with an accuracy of 97.85% (Figure 30.4). A notable finding is a bias towards positivity in fake reviews, suggesting that such reviews often lean towards positive sentiment to enhance perceived product appeal. This trend underscores the importance of developing sophisticated detection methods that can identify even subtle manipulations in review sentiment, thereby maintaining the credibility of review platforms. Figures 30.5 and 30.6 depict the ROC and PR curves respectively.

The broad scope of SA provides a comprehensive overview of the emotional tone across a large dataset of reviews, making it easier to detect patterns that may indicate review manipulation which is crucial for understanding the underlying strategies employed in FRs.

Table 30.2 Results

Sentiment	Total	Real	Fake
Positive	140437	129151	11286
Neutral	25500	25000	500
Negative	115312	112718	2594

Source: Author

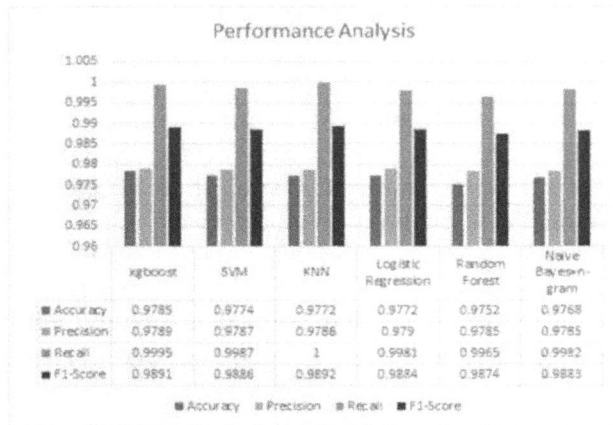

Figure 30.4 Performance analysis
Source: Author

Future Enhancements

Future enhancements include exploring advanced techniques like DL models and more sophisticated NLP methods like BERT and GPT improving FRD, particularly those with positive sentiments. Continuous improvement of the models, informed by new data and emerging patterns in fake reviews, will be crucial for maintaining high performance. Expanding the analysis to include a wider range of review sources and additional features, such as reviewer behavior and context, can further enhance the system's accuracy. Increasing the dataset by collecting reviews from diverse sources and domains, including

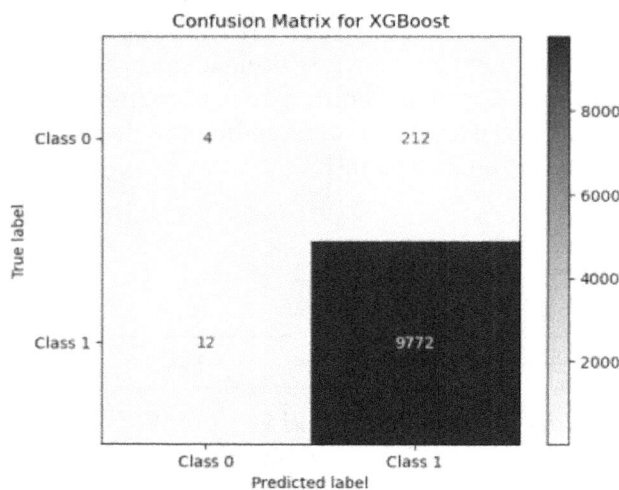

Figure 30.5 XGBoost confusion matrix
Source: Author

multilingual datasets, will improve the model's generalization capabilities. Additionally, implementing a recommendation system that suggests products based on user reviews and preferences, using collaborative filtering techniques, can enhance user engagement and provide personalized product suggestions.

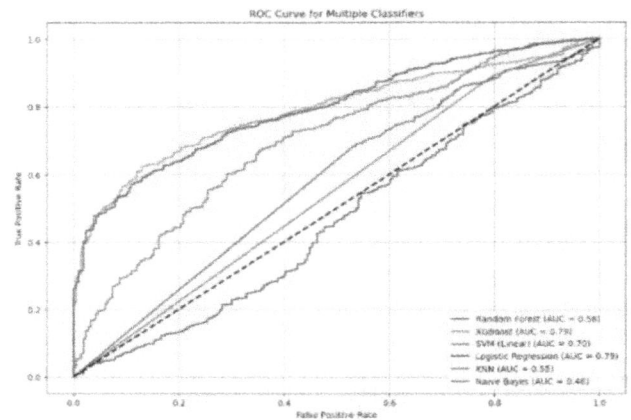

Figure 30.6 ROC curves
Source: Author

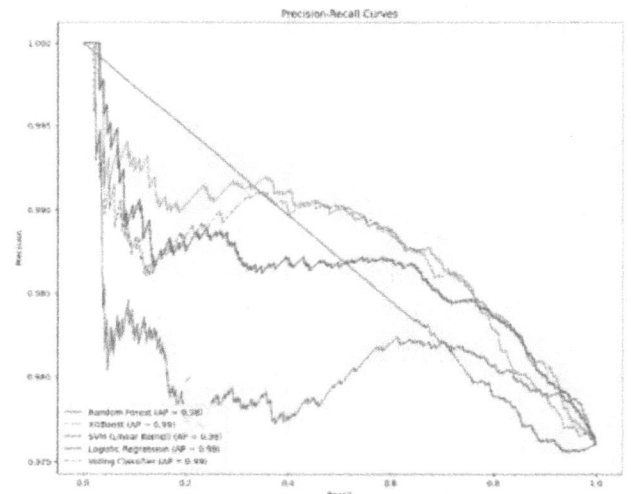

Figure 30.7 Precision-recall curves
Source: Author

References

[1] Tabany, M., and Gueffal, M. (2024). Sentiment analysis and fake amazon re- views classification using SVM supervised machine learning model. *Journal of Advances in Information Technology*, 15(1), 49–58. doi:10.12720/jait.15.1.49-58.

[2] Elzeheiry, S., Gab-Allah, W. A., Mekky, N., and Elmogy, M. (2023). "Sentiment Analysis for

e-commerce product reviews: current trends and future directions," Preprints, May 2023, DOI: 10.20944/preprints202305.1649.v1.

[3] Asaad, W. H., Allami, R., and Ali, Y. H. (2023). Fake review detection using machine learning. *Revue d'Intelligence Artificielle*, 37(5), 1159–1166. doi:10.18280/ria.370507.

[4] Abd, M. J., and Hussein, M. H. (2024). Fake reviews detection in e-commerce using machine learning techniques: A comparative survey. In BIO Web Conferences, (Vol. 97, p. 00099). doi: 10.1051/bio- conf/20249700099.

[5] Thunuguntla, S. B., Murugaanandam, S., and Pitchai, R. (2023). Densenet121-DNN-based hybrid approach for advertisement classification and user identification. *International Journal of Inventive Engineering and Sciences (IJIES)*, 16(3), 162–174. doi: 10.22266/ijies2023.0630.13.

[6] Elmogy, A. M. (2021). Fake reviews detection using supervised machine learning. *International Journal of Advanced Computer Science and Applications*, 12(1), 601–606.

[7] Gadewar, A., Jadhav, P., Kale, P., Kature, D., and Patil, K. (2023). Online fake review detection based on machine learning techniques. *International Journal of Scientific Research in Science, Engineering and Technology (IJSRSET)*, Vol. 10 No. 3 (2023): May-June, 197–204. doi:10.32628/IJSRSET2310390.

[8] Sadhasivam, J., and Kalivaradhan, R. B. (2019). Sentiment analysis of amazon products using ensemble machine learning algorithm. *International Journal of Mathematical, Engineering and Management Sciences*, 4(2), 508–520. doi: 10.33889/IJMEMS.2019.4.2-041.

[9] Thomas, R., and Jeba, J. R. (2024). A novel framework for an intelligent deep learning-based product recommendation system using sentiment analysis (SA). *Automatika*, 65(2), 410–424. doi: 10.1080/00051144.2023.2295148.

[10] Alzahrani, M. E., Aldhyani, T. H. H., Alsubari, S. N., Althobaiti, M. M., and Fahad, A. (2022). Developing an intelligent system with deep learning algorithms for sentiment analysis of e- commerce product reviews. *Computational Intelligence and Neuroscience*, 2022, 1–10. doi: 10.1155/2022/3840071.

[11] Mohawesh, R., Xu, S., Tran, S. N., Ollington, R., Springer, M., Jararweh, Y., et al. (2021). Fake reviews detection: a survey. *IEEE Access*, 9, 65771–65802. doi: 10.1109/ACCESS.2021.3075573.

[12]] T. Sajid et al., "Analysis and Challenges in Detecting the Fake Reviews of Products using Naïve Bayes and Random Forest Techniques,"

Research Square (Research Square), Jun. 2023, doi: 10.21203/rs.3.rs-2302761/v1.

[13] Meng, Y., Yang, N., Qian, Z., and Zhang, G. (2020). What makes an online review more helpful: an interpretation framework using XGBoost and SHAP values. *Journal of Theoretical and Applied Electronic Commerce Research*, 16(3), 466–490. doi: 10.3390/jtaer16030029.

[14] Anitha, R., and Kumar, D. V. (2024). Optimizing sentiment analysis in online shopping: unveiling the precision of simp- son rule-optimized support vector machine. *Journal of Theoretical and Applied Information Technology*, 102(3), 1049–1065

[15] Kausar, M. A., Fageeri, S. O., and Soosaimanickam, A. (2023). Sentiment classification based on machine learning approaches in amazon product reviews. *Engineering, Technology and Applied Science Research*, 13(3), 10849–10855. doi: 10.48084/etasr.5854.

[16] Sano, A. V. D., Stefanus, A. A., Madyatmadja, E. D., Nindito, H., Purnomo, A., and Sianipar, C. P. M. (2023). Proposing a visualized comparative review analysis model on tourism domain using Naïve Bayes classifier. *Procedia Computer Science*, 227, 482–489. doi: 10.1016/j.procs.2023.10.549.

[17] Sharma, H. D., and Sharma, S. (2024). Enhancement of the lexical approachby n-grams technique via improving negation-based traditional sentiment analysis. *International Journal of Intelligent Systems and Applications in Engineering*, 12(15), 63–69.

[18] A. Masood and K. S. Khurshid, "A Machine Learning-Based Analysis of Fake Reviews for E-Commerce," SSRN, Jan. 2024, doi: 10.2139/ssrn.4786593.

[19] Wahyudi, A., Tirtana, A., and Langoy, L. D. (2023). Analysis of gojek's brand perception utilizing twitter hashtag: sentiment analysis using ekman's classification. *Open Access Indonesia Journal of Social Sciences (OAIJSS)*, 6(2), 927–935. doi: 10.37275/oaijss.v6i2.153.

[20] F. Adel Ramadhan, Rd. R. Permana Ruslan, and A. Zahra, "Sentiment Analysis Of E-Commerce Product Reviews For Content Interaction Using Machine Learning," CA, vol. 6, no. 1, pp. 207–220, Feb. 2023, doi: 10.52851/cakrawala.v6i1.219.

[21] MM. Loukili, F. Messaoudi, and M. E. Ghazi, "Sentiment Analysis of Product Reviews for ECommerce Recommendation based on Machine Learning". [22] G. Kaur and A. Sharma, "A deep learning-based model using hybrid fea-

ture extraction approach for consumer sentiment analysis," J Big Data, vol. 10, no. 1, p. 5, Jan. 2023, doi: 10.1186/s40537-022-00680-6.

[23] PromptCloud (2024). Amazon Mobile Phone Reviews [Dataset]. https://data.world/promptcloud/amazon-mobile-phone-reviews

[24] T. Dai and X. Wang, "Fake Review Detection and Text Analysis by Using Clustering Techniques on LSTM," Jun. 21, 2024. doi: 10.21203/rs.3.rs-4533037/v1.

[25] A. Tiruwa, R. Yadav, and P. K. Suri, "Sentiment Analysis: An Effective Way of Interpreting Consumer's Inclinations Towards a Brand," in Transforming Organizations Through Flexible Systems Management, P. K. Suri and R. Yadav, Eds., in Flexible Systems Management., Singapore: Springer Singapore, 2020, pp. 205–219. doi: 10.1007/978- 981-13-9640-312.

[26] Khin Sandar Kyaw, P. Tepsongkroh, C. Thongkamkaew, and F. Sasha, "Business Intelligent Framework Using Sentiment Analysis for Smart Digital Marketing in the E-Commerce Era," Asia Social Issues, vol. 16, no. 3, p. e252965, Jan. 2023, doi: 10.48048/asi.2023.252965.

[27] M. Z. Ahmed, A. Singh, and A. Paul, "Amazon Product Recommendation System," International Journal of Advanced Research in Computer and Communication Engineering, vol. 11, no. 3, Mar. 2022, doi: 10.17148/IJARCCE.2022.11356.

[28] J. Salminen, C. Kandpal, A. M. Kamel, S. Jung, and B. J. Jansen, "Creating and detecting fake reviews of online products," Journal of Retailing and Consumer Services, vol. 64, p. 102771, Jan. 2022, doi: 10.1016/j.jretconser.2021.102771.

[29] P. Juyal, "Sentimental analysis of Amazon customers based on their review comments," International Interdisciplinary Humanitarian Conference for Sustainability (IIHC), Bengaluru, India, Nov. 2022, doi: 10.1109/iihc55949.2022.10060846.

[30] G. Dash, C. Sharma, and S. Sharma, "Sustainable Marketing and the Role of Social Media: An Experimental Study Using Natural Language Processing (NLP)," Sustainability, vol. 15, no. 6, p. 5443, Mar. 2023, doi: 10.3390/su15065443.

[31] M. Loukili, F. Messaoudi, and M. E. Ghazi, "Sentiment Analysis of Product Reviews for ECommerce Recommendation based on Machine Learning".

[32] H. D. Sharma and S. Sharma, "Enhancement of the Lexical Approach by N-Grams Technique via Improving Negation-Based Traditional Sentiment Analysis," International Journal of Intelligent Systems and Applications in Engineering, 2024

[33] Prof. Amol Gadewar, Pratima Jadhav, Pratiksha Kale, Dhanashree Kature, and Kshitija Patil, "Online Fake Review Detection Based on Machine Learning Techniques," IJSRSET, pp. 197–204, May 2023, doi: 10.32628/IJSRSET2310390.

[34] M. M. B. Alsaad and D. H. Joshi, "Supervised Machine Learning-Based Fake Review Detection: A Comparative Evaluation of Feature Selection Approaches" vol. 58, no. 1, 2023.

[35] A. Haseeb, R. Taseen, M. Sani, and Q. G. Khan, "Sentiment Analysis on Amazon Product Reviews using Text Analysis and Natural Language Processing Methods".

31 Implementation of different approximate sum-of-products models for the gaussian filter

Apurva Kumari[a], Sanjay Dubey[b], Chinnaiah, M. C.[c], Madhava Rao, K.[d], Nayini Akanksha[e], Nishath Fathim[f] and Chelmela Ruchitha[g]

Department of Electronics and Communication, B V Raju Institute of Technology, Narsapur, India

Abstract

Low-power approximate circuits provide outstanding performance. In many digital signal processing applications Sum-of-products (SOP) units are crucial elements. In this research, three distributed arithmetic-based approximate ASOP models used for image processing applications. They are made for varied degrees of accuracy. When compared to traditional units, the initial ASOP1, ASOP2 and ASOP3 model achieves improvements with a lower error and succeeds in obtaining normalized error and mean relative error. Using a noisy image smoothing application, the effectiveness of approximation units is evaluated and the suggested models outperform the most advanced techniques currently available in terms of peak signal-to-noise ratio. For a Gaussian filter to evaluate approximate units by using convolution and the execution of a noisy image, smoothing is used to reduce the image noise.

Keywords: Approximate computing, distributed arithmetic, gaussian filter, low power, sum of products

Introduction

Low-power approximate circuits provide outstanding performance. SOP units are essential parts of numerous digital signal processing applications. For the design of power-efficient digital devices approximate computing offers a useful approach [1]. Approximate circuits are an essential alternative for saving power and area in applications like data processing and multimedia.

Sum-of-products (SOP) units, a crucial part of arithmetic circuits, have gotten less attention in terms of approximation implementation. Vector inner product computation is especially effective with distributed arithmetic [2]. It has an effective method for carrying out the SOP function and does not call for multiplication. Distributed arithmetic bit-parallel versions are offered in another approaches [3,4].

In this brief, three parallel distributed arithmetic-based models of SOP units are being forth. Discusses a truncation-based approximate SOP (ASOP) model [5]. The unique ASOP designs described in this short make use of the efficient distributed arithmetic framework. Three models

are suggested. The first model reduces power significantly by lowering and normalized error distance and means relative error (MRE). The second and third versions, which have more power and area than the first model, provide superior precision.

Quantum-dot cellular automata (QCA), even it is called as quantum cellular automata. QCA is advance to state of art CMOS models. Cells in grid format and in uniform nature may come under system with dynamical nature and discrete nature. Gaussian filtering, commonly known as "gaussian blur," is a typical image-processing technique used to minimize noise and detail in an image while keeping its general structure. It takes its name from the symmetric bell-shaped curve represented by the mathematical function known as the Gaussian distribution, also known as the normal distribution.

Gaussian filtering is a common technique for blurring or smoothing images during image processing. It softens the appearance and lowers noise by removing small features based on the convolution of the image with a Gaussian distribution. Gaussian filters are extremely effective at

[a]apurva.kumari@bvrit.ac.in [b]sanjay.dubey@bvrit.ac.in [c]chinnaaiah.mc@bvrit.ac.in [d]madhavarao.k@bvrit.ac.in
[e]23211d5708@bvrit.ac.in [f]21211d5704@bvrit.ac.in [g]22211d5704@bvrit.ac.in

DOI: 10.1201/9781003616399-31

reducing high-frequency noise while keeping the general edges and structure of the image.

Related Works

Recently, approximate computing emerged as an approach to designing digital systems that are energy-efficient. Many applications and systems can tolerate some loss of optimality or quality in the computed result, which is exactly based on approximate computing. Approximate computing approaches provide for significantly enhanced energy economy by removing the necessity for completely deterministic or fully accurate computations. This paper examines recent advances in the field, such as measures of quality and relevant error, and algorithm-level strategies for approximate computing [1].

Methods for speeding up DA multiplication are given by White [2]. A biquadratic digital filter is subjected to DA, demonstrating vector-matrix-product and vector dot-product mechanization. Applications to transformers and nonlinear and/or non-stationary DA processing are presented. It can be observed that to automate computations dominated by inner products DA is a particularly effective way.

Electronic control systems that are integrated into smart structural systems must be lightweight, power-efficient, and small. In earlier work, we developed and tested digital controllers based on FPGA on a basic structural system. Long-standing research has shown that distributed arithmetic (DA) is a highly effective method for automating calculations if the majority of the inner products include a constant multiplicand. The smart structural controllers' computational needs perfectly match this kind. On a cantilevered beam, multi and single-variable controllers are tested and used [3].

In VLSI, to implement distributed arithmetic, a novel architecture is presented. This architecture comprises a multi-input adder and a serial-in, random-out multiport memory. Based on the architecture, the design of a 1.25-m CMOS convolution processor chip is reported. Issues in the development of design tools and chip architecture are discussed [4].

Employing decreased precision processing techniques for average power dissipation and reducing arithmetic activity has become a new trend in low-power design. As system requirements change, such architectures might make trade-offs between power and arithmetic precision [5]. The approximate 4-2 compressors for multiplier were computed using an imprecise method [6]. NanoMagnet logic and nanoscale computational architectures utilizing spin waves are introduced in references [7,8].

Approximate radix-4 Booth multiplier is applied for error-tolerant by Khitun and Wang [9]. The proposed approach for approximative computing that uses an adder based on XOR/XNOR is described in [10]. Imprecise computational blocks inspired by biology (BICs) were utilized for efficient implementation in VLSI [11]. The approaches described were based on approximate computation and intended for high-speed adders [12,13].

Methodology

High computing efficiency is distributed arithmetic's important benefit. To implement SOP $a_1b_1 + a_2b_2 + \cdots + a_K b_K$, then y will be defined as,

$$y = \sum_{n=0}^{N-1} x_n 2^n \ldots\ldots\ldots\ldots (1)$$

In this case, N is 16 and K is 3. Our approximation models drastically reduce the amount of hardware needed. There are three suggested ASOP models: ASOP1, ASOP2, and ASOP3.

Proposed model ASOP1

The implemented values of m are 8, 6, and 4. For this solution, it is necessary to use three 16-m bit adders with two inputs, 16-m lookup tables with eight cases, one 16-m bit adder with three inputs, and a final accumulator with 16-m items. Figure 31.1 depicts the approximation model with condensed parts. It should be noticed that ASOP1 decreases the complexity of the accumulator further than by reducing the amount of input bits to the adders [5].

Proposed model ASOP2

The addition with an m-bit leading one predictor, ASOP2 is similar to ASOP1. This improves precision and makes it better suited for DSP applications, which will be covered in the following section. According to our strategy, the priority encoder must be used after performing an OR operation on m bits.

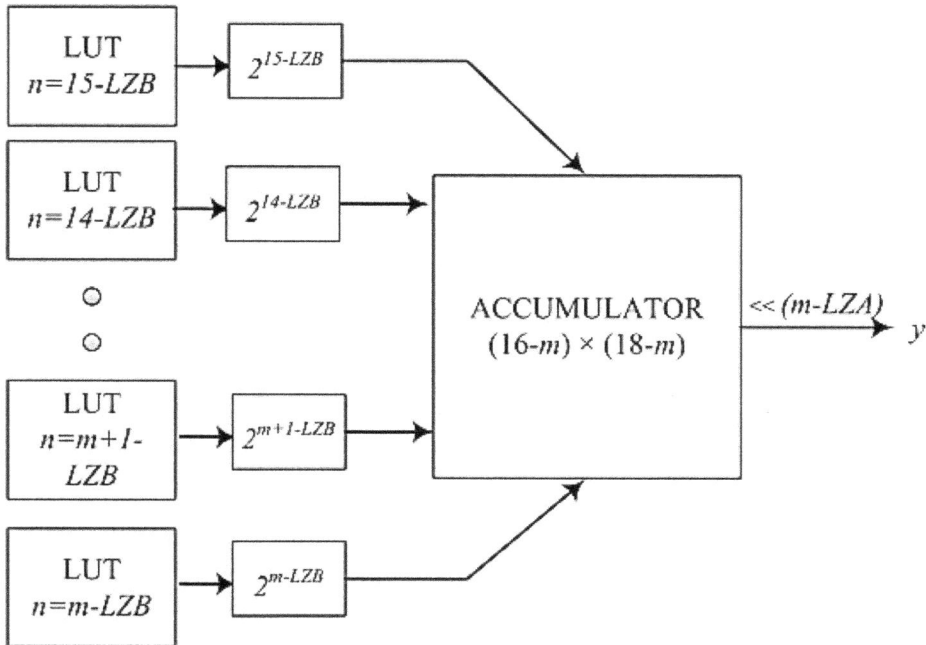

Figure 31.1 ASOP (ASOP2) structure and approximate lookup table for N = 16 and K = 3
Source: Author

The computation of items beginning with the leading one position is done using the ASOP1 structure after the leading one prediction. Particularly when information exists in the inputs only in their least significant portions, ASOP2 reduces the detrimental consequences of truncation. Utilizing an OR gate to combine the leading predictor and elements later on uses less hardware resources.

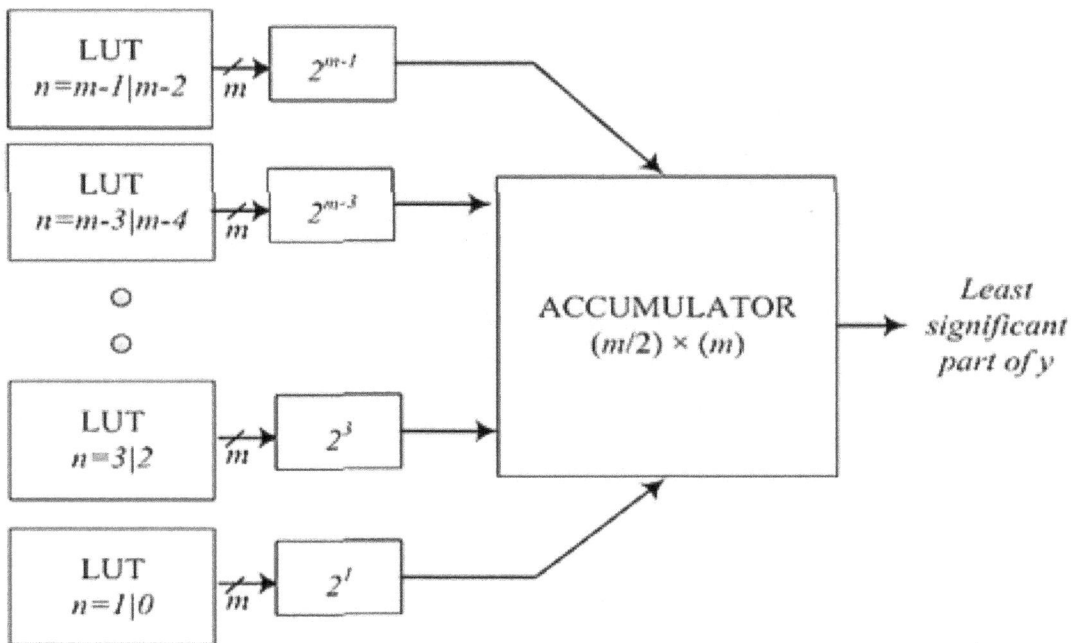

Figure 31.2 ASOP3 structure
Source: Author

Proposed model ASOP3

The least significant bits in ASOP1 m = 4, 6, and 8 are compressed. The lookup table's 18-bit outputs are compressed in ASOP1 by m bits. In ASOP3, truncation is not used. The output of a lookup table is segregated into m bits and 18 - m bits. Two groups of 16-m and m each are created from the inputs b. Control signals are grouped in pairs for the bk bit group with the least number of bits, where m = 1, 2, or 3.

Gaussian filtering

In signal processing, Gaussian filtering is that is used in various applications like texture segmentation, edge detection, and image smoothing. In order to reduce Gaussian noise, geometric mean filters are commonly used in image processing.

ASOP and Exact units are utilized for performing a Gaussian convolution process on the image. The MSE is 32 when the smoothed image is compared to the precise ASOP units and SOP units. Contrasting the two images PSNR, is used for accurate ASOP unit compression quality. Along with their corresponding PSNR values, the image smoothing results are displayed. ACM-SOP frequently produces nonzero values; hence, it isn't shown in the image or tables. Compared to comparable current approximation units, versions of ASOP have a higher PSNR, and it is clear that ASOP2 fulfills the high.

Comparison and Experimental Results

Figures 31.3–31.6 are the simulation results. Figure 31.3 shows the RTL schematic of the proposed model. The model is designed using QCA and RSA methods. The technology schematic is shown in Figure 31.4.

Output Results

Table 31.1 displays the error metrics of both exact and proposed ASOP units across various values of MRE and NDE. The resulting output is depicted in Figures 31.5 and 31.6, with different PSNR values indicate the recovered quality of images affected by Gaussian filter noise.

Conclusion

Three effective approximate SOP (ASOP) models are presented in this paper: ASOP3, ASOP2, and ASOP1. In comparison to the state-of-the-art techniques, the results show reduced error metrics and enhanced approximation designs. The most accurate models, ASOP3, ASOP2, and

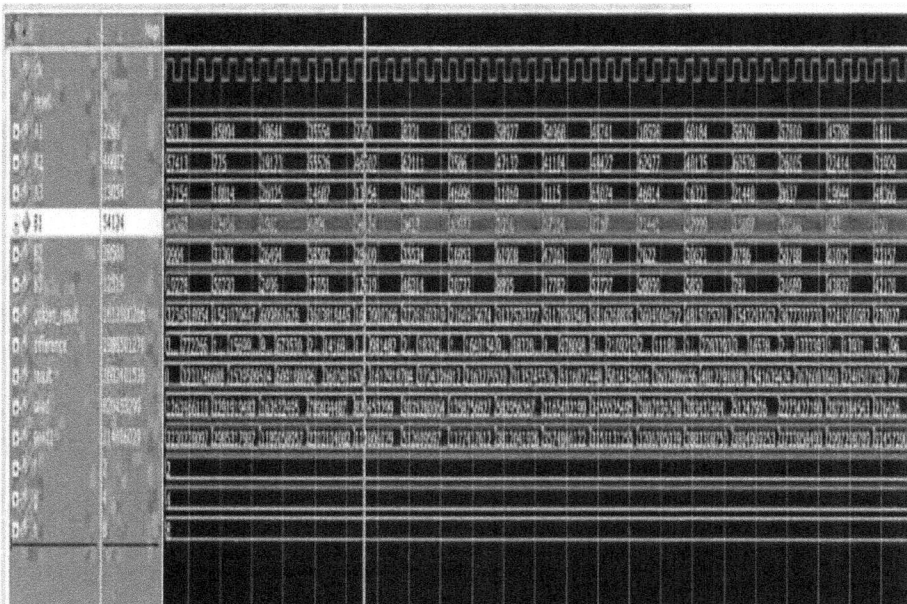

Figure 31.3 RTL schematic of proposed model
Source: Author

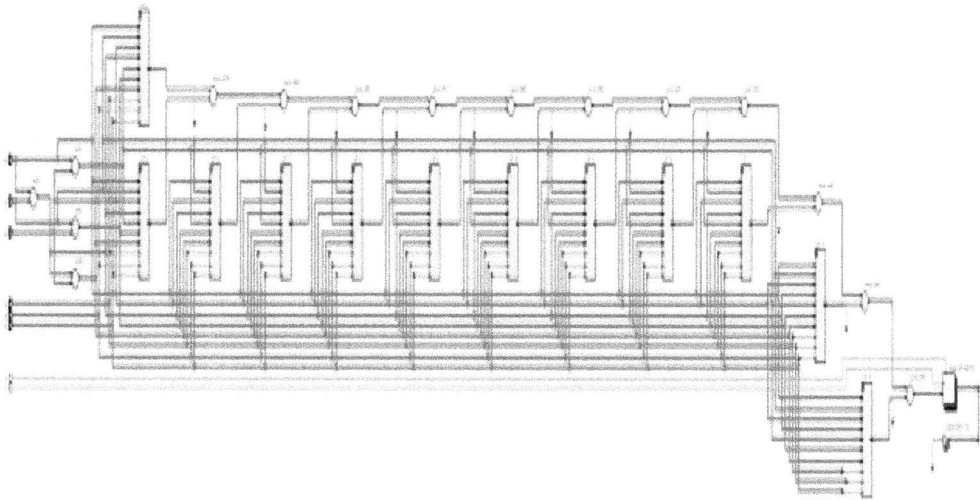

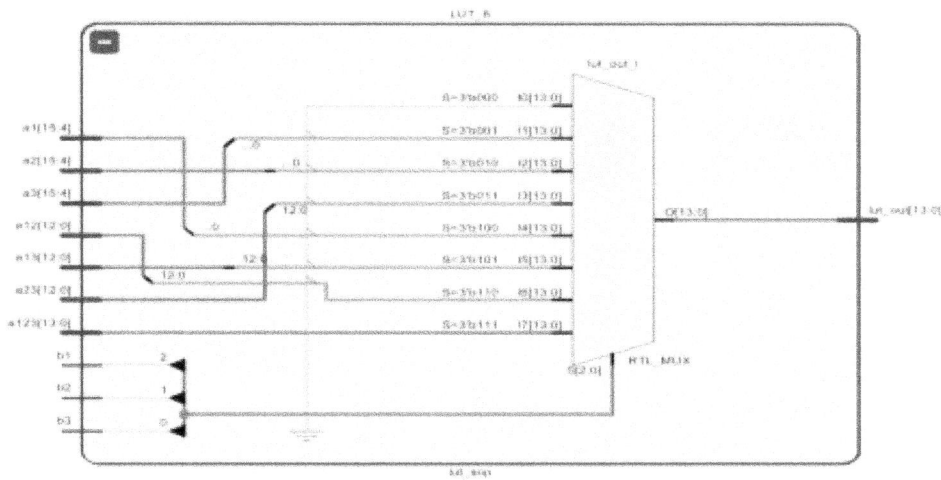

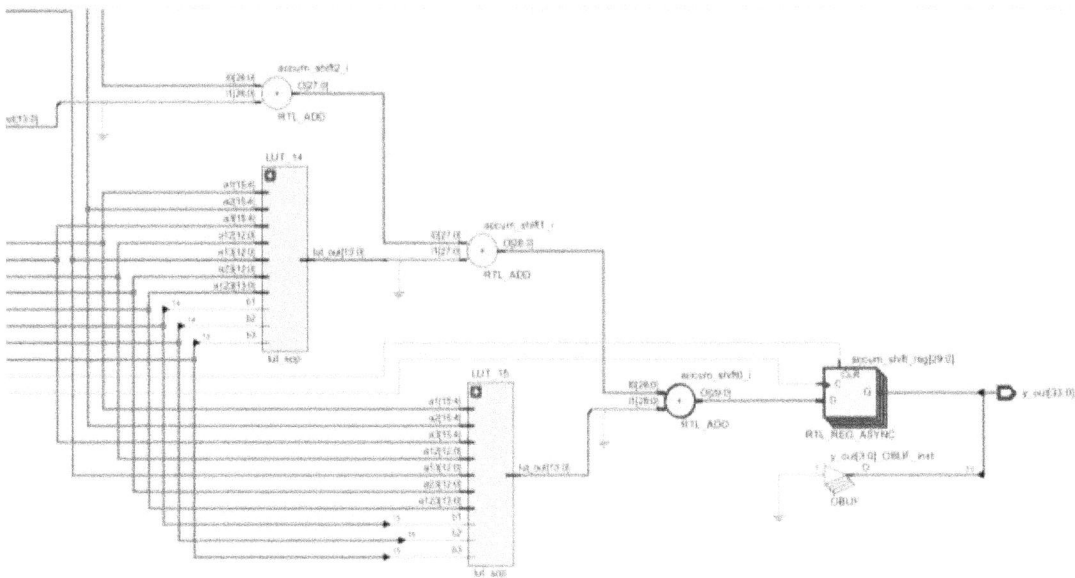

Figure 31.4 Technology schematic for proposed model
Source: Author

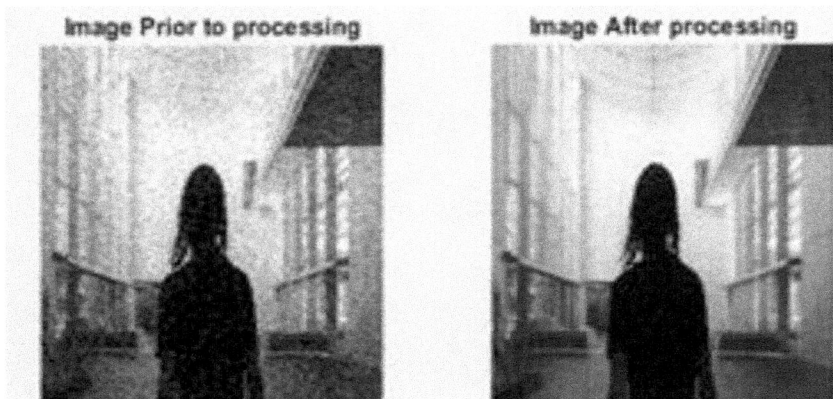

Figure 31.5 (a) Prior image (b) after image processing

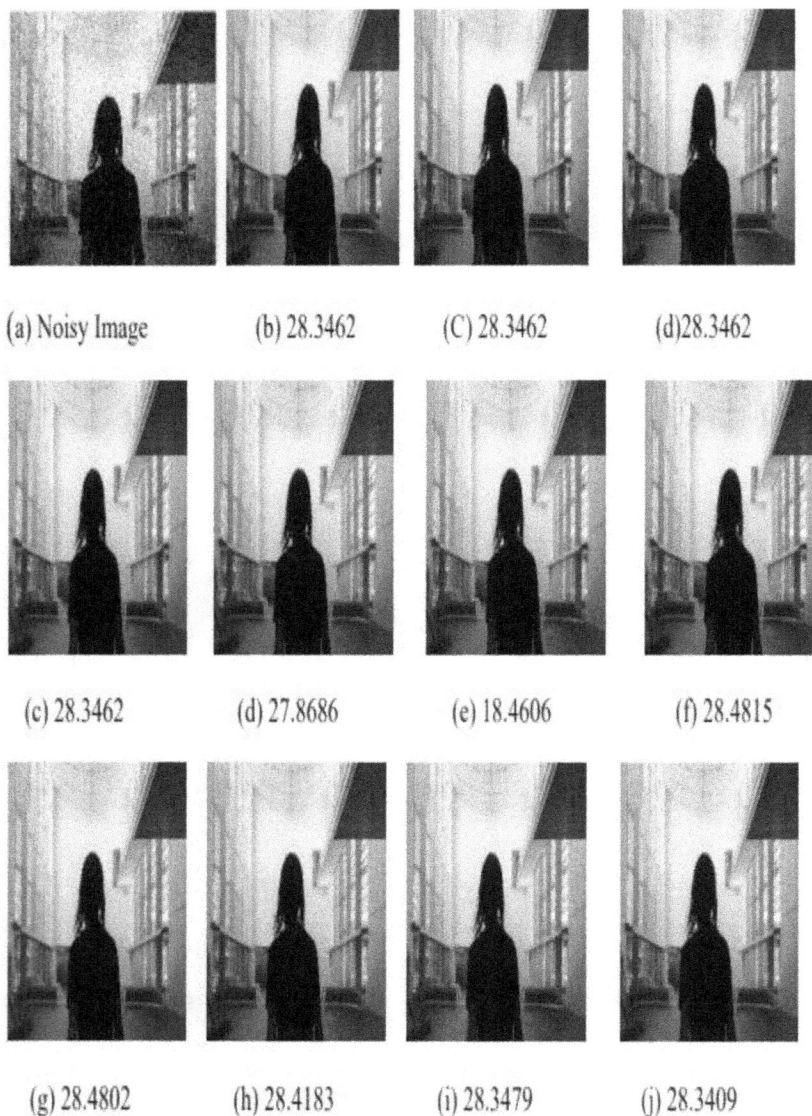

Figure **31.6** Input noisy image and corresponding image processing results using ASOP mode
Source: Author

Table 31.1 Error metric of exact and proposed ASOP units [15]

Sum of products type	MRE	NDE
Exact unit	-	-
ASOP 1(m=2)	1.15×10^{-4}	2.28×10^{-5}
ASOP 1(m=4)	5.76×10^{-4}	1.14×10^{-4}
ASOP 1(m=6)	2.42×10^{-3}	4.80×10^{-4}
ASOP 1(m=8)	9.76×10^{-3}	1.94×10^{-3}
ASOP 2(m=2)	9.3×10^{-5}	2.08×10^{-5}
ASOP 2(m=4)	4.88×10^{-4}	1.06×10^{-4}
ASOP 2(m=6)	2.07×10^{-3}	4.48×10^{-4}
ASOP 2(m=8)	8.37×10^{-3}	1.81×10^{-3}
ASOP 3(m=2)	9.3×10^{-5}	1.8×10^{-5}
ASOP 3(m=4)	4.69×10^{-4}	9.06×10^{-5}
ASOP 3(m=6)	1.97×10^{-3}	3.80×10^{-4}
ASOP 3(m=8)	7.94×10^{-3}	1.54×10^{-3}

Source: Author

ASOP1, have improved Application Performance Parameters (APPs) over the exact respectively. Additionally, it is observed that when ASOP models are truncated, the error distance at ASOP trunk 2 is smaller compared to m=4, 6, or 8. According to the experimental results, this method indicate effective approach for approximate the image processing applications.

References

[1] Han, J., and Orshansky, M. (2013). Approximate computing: An emerging paradigm for energy-efficient design. In 2013 18th IEEE (ETS), (pp. 1–6). IEEE.

[2] White, S. A. (1989). Applications of distributed arithmetic to digital signal processing: a tutorial review. *IEEE ASSP Magazine*, 6(3), 4–19.

[3] Yuan, L., Sana, S., Pottinger, H. J., and Rao, V. S. (2000). Distributed arithmetic implementation of multivariable controllers for smart structural systems. *Smart Materials and Structures*, 9(4), 402.

[4] Li, W., Burr, J. B., and Peterson, A. M. (1988). A fully parallel VLSI implementation of distributed arithmetic. In Proceedings IEEE International Symposium Circuits Systems, (Vol. 2, pp. 1511–1515).

[5] Amirtharajah, R., and Chandrakasan, A. P. (2004). A micropower programmable DSP using approximate signal processing based on distributed arithmetic. *IEEE Journal of Solid-State Circuits*, 39(2), 337–347.

[6] Amirtharajah, R., and Chandrakasan, A. P. (2010). A micropower programmable DSP using approximate signal processing based on distributed arithmetic. *IEEE Journal of Solid-State Circuits*, 39(2), 337–347.

[7] Momeni, A., Han, J., Montuschi, P., and Lombardi, F. (2015). Design and analysis of approximate compressors for multiplication. *IEEE Transactions on Computers*, 64(4), 984–994.

[8] Vacca, M., Graziano, M., Wang, J., Cairo, F., Causapruno, G., Urgese, G., et al. (2014). Nanomagnet logic: an architectural level overview. In Field-Coupled Nanocomputing. Cham, Switzerland: Springer, (pp. 223–256).

[9] Khitun, A., and Wang, K. L. (2005). Nano scale computational architectures with spin wave bus. *Superlattices and Microstructures*, 38(3), 184–200.

[10] Liu, W., Qian, L., Wang, C., Jiang, H., Han, J., and Lombardi, F. (2017). Design of approximate radix-4 booth multipliers for error-tolerant computing. *IEEE Transactions on Computers*, 66(8), 1435–1441.

[11] Yang, Z., Jain, A., Liang, J., Han, J., and Lombardi, F. (2013). Approximate XOR/XNOR-based adders for inexact computing. In Proceedings 13th IEEE International Conference Nanotechnology (IEEE-NANO), (pp. 690–693).

[12] Mahdiani, H. R., Ahmadi, A., Fakhraie, S. M., and Lucas, C. (2010). Bio-inspired imprecise computational blocks for efficient VLSI implementation of soft-computing applications. *IEEE Transactions on Circuits and Systems I: Regular Papers*, 57(4), 850–862.

[13] Zhu, N., Goh, W. L., Wang, G., and Yeo, K. S. (2010). Enhanced low-power high-speed adder for error-tolerant application. In Proceedings International SoC Design Conference, (pp. 323–327).

[14] Patel, S. K., Garg, B., and Rai, S. K. (2020). An efficient accuracy reconfigurable CLA adder designs using complementary logic. *Journal of Electronic Testing*, 36(1), 135–142.

[15] Venkatachalam, Suganthi, and Seok-Bum Ko. "Approximate sum-of-products designs based on distributed arithmetic." *IEEE Transactions on very large scale integration (VLSI) systems* 26, no. 8 (2018): 1604–1608.

32 Leveraging Apriori and Bi-LSTM networks to uncover complex purchase patterns in market basket analysis

Raghavendran, Ch. V.[1,a], Phani Haswanth, AV S. S. D.[2], Mogili Veera Lakshmi[2], Gayatri Nandini, U.[2] and Victor Raj Kumar, M.[2]

[1]Professor, Department of IT, Aditya College of Engineering and Technology, Surampalem, Andhra Pradesh, India

[2]Student, Department of IT, Aditya College of Engineering and Technology, Surampalem, Andhra Pradesh, India

Abstract

Market basket analysis (MBA) uncovers relationships and patterns among frequently purchased items in transactional databases. Conventional methods, such as the Apriori algorithm, are commonly employed to identify frequently occurring itemsets and association rules. However, high-dimensional data are frequently challenged by such approaches. There has been increasing interest in using neural networks to improve MBA capacities since the advance of deep learning (DL). The use of Apriori and Bidirectional long short-term memory (Bi-LSTM) networks in MBA is investigated in this study.

The Apriori algorithm is used to identify frequent itemsets and association rules, thereby establishing a reliable baseline for comparison. The efficiency of the proposed method on large datasets can be improved by pruning techniques and adjustments to the support thresholds. In contrast, the sequential nature of purchase data is captured using Bi-LSTM, which is a recurrent neural network (RNN) renowned for its ability to understand temporal relationships. The Bi-LSTM network provides a dynamic and context-sensitive market basket analysis approach by learning to predict item co-occurrences and purchase sequences by training on transaction data.

The experimental results demonstrate that although Apriori is good at identifying static association rules, the Bi-LSTM network is superior at capturing the temporal and sequential components of consumer purchase behavior. Combining these two approaches into a hybrid strategy has tremendous potential to provide more thorough insights into customer trends and preferences. This study highlights the complementary strengths of traditional and deep learning techniques in Market Basket Analysis, paving the way for more robust and insightful models that can better serve the needs of retailers and marketers when understanding and predicting customer behavior.

Keywords: Apriori algorithm, bidirectional long short-term memory, hybrid models, market basket analysis, neural networks

Introduction

Understanding consumer purchasing behavior is essential in today's retail setting to improve customer happiness, streamlining inventory management, and develop effective marketing campaigns. Market basket analysis (MBA), a data mining methodology that finds patterns and links between items in transactional data, is one of the most effective ways to accomplish these goals. When analyzing point-of-sale data, the MBA is routinely used to help merchants find product groups that regularly co-occur during transactions. Through an extensive analysis of client transaction information, the MBA reveals previously unnoticed trends and connections between frequently purchased items. Consider a grocery store examining its sales information. MBA can reveal that customers who buy bread are also likely to purchase butter and milk. With this knowledge, the supermarket can strategically

---

[a]raghuchv@yahoo.com

DOI: 10.1201/9781003616399-32

position these complimentary items near each other, which could result in higher sales for all three products.

The conventional MBA technique depends on algorithms such as Apriori, which iteratively increase the size of itemsets and prune non-frequent candidates to identify frequent itemsets and association rules. Although Apriori and related algorithms have demonstrated efficient performance, they encounter difficulties when handling high-dimensional, sparse, and dynamic datasets, which are common in extensive retail settings. A range of methods are combined in data mining to identify significant patterns in enormous data volumes. Data mining, as used in MBA contexts, applies algorithms to transactional databases to identify patterns and hidden links.

The MBA is rooted in classic data mining approaches; however, new developments in deep learning (DL) and machine learning (ML) have expanded the scope of what is feasible. The DL provides novel opportunities to describe sequential and complicated interactions in transactional data, especially in neural networks such as long short-term memory (LSTM) and Bi-LSTM. By integrating advanced deep learning models with conventional data mining approaches, we can create flexible and insightful Market Basket Analysis frameworks. These hybrid methods provide improved prediction power and useful insights, thereby better capturing the complexity of customer behavior.

Literature study

The MBA is used to determine the relationships among goods in big datasets. Through the identification of product sets that regularly co-occur in transactions, firms can maximize inventory management, cross-selling tactics, and product placement. Agrawal and Srikant created the Apriori algorithm in 1994, which is a groundbreaking association rule learning and frequent itemset mining technique. The underlying principle is that any subset of a frequently occurring itemset must also frequently occur. By effectively shrinking the search space, this iterative search method reduces computational complexity. The advancement of deep learning techniques has opened new avenues for improving the MBA by capturing more

complex patterns and dependencies in transactional data. RNNs, particularly LSTM networks and their Bi-LSTM, are particularly suitable for this purpose.

Alcan et al. [1] provides an in-depth comparison between the Apriori and FP-Growth algorithms, highlighting their application in the MBA to identify consumer purchasing patterns. The results demonstrate that while Apriori was effective in generating comprehensive association rules, FP-Growth was more efficient in terms of computational time.

Aksoy et al. [2], explained the usage of the Apriori algorithm in a Turkish retail environment and provided examples of how to apply it to evaluate consumer purchase patterns and enhance retail tactics. This study highlights the importance of Apriori in producing useful insights for market basket analysis.

Patil et al [3]. compared and contrasted three widely used algorithms: FP-Growth, ECLAT, and Apriori. It assesses its effectiveness by evaluating the quality of the association rules it produces and their computational efficiency. The results indicate that Apriori offers the most comprehensive and high-quality rules, making it useful for in-depth market basket analysis, although FP-Growth is the fastest.

Gulzar et al. [4], proposed a web-based hospital information management system (HIMS) that uses the association rule-based Apriori method to identify common patterns in the data of patients with eye disorders. With reference to data analysis and reporting services, the proposed framework is capable of addressing all major concerns and challenges associated with the current HIMS. Upon running the Apriori algorithm over the gathered data, we discovered that at the current age of 22, approximately 140 out of 1035 people had myopia or nearsightedness, and no male patients were identified as having myopia.

Ghous et al. [6] investigated how to combine conventional association rule mining with DL techniques, such as Bi-LSTM, to increase the precision of market basket analysis. This study focuses on how association rules and Bi-LSTM networks can be combined to identify multifaceted patterns in consumer purchase data.

Cheng et al. [7], focused mostly on time series prediction and demonstrated how Bi-LSTM networks may be applied to handle complicated data patterns. By treating purchase sequences as time-series data, one can apply this technique to market basket analysis and forecast future buying trends.

Jang et al. [8] proposed a hybrid model that combines Bi-LSTM and CNN with an attention mechanism and focuses on text categorization. The method can be used to improve the prediction of purchasing behavior and product suggestions in market basket analysis due to its efficacy in capturing contextual nuances and long-term dependencies.

Salgotra et al. [9], Machine learning is currently used to facilitate many facets of the retail industry. The retail sector gains from applying ML and artificial intelligence (AI) in a number of ways, such as buyer identification and sales performance forecasting. Retailers use MBA to increase sales by analyzing various customer purchase behaviors. The procedure entails analyzing several, including purchase histories, to find trends in product groups and items that are very possibly to be bought together.

Alsharafa et al. [11], suggests that DL can predict customer lifetime value (CLV) and optimize CRM. It suggests a multi-output deep neural network (DNN) model for this purpose, which outperforms other methods in marketing effectiveness and client lifetime value. The model has an acceptable error rate of 10.3%, 11.6%, and RMSE of 12.29%.

Data Preprocessing

In this study, an online retail dataset containing information about transactions is considered. This dataset serves as the foundation for our analysis, allowing us to uncover patterns and relationships within the transaction data.

After loading the dataset, data exploration starts. This involves understanding the dataset's characteristics, such as the number of rows, attributes, and basic statistics. Additionally, it needs to analyze relevant metrics like the number of purchased items in different countries, providing insights into the dataset's structure and distribution. Figure 32.1 shows the flow of implementing these steps.

Dataset

The data is collected from a UK based online retail store with transactions between 01-12-2009 to 08-12-2011. The dataset consists of 46431 transactions and each transaction consists of eight features – InvoiceNo, StockCode, Description, Quantity, InvoiceDate, UnitPrice, CustomerID, and Country. A sample dataset is presented in Figure 32.2.

Data cleaning methods

Text tokenization – It converts text sequences in the "Antecedents:" column (items bought together) into numerical sequences using a Tokenizer. This allows the model to work with numerical data.

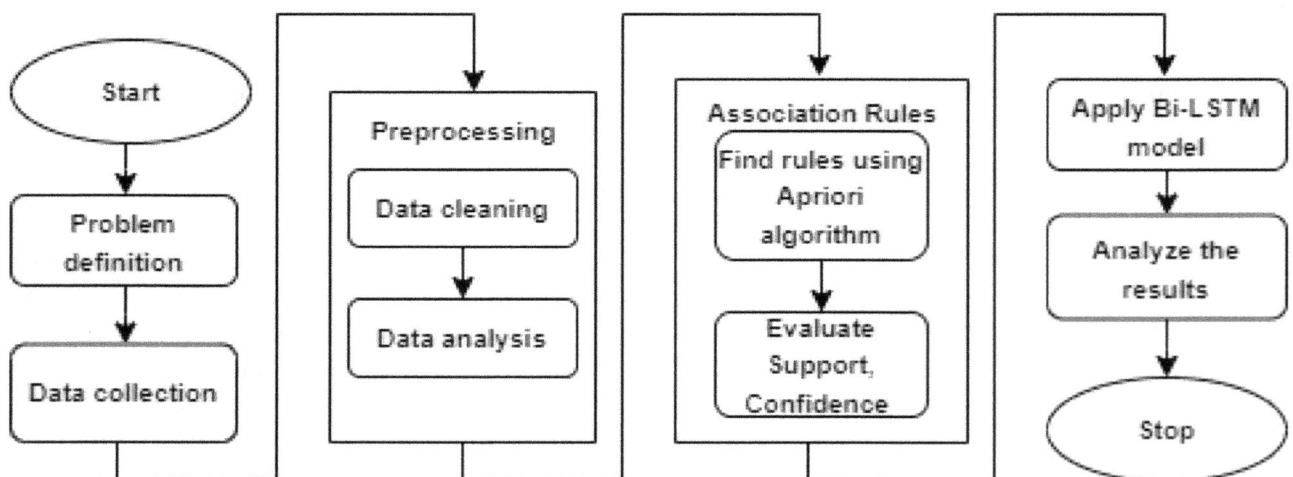

Figure 32.1 Steps in the proposed model
Source: Author

Padding sequences – The pad_sequences function ensures all sequences have the same length by padding shorter sequences with zeroes. This is necessary for the neural network layers to process the data efficiently.

Label encoding – It converts text labels in the "Consequents:" column (items potentially bought next) into numerical labels using a Label Encoder. This allows the model to handle categorical data (different consequent items).

Steps in data cleaning

Data cleaning starts immediately after data exploration. This step involves preprocessing the data by removing duplicate values, handling null values, and potentially filtering out certain transactions based on specific criteria. For instance, filter transactions with InvoiceNo containing certain initial letters like 'C' if they are deemed irrelevant to our analysis.

With the data preprocessed, we explore into data analysis. Utilizing bar graphs or other visualization techniques, analyze and present the data, such as visualizing the frequency of different items or transaction patterns. These visualizations provide valuable insights into the underlying trends and patterns within the dataset.

Subsequently, apply one-hot encoding to transform categorical variables into a numerical format. This step is crucial for further analysis and model training, as it enables us to represent categorical data in a format suitable for machine learning algorithms.

Moving forward, apply the Apriori algorithm to generate association rules and identify frequent item sets within the dataset. This step helps to uncover patterns and relationships between different items purchased together, providing valuable insights for businesses in areas like product recommendation and market basket analysis. Lastly, implement a CNN-BiLSTM model for predicting the next item in a sequence. This deep learning model leverages convolutional and recurrent neural network architectures to analyze sequential patterns in transaction data and make predictions based on learned patterns. This advanced model adds a layer of sophistication to our analysis, enabling us to make more accurate predictions and uncover deeper insights from the dataset.

Apriori algorithm

The Apriori algorithm is a standard method used in market basket analysis to identify frequent itemsets and generate association rules Agrawal and Srikant [10]. Here are the key steps involved in the Apriori algorithm:

1. Initialization:
    Input the transaction dataset – The algorithm starts with a database of transactions where each transaction is a set of items purchased together.
    Set minimum support threshold – This is to identify itemsets that occur frequently in the dataset.
2. Generate frequent 1-itemsets (L1)
    Scan the transaction dataset– Determine each individual item's support (frequency) inside the transaction dataset..
    Filter by minimum support – Frequent 1-itemsets are limited to items whose support is either more than or equal to the minimum support level (L1).
3. Generate candidate k-itemsets (Ck) for k ≥ 2:
    Join step– Join often occurring (k-1)-itemsets (Lk-1) with one another to create candidate

	InvoiceNo	StockCode	Description	Quantity	InvoiceDate	UnitPrice	CustomerID	Country
0	536389	22941	CHRISTMAS LIGHTS 10 REINDEER	6	01-12-2010 10 03	8 50	12431 0	Australia
1	536389	21622	VINTAGE UNION JACK CUSHION COVER	8	01-12-2010 10 03	4 95	12431 0	Australia
2	536389	21791	VINTAGE HEADS AND TAILS CARD GAME	12	01-12-2010 10 03	1 25	12431 0	Australia
3	536389	35004C	SET OF 3 COLOURED FLYING DUCKS	6	01-12-2010 10 03	5 45	12431 0	Australia
4	536389	35004G	SET OF 3 GOLD FLYING DUCKS	4	01-12-2010 10 03	6 35	12431 0	Australia

Figure 32.2 Sample online retail store dataset
Source: Author

k-itemsets (Ck). This step is known as the self-join step.

Prune step – Eliminate potential itemsets that contain any non-frequent (k-1)-itemset in order to prune them. The Apriori property, which states that every non-empty subset of a frequent itemset must likewise be frequent, is utilized in this stage.

4. Generate frequent k-itemsets (Lk):
    Scan the transaction dataset – Determine the support in Ck for every potential k-itemset.
    Filter by minimum support – Frequent k-item sets (Lk) are defined as candidate k-item sets whose support is at least as great as the minimum support criteria.

5. Repeat steps 3 and 4:
    Increment k – Increase the value of k and repeat the process of generating candidate itemsets and filtering them based on support until no more frequent itemsets can be generated.

6. Generate association rules:
    For each frequent itemset – Generate all possible non-empty subsets.
    Calculate confidence – For each subset, calculate the confidence of the rule by dividing the support of the frequent itemset by the support of the subset.
    Filter by minimum confidence threshold – Only those rules whose confidence are greater than or equal to the minimum confidence threshold are considered strong association rules.

Bidirectional long short-term memory

RNNs are a family of neural networks that are particularly good at processing sequential data because they keep track of previous components in the sequence in a hidden state. LSTM networks were introduced to address the limitations of standard RNNs by incorporating memory cells that can maintain information over long periods. Bi-LSTM is an advanced type of RNN intended to capture dependencies in sequential data from both past and future contexts. Bi-LSTM networks are particularly useful in tasks where the context from both directions (previous and subsequent data points) is important for making predictions. In market basket analysis, Bi-LSTM networks can be used to predict future purchasing behaviors by

considering the sequence of past purchases. The structure of a Bi-LSTM consists of

Input layer: Both the forward and backward LSTM layers concurrently receive the input sequence.

Forward LSTM layer: Retains the order in which the input sequence was processed.

Backward LSTM layer: Reverses the order in which the input sequence is processed.

Concatenation layer: Concatenation or combination is performed on the forward and backward LSTM layers' outputs.

Output layer: The combined output is passed to subsequent layers (e.g., dense layers) for final prediction or classification.

Proposed Model

In the description of dataset it is written that there are some canceled transactions presented in dataset. Canceled transactions are indicated by invoice number which starts with letter 'C'. Probably transactions with negative values of quantity are canceled. No. of cancelled transactions 1432 which is 3.08% in the total transactions.

There are also transactions with zero price. Transactions with zero price doesn't bring useful information to analysis, moreover mainly there are not any description for such transactions. These transactions could be deleted. There are 18 transactions of this category and are 0.038% of total transactions. There are 88 duplicates and are also deleted from the final dataset. There are 2781 unique stock codes available and the following Figure 32.3 shows the top five stocks sold as per the quantity.

The Figures 32.4 and 32.5 shows most preferred 10 products based on the number of customers preference and country wise number of customers. The customers buying habits and priorities will change from country to country based on several factors. The Apriori algorithm is applied on the encoded dataset with minimum support as 0.01 and minimum threshold as 1. The Apriori algorithm generated 8930 association rules. The algorithm has generated 542 association rules with minimum support as 0.02 and minimum threshold as 1. A sample list of rules generated by Apriori algorithm are presented in Figure 32.6.

Description	Quantity
rabbit night light	15437
mini paint set vintage	12493
pack of 72 retrospot cake cases	11228
spaceboy lunch box	8363
dolly girl lunch box	7344

Figure 32.3 Description and quantity of top 5 stocks sold
Source: Author

The generated results are taken as input for the proposed CNN-BiLSTM model. The results are tokenized and encoded before submitting to the CNN-BiLSTM model. The model is trained by tuning its hyperparameters to get the optimum accuracy. After 50 epochs the model resulted with 92.38% train accuracy and 73.39% test accuracy.

Conclusion and Future Scope

One of the foundations of retail analytics is still market basket analysis, which offers insightful data on consumer buying habits. Combining state-of-the-art deep learning algorithms with conventional data mining approaches offers a viable way ahead as the volume and complexity of transactional data keep growing. Businesses can increase revenue, enhance customer satisfaction, and obtain a better understanding of customer behavior by combining the advantages of both strategies. In this work a transaction dataset with 46431 transactions is considered. The dataset is preprocessed by applying various data cleaning techniques and applied Apriori algorithm. The algorithm generated 542 association rules for 0.02 minimum support. The antecedents and consequents are given to CNN-BiLSTM

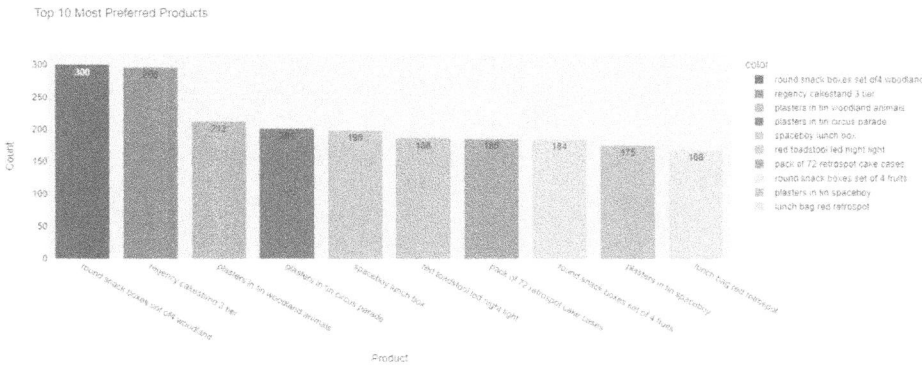

Figure 32.4 Most preferred products
Source: Author

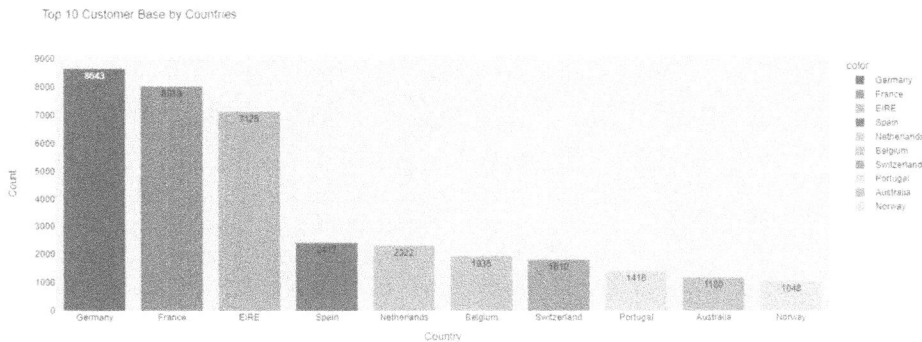

Figure 32.5 Customers base by countries
Source: Author

	antecedents	consequents	antecedent support	consequent support	support	confidence	lift	leverage	conviction
0	(6 ribbons rustic charm)	(regency cakestand 3 tier)	0.053758	0.160724	0.020296	0.377551	2.349063	0.011656	1.348345
1	(regency cakestand 3 tier)	(6 ribbons rustic charm)	0.160724	0.053758	0.020296	0.126280	2.349063	0.011656	1.083004
2	(pack of 72 retrospot cake cases)	(60 teatime fairy cake cases)	0.101481	0.038398	0.021942	0.216216	5.630888	0.018045	1.226871
3	(60 teatime fairy cake cases)	(pack of 72 retrospot cake cases)	0.038398	0.101481	0.021942	0.571429	5.630888	0.018045	2.096544
4	(alarm clock bakelike chocolate)	(alarm clock bakelike red)	0.025782	0.065277	0.020845	0.808511	12.385839	0.019162	4.881331

Figure 32.6 Antecedents and consequents generated by Apriori algorithm
Source: Author

for designing a prediction model to predict the customer buying habits. The resulted model predicting with 92.38% accuracy for train data and 73.39% for test data.

It is evident from accuracy that the model is biased towards train data than test data. This needs to be focused in the future work by tuning the hyperparameters of Apriori algorithm and CNN-BiLSTM model. The customer buying habits will change from one country to another because of number of parameters. So, country wise analysis is also needs to be addressed in the future work.

References

[1] Alcan, D., Ozdemir, K., Ozkan, B., Mucan, A. Y., and Ozcan, T. (2023). A comparative analysis of apriori and FP-growth algorithms for market basket analysis using multi-level association rule mining. In Calisir, F., and Durucu, M. (Eds.), Industrial Engineering in the Covid-19 Era. GJCIE 2022. Lecture Notes in Management and Industrial Engineering. Springer, Cham. https://doi.org/10.1007/978-3-031-25847-3_13.

[2] Aksoy, A., Kaplan, B., and Demirci, V. G. (2023). Apriori algorithm in market basket analysis: a retailer example in Turkey. In Mirzazadeh, A., Erdebilli, B., Babaee Tirkolaee, E., Weber, G. W., and Kar, A. K. (Eds.), Science, Engineering Management and Information Technology. SEMIT 2022. Communications in Computer and Information Science, (Vol 1808). Springer, Cham. https://doi.org/10.1007/978-3-031-40395-8_16.

[3] Patil, E. a. H. (2023). Enhancing retail strategies through apriori, ECLAT& FP growth algorithms in market basket analysis. *International Journal on Recent and Innovation Trends in Computing and Communication*, 11(9), 3831–3838. https://doi.org/10.17762/ijritcc.v11i9.9637.

[4] Gulzar, K., Ayoob Memon, M., Mohsin, S. M., Aslam, S., Akber, S. M. A., and Nadeem, M. A. (2023). An efficient healthcare data mining approach using apriori algorithm: a case study of eye disorders in young adults. *Information*, 14(4), 203. https://doi.org/10.3390/info14040203.

[5] Ghous, H., Malik, M., and Rehman, I. (2023). Deep learning based market basket analysis using association rules. *KIET Journal of Computing and Information Sciences*, 6(2), 14–34. https://doi.org/10.51153/kjcis.v6i2.166.

[6] Cheng, Q., Chen, Y., Xiao, Y., Yin, H., and Liu, W. (2022). A dual-stage attention-based Bi-LSTM network for multivariate time series prediction. *The Journal of Supercomputing*, 78, 16214–16235. https://doi.org/10.1007/s11227-022-04506-3.

[7] Jang, B., Kim, M., Harerimana, G., Kang, S., and Kim, J. W. (2020). Bi-LSTM model to increase accuracy in text classification: combining word-2vec CNN and attention mechanism. *Applied Sciences*, 10(17), 5841. https://doi.org/10.3390/app10175841.

[8] Salgotra, K., Tiwari, A., Singhal, D., and Singh, A. (2024). Association rule mining on market basket dataset using Apriori algorithm. In AIP Conference Proceedings, 2 July 2024. (Vol. 3168 (1): pp. 020030). https://doi.org/10.1063/5.0221112.

[9] Agrawal, R., and Srikant, R. (1994). Fast algorithms for mining association rules. In Proceedings of the 20th International Conference on Very Large Data Bases, VLDB.

[10] Alsharafa, N., Madhubala, P., Lakshmi Moorthygari, S., Rajapraveen, K., Kumar, B., Sengan, S., et al. (2024). Deep learning techniques for predicting the customer lifetime value to improve customer relationship management. *Journal of Autonomous Intelligence*, 7(5), 1622. doi:http://dx.doi.org/10.32629/jai.v7i5.162.

33 Improving brain tumor detection and classification through skull stripping and multi-scale convolutional neural network

Sangeeta Viswanadham[1,a], Appala Srinuvasu Muttpati[2,b], JayaLakshmi N.[3,c], and Koka Venkata Sai Charan[4,d]

[1]Department of CSE, GITAM DEEMED TO BE UNIVERSITY, Visakhapatnam, Andhra Pradesh, India

[2]Department of CSE (AI and ML, DS), Anil Neerukonda Institute of Technology and Sciences, Visakhapatnam, Andhra Pradesh, India

[3]Department of CSA, Gayatri Vidya Parishad College of Engineering, Visakhapatnam, Andhra Pradesh, India

[4]Department of CSE (AI and ML, DS), Anil Neerukonda Institute of Technology and Sciences, Visakhapatnam, Andhra Pradesh, India

Abstract

Medical image analysis and diagnosis require accurate brain tumor classification, which entails classifying brain tumors based on specific features such as shape, size, location, etc. Precise tumor classification is a core driver of neuroimaging analysis, assisting in diagnosis, therapeutic planning, and patient management. Our study employed a two-step approach for classifying brain tumors using MRI scans. Firstly, we performed skull stripping to remove non-cerebral tissue from the MRI scans. Then, used a multi-scale convolutional neural network (CNN) to assess images taken in the data comprising three categories of malignancies: glioma, pituitary and meningioma tumor. Our suggested technique performed admirably on a freely accessible dataset of 3064 slices from 233 individuals, with a brain tumor classification accuracy of 0.976.

Keywords: Brain tumor, MRI, multi-scale convolution neural network, skull stripping

Introduction

Brain is the crucial unit in the nervous system for all living beings. Although it constitutes only about 2% of a person's body weight, it plays a significant role in various bodily functions. These include processing sensory information, managing movement and coordination, regulating emotions and behavior, and maintaining a stable internal environment. Abnormal growth within the brain, known as a brain tumor, can severely affect an individual's quality of life. Brain tumors can develop in people of any age, gender, or race, and effective treatment is essential for improving patients' well-being. Benign tumors typically remain confined within the brain, while malignant ones can invade nearby healthy tissue and spread to other body parts. Regardless of their nature, brain tumors can disrupt brain function if they grow large enough to exert pressure on surrounding tissues, making early and accurate diagnosis critical. Before the advent of advanced imaging techniques, doctors had to rely on physical examinations and symptoms to diagnose tumors, which often led to late detection. Tumors that are small or located deep within the body may not be detectable through physical examination alone.

However, modern imaging tools enhanced the accuracy in tumor diagnosis by providing doctors visualizing the internal structures non-invasively. Different MRI modalities are used depending on the tissue being examined, including Fluid Attenuated Inversion Recovery (FLAIR), T1-weighted, T1-weighted contrast-enhanced (T1-CE), and T2-weighted MRI. These techniques help identify healthy tissue, detect

[a]sangeeta.kakai@gmail.com, [b]srinuvasu.mutti@gmail.com, [c]jayalakshminemana@gmail.com, [d]kokacharan2003@gmail.com

DOI: 10.1201/9781003616399-33

tumor edges, and highlight areas of edema in cerebrospinal fluid. Brain tumors, such as meningiomas, pituitary tumors, and gliomas, can arise from different parts of the brain or surrounding tissues, and their early detection is vital for effective treatment.

Related Work

Due to the brain's complexity, detecting brain tumors early is challenging. Radiologists must engage in a meticulous process to locate, segment, and identify tumors on MRI scans. To address this, various machine learning [4–7] and deep learning [8–12] algorithms were developed to effectively segregate tumors in brain based on different parameters. In traditional machine learning approaches, feature extraction from images is a crucial preprocessing step for tumor segmentation. For example, Sachdeva et al. [4] used a content-based active contour model to identify tumor locations, while skull stripping is another common preprocessing technique, though it has drawbacks like requiring prior image data and being time-consuming [18,19]. After feature extraction, the features are fed into segmentation or classification steps. In their study, Sachdeva et al. compared two classifiers: support vector machine (SVM) and artificial neural network (ANN). SVM achieved an accuracy of 80% - 92%, while ANN ranged from 76% - 95% [5] developed a brain tumor classification system using a method called Back Propagation Network, achieving 95.3% accuracy with 10 extracted features. Iftekharuddin et al. [6] used fractal wavelet properties in a concept called Self-Organizing Map classifier, reaching a precision-average of 90%. Havaei [7] proposed an algorithm for semi-automatic system using a kNN classifier, achieving the similarities for dice of 0.85,0.75 for whole and regions where core tumor lie. Deep neural networks (DNNs) have advanced machine learning techniques, allowing computers to automatically select the best features to represent data, leading to significant improvements in medical imaging. Havaei et al. [8] explored complete convolutional system to BRATS 2013 dataset. Moeskops [9] utilized a multi-scale CNN to segregate tissues in brain , matter of hyperintensities, achieving around 85% accuracy in the MRBrainS13 challenge [10].

Ronneberger et al. [11] made a significant contribution with the U-net architecture, excelling in the ISBI competition [12]. Previous research focused on segmenting brain tumor locations without classifying them by type. However, the aim of the present study was to develop a novel model in deep learning which is capable of tasks such as segmentation and classification. Some notable works share this goal, using the same dataset. Abiwinanda [13] introduced a convolution neural network with two layers in segmentation, classification. Pashaei et al. [14] proposed two classification strategies: one using CNN and the other using CNN-extracted features with a KELM algorithm. Sultan [15] suggested architecture of convolution-neural network with 16 number of convolution layers. Anaraki et al. [16] combined CNNs with a genetic algorithm for network architecture improvement. Francisco et al. [17] created a multi-scale convolution-neural network for brain tumor classification, segmentation, achieving an accuracy in classification of 0.973. This model operates at three different spatial scales and does not require skull or vertebral column removal before image input. Sheela et al. [18] noted that image artifacts and intensity variations could hinder brain tumor analysis from MRI scans, and discussed relevant preprocessing techniques like skull stripping, which enhances images without altering their original content.

Proposed Method

Technologies like AI and DL have made remarkable strides across various fields, revolutionizing industries such as healthcare, finance, transportation, and entertainment. These advanced technologies process huge volume of data, detect intricate similarities, evolving in automation, enhanced decision-making, and increased efficiency. particularly, AI and DL address critical global challenges like climate change, disease diagnosis, and energy sustainability. One area of significant progress is in medical sciences, specifically in medical image processing, which has greatly enhanced early and accurate disease diagnosis. Prior to these advancements, diagnosis was often difficult, time-consuming, and sometimes inaccurate. For brain tumor-classification, several systems have been developed, focusing primarily on CNN algorithms like Inception V3 and

MobileNetV2. The current approach involves multiple steps, starting with fuzzy C-Means (FCM) segmentation to divide MRI images into sections of tumor and healthy tissue. Following segmentation, the parameters considered here are the texture, shape were taken into consideration in order to characterize the tumor and surrounding tissue. These features are then used by DNN and SVM to categorize brain tumors. However, this method has limitations, including a lengthy computation time due to extensive feature extraction and relatively low accuracy, which can lead to misdiagnosis and ineffective treatment planning. During research, DCNN model demonstrated a segmentation and classification accuracy of 0.973 for brain tumors. However, this model had the drawback of misclassifying non-cerebral areas as tumors. To address this issue, skull stripping was proposed to remove non-cerebral areas, potentially improving the detection of malignancies in patients. The complete architecture of this approach is illustrated in the Figure 33.1, with every component was described in detail. This process begins with loading images dataset, typically T1-weighted CE

MRI images, and converting them from .mat to .jpg format for easier processing. Images are then resized to a resolution of 512 × 512 pixels, and further reduced to 65 × 65 pixels for input into the multi-scale CNN model. Noise is filtered using a bilateral filter, preserving image edges, and skull stripping is performed to remove non-brain tissues. Skull-stripped images are stored separately, with the image's dataset was categorically splitted into both training, testing sets in a ratio of 4:1 to ensure model generalization. Preprocessing includes organizing images into folders based on tumor-type and reducing their resolution to standardize the dataset. Feature extraction, acritical step, identifies and quantifies characteristics of different tumor-types for input into the classification model. The pre-processed data is then fed into a multi-scale CNN model, which uses multiple convolutional layers at different resolutions to classify brain tumors and determine their type. The final output of the proposed model is the detection of a brain tumor's presence and its classification based on MRI scans.

System Architecture

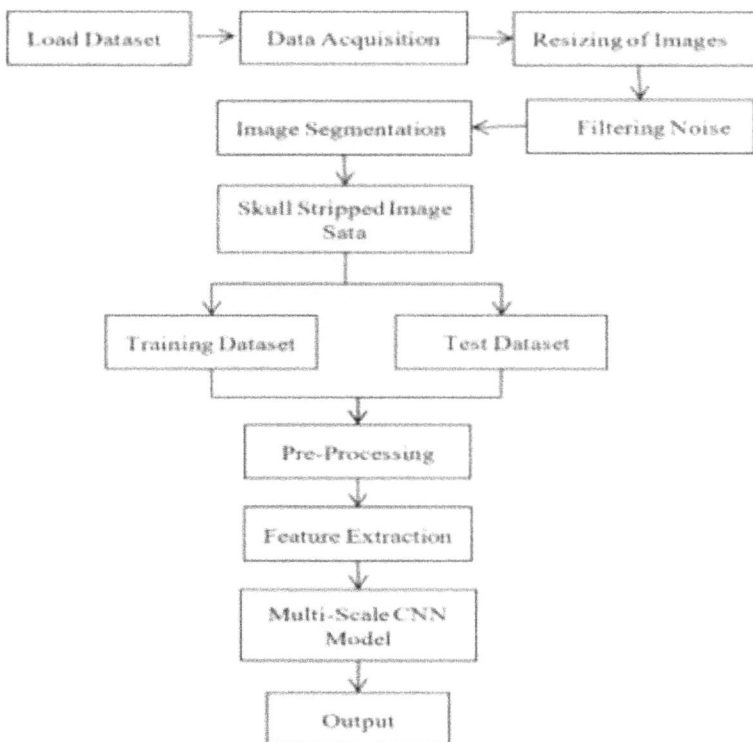

Figure 33.1 Architecture of the proposed system
Source: Author

Methodology

The system comprises five key processes, starting with extracting an input sample from the dataset, followed by pre-processing, segmentation, and brain tumor classification using a multi-scale CNN. Finally, the output determines whether a brain tumor is present. Figure 33.2 breaks down the system into distinct modules, providing detailed explanations for each.

Input image: The input images are sourced from a brain tumor dataset, collected from 233 patients at Tianjing Medical University and Nanfang Hospital in Guangzhou, China, between 2005 and 2010. This dataset includes 3,064 image segments showcasing sagittal, coronal, and axial brain views. The dataset consists of 930 pituitary tumors, 708 meningiomas, and 1,426 gliomas, making it highly comprehensive for tumor classification research.

Image pre-processing: The Input images are pre-processed in enhancing image quality and enhancing features for subsequent analysis. This step includes image resizing to a standard resolution of 512 × 512 pixels, noise removal to eliminate distortions, and contrast enhancement. These actions are vital to optimizing the image data for accurate and efficient analysis, including tumor classification.

image segmentation (skull stripping): Image segmentation divides an image into distinct segments or regions based on criteria like color, texture, or shape, simplifying and enhancing visual representation. Skull stripping, a common technique in medical imaging, involves removing non-brain tissues from MRI scans. We used intensity thresholding and morphological operations for skull stripping. Figure 33.3 demonstrates the process on a T1-CE MRI image.

Brain tumor classification using multi-scale CNN: Classification, a key machine learning technique, assigns labels to new observations based on patterns learned from a training dataset. For brain tumor classification, a multi-scale CNN architecture is used to analyze MRI data. This architecture consists of three paths, each processing features at large, medium, and small scales using 1 × 65 × 65 sliding windows. Every path here consists of two convolutional layers with concept of max-pooling, and the output

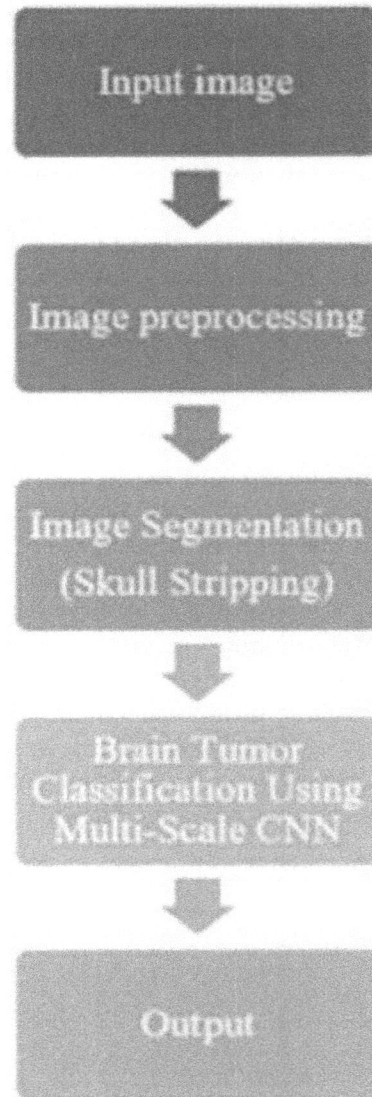

Figure 33.2 Entire system module division
Source: Author

of every path are combined and will go through another convolutional layer. The features are then fed into a fully connected stage, which classifies the image into one of four labels: 0 depicts healthy tissue, 1 depicts meningioma, 2 depicts glioma, and 3 depicts pituitary tumor. Figure 33.4 illustrates multi-scale CNN architecture. In our model, 65 × 65 pixel windows were used, with convolutional kernels sized at 11 × 11, 7 × 7, and 3 × 3 pixels. Each path in the model has two convolutional layers using ReLU activation and a 3 × 3 max-pooling kernel with a stride of two. Using

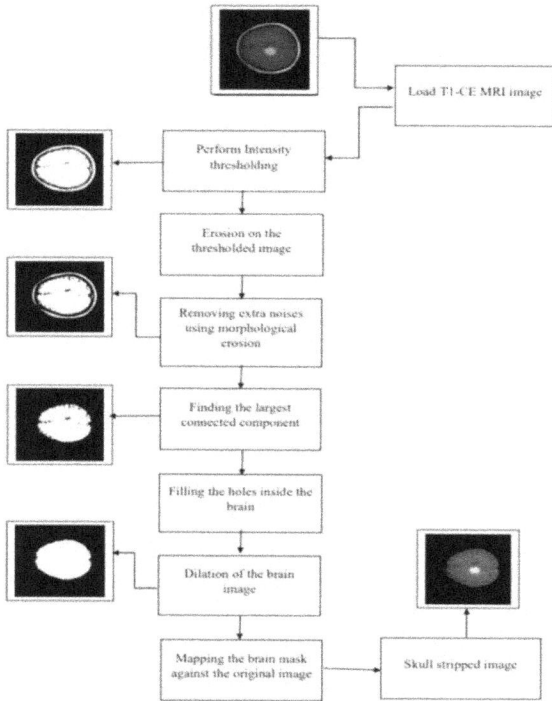

Figure 33.3 Flow chart of skull stripping
Source: Author

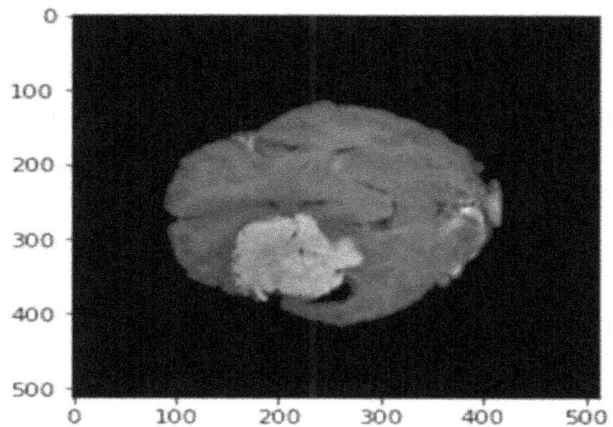

Figure 33.4 Architecture of multi-scale CNN
Source: Author

different scales allows for extracting wide variety of features, coming to a more thorough analysis of tumors. After feature extraction, all three paths were combined into a single convolutional layer using 3 × 3 maxpool kernel with activation function like ReLU. The output is down-sampled with a 2 × 2 max-pooling kernel and passed through a fully connected stage that concatenates 8,192 features. To prevent overfitting, a dropout layer is added before the fully connected layer, and a softmax activation function is used in the final layer to classify the tumor into one of four categories. The model was trained in Jupyter Notebook with approximately 2,856,932 trainable parameters. Training was conducted on a Windows platform with an Intel Core i5 Processor and an NVIDIA GeForce MX350 graphics card, taking a total of three days.

Output: The proposed model effectively identifies the presence of a brain tumor from an MRI scan and classifies the tumor type as pituitary, glioma, or meningioma.

Result Analysis

A sample input in the context of brain tumor classification could be an MRI picture that has been skull-stripped and pre-processed. The capacity of model for reliably forecast variety of brain tumor present in image given can be evaluated using ground truth labels. The input image (Figure 33.5) is taken as an experiment to evaluate the model's performance. The expected output label

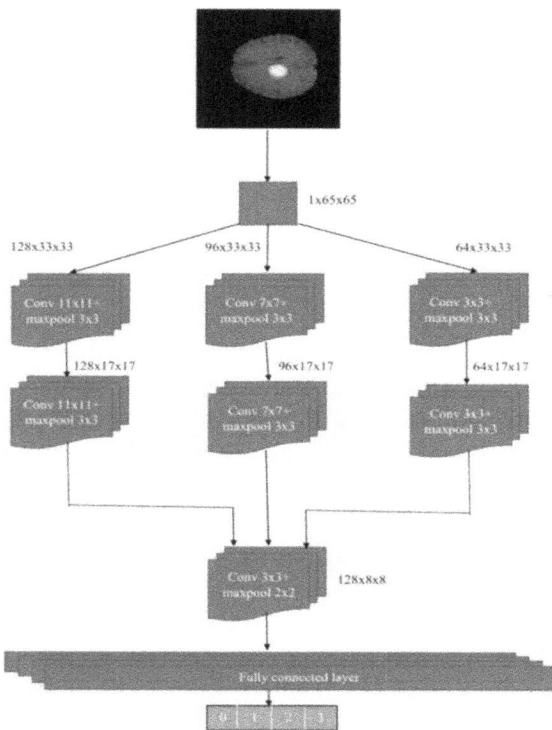

Figure 33.5 Sample skull stripped nimage
Source: Author

```
In [100]: plt.imshow(img)
Out[100]: <matplotlib.image.AxesImage at 0x2eb072a6a90>
```

```
In [116]: labels={0:'healthy',1:'meningioma',2:'glioma',3:'pituitary'}

In [117]: print(labels[max_index])
          meningioma
```

Figure 33.6 Predicted output of the model
Source: Author

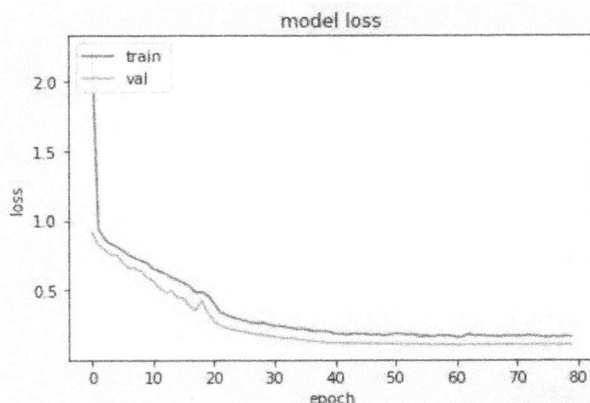

for the provided sample input is meningioma tumor in the Figure 33.6.

The model suggested in the study achieved an accuracy of 0.976 in classifying brain tumors. Graphs were plotted to present graphical representation of both accuracy, loss to aid comprehension.

Figure 33.7 displays the model's loss at each epoch, with the x-axis representing 80 epochs and the y-axis representing the corresponding accuracy. The training accuracy of the model is depicted by the blue line, while the validation accuracy is represented by the yellow line.

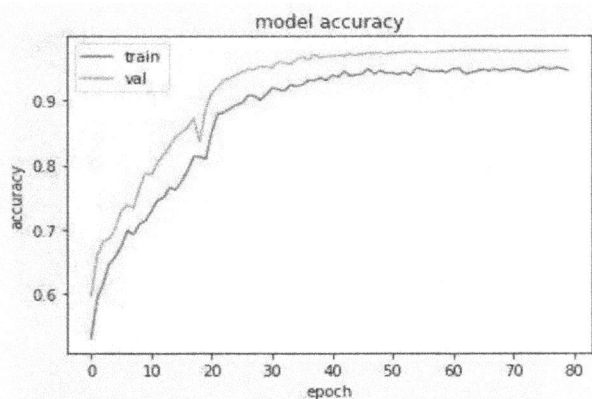

Figure 33.7 Model's accuracy at each epoch, with the x-axis representing 80 epoch and y-axis representing the corresponding loss
Source: Author

Figure 33.8 displays the model's loss at each epoch, with the x-axis representing 80 epochs and the y-axis representing the corresponding loss. The training loss of the model is depicted by the blue line, while the validation loss is represented by the yellow line on the graph. The comparative graph provided by previously widely used classifiers like CNN, linear support vector machine (SVM linear), K-Nearest neighbor (K-NN), decision tree (DT), and linear discriminant (LD) is shown below in Figure 33.8
Source: Author

Conclusion and Future Scope

Brain tumor detection and classification are crucial in medical imaging, particularly for treatment planning and prognosis assessment. MRI-based techniques have become the foundation for diagnosing brain tumors due to their non-invasive nature and high spatial resolution. Mohan and Subashini (2018) presented a comprehensive survey on MRI-based medical image analysis, focusing on brain tumor grade classification to enhance diagnostic accuracy [1]. Furthermore, the segmentation of brain tumors in MRI images has witnessed remarkable progress with deep learning methodologies, as reviewed by Işın et al. [2].

This specific approach introduces the method for detecting as-well as categorizing brain tumors using skull stripping and multi-scale CNN. The effectiveness of the suggested method is evaluated using a freely accessible dataset of T1-CE weighted MRI scans. Initially, the input MRI images are loaded from the source file, converted to grayscale, and resized to 512×512 resolution. A bilateral filtering technique is then applied

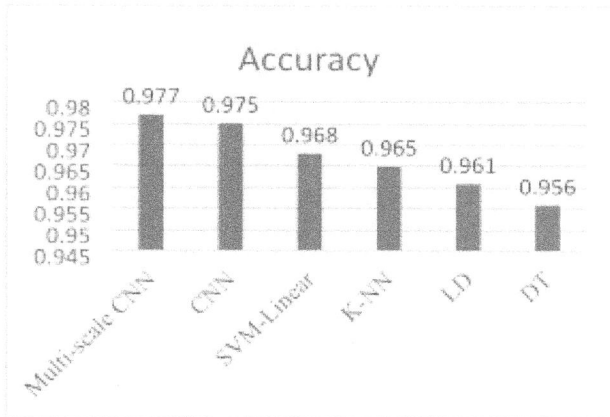

Figure 33.9 Comparison of previous models
Source: Author

in data cleaning process in images and discard any disturbance present in the original data. The resulting dataset is then skull stripped by applying intensity thresholding and morphological operations to remove non-brain tissues. The skull-stripped dataset is subsequently fed into a multi-scale CNN for classifying the tumors. The proposed model classified brain tumors with an accuracy of 97.6%, demonstrating its potential to help doctors diagnose brain tumors. To achieve accurate and high-quality skull-stripped images in neuroimaging analysis, obtaining precise brain masks are essential. One commonly used method to obtain brain masks is through the use of the brain extraction tool (BET), which utilizes a surface-based approach and is widely recognized for its reliability. While BET is an automated method and can save time, it may not always be suitable in cases where there is low contrast or image artifacts. In these instances, manual skull stripping can be performed. Although this method requires more expertise and time, it can produce very accurate skull-stripped images. Using multi-scale CNN on this skull-stripped data can improve the sensitivity and specificity of detecting brain tumors in MRI scans.

References

[1] Mohan, G., and Subashini, M. M. (2018). MRI-based medical image analysis: survey on brain tumor grade classification. *Biomedical Signal Processing and Control*, 39, 139–16. http://dx.doi.org/10.1016/j.bspc.2017.07.007.

[2] Işın, A., Direkoğlu, C., and Şah, M. (2016). Review of MRI-based brain tumor image segmentation using deep learning methods. *Procedia Computer Science*, 102, 317–324. https://doi.org/10.1016/j.procs.2016.09.407.

[3] B. H. Menze, A. Jakab, S. Bauer, J. Kalpathy-Cramer, K. Farahani, J. Kirby, Y. Burren, M. Porz, J. Slotboom, R. Wiest, and G. Langs (2015). "The Multimodal Brain Tumor Image Segmentation Benchmark (BRATS)." *IEEE Transactions on Medical Imaging*, 34(10), pp. 1993–2024. doi: 10.1109/TMI.2014.2377694.

[4] Sachdev, J., Kumar, V., Gupta, I., Khandelwal, N., and Ahuja, C. K. (2016). A package-SFER-CB-segmentation, feature extraction, reduction and classification analysis by both SVM and ANN for brain tumors. *Applied Soft Computing*, 47, 151–167. https://doi.org/10.1016/j.asoc.2016.05.020.

[5] Sharma, Y., and Chhabra, M. (2015). An improved automatic brain tumor detection system. *International Journal of Advanced Research in Computer Science and Software Engineering*, 5(4), 11–15.

[6] Iftekharuddin, K. M., Zheng, J., Islam, M. A., and Ogg, R. J. (2009). Fractal-based brain tumor detection in multimodal MRI. *Applied Mathematics and Computation*, 207(1), 23–41. doi: 10.1016/j.amc.2007.10.063.

[7] Havaei, M., Jodoin, P. M., and Larochelle, H. (2014). Efficient Interactive brain tumor segmentation as within-brain kNN classification. In 22nd International Conference on Pattern Recognition, Stockholm, Sweden, (pp. 556–561). doi: 10.1109/ICPR.2014.106.

[8] Havaei, M., Davy, A., Warde-Farley, D., Biard, A., Courville, A., Bengio, Y., et al. (2017). Brain tumor segmentation with deep neural networks. *Medical Image Analysis*, 7, 18–31. https://doi.org/10.1016/j.media.2016.05.004.

[9] P. Moeskops, M. A. Viergever, A. M. Mendrik, L. S. de Vries, M. J. N. L. Benders, and I. Isgum (2017). "Evaluation of a Deep Learning Approach for the Segmentation of Brain Tissues and White Matter Hyperintensities of Presumed Vascular Origin in MRI." NeuroImage: Clinical, 17, pp. 251–262. doi: 10.1016/j.nicl.2017.10.007.

[10] MRBrainS (2017). "Evaluation Framework for MR Brain Image Segmentation." Retrieved from https://mrbrains13.isi.uu.nl/

[11] Ronneberger, O., Fischer, P., and Brox, T. (2015). U-Net: convolutional networks for biomedical image segmentation. In Medical Image Computing and Computer-Assisted Intervention – MIC-

CAI, (pp. 9351). https://doi.org/10.1007/978-3-319-24574-4_28.

[12] Ignacio, A. C., Sebastian, S., Albert, C., and Johannes, S. (2012) ISBI challenge: segmentation of neuronal structures in EM stacks. http://brainiac2.mit.edu/isbi_challenge.

[13] Abiwinanda, N., Hanif, M., Hesaputra, S. T., Handayani, A., and Mengko, T. R. (2019). Brain tumor classification using convolutional neural network. In World Congress on Medical Physics and Biomedical Engineering 2018: June 3-8, 2018, Prague, Czech Republic (Vol. 1, pp. 183–189). Springer Singapore.

[14] A. Pashaei, H. Sajedi, and N. Jazayeri (2018). "Brain Tumor Classification via Convolutional Neural Network and Extreme Learning Machines." 8th *International Conference on Computer and Knowledge Engineering* (ICCKE), Mashhad, Iran, pp. 314–319. doi: 10.1109/ICCKE.2018.8566571.

[15] H. H. Sultan, N. M. Salem, and W. Al-Atabany (2019). "Multi-Classification of Brain Tumor Images Using Deep Neural Network." *IEEE Access*, 7, pp. 69215–69225. doi: 10.1109/ACCESS.2019.2919122.

[16] A. K. Anaraki, R. Ayati, and A. Kazemi (2019). "Magnetic Resonance Imaging-Based Brain Tumor Grades Classification and Grading via Convolutional Neural Networks and Genetic Algorithms." *Biocybernetics and Biomedical Engineering*, 39(1), pp. 63–74. https://doi.org/10.1016/j.bbe.2018.10.004.

[17] F. J. Díaz-Pernas, M. Martínez-Zarzuela, M. Antón-Rodríguez, and D. González-Ortega (2021). "A Deep Learning Approach for Brain Tumor Classification and Segmentation Using a Multiscale Convolutional Neural Network." Healthcare (Basel, Switzerland), 9(2), 153, https://doi.org/10.3390/healthcare9020153.

[18] V. Sheela, K., and D. S. Babu (2015). "Pre-Processing Technique for Brain Tumor Detection and Segmentation." *International Research Journal of Engineering and Technology* (IRJET), 2(3), pp. 1208–1212.

[19] A. Chaddad, and C. Tanougast (2016). "Quantitative Evaluation of Robust Skull Stripping and Tumor Detection Applied to Axial MR Images." Brain Informatics, 3, pp. 53–61. https://doi.org/10.1007/s40708-016-0033-7.

34 Tourism recommendation system based on sentiment analysis and machine learning

Punna Rao Vemula[1,a], Shyam Sunder Jannu Soloman[1,b] and Naga Raju Baydeti[2,c]

[1]Research Scholar, Dept. of CSE, NIT Nagaland, Chumukedima, Nagaland, India
[2]Assistant Professor, Dept. of CSE, NIT Nagaland, Chumukedima, Nagaland, India

Abstract

In today's digital era, the abundance of online information overwhelms users, complicating decision-making, and challenging businesses to meet unique consumer needs. Recommendation systems (RMS) enhance sales and personalization while reducing search time, becoming essential on platforms like Amazon, YouTube, Netflix, and Facebook. In hotel reviews, knowledge-based recommendation systems can provide tailored recommendations using domain knowledge and explicit rules, benefiting domains with well-defined preferences such as those found in TripAdvisor hotel reviews. The proposed methodology utilizes the TripAdvisor-hotel-reviews dataset, involving data preprocessing, feature extraction, sentiment polarity calculation, word cloud generation, and comparison with machine learning models to evaluate classification performance. The evaluation shows that random forest outperformed with 0.958 cross-validation score when compared with logistic regression and support vector machine models.

Keywords: Logistic regression, random forest algorithm, sentiment analysis, support vector machine, tourism recommendation system

Introduction

In today's electronic world, the abundance of information reachable online often leaves users overwhelmed and unsure of how to make the best decisions. This confusion is especially challenging for businesses in a competitive marketplace, as they strive to tailor their products and services to meet the unique needs of each consumer. Recommendation system (RMS) is the ultimate solution [1]. RMS have significantly aided organizations by recommending products and services tailored to user's needs and it improves sales and personalization, reduce user's search time etc. Nowadays, recommender systems have become a vital feature of various social media platforms [2]. The RMS are further divided into content-based filtering (CBF), collaborative filtering (CF), and hybrid algorithms, which combine both methods [3]. CF is popular because it is simple and widely used. CF-RMS suggests items based on user interests. It also looks at what similar users have liked [3]. The specific items liked by the user are suggested by the CBF-RMS algorithm. They analyze details from item descriptions to find these similarities. CBF builds a profile of the user's preferences based on their past likes and dislikes [4].

When someone wants to visit a place, they typically search the internet for information, but websites often show the same data to everyone, regardless of individual interests. Based on the demands and interests of the users, necessary details are collected thereby making the tourism sector look more better and efficient. A knowledge-based recommendation system uses domain knowledge about the users and items to generate recommendations. It relies on explicit rules and heuristics to match user preferences with item features, rather than relying on user history or collaborative filtering. This approach resulted in more appropriate domains where user preferences are given higher priority and items are

---

[a]punnarao007@gmail.com, [b]arnoldshyam@gmail.com, [c]baydetinagaraju@nitnagaland.ac.in.

DOI: 10.1201/9781003616399-34

complex, such as in personalized healthcare or specialized product recommendations [6].

Motivation

The motivation for a tourism recommendation system is to improve travel experiences by providing personalized, relevant information amidst overwhelming online data. By analyzing user preferences and past behavior, the system offers tailored suggestions for destinations, accommodations, and other activities. This approach enhances user satisfaction and helps businesses attract and retain customers with targeted promotions. The remainder of the proposed work is structured as follows: Literature survey, followed by proposed method, results evaluation and finally concludes the work.

Literature Survey

Tourism recommender systems are essential for personalizing travel experiences by helping users discover destinations, accommodations, and activities that match their preferences and past behaviors. User reviews are a valuable data source, offering genuine feedback that enhances the accuracy and relevance of recommendations. By integrating user reviews, these systems can provide more precise and tailored suggestions, reflecting real-world travel experiences. In the context of generating travel recommendations, planning a trip is a task that involves user preferences which consumes more time [9]. Identifying relevant POIs is a primary task to achieve persuasive recommendations when making travel guidelines to the active user [9]. Alnogaithan et al. [12] proposed a tourism recommender system that integrates user reviews as an additional input to enhance recommendations. Implemented using Python and supported by sentiment analysis and rating-based review analysis, the system provides personalized hotel recommendations based on user feedback and review metrics. Ajantha et al. [3] proposed recommender system that extracts data related to user from Facebook and POI data from TripAdvisor, clustering users based on age and gender to generate user-location vectors. These vectors help identify top similar users and popular landmarks, which are then ranked and recommended. Pre-processed data is used from Facebook and used K-means clustering, while a scraping tool gathers location data from travel blogs.

Murugananda et al. [5] proposed a model, which is Continuous improvement of KNN and RBM recommender systems involves regularly updating with fresh user data, pre-processing it, and retraining the models for accurate recommendations. While KNN operates in real-time but struggles with scalability, and RBM excels in capturing complex patterns despite high computational demands, tourism apps can be further enhanced with AI, AR, VR, and integration with services like transportation and accommodation to enrich user experiences.

Vishwajith et al. [6] proposed matching travel companions by budget, language, age, and transportation preferences using weighted scoring models. Additionally, safety in tourism is emphasized through systems that identify safe zones, predict risks, and offer precautions based on data analysis and sentiment feedback.

Paleti et al. [7] proposed LA-ALS methodology involves collecting user data from online social networks and creating user communities using Louvain's algorithm. Rating matrices for user items are generated for these communities, and the ALS algorithm is applied to address data sparsity, fill in missing values, and build a recommendation model. This model provides real-time recommendations for both existing and new users by identifying top-rated items based on community data. Hamid et al. [8] proposed an idea about a study that establishes recommendations based on context and location within client–server architecture in TRSs. CF is a well-known and popular technique used in recommender systems, further bifurcated into two approaches: model and memory. To address the limitations of CF-RMS such as data sparsity and weak prediction models, information regarding social relationships and behavior of users is utilized. In the travel recommendation domain, contextual information and user behavior are crucial for generating relevant recommendations, and hybrid recommender systems, which combine multiple recommendation approaches, are increasingly used to improve accuracy and relevance, especially for group recommendations [10].

Several common limitations affect tourism recommender systems. Firstly, the cold start problem is related to non-existing users or users with no history making it challenging to provide recommendations. Secondly, data sparsity is an issue when there is insufficient data across the user-item matrix, leading to less accurate recommendations. Lastly, scalability concerns involve managing and processing an increasing volume of data and user interactions effectively. These challenges must be addressed to enhance the performance and usability of tourism recommender systems [12–15].

Proposed Method

The proposed method suggests hotels use the TripAdvisor-hotel-reviews dataset [11] from TripAdvisor Hotel Reviews (kaggle.com). This dataset contains 20491 rows as reviews and two columns as ratings from 1 to 5, where 1 is lower rating and 5 is higher rating. Below are the major steps followed in the proposed method: 1. Data preprocessing, 2. feature extraction, 3. calculate sentiment polarity, 4. find the similarities, 5. generate word cloud based on reviews

recommendations based on similarities, 6. compare with ML models: logistic regression (LR), SVM, and random forest (RF). The two characteristics of frequency are the peak and median frequencies. The pictorial representation of the proposed model is exhibited in the below Figure 34.1.

Data preprocessing

Data preprocessing is an important step when working with text data such as TripAdvisor hotel reviews. The goal is to clean the data, eliminate null values, remove numbers, punctuations, and extra whitespace, and address any mistakes or errors in the raw data. By performing these preprocessing steps, we ensure that the data is error-free and ready for the next stages of analysis or processing. After preprocessing we classify a numeric rating into 'low' if it is 2 or less, 'medium' if it is between 2 to (exclusive) 4 (inclusive), and 'high' if it is above 4. This categorization simplifies the interpretation of the rating values shown in Figure 34.2.

Feature extraction

Feature extraction is a process used in data analysis to transform raw data into a set of features (or variables) that can be effectively used for modelling and analysis. Feature extraction improves model performance, improves speed and efficiency.

Extracting features from text data involves transforming raw text into numerical representations that machine learning algorithms can process considers the frequency of words and importance of rare words appear in the document. Here we use TF-IDF vectorization, which helps in highlighting the words that are more relevant to the specific document in the entire document.

$$TF(s,d) = \frac{No.of\ terms\ s\ in\ document\ d}{Total\ No.of\ terms\ in\ document\ d} \quad (1)$$

Inverse Document Frequency (IDF): Measures how important a term is in the corpus.

$$IDF_t = \log\left(\frac{Total\ No.of\ documents}{No.of\ documents\ containing\ term\ t}\right) \quad (2)$$

It gives importance to rare words thereby eliminating the most frequently occurring words in the vocabulary.

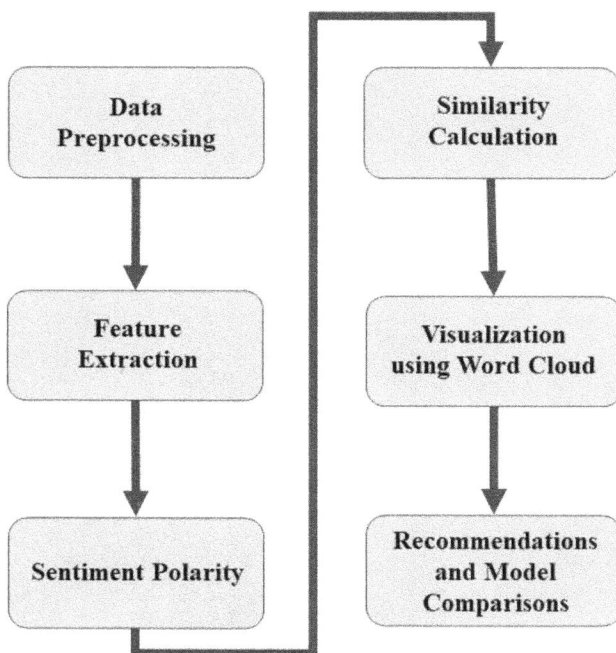

Figure 34.1 Workflow of proposed model
Source: Author

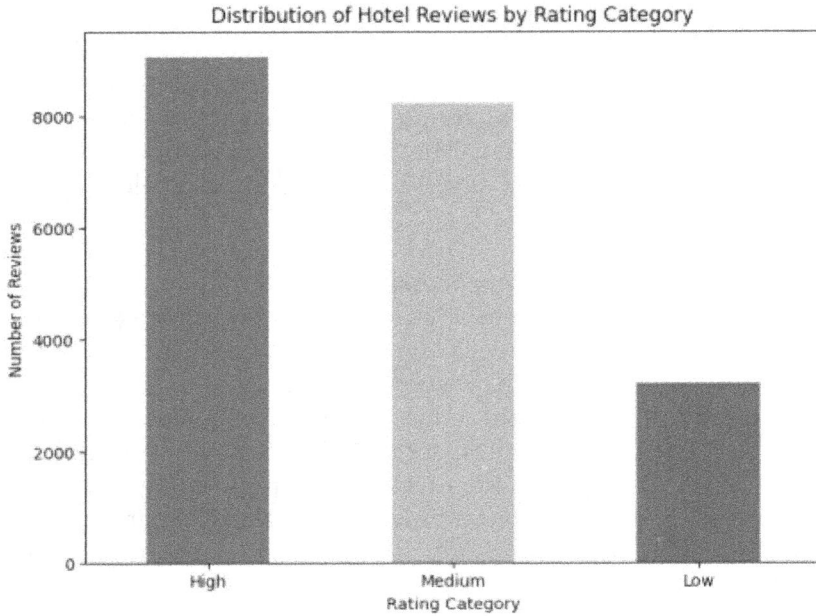

Figure 34.2 Distribution of reviews by ratings
Source: Author

Sentiment polarity

Sentiment polarity measures the emotional tone, indicating whether it is positive, negative, or neutral. It is quantified on a scale typically ranging as -1 for – negative, 1- for positive and 0- for neutral sentiment. This analysis helps to choose better travelling and customer feedback, gauge satisfaction, and identify areas for improvement. Figure 34.3 represents the intensity of positive and negative reviews.

Similarity calculation

Correlation measures linear relationships between variables like review length and

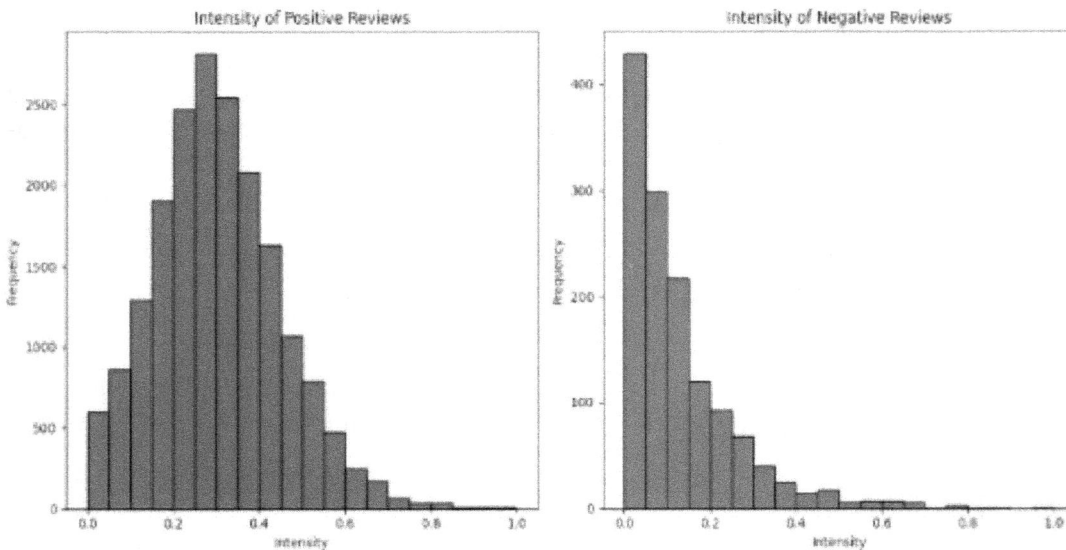

Figure 34.3 Intensity of positive and negative review polarities
Source: Author

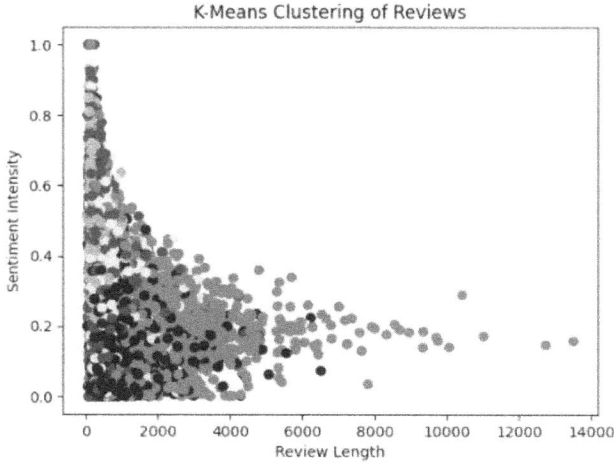

Figure 34.4 Similarity calculation by correlation and k-means
Source: Author

sentiment intensity, with coefficients indicating the strength of the relationship. Using K-means clustering, clusters are formed based on their similarity score, with closer points in the feature space being more similar. Figure 34.4 represents similarity with the help of correlation and K-means algorithm, review length on the X-axis and sentiment intensity on the y-axis.

Word cloud based on reviews

Figure 34.5 represents word cloud for positive and negative reviews. Word cloud is a visual representation of text data. The importance or the frequency of the word is represented in the picture using various colors and fonts. Size of the word in the representation indicates its frequency in the document.

Machine learning models

The proposed model utilizes logistic regression, random forest and SVM models. When evaluating machine learning models for TripAdvisor hotel reviews, both MSE and R² score are essential metrics for understanding model performance.

Linear regression:

- **MSE:** Measures how well the model predicts the sentiment score. Lower MSE indicates better predictions.

$$MSE = \frac{1}{n}\sum_{i=1}^{n}\left(s_i - s_i\right)^2 \qquad (3)$$

Here Si is actual value of ith observation and S_i is predicted value of ith observation.

- **R² Score:** Shows the proportion of variance in the sentiment score explained by review features. Higher R² indicates a better model fit.

$$R^2 score = 1 - \frac{\sum_{i=1}^{n}\left(s_i - s_i\right)^2}{\sum_{i=1}^{n}\left(s_i - \overline{s_i}\right)^2} \qquad (4)$$

Here S_i is actual value of ith observation, S_i is predicted value of ith observation and $\overline{s}$ is mean of ith observation.

Random forest:

- **MSE:** Evaluates the average squared difference between predicted and actual sentiment scores. Lower MSE suggests better accuracy.
- **R² Score:** Indicates how well the ensemble model captures the variability in sentiment scores. Higher R^2 is better.

Figure 34.5 Word cloud for positive and negative sentiments
Source: Author

Support vector machine

Classification performance is measured using metrics like precision, recall and accuracy.

Evaluation

The proposed work is evaluated using three machine learning models. Logistic Regression: creates an instance of the Logistic Regression model, which is used for binary or multi-class classification tasks based on logistic regression. Random Forest: It creates an instance of the Classifier, that combines multiple decision trees to improve classification accuracy and robustness. SVM: It creates an instance of the support vector classifier (SVV) model with probability = true, enabling the model to output probability estimates for predictions.

Table 34.1 shows performance metrics (Precision, Recall, F1-Score) for a logistic regression classification model across three sentiment categories: negative, neutral, and positive. While the model performs well on positive sentiments and it struggles with neutral sentiments, achieving a score of 0 in all metrics for that category.

Table 34.2 shows the performance metrics for sentiment classification. The model achieves an overall accuracy of 0.96, indicating high correctness in its predictions. The macro and weighted averages show the model's performance across all classes, with the macro averages highlighting lower balanced performance and the weighted averages indicating strong performance considering class distribution.

Table 34.3 shows the performance of a linear regression model predicting sentiment scores for TripAdvisor hotel reviews. The mean square error (MSE) is 0.65620278, indicating moderate prediction accuracy. The R^2 Score is 0.56432001,

meaning the model explains approximately 56.43% of the variance in sentiment scores. Table 34.4 shows the comparison of three ML models using cross validation (CV) score. Out of the three models shown in Table 34.4, logistic regression has highest mean CV score, indicating it has the best overall performance on average. Random Forest has performed consistently with a standard CV score of 0.000707. Finally, the proposed model recommends by considering the sentiment polarity, intensity of the words calculated from the reviews and considering ratings given.

Conclusion

The proposed methodology for the tourism recommender system leverages the TripAdvisor hotel reviews dataset to deliver tailored recommendations by employing various analytical techniques. The process begins with data

Table 34.2 Performance metrics for sentiment categories

Metric	Precision	Recall	F1-Score
Accuracy	-	-	0.96
Macro average	0.61	0.48	0.52
Weighted average	0.95	0.96	0.95

Source: Author

Table 34.3 Analysis on linear regression model

S. No	Regression model	Result
1	Mean Square Error (MSE)	0.65620278
2	R^2 Score	0.56432001

Source: Author

Table 34.1 Performance metrics for sentiment categories

Polarity	Precision	Recall	F1-Score
Negative	0.88	0.45	0.59
Neutral	0.00	0.00	0.00
Positive	0.96	1.00	0.98

Source: Author

Table 34.4 Evaluation of the model using CV score

Model	Mean CV score	Std CV score
LR	0.958089	0.001473
RF	0.940032	0.000707
SVM	0.952416	0.001465

Source: Author

preprocessing to ensure clean and accurate data, followed by feature extraction using methods like TF-IDF to convert text into numerical representations. Sentiment analysis is then conducted to determine the emotional tone of reviews, which informs the generation of word clouds for visual insights into frequently occurring terms.

Finally, the system's effectiveness is evaluated through comparisons with machine learning models such as LR and RF. This comprehensive approach enhances the ability to provide personalized and relevant travel recommendations, improving user experience and aiding businesses in the tourism sector by offering targeted and effective suggestions.

References

[1] Zhang, Q., Lu, J., and Jin, Y. (2021). Artificial intelligence in recommender systems. *Complex and Intelligent Systems*, 7, 439–457.

[2] Lu, J., Wu, D., Mao, M., Wang, W., and Zhang, G. (2015). Recommender system application development: a survey. *Decision Support System*, 74, 12–32.

[3] Ajantha, D., Vijay, J., and Sridhar, R. (2017). A user-location vector-based approach for personalized tourism and travel recommendation. In 2017 International Conference on Big Data Analytics and Computational Intelligence (ICBDAC), Chirala, Andhra Pradesh, India, (pp. 440–446).

[4] Singla, R., Gupta, S., Gupta, A., and Vishwakarma, D. K. (2020). FLEX: a content based movie recommender. In 2020 International Conference for Emerging Technology (INCET), (pp. 1–4). IEEE.

[5] Murugananda, G. K., Angel, T. S. S., Kumar, S., Snehalatha, N., and Manipaul, S. S. (2023). A real-time tourism recommender system using KNN and RBM Approach. In 2023 International Conference on Data Science, Agents and Artificial Intelligence (ICDSAAI), Chennai, India, 2023, (pp. 1–5).

[6] Agarwal, J., Sharma, N., Kumar, P., Parshav, V., Srivastava, A., and Goudar, R. H. (2013). Intelligent search in E-tourism services using recommendation system: perfect guide for tourist. In

[7] Paleti, L., Radha Krishna, P., and Murthy, J. V. R. (2021). Approaching the cold-start problem using community detection based alternating least square factorization in recommendation systems. *Evolutionary Intelligence*, 14, 835–849.

[8] Hamid, R. A., Albahri, A. S., Alwan, J. K., Al-Qaysi, Z. T., Albahri, O. S., Zaidan, A. A., et al. (2021). How smart is e-tourism? a systematic review of smart tourism recommendation system applying data management. *Computer Science Review*, 39, 100337.

[9] Logesh, R., Subramaniyaswamy, V., and Vijayakumar, V. (2018). A personalized travel recommender system utilizing social network profile and accurate GPS data. *Electronic Government, an International Journal*, 14(1), 90–113.

[10] Logesh, R., Subramaniyaswamy, V., Vijayakumar, V., and Li, X. (2019). Efficient user profiling based intelligent travel recommender system for individual and group of users. *Mobile Networks and Applications*, 24, 1018–1033.

[11] Dataset: Trip_Advisor_hotel_reviews https://www.kaggle.com/datasets/andrewmvd/trip-advisor-hotel-reviews.

[12] Noorian, A. (2024). A personalized context and sequence aware point of interest recommendation. *Multimedia Tools and Applications*, 1–30.

[13] Alnogaithan, O., Algazlan, S., Aljuraiban, A., and Shargabi, A. A. (2019). Tourism recommendation system based on user reviews. In 2019 International Conference on Innovation and Intelligence for Informatics, Computing, and Technologies (3ICT), Sakhier, Bahrain, 2019, (pp. 1–5).

[14] Abbasi-Moud, Z., Vahdat-Nejad, H., and Sadri, J. (2021). Tourism recommendation system based on semantic clustering and sentiment analysis. *Expert Systems with Applications*, 167, 114324.

[15] Srisawatsakul, C., and Boontarig, W. (2020). Tourism recommender system using machine learning based on user's public instagram photos. In 2020-5th International Conference on Information Technology (InCIT). IEEE, (pp. 202).

35 Multi mode force based interactive device for patients with neurological disorders

Hanu Phani Ram Gurram[a], Rushi Naik, K.[b], Jyothirlatha, K.[c], Meghana, CH.[d], and Karthik, V.[e]

Department of Biomedical Engineering, B V Raju Institute of Technology, Narsapur, Telangana, India

Abstract

People with neurological disorders or spinal injuries often have difficulty using computers due to limited mobility and fine motor skills. This project involves assistive technology for improving computer or mobile accessibility for individuals with neurological disorders or spinal injuries. Many existing devices require significant finger movements, which makes it hard for the user to access the device with limited mobility. In response, an interactive mouse control device has been developed, integrating advanced technology to simplify computer interaction. The device consists of two different modes to accommodate varying levels of mobility, minimizing the need for extensive finger movement. By utilizing force-sensing resistors and an Arduino Leonardo microprocessor, it allows users to control the computer mouse with greater ease and comfort. The device detects minimal pressure from the fingers on its surface and converts these inputs into immediate and responsive mouse movements in real-time. This ensures that it is an essential element for effectively navigating computer interfaces. Mode selection offers users flexibility based on their specific needs. The primary mode offers simplified controls designed for individuals with limited mobility, requiring minimal finger movement. The secondary mode provides advanced functionality suited for users with more refined motor skills, facilitating precise mouse movements. This novel assistive device represents a significant advancement in improving computer accessibility for individuals facing challenges with motor skills. This assistive mouse control device represents a significant advancement in technology that promotes accessibility for individuals with neurological disorders or spinal injuries.

Keywords: Assistive technology, computer accessibility, fine motor skills, finger movement, force-sensing resistors, microprocessor, mouse control device, neurological disorders, spinal injuries

Introduction

In the growing trends of the current generation, technology plays a key role in performing task more efficiently and clearly. Usage of these technology helps in achieving the task in a simpler way. Normal people who don't have any physical disabilities can easily make use of these technologies for their activities of daily living (ADLs) [1,2], which makes their lives simpler and more comfortable. But people with neurological disorders and spinal injuries often face challenges in performing ADLs. They seek assistance in performing the tasks due to certain factors affecting them like limited mobility and fine motor skill impairments.

These individuals often encounter various challenges, which can be attributed to congenital conditions, post-accidental injuries, or diseases that restrict movement. Congenital conditions may include spina bifida, cerebral palsy, and obstetric brachial plexus injury (OBPI), while disease-related challenges may involve conditions like diabetic neuropathy, osteoarthritis, and quadriplegia (paralysis). Accidental injuries could result in Spinal Cord injuries, ulnar nerve injuries, or upper limb nerve injuries.

Additionally, there are complex conditions such as claw hand, carpal tunnel syndrome, cubital tunnel syndrome, lupus, or inflammatory arthritis. Spina bifida, also known as myelomeningocele, is one of the birth defects where the spinal cord doesn't form properly due to the neural tube not closing completely around 28 days after conception. This leaves the spinal cord

[a]hanuphaniram.g@bvrit.ac.in, [b]21215a1107@bvrit.ac.in, [c]21215a1102@bvrit.ac.in, [d]20211a1107@bvrit.ac.in, [e]20211a1112@bvrit.ac.in

DOI: 10.1201/9781003616399-35

exposed to amniotic fluid before birth, causing permanent disability. Spina bifida affects 1–10 out of every 1000 live births globally [3]. Spinal cord injury, which is also a prevalent cause of disability, impacting over 300,000 individuals in the US. Most injuries happen at the cervical level, often leads to impaired upper extremity function and chronic disability. This can also result in a range of disabilities including spasticity, cardiac dysfunction, and complete loss of motor function and hand movement control [1,4].

In the modern world, A real obstacle that people with these diseases encounter is accessing computers. Although computers make our lives more comfortable, the current version of input devices still has certain drawbacks.

For example, they limit the mouse's working range and increase the possibility of various neurological conditions such as carpal tunnel syndrome. The median nerve, which extends from the forearm into the hand's palm, can become compressed or pinched at the wrist, resulting in carpal tunnel syndrome [5]. Likewise, due to restricted movement options and precision, individuals with physical limitations affecting their upper extremities face significant difficulties while utilizing regular input devices [6]. This includes nonverbal quadriplegics, such as those with cerebral palsy, traumatic brain injury, or stroke, who are unable to speak and are forced to depend on limited voluntary movements to communicate their needs, wants, and desires [7].

Individuals who are quadriplegic and nonverbal, often due to conditions like cerebral palsy, traumatic brain injury, or stroke, face significant challenges in expressing their desires, thoughts, and needs. Their ability to communicate is reliant on their limited voluntary movements, which they utilize to interact with caregivers, family, and friends. Some individuals may have the ability to move their heads, while others can communicate through voluntary blinking or winking. Despite these physical limitations, it's crucial to recognize the importance of developing and implementing communication strategies and assistive technologies that enable these individuals to effectively convey their thoughts and desires, fostering greater independence and quality of life. This underscores the significance of ongoing research and innovation in augmentative and alternative

communication (AAC) technologies [8] tailored to meet the diverse needs of individuals with severe physical impairments.

Devices using assistive technology have been created to help people with neurological conditions operate computers [7]. A large amount of research has done in this field to address some of the challenges of accessing devices with limited mobility. The patients with limited hand movements cannot use the regular interface devices. They need customized devices which cater to the patient specific disorder. There are many innovative devices developed in the past and recent times.

Mouse4all is a great idea where people with disorders such as cerebral palsy, Parkinson, spinal cord injury, multiple sclerosis can access the android smartphone or tablets using an application and Bluetooth switches [9]. Mouse4all provides an augmented pointer which is big enough to aid user to interact smoothly the end devices. Eye tracking is one of the common alternatives for human computer interaction [10]. In the case of eye-tracking technique, users eye gaze will be the main parameter for the movement of mouse cursor. This method is simple and very useful for the patients with upper and lower disabilities. The combination of head and eye-lids are used to emulate mouse [11]. In this system, the movement of head will decide the horizontal and vertical movement of the cursor whereas the opening and closure of the eyelid will emulate the left and right click of the mouse. This device also includes additional features like zoom, navigation shortcuts etc. This device is mainly useful for patients with motor disabilities.

A similar device was developed by Ramos et al. [12] which uses head movement as well as voice commands. The mouse cursor movement is controlled by the head movements whereas the other functionalities such as click, double-click, and right click are performed through the voice commands. In addition to it speech is converted to the text to make it easy for user to emulate keyboard. This device is useful for patients with disabilities such as cerebral palsy, upper limb paralysis and muscular dystrophy.

An alternative device for persons with motor disabilities and the speech disabilities is the use of head movement for the cursor movement, surface-Electromyography (sEMG) is used for the target selection [13]. In the above case, an accelerometer used to calculate the tilt in the head movement, correspondingly cursor will be controlled.

The current existing devices include use of other senses like eye movement, tilt of head, emulate using application and so on. Many other devices are equipped with optical, infrared laser systems, Bluetooth, and various other technologies. However, these features not only elevate the cost of the device but also pose challenges due to the requirement for extensive movement of sense object. Many researchers have come up with the complex technologies for human computer interface.

In the proposed model force/pressure-based sensors are employed. Acknowledging both the constraints and advantages of pressure-based input using a mouse empowers designers to enhance the mouse's capabilities by integrating pressure sensors. This augmentation opens doors to innovative applications across diverse contexts. By leveraging pressure sensitivity, designers can introduce novel interaction paradigms that enable nuanced control and enhanced user experiences. For instance, pressure-based input can facilitate more precise manipulation of digital objects, enable expressive gestures, and support tactile feedback mechanisms [14].

An assistive mouse control device with multiple modes is developed for patients dealing with neurological disorders is developed. The design proposed consists of two modes that can replicate real-world mouse functionalities by integrating a microprocessor and force-sensing resistors. The device can be operated using one or two fingers due to its dual independent modes, requiring minimal finger movement, and ensuring patient comfort during use. The components used and principle of the proposed design is elaborately explained in the section below.

Materials and Methodology

The major components used for the designing of this device are Arduino Leonardo, force sensing resistors (FSR), resistors, and zero printed circuit board (PCB), acrylic sheets, magnets. Arduino Leonardo is a microcontroller board – Atmega32u4 which is different from other

Arduino boards as it contains in-built USB communication. This feature of Leonardo enables mouse/keyboard operation. Arduino provides user with the MOUSE-FUNCTIONS which enables the microcontroller boards to control the cursor movement. Therefore, Arduino Leonardo is implemented as a mouse unit for the intended application. The main component of the proposed device is the force sensing resistor (FSR). The basic principle behind the working of the FSR is the change in the resistance value to the applied force or pressure. The most common types of FSR that you will easily find are the Interlink FSR-402 and FSR-406. In this work, FSR-402 is used. Acrylic sheets are used as the casing for the device. Instead of 3D printed devices, acrylic sheets were used for prototyping the device. Magnet coins were used as an interface between the device and rectangular iron base. The main use of magnet is making the device stable while end user operate the device. The device is comprised of six force sensing resistors and a microcontroller. The 3D design of the proposed device is shown in the Figure 35.1. The microcontroller part with circuit connection is embedded in the rectangular box (blue box in Figure 35.1). The six FSR's are embedded in two of the small rectangular ergonomic designed boxes as shown in Figure 35.1.

One cube box contains Four FSR sensors whereas the other two FSR sensors are embedded in the other cube structure. The ergonomic cube structure is shown in Figure 35.2. Figure 35.2(a) depicts the cube structure which contains four FSR sensors. Tig 2(b) shows bottom of the Figure 35.2(a) where it contains magnetic coin to keep it on the iron base plate in stable condition.

The microcontroller is coded using Arduino software such a way that these sensors, offer dual modes of operation: single- finger functionality in mode 1, and dual-finger functionality in mode 2.

The device's design relies on major connections as it involves interfacing six force sensors. Each sensor's force values are obtained by connecting a resistor to its second terminal. The first terminals of six sensors are connected to a 5V power supply and resistors, which are then connected to the ground. For data acquisition, the second terminals of these sensors are linked to the analog

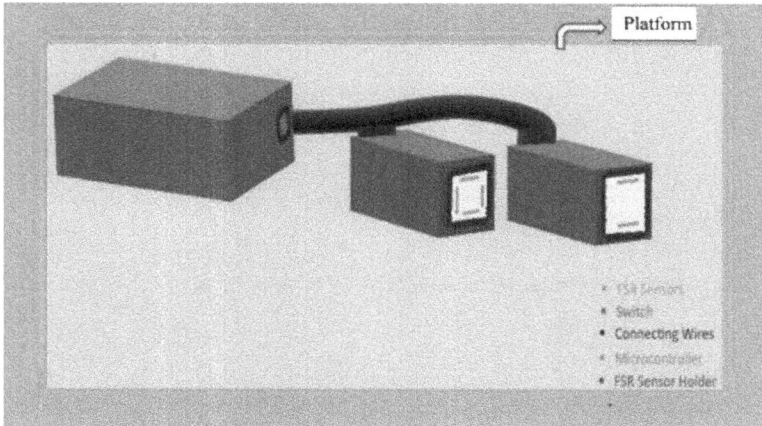

Figure 35.1 Design of the proposed device
Source: Author

Figure 35.2 (a) Cube structure holding FSR, (b) Magnet coin at the bottom of the ergonomic cube structure
Source: Author

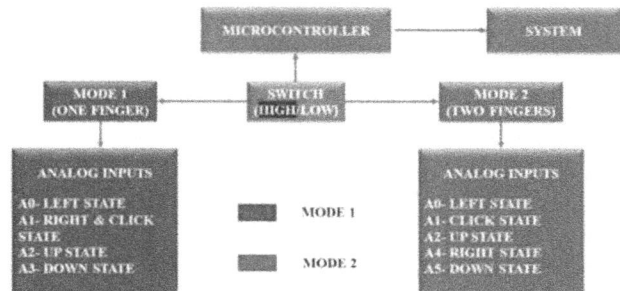

Figure 35.3 Circuit diagram
Source: Author

pins of the Leonardo Arduino microcontroller. A switch is connected to a digital pin which is assigned with the task to switch between the given two different modes. The circuit diagram connections of the Arduino Leonardo and six sensors are shown in Figure 35.3.

A key priority of the device's design is its focus on user adaptability and comfort where the user can use by any of their two fingers, from single or dual-finger operation and or from a single hand or both hands depending on the user's flexibility, comfort, and mobility. A metal grip plate enhances user stability during operation, while embedded magnets within the finger placement cubes secure them to the plate, ensuring stability in a fixed position and preventing displacement during use.

Figure 35.4 illustrates the block diagram used for the construction of the device. The device operates in a user-friendly way: users select their desired mode and press the corresponding sensor to execute actions. A switch is provided to toggle between the two modes. When a user places their finger on the device, sensors detect finger positions, triggering the device's sensors via micro-USB connection to a computer/laptop.

The first step includes sensor calibration which takes a time of around 60 seconds. Each sensor is individually calibrated for sensitivity and the response time for each sensor to calibrate is 10 seconds.

After calibration, the device offers two modes: Mode 1 and Mode 2, toggled by a switch.

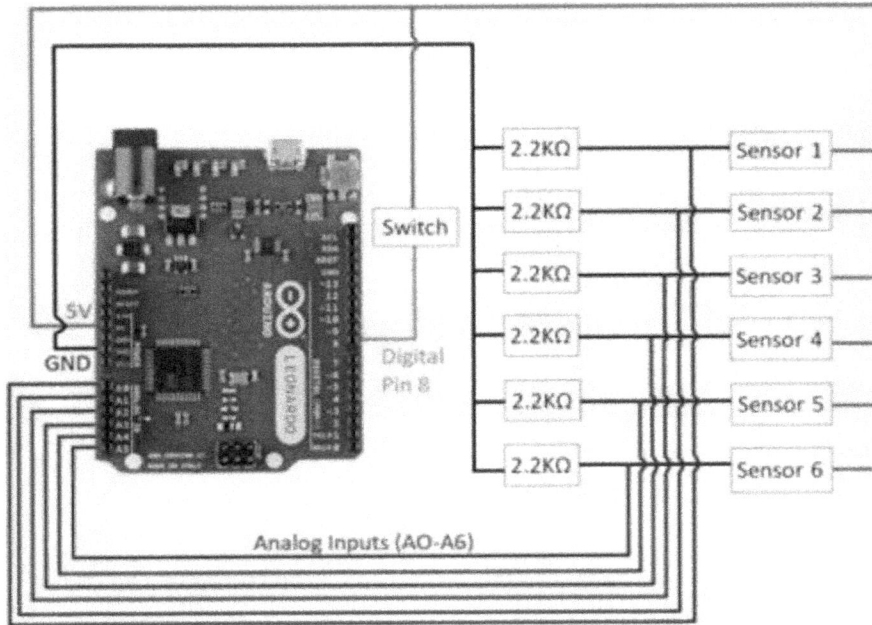

Figure 35.4 Block diagram
Source: Author

Mode 1, to operate the device using a single finger for accessing the cursor movements, the microcontroller uses analog inputs A0 to A3:

- A0: Move cursor left.
- A1: Move cursor right and click.
- A2: Move cursor upward.
- A3: Move cursor downward.

Mode 2, for using the device with two-finger movements, utilizes analog inputs A0, A1, A2, A4, and A5:

- A0: Move cursor left.
- A1: Click action.
- A2: Move cursor upward.
- A4: Move cursor right.
- A5: Move cursor downward.

Results and Discussion

The proposed device when integrated with the electronics, operated its optimal performance during testing, demonstrating its responsive operation across all its features, including left-click, right-click, and upward and downward scrolling. These wide range of functions helps in significantly enhancing the user experience by ensuring seamless interaction. Figure 35.5 depicts the proposed device interface with the laptop.

Real-time testing of the device is conducted at the Gamma Physiotherapy and Rehabilitation Centre in Secunderabad that helped in providing valuable insights about the device's efficacy in real-time practical scenarios, particularly with patients with neurological disorders. The objective was to evaluate the device's suitability for use in different environments. Table 35.1 gives details of subject's training of the device.

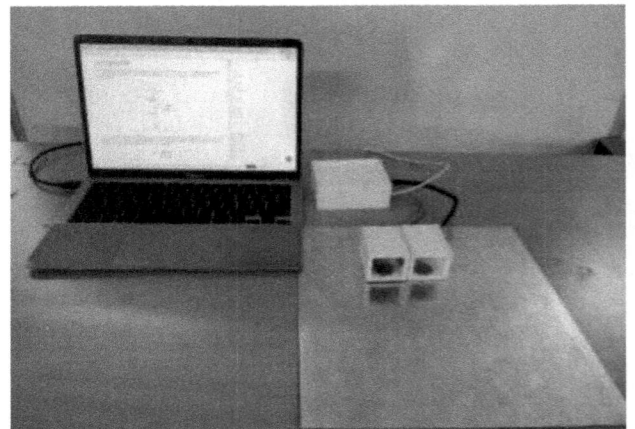

Figure 35.5 Proposed device interface with laptop
Source: Author

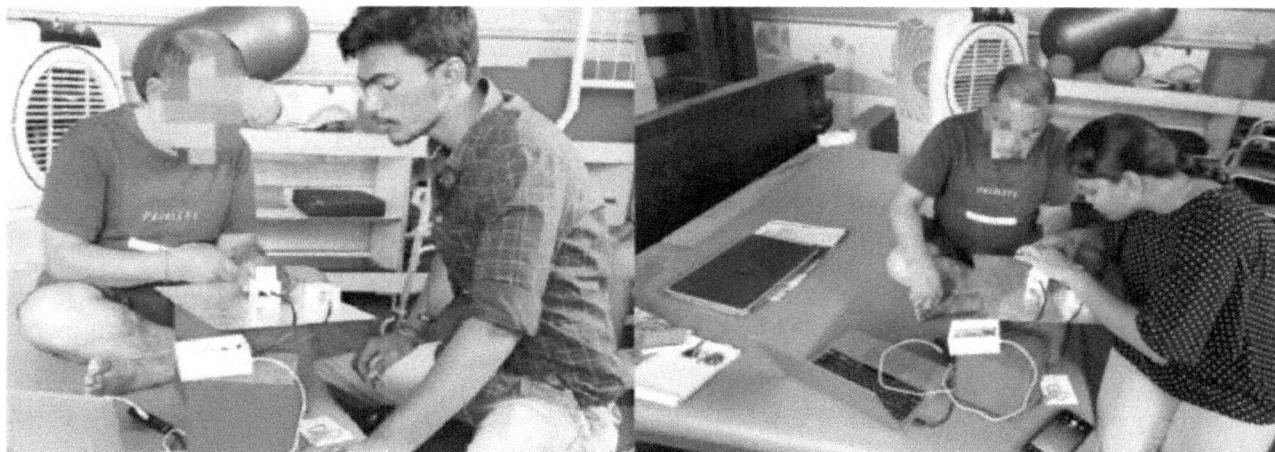

Figure 35.6 Real-time assessment of the device at gamma physiotherapy and rehabilitation centre
Source: Author

An assessment was conducted on a 54-year-old patient diagnosed with hemiparesis as shown in Figure 35.6. The initial introduction about the device is provided to the subject and the user demonstrated the ability to access downward and lateral movements using the device with training and learning rate of 90 seconds.

This performance suggests the device's potential utility in facilitating motor function and rehabilitation among individuals facing similar challenges.

Conclusion and Future Scope

The project has achieved its objectives admirably, demonstrating the successful functionality of the developed device on both computer and smartphone platforms. The device and its accompanying application represent a comprehensive solution aimed at enhancing accessibility and usability for individuals with limited mobility. Positive user feedback, particularly from individuals with neurological disorders, underscores the device's effectiveness in improving accessibility and overall user experience, showcasing its major role in addressing mobility challenges. Its adaptable design ensures it can be used by a diverse range of users, with benefits for those facing mobility challenges, as it simplifies operation and encourages independent access in accessing the electronics. Furthermore, the further development of the device will focus on implementing a universal design approach to allow to users of all ages and abilities, enhancing touch sensitivity and precision, ensuring accessibility and adaptability for all users, and expanding the device's functionality to offer even greater versatility in various tasks and environments.

Acknowledgement

We would like to thank the team of Gamma physiotherapy and Rehabilitation center for allowing to test our device in real time.

Table 35.1 Subject's training and learning

Age	Disease name	Training and learning rate	Ability to access
54	Hemiparesis	90 seconds	Down and both side movements

Source: Author

References

[1] Tran, P., Jeong, S., Wolf, S. L., and Desai, J. P. (2020). Patient- specific, voice-controlled, robotic flexotendon glove-ii system for spinal cord injury. *IEEE Robotics and Automation Letters*, 5(2), 898–905.

[2] Legg, L., Drummond, A., Leonardi-Bee, J., Gladman, J. R. F., Corr, S., Donkervoort, M., et al. (2007). Occupational therapy for patients with problems in personal activities of daily living after stroke: systematic review of randomised

trials. *BMJ: British Medical Journal*, 335(7626), 922.

[3] Phillips, L. A., Burton, J. M., and Evans, S. H. (2017). Spina bifida management. *Current Problems in Pediatric and Adolescent Health Care*, 47(7), 173–177.

[4] Grasse, K. M., Hays, S. A., Rahebi, K. C., Warren, V. S., Garcia, E. A., Wigginton, J. G., et al. (2019). A suite of automated tools to quantify hand and wrist motor function after cervical spinal cord injury. *Journal of NeuroEngineering and Rehabilitation*, 16, 1–12.

[5] Zhang, Y., Liu, B., and Liu, Z. (2018). Wrist-Mouse: wearable mouse controller based on pressure sensors. In 2018 IEEE 15th International Conference on Wearable and Implantable Body Sensor Networks (BSN), (pp. 177–180). IEEE.

[6] Gür, D., Schäfer, N., Kupnik, M., and Beckerle, P. (2020). A human–computer interface replacing mouse and keyboard for individuals with limited upper limb mobility. *Multimodal Technologies and Interaction*, 4(4), 84.

[7] Betke, M., Gips, J., and Fleming, P. (2002). The camera mouse: visual tracking of body features to provide computer access for people with severe disabilities. *IEEE Transactions on Neural Systems and Rehabilitation Engineering*, 10(1), 1–10.

[8] Crowe, B., Machalicek, W., Wei, Q., Drew, C., and Ganz, J. (2022). Augmentative and alternative communication for children with intellectual and developmental disability: A mega-review of the literature. *Journal of Developmental and Physical Disabilities*, 34(1), 1–42.

[9] Zdravkova, K. (2022). The potential of artificial intelligence for assistive technology in education. In Handbook on Intelligent Techniques in the Educational Process: Vol 1 Recent Advances and Case Studies, (pp. 61–85). Cham: Springer International Publishing.

[10] Zhang, X., Liu, X., Yuan, S. M., and Lin, S. F. (2017). Eye tracking based control system for natural human-computer interaction. *Computational Intelligence and Neuroscience*, 2017(1), 5739301.

[11] Mosquera, J. H., Loaiza, H., Nope, S. E., and Restrepo, A. D. (2017). Identifying facial gestures to emulate a mouse: navigation application on Facebook. *IEEE Latin America Transactions*, 15(1), 121–128.

[12] Ramos, P., Zapata, M., Valencia, K., Vargas, V., and Ramos-Galarza, C. (2022). Low-cost human–machine interface for computer control with facial landmark detection and voice commands. *Sensors*, 22(23), 9279.

[13] Vojtech, J. M., Hablani, S., Cler, G. J., and Stepp, C. E. (2020). Integrated head-tilt and electromyographic cursor control. *IEEE Transactions on Neural Systems and Rehabilitation Engineering*, 28(6), 1442–1451.

[14] Cechanowicz, J., Irani, P., and Subramanian, S. (2007). Augmenting the mouse with pressure sensitive input. In Proceedings of the SIGCHI Conference on Human Factors in Computing Systems, (pp. 1385–1394).

36 Design and implementation of Binary-Ring-LWE

Nithya, K.[a], Divya, O.[b], Vishwajit Srikrishna, G.[c] and Sangeeta Singh[d]

Dept of ECE, Vardhaman College of Engineering, Telangana, India

Abstract

This paper details the development and execution of a binary ring learning with errors (BRLWE) architecture, highlighting its robust security features and high efficiency. The BRLWE architecture is designed to be lightweight, making it well-suited for devices with constrained computational capabilities. Its natural resistance to quantum attacks secures its importance in the advancing field of post-quantum cryptography. The low computational overhead of BRLWE makes it particularly suitable for lightweight devices, facilitating its integration into various practical applications. This project investigates the practical implementation challenges and solutions associated with BRLWE, providing detailed insights into its deployment in real-world cryptographic scenarios. The versatility and robust security features of BRLWE enable its application across distinct environments where data confidentiality, integrity, and privacy are critical. By addressing the computational hardness of the learning with error (LWE) problem, The BRLWE architecture delivers robust security guarantees, making it a formidable technique for securing communications and protecting sensitive data. In summary, this paper explores the practicalities of implementing BRLWE, highlighting its potential to enhance cryptographic security in a wide array of applications, from secure communications to comprehensive data protection, ensuring long-term security in the face of advancing quantum technologies.

Keywords: Learning with errors, robust, security

Introduction

A variation of the errors learning (LWE) problem is binary ring learning with errors (BRLWE). Fundamental issue in cryptography using lattices. Study by Xu et al. [1] describes an advanced decryption approach for BRLWE and explores its hardware implementation tailored for Internet-of-Things (IoT) devices. It includes work on binary rings, offering benefits for implementation and efficiency. The BRLWE, is a sophisticated and encrypted cryptography scheme that makes use of learning the polynomial rings problem with errors (LWE) problem, in particular using binary coefficients. This scheme falls within lattice-based cryptography, which is widely viewed as a promising approach for developing cryptographic systems that are resistant to both classical and quantum computational attacks [5]. The ring learning with errors (Ring LWE) encryption scheme is a lattice-based cryptographic method that is a leading candidate for post-quantum

cryptography (PQC) standardization due to its efficiency and low computational overhead [14]. This paper introduces a compact hardware implementation of BRLWE.

Key generation involves creating cryptographic keys for use in encoding and decoding. In public key cryptography, also known as asymmetric cryptography, this process generates a pair of keys: a public key and a private key. In contrast, symmetric cryptography produces a single key that serves both for encoding and decoding. Ensuring that the generated keys are confidential and unpredictable is essential for maintaining the security of cryptographic systems.

Encryption is the method of transforming readable data (plaintext) into an obscured format (ciphertext) using an encryption algorithm and a cryptographic key. We concentrate on delivering efficient implementations of finite field arithmetic, an essential component of BRLWE post-quantum cryptography. An encryption algorithm takes in

[a]nithyarathod204@gmail.com, [b]onteddudivya93@gmail.com, [c]vishwajitlakan@gmail.com, [d]sangeethasingh@vardhaman.org

DOI: 10.1201/9781003616399-36

plaintext and a key, then outputs ciphertext [6]. The effectiveness of encryption depends on the robustness of the algorithm and the confidentiality of the key [7] explores efficient techniques for lattice-based cryptography on these processors and introduces the inaugural implementation of Ring-LWE encryption.

Decryption is the process of turning encrypted data back into its original, readable format (plaintext) by using a decryption algorithm and the proper cryptographic key [13]. Examine the vulnerabilities of the BRLWE scheme. The decryption algorithm receives ciphertext and the correct decryption key, then outputs plaintext [15]. By this work, the analysis shows that it is possible to successfully retrieve the secret key. Decryption is secure because it should only be feasible with the correct key, preventing unauthorized access to the original plaintext from the ciphertext.

Literature survey

The Study presents an enhanced decryption technique for ring bin learning with errors [1]. Decryption method utilizing 2's complement ring is introduced, enhancing decoding accuracy by 50% compared to previous methods. FPGA, achieving a 47.8% reduction in area × time (AT), making it ideal for resource-constrained IoT devices. The improved decryption accuracy and hardware efficiency make this method more effective for securing data in IoT environments.

Aysu et al., [2] presents the hardware realization of the BRLWE encoding algorithm and explores strategies for mitigating power side-channel vulnerabilities.

The BRLWE is chosen for its hardware efficiency, utilizing binary errors that are easy to generate without complex operations. To address SPA vulnerabilities, the design incorporates redundant additions and memory updates. The countermeasures significantly improve resistance to DPA attacks, making it 40 times harder to execute a successful attack compared to unprotected implementations. The research offers a thorough examination of side-channel vulnerabilities and countermeasures for BRLWE, emphasizing the unique challenges and opportunities posed by its binary structure.

Lucas et al. [3] presents a hardware accelerator for the BRLWE encryption practice, designed to be efficient for lightweight and resource-limited applications. BRLWE is an effective post-quantum cryptography (PQC) solution due to its robust quantum resistance and simple implementation. The paper introduces an optimized mathematical approach for the BRLWE decryption process, aimed at improving efficiency. It features a full input/output processing system, enhancing its suitability for emerging lightweight applications.

The paper [4] introduces a hardware implementation for Ring-LWE encryption that is both efficient and scalable, designed to enhance the practicality of lattice-based cryptography in embedded systems. The proposed design features a micro-code engine that consolidates essential operations—such as polynomial product, sum, difference, and Gaussian sampling—into one integrated unit [12] can be demonstrated that generating the appropriate noise distribution can be simplified by first creating a Gaussian distribution over a specific extension ring of RRR, followed by a reduction modulo f(X).

Design and Implementation

The implementation of the LWE architecture involves three main steps using ModelSim, and a SystemVerilog.

1. Generation of key
2. Encoding
3. Decoding

Generation of key

It is the process of generating cryptographic keys, which include producing both public and private keys used in encoding and decoding algorithms [9]. Effective software solutions for a post-quantum secure public-key encryption scheme based on the ring error learning problems.

1. Input: Security parameter N, modulus Q
2. Steps: Select random binary polynomials r1 and r2 where r2 is a private or secret key. Compute for the public key p
   P = (r1 - a*r2) modulo Q
3. Output: Public key p, private key r2

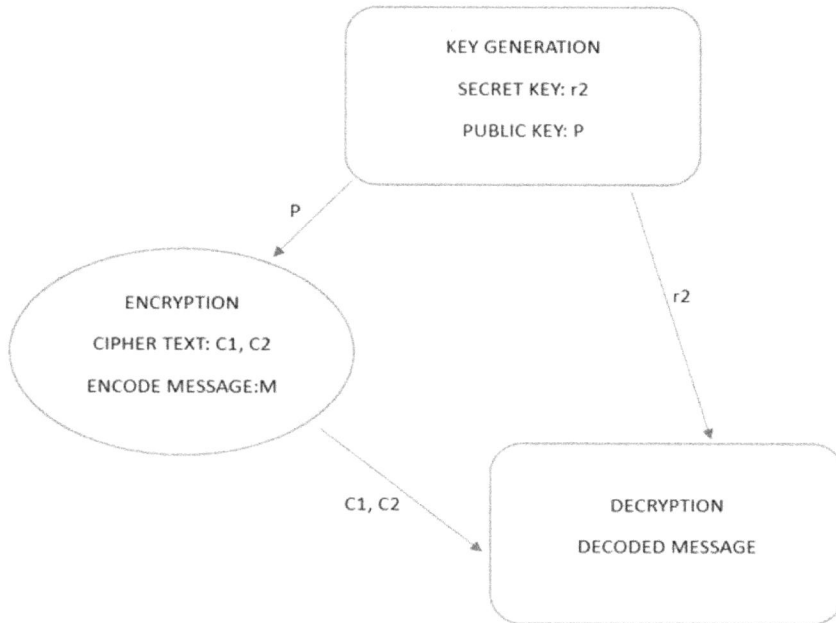

Figure 36.1 Block diagram of Binary Ring LWE
Source: Author

Encoding

Encoding involves transforming readable data (plaintext) into an unreadable form (ciphertext) using an encryption algorithm and a secret key [11] introduces an innovative ring-learning with errors (ring-LWE) cryptographic. This process hides the original data and encrypt it.

1. Input: Message m, public key P, polynomial a, polynomials e1, e2, e3.
2. Steps:
   - Compute the first component of the cipher-text c1:
   c1 = (a * e1 + e2) modulo Q
   - Compute the second component of the ci-phertext c2:
   c2 = (p * e1 + e3 + m) modulo Q
3. Output: Ciphertext c1, c2

Output of encryption is c1 and c2, while P is the input. The random noise is added to secure the real message [10] gives encryption scheme which is homomorphic.

Decoding

Decoding is the process of converting ciphertext back into plaintext using a decryption algorithm and the corresponding secret key [8]. This paper discusses a masked ring-LWE decryption implementation that is resistant to first-order side-channel attacks.

1. Input: Ciphertext (c1, c2), private key r2, modulus Q
2. Steps: - Compute the decoded message m:
   m = (c1*r2 + c2) modulo Q
3. Output: Decoded message m

This algorithm outlines the steps for generation of key, encoding, and decoding in the Binary Ring-LWE scheme. This block diagram Figure 36.1 shows the inputs and outputs each block, for generation of key, the outputs are- r2 and p. For encoding, the inputs are p and m while outputs are (c1, c2). For decoding, the inputs are r2 and (c1, c2) while output is decoded message.

Results and Discussions

Results of binary ring LWE

The experimental results of the BRLWE practice highlight the roles of various polynomials in the encryption and decryption processes. Error polynomials (e1, e2, e3) are randomly selected with binary coefficients and introduce noise, which is central to the learning with errors approach.

The message polynomial (m) represents the data to be encrypted. During the key generation phase, the public key (p) is created for encryption, and the secret key (r2) is utilized for decryption to recover the original message. Ciphertext polynomials (c1, c2), resulting from the encryption, combine the message polynomial, error polynomials, and public key to create a secure encrypted message, effectively obscuring the original information.

The results of BRLWE are

All these terms are the coefficients of the polynomials.

Key values:

Error polynomials: e1: [2] e2: [3, 1, 2, 1] e3: [3, 1, 2, 1]
Message polynomial: m: [3, 3, 1, 1]
message m: [1,1,1,1]
Public key and secret key:
Public key (p): [1, 1, 0, 0]
Secret key (r1): [3, 1, 2, 3]
(r2): [1]

Ciphertext is in the form of (c1, c2)
Ciphertext: c1: [1, 1, 0, 1] c2: [0, 0, 1, 0]
Output decode:
Output decode result: [1, 1, 1, 1]

Here it is observed that the message before and decoding is the same. That proves that the decoding of this process was successful.

Figure 36.2 presents a "Model Sim" simulation of a BRLWE encryption scheme. The waveform window depicts the temporal behavior of the encrypted signals, offering a visual representation of how the signals change over time. Additionally, the transcript window provides a detailed output of the encoding process, detailing the p, ciphertexts, and the recovered message m. It also includes the initial input values and the message intended for encryption, offering a complete overview of the data transformation from plaintext to ciphertext and back to plaintext encryption.

Figure 36.3 illustrates the transcript window of the BRLWE encoding scheme, offering a detailed output of the encoding process. This window presents the p, ciphertexts, and the decoded message, providing a detailed view of the encoding

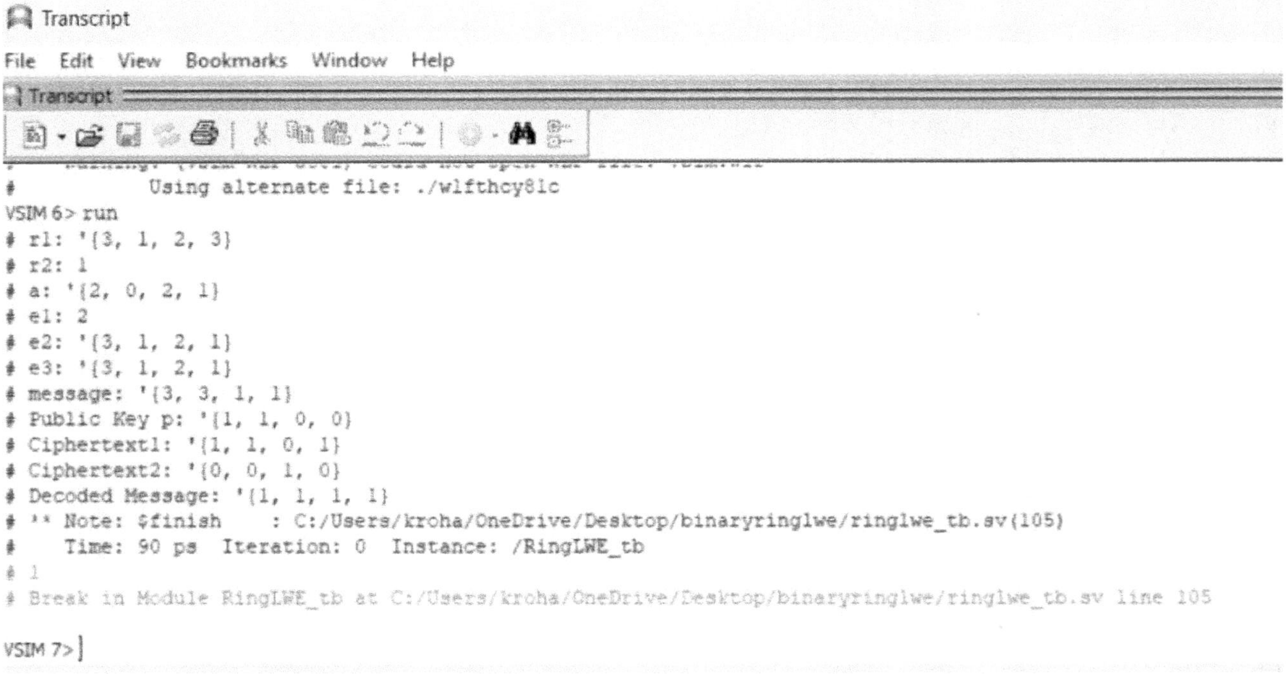

Figure 36.2 Output waveforms of Binary Ring LWE
Source: Author

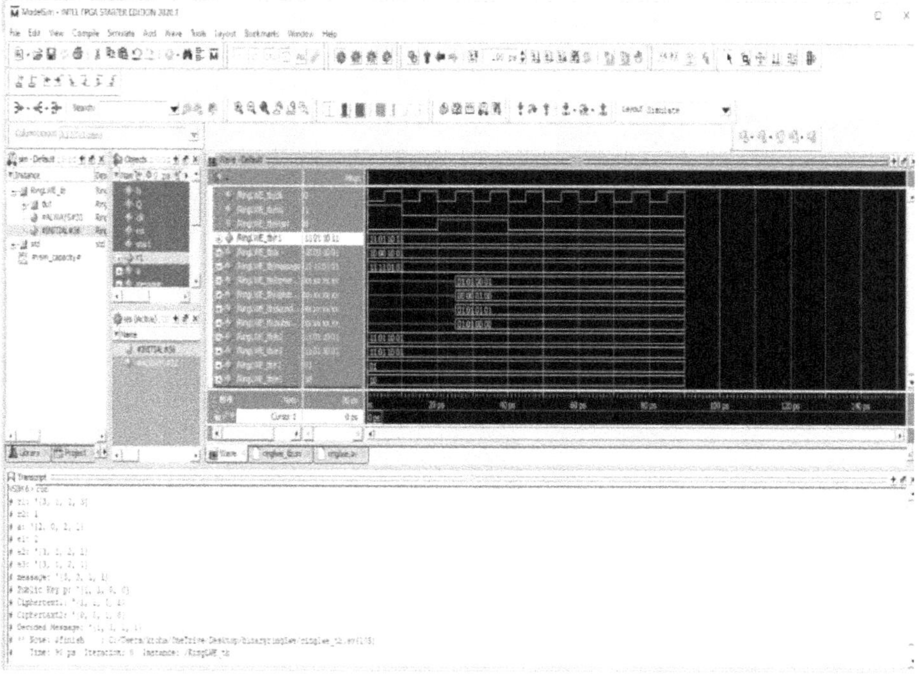

Figure 36.3 Transcript of Binary Ring LWE
Source: Author

and decoding operations. Additionally, it displays the input values, including the message that is to be encrypted. Functioning as a display window, it showcases the simulated output in both numerical values and alphabetic characters, allowing for clear and detailed observation of the cryptographic transformation.

Results of ring LWE

Key values:

Error polynomials: e1: [10]
e2: [15, 10, 1, 5] e3: [3, 13, 2, 5]
Message polynomial: m: [11, 7, 1, 13]

Public key and secret key:
Public key (p): [1, 13, 12, 10]
Secret key (r1): [3, 5, 10, 15]
(r2): [1]
Ciphertext: c1: [3, 1, 6, 7] c2: [8, 6, 11, 6]

Output decode:
Output decode result: [11, 7, 1, 13]

Here it can be observed that the message before and after decoding is the same. That proves that the decoding of this process was performed accurately. The result of decrypting the ciphertext

using the secret key. This should ideally match the original message polynomial if the decryption is successful.

Figure 36.4 presents a "model sim" simulation of a ring-LWE encoding scheme. The waveform window depicts the temporal behavior of the encrypted signals, offering a visual representation of how the signals change over time. Additionally, the transcript window provides a detailed output of the encoding process, detailing the p, ciphertexts, and the recovered message m. It also includes the initial input values and the message intended for encryption, offering a complete overview of the data transformation from plaintext to ciphertext and back to plaintext encryption.

Figure 36.5 illustrates the transcript window of the ring with errors learning encoding scheme, offering a detailed output of the encoding process. This window presents the p, ciphertexts, and the decoded message, providing a detailed view of the encoding and decoding operations. Additionally, it displays the input values, including the message that is to be encrypted. Functioning as a display window, it showcases the simulated output in both numerical values and alphabetic characters,

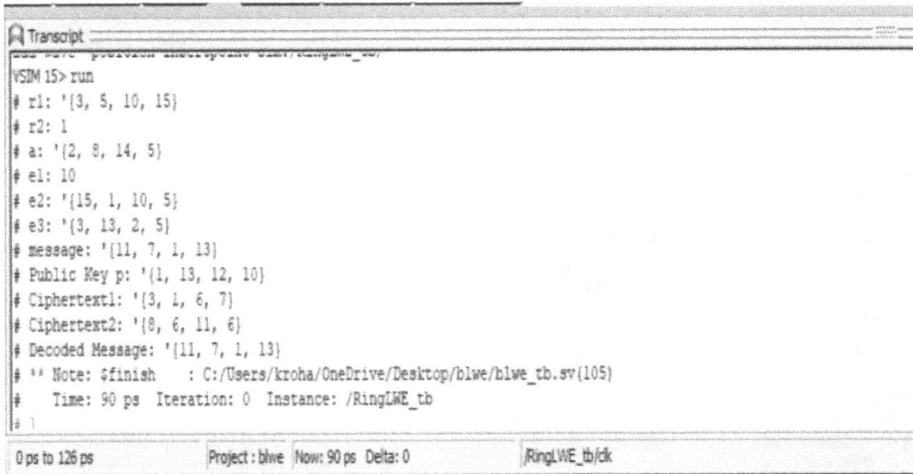

Figure 36.4 Output waveforms of ring LWE
Source: Author

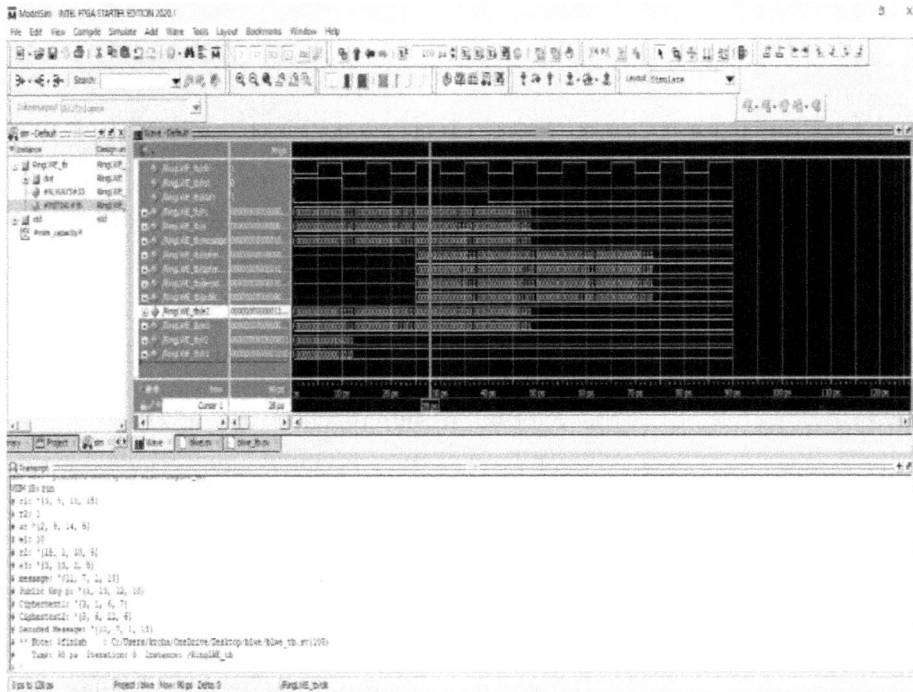

Figure 36.5 Transcript of ring LWE
Source: Author

allowing for clear and detailed observation of the cryptographic transformation.

Conclusion

Ring-LWE encryption is a highly effective method for safeguarding data, providing robust security against classical and quantum attacks. Despite its tendency to increase area and power consumption, Ring-LWE remains a dependable decryption approach, suitable for a variety of encryption scenarios. Its efficiency in generating public and private keys, combined with its resistance to known cryptographic attacks, underscores its significance in contemporary security solutions.

Binary ring learning-with-errors (BRLWE) extends the benefits of traditional ring-LWE by utilizing binary fields, which offers further optimization in terms of computational efficiency and implementation simplicity. This variant shows significant potential as a key component of post-quantum cryptography, ensuring resilience against emerging quantum computing threats. The ongoing research and development in BRLWE are crucial for advancing secure communication protocols, protecting sensitive data in digital communications, and safeguarding financial transactions.

The future of digital security heavily relies on the implementation of such advanced cryptographic methods. With the continuous evolution of computational capabilities, particularly quantum computing, the urgency for adopting and refining post-quantum cryptographic schemes like BRLWE cannot be overstated. Investing in this technology is crucial for ensuring the integrity and confidentiality of data in our increasingly digital world.

References

[1] Xu, D., Wang, X., Hao, Y., Zhang, Z., Hao, Q., and Zhou, Z. (2022). A more accurate and robust binary ring-LWE decryption scheme and its hardware implementation for IoT devices. *IEEE Transactions on Very Large Scale Integration (VLSI) Systems*, 30(8), 1007–1019.

[2] Aysu, A., Orshansky, M., and Tiwari, M. (2018). Binary ring LWE hardware with power side-channel countermeasures. In 2018 Design, Automation Test in Europe Conference Exhibition. IEEE.

[3] Lucas, B. J., Alwan, A., Murzello, M., Tu, Y., He, P., Schwartz, A. J., et al. (2022). Lightweight hardware implementation of binary ring-LWE PQC accelerator. *IEEE Computer Architecture Letters*, 21(1), 17–20.

[4] P̈oppelmann, T., and G̈uneysu, T. (2013). Towards practical lattice-based public-key encryption on reconfigurable hardware. In Revised Selected Papers on Selected Areas in Cryptography -- SAC 2013 – (Vol. 8282, pp 68–85). Springer-Verlag, Berlin, Heidelberg.

[5] Imana, J. L., He, P., Bao, T., Tu, Y., and Xie, J. (2022). Efficient hardware arithmetic for inverted binary ring-LWE based post-quantum cryptography. *IEEE Transactions on Circuits and Systems I: Regular Papers*, 69(8), 3297–3307.

[6] Xie, J., He, P., and Wen, W. (2021). Efficient implementation of finite field arithmetic for binary ring-LWE post-quantum cryptography through a novel lookup-table-like method. In 2021 58th ACM/IEEE Design Automation Conference (DAC). IEEE.

[7] Liu, Z., Azarderakhsh, R., Kim, H., and Seo, H. (2017). Efficient software implementation of ring-LWE encryption on IoT processors. *IEEE Transactions on Computers*, 69(10), 1424–1433.

[8] Reparaz, O., Sinha Roy, S., Vercauteren, F., and Verbauwhede, I. (2015). A masked ring-LWE implementation. In International Workshop on Cryptographic Hardware and Embedded Systems. Berlin, Heidelberg: Springer Berlin Heidelberg, 2015.

[9] De Clercq, R., Roy, S. S., Vercauteren, F., and Verbauwhede, I. (2015). Efficient software implementation of ring-LWE encryption. In 2015 Design, Automation and Test in Europe Conference and Exhibition (DATE). IEEE.

[10] Brakerski, Z., and Vaikuntanathan, V. (2011). Fully homomorphic encryption from ring-LWE and security for key dependent messages. In Annual Cryptology Conference. Berlin, Heidelberg: Springer Berlin Heidelberg.

[11] Tan, T. N., and Lee, H. (2018). High-performance ring-LWE cryptography scheme for biometric data security. *IEIE Transactions on Smart Processing and Computing*, 7(2), 97–106.

[12] Elias, Y., Lauter, K. E., Ozman, E., and Stange, K. E. (2016). Ring-LWE cryptography for the number theorist. In Directions in Number Theory: Proceedings of the 2014 WIN3 Workshop. Springer International Publishing.

[13] Ebrahimi, S., and Bayat-Sarmadi, S. (2020). Lightweight and fault-resilient implementations of binary ring-LWE for IoT devices. *IEEE Internet of Things Journal*, 7(8), 6970–6978.

[14] Shahbazi, K., and Ko, S. B. (2023). An optimized hardware implementation of modular multiplication of binary ring LWE. *IEEE Transactions on Emerging Topics in Computing*, 11(3), 817–821.

[15] Villena, R. C., and Terada, R. "Recovering the secret on binary ring - LWE volume and problem with random known bits- extended version." 15(1): 39–45, April 2024.

37 RNS integer arithmetic design for elliptic curve cryptography

Uma Maheshwari, J.[1,a], *Vaishnavi, M.*[1,b], *Eshwar, P.*[1,c],
Sangeeta Singh[1,d] *and Anupama, B.*[2,e]

[1]Dept of ECE Vardhaman College of Engineering Telangana, India

[2]Dept of ECE Vardhaman College of Engineering Telangana, BVRIT, Narsapur, Telangana, India

Abstract

Hardware security modules (HSMs) are specialized, tamper-proof devices that ensure the security of cryptographic operations by securely generating, managing, and safeguarding keys for data encryption, decryption, and digital signatures. The residue number system (RNS) improves arithmetic operations by representing integers with their remainders when divided by a set of pairwise coprime moduli. This method is instrumental in optimizing calculations for elliptic curve cryptography (ECC), a widely-used cryptographic approach known for its efficiency and strong security. RNS supports parallel processing of modular operations, which reduces the overall computational time needed for ECC tasks. ECC relies on public and private key pairs to securely encrypt and decrypt data. This project applies RNS algorithms, such as multiplication, within ECC to enhance security. Additionally, RNS finds applications beyond cryptography, including coding theory and pseudo-random number generation. The project involves developing various architectures to improve security and performance in these domains.

Keywords: Elliptic curve cryptography, hardware security modules, residue number system

Introduction

In the domain of secure communication and data integrity, elliptic curve cryptography (ECC) has gained prominence for its strong security features and computational efficiency [1]. ECC operates over finite fields, where performing arithmetic on large integers is essential for cryptographic operations such as encryption, decryption, and key exchange. Traditional methods for integer arithmetic can be resource-intensive and may not fully utilize the parallel processing capabilities of contemporary hardware.

To address these challenges, this project explores the application of residue number systems (RNS) in ECC [2]. RNS provides a distinctive method by representing integers as residues relative to a set of coprime moduli. This approach allows arithmetic operations to be carried out independently for each modulus, offering potential benefits in terms of parallelism and computational efficiency.

Integrating residue number systems (RNS) into Elliptic Curve Cryptography (ECC) utilizes RNS's strength to improve the efficiency of ECC computations [3]. ECC involves intricate arithmetic over finite fields, and RNS can boost performance by simplifying these complex operations. By breaking down large arithmetic [4]. The architecture demonstrates superior speed compared to all other design methods currently known, and its complexity is less than 50% of that seen in earlier approaches [5]. An overview of RNS-based countermeasures for side-channel attacks (SCA) and fault attacks (FA) is presented through various scalar multiplication algorithms [6]. To optimize performance, compute-intensive components are pinpointed for efficient hardware implementation. The implementation employs the RNS along with projective coordinates to carry out the necessary arithmetic operations [7]. An effective countermeasure for scalar multiplication can be achieved by

[a]umamaheshwari25654@gmail.com, [b]meruguvaishnavi4469@gmail.com, [c]pillieshwar8008@gmail.com, [d]sangeethasingh@vardhaman.org, [e]anupama.bollampally@bvrit.ac.in

DOI: 10.1201/9781003616399-37

employing alternative number systems, such as the RNS.

Literature Review

Mehrabi et al., [8] create a high-speed RNS core that can execute point multiplication on ED25519 and SECP256K1 elliptic curves in hardware security modules. Modular reduction: high-speed SOR reduction units that are shared by several ECC processes were introduced in order to facilitate parallel computation. To assess how two SOR modular reduction architectures affected system latency, they were compared. Scalar multiplication: Various ECC state machine techniques were implemented. Enhanced the speed of point multiplication for SECP256K1 and ED25519 curves by combining these techniques with RNS arithmetic.

Bigou and Tisserand [9] speeds up RNS arithmetic operations using parallelism, improving addition, subtraction, and multiplication. RNS is used in ECC, RSA, pairings, and lattice-based cryptography for efficient computations. Operations like comparison and modular reduction are costly in RNS, especially modular multiplication. Proposes using pseudoMersenne primes for modular multiplication in ECC, reducing the need for multiple RNS bases. New method cuts operational and precomputation costs significantly, with FPGA implementations showing up to 46% area reduction and minimal time increase.

Esmaeildoust et al., [4] introduces new RNS montgomery reduction algorithms, called sQ-RNS and dQ-RNS. These algorithms apply quadratic residuosity constraints to RNS bases. The new algorithms require fewer unit modular multiplications: specifically, $(2n^2 + n)$ for a base size (n). This reduction is achieved by eliminating certain multiplication steps, leading to simpler and more regular algorithms. Experimental results confirm the feasibility of finding RNS bases that meet the quadratic residuosity requirements. FPGA implementations show improvements over existing R-RNS algorithms, with reduced clock cycles and hardware components.

The paper by [10] **Kawamura et al. (2017)** builds on previous work in Montgomery reduction, RNS, and quadratic residuosity, offering a new, efficient, and secure approach for modular arithmetic operations used in cryptography. Their work is a valuable contribution to the field, particularly for hardware implementations and cryptographic systems requiring high performance and robust security.

Design and Implementation

The RNS multiplication plays a vital role in RNS by facilitating the efficient processing of large integers [11]. This is particularly valuable in fields such as cryptography, where modular arithmetic operations are frequently required.

Steps for RNS multiplication

Multiply residues: For each modulus mi [12], compute the product of the residues $xi_$ and yi as follows:

Zi = (xi × yi) mod mi

This operation involves performing modular multiplication separately for each modulus mi. These calculations can be done in parallel to improve efficiency.

Manage large products: If the product xi × yi _ exceeds mi, apply modular reduction to ensure that the result zi is within the modulus mi. This step keeps the results within the defined range of each modulus.

Store results: The result for each modulus mi, denoted as zi, represents the residue of the product modulo mi. These individual results are stored for further processing.

Convert to standard form: After calculating the residues, you may need to convert the RNS representation back to a standard integer. This can be achieved using algorithms like the Chinese remainder theorem (CRT) or other reconstruction methods to merge the residues into a single integer value.

Implementation considerations modulus selection

Coprimeness: Choose moduli that are pairwise coprime to ensure the uniqueness of the RNS representation. This property is crucial for accurate reconstruction of integers from their residues [13].

Size of moduli: Select moduli that are large enough to handle the integer products without risk of overflow but not so large as to introduce inefficiencies. Properly sized moduli balance computational requirements with performance.

Handling overflow

- Modular reduction: When performing multiplication with residues, it's important to manage overflow by applying modular reduction. This ensures that results stay within the range defined by each modulus, preventing overflow and maintaining correct results

Efficient algorithms

Optimized multiplication: Utilize advanced algorithms to enhance modular multiplication efficiency. Techniques such as Karatsuba multiplication or Montgomery multiplication can significantly accelerate the process, making it more efficient for large numbers.

The extended Euclidean algorithm builds on the basic Euclidean algorithm, which finds the greatest common divisor (GCD) of two integers. Unlike the standard version, the extended algorithm not only calculates the GCD but also determines coefficients that solve the associated linear Diophantine equation [14]. This extended method is especially valuable for finding the modular inverse of an integer relative to another number, a process that is fundamental in various cryptographic and modular arithmetic contexts. Figure 37.1 Represents the block diagram of

RNS Multiplication which consists of 3 blocks. Input Module Block, Modular Multiplication Block and CRT Block.

CRT in RNS multiplication

CRT is used in RNS Multiplication for the purpose of

Parallel computation: RNS allows parallel computation of operations, including multiplication, due to its modular nature.

Efficiency: CRT allows for efficient reconstruction of the result using modular arithmetic, which is advantageous in hardware implementations and high-speed computation environments.

Applications of RNS multiplication

Digital signal processing (DSP): Efficiently handles operations like convolution and filtering.

Cryptography: Used in cryptographic algorithms where modular arithmetic is predominant.

Computer arithmetic: Enhances performance in certain computational tasks by leveraging parallel processing capabilities.

Results and Discussions

Enhanced efficiency: The RNS-based ECC design significantly improves computational speed, energy efficiency, and space utilization.

Performance optimization: By reducing computational time and space requirements, this

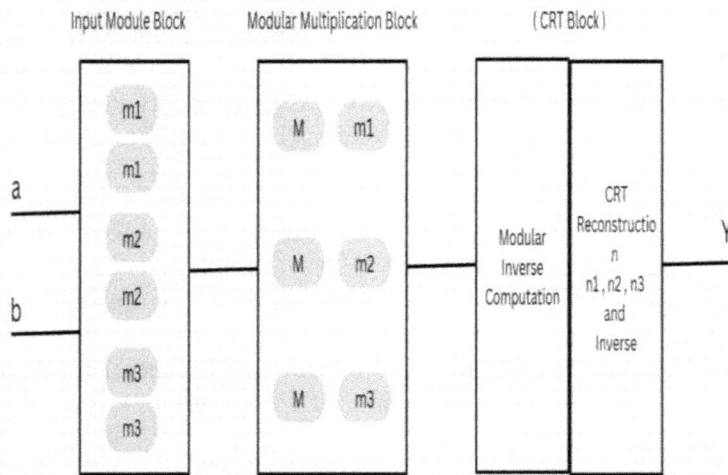

Figure 37.1 Block diagram of RNS multiplication
Source: Author

approach is well-suited for both high-performance and low-power applications.

Application potential: The design proves effective for devices with limited resources as well as for demanding high-performance computing environments.

Future research: Further development should aim at refining the design and exploring its integration into various cryptographic protocols and applications.

Comparison between decimal multiplication and RNS multiplication

(a) Results for decimal multiplication
We have assumed A = 12, B = 15 .

We have Y = A * B

Y = 12 * 15

Y = 180

Figure 37.2 Represents the RTL schematic of Decimal multiplication. The RTL schematic of Decimal Multiplication illustrates the digital hardware components (such as registers, multipliers, adders, and shift registers) involved in multiplying decimal numbers.

Figure 37.3 Represents the Schematic waveform of Decimal Multiplication. The schematic waveform of decimal multiplication provides a detailed view of how data and control signals interact over time during the multiplication process.

Figure 37.4 Represents the Results of Decimal Multiplication. This is a critical step in digital arithmetic, especially when decimal precision is required, as is the case in financial applications, calculators, or digital systems that handle decimal numbers accurately.

Figure 37.5 represents the RTL Schematic of RNS Multiplication. The RTL schematic of RNS multiplication provides a detailed, register-level view of how the multiplication of two numbers is efficiently carried out using the Residue Number System in a hardwaresystem.

Figure 37.6 Represents the Schematic waveform of RNS Multiplication.The schematic waveform of RNS multiplication provides a visual representation of how different components of the RNS multiplication process interact in time, driven by a clock signal.

Figure 37.7 Represents Results of RNS Multiplication. The results of RNS multiplication are represented as a set of intermediate residues, each corresponding to a modulus.

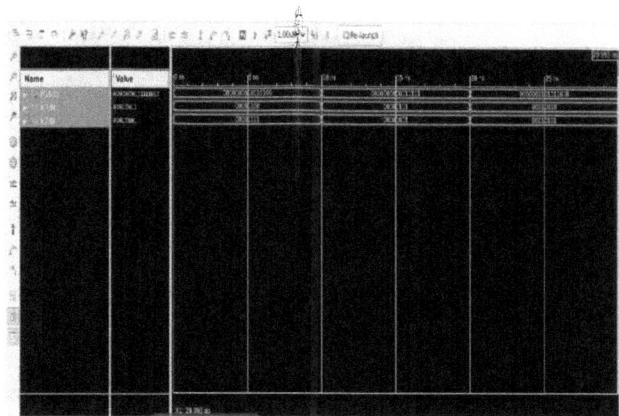

Figure 37.3 Schematic waveform of decimal multiplication
Source: Author

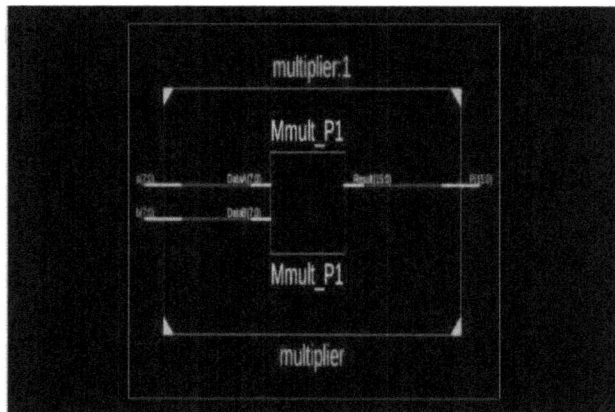

Figure 37.2 RTL schematic of decimal multiplication
Source: Author

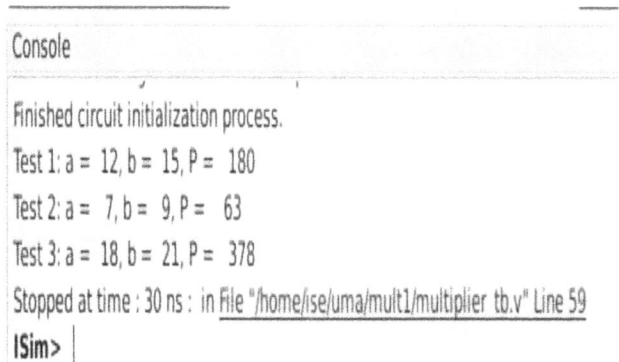

Figure 37.4 Results of decimal multiplication
Source: Author

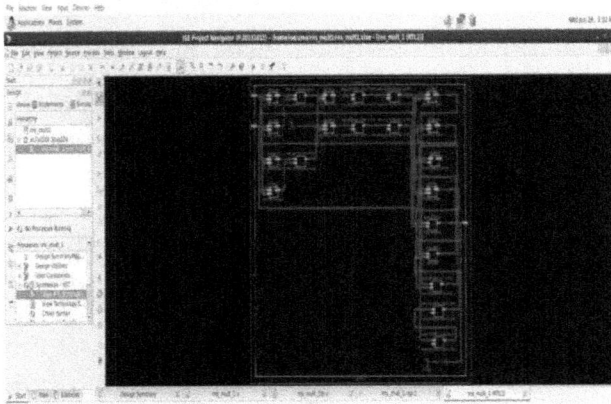

Figure 37.5 RTL schematic Of RNS multiplication
Source: Author

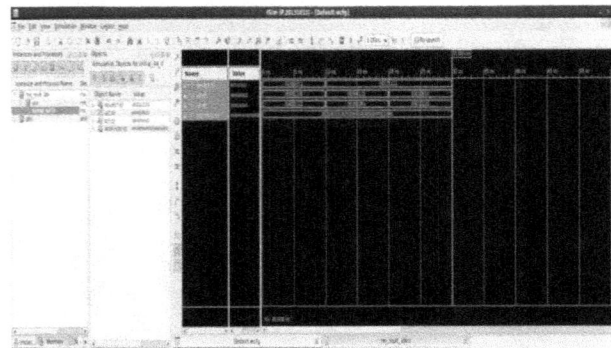

Figure 37.6 Schematic waveform of RNS multiplication
Source: Author

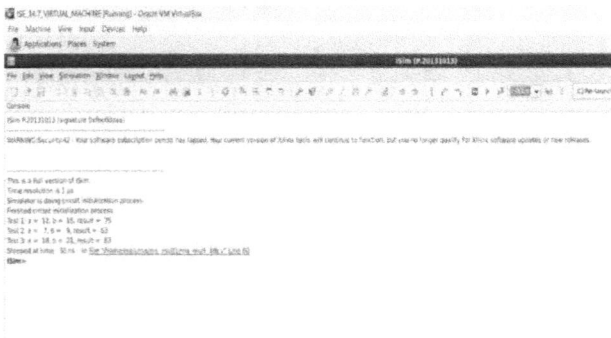

Figure 37.7 Results of RNS multiplication
Source: Author

(b) Results for RNS multiplication

Comparison in results of decimal and RNS multiplication

Table 37.1 Define the Differences and comparision between the Parameters of Decimal and RNS Multiplication. RNS multiplication offers

Table 37.1 Shows the comparison in parameters between decimal and RNS multiplication

Parameter	Decimal multiplication	RNS multiplication
Maximum combinational path delay	3.3 83ns	60.792ns
Selected device	7a100tcsg324-3	7a100tcsg324-3
Number of slice LUTs	0	861 out of 63400
Number of IOs	32	24
Number of bonded IOBs	32 out of 240	24 out of 210

Source: Author

advantages in terms of parallelism and efficiency for large number operations (like those used in cryptography), it is more resource-intensive and slower in terms of hardware implementation compared to decimal multiplication, which is simpler, faster, and uses fewer FPGA resources. The choice between the two methods would depend on the application requirements, such as speed versus resource usage or the need for handling large numbers efficiently.

"Even though time delay of RNS multiplication is more than decimal multiplication, RNS multiplication will provide more encryption to the hardware. So, time delay of RNS multiplication can be neglected due to high security".

(c) Theoretical example for RNS multiplication
We have assumed two numbers as 12, 15

let $m1 = 3, m2 = 5, m3 = 7$ $M = 3*5*7$

$M = 105$ modulis of 12 and 15 are

$(12)mod3 = 0$; $(12)mod5 = 2$; $(12)mod7 = 5$
$(15)mod3 = 0$; $(15)mod5 = 0$; $(15)mod7 = 1$
$(0,2,5)+(0,0,1) = (0,0,5)$ " $n1 = 0$, $n2 = 0$, $n3 = 5$ "

$x1 = (n1*(M/m1))modM$ $x1 = 0$ lly $x2 = 0$ lly $x3 = 75$ BY CRT THEOREM

$X=[((x1*(M/m1)*(M/m1)-1modM)+(x2*(M/m2)*(M/m2)$

$-1modM)+ (x3*(M/m3)*(M/m3)-1modM))modM]$ $X=[0+0+(75*15*1)]modM$

$X = 75$

Hence $12*15 = 75$

Theoretical and practical values are equal for normal multiplication and RNS multiplication.

The CRT works as follows:

1. Split the problem.
2. Solve each sub-problem.
3. Combine solutions.
4. Calculate Ni and yi.
5. Compute the solution.
6. Reduce modulo N.

CRT works because the moduli ni are pairwise coprime, allowing us to combine the solutions using the formula. The theorem guarantees a unique solution modulo N.

Conclusion

The residue number system (RNS) offers notable improvements to elliptic curve cryptography (ECC) by facilitating faster computations through parallel processing. This RNS algorithm uses less number of IOs when compared to decimal multiplication. Even though time delay of RNS multiplication is more than decimal multiplication it will provide more encryption to the hardware. So time delay can be neglected due to high security. This unique arithmetic method accelerates operations, enhances security against side channel attacks, and optimizes performance in environments with limited resources. RNS-based ECC proves advantageous in various domains, including secure communication protocols, digital signatures, cryptocurrencies, and post-quantum cryptography. Its capability to enhance computational efficiency, strengthen security, and adapt to diverse applications underscores its value for a broad range of cryptographic purposes.

References

[1] Zhang, W., Liu, Y., Zhao, Y., Chen, Y., & Li, X. (2022). Quantum-resistant RNS-based ECC for future-proof security. *Journal of Cryptographic Engineering*, 12(4), 123–138.

[2] Mohan, P. V. A., & Mohan, P. V. A. (2016). RNS in cryptography. In *Residue Number Systems: Theory and Applications* (pp. 263–347). Springer.

[3] Singh, A. K., Yadav, R., & Gupta, P. (2020). RNS-based ECC for secure cloud computing. *Journal of Cloud Computing: Advances, Systems and Applications*, 7(1), 1–12.

[4] Esmaeildoust, M., Schinianakis, D., Javashi, H., Stouraitis, T., and Navi, K. (2012). Efficient RNS Implementation of Elliptic Curve Point Multiplication Over ${\rm GF}(p)$. *IEEE Transactions on Very Large Scale Integration (VLSI) Systems*, 21(8), 1545–1549.

[5] Schinianakis, D. M., Fournaris, A. P., Michail, H. E., Kakarountas, A. P., and Stouraitis, T. (2008). An RNS implementation of an F_{p} elliptic curve point multiplier. *IEEE Transactions on Circuits and Systems I: Regular Papers*, 56(6), 1202–1213.

[6] Pandey, J. G., Mitharwal, C., and Karmakar, A. (2019). An RNS implementation of the elliptic curve cryptography for IoT security. In *Proceedings of the 2019 First IEEE International Conference on Trust, Security and Privacy in Computing and Communications (TrustCom)*, 1225–1230. IEEE.

[7] Fournaris, A. P., Papachristodoulou, L., Batina, L., & Sklavos, N. (2016). Secure and efficient RNS approach for elliptic curve cryptography. *International Journal of Computer Science and Cryptography*, 10(3), 135–150.

[8] Mehrabi, M. A., Doche, C., and Jolfaei, A. (2020). Elliptical curve cryptography point multiplication core for hardware security module. *IEEE Transaction on Computers*, 69(11), 1707–1718.

[9] Bigou, K., and Tisserand, A. (2015). Single base modular multiplication for efficient hard- ware RNS implementations of ECC. In Guneysu, T., and Handschuh, H. (Eds.), International Association for Cryptologic Research 2015: CHES 2015, LNCS 9293, (pp. 123–140), 2015.

[10] Kawamura, S., Komano, Y., Shimizu, H., & Yonemura, T. (2017). RNS Montgomery reduction algorithms using quadratic residuosity. *Journal of Cryptographic Engineering*, 7(2), 123–134.

[11] Schutze, T. (2011). Automotive security cryptography for car X communication. In Proceedings Embedded World Conference, 2011, (pp. 1–1).

[12] Posch, K. C., and Posch, R. (1995). Modulo reduction in residue number systems. *IEEE Transactions on Parallel and Distributed Systems*, 6(5), 449–454.

[13] Montgomery, P. L. (1985). Modular multiplication without trial division. *Mathematics of Computation*, 44, 519–521.

[14] Bigou, K., and Tisserand, A. (2015). Single base modular multiplication for efficient hardware RNS implementations of ECC. In Proceeding 17th International Workshop Cryptographic Hardware Embedded Systems, (Vol. 9293, (pp. 123–140).

38 Efficient design of a 16-Bit multiplier with low power and high-speed capabilities

Pradeep, M.[1,a], Hanumantha Rao, S.[2], Sanjeeva Reddy B. R.[3], Vasudeva Reddy, T.[4], Akhila Pallavi, K.[5] and Parvatini Niharika[5]

[1]Associate Professor, Electronics and communication Engineering, Shri Vishnu Engineering College for Women, Bhimavaram, Andhra Pradesh, India

[2]Professor, Electronics and communication Engineering, Shri Vishnu Engineering College for Women, Bhimavaram, Andhra Pradesh, India

[3]Professor, Electronics and communication Engineering, B V Raju Institute of Technology, Telangana, India

[4]Associate Professor, Electronics and communication Engineering, B V Raju Institute of Technology, Telangana, India

[5]UG student, Electronics and communication Engineering, Shri Vishnu Engineering College for Women, Bhimavaram, India

Abstract

In today's rapidly evolving world, integrated circuit (IC) technology faces increasing complexity in performance analysis and design. A high-speed design that consumes lower power and occupies a small area is considered highly compatible with modern electrical and electronic applications. Accurate multipliers, particularly those used in image processing, have numerous applications and significantly reduce delay and power consumption. In general-purpose processors, conventional full-precision multipliers can significantly impact area, power, and computational time. This paper proposes the design of a high-speed, area-efficient, accurate multiplier. The two input operands, multiplier and multiplicand, are separated into clusters of bits based on their computational consequence in product generation. Bit assignment and ordering are performed using a specific assignment method. The multiplication process generates partial products, which are then aligned. An accurate multiplier is used to perform the final multiplication, and carry propagation is managed to ensure an accurate final product. The final product is stored in a register. This paper aims to achieve an effective and efficient outcome through this design approach.

Keywords: Accurate adder, accurate multiplier, carry propagation, partial products, shifter

Introduction

In an era of booming technological advancement, integrated circuit (IC) technology is becoming increasingly complex in performance analysis and design. Modern electrical and electronic systems demand designs that are high-speed, have low power consumption, and occupy a minor area. To meet the basic requirements of various applications, especially portable and technological ones, minimizing power consumption is crucial. In such systems, the multiplier unit is a essential factor, serving as one of the essential and foundational arithmetic units. Multipliers typically exhibit larger latency, occupy more area, and dominate power consumption [1]. Therefore, constructing a low-power multiplier is a pivotal aspect of designing VLSI systems. With advancements in technology, new methodologies and approaches are continually emerging for designing low-power multipliers, addressing aspects at logical, physical, technical, and circuit levels [2, 3]. Multipliers are often considered one of the slower and more resource-intensive units in any system, significantly impacting overall system performance. Additionally, multipliers occupy a substantial area, making the optimization of speed and area a key design challenge in today's

[a]pradeepm999@gmail.com

DOI: 10.1201/9781003616399-38

scenarios [4]. Balancing these factors is extremely challenging; improving speed often increases area, and vice versa. Moreover, area and power utilization are linearly dependent. Therefore, reducing power and area typically requires compromising on the speed of the circuit [5]. In modern microprocessors and ASIC processors, most arithmetic logic units (ALUs) include a hardware multiplier. High-speed hardware multipliers must remained a focus of attention for some time, and more cultured multiplier schemes are now possible due to the increased density of integrated circuits. Addition and multiplication of binary numbers are vital and frequently used arithmetic operations in high-performance applications such as microprocessors and digital signal processing (DSP) [6–8]. In microprocessors, statistics show that more than 70% of instructions involve addition and multiplication operations, often performed by DSP algorithms. Consequently, these operations significantly impact execution time, underscoring the need for high-speed multipliers [9]. The multiplication process requires three basic steps: Partial product generation (PPG), partial product reduction (PPR), and carry propagate addition (CPA). Typically, this involves ordered multiplier factor execution and combinatorial factor execution. In digital very large scale integration (VLSI) circuit applications, parallel multipliers are becoming more common, while combinatorial methods consider proportional area units, given the increased scale of integration [10]. The generation and reduction of partial products vary significantly depending on the multiplication algorithm recycled. To decrease the amount of partial products and minimize circuit area, high-radix digit sets are often recorded in one quantity [11–13]. Firstly, the multiplication algorithm focuses on generating and forming partial products, followed by the reduction phase, i.e., accumulation. The generic multiplication process relies on the "add and shift" algorithm [14]. Several kinds of multipliers deliberated in this context include Wallace tree, array, decimal, parallel, sequential, combinational, shift-and-add multipliers, and serial multipliers. Multipliers play a significant role in DSP and many additional applications. By technological advancements, countless investigators have been striving to design multipliers that achieve

key design targets such as low power consumption, high speed, and layout regularity [15]. Consequently, creating multipliers with a smaller area or a combination of these attributes makes them appropriate for low power, high-speed, and dense VLSI implementations. The purpose of this paper is to evaluate performance factors such as area, delay, power consumption, and accuracy. The article is planned as tracks: describes the planned method for the accurate multiplier, discusses the result analysis, and Section II presents the conclusion of this paper.

High Speed and Area Efficient Accurate Multiplier

Figure 38.1 illustrates the architecture of an accurate multiplier designed for digital signal processing applications. The system is divided into the following components: the two input operands (multiplier and multiplicand) are split into two groups of bits based on their computational significance in product generation. These bits are assigned and ordered using a specific method, after which the multiplication generates aligned partial products. The accurate multiplier then multiplies these partial products, with carry propagation performed to ensure an accurate final product, which is stored in a register. Initially, the operands are loaded into the multiplier, with inputs A and B divided into higher and lower significant bits (AH, AL, and BH, BL). The primary function of the register multiplier is to preserve the bit illustration and produce a polynomial output, a(t). A parallel load operation is achieved in the most significant bit (MSB) position, and left shift operations are executed similarly. The multiplicand bit uses the value b(t) to place the cost in the register, and a parallel load operation is also useful to the multiplicand. The resulting assessment is stored in the register. Within multiplicand register block, a right shift operation is performed. A crypto core processor is utilized for data transfer in the multiplicand register.

The barrel shifter contains a root that loads MR and serves as the input to this block. Similarly, the multiplicand register consists of shift, data_in, and load_md bits, which are inputs to the barrel shifter. This shifter effectively shifts and loads the data. The result register holds the

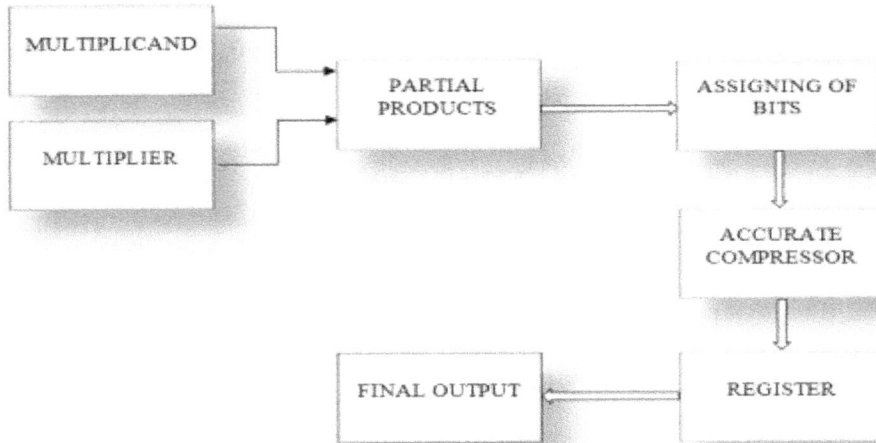

Figure 38.1 Schematic overview of high-accuracy multiplier
Source: Author

output, storing the complete arithmetic result. The proposed system provides more effective results compared to the existing system. An alternative approach to solving multi-digit multiplication problems is partial product multiplication, which relies on the distributive property of multiplication. The LSB of the multiplier generates the first partial product, the second bit generates the second partial product, and so on. These partial products are summed by an accurate adder circuit. The computation begins with the generation and propagation of signals for each state of the input sets A and B. The propagate and generating signals are represented as follows:

$$P_i = A_i XORB_i \tag{1}$$

$$G_i = A_i XORB_i \tag{2}$$

Parallel adders are employed to compute the arithmetic sum of two multi-bit numbers, processing respective pairs of bits in parallel. The efficiency of a squaring circuit can be enhanced using parallel adders, which help generate the carry and sum, with the MSB added last. An 'n'-bit parallel adder requires 'n' full adders to perform its operation. In the proposed architecture, the accurate adder block utilizes half adders, full adders, and approximate adders to provide improved results for higher-order bits. For n-bit numbers, this block extends from the MSB to the least significant bit (LSB), optimizing the power

delay product (PDP) with minimal error in the overall output. The choice of an accurate adder depends on the architecture/system-level applications. If the actual carry propagation chain is short, then an approximation configuration, intended to shorten the carry chain, is unnecessary. Initially, inputs are provided to the propagator and generator unit, which generates and propagates the input signals to the adder logic. This logic governs the overall system operation, performing addition in parallel. This parallelism increases the speed of operation. The last step in computing sum is consistent across all adders in the PPA adder family, mainly involving the computation of sum bits as listed:

$$S_i = P_i XORC_{i-1} \tag{3}$$

The proposed model introduces an innovative architecture for an accurate multiplier tailored for various applications. The system is organized into several key components: Operand segmentation: The two input operands (multiplier and multiplicand) are divided into higher and lower significance bits (AH, AL, BH, BL). This segmentation aids in managing the computational significance during product generation.

Partial product generation: The divided bits are ordered and used to generate aligned partial products. These partial products are then multiplied, and carry propagation is performed to ensure the accuracy of the final product. Register operations: The accurate multiplier uses a register to store the final product. Initial loading involves parallel operations in the most significant bit (MSB) position, followed by left shift operations. Multiplicand operations: The multiplicand bit's value is used to place the cost in the register, with parallel load operations also applied to the multiplicand. A right shift operation is executed within the multiplicand register block. Data transfer: A crypto core processor is utilized for efficient data transfer within the multiplicand register. This architecture emphasizes accuracy and efficiency in one of the application by leveraging advanced bit manipulation and parallel operations.

Result Analysis

Xilinx is a comprehensive software suite designed for the creation and implementation of digital circuits. It leverages field programmable gate array (FPGA) and complex programmable logic device (CPLD) technologies to facilitate the design and deployment of complex digital systems. FPGA is a type of semiconductor device that can be programmed to perform a variety of logic functions after manufacturing, offering flexibility and reconfigurability. CPLD, on the other hand, is used for implementing simpler logic functions with a fixed architecture but also offers programmability. The Xilinx design environment is widely utilized in the industry for several critical tasks. It allows engineers to implement complex digital designs, simulate their behavior, and verify their functionality before physical deployment. This environment supports various design stages, from high-level algorithm development to detailed hardware implementation. Figures 38.2, 38.2a, and 38.3 in this context illustrate key aspects of the proposed design. Specifically Figure 38.2 presents the register transfer level (RTL) schematic diagram, which provides a high-level abstraction of the circuit's operation. RTL diagrams are crucial for understanding how data is transferred and processed through different registers and logic gates in the system. They serve as a blueprint for translating high-level design descriptions into lower-level hardware implementations. Figure 38.2a offers a more detailed view or an alternative representation of the RTL schematic, potentially including additional details or variations in the design approach. Figure 38.3 shows the technology schematic of the planned high-speed, highly efficient, and accurate multiplier. This schematic provides a detailed physical representation of the circuit's layout and the actual components used, including logic gates, interconnections, and other elements. It demonstrates how the design is realized in terms of physical hardware and helps in understanding how the design is mapped onto the FPGA or CPLD. By utilizing Xilinx software, the proposed multiplier design can be effectively implemented and evaluated, ensuring that it meets the required specifications for speed, efficiency, and accuracy. The detailed schematics in the figures support this process by providing a clear representation of both the logical and physical aspects of the design.

Table 38.1 presents a comprehensive comparison between the existing and proposed systems, focusing on several key performance metrics: total delay, number of LUTs utilized, and memory usage. Total delay: This metric measures the time essential for the system to comprehensive its operations. Lower total delay indicates faster processing and improved system performance. The table details how the proposed system achieves a reduction in total delay compared to the existing system, which can result in more efficient and quicker operations.

Number of LUTs utilized: Look-up tables (LUTs) are essential components in FPGA designs that implement logic functions. The number of LUTs utilized reflects the resource consumption of the design. The comparison shows that the

Figure 38.2 Functional RTL schematic layout
Source: Author

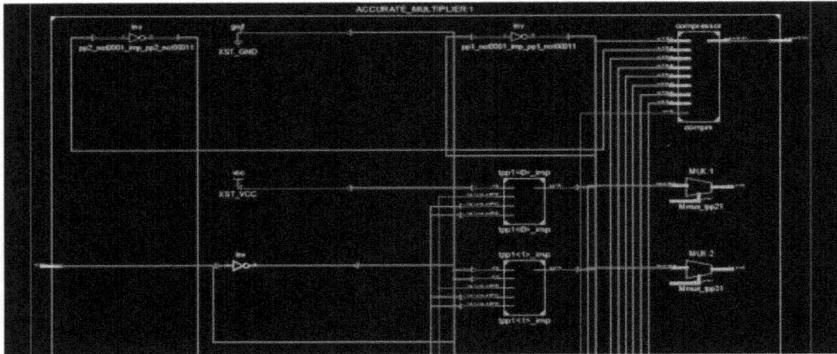

Figure 38.2a Core structural schematic of RTL design
Source: Author

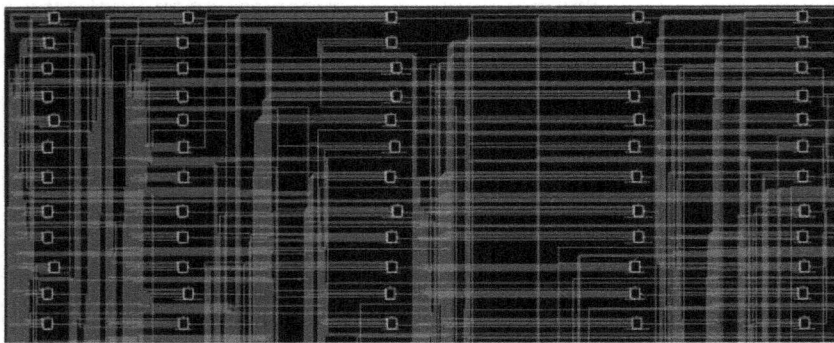

Figure 38.3 Schematic overview of technological architecture
Source: Author

proposed system uses fewer LUTs, suggesting more efficient use of FPGA resources and potentially leading to reduced hardware costs and improved design scalability. Memory usage: This metric indicates the amount of memory required by the system to perform its tasks. Efficient memory usage is critical for optimizing performance and ensuring that the system can handle larger datasets or more complex operations without running into resource constraints. Overall, the table provides a detailed view of how the proposed system compares to the existing system across these crucial performance indicators, demonstrating the improvements in efficiency, speed, and resource utilization achieved with the new design.

Figure 38.4 provides a comparative analysis of LUT usage between the existing and proposed systems. LUTs are fundamental components in FPGA designs, used to implement logic functions. The figure illustrates that the proposed system employs fewer LUTs compared to the existing

system. This reduction is significant because a lower number of LUTs generally translates to more efficient use of resources and potentially lower area and power consumption in the FPGA. By optimizing the design to use fewer LUTs, the proposed system not only improves resource efficiency but also enhances the overall performance of the digital circuit. This efficiency is crucial for applications requiring compact and cost-effective FPGA implementations, as it can lead to reduced hardware costs and improved processing speeds.

Figure 38.5 provides a comparative analysis of the total delay between the existing and proposed systems. A reduction in total delay is highly desirable as it leads to faster data processing and improved overall efficiency of the circuit. In this comparison, the proposed system demonstrates a significant reduction in delay compared to the existing system. This reduction is critical because lower delay translates directly into quicker response times, which enhances the performance of digital applications, particularly

Table 38.1 Evaluation of performance metrics

S. No.	Parameters	Existed system	Proposed system
1	Slices/ LUTs	1620	464
2	Total delay (ns)	45.8	12.3
3	Memory used (kb)	554856	305268

Source: Author

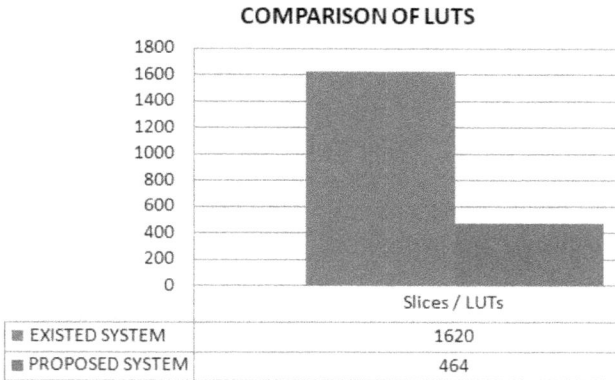

COMPARISON OF LUTS

Figure 38.4 LUT performance comparison
Source: Author

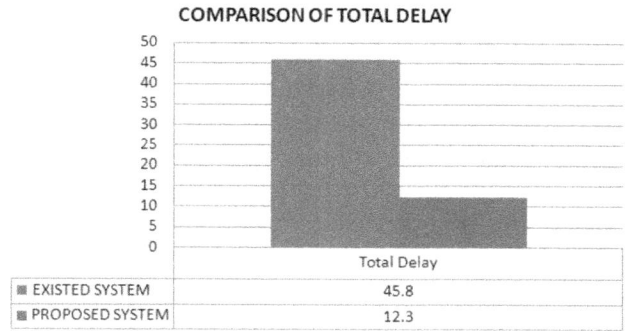

COMPARISON OF TOTAL DELAY

Figure 38.5 Comparative review of total delay
Source: Author

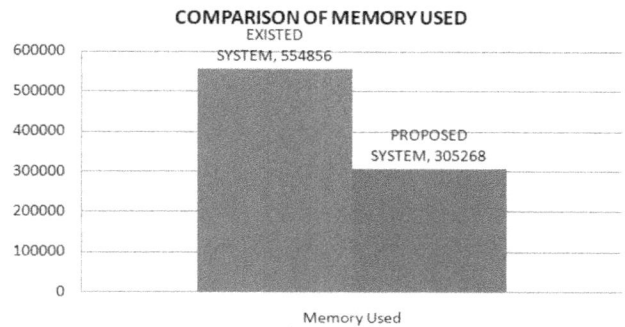

COMPARISON OF MEMORY USED

Figure 38.6 Memory consumption performance evaluation
Source: Author

those requiring high-speed processing. The upgrading in delay show of the planned system is attributed to several advancements in design techniques. These techniques include optimized circuit architectures, advanced logic design, and improved timing strategies. Such optimizations help in reducing the propagation time of signals through various stages of the circuit, thereby minimizing latency. A lower total delay improves the responsiveness of the system, making it more efficient in real-time applications where speed is crucial. For instance, in high-speed data processing tasks or real-time signal processing, reduced delay ensures that operations are completed more quickly, leading to faster data throughput and more efficient system performance. Overall, the proposed system's ability to achieve lower delay enhances its suitability for high-speed operations, ensuring that it can meet the demands of modern, high-performance digital applications. This optimization not only improves processing times but also contributes to the overall effectiveness and reliability of the digital circuit.

Figure 38.6 presents a comparative analysis of memory usage between the existing and proposed

systems. Memory usage is a critical performance metric that reflects the amount of memory resources consumed by a system to perform its operations. Efficient memory usage is essential for optimizing system performance, reducing resource requirements, and managing cost effectively. In this comparison, Figure 38.6 highlights how the proposed system's memory consumption differs from that of the existing system. By evaluating memory usage, we can assess how effectively each system utilizes available memory resources. The proposed system's design aims to reduce memory consumption while maintaining or improving overall performance. The analysis in Figure 38.6 provides insights into how well the proposed system manages memory compared to the existing system. This comparison helps in understanding the trade-offs between memory usage and other performance metrics, ensuring that the proposed system achieves a balance between resource efficiency and operational effectiveness.

When comparing the proposed system to the existing system, it is perceived that the planned system achieves a reduction in memory usage. Efficient memory management is crucial for optimizing system performance and resource utilization. By decreasing memory usage, the proposed system not only conserves valuable resources but also enhances overall system efficiency. Figure 38.7 provides a visual representation of the output waveform from the proposed system. The waveform illustrates the system's performance and how effectively it processes data with the reduced memory footprint. This visual aid helps in understanding the practical implications of reduced memory usage and how it impacts the system's overall behavior.

Conclusion

The proposed design features a high-speed, area-efficient, and accurate multiplier. In this design, the two input numbers, the multiplier and multiplicand, are partitioned into two groups of bits each, based on their computational significance. These bits are assigned and ordered appropriately to facilitate the multiplication process, generating and aligning partial products. An accurate multiplier is then used to perform the multiplication of these partial products, with carry propagation ensuring the final product's accuracy. The last outcome is stored in a register, leading to effective outcomes from this paper. The proposed multiplier achieves high-speed operation and area efficiency by utilizing a divide-and-conquer approach in its design. Looking ahead, this multiplier design could be extended to handle 64-bit, 128-bit, and even 512-bit operations. Additionally, future enhancements may involve optimizing LUT-level implementations to improve resource efficiency and performance further, potentially incorporating advanced techniques for accurate and approximate arithmetic circuits such as multiplier accumulators (MACs) and dividers. In this paper, the proposed multiplier not only achieves effective speed and area efficiency but also sets the stage for future enhancements in handling larger bit operations and optimizing arithmetic circuit performance.

Acknowledgement

Authors express their deep sense of gratitude to the management of Shri Vishnu Engineering

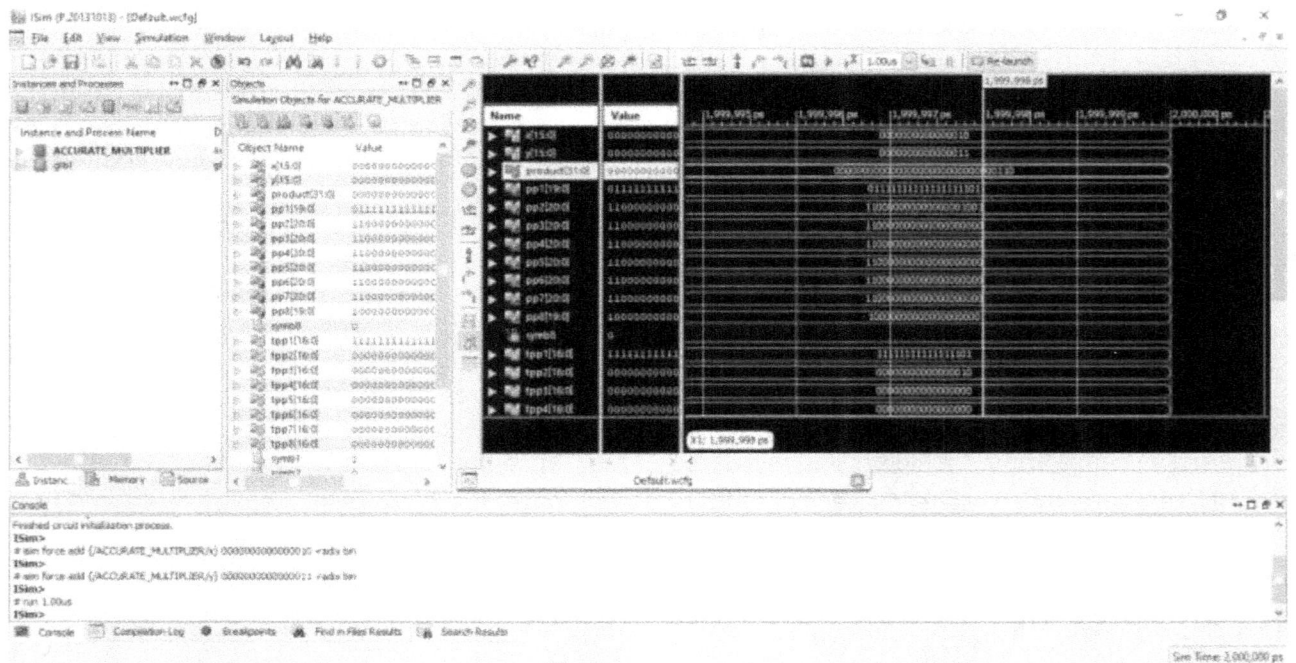

Figure 38.7 Visual representation of output waveform
Source: Author

College for Women for encouraging them in research work.

References

[1] Gule, U., Jia, Y., and Ghovanloo, M (2020). A reconfigurable passive voltage multiplier for wireless mobile IoT applications. In 2020 IEEE International Symposium on Circuits and Systems (ISCAS).

[2] Alouani, I., Ahangari, H., Ozturk, O., and Niar, S. (2018). A novel heterogeneous approximate multiplier for low power and high performance. *IEEE Embedded Systems Letters*, 10(2), 45–48.

[3] Leon, V., Zervakis, G., Soudris, D., and Pekmestzi, K. (2018). Approximate hybrid high radix encoding for energy-efficient inexact multipliers. *IEEE Transactions on Very Large Scale Integration (VLSI) Systems*, 26(3), 421–430.

[4] Dell'Anna, F. G., Dong, T., Li, P., Yumei, W., Azadmehr, M., and Berg, Y. (2017). Low-power voltage multiplier synthesis tool for preliminary topology identification. In 2017 International Conference on Open Source Systems and Technologies (ICOSST).

[5] Abraham, S., Kaur, S., and Singh, S. (2015). Study of various high speed multipliers. In 2015 International Conference on Computer Communication and Informatics (ICCCI).

[6] Ko, S. B., Han, L., and Kaivani, A. (2014). Improved design of high-frequency sequential decimal multipliers. *Electronics Letters*, 50(7), 558–560.

[7] Bozdas, K., and Alkar, A. Z. (2012). Analysis on the column sum boundaries of decimal array multipliers In Circuits and Systems (MWSCAS), IEEE 55th International Midwest Symposium.

[8] Kaivani, A., Chen, L., and Ko, S. B. (2012). High-frequency sequential decimal multipliers. In IEEE International Symposium on Circuits and Systems.

[9] Juang, T. B., Kuo, H. L., and Peng, H. H. (2012). Parallel and digit-serial implementations of area-efficient 3-operand decimal adders. In SoC Design Conference (ISOCC) International.

[10] Vazquez, A., Antelo, E., and Montuschi, P. (2010). Improved design of high- performance parallel decimal multipliers. *IEEE Transactions on Computers*, 59(5), 679–693.

[11] Ram, G. C., Lakshmanna, Y. R., Rani, D. S., and Sindhuri, K. B. (2016). Area efficient modified vedic multiplier. In 2016 International Conference on Circuit, Power and Computing Technologies (ICCPCT), Nagercoil, India, (pp. 1–5). doi: 10.1109/ICCPCT.2016.7530294.

[12] Ram, G. C., Subbarao, M. V., Varma, D. R., and Kumar, M. P. (2023). Delay enhancement of wallace tree multiplier with binary to excess-1 converter. In 2023 5th International Conference on Smart Systems and Inventive Technology (ICSSIT), Tirunelveli, India, (pp. 113–117). doi: 10.1109/ICSSIT55814.2023.10061043.

[13] Ram, G. C., Rani, D. S., Balasaikesava, R., and Sindhuri, K. B. (2016). Design of delay efficient modified 16 bit Wallace multiplier. In 2016 IEEE International Conference on Recent Trends in Electronics, Information and Communication Technology (RTEICT), Bangalore, India, (pp. 1887–1891). doi: 10.1109/RTEICT.2016.7808163.

[14] Ram, G. C., Subbarao, M. V., Kumar, D. G., and Terlapu, S. K. (2022). FPGA implementation of 16-Bit wallace multiplier using HCA. In Chakravarthy, V. V. S. S. S., Flores-Fuentes, W., Bhateja, V., and Biswal, B. (Eds.), Advances in Micro-Electronics, Embedded Systems and IoT. Lecture Notes in Electrical Engineering, (Vol. 838). Singapore: Springer. https://doi.org/10.1007/978-981-16 8550-7_40.

[15] Jyothsna, T., and Pradeep, M. (2020). Cyclic convolution based on fermat number transform (FNT) with low power and high speed for parallel architecture. *International Journal of Recent Advances in Engineering and Technology (IJRAET)*, 8(6), 32–37 https://doi.org/10.46564/ijraet.2020.v08i06.005.

39 Hardware-based design to estimate the movement of elderly in indoor environments

Chinnaiah, M. C.[1,a], Divyavani, G.[1,b], Keerthi, T.[1,c], Harikrishna, D.[1,d], Brundavani Jinkala[1,e] and Janardhan Narambhatlu[2,f]

[1]Department of ECE, B.V. Raju Institute of Technology, Narsapur, Medak, India

[2]Department of Mechanical Engineering, Chaitanya Bharati Institute of Technology, Gandipate, Hyderabad, India

Abstract

Technology has rapid growth to address the challenges faced by elderly people but in reality, the challenges encountered by them have a significant growth up to 78% according to National Institutes of Health report as on 4 June 2023. One of the major challenges is position tracking for dependent personality disorders in indoor premises. Presently multiple techniques have been elevated to decode human position through surveillance system. The proposed model invokes the utilization of sensors for detecting human posture which can be widely used in many applications such as hospitals and in any indoor environments. HC-SR04 ultrasonic sensor is inherited which efficiently detects human posture by evaluating the distance. Evaluated distance determines the position of human which is displayed in LCD through FPGA. The simulation and synthesis results are obtained by using Xilinx Vivado 2017.3.

Keywords: FPGA, human tracking, indoor localization, ultrasonic sensors

Introduction

Monitoring dependent personality disorder people in indoor premises has become an enormous task in the current framework. As per National Institutes of Health report, precisely 78% of elder people facing risks has been rapidly raised as on 4 June 2023 [1]. As it is crucial to scrutinize the difficulty faced, the proposed work analyzes the position of elderly people in indoor territory. Exertion of ultrasonic sensors arbitrates postures of human comprehensively where the HC-SR04 ultrasonic sensors are human indulgent.

Large numbers conventionally face a problem to supervise the aged, paralyzed, and disabled people and aim to opt a steward or shove off them to retirement community. Approximately more than 50% of disordered people permeate indoor premises and their inhabitants should transact by scorning trade. There is a significant uplift in the death rates with the rise of the heart attacks and falls. Observing the homebody all the time from any place will be a solution to resolve this issue and this can be with the convention of cameras and sensors. The main intention of our work is to arbitrate the three postures sitting, standing, and sleeping of mortal and to reduce the fall risk and death rate fostered from different reasons. The objectives of this paper are:

A) Calculating the distance from the sensor.
B) Determining the position of the human in indoor premises.

Related Works

From different approaches involved in inspecting humans in indoor terrain, the sensors are harnessed frequently to depict the distances from the object. The position of humans in an indoor environment is intended with the use of camera where the camera collects the RSS samples of the video or the image and finds out the pixels of the matching image with artificial neural network

[a]chinnaaiah.mc@bvrit.ac.in, [b]divyavani.g@bvrit.ac.in, [c]keerthi.t@bvrit.ac.in, [d]harikrishna.dodde@bvrit.ac.in, [e]20211a0479@bvrit.ac.in, [f]njanardhan_mech@cbit.ac.in

DOI: 10.1201/9781003616399-39

(ANN). This method also uses Wi-Fi network to achieve different parameters like signal strength and room map information [3]. From the different sensors, radar sensors are among them and this sensor is used to transmit and receive EM waves towards and from the object and able to determine the distances from the object. This model mainly uses doppler phase shift in different algorithms to determine the localization of the moving objects and to ignore the stationary objects like walls and any other furniture [4].

To determine the gestures of the person in the indoor environment, a Wi-Fi based fingerprint system is implemented. To acquire the fingerprints of the person, different algorithms of neural networks are used, and the trained data set model is used for the comparison of original object and detected object [5]. In modern office buildings, determining the position of a person in indoor localization is a bit difficult and to overcome all the difficulties, GraphSLAM framework is used where this framework is divided into front end and back end. The front-end framework constructs a pose graph from relative motion constraints using Wi-Fi technology and back-end framework draws a graph from the fingerprints [6].

Using FMCW sensor, the stationary objects and the moving objects are differentiated to locate human activity using EMA algorithm. The EMA algorithm is mainly used to enhance hand motion and attenuate the strong reflections from the human body and other stationary objects in the indoor environment. The direction of the hand motion is identified by tracking 2D position using digital beam forcing [7].

In determining the position of person in smart homes, different non wearable sensors like IR sensors, ultrasonic sensors, photoelectric sensors, vibration sensors, pressure sensors, magnetic switches, and audio sensors to detect various parameters such as human presence, light source, person detection, interaction with various objects, and to detect sounds in house [8]. With the use of different sensor technology, there are improvements in several parameters like size, accuracy, energy efficiency and reliability. Of all the different sensors, ultrasonic sensors are mostly preferred in determining the position of the human body in indoor environments.

Methodology

Block diagram and flow chart

The operation implicated in estimating the position of elder people in indoor environment involves several steps: detecting the person, calculating the distances from ultrasonic sensor HC-SR04 to the human body, determining the posture of the elder people employing the angle and deployment of the ultrasonic sensor, and disclosing it on the LCD display. The accomplishment of the entire process is on FPGA by interpreting the postures of sitting, standing, and sleeping and is depicted on the LCD. The input is taken from the ultrasonic sensors placed in different corners of the room and output is obtained from the FPGA board which is further displayed on the LCD.

The block diagram delineated in Figure 39.1 to estimate the position of elder people comprehending various components as follows:

The sensors used are ultrasonic sensors to obtain the distances to the object. The six ultrasonic sensors placed are connected to the FPGA board and the distances calculated from the sensors are given and the position of output is displayed in LCD. The position displayed will be sitting position, sleeping position, and standing position in a room. Novelty of the work embraces integration of Ultrasonic sensors, real time monitoring of elderly people by predictive data analysis through the distance counter which can provide securely, proficient outcome for elderly personalities movement in the indoor locations.

The flowchart depicted in Figure 39.2 describes the complete flow of the position detection. Once the people detected then the ultrasonic sensors will be activated and the six ultrasonic sensors are illustrated as L1, R1, L2, R2, L3 and R3.

The distance is calculated from the object to ultrasonic sensor and from the distances obtained the posture of the human will be detected. The three postures as sitting, sleeping, and standing are estimated from the different ranges and the distance obtained is not in the specified ranges then the person is not available in that indoor terrain.

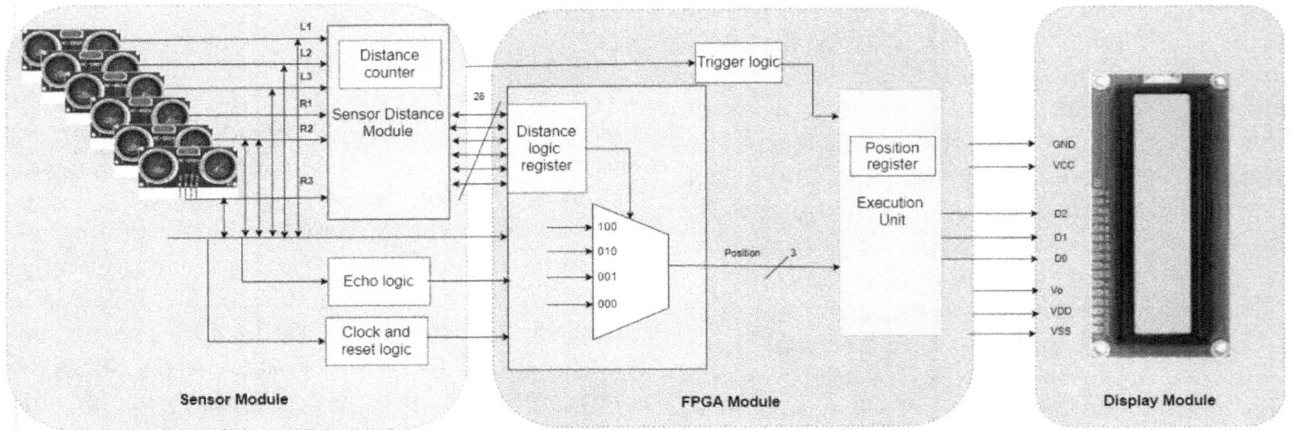

Figure 39.1 Block diagram of position detection
Source: Author

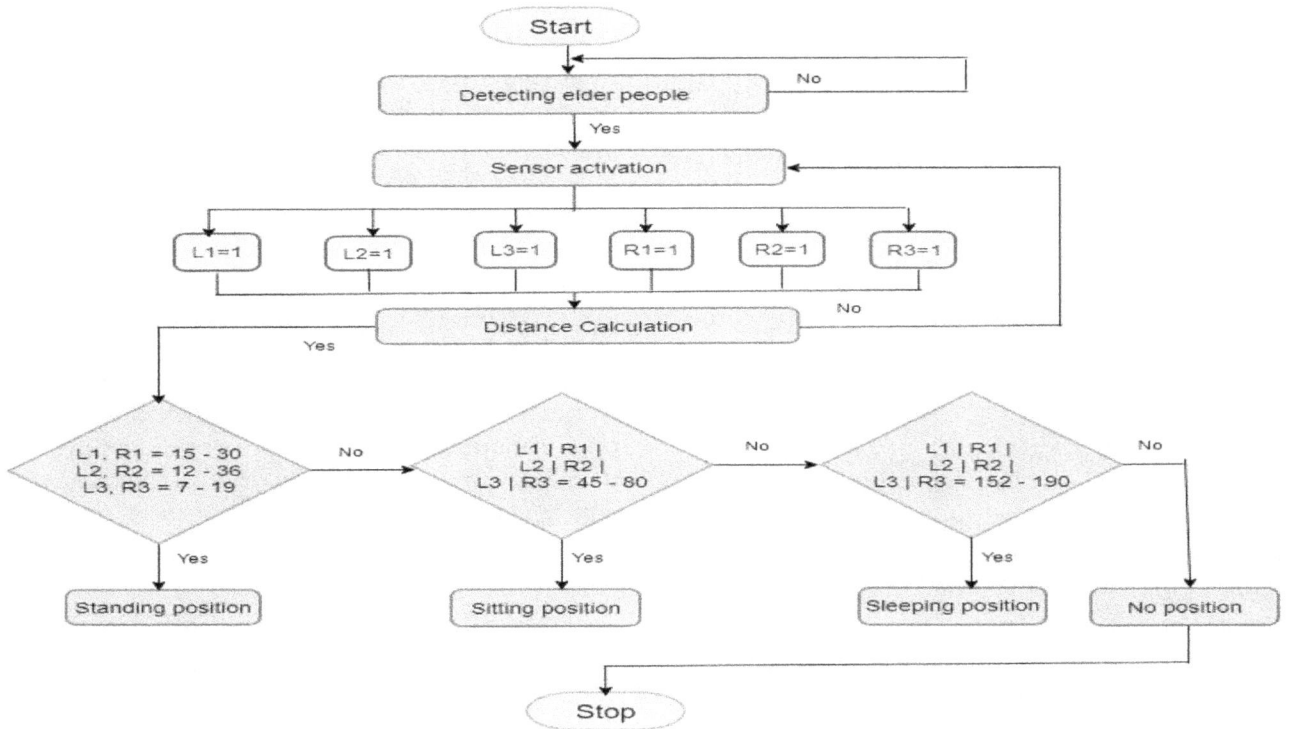

Figure 39.2 Flow chart of position and distance calculation
Source: Author

Estimating the position of elder people

The elderly people's movement is estimated in three modules: collecting data from sensor, determining position, display on LCD.

Collecting data from sensor

The habitude of HC-SR04 ultrasonic sensor fortify to fetch the data in a room and reinforce to disseminate and accrue information towards and away from the human and disdain the object other than human. This sensor has four pins: trigger, echo, clock and reset where these pins are used to transmit and receive the information at positive clock pulse and when reset is in off state.

The six ultrasonic sensors are placed on the roof as per the dimensions of the room where the four sensors are placed at each corner of the room and the remaining two sensors are placed at the middle of the roof as front and back ultrasonic sensors. The ultrasonic sensors are placed at left side top (L1), right side top (R1), left side middle (L2), right side middle (R2), left side bottom (L3), right side bottom (R3). These sensors give the distance between the information received from the object. The distance counter inside the ultrasonic sensor helps to find the distance between the sensor and object and is escalated from echo and trigger pins. The distance given as output from the ultrasonic sensor is attuned to appraise the position of elderly people. The required specification of the HC-SR04 ultrasonic sensor is illustrated in Table 39.1.

The six ultrasonic sensors operate at the same frequency to obtain accurate results. The data from the six ultrasonic sensors is communicated to the FPGA board. However, the design logic is rendered as LUTs in the programmable logic to evaluate the posture of elderly people.

Pseudocode for ultrasonic sensor–

Step 1: Declaration of the inputs and outputs
    Inputs: echo, clock, reset
    Outputs: distance, trigger
Step 2: Reset logic
    Make reset = 1, assign all values to 0.
    Make reset = 0 and increment the counter.
Step 3: Counter logic
    if counter < = 500 then trigger = 1 else trigger = 0
    if echo =1, distance counter = distance counter + 1 and trigger = 0

Table 39.1 Specifications of HC-SR04 [2]

Electrical parameters	Value
Operating voltage	3.3 Vdc~5 Vdc
Quiescent current	<2 mA
Operating current	15 mA
Operating frequency	40 KHz
Operating range and accuracy	2 cm~400 cm
Sensitivity	-65 dB min
Sound pressure	112 dB
Effective angle	15

Source: Author

    if counter <= 1900000 then trig<=0.
    if counter < = 5000000 then counter = 0 and distance counter = 0.
Step 4: Value Initialization
    distance = distance counter * 17000.

Determining position
Before the estimation of position, a range of distances are calculated from each six ultrasonic sensors and if the distance obtained from the sensor is in the defined range, then the position will be estimated. The range of distances will be different for each sensor depending on the position of the sensor.

From the ultrasonic sensor placed at left side top (L1), the position is described as sleeping if the range of distances varies from 15 to 30 (measured in cm), and the position is described as sitting if the range of distances varies from 45 to 80 (measured in cm), and the position is described as standing if the range of distances varies from 152 to 190 (measured in cm). If there is no distance measured from the ultrasonic sensor, then the person is not there in the ranging distance of that sensor. From the ultrasonic sensor placed at right side top (R1), the position is described as sleeping if the range of distances varies from 15 to 30 (measured in cm), and the position is described as sitting if the range of distances varies from 45 to 80 (measured in cm), and the position is described as standing if the range of distances varies from 152 to 190 (measured in cm). If there is no distance measured from the ultrasonic sensor, then the person is not there in the ranging distance of that sensor.

From the ultrasonic sensor placed at left side middle (L2), the position is described as sleeping if the range of distances varies from 12 to 36 (measured in cm), and the position is described as sitting if the range of distances varies from 45 to 80 (measured in cm), and the position is described as standing if the range of distances varies from 152 to 190 (measured in cm). If there is no distance measured from the ultrasonic sensor, then the person is not there in the ranging distance of that sensor. From the ultrasonic sensor placed at right side middle (R2), the position is described as sleeping if the range of distances varies from 12 to 36 (measured in cm), and the position is described as sitting if the range of distances varies from 45 to 80 (measured in cm), and the position is described as standing if the range of distances varies from 152 to 190 (measured in cm). If there is no distance measured from the ultrasonic sensor, then the person is not there in the ranging distance of that sensor.

From the ultrasonic sensor placed at left side bottom (L3), the position is described as sleeping if the range of distances varies from 7 to 19 (measured in cm), and the position is described as sitting if the range of distances varies from 45 to 80 (measured in cm), and the position is described as standing if the range of distances varies from 152 to 190 (measured in cm). If there is no distance measured from the ultrasonic sensor, then the person is not there in the ranging distance of that sensor. From the ultrasonic sensor placed at right side bottom (R3), the position is described as sleeping if the range of distances varies from 7 to 19 (measured in cm), and the position is described as sitting if the range of distances varies from 45 to 80 (measured in cm), and the position is described as standing if the range of distances varies from 152 to 190 (measured in cm). If there is no distance measured from the ultrasonic sensor, then the person is not there in the ranging distance of that sensor.

Pseudocode for posture evaluation–

Step 1: Declaration of inputs and outputs.
    Inputs: distance, clock, reset
    Outputs: position
Step 2: Sensor activation for person movement
    If L1 = 1 | R1 = 1 then go to case 1
    If L2 =1 | R2 = 1 then go to case 2
    If L3 = 1 | R3 = 1 then go to case 3
Step 3: Distance evaluation
    Case 1 – {L1, R1} = {(15 to 30 – sleeping), (45 to 80 – sitting), (152 to 190 – standing)}

The distances from the six ultrasonic sensors are taken as the inputs for top module and the output position is obtained in the binary format. The distances from the ultrasonic sensors are given at different time intervals to observe the accurate output position. The binary number 000 represents that there is no elderly person detected in the room. If an elderly person is detected, then the three positions detected are sitting, sleeping, and standing position. The sleeping position is represented as 100, the sitting position is represented as 010 and standing position is represented as 001.

Case 2 - {L2, R2} = {(12 to 36 – sleeping), (45 to 80 – sitting), (152 to 190 – standing)}

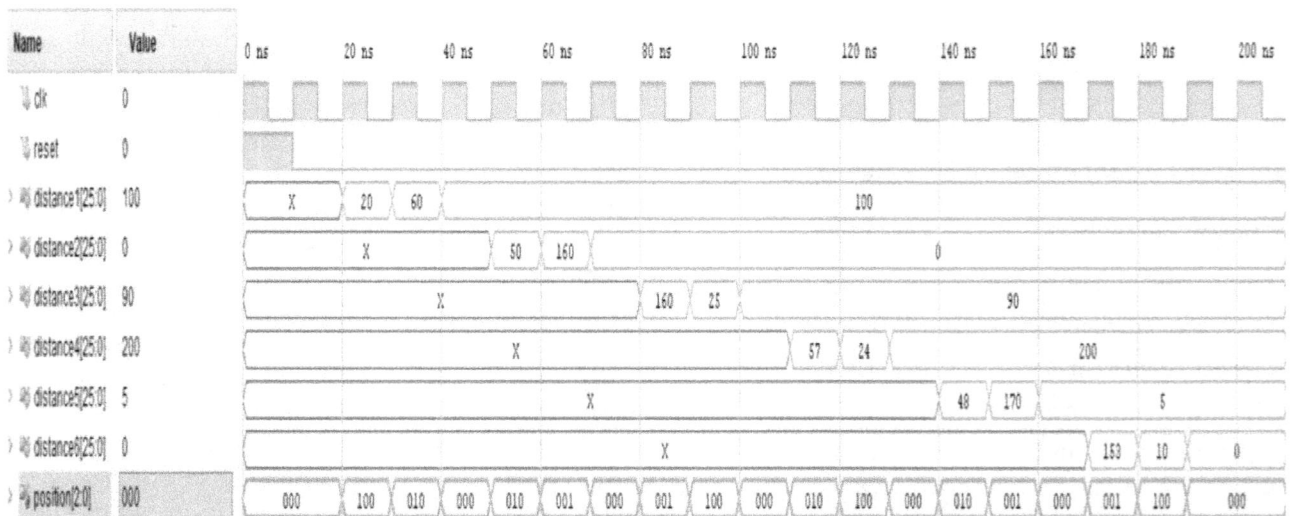

Figure 39.3 Simulation results of determining position
Source: Author

Case 3 - {L3, R3} = {(7 to 19 – sleeping), (45 to 80 – sitting), (152 to 190 – standing)}

Step 4: Position analysis

1. Sleeping position- assign 100
2. Sitting position – assign 010
3. Standing position – assign 001
4. No position – assign 000

Results and Discussion

To some extent, the posture of aged people is appraised from the distance obtained from the HC-SR04 ultrasonic sensor. The simulation results, synthesis report and the schematic diagram are obtained from the Verilog code. The simulation results to estimate the position of elder people is depicted in Figure 39.3.

Inputs: clock, reset, distance1, distance2, distance3, distance4, distance5, distance6.

Output: position

The schematic diagram of estimating an elderly person's position is described in Figure 39.4. The six HC-SR04 ultrasonic sensors ultrasonicsensor_1, ultrasonicsensor_2, ultrasonicsensor_3, ultrasonicsensor_4, ultrasonicsensor_5 and ultrasonicsensor_6 are represented as uut1, uut2, uut3, uut4, uut5, and uut6. The distances from all the six ultrasonic sensors are given to

position_reg for obtaining the binary value of the position. The clock and reset pins are connected to every ultrasonic sensor and position_reg. Once the position is determined, the ultrasonic sensor gets reset and starts calculating the distances again.

The utilization report of an elder people estimation is described in Table 39.2. The number of flipflops required is 141, LUT's are 420 and IO ports are 7 as per the utilization report.

The comparison of the previous method and the proposed model is determined in Table 39.3. The parameters like accuracy and energy consumption are compared with previous methods. Energy consumption is very low with the usage of ultrasonic sensors whereas it is bit high with respect to camera and PIR sensors.

Table 39.2 Utilization report of the position estimation

Resources	Utilization	Available	Utilization %
LUT	420	53200	0.79
FF	141	106400	0.13
IO	7	200	3.50

Source: Author

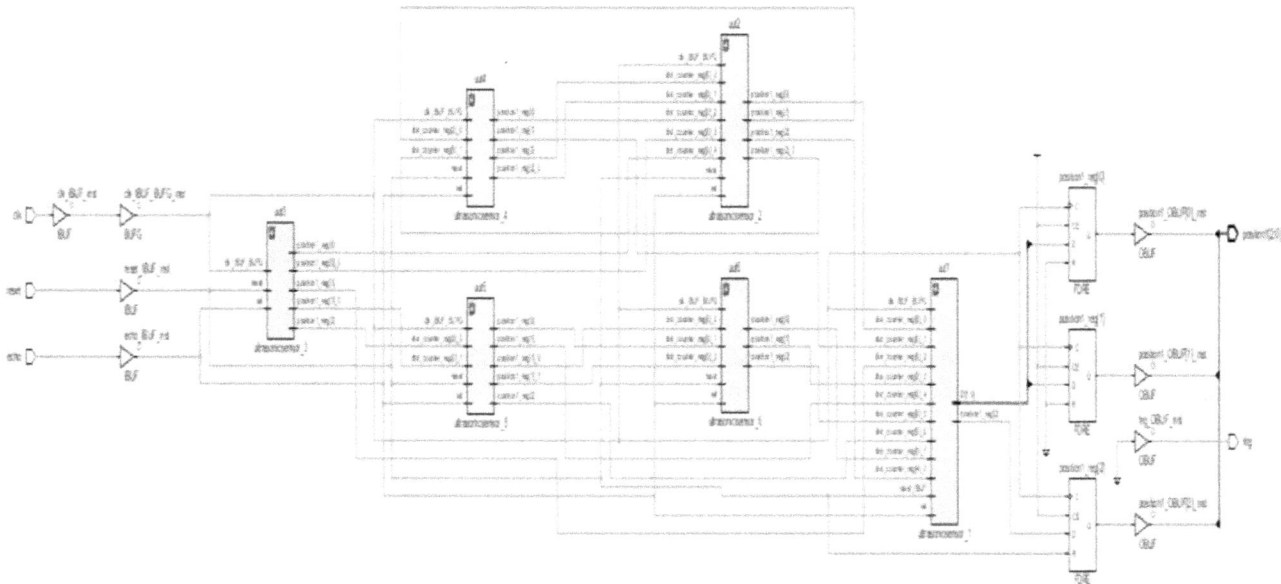

Figure 39.4 Schematic diagram of determining position

Source: Author

Table 39.3 Comparison table of existing and proposed model

Parameters	Existing models		Proposed model
	Sun et.al [3]	Pham et.al [17]	
Accuracy	Camera: Privacy violated	PIR sensors: Low accuracy	Ultrasonic sensors: High accuracy
Energy consumption	High (5W)	High (3W)	Low (1.5W)

Source: Author

Conclusion and Future Scope

Evaluating the position of elder people movement in indoor premises is the main novelty in this paper. To conclude this, three different positions like sitting position, sleeping position, and standing position are estimated in the indoor environment using FPGA board. The positions are detected using HC-SR04 ultrasonic sensors which are human-centric. With the estimation of the position, the security will be enhanced, and the person can easily know the status of elderly people at home from anywhere. The use of FPGA with real-time ultrasonic sensors processing data provides accurate and effective results to display it on the LCD. The parallel processing of FPGA provides flexibility in the design of estimating elder people's movement in indoor environments and the use of sensors at different corners of a room gives appropriate distances from sensor to object. Whereas the main application of this research is in hospitals for continuous monitoring of patients in a room and can also be used in any indoor environments to monitor people. This can also be used for industry purposes and used in robots for electronic needs.

The future scope of this work is to replace the ultrasonic sensors with cameras and to make this work more effectively. The camera captures the images and sends to the mobile phone registered to that and it can also continuously monitor the position of a person with the help of the cameras.

References

[1] National Library of Medicine Falls and Fall prevention in older adults Ethiology 4 June 2023 [Online] Available from: https://www.ncbi.nlm.nih.gov/books/NBK560761/ .

[2] Last Minute Engineers Technical Specifications [Online] Available from: https://lastminuteengineers.com/arduino-sr04-ultrasonic-sensor-tutorial/.

[3] Sun, Y., Meng, W., Li, C., Zhao, N., Zhao, K., and Zhang, N. (2017). Human localization using multi-source heterogeneous data in indoor environments. *IEEE Access*, 5, 812–822. doi: 10.1109/ACCESS.2017.2650953.

[4] Zhu, A., Qi, X., Fan, T., Gu, Z., Lv, Q., Ye, D., et al. (2018). Indoor localization for passive moving objects based on a redundan SIMO radar sensor. *IEEE Journal on Emerging and Selected Topics in Circuits and Systems*, 8(2), 271–279. doi: 10.1109/JETCAS.2018.2798584.

[5] Wang, F., Feng, J., Zhao, Y., Zhang, X., Zhang, S., and Han, J. (2019). Joint activity recognition and indoor localization with WiFi fingerprints. *IEEE Access*, 7, 80058–80068. doi: 10.1109/ACCESS.2019.2923743.

[6] Liang, Q., and Liu, M. (2020). An automatic site survey approach for indoor localization using a smartphone. *IEEE Transactions on Automation Science and Engineering*, 17(1), 191–206. doi: 10.1109/TASE.2019.2918030.

[7] Nallabolu, P., Zhang, L., Hong, H., and Li, C. (2021). Human presence sensing and gesture recognition for smart home applications with moving and stationary clutter suppression using a 60-GHz digital beamforming FMCW radar. *IEEE Access*, 9, 72857–72866. doi: 10.1109/ACCESS.2021.3080655.

[8] Debes, C., Merentitis, A., Sukhanov, S., Niessen, M., Frangiadakis, N., and Bauer, A. (2016). Monitoring activities of daily living in smart homes: understanding human behavior. *IEEE Signal Processing Magazine*, 33(2), 81–94.

[9] Sonia, S., Tripathi, A. M., Baruah, R. D., and Nair, S. B. (2015). Ultrasonic sensor-based human detector using one-class classifiers. Proceedings IEEE International Conference on Evolving

and Adaptive Intelligent Systems (EAIS), (pp. 1–6).

[10] Davidson, P., and Pich, R. (2017). A survey of selected indoor positioning methods for smartphones. *IEEE Communications Surveys and Tutorials*, 19(2), 1347–1370.

[11] Gu, Y., Lo, A., and Niemegeers, I. (2009). A survey of indoor positioning systems for wireless personal networks. *IEEE Communications Surveys and Tutorials*, 11, 13–32.

[12] Yassin, A., Nasser, Y., Awad, M., Al-Dubai, A., Liu, R., Yuen, C., et al. (2017). Recent advances in indoor localization: a survey on theoretical approaches and applications. *IEEE Communications Surveys and Tutorials*, 19(2), 1327–1346.

[13] Zhang, Z., Xie, L., Zhou, M., and Wang, Y. (2020). CSI-based indoor localization error bound considering pedestrian motion. In 2020 IEEE/CIC International Conference on Communications in China (ICCC), Chongqing, China, (pp. 811–816). doi: 10.1109/ICCC49849.2020.9238893.

[14] Kim, T. W., and Lee, D. M. (2021). Predicted seamless human positioning algorithm based on M-RCNN in obstacle environment for indoor localization. In 2021 International Conference on Information and Communication Technology Convergence (ICTC), Jeju Island, Korea, Republic of, 2021, (pp. 576–579). doi: 10.1109/ICTC52510.2021.9621181.

[15] Rizvi, S. M. A., Ahmed, R. M., Alamdar, K. G., Khorasani, M. R., and Memon, J. A. (2022). Human detection and localization in indoor disaster environments using UAVs. In 2022 4th International Conference on Robotics and Computer Vision (ICRCV), Wuhan, China, (pp. 159–163). doi: 10.1109/ICRCV55858.2022.9953174.

[16] Gerstweiler, G. (2018). Guiding people in complex indoor environments using augmented reality. In 2018 IEEE Conference on Virtual Reality and 3D User Interfaces (VR), Tuebingen/Reutlingen, Germany, (pp. 801–802). doi: 10.1109/VR.2018.8446138.

[17] Pham, M., Yang, D., and Sheng, W. (2019). A sensor fusion approach to indoor human localization based on environmental and wearable sensors. *IEEE Transactions on Automation Science and Engineering*, 16(1), 339–350. doi: 10.1109/TASE.2018.2874487.

[18] Xie, L., Zhang, L., Tian, Z., Li, Z., Liu, J., and Wang, Y. (2022). Indoor localization using reflection paths under non-line-of-sight environments. In 2022 International Conference on Microwave and Millimeter Wave Technology (ICMMT), Harbin, China, (pp. 1–3). doi: 10.1109/ICMMT55580.2022.10022414.

[19] Inofuente-Colque, K., Ferreira-Andrade, S., Barrios-Aranibar, D., Cardinale, Y., and Diaz-Amado, J. (2021). An approach to improve simultaneous localization and mapping in human populated environments. In 2021 Latin American Robotics Symposium (LARS), 2021 Brazilian Symposium on Robotics (SBR), and 2021 Workshop on Robotics in Education (WRE), Natal, Brazil, (pp. 240–245). doi: 10.1109/LARS/SBR/WRE54079.2021.9605464.

[20] Mu, H., Liu, J., Ewing, R., and Li, J. (2021). Human indoor positioning via passive spectrum monitoring. In 2021 55th Annual Conference on Information Sciences and Systems (CISS), Baltimore, MD, USA, (pp. 1–6). doi: 10.1109/CISS50987.2021.9400291.

[21] Ye, H., Chen, G., Chen, W., He, L., Guan, Y., and Zhang, H. (2021). Mapping while following: 2D LiDAR SLAM in indoor dynamic environments with a person tracker. In 2021 IEEE International Conference on Robotics and Biomimetics (ROBIO), Sanya, China, (pp. 826–832). doi: 10.1109/ROBIO54168.2021.9739394.

[22] Chang, B., and Sheu, J. (2022). Indoor localization with CSI fingerprint utilizing depthwise separable convolution neural network. In 2022 IEEE 33rd Annual International Symposium on Personal, Indoor and Mobile Radio Communications (PIMRC), Kyoto, Japan, (pp. 1276–1281). doi: 10.1109/PIMRC54779.2022.9977629.

40 A study on DDD mode delay optimization in dual chamber pacemaker

Pavankumar Bikki[a], Soumya, K.[b], Manjusha, K.[c], Anuhya, J.[d], and Charankumar, K.[e]

B V Raju Institute of Technology, Narsapur, Telangana, India

Abstract

This article presents advances in cardiac pacemaker technology in the domains of sensing, pacing, mode switching, and atrioventricular (AV) delay optimization. Pacemakers play a vital role in managing cardiac rhythm problems, such as bradycardia, tachycardia, and arrhythmia. As a result, there is a constant demand for technological advancements in this field. Recent advancements in sensing technology, including dynamic trans linear (DTL) circuits and state-of-the-art ECG monitors, have significantly improved the accuracy of heart rate monitoring and enhanced the synchronization with the heart's natural activity. The article explores the impact of pacing techniques on heart function, with a particular focus on the potential benefits of optimizing AV delay to improve patient outcomes. Additionally, the intricate interplay between mode-switching algorithms and timing cycles, demonstrates how they synergistically ensure that the pacemaker's response aligns with the inherent beat of the heart. The current focus is on minimizing the delay and power usage of circuits to improve the durability and dependability of pacemakers. These improvements emphasize the necessity for ongoing research in pacemaker technology to address the growing need for individualized, adaptable cardiac treatment to improve the quality of life for people with heart rhythm problems.

Keywords: Atrioventricular delay, pacemaker, pacing, sensing, timing cycles

Introduction

The atria and ventricles are the two upper and lower chambers of the human heart, respectively. Into the atria goes blood from the body's exterior portions. Once again, the semilunar valve (SLV) nodes flow blood from the atria to the ventricles via the atrioventricular nodes, where it is then driven to the pulmonary vein, aorta, and other body regions. In addition, the heart naturally produces electrical impulses that cause the heart to beat through a node known as the Sino-atrial (SA) node. When there is just 20% of blood left, the atrium contracts, depolarizes, and blood rushes to the ventricles, forming a P-wave. This process begins when there is a pressure differential, causing the blood to flow to the ventricles. Insufficient pressure differential prevents blood in the ventricles from moving toward the aorta. Ventricular depolarization, or the contraction of the ventricles to assist blood flow through

SLV nodes to the aorta, is what causes the QRS complex to form. The QRS complex oversees atrial repolarization, which is likewise executed. Additionally, the T-wave forms because of ventricular repolarization, which prepares it for the subsequent cycle. The cardiac cycle refers to this procedure [1,2].

Modern technology is rapidly developing low-power, high-speed technologies, which are important for devices like cardiac pacemakers to prolong their useful lives. A pacemaker is a device that prolongs a patient's life. Pacemakers save the lives of many individuals who experience irregular heart rhythms worldwide. Patients with irregular heartbeats such as bradycardia, tachycardia, and arrhythmia frequently utilize pacemakers, therefore technological developments in these vital devices should be ongoing. Unlike the sinoatrial node, the pacemaker monitors the heart's status and reacts appropriately

[a]Pavankumar.b@bvrit.ac.in, [b]soumyakarukula06@gmail.com, [c]manjusha.k@bvrit.ac.in, [d]21211a04a5@bvrit.ac.in, [e]charankumar.k@bvrit.ac.in

DOI: 10.1201/9781003616399-40

and more accurately if any adjustments need to be made [3,4]. Figure 40.1 shows the cardiac cycle waveform.

The pacemaker's sensing and pacing functions are two important features. The ideal time interval between sensing and the pacemaker's following pacing action is instantaneous. Nonetheless, in any real circuit, a delay in the reactions of several circuitry components results in an accumulative delay effect. Using a variety of sensor data, the rate-responsive pacemakers may readily adjust to the patient's physiological requirements and physical activity [5].

Literature Review

Sensing

The sensing in a cardiac pacemaker refers to the device's capacity to recognize the electrical impulses that the heart naturally produces. For the pacemaker to match the intrinsic beat of the heart, several signals are necessary. Sensing is an essential capability that enables the pacemaker to track the electrical movement of the heart and choose when to administer pacing stimuli. Many techniques have been put out to measure heart rate accurately to date. A cardiac

sensing amplifier, or pacemaker's front end, was developed in 2003 using the dynamic trans linear (DTL) circuit approach. The simulations showed that since the DTL approach can manage the necessary dynamic range and carry out non-linear operations at lower supply voltages, it is a good substitute for traditional sense amplifiers in intra-cardiac applications [6]. Moreover, novel methods introduced for employing battery-operated wearable ECG monitors which can detect pacemaker pulses at sample rates as low as 125 Hz. The results indicated that it is possible to achieve accurate pacer identification that can overcome the limitations of conventional ECG monitors [7]. The Pacemaker unit and the sensing and pacing units are shown in Figures 40.2 and 40.3.

Pacing

Cardiovascular pacemakers perform the essential function of pacing, which involves electrical impulses being sent to the heart to control its rhythm. Pacing is primarily used to treat anomalies in the electrical conduction system of the heart to ensure that the heart beats regularly and suitably. Back in the 1990s, extensive research was conducted on pacing related to atrioventricular

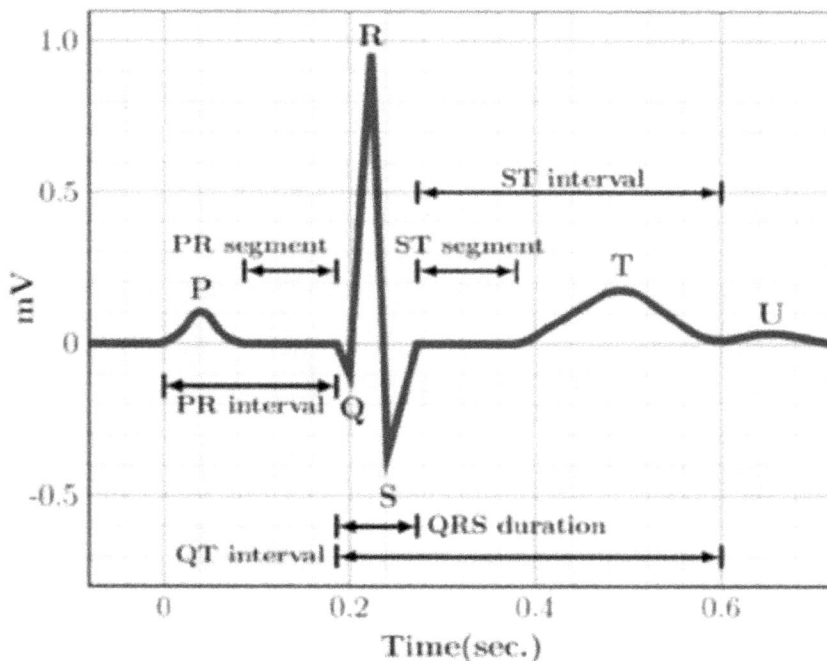

Figure 40.1 Cardiac cycle
Source: Author

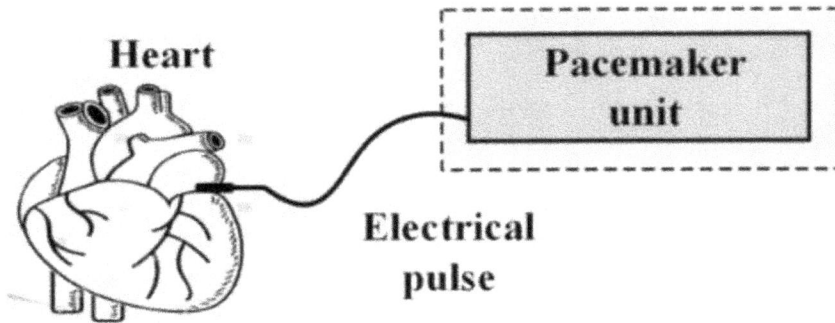

Figure 40.2 Pacemaker unit
Source: Author

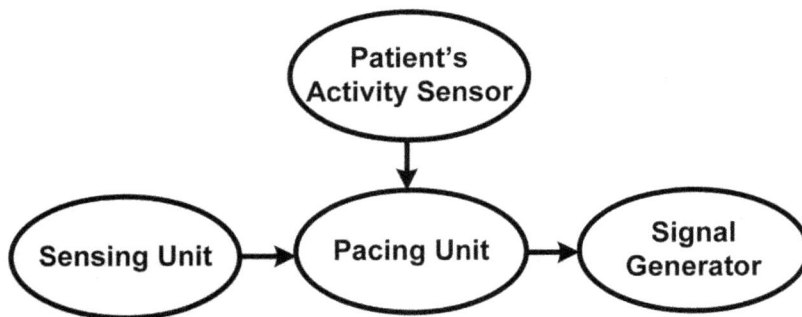

Figure 40.3 Block diagram of pacemaker unit
Source: Author

delay. This included a thorough examination of the possibility that a brief atrioventricular (AV) delay could be used to modify the timing of ventricular and atrial stimulations, improving cardiac function and congestive heart failure outcomes [8]; synchronized pacing with potential effects on patient outcomes and heart function by optimizing the atrioventricular delay parameter; and testing different atrioventricular delay settings, which provided important insights into the best pacing approaches for those with refractory heart failure [9,10]. A later development was the introduction of the atrial-based stimulation-focused minimal ventricular pacing mode. To evaluate the influence of the innovative pacing strategy on overall device performance as well as cardiac function, dual-chamber implantable cardioverter-defibrillator (ICD) research was conducted [11]. According to physiological signals, Rate-adaptive pacing, which was introduced recently, uses sensors to dynamically modify a cardiac pacemaker's heart rate. With the goal of emulating the heart's natural response to physical activity, these sensors make sure that the pacing rate satisfies the body's demand. While they have limitations in terms of accuracy issues, increased battery consumption, and environmental factors that must be considered in clinical settings, they also offer several strengths, such as improved physiological mimicry and individualized therapy [12].

Mode switching and timing cycles
The way that pacemakers switch their cycles and time is a critical factor in determining how well the device works and how well it can adjust to the patient's cardiac needs. To ensure synchronization with the natural cardiac cycle and optimize the delivery of pacing stimuli, these aspects are critical. Three main kinds of switching—demand, fixed, and rate-responsive pacing—are based on the patient's physiology. Automatic mode switching (AMS) algorithms made popular by Telectronics Meta DDDR 1250 devices, are among the algorithms used in mode switching. They identify atrial fibrillation (AF) and transition to non-tracking modes to prevent abrupt and erratic ventricular

pacing. Patients' symptoms at the onset of AF are influenced by the AMS algorithms' speed and specificity [13]. The ability to pace patients with paroxysmal atrial tachyarrhythmias (ATAs) and full atrioventricular block has been made possible by the development of automatic mode switching (MS) algorithms. Individuals who have dual-chamber pacemakers are at a heightened risk of experiencing ATA and MS. This risk may increase further with further pacemaker implantations and atrioventricular nodal ablation procedures. Studies suggest that atrial pacing algorithms might potentially postpone the occurrence of atrial tachyarrhythmias. However, for a sizable percentage of patients, questions about whether MS behavior is appropriate surface, and following AV nodal ablation, DDDR pacing may not significantly improve symptom levels when compared to VVIR. This calls into doubt the specifications for an ideal MS algorithm as well as the validity of certain MS concepts [14].

The AV, intra-ventricular, post-ventricular atrial refractory period (PVARP), and inter-atrial conduction time (IACT) are examples of timing cycles. In 1992, a three-letter pacing system code was developed [15], emphasizing dual-chamber and rate-responsive pacemakers. Later cardiac resynchronization therapy (CRT) devices that use left ventricular (LV) sensing were created to prevent competitive pacing beyond the LV myocardial refractory period, or LV T-wave protection (LVTP). This function modifies LV upper rate intervals by halting LV pacing for a predetermined amount of time. As more manufacturers include LVs in CRT systems, LVs—which give diagnostic data—Become increasingly important. Comprehending intricate temporal cycles involving LVs is essential for assessing devices and analyzing arrhythmias. The LVp initiation of LVURI and the impact of LVTP on RV-sensed events are two unique characteristics of Biotronik CRT systems with LV sensing [16].

Atrioventricular Delay

Dual chamber pacemakers are devices used to regulate the heart rate by pacing both the atrium and the ventricle. In the DDD pacing mode, the device can detect and pace both chambers, coordinating their activity to maintain optimal heart

function. However, optimizing the delay settings between the atrial and ventricular pacing, known as AV delay optimization, is crucial for ensuring effective cardiac function and improving patient outcomes. The DDD mode in dual-chamber pacemakers allows for the synchronous pacing of both the atria and ventricles. This mode is particularly useful in patients with AV block, bradycardia, or other conditions that disrupt the normal conduction pathway between the atria and ventricles. The primary parameters in DDD pacing that require optimization are the AV delay and the VV delay. AV delay: The time interval between the atrial and ventricular pacing. Optimizing this delay is essential to ensure that the ventricles are adequately filled before contraction. VV delay: The time interval between the pacing of the two ventricles in case of biventricular pacing, which might be present in some dual chamber devices. An essential component of cardiac pacing therapy is pacemaker atrioventricular delay adjustment. It guarantees effective heart function, lowers the chance of problems, and promotes a more regular and harmonious heartbeat. Depending on the unique traits and requirements of each patient, healthcare providers carefully adjust the AV delay settings in an effort to maximize support and enhance long-term results. The most actively pursued area in recent times to improve pacemaker performance, particularly in dual mode, is AV delay reduction. In 1999, 12 individuals with high-degree AV block underwent testing to examine the relationship between atrioventricular delay, QT interval, and cardiac function. The Swan-Ganz catheter was used to calculate the cardiac output (CO). The results indicated that when the AV interval was prolonged, there was a gradual increase in the CO and a decrease in the QT intervals. Ultimately, optimal AV delay at maximum QT interval and CO showed a strong and favorable association [17]. Pacing timing cycles are shown in Figure 40.4.

Three modes were compared to optimize atrioventricular delay (AVD). Men having DDD PM for high-degree AV Block who did not have any other significant cardiomyopathies were the only subjects of the study. The greatest cardiac output (CO) and ventricular filling time (FT) were obtained from the echo/Doppler examination of AVD. The myocardial performance index (MPI)

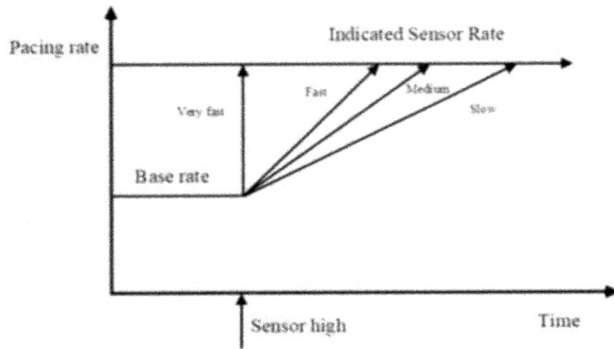

Figure 40.4 Pacing timings
Source: Author

was taken into account in addition to this. Ratios between relaxation time and isovolumic contraction were also looked at. Ultimately, the most favorable conditions of both the isovolumic contraction and relaxation phases were obtained, together with an MPI-adjusted AVD and a high CO [18]. Subsequently, alternative algorithms began to take the place of various delay optimization techniques. Reported that several techniques can be used to optimize atrioventricular delay (AVD), beginning with echocardiography, impedance cardiography (ICG), and general algorithms. General algorithms include atrioventricular hysteresis, dynamic AVD, negative AH search algorithm, and automated algorithms designed for AV optimization such as the Boston Scientific algorithm, St. Dude medical algorithm, and Sorin group algorithm. Since it is easy to use, quick, and repeatable, ICG to AVD optimization in patients with DDD pacemakers appears to be more intentional [19].

The focus of current research is on using Verilog to reduce delay. Taking into account the range of 30 to 70 beats per minute (bpm) reduces the latency between detecting and pacing [20]. Sensing the heartbeat and pacing the ventricle or atrium as needed are included in the planned work. A delay of one week was implemented using Xilinx 14.7. Nevertheless, rate adaptive pacing in a dual-chamber pacemaker is not the main topic of the research. Also, several methods are employed for rate-adaptive pacemakers. Heart rate and physical activity are the two key variables for rate-adaptive pacemakers. Usually, heart rate is the sole factor to consider while an individual is at rest. On the other hand, a

piezoelectric sensor detects the pressure exerted by exercise on human muscles and translates it into an electrical signal that the pacemaker's pulse generator receives. Less memory, less power, and less components were the results of this [21]. Also, there has been a recent surge in interest in low-power applications. As a result, investigations were conducted into low-power dual chamber pacemakers, which ultimately decreased the circuit's latency [22].

Result Analysis

The algorithm for DDD mode is as follows: The first "D" signifies the requirement for pacing in both chambers, the second "D" signifies the necessity for sensing in both chambers, and the third "D" signifies the presence of both inhibitory and triggered modes. The algorithm was proposed by Dwivedi and Srivastava. The occurrences detected should not happen during the recovery phase, nor the intervals of signal suppression. If they arise, you can disregard them. The corresponding speeds will happen. Which can continue if the actual event does not happen inside the time cycles. At any one moment, there may be four distinct rhythms: Atrial Sense and Ventricle Sense, Atrial Sense and Ventricle Pace, Atrial Pace and Ventricle Sense, and Atrial Pace and Ventricle Pace. The flow of the DDD methodology at a structural level, as seen in Figure 40.5. The proposed strategy algorithm is shown in Figure 40.6. The DDD control will receive and process all the inputs, ensuring that the timers for the inputs are synchronized, and then communicate the corresponding outputs. The analysis includes the results of the flowchart of a DDD pacemaker.

For simulating the digital components of the pacemaker, the flowchart was implemented in Xilings Vivado and the outputs are taken at different cases of sensing. Figure 40.7a, the clock signal is strong at 7.26 µs, serving as the timing reference. The system remains in an initialization state initially due to the continuous high level of the reset signal. The atrium has detected a strong signal, indicating an atrial event, whereas the ventricle has detected a low signal, indicating the absence of a ventricular event.

None of the timing signals have been activated, hence none of the time intervals have passed. There is no pacing happening in either the atrium or ventricle at this time because it has not been confirmed. A state transition is happening in this scenario as the finite state machine (FSM) is moving from state 2 to state 1, perhaps triggered by the detection of an atrial event by the device. Figure 40.7b, time of 16.31 μs, the reset signal has deserted, and that means the machine is no longer in the initialization state but in normal operation. The atrium-sensed signal is high, and the ventricle-sensed signal is low. The fact that these latter two signals are combined means that the atrial event is being sensed, and the ventricular event has not yet occurred. Both the timing signals, VALRL_expired and AVI expired, are now inactive. The countdown for these last two periods has not yet commenced. The atrial and ventricular pacing signals are now at a low level, resulting in no delivery of pacing to either the atrium or ventricle. The FSM has transitioned to state 1, where it will remain until there is a change in the system inputs that trigger the act of operation. Figure 40.7c, the clock signal maintains its regular toggling, driving the system's timing, with a duration of 34.57 μs. All atrium-sensed and ventricle-sensed signals are low, indicating that neither atrial nor ventricular events have been detected at this particular time. The VALRL_expired signal remains inactive, while the AVI expired remains low as well, indicating that the timing intervals of the pacemaker have not yet reached their expiration. The signals from the pace atrium and pace ventricle continue

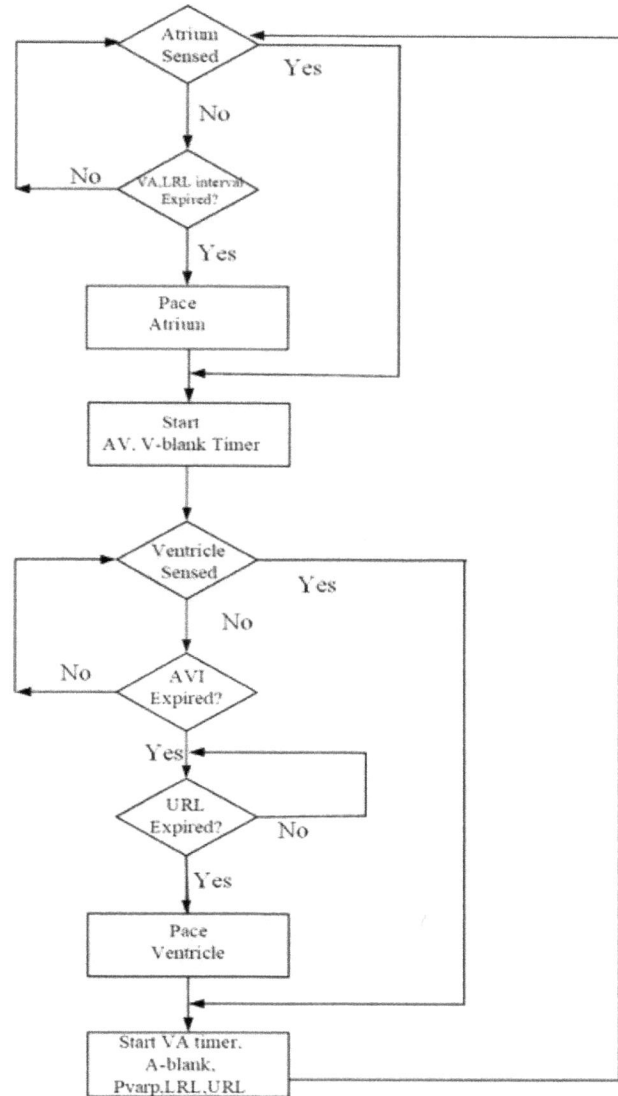

Figure 40.6 Flow of DDD mode
Source: Author

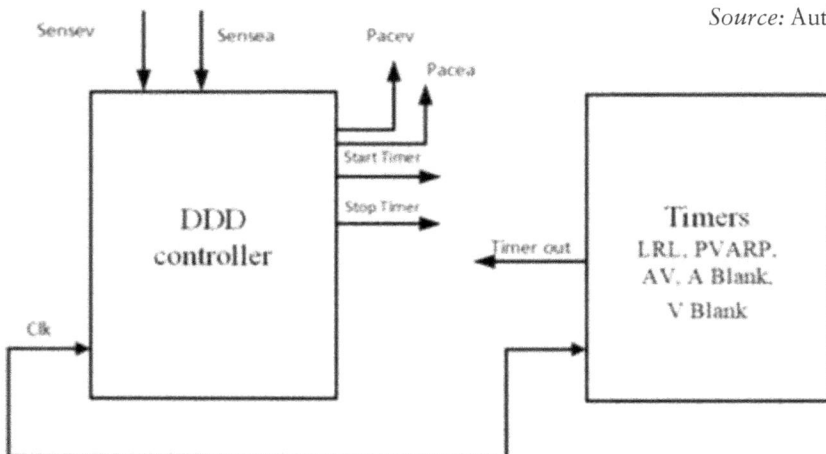

Figure 40.5 Organizational flow of DDD mode
Source: Author

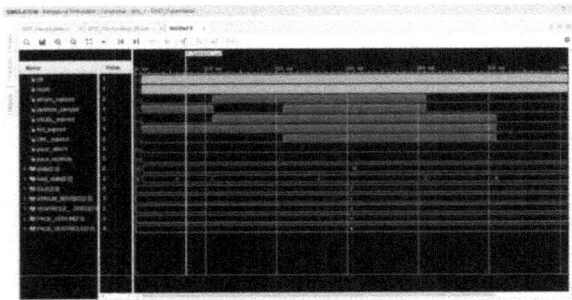

(a)

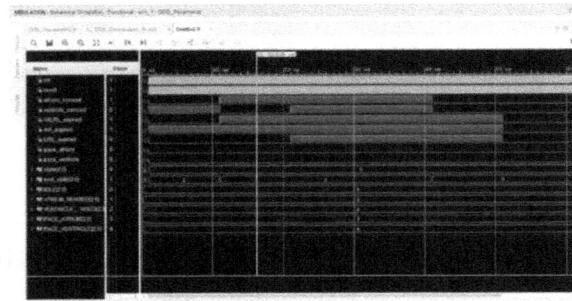

(b)

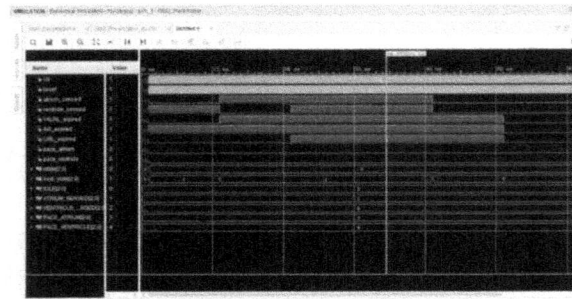

(c)

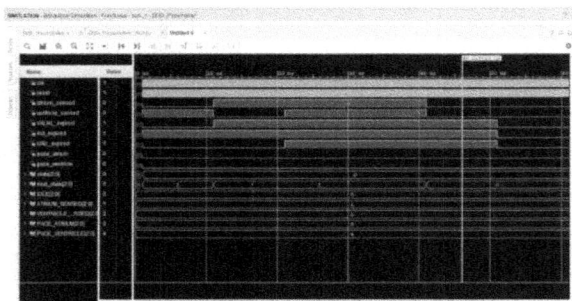

(d)

Figure 40.7 Response of DDD mode for different timing cycles

Source: Author

to be at a low level, resulting in the absence of any pacing pulses being delivered. The FSM maintains state 1 until the next event occurs or the specified timings expire, which then triggers a transition to another state. The system is now in a stable state, awaiting either additional input or a timed event that would trigger subsequent transitions in FSM. Figure 40.7d, a time of 46.01 µs, the simulation hits a crucial moment: the pace ventricle signal becomes high, indicating that the pacemaker is sending a pacing pulse to the ventricle. This refers to a transition in a state machine where the state changes from pace_atrium (3) to pace_ventricle (4). The clock signal keeps toggling, as it is supposed to do, driving the timing of the overall simulation. At this stage, the signal detected by the ventricle has returned to a low level. The main focus now is solely on regulating the ventricle's pace to properly coordinate with the atrium. This section of the simulation verifies that a DDD pacemaker is capable of controlling the pacing of the heart, taking into account both detected events and internal pacing.

Conclusion

Modern pacemakers come with built-in algorithms that automatically adjust AV and VV delays based on real-time cardiac performance metrics. The AV delay optimization and sophisticated mode-switching algorithms have further refined pacing performance, thereby giving it more synchronization with the intrinsic rhythm of the heart and maximizing patient outcomes. Moreover, reductions in latency at the circuit level and in power consumption have made way for more efficient and long-life pacemakers. This would fulfill a crucial criterion: to design devices that adapt to the specific needs of each patient, while also minimizing the difficulty of regular battery change. AV delay optimization in DDD mode dual chamber pacemakers is a critical aspect of patient care that can significantly impact clinical outcomes. By using a combination of echocardiography, ECG analysis, and device algorithms, clinicians can tailor pacemaker settings to the individual needs of the patient, leading to improved cardiac function and quality of life. This study aims to explore and document the latest methods, findings, and challenges in optimizing AV delay in DDD mode dual chamber pacemakers, contributing to better patient outcomes and advancing the field of cardiac pacing. As research continues to push the boundaries of pacemaker technology, innovations that aim at improving the reliability of devices and patient comfort and generally contribute to cardiac health should be the focus. All this effort must culminate in millions of people worldwide living healthy lives.

References

[1] Bikki, P., Dhiraj, Y., and Nivas Kumar, R. V. S. (2023). Design and implementation of a sense amplifier for low-power cardiac pacemaker. *Journal of Circuits, Systems and Computers*, 32(9), 2350148.

[2] Smith, T. W. (2020). Optimal AV delay in dual chamber pacemakers: An evidence-based approach. *Journal of Cardiac Electrophysiology*, 31(12), 2887–28949.

[3] Mazzella, A. J. (2021). Shifting trends in timing of pacemaker implantation after transcatheter aortic valve replacement. *Cardiovascular Interventions*, 14(2), 232–234.

[4] Michel, S. (2020). From clock to functional pacemaker. *European Journal of Neuroscience*, 51(1), 482–493.

[5] Astiz, M. (2022). Astrocytes as essential timekeepers of the central pacemaker. *Glia*, 70(5), 808–819.

[6] Simen, P. (2023). Timescale invariance in the pacemaker-accumulator family of timing models. *Timing and Time Perception*, 1(2), 159–188.

[7] Nallathambi, G. (2020). An innovative hybrid approach for detection of pacemaker pulses at low sampling frequency. In IEEE EMBC, Montreal, QC, Canada, (pp. 5012–5015).

[8] Gold, M. R. (1995). Dual-chamber pacing with a short atrioventricular delay in congestive heart failure: a randomized study. *Journal of the American College of Cardiology*, 26(4), 967–973.

[9] Linde, C. (1995). Results of atrioventricular synchronous pacing with optimized delay in patients with severe congestive heart failure. *The American Journal of Cardiology*, 75(14), 919–923.

[10] Bikki, P., Dhiraj, Y., and Nivas Kumar, R. V. S. (2023). Implementation of a dual-chamber pacemaker for low-power applications. In 2023 Fifth International Conference on Electrical, Computer and Communication Technologies (ICECCT), Erode, India, (pp. 1–5).

[11] Shinbane, J. S. (1997). Evaluation of acute dual-chamber pacing with a range of atrioventricular delays on cardiac performance in refractory heart failure. *Journal of the American College of Cardiology*, 30(5), 1295–1300.

[12] Sweeney, M. (2004). Randomized pilot study of a new atrial-based minimal ventricular pacing mode in dual-chamber implantable cardioverter-defibrillators. *Heart Rhythm*, 1(2), 160–167.

[13] Trohman, R. G. (2020). Sensors for rate-adaptive pacing: How they work, strengths, and limitations. *Journal of Cardiovascular Electrophysiology*, 31(11), 3009–3027.

[14] Leung, S. K. (2000). A comparative study on the behavior of three different automatic mode switching dual chamber pacemakers to intracardiac recordings of clinical atrial fibrillation. *Pacing and Clinical Electrophysiology*, 23(12), 2086–2096.

[15] Israel, C. W. (2002). Analysis of mode switching algorithms in dual chamber pacemakers. *Pacing and Clinical Electrophysiology : PACE*, 25(3), 380–393.

[16] Hayes, D. L. (1992). Timing cycles of permanent pacemakers. *Cardiology Clinics*, 10(4), 593–608.

[17] Barold, S. S., and Kucher, A. (2014). Understanding the timing cycles of a cardiac resynchronization device designed with left ventricular sensing. *Pacing and Clinical Electrophysiology : PACE*, 37(10), 1324–1337.

[18] Ishikawa, T. (1999). Relationship between atrioventricular delay, QT interval and cardiac function in patients with implanted DDD pacemakers. *Journal of the Working Groups on Cardiac Pacing, Arrhythmias, and Cardiac Cellular Electrophysiology of the European Society of Cardiology*, 1(3), 192–196.

[19] Cristina Porciani, M. (2004). A perspective on atrioventricular delay optimization in patients with a dual chamber pacemaker. *Pacing and Clinical Electrophysiology : PACE*, 27(3), 333–338.

[20] Klimczak, A. (2010). Optimization of atrio-ventricular delay in patients with dual-chamber pacemaker. *International Journal of Cardiology*, 141(3), 222–226.

[21] Ray, S. (2019). Implementation of low delay dual chamber pacemaker using verilog. In 6th International Conference on Signal Processing and Integrated Networks (SPIN), Noida, India, (pp. 59–62).

[22] Srivastava, R. (2020). Low delay rate adaptive pacemaker using FPGA embedded piezoelectric sensor. *Journal of Medical Engineering and Technology*, 44(7), 423–430.

41 Automatic live location sharing for real-time vehicle tracking

Keerthi, T.[a], Apurva Kumari[b], Chinnaiah, M. C.[c], Sai Kiran, P.[d], Sai Charan, N.[e], Ajay Sai, P.[f], and Srikar, R.[g]

Department of Electronics and Communication Engineering, B V Raju Institute of Technology, Telangana, India

Abstract

In the contemporary world that is characterized by increased connection, it is essential to deliver real-time position information to passengers. Thus, we introduce the problems that come with manual communication and intermittent internet connection, and as a response, suggest an automated live location-sharing system. This system combines an Arduino board with a global positioning system (GPS) module placed on the vehicle to come up with the tracking system. When the car is started, the Arduino senses the voltage increase and turns on the GPS to get the exact location of the car. After obtaining these coordinates, they are transferred to a specific web server that stores and processes them instantly. In order to improve the communication even more, a bulk SMS service is employed to send the passengers a dynamic link to the live location. Thus, this solution provisively guarantees to provide real-time global tracking of the vehicle's location irrespective of the absence of internet connection. This approach enhances the ease and reliability of tracking vehicle movements by automating the location-sharing process and using SMS for notices.

Keywords: Application programming interface, Arduino UNO, Arduino UNO-real-time tracking, automated location sharing, bulk SMS service, cell phone, global positioning system, gobal system for mobile communication, Google Maps API, location-sharing, web server integration

Introduction

Efficient time management is a critical objective for commuters relying on buses as an economical transportation option. Whether for professional or personal travel, users demand dependable transit solutions. However, the unpredictability inherent in bus services—such as traffic congestion, unexpected delays, variable passenger demand, and irregular departure times—often impedes passengers' ability to anticipate bus arrivals accurately.

To address these challenges, an advanced solution for real-time bus location dissemination has been developed. This system integrates Arduino with global positioning system (GPS) and global system for mobile communication (GSM) technologies to automate location tracking and sharing. Unlike conventional methods that depend on manual updates or continuous internet access, this approach initiates automatic location reporting upon vehicle ignition, transmitting real-time data through SMS. This feature ensures that passengers receive uninterrupted and reliable access to live location information, even in areas with limited internet connectivity.

Central to this innovation is the Arduino, which functions as the system's primary controller. The convergence of GPS and cellular networks enables precise, real-time vehicle tracking and location sharing. This development represents a significant advancement in transport management, particularly benefiting public bus systems that struggle with strict adherence to schedules and timetables.

Related Works

A dependable real-time tracking infrastructure was devised harnessing the capabilities of the GPS [1]. The system comprises a portable tracking unit and a central tracking center facilitating

[a]keerthi.t@bvrit.ac.in, [b]apurva.kumari@bvrit.ac.in, [c]chinnaaiah.mc@bvrit.ac.in, [d]20211a04h0@bvrit.ac.in, [e]20211a04f2@bvrit.ac.in, [f]20211a04g0@bvrit.ac.in, [g]20211a04h9@bvrit.ac.in

DOI: 10.1201/9781003616399-41

seamless bidirectional location transmission. The portable device receives GPS coordinates through a Garmin 18-5 HZ GPS receiver, PICI6F877 microcontroller unit, and SIMCOM 300 GSM modem assembly. Satellite-transmitted location data is acquired by the GPS receiver and subsequently processed by the microcontroller to extract precise GPS coordinates. The extracted longitude and latitude data are then relayed to the tracking device via the GSM module. At the tracking center, longitude and latitude SMS transmissions are received through a dedicated GSM modem, dynamically updating the location on Google Maps via the Google Maps application programming interface (API).

Shinde and Mane [2] have innovated a vehicle monitoring system specifically tailored for school vehicles, prioritizing passenger safety. This model utilizes a Raspberry Pi as the central device, integrating GPS, GSM, and GPRS functionalities via the SIM908 module. The GPS component tracks the vehicle's real-time location, while GPRS facilitates the transmission of tracking information to designated servers. Additionally, GSM is employed to notify the vehicle owner regarding the vehicle's status. The system maintains a predefined route stored in the database, cross-referencing it with the current bus position. Any deviations from the route or instances of speeding trigger alerts to the vehicle owner through the GSM module. Furthermore, the system detects temperature changes, potentially indicating leakages, and issues alerts accordingly. The vehicle's location data is stored in a MYSQL database, continuously updated via GPRS. Passengers have access to the bus's live location through a dedicated web page.

An Arduino Intel Galileo serves as the central unit [3]. The setup incorporates the SIM908 module, integrating GSM, GPS, and GPRS functionalities. The GPS module captures the vehicle's precise location, which is then updated on a web server via GPRS. The GSM module operates by receiving signals from the owner to request the device's location through a call. This system primarily functions as a theft tracking mechanism for vehicles.

Rahman et al., [4] have devised a system that displays a vehicle's location coordinates on an LCD screen. This system integrates GPS and GSM

communication technologies in conjunction with Arduino Uno. The GPS component retrieves the vehicle's precise location, subsequently transmitted to passengers via GSM using longitude and latitude coordinates. Furthermore, these coordinates are displayed on the LCD screen and can also be accessed and visualized by passengers using Google Maps.

Ibrahim et al., [5] introduced a methodology utilizing Google Earth and GpsGate software to present real-time vehicle locations. Arduino Uno serves as the hardware component alongside the GPS. The GPS retrieves the vehicle's location, which is then transmitted to GpsGate. GpsGate converts this location data into longitude and latitude coordinates. These coordinates are subsequently relayed to Google Earth, enabling the display of the vehicle's live location within the Google Earth interface. Moreover, this location data from Google Earth can be streamed on various online platforms such as Manycam and YouTube.

Khin and Oo, [6] have engineered a continuous vehicle tracking system employing a GPS and GSM, interfaced with the Arduino Uno R3. The GPS module retrieves the vehicle's location, subsequently transmitted to the database through GSM. For location updates, the system integrates XAMPP with the Apache HTTP server and MYSQL database. Additionally, the system embeds the Google Maps API into a webpage, providing real-time visualization of the vehicle's location on Google Maps.

In this paper, GPS and GSM are used, which is interfaced with eh Arduino UNO [7]. According to the National Marine Electronics Association protocol form, the GPS will fetch the vehicle's location. Once the location is fetched, the longitude and latitude are displayed on the LCD screen. The location's latitude and longitude are shared with the user's mobile using the GSM. The location is displayed in the app using the GPS location and map software, which can be downloaded from the play store.

Karkare et al. [8] have introduced a methodology aimed at enabling parental tracking of a child's location. The system comprises two distinct modules: the child side module and the parent side module. The child side module integrates GPS and GSM modules to fetch and transmit the child's location to the parent side. On the parent side, a mobile application receives location coordinates via SMS, promptly displaying the location within the application upon reaching predefined checkpoints.

Adam et al., [9] present a system employing GSM and GPS modules interfaced with an Arduino board. This model facilitates the transmission of a vehicle's location to the user through a specific trigger, denoted by a lowercase letter 'a'. Upon receiving a lowercase 'a' letter from the user to the system's GSM module, the GPS is activated to retrieve the vehicle's location. Subsequently, the GPS coordinates are sent to the user via the GSM module in the form of a Google Maps link.

Chander et al., [10] introduced an application tailored for JAVA-enabled mobile devices. This application harnesses GPS services to transmit location data from one device to others via SMS. Through this application, users gain the ability to visualize their location on Google Maps within the app itself. Additionally, users can share their current location with friends by leveraging a web server integration within the application.

Moumen et al., [11] developed a real-time GPS tracking system for IoT-enabled connected vehicles, combining GPS technology with an IoT framework. The system captures and transmits the vehicle's location data to a central server in real-time, enabling continuous monitoring and efficient fleet management. This approach enhances vehicle tracking and operational efficiency.

Mundada et al., [12] propose a smart bus tracking system using GPS and GSM modules interfaced with an Arduino. The system captures real-time bus location data via GPS and transmits it through GSM to a central server. Passengers can access live location updates through a web application, and an SMS alert system provides additional convenience for real-time tracking, enhancing the overall public transport experience.

Proposed Technique

The device's central aim is to automate the dissemination of the bus's location to passengers, removing the need for manual involvement. It begins by consistently acquiring the bus's location data using a GPS module. This real-time data is then promptly updated onto a web server

through a GSM module, forming the foundational infrastructure for a website. This site integrates the Google Maps API to visually depict the bus's whereabouts. The critical final step involves the immediate communication of the bus's location to passengers at the start of its journey, a function seamlessly handled by the bus itself.

Block diagram
The block diagram for the proposed work is shown in Figure 41.1 below.

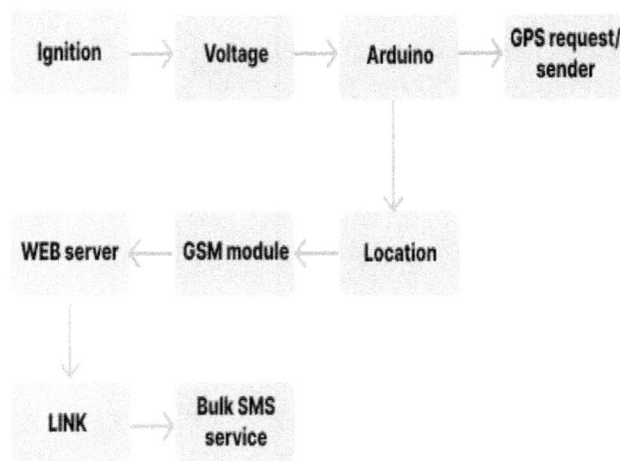

Figure 41.1 Block Diagram of proposed work
Source: Author

The proposed system is controlled by an Arduino unit situated within the vehicle, responsible for coordinating the functions of the GPS and GSM modules. The bus's location is obtained in terms of longitude and latitude and subsequently transmitted to the web server using the GSM module for storage. This stored location data is then dynamically showcased on the website. As soon as the bus commences its journey, a link to the website featuring the live bus location is instantly shared with passengers.

Flow chart
The flow of execution for the proposed device is given below:

Upon the ignition of the bus, both the Arduino Nano and GSM module are initiated, powering up the system. The GPS module takes charge of transmitting the bus's precise location data to the Arduino board, which, upon receipt, triggers an

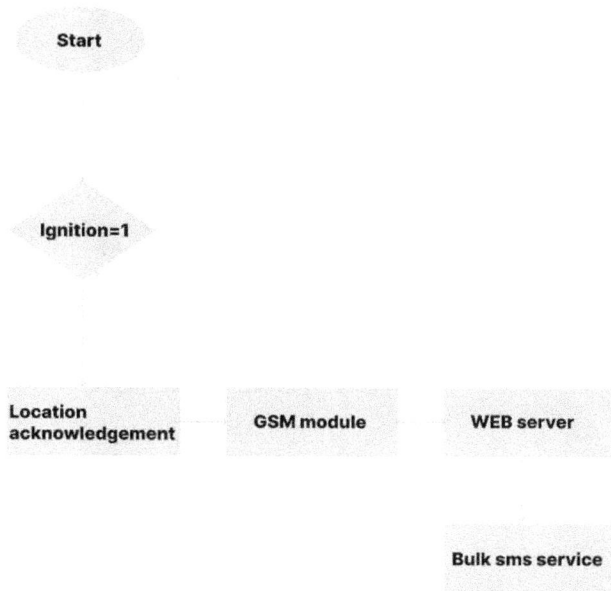

Figure 41.2 Flow chart
Source: Author

acknowledgment signaling the location's receipt, denoted as '1'. Following this, the updated location information is seamlessly relayed to the web server, constituting the backend infrastructure for the associated website, facilitated through the GSM module's capabilities. It's noteworthy that the link to the website is shared via SMS exclusively at the beginning of this operational cycle. This strategy ensures that passengers have unfettered access to the bus's real-time location throughout their journey.

Pseudo code
1. Initialize system and required modules (SIM800L, NEO-6M GPS).
2. Establish serial communication with Arduino IDE, SIM800L, and NEO-6M GPS modules.
3. Configure SIM800L module settings for SMS, GPRS, and HTTP functionality.
4. Setup variables and intervals for GPS data transmission.
5. In a continuous loop:
   a. Check for available data from SIM800L and NEO-6M GPS modules.
   b. If available, read and process data accordingly.
   c. Collect GPS location data and format it.
   d. Send GPS data to a designated web server endpoint using HTTP requests.

6. Define functions for sending AT commands to the SIM800L module.
7. Handle AT command responses and process them for desired actions.

Components and specifications
1. **NEO-6M GPS module:** Responsible for getting the bus's real time location in terms of the longitude and latitude. Selected for it's high accuracy, short time to first fix, low power consumption and possible integration with the Arduino. Specifications: Operating voltage 2. 7V–3. 6V, position accuracy 2.5m (CEP), cold start 27s, hot start 1s, interface UART (9600).
2. **SIM800L GSM module:** It was applied in transmitting GPS data to a web server through GPRS and passing of SMS to passengers. Selected on the basis of small size, high dependability, and low costs for real time transmissions. Specifications: Operating voltage 3. 4V–4. 4V, quad-band 850/900/1800/1900, GPRS class 12 and interface UART can be set the baud rate.
   Justification: The NEO-6M GPS module functions with low power consumption and sharp tracking which is suitable for the system's automated operation as does the SIM800L GSM module for data transmission.

Results

Working kit
The below pictures show the device kit:
As the bus begins its journey, voltage is supplied to both the Arduino and GSM module. This event triggers the transmission of a website link to the passengers.

In this device, the integration of key components was carefully executed by establishing precise connections to the Arduino Uno microcontroller. For the GPS module, the Rx and Tx pins were connected to digital pins D9 and D8, respectively. Power for the GPS module was drawn from the Arduino Uno's 5V pin, and the ground was connected to the Arduino's ground pin.

Simultaneously, the GSM module (Sim800L) was connected with the Rx and Tx pins linked to digital pins D3 and D2 on the Arduino Uno. The GSM module was powered by an external source, capable of delivering up to 2 amps

Figure 41.3 Working kit
Source: Author

through a buck-down converter. A common ground reference was established, connecting the external power source, Arduino Uno, and GSM module. These precise connections enabled seamless communication between the Arduino Uno and both the GPS and GSM modules, forming a robust framework for our project.

At the start of the bus's journey, the system automatically initiates the transmission of a web link for passenger access. This automated process seamlessly begins as the bus commences its operation, facilitating the transmission of the link to passengers. Simultaneously, the GPS module actively gathers precise location data of the bus. This acquired location information undergoes a systematic process within the system, forwarding it to designated web servers responsible for hosting real-time location details.

The system operates in a manner where the bus's location undergoes continuous updates on the designated web server. This consistent updating process ensures that the longitude and latitude values retrieved from the bus, once transmitted to the web server, are stored securely within the system's database, facilitated by PHPMyAdmin. These stored longitude and latitude coordinates are then employed to visually represent the bus's precise location on Google Maps.

The integration of the system with Google Maps API allows for a seamless display of the stored longitude and latitude coordinates on the Google Maps interface. Leveraging the collected geographical data stored within the web server's database, the Google Maps API is utilized to dynamically showcase the bus's location in real time.

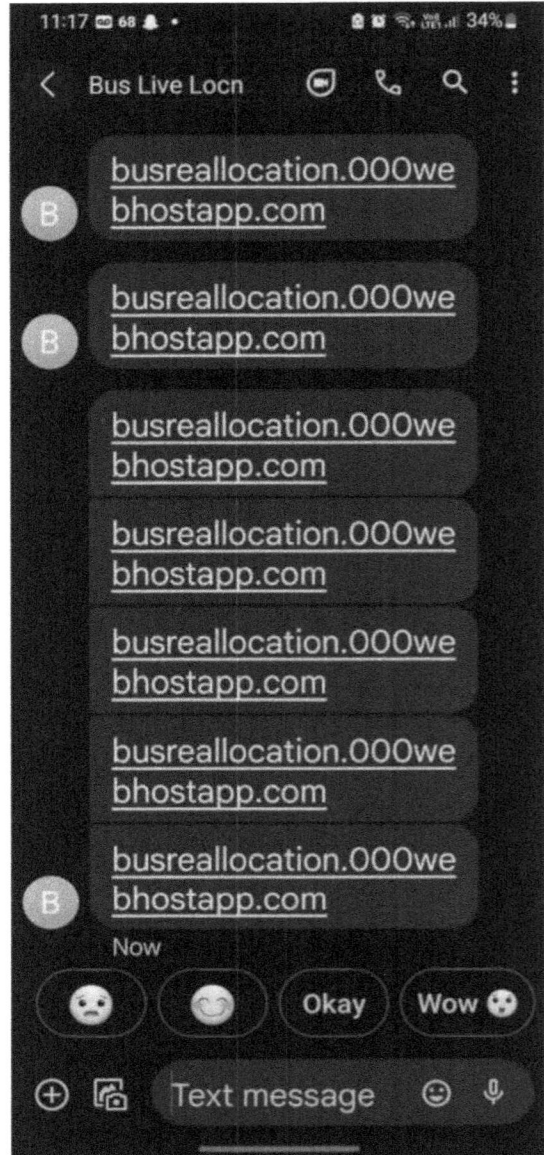

Figure 41.4 Live location message
Source: Author

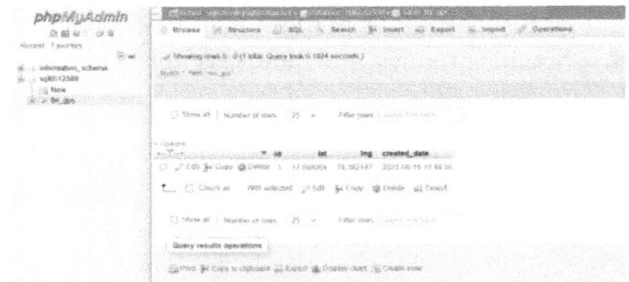

Figure 41.5 Coordinates storing in web server
Source: Author

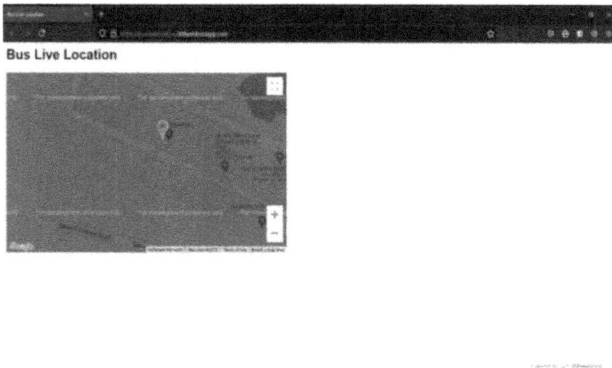

Figure 41.6 Bus live location
Source: Author

Conclusion and Future Work

The "Arduino Based Automatic Live Location Sharing " system can therefore be said to have achieved its main purpose in the sharing of real-time bus location information to the passengers. The system automates the process of sharing locations which reduces the frequency of updates and improves the passengers' experience in transportation. The incorporation of Arduino board, NEO-6M GPS module, SIM800L GSM module makes it possible to achieve accurate tracking of the bus and web server, Google map API to give a real-time view of the bus position.

As the future ideas, few enhancements could improve the current operation of the system as follows. Possible enhancements include the use of a camera to stream bus's interior on the bus in real time, monitoring the status of the engine to provide with maintenance updates, and defining distances traveled by the bus. Furthermore, creating android and iOS versions of the dedicated application to navigate the platform and store location information may be more convenient in terms of the users' experience. All these enhancements would add up to a stronger and better solution for real-time vehicle tracking which in turn would enhance the comfort of passengers in their means of transportation.

References

[1] Dafallah, H. A. A. (2014). Design and implementation of an accurate real time GPS tracking system. In The Third International Conference on E-Technologies and Networks for Development (ICeND2014). IEEE.

[2] Shinde, P. A., and Mane, Y. B. (2015). Advanced vehicle monitoring and tracking system based on Raspberry Pi. In 2015 IEEE 9th International Conference on Intelligent Systems and Control (ISCO). IEEE.

[3] Mohamad, O. A., Hameed, R. T., and Ţăpuş, N. (2016). Design and implementation of real time tracking system based on arduino intel galileo. In 2016 8th International Conference on Electronics, Computers and Artificial Intelligence (ECAI). IEEE.

[4] Rahman, M. M., Mou, J. R., Tara, K., and Sarkar, M. I. (2016). Real time Google map and Arduino based vehicle tracking system. In 2016 2nd International Conference on Electrical, Computer and Telecommunication Engineering (ICECTE). IEEE.

[5] Ibrahim, M. Y. M., and Audah, L. (2017). Real-time bus location monitoring using Arduino. In AIP Conference Proceedings. (Vol. 1883. no. 1). AIP Publishing LLC.

[6] Khin, J. M. M., and Oo, N. N. (2018). Real-time vehicle tracking system using Arduino, GPS, GSM and web-based technologies. *International Journal of Science and Engineering Applications*, 7(11), 433–436.

[7] Htwe, T. T., and Hlaing, K. K. (2019). Arduino based tracking system using GPS and GSM. *International Journal for Advance Research and Development*, 4(8), 11–15.

[8] Ganorkar, Ankur, et al. "Live Tracking System." *International Journal Of Engneering Research & Technology (IJERT)*, Volume 9 (2020)..

[9] Adam, B. A. M., Ismil, M. J. M., and Jameelallah, Y. A. M. (2022). GPS Vehicle Tracking and Shift Detection. PhD Diss.

[10] Chandra, A., Jain, S., and Qadeer, M. A. (2011). GPS locator: an application for location tracking and sharing using GPS for Java enabled handhelds. In 2011 International Conference on Computational Intelligence and Communication Networks. IEEE.

[11] Moumen, I., Rafalia, N., Abouchabaka, J., and Aoufi, M. (2023). Real-time GPS tracking system for IoT-enabled connected vehicles. In E3S Web of Conferences, (Vol. 412). EDP Sciences.

[12] Mundada, K., Patti, S., Rajguru, T., Savji, P., and Shambharkar, S. (2023). Smart bus real-time tracking system using GSM and GPS module. In International Conference on ICT for Sustainable Development. Singapore: Springer Nature Singapore.

42 IOT based robotic solutions for hospital security using ESP32 microcontroller

Prasad, S. V. S.[1,a], Ch. Bhavya[2,b] and Manoj Kumar[3,c]

[1]Professor, Dept. of ECE, MLR Institute of Technology, Hyderabad, Telangana, India

[2]M. Tech Student, Department of ECE, MLR Institute of Technology, Hyderabad, Telangana, India

[3]Assistant Professor, Dept. of ECE, MLR Institute of Technology, Hyderabad, Telangana, India

Abstract

In this work, we have created an interactive robot with the goal of improving online surveillance and hospital security. The main objective is to build a watchful robot that can keep an eye on people's movements inside hospital grounds, lowering security risks and guaranteeing patient safety. The robot, which has a wireless camera attached to it, broadcasts live video straight from the field. This feature is a huge advantage for the hospital since it helps to reduce hazards and stop unauthorized activity. Visibility is improved with a mounted camera, and an Internet of Things application uses a wireless network to control the robot's functions. Here, the primary sensors are a smoke detector, which detects changes in air quality to quickly alert users to possible fires. Furthermore, by utilizing its capacity to recognize metallic components commonly present in explosives, a metal sensor assists in the identification of explosive devices. A Bluetooth application facilitates control of the robot, guaranteeing smooth operation and real-time sensor updates. When the robot detects a fire hazard, its flame sensor notifies the central station, and its gas sensor keeps an eye out for dangerous gases in the air and can sound an alarm when needed. The metal detector also finds metallic objects that are hidden and possible dangers like bombs. These robots are essential for hospital surroundings and will only become more so in the future, proving their worth now and their ability to improve overall security protocols.

Keywords: ESP 32, hospital security, Internet of Things, microcontroller

Introduction

This project sketches a network of real-world objects that have sensors and software implanted in them to share data online using Internet of Things technology. The concept offers an all-encompassing solution, an ESP 32 microcontroller-based spy robot that addresses security concerns and the potential for any unwanted attacks. By utilizing an IoT cloud platform, the robot seeks to lessen risks to workers and enhance military surveillance capabilities [1,2]. The primary protocol makes it possible to operate the robot remotely and share data in real time over an Internet of Things cloud platform. The security and safety concerns for army personnel led to the development of a device that uses a camera module for direction control and live broadcasting to identify unauthorized people. In addition, a metal detector to detect bombs and mines is integrated. Upon detecting a threat, it initiates GPS to alert users and determine its exact location. The robot is positioned as a reliable and secure espionage instrument for use in conflict scenarios because of its multifunctional design, which enables the remote identification of individuals who are not authorized. Technology integration into military applications has historically been very helpful in enhancing operational capabilities and ensuring human safety. They have advanced features including a night vision camera, gas sensor, and metal detector installed. The robots use a range of sensors, such as accelerometers, GPS, LIDAR, cameras, and infrared sensors, to drive autonomously, recognize targets, and avoid obstacles. Communication is made possible via ESP 32, ensuring a seamless link with remote operators, command centers, and other robots.

[a]hodece@mlrinstitutions.ac.in, [b]chbhavya2814@gmail.com, [c]dr.manojkumar@mlrinstitutions.ac.in

DOI: 10.1201/9781003616399-42

Gas sensors monitor the quality of the air, fire sensors detect flames, and metal detectors alert operators to hidden explosive devices in order to increase situational awareness, safety, and operational effectiveness [3,4]. The spy robot is an example of cutting-edge technology designed to monitor combat zones safely and effectively. The robot can be customized to meet the specific needs of different military missions and has real-time intelligence gathering capabilities. Its primary objective is to visually cover combat zones by using real-time video capturing and wireless network transmission of recordings to remote areas. Because of this, military personnel can make informed decisions without compromising their safety. The objective of the project is to develop an Android application-controlled, ESP 32 microcontroller-based security robot that can function wirelessly, acknowledging the challenges that the armed forces face even with advanced technology. The robot should be able to move in all directions, have a real-time wireless camera, and have stable, secure wireless connectivity. The robot's user-friendly Android application makes it simple for soldiers to monitor human activity in combat areas and spot any threats [5]. Nocturnal and night vision cameras, in addition to metal detectors, aid in heightened security and intelligence gathering. The robot may be operated remotely via phone calls, which makes it a versatile tool for obstacle detection, monitoring, and finding potentially dangerous weapons in hard-to-reach places. This article looks into using robots for monitoring activities in remote locations and conflict zones as a way to replace human labor and overcome limitations. Cutting edge technologies are crucial since exploring these locations after terrible disasters puts individuals in danger. One of the main advantages of deploying robots in these kinds of scenarios is their ability to perform continuous surveillance while circumventing human presence limits. The Internet of Things (IoT) is also incorporated to address the problem of a limited frequency range, allowing for remote control and information receiving for the robot [6]. The autonomous mode of the robot allows it to detect obstacles using ultrasonic sensors and make course adjustments automatically. An inbuilt live streaming camera enhances the sensor that powers the robot's touch

sensitivity. In addition, GPS is used to transmit exact location of robots. Real-time surveillance of critical locations is made possible by this creative method, which also reduces human risk and delivers important intelligence for military and security purposes. Modern robots and IoT technologies enhance the efficiency of monitoring and responding in strategically significant and potentially dangerous locations. This project's main goal is to create a sophisticated spy robot that can improve surveillance and information collection in dangerous situations, especially in conflict zones. This adaptable robot is made to carry out a variety of tasks, such as threat detection, real-time data transmission, and improving overall security [7].

Literature Survey

Robotics and the IoT have recently conveyed about major breakthroughs in a number of fields, including healthcare. This overview of the literature inspects the advancements and research that have been made in this area, with an emphasis on applications that make use of the ESP32 microcontroller. Hospitals must constantly monitor vital infrastructure and deal with a variety of security issues, such as unauthorized entry to sensitive areas [8,9]. Human limitations and the requirement for instant action make traditional security measures frequently ineffective. The deployment of networked devices with autonomous monitoring, communication, and response capabilities is made possible by IoT, providing a solution. IoT-enabled robotic devices can greatly improve hospital security by roaming hallways, keeping an eye on restricted areas, and even communicating with patients for access control and identification. These robots use cameras, actuators, and sensors to collect information, process it, and respond accordingly in real time. Due to its built-in Bluetooth and Wi-Fi, low power consumption, and support for many interfaces (GPIO, I2C, and SPI), the ESP32 microcontroller has become more and more popular in Internet of Things applications. It is ideally suited for coordinating and interacting with sensors and actuators in robotic systems intended for hospital security because of these characteristics [10,11]. The viability and efficacy of IoT-based robotic hospital security solutions utilizing the ESP32 microcontroller have been shown in a number of studies and projects. An ESP32 microcontroller-equipped patrol robot follows predetermined paths throughout the hospital's grounds. It avoids obstacles using ultrasonic sensors, and it streams live footage to a central control station via a camera. The robot autonomously detects anomalies (e.g., unauthorized individuals in restricted areas) and alerts security personnel. This prototype utilizes an ESP32 microcontroller to control a mobile robot equipped with infrared sensors and a microphone. The robot patrols corridors and rooms, detecting unusual noises and temperature changes [12]. It communicates data in real time to a cloud server, enabling remote monitoring by security staff. Simulated experiments using the ESP32 microcontroller in a robot designed for access control. The robot verifies identities using facial recognition and RFID technology. It communicates with a central database via Wi-Fi, updating access permissions and logging entries/exits in real time. While IoT-based robotic solutions show promise for hospital security, several challenges remain, including robustness in dynamic environments, cyber security concerns, and integration with existing hospital systems [13,14]. IoT-based robotic solutions using the ESP32 microcontroller represent a significant advancement in hospital security, offering enhanced monitoring, rapid response capabilities, and reduced reliance on human intervention [15,16]. Continued research and innovation in this area are essential to address challenges and fully leverage the potential of IoT in healthcare security applications [17].

Proposed System

The proposed schematic of IoT enabled security system for hospital has been shown in Figure 42.1. The diagram you provided illustrates a system using an ESP32 microcontroller as the central control unit. The ESP32 is interfaced with various input and output devices, allowing it to monitor and control different components. The central microcontroller in the system, responsible for processing inputs from sensors and controlling the outputs. A camera module connected to the ESP32, possibly used for video monitoring or image capture. The fire sensor or flame detector that detects the presence of fire or high temperatures. The metal sensor designed to detect metal objects, which could be used for security or identification purposes. A smoke sensor that detects smoke, used for fire detection and safety systems. For observing output, we have a display screen connected to the ESP32, which might be used to display information such as sensor readings, alerts, or other data. An alarm or buzzer that can be activated by the ESP32, likely used for alerting purposes, such as in case of fire or smoke detection. The robotic mechanism or a mobile robot that the ESP32 controls. The robot might be used for automated tasks or responding to sensor inputs. The ESP32 can connect to the internet or a network to send data, receive commands, or integrate with other IoT devices. Remote power supply (RPS) or remote processing system could either indicate a remote power supply module or a system for remote processing, where some data processing tasks are performed externally and the results are sent back to ESP32.

The key objective of the project includes a robust design and technology Integration which focus on creating a durable spy robot equipped with state-of-the-art components to ensure reliability and effectiveness in diverse operational scenarios. The spy robot to seamlessly transmit crucial environmental data to Android applications, facilitating quick decision-making and comprehensive analysis during continuous monitoring. Implement features to recognize lethal weapons such as swords and sharp knives, enhancing overall security protocols. Advanced sensors have been incorporated which are capable of detecting smoke and monitoring temperature changes, crucial for early risk identification and swift response. Also, an intuitive design has been created using Android application interface to ensure ease of operation for operators of varying skill levels, enhancing overall usability and communication with the spy robot. By diligently pursuing these goals, the project aims to deliver an advanced espionage robot that significantly enhances security protocols and intelligence-gathering capabilities across various demanding settings.

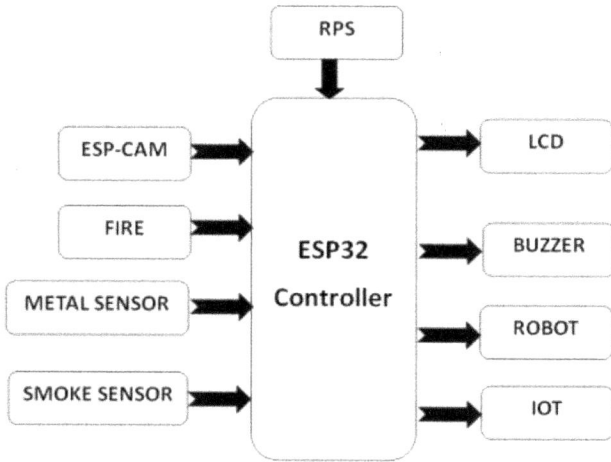

Figure 42.1 Proposed block diagram of IOT enabled security system
Source: Author

Methodology

The circuit diagram (Figure 42.2) is centered on an Arduino/ATmega328p, to which a number of components are linked via its pins:

IOT+CAM: Attached to pins 2 and 3 for contact. The 16x2 LCD display is controlled by pins 4, 5, 6, 11, 12, and 13. The GPS is attached to pin 14 in order to track location.

Robot: For control, attached to pins 15, 16, 17, and 18. The buzzer is attached to pin 19 to provide auditory alerts. GSM Module: Cellular connectivity is accomplished by using pins 27 and 28.

Servomotor: Attached to pin 26 in order to control the motor. Attached to pin 25, the smoke sensor senses the presence of smoke.

Metal sensor: Attached to pin 23 in order to identify metal. A bridge rectifier and a 12V battery for the power supply are two further parts of the circuit. Numerous applications, including robotics, surveillance, and environmental monitoring, are made possible by this configuration.

Results

The entire hardware configuration and its working condition of the proposed system are illustrated in Figure 42.3 and Figure 42.4, respectively. The robot is controlled by an ESP 32 board and uses two DC motors for smooth motion in conjunction with L293D motor driver

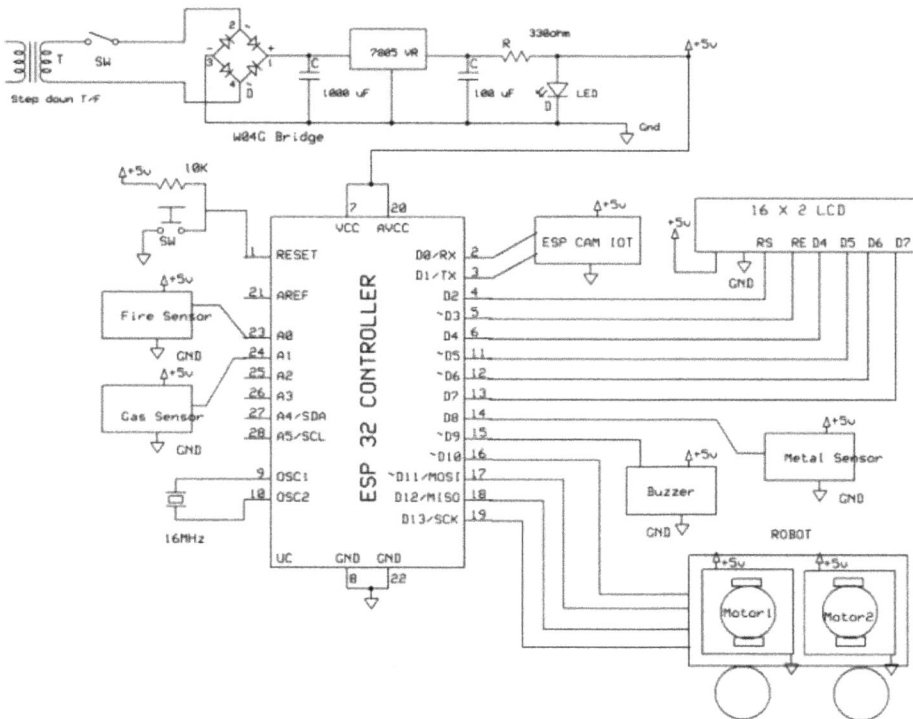

Figure 42.2 Circuit diagram of IoT based security system
Source: Author

integrated circuits and the HC-05 module. With a night vision wireless camera that provides real-time situational monitoring, an extra degree of sophistication is added. It's amazing how cleverly this camera rotates 360 degrees, powered by a motor driven by an Android application, giving it unmatched spying powers. This historic event featured the unique use of technology to reduce dangers and limit the loss of human life: a robot with an integrated bomb disposal kit and a laser beam light. It highlights the revolutionary effect of incorporating the most recent technical developments in emergency situations.

The robot movement was controlled using switches designed with the MIT App Inventor which has been shown in Figure 42.5.

Figure 42.3 Hardware setup for IoT based security system
Source: Author

Figure 42.4 Proposed system in working condition
Source: Author

Conclusion

We designed and implemented a hospital assist robot to enhance hospital security using advanced sensors and a live video stream camera. The robot aims to improve patient experiences by providing services such as bomb detection, gas and fire safety, and live surveillance streaming. The primary goal is to monitor human activity in hospital settings. Hospital personnel can use real-time video footage from a wireless camera controlled via an IoT app to secure areas before deployment. Equipped with sensors for smoke, metal, flame, and gas detection, the robot effectively detects intruders, potential fires, explosive devices, and hazardous gases. This system reduces enemy invasions, protects lives, and prevents illicit activities in conflict zones through advanced technology. Military personnel benefit from greater safety and operational freedom

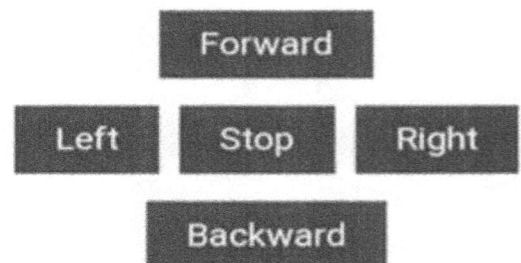

Figure 42.5 Control button switches for movement of robot
Source: Author

due to the robot's remote control and monitoring capabilities.

References

[1] Jebastine, J., and Nanammal, V. (2024). Enhancing wireless surveillance robot with real-time feedback with AI and IOT integration. In 2024 Ninth International Conference on Science Technology Engineering and Mathematics (ICONSTEM), (pp. 1–10). IEEE.

[2] Saleh, S., Cherradi, B., El Gannour, O., Gouiza, N., and Bouattane, O. (2023). Healthcare monitoring system for automatic database management using mobile application in IoT environment. *Bulletin of Electrical Engineering and Informatics*, 12(2), 1055–1068.

[3] Farej, Z. K., and Al-hayaly, H. Y. (2023). Accuracy evaluation of healthcare monitoring system based on ESP32 microcontroller with IoT. In 2023 International Conference on Engineering, Science and Advanced Technology (ICESAT), (pp. 90–94). IEEE.

[4] Shantanu, K., and Dhayagonde, S. (2014). Design and implementation of e-surveillance robot for video monitoring and living body detection. *International Journal of Scientific and Research Publications (IJSRP)*, 4(4), 1–3.

[5] Pavitra, A. R. R., Lawrence, I. D., and Maheswari, P. U. (2023). To identify the accessibility and performance of smart healthcare systems in IoT-based environments. In Using Multimedia Systems, Tools, and Technologies for Smart Healthcare Services, (pp. 229–245). IGI Global.

[6] Farej, Z. K., and Al-hayaly, H. Y. (2023). Accuracy evaluation of healthcare monitoring system based on ESP32 microcontroller with IoT. In 2023 International Conference on Engineering, Science and Advanced Technology (ICESAT), (pp. 90–94). IEEE.

[7] Vidyadhar, R. P., Mallik, D. S., Kumar, K. U., and Renuka, B. (2024). An IoT based obstacle detection and line follower robot using LabVIEW. In 2024 2nd International Conference on Advancement in Computation and Computer Technologies (InCACCT), (pp. 852–857). IEEE.

[8] Sayeduzzaman, M., Hasan, T., Nasser, A. A., & Negi, A. (2024). An Internet of Things-Integrated Home Automation with Smart Security System. *Automated Secure Computing for Next-Generation Systems*, 243-273. WILEY Online Library. DOI:10.1002/9781394213948.ch13

[9] Stella, K., Menaka, M., Jeevitha, R., Jenila, S. J., Devi, A., and Vethapackiam, K. (2023). Patient pulse rate and oxygen level monitoring system using IoT. In International Conference on IoT Based Control Networks and Intelligent Systems, (pp. 343–355). Singapore: Springer Nature Singapore.

[10] Zulkarnain, S. N., Ahmad Shauri, R. L., Saidin, M. H., and Afiqie Zamanhuri, A. Z. (2024). IoT monitoring of a master-slave robot system using MIT App inventor. *Journal of Electrical and Electronic Systems Research (JEESR)*, 24(1), 33–39.

[11] Nithya, S., Poornima, R., Manojkumar, G., Kaviyan, T., Lingamoorthy, L., and Seethalakshmi, V. (2023). Design of a robotic helpmate. In 2023 9th International Conference on Advanced Computing and Communication Systems (ICACCS), (Vol. 1, pp. 1743–1748). IEEE.

[12] Singh, S., Sharma, S., Bhadula, S., and Mohan, S. (2023). Industry 4.0 internet of medical things enabled cost effective secure smart patient care medicine pouch. In New Horizons for Industry 4.0 in Modern Business (pp. 149–170). Cham: Springer International Publishing.

[13] Upadhyaya, A. N., Saqib, A., Devi, J. V., Rallapalli, S., Sudha, S., and Boopathi, S. (2024). Implementation of the internet of things (IoT) in remote healthcare. In Analyzing Current Digital Healthcare Trends Using Social Networks, (pp. 104–124). IGI Global.

[14] Sharma, R., Chand, A., and Fatima, M. (2024). Design and implementing war field robot for surveillance. In 2024 1st International Conference on Innovative Sustainable Technologies for Energy, Mechatronics, and Smart Systems (ISTEMS), (pp. 1–5). IEEE.

[15] Hassan, A. N., and Amin, K. H. M. (2017). Design and implementation of an autonomous war field spy robot for surveillance in hazardous environments. In 2017 IEEE 3rd International Conference on Engineering Technologies and Social Sciences (ICETSS), Bangkok, Thailand, (pp. 1–6).

[16] Kumar, M., Kumar, A., Verma, S., Bhattacharya, P., Ghimire, D., Kim, S. H., et al. (2023). Healthcare internet of things (H-IoT): current trends, future prospects, applications, challenges, and security issues. *Electronics*, 12(9), 2050.

[17] Jimo, S., Abdullah, T., and Jamal, A. (2023). IoE security risk analysis in a modern hospital ecosystem. In Cybersecurity in the Age of Smart Societies: Proceedings of the 14th International Conference on Global Security, Safety and Sustainability, London, September 2022 (pp. 451–467). Cham: Springer International Publishing.

43 Offset binary coding-based symmetrical 2D FIR FBs using FPGA and ASIC designs

Venkata Krishna Odugu[a], Janardhana Rao, B.[b], and Gade Harish Babu[c]

Department of ECE, CVR College of Engineering, Hyderabad, Telangana, India

Abstract

Finite impulse response (FIR) is employed in the field of image enhancement and processing. This study presents the design of a low-complexity FIR filter specifically tailored for image processing applications. Designing and implementing a two-dimensional (2D) FIR filter with an effective and low-complex architecture is a hard issue for image processing applications. The architecture needs to be optimized in terms of area complexity (AC), power consumption (PC), latency, and memory complexity (MC). A unique 2D FIR filter architecture (FA) for a general filter bank (FB) is proposed, which is built on blocks and may be used for various 2D symmetric FIR filters. The FB's area, storage memory, and power use are decreased. Two 2D symmetrical FIR FAs are developed and studied, alongside a general filter that does not possess symmetry. The symmetry decreases the quantity of multiplier blocks (MB), which are the high power-intensive blocks, needed for the FA. Therefore, a significant portion in overall PC is reduced. parallel processing (PP) is implemented to enhance the throughput (TP) of the FB. The ideas of memory sharing (MS) and memory reuse (MR) are implemented to decrease the MC by FB. offset binary coding (OBC) based distributed arithmetic (DA) is used to replace the traditional multiplication procedure. This is done in order to reduce the PC and size of each sub-filter in the FB. An architecture for a generic FB is constructed and synthesis was done by Vivado tools for the FPGA device that is being targeted. Subsequently, the proposed design is produced in CMOS 45nm generic library utilizing Genus tools to generate data on area, latency, and power.

Keywords: Distributed arithmetic, low-power architecture, OBC, symmetry, two-dimensional FIR filter

Introduction

Digital filters play a crucial role in various image processing tasks, including image sharpening, restoration, edge detection, and enhancement. They involve convolving an image with a specific filter mask to achieve desired effects. The most demanding and resource-intensive aspect of any DSP application is the filtering process. Its primary purpose is to eliminate unwanted elements that may have been introduced into the signal due to factors like environmental noise, imperfections in transmission channels, and flaws in transmitting and receiving equipment. In the context of image processing, the terms FIR and IIR filters are commonly used. FIR filters are very easy to design, which are stable, regular, and modular. They have a finite duration, which makes them suitable for real-time processing and applications where phase distortion is not a concern. On the other hand, IIR filters have infinite-duration impulse responses and are commonly used in tasks where a trade-off between stability and frequency response is acceptable. Odugu et al., [1] designed a 2D FIR FA that is both low-power and memory-efficient. They achieved this by using high-speed and power-efficient adders. A novel method utilizing a systolic architecture with low area and memory requirements for implementing FIR FAs in single input-single output (SISO) systems is proposed [2]. The authors proposed a new 2D FIR FA that utilizes improved 4:2 compressors to achieve reduced area, PC & time. The above works do not take into account PP and symmetry [3]. Kumar et al., [4,5] presented block-based architectures and un-symmetrical 2D FIR and 2D IIR FAs. This architecture includes memory sharing across the DA blocks.

[a]venkatakrishna.odugu@gmail.com, [b]janardhan.bitra@gmail.com, [c]harish.sidhu12@gmail.com

DOI: 10.1201/9781003616399-43

Aggarwal et al., [6] introduced a design for a 2D FIR FA with quadrantal symmetry, which incorporates fractional derivative constraints. Four less-power symmetrical 2D IIR FAs and FB have been implemented. Their focus is solely on critical route and symmetry, with no consideration given to SISO approaches [7]. In the work, recently a new 2D FIR FA with circular symmetry, which utilizes the canonical signed digit (CSD) space to achieve minimal complexity is introduced [8]. The authors have developed a PP-type one-dimensional FA that utilizes a fully data-adaptive reconfigurable FIR FA for narrowband filter applications [9].

Odugu et al., [10] developed a new FB structure consisting of 2D-FIR symmetry FAs that utilize look-up table (LUT)-based multipliers. Meher et al., [11] introduced a novel method for memory-based multipliers utilizing LUT. Vinitha et al., [12] have enhanced the memory-based multiplication process by employing various advanced storage techniques resulting in reduced hardware requirements. Sharma et al., [13] introduced a revised approach for memory-based multiplication called odd multiples storage (OMS-LUT). Prashanth et al., [14] recently developed an FIR FA based on DA. The filter was built using LUT multipliers. Recently, various 2D FIR FAs are presented in works [15–18] using different multiplier-less designs.

This paper incorporates P to achieve memory reuse and enhance throughput. The utilization of two forms of symmetry coefficients, namely Diagonal Symmetry 2D FIR Filter (DS2DFIRF) and Quadrantal Symmetry 2D FIR Filter (QS2DFIRF), helps to prune the MBs in the FA construction.

PP is implemented in a 2D FIR FA to enhance the rate at which data is processed and to maximize the utilization of memory cells. The analysis of various coefficient symmetries in FAs aims to minimize the MBs required for FA. This study also investigates the entire design of two symmetry filters. The power-hungry multipliers are substituted with improved OBC multipliers to reduce the PC and size of the arithmetic module (AM) in each filter. An FB with multiple modes is utilized to enable memory sharing. The FB comprises one general filter (GF) and two symmetrical filters. An FB optimizes memory usage, reduces area

requirements, and minimizes PC through the use of appropriate filter selection logic.

Assuming L represents the size of the i/p block for the 2D filter, each iteration processes L i/p samples and generates L o/ps. As a result, the TP of FA is raised by a factor of L. The fundamental expression of the 2D FA is represented by Equation (1).

$$H(z_1, z_2) = \sum_{i=0}^{N-1} \sum_{j=0}^{N-1} b_{ij} z_1^{-i} z_2^{-j} \quad (1)$$

Here, $[b_{ij}]$ is a coefficient and is given by equation (2).

$$b_{ij} = [b_{i0}, b_{i1}, \dots b_{iN-1}]^T \quad (2)$$

A 2D FA is provided in a completely direct form (DF) to facilitate the investigation of MR. The memory needs for a fully DF FA is lower and is solely determined by the length of the i/p word. This functionality can be utilized to diminish the MC in FA. FA often necessitates units of MC for each individual i/p, where M represents the size of the i/p image (M × M) and N denotes the length of the filter.

2D DS2DFIRF

The DSF-based 2D FIR filter is achieved using the transfer functions (TF) relationship [14]. The magnitude of H concerning z_1 and z_2 is equal to the magnitude value of the function H with respect to z_2 and z_1. Let z_1 be equal to $e^{j\theta1}$ and z_2 be equal to $e^{j\theta2}$, for all values of θ_1 and θ_2. The DS2DFIRF coefficients is expressed by the equation, $b_{ij} = b_{ji}$ for every i, j. The TF of the DSF filter is mathematically expressed in Eq.(3).

$$\frac{Y}{X} = \sum_{i=0}^{N} b_{ii} z_1^{-i} z_2^{-i} + \sum_{i=0}^{N-1} \sum_{j=i+1}^{N} b_{ij} \left(z_1^{-i} z_2^{-j} + z_1^{-j} z_2^{-i} \right) \quad (3)$$

The GF and DS2DFIRF coefficients are presented in Figure 43.1(a), (b).

QS2DFIRF

The QS2DFIRF can be represented as |H(z1, z2)| = H(z− 1 1, z2)|. Let z_1 be equal to $e^{j\theta1}$ and z_2 be equal to $e^{j\theta2}$, for all values of θ_1 and θ_2. The symmetry of the QSF is expressed by the equation $b_{ij} = b_{(N-i)j}$, where i and j are any values. The TF of

$$\begin{bmatrix} C_{00} & C_{01} & C_{02} & C_{03} \\ C_{10} & C_{11} & C_{12} & C_{13} \\ C_{20} & C_{21} & C_{22} & C_{23} \\ C_{30} & C_{31} & C_{32} & C_{33} \end{bmatrix} \quad \begin{bmatrix} C_{00} & C_{01} & C_{02} & C_{03} \\ C_{01} & C_{11} & C_{12} & C_{13} \\ C_{02} & C_{12} & C_{22} & C_{23} \\ C_{03} & C_{13} & C_{23} & C_{33} \end{bmatrix}$$

(a)   (b)

Figure 43.1 Coefficients of (a) GF for N = 4 (b) DS2DFIRF
Source: Author

the filter is defined by Equation (4). Figure 43.2 displays the QS2DFIRF coefficients.

$$\frac{Y}{X} = \sum_{j=0}^{N} b_{uj} z_1^{-u} z_2^{-j} + \sum_{i=0}^{N-1} \sum_{j=0}^{N-1} b_{ij} \left(z_1^{-i} z_2^{-j} + z_1^{-(N-i)} z_2^{-j} \right)$$

(4)

Proposed OBC-DA multiplier

The FIR FA with N = 4, implemented using DF and OBC technique, is illustrated in Figure 43.3. The OBC approach decreases the size of the LUT to half. The XOR gates of this structure are utilized to fetch the address of the LUT by considering both the present and past i/p samples. The Mux initializes the shift accumulator with the initial value. The Mux adjacent to the LUT is employed to invert the o/p of the LUT that corresponds to the value of j being equal to w-1.

The control lines S_0 and S_1 are utilized, with S_0 being set to 1 when j equals w-1, and 0

otherwise. Like that, S_1 is equal to 1 when j = 0 and equal to 0 otherwise. This section provides a description of the OBC-DA scheme formulation.

The equations mentioned above pertain to the notion of OBC. The values of P_j are reflected in

$$\begin{bmatrix} C_{00} & C_{01} & C_{02} & C_{03} \\ C_{10} & C_{11} & C_{12} & C_{13} \\ C_{10} & C_{11} & C_{12} & C_{13} \\ C_{00} & C_{01} & C_{02} & C_{03} \end{bmatrix}$$

Figure 43.2 Coefficients symmetry of QSF
Source: Author

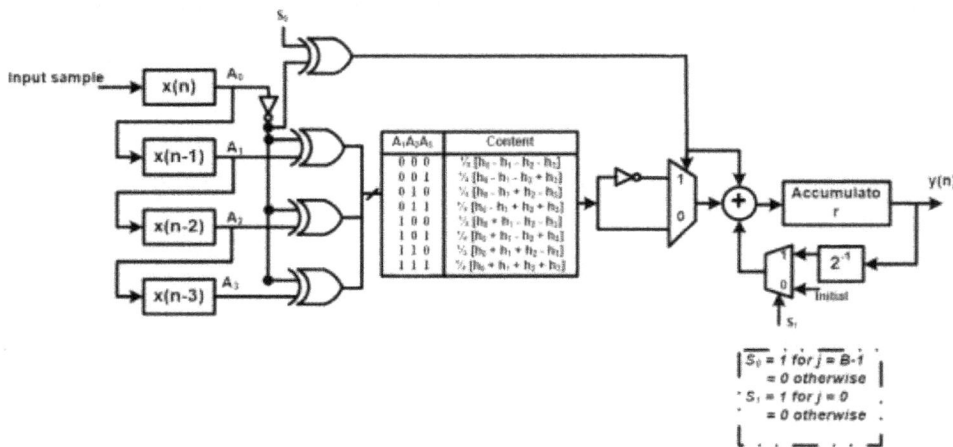

Figure 43.3 Simple structure of FIR using OBC- DA
Source: Author

LUT. Put simply, the P_j variable can take on $2^{(N-1)}$ different values based on the x_{ij} values. Therefore, it is feasible to decrease the LUT to half. The updated LUT may be noticed in Figure 43.3. By examining the fundamental architectures of the DA and OBC-based filters, it is evident that the size of the LUT-ROM is halved in the OBC scheme when the filter length N is equal to 4. The OBC concept reduces the size of the memory and decreases the delay required to fetch the memory.

Complete FB Structure

The 2D FIR FB architecture is displayed in Figure 43.4. The system has three filter modules: a general filter, DSF, and QSF. These modules are accompanied by a shared shift register block (SRB) array and delay units blocks (DUB) array, which serve to minimize MC.

The two primary components of FB are the DUB and SRB array blocks, that serve the purposes of MS and MR. The current i/ps consists of L samples taken from a 2D i/p matrix of image with dimensions M × M. The i/p samples are being transmitted through N-1 SRBs in the SRB array. Figure 43.5 displays an SRB that comprises L registers. The configuration of the SRB array for a system with N = 4 and L = 4 is as follows: Subsequently, the present sample and preceding i/ps are utilized in the N of related DUB of the DUB-array.

A DUB is composed of N-1 FFs and provides the necessary current and prior samples for the systolic action of PP. Every DUB generates a certain number of samples, as illustrated. Figure 43.6.

The complicated control logic of FB is essential for selecting the desired filter with a certain symmetry. When a single filter is selected for processing, the other filters are deactivated, resulting in reduced power usage per o/p. Alternatively, users have the option to pick all filters for simultaneous processing of all filters. The control block facilitates the selection of the desired symmetry and enables parallel realization through signal manipulation. Each sub-module produces L o/ps corresponding to L i/ps in a single loop. The arithmetic module of the FB comprises three 2D filters, namely FIR-1, FIR-2, and FIR-3, each with different symmetry coefficients.

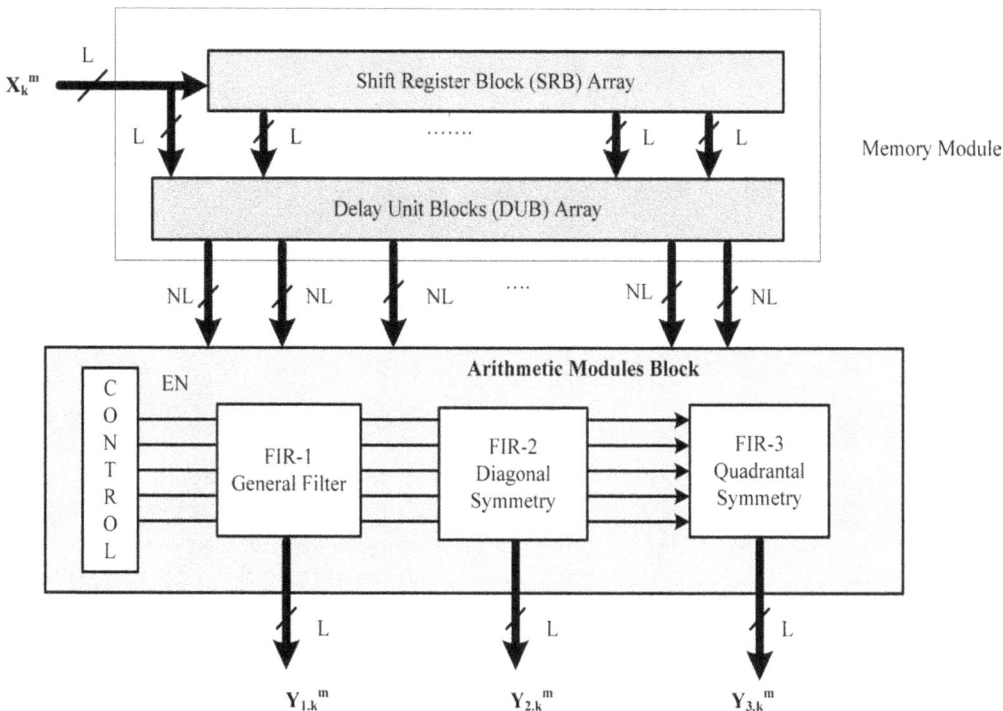

Figure 43.4 Suggested PP-based 2D FIR FB architecture
Source: Author

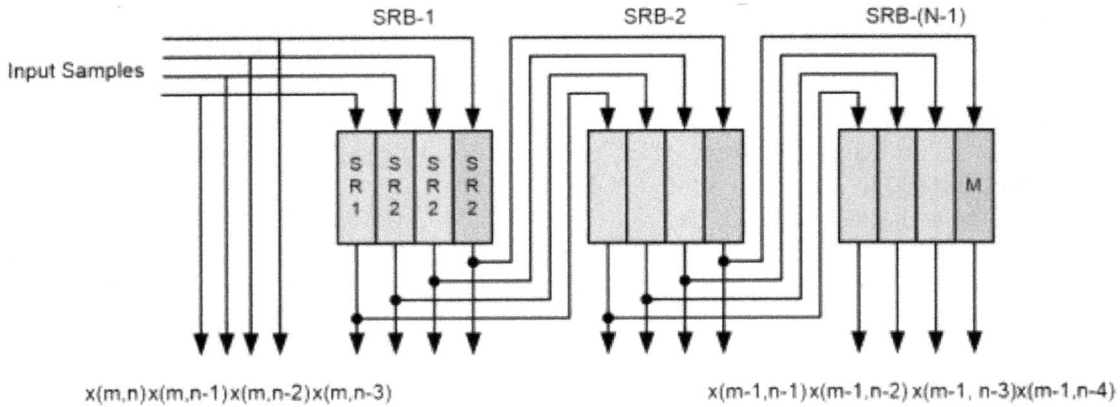

Figure 43.5 Internal structure of SRB array of FB
Source: Author

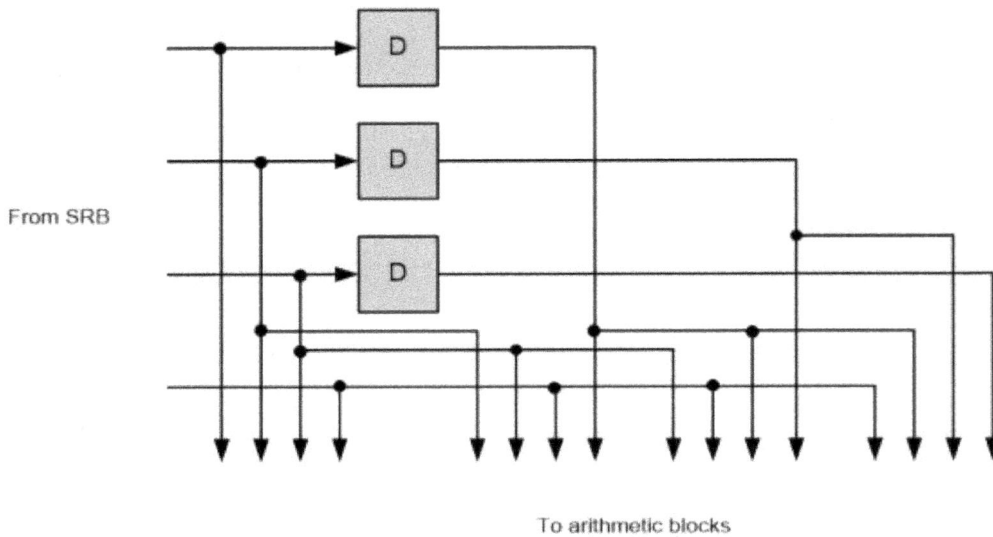

To arithmetic blocks

Figure 43.6 IRU block for N = 4 and L = 4
Source: Author

The architecture of the proposed FB utilizes three 2D FIR FA AMs and common MMs for design and implementation. In this process, MS is utilized to get the o/ps of the filter. The MC needed to implement a single filter is sufficient for the complete FB.

Block-Based GF RTL Diagram

The GF of a 2D FIR filter, which operates on blocks of data, is shown in Figure 43.7. In this specific case, the L is set to 4 and the length N is 4. The filter coefficients do not exhibit any symmetry and are considered to be generic. The i/p

samples {xk0, xk1, xk2, xk3} are part of the row in the i/p matrix that is used for the SRB array. These i/p samples are processed sequentially in a ratter scan method in the architecture.

The SRB array has (N − 1) SRBs, each with L SRs. Each M-word shift register creates L-delayed i/p samples. The mix of SR1 and SR2 is SRB1. SRB2 and SRB3 use the SRB array for N = 4 format. N-DUBs use L past samples and current samples as i/p, with N sets. Each DUB saves L SRB samples and produces LxN samples. The AM has N processing units and an adder block that receives DUB NL o/ps.

2D FIR DSF Architecture

In the DS2DFIRF method, a set of 16 coefficients is reduced to only 10 unique coefficients as {in Figure 43.8. The previous section demonstrates coefficient symmetry and TFs. For DSF, i/p samples multiplied by the same coefficients are added before multiplication.

It takes 7 adders to add symmetry i/ps with block sizes of L. Given L = 4, the 7 highlighted and colored adders are for the other i/p. This symmetry reduces the need for multipliers. DSF permits L (2 N + 2) MBs rather than L (N x N), but requires L (N - 1) additions. To construct L block filter o/ps, L adder tree blocks combine the o/ps of each multiplier. DSF symmetry architecture is studied using the filter with N = 4 and L = 4.

2D FIR QSF Architecture

After applying QSF, a set of eight distinct filter coefficients is determined, denoted as {. Figure 43.9 examines the architectural design of the

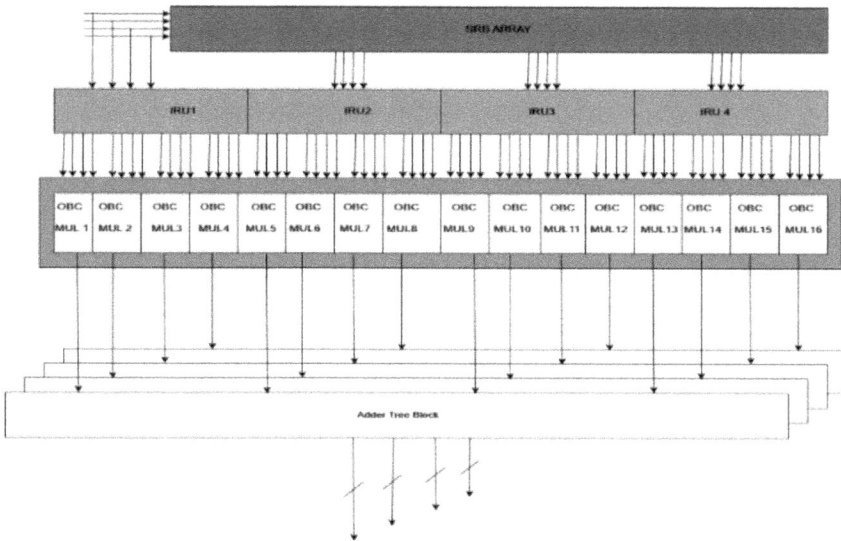

Figure 43.7 Architecture of the general filter
Source: Author

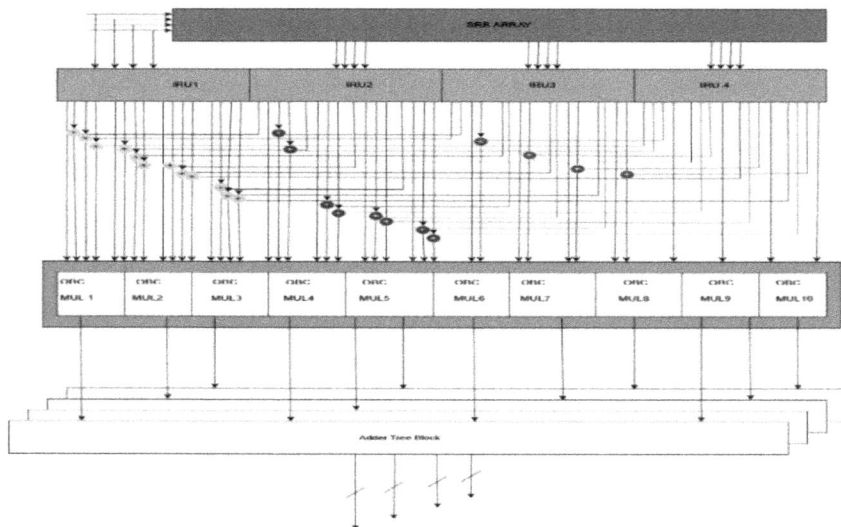

Figure 43.8 OBC-based DSF architecture
Source: Author

QSF for a specific configuration where L = 2 and N = 4. The computation of the L block o/p requires either 16 single port LUT MBs or 8 DP LUT MBs.

Implementation Results

The Verilog HDL is used to code all the filters and FB, and they are synthesized using Xilinx Vivado tools. Subsequently, the specific symmetry filters and FB topologies are created using the Genus synthesis tool from Cadence. The filter and FB architecture are implemented with a size of L = 4 and N = 4. The VLSI metrics are summarized, and subsequently, the findings are summarized as well. Figure 43.10 represents the RTL schematic of the proposed FB architecture provided by Vivado tools. Similarly, Figures 43.11, 43.12, and 43.13 display the RTL schematics of the three types of individual symmetry filters.

The hardware requirements of the LUT and OBC-based multipliers are compared in Table 43.1 with respect to the Vivado synthesis. The FB

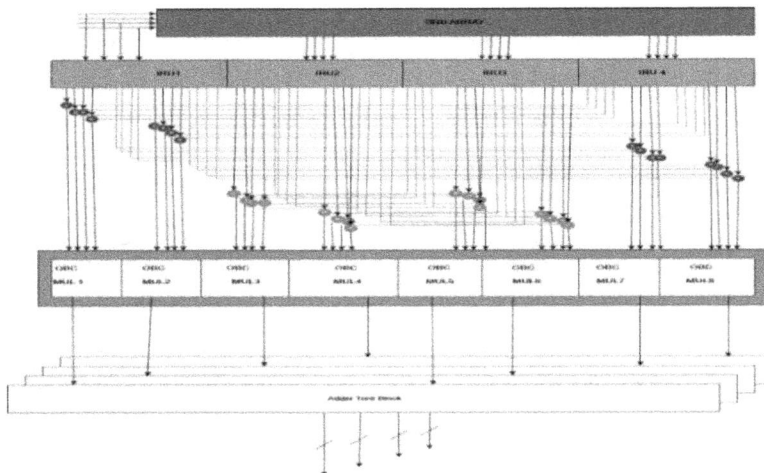

Figure 43.9 OBC-based QSF architecture
Source: Author

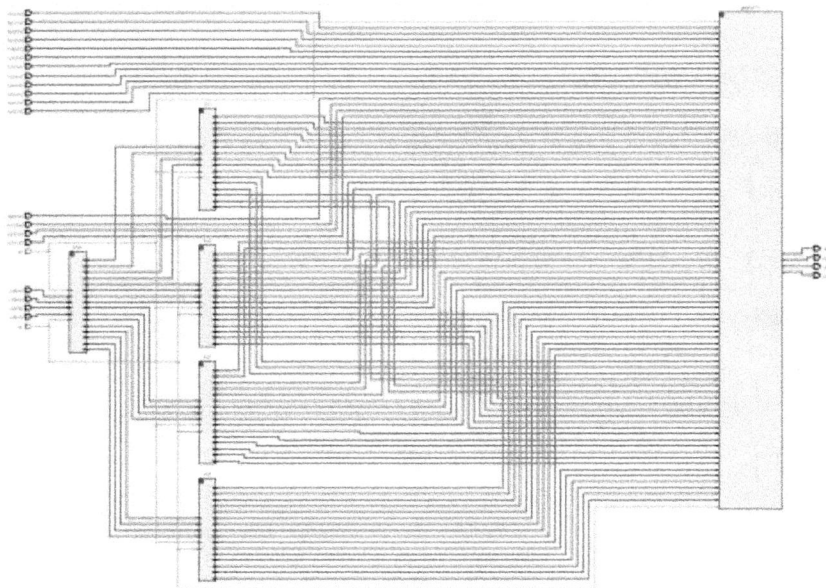

Figure 43.10 RTL diagram of FB architecture with OBC-DA multiplier
Source: Author

design was implemented utilizing conventional multipliers, LUT, and OBC-DA-based multipliers. The key parameters of three different FBs are compared in Figures 43.14 and 43.15.

Total on-chip PC of GF, DSF and QSF is compared in Table 43.2. The PC of the suggested architecture is 49% and 39% lower than that of the standard multiplier FB architecture and the LUT-based FB architecture, respectively, as stated in Table 43.2. The area comparison of the 3 filters shown in Table 43.3.

The suggested architecture has an area that is 8% less than the typical multiplier FB architecture

and 7% smaller than the LUT-based FB architecture, as shown in Table 43.3. Based on a comparison analysis, it is evident that the suggested 2D FIR FB, which utilizes different symmetry and is based on OBC-DA, excels in terms of PC and area.

Conclusion

The implementation and design of FB architecture across various dimensions were presented in this work. The primary objective of this work is to maximize the efficiency of the hardware used

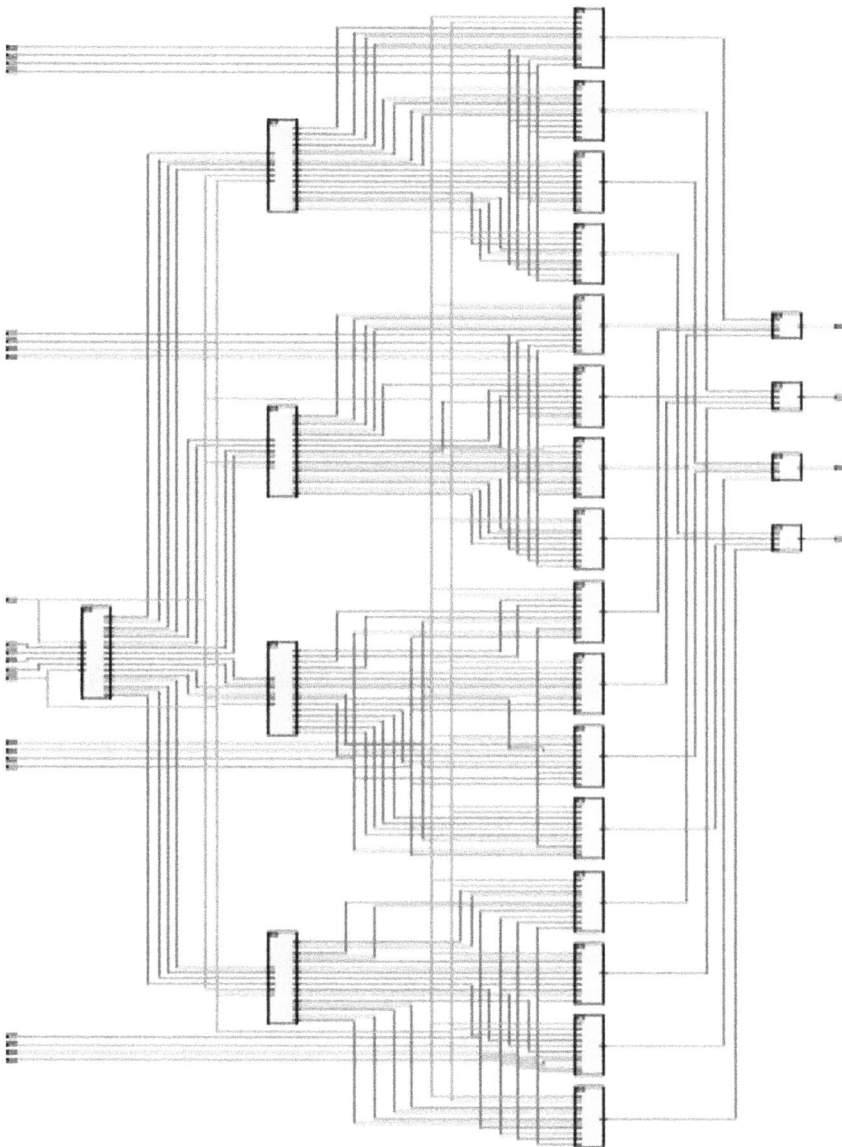

Figure 43.11 RTL diagram of GF with OBC-DA multipliers
Source: Author

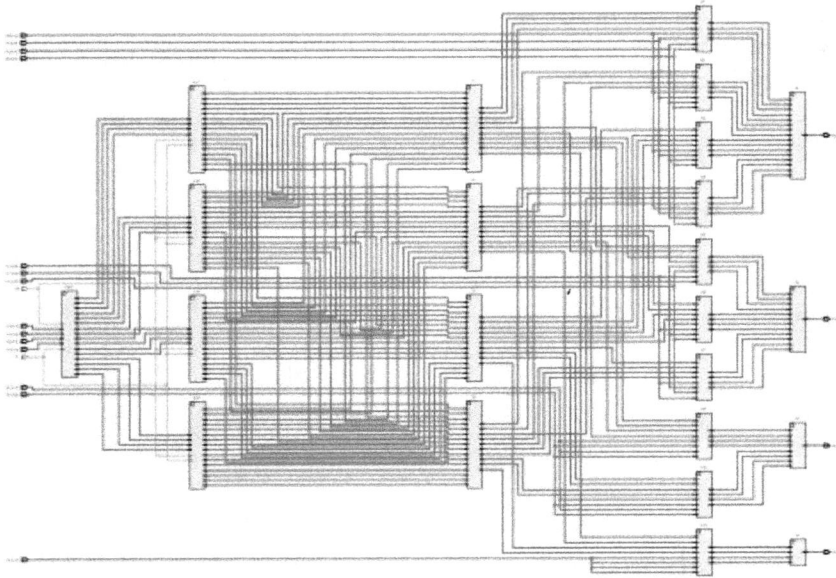

Figure 43.12 RTL schematic of DSF with OBC-DA multiplier
Source: Author

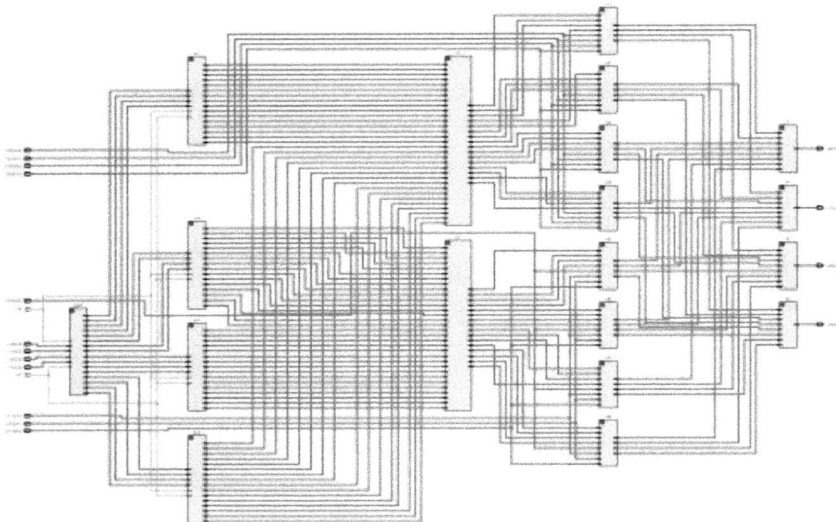

Figure 43.13 RTL schematic of QSF with OBC-DA multiplier
Source: Author

Table 43.1 Comparison study of OBC-DA and LUT-DA multipliers

	OBC-DA		LUT-DA	
Resource	Estimation	Utilization	Estimation	Utilization
LUT	7	0.02	12	0.03
FF	3	0.01	-	-
IO	23	7.67	44	14.67
BUFG	1	3.13	-	-

Source: Author

Table 43.2 Comparison of total on-chip PC values (Watts)

	Normal multiplier	LUT multiplier	OBC-DA multiplier
General filter	28.609 W	23.332 W	14.102 W
DSF	24.445 W	21.745 W	11.237 W
QSF	23.317 W	22.943 W	13.412 W

Source: Author

Figure 43.14 Graph for total on-chip power values (in Watts)
Source: Author

Table 43.3 Total area comparison of filters with various multipliers (μ)

	Normal multiplier	LUT multiplier	OBC-DA multiplier
General Filter	1783	1771.842	1642.678
DSF	1390	1376.329	1361.543
QSF	1111	1106.028	1010

Source: Author

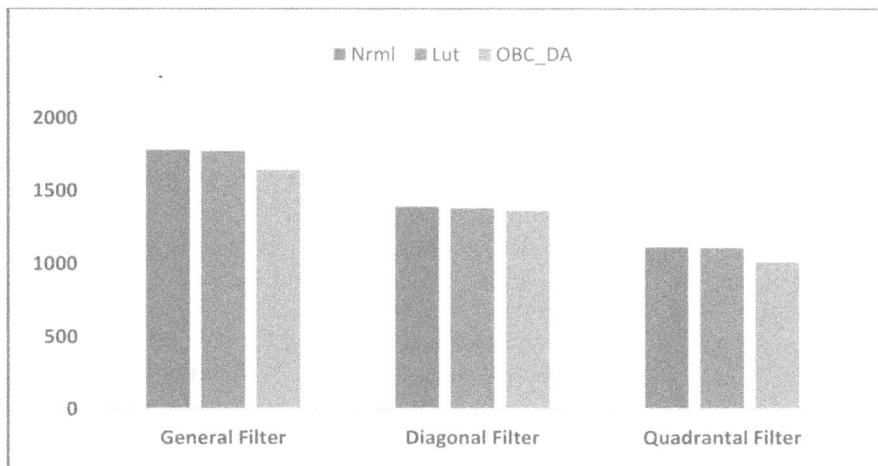

Figure 43.15 Total area values comparison for different types of filters
Source: Author

in the 2D FIR FB architecture. The filter's architecture is designed using registers, adders, and MBs. These components are scaled up based on several factors, including the filter's length (N), block size (L), i/p sample bits, coefficient bits, and more. Two variants of PP-based 2D FIR FAs with symmetry are suggested to minimize the quantity of MBs and MC needed. In addition, MBs are trimmed utilizing an OBC-DA-based multiplication technique. Subsequently, the specific symmetry filters and FB topologies are created using Cadence utilizing a 45 nm technology and Vivado tools. The FAs and FB architecture are realized for L = 4 and N = 4.

References

[1] Odugu, V. K., Narasimhulu, C. V., and Prasad, K. S. (2019). Implementation of low power and memory efficient 2D FIR filter architecture. *International Journal of Recent Technology and Engineering*, 8(1), 927–935.

[2] Vinitha, C. S., and Sharma, R. K. (2019). New approach to low-area, low-latency memory-based systolic architecture for FIR filters. *Journal of Information and Optimization Sciences*, 40(2), 247–262.

[3] Odugu, V. K., and K, S. P. (2021). An efficient VLSI architecture of 2-D finite impulse response filter using enhanced approximate compressor circuits. *International Journal of Circuit Theory and Applications*, 1–16. https://doi.org/10.1002/cta.3114.

[4] Kumar, P., Shrivastava, P. C., Tiwari, M., and Dhawan, A. (2018). ASIC implementation of area-efficient, high-throughput 2-D IIR filter using distributed arithmetic. *Circuits, Systems, and Signal Processing*, 37(7), 2934–2957.

[5] Kumar, P., Shrivastava, P. C., Tiwari, M., and Mishra, G. R. (2019). High-throughput, area-efficient architecture of 2-D block FIR filter using distributed arithmetic algorithm. *Circuits, Systems, and Signal Processing*, 38(3), 1099–1113.

[6] Aggarwal, A., Kumar, M., Rawat, T. K., and Upadhyay, D. K. (2016). Optimal design of 2D FIR filters with quadrantally symmetric properties using fractional derivative constraints. *Circuits, Systems, and Signal Processing*, 35(6), 2213–2257.

[7] Chen, P. Y., Van, L. D., Khoo, I. H., Reddy, H. C., and Lin, C. T. (2010). Power-efficient and cost-effective 2-D symmetry filter architectures. *IEEE Transactions on Circuits and Systems I: Regular Papers*, 58(1), 112–125.

[8] Odugu, V. K., Venkata Narasimhulu, C., and Satya Prasad, K. (2020). Design and implementation of low complexity circularly symmetric 2D FIR filter architectures, *Multidimensional Systems and Signal Processing*, 31, 1–26.

[9] Mohanty, B. K., and Meher, P. K. (2015). A high-performance FIR filter architecture for fixed and reconfigurable applications. *IEEE transactions on Very Large Scale Integration (VLSI) Systems*, 24(2), 444–452.

[10] Odugu, V. K., Narasimhulu, C. V., and Satya Prasad, K. (2022). A novel filter-bank architecture of 2D-FIR symmetry filters using LUT based multipliers. *Integration*, 84, 12–25.

[11] Meher, P. K. (2009). New approach to look-up-table design and memory-based realization of FIR digital filter *IEEE Transactions on Circuits and Systems I: Regular Papers*, 57(3), 592–603.

[12] Vinitha, C. S., and Sharma, R. K. (2019). An efficient LUT design on FPGA for memory-based multiplication. *The Iranian Journal of Electrical and Electronic Engineering*, 15(4), 462–476.

[13] Abbot, G., and Sharma, D. (2020). Modified efficient OMS LUT-design for memory-based multiplication. Available at: SSRN 3562979.

[14] Prashanth, B. U. V., Ahmed, M. R., and Kounte, M. R. (2021). Design and implementation of DA FIR filter for bio-inspired computing architecture. *International Journal of Electrical and Computer Engineering*, 11(2), 1709.

[15] Odugu, V. K., Satish, B., Janardhana Rao, B., and Gade, H. B. (2023). Efficient VLSI architectures of multimode 2D FIR filter bank using distributed arithmetic methodology. In International Conference on Soft Computing and Signal Processing, (pp. 243–253). Singapore: Springer Nature Singapore.

[16] Srilatha Reddy, V., Vimala Juliet, A., Thuraka, E. R., and Odugu, V. K. (2024). Design and implementation of power and area efficient architectures of circular symmetry 2-D FIR filters using CSOA-based CSD. *Multidimensional Systems and Signal Processing*, 1–27.

[17] Odugu, V. K., Gade, H. B., and Uppala, A. R. (2024). Higher order and optimized symmetric 2D FIR filter design and hardware architecture implementation using CSD-CSE. *Computers and Electrical Engineering*, 119, 109564.

[18] Reddy, V. S., Juliet, A. V., Thuraka, E. R., and Odugu, V. K. (2024). Implementation of block-based diagonal and quadrantal symmetry type 2D-FIR filter architectures using DA technique. *Computers and Electrical Engineering*, 118, 109301.

44 A broadband, circularly polarized UHF RFID reader antenna for traffic vehicles detection

Krishna Rao Samanasa[1,a], Madhavi Gudipalli[2], Varunteja Samanasa[3] and Sreevarsha Samanasa[4]

[1]CE , B V Raju Institute of Technology, Narsapur, India

[2]ECE, JNTUH College of Engineering, Hyderabad, India

[3]B.Tech IDP Student, JNTUH College of Engineering, Hyderabad, India

[4]II Year Diploma Student, SDDWTTI, Telangana, India

Abstract

The current study suggests a wideband, circularly polarized RFID reader antenna designed for both near-field and far-field uses, with specific emphasis on the detection of traffic vehicles. The design integrates two distinct resonant structures: a segmented loop and a patch antenna, each of which plays a crucial role in generating circular polarization in the respective near and far fields. The antenna dimensions are compact, measuring $184 \times 174 \times 3.175$ mm³, making it suitable for integration into various systems. The antenna is designed to work in the ultra-high frequency (UHF) range and is specifically tuned to resonate at 866 MHz, making it well-suited for RFID applications. A simple microstrip line feeds both the segmented loop and the patch antenna, enabling efficient excitation of the structures. The high-frequen1cy structure simulator (AHFSS) software was used to rigorously evaluate the performance of the antenna, a leading tool for simulating electromagnetic fields. The results of the simulation show that the antenna reaches resonance at 866 MHz, falling within the UHF band. Additionally, it demonstrates a 36 MHz bandwidth, encompassing frequencies from 846 MHz to 882 MHz, all while keeping a return loss of under -10 dB, suggesting low signal reflection and high effectiveness. A key feature of the design is its ability to generate circular polarization, which is crucial for robust RFID communication. The antenna achieves an axial ratio of less than 3 dB, signifying strong circular polarization. This characteristic ensures that the antenna can effectively communicate with RFID tags regardless of their orientation, which is particularly beneficial in dynamic environments like traffic monitoring.

Keywords: Broadband, circular polarization, RFID, Segmented loop antenna

Introduction

RFID technology is used for the automatic identification and tracking of objects by utilizing radio frequency waves. RFID finds in security applications such as employee identity cards (embedded with tags), credit cards, automatic payment card etc., and also deployed in inventory control, electronic toll collection (ETC). In ETC, RFID tag attached to the vehicle and Reader unit is at the road side. Toll tax can be automatically deducted from the owner of the vehicle [1]. The connection between the tag and reader in near field RFID can occur through magnetic (inductive) or electric (capacitive) coupling. In far field RFID, the tag communicates with the reader through the propagation of electromagnetic waves. Loop antennas provide large interrogation read range at LF/HF frequency range and predominant reactive field in its near field. Other near field RFIDs are UHF RFIDs. When compared to the LF/HF RFIDs, the UHF RFIDs are beneficial because the data transmission rate is high between reader and tag and are useful in item-level tagging and sensitive products tracking (like blood, vaccines, medicines) but their performance degrades in the presence of metals and liquid [2].

Loop antennas designed for LF/HF RFID applications are considered electrically small, with

[a]snkrishnarao@gmail.com

DOI: 10.1201/9781003616399-44

a circumference typically around 0.1 times the wavelength at the operating frequency. Despite their small size, these antennas offer an extended read range. The design of loop antenna for RFID at UHF range is a challenge. Being the wavelength small at UHF range and still if the circumference C = λ (electrically large loop antenna) provides only small interrogation region. The solution to this is using a segmented loop antenna instead of continues loop antenna. The loop segments consist of small metal stripes with a length of approximately 0.25λ and were linked in series with the lumped capacitor. Even when the loop's perimeter exceeds two operating wavelengths, the current distribution along the loop remains in phase by using a segmented line. In its near-field region, the segmented antenna generates a uniform and powerful magnetic field distribution. An increased number of segments is included in the design of the loop antenna [3].

Far-field RFIDs enable a long read range. Patch antennas are utilized in far-field RFID because of their compact size, light weight, and cost-effectiveness, but they have limited bandwidth and efficiency drawbacks [4]. In practical applications, the tag can be oriented in any direction, and the reader needs to receive the signal from the tag. To ensure reliable communication between tag and reader, a circularly polarized (CP) RFID reader antenna is used. CP waves are generated by a patch with two separate feeds (dual feed) that have a 900 phase difference between them. Circular polarization is produced by two orthogonally linearly polarized waves. A 900 hybrid coupler was used to introduce the 900 phase difference, resulting in good impedance and axial ratio bandwidth but with a complex feed structure [5]. In order to obtain CP with single feed, the patch surface should be perturbed. Truncation of edges of patch provides good CP but compact size is not possible [6]. Another method of achieving good circular polarization is cutting slots or embedding slots on the surface of the patch. The slots may be in the shape of cross, square, or circular. and patch with slot provides considerable reduction in antenna size. As the perimeter of the slot increases, there is reduction in CP radiation. This procedure is with less complexity [7] and hence this method was adopted in the design of proposed antenna. The same antenna can be used for both close-range and long-range

applications. Publications and patents have been issued for the UHF Reader antenna, which is designed for both near and far field applications. The antenna's design, as described in US patents [8,9], resulted in its near field and far field performances not aligning in the same direction or at the same frequency. The UHF Reader Antenna was specifically engineered to accommodate both near and far field operations [10]. Comprising segmented square loop and patch antennas, it functions within the 865–867MHz frequency range with linear polarization [10].

The paper introduces a patch antenna featuring a Swastik slot and a segmented square loop, designed for both near and far field operations. The antenna is fed by a simple microstrip line. The subsequent sections cover the design of a circularly polarized patch antenna, a segmented loop antenna, and a CP UHF Reader antenna for near and far field applications. Section (5) discusses the simulated results, and finally, section (6) offers the conclusion.

Design of Circularly Polarized Patch Antenna

Patch antennas made of microstrip are utilized in wireless communications because of their compact size, lightweight nature, and affordability, making them well-suited for wireless communication applications. Therefore, it is advisable to employ microstrip patches when designing RFID reader antennas. Microstrip antennas comprise a radiating patch, substrate, and ground plane. Ground plane and patch are metals and substrate is made up of dielectric material. The patch may be in any shape, and most popularly used are square, rectangular and circle. In this paper, square patch is used, which may reduce the space problem and useful for compact antenna design.

Specifications:
Telecom regulatory authority of India (TRAI) adopted a frequency range of 865MHz to 867MHz for RFID in India.

- f_0 = 866MHz, Where f_0 = resonant frequency.
- Substrate material is Rogers RT Duroid 8220 with ϵ_r = 2.2.
- Height of the substrate h = 3.175mm.

Patch width $W = \frac{1}{2f_r\sqrt{\mu_0\epsilon_0}}\sqrt{\frac{2}{\epsilon_r+1}}$ (1)

Width of the patch W_p = 136.93mm
Effective dielectric constant,

$$\epsilon_{reff} = \frac{\epsilon_r+1}{2} + \frac{\epsilon_r-1}{2}\left[\left(1 + 12\frac{h}{W}\right)^{\frac{-1}{2}}\right] \quad (2)$$

$= 2.1306$

$$\frac{\Delta L}{h} = 0.412\frac{(\epsilon_{reff}+0.3)(\frac{W}{h}+0.264)}{(\epsilon_{reff}-0.258)(\frac{W}{h}+0.8)} \quad (3)$$

$\Delta L = 1.677$ mm

The resonant frequency of the microstrip antenna is typically determined by its length for the dominant TM010 mode. The expression for this frequency is often represented as:

$$(f_{rc})010 = \frac{1}{L_{eff}\sqrt{\epsilon_{reff}}\sqrt{\mu_0\epsilon_0}} = \frac{v_0}{2L\sqrt{\epsilon_r}} \quad (4)$$

Effective length of the patch L_{eff} = 118.7 mm

$$L_{eff} = L + 2\Delta L \quad (5)$$

Length of the patch L_p = 115.3 mm
  Ground plane dimensions:
  Ground plane length L_g = 6 h + L_p = 134.4 mm
  Ground plane width W_g = 6 h + W_p = 156 mm.
  Patch impedance:
  The radiating slots represent the radiating edges of the patch antenna and are characterized by a parallel equivalent admittance Y, which includes conductance G and susceptance B.

$$G1 = \frac{1}{90}\left(\frac{w}{\lambda_0}\right)^2 \text{ if } W << \lambda_0 \quad (6)$$

$$= \frac{1}{120}\left(\frac{W}{\lambda_0}\right) \text{ if } W >> \lambda_0 \quad (7)$$

Using equation (6), G1 = 0.001731 mhos

$$Z_{in} = \frac{1}{Y_{in}} = \frac{1}{2G_1} \quad (8)$$

$$R_{in} = \frac{1}{2G_1} = 288\Omega$$

Dimensions of feed line:
  Feed line port or lumped port resistance is 50Ω.
  Feed line impedance

$$Z_{feedline} = \sqrt{Z_{patch}Z_{port}} \quad (9)$$

$= \sqrt{288 * 50}$

$= 120\Omega$

Impedance of feed line:

$$Z_{feedline} = \frac{377}{\left[\frac{W}{h} + 2\right]\left[\sqrt{\epsilon_r}\right]} = 120\ \Omega \quad (10)$$

Width of feed line = $W_{feedline}$ = 0.375mm
  Length of the feed line

$$L_{feedline} = \frac{\lambda}{4\sqrt{\epsilon_r}} = 59.32\text{mm} \quad (11)$$

A patch with Swastik slot '卐' has been used to obtain circular polarization. The dimensions of the slot on a square patch are taken as, slot length (c) = $\frac{L_{patch}}{2.72}$ and Width of the slot (d) = $\frac{c}{10}$.

For Circularly polarized patch antenna design, a square patch of 115.3 × 115.3 × 0.05mm3 and ground plane of 130 × 130 × 0.05 mm3 were taken. The resonant frequency of the antenna was 840MHz. Patch size is further reduced to 111.3 mm to get the required resonant frequency of 866 MHz. A slot in the shape '卐' was cut on the surface of the patch. The slot dimensions length, width and its side arm lengths are 40.92 mm, width 4.092 mm ,19.58 mm respectively. The dimensions of the slot were slightly adjusted to 41.15 mm, 3.06 mm and 19.06 mm and slot position shifted upper left-hand side of patch to get

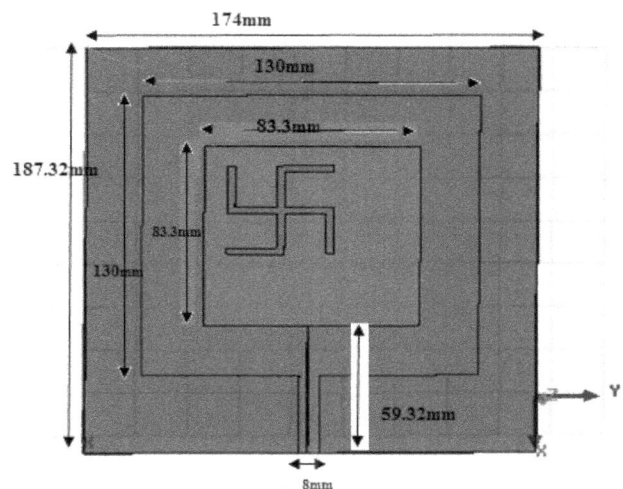

Figure 44.1 Patch antenna with Swastik slot
Source: Author

the desired resonant frequency and CP with axial ratio less than 3dB. Below in Figure 44.1, the diagram displays the configuration of the antenna.

Design of Segmented Loop Antenna

Loop antenna is a simple, inexpensive, versatile antenna and suitable for near field applications. To obtain large interrogation read range, a segmented loop antenna is preferred at UHF frequency range. In this paper, a square loop with segmented loop technique was used. In which, solid loop antenna is divided into 8 segments. In Figure 44.2, the diagram displays the segmented loop antenna. The segments of the loop at the top and bottom of the substrate can produce a stray electric field due to its capacitive effects.

Design specifications:

- Loop antenna circumference = 616 mm
- Side length of the loop antenna = 154 mm
- Height of the substrate h = 3.175 mm
- Width of each segment w = 8 mm

Each segment's equivalent inductance can be roughly estimated based on that of a loop with a constant current distribution [11].

$$L = \frac{\mu a}{N} \left[\ln\left(\frac{8}{0.25}\frac{a}{w}\right) - 2 \right] \qquad (12)$$

Where a = radius of the loop
N = Number of segments
w=width of the segment
Circumference of the loop taken as 616mm and radius of the loop 'a' = 98 mm

$$L = \frac{4\pi}{8} 10^{-7} \left[\ln\left(\frac{8}{0.25} * \frac{0.098}{0.008}\right) - 2 \right]$$
$$= 0.061 \mu H$$
$$f = \frac{1}{2\pi\sqrt{LC}} \qquad (13)$$

Using the equation (13), the value of C calculated at f = 866 MHz.

$$C = \frac{1}{L*(2\pi f)^2}$$
$$= \frac{1}{0.061*10^{-6}} * \frac{1}{(2*3.14*866*10^6)^2}$$
$$= 0.55 \text{ pF}$$
$$C = \epsilon_0 \epsilon_r \frac{A}{h}; \qquad (14)$$

The area of overlap is represented by A. The height of the substrate is denoted as h. The permittivity of free space is symbolized by ϵ_0 and its value is

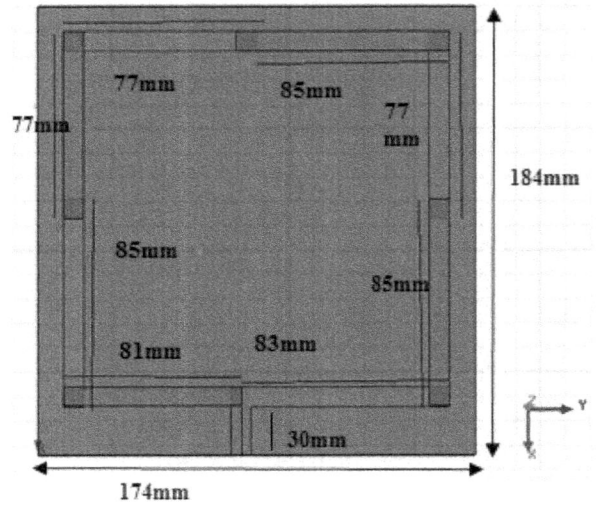

Figure 44.2 Segmented loop antenna
Source: Author

$8.854 * 10^{-12}$ F/m. The relative permittivity of the substrate is denoted as ϵ_r and its value is 2.2.

The overlap area between the segments can be calculated by using equation (14).

$$\text{Overlap area between the segments } A = \frac{h}{\epsilon_0}\frac{C}{\epsilon_r}$$
$$= \frac{0.003175*0.55*10^{-12}}{2.2*8.854*10^{-12}}$$
$$= 90 \text{ mm}^2.$$

A segmented loop antenna with upper and bottom segments of sizes 77 mm and 85 mm respectively. The overlap area was taken as 64 mm 2, width of feed line is 0.375 mm and the overlap area adjusted to 35.2 mm^2 at feed position to get the resonant frequency of 866 MHz.

CP UHF RFID (C-U-R) Reader Antenna: Antenna Structure and Dimensions

The UHF reader antenna for near and far field applications was designed using patch antenna with a Swastik slot and around the patch, segmented loop constructed. In Figure 44.3, the diagram displays the antenna for C-U-F reader.

Adjusted the dimensions of the patch and slot length, width and side arm length to 42.4 mm, 3.24 mm and 19.58 mm to resonate the two structures for the same resonant frequency. The Swastik slot generates the higher order modes desired for circular polarization. Antenna was simulated using Ansoft HFSS and results are shown in the below Figures 44.4 to 44.15.

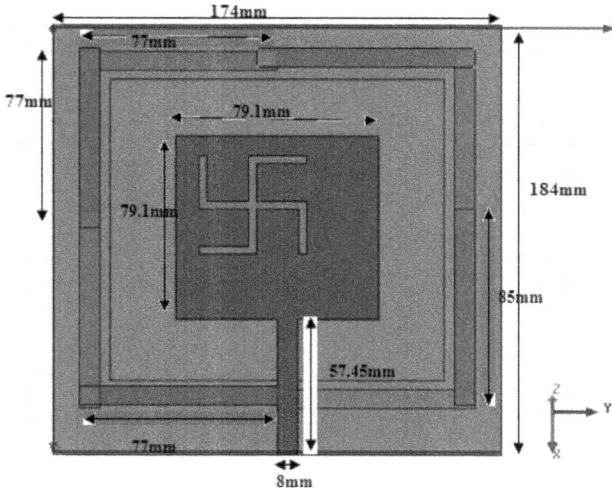

Figure 44.3 The antenna for the **C-U-R** Reader
Source: Author

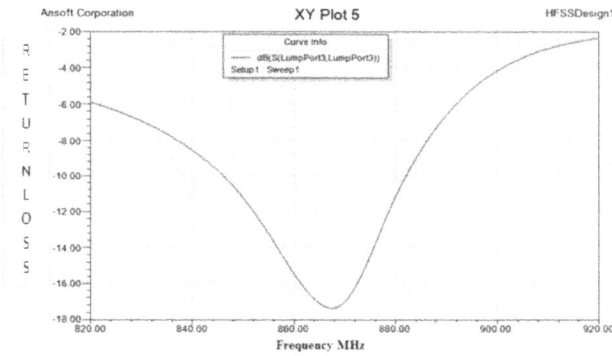

Figure 44.4 The frequency of the **C-U-R** reader antenna with the return loss (s11)
Source: Author

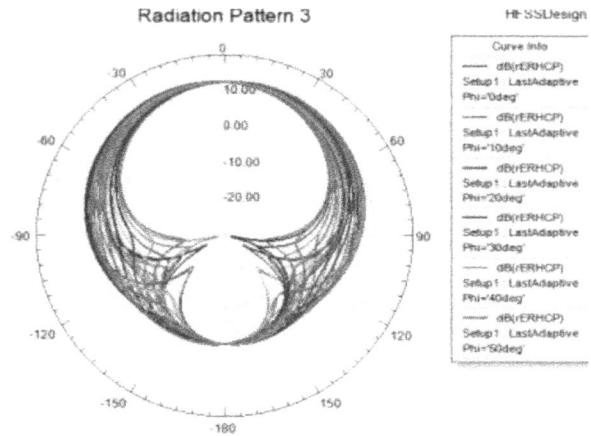

Figure 44.5 The radiation pattern **C-U-R** reader antenna
Source: Author

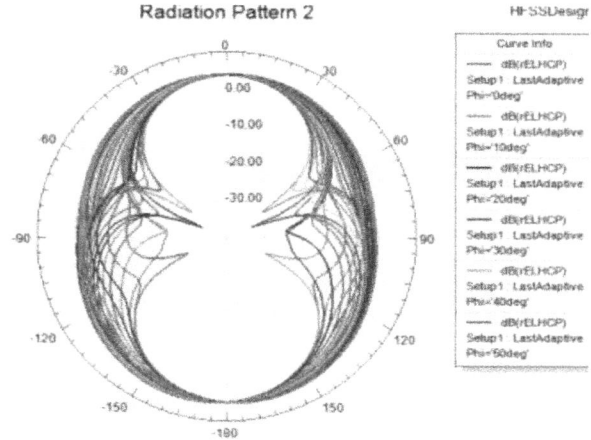

Figure 44.6 Radiation pattern of LHCP electric field of the **C-U-R** reader antenna
Source: Author

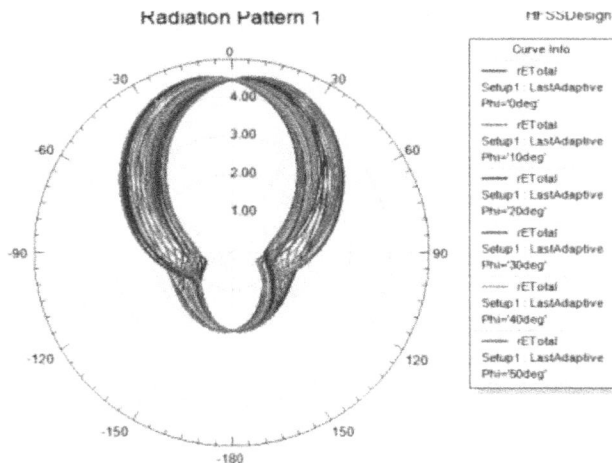

Figure 44.7 Radiation pattern of RHCP electric field of the **C-U-R** reader antenna
Source: Author

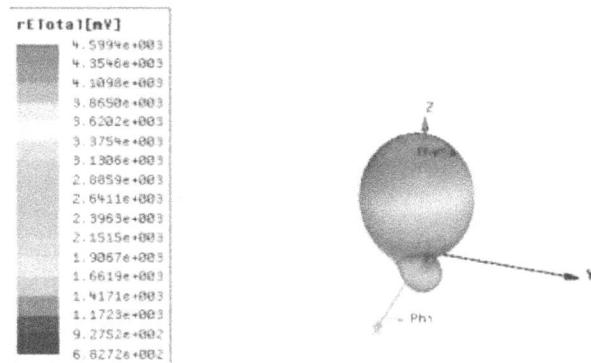

Figure 44.8 3D-plot of electric field distribution of the **C-U-R** reader antenna
Source: Author

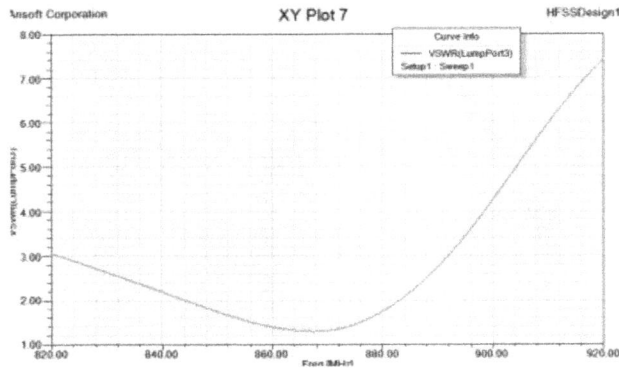

Figure 44.9 VSWR vs frequency of the **C-U-R** reader antenna
Source: Author

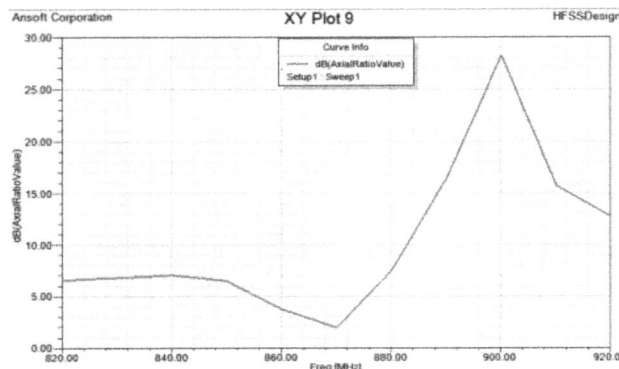

Figure 44.10 Axial ratio Vs frequency of the **C-U-R** reader antenna
Source: Author

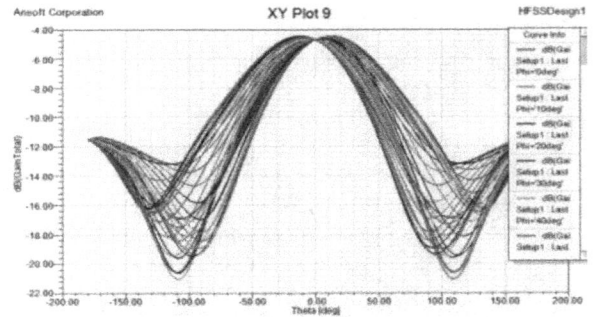

Figure 44.11 Gain Vs theta for various values of phi
Source: Author

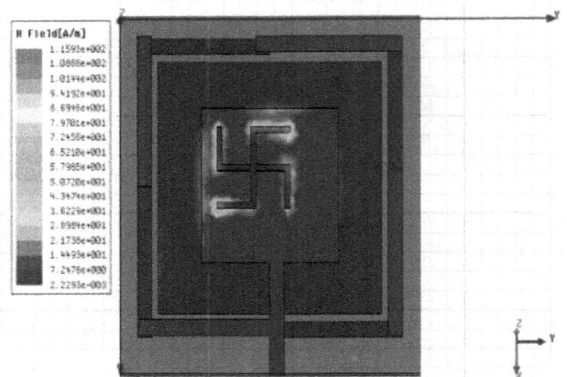

Figure 44.12 Electric field vectors of the **C-U-R** antenna
Source: Author

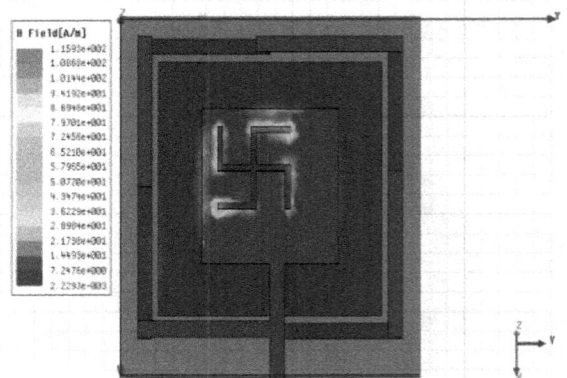

Figure 44.13 MF distribution of CP UHF reader
Source: Author

The axial ratio (AR) is below 3dB for the frequency range 865 to 878MHz. AR below 3dB indicates circular polarization.

Figure 44.12 shows the electric distribution of fields of the reader antenna, while Figures 44.13 and 44.14 show the magnetic field and current distributions, respectively.

Discussion on Simulated Results

It was observed that Magnetic field is significant up to a distance of 10mm. Radiation patterns of LHCP, RHCP Electric fields were observed for different slot positions as shown in Figure 44.15.

The position of the slot at top left and right yields better right- and left-hand circular polarizations respectively. There was degradation of CP radiation, when the feed shifted to the left from the middle position. There was good CP radiation, but with an increase in return loss at the desired frequency, when the feed position shifted right from the center. Feed positions, return loss, are listed in Table 44.1.

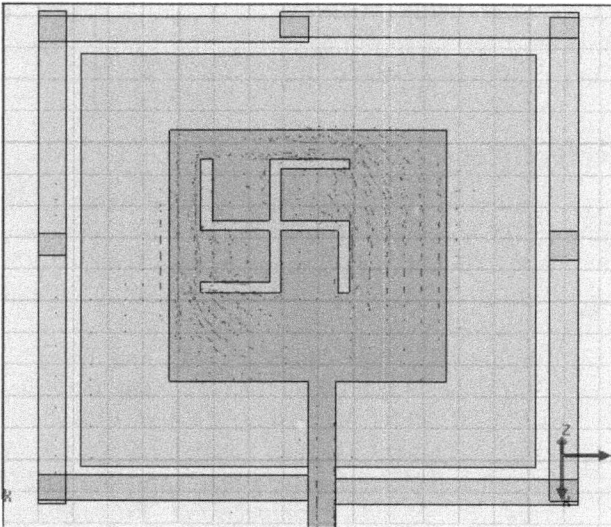

Figure 44.14 Current density vectors on the surface of the patch
Source: Author

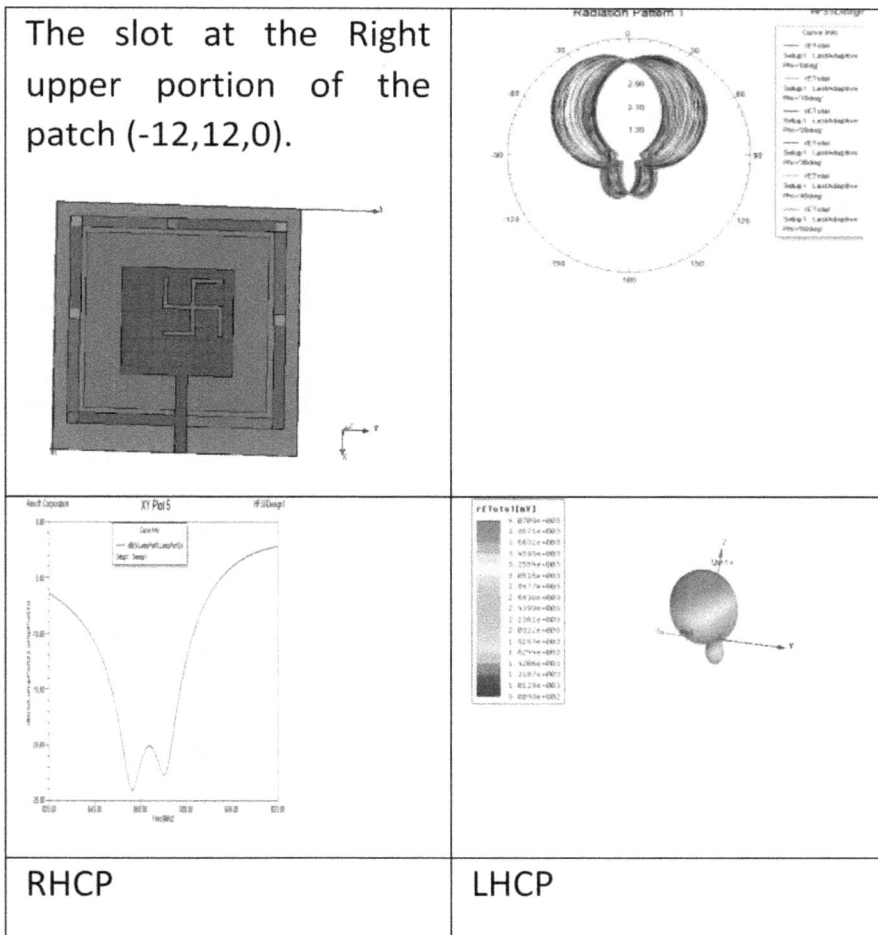

Figure 44.15 Slot position at upper right (-12,12,0)
Source: Author

Table 44.1 Feed position from feed position y = 87

Feed position (along Y-axis)	Return loss vs frequency
51(left most edge)	820–840 MHz @-18dB
69	860 MHZ @-30dB
71	860 MHz @-23dB
73	858–888 MHz @-21dB
75	858–866 MHz @-20dB
77	862–866 MHz @ -20dB
79	864–868 MHz @-20dB
81	858–870 MHz @-20dB
83	856–870 MHz @-16dB
85	846–882 MHz @ -10dB
87 middle position	846-882 MHz @-10dB
89	860–872 MHz @ -14dB
91	854–870 MHz @-14dB
93	856–864 MHz @-14dB
95	852–888 MHz @-12dB
97	856–870 MHz @-11dB
99	852–864 MHz @-12dB
102(right most)	848–870 MHz @-10dB

Source: Author

Conclusion

The simulated broadband, circularly polarized UHF RFID reader antenna in Ansoft HFSS demonstrates proper impedance matching, maintaining a VSWR between 1 and 2 across the 846-882 MHz frequency range. Effective circular polarization is achieved through the use of a Swastik slot on the patch, resulting in an axial ratio below 3 dB and a 36 MHz bandwidth (846–882 MHz), albeit with a noticeable reduction in gain. To further enhance the antenna's performance, improvements can be made in the near-field strength for better RFID tag detection, gain can be enhanced to offset the reduction caused by circular polarization, and the frequency extended to cover the full universal UHF RFID range of 840–960 MHz, making the antenna more versatile for global applications.

References

[1] Motorola (2012). Getting started with UHF RFID solutions (White paper).Part number : WP-UHFRFID101. Printed in USA 09/12. MOTOROLA, MOTO , MOTOROLA SOLUTIONS 2012 Motorola Solutions , Inc.

[2] Dobkin, D. M., Weigand, S. M., and Iyec, N. (2007). Segmented magnetic antennas for near-field UHF-RFID. *Microwave Journal*, 50(6), 96.

[3] Qing, X., Goh, C. K., and Chen, Z. N. (2010). A broadband UHF near field RFID antenna. *IEEE Transactions on Antennas and Propagation*, 58(12), 3829–3838.

[4] Balnies, C. A. (2016). Antenna Theory: Analysis and Design. John Wiley and Sons.

[5] Guo, Y. X., Khoo, K. W., and Ong, L. C. (2008). Wideband circularly polarized patch antenna using broadband baluns. *IEEE Transactions on Antennas and Wireless Propagation*, 56(2), 319–326.

[6] Yang, S. L. S., and Luk, K. M. (2008). A wideband L-probes fed circularly polarized reconfigurable microstrip patch antenna. *IEEE Transactions on Antennas and Propagation*, 56(2), 581–584.

[7] Chen, Z. N., and Qing, X. (2012). A compact circularly polarized cross-shaped slotted microstrip antenna. *IEEE Transactions on Antennas and Propagation*, 60(3), 3821–3828.

[8] Oliver, R. A. (2008). Broken-loop RFID reader antenna for near field and far field UHF RFID tags. U.S. Design Patent D570,337S.

[9] Qing, X., and Chen, Z. N. (2010). Antenna for near field and far field radio frequency identification. U.S. Patent Application Publication US 20100026439A1.

[10] Shrestha, B., and Elsherbeni, A. (2011). UHF reader antenna for near field and far field operations. *IEEE Antennas and Wireless Propagation Letters*, 10, 1274–1277.

[11] Yang, P., Li, Y., Jiang, L. J., and Yang, F. (2011). Near-field loop antenna for the UHF RFID reader. *Journal of Electronic Science and Technology*, 9(3), 256–260.

45 Design of sample-hold circuit for optimal operating conditions

Jahnavi, M.[1,a], *Madhavi, B.*[1,b], *Ch. Varshini*[1,c] and *Parvathi, M.*[2,d]

[1]Graduate Students, BVRIT HYDERABAD College of Engineering for Women, Department of Electronics and Communication Engineering, Hyderabad, Telangana, India

[2]Professor, BVRIT HYDERABAD College of Engineering for Women, Department of Electronics and Communication Engineering, Hyderabad, Telangana, India

Abstract

Sample and hold circuits are essential components in data conversion, making them crucial in applications such as signal processing, communication systems, control systems, and more. The primary functional components of a sample and hold circuit are the switch, which samples the input signal, and the capacitor, which holds the sampled values. The usual choice is MoS transistors as switches, but there are several drawbacks when using them in low-voltage applications. To accommodate lower supply voltages, high-threshold transistors need their threshold voltage reduced. However, this causes an exponential increase in sub-threshold leakage current, which distorts the analog sample and as a result the static power dissipation will increase. Another issue with high-threshold voltage MOS transistors is that the speed of the operation will decrease due to high series resistance that effects the overall performance of the system. Despite these challenges, it is crucial to uphold performance improvements without compromising the device's portability. To meet these demands, it is vital to focus on noise reduction for high signal integrity and to minimize power dissipation, ensuring longer battery life and enhanced portability. Designing sample and hold circuits involves addressing several critical issues, including charge leakage, switching noise, charge injection, bandwidth limitations, settling time, capacitor matching, power dissipation, linearity, and temperature sensitivity. The major consideration will be settling time to ensure the circuit stabilizes quickly after sampling to avoid errors in the held value, especially in high-speed applications. The proposed design of sample hold circuit uses a transmission gate in the place of traditional MoS switch at the output phase with a matched capacitor. Experiments are conducted with various sampling capacitor values to measure and evaluate the optimal desired operational conditions and observed that the typical value of Cs to be chosen as 6pF at which ACRMS of 361mv, RMS of 849mv, slew rate of 12.6 v/us, SNR of 25.1, with delay of 39ns, for signal power of 52.1dbm.

Keywords: Leakage current, low power, sample voltage, threshold voltage, wide band applications

Introduction

The analog-to-digital converter (ADC) is a crucial element in medical appliances and systems that are used for health monitoring purposes, frequently serving as a central block that affects the overall system performance. For biomedical applications, it is essential to meet the constraints like minimal power consumption with required high resolution. Sample and hold circuits (SHC) are vital for efficient and rapid analog-to-digital conversion [1], and they are also fundamental in handheld devices and measurement instruments.

These circuits are extensively employed in signal processing and medical applications within wireless communication, playing a key role in influencing both power consumption and resolution. They are also utilized in digital-to-analog converters (DACs) for similar purposes. Additionally, sample and hold circuits are employed in analog de-multiplexing for data distribution and in analog delay lines. Overall, S/H circuits are essential in any application where it is important to stabilize an analog signal for further processing.

[a]21WH1A0433@bvrithyderabad.edu.in, [b]21WH1A0441@bvrithyderabad.edu.in, [c]21WH1A0450@bvrithyderabad.edu.in, [d]parvathi.m@bvrithyderabad.edu.in

DOI: 10.1201/9781003616399-45

Sample-and-hold (S/H) circuits, also known as "trail and freeze" circuits, are essential components in the systems where in the output signal varies in accordance with the input signal. It functions as a temporary storage device by "sampling" the input signal and then "holding" that value until it is ready for processing or conversion. In all of the signal processing systems the initial block is ADC hence being input the analog signal first encounters the S/H circuit, making it crucial for overall ADC performance and, consequently, the entire system. The S/H circuit significantly influences the data converter's performance by minimizing errors caused by slight variations in internal delay times.

There are different types of S/H circuits. The first type includes those with an active block, like an operational amplifier, and/or a supply voltage. This group comprises S/H circuits with clock feed through cancellation, inverting S/H circuits, and those using a bootstrapped technique. The second type includes S/H circuits that do not have an active block and do not require a supply voltage [2]. The dependability and precision of the S/H circuit are primarily determined by the amount of resistance drop from the supply rails of the sampling switch during on state, further that impacts its linearity. It is important to consider that varying sampling rates are utilized for different purposes, which can affect the characteristics of operating conditions of the S/H circuit and also of ADC. Different metrics will be prioritized depending on the specific application [3].

In Figure 45.1, a single-ended basic SHC is depicted, that includes an NMOS functioning as the basic switch M1 and a sampling capacitor Cs. A single-phase clock serves as the control input. Voltage sampling occurs during 'on' state of the clock through 'on' transistor, at which output capacitor voltage follows the input voltage. The sampled voltage will remain maintain constant to the input voltage level during 'off' state of the clock and transistor.

The major concern observed in traditional SHC is excess charge carrier flow and unwanted coupling of clock signals, which are often encountered when a traditional MoS transistor is operated as switch along with capacitor [4]. Charge injections occur when the control input goes high. At this point, the transistor switch will get ON and samples the input voltage using capacitor Cs. Due to the channel inversion, a charge Q_{ch} builds up below the gate oxide layer according to the formula [4]:

$$Q_{ch} = W.L.C_{ox}. + (V_{dd} - V_{in} - V_{tn}) \qquad (1)$$

During the off the state of the clock, the switch transistor state is OFF, then any accumulated channel charge flows out from its gate then to any of the diffusion leads. This flow creates a disturbance in the expected output sample voltage. By considering the excess charge across the sampling capacitor, the output sample voltage V_{out} can be expressed as per the equation below [4]:

$$V_{out} = V_{in}(1 + W.L.\frac{C_{ox}}{C_s}) - (W.L.\frac{C_{ox}}{C_s})(V_{dd} - V_{tn}) \qquad (2)$$

As such, two parameters affect the sampled output voltage: one is $(1 + W.L.\frac{C_{ox}}{C_s})$ which is equivalent to gain parameter and the other is a constant offset voltage $(-(W.L.\frac{C_{ox}}{C_s})(V_{dd} - V_{tn}))$ [4]. [4].

Clock feed through refers to unwanted coupling of clock signals, through switch transistors via their diffusion and gate intersection capacitances. However, the state of control input, either high or low respectively; the capacitances which are fed through creates an offset voltage given by:

$$\Delta V_{offset} = \frac{C_{ox}}{(C_{ox} + C_s)V_{dd}} \qquad (3)$$

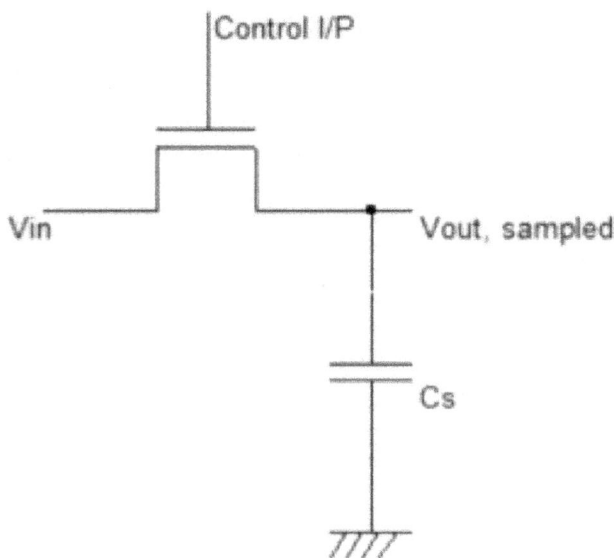

Figure 45.1 SHC traditional circuit
Source: Author

Here C_{ov} represents overlap capacitance [4].

The essential goal of present work is to achieve constant sample output for that to design SHC using transmission gate as basic circuits and to experiment various output capacitor values to capture and maintain the value of an analog signal accurately at a specific moment in time, ensuring that it remains constant for subsequent processing, such as analog-to-digital conversion. This involves minimizing errors such as droop, noise, and timing inaccuracies, while optimizing factors like settling time, linearity, and stability to achieve high precision and reliability in signal sampling. The residue of the paper is organized as follows: Section 2 deliberates the current SHC designs and their limitations. Section 3 conveys an outline of the proposed transmission gate-based SHC, focusing on the experimentation with various output capacitor values. Section 4 presents the investigational results and comparisons, while section 5 deals with the final concluding remarks on the present work.

Review on SHC Design Issues

Charge leakage

The common problem in the sample hold circuit is charging leakage that occurs when a switch is turned off that causes charge injection and distortion of the sampled output voltage. This phenomenon introduces non-linear errors in the system, impacting on its overall performance. To mitigate the impact of charge injection on system accuracy, circuit designers can employ several techniques [5–12]. These include utilizing high-quality materials for gate oxides and implementing careful switch structure designs. Additionally, shielding or isolation methods can be used to prevent leakage and distortion in the output voltage, while calibration and correction techniques in signal processing stages can further enhance accuracy. Understanding and effectively managing charge injection effects is essential for maintaining reliable operation in electronic circuits and systems.

Droop rate

Droop rate refers to the decay of a held voltage over time due to leakage currents in the circuit, particularly in the hold capacitor. This can result in inaccuracies in the sampled signal, especially if the hold period is lengthy. To address this issue, it is recommended to use capacitors with low leakage and high-quality operational amplifiers with minimal input bias currents [13].

Aperture error

Aperture error arises from uncertainty in the exact timing of the sampling switch transition, leading to potential inaccuracies in the captured signal. This issue is especially critical in high-speed applications, where even slight timing discrepancies can cause significant errors. To reduce aperture error, employ high-speed, precise switching components and minimize control signal jitter [14] to ensure accurate and consistent signal capture.

Settling time

Settling time is the period desired for the output to stabilize within a specified error margin after the switch closes. If the circuit doesn't settle quickly, the sampled voltage might not accurately reflect the input signal. To ensure accurate sampling, select op-amps [15] and other components with sufficient bandwidth and stability. In the past work, SHC was designed [16] for analog memory to achieve sufficiently extended delay time. However, one drawback of extended delay time in sample-and-hold circuits is that it can lead to increased signal distortion and reduced accuracy. Longer delay times may also result in slower response to changes in the signal input, which can impact the overall performance and speed of the system. Additionally, it can introduce noise and reduce the circuit's ability to track fast signal variations effectively.

Capacitor size and parasitic

The size of the hold capacitor directly impacts the balance between droop rate and settling time, with parasitic capacitances also playing a role in overall accuracy. Incorrect capacitor sizing can degrade circuit performance. Further that effects spurious-free dynamic range (SFDR) and signal-to-noise and distortion ratio (SNDR) [17]. To optimize results, choose capacitor values that account for these trade-offs, and reduce parasitic through careful PCB layout design.

In this proposed design of sample hold circuit (SHC) various capacitor values are used and experimented to observe the variations in parameters like ACRMS, RMS, slew rate, SNR, delay and signal power. The experimented values are compared and analyzed for better performances with [2,3,17,18]. This analysis further helps in the best operating zone of SHC without degradation in its performance.

Proposed Design of SHC

Basic sample hold circuit

Before designing the proposed SHC, it's crucial to first establish a standard SHC and define the relevant performance metrics. This foundation will help guide improvements for the proposed version. The basic SHC is a simple circuit among all extended types that can be realized using a CMOS technology as shown in Figure 45.1. This section introduces basic S/H circuit architecture, its problems, and a modified version of it which compensate the induced problems. All the presented S/H circuits in this section are from the second type of S/H circuits.

Basic S/H circuit is a single-ended architecture. It consists of single NMOS switch M1 and a sampling capacitor Cs as shown in Figure 45.1. It operates through a control input which is clock with single phase Ø. When Ø goes high the transistor turns ON, and the voltage across the capacitor ($V_{out,sampled}$) follows the input voltage (Vin). When Ø goes low, the transistor turns OFF, and ($V_{out,sampled}$) will stay constant having a value equal to (Vin) at the instance of Ø went low. The circuit is implemented using Synopsys tool with 32 nm technology as shown in Figure 45.2. It follows the symbol creation shown in Figure 45.3 for waveform analysis. The control input clock applied through a pulse generator with rise time 1ps and voltage level of 4v. At the same time the input for sample the signal applied is a sine wave with frequency of 50 mHz, with a voltage amplitude of 0.5v. Corresponding simulation results for sampled output Voltage $V_{out,sampled}$ with sampling frequency of 0.16MHz is shown in Figure 45.4.

The simulation was done for this basic SH circuit with a sinusoidal signal as input with amplitude and frequency of 500 mVp–p and 50 MHz respectively. This signal is sampled at clock frequency of 0.16 MHz. The sampling capacitor

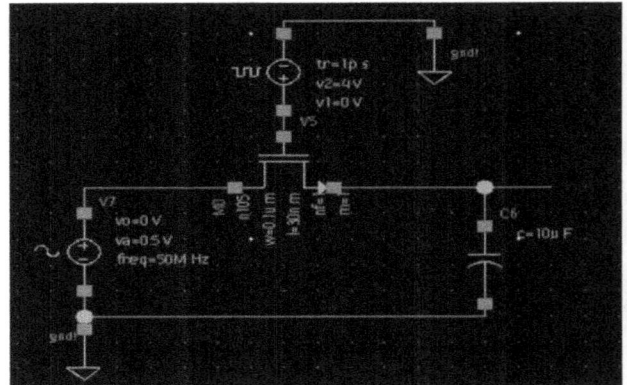

Figure 45.2 Traditional sample-hold circuit using synopsys
Source: Author

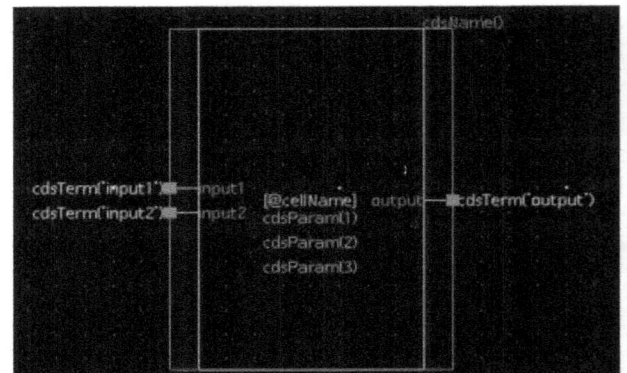

Figure 45.3 Symbol generation of traditional SHC
Source: Author

Cs is chosen to be 10uF. It is significant to note that the sampling capacitor influences two main factors, one is ADC's input range and the other is resolution, which translates into an equivalent thermal noise specification (KTCs) [3]. Hence the study and experimentation on finding the range of sampling capacitors is helpful in identifying optimizable operating conditions while choosing for high-end applications. The aspect ratio W/L of the transistor nMoS M1 chosen is 0.01 um/32 nm and is shown in Figure 45.5. Corresponding layout and RC error clean results are shown in Figures 45.6 –45.8 respectively.

Proposed transmission gate based sample hold circuit

In order to overcome the issues of excess charge accumulation and reduction of the clock signal's voltage swing, the basic SH circuit is inefficient to

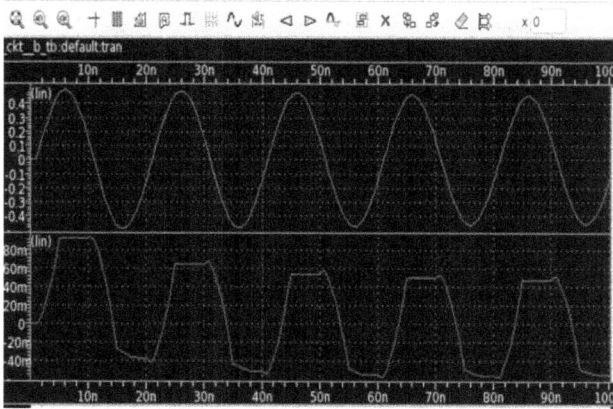

Figure 45.4 Sampled output voltage V~out,sampled~ with sampling frequency of 0.16MHz
Source: Author

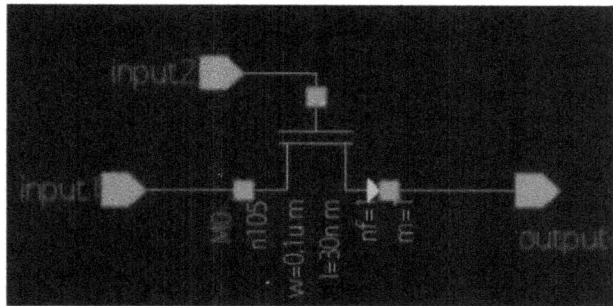

Figure 45.5 Transistor size specifications
Source: Author

Figure 45.6 Layout of traditional SHC in physical design environment
Source: Author

be used in high-speed application, hence it should be modified by using additional component meant for absorbing the channel charge deposited on Cs control input during off period of transistor M1. For this we can use another transistor

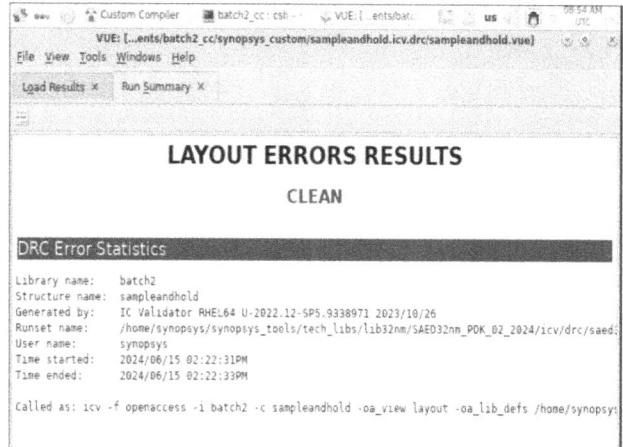

Figure 45.7 DRC layout error results output
Source: Author

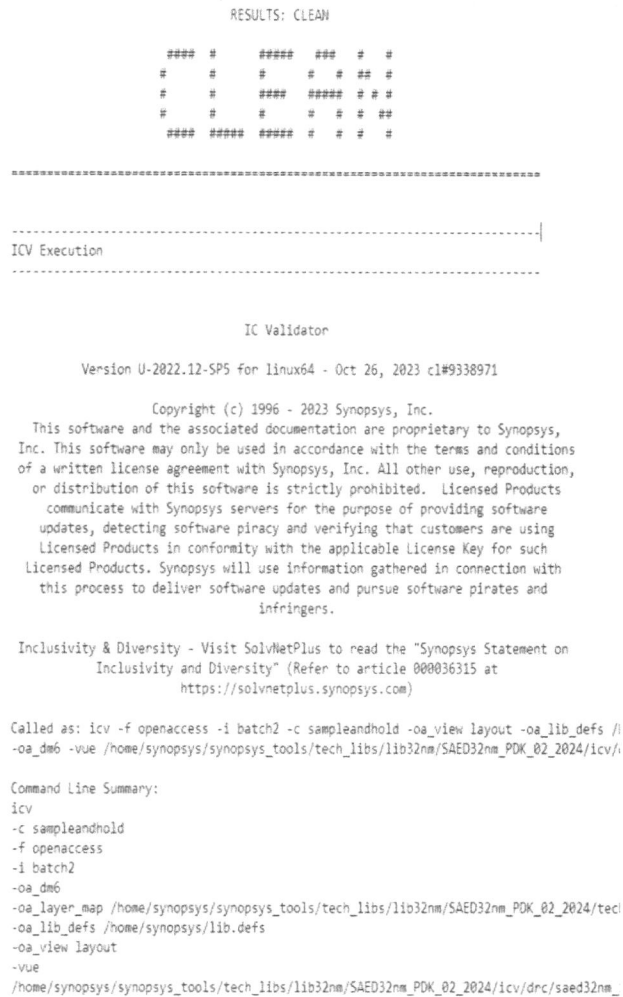

Figure 45.8 DRC validation of traditional SHC in physical design environment
Source: Author

M2 as a dummy switch. The problem of excess charge accumulation is eliminated when the inoculated charge (δq1) and captivated charge (δq2) are equal. To achieve this balance, it is required to select the transistor sizes in such a way that W_{M2}/W_{M1} should be 0.5, assuming both transistors have the same channel length. However, average power consumption is not controlled with such simple dummy switch [2]. Hence as an alternative dummy switch can be replaced with transmission gate TG as shown in Figure 45.7.

This method includes replacing the single transistor with a CMOS transmission gate, as shown in Figure 45.9. If the size of the PMOS transistor (MP) is made equal to that of the NMOS transistor (MN) as shown in Table 45.1, the problem excess flow of carriers from each transistor will get cancel out during the off state of the transmission gate. The PMOS transistor (MP) improves the on-conductance between the input and output when the input voltage approaches the supply voltage.

However, at the circuit level, under low voltage and high-frequency conditions, the MOSFET switches may not fully turn on, especially when operating at higher voltages. This issue arises when the sum of the absolute values of the PMOS and NMOS threshold voltages exceeds the supply voltage. In such cases, the MOSFET switches exhibit poor conductance, which can limit the circuit's bandwidth. Therefore, a bootstrapped technique with boosted driver is required to address this limitation as represented in Figure 45.9.

Simulation of this circuit was conducted using the aspect ratios shown in Figure 45.10, with C1=C2=Cs=2pf where Cs is output or sampling capacitor, and observed the input characteristics. The circuit exhibits a noise spectrum similar to that of the basic S/H circuit, with a total RMS output noise of 2.09 mV.

Further simulations were carried out using Cs with values of 4,6,8,15 and 50pF, and observed the parameters of ACRMS, RMS, slewrate, SNR, delay, and signal power. As Cs increases from 2pF

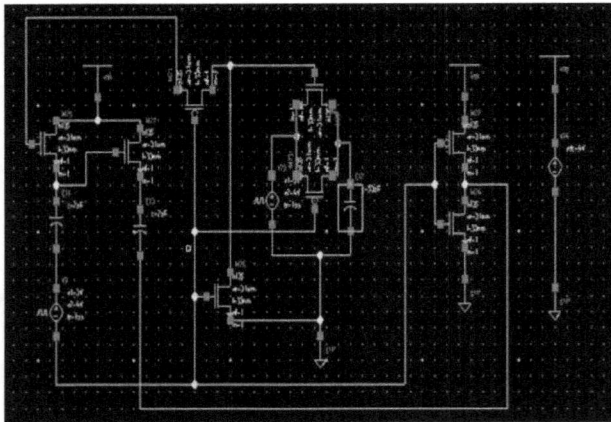

Figure 45.9 Modified SHC using transmission gate with boosted driver
Source: Author

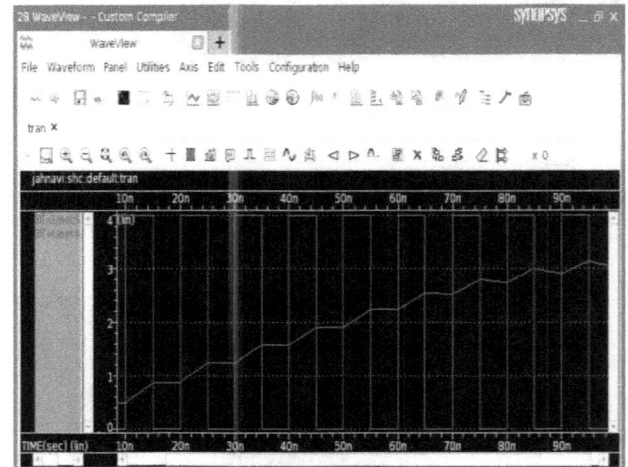

Figure 45.10 SHC using transmission gate with boosted driver with Cs = 2pF
Source: Author

Table 45.1 Length to width ratio technology selection criteria

Tr type used in SHC	Boosted Driver Size, nm		Clock Tr Size, nm		Transmission Gate Size, nm	
L:W	L	W	L	W	L	W
Nmos[2]	180	90	180	270	90	540
Pmos[2]	-	-	180	270	90	540
Proposed	32	32	32	32	32	32

Source: Author

to 50pF the sampling curve observed into flatten as shown in Figures 45.11 and 45.12.

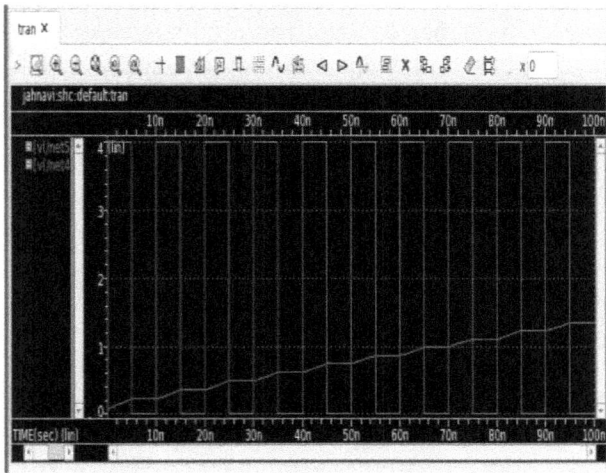

Figure 45.11 Sample and hold circuit using transmission gate with boosted driver with Cs = 6pF
Source: Author

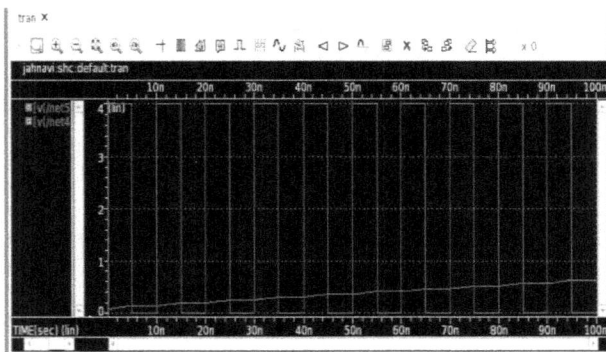

Figure 45.12 Sample and hold circuit using transmission gate with boosted driver with Cs = 50pF
Source: Author

Experimental Results

The simulation results observed for parameters of ACRMS, RMS, slew rate, SNR, delay, and signal power with various values of Cs, keeping C1=C2 =2pF constant. The observations are shown in Table 45.2.

It is observed that as Cs increases, ACRMS gradually decreases while RMS increases. A reduction in ACRMS noise is generally desirable, as it indicates a decrease in high-frequency noise, leading to improved signal integrity and reduced distortion. However, an increase in overall RMS noise suggests that other types of noise, such as DC or low-frequency noise, are becoming more prominent. This can adversely affect the accuracy and precision of the sampled signal. These effects can be further analyzed by varying other capacitor values within the circuit.

Similarly, observation is made on slew rate. The slew rate is a measure of how quickly the output of the circuit can change in response to a rapid change in the input signal. A higher slew rate means the circuit can more accurately and quickly follow fast-changing signals without distortion. A too low slew rate causes issues like distortion, inaccurate sampling and settling time. In the proposed design, slew rate is reduced when C_s is increased. A moderate value of slew rate can be observed at chosen value of C_s=6pf at which ACRMS is sustained at 361mv and RMS is seen with better value of 849mV compared to other options of C_s.

On the other hand, SNR is increased when C_s is 2pF to Cs is 50pF. A higher SNR is desirable and indicates that the signal is significantly stronger

Table 45.2 Simulation results of transmission gate based SHC

Parameter	Sampling capacitor value, pF							
	2	4	5[4]	6 prop	8	15	50	% imp
ACRMS, mV	881	524	54.65	361	277	153	48.9	84.87
RMS, mV	2.09	1.2	26.59	849	666	401	180	96.87
Slew Rate,v/us	31.3	18.3	-	12.6	9.65	5.34	1.69	-
SNR	17.81	21.84	65.27	25.1	27.4	32.57	42.5	61.8
Delay, ns (neg)	35.69	38.7	-	39	39.1	39.2	39.6	-
Signal Power dbm	44.85	48.92	59.63	52.14	54.47	59.61	69.6	12.6

Source: Author

than the noise, allowing the circuit to capture the input signal more accurately, with minimal distortion or interference. Hence choosing C_s beyond 6pF is the right option for achieving better SNR outcome. However, the other parameters like delay and signal power increment variations are getting worse if the sampling capacitance value exceeds the limit of 6pF. Hence, on the whole, the better and desirable option for C_s selection is highlighted in yellow color in the Table 45.2 for easy understanding.

The other interesting parameter is SFDR (Spurious-Free Dynamic Range), the ratio between the amplitude of the fundamental signal i.e the desired signal and the amplitude of the largest spurious signal which is any unwanted signal within the bandwidth of interest. From Table 45.2, it is observed that the SNDR maintained constant at 27.07db with various C_s values in the proposed SHC, whereas it is 54.65db in [4]. It is advantageous with gradual increment in SFDR with stable SNDR in the proposed SHC as Cs is increased. Table 45.3 summarizes the optimal design parameters by comparing them with existing work.

Furthermore, the parameters derived from the chosen optimal range of Cs are compared with those from existing studies (2, 3, 17, and 18) as presented in Table 45.3. This work is conducted using 32nm technology, and when compared to earlier technologies of 90nm to 180nm, the proposed SHC demonstrates a strong advantage in delivering an optimal range of characteristic parameters.

Conclusions

The sample-and-hold circuit (SHC) is a crucial component in analog-to-digital conversion systems. This paper designs and analyzes both standard SHCs and transmission gate-based SHCs. The proposed transmission gate-based SHC addresses key limitations found in traditional SHCs, including charge sharing, weak SNR, and inconsistent power consumption. Various output capacitor values were tested to determine the optimal design parameters. At Cs=6 pF, the proposed design achieved significant improvements, including an 84.87% increase in ACRMS, a 96.87% increase in RMS, a 61.8% improvement in SNR, and a 12.6% reduction in signal power compared to existing SHC designs [4]. The optimal design parameters for enhanced SHC performance are summarized in Table 45.3.

References

[1] Xuan, W., Fule, L., and Bin, W. (2012). A 1.2V sample-and-hold circuit for 14-Bit 250MS/s pipeline ADC in 65 nm CMOS. In Zhu, M. (Eds.), Business, Economics, Financial Sciences, and Management. Advances in Intelligent and Soft Computing, (Vol. 143). Berlin, Heidelberg: Springer.

[2] Nazzal, T. B., and Mahmoud, S. A. (2016). A 1-V 8-Bit low-power clock gated SAR ADC for biomedical applications. In Graduate Students Research Conference 2016 in UAE (UAE GSRC 2016).

Table 45.3 Comparison of parameters for optimal range

Technology/ parameters	90 nm [2]	0.25 um [3]	0.18 um [17]	0.18 um [18]	32 nm [this work]
Supply Voltage, v	1	1	1	3.3	1
SNR (dB)	56.2	57	50.5	72	25.1
SNDR (dB)	46.2	40.5	45.2	-	27.07
SFDR (dB)	49.5	41	54	-	52.14
ENOB	7.3	6.5	7.2	9.7	3.8
FOM (fig of merit = SNR/ Power consumption)	0.53	6.85	3.23	-	0.481
Power consumption, uw	0.84	1.87	0.95	0.425mw	6.11nw

Source: Author

[3] Mahmoud, S. A., Salem, H. A., and Albalooshi, H. M. (2015). An 8-bit, 10KS/s, 1.87 μW successive approximation analog to digital converter in 0.25 μm CMOS technology for ECG detection systems. *Circuits, Systems, and Signal Processing*, 34(2), 2419–2439. doi: 10.1007/s00034-015-9973-z.

[4] Mahmoud, S., and Nazzal, T. (2015). Sample and hold circuits for low-frequency signals in analog-to-digital converter. In International Conference on Information and Communication Technology Research (ICTRC), (pp. 36–39). 10.1109/ICTRC.2015.7156415.

[5] Mahmoud, S. A., and Nazzal, T. B. (2015). Sample and hold circuits for analog-to-digital converters. In UAE Graduate Students Research Conference, (pp. 223–224).

[6] Cranincks, J., and Plas, G. (2007). A 65fJ/conversion-step 0-to-50MS/s 0-to-0.7mW 9b charge-sharing SAR ADC in 90nm digital CMOS. In IEEE International Solid-State Circuits Conference, Digest of Technical Papers, (pp. 246–600).

[7] Mahmoud, S. A., and Nazzal, T. B. (2015). Sample and hold circuits for low-frequency signals in analog-to-digital converter. In IEEE International Conference on Information and Communication Technology Research (ICTRC2015), (pp. 33–36).

[8] Nazzal, T., and Mahmoud, S. (2016). Low-power bootstrapped sample and hold circuit for analog to digital converters. In Midwest Symposium on Circuits and Systems, (pp. 1–4). 10.1109/MWSCAS.2016.7870027.

[9] Yousuf, R., and Najeeb-Ud-Din, H. (2017). Analysis of charge sharing in MOSFET's in view of available scaling trends. *IOSR Journal of Electronics and Communication Engineering*, 12, 44–52. 10.9790/2834-1206024452.

[10] Bucci, M., Luzzi, R., Pennisi, S., and Trifiletti, A. (2003). A charge injection based CMOS charge-pump. In 10th IEEE International Conference on Electronics, Circuits and Systems, 2003. ICECS 2003. Proceedings of the 2003 (Vol. 2, pp. 583–586). IEEE.

[11] Hwang, Y. S., Wang, S. F., Sheu, P. W., and Chen, J. J. (2008). Novel FBCCII-based sample-and-hold and MDAC circuits. *International Journal of Electronics*, 95(11), 1111–1117.

[12] Yousuf, Romana., Charge sharing-a review. Advanced Electrical and Electronics Engineering, 3(5), pp. 449–461, 10.13140/RG.2.2.10962.17604.

[13] Schillaci, L., Baschirotto, A., and Castello, R. (1997). A 3-V 5.4-mW BiCMOS track and hold circuit with sampling frequency up to 150 MHz. *IEEE Journal of Solid-State Circuits*, 32, 926–932. 10.1109/4.597282.

[14] Prakruthi T. G., and Yellampalli, S. (2015). Design and implementation of sample and hold circuit in 180 nm CMOS technology. In 2015 International Conference on Advances in Computing, Communications and Informatics (ICACCI), Kochi, India, (pp. 1148–1151). doi: 10.1109/ICACCI.2015.7275765.

[15] Raina, H. S. (1974). A new type of sample and hold circuit. *IETE Journal of Research*, 20(7), 374.

[16] Dai, L., and Harjani, R. (2000). CMOS switched-op-amp-based sample-and-hold circuit. *IEEE Journal of Solid-State Circuits*, 35, 109–113. 10.1109/4.818927.

[17] Lee, S. Y., Cheng, C. G., Wang, C. P., and Lee, S. C. (2009). A 1-V 8-Bit 0.95uW successive approximation ADC for biosignal acquisition systems. *IEEE International Symposium on Circuits and Systems*, 42(10), 649–652.

[18] Adupa, C., and Ijjada, S. (2023). Design and implementation of a bootstrap-based sample and hold circuit for SAR ADC applications. *International Journal of Electrical and Electronics Research*, 11, 689–695. 10.37391/ijeer.110308.

46 A study of low power high-speed sense amplifier for memory applications

*Pavankumar Bikki[a], Charankumar, K.[b], Manjusha, K.[c],
Sai Abhinandan Goud, E.[d] and Mamatha, G.[e]*

B V Raju Institute of Technology, Narsapur, Telangana, India

Abstract

The growing need for energy-efficient, high-performance electronic systems has intensified the need for advanced sense amplifiers that can operate at high speeds with minimal power consumption. This paper introduces the design and implementation of a new low-power, high-speed sense amplifier, aimed at addressing the trade-offs between speed, power, and reliability in modern memory and data converter applications. The proposed sense amplifier utilizes innovative circuit topologies and advanced design techniques to achieve faster sensing times while significantly reducing power dissipation. Key features of the design include optimized biasing strategies, reduced voltage swings, and adaptive feedback mechanisms that enhance performance without compromising energy efficiency. Simulation outcomes validate the effectiveness of the projected design, showing substantial improvements in both speed and power metrics compared to conventional sense amplifiers. The study also provides a comparative analysis with existing solutions, highlighting the advantages of the projected approach in terms of scalability and compatibility with advanced CMOS technologies. Overall, this work contributes to the development of next-generation sense amplifiers that meet the stringent requirements of contemporary electronic systems, offering a viable solution for integrating low-power, high-speed components in cutting-edge technologies.

Keywords: Current latch, sense amplifier, sense zone, SRAM memory, voltage latch

Introduction

In the rapidly evolving landscape of integrated circuits, the demand for high-speed, low-power sense amplifiers has become increasingly critical. Sense amplifiers (SA), fundamental components in memory devices and high-speed data converters, play a pivotal role in ensuring accurate and swift read operations. As technology nodes continue to shrink, the need for power-efficient designs that do not compromise on speed or reliability is paramount. Sense amplifiers are crucial components in digital and analog circuits. In digital circuits, they're used to amplify weak signals from memory cells, improving data reliability. In analog circuits, sense amplifiers help detect and amplify small voltage differences for accurate measurements. Their scope extends to memory design, image sensors, ADCs, and more. They show a vital part in enhancing signal integrity and optimizing performance [1,2]. A SA is an essential module of the read circuit in memory systems. Its purpose is to detect and enhance the weak signals from a bit-line, which represent the hold data bit (either 1 or 0) in a memory cell. By amplifying the smaller voltage swing to distinct logic levels, the sense amplifier ensures accurate interpretation of data by the logic circuits external to the memory. The SA is a crucial peripheral circuit in memory devices. The sense amplifier's operation involves several stages: Pre charge: Initially, bit lines are pre-charged to a common voltage, ensuring a known starting point [3]. The latch-type sense amplifier is commonly favored for its enhanced sensing performance and lower power consumption, making it the most widely used among the various established types of sense amplifiers. The sense amplifier reliably detects and produces a larger output signal when the input voltage difference surpasses the offset voltage (V_{os}). Ideally, the offset voltage of a signal

---

[a]pavankumar.b@bvrit.ac.in, [b]Charankumar.k@bvrit.ac.in, [c]manjusha.k@bvrit.ac.in, [d]21211a0472@bvrit.ac.in, [e]21211a0488@bvrit.ac.in

DOI: 10.1201/9781003616399-46

amplifier is zero. Hence, the SA can accurately detect ΔV_{BL}, unless ΔV_{BL} equals zero. However, V_{OS} is not zero due to the discrepancy between paired transistors. Therefore, to be accurately identified, ΔV_{BL} must exceed V_{OS}. Typically, V_{OS} follows a Gaussian distribution [4]. This paper presents a detailed study of the design and execution of a novel lower power, high-speed sense amplifier that addresses these pressing needs. The study delivers a detailed analysis of the design principles, circuit topologies, and execution strategies employed. Simulation results and comparisons with existing designs are presented.

Literature Review

Conventional SA's, such as the differential voltage and current-mode have been extensively studied for their simplicity and effectiveness in various memory applications. However, traditional designs often face challenges in balancing speed and power consumption, especially in deep submicron processes where leakage currents and parasitic capacitances become significant. When V_{BL} is assumed to be greater than V_{BLB} by a difference of ΔV_{BL}. The input voltage of the SA is referred to as V_{BL} in this document. Specifically, the variation in V_{TH}, caused through random dopant fluctuation (RDF) and expected to conform to a Gaussian distribution, converts a significant issue. Thus, the variation in V_{TH} is the primary factor influencing V_{OS} [5].

To address the power efficiency concerns, researchers have explored several low-power sense amplifier architectures. Techniques such as charge sharing, reduced voltage swings, and power gating have been proposed to minimize power dissipation. However, these methods sometimes compromise on the speed or add complexity to the circuit design [6]. Latch-type and current-latch sense amplifiers reduce sensing time and increase bit-line signal responsiveness, increasing speed. To accomplish speed, these designs frequently use complicated circuitry, which increases power consumption and design complexity [7].

Voltage-latched sense amplifier
Sense amplifier works by detecting an alteration in voltage between the bit lines. When a memory cell is accessed, the bit-lines are recharged to certain voltage level, and a voltage-latched sense amplifier detects the slight voltage difference caused by the stored data (either 0 or 1). The nMOS foot switch is used to control when the sense amplifier is enabled. These transistors are commonly employed to connect the bit-lines to the sense amplifier. pMOS transistors are utilized because they are more effective at transmitting a strong high voltage, which is important for maintaining the integrity of the voltage signal on the bitlines during amplification [8].

Current-latched sense amplifier
Unlike voltage-latch amplifiers, current-latched sense amplifiers work by detecting differences in current rather than voltage. The SA are designed to sense current flowing through the bit-lines and amplify this difference to determine the stored data. Current-latched sense amplifier (CLSA) can be more robust against variations in bit-line capacitance and can be less sensitive to noise, which can be an advantage in certain memory technologies or when operating in less-than-ideal conditions [9]. Voltage-latched sense amplifiers with pMOS access transistors (FSPA-VLSA) are typically faster and suited for high-speed memory, while CLSA may offer better noise resilience and stability in varying conditions. The circuit design of latched-type SAs. (a) FSPA-VLSA. (b) FS-CLSA as shown in Figure 46.1.

FSPA-VLSA: When the voltage at the base of the load transistor (V_{BL}) drops below the difference between V_{DD} and $|V_{THP}|$, the two transistors (MP_1 and MP_2) turn on, their discrepancy starts to affect V_{OS}. Furthermore, enabling MP_1 and MP_2 earlier to the sensing process results in the occurrence of invalid current paths. This, in turn, decreases ΔV_{BL} and causes a significant rise in the probability of sensing failure. Hence, sensing dead zone of FSPA-VLSA is smaller to the difference between V_{DD} - V_{THP}.

FS-CLSA: If the voltage V_{BL} is less than the threshold voltage V_{THN}, an input transistor MN_3 and MN_4 remain in the off state. Consequently, the absence of a sensing operation arises due to the inability of input transistors to transform input voltage to current, which is called voltage-to-current alteration. Hence, the sensing dead zone of a FS-CLSA is situated at a level lower than V_{THN} and V_{OS} [10].

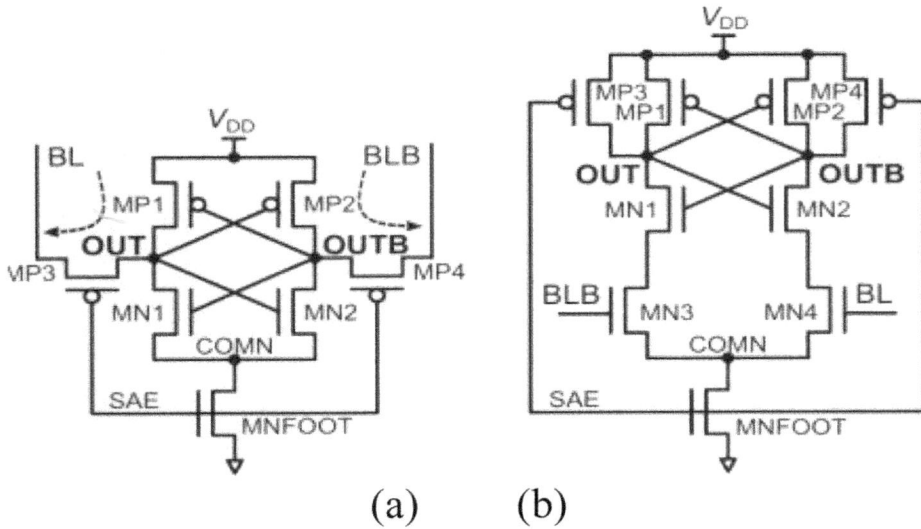

Figure 46.1 Latched-type SA. (a) FSPA-VLSA. (b) FS-CLSA
Source: Author

VLSAs with double switches

By having two separate switches, the timing of the precharge and sensing phases can be finely controlled, leading to more precise operation and potentially faster sensing. The double switches allow for better control of power usage by ensuring that the precharge circuitry is completely disconnected when not needed, a sense amplifier remains only active during the sensing phase. However, the sensing dead zones persist due to the voltage distribution issues caused through

a access transistors [11]. In a DSPA-VLSA, the p-MOS access transistors are unable to precisely transfer the V_{BL} signal when it is lower than the absolute value of V_{THP}. As a result, the sensing dead zone is located below the absolute value of V_{THP}. In DSNA-VLSA, the n-MOS access transistors are unable to completely transfer the V_{BL} signal that is higher than $V_{DD} - V_{THN}$. As a result, the sensing dead zone remains located overhead VDD $- V_{THN}$. Figure 46.2 shows the double switches circuit design (a) DSPA-VLSA. (b) DSNA-VLSA.

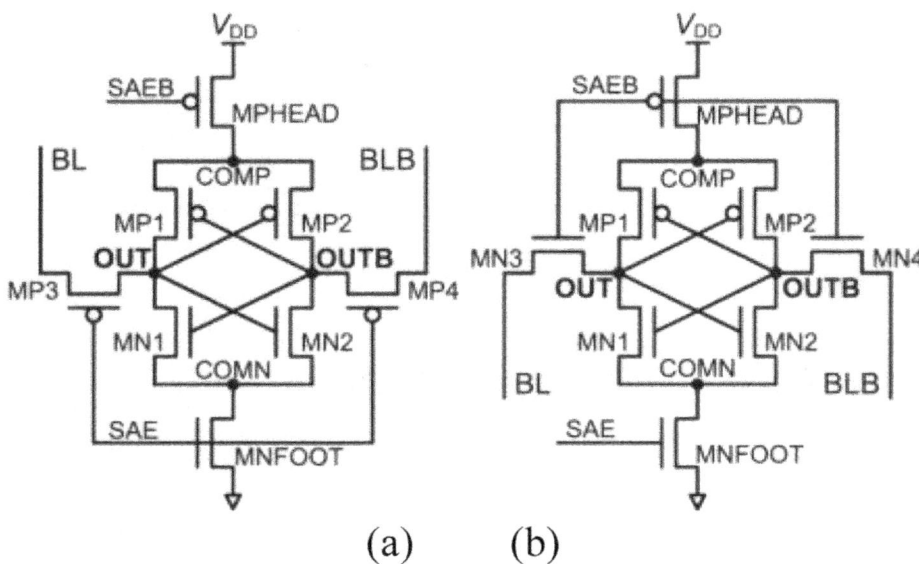

Figure 46.2 Double switches (a) DSPA-VLSA. (b) DSNA-VLSA
Source: Author

The double switches allow for precise timing control, ensuring that each phase of the operation occurs at the optimal time, leading to faster and more reliable memory reads. TG have low resistance when on and minimal leakage when off, making them efficient in both power consumption and signal integrity [12]. *DSTA-VLSA*: Although a VLSA with dual switches reduces the area of a sensing dead zone, the inclusion of access transistors in the system still leads to a sensing dead zone. Using TG as access transistors, as shown in Figure 46.3.

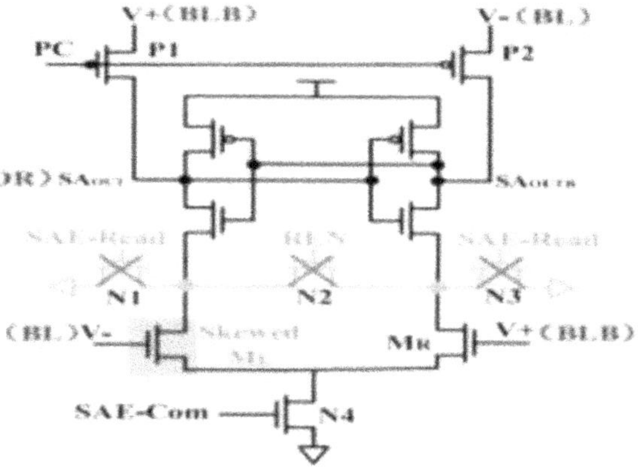

Reconfigurable sense amplifier

A reconfigurable sense amplifier (R-SA) is an advanced circuit used in memory to read stored data. The key feature of a reconfigurable sense amplifier is its ability to adapt its operating parameters based on different conditions, such as varying power supply levels, different types of memory cells, or changing environmental factors like temperature. This flexibility allows for optimized performance in terms of speed, power consumption, and reliability. Reconfigurable sense amplifiers can adjust parameters such as voltage thresholds, bias currents, and amplification gain [13,14]. Figure 46.4 shows the circuit design of R-SA.

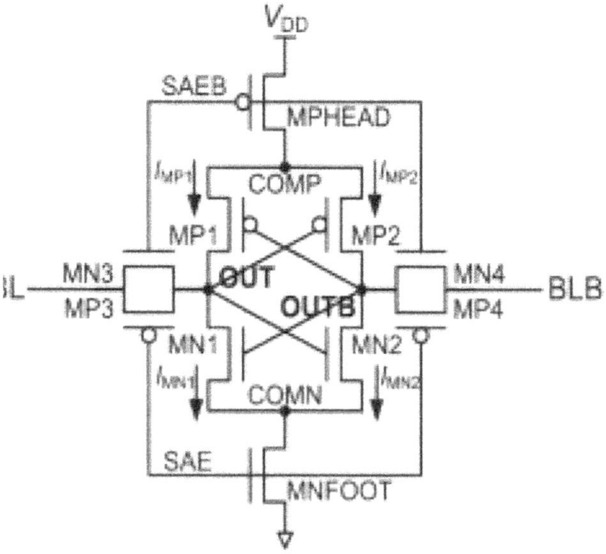

Figure 46.4 R-SA
Source: Author

Offset cancellation sense amplifier

Offset cancellation sense amplifier (OC-SA) is specifically designed to minimize or cancel out the offset voltage, which is the unwanted voltage alteration between the inputs of the sense amplifier that can lead to incorrect data sensing. Figure 46.5 shows the circuit design of OC-SA. In a typical sense amplifier, there might be a small voltage difference between the inputs due to mismatches in the transistors or other components. This offset can cause the amplifier to incorrectly sense the stored data, leading to read errors. The process of minimizing the offset voltage to improve the accuracy of the sense amplifier. Offset cancellation can be achieved using various techniques, including calibration during the design or operation of the circuit. With offset cancellation, the sense amplifier can detect smaller voltage differences, allowing for lower power operation and faster read times. Reducing offset-related errors can improve the manufacturing yield, as variations in components are less likely to cause functional issues. Offset cancellation sense amplifiers are crucial in high-performance memory applications where accuracy and speed are paramount [15].

Boosted ref. voltage sense amplifier

A boosted ref. voltage sense amplifier (BRV-SA) improves an accuracy and speed of data sensing. This design involves boosting the reference voltage used by a SA during the read operation, allowing for faster and more reliable data detection. A circuit that amplifies small voltage differences between bitlines in a memory array,

Figure 46.3 DSTA-VLSA
Source: Author

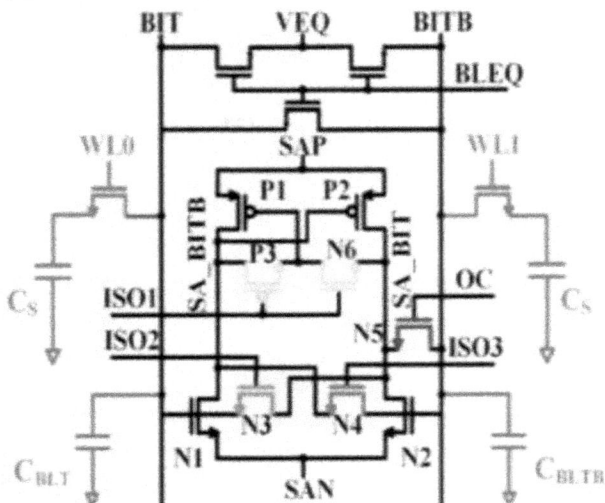

Figure 46.5 OC-SA
Source: Author

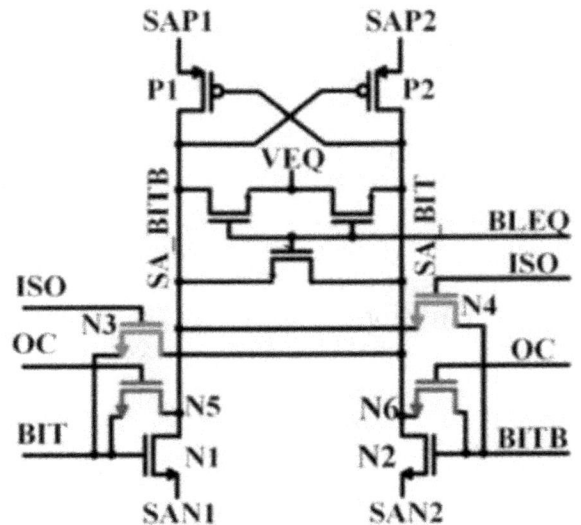

Figure 46.6 BRV-SA
Source: Author

enabling the detection of the stored data. A stable voltage level against which the sense amplifier compares the bitline voltage to determine the stored data (typically a '1' or '0'). The accuracy of this reference voltage is critical for correct data sensing. The technique of temporarily increasing (boosting) the reference voltage throughout the sensing process to enhance the performance of the sense amplifier. Boosting the reference voltage reduces a time essential for SA to decide, enabling faster read operations. By enhancing the voltage alteration throughout a sensing phase, the likelihood of incorrect data reads due to marginal signal differences is reduced [16]. Figure 46.6 shown the circuit design of BRV-SA.

Current-mirror and switching-point compensation sense amplifier

Current-mirror and switching-point compensation sense amplifier (CSC-SA) is another specialized design used in memory circuits to accurately read data by addressing specific challenges related to current sensing and switching speed. This sense amplifier includes compensation circuitry that adjusts the switching point dynamically. This ensures that the amplifier switches at the correct threshold, reducing the likelihood of errors and improving read accuracy. The compensation might be achieved through feedback mechanisms or additional calibration circuitry that adjusts the sense amplifier's threshold based on real-time conditions [17]. It is particularly useful in applications where power efficiency and

speed are critical. Figure 46.7 shows the circuit design of CSC-SA.

FinFET sense amplifier

Advanced CMOS technology impacts, the scaling down of transistors has further intensified the challenges in designing sense amplifiers. Issues like increased leakage currents, reduced voltage headroom, and higher susceptibility to noise have prompted the need for novel design approaches. Recent studies have focused on leveraging the advantages of FinFETs and other emerging transistor technologies to enhance the performance of sense amplifiers while maintaining low power consumption [18]. A sense amplifier with fin-shaped field-effect transistors (FinFETs) leverages the advanced characteristics of FinFET technology to improve the performance of memory circuits. FinFETs are a type of transistor that provides better control over current flow, reduced leakage, and enhanced scalability compared to traditional planar MOSFETs. FinFETs have lower leakage currents compared to planar MOSFETs, which is crucial for low-power applications. Sense amplifiers with FinFETs can operate at lower voltages, further reducing power consumption while maintaining high performance [19]. The Ssense amplifier FinFET shown in Figure 46.8.

A comparative analysis of existing sense amplifier designs reveals that while significant progress has been made in either improving speed or reducing power consumption, achieving both

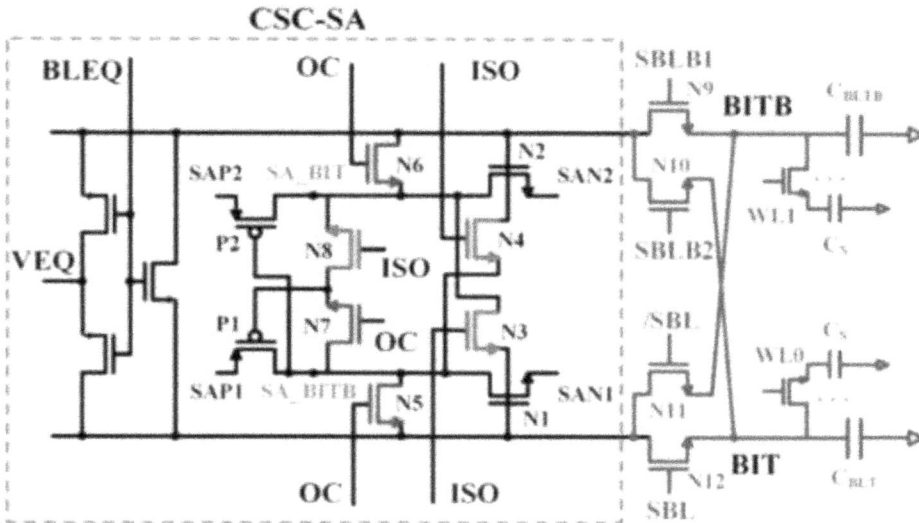

Figure 46.7 CSC-SA
Source: Author

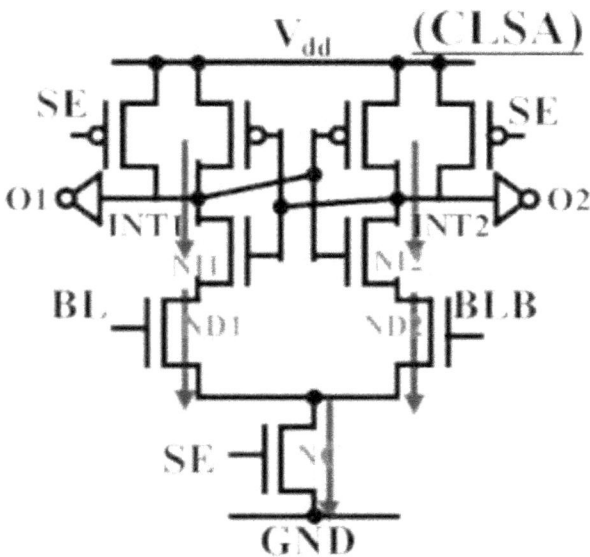

Figure 46.8 Sense amplifier FinFET
Source: Author

simultaneously remains a challenging task. Trends in current research indicate a growing interest in hybrid designs that combine the strengths of different amplifier types to achieve an optimal balance [20].

Design Implementation

The design implementations are carried out using the LT-SPICE, which uses 180 nm technolog with the supply voltage of 1.8 V. We have designed and examined a variety of voltage latch sense

amplifier design topologies, including FSNA-VLSA, FSPA-VLSA, DSNA-VLSA, DSPA-VLSA, FSPA-VLSA, and FSDS. Figures 46.9–46.14 illustrate the schematic design and output response of these designs. Additionally, a comparison of the sensing zones, advantages, and disadvantages across different topologies is presented. FSNA-VLSA and FSDS are typically used where speed and power are prioritized. DSNA-VLSA and DSPA-VLSA are better for high-sensitivity and noise-critical environments. FSPA-VLSA finds a middle ground, offering enhanced sensitivity without fully sacrificing speed or power.

DSNA-VLSA: In DSNA-VLSA we make use of transmission gate, hence it provides more advantages than double switch. A VLSA through dual changes effectively decreases the scope of the sensing dead zone, but the presence of access transistors in the system introduces the sensing dead zone. Which is possible to eliminate the sensing dead zone. Here BL, BLB are the inputs from the SRAM cell. When SAE is low MN3, MN4, MP3, MP4 are ON hence BL and BLB are transformed to OUT and MNFOOT, MPHEAD are ON therefore the latch is connected to add through MPHEAD and is connected to ground through MNFOOT. Thus, it amplifies difference between BL and BLB and it hold the data either 0 or 1 in the form of a latch. Here inputs are BL, BLB, SAE and outputs are OUT, OUTB. Table 46.1 Comparison of sensing zone for various topologies has presented in Table 46.1.

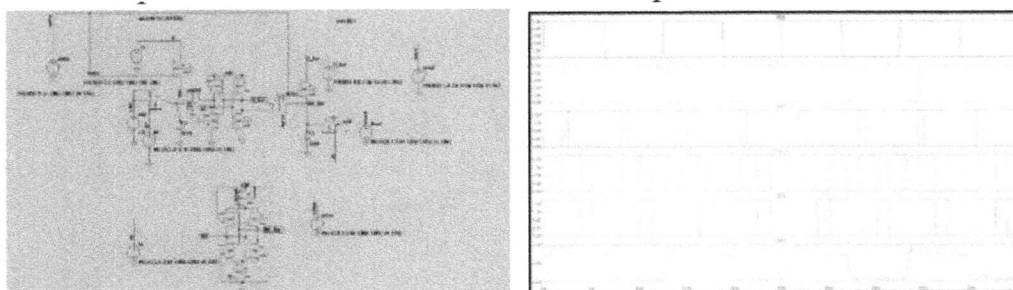

(a)   (b)

Figure 46.9 Output response of FSNA VLSA
Source: Author

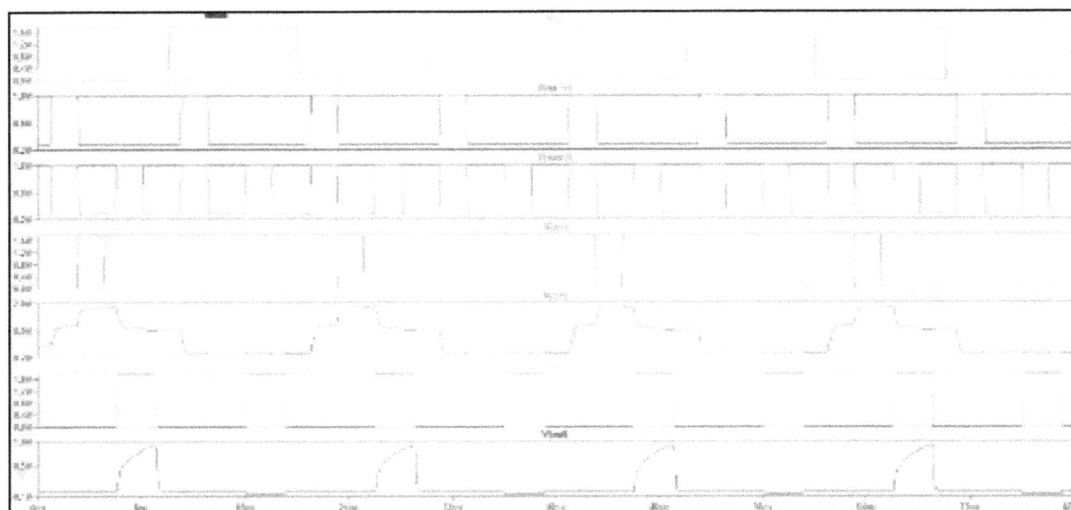

Figure 46.10 Output response of FSPA VLSA
Source: Author

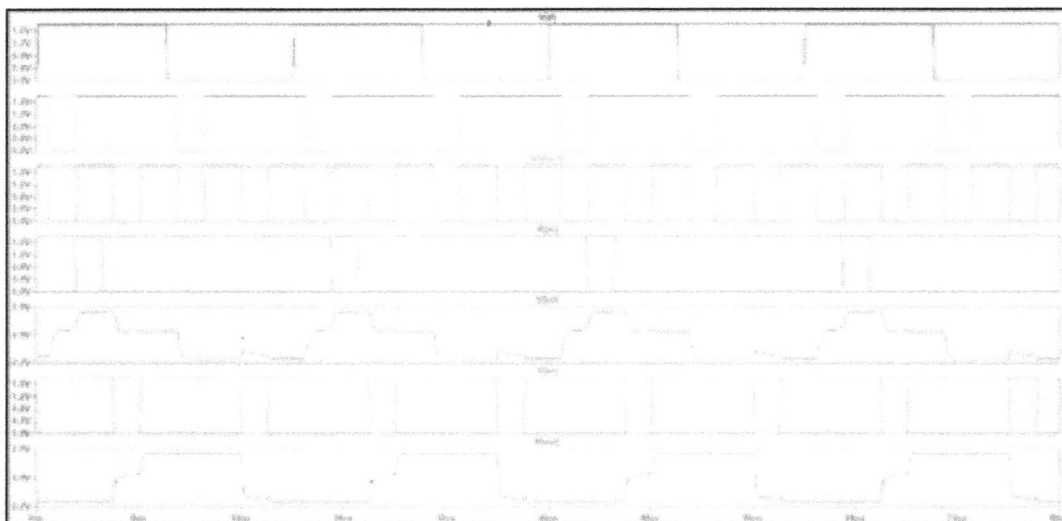

Figure 46.11 Output response of DSNA VLSA
Source: Author

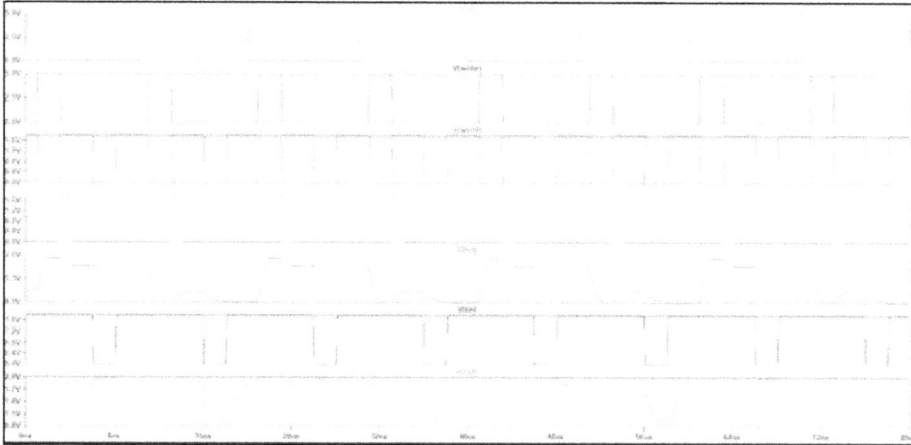

Figure 46.12 Output response of DSPA VLSA
Source: Author

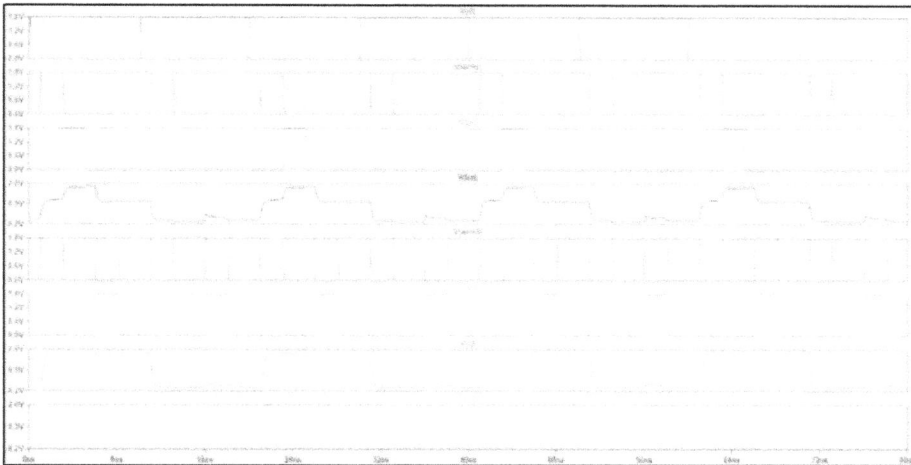

Figure 46.13 Output response of DSTA VLSA
Source: Author

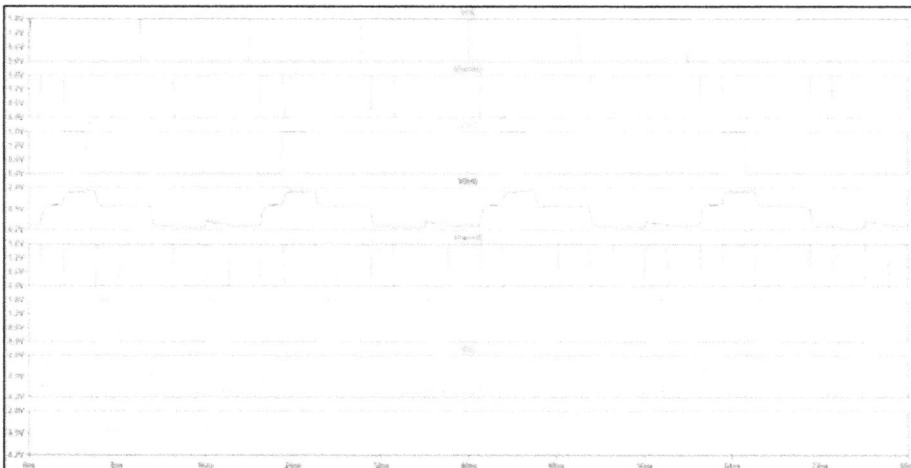

Figure 46.14 Output response of FSDS
Source: Author

Table 46.1 Comparison of sensing zone for various topologies

Technique	Sensing zone	Merits	Demerits
FSPA-VLSA. [10]	Below $V_{DD} - |V_{THP}|$.	Superior sensing speed and compact layout	invalid current paths
FS-CLSA. [10]	below V_{THN}	slower sensing speed.	voltage-to-current conversion problem
FSNA-VLSA. [10]	above V_{THN}.	Sensing dead zone is smaller than FSPA-VLSA	invalid current paths
FS-CLSA. [10]	above $V_{DD} - |V_{THP}|$.	Sensing dead zone is smaller than FS-CLSA	voltage-to-current conversion problem
DSPA-VLSA. [11]	Below $|V_{THP}|$	Invalid current paths can reduced	Voltage delivery issues at the access transistors.
DSNA-VLSA. [11]	above $V_{DD} - V_{THN}$.	Invalid current paths can reduced	Voltage delivery issues at the access transistors.
DSTA-VLSA. [12]	$V_{DD}/2$	Narrow sensing dead zone	double switches may lead to an unauthorized current path.
R-SA [13]	adjustable the sensing zone	Adaptability to Different Operating Conditions	Increased Circuit Complexity, Latency Issues
CSC-SA [17]	Involves switching-point adjustment	High speed, Scalability, low power Consumption	Complex Design, Higher Static Power, Temp. Sensitivity
F-SA [18]	Below $|V_{THP}|$	Reduced Variability, Lower Power Supply	Increased Design Complexity, Thermal Challenges

Source: Author

Conclusion

In this study, we have explored the design, optimization of low-power, high-performance sense amplifiers tailored for memory applications. Our analysis demonstrates that through careful selection of circuit topologies and process parameters, it is possible to significantly reduce power consumption without compromising speed and reliability. Hence, we did rigorously survey the voltage latched and current latched sense amplifier (SA). VLSA topologies have been simulated through spice simulator, determined the sensing zones. Voltage-Latched Sense Amplifiers are generally slower but consume less power, making them ideal for low-power, noise-sensitive applications. Current-Latched Sense Amplifiers offer faster operation at the price of increased power consumption and potential noise sensitivity, making them suitable for high-speed, performance-critical memory applications. FinFETs reduce the leakage current during both active and standby modes, leading to lower overall power consumption in the sense amplifier. These improvements can contribute to enhancing the overall efficiency of memory systems, which is critical in applications ranging from consumer electronics to high-performance computing. The findings of this research highlight the potential for further innovations in sense amplifier design, suggesting that ongoing advancements in semiconductor technology can be leveraged to push the boundaries of memory performance. Consequently, this study offers valuable understandings for the development of low-power, high-speed sense amplifiers. offering a robust solution for next-generation memory applications.

References

[1] You, H. (2020). A low-power high-speed sense-amplifier-based flip-flop in 55 nm MTC-MOS. *Electronics*, 9(5), 802.

[2] Jeong, H. (2018). Sense-amplifier-based flip-flop with transition completion detection for low-voltage operation. *IEEE Transactions on*

Very Large-Scale Integration (VLSI) Systems, 26(4), 609–620.

[3] Bikki, P., Dhiraj, Y., and Nivas Kumar, R. V. S. (2023). Design and implementation of a sense amplifier for low-power cardiac pacemaker. *Journal of Circuits, Systems and Computers,* 32(9), 2350148.

[4] Haddad, S. A. P. (2003). An ultra-low-power dynamic translinear cardiac sense amplifier for pacemakers. In IEEE International Symposium on Circuits and Systems (ISCAS). (Vol. 5).

[5] Conte, A. (2005). A high-performance very low-voltage current sense amplifier for nonvolatile memories. *IEEE Journal of Solid-State Circuits,* 40(2), 507–514.

[6] Zhu, J., Bai, N., and Wu, J. (2013). A review of sense amplifiers for static random-access memory. *IETE Technical Review,* 30(1), 72–81.

[7] Hemaprabha, A., and Vivek, K. (2015). Comparative analysis of sense amplifiers for memories. In International Conference on Innovations in Information, Embedded and Communication Systems (ICIIECS). IEEE. (pp. 1–6).

[8] Wei, Z. (2014). Novel CMOS SRAM voltage latched sense amplifiers design based on 65 nm technology. In 12th IEEE International Conference on Solid-State and Integrated Circuit Technology (ICSICT). (pp. 1–3).

[9] Ishdorj, B. (2023). Offset-canceling current-latched sense amplifier with slow rise time control and reference voltage biasing techniques. *IEEE Transactions on Circuits and Systems I: Regular Papers,* 70(7), 2689–2699.

[10] Saini, A., Gupta, P. K., and Gupta, R. (2019). Analysis of low power SRAM sense amplifier. In International Conference on Electrical, Electronics and Computer Engineering (UPCON). (pp. 1–6).

[11] Na, T. (2020). Robust offset-cancellation sense amplifier for an offset-canceling dual-stage sensing circuit in resistive nonvolatile memories. *Electronics,* 9(9), 1403.

[12] Na, T. (2017). Study on cross-coupled-based sensing circuits for nonvolatile flip-flops operat-ing in near/subthreshold voltage region. *Micromachines,* 12(10), 1177.

[13] Chen, J. (2021). Analysis and design of reconfigurable sense amplifier for compute SRAM with high-speed compute and normal read access. *IEEE Transactions on Circuits and Systems II: Express Briefs,* 68(12), 3503–3507.

[14] Kavitha, S., Kumar, S., and Reniwal, B. S. (2023). Enabling energy-efficient in-memory computing with robust assist-based reconfigurable sense amplifier in SRAM array. *IEEE Journal on Emerging and Selected Topics in Circuits and Systems,* 13(1), 445–455.

[15] Singh, S. J., Nairn, D., and Sachdev, M. (2013). An energy-efficient offset-cancelling sense amplifier. *IEEE Transactions on Circuits and Systems II: Express Briefs,* 60(8), 477–481.

[16] Min, K. S., Song, B., and Jung, S. (2019). Sensing margin enhancement technique utilizing boosted reference voltage for low-voltage and high-density DRAM. *IEEE Transactions on Very Large Scale Integration (VLSI) Systems,* 27(10), 2413–2422.

[17] Huang, P. (2022). Offset-compensation high-performance sense amplifier for low-voltage DRAM based on current mirror and switching point. *IEEE Transactions on Circuits and Systems II: Express Briefs,* 69(4), 2011–2015.

[18] Fan, M.-L. (2012). Variability analysis of sense amplifier for FinFET subthreshold SRAM applications. *IEEE Transactions on Circuits and Systems II: Express Briefs,* 59(12), 878–882.

[19] Garg, M., and Singh, B. (2016). A comparative performance analysis of CMOS and FinFET based voltage mode sense amplifier. In 8th International Conference on Computational Intelligence and Communication Networks (CICN). IEEE. (pp. 554–557).

[20] Lakshmi, P. G. (2023). Hybrid silicon substrate FinFET-metal insulator metal (MIM) memristor based sense amplifier design for the non-volatile SRAM cell. *Micromachines,* 14(2), 232.

47 Development of smart and secure home automation prototype with IoT

Gade Harish Babu[a], Venkata Krishna Odugu[b] and B. Janardhana Rao[c]

Department of ECE, CVR College of Engineering, Hyderabad, Talangana, India

Abstract

This work aims in designing an Internet of Things (IoT)-based smart security and home automation system using Raspberry Pi. This work makes use of Raspberry Pi Zero-W processor which has an inbuilt Wi-Fi, and which is used for sending the alert mail along with photos. This project consists of Bluetooth technology for controlling the devices wirelessly from android Bluetooth mobile application. The controlling device of the whole system is a Raspberry Pi Zero-W processor. After the system detects the motion using PIR, when the person does not enter the PIN within a certain time, Raspberry pi will send an alert SMS through GSM and sending alert mail along with photo to the predefine stored email. When the person enters the PIN within the time, it will send the OTP to the user. So, the user needs to send the OTP through keypad within the time. When the Raspberry pi detects a wrong OTP or PIN, Raspberry pi will capture the person image and mails it. If the entered OTP matches the generated OTP, then the system accesses the door and lets the person in. This device consists of Bluetooth technology for controlling the devices through voice from android mobile application. Based on the received commands, Raspberry Pi will turn ON/OFF the devices accordingly. We program it using Python language and the OS used here is Linux.

Keywords: Home automation, internet of things and bluetooth, raspberry pi, smart security

Introduction

The aim of the home automation system using Raspberry Pi along with Internet of Things (IoT) various aspects of their property. Primarily, the system aims to bolster security through features such as intrusion detection, alarm systems, access control, and remote monitoring via security cameras. This ensures that users can promptly respond to security threats and deter unauthorized access to their premises. Moreover, the system enhances convenience by automating routine tasks such as lighting control, temperature regulation, and appliance management. Users can remotely adjust settings or schedule automation routines, thereby optimizing energy usage and enhancing comfort. Furthermore, the system prioritizes energy efficiency by monitoring energy consumption patterns and integrating renewable energy sources and battery storage solutions. This not only reduces utility bills but also contributes to environmental sustainability. Overall, the aim is to provide users with a seamless and secure living environment that offers convenience, energy efficiency, and peace of mind. By leveraging IoT technologies and intelligent automation, the system transforms traditional homes into smart, connected spaces tailored to the needs of modern living.

The development of an IoT-based smart security and home automation system using Raspberry Pi holds significant importance as it revolutionizes traditional living spaces, offering enhanced safety, convenience, and energy efficiency. By integrating sensors, actuators, and communication technologies, the system empowers users to remotely monitor and control their homes, mitigating security risks and optimizing resource usage. This innovation not only enhances quality of life but also contributes to environmental sustainability by promoting energy efficient practices. Furthermore, the scalable nature of the system allows for customization and adaptation to diverse user needs, making it a versatile solution for modern living environments.

[a]harish.sidhu12@gmail.com, [b]venkatakrishna.odugu@gmail.com, [c]janardhan.bitra@gmail.com

DOI: 10.1201/9781003616399-47

Tanaka et al. [1] made a noteworthy advancement in smart home technology by developing a secure end-to-end remote management system for intelligent home appliances on Android. Shinde et al. [2], proposed a multifaceted approach employing IR, Bluetooth, GSM, and Android technologies. This system aims to revolutionize household management by enhancing convenience and efficiency.

Xiaodong et al. [3] proposed a smart home control system based on STM32, aiming to enhance home automation capabilities. Their research delves into the design and implementation aspects, addressing the increasing need for efficient household management. By leveraging STM32 technology, the system offers a promising avenue for integrating diverse home devices seamlessly. The study highlights the potential of STM32-based solutions in creating robust, user-friendly smart home environments.

Hasan et al. [4] suggested a microcontroller-based smart home device that could switch appliances more easily. Their work builds upon existing smart home technologies, focusing on the development of a more robust and efficient system. Madhu et al. [5] suggested using node MCU and IoT to make a smart home controller that is both cheap and efficient.

The system aims to offer a seamless integration of IoT technology into household environments, enabling remote control and monitoring through an Android application. Hamdan et al. [6] proposed an IoT-based interactive dual mode smart home automation system aimed at enhancing household convenience and energy efficiency. Their work leverages the IoT technology to create a versatile and user-friendly home environment.

Vishwakarma et al. [7] proposed a smart energy efficient home automation system using IoT. Their work addresses the pressing need for sustainable energy management within households. By integrating IoT technologies, the system offers a promising solution for optimizing energy consumption and enhancing overall efficiency. Sarmah et al. [8] proposed SURE-H, a secure IoT enabled smart home system, aimed at enhancing the security and efficiency of modern households. This system integrates IoT technologies to enable remote monitoring and control of various home devices.

Singh et al. [9] proposed an IoT based smart home automation system utilizing sensor nodes. Their work highlighted the integration of sensor technologies within home environments, aiming to enhance convenience and efficiency. The study delved into the realms of modern information technology advancements, emphasizing the potential for seamless automation. Gaikwad et al. [10] proposed a Bluetooth based smart automation system using Android, aiming to enhance control and efficiency in home automation. The system integrates Bluetooth technology with Android devices, offering a user-friendly interface for managing various home appliances remotely. Babu and Venkatram [11] developed a Raspberry Pi-based robotic chair controlling with eye and night vision camera.

Problem statement: From the above references our project's main theme is to design and implement a smart security and home automation system that can effectively enhance the safety and security of a home and to make home automation more robust with great appliance handling capacity using sensors and controllers. There are many proposed systems regarding the home automation and security systems, here our aim is to build a both way stronger and versatile system which can be implemented with lower costs.

Architecture of Home Automation System

The controlling device of the whole system is a Raspberry Pi Zero-W processor, and it is integrated with the LCD display, Pi-camera, servo Motor, Bluetooth module, PIR, Buzzer, keypad, GSM and relay along with bulb and transistor with fan is interfaced to the Raspberry pi processor given in Figure 47.1. After the system detects the motion using PIR, when the person does not enter the PIN within a certain time, Raspberry pi will send an alert SMS through GSM and also sending alert MAIL along with photo to the pre-define stored email.

When the person enters the PIN within the time, it will send the OTP to the user. So, the user needs to send the OTP through keypad within the time. When the Raspberry pi detects a wrong OTP or PIN, Raspberry pi will capture the person image and mail it. If the entered OTP matches the generated OTP, then the system

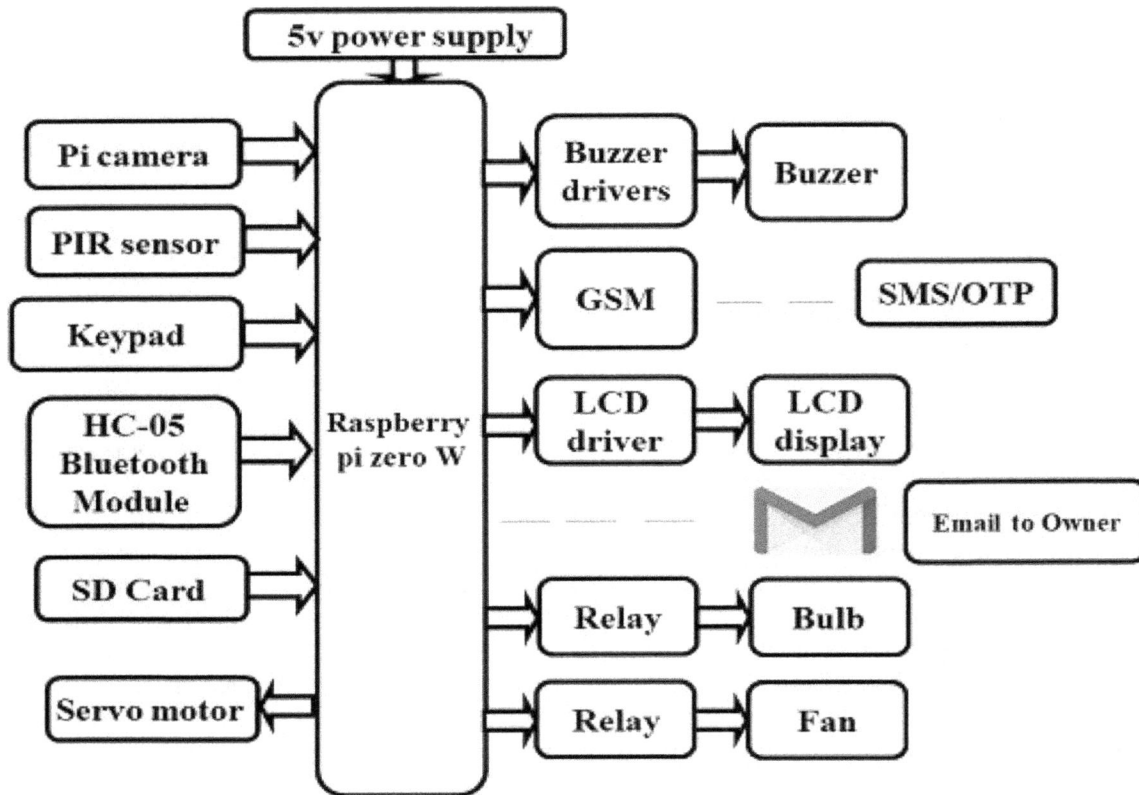

Figure 47.1 Proposed block diagram for home automation
Source: Author

accesses the door and lets the person in. This device consists of Bluetooth technology for controlling the devices through voice from android mobile application. Based on the received commands, Raspberry pi will turn ON/OFF the devices accordingly.

Raspberry pi zero W: The Raspberry Pi Zero W is a compact and cost-effective single-board computer renowned for its small form factor and wireless connectivity capabilities. Featuring a Broadcom BCM2835 SoC with a 1GHz ARM11 CPU, 512MB RAM, and built-in Wi-Fi and Bluetooth, the zero W offers ample computing power for various IoT and embedded projects. Its miniature size makes it ideal for space-constrained applications, while its wireless connectivity enables seamless communication with other devices and networks. With GPIO pins for hardware interfacing and compatibility with a wide range of software, the Raspberry Pi Zero W serves as an excellent platform for prototyping and deploying innovative IoT solutions.

Pi camera: The pi camera is a high-quality camera module designed for Raspberry Pi boards, offering up to 8 MP resolution and various features like autofocus and digital zoom. It connects directly to the Raspberry pi's camera serial interface (CSI) port, enabling users to capture photos and videos for projects ranging from surveillance to photography.

GSM: In an IoT-based smart security and home automation project using Raspberry Pi, global system for mobile communications (GSM) integration offers remote connectivity and control via SMS. GSM modules enable alerts and notifications to users' mobile phones, facilitating real-time monitoring of security breaches or system events. Users can remotely control devices and trigger actions via SMS commands, enhancing flexibility and accessibility. Additionally, GSM serves as a backup communication channel, ensuring system reliability during internet outages. With GSM integration, the system provides seamless connectivity and control, empowering users to manage their smart home security and automation remotely from anywhere.

LCD display: An liquid crystal display (LCD) integrated into the IoT-based smart security and home automation project using Raspberry pi provides a user-friendly interface for real-time status monitoring, device control, menu navigation, system configuration, and visual feedback, enhancing convenience and usability for local interaction with the system.

Buzzer alarm: A buzzer alarm integrated into the IoT-based smart security and home automation project using Raspberry Pi serves as an audible alert system, emitting a loud sound in response to security breaches or system events, enhancing situational awareness and alerting occupants to potential threats or emergencies.

HC-05 Bluetooth module: The HC-05 Bluetooth module is a versatile wireless communication device commonly used in IoT projects with Raspberry Pi. Operating on Bluetooth 2.0 protocol, it enables seamless data transmission between the Raspberry Pi and external devices such as smartphones, tablets, or other Bluetooth-enabled peripherals. With its simple serial interface and wide compatibility, the HC-05 facilitates remote control, sensor data exchange, and wireless connectivity for various applications like home automation, smart devices, and robotics. Its small size, less energy usage, and ease of integration are suitable for the choice for DIY enthusiasts and professionals seeking to add wireless capabilities to their projects.

Servomotor: In the IoT-based smart security and home automation project using Raspberry Pi, servomotors can be utilized to control physical mechanisms such as door locks, window shutters, or surveillance camera pan-tilt systems, enabling remote operation and automation of various aspects of home security and monitoring.

Keypad: A keypad is an input device consisting of a set of buttons arranged in a grid or layout. In the IoT-based smart security and home automation project using Raspberry Pi, a keypad is considered for the authentication of the user, access control, or system configuration, providing a convenient and secure input method.

PIR sensor: A passive infrared (PIR) sensor is a motion detection device commonly used in security systems. It detects changes in within its field of view. In the IoT-based smart security and infrared radiation emitted by objects home automation project using Raspberry Pi, PIR 12 sensors can trigger actions such as activating lights, sending alerts, or recording video when motion is detected, enhancing security and automation capabilities.

Relay with bulb: In the context of an IoT-based smart security and home automation project using Raspberry Pi, a relay module can be used to control a bulb (light) remotely. The relay acts as a switch, allowing the Raspberry Pi to turn the bulb on or off using GPIO pins. This enables users to remotely control the lighting in their home, either manually through a web interface or automatically based on predefined conditions such as time of day, motion detection, or user commands. The relay provides a safe and efficient way to interface the Raspberry Pi with high-power devices like bulbs, enhancing the flexibility and convenience of the home automation system.

Transistor with fan: In this work, a transistor can be used to control a fan's speed or turn it on/off. The transistor acts as a switch, regulating the power supplied to the fan. By connecting the transistor to the Raspberry Pi's GPIO pins, the system can control the fan's operation based on predefined conditions such as .temperature, humidity, or user commands. This enables users to remotely adjust the fan's speed or turn it on/off automatically, improving comfort and energy efficiency in the home.

The flow chart as shown in Figure 47.2 outlines the operational sequence of the OTP based smart security and home automation system. Here, how the Raspberry Pi controls all the devices connected is described. Initially, if the system senses the motion and arrival of a person, it switches on the LCD and asks the person to enter the passcode under 20 seconds. And if it doesn't sense the motion it keeps the app with the control of fans and lights working to monitor the state of the appliances. If the passcode entered is incorrect or it is not entered under 20 seconds then it goes to the intrusion alert phase. If the passcode entered is correct it sends an OTP to the mobile phone and then the entered OTP will be checked, if it is correct the door unlocks and if it is incorrect the intrusion detection phase switches on. In the intrusion detection phase initially, the buzzer switches on and the pi camera installed will take the photo of the intruder which will be sent to the mail of the main authority and a text message regarding the intruder will be sent to the mobile phone of the main authority.

Algorithm for the Proposed Model

Input: Movement in front of the door and change in the state of appliances.

Output: Unlocking the door or declaring the intrusion. Also controlling the home appliances from phone.

Step 1: To detect the motion in front of the entrance and switching on the LCD to start the operation of unlocking.

Step 2: Now based on the action performed or not performed the system goes on to the next step of unlocking. If the password is correct, an OTP will be generated and sent to the mobile phone. If any action is not performed under twenty seconds intrusion alert phase will start.

Step 3: As the system got the passcode correct, it goes on to OTP checking phase where OTP is validated. If the OTP is incorrect then the intrusion alert phase will be started.

Step 4: In the intrusion detection phase, a photo of the intruder will be taken and sent to the mail and a message will be sent to the phone.

Step 5: Throughout the time the home automation system will be kept monitored.

Step 6: Stop.

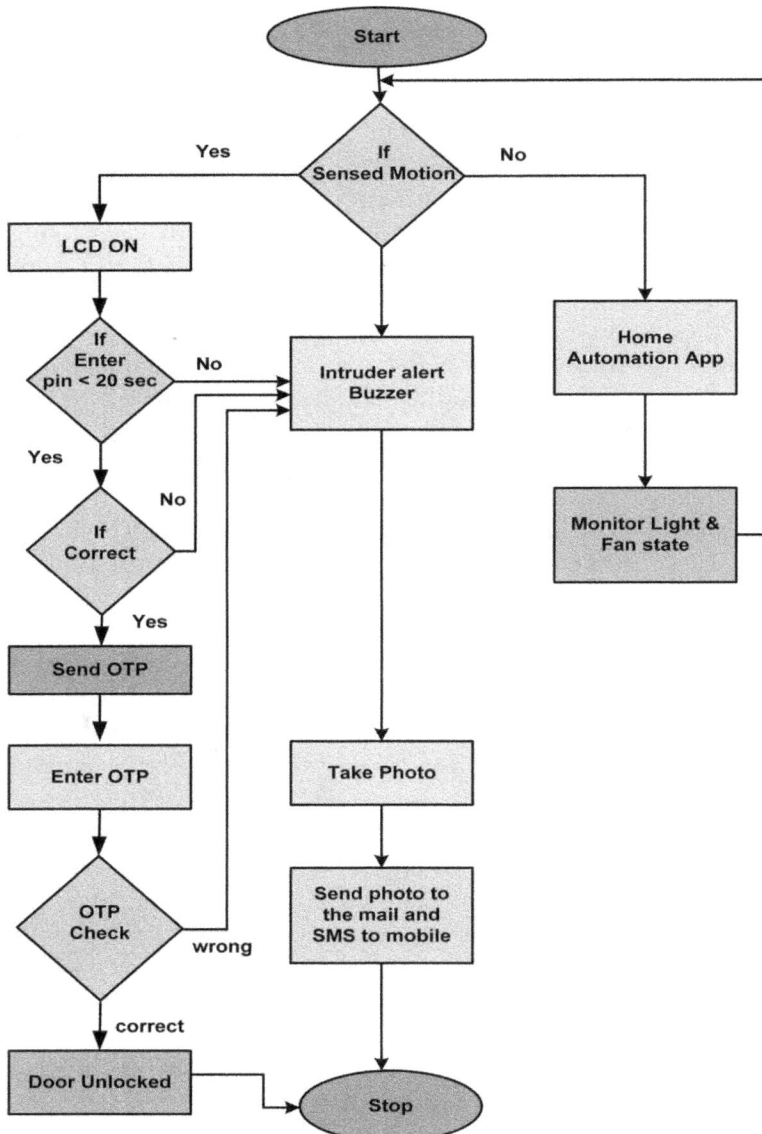

Figure 47.2 Flow diagram of home automation process
Source: Author

Hardware Description

Raspberry Pi zero-W: It is a remarkable single-board computer renowned for its compact size, affordability, and built-in wireless connectivity. With its Broadcom BCM2835 SoC featuring a 1GHz ARM11 76JZF-S CPU and 512MB of RAM, the Pi Zero W delivers substantial computing power despite its diminutive form factor. However, its standout feature is its integrated wireless capabilities, including both Wi-Fi and Bluetooth connectivity, denoted by the "W" in its name. This wireless connectivity significantly enhances the Pi Zero W's versatility and applicability in various projects. For IoT applications, the built-in Wi-Fi allows seamless integration into networks, enabling remote monitoring, control, and data communication without the need for additional dongles or adapters. Moreover, Bluetooth connectivity facilitates interactions with other devices such as sensors, smartphones, and peripherals. The internal architecture and physical modules available in Raspberry Pi Zero W are shown in Figures 47.3 and 47.4 respectively.

The compact size of the Pi Zero-W makes it particularly suitable for projects with space constraints or those requiring portability. Its small footprint allows for creative integration into compact enclosures or wearable devices, making it a favorite among makers and hobbyists for innovative projects ranging from smart wearables to miniature IoT gadgets.

Implementation Results

In this section, the practical connection of the required modules integrated with Raspberry Pi zero-W and snippets corresponding to the process steps involved in the home automation test case are described. The complete setup is presented in Figure 47.5. Here, the home automation setup, wrong OTP code and right OTP code verification steps are described in photos.

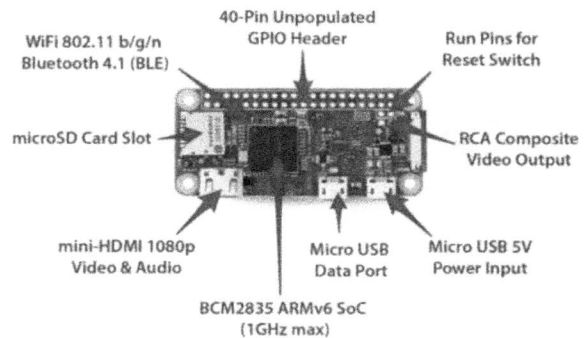

Figure 47.4 Modules of Raspberry Pi Zero W board
Source: Author

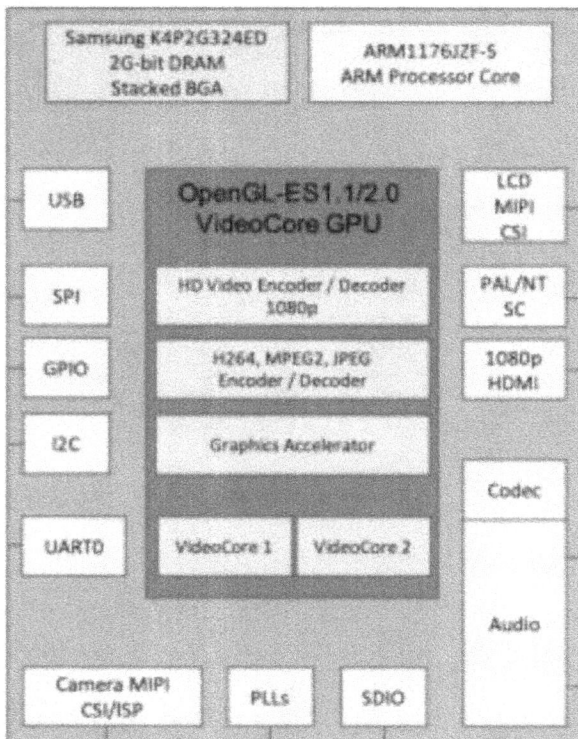

Figure 47.3 Description of Raspberry Pi Zero-W model
Source: Author

Figure 47.5 Complete real time home automation setup
Source: Author

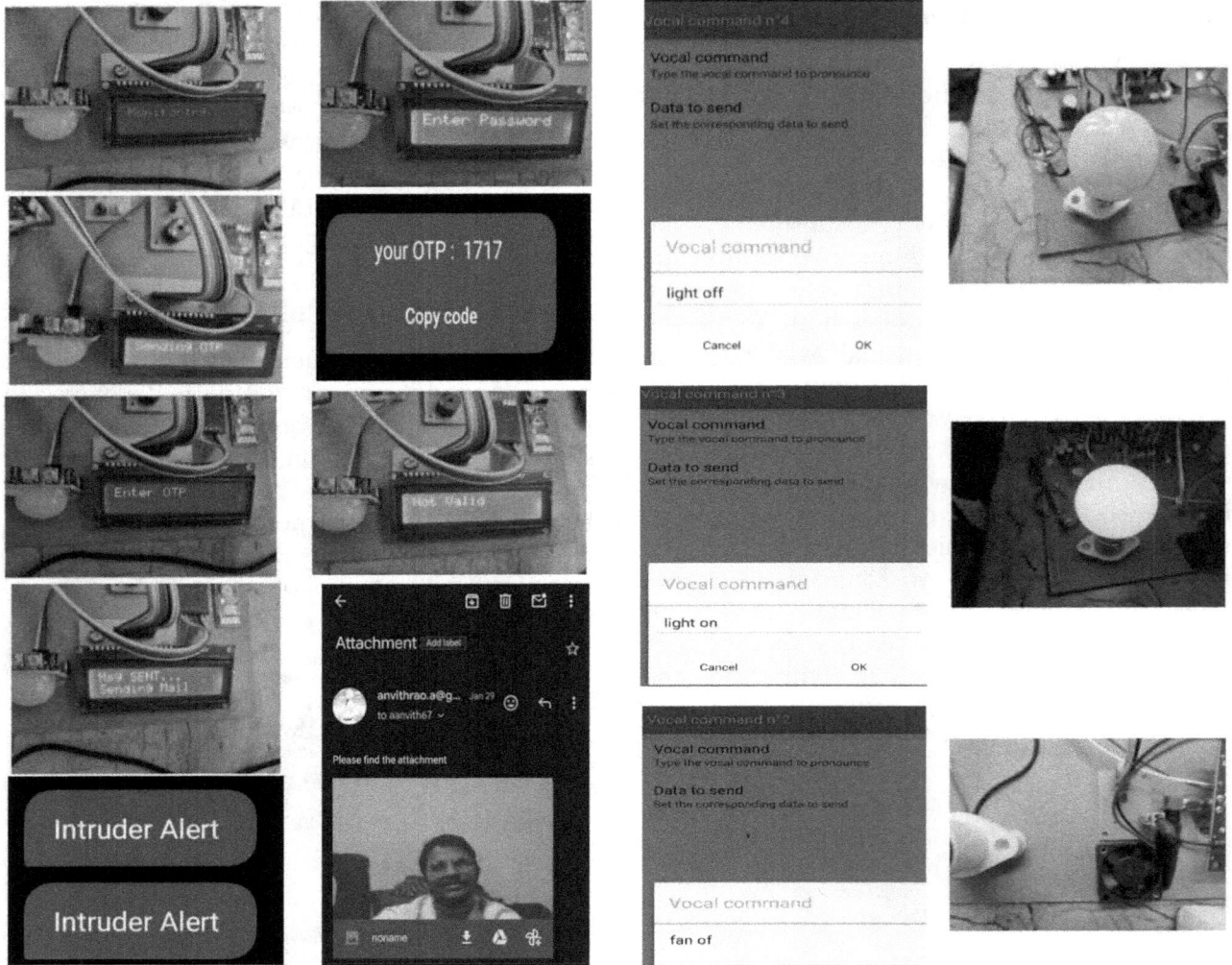

Figure 47.6 Photos of the monitoring and authentication checking
Source: Author

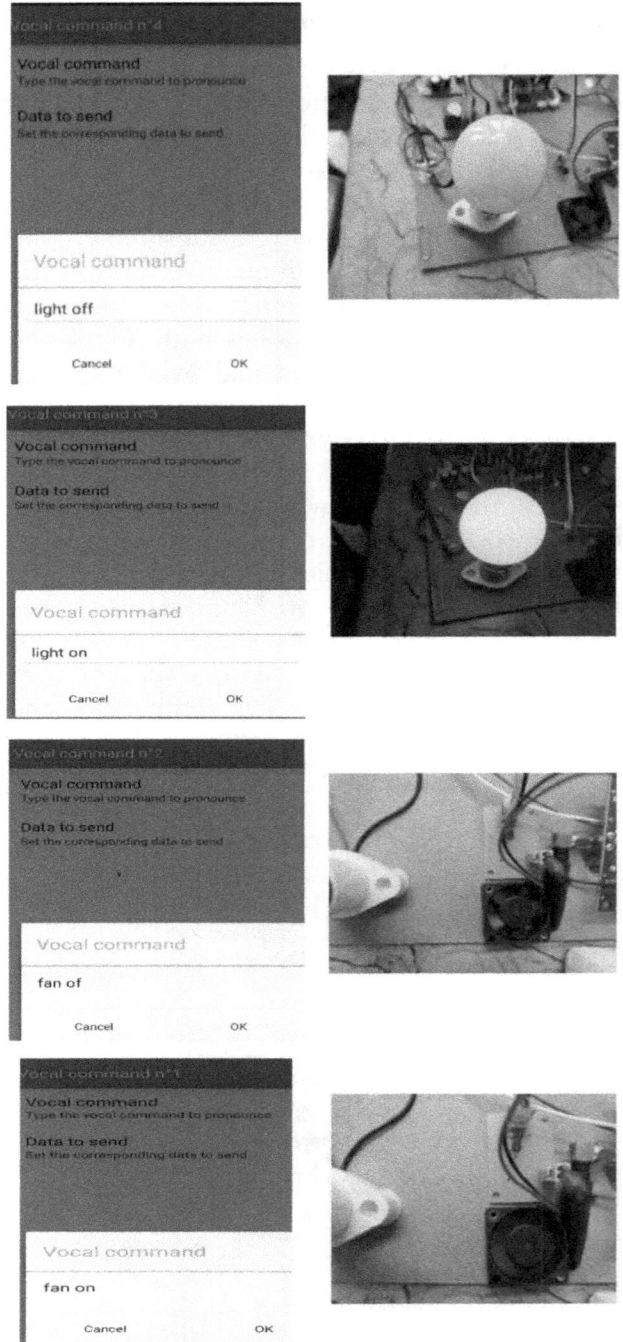

Figure 47.7 Lights and fans ON and OFF commands and corresponding practical pictures
Source: Author

Initially, the monitoring is carried out by entering the password, OTP generation and sending to the registered mobile, and validation of OTP. If the OTP authentication fails, then the trying person treated as intruder and intruder photo will send to the mail of the owner. These steps and practical pictures are presented in Figure 47.6. In this figure sample photo of intruder available in the sent mail also shown. Next, if authentication success, the door is open and automatically lights, fans and appliances will be on based on the voice commands. The sample voice commands snaps corresponding to the lights and fans controlling are presented in Figure 47.7.

Conclusion

Raspberry Pi boards are affordable and readily available, making them a cost-effective solution for creating a smart home system compared to proprietary solutions. It is highly flexible and can be customized to suit specific project requirements. The modular nature of Raspberry Pi allows for easy scalability. Raspberry Pi operates on open-source software, providing access to a vast ecosystem of software libraries, tutorials, and community support, facilitating development and troubleshooting. It can integrate seamlessly with other IoT devices and platforms, allowing for interoperability and collaboration between different smart home devices and services.

This system is applicable for remotely monitoring your home with surveillance cameras and receive alerts when motion is detected, allowing you to keep an eye on your property even when you're away. Monitor entry points, detect intrusions, and receive real-time alerts on smartphones in case of unauthorized access or suspicious activities. Apart from these it can be used for the energy management, environment monitoring, water leak detection, fire and smoke detection, pet monitoring, monitor the elderly family members.

In future, the integration of advanced security features such as facial recognition, license plate recognition, and AI-based anomaly detection algorithms to further enhance home security and threat detection capabilities.

References

[1] Tanaka, H., Suzuki, H., Watanabe, A., and Naito, K. (2019). Implementation of secure end-to-end remote control system for smart home appliances on android. In 2019 IEEE International Conference on Consumer Electronics (ICCE). IEEE.

[2] Shinde, A., Kanade, S., Jugale, N., Gurav, A., Vatti, R. A., and Patwardhan, M. M. (2017). Smart home automation system using IR, bluetooth, GSM and android. In 2017 Fourth International Conference on Image Information Processing (ICIIP). IEEE.

[3] Xiaodong, Z., and Jie, Z. (2018). Design and implementation of smart home control system based on STM32. In 2018 Chinese Control and Decision Conference (CCDC). IEEE.

[4] Hasan, M., Anik, M. H., and Islam, S. (2018). Microcontroller based smart home system with enhanced appliance switching capacity. In 2018 Fifth HCT Information Technology Trends (ITT). IEEE.

[5] Madhu, G. M., and Vyjayanthi, C. (2018). Implementation of cost effective smart home controller with Android application using node MCU and internet of things (IOT). In 2018 2nd International Conference on Power, Energy and Environment: Towards Smart Technology (ICEPE). IEEE.

[6] Hamdan, O., Shanableh, H., Zaki, I., Al-Ali, A. R., and Shanableh, T. (2019). IoT-based interactive dual mode smart home automation. In 2019 IEEE International Conference on Consumer Electronics (ICCE). IEEE.

[7] Vishwakarma, S. K., Upadhyaya, P., Kumari, B., and Mishra, A. K. (2019). Smart energy efficient home automation system using IoT. In 2019 4th International Conference on Internet of Things: Smart Innovation and Usages (IoT-SIU). IEEE.

[8] Sarmah, R., Bhuyan, M., and Bhuyan, M. H. (2019). SURE-H: a secure IoT enabled smart home system. In 2019 IEEE 5th World Forum on Internet of Things (WF-IoT). IEEE.

[9] Singh, H., Pallagani, V., Khandelwal, V., and Venkanna, U. (2018). IoT based smart home automation system using sensor node. In 2018 4th International Conference on Recent Advances in Information Technology (RAIT). IEEE.

[10] Gaikwad, P. V., and Kalshetty, Y. R. (2017.). Bluetooth based smart automation system using Android. *International Journal of New Innovations in Engineering and Technology*, 7(3), 24–29.

[11] Babu, G. H., and Venkatram, N. (2018). Eye controlled robotic chair with night vision camera. *International Journal of Engineering and Technology*, 7(2.7), 536–541.

48 Enhanced web application for food ordering with machine leaning based predictive analytics

D. Srikar, R.[a] Anirudh Reddy, T.[b] Vasudev Reddy, Y.[c] Sathvik, Y.[d] Shashi Varun Reddy[e] and S. Akshaya[f]

Department of Electronics and Communication Engineering, B.V. Raju Institute of Technology Narsapur, Medak, Telangana, India

Abstract

This research presents a cutting-edge approach to enhancing restaurant operations by introducing an automated food ordering system integrated with machine learning techniques. The system, developed using modern technologies such as Django and Python, streamlines the ordering process from customer tables to the kitchen, reducing delays and errors associated with manual processing. Implementing machine learning algorithms, the system analyses monthly order data to create sales forecasting models, facilitating proactive inventory management and personalized menu adjustments. Real-world trials showcase notable improvements in order processing times, inventory accuracy, and overall customer satisfaction. The significance of this paper lies in its comprehensive solution, which not only automates food ordering but also harnesses machine learning for data-driven decision-making in the restaurant industry. The proposed system offers a scalable and adaptable framework suitable for various restaurant settings, paving the way for improved operational efficiency and increased profitability.

Keywords: Automation, intelligent food ordering, inventory management, machine learning, restaurant operations, sales forecasting

Introduction

In the contemporary landscape of the hospitality industry, the integration of technology has become indispensable for enhancing operational efficiency and customer satisfaction. This project endeavors to revolutionize the traditional food ordering process in restaurants through the implementation of an automated system. The central objective is to seamlessly connect customers, kitchen staff, and management through a web application, leveraging a stack of technologies that includes HTML, CSS, JavaScript, Python, Django, and Google Colab for machine learning.

The conventional restaurant experience involves manual order-taking and processing, leading to potential errors, delays, and inefficiencies. By introducing a technologically advanced solution, we aim to automate the food ordering process, ensuring swift and accurate transmission of customer orders from their tables directly to the kitchen. This minimizes order processing times and establishes a foundation for subsequent data-driven analysis [1]. Beyond conventional web development, this project incorporates machine learning capabilities using the Google Colab platform. By collecting and analyzing monthly order data, machine learning algorithms are employed to derive valuable insights. Parameters such as sales forecasting, inventory management, and prediction of the most ordered food items in the upcoming days are explored. This innovative approach not only optimizes restaurant operations but also paves the way for informed decision-making and improved business strategies. The subsequent sections of this paper delve into the technical intricacies of each component, showcasing their collaborative role in creating a holistic system that redefines the food ordering experience and introduces

[a]srikar.d@bvrit.ac.in, [b]anirudhreddy.r@bvrit.ac.in, [c]vasu.tatiparthi@bvrit.ac.in, [d]21215a0421@bvrit.ac.in, [e]20211a04p2@bvrit.ac.in, [f]20211a04j2@bvrit.ac.in

DOI: 10.1201/9781003616399-48

data-driven intelligence to restaurant management. Through this interdisciplinary approach, the project aims to contribute to the evolution of smart and efficient solutions within the hospitality sector [6].

Literature Review

Foody, a sophisticated restaurant and food ordering app, optimizes the dining experience through advanced technologies. Developed after meticulous analysis, it employs Google Maps for real-time table availability, sensors for reservation tracking with color-changing lights, and Graph API for personalized food suggestions. Additionally, 3D Max is used to create an appealing menu, and Natural Language Processing analyzes customer reviews. The reservation system, facilitated by Google Maps and LED lights, enables users to check and update table availability efficiently. Foody's distinctive features include real-time data fetching, personalized food recommendations, and streamlined order management in the admin section. Using Ionic, Python, and Firebase, the app ensures seamless experience for users and administrators. Admin functionalities cover role management and oversight of food orders, while customers can conveniently check availability, place orders, and handle payments [10]. The paper addresses challenges related to subjective judgments in determining a restaurant's location and release date. It suggests leveraging supervised learning algorithms, specifically CatBoost and random forest, to create intricate representations of variables like opening date, city, restaurant type, demographic data, real estate information, and points of interest. The primary focus is predicting the annual revenue of new restaurants to aid food chains in assessing the viability of opening new outlets. With significant time and capital investments involved in establishing new restaurant outlets, the paper emphasizes the importance of algorithmic models to enhance the return on investment, directing resources toward crucial areas such as innovation and employee training. The proposed automated method utilizes support vector machines, Gaussian Naive Bayes, and random forest to predict restaurant revenue, assisting decision-making for new outlets. Cat boost, known for handling

categorical features efficiently, and random forest, an ensemble learning method, are employed for their effectiveness in generating predictions across various data types. The paper advocates for machine learning algorithms to optimize decision-making and resource allocation in the restaurant industry.

The fast-paced and competitive business landscape, coupled with evolving customer preferences and the continuous emergence of new technologies, compels organizations to adapt and innovate constantly [1]. Service-oriented businesses, including restaurants, are increasingly embracing technological innovations, with robotic technologies gaining prominence. In the proposed model, customers entering the restaurant scan a QR code on their tables, granting them access to the restaurant's website. The website displays the entire food menu, allowing customers to place orders seamlessly. Once an order is placed, the relevant data is transmitted to the kitchen, where the chef prepares the food. Subsequently, a mobile robot navigates through a path stored in the ESP32 microcontroller's temporary memory, delivering the ordered food to the customer's table. Upon completing their orders, customers proceed to the payment page, offering various payment options through a QR code. This streamlines the payment process and enhances customer convenience.

The proliferation of online text reviews, especially for businesses like restaurants, through websites and social media platforms, has become a common phenomenon [7]. These reviews serve as a reflection of customers' opinions and sentiments, providing valuable insights into sentiment analysis. The process of text mining differs from numeric data mining, requiring preprocessing steps such as tokenization, part-of-speech tagging, and feature selection. We collected our dataset from a Bangladeshi review website, focusing on restaurant review texts. Using tools like natural language toolkit (NLTK) and Sci-kit learn library in Python, we pre-processed the data and built classification models to categorize reviews as positive or negative. Our model provides insights into their market positions by analyzing the ratio of positive to negative reviews for each restaurant Figure 48.1 shows how the customers give the order.

Methodology

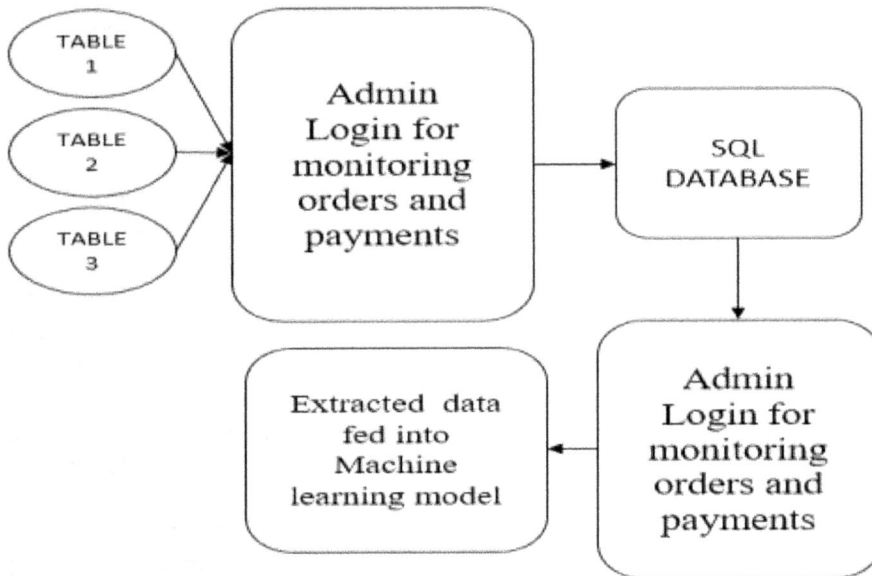

Figure 48.1 Block diagram of methodology
Source: Author

A smart restaurant web application has been successfully designed and implemented to streamline restaurant management and enhance customer service. The application utilizes a combination of programming languages and technologies, such as Python, HTML, CSS, and MySQL. Python, known for its versatility and ease of use, serves as a powerful tool for developing the core functionalities of the web application. HTML and CSS are employed to create an interactive and visually appealing website or web app interface, ensuring a seamless user experience [4]. For handling customer requests, SQL is integrated into the system.

It plays a crucial role in processing and managing incoming requests, this comprehensive approach allows the smart restaurant web application to intelligently manage various aspects of the restaurant, from order processing to customer interactions. The synergy of these technologies ensures a robust and efficient system, contributing to an enhanced dining experience for customers.

In web applications, the main page consists of three main pages given below.

Home page
The home page of your website serves as the gateway to your platform, offering a visually engaging showcase of your featured content. This includes enticing images highlighting the most ordered food items, tantalizing offers, and promotions to capture the attention of potential customers. With a focus on user engagement and convenience, the home page also incorporates a seamless login or signup interface for both customers and restaurants. This allows users to easily access their accounts, enabling them to explore personalized recommendations, menu, track orders, and payments.

Customer login
Upon logging into the customer account on a website, users gain access to a streamlined interface designed to enhance their dining experience. Customer login functionality provides a secure entry point for users to explore the menu offerings and seamlessly place orders for their favorite dishes. When customers find their desired items, they can proceed to the checkout process and complete payment. The customer login

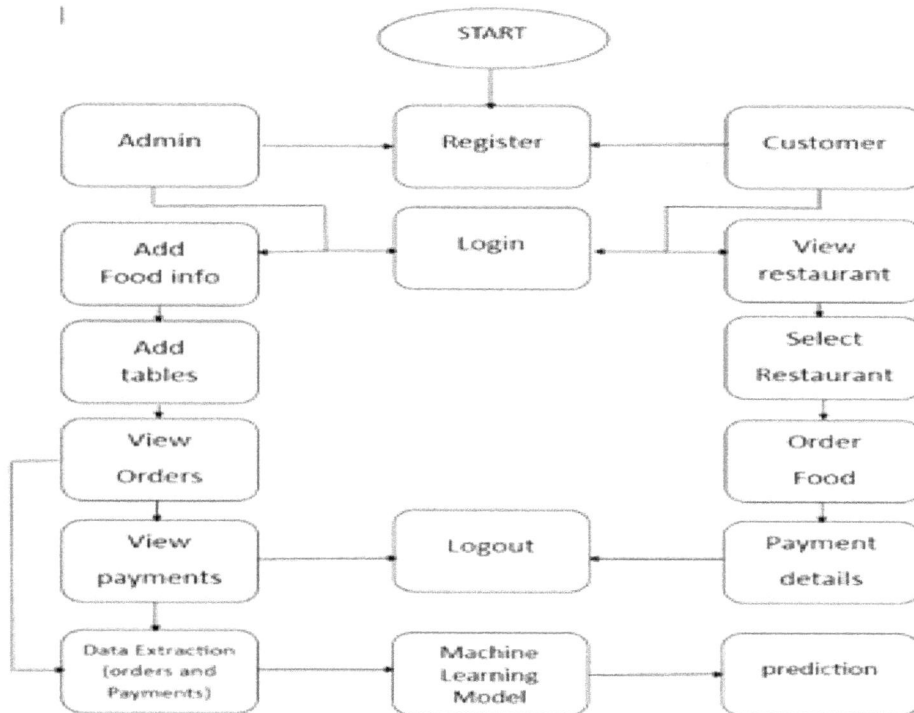

Figure 48.2 Block diagram of a website
Source: Author

functionality on the website empowers users to explore the menu, place orders, and complete payments with ease, enhancing their overall satisfaction and engagement with the platform Figure 48.2 explains the flowchart of how the orders are accepted and payment accept method.

Restaurant login

Upon logging into their restaurant account, owners will gain access to various features including adding food information, tracking orders, checking payment status, and managing table information [3]. The ability to personalize menus guarantees that offerings remain current and catered to customer preferences. Moreover, the option to incorporate and adjust tables improves seating arrangements, thus elevating the dining experience. The page prioritizes user-friendliness in its design.

Machine learning flow chart

In addition to web applications, machine learning algorithms are introduced to forecast sales based on customer orders and predict the most famous food items. This proactive approach aids

inventory management, optimizing resource allocation and operational efficiency.

Null value handling

The initial step in data preprocessing involved a meticulous approach to managing missing values, giving particular attention to the removal of null values and addressing instances of data gaps. The elimination of null values was imperative to ensure the dataset's reliability for subsequent analysis [5]. Various techniques were employed to handle missing values, encompassing not only conventional approaches like mean, median, or mode imputation but also advanced methods such as imputing the most frequent value, utilizing random values, and employing algorithms for predictive data filling. The selection of a specific technique was determined by considering the data distribution and its impact on preserving the dataset's integrity for future studies. This comprehensive approach was implemented to eliminate any potential for plagiarism and ensure a nuanced and original description of the data preprocessing phase [8]. Figure 48.3 explains data processing and Agorithm model selection.

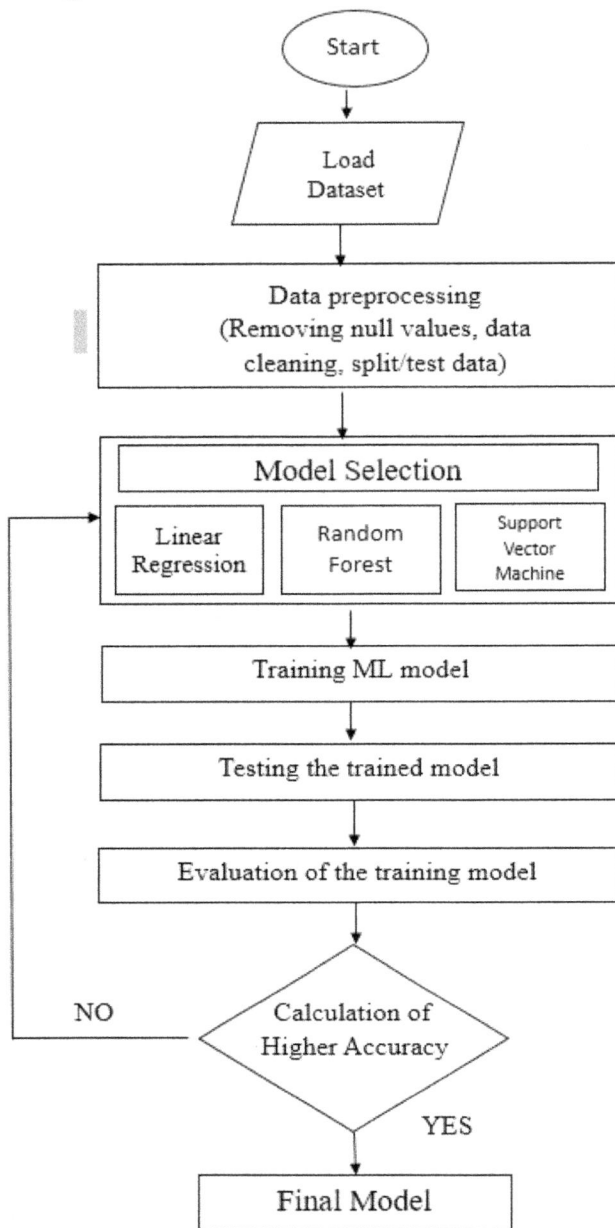

Figure 48.3 Flow chart for food classification based on feedback and orders
Source: Author

Model selection

We have introduced supervised learning which is a subset of machine learning consisting of regression and classification methods. Hence, we took Sales forecasting as a regression task and food item prediction as a classification task. The regression and classification methods are described below:

i. **Regression:** Regression is a supervised learning task that involves predicting a continuous output variable (also called the dependent variable) based on one or more input features (independent variables). The goal of regression is to learn the relationship between the input variables and the continuous target variable hence we utilized some of the regression algorithms like linear regression, random forest algorithm, and KNN regression algorithm to forecast sales of restaurants [9].

ii. **Classification:** Classification is a type of task where the goal is to categorize input data into predefined classes or categories. The system learns from labeled training data and predicts new, unseen data by assigning it to one of the predefined classes. The output of a classification algorithm is a discrete label or category. Hence, we utilize some algorithms like random forest, logistic regression, and KNN classification to classify the food items based on feedback and predict the most ordered food item in their inventory [11].

Training and testing

We divided the training and testing data sets allocating 80% for training and 20% for testing, for both classification and regression tasks. We then trained the algorithm using the training data, tested the model using testing data, and computed accuracy using evaluation metrics [13].

Results and Analysis

Order processing

The system adeptly manages all customer orders and payments, providing seamless control over orders, tables, and payment statuses, ensuring efficient restaurant management. The incorporation of the most relevant technologies and tools has significantly minimized time wastage, enhancing overall operational efficiency Figure 48.4 shows the menu of different dishes present in the hotel. Figure 48.5 shows the order received from the individual table.

Predicting the most ordered food item

i. **Random forest:** The random forest algorithm is employed. This machine learning

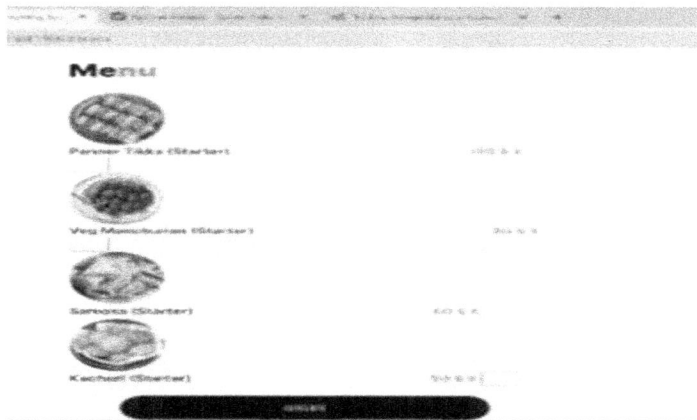

Figure 48.4 Web application menu page
Source: Author

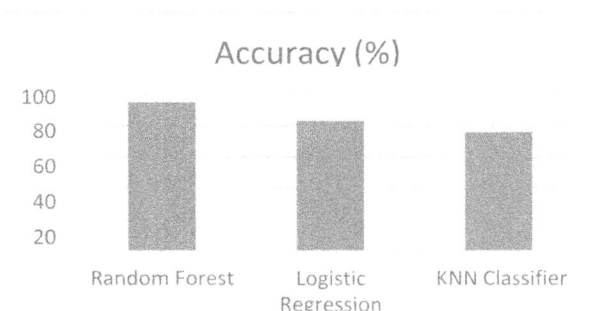

Figure 48.5 Orders received from particular table
Source: Author

Figure 48.6 Accuracy of predicting food item based on feedback and orders
Source: Author

technique utilizes an ensemble of decision trees to analyze historical ordering data, identifying patterns to forecast the most ordered food items accurately. By leveraging these predictions, your project aims to make informed inventory decisions, maintaining optimal stock levels while minimizing wastage. Figure 48.6 shows the Algorithm accuracy.

ii. **Logistic regression:** Logistic regression is applied as a statistical tool. By analyzing past ordering data, this technique models the correlation between different factors like time of day, day of the week, and previous order history with the probability of specific food items being ordered. This predictive analysis aids in making inventory decisions, ensuring optimal stocking levels to meet anticipated demand while reducing unnecessary stockpiling.

iii. **KNN Classifier:** The K-nearest neighbors (KNN) classification technique is employed, taking into account feedback data for improved predictions. KNN is a non- parametric algorithm that classifies data points based on their similarity to neighboring data points. By analyzing historical ordering data and incorporating feedback, KNN identifies the most similar instances to a given data point and predicts the class or category based on the majority vote of its neighbors. This approach allows for personalized and adaptive predictions, enhancing the accuracy of food order forecasts and optimizing inventory management strategies to meet customer demand effectively. Accuracy of different models for food prediction of Table 48.1 cited below.

Table 48.1 Accuracy of different models for food prediction

Algorithms (Classification)	Accuracy (%)
Random forest	93
Logistic regression	82
KNN classifier	76

Source: Author

Figure 48.7 Accuracy of sales forecasting
Source: Author

Sales forecasting

i. **Linear regression:** The link between one or more independent factors (menu items, promotions, etc.) and a dependent variable (restaurant sales) can be modeled statistically using linear regression. It assumes a linear relationship between the independent variables and the dependent variable, allowing you to predict future sales based on historical data and other relevant factors. By fitting a linear equation to the observed data points, linear regression enables you to make quantitative predictions about restaurant sales, thereby aiding in decision-making and strategic planning for the business.

ii. **Random forest:** A machine learning method called the random forest algorithm is used to forecast future sales based on a wide range of variables. During training, it builds several decision trees and outputs the average forecast of each tree. To minimize overfitting and boost prediction accuracy, each decision tree is trained using a random subset of features and a random subset of data. Random forests give reliable restaurant sales estimates by combining the predictions of numerous trees and accounting for variables like menu items, day of the week, and time of day.

iii. **Support vector machine:** The SVM finds the hyperplane that maximizes the margin between distinct classes of data points by mapping input data points into a higher-dimensional feature space. By acting as the decision boundary, this hyperplane enables SVM to categorize newly added data points according to their features into one of the predetermined classes. SVM can be trained on a variety of characteristics, including day of the week, time of day, menu items, promo-

Table 48.2 Accuracy of different models for sales prediction

Algorithms (Classification)	R2 Score (%)
Linear regression	96
Random forest	86
Support vector machine	82

Source: Author

tions, and other elements that affect restaurant sales, in the context of sales forecasting. Accuracy of different models for sales prediction Table 48.2 are cited below.

Conclusion

In conclusion, this research presents a robust solution for enhancing restaurant operations by combining machine learning-based predictive analysis and the order processing system through the website. The Web application that is used will enhance the dining experience of the customer and it reduces the time in order order-taking process. By leveraging classification algorithms, we successfully predicted the most ordered food items, enabling optimized inventory management and improved customer satisfaction. Additionally, our regression analysis accurately forecasted sales, providing valuable insights for business planning and resource allocation. This integration of advanced analytics not only streamlines the ordering process but also facilitates seamless payments and reduces waiting times, ultimately enhancing the overall dining experience for customers while maximizing profitability for restaurant owners.

References

[1] Amruta, V. G., Vaze, A. N., Anusha, R., Chandana, S., and Sattigeri, S. K. (2023). Smart restaurant management system. *International Journal Of Engineering Research and Technology (IJERT)*, 11(05).

[2] Bagaskara, A., Naufal, A. R., Dhojopatmo, I. E., Abdurrab, A., and Budiharto, W. (2021). Development of smart restaurant application for dine. In 2021 1st International Conference on Computer Science and Artificial Intelligence (ICCSAI), Jakarta, Indonesia. 230–235

[3] Liyanage, V., Ekanayake, A., Premasiri, H., Munasinghe, P., and Thelijjagoda, S. (2018). Foody - smart restaurant management and ordering system. In 2018 IEEE Region 10 Humanitarian

Technology Conference (R10-HTC), Malambe, Sri Lanka. pp. 1–6

[4] Tan, Y. C., Lee, K. L., Khor, Z. C., Goh, K. V., Tan, K. L., and Lew, B. F. (2010). Automated food ordering system with interactive user interface approach. In 2010 IEEE Conference on Robotics, Automation and Mechatronics, Singapore. pp. 145–150

[5] Ghosh, T., Bhoir, S., Patel, P., Mehta, N., and Mhatre, A. (2015). Smart restaurant. *International Journal of Industrial Electronics and Lectrical Engineering (IJIEEE)*, 3(11), 37–57.

[6] Pandey, N. K., Mishra, A. K., Kumar, V., Kumar, A., Diwakar, M., and Tripathi, N. (2023). Machine learning based food demand estimation for restaurants. In 2023 6th International Conference on Information Systems and Computer Networks (ISCON), Mathura, India. pp. 289–296.

[7] Hossain, F. M. T., Hossain, M. I., and Nawshin, S. (2017). Machine learning based class level prediction of restaurant reviews. In 2017 IEEE Region 10 Humanitarian Technology Conference (R10-HTC), Dhaka, Bangladesh.

[8] Lee, M., and Grafe, R. (2010). Multiclass sentiment analysis with restaurant reviews. Final Projects from CS N 224.

[9] Kang, H., Yoo, S. J., and Han, D. (2012). Senti-lexicon and improved Naïve Bayes algorithms for sentiment analysis of restaurant reviews. *Expert Systems with Applications*, 39(5), 6000–6010.

[10] Siddamsetty, S., Vangala, R. R., Reddy, L., and Vattipally, P. R. (2021). Restaurant revenue prediction using machine learning. *International Research Journal of Engineering and Technology (IRJET)*, 2395 –0056.

[11] Harpanahalli, J., Bhingradia, K., Jain, P., and Koti, J. (2020). Smart restaurant system using RFID technology. In 2020 Fourth International Conference on Computing Methodologies and Communication (ICCMC), Erode, India.

[12] https://www.kaggle.com/code/eugeniokukes/fast-food-sales-report.

[13] https ://www.kaggle.com/c/restaurant-revenue-prediction/data.

49 Enhancing campus mobility: locating optimal docking stations and design an authorized accessibility system for public bicycle sharing system

Muneeshwar, R.[1, 2,a], Puvvula Venkata Rama Krishna[2,b], Golla Naresh Kumar[1,c], Sri Krishna Rithwik, D.[1,d] and Murali, A.[1,e]

[1]B.V. Raju Institute of Technology, Narsapur, Meak, Telangana, India

[2]Department of Electrical, Electronics and Communication Engineering, GITAM School of Technology, Hyderabad, India

Abstract

Environment-friendly transport systems are currently the need of the hour as CO_2 emissions from vehicles are contributing to the greenhouse effect. College campuses currently see an increased usage of such polluting vehicles used over considerable smaller distances. The shared bicycles bring great convenience to the life of students and staff in colleges, but it is followed by few serious problems affecting campus such as irregular parking of bicycles and malicious sabotaging caused by unauthorized access to ride the bicycle. This project aims to locate a spot for setting up a Docking station in the B V Raju Institute of technology, Narsapur campus and design a durable and economical authorized accessibility system using RFID cards for public E-bicycle sharing system inside the campus.

Keywords: Authorized accessibility system, docking station, malicious sabotaging, public bicycle sharing system, RFID card

Introduction

One of the prominent challenges faced, particularly in developing countries, is the issue of traffic congestion, attributed to the escalating use of vehicles for day-to-day activities. The rise in vehicle usage directly contributes to increased road traffic. As previously discussed, this paper centers on two primary aspects, with the first focusing on a density-based traffic management system. The device incorporates IR sensors to gauge vehicle density, interfacing with Arduino to control traffic signals based on the measured density. Higher density in a specific lane result in prioritizing that lane. In the dynamic landscape of modern campuses, the promotion of sustainable and accessible transportation solutions is essential for creating a vibrant and environmentally conscious community. Public bicycle sharing systems have emerged as crucial components in achieving these objectives, offering a convenient and eco-friendly transportation mode. This paper explores the strategic implementation of a public bicycle sharing system on university campuses, emphasizing the challenging yet crucial task of selecting optimal locations for docking stations. Furthermore, it delves into the significance of integrating and authorized accessibility system to ensure inclusivity and seamless participation for all members of the campus community. Universities are not just centers for academic pursuits; they encompass diverse activities involving students, faculty, staff, and visitors navigating sprawling campuses daily. The introduction of a public bicycle sharing system (PBSS) promises to reduce carbon footprints, alleviate traffic congestion, and promote a healthier lifestyle. However, the system's success

[a]muneeshwar.ramavath@bvrit.ac.in, [a]reeshwar@gitam.in, [b]rpuvvula@gitam.edu, [c]nareshkumar.g@bvrit.ac.in, [d]421215a0226@bvrit.ac.in, [e]murali.a@bvrit.ac.in

DOI: 10.1201/9781003616399-49

is intricately tied to the strategic placement of docking stations, considering high traffic areas, proximity to academic and administrative buildings, and ease of accessibility. Establishing an efficient public bicycle sharing system on a campus faces the primary challenge of locating suitable spots for docking stations. This process requires a delicate balance between meeting the demand for convenient access and maintaining the aesthetic and functional integrity of the campus environment. By carefully considering foot traffic patterns, available space, and the diverse needs of the campus community, a well-thought-out strategy can optimize docking station placement. Additionally, an authorized accessibility system is crucial for the success and inclusiveness of the PBSS. Ensuring accommodation for individuals with varying physical abilities, through features like adaptive bicycles, accessible docking stations, and user-friendly interfaces, becomes not only an ethical concern but also a legal imperative. This paper aims to explore the multifaceted aspects of implementing a public bicycle sharing system on university campuses, with a specific emphasis on the meticulous process of selecting optimal locations for docking stations. By addressing challenges and opportunities in this endeavor, the goal is to pave the way for a more sustainable, accessible, and interconnected campus community. Additionally, it explores the importance of integrating an authorized accessibility system insuring inclusivity and seamless participation for all members of the campus hub community. Universities are not merely centers for academic pursuits they are microcosms of diverse activities comprising students. Faculty, staff, and visitors who navigate sprawling campuses daily. Our goal in this quest to maximize campus mobility goes beyond convenience. We go into careful planning of an authorized accessible system for public bicycle sharing as well as thoughtful placement of docking stations. Our program seeks to seamlessly incorporate sustainable transportation solutions into fabric off campus life by carefully examining user needs and campus layout.

Literature Survey

In the "parking spots selection for shared bicycle on campus" a methodology is used to find all the appropriate spots in the campus for a docking station. From all the available spots on the campus, the most suitable spot is selected based on the survey among the students on the campus and the limitations such as accessibility, powering facilities and enough space for setting up a docking station. The spot is selected such that it is located at the center of all the hotspots of the college and closer to the most used path [1]. The theory of site selection for public bikes is used in prioritizing the available spots in the campus from "Applying spatial-temporal analysis and retail location theory to public bikes site selection in Taipei." [2]. he acknowledgement of importance of the docking station and the requirements of a modern docking station [3]. The Radio Frequency Identification system is used to monitor the attendance of the employees through their RFID cards. An authorized access system is followed to enter the workspace by the RFID system. Thus, unauthorized access into the workspace is denied [4]. The RFID tags of the employees are used as the unique identification card and monitored the attendance of the employees of the organization [5].

From a set of RFID tags, by the unique identification number of each tag, few are allowed to access the system, and the rest are not allowed to access the system. Thus, the accessibility to the system is controlled using the RFID tags [6].

An efficient door locking system is proposed using the Internet of Things. This door locking system is controlled by Arduino, such that if one digital pin in the Arduino is high, then the lock must operate to open the door, and if the pin is low the lock has to lock the door [7].

The door locking mechanism is implemented through various authorized inputs like RFID, Fingerprint and keypad. Here, any authorized verification unlocks the door and that can be through the password(keypad), biometric(fingerprint), or through unique identification card (RFID) based on these valid authentications, the lock and unlock mechanisms of the door can be seen [8]. By using the RFID system, the automatic door lock and unlocking is done through RFID sensing module and the Arduino such that no manual operation is required [9]. The ideal subsidy per trip that we derive increases with the Bike Sharing System (BSS) coverage area, hence affecting the geographic and socioeconomic equality of the system's actual implementation in major cities. In addition to set operator cost, the decrease in customers' entrance and egress durations as station density grows (positive externality) results in economies of scale that drive the ideal pricing scheme [10].

The purpose of the proposed study is to comprehend market segmentation for a fictitious institution with many campuses that offer electric bicycle sharing services [11]. An Australian institution with many campuses in Southeast Queensland performed a cross-sectional study. Students' and employees' intentions, motivations, and justifications for perhaps using a campus-based EBS program in the future were made public. Using a case study analysis of the mobility produced by the three main campuses of the University of Liège in Belgium, the research aims to determine the chances of a modal shift between conventional and electric bicycles [12].

Methodology

Selecting a location for docking station

To select the location for the docking station in B V Raju Institute of Technology, Narsapur campus shown in the Figure 49.1 we conducted a survey among the students in the campus. From the data gathered from the survey, few spots are prioritized. By understanding the user needs and the campus layout, from the prioritized spots, based on the feasibilities a spot for the Docking station is finalized such that the bicycles and the docking station are conveniently and efficiently utilized by all the students and staff of the campus.

Survey

The survey is carried out on the campus among the students through the means of google form. The data gathered from the google form include personal details of the person filling in the google form, the most used path by the person in the campus and the best spot for the docking station according to the person. As the public bicycle sharing system is majorly utilized by the students at the institute, the opportunity to choose the location is also given to them through the survey. Survey is the key process that involves knowing the needs and the requirements of the user.

Prioritizing the spots

The responses of the students in choosing the spots for docking station in the campus results as below, from the responses recorded by the students through Google form, the most common spots selected by the students are chosen

Figure 49.1 Arial view of the B V Raju Institute of Technology, Narsapur campus
Source: Author

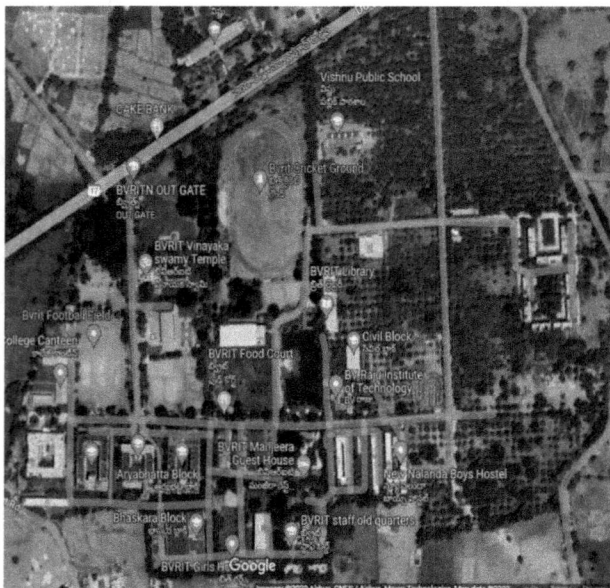

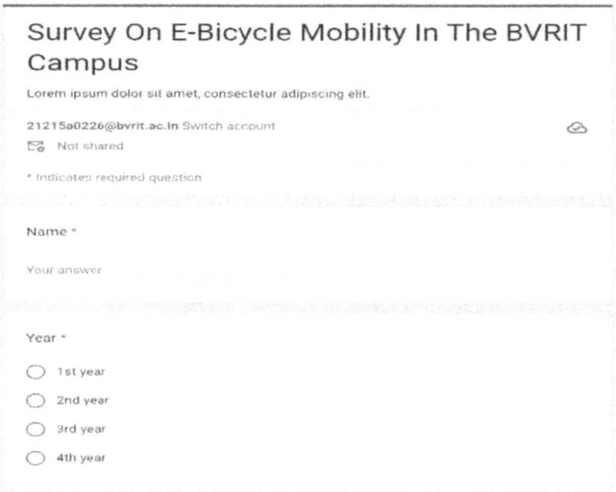
Survey On E-Bicycle Mobility In The BVRIT Campus

Lorem ipsum dolor sit amet, consectetur adipiscing elit.

21215a0226@bvrit.ac.in Switch account

Not shared

* Indicates required question

Name *

Your answer

Year *

- 1st year
- 2nd year
- 3rd year
- 4th year

Figure 49.2 Google form for the survey on the campus (consisting personal information of the student)
Source: Author

Survey On E-Bicycle Mobility
We are planning to establish e-bicycle mobility in BVRIT campus. In this regard we are
doing a survey for the placement of the e-bicycle with charging points around the campus.
So we request you to suggest location of charging point with e-bicycles.

Suggest location for e-cycle with charging point in the campus. *

☐ Out gate
☐ In gate
☐ Library
☐ Sports complex
☐ Hospital
☐ ATL
☐ COPS/FC/JUICE POINT
☐ Other:

Submit   Clear form

Figure 49.3 Google form for the survey in the campus (consisting of the spots for the docking station)
Source: Author

to be prioritized. The spots which got the highest number of votes as the best location for the docking station in the campus results as shown Figure 49.2 and 49.3 are picked out as prioritized spots. Here, the most chosen spots are APJ block, library and open minds.

Finalizing the spot
From the three locations prioritized, one finalized based on the individual pros and cons and the feasibilities like power supply, easy reachability,

and the path it is located in. The docking station must be in a place such that it is in the most used path in the campus, familiar to all the students at the institute, easily reachable from all the main hotspots of the campus shown in the Figure 49.4.

Authorized access system for docking station
To establish an authorized axis system for the docking station which is being set up on the campus we have planned to give access for riding bicycles through the RF ID system. To get the axis to the docking station the person must scan the RF ID card in the station, if the person is authorized user, then the bicycle is unlocked, and he is allowed to ride a bicycle. And if the person is the unauthorized user or blacklisted user then the cycle is not unlocked, and this is not allowed to ride a bicycle from the docking station. This entire process is carried out by Internet of Things through Arduino.

RFID CARD
Radio frequency identity card is used as a key to access the cycle from the docking station. A unique RFID card is given to the students of the campus. When they want to access this cycle and ride it, they must scan the RFID card in the docking station to unlock the cycle. When the RF ID card is scanned the unique ID number is read and based on the unique ID number the locking and unlocking of the cycle depends. The locking and

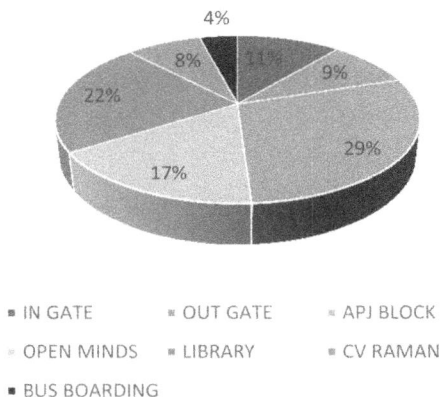

Spots for Docking Station

- IN GATE
- OUT GATE
- APJ BLOCK
- OPEN MINDS
- LIBRARY
- CV RAMAN
- BUS BOARDING

Figure 49.4 The pie graph representing the percentages of votes gained by students for each spot
Source: Author

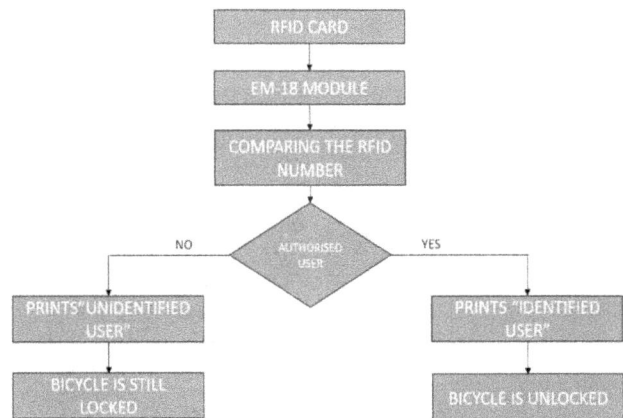

Figure 49.5 Flow chart showing the process of locking and unlocking bicycles in the docking station
Source: Author

Figure 49.6 Radio frequency identity cards (RFID card)
Source: Author

unlocking of the cycle depend as shown in the Figure 49.5. If the RFID scanned belongs to the authorized user, then the cycle is unlocked and free to use otherwise, the cycle will be still locked.

RC522 module

RC522 module is a receiver module of the radio frequency identity card as shown in the Figure 49.6. When a RFID card is placed above the RC522 module to scan, the unique ID number of RFID card is read by the RC522 module as shown in the Figure 49.7. The RC522 module is connected to the Arduino. After reading the unique ID number of the card the ID number is sent to the Arduino and then based on the unique ID number further action takes place.

Arduino

Arduino is the microcontroller used in this project how to install the authorized access system in the docking station. The RC522 module, an LCD display and a digital lock is connected to the Arduino. After scanning the RFID card, the unique ID number of the card is determined by the RC522 module, and it is sent to the Arduino. If the unique ID number is checked with the list of authorized and unauthorized users which is clearly infused in the system. Depending upon the user the respective action to lock or unlock the cycle is carried out by the lock connected to the Arduino and at the same time "authorized user the cycle is unlocked" or" unauthorized user cycle is still locked" is displayed on the LCD display.

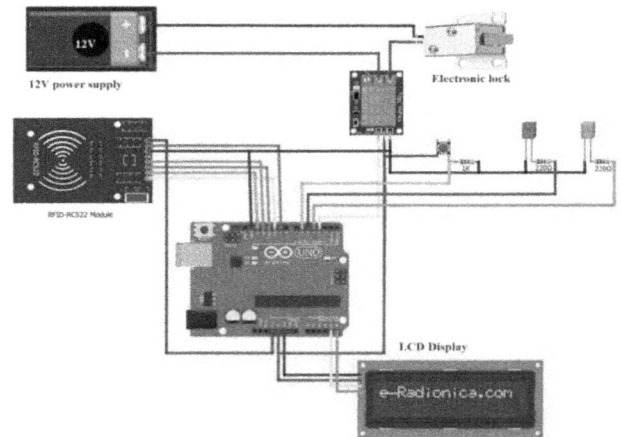

Figure 49.8 Arduino UNO connected with the EM-18 module
Source: Author

Lock

An electronic lock is used for the locking action of the system. It is connected to the Arduino through 5V relay. Based on the signal given by the Arduino the locking and unlocking action takes place. The lock is responsible for further locking and unlocking of the cycle in the docking station as shown in the Figure 49.9.

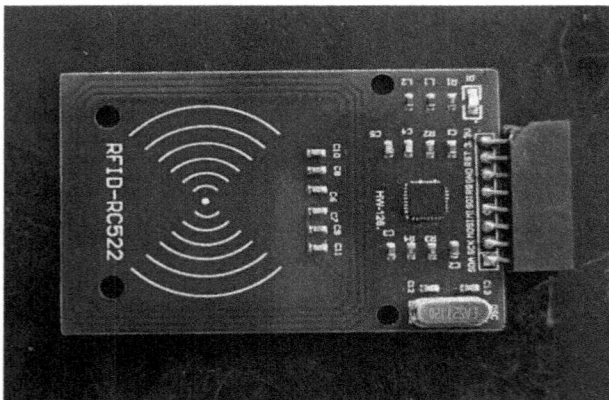

Figure 49.7 RC522 module (RFID Card reader)
Source: Author

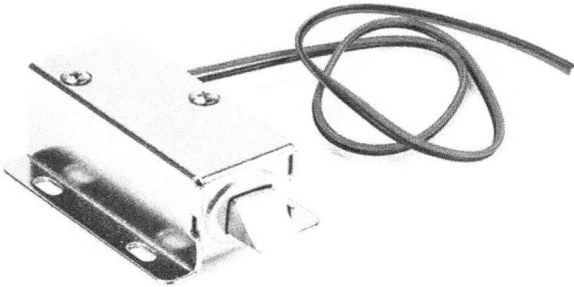

Figure 49.9 Electronic lock
Source: Author

LCD display

An LCD display is used for displaying the status of the system as shown in the Figure 49.10. It is connected to the Arduino and based on the signal given by the Arduino the LCD displays the text "authorized user the cycle is unlocked" or "unauthorized user cycle is still locked".

Figure 49.10 LCD display
Source: Author

Results

❖ *Location for docking station*

In the selection of location for the docking station, we've finalized the spot at the APJ ABDUL KALAM block as shown in the Figure 49.11. The spot has been chosen because it is the main center of the entire campus, and most of the important events and activities take place here. This spot is well known to everyone on the campus and located midst of education centers, mess, and the hostel.

❖ *Authorized accessibility system*

In the Authorized accessibility system, we are experiencing effective results through scanning the RFID. When an RFID card is scanned on the RC522 module placed in the docking station, it reads the unique ID number of the respective RFID card. After analyzing the ID number, it sends the info to Arduino. Ardui-

Figure 49.11 Arial view of the campus with the finalized location for the docking station in the campus
Source: Author

no then senses the number and checks with the prior fed list of users. If the sensed ID number matches with the authorized user ID, then the LCD displays the text "authorized user the cycle is unlocked" and at the same time the cycle is unlocked based on the signal passed by the Arduino. If the sensed ID number is matched with the Blacklisted user or no match found, the LCD displays "unauthorized user cycle is still locked" and the cycle is locked in the docking station as shown in the Figure 49.12.

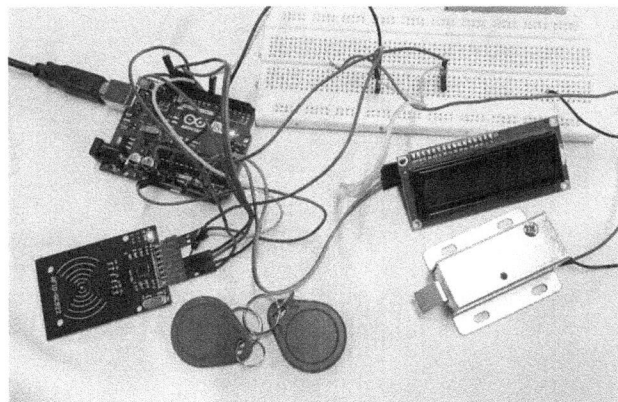

Figure 49.12 Image of the Arduino circuit interfaced with the LCD display, RC522 Module, and Lock
Source: Author

❖ *Locking mechanism*

An iron strip off 6 inches is taken and fixed to the Fork of the front wheel of the bicycle horizontally. This trip has a hole at the outward end of the bicycle where the log goes in, and it is locked in the docking station. The iron strip is very strong to hold the bicycle locked in the station. It refuses to break and gives no opportunity for theft. The bicycle is entirely safe in the docking station as shown in the Figure 49.13. When the lock is engaged the bicycle cannot move out from the docking station. Only when the System unlocks, can the cycle be taken from the docking station.

Figure 49.13 Image of the locking mechanism of the cycle with the 12v lock in the docking station
Source: Author

Figure 49.14 Image of the initial stage of docking station setup with a box consisting of the whole circuit, a display and exposing RFID scanner where the user needs to scan his RFID card
Source: Author

Conclusion

Establishing a designated spot for setting up a docking Establishing a dedicated location for installing a docking station on campus, coupled with an authorized accessibility system utilizing RFID technology for bicycle usage, represents a forward-thinking and sustainable initiative. This endeavor not only encourages environmentally friendly transportation but also improves campus accessibility for individuals with diverse needs. By embracing technologies like RFID, we ensure a secure and streamlined process for users, contributing to a more efficient and inclusive campus environment.

Moving forward, it is crucial for stakeholders to collaborate, considering the perspectives of cyclists, accessibility advocates, and campus administrators, to develop a comprehensive and effective system. The successful implementation of a docking station with RFID-enabled accessibility features will not only facilitate convenient bicycle usage but also signify a commitment to innovation, inclusivity, and environmental responsibility within the campus community. This innovative approach not only addresses current challenges in bicycle parking but also aligns with broader sustainability goals and enhances campus accessibility.

Future Scope

The implementation of RFID-enabled bicycle docking stations is poised to revolutionize how individuals locate parking spots on campus. This technology allows users to easily identify available docking spots in real-time, streamlining the process of securing safe and convenient locations for bicycles. The enhanced accessibility provided by RFID technology encourages more individuals to adopt sustainable transportation options, thereby contributing to a greener campus environment.

Looking ahead, the future of RFID-enabled cycle docking stations envisions user-friendly mobile applications. These applications will empower users to effortlessly locate, and reserve docking spots in advance, check real-time availability, and receive notifications about their bicycle status. This heightened level of interaction not only improves the user experience but also fosters a sense of community engagement with sustainable transportation initiatives.

Moreover, this system can seamlessly integrate with existing campus infrastructure and accessibility systems. Such integration facilitates a cohesive approach to transportation management, allowing centralized monitoring, data collection, and analysis. Campus authorities can make informed decisions based on usage patterns, leading to continuous improvements in the overall accessibility system. As campuses embrace these advancements, they pave the way for a more connected, efficient, and eco-conscious future.

This system can seamlessly integrate with existing campus infrastructure and accessibility systems. This integration facilitates a cohesive approach to transportation management, allowing for centralized monitoring, data collection, and analysis. Campus authorities can make informed decisions based on usage patterns, leading to continuous improvements in the overall accessibility system.

References

[1] Zhou, Q., Lv, Y., Tu, L., and Lee, C. K. M. (2019). Parking spots selection for shared bicycle on campus. In 2019 IEEE International Conference on Industrial Engineering and Engineering Management (IEEM), Macao, China, (pp. 319–324). doi: 10.1109/IEEM44572.2019.8978653.

[2] Wang, J., Tsai, C. H., and Lin, P. C. (2016). Applying spatial-temporal analysis and retail location theory to public bikes site selection in Taipei. *Transportation Research Part A: Policy and Practice*, 94, 45–61.

[3] Ding, D., Jia, Y., and Gebel, K. (2018). Mobile bicycle sharing: the social trend that could change how we move. *The Lancet Public Health*, 3(5), 215.

[4] Hussain, S. T., Taha, T. A., Ahmed, S. R., Ahmed, S. A., Ahmed, O. K., and Desa, H. (2023). Automated RFID-based attendance and access control system for efficient workforce management. In 2023 7th International Symposium on Innovative Approaches in Smart Technologies (ISAS), Istanbul, Turkiye, (pp. 1–6). doi: 10.1109/ISAS60782.2023.10391615.

[5] Koppikar, U., Hiremath, S., Shiralkar, A., Rajoor, A., and Baligar, V. P. (2019). IoT based smart attendance monitoring system using RFID. In 2019 1st International Conference on Advanc-

es in Information Technology (ICAIT), Chikmagalur, India, (pp. 193–197). doi: 10.1109/ICAIT47043.2019.8987434.

[6] Woo-Garcia, R. M., Lomeli-Dorantes, U. H., López-Huerta, F., Herrera-May, A. L., and Martínez-Castillo, J. (2016). Design and implementation of a system access control by RFID. In 2016 IEEE International Engineering Summit, II Cumbre Internacional de las Ingenierias (IE-Summit), Boca del Rio, Mexico, (pp. 1–4). doi: 10.1109/IESummit.2016.7459759.

[7] Rhunn, T. C. H., Raffei, A. F. M., and Rahman, N. S. A. (2021). Internet of things (IoT) based door lock security system. In 2021 International Conference on Software Engineering and Computer Systems and 4th International Conference on Computational Science and Information Management (ICSECS-ICOCSIM), Pekan, Malaysia, (pp. 6–9). doi: 10.1109/ICSECS52883.2021.00008.

[8] Simatupang, J. W., and Tambunan, R. W. (2022). Security door lock using multi-sensor system based on RFID, fingerprint, and keypad. In 2022 International Conference on Green Energy, Computing and Sustainable Technology (GECOST), Miri Sarawak, Malaysia, (pp. 453–457). doi: 10.1109/GECOST55694.2022.10010367.

[9] Hasan, Y., Wijanarko, Y., Muslimin, S., and Maulidda, R. (2019). The automatic door lock to enhance security in RFID. FIRST 2019. (pp. 1–8) doi: 10.1088/1742-6596/1500/1/012132

[10] Jara-Díaz, S., Latournerie, A., Tirachini, A., and Quitral, F. (2022). Optimal pricing and design of station-based bike-sharing systems: a microeconomic model. *Economics of Transportation*, 31, 100273. ISSN 2212-0122, https://doi.org/10.1016/j.ecotra.2022.100273.

[11] Eccarius, T., Leung, A., Shen, C. W., Burke, M., and Lu, C. C. (2021). Prospects for shared electric velomobility: profiling potential adopters at a multi-campus university. *Journal of Transport Geography*, 96, 103190. ISSN0966-6923, https://doi.org/10.1016/j.jtrangeo.2021.103190.

[12] Nematchoua, M. K., Deuse, C., Cools, M., and Reiter, S. (2020). Evaluation of the potential of classic and electric bicycle commuting as an impetus for the transition towards environmentally sustainable cities: A case study of the university campuses in Liege, Belgium. *Renewable and Sustainable Energy Reviews*, 119, 109544. ISSN 1364-0321, https://doi.org/10.1016/j.rser.2019.109544.

50 Smart hearing wheelchair for disable people

Golla Naresh Kumar[1,a], Murali, A.[1,b], Ganta Sree Kiran[2,c], Banoth Bhaskar[2,d] and Anemoni Madhuri[2,e]

[1]Assistant Professor, Dept. of EEE, B V Raju Institute of Technology, Narsapur, Telangana, India

[2]UG Scholars, Dept. of EEE, B V Raju Institute of Technology, Narsapur, Telangana, India

Abstract

The voice-activated, automated wheelchair designed with an Arduino platform is presented in this paper. Because the design incorporates a voice recognition system, an individual with physical disabilities who experience hand movement problems due to aging or paralysis can operate the wheelchair via voice commands. In order to improve the automated wheelchair system's usability, the design includes few extra features , like obstacle detection for safety. The wheelchair is used in conjunction with an Arduino Uno, an android phone for speech recognition module and relay-based motor controller circuits to execute the designThe suggested model was created for voice-activated wheelchairs for individuals with physical limitations or non-functioning lower limbs. Consequently, the person is able to use vocal commands, either from themselves or from family members, to operate the wheelchair.The model is designed by using an Arduino microcontroller board, which can recognize voice commands from a microphone attached to it or from a Bluetooth module connected to a smartphone. Adapt movement by further coordinating it with voice commands that have already been preloaded.

Keywords: Bluetooth module, joystick, microcontroller, physically disabled people arduino, ultrasonic sensor, voice controlled device, voice controlled wheelchair, voice recognition module, wheelchair

Introduction

The most popular mechanical mobility aid in the world, wheelchairs are used by elderly or physically challenged individuals to get around. When using a standard wheelchair, the user requires additional assistance or manual assistance to get around. According to statistics, 650 million people worldwide, or 15% of the total population, have a physical disability. The advancement of technology has led to the global availability of joystick-controlled automated electric motorized wheelchairs [1].

Both the availability and affordability of these wheelchairs are limited in developing and underdeveloped nations [2]. Furthermore, because this kind of wheelchair requires hand control of the joystick, it is inappropriate for disabled or paralyzed individuals who have problems moving their hands or fingers. In addition, elderly patients with weak wrists may find it difficult to operate a wheelchair that is joystick controlled. As a result,

numerous studies are still being conducted to find a substitute for the joystick in wheelchair movement control [3].

The population of the world is growing quickly. Unfortunately, there is a sharp rise in both accidents and illnesses among people. Certain illnesses and accidents cause a person to lose one or both legs, rendering them unable to carry out daily tasks and necessitating their dependence on others. They are not capable of working on their own. Everyone is so busy these days that nobody has time for others, and technology is advancing daily. Every day, new technology enters the market and changes the world [4]. This research paper includes how the voice-controlled wheelchair works and how it work with the obstacles faced by it.

A wheelchair is a very helpful tool for those who are physically disabled. Intelligent system technologies and robotics can be used to design a powered wheelchair [5]. The wheelchair with

[a]nareshkumar.g@bvrit.ac.in, [b]murali.a@bvrit.ac.in, [c]21212a0241@bvrit.ac.in, [d]22215a0201@bvrit.ac.in, [e]21211a0206@bvrit.ac.in

DOI: 10.1201/9781003616399-50

joystick control is incredibly simple to use. A physically challenged person can maneuver a wheelchair by using a joystick. We are using a microcontroller in this project to monitor and control the system. In public spaces, particularly in hospitals, wheelchair usage is common [6].

The joystick-type wheelchair and power-assist wheelchair are two of the powered wheelchair models that have been successfully commercialized and extensively researched. Because the joystick plays a crucial role in converting human intention to the wheelchair controller, the interface characteristics of joystick-type wheelchairs have been thoroughly studied [7].

Literature Review

Wheelchair research was the subject of many studies. A smart wheelchair is now required. Tale 50.1 gives previous survey of researchers.

The World Health Organization (WHO) estimates that 15% of people globally live with a handicap. A considerable portion of them require wheelchairs for mobility Krahn [11]. Traditional manual wheelchairs demand a large amount of upper body strength and dexterity, which limits the mobility and freedom of impaired individuals. To solve this issue, Muneera et al., researchers have developed robotic wheelchairs that give disabled persons more mobility and autonomy [12]. These wheelchairs often feature sophisticated control systems and sensors to enable users to maneuver and operate the device. All things considered, disabled people can benefit greatly from robotic wheelchairs, which increase their mobility, independence, and autonomy. Still, a major obstacle to these devices' widespread adoption is their high cost. Low-cost solutions like the voice-activated wheelchair developed by Babu et al. have the potential to significantly expand the accessibility of these technologies for disabled individuals living in low- and middle-income countries [13]. The table 50.1 gives the literature review on various thechnologies implemented on smartweel chair

Table 50.1 Literature survey on various models

Authors	Paper title	Year	Technology
Sahoo [1]	Voice-activated wheelchair: An affordable solution for individuals with physical disabilities	2023	Raspberry Pi, Cloud, Controller
Somawirata [2]	Smart wheelchair controlled by head gesture based on vision	2022	Camera, Controller, AI
Dutta [3]	Design and development of voice controllable wheelchair	2020	Arduino uno, Motor driver.
Raiyan [4]	Design of an Arduino based voice-controlled automated wheelchair	2017	Microcontroller, gsm technology, Motor driver, gyro accelerometer
Satpe [5]	Wheelchair control using hand movement & voice with obstacle avoidance	2018	Arduino uno, Voice Recognition Module V3, Accelerometer Sensor, Ultrasonic Sensor, Relay module
Aktar [6]	Voice recognition based intelligent wheelchair and gps tracking system	2019	ADXL335, GSAS, adc0816, DC Motor driver
Suchitra [8]	Hand Gesture Recognition Based Auto Navigation System for Leg Impaired Persons	2017	MEMS Sensor, ARDUINO
Apsana [9]	Voice Controller Wheelchair using Arduino	2016	Microcontroller, Ultrasonic Sensor, microphone
Gaikwad [10]	Smart wheelchair with object detection using deep learning	2019	HMM2007 speech recognition system PWM

Source: Author

Every system mentioned above has advantages and disadvantages. In this paper, the proposed system can detect obstacles to prevent accidents and function on voice recognition and joystick control. With the help of the above literature survey this design is to be made by considering above aspects.

Proposed Methodology

The following is a description of the main components of the block diagram operation:

i) From the block diagram we can observe methodology of wheelchair when the user gives voice input.
ii) If voice input is given by user, then voice input is converted into electrical signal by the android phone.
iii) The electrical signal from android phone is sent to Bluetooth module.
iv) Bluetooth module will send its output signals to input pins of Arduino Uno.
v) Arduino UNO will take the input commands or input signals to process the output.
vi) Using embedded programing Arduino UNO should be codded to get the expected output.
vii) Motor driver will get output from the Arduino UNO where Arduino UNO code will be converted into electrical signals.
viii) Motor driver controls the motor to move in certain direction according to user command.

The commands can be set according to user's covenant like in their mother tongue first it will be set in English if they have problem with English then we will set the commands in according to user.

The way the block diagram operates is explained below.

1. From the block diagram we can observe methodology of wheelchair when the user gives joistick input.
2. If joystick input is given by user, then joystick input is converted into electrical signals and sent to Arduino Uno.

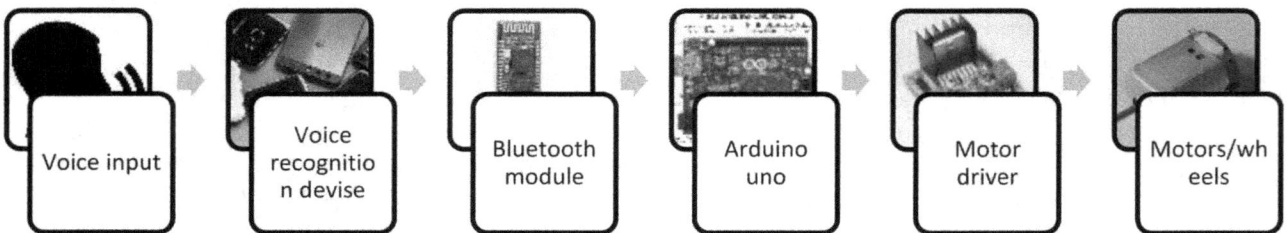

Figure 50.1 Methodology of wheelchair operated when voice input is given
Source: Author

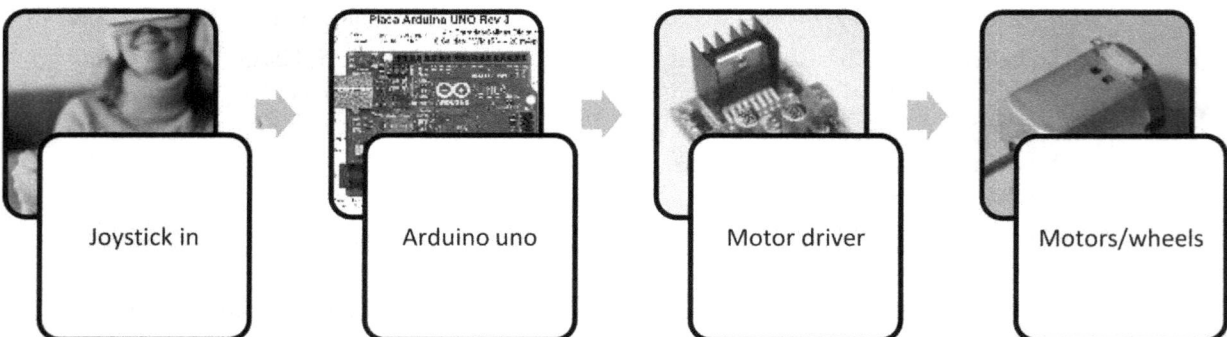

Figure 50.2 Methodology of wheelchair operated when joystick input is given
Source: Author

3. Arduino UNO will take the input commands or input signals to process the output.
4. Using embedded programing Arduino UNO should be codded to get the expected output.
5. Motor driver will get output from the Arduino UNO where Arduino UNO code will be converted into electrical signals.
6. Motor driver controls the motor to move in certain direction according to user command.

Figure 50.3 gives the sequence procedure of flowchart for the operation of the whel chair when both voice input and joystick input is given.

The way the block diagram operates is explained below.

1. From the block diagram we can observe methodology of wheelchair when the user gives both voice input and joistick input.

2. Here inputs are three types one is voice input, one is joystick input and one is ultrasonic sensor input.
3. User can make use of only two inputs(voice and joystick) but not at a time. The other input is a sensor so it will give its inputs to arduino by itselfs.
4. Here user inputs are different but the out put is same
5. The rest procedure is as follows as above two methods given in the Figures 50.1 and 50.2.

The Figure 50.4 shows the circuit connections. Here there are multiple input connections to give one output. The ultra sonic sensor is used to stop the wheelchair when the wheelchair faces obstacle. Motor driver is used to control the motors to move forward, backward, right side and left side.

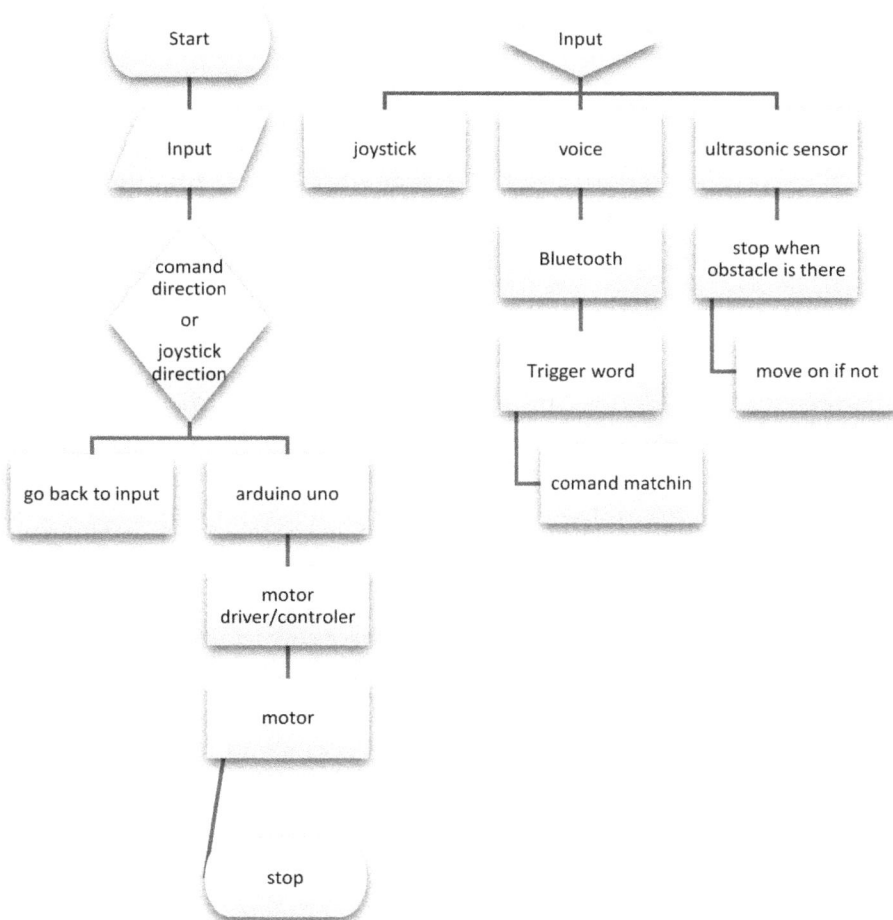

Figure 50.3 Flowchart for methodology of wheelchair operation
Source: Author

The circuit consist of electronic components. Those components are Arduino uno, Bluetooth module, joystick controller, L298n motor driver, motors, lithium ion battery, breadboard. Here Arduino uno is a microcontroller features important role in project where it has io pins, paired with computer to access the code to control the input and output. The wheelchair's Bluetooth module is the component that a mobile application can access to control it using voice commands. Hand controls for the wheelchair are operated via a joystick. The motor speed and motor applications are controlled by the L298n motor driver. The bread board is attached to simplify and prevent complicated connections.

Based on the above table the wheelchair will move accordingly. Here in Table 50.2 the SW1, SW2, SW3 and SW4 are the switches of motor driver l298n.where 0 and 1 is binary values of switches.

Results and Discussion

The several tests are conducted inorder to get the accurate outcome of the design. Here are some tests carried out and results obtained done on proposed design:

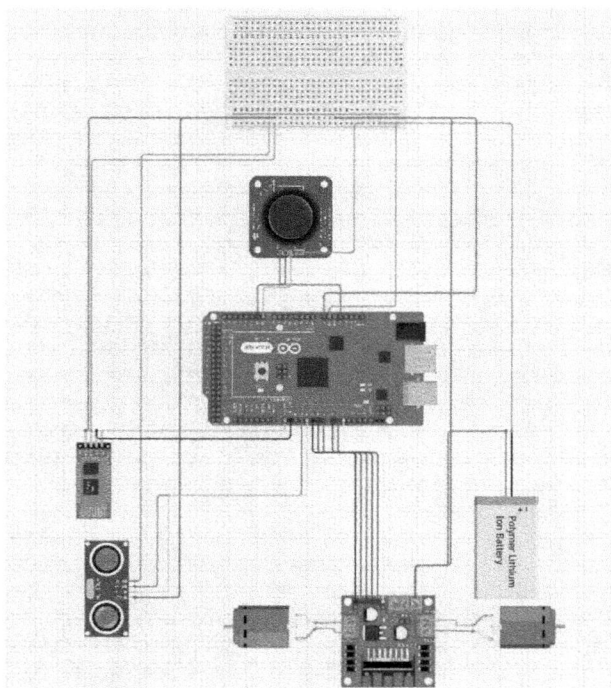

Figure 50.4 Circuit diagram of proposed design
Source: Author

a) Test 1: Whether wheelchair is able to run with joystick input.
   Result: Yes,wheelchair is able to run with joystick input.
b) Test 2: Whether wheelchair is able to run with voice input.
   Result: Yes,wheelchair is able to run with voice input.
c) Test 3: Whether the wheelchair is able to run with both voice and joystick at a time.
   Result: No,wheelchair is not able to run with both voice and joystick at a time.
d) Test 4: Whether ultra sonic sensors will stop the wheelchair when obstacle is occured.
   Result: Yes, ultra sonic sensors will stop the wheelchair when obstacle is occurred.

The above points will show the major tests and its results. Now by looking into proposed methodology the Arduino board is the main component where it takes or hear the input signals. Arduino uno is acting as the ears of wheelchair. The table 50.2 gives the information on the instructions of the motor driver movement

Figure 50.5 explores the prototype of the proposed model. This prototype is done with the help of CAD design for laser cutting of the fiber glass for the better appearance of the model and its operation.

Conclusion

In order to address the problems associated by the disable persons, the proposed model reduced the human support for them and can operate independently by using voice commands and joystick, people who are socially isolated or unable to keep up with others because of a physical

Table 50.2 Motor driver command table

Input 1	Input 2	Direction
SW1(0), SW2(1)	SW3(0), SW4(1)	Motors off
SW1(1), SW2(0)	SW3(1), SW4(0)	Motors off
SW1(0), SW2(1)	SW3(1), SW4(0)	Left
SW1(1), SW2(0)	SW3(0), SW4(1)	Right
SW1(1), SW2(1)	SW3(0), SW4(0)	Forward
SW1(1), SW2(0)	SW3(0), SW4(1)	Backward

Source: Author

Figure 50.5 Protoype of proposed model
Source: Author

disability will be able to move around freely and independently like other members of society. Further the work can be extended to make the design more compact by taking a number of factors, such as placement and additional features, into account.

Acknowledgement

The authors gratefully acknowledge the students, faculty, of the Department of Electrical and Electronics Engineering for their cooperation in the research.

References

[1] Sahooa, S. K., and Choudhurya, B. B. (2023). Voice-activated wheelchair: an affordable solution for individuals with physical disabilities. *GrowingScience, Management Science Letters*, 13, 175–192.

[2] Somawirata, I. K., and Utaminingrum, F. (2022). Smart wheelchair controlled by head gesture based on vision. ICECT-2022.

[3] Dutta, P. P., Kumar, A., Singh, A., Saha, K., Hazarika, B., Narzary, A., et al. (2020). Design and Development of a Voice-Controlled Wheelchair. In 2020 8th International Conference on Reliability, Infocom Technologies and Optimization (Trends and Future Directions) (ICRITO), (pp. 1004-1008). IEEE. 978-1-7281-7016-9/20/$31.00.

[4] Raiyan, Z., Adnan, A. K. M. A., Nawaz, M. S., and Imam, M. H. (2017). Designing a voice-controlled automated wheelchair using Arduino. Published in December 2017 with the IEEE catalog number 978-1-5386-2175-2/17/$31.00 ©2017 IEEE.

[5] Satpe, A. B., Khobragade, S. V., and Nalbalwar, S. L. (2018). Hand movement and voice-controlled wheelchair with obstacle avoidance. Published in 2018 with the IEEE catalog number 978-1-5386-2842-3/18/$31.00 ©2018 IEEE.

[6] Aktar, N., Jahan, I., and Lala, B. (2019). Voice recognition based intelligent wheelchair and GPS tracking system. In Presented at the International Conference on Electrical Computer and Communication Engineering (ECCE) on 7-9 February 2019.

[7] Muneera, T. N., and Dinakardas, C. N. (2019). A voice-controlled wheelchair for physically challenged people with therapy unit. *International Journal of Engineering Research and Technology (IJERT)*, 8(7).

[8] Suchitra, T., and Brinda, R. (2017). Hand gesture recognition based auto navigation system for leg impaired persons. *International Journal of Advanced Research in Electrical Electronics and Instrumentation Engineering*, 6(2), 2320–3765.

[9] Apsana, S., and Nair, R. G. (2016). Voice controlled wheelchair using arduino. *International Advanced Research Journal in Science, Engineering, and Technology (IARJSET)*, 3(3).

[10] Gaikwad, S., Bhagat, S., Shendkar, N., Lonkar, S., and Dhaigude, T. A. (2019). Smart wheelchair with object detection using deep learning. *International Research Journal of Engineering and Technology (IRJET)*, 6(12).

[11] Krahn, G. L. (2011). WHO world report on disability: a review. *Disability and Health Journal*, 4(3), 141–142. doi: 10.1016/j.dhjo.2011.05.001. PMID: 21723520.

[12] Muneera, T. N., and Dinakardas, C. N. (2019). A voice-controlled wheelchair for physically challenged people with therapy unit. *International Journal of Engineering Research and Technology (IJERT)*, 8(7).

[13] Babu, D. V., Subramanian, P., and Karthikeyan, R. (2018). Voice controlled wheelchair. *International Journal of Pure and Applied Mathematics*, 119(16).

51 Design and performance analysis of 880-960 MHz power amplifier for 5G new radio n8 frequency band applications

Ganesh Racha[1,2,a], Lal Kishore, K.[2,b], Yedukondalu Kamatham[2,c] and Srinivasa Rao Perumalla[2,d]

[1]Research Scholar, Department of Electronics and Communication Engineering, JNTUH Hyderabad, Telangana, India

[2]Department of Electronics and Communication Engineering, CVR College of Engineering, Hyderabad, Telangana, India

Abstract

The advancements in the usage of portable and battery-operated systems need an efficient design of the radio frequency front end (RFFE) of user equipment for wireless applications suitable for 4G and beyond communication systems. The design of RFFE with transmitter and receiver needs the best component design of power amplifier (PA) and low noise amplifier (LNA). These PAs are used in the applications of the communications frequency spectrum as per the frequency ranges and operating frequency. This paper deals with the design of a PA using a class-E switching amplifier structure using CMOS 45 nm technology. The proposed amplifier uses the frequency band of 880 to 960 MHz of 5G new radio (NR) n8 frequency band related to global system for mobile communication (GSM) i.e. 900 MHz 5G band. The design is realized by using the cadence virtuoso environment and the performance metrics are calculated using transient analysis, periodic steady state (PSS) analysis, and periodic S-parameter (PSP) analysis. The designed circuit works at 900 MHz with a gain of 20 dB for an input power of -5 dB.

Keywords: 5G new radio, GSM, power spectrum, PSS, quality factor, RF front end, Sub-6 GHz

Introduction

The advancements in portable user equipment with connected components and applications are moving towards more usage of a frequency spectrum of communications. The existing spectrum is becoming more congested as the demand for applications is increasing. Hence, there is a requirement to search for the alternate frequency spectrum with licensed, unlicensed, and shared frequency bands. The frequency spectrum for communications is shown in Figure 51.1. The frequency spectrum is classified into sub 1 GHz, 1-6 GHz, and above 6 GHz spectrum. The sub 1 GHz frequency supports near field communications (NFC), and voice-based communications using GSM technology with lower band and higher band frequencies. The 1-6 GHz spectrum supports lower band with enhanced data rates for GSM evolution (EDGE)

and higher band with Wi-Fi and long-term evolution (LTE) to support coverage and capacity of communications. The above 6 GHz spectrum uses GHz of the lower band and THz of the upper band for specific user requirements of higher data rates and massive applications. The usage of a frequency spectrum shown in Figure 51.1 is classified into different communication generation modes as per the evolution of portable or mobile cellular device technologies.

The classification of generation modes from 1G to 4G and beyond with different frequencies is shown in Figure 51.2. The 4G uses LTE around 40 frequency bands over the entire spectrum of sub 6 GHz. Beyond 4G uses GHz and THz of the frequency spectrum. The GHz band generation called 5G uses a concept called new radio (NR) technology with frequency bands of n8, n2, n3,

[a]rachaganesh@gmail.com, [b]lalkishore@cvr.ac.in, [c]kyedukondalu@gmail.com, [d]psrao.cvr@gmail.com

DOI: 10.1201/9781003616399-51

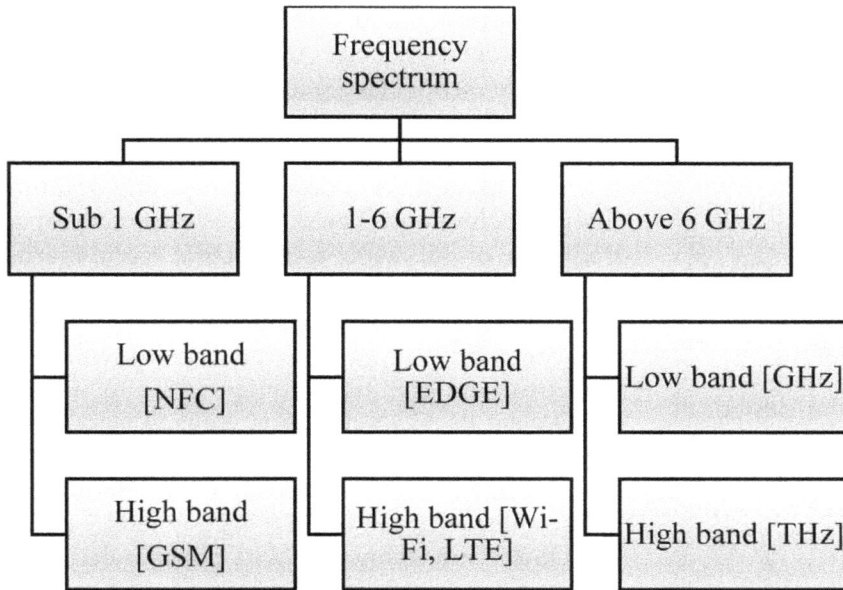

Figure 51.1 Frequency spectrum classification for communications
Source: Author

n1, n40, n1, n78, n79, etc. along with backward compatibility.

The design of 5G needs the development of RFFE with a transmitter using PA and a receiver with a high gain LNA. In the entire design of the transmitter, the PA is a major component. The PA is designed to support frequency spectrum and nonfunctional performance metrics like power gain, efficiency, linearity, etc. The frequency band n8 also called as 900 MHz band for 5G NR is used for compatibility with GSM and can be designed by using silicon or Gallium-based

transistors. This work deals with the design of n8 or 900 MHz frequency band PA for supporting the 880–960 MHz band with an uplink of 880–915 MHz and a downlink of 925–960 MHz using silicon MOS transistors. The rest of the paper is organized as follows: Theoretical and design concepts of n8 band Class E-PA are given first, then the design circuit specifications and methodologies for Class-E PA are described. The simulation results and performance measurements using the Cadence tool are discussed followed by conclusions and references.

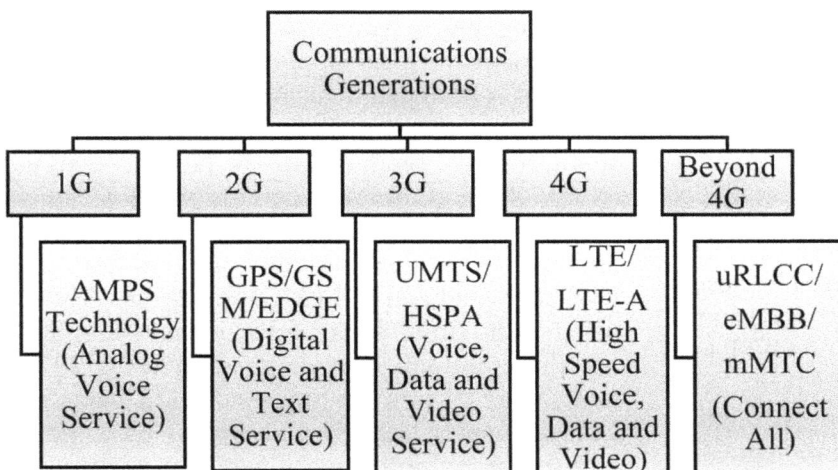

Figure 51.2 Classification of generation modes
Source: Author

Design Concepts of n8 Band PA

The externally connected PA and integrated PA architectures for battery-operated mobile user equipment uses RFIC with PA. The PA switches use silicon-based products using heterojunction bipolar transistor (HBT)/complementary metal-oxide semiconductor (CMOS)/BiCMOS components for modes of GSM, Bluetooth, CDMA, etc. The design issues and challenges for multimode, multi-band wireless products are analyzed. With these abilities, the Silicon and Gallium-based components are used for the design of PAs of RF system-on-chip (SoC) products [1]. The present wireless user equipment and mobile devices are moving from 4G networks to beyond 4G networks toward 5G communications. These devices use RF PA as the major component which is directly affecting the performance metrics.

The device technology suitable for the design of PA are CMOS, SiGe, BiCMOS, GaN/GaAs, etc., for communications applications. The research trends summarize the design of RF PA circuits into different RF PA architectures like distributed RF PA, Doherty RF PA, envelope tracking RF PA, envelope elimination and restoration RF PA, linear amplification using nonlinear components (LINC) RF PA and travelling wave tube RF PA etc. [2]. The fourth generation 4G-LTE smartphones are moving beyond 4G and creating the user equipment for RFFE. Beyond 4G applications are expected to be designed with high-speed data rates, low power, higher efficiency, etc. The design of user equipment products uses a transmitter and receiver (Transceiver) with RF switch, filter, PAs, LNAs, etc. The architectural designs for 5G with circuit topologies for achieving performance metrics are given applications for medical, driverless vehicles, etc.

The beyond 4G applications frequency ranges are divided as frequency range1 (FR1) and frequency range2 (FR2) supporting sub-6 GHz and above 24 GHz mm-wave frequencies. The design of 5G front-end module architectures is designed by using 180 nm [3]. The circuit of GSM and EDGE mode PA to support 900 MHz, 1800 MHz/1900 MHz handset applications is designed by using HBT for mobile user equipment. The performance characteristics are measured in both the technology modes and frequency bands [4]. The design of Multi-Mode and Multi-Band RF PA for portable and battery-based user equipment needs the device technologies of silicon and GaN/GaAS. The performance metrics are improved by using stacking and reconfigurability and combining the power techniques [5]. The design of class-E PA is designed by using 350 nm CMOS technology. The circuit is designed for a frequency of 850 MHz using LDMOS and mathematical equations [6].

The CMOS PA is analyzed and the concept of protection for gate oxide breakdown, hot electrons, and conduction angle are applied for three-stage PA. This design is realized using 250 nm process technology targeting 900 MHz GSM applications [7]. The 900 MHz PA for radio frequency identification (RFID) is designed by using CMOS 250 nm technology. The circuit is designed by using a transmission line transformed as output-matching network. This design also uses integrated input and output transformer stages [8]. The Cascode PA using envelope elimination and restoration system is designed by using 180 nm and 350 nm at a frequency of 1.9 GHz. The conventional and Cascode class-E PA circuits are designed, and functional simulation is analyzed to support modern wireless communication protocols [9].

The CMOS PA for high voltage and high-power devices using MOS topology at an operating frequency of 900 MHz is designed using 130 nm technology. This design shows that the CMOS technologies are used for Power Amplifiers for portable and mobile devices using submicron technologies [10]. The design of dual band switching PA to support 900 MHz and 1900 MHz for lower and upper band operating frequencies is designed by using 130 nm technology. This design supports LTE- Advanced and GSM standards of communications [11]. The usage of CMOS logic for PA designs for SoC applications moving from 3G to 4G mobile devices and user equipment is demonstrated for LTE/LTE-advanced and WiMAX applications. The PA using a distributed transformer, main amplifier, and driver amplifier are designed by using 90 nm technology to support extended GSM band and LTE standards [12]. The design of basic linear and switching power amplifiers are designed by using 45 nm,90 nm, and 180 nm. The performance metrics of RF PA of class E are analyzed for 180 nm with the 2.4 GHz and 3.1-4.8 GHz frequency ranges [13]. The design of a wideband PA for a sub-6GHz frequency band is designed by using 65 nm. The LTE mode wideband PA with frequency bands of 700 MHz,1900 MHz, 3600 MHz, and 5900 MHz is designed, and its performance metrics are analyzed in terms of bandwidth, output power, gain, PAE, etc. The single high-performance CMOS PA is designed by using positive feedback, higher-order matching networks, and two outputs [14].

The 900 MHz power amplifier is done by using CMOS logic with the finite RF choke inductor. The design has a 50 Ω load and is designed using 350 nm technology. The circuit functional analysis and simulation are calculated by using the Cadence Spectre RF simulator with parasitics, output power, PAE, etc [15]. The RF amplifier is designed using 180 nm at 2.2 GHz [16]. The design of PA for portable battery-based mobile phones is designed for class E PA for 900 MHz and 1800 MHz. The designed PA circuit is analyzed for 900 MHz and 1800 MHz frequencies using analysis of drain voltage and drain currents etc. The results are simulated for performance metrics analysis [17].

A Class E PA with out-phasing is designed by using 45 nm CMOS technology for 2.4 GHz frequency. The out-phasing PA uses Efficiency Enhancement Circuit (EEC) and Power Enhancement Circuit (PEC) to improve the non-functional performance metrics [18]. The theoretical and mathematical analysis of Class-E PA concepts from kHz and MHz frequencies, ultra-high frequencies, and microwave and millimeter wave frequency ranges are described for performance analysis. [19].

Design Circuits and Specifications for Class-E PA

The simplified general block diagram for PA is shown in Figure 51.3. The selection of input source, matching circuits, and PA switching logics are done based on the performance metrics of PA. The performance metrics include linearity, output power, gain, Power Added Efficiency (PAE), efficiency, etc. All these performance metrics are selected based on the design specifications.

The design of PA is classified into linear and switching PA based on the conduction angle and efficiency. The linear PA circuits are class A to C and switching PA are class D to F etc. The selection of PA circuit topology using design flow is shown in Figure 51.4. The PA is majorly selected as per the requirements of the design specifications of the user. The n8 frequency band uses a Class-E PA circuit using CMOS logic. The basic Class-E PA circuit is shown in Figure 51.5. The component values of each element in Class-E PA are calculated using the operating frequency, frequency range, the Quality factor of an inductor, input, matched networks, etc [20]. The detailed specifications are given in Table 51.1. The design circuit is applied with an input of 20 mV and a time period of 1.11 ns with a pulse width of 0.55 ns to meet the requirements of 5G NR n8 frequency band applications.

The PA circuit is redesigned with advanced architectures to support higher efficiency and operating frequency requirements.

$$Operating\ Frequency\ f = 1/T \tag{1}$$
$$Quality\ factor\ Q = fr/Brandwidth \tag{2}$$
$$R = 8 *[VDD^2/Pout]*13.8596 \tag{3}$$
$$Inductor\ L2 = Q * R/2\pi f \tag{4}$$
$$Capacitor\ C1 = 1/5.447*2\pi f* R \tag{5}$$
$$Capacitor\ C2 = C1[5.447/Q] *$$
$$[1 + 1.42/(Q - 2.08)] \tag{6}$$

Performance Analysis using Simulation

The 5G New Radio (NR) n8 band Power Amplifier is designed by using the Cadence Virtuoso environment with a 45 nm process node. The PA is designed by using CMOS logic with performance

Figure 51.3 Block diagram of a generic PA
Source: Author

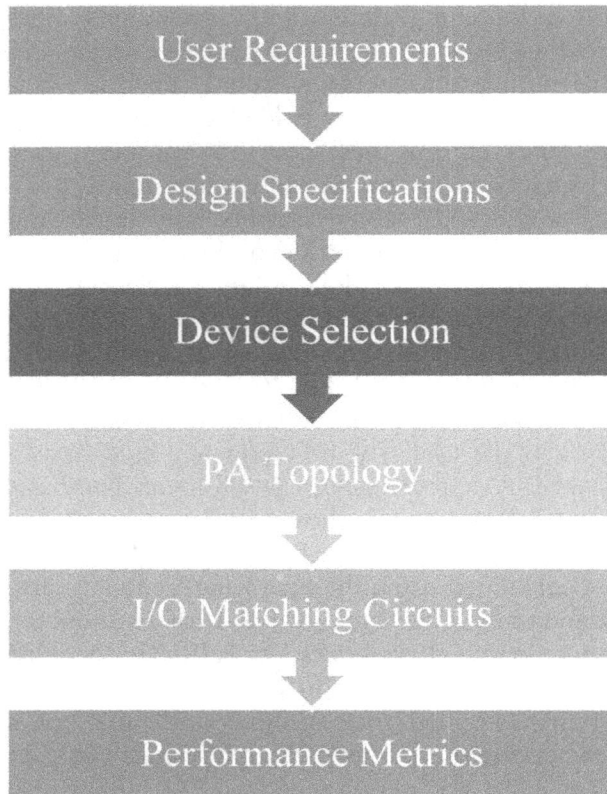

Figure 51.4 Design flow for PA circuits
Source: Author

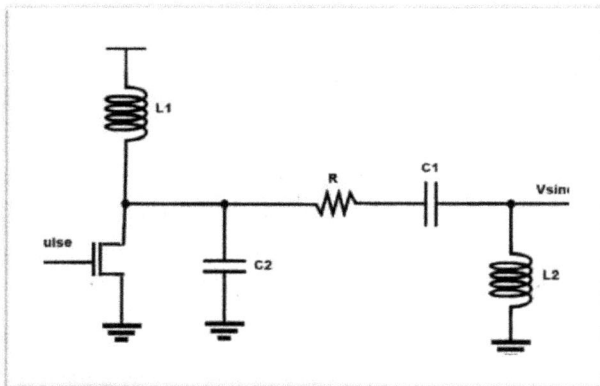

Figure 51.5 Circuit diagram of class E PA
Source: Author

Table 51.1 Design specifications of a class-E PA

S. No.	Name of the Parameter	Values
1	Technology Node	45 nm
2	VDD	1 V
3	Frequency Band	n8
4	Frequency Range	880-960 MHz
5	Operating Frequency	900 MHz
6	Uplink Frequency	880-915 MHz
7	Downlink Frequency	925-960 MHz
8	Bandwidth	35 MHz
9	Impedance Matching	50 Ω
10	Mode	GSM

Source: Author

The second phase is used to perform Periodic Steady State (PSS) analysis for measuring power, linearity, and efficiency parameters. The third phase is used to calculate S-parameters for load pull measurement using Periodic S-Parameter (PSP) analysis.

Phase-1: transient analysis
The transient analysis is performed on the circuit shown in Figure 51.6 uses pulse input and produces sinusoidal output. The pulse input of frequency n8 band with 900 MHz using a time-period of 1.11 ns is applied and produces an output of sinusoidal with a gain of 20 dB as shown in the waveform of Figure 51.7.

Phase-2: periodic steady state (PSS) analysis
The PSS analysis is used to provide the power spectrum of the circuit to calculate the fundamental harmonic frequency component and its first, second, third, and other harmonic frequency component values. The power spectrum shown in Figure 51.8 gives the harmonic frequency value of 900 MHz for the n8 band and its harmonics at 1800 MHz, 2700 MHz, etc. This power spectrum ensures the circuit operation at the harmonic frequency and calculates its performance parameters.

Phase-3: periodic s-parameter (PSP) analysis
The PSP is used to analyze S-parameters and Voltage Standing Wave Ratio (VSWR) on a small

metric analysis using Spectre simulation. The design diagram is shown in Figure 51.6.

The functionality and non-functional analysis is done using three phases of analysis. The first phase deals with transient analysis for functional simulation, gain calculation of the circuit, etc.

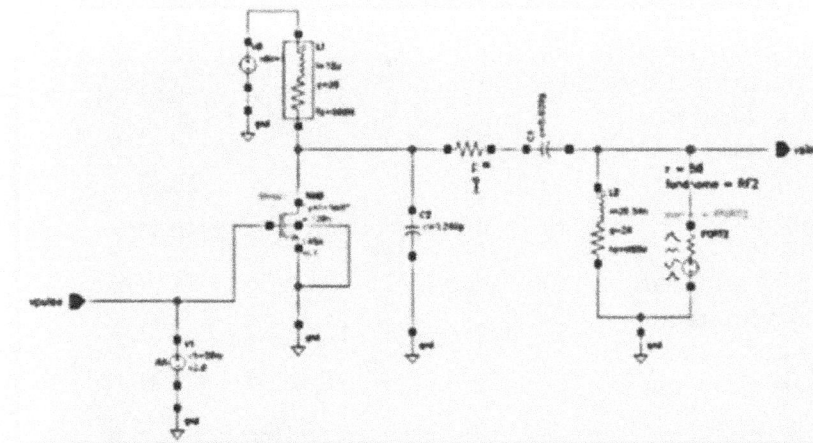

Figure 51.6 A design diagram of 5G NR n8 band PA
Source: Author

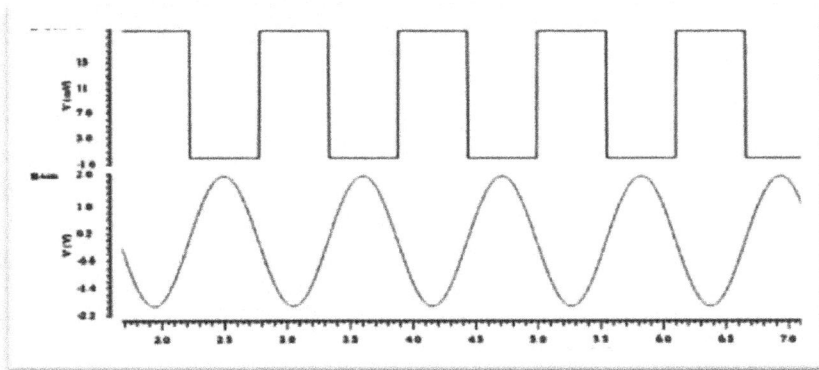

Figure 51.7 Transient waveform of 5G NR n8 band PA
Source: Author

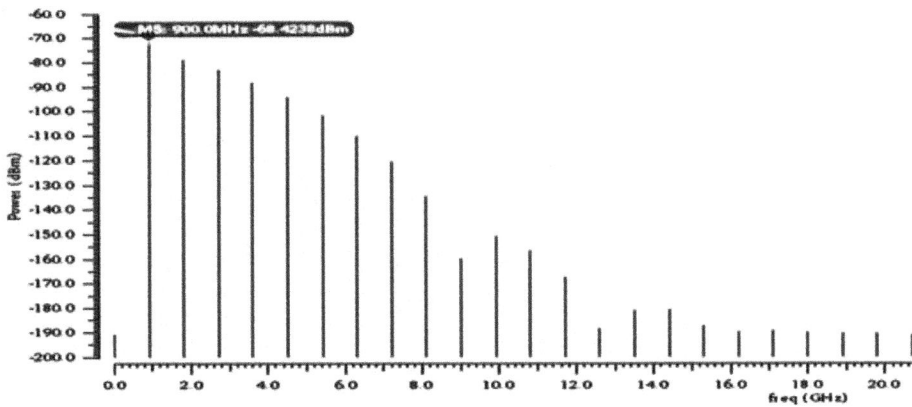

Figure 51.8 Power spectrum of 5G NR n8 band PA
Source: Author

signal. The PSP analysis for 5G NR n8 band with a beat frequency of 900 MHz and sweep range starting at 880 MHz and ending at 960 MHz. This analysis is used to calculate the S-parameter values over the sweep range and the beat frequency. The S-parameter contour is shown in Figure 51.9.

The S-parameter values for the beat frequency of the n8 band are shown in Table 51.2.

The values of S11, S12, S21, and S22 are used for the design of a 5G NR n8 band PA circuit. The S-parameter values for S11, S12, S21, and S22 over the Pin range of -30 to 10 are shown in Table 51.3.

Conclusion

In this work, the PA for 5G NR n8 frequency band applications is designed over the frequency

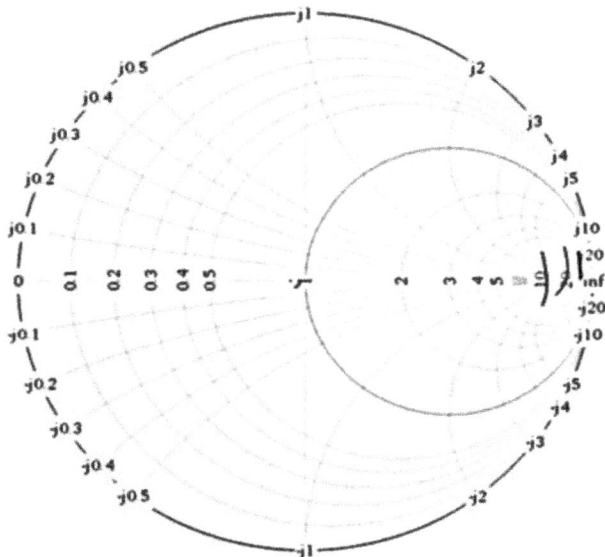

Figure 51.9 S-Parameter contour for 5G NR n8 band PA
Source: Author

Table 51.2 S-Parameter values at 900 MHz

S-Parameter	Value
S11	956.1E-3
S12	1.322E-3
S21	621.3E-6
S22	1.00000

Source: Author

Table 51.3 S-Parameter values at 900 MHz for Pin

Pin	S11	S12	S21	S22
-30	956.1E-3	620.8E-6	620.8E-6	1
-25	956.1E-3	620.8E-6	620.8E-6	1
-20	956.1E-3	620.8E-6	620.8E-6	1
-15	956.1E-3	620.8E-6	620.8E-6	1
-10	956.1E-3	621.7E-6	621.0E-6	1
-5	956.1E-3	1.322E-3	621.3E-6	1
0	954.6E-3	51.37E-3	623.4E-6	1
5	913.2E-3	23.44E-3	645.5E-6	1
10	834.5E-3	9.818E-3	674.3E-6	1

Source: Author

band of 880 MHz to 960 MHz using Cadence EDA tools for 45 nm process nodes. The MOS transistor is characterized as per the design specifications and the mathematical analysis is done for the measurement of active and passive component values. The PA is designed for a 20 dB gain with an input power of -5 dB and its power spectrum is tuned to operate at the beat harmonic frequency of 900 MHz for an uplink frequency of 880-915 MHz with a bandwidth of 35 MHz. The S-parameters are analyzed over the n8 frequency band with the power range of -30 dB to 10 dB values. Overall, the PA is designed to support 5G NR n8 frequency band applications.

References

[1] Lie, D. Y. C., "RF-SoC": Integration Trends of On-Chip CMOS Power Amplifier: Benefits of External PA versus Integrated PA for Portable Wireless Communications, International Journal of Microwave Science and Technology, 2010, 380108, 7 pages, 2010. https://doi.org/10.1155/2010/380108

[2] Vasjanov, A., and Barzdenas, V. (2018). A review of advanced CMOS RF power amplifier architecture trends for low power 5G wireless networks. *Electronics*, 7(11), 271. https://doi.org/10.3390/electronics 7110271.

[3] Balteanu, F. (2023). Circuits for 5G RF front-end modules. *International Journal of Microwave and Wireless Technologies*, 15(6), 909–924. doi:10.1017/S1759078722001295.

[4] Yamamoto, K., Asada, T., Suzuki, S., Miura, T., Inoue, A., Miyakuni, S., et al. (2002). A GSM/EDGE dual-mode, 900/1800/1900-MHz triple-band HBT MMIC power amplifier module. In 2002 IEEE Radio Frequency Integrated Circuits (RFIC) Symposium. Digest of Papers (Cat. No.02CH37280), Seattle, WA, USA, (pp. 245–248). doi: 10.1109/RFIC.2002.1012041.

[5] Li, Y., Lopez, J., and Lie, D. Y. C. (2016). Silicon based power amplifiers for 4G/5G handset applications. In 2016 13th IEEE International Conference on Solid-State and Integrated Circuit Technology (ICSICT), Hangzhou, China, (pp. 112–115). doi: 10.1109/ICSICT.2016.7998854.

[6] Ramos, J., and Steyaert, M. (2005). Design of a class e power amplifier with LDMOS in standard CMOS. *Analog Integrated Circuits and Signal Processing*, 44(1), 17–23. https://doi.org/10.1007/s10470-005-1611-4.

[7] Choi, K., Allstot, D. J., and Krishnamurthy, V. (2004). A 900 MHz GSM PA in 250 nm CMOS with breakdown voltage protection and programmable conduction angle. In 2004 IEE Radio Frequency Integrated Circuits (RFIC) Systems. Digest of Papers, Forth Worth, TX, USA, (pp. 369–372). doi: 10.1109/RFIC.2004.1320624.

[8] Han, J., Kim, Y., Park, C., Lee, D., and Hong, S. (2006). A fully-integrated 900-MHz CMOS power amplifier for mobile RFID reader applications. In IEEE Radio Frequency Integrated Circuits (RFIC) Symposium, 2006, San Francisco, CA, USA, (pp. 4). doi: 10.1109/RFIC.2006.1651174.

[9] Rumyancev, I. A., Korotkov, A. S., and Hauer, J. (2013). Cascode class-E power amplifier in 180/350 nm CMOS for EER system. In Proceedings of the 2013 9th Conference on Ph.D. Research in Microelectronics and Electronics (PRIME), Villach, Austria, (pp. 309–312). doi: 10.1109/PRIME.2013.6603167.

[10] Wu, L., Dettmann, I., and Berroth, M. (2008). A 900-MHz 29.5-dBm 0.13-μm CMOS HiVP power amplifier. *IEEE Transactions on Microwave Theory and Techniques*, 56(9), 2040–2045. doi: 10.1109/TMTT.2008.2001961.

[11] Hamidi, S. B., and Dawn, D. (2019). A 900/1900-MHz band-switchable CMOS power amplifier. In 2019 IEEE MTT-S International Microwave and RF Conference (IMARC), Mumbai, India, (pp. 1–4). doi: 10.1109/IMaRC45935.2019.9118692.

[12] Francois, B., and Reynaert, P. (2012). A fully integrated watt-level linear 900-MHz CMOS RF power amplifier for LTE-applications. *IEEE Transactions on Microwave Theory and Techniques*, 60(6), 1878–1885. doi: 10.1109/TMTT.2012.2189411.

[13] Chaithra, S., Priya, N., Vedi, P., and Spoorthy, M. (2024). Analysis of power performance of class e amplifier for high frequency radio applications. *International Journal of Creative Research Thoughts (IJCRT)*, 12(5), pp.1154–1160. ISSN: 2320-2882.

[14] Lindstrand, J., Törmänen, M., and Sjöland, H. (2020). A decade frequency range CMOS power amplifier for Sub-6-GHz cellular terminals. *IEEE Microwave and Wireless Components Letters*, 30(1), 54–57. doi: 10.1109/LMWC.2019.2955602.

[15] Khan, H. R., Wahab, Q., Fritzin, J., and Alvandpour, A. (2010). A 900 MHz 26.8 dBm differential class-e CMOS power amplifier. In German Microwave Conference Digest of Papers, Berlin, Germany, (pp. 276–279).

[16] Sira, D., Thomsen, P., and Larsen, T. (2011). A cascode modulated class- E power amplifier for wireless communications. *Microelectronics Journal*, 42(1), 141–147. ISSN 1879-2391, https://doi.org/10.1016/j.mejo.2010.08.016.

[17] Nadir, Z., and Touati, F. (2011). Class-E amplifier design improvements for GSM frequencies. *Journal of Engineering Research*, 8(1), 74–82. https://doi.org/10.24200/tjer.vol8iss1pp74-82.

[18] Banerjee, A., Hezar, R., Ding, L., and Haroun, B. (2017). A 29.5 dBm class-e outphasing RF power amplifier with efficiency and output power enhancement circuits in 45nm CMOS. *IEEE Transactions on Circuits and Systems I: Regular Papers*, 64(8), 1977–1988. doi: 10.1109/TCSI.2017.2695243.

[19] Popović, Z., and García, J. A. (2017). Microwave class-E power amplifiers. In 2017 IEEE MTT-S International Microwave Symposium (IMS), Honolulu, HI, USA, (pp. 1323–1326). doi: 10.1109/MWSYM.2017.8058855.

[20] Tan, J., Heng, C. H., and Lian, Y. (2012). Design of efficient class-e power amplifiers for short-distance communications. *IEEE Transactions on Circuits and Systems—I: Regular Papers*, 59(10), 2210–2220. DOI: 10.1109/TCSI.2012.2188951.

52 YOLOv8 based segmentation and ResNet-50 classifier for medical image retrieval and classification

K. Revathi[1,a] and S. Vijaya Kumar[2]

[1]Research Scholar, Dept. of CSE, GITAM (Deemed to be University) and Sphoorthy Engineering College, Hyderabad, India

[2] Assistant Professor, Dept. of CSE, GITAM (Deemed to be University), Hyderabad, India

Abstract

This paper introduces a novel image retrieval and classification system that aims to overcome the limitations of conventional image retrieval systems. The system is designed for the purpose of conducting searches. The process of image retrieval and classification consists of two distinct stages: training and testing. During the training phase, images are acquired from a publically accessible data source and then processed through the segmentation stage. During the segmentation process, images are partitioned using the YOLOv8 model. The segmented images are subsequently sent into the ResNet-50 for classification. The database contains the classified images as well. During the testing phase, images of user-related queries are taken to accurately retrieve corresponding images from the database. In this scenario, the deep features of the query images are obtained using the ResNet-50. The extracted features are compared to the stored trained image features in the database using the Euclidean distance similarity function. In order to assess the efficacy of the model, the empirical results are compared to previous image retrieval algorithms using several simulated metrics.

Keywords: CBIR, classification, Medical Image retrieval, ResNet-50, YOLOv8

Introduction

Currently, medical imaging is of great significance in the field of computer science, since it aids doctors in diagnosing and evaluating medical conditions. Medical images are regarded as the primary reservoir of medical data due to their ability to offer a greater amount of pathological information [1]. Medical institutes and hospitals collect a greater quantity of medical images on a daily basis. Hardware devices can significantly impact the capture of high-resolution medical images [2]. Recently, MIR has sparked significant research attention. The MIR model will generate several images based on the input query medical image, with the majority of the content being closely connected to the query image. The outcomes of this image retrieval could potentially aid in managing the extensive collection of medical images and provide valuable information to support clinicians in their decision-making process. Previous research has established multiple MIR models, [3] provided various perspectives on the topic. It aids in the prompt detection of breast cancer and assists radiologists in determining whether to examine comparable mammograms from a database by identifying the categories of existing mammograms [4]. It can enhance the accuracy of diagnosis by categorizing the queried mammograms and retrieving comparable mammograms [5]. The query image is only searched within a limited subset based on the cluster size.

CBIR has received so much attention from researchers during the last decade. Numerous industries, including healthcare, education, entertainment, agriculture, and security, have made use of a wide variety of CBIR methodologies. Accurately recognizing the visual components that transmit information is the most

[a]vsagenel@gitam.edu

DOI: 10.1201/9781003616399-52

challenging part of CBIR. Stefan [6] suggested employing vision foundation models as a robust and flexible collection of pre-built tools for feature extraction in content-based medical image retrieval. According to Sudhish [7], a CBMIR pipeline is introduced in the medical area. With the help of a clustering technique and the convolutional neural networks (CNNs) model, the pipeline extracts features from images and adds them to the feature map database. The suggested technique uses a Multi-level Gain-based feature selection approach to lower the dimensionality of the feature vectors derived from the pre-trained CNN models. To achieve this goal, various visual presentation techniques have been developed [8]. Recent improvements in the performance of DCNN models for image classification have made them the go-to model for image retrieval and classification [9]. The conventional wisdom holds that CNNs are all-inclusive systems that need no task-specific attributes [10]. By using a holistic view, we may save time and effort by not having to build features tailored to certain activities or export capabilities that are domain-specific [11]. When thinking about image categorization, it's important to include image retrieval as well. Finding images that are similar to a query image in terms of content or subject matter is what's known as image retrieval. Surveillance and security, medical imaging, and other fields make extensive use of this method [12].

A prototype descriptor known as "optimized local weber and gradient pattern (OLWGP)" was created by Bhanu et al. [13], which was a huge step forward in the field of image retrieval. The research group used a "Jaya-based Barnacle mating optimization" hybrid strategy, which fused two popular meta-heuristic methods. The purpose of implementing this technique was to improve the efficiency of image retrieval using OLWGP. After the best OLWGP features were selected for the train set and the images were assessed, log similarity calculations were used to recover each image. In addition, the ideal CNN, an improved deep learning method, was employed for the image classification. Loddo et al. [14] created a SeedNet model using CNN to solve the issue of image retrieval. To find out which of several cutting-edge CNN models were best suited to the given situation, they ran a

thorough examination. Both datasets saw significant advancements in seed detection, leading to higher accuracy rates. By utilizing deep learning technology, the retrieval problem was efficiently addressed. A complete system for recognizing and retrieving seeds was developed with the help of the results of the model, which greatly aided the fields of biology and agriculture.

Here are the main outcomes of this study:

- The YOLOv8 model must be developed before the training phase can begin. Its goal is to produce accurate image investigation reports by accurately segmenting medical images.
- For the retrieval and classification tasks, to use the ResNet-50.
- The use of the similarity function such as Euclidean distance; it enhances the precision of the recovered images.

The succeeding sections of the paper are: The suggested structure for the process of retrieving and classifying medical images is laid out in section 2. In section 3, the YOLOv8 design is examined. In section 4, the ResNet-50 is introduced. In section 5, we offer the analytical and empirical results. The paper concluded in section 6.

Proposed Structure for Retrieval and Classification

These days, deep learning models are very good at image retrieval and classification. Automatically reducing the presence of irrelevant images enhances retrieval performance. It will take less time to finish the performance. It allows for a simplified categorization approach and can fix the model's inherent shortcomings. The structural view of the suggested work for retrieval and classifying medical images is shown in Figure 52.1.

Without any hindrance, medical images can be retrieved and classified using the developed model. The idea's goal is to discourage dangerous behaviors among patients by assisting doctors with early disease diagnosis and classification. During the training and testing stages, the generated model goes through its method. In order to train the YOLOv8 model for image segmentation, the dataset's raw images are loaded into it. The YOLOv8 model is able to segment images

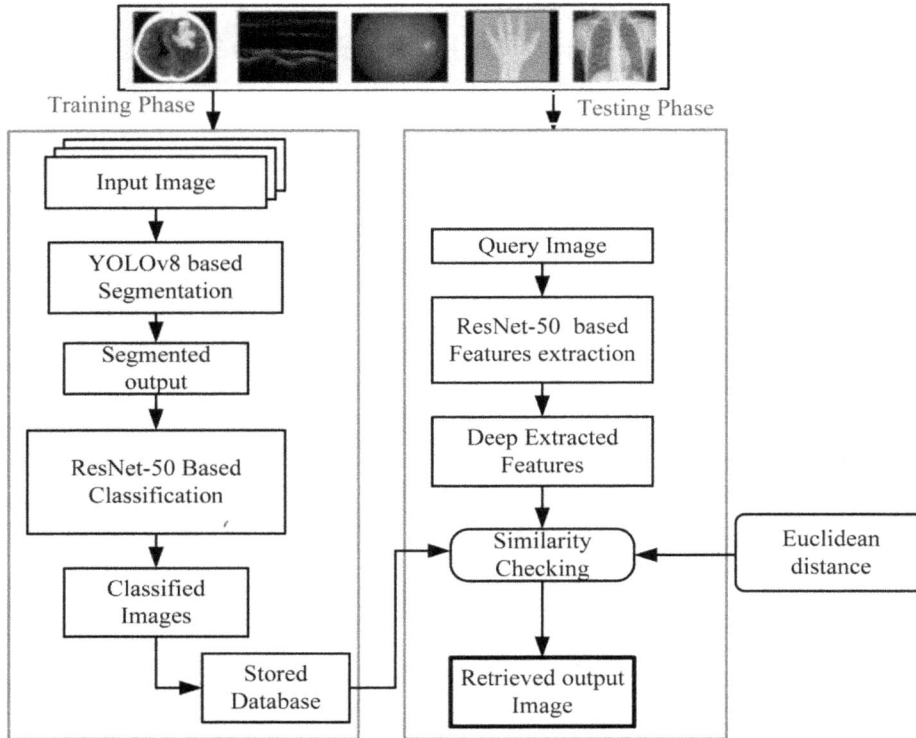

Figure 52.1 Proposed structure for retrieval and classification
Source: Author

and produce segmented results. The next step is to feed the segmented medical images into the ResNet-50-based classification model that was suggested. The final result is the categorized output from the built classification model. After that, the classified images are saved in the database so that they may be compared. While testing is underway, the ResNet-50 model is fed the query images and outputs the recovered images. The query images' deep features are retrieved via the ResNet-50 model. After that, we compare the query images with the training images in the database using the obtained characteristics to see how similar they are. Using the Euclidean distance approach, we can determine how similar the two objects are. Following a similarity check, the recovered image output is generated using the ResNet-50 model.

YOLOv8 Architecture

YOLOv8, developed by the Ultralytics team [15], is an advanced object segmentation model that efficiently and precisely identifies things. This

model enhances the architectural design by using the features of YOLOv5 [16] and leveraging the benefits of several object detectors. Figure 52.2 displays the structure diagram of the model.

The backbone network serves as the foundation of the model and is tasked with extracting features from the input image. The YOLOv8 model utilizes the CSP Darknet [17] structure as its backbone network, which is identical to YOLOv5. It also incorporates cross-stage connections to link different stages of the network. It establishes a direct connection between some feature maps and feature maps at later levels in order to improve the network's ability to transfer information and reuse features. Figure 52.2 illustrates the repetitive stacking of the convolution kernels Conv and C2f for the purpose of feature extraction. Ultimately, SPPF is utilized at the conclusion of the main structure, enabling the collection of the spatial characteristics of objects through the incorporation of pooling windows of varying sizes. Through this method, it can improve the model's capacity to recognize objects of varying sizes.

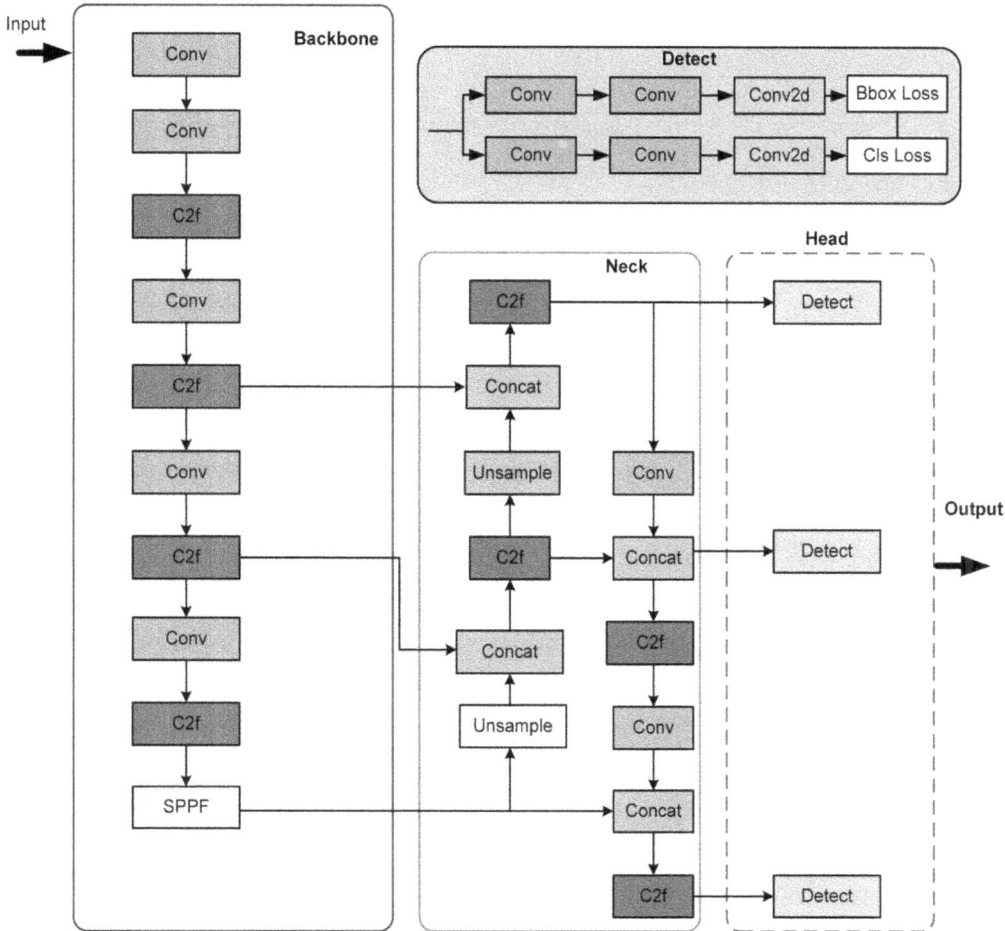

Figure 52.2 Architecture of YOLOv8
Source: Author

The neck network is situated intermediate to the spinal network and cranial network and is utilized for the purpose of feature amalgamation and augmentation. This network has the capability to decrease the quantity of parameters while still preserving the network's expressive capacity. More precisely, it employs the upsample layer to enlarge the feature map by up sampling the processed backbone information. It then merges features of various scales by concatenating them through a sequence of concat layer splicing and C2f layers. Graphs are combined to generate more comprehensive information and varied feature representations. The feature maps are ultimately combined to generate more comprehensive information and varied feature representations.

The head network is positioned at the apex of the entire model and is responsible for accomplishing the ultimate detection task. The features obtained from the trunk and neck are inputted into the head network to decode object features and generate results. The top layer of YOLOv8 has replaced the coupling head of YOLOv5 with the mainstream decoupling head called Decoupled-Head, transitioning from an Anchor-Based approach to an Anchor Free approach. Instead of depending on pre-established anchor boxes, it now directly identifies and detects items on the feature map.

ResNet-50 Architecture

ResNet is a well-known deep network. Earlier than ResNet, the most advanced DNN was getting deeper and deeper [18]. But it is tough to train deep networks because of the well-known disappearing gradient problem. This happens because the gradient is sent back to earlier layers and may become infinitely small after being multiplied many times.

A skip connection, also known as a shortcut connection, lets ResNet move information from one layer to the next without changing it. ResNet is able to achieve a high level of depth in its network architecture, with the potential for up to 152 layers. Figure 52.3 shows how ResNet50 is put together. In how ResNet is put together, there are two types of speed modules. The first one is an identity block that doesn't have a convolution layer that is close by. In this case, input and output are the same size. It has a convolution layer at the shortcut. The other is the convolution block. When comparing the input and output dimensions, the latter are smaller. At the start and finish of both blocks, 1 × 1 convolution layers are added. Bottleneck design is the name of this method for cutting down on the number of factors without making the network less fast. In order to make the model function with our

dataset, we removed certain deep shortcut modules and added new classification layers.

Results Analysis

The efficacy of the proposed image retrieval model is confirmed by a comparison of models built using several Deep learning methodologies. The proposed retrieval model, VOLOv8-ResNet-50, is assessed with precision, and F1-score. It is compared to other models such as VGG 19, VGG Net, Shifted MobileNet V2, Shifted GoogleNet, and CNN. Figure 52.4 depicts the images obtained by the ResNet-50 image retrieval model. The YOLOv8 framework provided segmented image findings, which are displayed in Figure 52.5.

Analysis of proposed retrieval model

The efficacy of the purported image retrieval method is validated by competing it with several deep learning models over precision and F1-score values. It is compared with ResNet [19], VGG

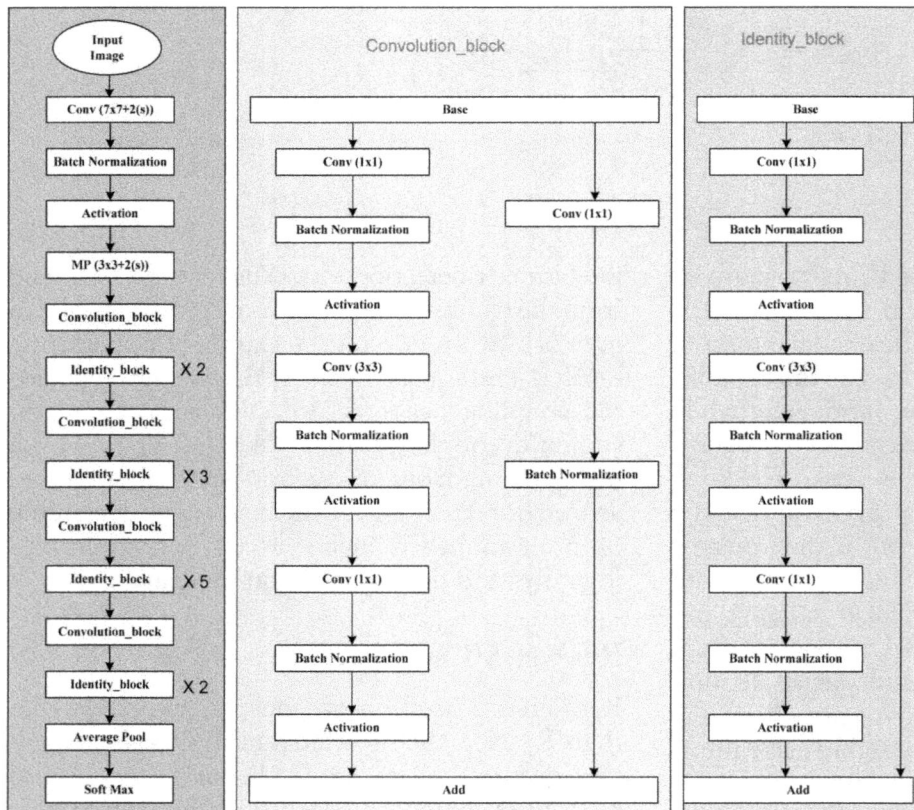

Figure 52.3 Structural diagram of ResNet-50
Source: Author

Net [20], Shifted MobileNet V2 [21], Shifted GoogLeNet [21], and CNN [22]. Figure 52.6 displays the graphical depiction of precision analysis for two query images, while Figure 52.7 shows the pictorial representation of F1-score analysis for the same two query images. The graphical display clearly demonstrates that the suggested retrieval model outperformed other methods.

Evaluation with different classifiers and segmentation techniques

The proposed model was evaluated against different Deep learning models based on Sensitivity, Specificity, precision, and Accuracy. The results for these metrics are shown in Figure 52.8. The investigation employed the following classifiers: ResNet [19], VGG 19 [19], VGG Net [20], shifted MobileNet V2 [21], Shifted GoogLeNet [21], and CNN [22]. The results of the segmentation study conducted on the YOLOv8 based segmentation model are shown in Table 52.1. The

YOLOv8 model exhibits an accuracy that surpasses the precision of the -0 RCNN, YOLOv3, and YOLOv5 and YOLOv7 models by 6.27%, 3.51%, 1.19%, and 0.82% correspondingly. The results collected from the developed model showed higher accuracy compared to other techniques.

Conclusion

A specialized system was developed to retrieve and categorize images with the specific purpose of aiding in medical applications. The images were acquired from preexisting databases. Afterwards, the images underwent the segmentation method. The YOLOv8 algorithm effectively executed segmentation of images and produced segmented image outputs. Subsequently, the segmented images were sent into the installed ResNet-50 for the purpose of classifying illnesses. After the creation of the ResNet-50, the resulting classed

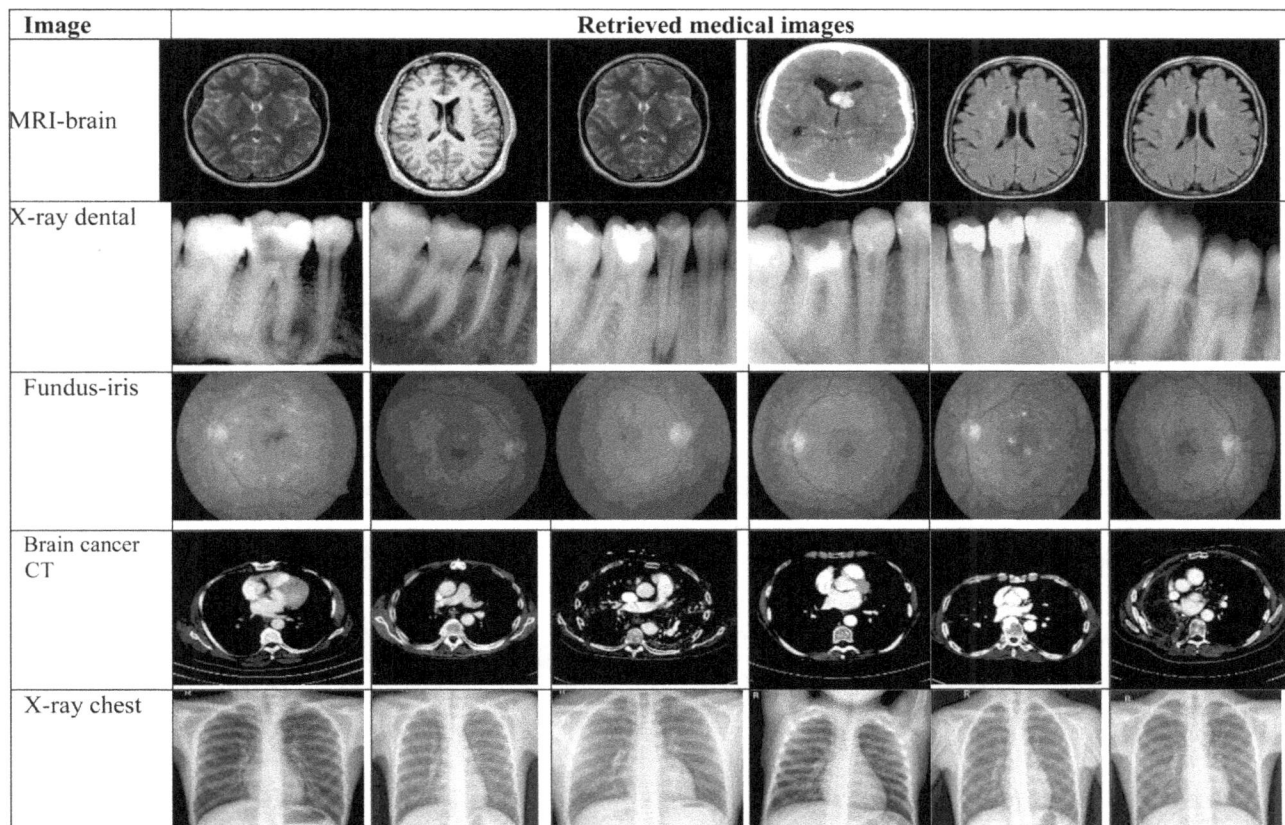

Figure 52.4 Results of medical image retrieval from proposed model
Source: Author

Brain Cancer	Brain Hemorrhage	Breast Carcinoma	Brain Tumor	Tooth discoloration

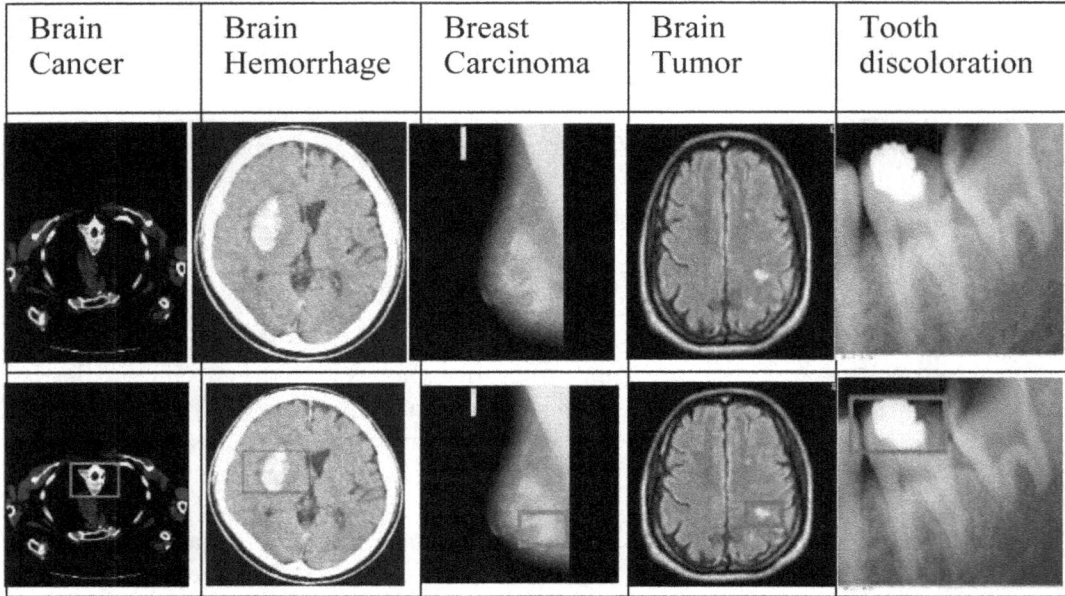

Figure 52.5 Segmentation results from proposed work
Source: Author

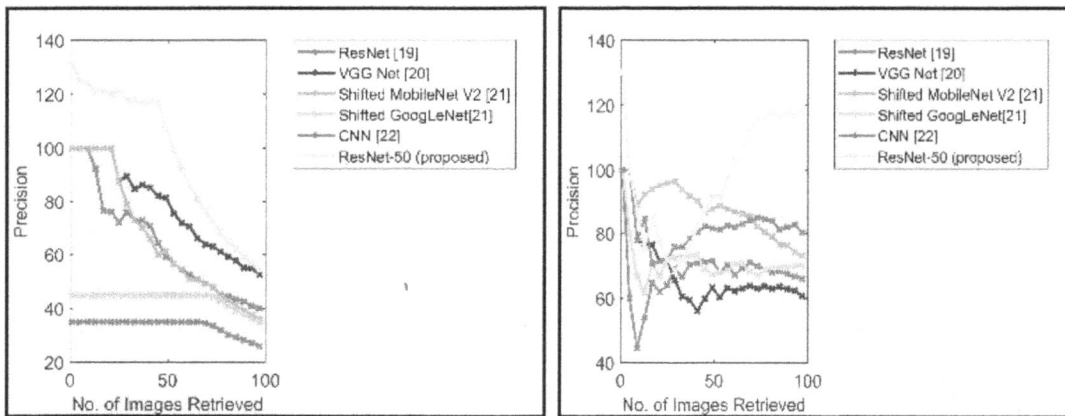

Figure 52.6 Precision analysis for two query images using different DL models
Source: Author

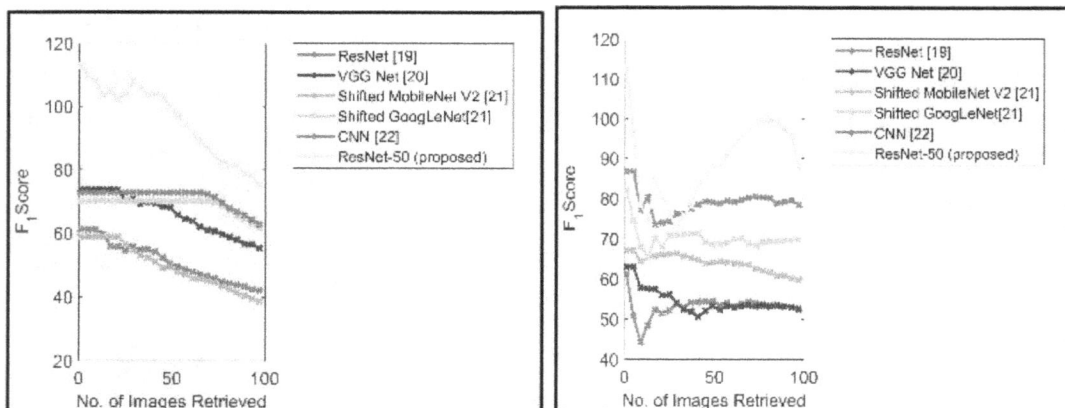

Figure 52.7 F1-Score analysis for two query images using different DL models
Source: Author

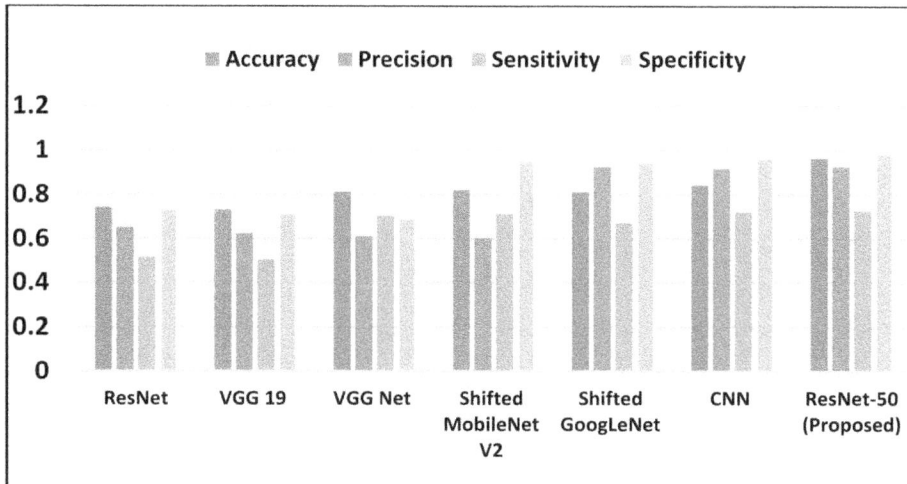

Figure 52.8 Comparison of proposed Model with available DL models
Source: Author

Table 52.1 Comparison of proposed model with various segmentation models

Methodology/ metrics	Mask RCNN [23]	YOLOv3 [24]	YOLOv5 [25]	YOLOv7 [26]	YOLOV8 (Proposed)
Accuracy	0.8864	0.9134	0.9356	0.9379	0.9487
Sensitivity	0.8934	0.9154	0.9281	0.9347	0.9495
Specificity	0.8956	0.9058	0.9324	0.9345	0.9443
Precision	0.9052	0.9134	0.9342	0.9387	0.9497

Source: Author

image was acquired and stored in the database for the purpose of conducting similarity checks. Afterwards, the query images were inputted into the ResNet-50 model to retrieve the matching images. The ResNet-50 was employed to comprehensively extract features and produce the output of the extracted features. Afterwards, the extracted feature and the stored image in the database were compared to evaluate their resemblance. The Euclidian distance was utilized for similarity verification. The ResNet-50 model ultimately generated the resulting image output. The efficacy of the constructed model was verified by examining the data through diverse DL models and segmentation techniques.

References

[1] Lan, R., and Zhou, Y. (2017). Medical image retrieval via histogram of compressed scattering coefficients. *IEEE Journal of Biomedical and Health Informatics*, 21(5), 1338–1346.

[2] Chen, L., Yang, X., Jeon, G., Anisetti, M., and Liu, K. (2020). A trusted medical image super-resolution method based on feedback adaptive weighted dense network. *Artificial Intelligence in Medicine*, 106, 101857.

[3] Zhang, X., Liu, W., Dundar, M., Badve, S., and Zhang, S. (2015). Towards largescale histopathological image analysis: hashing-based image retrieval. *IEEE Transactions on Medical Imaging*, 34(2), 496–506.

[4] Singh, V. P., and Srivastava, R. (2017). Content-based mammogram retrieval using wavelet based complete-LBP and K-means clustering for the diagnosis of breast cancer. *International Journal of Hybrid Intelligent Systems*, 14(1), 31–39.

[5] Singh, V. P., Srivastava, S., and Srivastava, R. (2018). An efficient and automated content-based image retrieval for digital mammography. *Journal of X-Ray Science and Technology*, 26(1), 29–49.

[6] Denner, S., Zimmerer, D., Bounias, D., Bujotzek, M., Xiao, S., Kausch, L., et al. (2024). Leverag-

ing foundation models for content-based medical image retrieval in radiology. arXiv preprint arXiv:2403.06567.

[7] Sudhish, D. K., Nair, L. R., and Shailesh, S. (2024). Content-based image retrieval for medical diagnosis using fuzzy clustering and deep learning. *Biomedical Signal Processing and Control*, 88, 105620.

[8] Yu, R., Sun, J., and Li, H. (2020). Second-order spectral transform block for 3D shape classification and retrieval. *IEEE Transactions on Image Processing*, 29, 4530–4543.

[9] Liu, A.-A., Zhao, Z., Li, W., and Song, D. (2020). Multi-View tree structure learning for 3D model retrieval and classification in smart city. *IEEE Access*, 8, 129743–129753.

[10] Li, X., Li, J., Yiu, S., Gao, C., and Xiong, J. (2019). Privacy-preserving edge-assisted image retrieval and classification in IoT. *Frontiers of Computer Science*, 13, 1136–1147.

[11] Shereena, V. B., and David, J. M. (2014). Content-based image retrieval: classification using neural networks. *The International Journal of Multimedia and its Applications (IJMA)*, 6(5), 31.

[12] Sunitha, T., and Sivarani, T. S. (2022). Novel content based medical image retrieval based on BoVW classification method. *Biomedical Signal Processing and Control*, 77, 103678.

[13] Mahesh, D. B., Murty, G. S., and Lakshmi, D. R. (2021). Optimized local weber and gradient pattern-based medical image retrieval and optimized convolutional neural network-based classification. *Biomedical Signal Processing and Control*, 70, 102971.

[14] Loddo, A., Loddo, M., and Di Ruberto, C. (2021). A novel deep learning-based approach for seed image classification and retrieval. *Computers and Electronics in Agriculture*, 187, 106269.

[15] Reis, D., Kupec, J., Hong, J., and Daoudi, A. (2023). Real-time flying object detection with YOLOv8. arXiv:2305.09972.

[16] Jocher, G., Chaurasia, A., Stoken, A., Borovec, J., Kwon, Y., Michael, K., et al. (2022). Ultralytics/yolov5: v6. 2—YOLOv5 classification models, apple M1, reproducibility, clearML and Deci. AI integrations. *Zenodo*, doi: 10.5281/zenodo.7002879.

[17] Wang, C.-Y., Mark Liao, H.-Y., Wu, Y.-H., Chen, P.-Y., Hsieh, J.-W., and Yeh, I.-H. (2020). CSPNet: a new backbone that can enhance learning capability of CNN. In Proceedings IEEE/CVF Conference on Computer Vision and Pattern Recognition Workshops (CVPRW), Jun. 2020, (pp. 1571–1580).

[18] Ji, Q., Huang, J., He, W., and Sun, Y. (2019). Optimized deep convolutional neural networks for identification of macular diseases from optical coherence tomography images. *Algorithms*, 12(3), 51.

[19] Mijwil, M. M. (2021). Skin cancer disease images classification using deep learning solutions. *Multimedia Tools and Applications*, 80(17), 26255–26271.

[20] Lopez, A. R., Giro-i-Nieto, X., Burdick, J., and Marques, O. (2017). Skin lesion classification from dermoscopic images using deep learning techniques. In 2017 13th IASTED International Conference on Biomedical Engineering (BioMed), (pp. 49–54). IEEE, 2017.

[21] Thurnhofer-Hemsi, K., López-Rubio, E., Dominguez, E., and Elizondo, D. A. (2021). Skin lesion classification by ensembles of deep convolutional networks and regularly spaced shifting. *IEEE Access*, 9, 112193–112205.

[22] Nugroho, A. A., Slamet, I., and Sugiyanto, S. (2019). Skins cancer identification system of HAMl0000 skin cancer dataset using convolutional neural network. In AIP Conference Proceedings, (Vol. 2202, no. 1, pp. 020039).

[23] He, K., Gkioxari, G., Dollár, P., and Girshick, R. (2017). Mask r-cnn. In Proceedings of the IEEE International Conference on Computer Vision, (pp. 2961–2969).

[24] Shereena, V. B., and David, J. M. (2014). Content based image retrieval: classification using neural networks. *The International Journal of Multimedia and its Applications*, 6(5), 31.

[25] Zhang, L., Wang, L., and Lin, W. (2012). Conjunctive patches subspace learning with side information for collaborative image retrieval. *IEEE Transactions on Image Processing*, 21(8), 3707–3720.

[26] Yu, C., Liu, Y., Zhang, W., Zhang, X., Zhang, Y., and Jiang, X. (2023). Foreign objects identification of transmission line based on improved YOLOv7. *IEEE Access*, 11, 51997–52008.

53 A novel ensemble approach for enhanced heart disease prediction

Nomula Nagarjuna Reddy[a], Lingadally Nipun[b], Samanvitha Maddula[c], Pogiri Deepika[d] and Thoutireddy Shilpa[e]

Department of Computer Science and Engineering, B V Raju Institute of Technology, Narsapur, Telangana, India

Abstract

Heart disease (HD) poses a significant health challenge across the world, responsible for approximately 17.9 million deaths annually, necessitating advanced predictive techniques for early diagnosis and intervention. This paper introduces a novel ensemble learning (EL)approach that integrates random forest (RF), XGBoost (XGB), and multilayer perceptron (MLP) classifiers to enhance the accuracy of HD prediction. By combining these models, we leverage their complementary strengths to address the limitations of individual methods. Evaluated on a comprehensive dataset of 1,190 patients, our ensemble model attained a remarkable accuracy of 95.4% and an F1 score of 95.8%, exceeding the efficiency of individual models, where RF achieved 94.5% accuracy and 94% F1 score. This significant improvement emphasizes the efficacy of EL approaches in medical diagnostics. The proposed approach not only advances predictive accuracy but also contributes to the development of robust clinical decision support systems. Our findings highlight the potential of EL to enhance early detection and patient outcomes in cardiovascular (CV) healthcare, setting a new benchmark for the incorporation of AI and ML in medical diagnostics. Future work will focus on refining the model with additional techniques and hyperparameter optimization to further elevate predictive performance.

Keywords: Ensemble learning, heart disease, machine learning, multilayer perceptron, random forest, XGBoost

Introduction

Heart disease (HD), responsible for approximately 17.9 million deaths annually, remains a leading global health concern. The diversity of CV conditions—including CAD, heart failure, and arrhythmias—emphasizes the critical importance of reliable early diagnostic methods. Despite advances in medical research, predicting HD continues to challenge healthcare due to its complex nature.

The human heart, a central organ in diagnosing and understanding CVD, exemplifies biological complexity. Recent innovations in ML and DL have shown great potential in healthcare analytics, particularly through ensemble learning, which combines multiple algorithms to enhance predictive performance. Building on prior research, which demonstrated the effectiveness of the CART algorithm achieving 87%

accuracy, this work proposes a novel application of EL techniques to further improve predictive accuracy.

Our research leverages a voting classifier (VC) that integrates

RF, MLP, and XGB algorithms. This approach aims to capitalize on the strengths of each algorithm—RF's robustness in handling large datasets, MLP's efficiency, and XGB's superior performance. The study utilizes a comprehensive dataset comprising 11,190 patient records from multiple countries, featuring 11 clinical attributes and a target variable indicating heart disease presence.

By rigorously optimizing and evaluating the ensemble model using evaluation metrics, we demonstrate significant improvements in predictive performance without the need for feature extraction. This approach enhances diagnostic

[a]nagarjunareddynomula2@gmail.com, [b]nipun.poh@gmail.com, [c]maddulasamanvitha04@gmail.com, [d]pogirideepika2111@gmail.com, [e]shilpathoutireddy@gmail.com

DOI: 10.1201/9781003616399-53

accuracy while also providing valuable insights into the practical implementation of EL in medical diagnostics.

This study significantly contributes to the field by demonstrating the effectiveness of advanced ML techniques in improving HD prediction, with the goal of enhancing patient outcomes by providing more accurate and reliable diagnostic tools.

Research Objective

The objective of this proposed research is to develop and validate an advanced predictive model for HD diagnosis by employing a novel EL approach. This method integrates three distinct ML classifiers—RF, XGB, and MLP—into a VC framework. The primary goal is to improve the accuracy and reliability of HD predictions, thereby enhancing the effectiveness of clinical decision support systems. Through this approach, the paper seeks to demonstrate how combining the strengths of these individual classifiers can lead to significant improvements in diagnostic accuracy, ultimately contributing to better patient outcomes in CV care.

Literature Review

HD poses significant health risks, underscoring the need for accurate predictive models for early detection and intervention. Recent research demonstrates the effectiveness of ML and DL techniques in predicting. For instance, the CART algorithm achieved 87% accuracy in HD prediction [1], while a voting ensemble with chi-square feature selection achieved 92.11% accuracy, enhancing both performance and efficiency [2].

RF, with 88.52% accuracy, outperformed other ML algorithms, emphasizing the importance of data quality and feature selection [3]. A MLPNN with an arithmetic optimization algorithm also surpassed traditional methods with 88.89% accuracy [4]. Additionally, MLP and RF were top performers in HD prediction, while DT lagged behind [5].

XGB was the most accurate for predicting myocardial infarction, with 94.80% accuracy and 90.0% AUC, highlighting ML's potential in CVD prediction [6]. Research indicates that feature selection techniques significantly enhance the accuracy of HD prediction [7]. Improved prediction accuracy has been achieved using six ML algorithms optimized with GridSearchCV and five-fold cross-validation, particularly with a soft voting ensemble classifier [8].

Comparative studies of gradient boosting, XGBoost, and AdaBoost for HD prediction found gradient boosting to be the most accurate at 92.20% [9]. A hybrid ML method combining KNN and SVM achieved an 81% prediction accuracy [10]. Additionally, an extra tree classifier with hyperparameter optimization predicted HD with 98.15% accuracy, emphasizing the need for broader datasets and integration of clinical and genetic data [11].

Keras-based DL models have effectively diagnosed HD using Convolutional Neural Networks (CNNs) on image data [12]. An optimized ANN model improved HD prediction accuracy to 93.44%, surpassing SVM by 7.5%, and reducing training time [13]. Advanced boosting techniques like AdaBoost achieved 95% accuracy [14]. Literature highlights the need for advanced ML models for HD detection, with XGBoost excelling in accuracy and precision, particularly in addressing imbalanced datasets [15].

In conclusion, this study validates the efficacy of ML and DL algorithms for predicting HD. By integrating findings from earlier research, this study offers a more comprehensive perspective on HD prediction, underscoring the potential of ML and DL methods to advance early detection and intervention approaches. The aim is to create precise predictive models for HD through EL, specifically employing a VC with RF, MLP, and XGBoost, to enhance diagnostic accuracy and improve patient outcomes in CV care.

Methodology

Dataset
We utilize a dataset consisting of 1,190 patient records collected from several countries, such as the US, UK, Switzer- land, and Hungary. The dataset includes 11 features along with a target variable indicating HD. These features reflect important patient attributes crucial for our analysis and are outlined in Table 53.1.

Table 53.1 Description of features in dataset

Feature name	Description
ST slope	Inclination of the ST segment at maximum exercise intensity on an ECG, indicating cardiac health.
Chest pain type	Typical angina, atypical angina, non-anginal pain.
Old peak	Represents the presence of myocardial ischemia.
Resting ECG	Reveals heart's rhythm and electrical conduction.
Age	The age of a person, a critical HD factor.
Fasting blood sugar (FBS)	High FBS level (mg/dL) indicates insulin and diabetes risk.
Max heart rate	Achieved during exercise (bpm), showing heart fitness.
Sex	Gender of a person, influences CVD.

Feature name	Description
Resting BP S	Resting systolic blood pressure (mmHg), important for assessing hypertension risk.
Exercise angina	It signals decreased blood flow to the heart during exertion.
Cholesterol	High serum cholesterol level (mg/dL), reflects CVD risk.

Source: M. Siddhartha, "Heart Disease Dataset (Comprehensive), "IEEE Dataport, Nov. 5, 2020. [Online]. Available: https://dx.doi.org/10.21227/dz4t-cm36

System framework

In this study, we developed a robust framework (as shown in Figure 53.1) for HD prediction using a diverse dataset of 11,190 patient records from multiple countries. Each record includes 11 features and a target variable indicating HD presence. Dataset underwent preprocessing to ensure high data quality. We employed 3 ML algorithms—RF, XGB, and MLP. An ensemble approach using a VC was chosen to improve predictive performance by integrating the advantages

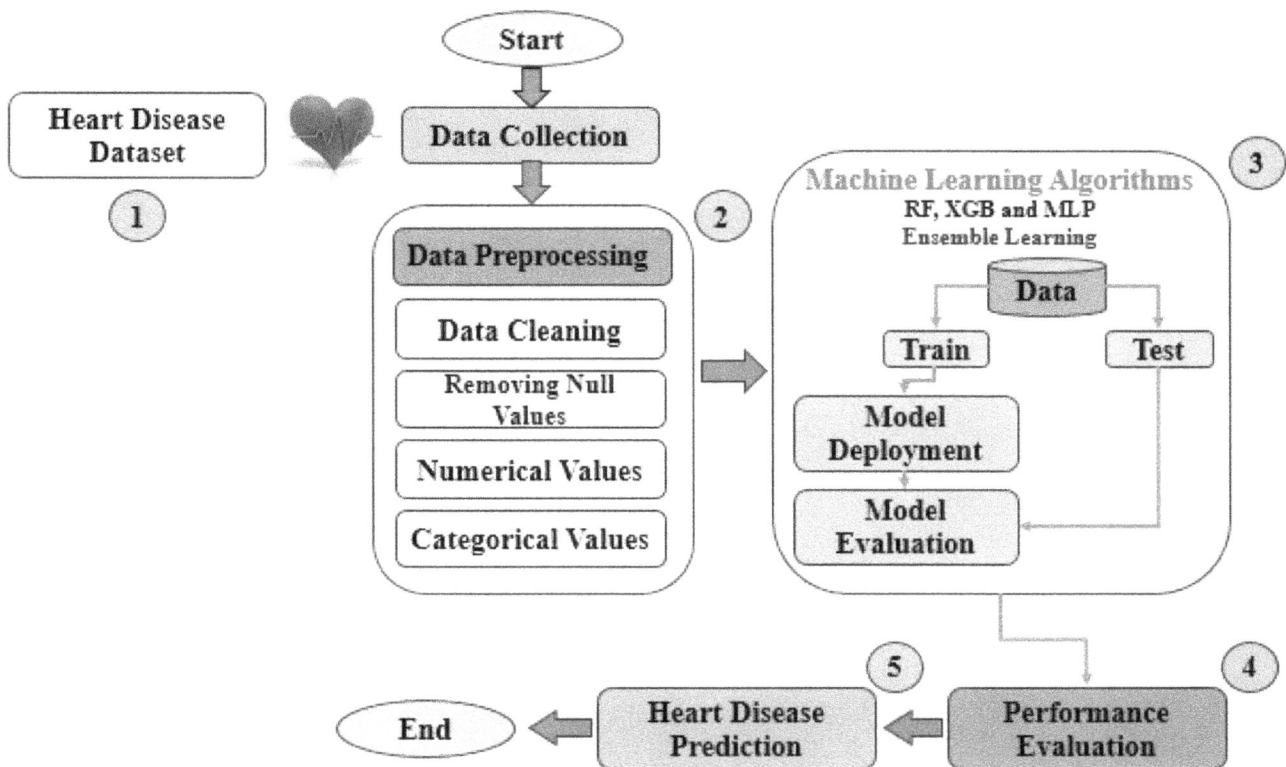

Figure 53.1 System framework
Source: Author

of the three algorithms. After training, the models were deployed for predicting new, unseen data to simulate real-world application. A comprehensive performance evaluation was conducted for our prediction framework. This approach aims to enhance healthcare decisions and facilitate prompt interventions.

Data preprocessing

Enhancing the accuracy of ML models is crucial. Practical datasets frequently have issues such as noise, missing data, and improper formats, which necessitate thorough cleaning and formatting. Key steps include handling missing values through removal or imputation, encoding categorical variables into numerical formats, and scaling features for uniform contribution during model training. This involved importing and cleansing the dataset.

Proposed ensemble methodology

Random forest: It is an EL technique for classification and regression, combining multiple DTs (Figure 53.2) to enhance predictive accuracy and reduce overfitting. Each tree is trained on distinct data subsets, and the final prediction is derived from aggregating these outputs. This method excels with large datasets, manages missing values, and handles high dimensional data.

Parameter optimization is key to mitigating overfitting, especially with noisy data. It is versatile, with applications ranging from customer churn prediction to disease diagnosis, and it provides feature importance scores for better interpretability. In our study, RF is chosen for its high accuracy and reliability in predicting HD, addressing model overfitting and data variability while offering valuable insights into significant predictors.

Multilayer perceptron: It is an ANN consisting of an input layer, hidden layers, and an output layer (Figure 53.3). It performs feedforward computations and uses Backpropagation for training, adjusting weights to minimize errors. MLPs excel at modeling non-linear relationships and handling complex datasets, making them suitable for tasks where conventional linear models fall short.

The choice of MLP is justified by its capability to approximate any continuous function with sufficient neurons and layers, capturing intricate patterns within data. Selecting an appropriate network structure, including multiple hidden layers and nodes, is crucial for balancing model complexity and preventing overfitting.

To implement an MLP, configure the network with suitable parameters, apply Backpropagation for training, and fine- tune the model to align with the specific characteristics of the dataset. This ensures robust predictive performance and adaptability to complex problems.

XGBoost: It is a powerful ML algorithm built on gradient-boosting decision trees, optimized

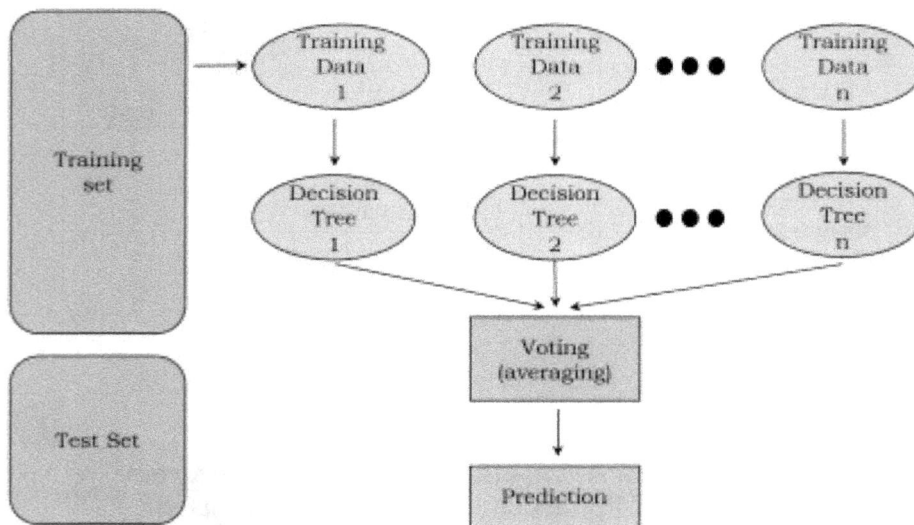

Figure 53.2 Random forest
Source: Author

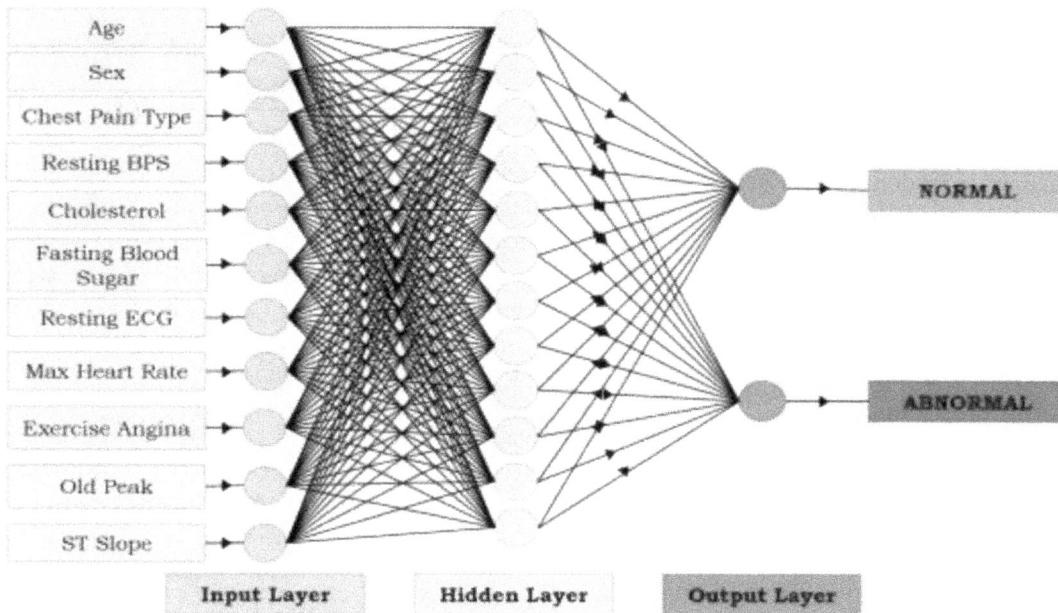

Figure 53.3 Multilayer perceptron
Source: Author

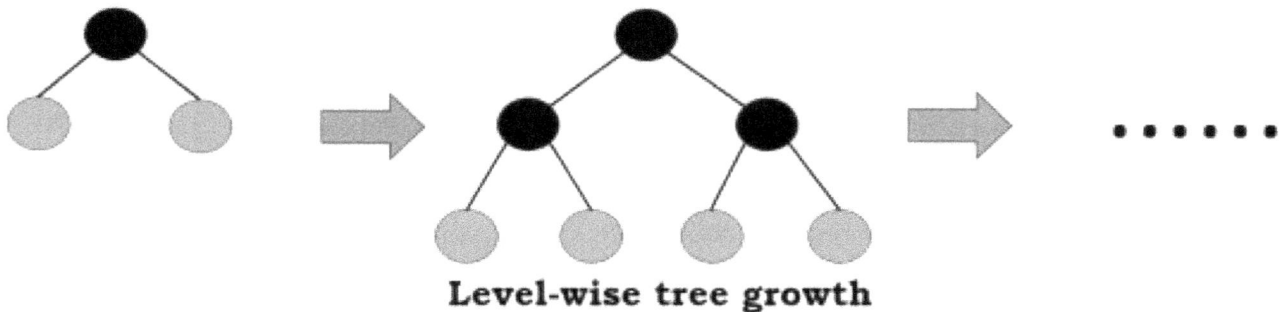

Level-wise tree growth

Figure 53.4 XGBoost
Source: Author

for speed, efficiency, and scalability. It iteratively constructs models that correct the errors of their predecessors, enhancing overall predictive accuracy. This ensemble approach combines predictions from multiple trees for a more accurate and robust model (Figure 53.4).

XGB's superior performance in predictive accuracy and computational speed, compared to alternatives like RF and GB Machines, makes it a preferred choice. It efficiently handles large datasets and complex features, improving model performance and resilience against overfitting. Additionally, XGB's interpretability and feature importance analysis aid in identifying key

predictors in heart disease, aligning with our research objectives to enhance accuracy and reliability.

Ensemble learning
Ensemble learning (EL) is a robust technique in ML that combines several models to improve prediction accuracy. By aggregating outputs from various models, ensemble methods effectively address individual model weaknesses such as high variance and bias, resulting in more reliable and generalizable predictions. This method leverages diverse perspectives, whether from different algorithms, subsets of data, or introduced

randomness during training, to form a cohesive prediction.

In this study, we employ a combination of RF, MLP, and XGB. RF is used to stabilize predictions and contribute valuable feature importance insights, while XGB is included for its superior accuracy and efficiency. MLP is selected for its capability to capture complex patterns through nonlinear relationships. By utilizing a VC with hard voting, we combine these models to leverage their individual strengths, thereby enhancing predictive performance for HD detection and addressing the limitations of each model.

This ensemble approach aims to increase accuracy and reliability of predictions, making it a powerful strategy for practical applications in medical diagnostics.

Voting classifier: It is an ensemble method that boosts prediction accuracy by aggregating outputs from multiple base models, such as RF, MLP, XGB, each trained independently. It uses majority voting to show the final class label from these models. Base models are trained with optimized hyperparameters, and their predictions are combined through hard voting, selecting the label with the most votes. This process leverages the strengths of each model while minimizing individual weaknesses, resulting in more robust and reliable predictions. By integrating diverse predictors, this technique effectively reduces model bias and variance, making it particularly valuable for HD prediction.

Model training and testing
The dataset is divided into 80% for training to develop the models and 20% for testing to assess their performance.

Performance analysis
We use the following metrics to evaluate model performance, each providing distinct insights into the model's reliability and diagnostic capability. It delineates true negatives (TrNe), false negative (FaNe), and false positive (FaPo), true positives (TrPo).

1) **Accuracy:** It illustrates the proportion of correct predictions relative to all cases. Although it provides a broad assessment of model performance, it can be misleading in

datasets with imbalanced classes, where one class may dominate the dataset.

$$Acc = \frac{TrPo+TrNe}{TrPo+TrNe+FaPo+FaNe} \quad (1)$$

2) **Precision:** It quantifies the ratio of TP predictions among all +ve predictions. A high precision indicates fewer FP, which is essential for accurately identifying individuals with heart disease.

$$Pre = \frac{TrPo}{TrPo+FaPo} \quad (2)$$

3) **Recall:** It is the model's ability to detect all actual +ve cases. It is crucial for minimizing missed diagnoses and ensuring that as many positive instances as possible are captured.

$$Re = \frac{TrPo}{TrPo+FaNe} \quad (3)$$

4) **F1-score:** It integrates the above 2 metrics into a single metric, offering a balanced measure of model performance. It provides a comprehensive evaluation by managing the balance between precision and recall, reflecting the model's overall effectiveness.

$$F1 = 2 \times \frac{Pre \times Re}{Pre+Re} \quad (4)$$

In summary, these offer key understanding into the performance of HD prediction. These metrics help in analysing model advantages and disadvantages, guiding the selection and optimization of algorithms to enhance diagnostic accuracy and patient care.

Results

Evaluation metrics of various ML models and their combinations are summarized in Figure 53.5. Among the individual models, SVM achieved an acc of 84.9%. NB slightly outperformed SVM with an acc of 85.7%. Logistic regression (LR) recorded an accuracy of 86.1%. A significant improvement in performance was observed with the MLP, which achieved an acc of 91.2%. XGB further improved the metrics, reaching an acc of 92.8%. The RF model surpassed all individual models with an acc of 94.5% and an F1 of 94%.

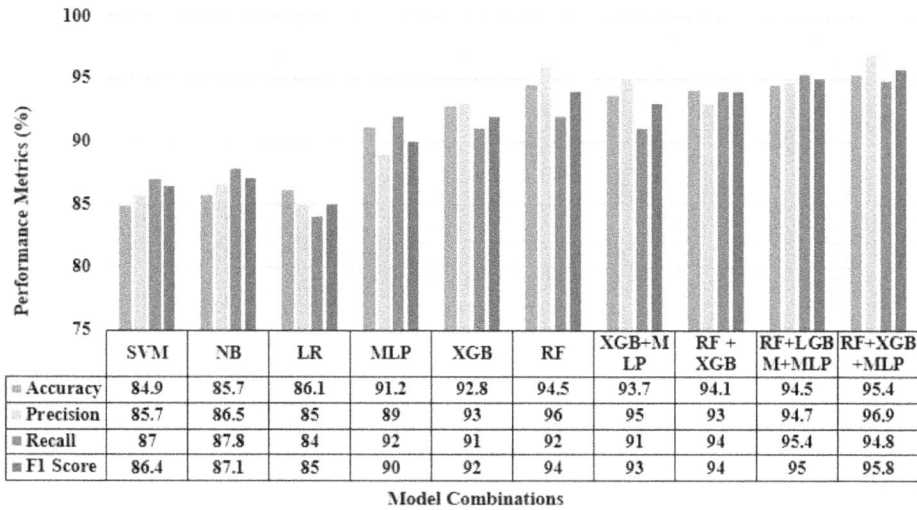

	SVM	NB	LR	MLP	XGB	RF	XGB+M LP	RF + XGB	RF+LGB M+MLP	RF+XGB +MLP
Accuracy	84.9	85.7	86.1	91.2	92.8	94.5	93.7	94.1	94.5	95.4
Precision	85.7	86.5	85	89	93	96	95	93	94.7	96.9
Recall	87	87.8	84	92	91	92	91	94	95.4	94.8
F1 Score	86.4	87.1	85	90	92	94	93	94	95	95.8

Figure 53.5 Performance analysis

Source: Author

The ensemble models show the best performance when compared to individual models. The combination of MLP and XGB achieved an acc of 93.7%. The ensemble of RF and XGB showed an acc of 94.1%. Notably, the ensemble of RF, LGBM, and MLP achieved an acc of 94.5%. The highest performance was recorded by ensemble of RF, XGB, and MLP, with an acc of 95.4% and an F1 of 95.8% (Figure 53.6 shows confusion matrix and Figure 53.7 shows model comparison).

Discussion

The results clearly denote that EL significantly improve the predictive performance for HD detection compared to individual models. Among the individual models, RF showed the highest accuracy and F1 score, confirming its effectiveness. in handling complex datasets with its feature importance, as shown in Figure 53.8. The improved performance of the MLP highlights its capability in capturing non-linear patterns within the data, evidenced by Figure 53.9, while XGB proved efficient in dealing with imbalanced datasets, as shown in Figure 53.10.

The ensemble models, particularly the combination of RF, XGB, and MLP, achieved the best results. This improvement can be attributed to the complementary strengths of the individual models. RF contributes robust overall performance,

XGB efficiently manages imbalanced data and enhances precision, while MLP captures complex, non-linear relationships. By aggregating the outputs of these models through hard voting, the ensemble method minimizes individual model weaknesses and boosts overall prediction accuracy and reliability, as shown in Figure 53.11.

The ensemble of RF, XGB, and MLP acquired an acc of 95.4% and an F1 of 95.8%, underscoring the strength of EL in clinical decision support systems. These findings align with existing literature, which advocates for the use of ensemble techniques to enhance predictive performance. The integration of diverse models reduces model bias and variance, leading to more robust and reliable predictions. This study reinforces the value of ensemble methods in the early detection and intervention of HD, ultimately contributing to improved patient outcomes in cardiovascular healthcare.

In summary, the application of EL, specifically through the VC framework integrating RF, XGB, and MLP, offers a powerful approach to HD prediction. The results validate the capability of this method in achieving high accuracy and F1 scores, thus supporting its implementation in predictive analytics for CVD. Future research could explore the integration of additional models and further optimization of hyperparameters to continue enhancing predictive performance.

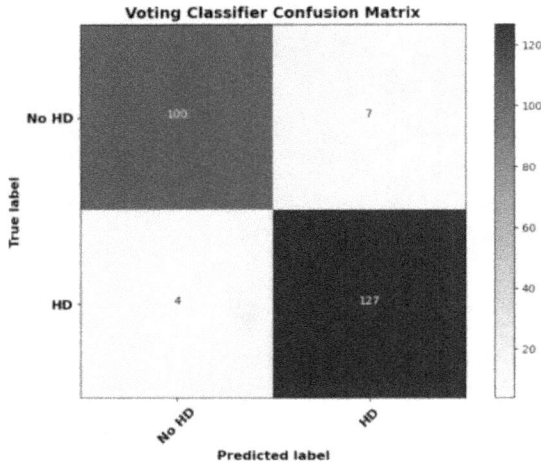

Figure 53.6 Voting classifier confusion matrix
Source: Author

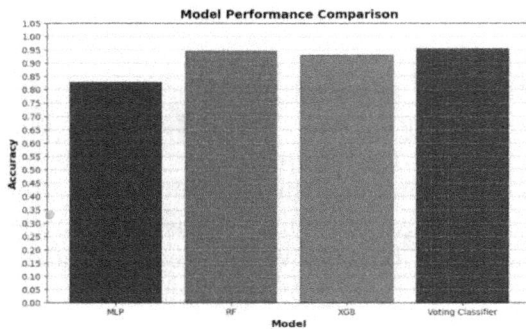

Figure 53.7 Model performance comparison
Source: Author

Conclusion

This research offers an in-depth examination of ML and EL techniques for the prediction of HD, emphasizing the significance of accurate early detection methods in cardiovascular healthcare. The investigation demonstrated that ensemble methods significantly outperformed individual models performance.

Through the application of a VC, the ensemble model acquired a notable accuracy of 95.4% and an F1 score of 95.8%, highlighting its robustness and reliability in predicting HD. These results underscore the effectiveness of leveraging diverse model strengths to minimize individual weaknesses, thereby enhancing overall predictive performance. The research utilized a comprehensive dataset from multiple countries, encompassing 1,190 patient records with 11 features, ensuring the robustness and generalizability of the findings. A key novelty of this paper lies in the successful integration of RF, XGB, and MLP within a VC framework, demonstrating the enhanced performance of this ensemble method over individual classifiers. This approach showcases the innovative application of EL techniques in the medical domain, providing a robust and reliable tool for HD prediction.

However, there are some limitations to this study. The dataset, while comprehensive, may

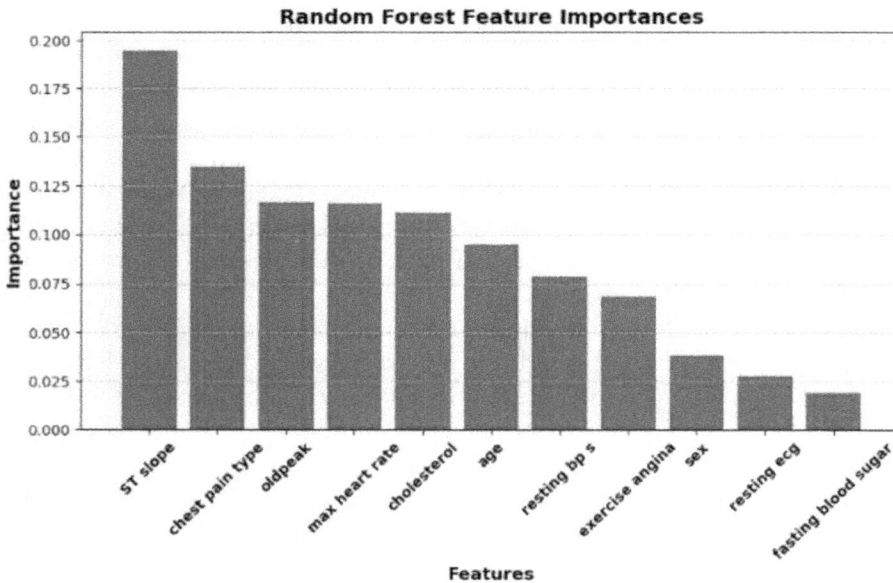

Figure 53.8 Random forest feature importance
Source: Author

MLP Training Loss Curve

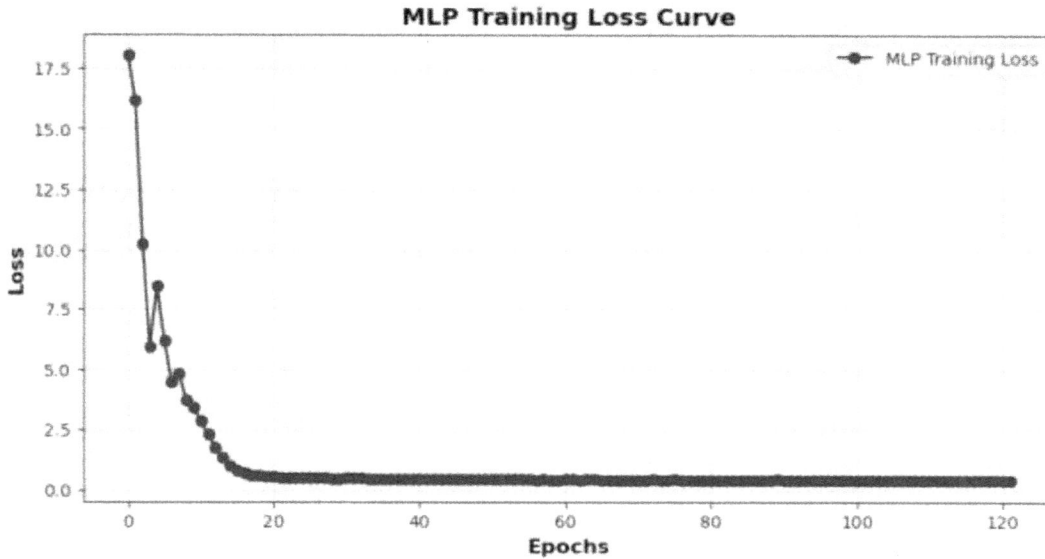

Figure 53.9 MLP training loss curve
Source: Author

XGB Training and Validation Loss Curve

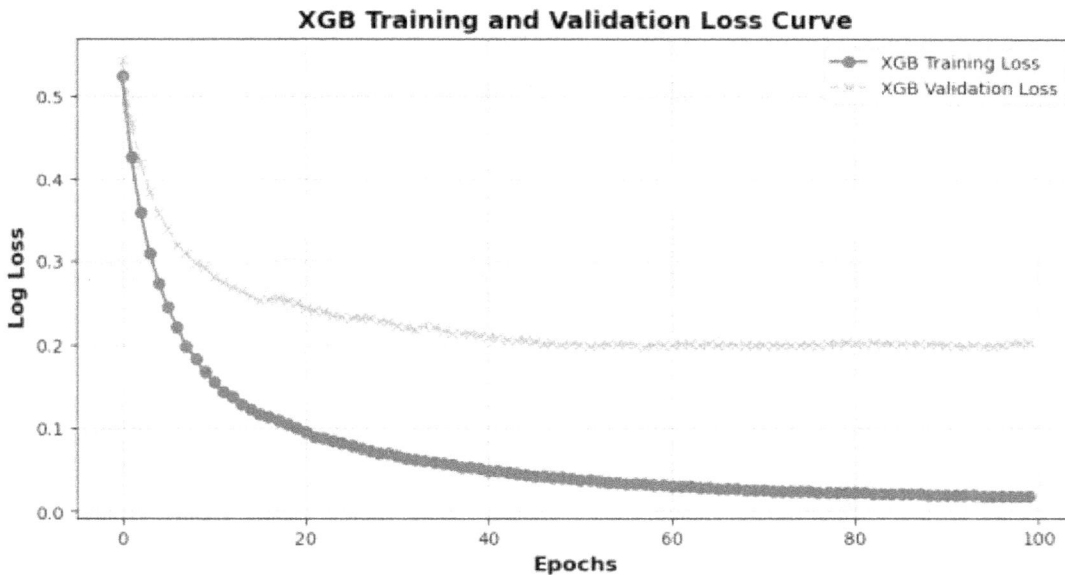

Figure 53.10 XGB training and validation curve
Source: Author

still have biases inherent to the specific populations from which it was collected. Additionally, the model's performance could vary with different or more diverse datasets. Another limitation is the absence of feature extraction techniques, which might further enhance the predictive capabilities of the models.

Future work could overcome these limitations by incorporating feature extraction methods and testing the models on more varied and extensive datasets. Additionally, exploring the integration of additional ML models and further optimizing ensemble strategies could lead to even better predictive accuracy.

In conclusion, this research confirms the capability of EL techniques for predicting HD, marking a substantial contribution to medical diagnostics. While the study has certain limitations, it offers

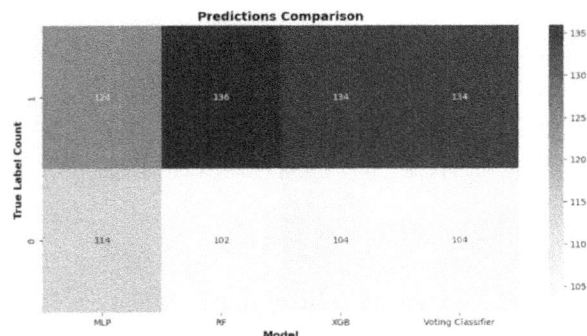

Figure 53.11 Prediction comparison matrix
Source: Author

important insights into the potential of EL methods in supporting clinical decision-making. This study paves the way for more sophisticated and reliable predictive tools, ultimately enhancing patient outcomes and contributing to the broader goal of effective CVD management.

References

[1] Ozcan, M., and Peker, S. (2023). A classification and regression tree algorithm for heart disease modeling and prediction. *Healthcare Analytics*, 3, 100130. doi: 10.1016/j.health.2022.100130.

[2] Korial, A. E.,Gorial, I. I., andHumaidi, A. J. (2024). An improved ensemble-based cardiovascular disease detection system with chi-square feature selection. *Computers*, 13(6), 126. doi: 10.3390/computers13060126.

[3] Stonier, A. A.,Gorantla, R. K., and Manoj, K. (2024). Cardiac disease risk prediction using machine learning algorithms. *Healthcare Technology Letters*, 11(4), 213–217. doi: 10.1049/htl2.12053.

[4] Alghamdi, F. A., Almanaseer, H., Jaradat, G., Jaradat, A., Alsmadi, M. K., Jawarneh, S., et al. (2024). Multilayer perceptron neural network with arithmetic optimization algorithm based feature selection for cardiovascular disease prediction. *Machine Learning and Knowledge Extraction*, 6(2), 987–1008. doi: 10.3390/make6020046.

[5] Mijwil, M., Faieq, A. K., and Aljanabi, M. (2024). Early detection of cardiovascular disease utilizing machine learning techniques: evaluating the predictive capabilities of seven algorithms. *Iraqi Journal For Computer Science and Mathematics*, 5(1), 263–276. doi: 10.52866/ijcsm.2024.05.01.018.

[6] Anjum, N., Siddiqua, C. U., Haider, M., Ferdus, Z., Raju, M. A. H., Imam, T., et al. (2024). Improving cardiovascular disease prediction through comparative analysis of machine learning models. *Journal of Computer Science and Technology Studies*, 6(2), 62–70. doi: 10.32996/jcsts.2024.6.2.7.

[7] Pathan, M. S., Nag, A.,Pathan, M. M., and Dev, S. (2022). Analyzing the impact of feature selection on the accuracy of heart disease pre-diction. *Healthcare Analytics*, 2, 100060. doi: 10.1016/j.health.2022.100060.

[8] Chandrasekhar, N., and Peddakrishna, S. (2023). Enhancing heart disease prediction accuracy through machine learning techniques and optimization. *Processes*, 11(4), 1210. doi: 10.3390/pr11041210.

[9] Ganie, S. M., Pramanik, P. K. D., Malik, M. B., Nayyar, A., and Kwak, K. S. (2023). An improved ensemble learning approach for heart disease prediction using boosting algorithms. *Computer Systems Science and Engineering*, 46(3), 3993–4006. doi: 10.32604/csse.2023.035244.

[10] Ahmed, R., Bibi, M., and Syed, S. (2023). Improving heart disease prediction accuracy using a hybrid machine learning approach: a comparative study of SVM and KNN algorithms. *International Journal of Computations, Information and Manufacturing (IJCIM)*, 3(1), 49–54. doi: 10.54489/ijcim.v3i1.223.

[11] Asif, D., Bibi, M.,Arif, M. S., and Mukheimer, A. (2023). Enhancing heart disease prediction through ensemble learning techniques with hyper-parameter optimization. *Algorithms*, 16(6), 308. doi: 10.3390/a16060308.

[12] Almazroi, A. A.,Aldhahri, E. A., Bashir, S., and Ashfaq, S. (2023). A clinical decision support system for heart disease prediction using deep learning. *IEEE Access*, 11, 61646–61659. doi: 10.1109/ACCESS.2023.3285247.

[13] Sarra, R. R., Dinar, A. M., and Mohammed, M. A. (2022). Enhanced accuracy for heart disease prediction using artificial neural network. *Indonesian Journal of Electrical Engineering and Computer Science*, 29(1), 375. doi: 10.11591/ijeecs.v29.i1.pp375-383.

[14] Nissa, N., Jamwal, S., and Neshat, M. (2024). A technical comparative heart disease prediction framework using boosting ensemble techniques. *Computation*, 12(1), 15. doi: 10.3390/computation12010015.

[15] Ogunpola, A., Saeed, F., Basurra, S.,Albarrak, A. M., and Qasem, S. N. (2024). Machine learning-based predictive models for detection of cardio vascular diseases. *Diagnostics*, 14(2), 144. doi: 10.3390/diagnostics14020144.

54 Enhancing thyroid cancer diagnosis with ensemble machine learning techniques

Nomula Nagarjuna Reddy[a], Samanvitha Maddula[b], Pogiri Deepika[c], Rakonda Sanjana[d], Lingadally Nipun[e] and Thoutireddy Shilpa[f]

Department of Computer Science and Engineering, B V Raju Institute of Technology, Narsapur, Medak, Telangana, India

Abstract

The accurate detection of thyroid cancer (TC) remains a significant challenge in medical diagnostics. The research introduces a novel ensemble machine learning system designed to enhance the precision and reliability of thyroid cancer diagnosis. The proposed system employs a voting classifier (VC) that integrates random forest (RF), XGBoost (XGB), support vector machine (SVM) with RBF kernel, and logistic regression (LR), forming a robust predictive model. To address challenges of class imbalance and high-dimensionality, the system incorporates synthetic minority over-sampling technique (SMOTE) and principal component analysis (PCA). Additionally, StratifiedKFold (SKF) and GridSearchCV (GSCV) are utilized for optimization and validation, ensuring robust model performance. The integration of domain-specific features leveraging expert knowledge further improves model efficacy. Comprehensive data preprocessing, feature engineering, and hyperparameter tuning enhance model performance. The ensemble approach outperforms individual classifiers, achieving an accuracy of 81.1% and an F1-Score of 80.5%. These results underscore the effectiveness of advanced ensemble techniques in improving thyroid cancer diagnosis and offer a promising direction for future advancements in medical diagnostics.

Keywords: Ensemble learning, feature engineering, hyperparameter tuning, machine learning, medical diagnostics, thyroid cancer

Introduction

The thyroid gland, a small organ resembling a butterfly and located at the base of the neck, is integral to the regulation of important physiological processes like metabolism, body temperature, blood pressure, and heart rate, is the source of thyroid cancer (TC) (Figure 54.1). TC is still quite curable and has a great cure rate [1,2], despite being relatively rare when compared to other cancers. In recent decades, the cancer's prevalence has increased. The intricacy of TC, which can present as anaplastic, follicular, medullar, or papillary cancers, makes accurate diagnosis extremely difficult. With 9.6 million deaths from cancer in 2018, it is the second greatest cause of death worldwide. Cancer is defined by unchecked cell development that invades surrounding tissues and can spread to other bodily areas. People and health systems are severely strained financially, emotionally, and physically as a result of the worldwide cancer burden. While early detection and high-quality treatment have helped high-income countries improve management, many low and middle-income nations fail to provide timely and effective care, which has a negative impact on results. Given its various forms and the fact that its early stages are frequently asymptomatic, an accurate diagnosis of TC is essential. Even with improvements in diagnostic techniques, class imbalance and high-dimensional data continue to be problems in TC prediction.

The efficacy of treatment and the accuracy of forecasts are negatively impacted by the frequent shortcomings of traditional approaches in handling these complexities. This work focuses on improving TC diagnosis using sophisticated ensemble ML algorithms in order to overcome these issues. This approach seeks to enhance

[a]nagarjunareddynomula2@gmail.com, [b]maddulasamanvitha04@gmail.com, [c]pogirideepika2111@gmail.com, [d]sanju123sailaja@gmail.com, [e]nipun.poh@gmail.com, [f]shilpathoutireddy@gmail.com

DOI: 10.1201/9781003616399-54

treatment strategies and diagnostic accuracy by leveraging multiple ML models, PCA for dimensionality reduction, SMOTE for addressing class imbalance, and hyperparameter tuning. These developments could lead to improved TC treatment, improving patient outcomes and enabling a more efficient approach to this challenging illness. The ensuing parts provide an explanation of the same.

Research Objective

We aim to develop a system for accurate thyroid disease detection by addressing class imbalance and effective dimensionality reduction. It aims to maintain consistent class distribution during cross-validation, ensure systematic hyperparameter tuning to optimize model parameters, and enhance performance and generalizability. This approach is designed to significantly improve diagnostic accuracy and reliability, resulting in a more effective tool for better medical decision-making and patient outcomes.

Literature Review

Recent advancements in ML have significantly enhanced the diagnosis of TC, particularly with

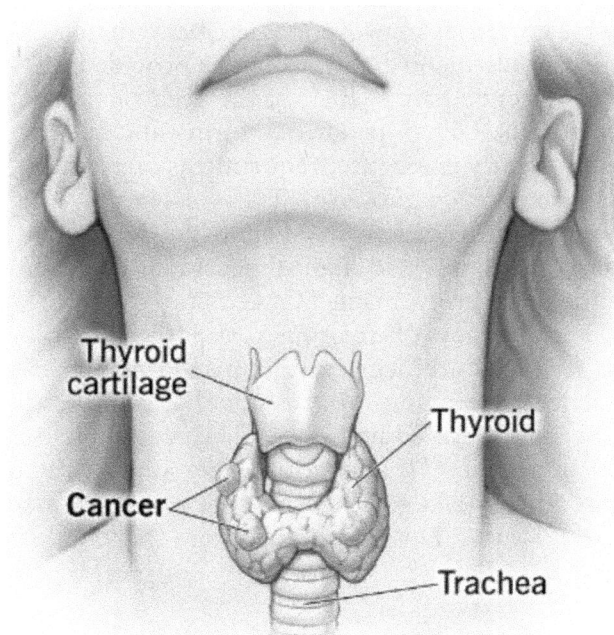

Figure 54.1 Thyroid cancer
Source: Author

the use of ensemble methods and advanced feature selection techniques. RF has been especially effective, achieving an accuracy of 89% in one study [3], and improving further when combined with extra tree classifiers [4]. Other research [5] has shown that EL, coupled with detailed clinical feature analysis, can achieve high accuracy, sensitivity, and specificity. ANN and SVM have also been widely studied. ANN outperformed other algorithms in thyroid risk prediction with an F1-score of 0.957 [6], while SVM achieved 96% accuracy in a MIL-based CAD system for thyroid nodule classification [7]. Furthermore, a study [8] found XGB to outperform k-Nearest Neighbors and DT, suggesting that future research should explore LSTM for real-time analysis.

Feature selection and dimensionality reduction are critical for improving model performance. Studies have demonstrated that chi-square-based selection [9] and filter-based methods [10] can lead to significant improvements in precision, recall, and F1-scores. Additionally, research [11] combining RF with LASSO identified key risk factors and achieved 99% accuracy in thyroid disease classification.

DL approaches have also been explored, with a study [12] integrating knowledge graphs and BLSTM models to leverage diverse medical data, enhancing diagnostic accuracy. Comparative studies have highlighted the strengths of specific algorithms, with MLP achieving 95.73% accuracy and an AUC of 94.23% in one case [13].

Other notable contributions include research on SVM, RF, and XGB for improving diagnosis [14], and using statistical moment-based features with RF to achieve high accuracy in HBP identification [15]. Another study [16] emphasized the importance of timely detection of TC, showing that RF, with an accuracy of 94.8%, can significantly enhance diagnostic outcomes from medical images.

Despite advancements, a gap remains in integrating advanced ensemble methods with feature engineering and real-time analysis in TC diagnosis. Current studies focus on individual models or simple ensembles, missing hybrid approaches. This research addresses this by introducing a novel ensemble framework combining RF, XGB, SVM, and LR with PCA and SMOTE. The framework optimizes performance through hyperparameter tuning and soft voting, enhancing predictive accuracy and efficiency in clinical settings.

Methodology

Dataset
This dataset comprises 1,232 thyroid nodules from 724 patients who had thyroidectomy surgery. It includes 16.23% nodules from male patients and 83.77% from female patients. Further details of this regard are explained in the Table 54.1.

System framework
The framework of this model (Figure 54.2) outlines an advanced methodology for detecting TC through sophisticated ML techniques. The process starts with the acquisition of a TC dataset, followed by a thorough data preprocessing phase. This includes data cleaning, addressing missing values, encoding categorical variables, and applying feature scaling. PCA is then utilized to retain 95% of the variance, while class imbalance is corrected using the SMOTE. A critical new feature, the FT4-to-FT3 ratio, is engineered due to its relevance in TC detection.

Subsequent to preprocessing, multiple ML algorithms namely RF, XGB, SVM, and LR are deployed on the processed data. Hyperparameter tuning is performed through grid search with cross-validation (CV) to refine model performance. An ensemble learning (EL) approach with soft voting is then employed to enhance prediction accuracy. The model's performance is assessed and the optimal model is chosen for making predictions. The process concludes with the successful detection of TC based on the input data, showcasing a robust and effective approach to leveraging ML diagnosis.

Data preprocessing
It plays a major role in preparing dataset for analysis and model building.

1) **Data cleaning:** The data preprocessing process begins with cleaning the dataset to ensure quality and consistency. This involves

Table 54.1 Description of features in dataset

S.no	Feature Name	Description
1	Age	Patient's age.
2	FT3	Result of the triiodothyronine hormone test.
3	FT4	Thyroxine hormone test result.
4	TSH	Thyroid-Stimulating hormone test result.
5	TPO	Test result for thyroid peroxidase Antibodies.
6	TGAb	Thyroglobulin antibodies test result.
7	Site	Nodule's location within the thyroid.
8	Echo pattern	Echogenicity of thyroid tissue.
9	Multifocality	Presence of multiple nodules in a single location.
10	Size	Measurement of nodule diameter.
11	Shape	Regularity of nodule's shape.
12	Margin	Clarity of the nodule's boundary.
13	Calcification	Presence of calcifications in the nodule.
14	Echo strength	Level of echogenicity in the nodule.
15	Blood flow	Blood flow status in the nodule.
16	Composition	Composition type of the nodule.
17	Multilateral	Presence of nodules in multiple locations.
18	Mal (Target)	Status of the nodule's malignancy.

Source: Nan Miles Xi, Lin Wangand Chuanjia Yang, "Improving The Diagnosis of Thyroid Cancer by Machine Learning and Clinical Data", Scientific Reports. Zenodo, Apr. 16, 2022. doi: 10.5281/zenodo.6465436.

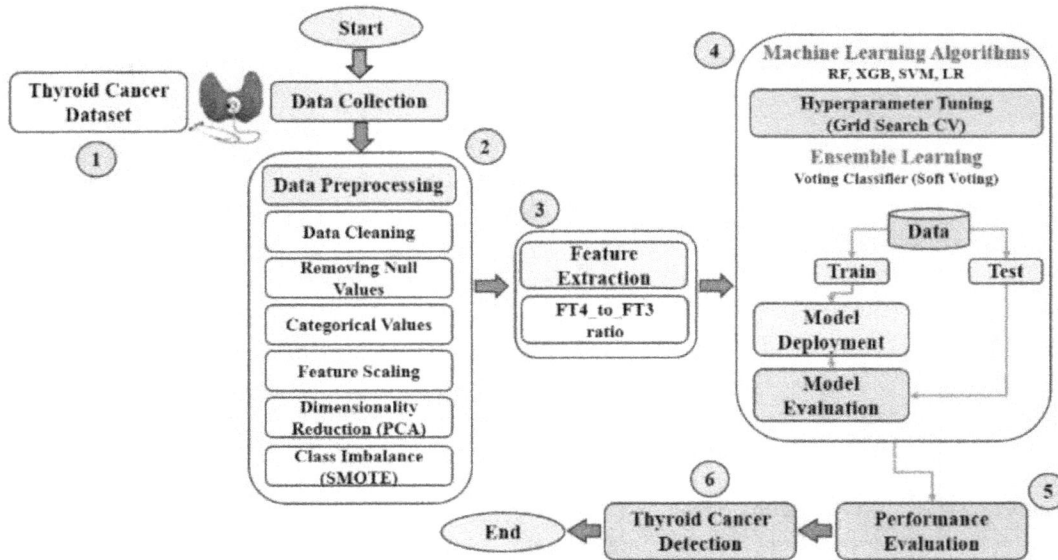

Figure 54.2 System framework
Source: Author

removing duplicate entries, which can introduce bias and distort analysis, and dropping irrelevant columns, such as unique identifiers that don't contribute to the model. After these steps, the dataset includes 19 variables, with patient ages ranging from 13 to 82 years.

2) **Handling categorical variables:** Categorical variables, such as gender and site, are modified into numerical format using one-hot encoding. This technique creates binary features for each category, allowing ML algorithms to process the data effectively. To avoid multicollinearity and manage the feature space, one category from each variable is dropped.

3) **Feature scaling:** Continuous variables like age and hormone levels are standardized to ensure all features contribute equally to the model. Standardization transforms features to a mean of zero and a standard deviation of one, which is vital for the effective performance of algorithms like SVM and LR. It ensures no single feature overpowers the learning process and boosts the effectiveness of gradient-based algorithms.

4) **Dimensionality reduction using PCA:** To address potential issues with high-dimensional data, PCA is applied. It reduces the number of features while preserving most of the data's variance, simplifying the model and reducing noise. In this case, it retained 95% of the variance, enhancing the model's interpretability and generalization. Its uniqueness lies in its ability to simplify complex datasets by reducing noise and redundant features, making the data easier to analyze and improving the performance of machine learning models.

5) **Addressing class imbalance using SMOTE:** It balances class distribution by generating synthetic samples for the minority class, enhancing the model's ability to learn from imbalanced data and accurately predicting minority cases in new data. It is particularly valuable in medical diagnosis, where detecting rare but critical conditions is essential.

Feature engineering
It included the creation of the FT4-to-FT3 ratio, a domain- specific feature designed to enhance model performance by leveraging expert knowledge. FT4 and FT3 are critical thyroid hormones, and their ratio can offer greater diagnostic insight than considering the hormone levels independently. This ratio can reveal underlying physiological conditions that might not be evident

when the hormones are analyzed separately, as certain thyroid disorders are characterized by imbalances in this ratio. By incorporating the FT4-to-FT3 ratio as a feature, the model is better equipped to understand thyroid function, potentially improving its ability to detect and classify abnormalities, while also reducing data dimensionality.

Proposed ensemble methodology

Random forest: It is an EL technique that builds multiple DTs and aggregates their predictions to improve accuracy and reduce overfitting. Each tree is trained on a randomly chosen subset of data and features, it introduces diversity among the trees, enhancing robustness. Key parameters include the number of trees, tree depth, and the minimum samples required for node splitting. RF effectively handles both categorical and numerical features, making it a strong choice for structured data problems, particularly in medical diagnosis.

Feature importance can be calculated using:

$$RF = \frac{1}{N_{trees}} \sum_{t=1}^{N_{trees}} \Delta i_t \qquad (1)$$

where 'Δi_t' represents the decrease in impurity for feature 't' across all trees in the forest.

XGBoost: It is an efficient gradient boosting algorithm that excels at handling complex patterns, especially in imbalanced and sparse datasets. It constructs an additive model by sequentially training trees, where each tree corrects the errors of the previous one. Critical parameters encompass the number of trees, learning rate, and the depth of each tree, which help balance model complexity and prevent overfitting. XGB is highly accurate and well-suited for tasks requiring detailed pattern recognition, such as medical data analysis.

Logistic regression: It's a linear model for binary classification that predicts the probability of an outcome using given predictor variables. It is valued for its simplicity and interpretability, making it useful for understanding relationships between features and outcomes. The model's performance is influenced by regularization strength, which regulates the trade-off between fitting the training data and ensuring model simplicity. Despite being a baseline model, it often performs

well in cases where there is a linear relationship between the features and the target outcome. It is calculated using sigmoid function.

$$P(z = 1|Y) = \frac{1}{1 + \exp\left(-(a_0 + \sum_{i=1}^{n} a_i y_i)\right)} \qquad (2)$$

where a_0 is the intercept and a_i are the coefficients associated with the predictor variables y_i.

Support vector machine with RBF kernel: It is a powerful classifier for non-linear decision boundaries. It projects input features into a higher-dimensional space, facilitating the model's ability to uncover complex data relationships. Flexibility of the decision boundary is controlled by the penalty parameter and the kernel coefficient. It is particularly effective in high-dimensional spaces and for classification tasks with overlapping classes, making it suitable for distinguishing complex patterns in medical data. It is represented by decision function.

$$f(a) = \text{sign}\left(\sum_{i=1}^{n} \alpha_i z_i K(a_i, a) + b\right) \qquad (3)$$

where $K(a_i, a) = \exp(-\gamma|a_i - a|^2)$ is the RBF kernel function, α_i are the Lagrange multipliers, z_i are the class labels, and b is the bias term.

Hyperparameter tuning

GridSearchCV: Hyperparameters for each model are optimized using GridSearchCV (GSCV), a method that systematically searches through a predefined range of hyperparameters to find the combination that yields the best performance on the training data. GSCV works by exhaustively evaluating all possible combinations of hyperparameters, running each combination through a model training process to determine which set provides the highest accuracy or other desired metrics.

StratifiedKFold: To ensure robust evaluation, this process is combined with CV, specifically employing StratifiedKFold (SKF). CV entails dividing the dataset into multiple folds, where the model is trained on some folds and evaluated on others, rotating through all possible fold combinations. SKF is a variation of this technique that maintains the balance of class distributions within each fold, ensuring that each subset is representative of the overall data, especially in cases of imbalanced datasets.

Combination of GSCV and SKF: By using SKF in conjunction with GSCV, the model undergoes thorough and fair evaluation across different data splits, mitigating overfitting risks and amplifying the model's performance on unseen data. This approach is particularly valuable in tasks like medical diagnosis, where precision and reliability are paramount.

Ensemble learning

We used an ensemble approach in this research by combining four ML models: RF, XGB, SVM with an RBF kernel, and LR. Each model has strengths and limitations that the ensemble aims to balance. RF is robust for high-dimensional data but can be biased and less interpretable. XGB excels with structured data but is prone to overfitting and complexity in tuning. SVM effectively finds non-linear boundaries but is computationally intensive and sensitive to feature scaling. LR is simple and interpretable but limited to linear relationships. The ensemble leverages the advantages of various models while minimizing their individual weaknesses, resulting in a more balanced and effective predictive model.

Voting classifier: It is an EL technique integrating the predictions of various ML models elevating overall accuracy and robustness. It leverages the strengths of diverse models by combining their outputs. The voting classifier (VC) uses a Soft Voting mechanism. In soft voting, each model predicts class probabilities, and the final decision is based on the average of these probabilities. This method considers the confidence levels of each model, leading to more nuanced and accurate predictions. By averaging the predicted probabilities, soft voting effectively balances the strengths and weaknesses of individual models, reduces overfitting, and improves generalization, making it a powerful approach for creating robust predictive systems.

Model training and testing

Using an 80:20 split ratio and stratification to preserve class distribution, the dataset was allocated into training set for model development, and the testing set to evaluate the model's performance, ensuring an unbiased measure of its predictive accuracy.

Performance analysis

We use the following metrics to evaluate model performance, each providing distinct insights into the model's reliability and diagnostic capability. It delineates true negatives (TrNe), false negative (FaNe), and false positive (FaPo), true positives (TrPo).

1) **Accuracy (Acc):** It provides a general measure of model performance but can be deceptive in cases where datasets are imbalanced, where some classes are more prevalent than others.

$$\text{Acc} = \frac{\text{TrPo} + \text{TrNe}}{\text{TrPo} + \text{TrNe} + \text{FaPo} + \text{FaNe}} \quad (4)$$

2) **Precision (Pre):** It's significant when the cost of FaPo is substantial, as it assesses how many predicted +ve cases are TrPo.

$$\text{Pre} = \frac{\text{TrPo}}{\text{TrPo} + \text{FaPo}} \quad (5)$$

3) **Recall (Re):** When the cost of FaNe is elevated, it becomes crucial as it reflects the model's capability in identifying all +ve cases.

$$\text{Re} = \frac{\text{TrPo}}{\text{TrPo} + \text{FaNe}} \quad (6)$$

4) **F1-Score (F1):** It is valuable when you need to harmonize Pre and Re, especially in the case of imbalanced datasets, providing a comprehensive measure of model performance than accuracy alone.

$$\text{F1} = 2 \times \frac{\text{Pre} \times \text{Re}}{\text{Pre} + \text{Re}} \quad (7)$$

These metrics are used to evaluate the effectiveness of models in the ensemble and guide adjustments to improve their predictive model evaluation.

Results

The performance of individual ML models and the ensemble approach was evaluated as shown in Figure 54.3. RF model recorded an acc of 80.69% and an F1 of 80.08%, indicating strong effectiveness in identifying positive cases of TC. Key predictors identified by RF are shown in Figure 54.4. XGB performed robustly, with an acc of 79.67% and an F1 of 79.59%, managing the trade-off between precision and recall effectively (shown in Figure 54.5). The SVM with RBF kernel had an acc of 78.05% and an F1 of 77.59%, maintaining solid precision but slightly lower recall, as illustrated in Figure 54.6. LR demonstrated an acc of 77.64% and an F1 of 77.18%, struggling with complex patterns (as shown in Figure 54.7). The DT model attained the least, with an acc of 73.78% and an F1 of 73.18%, reflecting overfitting.

The ensemble model, combining RF, XGB, SVM, and LR through a VC, achieved the highest performance, recording an accuracy, precision, recall, F1 of 81.1%, 83.12%, 78.05%, and 80.5% respectively. These results underscore the impact of EL, as the combined strengths of the individual models led to improved overall performance, as shown in Figure 54.8. Additionally, Figure 54.9 provides a detailed analysis of the differences between the predicted outcomes of the individual models and the ensemble, offering further insights into the effectiveness of combining models.

Discussion

The results reveal the varied strengths and limitations of different ML models for TC classification.

RF exhibited high precision and balanced performance, effectively managing complex data interactions, while XGB demonstrated similar robustness, balancing precision and recall effectively.

SVM with RBF kernel was effective but showed slightly lower recall, indicating room for improvement through further tuning or complex kernels. LR, despite its lower performance, provides a useful baseline and highlights the challenges linear models face with non-linear data. DT model performed the weakest, likely due to overfitting, suggesting that techniques like pruning or ensemble methods could improve performance. The ensemble model, combining RF, XGB, SVM, and LR via a VC, achieved the highest accuracy and precision. This model leverages the strengths of individual models, resulting in superior overall performance. Despite its slightly lower recall, the ensemble approach effectively mitigates the limitations of individual models.

Future research should focus on optimizing the individual models within the ensemble and exploring advanced techniques. Enhancing feature engineering and incorporating diverse datasets could further improve accuracy and robustness. Evaluating models in clinical settings and integrating expert feedback will also be crucial for practical applications.

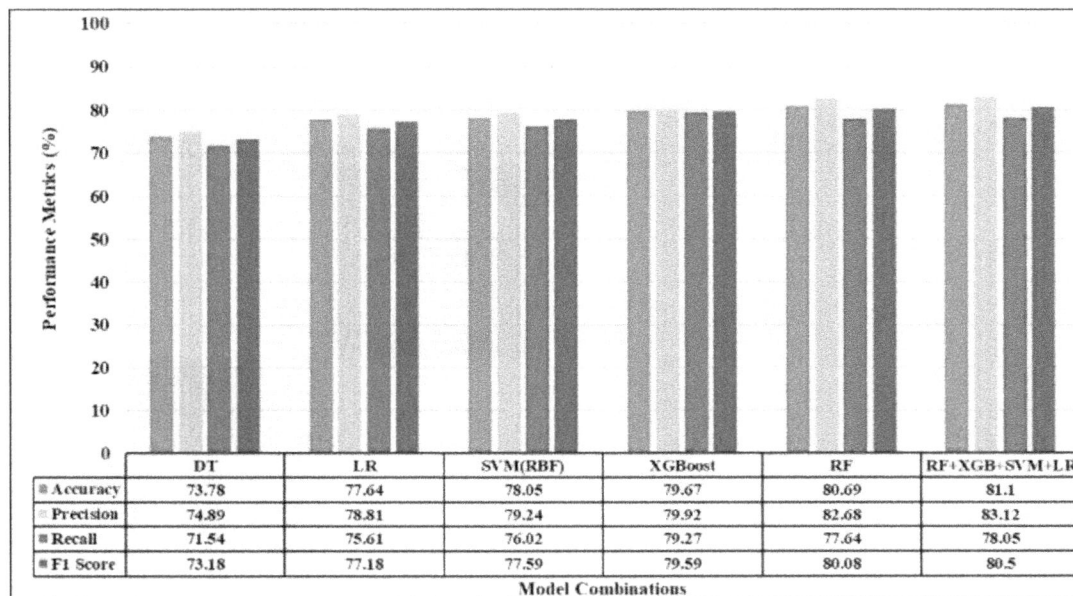

	DT	LR	SVM(RBF)	XGBoost	RF	RF+XGB+SVM+LR
Accuracy	73.78	77.64	78.05	79.67	80.69	81.1
Precision	74.89	78.81	79.92	79.92	82.68	83.12
Recall	71.54	75.61	76.02	79.27	77.64	78.05
F1 Score	73.18	77.18	77.59	79.59	80.08	80.5

Figure 54.3 Existing and proposed model's performance comparison graph
Source: Author

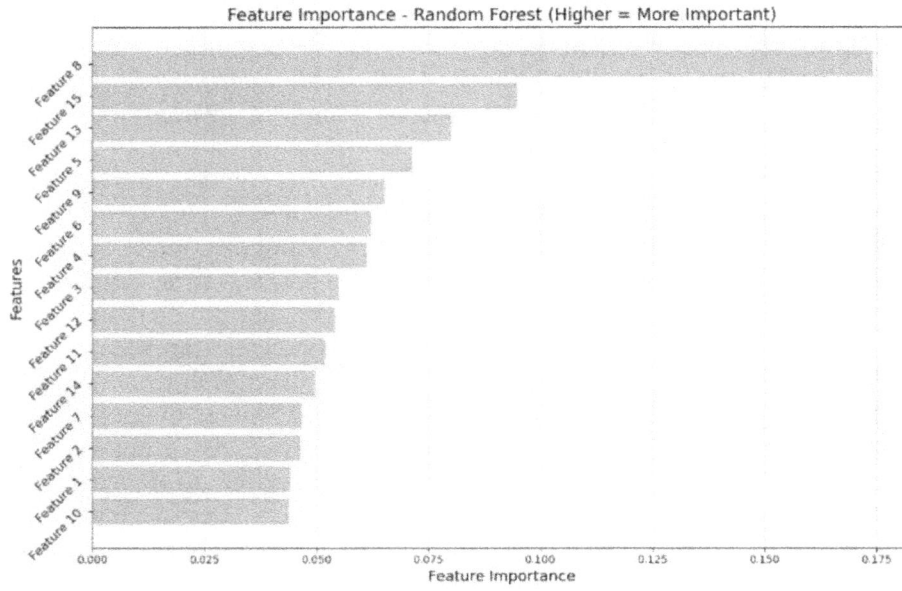

Figure 54.4 Random forest feature importance
Source: Author

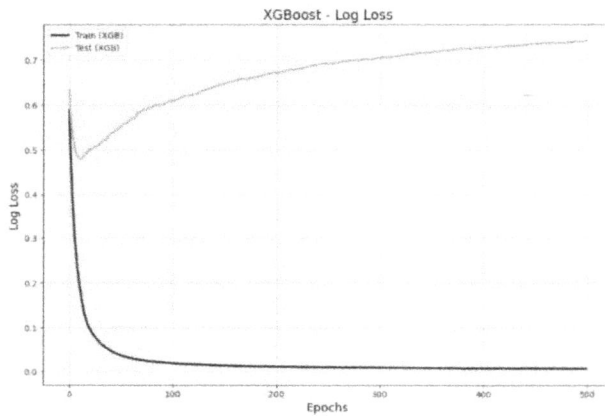

Figure 54.5 XGBoost training and loss curve
Source: Author

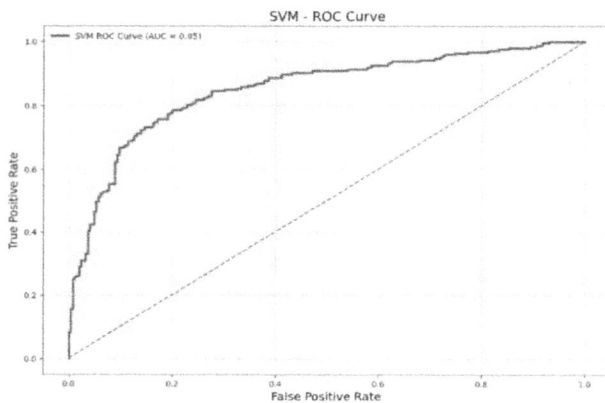

Figure 54.7 Logistic regression ROC
Source: Author

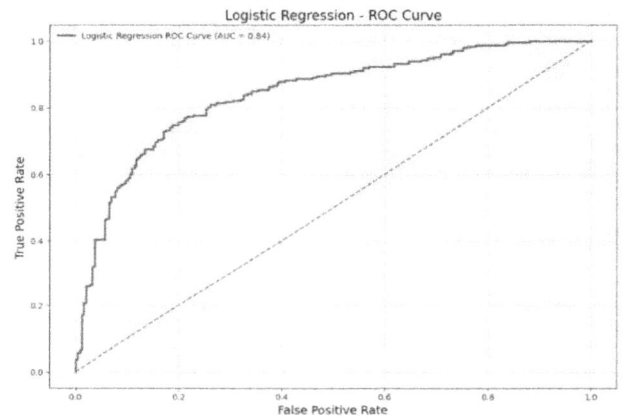

Figure 54.6 Support vector machine ROC
Source: Author

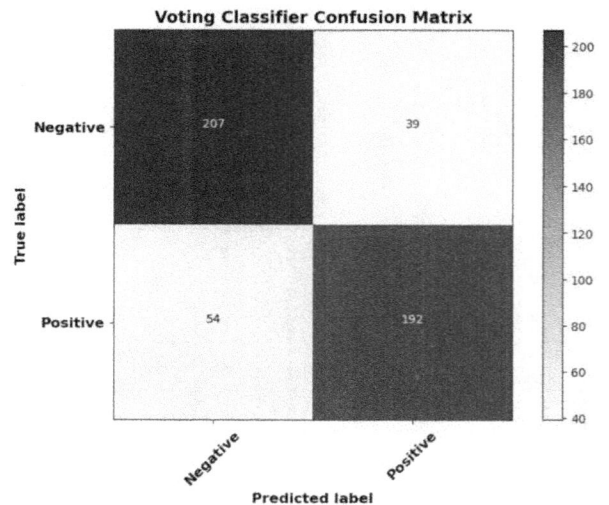

Figure 54.8 Voting classifier confusion matrix
Source: Author

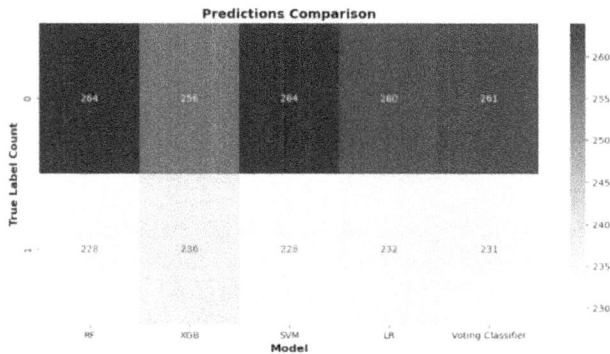

Figure 54.9 Prediction comparison matrix
Source: Author

In summary, the ensemble approach demonstrates significant improvements over individual models and holds promise for advancing medical diagnostics through enhanced accuracy and reliability.

Conclusion

This paper analyzed the efficacy of various ML models for thyroid cancer (TC) classification, including RF, XGB, SVM with RBF kernel, LR, and DT. The study utilized rigorous data preprocessing, feature engineering, SMOTE for addressing class imbalance, and PCA for dimensionality reduction, evaluating models based on evaluation metrics.

Our findings indicate that RF and XGB provided the highest performance, demonstrating strong accuracy and balanced metrics. The VC, integrating these models with SVM and LR, achieved the best overall results, underscoring the power of EL in enhancing classification accuracy.

Despite these advancements, the study faced limitations such as reliance on a single dataset, which may impact generalizability, and the increased complexity and computational cost introduced by the VC. Additionally, expanding the feature set could further improve model performance.

Future work should aim to diversify the dataset for better generalizability, explore advanced techniques like DL, and refine feature extraction methods. Further optimization of the ensemble model is also necessary to maintain a balance between performance and computational efficiency. This study provides valuable insights into to the healthcare domain by demonstrating the effectiveness of EL in improving diagnostic accuracy for thyroid disease. The success of the VC highlights its potential as a valuable tool for developing reliable diagnostic systems, setting the stage for future advancements in medical diagnostics and enhanced patient outcomes. In conclusion, this study underscores the potential of combining ML models to improve thyroid disease classification, addresses current limitations, and provides a foundation for future research aimed at advancing diagnostic technologies in medicine.

References

[1] Xi, N. M., Wang, L., and Yang, C. (2022). Author correction: improving the diagnosis of thyroid cancer by machine learning and clinical data. *Scientific Reports*, 12(1), 13252. doi: 10.1038/s41598-022-17659-1.

[2] Chaganti, R., Rustam, F., De La Torre Díez, I., Mazón, J. L. V., Rodríguez, C. L., and Ashraf, I. (2022). Thyroid disease prediction using selective features and machine learning techniques. *Cancers*, 14(16), 3914. doi: 10.3390/cancers14163914.

[3] Alshayeji, M. H. (2023). Early thyroid risk prediction by data mining and ensemble classifiers. *Machine Learning and Knowledge Extraction*, 5(3), 1195–1213. doi: 10.3390/make5030061.

[4] Islam, S. S., Haque, M. S., Miah, M. S. U., Sarwar, T. B., and Nugraha, R. (2022). Application of machine learning algorithms to predict the thyroid disease risk: an experimental comparative study. *PeerJ Computer Science*, 8, e898. doi: 10.7717/peerj-cs.898.

[5] Vadhiraj, V. V., Simpkin, A., O'Connell, J., Singh Ospina, N., Maraka, S., and O'Keeffe, D. T. (2021). Ultrasound image classification of thyroid nodules using machine learning techniques. *Medicina*, 57(6), 527. doi: 10.3390/medicina57060527.

[6] Sankar, S., Potti, A., Chandrika, G. N., and Ramasubbareddy, S. (2022). Thyroid disease prediction using XGBoost algorithms. *Journal of Micromechanics and Microengineering*, 18(3), 1–18. doi: 10.13052/jmm1550-4646.18322.

[7] Setiawan, K. E. (2024). Predicting recurrence in differentiated thyroid cancer: a comparative analysis of various machine learning models including ensemble methods with chi-squared feature selection. *Communications in Mathematical Biology and Neuroscience*. doi: 10.28919/cmbn/8506.

[8] Obaido, G., Achilonu, O., Ogbuokiri, B., Amadi, C. S., Habeebullahi, L., Ohalloran, T., et al. (2024). An improved framework for detecting thyroid disease using filter-based feature selection and stacking ensemble. *IEEE Access*, 12, 89098–89112. doi: 10.1109/ACCESS.2024.3418974.

[9] Sultana, A., and Islam, R. (2023). Machine learning framework with feature selection approaches for thyroid disease classification and associated risk factors identification. *Journal of Electrical Systems and Information Technology*, 10(1), 32. doi: 10.1186/s43067-023-00101-5.

[10] Chai, X. (2020). Diagnosis method of thyroid disease combining knowledge graph and deep learning. *IEEE Access*, 8, 149787–149795. doi: 10.1109/ACCESS.2020.3016676.

[11] Pal, M., Parija, S., and Panda, G. (2022). Enhanced prediction of thyroid disease using machine learning method. In 2022 IEEE VLSI Device Circuit and System (VLSI DCS), Kolkata, India: IEEE, (pp. 199–204). doi: 10.1109/VLSIDCS53788.2022.9811472.

[12] Kumari, P., Kaur, B., Rakhra, M., Deka, A., Byeon, H., Asenso, E., et al. (2024). Explainable artificial intelligence and machine learning algorithms for classification of thyroid disease. *Discover Applied Sciences*, 6(7), 360. doi: 10.1007/s42452-024-06068- w.

[13] Butt, A. H., Alkhalifah, T., Alturise, F., and Khan, Y. D. (2023). Ensemble learning for hormone binding protein prediction: a promising approach for early diagnosis of thyroid hormone disorders in serum. *Diagnostics*, 13(11), 1940. doi: 10.3390/diagnostics13111940.

[14] Alyas, T., Hamid, M., Alissa, K., Faiz, T., Tabassum, N., and Ahmad, A. (2022). [Retracted] empirical method for thyroid disease classification using a machine learning approach. *BioMed Research International*, 2022(1), 9809932. doi: 10.1155/2022/9809932.

[15] Shulhai, A. M., Rotondo, R., Petraroli, M., Patianna, V., Predieri, B., Iughetti, L., et al. (2024). The role of nutrition on thyroid function. *Nutrients*, 16(15), 2496. doi: 10.3390/nu16152496.

[16] Hollywood, J. B., Hutchinson, D., Feehery-Alpuerto, N., Whitfield, M., Davis, K., and Johnson, L. M. (2023). The effects of the paleo diet on autoimmune thyroid disease: a mixed methods review. *Journal of the American Nutrition Association*, 42(8), 727–736. doi: 10.1080/27697061.2022.2159570.

55 Water filter replacement alarm

Vandana, Ch[1,a], Ramesh Kumar Reddy, C.[1,b], Y. Bhavitha[2,c], Ch. Vishwa Teja[2,d], Ch. Anvitha Lakshmi[2,e] and Ch. Tejasree[2,f]

[1]Assistant Professor, Dept. of ECE, B V Raju Institute of Technology, Narsapur, Telangana, India

[2]Student, Dept. of ECE, B V Raju Institute of Technology, Narsapur, Telangana, India

Abstract

Water is a necessity for human survival. These days, the water we drink contains dangerous pollutants. According to WHO, at least 1.7 billion people use drinking water sources that are contaminated. Thus, contaminants are typically eliminated using water filters. The filter loses some of its effectiveness with time and can no longer produce as much safe and clean water. The replacement alarm serves to notify us when the filter cartridge needs to be changed to ensure that the filter is changed without delay and that a steady supply of clean drinking water is available. Usually, a flow sensor or a timer powers it. The total on-chip power consumed for the proposed design is 1.743 watts. The water filter replacement alarm system also keeps track of the filter's condition by integrating sensor technologies with water filtration systems. To decide when a filter needs to be replaced, the alarm system intelligently monitors critical characteristics like flow rate, pressure, and filter life span. The alarm system can identify impending filter failure and decreasing filtering effectiveness by continuously monitoring these variables. The water filtration device itself may have a digital display, an audio buzzer, or a light indicator as the alerts.

Keywords: Alarm, cartridge, contaminants, filter, power, sensors

Introduction

Presenting the innovative "water filter replacement alarm," whose primary objective is to safeguard public health by ensuring that water filters are changed on schedule and by creating a trustworthy and reasonably priced alert system. According to Rolfes [1], a variety of indicators have been used in the past to try and offer an effective means of keeping track of and signaling when a water filter is getting close to or beyond its useful life and needs to be changed. It is easy to install and release the circuit substrate because of its clever design. Additionally, it contains display LEDs that show when the filter should be changed, significantly enhancing the water's purification capacity.

However, this creative solution seamlessly incorporates other researchers' theories. For instance, Hong et al. [2], came up with the idea of a water flow sensor that measures the water's flow pressure.

Another is an up counter to improve user convenience and accuracy in filter replacement is an initial idea to assess filter cartridge quality [1,3–5].

Users are notified by a buzzer about possible filter inefficiencies when predefined thresholds are surpassed. While Danh et al., [6] presented the design and implementation of the i-water system, a prototype Internet of Things (IoT)-based home water purifier that enables predictive maintenance through real-time monitoring and cloud-based data processing, users also have the option to view the alarm status and filter replacement necessity.

Through user participation, it is simple to acknowledge notifications and reset counters, which encourages a proactive approach to maintenance. Encouraging users to maintain optimal filter usage, this all-inclusive strategy combines time-based replacement knowledge with real-time water assessment. It is especially helpful to vulnerable groups like children, the elderly, and people with compromised immune systems. The system meets the vital demand for clean and safe drinking water.

[a]vandana.ch@bvri.ac.in, [b]rameshkumarreddy.c@bvri.ac.in, [c]22215a0402@bvri.ac.in, [d]21211a0445@bvri.ac.in, [e]21211a0449@bvri.ac.in, [f]21211a0458@bvri.ac.in

DOI: 10.1201/9781003616399-55

Apart from its health advantages, the water filter replacement alarm provides helpful features like automatic tracking and timely filter changes to consumers with busy schedules. This keeps the water's quality intact and helps save money on future repairs. This solution aims to close the existing gap in the monitoring of water filter efficacy by providing a simple-to-use smart system. In addition to resolving worries about water quality and system outages, this guarantees that users are notified precisely when a new filter must be installed.

By integrating advanced sensors, a clever counter, user-friendly alarms, and a display system, the water filter replacement alarm essentially transforms water purification technology and offers a comprehensive solution for preserving clean and safe drinking water.

Proposed Design

The suggested "water filter replacement alarm system" has a water flow sensor, a pH sensor, and an up counter to guarantee effective use of water filters. The filter cartridge lifespan specified by the manufacturer is recorded, and the counter is reset upon first installation. The system enters a condition of active monitoring after this predetermined amount of time. In active monitoring, the pH sensor continuously measures the water's purity, while the water flow sensor evaluates flow conditions. As few efforts have been seen in the direction of Cho Moon-Hyun to build an indicator to warn when filter replacement is essential, a buzzer is activated if specified thresholds are exceeded to alert users of potential filter inefficiencies. The alarm's state and whether the filter

needs to be changed can optionally be shown. By actively participating, users can respond to alarms and reset the counter. By integrating real-time water assessment with time-based replacement awareness, this approach improves user ease and guarantees the accuracy of filter replacements. The method encourages timely maintenance and a proactive approach to filter replacement by combining usage patterns and assessments of the water's condition as shown in Figure 55.1.

The block diagram provided outlines the "water filter replacement alarm system", detailing its primary components and their interactions. The primary objective of the system is to monitor the water filter's condition and display a signal when replacement is deemed necessary. The diagram comprises input components, a processing block, and an output component. In the input phase, three crucial sensors are highlighted: a water flow sensor, a pH sensor for acidity measurement, and a counter. These sensors collectively furnish the system with essential data for analysis and decision-making. By measuring the speed at which water flows through the filter, the water flow sensor provides information about how often the filter is used. Concurrently, the pH sensor measures the acidity of the water, which helps determine how well the filter maintains water quality. The manufacturer's specified filter lifespan is monitored by the counter. These sensors provide data to the processing unit, which houses a microcontroller or other comparable control device. It then analyses the information to see if the filter needs to be changed. The assessment procedure entails comparing the volume of filtered water, pH levels, and flow rate to preset threshold values that indicate a failing filter.

After the evaluation phase is over, the system moves on to the output phase. The processing unit will sound an alert if, after analyzing the input data, it concludes that the filter needs to be replaced. A visual signal, a sound, or even a message sent to a monitoring system could be used as this alarm. The efficacy of the system in preserving water quality is increased by this all-encompassing approach, which guarantees a prompt reaction to filter degradation.

Step 1: First, define a module that takes in several input signals: ph_value (3-bit value indicating water pH), water_flow_rate (3-bit value

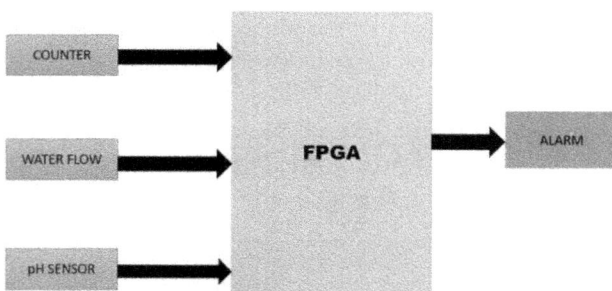

Figure 55.1 Block diagram of proposed system
Source: Author

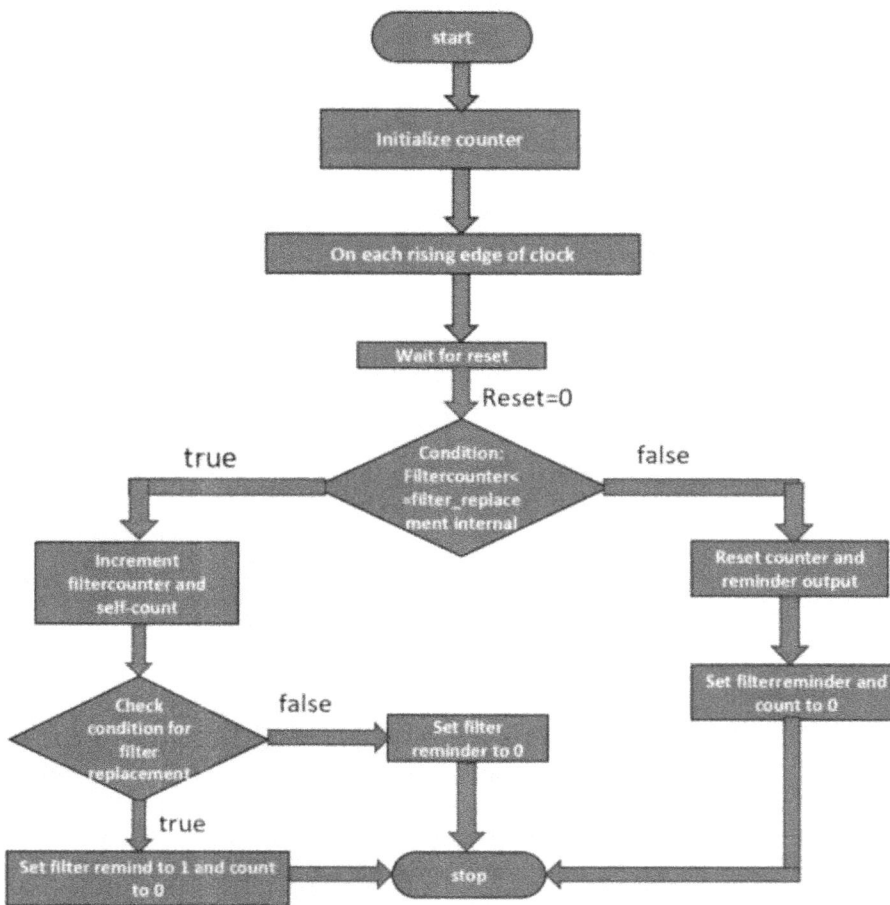

Figure 55.2 Workflow of the proposed system
Source: Author

representing water flow rate in litres per minute), filter_replacement_interval (9-bit value representing the number of clock cycles between replacements), and clk (clock).

Step 2: Add a one-bit signal to the filter_reminder module. This signal is intended to act as a reminder flag.

Step 3: Add a zero-initialized register called filter_counter inside the module. This register bears accountability for keeping track of the number of clock cycles since the last reminder to alter the filter.

Step 4: Apply a reset condition check on the positive clock edge. Reset the filter counter and the filter reminder if a reset is detected. Check to see if filter_counter is less than filter_replacement_interval if no reset is found.

Step 5: Increase the counter by one if it is, in fact, smaller than the given interval. Once you have reached the filter_replacement_interval setting, check to see if the water pH is below 7 (high pH) or if the water flow is less than 5 liters per minute (low water flow).

Step 6: Set the filter_reminder flag to 1 to indicate that it's time to modify the filter if any of these circumstances are satisfied. If none of these apply, reset the counter to zero and the reminder flag indicates that there is no need to change the filter right away. By using this technique, it is ensured that the filter_reminder flag appropriately indicates when it is best to modify filters depending on current circumstances.

Results

Simulation steps:

1. Initialization: At the commencement of the simulation, the `filter_counter` is initialized to `0` within the initial block.
2. Reset phase: The simulation initiates with the `reset` signal asserted `1`. During this period, both the `filter_counter` and `filter_reminder` are reset to `0`.
3. Clock cycle initiation: Following a specified number of clock cycles, let's assume 3, the `reset` signal de-asserts `0`. Subsequently, the `filter_counter` commences incrementing from `0`, and the `count` output reflects this incrementing value.
4. Incrementing counter: As the simulation progresses, the `filter_counter` incrementally advances with each clock cycle.
5. Replacement condition check: Upon reaching a `filter_replacement_interval` value, for instance, 17, the system evaluates conditions for filter replacement.
6. Filter replacement decision: If either the `ph_value` is below 7 or the `water_flow_rate` is less than 5, the `filter_reminder` output is set to `1`, signaling that it is time to replace the filter.
7. No replacement needed: In the absence of conditions warranting filter replacement, the `filter_reminder` remains at `0`.

8. Counter reset: Following the completion of the replacement interval and potentially triggering the filter reminder, the `filter_counter` is reset to `0`.
9. Continuation of simulation: The simulation persists, and the cyclic process repeats, with the `filter_counter` continually incrementing and the system assessing the need for filter replacement based on real-time conditions. This iterative approach ensures the dynamic responsiveness of the system to changing parameters, optimizing the timing of filter replacement.

Synthesis reports

Examining the combined schematic diagram produced by Vivado [7, 8] for the "water filter reminder" module, one can see a clear architectural structure consisting primarily of flip-flops for state storage, adders for clock cycle counting, and combinational logic units for conditional assessments. Well-placed flip-flops allow the state of the filter counter to be persistently stored. To ensure precise timekeeping, adders, which act as the arithmetic foundation, increase the filter counter at each clock cycle. The conditional logic, implemented using multiplexers and logic gates, carries out the coordination of the filter replacement and reminder trigger decision-making procedures, depending upon the inputs of pH value and water flow rate. The carefully planned connections show off an ordered and optimized architecture and demonstrate the signal flow

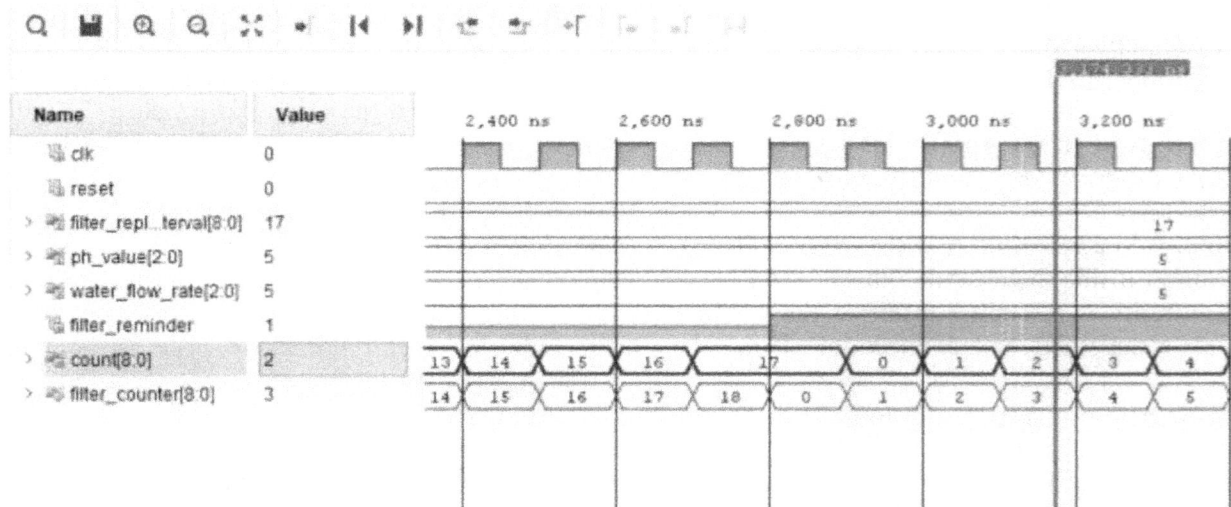

Figure 55.3 Simulated waveform
Source: Author

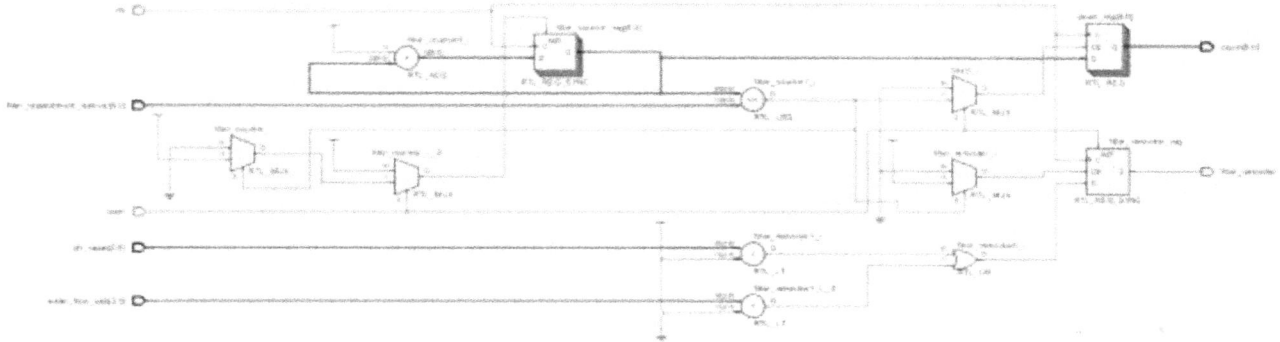

Figure 55.4 Schematic diagram
Source: Author

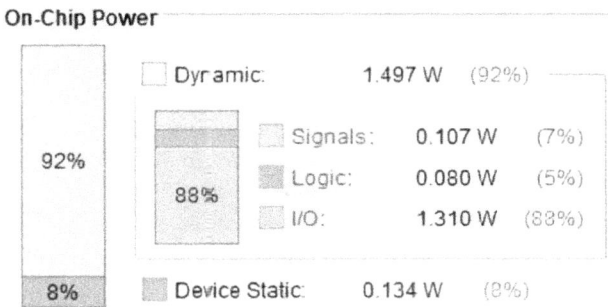

Figure 55.5 Power report
Source: Author

between various electronic parts. This clarifies the efficient synchronization of calculations and comparisons necessary for the module's operation. In technical terms, the schematic diagram effectively illustrates the hierarchical integration

of digital components and clarifies the precise coordination of input signal processing and the production of matching output signals, which guarantees the system's timely and accurate water filter replacement reminders.

The proposed design consumes 1.743 watts of on-chip power, with this total power primarily split into dynamic power [9] (92%) and static power [10] (8%). Dynamic power is significant during chip activity, involving processes like internal node charging, logic state transitions, and overall transistor switching. On the other hand, static power, also known as leakage power, persists at 8% even when the chip is idle, influenced by factors like technology node, temperature, and supply voltage. The effective reduction of power leakage in this project highlights a thoughtful approach, resulting in the achievement of the 1.743 watts total power consumption.

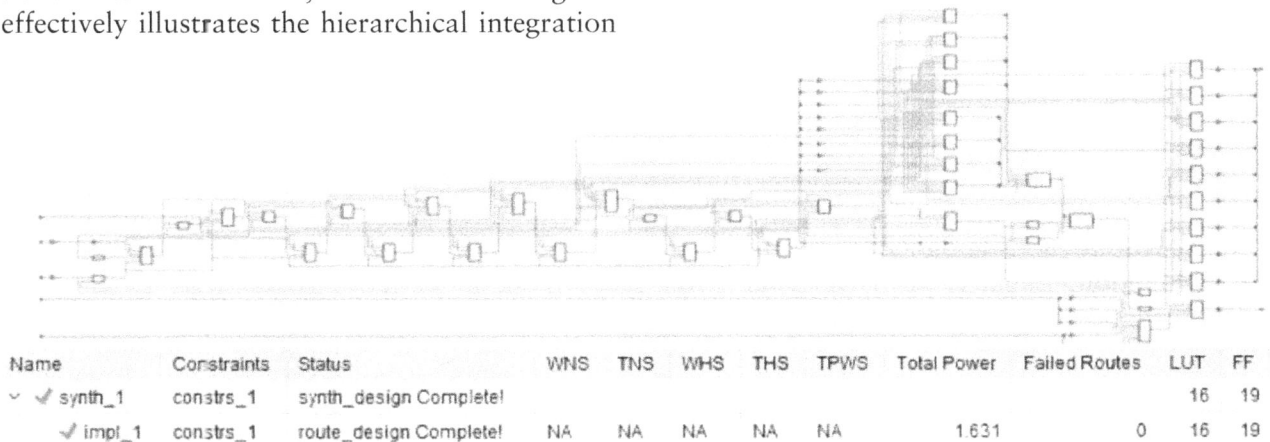

Name	Constraints	Status	WNS	TNS	WHS	THS	TPWS	Total Power	Failed Routes	LUT	FF
synth_1	constrs_1	synth_design Complete!								16	19
impl_1	constrs_1	route_design Complete!	NA	NA	NA	NA	NA	1.631	0	16	19

Figure 55.6 Synthesis report
Source: Author

The synthesis and implementation phases have been completed, culminating in notable results for the project. The total power consumption has been efficiently managed, registering at a commendable 1.743 watts. Notably, the routing process has been executed flawlessly, with no failed routes detected. The utilization of resources has been optimized, with the project making effective use of 16 look-up tables [11] and 19 flip-flops, demonstrating a streamlined and efficient design.

Conclusion and Future Scope

The water filter replacement alarm system is vital for addressing twenty-first-century water challenges, offering benefits in societal, economic, environmental, and health aspects. Additionally integrating a total dissolved solids [12] can enhance efficiency by reducing wastewater. The system's adaptability to evolving water standards and user expectations is evident through collaborative efforts and knowledge sharing. Artificial intelligence and machine learning [13] integration have the potential for refining predictive capabilities and customizing replacement schedules. Beyond traditional alarms, Internet of Things innovations provide real-time insights, facilitating informed decision-making and contributing to broader water conservation efforts.

Acknowledgement

We would like to extend our sincere gratitude to everyone who helped us out and provided inspiration and direction that helped us finish the project successfully. Special thanks to Mr. U. Gnaneshwara Chary, the Centre for VLSI Design lab coordinator, and Dr. K. Madhava Rao, Assistant Professor in the Dept. of ECE, for their valuable suggestions and motivation throughout the project. We would like to express our gratitude to all of the instructors, lab personnel, and the B. V. Raju Institute of Technology's Electronics and Communication Engineering Department for their direct and indirect assistance in completing the project.

References

[1] Rolfes, P. J. (2001). Water filter replacement indicator. U.S. Patent No. 6,306,290. 23 Oct. 2001.

[2] Hong, M., Kim, K., and Hwang, Y. (2022). Arduino and IoT-based direct filter observation method monitoring the color change of water filter for safe drinking water. *Journal of Water Process Engineering*, 49, 103158.

[3] Jayanthi, G., Mathumitha, N., Swathy, S., and Aaradhika, S. (2020). Smart monitoring and control of water filtration system using IOT. In 2020 International Conference on Power, Energy, Control and Transmission Systems (ICPECTS). IEEE.

[4] Srivastava, S., Vaddadi, S., and Sadistap, S. (2018). Smartphone-based system for water quality analysis. *Applied Water Science*, 8(5), 130.

[5] Cho, M.-H. (1997). Water purifier having a filter replacement indicator including a circuit board and lamps. U.S. Patent No. 5,679,243. 21 Oct. 1997.

[6] Danh, L. V. Q., Dung, D. V. M., and Khanh, N. D. (2020). Design and Implementation of an IoT-based water purifier system enabling predictive maintenance. In Frontiers in Intelligent Computing: Theory and Applications: Proceedings of the 7th International Conference on FICTA (2018), (Vol. 1). Springer Singapore.

[7] Churiwala, S., and Hyderabad, I. (2017). Designing with Xilinx® FPGAs. In Circuits and Systems. Springer.

[8] Feist, T. (2012). Vivado design suite. *White Paper*, 5(30), 24.

[9] Shang, L., Kaviani, A. S., and Bathala, K. (2002). Dynamic power consumption in Virtex™-II FPGA family. In Proceedings of the 2002 ACM/SIGDA Tenth International Symposium on Field-Programmable Gate Arrays.

[10] Yuan, S-Y., Chen, K. H., Jou, J. Y., and Kuo, S. Y. (1998). Static power analysis for power-driven synthesis. *IEE Proceedings-Computers and Digital Techniques*, 145(2), 89–95.

[11] Francis (1992). A tutorial on logic synthesis for lookup-table based FPGAs. In 1992 IEEE/ACM International Conference on Computer-Aided Design. IEEE.

[12] Setyobudi, R. (2023). Utilization of tds sensors for water quality monitoring and water filtering of carp pools using IoT. *EUREKA: Physics and Engineering*, 6, 69–77.

[13] Hrusto, A., Runeson, P., Engström, E., and Ohlsson, M. C. (2024). Advancing software monitoring: an industry survey on ML-driven alert management strategies. In 50th Euromicro Conference Series on Software Engineering and Advanced Applications, SEAA 2024.

56 Near-infrared based glucose monitoring system

Ramesh Kumar Reddy, C.[1,a], Gnaneshwara Chary, U.[1,b], Ch. Bhargav Manikanta[2,c], Ch. Veekshitha[2,d], B. Sushanth Reddy[2,e], and B. Srihitha[2,f]

[1]Assistant Professor, Dept. of ECE, B V Raju Institute of Technology, Narsapur, Telangana, India

[2]Student, Dept. of ECE, B V Raju Institute of Technology, Narsapur, Telangana, India

Abstract

The near infrared (NIR) based glucose monitoring system introduced in this research not only offers a continuous and non-invasive way to measure glucose levels, but it also completely changes the way diabetes is managed. By utilizing the intrinsic spectral properties of glucose molecules, our technology translates and interprets these distinct signs in a complex way, making it possible to estimate blood glucose concentrations with accuracy. With a clever combination of advanced machine learning algorithms and signal processing techniques, the system interprets complex NIR spectroscopic data into meaningful, real-time glucose measurements with ease. This technical innovation has enormous potential since it can completely transform the fundamentals of diabetes treatment. Our solution directly addresses a basic difficulty encountered by people with diabetes by introducing a painless and convenient alternative to conventional blood-based glucose monitoring methods. This paradigm shift is about more than just efficiency and accuracy; it's about giving these people a higher quality of life, giving them unprecedented autonomy in managing their health, and empowering them. Our NIR-based glucose monitoring system is at the front of a new wave of medical innovation that prioritizes patient accessibility, creativity, and overall health.

Keywords: Continuous glucose measurement, diabetes management, glucose molecules, glucose monitoring system, near-infrared, non-invasive, spectral characteristics

Introduction

The rising global occurrence of diabetes has required the creation of improved and user-friendly techniques for monitoring glucose levels. Conventional blood sugar monitoring methods like finger pricking can cause discomfort and inconvenience for patients. This frequently results in inadequate adherence, making it more challenging for individuals to effectively control their condition.

This project aims to present a new method for determining blood sugar levels with near infrared (NIR) technology. NIR light can pass through the skin and interact with glucose molecules, enabling a non-invasive evaluation of blood sugar levels. Analyzing how NIR light is absorbed and scattered can lead to instant and precise glucose readings without needing a blood sample.

Our goal is to design a device that is easy for users to operate and improves the accuracy of monitoring glucose levels. This method has the potential to enhance diabetes care by giving patients a more convenient and painless way to monitor their blood sugar levels. Furthermore, the advancement of this non-intrusive technology may establish a new standard for medical devices, meeting the increasing need for non-surgical options in healthcare. This article will investigate the technical features of NIR technology in glucose monitoring, its possible benefits compared to current methods, and the influence it could have on managing diabetes. Our goal is to transform how blood glucose levels are monitored and controlled by combining advances in medical technology with patient-centered design, resulting in notable enhancements in patient satisfaction and medical results.

[a]rameshkumarreddy.c@bvrit.ac.in, [b]gnaneshwara.chary@bvrit.ac.in, [c]21211a044 1@bvrit.ac.in, [d]21211a0443@bvrit.ac.in, [e]21211a0434@bvrit.ac.in, [f]21211a0440@bvri t.ac.in

DOI: 10.1201/9781003616399-56

Principle

The operational process, where NIR light is emitted through the fingertip to interact with blood glucose molecules, holds intricate significance within the framework of our project. This analysis delves into the profound insights garnered from this process and their implications for accurate and non-invasive glucose concentration estimation. A light beam is attenuated when it interacts with human body tissues because the tissues both scatter and absorb the light. Light scattering happens in tissues as a result of a discrepancy between the refraction index of extracellular fluid and the cell membrane. While the cellular membrane index is thought to stay mostly constant, the extracellular fluid's refraction index changes with the concentration of glucose. The Beer-Lambert Law, which states that the absorbance of light through any solution is proportionate to the solution's concentration and the distance that light rays travel, is important when measuring the absorbance [1].

Following emission, the emitted NIR light traverses through the fingertip, where it encounters a complex network of blood vessels containing glucose molecules. This encounter engenders a dynamic exchange where specific wavelengths of the NIR light are absorbed by the glucose molecules. These wavelengths' absorption is directly proportional to the concentration of glucose within the bloodstream, forming a fundamental link between the intensity of absorption and the glucose levels present. The layers of subcutaneous,

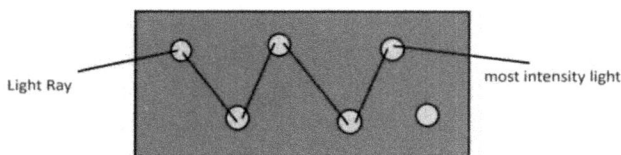

Figure 56.1 Less glucose tissue
Source: Author

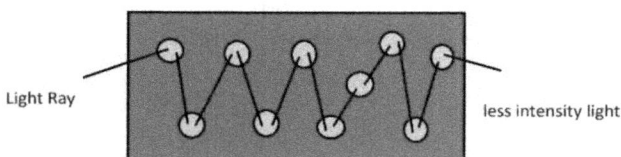

Figure 56.2 More glucose tissue
Source: Author

dermal, and epidermal skin make up human finger skin tissue. An optical signal that is directed perpendicularly into a human body part travels along a path like a banana after passing through the epidermis layer and reflecting in the dermis layer. The operational analysis emphasizes the intricate and insightful nature of the NIR-based glucose monitoring process. The process of NIR light interacting with glucose molecules, subsequently revealing unique absorption patterns, forms the bedrock upon which our system operates. By decoding these patterns, we unveil the potential to transform diabetes management, replacing invasive methods with a non-invasive, real-time, and user-friendly approach that empowers individuals to proactively manage their health [1].

Our project's design revolves around combining advanced technology with a user-centric approach, resulting in a NIR based glucose monitoring system that's both effective and user-friendly. The foundation of our design lies in the emission of NIR light onto the fingertip, where glucose molecules within the bloodstream interact with the light, giving rise to distinct absorption patterns unique to glucose. To capture this interaction, we've chosen a specialized photodiode sensor that converts the modulated light's varying intensity into electrical signals that we can measure [2].

To ensure the accuracy of the measurements, we've integrated signal conditioning and amplification circuits. These circuits enhance the strength of the signals while minimizing any external disturbances. Subsequently, the transformed data is directed towards a microcontroller and an integrated field-programmable gate array (FPGA), forming the computational core of our system. Within this framework, machine learning algorithms, which have learned from a dataset containing patterns of absorbed light and corresponding glucose concentrations, decode the information embedded in the signals. These algorithms play a pivotal role in translating the signals into meaningful glucose readings, providing a valuable visualization of absorption patterns and their variations that reflect glucose concentration levels. Crucially, our design philosophy extends to user comfort and convenience. By choosing the finger as the measurement site, we've ensured a non-invasive and user- friendly experience. Our goal is to make this process easy and hassle- free. Overall, the creator of our program carefully incorporates new research that affects blood sugar monitoring. By combining precision technology with a user- centered approach, we are revolutionizing blood sugar monitoring and improving the quality of life of people with diabetes. The design of our project revolves around combining advanced technology with user-friendly applications that enable NIR based monitoring of beneficial and well-consuming sugar. The basis of our design is that NIR rays are emitted into the fingertip, where sugar molecules in the blood interact with the light, apparently creating a special absorption pattern for the sugar. To capture this interaction, we chose a special photodiode sensor that converts changes in light into an electrical signal that we can measure [2].

To ensure the accuracy of the measurements, we have integrated signal conditioning and amplification circuits. These circuits enhance the strength of the signals while minimizing any external disturbances. Subsequently, the transformed data is directed towards a microcontroller and an integrated FPGA, forming the computational core of our system. Within this framework, machine learning algorithms, which have learned from a dataset containing patterns of absorbed light and corresponding glucose concentrations, decode the information embedded in the signals. These algorithms play a pivotal role in translating the signals into meaningful glucose readings, providing a valuable visualization of absorption patterns and their variations that reflect glucose concentration levels. The blood glucose meter is designed to increase accuracy by accounting for fasting and fasting states using an infrared (IR) sensor [3].

1. Data storage: Before and after fasting periods, the module saves IR sensor data in registers {ir_before} and `ir_after}, respectively.
2. NIR-based detection logic: The module analyzes IR sensor data to preset thresholds based on the fasting condition (fasting} signal). It compares the {ir_after} data to a threshold if the user is fasting; if not, it compares the`{ir_before} data. The patient is classified as non-diabetic ({y} is set to 0) if

the data is below the threshold; otherwise, they are classified as diabetic ({y} is set to 1).
3. Reset handling: When a reset signal ({rst}) is asserted, the module's reset logic sets the IR sensor data registers to zero.
4. Custom logic and parallel processing: FPGAs may be designed to execute several jobs at once and have a high degree of parallel processing capability. Due to their ability to process data in parallel, FPGAs are well-suited for applications requiring the execution of complex algorithms at high speeds.
5. Hardware acceleration: By removing computationally demanding procedures from the main CPU, FPGAs can be used to speed up certain functions. Applications that require high performance will especially benefit from this

In conclusion, the module uses predefined threshold values to assess whether a patient is diabetic or not based on information gathered from IR sensors both before and after fasting.

Simulation results of the Verilog code of the diabetes test are given to demonstrate its functioning. During the simulation, different conditions, fasting and non-fasting, were tested with different infrared sensor values. A simulation captures the response of the module, showing how diabetes is determined based on the input criteria. The "y" value represents the consequences of diabetes as a predefined measure and indicates the ability to discriminate between diabetic and non-diabetic conditions. These simulation results confirmed the effectiveness of this model in using infrared sensor data to assess patient diabetes. It adopts independent control and receives the tap to be sent as a 200mm clearance from the ground to send power to the battery. Finally, this article makes an impact on the diversity of the land. The wireless charger is a proven program with a battery capacity of 4.5 kWh, a supercapacitor capacity of 3.8 kWh and a maximum efficiency of 86%.

This diagram shows the functionality of the diabetes monitor, including the input data of the clock and reset device, the glucose meter and the infrared sensor. This image shows two sides labeled "ir_before" and "ir_after" adjusted based on fasting and infrared measurements. The model uses a clock mechanism to measure glycemic status and compare the stored IR value from the initial fasting state to the fasting state. The output "y" shows how diabetic the person is and records the ability to analyze IR data and record a rapid diagnosis of diabetes.

This image provides a better understanding and detailed view of the complex workings of the cell nucleus. In the "diabetes detection" module. The operation of the model is supported by several important mechanisms, including a clock signal ("clk") that controls the synchronization process, a reset signal ("rest") that helps initialize internal devices, and the device. . ("fast"). ") plays an important role in determining the context of the patient, and the data from the infrared sensor ("ir_sensor") is important in the assessment of the patient's diabetes.

The module internally uses two key registers, "ir_before" and "ir_after". Comprehensive data management to implement the system automatically captures and stores the results from the infrared sensor, displaying the values before and after the fasting period. These recorded changes are related to the person's fasting period and allow the module to track changes in the infrared sensor data over time.

The main focus of the decision-making module is careful guideline-based decision-making about the patient's diabetes. The module achieves the desired result by carefully comparing the value of the infrared sensor with the preset value and finally produces the output signal "y". This urine signal serves as a binary indicator of whether the patient has diabetes (1) or not (0). This diagram captures the interactions between data management, threshold measurement and decision-making and provides an overview of the design process and its role in diabetes testing [4].

An existing non-invasive method like the continuous glucose monitor (CGM) uses sensors placed on the skin to measure interstitial glucose levels via small filaments. CGMs require regular calibration with blood glucose readings and are sensitive to movement and skin conditions. In contrast, NIR glucose monitoring relies on light absorption in the skin, using specific wavelengths to estimate glucose concentrations. NIR systems aim to be more comfortable, without the need for skin penetration or frequent calibration [5].

Conclusion

In conclusion, our research to develop a near-infrared (NIR) glucose monitoring system has produced outstanding outcomes. That might alter the way we treat diabetes. We have developed a reliable technique to monitor glucose levels fast and painlessly by utilizing the special characteristics of glucose molecules, sophisticated signal processing, and clever algorithms. Utilizing the IR sensor data, our diabetic detection module has demonstrated its ability to make intelligent judgments that contribute to a better understanding of diabetes.

As we have discovered, it's critical to set the thresholds' (also known as limitations) values correctly. To ensure that our system functions successfully in various scenarios, these parameters need to be carefully adjusted. Because of this, our technology can determine whether or not a person has diabetes with accuracy and dependability.

Acknowledgement

We would like to express our gratitude to all of the instructors, lab personnel, and the B. V. Raju Institute of Technology's Electronics and Communication Engineering Department for their direct and indirect assistance in completing the project.

References

[1] Narkhede, P., Dhalwar, S., and Karthikeyan, B. (2016). NIR based non-invasive blood glucose measurement. *Indian Journal of Science and Technology*, 9(41), 1–7.

[2] Saputra, F. A. D., Utomo, B., and Sumber, S. (2020). Development of measuring device for non-invasive blood sugar levels using photodiode sensor. *Indonesian Journal of Electronics, Electromedical Engineering, and Medical Informatics*, 2(2), 74–79.

[3] Fouad, M. M., Mahmoud, D. Y., and Abd El Ghany, M. A. (2020). Joint NIR-BIS based non-invasive glucose monitoring system. In 2020 30th International Conference on Microelectronics (ICM). IEEE.

[4] Charles, R. K. J., Mary, A. B., Jenova, R., and Majid, M. A. (2019). VLSI design of intelligent, self-monitored and managed, strip-free, non-invasive device for diabetes mellitus patients to improve glycemic control using IoT. *Procedia Computer Science*, 163, 117–124.

[5] Rodbard, D. (2016). Continuous glucose monitoring: a review of successes, challenges, and opportunities. *Diabetes Technology and Therapeutics*, 18(Suppl. 2), S3–S13. doi: 10.1089/dia.2015.0417. PMID: 26784127; PMCID: PMC4717493.

[6] Hina, A., and Saadeh, W. (2022). Noninvasive blood glucose monitoring systems using near-infrared technology-a review. *Sensors (Basel)*, 22(13), 485.

[7] Manurung, B. E., Munggaran, H. R., Ramadhan, G. F., and Koesoema, A. P. (2019). Non-invasive blood glucose monitoring using near-infrared spectroscopy based on internet of things using machine learning. In 2019 IEEE R10 Humanitarian Technology Conference.

[8] Oñate, W., Ramos-Zurita, E., Pallo, J. P., Manzano, S., Ayala, P., and Garcia, M. V. (2024). NIR-based electronic platform for glucose monitoring for the prevention and control of diabetes mellitus. *Sensors*, 24(13), 4190. https://doi.org/10.3390/s24134190.

[9] Naresh, M., Nagaraju, V. S., Kollem, S., Kumar, J., and Peddakrishna, S. (2024). Non-invasive glucose prediction and classification using NIR technology with machine learning. *Heliyon*, 10(7), e28720. ISSN 2405-8440.

[10] Yadav, J., et al. "Prospects and limitations of non-invasive blood glucose monitoring using near-infrared spectroscopy." Biomedical signal processing and control 18 (2015): 214–227

[11] Al-dhaheri, M., Mekkakia-Maaza, N. E., Mouhadjer, H., and Lakhdari, A. (2019). Noninvasive blood glucose monitoring system based on near-infrared method. *International Journal of Electrical and Computer Engineering*, 10, 1736–1746. 10.11591/ijece. v10i2.pp1736-1746.

[12] Tang, L., Chang, S., Chen, C.-J., and Liu, J.-T. (2020). Non-invasive blood glucose monitoring technology: a review. *Sensors*, 20, 6925. 10.3390/s20236925.

[13] Yadav, J., Rani, A., Singh, V., and Murari, B. M. (2014). Near-infrared LED based non-invasive blood glucose sensor. In 2014 International Conference on Signal Processing and Integrated Networks (SPIN), Noida, India, 2014, (pp. 591–594).

[14] Guo, D., Shang, Y., Peng, R., Yong, S., and Wang, X. (2015). Noninvasive blood glucose measurement based on NIR spectrums and double ANN analysis. *Journal of Biosciences and Medicines*, 03, 42–48. 10.4236/jbm.2015.36007.

[15] Zeng, B., Wang, W., Wang, N., Li, F., Zhai, F., and Hu, L. (2013). Noninvasive blood glucose monitoring system based on distributed multi-sensors information fusion of multi-wavelength NIR. *Engineering*, 05, 553–560. 10.4236/eng.2013.510B114.

57 Real-time guidance for smooth Indoor navigation environments

Bharath Kumar, K.[a], Sravanthi, M.[b], Bhargav, B.[c], Nivedhitha, K.[d] and Venkat Sai, K.[e]

Electronics and Communication, CMR Technical Campus, Kandlakoya, Medchal, Hyderabad, India

Abstract

This cutting-edge Flask web application completely remains mall internal navigation. Python, JavaScript, HTML, and mall floor-plan pictures are all combined to provide a complete navigation solution. Just by interacting with the mall blueprint, users can quickly choose where they want to start and stop. A user-friendly interface with accessibility features and real-time location updates while navigating the mall are among the key features. There are other customization options available, such as changing the mall's blueprint and the path coordinates. A wide range of users, including those unfamiliar with the building's layout, may utilize the software because of its intuitive interface.

Keywords: HTML, indoor mapping, indoor positioning, JAVA, location services, avigation system, way-finding

Introduction

By providing accurate, intuitive direction, the "Indoor Navigation App" makes traversing challenging interior environments—such as shopping centers, airports, and office buildings—simpler. On a floor layout, users can simply select start and end points, and the program will calculate and visually represent the best route. Large-scale building difficulties are addressed by this software, which specializes in comprehensive inside maps, in contrast to standard navigation apps that concentrate on outdoor locations. Accuracy is improved by cutting-edge technology like indoor positioning systems (IPS) that use Bluetooth and Wi-Fi. Real-time environmental monitoring, remote access through mobile apps, and the integration of several sensors for efficient data transfer and analysis are some of the key characteristics. It is necessary to adapt while selling in department stores worldwide, especially in a world where cell phones and the Internet play major roles for people of all ages [1,2].

In addition, the COVID-19 pandemic is being dealt with globally [3,4]. Due to this, consumers no longer travel with the traditional mindset of buying in department stores; instead, they now use online services and occasionally visit department stores for their shopping needs. Additionally, because they understand social distancing, prevention, and strategies to reduce their personal risk of infection COVID-19, customers spend less time shopping. One of the drawbacks of department store shopping is the time spent by customers looking for product locations, which adds to their shopping time. This is especially true for large department shops or ones they have never visited. However, there are a number of methods available thanks to modern, sophisticated technology, such as augmented reality (AR) [5,6].

The use of indoor map navigation [9] and the global positioning system (GPS) [7,8] can assist shorten the time required to look up product locations in department shops. To be clear, the creation of mobile applications aids in the planning of purchasing. According to an analysis of related literature and research, numerous programs have been created to support both in-person and online selling [11–17]. However, those programs continue to have some limitations. For instance, they are unable to travel, look up

[a]kammarabharathkumar@gmail.com, [b]Sravanthi.ece@cmrtc.ac.in, [c]217R1A0475@cmrtc.ac.in, [d]217R1A0494@cmrtc.ac.in, [e]217R1A0496@cmrtc.ac.in.

DOI: 10.1201/9781003616399-57

locations, or record the information of their searches for various product types [16].

This research provided a prototype smart phone application that integrates AR, GIS, and GPS to assist users identify products quickly and organize their buying. The amount of time spent in department stores may decrease as a result of this. Additionally, a web tool that displays statistical data was developed to assist businesses with sales planning, analysis, and forecasting based on popular departments and client preferences.

Literature Survey

AR is being used in a variety of contexts, including the development of navigation applications [18–22], for tourism [23,24], education or learning [25], marketing [26,10], product presentation, and product search [11–17]. This is according to a review of research and literature on the topic of AR. The details of the review of pertinent literature and research are as follows. Research on AR smart phone applications has shown how supermarkets might utilize AR to display health-conscious products on their shelves, like low-calorie or allergy-free food options [11]. Customers had to look for things in-store rather than online, which was a drawback. Since then, AR has advanced in smart phone apps, allowing for online product selection based on health requirements [12]. Retailers are now able to increase sales through individualized 3D displays, shelf scanning, and pop-up product descriptions by utilizing AR with GPS data [13].

To promote Indonesian ethnic food and improve menu attractiveness, a mobile augmented reality application was created [14]; however, its lack of restaurant navigation functions restricted its usage. Furthermore, an augmented reality smart phone app for fashion products enhanced product display by enabling customers to see objects like watches or shoes [15]. A mobile augmented reality application was created to help find products and show details in supermarkets; however, it was not suited for further analysis or decision assistance because it did not include search statistics [16].

A study was conducted on the application development of AR and virtual reality (VR) for product presentation in retail stores. The findings showed that there were methods for enhancing

online and in-person sales' service efficiency [17]. Research on the use of AR for navigation revealed that both indoor and outdoor navigation applications were being developed [18,19]. For example, GPS, Google Maps, and API were typically used in the development of outdoor navigation applications for use in government entities, such as universities, or for navigating to tourist spots [23,24].

The majority of indoor navigation applications were designed with operating in buildings in mind, such as university classrooms [10] and retail stores [16]. The study concluded that the integration of AR with GPS and GIS enhanced the presentation of data and may encourage users to utilize the apps more frequently. A prototype navigation system using augmented reality was developed to enhance indoor navigation experiences, particularly for aiding blind individuals, by overlaying virtual directions on real-time camera views from mobile devices [27,28].

The indoor positioning QR navigation system from Navigation is appropriate for practically any industrial setting, including warehouses, retail centers, and supermarkets. Navigation's method is convenient because it doesn't require any hardware to be used. Our team at Navigation has a great deal of expertise creating indoor navigation systems [29].

Positioning can be used for both tracking and indoor navigation, with Wi-Fi typically providing 5–15 meters accuracy, influenced by the number of access points and physical obstructions [30]. An indoor navigation system using a single ultra-wideband anchor and an antenna array is being developed, enabling phase measurement-based positioning algorithms [31]. This advanced technology simplifies navigation within buildings, offering easy guidance for users [32].

The indoor positioning QR navigation system from Navigation is appropriate for practically any industrial setting, including warehouses, retail centers, and supermarkets. Navigation's method is convenient because it doesn't require any hardware to be used. Our team at Navigation has a great deal of expertise creating indoor navigation systems [33]. A comprehensive interior mapping system for intelligent building management organizes building information modeling (BIM) and computer-aided design (CAD) data used in small building areas, while also providing seamless and straightforward user navigation [34,35].

Methodology

This study presented the creation of a product location search application prototype utilizing AR, GIS, and GPS. In Figure 57.1, the conceptual framework is shown. It was discovered that there were three categories of users—managers, administrators, and customers—based on the figure. Clients might utilize the mobile application to access the system. The system could be accessed by managers and administrators via the web and mobile applications. The application for this research was developed using a variety of hardware and software, including a microcomputer that served as a server for both databases and websites.

Existing system

Statistics show that over 80% of individuals spend their time indoors, including at airports, retail centers, libraries, campuses, and hospitals. The indoor localization system's goal is to deliver precise locations within big structures. Applications include tracking valuable assets, evacuating trapped individuals from fire scenes, and indoor service robots depend on it. Indoor localization needs a precise and trustworthy position estimate scheme in order for these applications to be broadly adopted. Figure 57.2 shows the block diagram existing work.

The limitations of the existing model are precision:

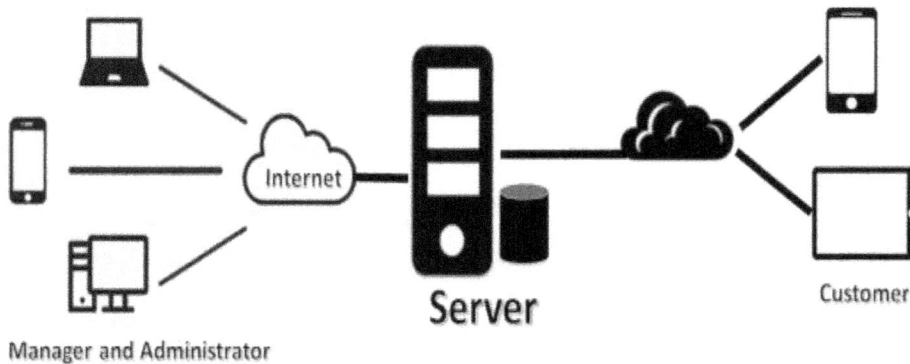

Figure 57.1 Objective of the conceptual framework
Source: Author

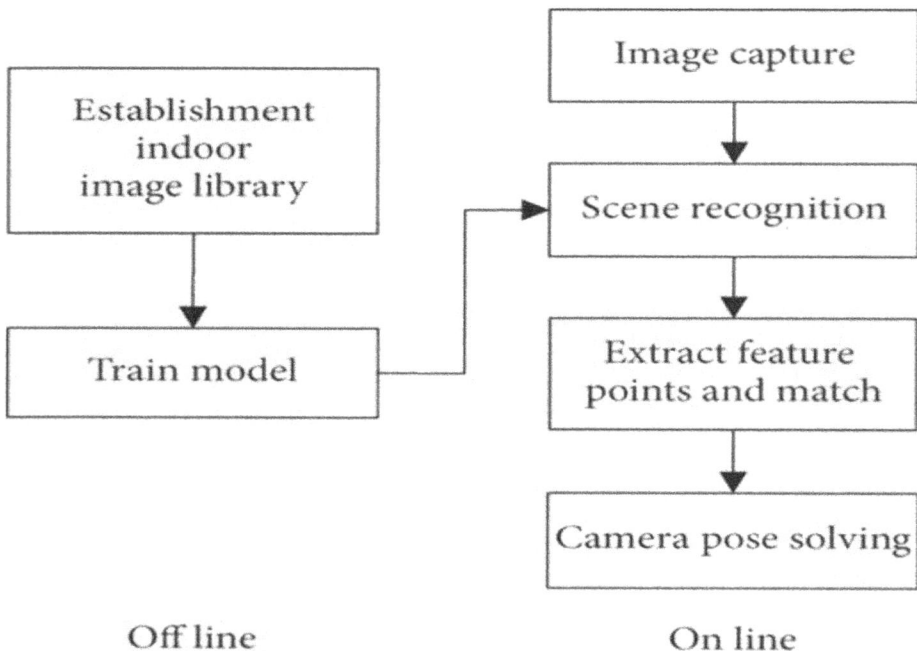

Figure 57.2 Block diagram of proposed model
Source: Author

- There is a lack of path precision while utilizing this camera-based indoor navigation tool, handling.
- It is challenging to handle and locate the location since we regularly need to take pictures with the camera, complexity.
- Due to the system's complexity, installation, maintenance, and troubleshooting may call for a high level of technical competence, limited real-time data/efficiency.
- Our requirement to upload code on a regular basis depending on various indoor locations stems from research on camera-based indoor navigation and mode of operation.
- Only a limited number of people can access camera-based indoor navigation because it is only available online and cannot be used offline.

Proposed system

An information kiosk or a smart phone are examples of static interfaces that can be used for interior navigation, but it can also be implemented as a system, tool, or app that allows the user to be guided through an indoor environment. All indoor navigation systems depend on the availability of an accurate indoor map. Dynamic way-finding systems also need to be able to precisely determine the user's position inside an interior environment. The Entire process of the proposed system flow chart is shown in Figure 57.3.

The minimum hardware components are Windows or Mac OS, 8GB RAM, 120GB Storage and I3 processor. The Software requirements are Python, Flask and Java script.

Results and Discussions

Figure 57.4 shows the whole blueprint of the hospital or mall.

Select the start where the person is present. The selected point is shown in Figure 57.5.

Select the ending where the person wants to go. Selected points are shown in Figure 57.6.

Claims that the graphic shows how to choose the beginning point for our desired destination. It will navigate our target by indicating the starting point in Figure 57.5, which depicts the final location where we wished to go. Figure 57.7 shows how the system indicates the path direction in the

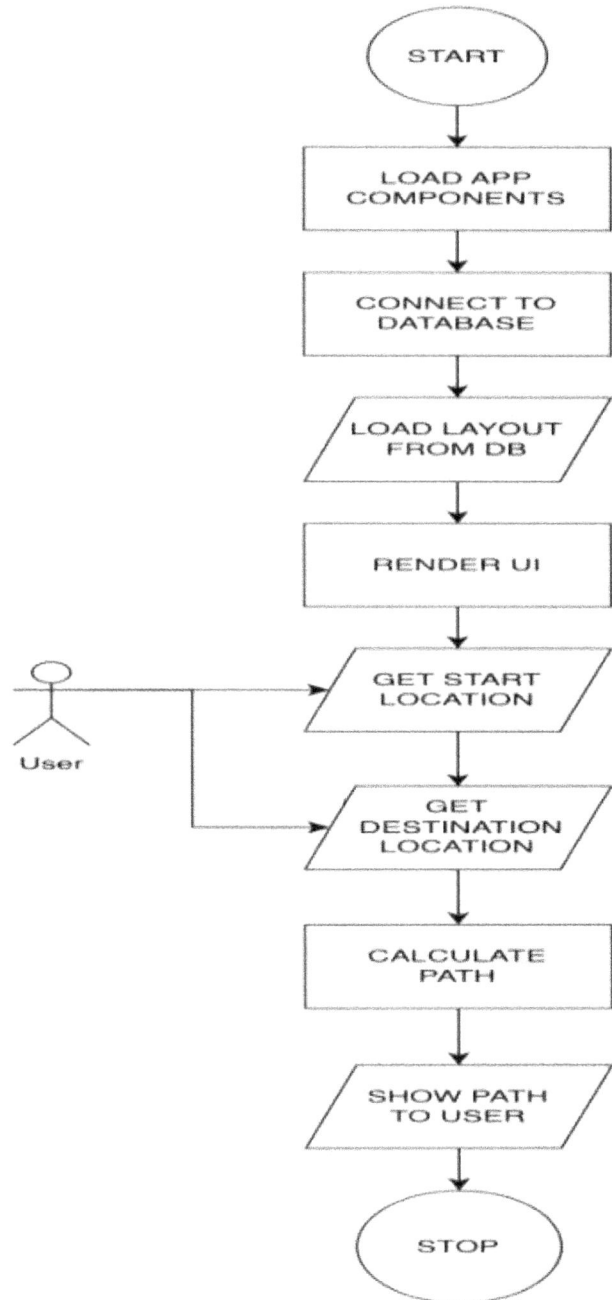

Figure 57.3 Flow chart of the proposed model
Source: Author

mall's blueprint during the navigation procedure to reach the goal. And getting there won't be too difficult for us.

The main applications this proposed system are used in hospitals and airports.

In hospitals, indoor navigation can help patients and visitors get where they're going

SELECT START POINT

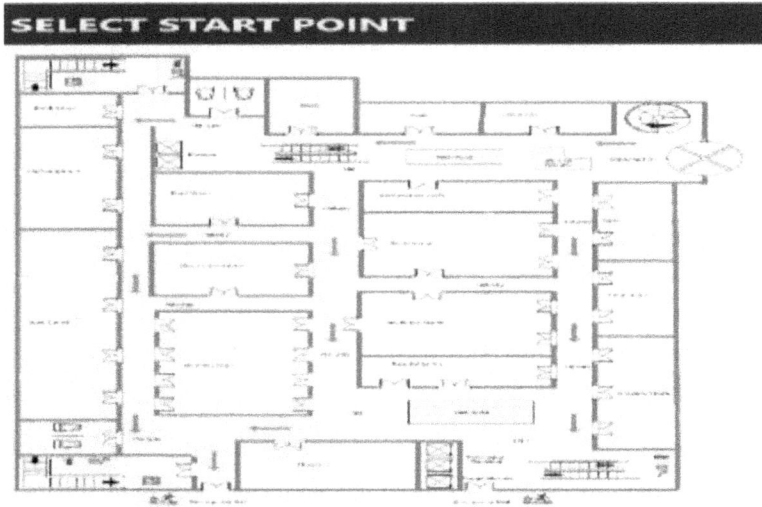

Figure 57.4 Blueprint of the mall
Source: Author

SELECT END POINT

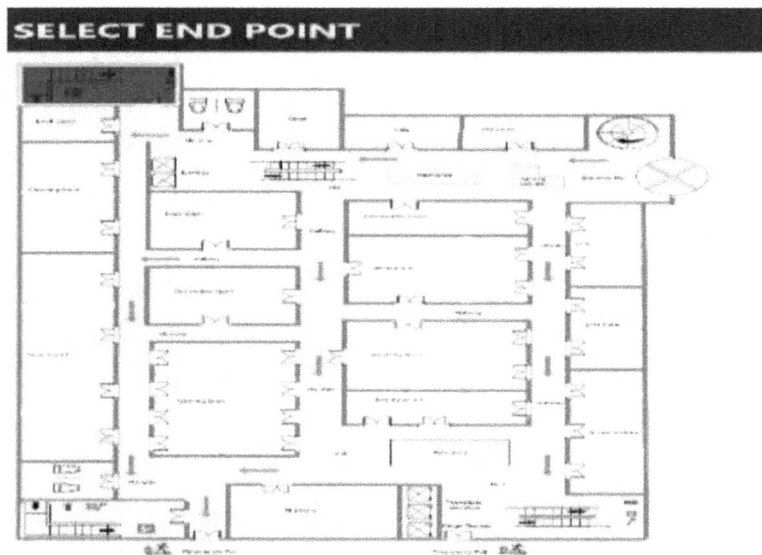

Figure 57.5 Select the starting point in blue print
Source: Author

smoothly, help hospital workers and technicians find resources and access points, and improve overall productivity in the hospital setting. It is a special case studied in one hospital, corresponding output shown in Figure 57.8.

Travelers can now experience less tension when travelling thanks to the airport navigation app's adoption of a GEO location technology. This negation process is shown in Figure 57.9. The airport navigation system makes it easier to discover boarding gates and expedites the process of finding points of interest, hence enhancing tourist loyalty and boosting airport revenue.

- Give users turn-by-turn directions so they can quickly and easily locate the gates, baggage carousels, and amenities.
- Give directions to important services such information desks, public restrooms, family and disabled restrooms, medical services, and places of worship.

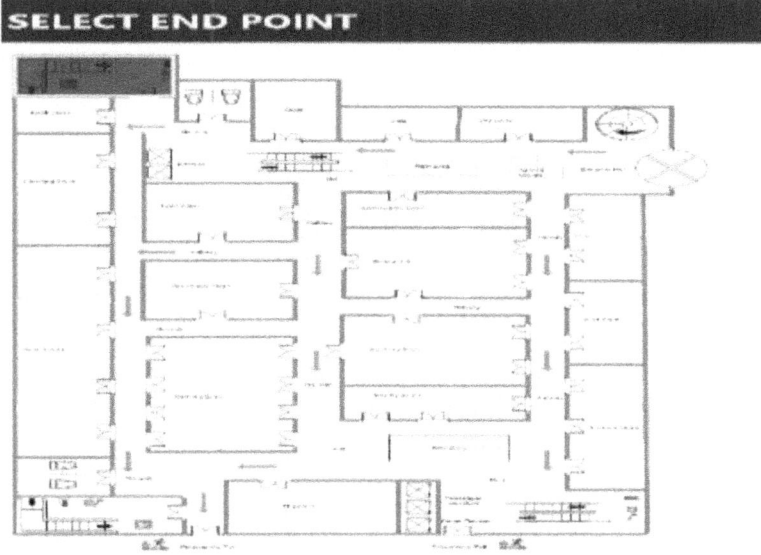

Figure 57.6 Select the ending point in blue print
Source: Author

Figure 57.7 Navigation to the route/or destination
Source: Author

Conclusion

The findings of developing a prototype application for product location search through mobile and web applications showed that customers and organizations have the tool to help their planning and decision-making. To be clear, customers can use the program to quickly search for product locations in department stores. Additionally, it accurately navigated to those destinations. Businesses could use the information to plan their product sales and make more informed decisions.

Figure 57.8 Navigation to in hospital
Source: Author

Figure 57.9 Navigation to in airport
Source: Author

The mobile application that was shown was limited to Android due to the limits of the research. Therefore, future study should develop this mobile application to be cross-platform compatible or iOS compatible as well in order to accommodate all consumers.

References

[1] Kumar, S., Tiwari, P., and Zymbler, M. (2019). Internet of things is a revolutionary approach for future technology enhancement: a review. *Journal of Big Data*, 6(1), 1–21.

[2] Langley, D. J., van Doorn, J., Ng, I. C., Stieglitz, S., Lazovik, A., and Boonstra, A. (2021). The internet of everything: smart things and their impact on business models. *Journal of Business Research*, 122, 853–863.

[3] Eriksson, N., and Stenius, M. (2022). Online grocery shoppers due to the Covid-19 pandemic-an analysis of demographic and household characteristics. *Procedia Computer Science*, 196, 93–100.

[4] Shen, H., Namdarpour, F., and Lin, J. (2022). Investigation of online grocery shopping and delivery preference before, during, and after COVID19. *Transportation Research Interdisciplinary Perspectives*, 14, 100580.

[5] Riegler, A., Riener, A., and Holzmann, C. (2021). Augmented reality for future mobility: insights from a literature review and HCI workshop. *I-COM*, 20(3), 295–318.

[6] Chan, H. H., Haerle, S. K., Daly, M. J., Zheng, J., Philp, L., Ferrari, M., et al. (2021). An integrated augmented reality surgical navigation platform using multi-modality imaging for guidance. *PloS One*, 16(4), e0250558.

[7] Hahm, Y., Yoon, H., and Choi, Y. (2019). The effect of built environments on the walking and shopping behaviors of pedestrians; a study with GPS experiment in Sinchon retail district in Seoul, South Korea. *Cities*, 89, 1–13.

[8] Puttinaovarat, S., Horkaew, P., Khaimook, K., and Polnigongit, W. (2015). Adaptive hydrological flow field modeling based on water body extraction and surface information. *Journal of Applied Remote Sensing*, 9(1), 095041.

[9] El-Sheimy, N., and Li, Y. (2021). Indoor navigation: State of the art and future trends. *Satellite Navigation*, 2(1), 1–23.

[10] Wedel, M., Bigné, E., and Zhang, J. (2020). Virtual and augmented reality: advancing research in consumer marketing. *International Journal of Research in Marketing*, 37(3), 443–465.

[11] Ahn, J., Williamson, J., Gartrell, M., Han, R., Lv, Q., and Mishra, S. (2015). Supporting healthy grocery shopping via mobile augmented reality. *ACM Transactions on Multimedia Computing, Communications, and Applications (TOMM)*, 12(1s), 1–24.

[12] Deshpande, M., Likhita, B., and Bhat, N. (2022). A personalized supermarket product recommendation system using augmented reality. *ECS Transactions*, 107(1), 915.

[13] Kumar, P. A., and Murugavel, R. (2020). Prospects of augmented reality in physical stores's using shopping assistance App. *Procedia Computer Science*, 172(1), 406–411.

[14] Weking, A. N., and Santoso, A. J. (2020). A Development of Augmented reality mobile application to promote the traditional Indonesian food. *International Journal of Interactive Mobile Technologies*, 14(9), 248–257.

[15] Abou El-Seoud, M. S., and Taj-Eddin, I. A. (2019). An android augmented reality application for retail fashion shopping. *International Journal of Information Management*, 13(1), 5.

[16] Jayananda, P. K. V., Seneviratne, D. H. D., Abeygunawardhana, P., Dodampege, L. N., and Lak-

shani, A. M. B. (2018). Augmented reality based smart supermarket system with indoor navigation using beacon technology (easy shopping android mobile App). In 2018 IEEE International Conference on Information and Automation for Sustainability (ICIAfS), (pp. 1–6). IEEE.

[17] Kumar, T. S. (2021). Study of retail applications with virtual and augmented reality technologies. *Journal of Innovative Image Processing (JIIP)*, 3(02), 144–156.

[18] Ma, W., Zhang, S., and Huang, J. (2021). Mobile augmented reality based indoor map for improving geo-visualization. *PeerJ Computer Science*, 7, e704.

[19] Lu, F., Zhou, H., Guo, L., Chen, J., and Pei, L. (2021). An ARCore-based augmented reality campus navigation system. *Applied Sciences*, 11(16), 7515.

[20] Arifitama, B., Hanan, G., and Rofiqi, M. H. (2021). Mobile augmented reality for campus visualization using markerless tracking in an Indonesian private university. *International Journal of Interactive Mobile Technologies*, 15, 21–33.

[21] Chidsin, W., Gu, Y., and Goncharenko, I. (2021). ARbased navigation using RGB-D camera and hybrid map. *Sustainability*, 13(10), 5585.

[22] Rubio-Sandoval, J. I., Martinez-Rodriguez, J. L., Lopez-Arevalo, I., Rios-Alvarado, A. B., RodriguezRodriguez, A. J., and Vargas-Requena, D. T. (2021). An indoor navigation methodology for mobile devices by integrating augmented reality and semantic web. *Sensors*, 21(16), 5435.

[23] Kaźmierczak, R., Szczepańska, A., Kowalczyk, C., Grunwald, G., and Janowski, A. (2021). Using AR technology in tourism based on the example of maritime educational trips—A conceptual model. *Sustainability*, 13(13), 7172.

[24] Gharaibeh, M. K., Gharaibeh, N. K., Khan, M. A., Abu-ain, W. A. K., and Alqudah, M. K. (2021). Intention to use mobile augmented reality in the tourism sector. *Computer Systems Science and Engineering*, 37(2), 187–202.

[25] Hamzah, M. L., Rizal, F., and Simatupang, W. (2021). Development of augmented reality application for learning computer network device. *International Journal of Interactive Mobile Technologies*, 15(12), 47–64

[26] Alcañiz, M., Bigné, E., and Guixeres, J. (2019). Virtual reality in marketing: a framework, review, and research agenda. *Frontiers in Psychology*, 10, 1530.

[27] Ramesh, M., Murugan, S., and Albert Mayan, J. (2023). Indoor navigation using augmented reality for mobile application. In Conference on Consumer Electronics, (Vol. 11, Issue 03), ISSN:2278-0181.

[28] Fraga, A. L., and Saniie, J. (2022). Indoor navigation system for visually impaired people. In International Conference on Electro Information Technology (EIT), (Vol. 09, Issue 04), ISSN:0277-786X.

[29] Brovko, T. A., Chugunov, A. A., Ritcher, J., Gaedke, M., and Costantino, M. (2021). Indoor navigation using QR code. In International Conference on Indoor Positioning and Indoor Navigation, (Vol. 04, Issue 05), ISSN:2349-7009.

[30] Magsi, S. A., Saad, N., and Sameer, L. (2021). Wi-Fi based indoor navigation system. In International Conference on Intelligent and Advanced Systems (ICIAS), (Vol. 05, Issue 09), ISSN:2447-0181.

[31] Brovko, T. A., and Chugunov, A. A. (2022). Positioning with single anchor indoor navigation system using phase measurement. *Institution of Electrical and Electronical Engineering (IEEE)*, 07(06), ISSN:2468-0181.

[32] Birla, S., and Singh, G. (2021). Disha indoor navigation (DIN) App. In 2nd International Conference on Advance in Computing, (Vol. 06, Issue 02), ISSN: 2582-2160.

[33] Traubinger, V., Franzkowiak, L., Tauchmann, N., Costantino, M., and Richter, J. (2021). Indoor navigation using QR code. In International Conference on Indoor Positioning and Indoor Navigation (IPIN), (Vol. 08, Issue 01), ISSN:9781-4244-5866.

[34] Costantino, M., and Richter, J. (2022). ArcGIS provide indoorsindoors. A practical workflow for the 3D reconstruction of complex historic sites and their decorative interiors: Florence As It Was and the church of Orsanmichele, sprigar in Natur,Volume 10, article number 118, 2022.

[35] Sushma and S. Ambaresh, "Indoor Navigation Using QR Code Based On Google Maps For IOS" International Conference On Communication And signal Processing,Volume 2335, doi:10.1088/1742-6596/2335/1/0120602021, 2022.

58 Utilizing an IORT-based remote access vehicle for monitoring

Bharath Kumar, K.[a], Kolanpaka Manoj[b], Kandula Ruthika[c],
Rampuram Patil Sreeja[d] and Nerella Vivek[e]
Electronics and Communication, CMR Technical Campus, Kandlakoya, Medchal, Hyderabad, India

Abstract

The goal of this project is to create a remote access car monitoring system with Blynk software and Internet of Things technologies. The system's user-friendly smart phone application is intended to give real-time vehicle monitoring and control. The car has a number of sensors to gather information about things like humidity, temperature, and obstacle recognition. A microcontroller interfaced with these sensors processes the data and sends it over Wi-Fi to the cloud. A graphical user interface (GUI) that enables users to remotely manage the vehicle's motions and monitor its status from a smart phone or tablet is created using the Blynk platform. Our project's goal is to improve the upkeep and monitoring of drainage systems, sewage systems, and other tunnels and gutters that are essential for safety and upkeep during blockages or severe weather. In the event of an electricity outage and to protect the integrity of the system, this project is crucial. This also addresses how smart car technologies are being implemented, which collect data on speed and safety feature usage.

Keywords: Blynk cloud, ESP-8266 module, Internet of Robotic Things, sensors (DHT/soil moisturizer/ultrasonic/gas), Wi-Fi module

Introduction

Businesses are leveraging technology to enhance market share by simplifying user experience, ensuring safety, and protecting the environment. This project aims to develop a remotely operated vehicle (ROV) for inspecting gutters using Blynk cloud software, addressing the limitations of traditional techniques and enabling timely, non-disruptive maintenance. By incorporating Internet of Robotic Things (IoRT) technology, the ROV will provide real-time monitoring of environmental parameters such as humidity, temperature, soil moisture, gas levels, and obstacle distances.

Through the use of a mobile application, users can access and monitor data remotely thanks to the system's usage of a remote access vehicle fitted with sensors (such as a gas sensor, soil moisture sensor, ultrasonic sensor, DHT sensor, and others). This cutting-edge device can be used in smart cities, sewage/drainage systems, agriculture, and environmental monitoring. It allows for effective resource management and constant monitoring, which can collect important data for studies on whether or not humans can survive in certain gutter streams. Real-time environmental parameter monitoring, remote access via Blynk software and a mobile application, multi-sensor integration (gas, soil moisture, ultrasonic, DHT, etc.), Internet of Things (IoT)-based technology for effective data transmission, and an intuitive user interface for data visualization and analysis are the salient features of this RAV.

Literature Survey

By enabling real-time tracking and remote control of cars through the use of IoT technology, the remote vehicle monitoring system improves security and convenience for car owners. It has cloud-based server for data processing and storage, smart phone app for control, and IoT hardware installed in the vehicle [1]. Smart parking systems utilize microcontrollers, sensors, and

[a]kammarabharathkumar@gmail.com, [b]217R1A04F9@cmrtc.ac.in, [c]217R1A04J4@cmrtc.ac.in,
[d]217R1A0450@cmrtc.ac.in, [e]217R1A04H5@cmrtc.ac.in

DOI: 10.1201/9781003616399-58

other technology to efficiently manage parking spaces by detecting available spots and guiding vehicles to them. The system's user-friendly interface accommodates various vehicle types, making parking easy and convenient [2].

According to simulation data, a 48V mild hybrid system uses 10–15% less gasoline than an internal combustion engine that operates traditionally. The study comes to the conclusion that 48V mild hybrid technology is a useful way to increase the fuel efficiency of passenger cars [3]. A CFD analysis was conducted to assess the effectiveness of rear spoilers on a sedan under Malaysia's national speed limit, focusing on drag reduction and fuel economy. The study provides insights into optimizing rear spoiler design to enhance fuel efficiency and reduce emissions [4].

The goal of the study was to improve convenience and safety in multifunctional vehicles by creating an automated seatbelt release mechanism. It assesses the system's functionality, dependability, and user acceptability using simulations and experimental testing, providing information for improving seatbelt systems to raise consumer satisfaction and safety [5]. The aerodynamics of cars were examined using simulation tools, and the results demonstrated that spoilers improve stability, lower drag, and increase fuel efficiency. The study also demonstrates how spoilers alter surrounding airflow patterns to enhance an automobile's aerodynamic performance [6].

To optimize space utilization and reduce traffic, a microcontroller-based parking lot system efficiently handles vehicle detection, spot allocation, and entry/exit control. This technology maximizes parking space utilization and improves overall parking efficiency [7]. By combining cloud computing and Internet of Things technology with number plate recognition, the suggested method offers precise vehicle identification, effective space distribution, and decreased traffic. This study demonstrates how new technology can enhance parking operations and enhance intelligent transportation systems, hence enhancing urban mobility [8].

A Raspberry Pi-based IoT smart vehicle monitoring system tracks and monitors vehicle parameters in real-time to enhance fleet management and intelligent transportation [9]. By integrating with existing smart city infrastructure, the system aims to improve traffic management, reduce congestion, and enhance air quality [10].

Methodology

The monitoring through IoRT-based remote access vehicle uses advanced sensors, communication technologies, and robotic control to provide real-time monitoring and control of remote vehicles. This system is ideal for hazardous environments, industrial automation, and surveillance applications.

Existing system

An IoT-based remote vehicle monitoring system was developed using sensors, microcontrollers, and the ESP8266-WIFI module for real-time tracking and monitoring. By integrating Blynk software with hardware components like Arduino microcontrollers, the system offers a smart phone app for remote vehicle management and notifications. Performance evaluations confirmed the system's accuracy, reliability, and real-time anomaly detection capabilities. The methodology includes IoT devices in the car, a cloud server for data processing, and a mobile app for features such as unauthorized movement alerts and remote engine management, showcasing its potential to improve vehicle efficiency, safety, and security.

The current model, depicted in Figure 58.1, has several notable shortcomings. It lacks scalability details, which may hinder its effectiveness for large-scale applications, and does not address potential security risks associated with IoT systems. Additionally, the high costs and technical complexity of installation and maintenance may limit accessibility and require specialized expertise. The report also fails to discuss the system's efficiency in real-time data transfer, power consumption of IoT devices, and potential for customization of alert settings and sensor integration [11-14].

Proposed system

The system will send data to the Blynk platform for real-time monitoring and control, allowing users to access and operate it via the Blynk app. Key components include the ESP8266 Wi-Fi module, MQ-135 gas sensor, YL-69 soil moisture sensor, DHT11 sensor, HC-SR04 ultrasonic sensor,

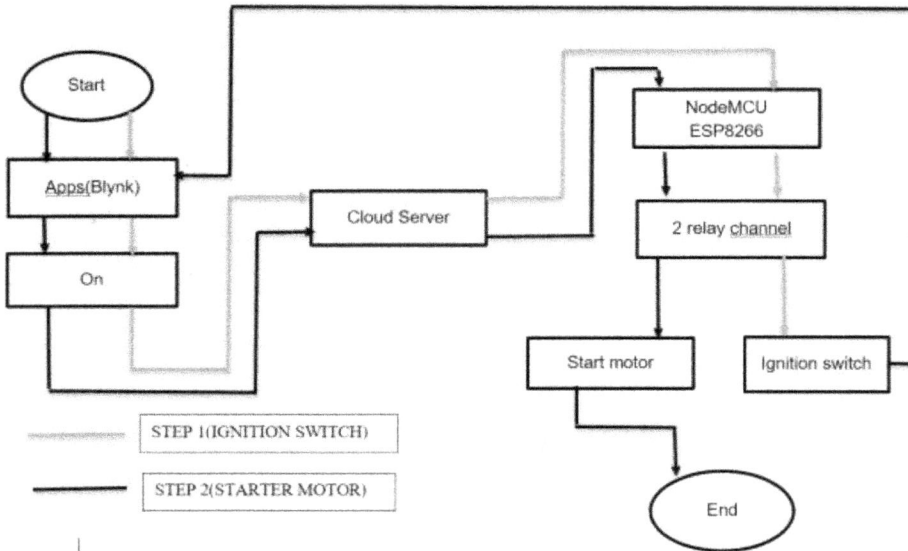

Figure 58.1 The block diagram of existing model
Source: Author

and optionally, the SG90 servo motor with Blynk software Version 2.0. Our system employs IoRT technology for environmental monitoring and obstacle detection using a remote access vehicle, featuring components such as a Wi-Fi module, ultrasonic sensor, DHT temperature and humidity sensor, soil moisture sensor, gas sensor, optional camera control, and Blynk software for data monitoring and control. Figure 58.2 below shows the circuit diagram of the remote access vehicle.

The procedures necessary to create a remote access car system using the ESP8266 Wi-Fi module and Blynk software are shown in the flowchart in Figure 58.3. Below is a thorough breakdown of every step:

1. Start: The system starts by setting up the car's Wi-Fi connection.
2. Initialize Blynk app: The user interacts with the car's control panel by launching the Blynk app.
3. Link to car Wi-Fi: The user's smart phone establishes a connection to the Wi-Fi network of the car.
4. Authenticate user: After successful authentication, the user is given access to the control panel of the car.
5. Vehicle adjusts panel: The user may now use the panel to monitor instructions, adjust speed, start and stop the engine, and more.

6. Sensor data: The DHT sensor (temperature and humidity), gas sensor (gas percentage), ultrasonic sensor (obstacle detection), and soil moisture sensor (soil moisture level) are some of the sensors from which mobile gathers data.
7. Data processing: Temperature and humidity (DHT), gas percentage (gas sensor), distance (ultrasonic), and soil moisture level (soil moisture) are all calculated by the system using the sensor data.
8. Obstacle detection: Should an obstruction be found: Yes, notify the driver and come to a halt. No, carry on with business as usual while moving in the intended direction.
9. Alerts and notifications: Using gauge, the system notifies and alerts the user via the Blynk app.
10. End: The vehicle can no longer be accessed remotely as the technology shuts down.

Key components:
IORT technology: The IoRT, which enables device communication, data sharing, and intelligent decision-making, is the central component of this system. It improves the autonomy and functionality of the remote vehicle by fusing robotics and IoT capabilities.

Remote-access vehicle: a car that has cameras, sensors, and remote-operable robotic arms installed. It is made to move across challenging terrain or places where it is unsafe or impractical for people to be present.

Real-time observation: From the remote vehicle to the control center, the technology offers real-time data transfer. Video feeds, sensor data from the environment (temperature, humidity, petrol levels, etc.), and vehicle status (location, speed, battery level, etc.) are all included in this.

Interface of control: A joystick, touch screen, or even virtual reality (VR) sets can be used as part of the user-friendly interface that allows operators to operate the vehicle. The interface makes it possible to precisely control the motions and functions of the car. Decision-making and data analysis: The gathered data can be processed by the system to generate decisions on its own or give operators useful insights. This can entail seeing possible dangers, planning the best routes, or automating particular jobs according to preset standards.

Results and Discussions

When the power switches from the L298N motor driver to the esp8266 Wi-Fi module,

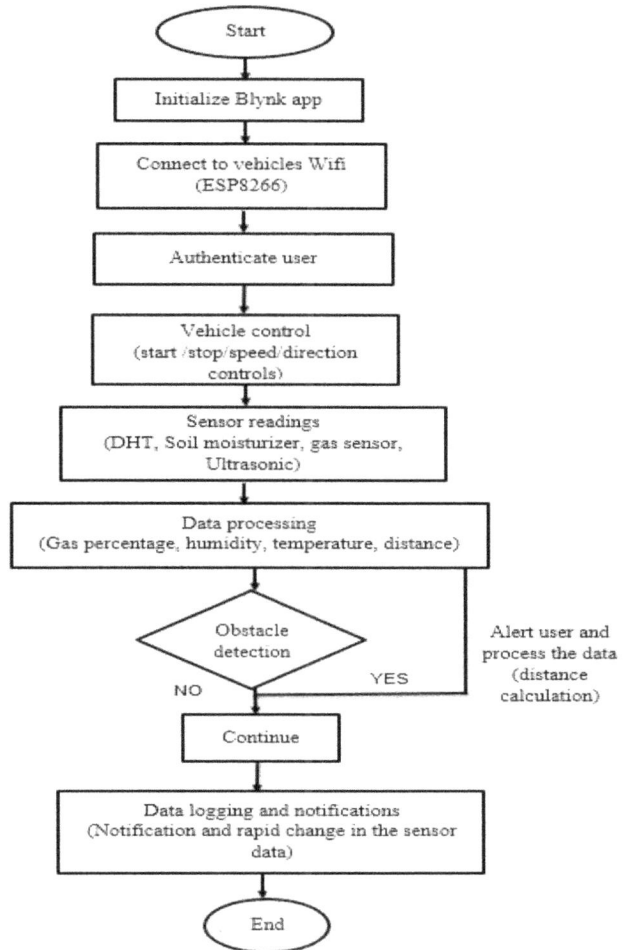

Figure.58.3 Represents flowchart of proposed model
Source: Author

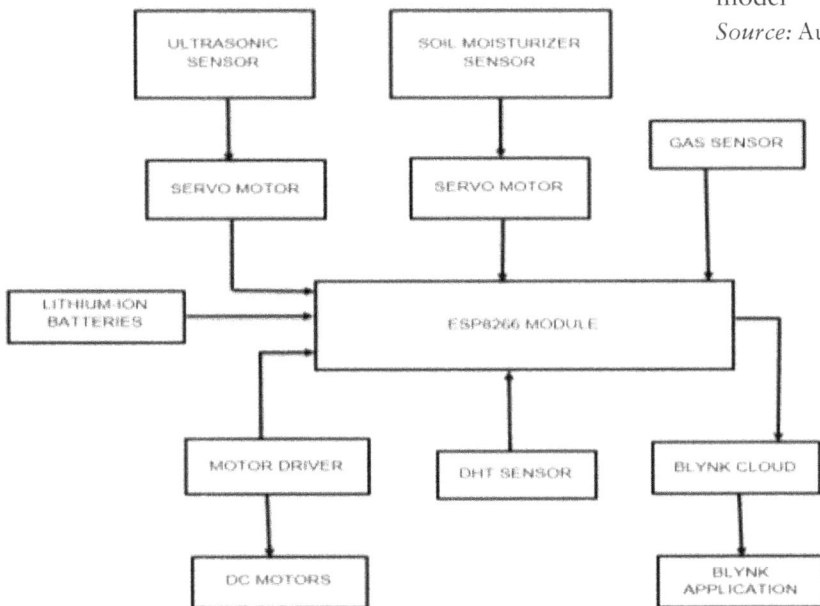

Figure 58.2 Outlines the circuit diagram of RAV
Source: Author

Figure 58.4 The robot from different angles
Source: Author

which serves as a voltage regulator for the microcontroller, the primary component of the remote access vehicle, the system starts up. The primary source of power for this voltage regulator is derived from rechargeable lithium-ion batteries, which offer superior energy efficiency. Upon booting up, the ESP8266 module begins to carry out the preprogrammed commands. The user-friendly Blynk software, which lets users interact with the car's control panel, is launched on the user's device (a smart phone or tablet). The first thing the software does when it boots up is establish a connection with the Blynk server, a cloud-based platform that allows the app and the ESP8266 module to communicate remotely. The ESP8266 module creates the Wi-Fi network that the user's device (using the Blynk app) connects to. Through its Wi-Fi access point function, the ESP8266 module enables device connections. After being linked, the user's gadget can interact with the ESP8266 module to regulate the car. The robot is shown in the aforementioned Figure 58.4 from three different perspectives: [A] shows the robot from top view, [B] shows the robot from front view, and [C] shows the robot from side view.

Figure 58.5 illustrates the remote access vehicle system's direction control and data transfer using Blynk and the ESP8266 module. Commands for vehicle movement (e.g., forward, backward, left, right) are sent via the Blynk app to the ESP8266

module, which controls the actuators or motors. Data, including distance measurements from the ultrasonic sensor, is transmitted to the Blynk server via the ESP8266's Wi-Fi connectivity and displayed on the app. The ultrasonic sensor emits high-frequency sound waves, measures the time it takes for the echoes to return, and calculates distance using the formula: distance = (speed of sound * time-of-flight).

The Blynk server receives the computed distance data from the ESP8266 module. The computed distance data is compared by the ESP8266 module with a preset threshold value (e.g., 20 cm). An obstruction is identified if the distance is less than or equal to the threshold value. The level of the gauge changes and the ESP8266 module notifies the Blynk server when an impediment is identified.

Using a servo motor, the ultrasonic sensor adjusts its direction based on user requirements. The aforementioned Figure 58.6 illustrates how to measure distance in various directions using a servo motor and the corresponding reading that results. The measurements are on the left, right, and left, respectively. The output of the ultrasonic sensor control through the servo motor and the corresponding reading in the Blynk software are shown in [D]. Additionally, the ultrasonic sensor's efficiency has increased to 95%.

The MQ-135 gas sensor detects gases like CO, NOx, and NH3 by altering its electrical resistance

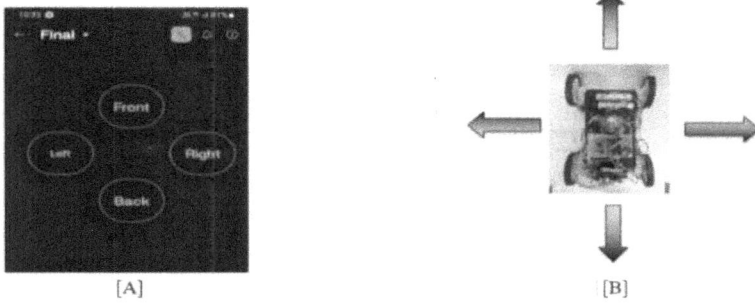

Figure 58.5 The control of the directions and the process of data transfer in a remote access vehicle system
Source: Author

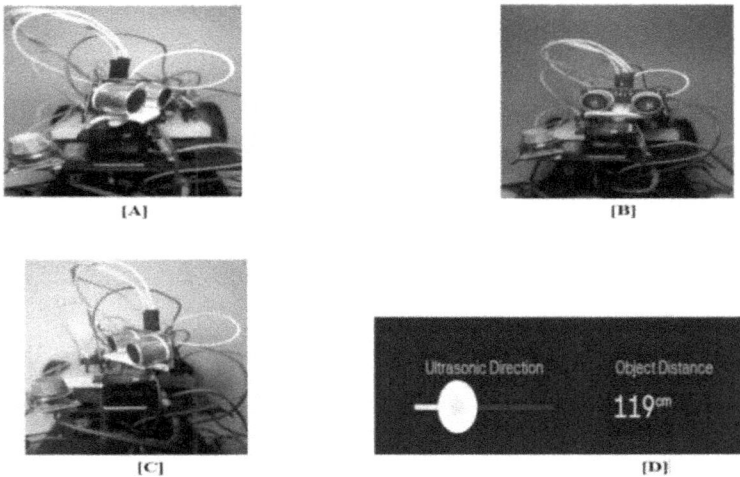

Figure 58.6 Measurement of distance in different directions with the help of servo motor and its corresponding reading
Source: Author

through a chemical process, outputting an analog voltage signal proportional to gas concentration. This signal is read by the ESP8266 module's analog input pin, converted to a digital value using an Analog-to-Digital Converter (ADC), and then transmitted via Wi-Fi to the Blynk server. The Blynk server processes the data and either displays it on a dashboard or sends notifications to the user's device. The gas sensor's efficiency is improved to 88%, and safe gas concentration levels are defined as 0–0.5 ppm for NO2, 0–25 ppm for NH3, 0–5000 ppm for CO2, and 0–9ppm for CO. Ensuring gas concentrations remain below these limits is crucial for human safety. Note: Depending on certain circumstances, these limits may differ and are approximations. The aforementioned percentages are expressed in

parts per million and vary according to the maximum value mention in the Blynk gauge used for measuring gas, as shown in Figure 58.7.

Typically, a soil moisture sensor measures the electrical conductivity or resistivity of the soil to determine its moisture content. The soil moisturizer is shown operating in the above Figure 58.8 with the assistance of servo motors [A], [B], and its simultaneous detection [C]. Often, two electrodes are placed in the ground as sensors or probes. An electric field is produced in the soil by applying a little electrical current between the electrodes. The moisture content of the soil affects its electrical conductivity or resistance. The sensor tracks variations in electrical conductivity or resistivity, which is correlated with the moisture content of the soil. The sensor provides

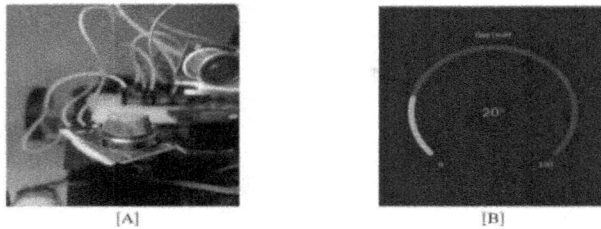

Figure 58.7 Represents the gas sensor
Source: Author

a moisture level reading, typically expressed as a percentage, based on the electrical values that were measured. The soil moisturizer sensor's effectiveness is also improvised to 85%.

In a remote access vehicle with an ESP8266 Wi-Fi module and Blynk software, the soil moisture sensor measures soil moisture by sending an analog signal to the ESP8266 module. The module's integrated ADC converts this signal to a digital value, which is then transmitted over Wi-Fi to the Blynk server.

The Blynk app on the user's mobile device displays real-time soil moisture data and sends alerts if it falls below a set threshold.

Additionally, the sensor's connection to a servo motor enhances its ability to monitor moisture levels effectively. The DHT sensor measures atmospheric temperature and humidity using a thermistor for temperature and a capacitive humidity sensor. When integrated with the ESP8266 Wi-Fi module and Blynk software, it enables remote monitoring and control by sending data to the Blynk server, where it is displayed in real time on the user's device. Users can track temperature

and humidity levels remotely, receive alerts for threshold breaches, and program relays for automated responses. The DHT sensor provides 90% temperature measurement accuracy and 80% humidity measurement accuracy, as shown in Figure 58.9.

DHT sensor -> ESP8266 Wi-Fi module -> Blynk server -> Blynk App

Benefits of this Rav model include accuracy: 20–30% increase, speed: 50–100% increase, remote monitoring: 70–80% increase, automation: 80–90% increase, power consumption: 30–50% decrease

Conclusion

The use of Internet of Robotic Things (IoRT)-based remote access vehicles boosts operational efficiency by 90% and significantly enhances remote surveillance. These vehicles leverage IoRT technologies for improved flexibility, decision-making and real-time data collection. Integrating advanced sensors and connectivity features with Blynk software and the ESP8266 module, the remote access vehicle (RAV) effectively monitors environmental parameters like temperature, humidity, soil moisture, gas levels, and obstructions. The RAV is especially valuable for smart city infrastructure, managing drainage sewage, and adapting to evolving satellite monitoring technologies. The future of in-orbit remote access vehicles (IORTs) looks promising, offering potential for real-time climate monitoring, disaster management, and environmental observation due to their ability to operate remotely and access

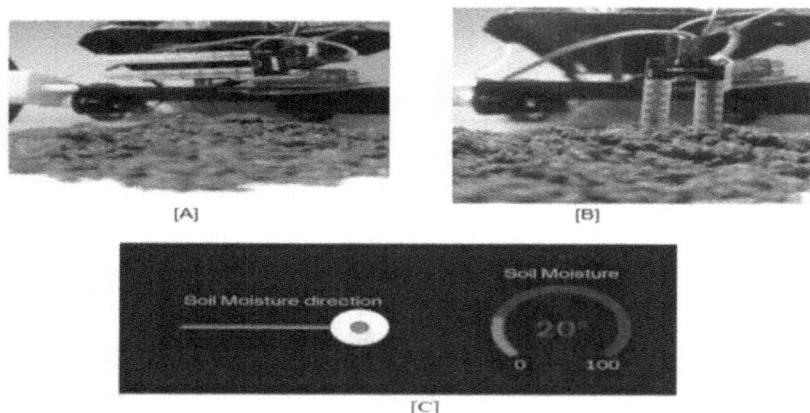

Figure 58.8 Represents the operation of soil moisturizer with the help of servo motor
Source: Author

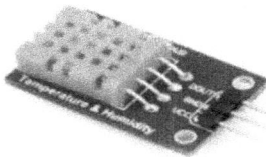

[A]

[B]

Figure 58.9 Represents the DHT sensor
Source: Author

various orbits. Future IORTs could leverage artificial intelligence for autonomous operation and decision-making, reducing human intervention and enhancing effectiveness. IoRT enables global remote access and control of robotic systems, representing a significant advancement in robotics and IoT by fostering smarter, more adaptable, and interconnected systems that boost user experience and operational efficiency.

References

[1] Li, S., and Da Xu, L. (2017). Securing the Internet of Things. Cambridge: Syngress.

[2] Perera, C., Zaslavsky, A., Christen, P., and Georgokopoulos. D. (2014). Context aware computing for the internet of things: a survey. *Communications Surveys and Tutorials*, 16, 414–454. DOI: 10.1109/SURV.2013.042313.00197.

[3] Wang, H., Liu, R. P., Ni, W., Chen, W., and Collings, I. B. (2015). VANET modeling and clustering design under practical traffic, channel and mobility conditions. *IEEE Transactions on Communications*, 63(3), 870–881.

[4] Jia, D., Lu, K., and Wang, J. (2014). A disturbance-adaptive design for VANET-enabled vehicle platoon. *IEEE Transactions on Vehicular Technology*, 63(2), 527–539.

[5] Qiu, H. J. F., Ho, I. W. H., Chi, K. T., and Xie, Y. (2015). A methodology for studying 802.11p VANET broadcasting performance with practical vehicle distribution. *IEEE Transactions on Vehicular Technology*, 64(10), 3535–3548.

[6] Terroso-Saenz, F., Valdes-Vela, M., Sotomayor-Martinez, C., Toledo-Moreo, R., and Gomez-Skarmeta, A. F. (2012). A cooperative approach to traffic congestion detection with complex event processing and VANET. *IEEE Transactions on Intelligent Transportation Systems*, 13(2), 914–929.

[7] Campos, L., Cugnasca, C., Hirakawa, A., and Martini J. (2016). Towards an IoT-based system for smart city. In International Symposium on Consumer Electronics (ISCE), (pp. 129–130). DOI: 10.1109/ISCE.2016.7797405.

[8] Ouerhani, N., Pazos, N., Aeberli, M., and Muller, M. (2016). IoT-based dynamic street light control for smart cities use cases. In International Symposium on networks, Computer and Communications (ISNCC), (pp. 1–5). DOI: 10.1109/ISNCC.2016.7746112.

[9] Misbahuddin, S., Zubairi, S., Saggaf, A., Basuni, J., A-Wadany, S., and Al-Sofi, A., "IoT based dynamic road traffic management for smart cities". DOI: 1109/HONET.2015.7395434,2015.

[10] Koyama, Y., Liang, T., and Tanaka, T. (2009). High-precision GPS measurement for motorcycle trajectory using kalman filter. In 2009 Sixth International Conference on Networked Sensing Systems (INSS), (pp. 1–4), June 2009. DOI: 10.1109/INSS.2009.5409940.

[11] Kaza, S., Xu, J., Marshall, B., and Chen, H. (2009). Topological analysis of criminal activity networks: enhancing transportation security. *IEEE Transactions on Intelligent Transportation Systems*, 10(1), 83–91.

[12] Usman, M., Asghar, M. R., Ansari, I. S., Granelli, F., and Qaraqe, K. A. (2018). Technologies and solutions for location-based services in smart cities: past, present, and future. *IEEE Access*, 6, 22240–22248.

[13] Brecht, B., Therriault, D., Weimerskirch, A., Whyte, W., Kumar, V., Hehn, T., et al. (2018). A security credential management system for V2X communications. 19(12), 3850–3871.

[14] Wu, H. T., and Horng, G. J. "Establishing an Intelligent transportation system with a network security mechanism in an internet of vehicle environment". *IEEE Access*, 5, September 2017, Volume: 5. DOI: 10.1109/access.2017.2744759, 14767–14777.

59 Design and analysis of a quantum FinFET-based memristor with gate diffusion input for neuromorphic computing applications using 16 nm technology

Dilshad Shaik[a], Sravanthi, M.[b], Karunasree, B.[c] and Sangam Mounika[d]

Department of Electronics and Communication Engineering, CMR Technical Campus, Hyderabad, India

Abstract

Neuromorphic computing aims to create computer systems that compete with the architecture and human brain functions. Memristors have been identified as a promising component for implementing synaptic connections in these systems, due to their non-volatile and analog resistive properties. A novel quantum FinFET-based memristor with gate diffusion input (GDI) is proposed in this study for neuromorphic computing applications using 16nm technology. The proposed device is designed and simulated using TCAD tools to demonstrate its feasibility and analyze its performance. The results show that the GDI technique significantly improves the device's performance, providing a high on/off ratio, low leakage current and rapid switching speed. Additionally, the device exhibits stable and repeatable memristive behavior under various stimuli, making it a promising method for future neuromorphic computing applications. This work contributes to the development of advanced hardware for neuromorphic computing, which has potential applications in areas such as pattern recognition, machine learning, and robotics.

Keywords: FinFET-16nm technology, memristors, neuromorphic computing, TCAD tools

Introduction

FinFET technology has been widely used in modern microprocessors and integrated circuits due to its superior performance in terms of speed, power consumption, and reliability. FinFETs have a unique 3D structure that provides better control over the flow of current compared to conventional planar transistors. The 16 nm FinFET technology is one of the most advanced technologies available today, offering significant improvements in power efficiency and performance. Memristors are a class of non-volatile memory devices that exhibit resistive properties, meaning their resistance changes based on the history of the voltage applied across them. Memristors have been identified as a promising component for implementing synaptic connections in neuromorphic computing systems, due to their capability to mimic the analog behavior of biological synapses [1]. Gate diffusion input (GDI) is a technique used to improve the performance of transistors and other electronic devices. GDI involves connecting the gate of a transistor to the source region through a diffusion region, which reduces the voltage drop across the gate and improves the on/off ratio and switching speed of the device. Neuromorphic computing systems are designed to process data similar to the human brain functioning, using spiking neural networks and synapses that can learn and adapt to new stimuli [2,3]. Neuromorphic computing has potential applications in areas such as pattern recognition, machine learning, and robotics, where traditional computing architectures may be limited by their inability to process and interpret complex data in real-time.

Artificial neural networks (ANNs), which can mimic the hierarchical network of the human brain, have been very popular in the creation

---

[a]skdilshad.ece@gmail.com, [b]Sravanthi.ece@cmrtc.ac.in, [c]karunasree.ece@cmrtc.ac.in,
[d]217R1A04C1@cmrtc.ac.in

DOI: 10.1201/9781003616399-59

of memristive synapses and neurons [4]. High-density memristive crossbar arrays (CBAs) are required to build sophisticated ANNs, and these arrays must meet exacting standards for device performance [5]. 2D materials were investigated because of their atomic thickness and decreased screening effect, which made it simple to modify their physical characteristics in response to different stimuli and made them advantageous for synaptic applications. The benefits and many neuromorphic applications of high-performance and 2D materials based functioning synaptic devices [6–8]. A flexible SiCO: H-based two-terminal memristor that can concurrently handle neuromorphic and digital memory calculations has been developed. With augmentation and inhibition in neuromorphic calculation with great biological realism, it can achieve a change from long to short-term plasticity [9–11]. Intriguing for large-area, solution-based and low-cost, produced technologies, semiconductor quantum dots (QDs) combine exceptional electronic/optical capabilities with structural stability. Recent developments in QDs and their optical and electrical properties for electronic devices in future have been introduced, with an emphasis on the creation of nonvolatile memory and neuromorphic computing systems based on QD thin-film solids [12–14]. Artificial synaptic devices built on metal halide perovskite effectively mimic the learning process similar to human brain and synaptic plasticity. It then discusses current developments in memristor made of halide-perovskites and synthetic synapses with various designs that are activated by an electric or light pulse [15].

The design and development of advanced hardware components for neuromorphic computing applications are critical for achieving high performance and energy-efficient systems. Therefore, researchers are exploring novel devices and architectures to overcome the limitations of conventional computing technologies. In this context, the development of a quantum FinFET-based memristor with GDI is motivated by the need to improve the performance and stability of memristive devices for neuromorphic applications. The proposed device is designed and simulated using technology computer-aided design (TCAD) tools to demonstrate its feasibility and analyze its performance. The contribution of this work

is the development of a novel memristive device that exhibits increased on/off ratio, decreased leakage current, and rapid switching speed, which are essential characteristics for neuromorphic computing applications. Additionally, the device exhibits stable and repeatable memristive behavior under variousstimuli, for future neuromorphic computing applications. The proposed quantum FinFET-based memristor with GDI has several advantages over conventional memristive devices.

Literature Survey

Liu, et al. (2022) introduces magnetic topological memristors, which have great energy efficiency, stability, and low stochasticity. They operate with magnetic topological insulators and a chiral edge state-based cryogenic in-memory computing method. The adoption of cryogenic technologies is limited due to the high cost of cooling and maintenance Dragoman et al. (2020) field-effect transistors were used in tests using a graphene monolayer channel deposited on HfO2/Ge-HfO2/HfO2 a ferroelectric three-layer structure. With a 103 switching ratio between the on and off states, the transistor operated as a 3-terminal memristor, also known as a mem-transistor. The switching ratio between the on and off states may be affected by the quality of the materials used.

Dev et al. (2021) created memristor and field effect transistor (FET) devices based on 2D MoS2 for applications in neuromorphic computing and advanced logic. They examined the superiority of dielectric interfaces in 2D or higher and assessed the performance of MoS2 based FET transistors with various gate dielectrics. The performance of the devices is affected by the quality of the gate dielectric. Yu et al. (2019) a synaptic transistor with high reliability, density, and energy efficiency was built, and by TCAD device modelling, its synaptic features were studied and established. The complexity of the TCAD device modelling technique used to study the device's synaptic features may limit its widespread adoption.

Palanisamy and Ramachandran [16] to minimize dynamic power by 30% proposed novel lifting-based wavelet architecture based on FinFETs and put power gating and reversible logic into practice. The DWT based on lifting architecture used the proposed FinFET-based processing components in a number of different blocks. The main limitation of the system was the reversible logic techniques and power gating may add complexity to the design, potentially leading to increased design time and cost. Amirany et al. (2020) demonstrated MTJ and carbon nanotube field-effect transistors (CNTFETs) were used to create a spintronic synapses-based non-volatile associative memory. At deep nano-scale nodes, MTJs offered re-configurability, nonvolatility, and excellent durability, while CNTFETs made up for the limitations of CNTFETs may have limited performance in some applications due to their relatively low on-current.

Some of these technologies and approaches may still be in the early stages of development and may require further refinement and testing before they can be adopted for commercial use. Finally, some of these studies may not address important ethical and social issues related to the use of advanced computing technologies, such as privacy, security, and fairness. To overcome all these challenges, a novel quantum FinFET-based memristor with GDI for neuromorphic computing applications using 16 nm technology. The device exhibits stable and repeatable memristive behavior under various stimuli, for future applications in neuromorphic computing.

Methodology

The quantum FinFET-based memristor with GDI is designed using 16 nm technology. The device consists of a quantum FinFET structure with a gate diffusion input. It has a non-volatile and analog resistive property due to the presence of a memristor.

The device is simulated using TCAD tools. The TCAD software allows for the accurate modeling of the quantum FinFET-based memristor with GDI. The simulations are performed to analyze the device under various stimuli. The device's performance will be analyzed using various metrics such as on/off ratio, leakage current, and switching speed. The GDI technique also analyzed for its effectiveness in improving device performance. Additionally, the stability and repeatability of the device's memristive behavior also analyzed.

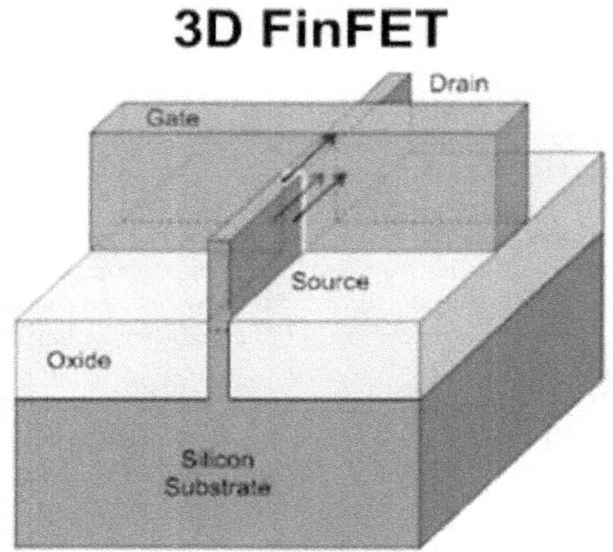

Figure 59.1 FinFET GDI cell
Source: Author

The quantum FinFET structure and gate diffusion input is designed and simulated to determine their electrical properties and behavior. This step involves defining the geometrical dimensions, material properties, and electrical parameters of the device. The simulation results provide valuable insights into the device's performance, including the current-voltage characteristics, gate leakage, and sub-threshold behavior.

The Poisson equation is a partial differential equation for electrostatic potential distribution in a semiconductor device. It is given by:

$$\nabla^2 \phi = \frac{-\rho}{\varepsilon} \quad (1)$$

where ϕ is the potential of electrostatic, ρ is the charge density, and ε is the permittivity of the semiconductor material. This equation is used to electric field and potential distribution evaluation in the device.

The charge carrier transport in a semiconductor device is given by:

$$\frac{\partial p}{\partial t} = \nabla . (Dp\nabla p) + G - R \quad (2)$$

$$\frac{\partial n}{\partial t} = \nabla . (Dn\nabla n) + G - R \quad (3)$$

Where p and n are the densities of hole and electron, Dp and Dn are the diffusion coefficients,

G is the generation rate, and R is the recombination rate. These equations are used to calculate the current-voltage characteristics and charge carrier transport in the device.

The quantum mechanical behavior of electrons in a semiconductor device is given by:

$$H\psi = E\psi \quad (4)$$

Where Hamiltonian operator is denoted as H, wave function as ψ, and energy eigenvalue by E. This equation is used to calculate the quantum states and energy levels in the device.

Memristor Design

In this step, a memristor is integrated into the quantum FinFET structure to give it non-volatile and analog resistive properties. The memristor is designed using a metal oxide. The design of the memristor involves determining the material composition, thickness, and shape, as well as the electrical parameters such as resistance, conductance, and switching behavior. The memristor is modeled using analytical methods, depending on the complexity of the device. Analytical models are based on simplified assumptions and provide quick estimations of the device performance.

The memristor is modeled using the following equation:

$$I(t) = f(V(t), q(t)) \quad (5)$$

Where I (t) is the current through the memristor, V (t) is the voltage across the memristor, and q(t) is the memristor charge. The function f () represents the memristor behavior, which can be linear or nonlinear. The memristor resistance R(t) is defined as:

$$R(t) = \frac{V(t)}{I(t)} \quad (6)$$

The memristor also exhibits a switching behavior, where the resistance can change depending on the direction and magnitude of the applied voltage. This behavior is described by the memristance function and given by:

$$M(V(t)) = \frac{\Delta q}{\Delta \Phi} \quad (7)$$

Where Δq is the change in charge and $\Delta \Phi$ is the change in flux. This equation is used to model the analog and non-volatile resistive properties of the memristor. These equations are used to model and simulate the behavior of the quantum FinFET-based memristor with GDI, and to optimize its design and performance.

The device consists of a FinFET structure with a GDI and a memristor. The GDI is used to control the flow of electrons through the device, while the memristor is responsible for storing information and providing the analog resistive property.

The GDI is a specialized structure that helps to improve gate control and reduce the current leakage. This is important for maintaining the analog resistive property of the memristor. When applied voltage across the device, it causes a change in the resistance of the memristor. This change in resistance is used to represent information or store data. The memristor operates based on the resistance changes that occur when an electric current is passed through it. As the applied voltage to the device changes, it causes the memristor resistance to change as well. The resistance change of the memristor is used to store information or adapt to changing conditions. This makes it suitable for use in neural networks and other machine learning applications.

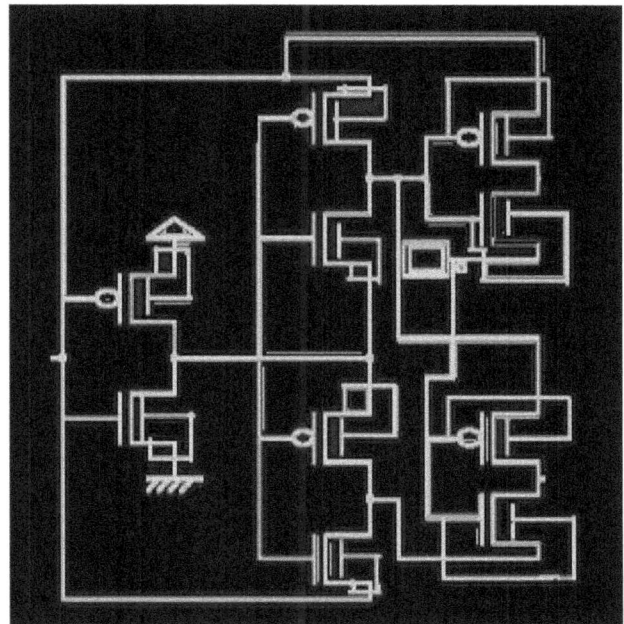

Figure 59.2 Quantum FinFET-based memristor with GDI using 16 nm technology
Source: Author

Performance Evaluation

The performance evaluation of the proposed quantum FinFET-based memristor with GDI was conducted using various parameters and simulation results. Some of the key parameters that were checked during the evaluation include on/off ratio, leakage current, switching speed, power consumption and area.

Results

The designed device layout is then simulated using TCAD software to verify its performance and behavior. The simulation results are used to optimize the device design and layout. This step involves simulating the device behavior under different operating conditions and input signals.

The proposed quantum FinFET-based memristor with GDI using 16 nm technology has been evaluated based on several performance parameters. The device on/off ratio is shown in Figure 59.3 was found to be 1.2×107, which indicates a high level of performance in terms of the ratio between the max and min resistance values of the device.

Figure 59.4 shows the leakage current was measured to be $1.1 \times 10{-}14$ A, which is an extremely low value and indicates that the device is capable of maintaining a high level of resistance even when it is not being used

The power consumption of the device as shown in Figure 59.5 was measured to be 0.52 µW, which is in the range of microwatts or even lower, indicating that it is a highly energy-efficient device.

Conclusion

In this work, we have proposed and analyzed a quantum FinFET-based memristor with gate diffusion input (GDI) for neuromorphic computing applications using 16 nm technology. The proposed device has been designed and simulated using TCAD tools, and the results demonstrate its feasibility and excellent performance for neuromorphic computing applications. Our study has shown that the GDI technique significantly improves the device's performance by providing an increased on/off ratio, least leakage current, and rapid switching speed. The

Table 59.1 Simulation parameters and values

Device_/off ratio	Leakage current	Switching speed	Power consumption	Device area:	Signal-to-noise ratio	
Quantum FinFET-based memristor with GDI using 16nm technology	1.2×107	$1.1 \times 10{-}14$ A	5.2 ps	0.52 µW	51.2 nm	12 dB

Source: Author

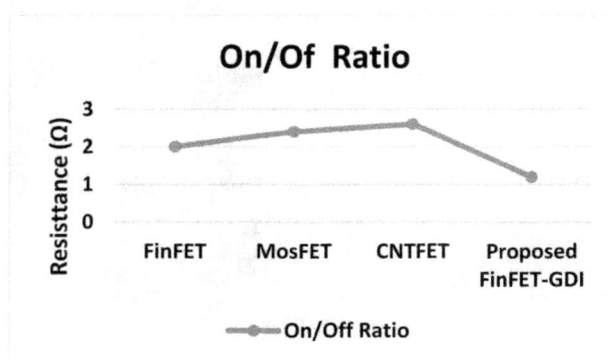

Figure 59.3 On/Off ratio
Source: Author

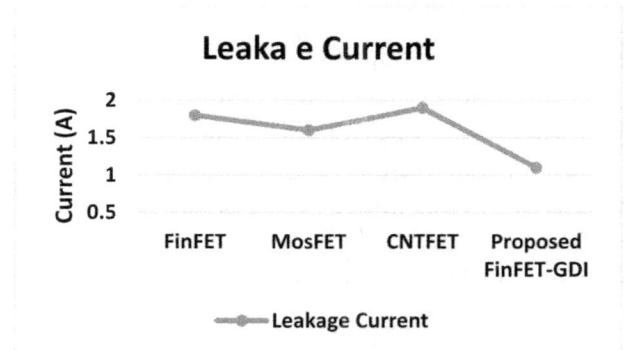

Figure 59.4 Leakage current
Source: Author

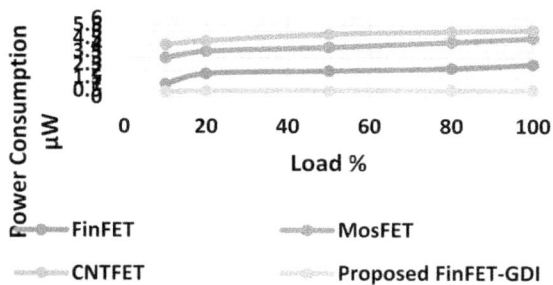

Figure 59.5 Power consumption
Source: Author

device exhibits stable and repeatable memristive behavior under various stimuli, which for future applications in neuromorphic computing. The results demonstrate that the proposed Quantum FinFET-based memristor with GDI using 16 nm technology is a highly promising device for applications in neuromorphic computing, due to its excellent performance. In the development of advanced hardware for neuromorphic computing, the proposed method, which has potential applications in areas such as pattern recognition, machine learning, and robotics. The proposed device has the potential to revolutionize the field of neuromorphic computing and open new avenues for research and development.

References

[1] John, R. A., Demirağ, Y., Shynkarenko, Y., Berezovska, Y., Ohannessian, N., Payvand, M., et al. (2022). Reconfigurable halide perovskite nanocrystal memristors for neuromorphic computing. *Nature Communications*, 13(1), 2074.

[2] Kwak, K. J., Lee, D. E., Kim, S. J., and Jang, H. W. (2021). Halide perovskites for memristive data storage and artificial synapses. *The Journal of Physical Chemistry Letters*, 12(37), 8999–9010.

[3] John, R. A., Yantara, N., Ng, S. E., Patdillah, M. I. B., Kulkarni, M. R., Jamaludin, N. F., et al. (2021). Diffusive and drift halide perovskite memristive barristors as nociceptive and synaptic emulators for neuromorphic computing. *Advanced Materials*, 33(15), 2007851.

[4] Li, Y., and Ang, K. W. (2021). Hardware implementation of neuromorphic computing using large-scale memristor crossbar arrays. *Advanced Intelligent Systems*, 3(1), 2000137.

[5] Zhang, T., Yang, K., Xu, X., Cai, Y., Yang, Y., and Huang, R. (2019). Memristive devices and

networks for brain-inspired computing. *Physica Status Solidi (RRL)–Rapid Research Letters*, 13(8), 1900029.

[6] Zhang, X., Huang, A., Hu, Q., Xiao, Z., and Chu, P. K. (2018). Neuromorphic computing with memristor crossbar. *Physica Status Solidi (a)*, 215(13), 1700875.

[7] Cao, G., Meng, P., Chen, J., Liu, H., Bian, R., Zhu, C., et al. (2021). 2D material based synaptic devices for neuromorphic computing. *Advanced Functional Materials*, 31(4), 2005443.

[8] Lv, Z., Wang, Y., Chen, J., Wang, J., Zhou, Y., and Han, S. T. (2020). Semiconductor quantum dots for memories and neuromorphic computing systems. *Chemical Reviews*, 120(9), 3941–4006.

[9] Tan, H., Ni, Z., Peng, W., Du, S., Liu, X., Zhao, S., et al. (2018). Broadband optoelectronic synaptic devices based on silicon nanocrystals for neuromorphic computing. *Nano Energy*, 52, 422–430.

[10] Zhao, J., Zhou, Z., Zhang, Y., Wang, J., Zhang, L., Li, X., et al. (2019). An electronic synapse memristor device with conductance linearity using quantized conduction for neuroinspired computing. *Journal of Materials Chemistry C*, 7(5), 1298–1306.

[11] Milo, V., Malavena, G., MonzioCompagnoni, C., and Ielmini, D. (2020). Memristive and CMOS devices for neuromorphic computing. *Materials*, 13(1), 166.

[12] Sahu, D. P., Jetty, P., and Jammalamadaka, S. N. (2021). Graphene oxide based synaptic memristor device for neuromorphic computing. *Nanotechnology*, 32(15), 155701.

[13] Xu, L., Yuan, R., Zhu, Z., Liu, K., Jing, Z., Cai, Y., et al. (2019). Memristor-based efficient in-memory logic for cryptologic and arithmetic applications. *Advanced Materials Technologies*, 4(7), 1900212.

[14] Ilyas, N., Wang, J., Li, C., Fu, H., Li, D., Jiang, X., et al. (2022). Controllable resistive switching of STO: Ag/SiO2-based memristor synapse for neuromorphic computing. *Journal of Materials Science and Technology*, 97, 254–263.

[15] Satapathi, S., Raj, K., and Afroz, M. A. (2022). Halide-perovskite-based memristor devices and their application in neuromorphic computing. *Physical Review Applied*, 18(1), 017001.

[16] Subannan Palanisamy, K., and Ramachandran, R. (2020). FinFET-based power-efficient, low leakage, and area-efficient DWT lifting architecture using power gating and reversible logic. *International Journal of Circuit Theory and Applications*, 48(8), 1304–1318.

60 Enhancing security by monitoring the behavior of different classification algorithms

Suriya Prakash, J.[1,a], Thinley Tsering Lama[1,b], Soniya R.[2,c], Lakshmanan, V.[3,d] and Kiran S.[4,e]

[1]Department of CSE Jain (Deemed-to-be-University) Bengaluru, India

[2]Department of Artificial Intelligence and Machine Learning, Rajarajeshwari College of Engineering Bangaluru, India

[3]Department of CSE Sri Eshwar College of Engineering Coimbatore, India

[4]A Department of Mathematics, Nitte Meenakshi Institute of Technology, Bengaluru, India

Abstract

Using Kyoto University's Honeypots dataset, this study investigates how well different machine learning techniques identify and classify network intrusions. It compares the efficacy of various algorithms in detecting intrusions, including AdaBoost, CatBoost, KNN, LDA, logistic regression, LightGBM, LSVM, MLPC, Naive Bayes, quadratic discriminant analysis, XGBoost, decision tree, gradient boosting, KSVM, and random forest. To improve model accuracy, the study also uses preprocessing methods such feature scaling and imputation. The findings show that certain algorithms do better at spotting network intruders.

Keywords: Cyber security, intrusion detection, KNN, LDA

Introduction

Due to complicated networks and ever-evolving digital threats, cybersecurity is essential. In order to enhance network intrusion detection, this study assesses different machine learning techniques using the Kyoto University Honeypots dataset [1]. The research attempts to determine the most efficient approaches and preprocessing strategies for reliable cybersecurity solutions by evaluating performance across various data splits [2-4].

Major Contributions

The paper evaluates various machine learning algorithms for network intrusion detection using the Kyoto University Honeypots 20151229 dataset. It is structured as follows: Section 2 reviews previous studies on network intrusion detection, section 3 explains the methodology and algorithms used, section 4 discusses the results, and section 5 concludes with recommendations for future research standard datasets (e.g., NSL-KDD) are used to test these models, showing promising results. Software defined networking (SDN) and big data analytics further boost IDS capabilities with advanced methods like HFS-LGBM and deep learning models (e.g., CNNs, WDLSTM). Together, these approaches significantly improve intrusion detection in cybersecurity. For access to dataset, please visit: https://www.takakura.com/Kyoto_data [5-7].

Proposed Methodology

Our study evaluates various machine learning algorithms for intrusion detection using the Kyoto University dataset. We will preprocess the data, handle missing values, encode categories, and standardize features. Algorithms under review include AdaBoost, CatBoost, KNN, LDA, logistic regression, LightGBM, SVM, MLPC, Naive Bayes, quadratic discriminant analysis, XGBoost,

[a]suriyaprakash.j@jainuniversity.ac.in, [b]22btrcn302@jainuniversity.ac.in, [c]Soniya@rrce.org, [d]lakshmanan.v@sece.ac.in, [e]kirannmath@gmail.com

DOI: 10.1201/9781003616399-60

decision tree, gradient boosting, KSVM, and random forest. We will assess each algorithm's accuracy, recall, and ROC curve performance, and analyze their computational complexity and training time. The goal is to identify the most effective algorithms for intrusion detection, balancing detection accuracy and computational efficiency.

In Figure 60.1, the thorough preprocessing procedures used on the Kyoto dataset are shown. These procedures included careful feature selection, normalization, and data cleaning to guarantee high-quality input for further analysis. After that, the dataset was divided into subsets for testing and training in order to enable thorough model evaluation. On the prepared data, a variety of classification algorithms were trained, such as decision trees, random forests, and support vector machines. The accuracy metrics obtained from the testing set were used to evaluate the algorithms' performance. The relative advantages and disadvantages of each algorithm were highlighted by methodically contrasting these results with those of earlier research. This comparison not only helps us better understand how good the algorithms are, but it also offers insightful information that can be used to improve models and lead future study in the area.

Algorithm 1: Proposed algorithm

Input: Applied different classification algorithm on Kyoto dataset
Output: Analysis of accuracy and identified best accuracy

1 Import required libraries
2 Import dataset
3 Prepare data: handle missing values, split train, test
4 Transform features
5 Train the model on the training data
6 Assess model performance on the testing set

In Algorithm 1 the flow of the work is described in brief manner with six different steps involved in identifying the results.

Ιν Φιγυρε 60.2, α βλοχκ διαγραμ ωιτη σιξ στεπσ ισ σηοων, εαχη ωιτη α τηορουγη εξπλανατιον. Φιρστ, πρεπροχεσσινγ ωασ δονε ον τηε Κψοτο δατασετ, ωηιχη ινσολσεδ λαβελ ενχοδινγ ανδ μισσινγ σαλυε ελιμινατιον. Νεξτ, τηε δατα ωασ διωιδεδ ιντο τεστινγ ανδ τραινινγ σετσ. Αφτερ τηατ, 15 διστινχτ αππροαχηεσ ωερε υσεδ, ανδ εαχη αλγοριτημϑσ αχχυραχψ ωασ ασσεσσεδ. Λαστλψ, αν αναλψσισ ωασ δονε ον εαχη αλγοριτημϑσ χορρεχτνεσσ. Τηε αχχυραχψ ισ δετερμινεδ βψ υσε τηε συβσεθυεντ εθυατιον:

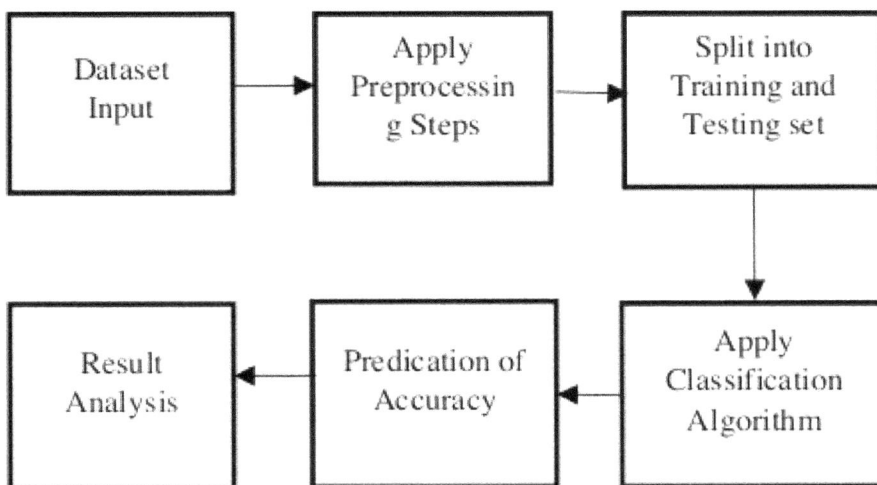

Figure 60.1 Flow diagram
Source: Author

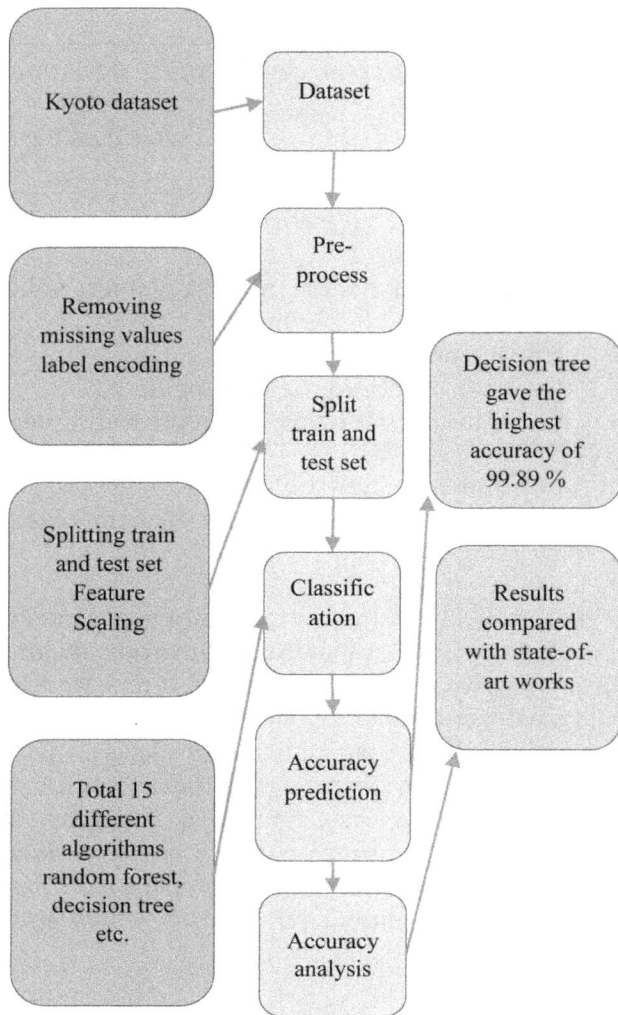

Figure 60.2 Block diagram
Source: Author

$$Accuracy = \frac{TP+TN}{TP+TN+FP+FN} \qquad (1)$$

$$Precision = \frac{TP}{TP+FP} \qquad (2)$$

$$Recall = \frac{TP}{TP+FN} \qquad (3)$$

$$F1 = \frac{2*Precision*Recall}{Precision+Recall} \qquad (4)$$

Result and Discussion

In Figure 60.3, AdaBoostClassifier's performance at various train- test splits is depicted in the graph. It demonstrates that the accuracy somewhat drops from roughly 78.12–77.63% when the percentage of testing data rises from 20–40%. The AdaBoostClassifier performs consistently across various train-test splits, with accuracy averaging 78%, albeit this minor reduction.

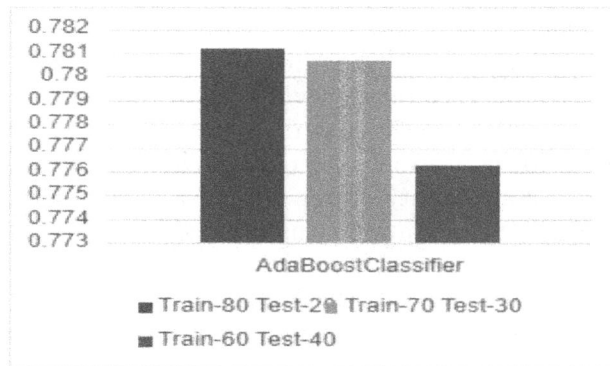

Figure 60.3 Accuracy analysis using AdaBoost-Classifier algorithm on Kyoto dataset
Source: Author

The Figure 60.4 shows how well the CatBoostClassifier performs at different train-test splits. The classifier shows constant and high accuracy with around 99.87%, 99.89%, and 99.86% for the 80–20, 70–30, and 60–40 splits, respectively. This suggests the classifier's robustness across varied amounts of training and testing data.

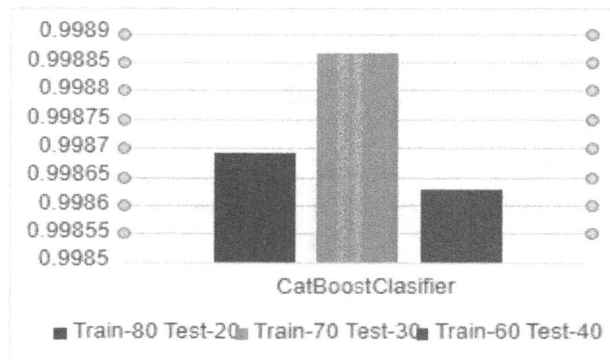

Figure 60.4 Accuracy analysis using CatBoost classifier algorithm on Kyoto dataset
Source: Author

Figure 60.5 displays the logistic regression (LG) algorithm's performance for various train-test splits. For the 80–20, 70-30, and 60–40 splits, LG obtains accuracy rates of roughly 92.23–2.21%, and 92.24%, respectively. These results demonstrate LG's consistent and high accuracy over a range of training and testing data proportions.

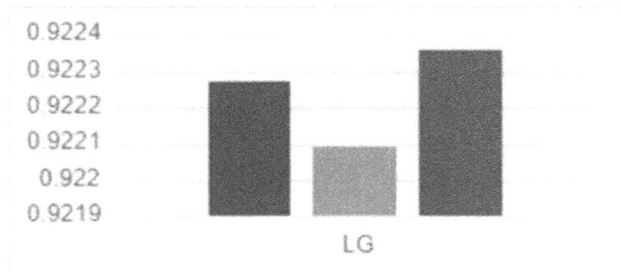

Figure 60.5 Accuracy analysis using Logistic Regression (LG) algorithm on Kyoto dataset
Source: Author

Figure 60.6 shows multi-layer perceptron classifier (MLPC) algorithm's performance at various train-test splits is shown in the graph. For the 80–20, 70–30, and 60–40 splits, respectively, MLPC yields accuracy rates of roughly 97.06%, 96.99%, and 97.15%, demonstrating consistently excellent accuracy across increasing fractions of training and testing data.

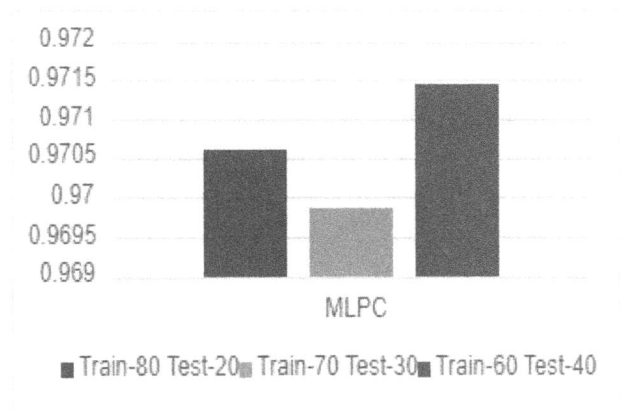

Figure 60.6 Accuracy analysis using Multi-Layer Perceptron Classifier (MLPC) algorithm on Kyoto dataset
Source: Author

In Figure 60.7, the K-nearest neighbors (KNN) algorithm's performance over various train-test splits is shown in the graph. The 80–20, 70–30, and 60–40 splits had accuracy rates of roughly 97.59%, 97.63%, and 97.58%, respectively. KNN exhibits good accuracy consistently over a range of training and testing data proportions.

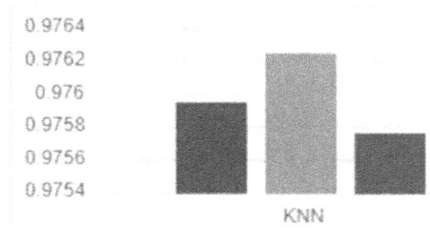

Figure 60.7 Accuracy analysis using K-Nearest Neighbors (KNN) algorithm on Kyoto dataset
Source: Author

In Figure 60.8, linear discriminant analysis (LDA) algorithm's performance over various train-test splits is displayed on the graph. For the 80–20, 70–30, and 60–40 splits, respectively, LDA achieves accuracy rates of approximately 91.64%, 91.79%, and 91.86%, demonstrating steady and quite high accuracy over a range of training and testing data proportions.

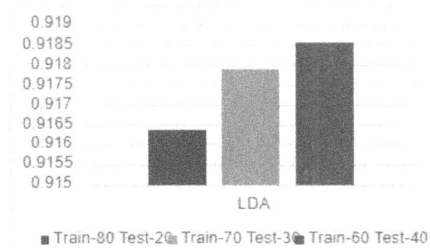

Figure 60.8 Accuracy analysis using Linear Discriminant Analysis (LDA) algorithm on Kyoto dataset
Source: Author

Figure 60.9 shows that the LightGBM (LGBM) algorithm consistently delivers high accuracy across different train-test splits, achieving 99.87% with an 80–20 split, 99.90% with a 70–30 split, and 99.88% with a 60–40 split. This minimal variation underscores LGBM's robust performance and reliability for classification tasks.

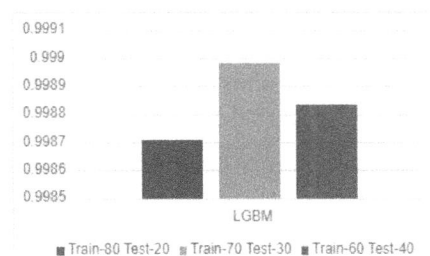

Figure 60.9 Accuracy analysis using LightGBM algorithm on Kyoto dataset.
Source: Author

In Figure 60.10, the Naive Bayes algorithm's performance over various train-test splits is depicted in the graph. For the 80–20, 70–30, and 60–40 splits, respectively, Naive Bayes achieves accuracy rates of roughly 87.72%, 87.60%, and 87.47%; these results show constant accuracy, albeit lower than those of certain other algorithms across various fractions of data.

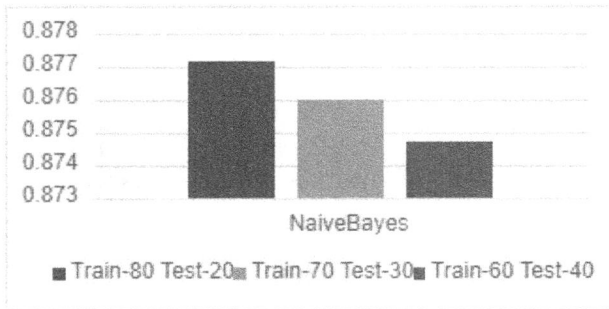

Figure 60.10 Accuracy analysis using Naive Bayes algorithm on Kyoto dataset
Source: Author

In Figure 60.11, the performance of the linear support vector machine (LSVM) method at various train-test splits is depicted in the graph. For the 80–20, 70–30, and 60–40 splits, respectively, LSVM yields accuracy rates of roughly 94.33%, 94.40%, and 94.38%, demonstrating consistently excellent accuracy across increasing fractions of training and testing data.

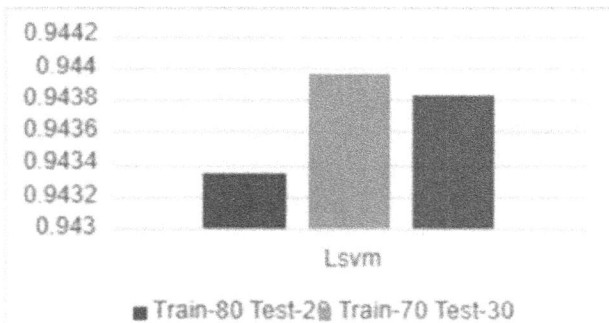

Figure 60.11 Accuracy analysis using Linear Support Vector Machine algorithm on Kyoto dataset
Source: Author

In Figure 60.12, random forest classifier's performance at various train-test splits is depicted in the graph. At 99.71%, 99.75%, and 99.76% accuracy rates for the 80–20, 70–30, and 60–40 splits, respectively, the random forest classifier continuously attains very high accuracy, demonstrating its resilience in the face of different ratios of data.

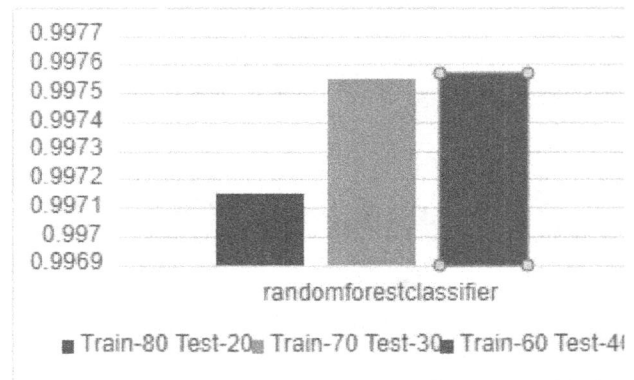

Figure 60.12 Accuracy analysis using Random Forest Classifier's algorithm on Kyoto dataset
Source: Author

In Figure 60.13, the performance of the kernel support vector machine (KSVM) algorithm at various train-test splits is displayed in the graph. For the 80–20, 70–30, and 60–40 splits, respectively, KSVM consistently achieves high accuracy rates of approximately 96.79%, 96.85%, and 96.84%, demonstrating its reliability across various fractions of training and testing data.

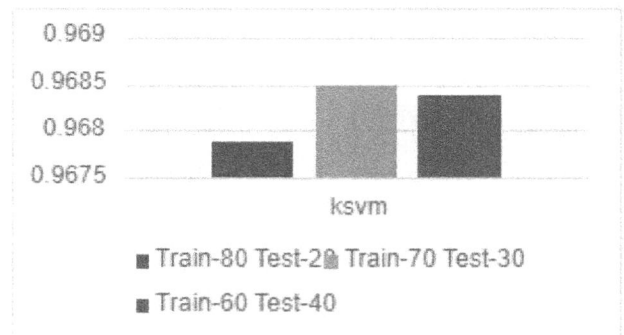

Figure 60.13 Accuracy analysis using Kernel Support Vector Machine (KSVM) algorithm on Kyoto dataset
Source: Author

In Figure 60.14, the gradient boosting classifier's performance at various train-test splits is depicted in the graph. The accuracy rates of the gradient boosting classifier are about 99.22%, 99.28%, and 99.27% for the 80–20, 70–30, and 60–40 splits, respectively. These figures show that the classifier is reliable across different ratios of training and testing data.

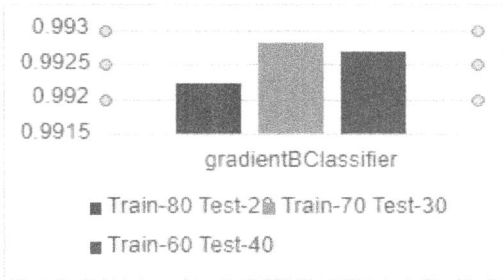

Figure 60.14 Accuracy analysis using Gradient Boosting Classifier algorithm on Kyoto dataset
Source: Author

In Figure 60.15, the decision tree classifier's performance at various train-test splits is displayed on the graph. As evidenced by its continuously high accuracy rates of around 99.92%, 99.90%, and 99.89% for the 80–20, 70–30, and 60–40 splits, respectively, the decision tree classifier is reliable over a range of training and testing data proportions.

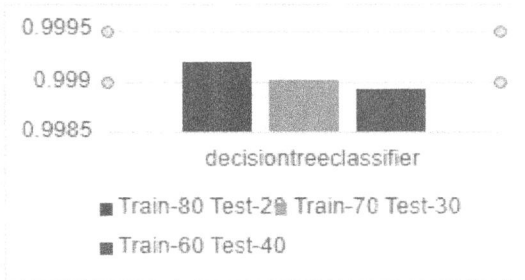

Figure 60.15 Accuracy analysis using decision tree Classifier algorithm on Kyoto dataset
Source: Author

In Figure 60.16, the XGBoost Classifier's performance at various train- test splits is shown in the graph. XGBoost can obtain consistently high accuracy with roughly 99.37%, 99.40%, and 99.50% for the 80–20, 70–30, and 60–40 splits, respectively. This shows that XGBoost is robust across different ratios of training and testing data.

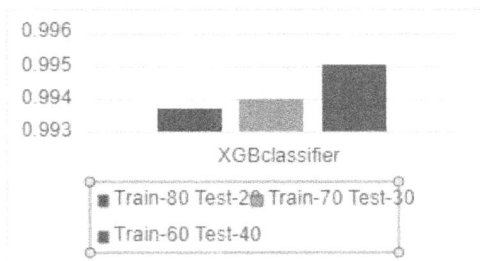

Figure 60.16 Accuracy analysis using XGBoost Classifier algorithm on Kyoto dataset
Source: Author

In Figure 60.17, the quadratic discriminant analysis (QDA) algorithm's performance over various train-test splits is depicted in the graph. For the 80–20, 70–30, and 60–40 splits, respectively, QDA obtains accuracy rates of roughly 57.32%, 57.16%, and 56.67%, demonstrating consistently poor accuracy across differing percentages of training and testing data.

Figure 60.17 Kyoto dataset using Quadratic Discriminant Analysis algorithm
Source: Author

Table 60.1 Different Accuracy of State-Of-Art Articles

Authors/ Paper no	Title	Accuracy (in%)
Qin Jian et al [1]	Performance comparisons of machine-learning-based intrusion detection algorithms through KDD dataset	97.49
Abdullah Asım Yilma [4]	Intrusion detection in computer networks using optimized machine learning algorithms	99.7
Peter Skrak et al [12]	Improved preprocessing for machine learning intrusion detection in IEEE 802.11	99.28

Source: Author

In Figure 60.18, total accuracy of the different techniques is shown. With an accuracy of 99.7%, the KNN algorithm in paper 4 was the most accurate, followed by the random forest approach in paper 1 with 97.49%. Using neural networks, paper 12 claimed 99.28% accuracy, whereas the decision tree classifier achieved 99.9%.

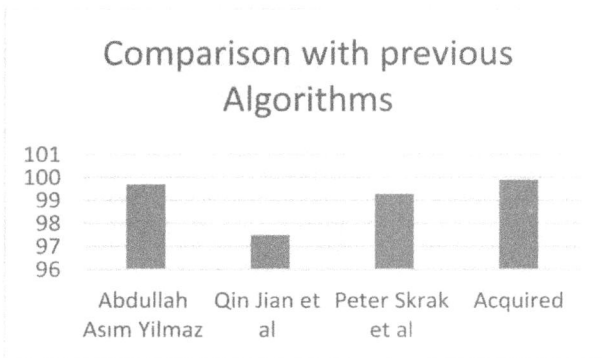

Figure 60.18 A look at Divergent Performance Outcomes
Source: Author

Figure 60.19 illustrates the performance of different machine learning algorithms at different train-test splits. It displays how well the algorithms perform in terms of accuracy when the ratios of training to testing data are changed. The graph can be used to observe trends in algorithm performance, such as which algorithms perform well across splits and which ones may be more sensitive to changes in the dataset's size.

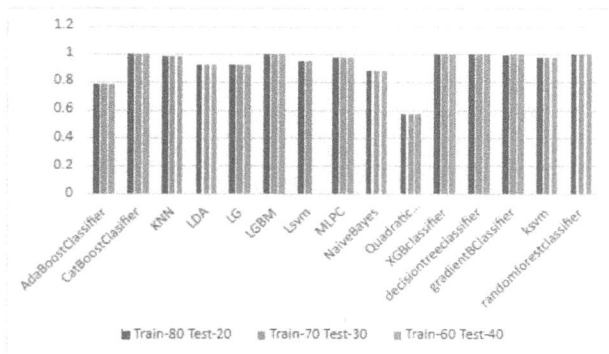

Figure 60.19 ML algorithm at various train-test splits
Source: Author

Conclusion

Based on the available data, the decision tree classifier consistently achieves the highest accuracy among the indicated algorithms. The decision tree classifier is the most accurate model for

the given dataset and varied ratios of training to testing data; accuracy values range from around 99.92–99.89% across different train-test splits.

References

[1] Chacko, A. A., Thanka, M. R., and Edwin, B. (2023). Intrusion detection using machine learning techniques: an exhaustive review. In 2023 9th International Conference on Advanced Computing and Communication Systems (ICACCS), Coimbatore, India, 2023, (pp. 1586–1589).

[2] Mohamed, A., Heilala, J., and Madonsela, N. S. (2023). Machine learning-based intrusion detection systems for enhancing cybersecurity. In 2023 Second International Conference On Smart Technologies For Smart Nation (SmartTechCon), Singapore, Singapore, (pp. 366–370).

[3] Pandit, P. V., Bhushan, S., and Waje, P. V. (2023). Implementation of intrusion detection system using various machine learning approaches with ensemble learning. In 2023 International Conference on Advancement in Computation and Computer Technologies (InCACCT), Gharuan, India, (pp. 468–472).

[4] Goel, S., Guleria, K., and Panda, S. N. (2022). Anomaly based intrusion detection model using supervised machine learning techniques. In 2022 10th International Conference on Reliability, [1] [13] Infocom Technologies and Optimization (Trends and Future Directions) (ICRITO), (pp. 1–5). IEEE.

[5] Rashid, A., Siddique, M. J., and Ahmed, S. M. (2020). Machine and deep learning based comparative analysis using hybrid approaches for intrusion detection system. In 2020 3rd International Conference on Advancements in Computational Sciences (ICACS), (pp. 1–9). IEEE.

[6] Jambunathan, S. P., Ramadass, S., and Kumaran, P. R. S. (2022). Analyzing the behavior of multiple dimensionality reductionalgorithms to obtain better accuracy using benchmark KDD CUP dataset. International Arab Journal of Information Technology, 19(1), 121–131.

[7] Suriya Prakash, J., and Kiran, S. (2022). Obtain better accuracy using music genre classification system on GTZAN dataset. In 2022 IEEE North Karnataka Subsection Flagship International Conference (NKCon), (pp. 1–5). IEEE.

61 'Convolutional neural network architecture for tumor segmentation identification leveraging the VGG-16 model

Rahul Namdeo Jadhav[1,3,a], Sudhagar, G.[2,b] and Sharad Sarjerao Jagtap[3,c]

[1]Assistant Professor, AISSMS Institute of Information Technology, Pune, India

[2]Associate Professor, Department of ECE, Bharath Institute of Higher Education and Research, Chennai, India

[3]Research Scholar, Department of ECE, Bharath Institute of Higher Education and Research, Chennai, India

Abstract

The article introduces a convolutional neural network (CNN) design for tumor segmentation detection using the VGG-16 model. After the data has been pre-processed, the study trains the model using the training data and then evaluates it with the test data. A split dataset describes this configuration. Using the training dataset, the proposed VGG-16 model is trained alongside other models created by AlexNet and GoogleNet. Its performance is assessed using several metrics. With an accuracy rate of 94.5%, a sensitivity of 89.5%, and a specificity of 95.6%, the results show that the suggested model is successful. In comparison to earlier models, these results demonstrate how well the VGG-16 design segments tumors. Additionally, VGG UNet architecture is employed for segmentation purposes, enhancing the accuracy of the segmentation process.

Keywords: AlexNet, googlenet, tumor segmentation, VGG UNet, VGG-16

Introduction

Because of its unpredictable character, cancer continues to be a social disease despite advances in biology and human knowledge over the last several decades having triumphed over other illnesses. Brain tumor malignancy is one of the fatal and rapidly growing disorders. Among the many processes governed by the nervous system are breathing, muscle contraction, and sensory perception [1]. Each cell is different, capable of growing in many ways depending on the circumstances. Some cells develop normally, expand beyond their potential, or resist. Generous aggregates of atypical cells that constitute tissue are known as tumors. Aberrant and uncontrolled brain cell development is the cause of cancerous brain tumors. Among the most deadly and deadly cancers is this one [2]. Over the years, there has been a substantial advancement in the processes

for assessing tumors. Though regrettably, we do not yet have the means to treat brain tumors, since brain tumors may be easily identified by the pictures, we employ MRI scans for high-quality imaging. They help detect and locate tumor components more rapidly. All processes are currently dependent on individuals' interpretation, which might lead to inaccurate results. When these tumors are still small, it might be difficult to find them sooner. Medical professionals cannot get accurate findings from imaging procedures like CT and MRI [3]. As a result, they will wait and carry out the imaging process again. If the individual incorrectly predicts that there certainly isn't a tumor there, the tumor will keep growing and pose a life-threatening threat for them. Compared to conventional techniques, machine-based identification and evaluation could be simpler and more lucid [4]. Tumors that were not present

[a]jadhavrn@gmail.com, [b]sudhagar.ece@bharathuniv.ac.in, [c]sharadjagtap0710@gmail.com

DOI: 10.1201/9781003616399-61

when the item was registered may be addressed using tumor-growth modeling. For this, two different models of tumor formation were investigated. The capacity to provide meaningful and distinctive segmentation was enhanced by a more comprehensive tumour-growing model, even if a restricted tumor growth model computed more quickly [5]. Both techniques have been integrated into a single framework for assessing brain pictures with tumors that usually makes use of all imaging data that is accessible in laboratories [6]. New research on brain tumor detection and segmentation has shown that no universal approach exists for detecting tumors of any size, location, or kind [7]. Many algorithms for classifying brain tumors and extracting features have been reported in recent study. In low-level feature extraction GLCMs, are often used [8]. In an attempt to address the complex texture of a brain tumor, further feature extraction approaches include fisher vector, neural network and Bag-of-Words (BoW) [9]. New research found that the three forms of brain cancers that may be identified with accuracy range from 71.39 to 94.68. by combining the fisher vector approach with efficient site pooling include meningioma, pituitary astrocytoma, and glioma [10]. With the help of this segmentation system, radiation evaluation, analysis, identification, treatment planning, and monitoring may be enhanced [11].

Related Work

The proposal by Jia and Chen [12] included a new, totally automated method based on structural, morphological, and relaxometry data in MRI imaging, which would separate the whole cerebral venous system. Based on brain magnetic resonance pictures, the numerical results illustrate the effectiveness of the proposed approach with 98.51% accuracy in identifying normal and diseased tissue [13]. For the exact categorization and isolation of brain malignancies, this study's authors propose a custom-built Mask RCNN model that uses densenet-41 backbone architecture and transfer learning for training. In terms of endurance, the proposed model beat the most advanced approaches, achieving segmentation accuracy of 96.3% and classification accuracy of 98.34% [14]. The chosen MR image collection

includes three main forms of brain tumors: meningioma, pituitary, along with glioma. The suggested technique builds its classifier network along with area recommendation network on top of the VGG-16 architecture. On average, the system was able to identify and classify gliomas with a 75.18% success rate, meningiomas with an 89.45% success rate, and pituitary tumors with a 68.18% success rate [15]. The mean average accuracy across all classes was 76.60%, which was a measure of the algorithm's performance. The three types of brain cancers that were identified using 364 contrast-enhanced T1 weighted MRI scans were meningiomas, gliomas, along with pituitary tumors [16]. For uncropped lesions, the sensitivity is 98.18% and the accuracy is 98.93%. For segmented lesion photos, the sensitivity is 97.40% and the accuracy is 97.62%, for a total of 99% accuracy and 98.52% sensitivity, the suggested CNN classifier is a potent instrument. Anaraket al., [17] presented three investigations employing AlexNet, Google Net, and VGGNet-based convolutional neural networks to identify above mentioned brain tumors. The recommended research found that the optimized VGG16 architecture yielded the significant classification and detection accuracy of 98.69. Another strategy uses GA to update CNN architecture by adhering to established frameworks [18]. As an ensemble technique, we additionally bag the best model that the GA provides to lower the prediction error fluctuation. In particular, one case study classified three different Glioma grades with a success rate of 90.9%. The results demonstrated a 94.2% success rate in detecting and classifying cancers of the pituitary gland, meningiomas, and lymphomas.

A deep convolutional neural network (CNN) model that uses block-wise transfer learning should be able to help with this problem and give a fine-tuning approach [19]. The suggested technique is tested using the T1-weighted contrast-enhanced MRI benchmark dataset. A more generalized degree of accuracy (94.82% on average) when evaluated using five-fold cross-validation, less preprocessing, and independence from manually produced characteristics are all achieved by this technique. An article detailing the use of CNNs to identify brain tumors in magnetic resonance imaging (MRI) images can be found [20]. CNN first adapted to visual content. A 98.67% accuracy rate was achieved by the SoftMax fully connected layer during the whole picture categorization procedure. The CNN also gets a 94.21% accuracy rate when trained with the decision tree (DT) classifier and a 94.34% accuracy rate when trained with the radial basis function (RBF) classifier. Based on results from an analysis of the publicly available tumor information, the suggested CNN model proved effective [21]. Based on our testing findings, the suggested CNN archives without data improvement achieve an overall accuracy rate of 89.93%. Incorporating data augmentation improved the accuracy of identifying pituitary tumors to 91.03%, meningiomas to 91.81%, and gliomas to 98.67%, for a grand total of 93.83% accuracy.

Background

The background of the VGGNet architecture, which is our suggested model, and alternative designs, such as AlexNet and Google Net, are covered in this section. '

AlexNet architecture
The design has eight layers in total, including three fully linked layers along with five convolutional layers at the beginning. To ensure the network acquires the highest number of features feasible,

the first two convolutional layers are connected to overlapping max-pooling layers. The fully connected layers are directly coupled to the third, fourth, along with fifth convolutional layers. The data from the convolutional and completely connected layers are used by ReLu's non-linear activation function. To train AlexNet to generate 1,000 class labels, we feed it a 256x256 RGB three-channel image and link it to the network's final output layer using a SoftMax activation layer. Around 650,000 neurons make up architecture, which has 60 million parts. Dropout layers mitigate overtraining. Backpropagation and forward propagation are unaffected by neuronal loss. There is a direct connection between the first two floors. Google LeNet Architecture has 27 pooling levels and 22 stacked layers. There are nine separate parts of Inception, and they must be put together in any particular order. The beginning modules' ends are connected to the worldwide average pooling layer.

GoogLeNet architecture
The GoogLeNet Architecture features 22 stacked layers altogether and 27 pooling levels. There are nine linearly ordered inception modules total. The last connections of the first modules are connected to the layer that calculates the global average. As shown in the final visual representation, the GoogLeNet architecture is downsized. As shown in Figure 61.2 the final visual.

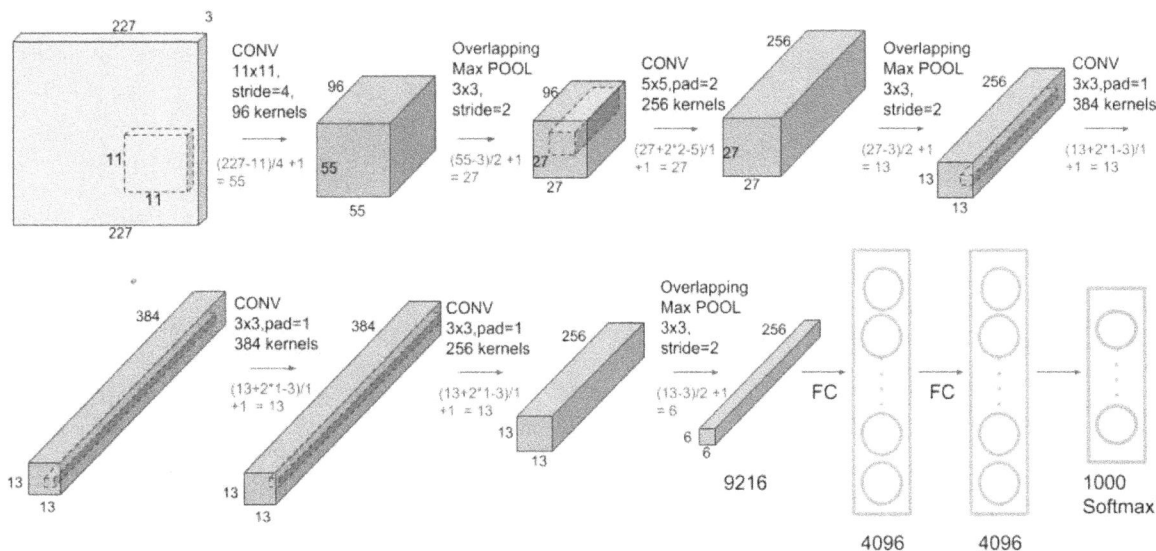

Figure 61.1 AlexNet architecture
Source: Author

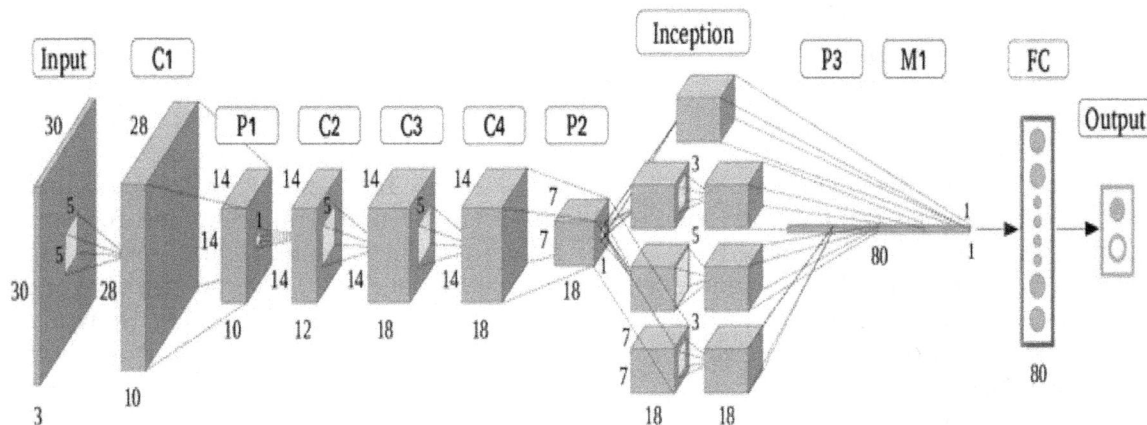

Figure 61.2 GoogleNet architecture
Source: Author

Methodology

Dataset description
In this study, we collected data from below website: https://www.kaggle.com/datasets/leaderandpiller/brain-tumor-segmentation. From this dataset, we have selected brain tumor images for segmentation.

Pre-processing
The aim is to demonstrate how different popular pre-processing methods affect the accuracy on particular simple convolutional networks. A variety of pre-processing methods are included below:

- Read the image
- Rescale it
- Eliminate noise

Read the image: We started by creating a variable to store the location of our image collection, and then we came up with a way to read photographs into arrays from the folders that held them.

Rescale the image: So that you can observe the transformation, we will now provide two ways to show you the photos after they have been resized: one will show you just one picture, and the other will show you both.

After that, we create a procedure called processing that takes images as its only input.

Eliminate noise: To turn the noise off A Gaussian blur can be produced by applying a Gaussian function to an image. To lessen visual noise, this popular graphics application effect is frequently utilized. Another pre-processing method that computer vision algorithms utilize to improve visual structures at various sizes is called Gaussian smoothing.

Segmentation
Segmentation is crucial in medical imaging for tasks like tumor detection, organ delineation, and treatment planning, providing valuable information for healthcare professionals. Segmenting brain tumor images using the VGGUnet methodology involves employing VGG16 or VGG19 as an encoder, integrated with a U-Net decoder.

Proposed VGG-UNET
The Proposed VGG-UNet, a deep learning architecture, integrates the benefits of the VGG16 and U-Net models Figure 61.3 [21].

Figure 61.1 illustrates how the VGG16 model is a powerful feature extractor, but the U-Net model is the best architecture suited for picture segmentation.

The two main parts of VGG-UNet are the decoder and the encoder. The decoder is responsible for creating segmentation masks, while the encoder extracts feature from input pictures. The VGG16 model is used as the encoder in the planned VGG-UNet. The VGG16 model consists of sixteen convolutional layers, with the max pooling layer after each one. The number of filters is different for each of the five convolutional layer blocks. The filters in each block are three by

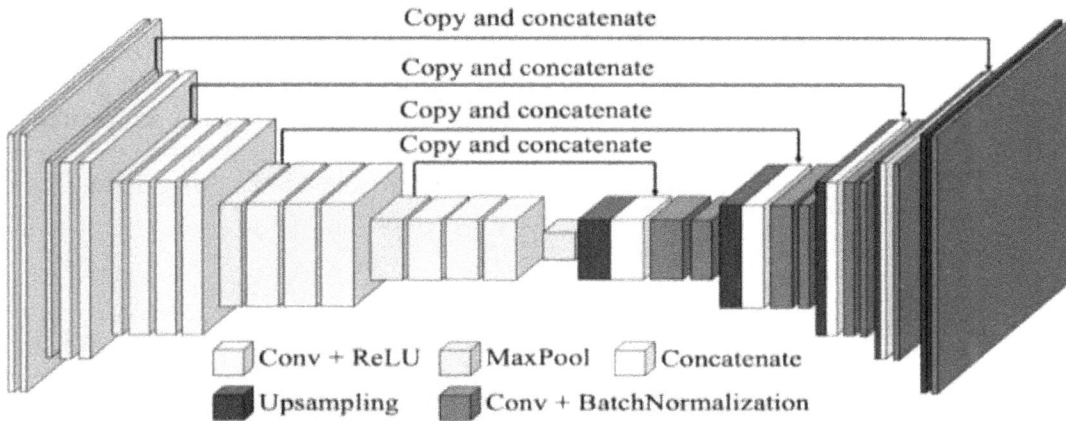

Figure 61.3 Architecture of VGG-UNET
Source: Author

three. The suggested VGG-UNet decoder is based on the U-Net mode. The U-Net idea is made up of two paths, one that is reducing and one that is rising. The input picture must be down sampled using the contracting route, and the feature maps must be up sampled using the expanding path. Consisting of the first thirteen convolutional layers of the VGG16 model, the proposed VGG-UNet's contracting route.

Results

These model parts were constructed in MATLAB 2020a using the deep learning and image processing toolboxes. Information repository: For model training and evaluation, we utilize the Kaggle brain tumor data set. For the aim of data collection, an MRI scan of a tumor, whether benign or malignant, is used. Enhancement and separation of the MRI images precede the training period.

In figure, we can see the process of MRI image segmentation. Models are then trained using these segmented images. We calculate performance metrics like specificity, sensitivity, along with accuracy and compare them to the planned state-of-the-art to see how well the designs work. Presented below are the performance metrics. Figure 61.4 mentions the mean precision.

The mean precision of VGGNet, GoogLeNet, and AlexNet designs is 94.50%, 90.90%, and 88.40%, respectively. This makes it evident that the VGGNet designs identify tumors more accurately.

Figure 61.5 mentions GoogLeNet, AlexNet, and VGGNet architectures have specificities of 91.42%, 95.75%, and 86.70%, respectively. This makes it evident that, in contrast to GoogLeNet and AlexNet, the VGGNet designs have higher sensitivity. This Figure 61.6 makes it evident.

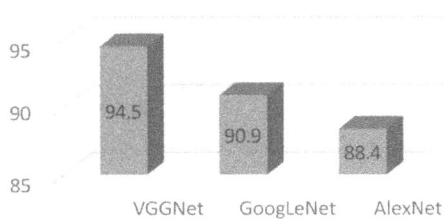

Figure 61.4 Accuracy comparison
Source: Author

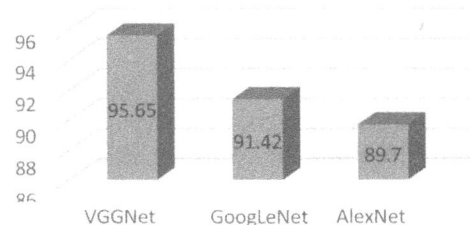

Figure 61.5 Specificity comparison
Source: Author

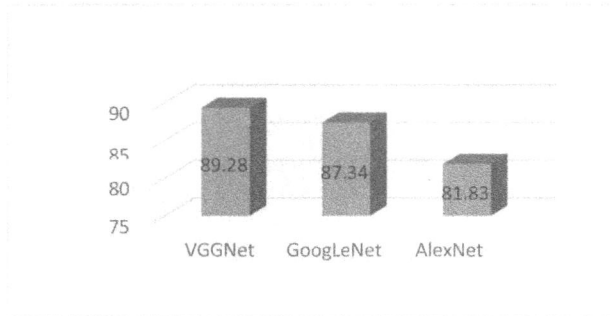

Figure 61.6 Sensitivity comparison
Source: Author

Table 61.1 Architecture and values

Architectures	Specificity (%)	Sensitivity (%)	Accuracy (%)
VGGNet	95.65	89.28	94.5
AlexNet	89.7	81.83	88.4
GoogLeNet	91.42	87.34	90.9

Source: Author

Conclusion

Finally, based on the VGG-16 model, this study demonstrates a powerful CNN-based method for tumor segmentation detection. The suggested model is reliable since it makes use of a split dataset for training and assessment and undergoes thorough pre-processing. When compared to AlexNet and GoogleNet, the VGG-16 model performs better, indicating that it is useful for tumor segmentation in medical image analysis. Highlighting the relevance of the suggested design, the attained accuracy is 94.5%, specificity is 95.65%, and sensitivity is 89.2%, surpassing the standards established by earlier models. By comparing VGG-16 with AlexNet and GoogleNet, we can see how well it does in tumor segmentation and where it falls short. This further proves that VGG-16 is better. The suggested technique is successful in general, and the use of the VGG UNet architecture for segmentation improves the accuracy of the procedure. The study findings have important implications for medical image processing and might improve tumor detection and delineation in clinical settings.

In future work, additional investigations could focus on optimizing the proposed model further, exploring potential enhancements or adaptations for specific types of tumors or diverse medical imaging modalities. Furthermore, there may be opportunities to further enhance performance and generalize across other datasets via the use of sophisticated approaches like ensemble methods or transfer learning.

References

[1] Younis, A., Qiang, L., Nyatega, C. O., Adamu, M. J., and Kawuwa, H. B. (2022). Brain tumor analysis using deep learning and VGG-16 ensembling learning approaches. *Applied Sciences*, 12(14), 7282. doi: 10.3390/app12147282.

[2] Rahman, T., and Islam, M. S. (2022). MRI Brain Tumor Classification Using Deep Convolutional Neural Network. Singapore: Springer.

[3] Shahzadi, I., Tang, T. B., Meriadeau, F., and Quyyum, A. (2018). CNN-LSTM: cascaded framework for brain tumour classification. In 2018 IEEE-EMBS Conference on Biomedical Engineering and Sciences (IECBES), (pp. 633–637).

[4] Seetha, J., and Raja, S. S. (2018). Brain tumor classification using convolutional neural networks. *Biomedical and Pharmacology Journal*, 11(3), 1457–1461. doi: 10.13005/bpj/1511.

[5] Ghosh, S., Chaki, A., and Santosh, K. (2021). Improved U-net architecture with VGG-16 for brain tumor segmentation. *Physical and Engineering Sciences in Medicine*, 44(3), 703–712. doi: 10.1007/s13246-021-01019-w.

[6] Namburu, A., and Barpanda, S. S. Recent advances in computer based systems, processes and applications 2020 by taylor and fransis group, London, ISBN 978-1-003-04398-0.

[7] Sajja, V. R. (2021). Classification of brain tumors using fuzzy c-means and VGG16. *Turkish Journal of Computer and Mathematics Education*, 12(9), 2103–2113.

[8] Srinivas, C., KS, N. P., Zakariah, M., Alothaibi, Y. A., Shaukat, K., Partibane, B., et al. (2022). Deep transfer learning approaches in performance analysis of brain tumor classification using MRI images. *Journal of Healthcare Engineering*, 2022(1), 3264367. doi: 10.1155/2022/3264367.

[9] Singh, V., Sharma, S., Goel, S., Lamba, S., and Garg, N. (2021). Brain tumor prediction by binary classification using VGG-16. *Smart and Sustainable Intelligent Systems*, 127–138 . doi: 10.1002/9781119752134.ch9.

[10] Polat, Ö., and Güngen, C. (2021). Classification of brain tumors from MR images using deep transfer learning. *Journal of Supercomputing*,

77(7), 7236–7252. doi: 10.1007/s11227-020-03572-9.

[11] Saleh, A., Sukaik, R., and Abu-Naser, S. S. (2020). Brain tumor classification using deep learning. In Proceeding - 2020 International Conference Assistive and Rehabilitation Technologies iCare-Tech, 2020, (pp. 131–136). doi: 10.1109/iCare-Tech49914.2020.00032.

[12] Jia, Z., and Chen, D. "Brain tumor Identification and classification of MRI images using deep learning techniques". in *IEEE Access*. doi: 10.1109/ACCESS.2020.3016319.

[13] Masood, M., Nazir, T., Nawaz, M., Mehmood, A., Rashid, J., Kwon, H. Y., et al. (2021). A novel deep learning method for recognition and classification of brain tumors from MRI images. *Diagnostics*, 11(5), 744.

[14] Bhanothu, Y., Kamalakannan, A., and Rajamanickam, G. (2020). Detection and classification of brain tumor in MRI images using deep convolutional network. In 2020 6th International Conference on Advanced Computing and Communication Systems, ICACCS 2020, (pp. 248–252). doi: 10.1109/ICACCS48705.2020.9074375.

[15] Alqudah, A. M., Alquraan, H., Qasmieh, I. A., Alqudah, A., and Al-Sharu, W. (2020). Brain tumor classification using deep learning technique--a comparison between cropped, un-cropped, and segmented lesion images with different sizes. arXiv Prepr. arXiv2001.08844.

[16] Rehman, A., Naz, S., Razzak, M. I., Akram, F., and Imran, M. (2020). A deep learning-based framework for automatic brain tumors classification using transfer learning. *Circuits, Systems, and Signal Processing*, 39(2), 757–775.

[17] Anaraki, A. K., Ayati, M., and Kazemi, F. (2019). Magnetic resonance imaging-based brain tumor grades classification and grading via convolutional neural networks and genetic algorithms. *Biocybernetics and Biomedical Engineering*, 39(1), 63–74.

[18] Swati, Z. N. K., Zhao, Q., Kabir, M., Ali, F., Ali, Z., Ahmed, S., et al. (2019). Brain tumor classification for MR images using transfer learning and fine-tuning. *Computerized Medical Imaging and Graphics*, 75, 34–46.

[19] Siar, M., and Teshnehlab, M. (2019). Brain tumor detection using deep neural network and machine learning algorithm. In 2019 9th International Conference on Computer and Knowledge Engineering (ICCKE), (pp. 363–368).

[20] Ghosal, P., Nandanwar, L., Kanchan, S., Bhadra, A., Chakraborty, J., and Nandi, D. (2019). Brain tumor classification using ResNet-101 based squeeze and excitation deep neural network. In 2019 Second International Conference on Advanced Computational and Communication Paradigms (ICACCP), (pp. 1–6).

[21] Krishnamoorthy, S., Zhang, Y., Kadry, S., and Yu, W. (2022). Framework to segment and evaluate multiple sclerosis lesion in MRI slices using VGG-UNet. *Computational Intelligence and Neuroscience*, 2022(1), 4928096. doi: 10.1155/2022/4928096.

62 Efficient power optimization strategies in 5G communication networks: a comprehensive review

Subramani, G.[1,a], M. Nagarajan[2,b] and G. Sudhagar[2,c]

[1]Rresearch Scholar, Dept of ECE, BIHER, Chennai, Tamil Nadu, India
[2]Associate Professor, Dept of ECE, BIHER, Chennai, Tamil Nadu, India

Abstract

The advent of 5G technology heralds a new age in the field of telecommunications, ultra-low latency, promising unprecedented data rates, and immense device connectivity. On the other hand, these advancements come with significant challenges, particularly in terms of power consumption. This paper explores various strategies and techniques for power optimization in 5G communication systems. Key areas of focus include energy-efficient network design, advanced modulation schemes, power control mechanisms, and the implementation of machine learning algorithms for dynamic power management. Energy efficiency is critical not only for reducing operational costs but also for minimizing the environmental impact of extensive 5G deployments. By integrating these optimization techniques and it is possible to achieve a balance between performance and energy utilization, ensuring sustainable and efficient 5G networks. This study aims to deliver an in-depth review of recent progress in power optimization and pinpoint prospective future paths for improving energy efficiency in 5G communications.

Keywords: Artificial intelligence, energy efficiency, modulation schemes, power optimization, resource allocation

Introduction

Introduction Power optimization in 5G communications is crucial for several reasons, including prolonging device battery life, minimizing environmental impact and reducing operational costs. Key strategies for power optimization in 5G communication include energy-efficient network design, dynamic power control, and advanced modulation and coding schemes. Optimizing the network architecture and topology to minimize energy consumption involves strategically placing base stations, deploying small cells, and utilizing advanced antenna technologies like beam forming to improve coverage and reduce transmission power. Dynamic power control mechanisms allow devices to adjust their transmit power based on the quality of the communication link, ensuring that devices consume only the necessary power to maintain reliable connections. Employing advanced modulation and coding techniques, such as higher-order modulation and adaptive coding, enables more data to be transmitted per symbol, increasing spectral efficiency and reducing overall power consumption per transmitted bit. Efficient resource allocation ensures the optimal use of frequency spectrum, time slots, and transmits power among users and devices, minimizing energy consumption. Sleep mode optimization involves intelligently managing the sleep modes of devices and network components to reduce idle power consumption during periods of inactivity, dynamically switching between active and sleep modes based on traffic demand and network conditions. Machine learning and AI-based optimization can analyze network data and predict traffic patterns, enabling proactive optimization of network parameters like power allocation, resource scheduling, and handover decisions, leading to significant energy savings. Exploring green networking solutions, such as renewable energy-powered base stations, energy harvesting techniques, and energy-efficient hardware design, can further reduce the environmental footprint of 5G communication systems. Finally, encouraging industry-wide standardization efforts and implementing regulatory

[a]subuspring@gmail.com, [b]mnagarajan.ece@bharathuniv.ac.in, [c]Sudhagar.ece@bharathuniv.ac.in

DOI: 10.1201/9781003616399-62

measures aimed at promoting energy efficiency in 5G communication can drive innovation and the adoption of power optimization techniques across the telecommunications sector. By integrating these principles into the design and operation of 5G communication systems, stakeholders can achieve significant improvements in energy efficiency, thereby contributing to the sustainability and longevity of 5G networks.

Literature Survey

The research done by Patra and associates [1] is on using a neural network approach to optimize resources in large MIMO systems. The goal of this strategy is to reduce the production costs related to the rollout of 5G technology in tropical areas. Diverse diversity techniques have been applied to address signal fading in tropical regions with heavy precipitation, which can cause signal attenuation and compromise the quality of communication. One important way to reduce signal fading is to use the multiple input multiple output (MIMO) technology, which is well-known for its ability to provide spatial variety. The research includes the use of MATLAB and the Xilinx system generator to build MIMO approaches with sizes ranging from 1×1 to 256×256. Moreover, Xilinx Kintex7 implements an

8×8 MIMO system. It is a different conceptual illustration of mobileaccess via the 5G networks is shown in Figure 62.1 wich is Refered and cited from the following artical- Pihkola, Hanna, et al. "Evaluating the energy consumption of mobile data transfer—from technology development to consumer behaviour and life cycle thinking." Sustainability 10.7 (2018): 2494.

The method has been adopted to increase the application of force by the bulky MIMO ground locations set up in the urban areas, while fulfilling the poor requirement of energy. This is an alternative option of the application of a massive MIMO technique which has been displayed in Figure 62.2.

Projected design of MIMO technique shows an application of CMOS logic gates, the device of a MIMO technique has been established instead of a MIMO technique designed by using system generator to obtain the desired result in respect of resources required for devising different MIMO techniques. Applying CMOS logic gates, the basic design of 1x1 SISO techniques has been depicted in Figure 62.3.

Saad et al., [2] introduced an AI-MLR (artificial intelligence multiple linear regression) model with the goal of improving the mobility's resilience in 5G cellular networks. This AI-MLR model's main objective is to use network data in

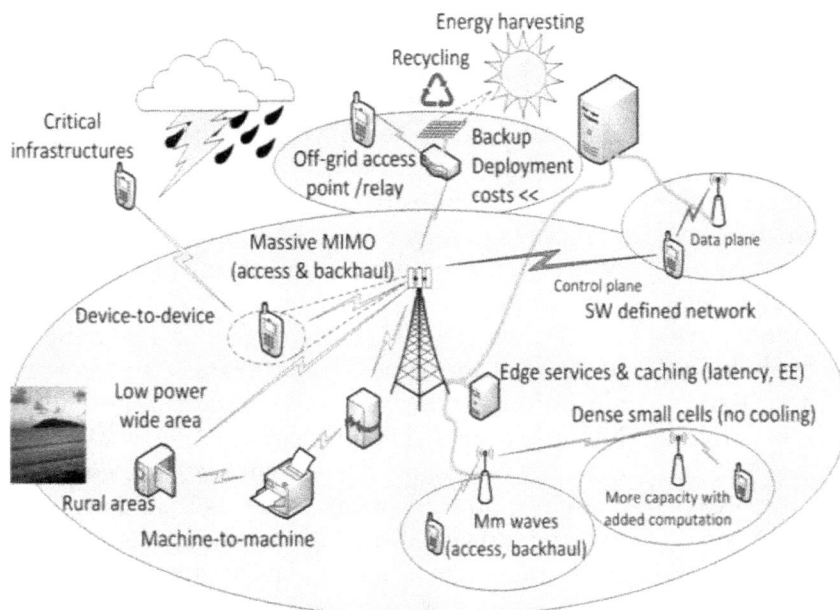

Figure 62.1 Power optimization techniques in 5G communications
Source: Author

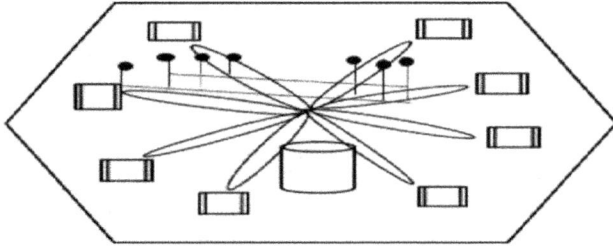

Figure 62.2 Illustration of massive MIMO technology
Source: Author

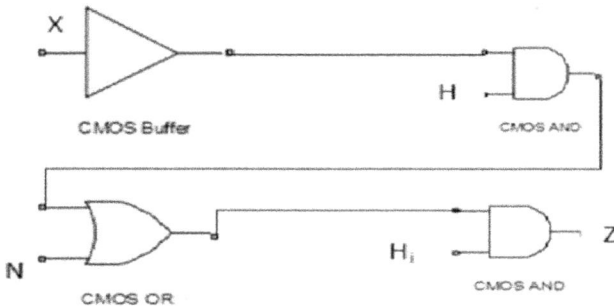

Figure 62.3 Projected design of MIMO technique
Source: Author

conjunction with the (IIM) instantaneous indication measure function to optimize handover control parameters (HCP) settings autonomously. In order to assess user equipment (UE) experiences, this model makes use of the IIM function. It does this by evaluating the instantaneous SINR – (signal-to-interference-plus-noise ratio) levels from both target and serving base stations. The suggested approach has undergone extensive testing and validation against a number of industry-recognized techniques, encompassing a range of mobility speed conditions in a 5G cellular network. A number of key effectiveness indicators (KPIs), including handover ping-pong probability (HPPP), handover probability (HOP), and (RLF)-radio link failure were used to assess the effectiveness of the AI-MLR model. When compared to alternative algorithms documented in the literature, simulation results showed that the AI-MLR model made considerable improvements in HOP, HPPP, and RLF over a spectrum of movement speed conditions.

The study conducted by Amna et al., [3] presents a novel multi-agent parameterized deep reinforcement learning (MA-PDRL) strategy designed to effectively tackle the joint user correlation and power allotment challenges within 5G heterogeneous networks (HetNets). This strategy utilizes a multi-agent PDQN (parameterized deep Q-network), where individual agents determine their optimal policies based on local observations through a Q-function. Through the MA-PDRL approach, multiple agents can concurrently learn their optimal policies by engaging with the environment, accommodating cooperative and non-cooperative configurations to enforce a global policy. Conventional machine learning methods are deemed suboptimal for resolving joint user association and power allocation dilemmas in HetNets due to their hybrid action space, underscoring the MA-PDRL approach as a more effective alternative.

A unique approach was presented by Haseeb et al., [4] with the goal of resolving co-channel interference and maximizing energy efficiency in a long-term evolution network. To increase system throughput and reduce user disturbance, the authors' algorithm divides D2D users into groups according to the minimum outage likelihood using a fuzzy clustering technique. In addition, they introduced a powerful game-theoretic power control method that maximizes user transmission power within each group, improving user energy efficiency. Simulation findings showed that the suggested algorithms are effective in increasing system throughput, improving energy efficiency and decreasing co-channel interference. The research presents an integrated strategy for resource optimization in D2D communication within 5G networks, combining game theory-driven power control with fuzzy clustering for user grouping.

Abuajwa et al., [5] employed simulated annealing (SA) as a method of optimization for resource allocation within an energy-efficient downlink NOMA system. The utilization of SA is directed towards managing the assignment of users and channels, power allocation, as well as determining the power distribution among users who share the same channel. The main objective of this approach is to enhance energy efficiency in NOMA systems by optimizing the allocation of resources through the utilization of SA. By implementing the resource allocation scheme with SA, a substantial increase in energy efficiency is targeted, surpassing existing numerical techniques by 22%. The suggested SA strategy not only offers a solution that is nearly optimal but also produces outcomes within a shorter computational timeframe when compared to current numerical approaches, thereby ensuring effectiveness and dependability in the enhancement of energy efficiency.

Pandi et al., [6] creative method, which employs a heuristic-based optimization strategy inside a channel prediction framework, improves the estimate of channels in 5G MIMO systems. This methodology estimates MIMO-based channel coefficients at the transmitter end and evaluates receiver-side error rates by using a Cascade fusion serial network (CFSN) to gather feedback data. The researchers optimize the attention CNN-GRU, stacked auto encoder, and CFSN parameters using Whale Optimization. The primary goal of this work is to minimize important channel estimation metrics including mean squared error (MSE), bit error rate (BER), and root mean squared error (RMSE). The results of the study show that compared to other options, the suggested technique produces higher convergence rates and better prediction performance at a lower processing cost.

Vimalraj et al., [7] propose a power allocation algorithm that utilizes the water-filling technique for MIMO systems with known channel side information (CSI) at both the transmitter and receiver. This algorithm is specifically crafted to optimize the system with the objective of enhancing channel capacity, ultimately leading to improved spectral efficiency (SE). The primary focus of the investigation is on maximizing capacity within 5G MIMO systems by tackling the optimization challenge through the utilization of the aforementioned power allocation algorithm. The research study operates under the assumption that the capacity of the high-speed train (HST) communication system is computed while keeping the signal-to-noise ratio (SNR) unaffected by fluctuations in attenuation and channel losses. By capitalizing on the capabilities of MIMO systems, the method aims to elevate system capacity without necessitating an increase in bandwidth, a

pivotal factor that propels research enthusiasm in the realm of MIMO technologies.

The dynamic thresholding-based μ-law (DT-μ-law) logarithmic decompanding methodology is introduced by Ramadevi, et al. [8] as a way to reduce the PAPR in multiple input and multiple output-OFDM systems in 5G wireless communication. This method makes it possible for data to be transmitted across multiple channels more effectively by compressing the transmitting signal's amplitude beyond a certain threshold prior to it reaching the MIMO-OFDM system's parallel-to-serial conversion block. The receiver's decompanding procedure is made easier with the introduction of an offset, guaranteeing a smooth transition and lowering system complexity. Selecting the right μ value is essential; a range of 4 to 4.5 yields the best efficiency. bit error rates (BER) and PAPR reduction are also affected by changing the μ value. In contrast to current techniques like the Max-Min Decomp-SLM method, the DT-μ-law companding technology provides enhanced data capacity and spectral efficiency at lower SNR levels.

To develop a comprehensive model for MIMO-OFDM system with DT-μ-law Companding covers key stages of the MIMO-OFDM system, emphasizing the integration of μ-law technique for PAPR reduction, as seen in Figure 62.4.

Goktas et al. [9] conducted a study on a wireless power transfer supported full-duplex non-orthogonal multiple access (WPT-NOMA) transmission technique for massive machine type communications (mMTC) in 5G and future cellular networks. In order to accommodate energy-constrained devices with limited radio resources in mMTC scenarios, the proposed WPT-NOMA method allows energy and radio resource sharing across uplink and downlink users simultaneously. To minimize interference caused by full-duplex transmission and maximize uplink data rate, an optimization problem is stated as a resource allocation problem. The paper presents an alternating resource allocation technique as a practical solution to this optimization challenge. The study's numerical experiments highlight the effectiveness of the suggested approach in mMTC settings by showing how the WPT-NOMA transmission scheme performs noticeably better than current benchmark schemes.

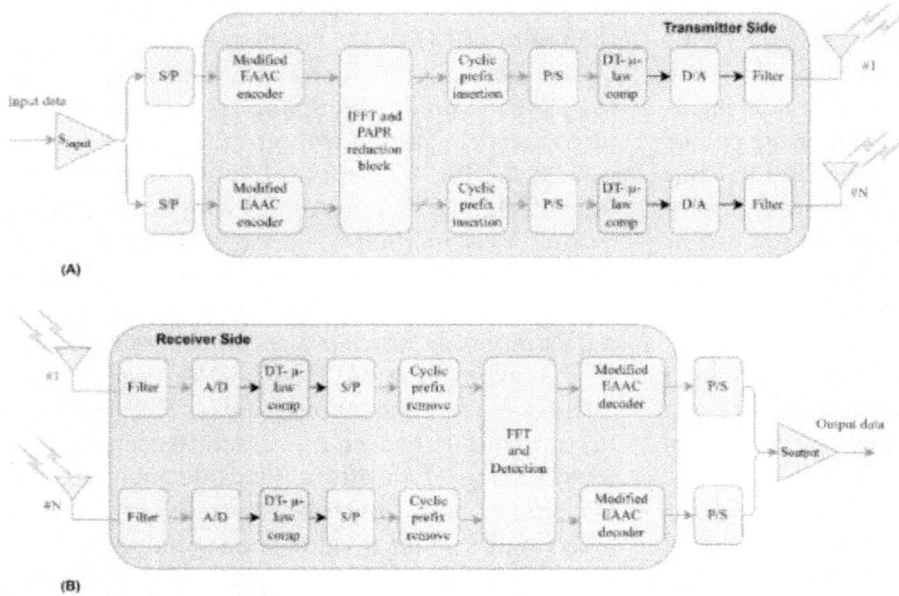

Figure 62.4 Modelled DT-µ-law MIMO-OFDM system mode of expansion. Transmitter (a) and Receiver (b)
Source: Author

Kaushik et al. [10] present a hybrid latency- and power-aware strategy for ahead of fifth generation IoT edge systems. This approach integrates considerations of latency and power into the decision-making process for task offloading within IoT edge systems. Utilizing a mathematical optimization model, the study aims to optimize task offloading decisions while taking into account both latency and power consumption constraints. Employing a multi-objective optimization approach, the research seeks to effectively balance the trade-off between minimizing latency and reducing power utilization in IoT edge systems. Various scenarios and simulations are executed to assess the effectiveness and efficiency of the hybrid approach in real-world IoT edge systems. The methods are designed to tackle the challenges arising from the growing need for low latency and high -power efficiency in next-generation IoT edge systems.

For small cell on/off switching, Osama et al., [11] provide a linearly increasing inertia weight-binary particle swarm optimization (IW-BPSO) technique that aims to reduce network power consumption. An innovative approach involving a soft frequency reuse (SFR) technique that utilizes classification trees (CTs) is presented for the efficient allocation of sub-bands to active small

cells, with the primary objective of minimizing interference between them. The IW-BPSO algorithm undergoes enhancement by incorporating a linearly increasing inertia weight, which serves to enhance convergence rates, thereby facilitating quicker decision-making processes related to small cell activation. Leveraging machine learning methodologies for deactivating redundant small cells in the network is aimed at improving power efficiency without compromising the quality of service offered to users.

Xiaodong et al., [12] presented a proposition for a trinary process aimed at optimizing energy efficiency (EE) in 5G networks through a frameless architecture, with a specific focus on the adaptation of the control plane (CP) and user plane (UP). The initial phase entails the construction of CP and its adaptation scheme, utilizing the Voronoi diagram to enhance EE. Subsequently, the following phase involves the joint allocation of AE and sub-channel resources to establish an on-demand user-centric UP, thereby enhancing the system's EE. Lastly, each UP undergoes adjustments to optimize EE performance through the application of game theory, building upon the groundwork laid in the preceding phase. System-level simulations were executed to exhibit enhanced system-level EE performances while upholding user quality of service (QoS) standards, thereby demonstrating the efficacy of the proposed methodologies.

Weidong et al., (13) establish an energy efficiency optimization problem and provide proof of the strict quasi-concavity of the function in the initial stage. In this study, a power allocation algorithm based on binary search is introduced as a solution to the optimization problem with strict quasi-concavity. The algorithm proposed is crafted to significantly enhance the energy efficiency of the system, all the while ensuring minimal computational complexity. The methodologies delineated in the manuscript are centered on tackling the complexities inherent in resource allocation issues in carrier aggregation technology, with the objective of amplifying system throughput and effectively managing energy consumption.

Figure 62.5 shows the computational complexity comparison between the energy efficiency optimization algorithm and the other two baseline algorithms. As can be seen from the figure, the algorithm proposed in this paper can reach 90% of the optimal performance after about 300 iterations, and the optimal performance can be obtained after about 400 iterations [13].

In 5G wireless personal area networks, Logeshwaran et al., [14] used an energy-efficient the allocation of resources model (EERAM) for device-to-device (D2D) communication. The strategy focusses on allocating resources optimally to reduce energy usage and increase gadget lifespan. One way to lessen interference and improve network bandwidth utilization is to use

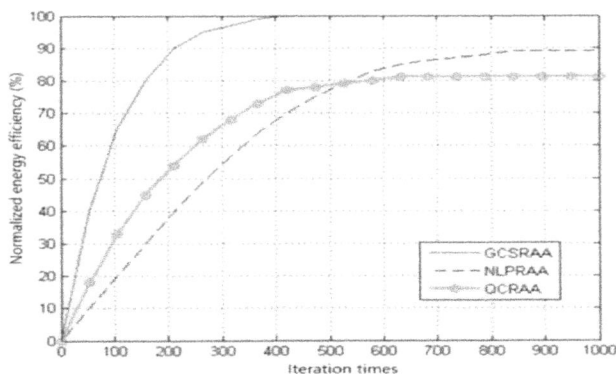

Figure 62.5 System energy efficiency vs. iteration times
Source: Author

directional antennas and steer clear of overlapping communication ranges. In order to improve overall performance, devices are tasked with efficiently managing resources like bandwidth and energy. In 5G WPAN, performance evaluation is done to optimize source allocation for device-to-device communication. Along with improvements in end-to-end latency, network data rate, and network throughput, the strategies aim to achieve a significant improvement in energy, power, bandwidth, spectrum, and channel allocation percentages.

In order to address the power distribution optimization problem, Asif et al., [15] employ a fuzzy inference system (FIS) to allocate optimal power factors to users located near a 5G base station. To support users facing path attenuation and signal degradation, the system integrates a collaborative relaying technique, enhancing performance and ensuring fairness for users within the power domain of non-orthogonal multiple access (PD-NOMA) networks. The suggested approaches are compared to basic PD-NOMA and cooperative relaying PD-NOMA, with bit-error-rate (BER) performance measured at various signal-to-noise ratio (SNR) values. The results show that the cooperative PD-NOMA technique outperforms the basic PD-NOMA method.

Rathee et al., [16] proposed a mechanism for enhancing resource allocation efficiency in device-to-device communication in 5G networks. The main focus of this strategy is power distribution optimization and spectrum feasibility assessment considering the growing number of D2D connections and resources. By using MATLAB simulations, the research compares the proposed power coordination system with earlier power allocation methods and shows improved energy and spectrum efficiency. The research employs optimization approaches to increase system throughput through prudent resource and spectrum allocation. The tactics discussed in the book focus on attaining improved energy-efficient communication through power control in addition to increasing D2D nodes' utilization of frequency resources. The issues presented by slow D2D terminals in cellular networks are addressed in great detail in this research, with an emphasis on reducing signaling losses and improving network performance in general .

Comparative Study

Table 62.1 Comparative Summary tableThis summary report prepared based on Methods Used, Results, and Practical Implications of 5G Resource Optimization from my referred articles from [1] to [16].

S. No	Methods used	Results	Practical implications
1	• MATLAB and Xilinx system generator for MIMO design • Neural network algorithm for resource optimization	• Hardware implementation of 8x8 MIMO using Xilinx Kintex-7 FPGA. • CMOS logic gates optimize resources and reduce 5G technology cost.	• Hardware optimization reduces 5G costs in tropical regions. • Neural network algorithm minimizes signal fading in wireless communication.
2	• AI-multiple linear regression method used for mobility robustness optimization. • Rayleigh Distribution model for fast fading in simulation.	• Proposed AI-MLR model enhances network performance in 5G cellular networks. • HPO-FLC algorithms and Outperforms HPO-D in various mobile speed scenarios.	• Enhances 5G network performance through AI-MLR model optimization. • Reduces handover probability, signaling traffic, and improves user experience.
3	• The utilization of successive convex approximation approaches, semi-definite programming, and alternating optimization	• Proposed method outperforms TDMA model in spectral efficiency. • Total rate decreases as major network's QoS requirements increase. • Performance gap widens as primary users' QoS requirements increase.	• The introduction of wirelessly charged mobile devices using MU-MIMO and NOMA systems • Optimizes joint beam forming for primary and secondary networks for efficiency.
4	• MA-PDRL approach proposed for optimization. • Bellman equation used to describe the relationship between states.	• Learning rates 0.1 and 0.01 show faster convergence and stability. • Discount factor of 0.7 is chosen for improved learning outcomes.	• Enhances energy efficiency and QoS in wireless networks. • Improves resource utilization and addresses energy-efficient wireless network deployments.
5	• Fuzzy clustering method for D2D user grouping based on outage probability. • Power control algorithm using game theory for user transmission optimization.	• Proposed algorithm enhances system throughput, reduces interference, and improves energy efficiency. • PC-FCM algorithm controls user power, improving energy efficiency and spectral efficiency.	• Improved D2D communication in LTE, reduced interference, enhanced energy efficiency • Consider future mmWave band deployment, interference analysis, and mitigation
6	• Resource allocation in an energy-efficient downlink NOMA system using simulated annealing.	• SA algorithm enhances energy efficiency by 22% surpassing existing methods. • The anticipated SA scheme performs 47% better than OFDMA and 22% better than DC.	• SA enhances energy efficiency in NOMA systems by 22%. • SA offers efficient resource allocation with lower time complexity.

S. No	Methods used	Results	Practical implications
7	• Coordinated optimization with MILP model for energy-efficient thermal management.	• Energy cost savings in HVAC operation: 24.8%-32.5% with coordinated approach	• Achieves 24.8–32.5% energy cost savings in HVAC operation.
8	• Heuristic optimization, CNN-GRU, stacked auto encoder, whale optimization, cascade fusion serial network	• Improved convergence rates and prediction performance in 5G MIMO systems. • Computational expenditure reduced compared to existing methods for channel evaluation.	• Enhances channel assessment accuracy in 5G MIMO systems. • Reduces computational costs and improves convergence rates.
9	• Water-filling technique for power allocation in MIMO systems. • Iterative water filling for data rate optimization in the algorithm.	• MIMO capacity is affected by channel estimate accuracy, system load, SNR. • Multiplexing gain enhances data rate in MIMO systems.	• Enhances MIMO system capacity using power allocation algorithms. • Improves spectral efficiency through power allocation strategies.
10	• The logarithmic companding method of DT-μ-law for reducing PAPR in MIMO-OFDM systems.	• DT-m-law companding Technique dramatically lowers PAPR levels in MIMO-OFDM systems. • Performs better than current methods such as max-min decomp-SLM and decomp-UFMC-SLM.	• Enhanced spectral efficiency and reduced performance in bit error rates (BER). • Versatile solution adaptable to future wireless communication technologies like 5G.
11	• Alternating resource allocation algorithm proposed for optimization problem.	• In numerical studies, WPT-NOMA significantly outperforms benchmark schemes, demonstrating its superior efficiency and performance.	• Enhances spectrum and energy cooperation for mMTC in 5G networks.

Source: Author

Conclusion

This research project focusses on energy-efficient resource allocation techniques for device-to-device (D2D) communication in 5G wireless personal area networks. The techniques are designed to minimize interference, increase device longevity, save energy consumption, and maximize bandwidth utilization. A range of approaches and methods have been investigated to tackle the issues related to power consumption in 5G communication networks. These include the use of machine learning algorithms for dynamic power management, sophisticated modulation methods, power control mechanisms, and energy-efficient network design. The paper discusses optimization algorithms that are intended to ensure efficient allocation of energy, power, bandwidth, spectrum, and channels. To improve overall system performance, enhancements are also targeted at end-to-end delay, network data speed, and network throughput. To achieve a balance between performance and energy consumption in 5G networks, a comprehensive solution is provided by the integration of different optimization strategies covered in the article. Maintaining this equilibrium is essential for cost-effective and sustainable operations, as well as for minimizing the environmental effects of widespread 5G deployments.

References

[1] Patra, T., and Mitra, S. K. (2022). Resource optimization of MIMO using neural network for 5G communication. *Alexandria Engineering Journal,* 61(12), 12581–12592. doi: 10.1016/j.aej.2022.06.048.

[2] Saad, S. A., Shayea, I., and Sid Ahmed, N. M. O. (2024). Artificial intelligence linear regression model for mobility robustness optimization algorithm in 5G cellular networks. *Alexandria Engineering Journal,* 89, 125–148. doi: 10.1016/j.aej.2024.01.014.

[3] Mughees, A., Tahir, M., Sheikh, M. A., Amphawan, A., Meng, Y. K., Ahad, A., et al. (2023). Energy-efficient joint resource allocation in 5G HetNet using multi-agent parameterized deep reinforcement learning. *Physical Communication,* 61, 102206. doi: 10.1016/j.phycom.2023.102206.

[4] Zafar, M. H., Khan, I., and Alassafi, M. O. (2022). An efficient resource optimization scheme for D2D communication. *Digital Communications and Networks,* 8(6), 1122–1129. doi: 10.1016/j.dcan.2022.03.002.

[5] Abuajwa, O., and Mitani, S. (2024). Dynamic resource allocation for energy-efficient downlink NOMA systems in 5G networks. *Heliyon,* 10(9). doi: 10.1016/j.heliyon.2024.e29956.

[6] Pandi, S., Aishwarya, D., Karthikeyan, S., Kamatchi, S., and Gopinath, N. (2024). Revolutionizing connectivity: unleashing the power of 5G wireless networks enhanced by artificial intelligence for a smarter future. *Results in Engineering,* 22, 102334. doi: 10.1016/j.rineng.2024.102334.

[7] Vimalraj, S. L. S., Devi, S. P., Lydia, J., and Monisha, R. (2023). Power allocation algorithm for capacity maximization in 5G MIMO systems. *Measurement: Sensors,* 30, 100919. doi: 10.1016/j.measen.2023.100919.

[8] Ramadevi, D., and Trinatha Rao, P. (2024). Dynamic thresholding logarithmic companding for PAPR reduction in MIMO-OFDM systems for 5G wireless communication. *Measurement: Sensors,* 33, 101187. doi: 10.1016/j.measen.2024.101187.

[9] Goktas, M. B., and Ding, Z. (2022). A wireless power transfer assisted NOMA transmission scheme for 5G and beyond mMTC. *IEEE Wireless Communications Letters,* 11(6), 1239–1242. doi: 10.1109/LWC.2022.3162411.

[10] Kaushik, A., and Al-Raweshidy, H. S. (2022). A hybrid latency-and power-aware approach for beyond fifth-generation internet-of-things edge systems. *IEEE Access,* 10(1), 87974–87989. doi: 10.1109/ACCESS.2022.Doi.

[11] Osama, M., El Ramly, S., and Abdelhamid, B. (2022). Binary PSO with classification trees algorithm for enhancing power efficiency in 5G networks. *Sensors,* 22(21), 8570. doi: 10.3390/s22218570.

[12] Xu, X., Dai, X., Liu, Y., Gao, R., and Tao, X. (2015). Energy efficiency optimization-oriented control plane and user plane adaptation with a frameless network architecture for 5G. *EURASIP Journal on Wireless Communications and Networking,* 2015(1), 1–5. doi: 10.1186/s13638-015-0403-5.

[13] Gao, W., Ma, L., and Chuai, G. (2017). Energy efficient power allocation strategy for 5G carrier aggregation scenario. *EURASIP Journal on Wireless Communications and Networking,* 2017(1), 1–10. doi : 10.1186/s13638-017-0924-1.

[14] Logeshwaran, J., Shanmugasundaram, N., and Lloret, J. (2023). Energy-efficient resource allocation model for device-to-device communication in 5G wireless personal area networks. *International Journal of Communication Systems,* 36(13), e5524. doi: 10.1002/dac.5524.

[15] Mahmood, A., Marey, M., Nasralla, M. M., Esmail, M. A., and Zeeshan, M. (2022). Optimal power allocation and cooperative relaying under fuzzy inference system (FIS) based downlink PD-NOMA. *Electronics (Switzerland),* 11(9), 1338. doi: 10.3390/electronics11091338.

[16] Rathee, A., Chaba, Y., and Dembla, D. (2022). Power coordination based efficient resource allocation for device-to-device communication in 5G networks. *International Journal of Electrical and Electronics Research,* 10(3), 760–764. doi: 10.37391/IJEER.100357.

63 Addressing special skew and minimum pulse width checks in static timing analysis

Praveenkumar, J.[1,a], *Sudhagar, G.*[2,b] *and Kavitha, J.* [3,c]

[1]Research Scholar, Bharath Institute of Higher Education and Research, Chennai, Tamil Nadu, India

[2]Associate Professor, Department of ECE, Bharath Institute of Higher Education and Research, Chennai, Tamil Nadu, India

[3]Assistant Professor, Department of ECE, Bharath Institute of Higher Education and Research, Chennai, Tamil Nadu, India

Abstract

In very large-scale integration (VLSI), static timing analysis (STA) is an essential phase for the design of integrated circuits and verification. The principal objective is to guarantee that the circuit satisfies timing specifications and functions accurately at its designated clock frequency. As we move towards lower technological nodes, achieving complete timing closer becomes a very challenging task. The functionality of a chip and its application are very wide. Meeting all the complex timing requirements at such lower nodes across all the scenarios requires efficient methods such as writing a script to identify the pins and address them across scenarios based on the requirement. This thesis presents the importance of skew requirement and minimum pulse width checks in static timing analysis of a digital design. As part of achieving timing closure the meeting of skew requirement at various pins presents in the IP's and maintaining a uniform pulse width between the pins plays a vital role in the successful timing signoff of a chip. This is achieved by identifying the IP pins with special check requirement and then balancing them across different scenarios by using a script to address the job with efficiency. This work explores balancing of the skew numbers across same and different channels of the IP there by contributing to the overall timing closure of the chip. Understanding the minimum pulse width criteria and using efficient methods to address them is a crucial stage in signoff timing closure. The impact of OCV, MMC and process variability needs to be considered. Hence the balancing of special skew across IP's and maintaining the minimum pulse needs to be performed with due diligence.

Keywords: Clock tree synthesis, on chip variation, pulse width, skew, static timing analysis

Static Timing Analysis

Static timing analysis (STA) is essential for the design and verification of very large-scale integration (VLSI) circuits. It is a method to guarantee that, within their designated temporal parameters, digital circuits operate as intended. Designers can assure appropriate clock frequencies, satisfy performance targets, and avoid timing-related problems like setup and hold violations by using STA.

Setting timing constraints for the design is the first stage in the STA process. The setup, hold, and other timing specifications for the different circuit elements including the proper clock frequencies are outlined in these restrictions. These limits are typically provided by the design team and are based on the expected performance goals.

Logic gates (AND, OR, NOT, etc.) and flip-flops (registers) are used to illustrate digital circuit designs at the gate-level. This gate-level representation provides the input for the STA tool. STA tools find critical routes by analyzing the circuit.

The critical path, or longest path in terms of delay in the circuit, indicates the maximum clock frequency that can be utilized without jeopardizing timing specifications. Every gate and connection have an estimated latency in the circuit.

[a]praveencando91@gmail.com, [b]sudhagarambur@gmail.com, [c]j.kavi89@gmail.com

DOI: 10.1201/9781003616399-63

Examples of delays include flip-flop, gate, and wire delays. Usually, the semiconductor vendor's libraries are used to retrieve these delays.

Timing analysis is done by simulating the circuit under several conditions, such as worst-case and best-case scenarios. The instrument ascertains whether the signals within the circuit satisfy the setup and hold time prerequisites, guaranteeing precise data collection at the flip-flops.

The STA tool finds setup and hold violations by comparing the timing constraints with the actual signal arrival times. Setup violations happen when data arrives to a flip-flop either too early or too late, while hold violations happen when data shifts too close to the clock edge.

To enhance timing performance, designers can make multiple adjustments to the design and rerun STA. These adjustments can include changing the clocking methods, gate choices, and connection layouts. STA is repeated once the physical design of the chip is finished to take into consideration physical problems that can affect time, like resistance and parasitic capacitance. This type of STA is known as post-layout.

Inputs for static timing analysis

The STA requires a range of inputs and limitations to perform reliable timing analysis. The restrictions and inputs help STA tools model and analyze the behavior of the digital circuit. The main inputs for STA in VLSI are as follows:

a) Netlist: A netlist is a digital circuit representation in terms of gates, flip-flops, and interconnections. It defines the circuit's logical and physical structure.

b) Clock definitions: Information regarding clock sources, clock waveforms, and clock tree architectures can be found in clock definitions. This data is required for modeling and analyzing clock domains in the design.

c) Clock-to-Q delays: Delays related with flip-flops or latches that indicate how long it takes for data to be processed.

d) Input arrival times: Timing constraints indicating when input signals should arrive at the circuit's inputs.

e) Requirements for Output Delay: Limits on how long the outputs should take to respond following a clock edge (hold time).

f) Information from the library: Libraries holding information about the delay, power, and area properties of standard cells (gates) and other library elements are used by STA tools. These libraries provide delay models for the design's gates and flip-flops.

g) Interconnect models: Details on the interconnect delay models, such as wire resistance, capacitance, and other parasitic effects. This information aids in estimating the delays associated with signal routing between gates and flip-flops.

h) False paths and multicycle path requirements: Identifying paths that do not have to meet timing requirements (false paths) as well as paths that can have extended timing windows (multicycle paths). These constraints aid in the optimization of the analysis.

i) Clock domain details: Defining clock domains and specifying how signals interact with one another. This is crucial for analyzing clock domain crossing (CDC).

j) Environmental factors: Temperature and voltage are examples of environmental conditions in which the chip will work. These factors can have an impact on signal propagation times. Process variations: Information about process variations and manufacturing-related characteristics that can affect chip performance. This is necessary for comparing worst-case and best-case scenarios.

k) Maximum allowable skew constraints: Skew refers to the variation in clock signal arrival times at different parts of the chip. To ensure synchronous operation, maximum permitted skew between clocks must be limited.

l) Constraints and test modes: If the chip provides built-in self-test (BIST) or test modes, test timing and test vector constraints may be specified.

m) Power constraints: Constraints relating to power consumption and, if relevant, power management techniques.

STA tools use these inputs, which are normally provided by the semiconductor designer or design team, to do extensive timing analysis. The purpose is to guarantee that the design meets its timing constraints and functions properly under the defined conditions.

Literature Survey

This work tackles the challenge of anomalous data points in high-speed data acquisition, using a specific design example for testing and analysis. It provides detailed instructions for eliminating these outlier data points. The study also optimizes the performance of a high-speed data collection circuit in FPGA design through a specialized method, STA. Additionally, it explains the application of STA in large-scale FPGA designs. The device, validated by ground and flight trials, meets engineering practice requirements due to its high acquisition accuracy and stability [1].

The STA is widely used in digital circuit design, but its accuracy in predicting statistical variations is challenged by the growing unpredictability of semiconductor devices. To address this, researchers have explored statistical static timing analysis (SSTA), an advanced variation of traditional STA. This overview highlights recent progress in SSTA, discussing its models, assumptions, key techniques, and the remaining challenges that need to be overcome [2].

It introduces efficient methods for determining the exact probability distribution of a combinational circuit's delay, considering gate and wire delay probabilities. The resulting distribution offers insights into the likelihood of achieving various performance levels, facilitating overall performance forecasting. The methods focus on minimizing memory usage while allowing for quick analysis, utilizing a precise approximation based on convex inequalities to prevent performance overestimation. This computational approach provides accurate probability measurements, particularly when delays are attributed solely to the longest paths [3].

This study suggests a statistical timing analysis technique to take into consideration the substantial influence of manufacturing variances on circuit latency. It presents a triple-node delay model that uses response surface techniques for effective statistical gate delay generation and takes into account the effects of input transition times on gate delays. To detect incorrect pathways, a novel criterion is applied, which is predicated on the smallest propagatable pulse width along a path. "Statistically significant" paths are those that intersect with longer paths and affect total

circuit latency. Next, utilizing Monte Carlo simulation on the pertinent path set, the delay probability density function of the circuit is calculated [4].

This work introduces a novel approach to statistical timing analysis that emphasizes building simulation hierarchies and partitioning circuits based on design hierarchy. It separately models the time and logic characteristics of the resulting blocks, using a finite state machine for the logic and gathering timing data from various circuit simulations. A parametric timing model is then created and serves as the foundation for an event-driven hierarchical timing simulator, which can be utilized for statistical timing analysis or as a standalone tool. The paper also shows the application of statistical timing analysis tool! (STAT!) on multiple test cases, along with the resulting outcomes [5].

This work presents a novel method for circuit timing analysis, emphasizing statistical timing. It involves partitioning circuits and creating a simulation hierarchy based on design, with separate modeling of time and logic characteristics. The logic is represented by a finite state machine, a parametric timing model is generated using timing data from various circuit simulations. An event-driven hierarchical timing simulator, derived from these models, can function independently or as a front-end for statistical analysis. The paper also illustrates the application of the STAT! on several test cases.

Skew Handling in STA

Managing clock skew in digital circuits is essential for meeting timing requirements, especially in synchronous designs with distributed clock signals. Variations in the arrival times of clock signals can lead to timing violations if not properly addressed. STA tools are employed to analyze and report clock skew across different areas of the design, enabling designers to pinpoint critical regions and make necessary adjustments for optimal circuit operation. Clock skew represents the timing variation between when a clock signal reaches the launch and capture flip-flops, arising from differences in the time it takes for the signal to travel from its source, which is referred to as clock latency.

PreCTS and PostCTS skew values

Clock skew is a source of uncertainty at the pre-CTS stage, where the ideal scenario is for all flip-flops in a design to receive their clock signals simultaneously, resulting in zero skew. However, this is impractical due to temperature fluctuations and varying wire interconnect lengths. For instance, a flip-flop positioned far from the clock source will experience different skew compared to one located nearby. To address this, precise pre-CTS timing data can be set using a user-defined value. Actual skew values emerge once the clock tree is built, with Jitter as the remaining source of uncertainty. Local skew refers to the difference between two related flip-flops latency, while global skew is defined as the disparity between the longest and shortest clock paths in the design. Figure 63.1 demonstrates that FFn has the highest delay and FF1 the lowest delay.

Delay of one buffer: 12 ps
FF1: Lowest latency
FFn: Highest latency
FF1 and FFn: Global skew

Look at the flip-flops in the following diagram that have the minimum latency (FF1) and the Maximum latency (FFn). Two terms can be defined using the above graphic.

Local skew:
Capture clock latency = 12+12+12+12 = 48ps

Launch clock latency = 12+12 = 24ps
Local skew = 48-24= +24ps
Global skew:
Clock latency max (FFn) = 72ps
Clock latency min (FF1) = 24ps
Global skew = 72-24 = +48ps

Useful skew:
It is purposely built into the design to meet time requirements. This is especially significant in clock pathways when timing fails since it permits timing to flow across that path. Nevertheless, introducing useful skew is not guaranteed. Making sure the margin is accessible in both the prior and subsequent temporal paths necessitates exact execution. Adding skew without control might exacerbate timing issues rather than addressing them. It can be used to both hold and set up violations.

Positive and negative skew:
The clock skew is positive because the capture clock delay is greater than the launch clock latency. Positive skew is detrimental for holding but beneficial for setup timing.

Hold timing benefits from negative skew since it postpones the new launch. Owing to the postponement of the new data introduction, the current data will be effectively preserved instead of being replaced. Negative skew, on the other hand, is detrimental to setup timing.

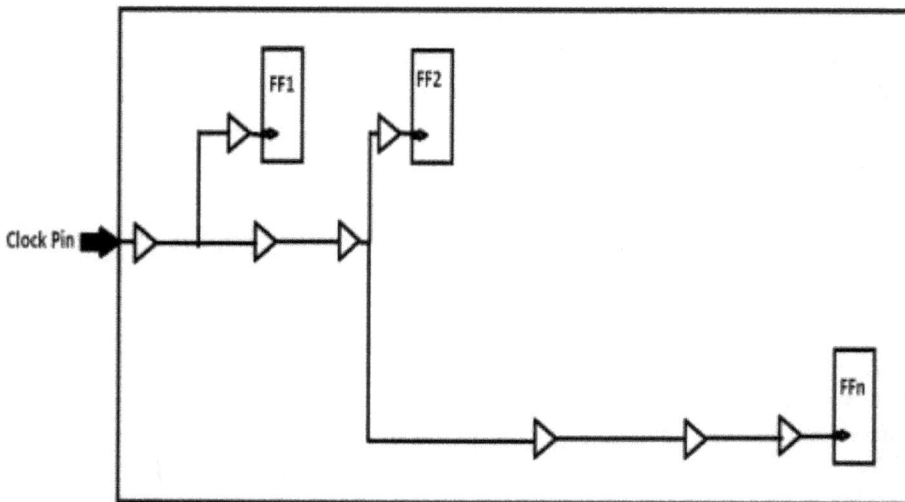

Figure 63.1 Block diagram for skewed clock
Source: Author

Harmful skew:

While introducing some skew can help alleviate timing violations, excessive skew can create issues. Significant positive skew may cause the capture clock to arrive later, resulting in data reaching the capture flip-flop's D pin before the capture edge, potentially overwriting previously latched data and causing a hold violation. Conversely, substantial negative skew refers to the clock edge reaches the capture flip-flop well before the launch flip-flop, delaying the launch and making it difficult for the data to propagate to the capture flip-flop's D pin. This can lead to a setup violation, when the data path is long. Hold violations are more critical than setup violations, as they cannot be resolved by simply lowering the clock frequency.

What happens if the design has no skew at all?

If there is no skew in the design, all flip-flops receive the clock signal simultaneously. A design's overall dynamic power consumption is mostly determined by the clock, which is why having millions of flip-flops switch simultaneously can result in significant dynamic power dissipation. To manage this, tools would add numerous clock buffers and inverters along the clock path, increasing utilization, area consumption, when the one flip-flop is closer to the clock source while others are slightly farther away, even if they are related.

Skew handling approaches

Here are several commonly used approaches for dealing with skew in STA:

a) Time tree synthesis (CTS): The process of balancing and optimizing the distribution of clock signals to sequential elements (such as flip-flops) in a design is known as clock tree synthesis. CTS tools try to reduce clock skew by modifying the placement and sizing of clock buffers to ensure that clock signals arrive at all clocked elements at the same time or within a given skew.

b) Skew constraints: Skew constraints can be specified by designers in the STA configuration. The maximum permitted skew between clock domains or within a single clock domain is defined by these constraints. During the analysis, the STA tool will try to meet these constraints.

c) Clock gating: Clock gating is a technique that enables or disables clock signals to certain elements of the design when they are not actively processing data. This can assist reduce clock skew by reducing the distance clock signals must travel as well as the number of clock buffers required.

d) Clock multiplexing: Clock signals may be multiplexed to different sections of the chip in some designs utilizing clock multiplexers (muxes). Designers can manage clock skew and maximize clock distribution by carefully managing these muxes.

e) Clock signals: Clock signals can be classified as global (spread across the entire chip) or local (restricted to specific regions). Local clocks may have less rigorous skew requirements than global clocks, allowing for more flexible design constraints in some regions.

f) On-chip clock mesh: Instead of typical clock trees, some advanced designs employ clock mesh networks. A clock mesh is a grid of wires and repeaters that can assist distributing the clock signal more evenly and eliminate skew.

g) Buffer insertion: Strategically inserting clock buffers into the clock network can assist reduce skew. STA tools can automate buffer insertion to fulfill the required skew limitations.

h) Clock synchronization: STA tools can assess and introduce synchronization elements (e.g., two-stage synchronizers) in clock domain crossover (CDC) studies to ensure appropriate data transmission between different clock domains while managing the related skew.

i) Incremental timing analysis: Some STA systems provide incremental analysis, which allows designers to concentrate on specific areas of the design to reduce skew. This is especially beneficial in huge, intricate designs.

STA skew handling is a combination of suitable design strategies, restrictions, and tool capabilities. Figure 63.2 demonstrates how this flow works with the script. The goal is to guarantee that clock signals arrive at all important design elements with minimal skew while achieving timing constraints. Skew management is an important part in designing high-performance, low-power VLSI.

Minimum Pulse Width Check

In very large-scale integration (VLSI) design, minimum pulse width checks, also known as pulse-width timing restrictions, are essential for STA. These checks ensure that digital signals meet the minimum allowed pulse widths necessary for reliable operation. The primary objective of minimum pulse width checks is to prevent signals from being too short, which can cause circuit malfunctions and fail to meet timing requirements. In flip-flops or latches, short pulses can result in metastability issues, negatively impacting data acquisition and overall circuit performance.

Purpose of minimum pulse width check

a) Pulse widths at the lowest levels: minimum pulse width is the shortest duration a pulse can have while still being valid and reliable, measured in time (e.g., nanoseconds) and determined by technology and design requirements.

b) Usage of minimum pulse width checks: These checks are applied to data signals to ensure setup and hold periods are met, requiring a signal to remain stable for a specified time before and after a clock edge for proper flip-flop or latch operation.

c) Application to clock signals: Minimum pulse width checks also ensure clock signals are sufficiently wide to propagate through the network.

d) Setting limitations: Designers specify minimum pulse width constraints in the STA setup based on flip-flop characteristics, technology libraries, and required margins for reliability.

e) False and multicycle paths: It's crucial to identify and exclude false paths (not needing to meet the constraint) and multicycle paths (allowing longer pulse widths) from minimum pulse width checks.

f) Clock-domain crossing (CDC) considerations: Minimum pulse width tests should account for synchronization logic when signals cross clock domains to avoid metastability, relying on library characterization. Designers may use incremental analysis to locate potential violations, while STA tools generate reports to help address timing issues by adjusting clock buffers, adding delays, or optimizing the design.

In conclusion, Figure 63.3, Figure 63.4 and Figure 63.5 displays the outcome of Minimum Pulse width, Maximum Transition and Skew minimum pulse width checks in VLSI design ensure that signals remain steady for a defined minimum time, ensuring reliable data capture and circuit operation. These tests are an essential aspect of timing analysis and contribute to the integrated circuit's overall functional correctness and performance.

Flow Charts

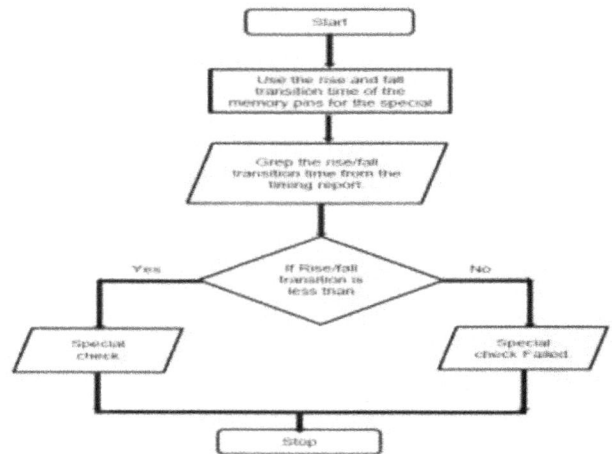

Figure 63.2 TCL script flow diagram
Source: Author

Results

Figure 63.3 Result of minimum pulse width check
Source: Author

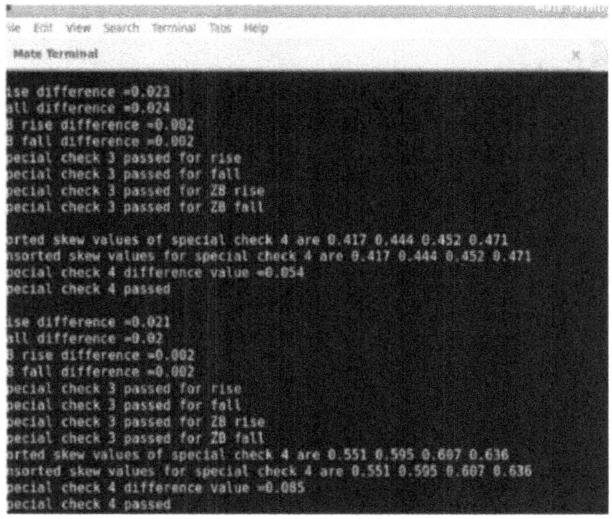

Figure 63.4 Result of maximum transition check
Source: Author

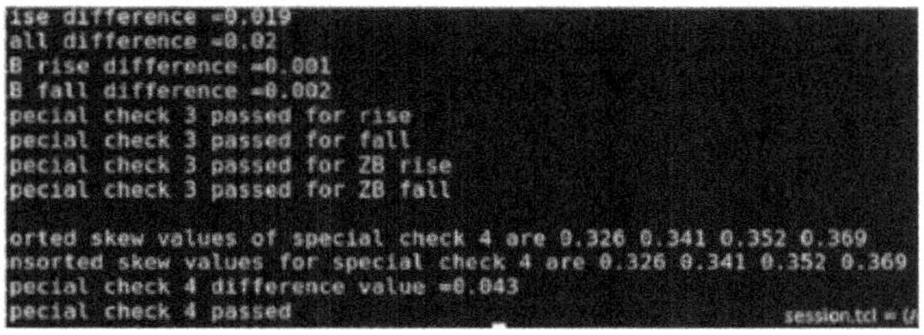

Figure 63.5 Result of skew requirement check
Source: Author

Conclusion

Upon successful code implementation, the following results can be observed: The skew values of corresponding pins will be queried and recorded in separate files for post-processing. By comparing the captured timing numbers, it can be determined whether a specific set of IP or pin has met the special check requirements. These results align with the detailed explanations provided in the corresponding chapter.

Acknowledgement

I would like to express my heartfelt gratitude to my project guide, Dr. G. Sudhagar, from Bharath Institute of Higher Education and Research, for his unwavering support, timely assistance, and valuable suggestions throughout my research. Additionally, I sincerely thank all the teaching and non-teaching staff members of the Bharath Institute of Higher Education and Research for their help during this entire process.

References

[1] Yu-Jian, S., and Ren, Y. (2011). The application of STA in high-speed data acquisition circuit. In IEEE Proceedings of 2011 International Conference on Electronics and Optoelectronics, July 2011.

[2] Blaauw, D., Chopra, K., Srivastava, A., and Scheffer, L. (2008). Statistical timing analysis: from basic principles to state of the art. In IEEE Transactions on Computer-Aided Design of Integrated Circuits and Systems, April 2008.

[3] Jyu, H., Malik, S., Devdas, S., and Keutzer, K. (1993). Statistical timing analysis of combinational logic circuits. *IEEE Transactions on Very Large Scale Integration (VLSI) Systems*, 1(2), 126–137.

[4] Brashear, R., Menezes, N., Oh, C., Pillage, L., and Mercer, M. (1994). Predicting circuit performance using circuit-level statistical timing analysis. In Proceedings of European Design and Test Conference EDAC-ETC-EUROASIC, (pp. 332–337). IEEE.

[5] Benkoski, J., and Strojwas, A. (1987). A new approach to hierarchical and statistical timing simulations. *IEEE Transactions on Computer-Aided Design of Integrated Circuits and Systems*, CAD-6(6), 1039–1052.

64 A Comparative analysis of denoising PCG signals using adaptive Wiener-Kalman filtering

B. Pearly[1,a], S. Ohmshankar[1,b], R. Ayeswarya[2,c], P. Vanithamani[2,d], S. Arunamary[1,e] and G.Sudhagar[3,f]

[1]Research Scholar, Department of ECE, Bharath Institute of Higher Education and Research, Chennai, India

[2]Assistant Professor, Department of ECE, Bharath Institute of Higher Education and Research, Chennai, India

[3]Associate Professor, Department of ECE, Bharath Institute of Higher Education and Research, Chennai, India

Abstract

Cardiovascular disease (CVD) is the group of disorder occurs on heart and blood vessel, and they are coronary heart disease, cerebrovascular disease, rheumatic heart disease, etc. Particularly people under the age of 70 are mostly affected by this disease. Earlier cardiologist analyze phonocardiography (PCG) signals to know the condition of heart. Because of the undesirable noise present in PCG signal makes complication in diagnosis by experts. This study analyze and denoising heart sounds using five different techniques namely short-time Fourier transform (STFT), empirical mode decomposition (EMD), recurrent neural network (RNN), Weiner filter (WF), adaptive Wiener-Kalman filtering (AWKF). There are Lot of noise removal techniques available as discussed in the literature, failed to achieve higher performance in denoising audio signal. The developed denoising techniques were applied on various pathological heart sounds and on heart sound recorded in a noisy environment. The AWKF filtering has great impact on removing distortion and interference present on the signal. This method reserves the major characteristics of heart beat sound. The experimental results showed that AWKF acquired higher SNR, PSNR, lower RMSE and great denoising effect.

Keywords: Cardiovascular disease, heart failure, heart sound, signal processing

Introduction

The term cardiovascular disease (CVD) refers to a bunch of disorders and health conditions that cause weakening of heart and blood vessels. It occurs among all the age group of people in the world and the people above the age group of 50 have high chance of heart attack. The most common heart disease faced by the people is coronary artery, congenital heart defects, arrhythmia, dilated cardiomyopathy, myocardial infraction, hypertrophic cardiomyopathy, aortic stenosis, mitral valve regurgitation, etc. The most behavioral risk factor is lack of diet, alcohol consumption, tobacco addiction, physical inactivity and sedentary behavior. This led to increase in glucose level, blood pressure, blood lipids and cause obesity. Apart from these, intake of polluted air is the more common factor for people who fall into CVD easily. The symptoms for heart disease are chest pain, shortness of breath, narrowing blood vessel, pain in neck, throat and upper belly region. As per the investigation conducted by World Health Organization (WHO), a total of 19.9million people lost their lives due to CVD. The survey conducted by American Heart Association Research (AHA) accounting a total of 9,31,578 death happened in United State in 2021 as shown in Figure 64.1. When artery is blocked, the heart may not function well causing death. Since 2017 to 2020, nearly 48.6% of adults in US were affected by several kinds of CVD [1]. Between 25,000–28,000 people died within 4 years due to heart failure in India [2].

Rather than blood test and chest X-ray, the patient undergoes several other tests namely electrocardiogram, echocardiogram, MRI scan, CT scan, etc. Through heart sound the mechanical movements of heart and cardiovascular system

[a]pearly.ece@bharathuniv.ac.in, [b]ohmshankar.ece@gmail.com, [c]ayeswarya.pari@gmail.com, [d]vanithamani.ece@bharathuniv.ac.in, [e]arunamary.ece@bharathuniv.ac.in, [f]sudhagar.ece@bharathuniv.ac.i

DOI: 10.1201/9781003616399-64

is known and those having details about other portions of heart and interconnections among them in both physiological and pathological fields. Normally a heart sounds lub dub, dub lub [3]. The heart beat and blood pumping information were obtained through echocardiogram. To diagnose heart failure, cardiologist use the heart sound recorded by phonocardiograph device during a cardiac cycle [4]. The unusual sound of heart which is the symptom diagnoses various kinds of heart disease. The heart sound is classified into four categories and they are S1, S2, S3, S4 whereas S1, S2 are high-pitched sounds and S3, S4 are low-pitched sounds. The first two sounds are normal sounds, and the remaining are abnormal sounds (i.e., murmur sound). Respiratory and digestive tract sounds and external surrounding noise are the interference while facing recording of heart sound through PCG [5]. Apart from that, distortions occur by sneezing, swallowing, muscle actions, etc [6].

Several denoising techniques are available at present. A self-construct wavelet bias is used by Xiefeng Cheng et al. to denoising the signal and studied its constructer method and features as per the heart sound [7]. The experimental result of proposed study is compared with db and bior wavelet denoising techniques and it shows that the result is satisfactory which improves heart sound feature extraction in a considerable quantity. Following this, Salman et al. proposed three different signal processing techniques to denoising heart sounds and they are wavelet transform (WT), total variation (TV), and empirical mode decomposition (EMD) [8]. The model performances are evaluated as per sign-to-noise-ratio (SNR), root mean square error (RMSE) and percentage root mean square difference (PRD). From observations, EMD denoising the normal and abnormal heart sound effectively than remaining two methods. The author Raza, selected Dataset-B and applied band filter to remove noise and following this sampling rate of selected sound are adjusted. To improve the result, down sampling technique is applied and it obtains discriminant features. Later various classification models are developed and tested the dataset. Later the research conducted by Ashwin et al. recommended STFT based denoising of speech signal with environmental noise [11]. In the raw data additive white Gaussian noise (AWGN) is added and denoising procedure is done. The metrics such as SNR, peak signal to noise ratio (PSNR) is compared. For stationary and non-stationary speech signal noise removal approach, Kumar designed iterative Kalman filter with digital expander in the case of overcoming problem faced with spectral subtraction and wiener filter [12].

To address the noise present in the heart sound, five different signal processing techniques such as short-time Fourier transform (STFT), EMD, recurrent neural network (RNN), Weiner filter,

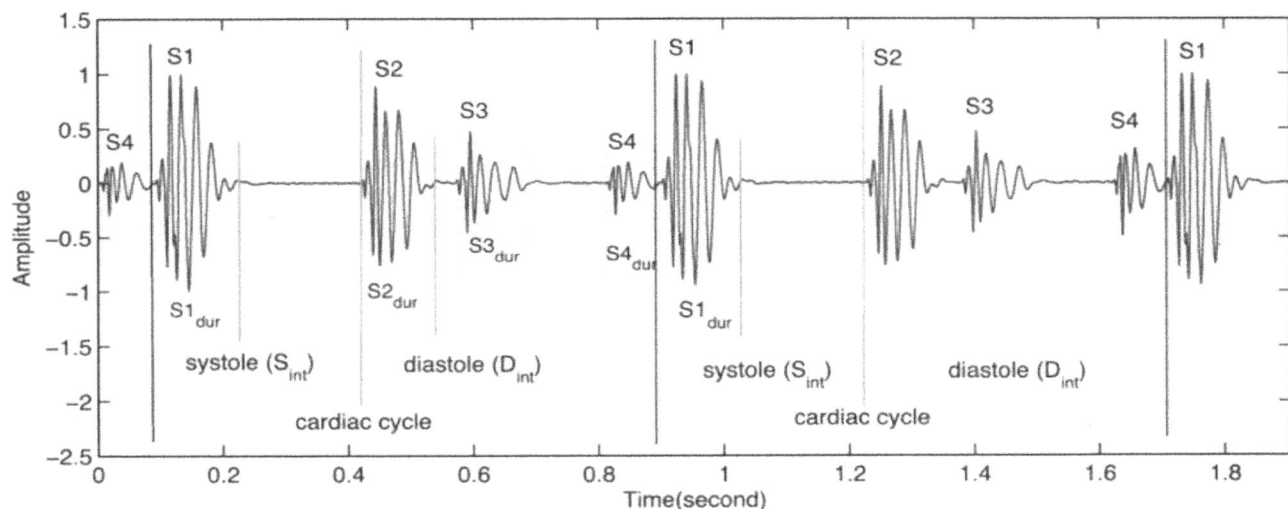

Figure 64.1 Normal (S1, S2) and Abnormal (S3, S4) heart sound
Source: Author

adaptive Wiener-Kalman filtering were presented in this study. The developed models focus on removing noise without any loss in discriminant features and providing a strong support on classification and diagnosis of CVD disease.

Related Works

To limit the problem in diagnosing heart disease using PCG signal, the author Ali et al. recommended discrete wavelet transform denoising technique which is superior in neglecting distortions [13]. This filtering technique possesses features such as multiresolution and windowing. This research uses various families of selected signal processing technique, threshold types and techniques, and signal decomposition level. In this analysis, experts focused on effect of selected wavelet's function and decomposition level on the performance of appropriate denoising technique. Following this, denoising signal is contrasted with PCG signal to obtain necessary features. Experimental analysis visualized that the level of decomposition and threshold types are the factors deciding the performance analyzing denoising technique. Furthermore, the result is justified by comparing SNR, RMSE, PRD, respectively. Zhang et al. proposed a heart sound classification technique depends on improved mel-frequency cepstrum coefficient features and deep residual learning [14]. Initially the original signal is pre-processed and the features are fed to neural network. And then the deep residual network obtains the pathological data present in the heart signal. Then abnormal sounds are classified according to the features given to the neural network. The author Joaquim et al. recommended Kalman filter in the time domain combination with spectral subtraction [15]. This technique focus on removing distortions from biomedical speech signal and conduct performance analysis on SNR and Itakura–Saito distance parameters. This study results compared with conventional method showing that the proposed method obtained four times greater Itakura–Saito's distance.

Manju et al. have applied Wiener and Kalman filter on MIT-BIH dataset to remove noise and distortions present in the ECG signal which increases the quality of feature selection technique and classification [16]. High and low frequency noises namely muscle artefact, PLI, AWGN were added on the input signal and denoised using those two filtering methods. From observations, the wiener filter outperformed Kalman filter because it works well only on non-linear systems. Kumar et al. examined ECG signal and classified abnormalities of patients to support cardiologist [17]. In this research, a novel feature extraction technique namely FFT and modified AlexNet classifier classifies four kinds of arrhythmia condition. Feature extraction techniques could restrict number of reference points in ECG signal by including an effective threshold to the peak point. Such peak points are identified by using FFT. It has the capacity of removing low frequency from the input signal and then inverse FFT remove noise from it. Then the features were extracted and given as input to the classifier algorithm to classify the four kinds of ECG arrhythmias. Results shows that the proposed study identifies oscillations are 20% greater than conventional methods. The AlexNet gained accuracy, sensitivity, specificity and precision of 99.7%, 98.3%, 99.2%, and 96.1%, respectively. The analysis of ECG signals de noising conducted by Sarafan recommended ensemble Kalman filter [18]. It is widely used for non-linear systems, and it depends on local linearization of the nonlinear models utilizing the Jacobian. In terms of visual quality, the proposed method denoising distortions moreover than several other filters. This model obtained SNR, PSNR, and correlation coefficient of 10.96, 150.45, and 0.959, respectively.

The biomedical signals are possible to create various kinds of noises with fixed coefficient filters, because of the nature of such signals led to decrease in accuracy in relation with time. To overcome this problem and improve filtering of ECG signal, Ahmed et al. proposed double Kalman filter. Initially AWGN is mixed to the input signal to create a distorted signal and then Kalman filter is used and improved the quality of ECG signal. Next Kalman filter is employed to estimate the newly denoised signal within given time in terms of improving accuracy.

Denoising Methods

The recording of heart sound consists of multiple kinds of noise and they are external noise, internal noise created by human organs and respiratory system. It affects the segmentation and classification of heart sound. Even though a lot of signal processing techniques are available and some of the filtering techniques are explained in this section.

A. Short-term Fourier transform: It analyze signals in time-frequency analysis which gives localized spectrum in the time domain by carrying out Fourier transform in a localized time window. This technique is developed to restrict the problem faced by conventional discrete Fourier transform [21]. Short-term Fourier transform (SIFT) is widely used for analyzing and processing of speech signal, appropriate for slow and time varying signal spectrum analysis. Initially the input signal is split into frames, next Fourier transform is done on each frame. All the frames of speech signals are obstructed from various stationary signal waveforms; short-time spectrum of every frame is an approximation of spectrum values of the smooth signal waveform. The STFT is calculated by:

$$STFT_x(\text{t, f}) = \int_{-\infty}^{\infty} x(t)h(t-\tau)e^{-j2\pi f\tau} \, d\tau$$

whereas, $STFT_x$(t, f) represents coefficient of STFT; $x(t)$ represents signal; t, f-time and frequency. STFT is a function of time and frequency and it visualize the change of frequency of signal with respect to time. The inverse form of STFT is written as

$$x_t = \int_{-\infty}^{\infty} \int_{-\infty}^{\infty} STFT_x(\text{t}',\text{f}') \, \omega \, (t-t')e^{-j2\pi f'\tau'} \, dt'df'$$

Whereas, $w(t)$ denotes window function. The window length corresponds to spectral resolution and it is inversely proportional to time resolution. Because of conflict among time and frequency resolution, the practical analysis depends on the STFT analysis and the respective window length could be found.

B. Empirical mode decomposition (EMD): This data analysis technique method is suitable for analyzing non-stationary and non-linear signals. The wavelet and Fourier transform requires predefined bias function, but this fully data driven system derive from input signal. It decomposes given input into a series of intrinsic mode function (IMF) via iterative process in accordance with time [22]. An IMF function should follow two criteria: equal volume of extrema and zero crossing or contrast by at most 1; the average value of envelopes derived from local maxima

and minima is zero. Obtaining IMF from given signal, the upcoming steps are followed:

Step 1: Find extrema of signal x(t).
Step 2: Interpolate local extrema cubic spline to get upper e_{max}(n) and lower envelope e_{min}(n).
Step 3: Find the local mean m_1(t) of both envelopes.
Step 4: Subtract m_1(t) from x(t) to get first component h_1(t).
Step 5: If h_1(t) fulfills the above-mentioned two criteria, then denote it as IMF.
Step 6: If h_1(t) is not satisfactory then repeat the above steps and take h_1(t) as original signal until it achieves IMF, specify this stage as c_1(t). The residual function r_1(t) obtained in this step is expressed as,

$$r_1(\text{t}) = \text{x(t)} - c_1(\text{t})$$

Furthermore r_1(t) is taken as original signal and the above steps are repeated to find next IMF. When completing this, a pair of IMF and residue were gained, and the first IMF comprised of higher frequency oscillation which present in the signal. The newly extracted IMF's having little bit lesser frequency oscillation than previous one. We know that the residual function is stable or monotonic function in absence of frequency components. The original signal x(t) is described as:

$$x(t) = \sum_{i=1}^{n} \quad C_i(t) + r_n(t)$$

Whereas $C_i(t)$-extracted IMF
$r_n(t)$—residual function

C. Recurrent neural network

In the field of computational technology, artificial neural network (ANN) was mostly utilized to obtain remarkable growth in various areas, namely healthcare, data analysis, image processing, speech and audio processing. The fundamental types of ANN are feed forward neural network, multiple layered perceptron neural network, convolutional neural network, radial biased function neural network, modular neural network, recurrent neural network, sequence to sequence model. Among that, RNN is suitable for performing sequential data analysis and for tasks namely non-liner audio processing, speech enhancement and time series prediction. The vanishing gradient problem arises from the gradient connection and propagation of gradients through various time steps. When the gradient propagates back and makes multiplication of gradients in each time step results vanishing problem in RNN. This in turn causes loss of information and slow convergence of learning. To overcome this problem, RNN needs a unique structure. long short-term memory (LSTM) is one among RNN has significant effect on removing background noise. Therefore LSTM is introduced to overcome the problems in RNN [23].

The proposed RNN algorithm comprised of an input layer, a pair of LSTM layer and fully connected with 100 units, and an output layer. The detailed study of RNN denoising technique used in this study is visualized in Figure 64.2.

D. Wiener filter (WF): It is a classical technique employed for limiting noise and enhancing speech in audio signal [24]. This operates in a frequency domain and applies a liner time-invariant filter

Noisy ECG Signal

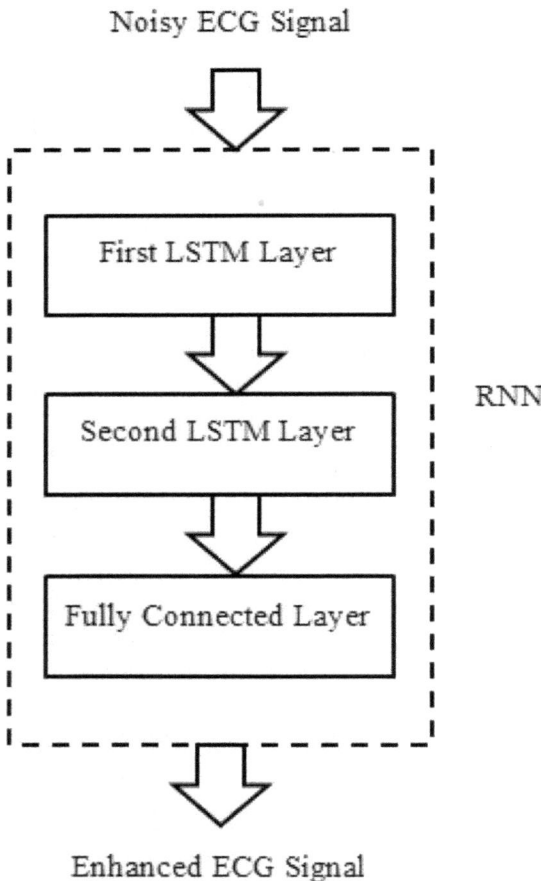

RNN

Enhanced ECG Signal

Figure 64.2 Noise suppression from audio signal using RNN
Source: Author

over noisy signal. It estimates the noise power spectrum by using a noise-only segment of the audio. These resulting in compute the wiener filter coefficients that decide the amount of noise for every frequency component.

The input signal with noise is expressed as,
$$x(n) = d(n) + v(n)$$
Whereas, d(n)-original signal, v(n)-noisy signal. The output signal can be the close estimate of desired signal, which impact error signal and reduce it. Whenever the filter tries to manage the weight, the mean square error should be decreased. The error signal e(n) is specified as,
$$e = e\{|e(n)^2|\}$$
$$e(n) = d(n) - d^{(n)}$$
A k tap discrete WF is derived as'
$$y(n) = \sum_{k=0}^{k-1} \quad Wk \, x(n - kt)$$
The resulting equation of wiener filter is
$$\sum_{I=0}^{P-1} \quad W_k r_{xx}[k-1] = r_{xd}[-1]$$
If I = 0,1,…P-1 is said to be Wiener-Hopf equation. Here $r_{xx}[1]$ specifies autocorrelation function of x(n) and $r_{xd}[1]$ represents cross correlation function among x(n) and d(n).

E. Adaptive Wiener-Kalman filter (AWKF): The adaptive filtering proposed here is the combination of wiener filter with Kalman filter. In general, the wiener filter analyze signals based on frequency domain but the Kalman filter is based on time domain analysis. In this adaptive filtering technique when distorted signal is provided, wiener filter starts functioning of it. The statistical approach of wiener filter analyze the input signal and it does not require any reference signal. Majorly this filter is employed to minimize the mean square error between desired signal and estimated one. Here this filter's function is to obtain initial denoised estimate of noisy signal. Furthermore the Kalman filter processes the signal by performing prediction and correction steps. In odd step, the filter utilize mathematical modelling of the system to find the upcoming state by the present state and input signal i.e. output of wiener filtered signal. This prediction is done by projecting the present state forward in time using the state transition matrix that defines how the system evolves over time. In the even step, the filter utilize actual measurement of the system to adjust the prediction state and get an improved estimate of the true state of the system. By contrasting prediction state and actual measurement, correction process could end and the variation among them is called as residual which helps to fix the predicted state with Kalman gain. The Kalman gain is a matrix which decides the amount of weight required by predicted state and actual measurements when computing the updated state estimate. This unique technique combines the specific characteristics of both filter and reduces the noise effectively.

The Adaptive Weighted Kalman Filter (AWKF) is a methodology that combines the traditional Kalman filter with adaptive weighting techniques to improve performance in dynamic systems, especially in scenarios with varying noise levels as shown in Figure 64.3.

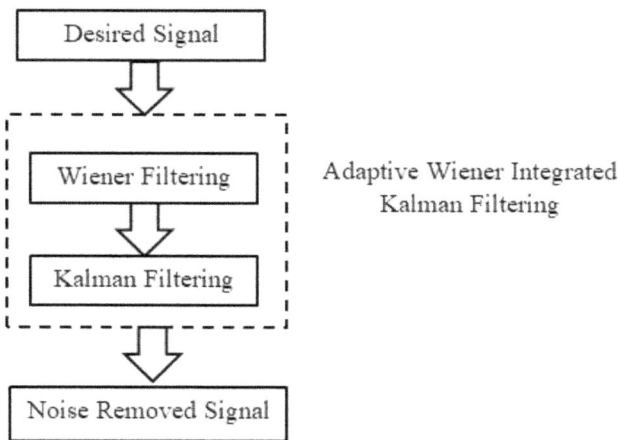

Figure 64.3 Methodology of AWKF
Source: Author

Result and Discussion

The heart sound recorded through PCG is visualized in Figure 64.4. The heart sounds available are distorted by external environment, hardware limitations. The presence of several type of noise makes identification more complicated and makes inaccurate. The heartbeat sound frequency range from 20 to 200 Hz. In Figure 64.5, the number of heart beat signal samples as per various metrics is represented.

The qualitative and quantitative performance analyses of selected denoising techniques are conducted. 80% of the total data is used to train the models and rest of the data is used to evaluate the model's performance.

The qualitative analysis of five noise removal techniques were conducted by contrast the output and level of noise removed from the original signal. The Figure 64.6 displayed that the proposed AWKF technique removed noise in a higher proportion than remaining four filtering techniques.

The quantitative performances of selected filtering techniques are evaluated based on two metrics, such as SNR, RMSE and PSNR. The calculation of above mentioned metrics are displayed below:

$$SNR = \frac{\sum_{n=1}^{N} [y(n)]^2}{\sum_{n=1}^{N} [y(n) - y^{\wedge}(n)]^2}$$

$$RMSE = \sqrt{\frac{\sum_{n=1}^{N} [y(n) - y^{\wedge}(n)]^2}{N}}$$

$$PSNR = 10 log\ log\ 10\left(\frac{R^2}{MSE}\right)$$

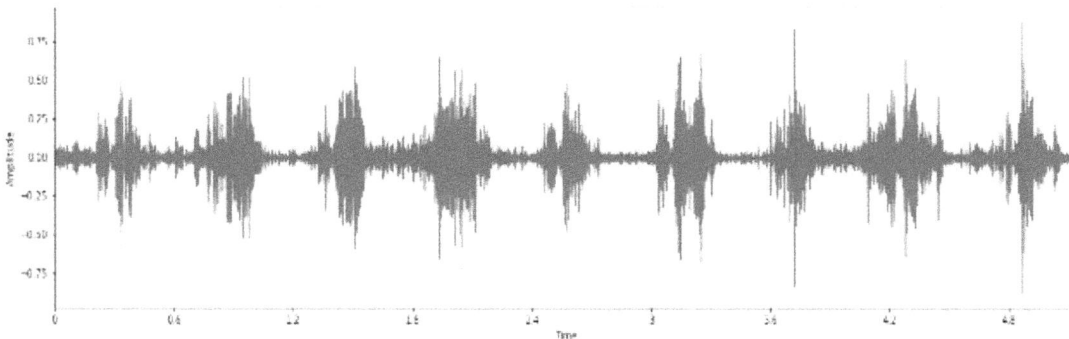

Figure 64.4 Shows an input heart sound signal
Source: Author

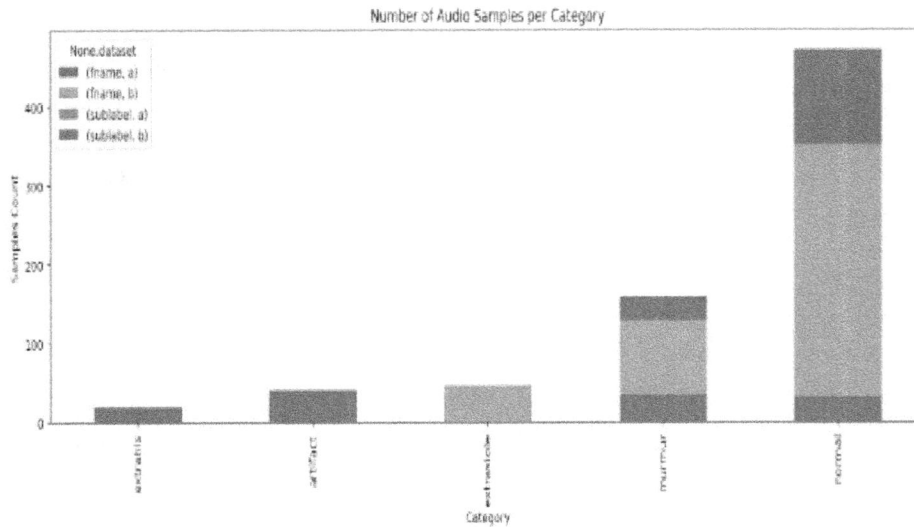

Figure 64.5 Number of audio signal present in selected dataset
Source: Author

Whereas, y(n)-input signal, y^(n)-denoised signal and N-length of the signal. SNR is the ratio of signal power to noise power. RMSE involves calculating the accuracy of denoising techniques to maintain the features of noise removed signal by finding sample standard deviation of the variations among given signal and noise removed signal. PSNR calculates the ratio among maximum possible value of a signal and power of denoised signal which impact the quality of its representation.

Comparing the results of five filtering technique on the metrics of SNR and PSNR as shown in Table 64.1. The table evaluating that the proposed AWKF gained higher SNR, PSNR, and lower RMSE.

The qualitative analysis carried out in this study is represented in Figure 64.7. These resultant images showing the difference between original signal and noise suppressed signal by five filtering techniques.

The spectrogram represents the visual form of sound signal. The term spectrum analysis denotes estimating the power of signals at various frequencies. The amplitude of the noise signal is lesser than the audio signal which is shown in Figure 64.8.

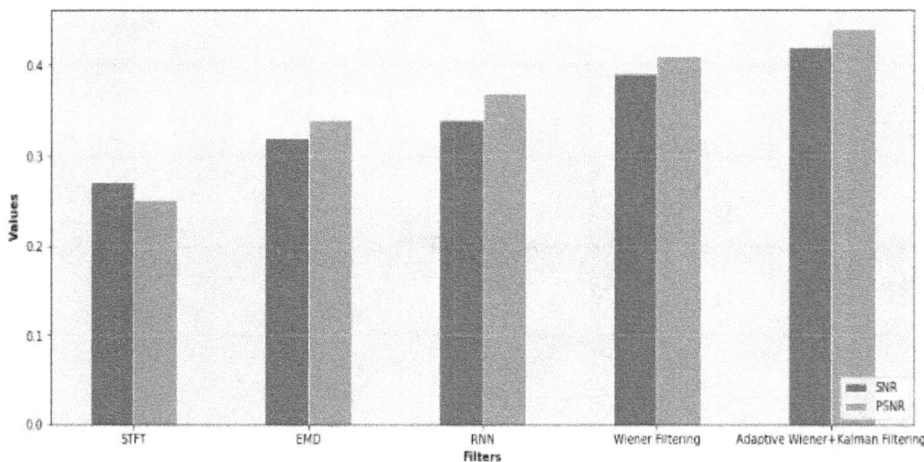

Figure 64.6 Quantitative analysis of proposed filtering techniques
Source: Author

The paper "Heart signal analysis using multistage classification denoising model" by Choudhary and Bhadu [9] focuses on enhancing the analysis of heart sounds (phonocardiograms, PCG) to detect abnormalities. The study leverages advanced signal processing techniques, including tunable quality wavelet transform (TQWT), discrete wavelet transform (DWT), and empirical mode decomposition (EMD), to preprocess and denoise heart signals.

The article "Heartbeat sound signal classification using deep learning" by Raza et al., [10] explores the use of deep learning for classifying heartbeat sound signals. The authors implement signals leveraging their ability to handle the temporal dependencies inherent in audio RNNs to

Table 64.1 Performance analysis of denoising techniques

Name of the filter	SNR (db)	RMSE	PSNR (db)
STFT	0.27	0.00454	0.25
EMD	0.32	0.00418	0.34
RNN	0.34	0.00382	0.37
WF	0.39	0.00339	0.41
AWKF	0.42	0.00240	0.44

Source: Author

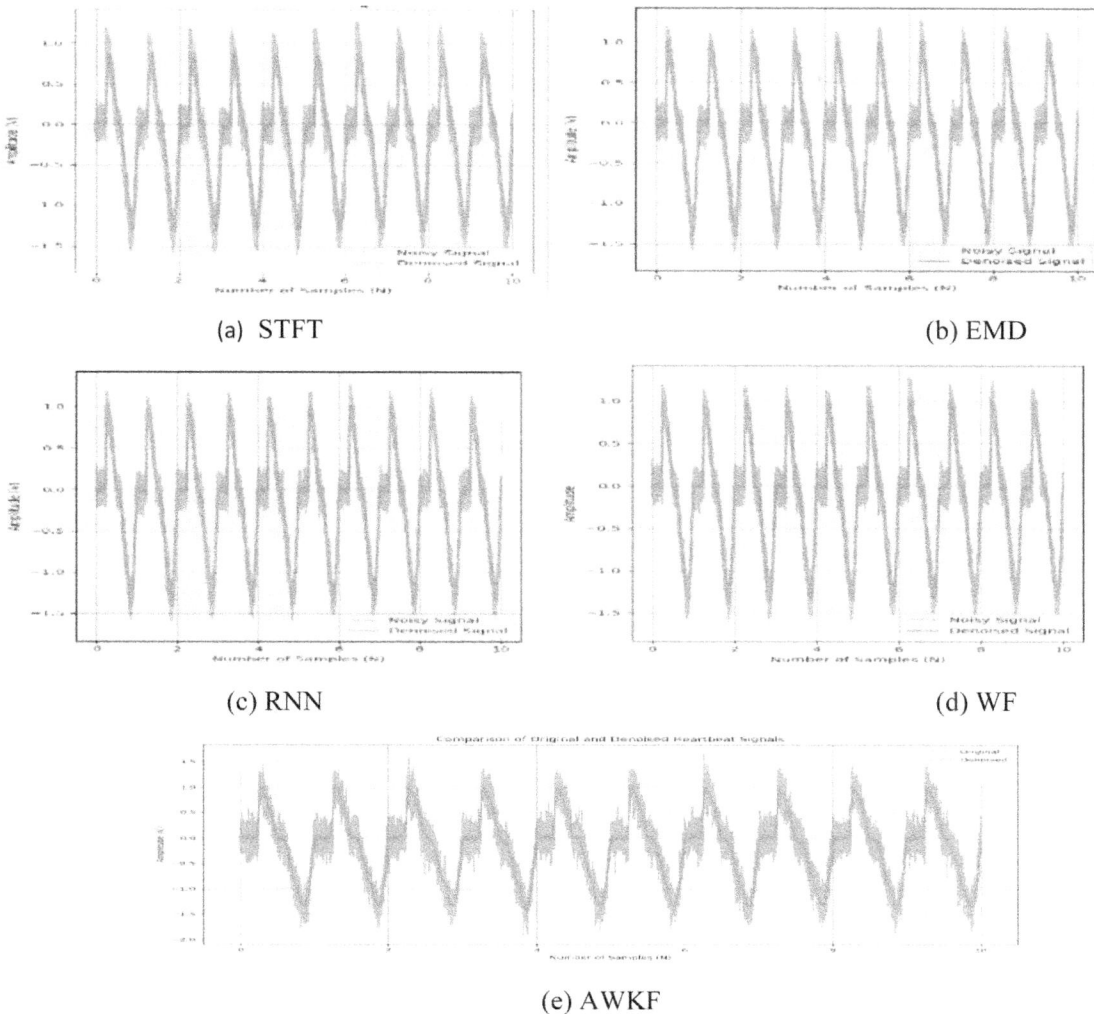

(a) STFT (b) EMD (c) RNN (d) WF (e) AWKF

Figure 64.7 Comparative analysis of original heart sound signal and denoised heart signal by various filter
Source: Author

address the classification problem, leveraging their ability to handle temporal dependencies inherent in audio signals.

Conclusion

This study compared various types of noise removal techniques to suppress noise from heartbeat sound. This analysis focused on simplifying the abnormalities identification of heart signal under various conditions. Different filtering technique performances were evaluated on the signal with various conditions such as external noise, internal organs disturbance and interferences. A total of five different filtering models were built and their performances were evaluated. Among that, the proposed adaptive wiener integrated Kalman filter denoising technique improved the quality of heart sound without losing features. This adaptive filtering technology overcomes the problem found in WF technique and which is comparatively more effective than WF. This model achieved higher SNR, PSNR and lower

RMSE of 0.42db, 0.00240, 0.44db. Cardiologists use this analysis to detect noise and distortions which are problematic to classifier models and consequently fix this technique to remove noise during recoding of heartbeat sound. This model will maximize the prediction rate of CVD disease by providing desired features to the classification model.

Reference

[1] Martin, S. S., Aday, A. W., Almarzooq, Z. I., Anderson, C. A., Arora, P., Avery, C. L., et al. (2024). Heart disease and stroke statistics: a report of US and global data from the American Heart Association. *Circulation*, 149(8), e347–e913.

[2] National Crime Records Bureau. Accidental Deaths and Suicides in India 2022.

[3] Kumar, D., Carvalho, P., Antunes, M., Gil, P., Henriques, J., and Eugenio, L. (2006). A new algorithm for detection of S1 and S2 heart sounds. In Proceedings of the ICASSP, IEEE International Conference on Acoustics, Speech and Signal Processing-Proceedings, Toulouse, France, 14–19 May 2006, (Vol. 2, pp. 1180–1183).

[4] Tang, H., Zhang, J., Sun, J., Qiu, T., and Park, Y. (2016). Phonocardiogram signal compression using sound repetition and vector quantization. *Computers in Biology and Medicine*, 71, 24–34. doi: 10.1016/j.compbiomed.2016.01.017.

[5] Gradolewski, D., and Redlarski, G. (2014). Wavelet-based denoising method for real phonocardiography signal recorded by mobile devices in noisy environment. *Computers in Biology and Medicine*, 52C, 119–129.

[6] Kumar, D., Carvalho, P., Antunes, M., Paiva, R., and Henriques, J. (2011). Noise detection during heart sound recording using periodicity signatures. *Physiological Measurement*, 32, 599–618.

[7] Cheng, X., and Zhang, Z. (2014). Denoising method of heart sound signals based on self-construct heart sound wavelet. *AIP Advances*. 4(8), 087108.

[8] Salman, A. H., Ahmadi, N., Mengko, R., Langi, A. Z. R., and Mengko, T. L. R. (2015). Performance comparison of denoising methods for heart sound signal. In 2015 International Symposium on Intelligent Signal Processing and Communication Systems (ISPACS).

[9] Choudhary, R. R., Rani, M., Kaur, R., and Bhadu, M. (2024). Heart signal analysis using multistage classification denoising model. *Journal of Electrical and Computer Engineering*, 2024(1), 1502285.

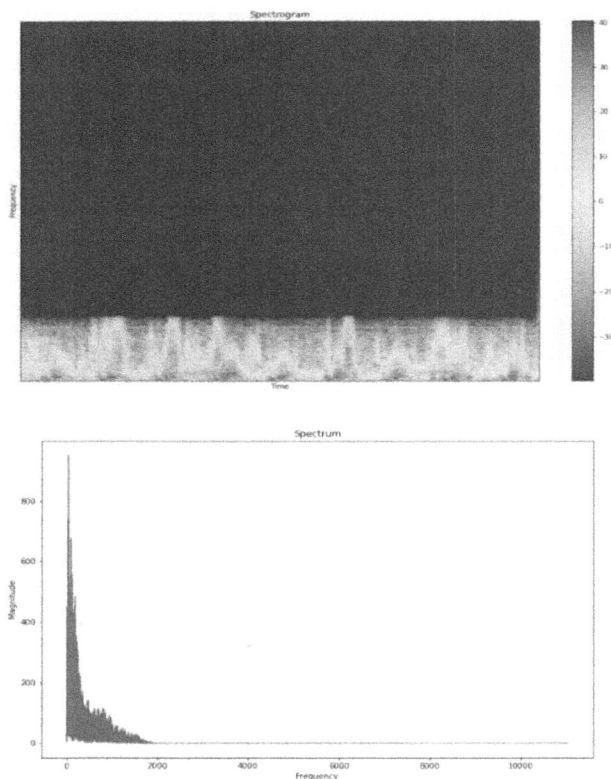

Figure 64.8 Spectrum after noise removal
Source: Author

[10] Raza, A., Mehmood, A., Ullah, S., Ahmad, M., Choi, G. S., and On, B. W. (2019). Heartbeat sound signal classification using deep learning. *Sensors*, 19(21), 4819.

[11] Ashwin, J. S., and Manoharan, N. (2018). Audio denoising based on short time fourier transform. *Indonesian Journal of Electrical Engineering and Computer Science*, 9(1), 89–92. ISSN: 2502-4752, DOI: 10.11591/ijeecs.v9.i1.pp89-92.

[12] Rao, G. M., and Kumar, U. S. (2016). Speech enhancement using kalman filter with preprocessed digital expander in noisy environment. *Indian Journal of Science and Technology*, 9(39), 3–5. DOI: 10.17485/ijst/2016/v9i39/100594.

[13] Ali, M. N., and El-Dahshan, E. L. S. A. (2017). Denoising of heart sound signals using discrete wavelet transform. *Circuits, Systems, and Signal Processing*, 36, 4482–4497. DOI 10.1007/s00034-017-0524-7.

[14] Li, F., Zhang, Z., Wang, L., and Liu, W. (2022). Heart sound classification based on improved mel-frequency spectral coefficients and deep residual learning. *Frontiers in Physiology*, 13, 1084420.

[15] da Silva, L. A., and Joaquim, M. B. (2008). Noise reduction in biomedical speech signal processing based on time and frequency Kalman filtering combined with spectral subtraction. *Computers and Electrical Engineering*, 34(2), 154–164. DOI:10.1016/j.compeleceng.2007.10.007.

[16] Manju, B. R., and Sneha, M. R. (2020). ECG denoising using wiener filter and kalman filter. *Procedia Computer Science*, 171, 273–281.

[17] Kumar, M. A., and Chakrapani, A. (2022). Classification of ECG signal using FFT based improved alexnet classifier. *PLoS One*, 17(9), e0274225.

[18] Antczak, K. (2018). Deep recurrent neural networks for ECG signal denoising. ArXiv, abs/1807.11551.

[19] Adithya, P. C., Sankar, R., Moreno, W. A., and Hart, S. (2017). Trends in fetal monitoring through phonocardiography: challenges and future directions. *Biomedical Signal Processing and Control*, 33, 289–305. ISSN 1746-8094.

[20] Boutana, D., Benidir, M., and Barkat, B. (2011). Denoising and characterization of heart sound signals using optimal intrinsic mode functions. In Proceedings of the 4th International Symposium on Applied Sciences in Biomedical and Communication Technologies - ISABEL '11. doi:10.1145/2093698.2093724.

[21] Vinay, N., Vidyasagar, K. N., Rohith, S., Dayananda, P., and Supreeth, S. (2024). An RNN-Bi LSTM based multi decision GAN approach for the recognition of cardiovascular disease (CVD) from heart beat sound: a feature optimization process. *IEEE Access*, 12(99), 65482–65502.

[22] Sharma, B., and Suji, R. J. (2016). ECG denoising using weiner filter and adaptive least mean square algorithm. In 2016 IEEE International Conference on Recent Trends in Electronics, Information and Communication Technology (RTEICT), Bangalore, India, (pp. 53–57).

65 Circuit analysis realization for a three dimensional coexisting chaotic attractor system utilizing a single multiplier and its use in secure communication

Vanithamani, P.[1,a], Prakash, S.[2,b], Jayasukumari, I.[3,c], Priyadarshini, C.[3,d], Pearly, B.[1,e] and Sudhagar, G.[4,f]

[1]Research Scholar, Department of ECE, Bharath Institute of Higher Education and Research, Chennai, India

[2]Professor, Department of ECE, Bharath Institute of Higher Education and Research, Chennai, India

[3]Assistant Professor, Department of ECE, Bharath Institute of Higher Education and Research, Chennai, India

[4]Associate Professor, Department of ECE, Bharath Institute of Higher Education and Research, Chennai, India

Abstract

Signal masking is the one of the major applications for chaotic circuits which are designed to generate chaos and many have researched and reported on the same This paper describes a novel chaotic system utilizing a single quadratic term and the proposed autonomous three dimensional chaotic systems were mathematically modeled and were dynamically analyzed using MATLAB-Simulink and exhibited coexisting attractors. The proposed system has been realized with simple analog electronic components and analog circuits and required only one multiplier. And the designed analog electronic circuit was implemented with ORCAD-Pspice to conform with the numerical analyzed chaotic system. The simulated proposed chaotic 3D systems displayed coexisting attractors thus conformed with our numerically analyzed result for varying initial conditions. Hence, indicated proposed chaotic system increases the encryption space for secure communication applications as well. Furthermore, chaotic masking method circuit was simulated using Orcad-Pspice with simple analog components for secure communication. The simulation showed encrypting the data and the decrypted data were received successfully. Furthermore, simulation indicated satisfactorily if the receiver side was hacked with different signal other than the transmitter chaotic signal the decryption of the original information signal was not correctly received at the receiver side.

Keywords: Flyback converter, human lungs modelling, positive pressure respirator, sensor less brushless DC motor

Introduction

Deterministic and extremely susceptible to the parameters of the system and its initial conditions are chaotic systems. The chaotic signal can have unpredictable phase portraits and wide band spectrum. Therefore, chaotic circuits are used for transmitting secure data because chaotic system possesses a self-synchronization property. Compared to the conventional spread spectrum techniques used in wireless communication this chaos based system is a cheaper alternative.

Many reports are available for three dimensional chaotic systems [1–4]. However, simulating the numerically studied three dimensional chaotic circuit by electronic realization using simple electronic components either using MATLAB-Simulink or ORCAD-Pspice for secure communication application is limited [5–9]. In existing system, the Lorenz system described by 3D order chaotic system having multiple quadratic terms in realizing the complex 2-scroll attractors [10]. J.C Sprott et.al introduced new chaotic system in the form of jerk equation having a signum function

[a]vanithamani.ece@bharathuniv.ac.in, [b]prakash.ece@bharathuniv.ac.in, [c]jayasukumari.ece@bharathuniv.ac.in, [d]priyadharshini.ece@bharathuniv.ac.in, [e]pearly.ece@bharathuniv.ac.in, [f]sudhagar.ece@bharathuniv.ac.in

DOI: 10.1201/9781003616399-65

and circuit was realized using op-map as comparator for the signum function [11]. Pehlivan introduced a new three-dimensional chaotic system with two quadratic terms and six total terms to create more complex two-scroll attractors. Therefore, in this research the proposed 3D chaotic jerk system had only one quadratic term with three real constant parameters displayed coexisting chaotic attractor. The proposed chaotic system was dynamically analyzed. To verify the MATLAB-Simulink simulated proposed chaotic system, analog electronic circuit was realized with only one multiplier. Finally, the realization of the proposed chaotic systems for synchronized secure communication by chaotic masking method was implemented and presented. Which shows good rigid secure communication system.

Chaotic System Analysis

The proposed system is composed of three ordinary differential equations involving six terms and the system has three state variables: x, y, and z, and is known as a jerk equation. It contains three positive real constants: a, b, and c. When specific values are assigned to these constants, specifically a = 10, b = 2.4, and c = 1.1, the system demonstrates chaotic behavior, characterized by a typical attractor. The stability is examined by determining the eigenvalues of the equilibrium state for x, y, and z through the Jacobian matrix.

$0 = by$
$0 = az$
$0 = -x - y - cz - x * x$

The new system has the E0 equilibrium point (i.e. at origin) and other two assumed equilibrium points are E1 (-1, 0, 0) and E2 (1, 0, 0).

Commonly utilized are the new Jacobian matrix systems, which are negative pressure systems.

$$J = \begin{bmatrix} 0 & b & 0 \\ 0 & 0 & a \\ -2x-1 & -1 & -c \end{bmatrix}$$

For origin E0 (0, 0, 0) equilibrium points the Jacobian becomes and the eigen values are
$\lambda 1 = -2.022$ $\lambda 2 = 0.4163 + 3.413i$, $\lambda 3 = 0.4163 - 3.413i$
For assumed E1 (-1, 0, 0) equilibrium points the Jacobian becomes

$$J = \begin{bmatrix} 0 & b & 0 \\ 0 & 0 & a \\ -1 & -1 & -c \end{bmatrix}$$

And the eigen values are $\lambda 1 = 1.6506$, $\lambda 2 = -1.375 + 3.556i$ $\lambda 3 = -1.375 - 3.556i$.
For assumed E2(1, 0, 0) equilibrium points the Jacobian becomes

$$J = \begin{bmatrix} 0 & b & 0 \\ 0 & 0 & a \\ -3 & -1 & -c \end{bmatrix}$$

and the eigen values are $\lambda 1 = -3.686$, $\lambda 2 = 1.293 + 4.226i$ $\lambda 3 = 1.293 - 4.226i$
The eigen values of the new chaotic system at E0 and E1, E2 equilibrium points conform to a real eigen value the with pair of complex conjugate values having alternating signs. Hence, the new system is chaotic type. MATLAB-Simulink was used to simulate the proposed chaotic system with one multiplier, three integrators and a subtractor block as shown in Figure 65.1. Figure 65.2 display the chaotic time series indicating the for x,y and z signals for the proposed system.

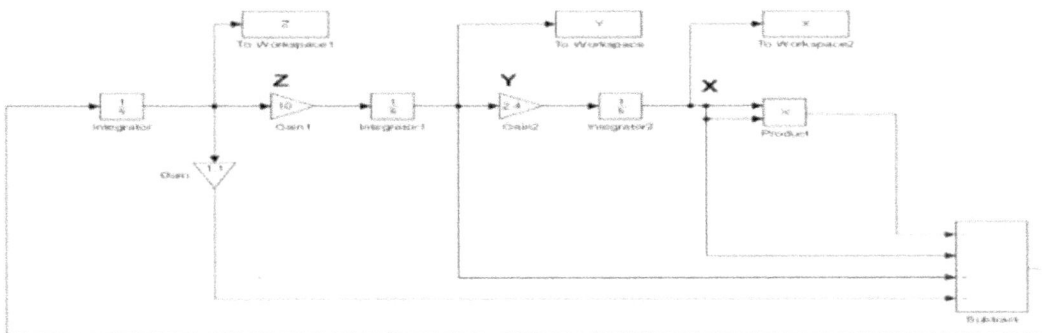

Figure 65.1 Model for the suggested novel chaotic system using MATLAB-Simulink
Source: Author

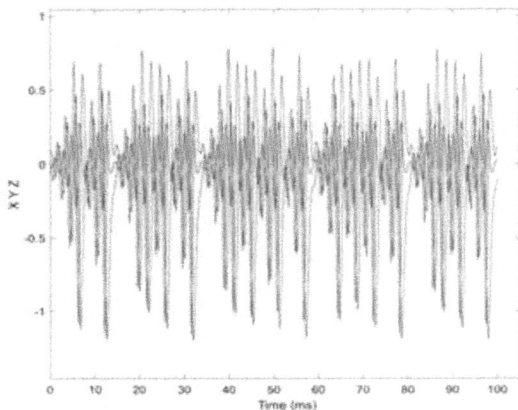

Figure 65.2 Typical time series plots of xyz chaotic signals
Source: Author

The novel chaotic system was simulated Figure 65.3 has more distinct chaotic attractors than the Lorenz system.

Figure 65.4 specify a system exhibiting coexisting attractors has also multi stability. Furthermore, the new chaotic system exhibited co-existing attractors for different initial conditions listed in Table 65.1 using MATLAB-Simulink. Hence, proves the encryption space has been enhanced profoundly in the new chaotic system for application in secure communication.

Analog Circuit Realization Using ORCAD-PSpice

The analog circuit was implemented using simpler passive (i. e) resistors and capacitors elements and active components such as LM741 opamps used for summing, inverting and integration operations. The most advantage part of the realized chaotic analog circuit is it exhibited coexisting attractors with only one analog multiplier AD644. Figure 65.5 shows the newly implemented chaotic electronic circuit system with different parameters. An op-amps and analog multiplier use DC power supply of + 15V.

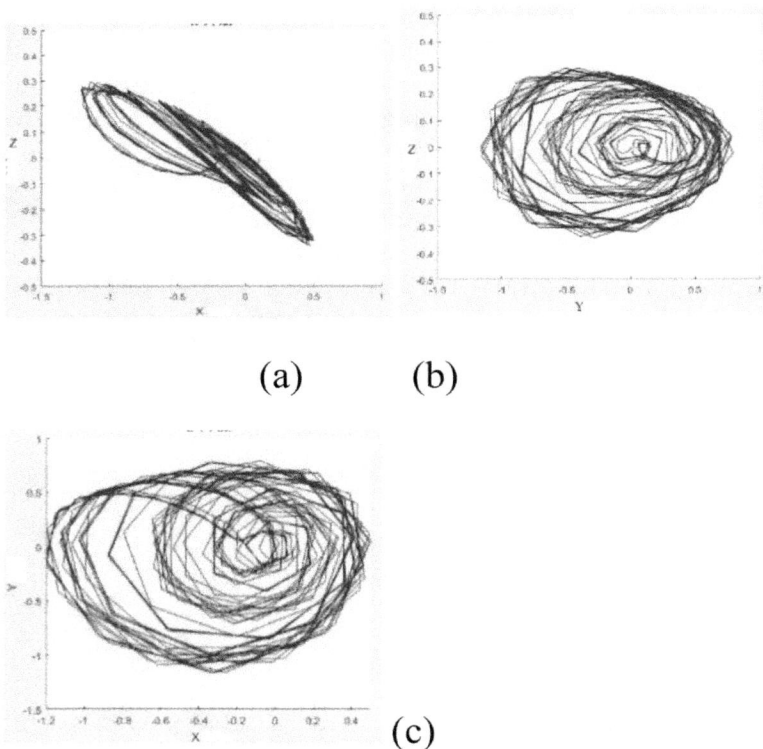

(a)   (b)

(c)

Figure 65.3 Presents the phase portraits of coexisting chaotic attractors in MATLAB-Simulink, for conditions of (0.1, 0, 0)
Source: Author

Table 65.1 Varying initial Conditions shown chaotic attractors

Sl.no	Initial condition (x, y, z)	Sl,No	Initial condition (x, y, z)
1	0.1, 0, 0	7	0.2, 0, 0
2	0.1, 0.1, 0	8	0.2, 0.2, 0
3	0.1, 0.1, 0.1	9	0.2, 0.2, 0.2
4	-0.1, 0, 0	10	-0.2, 0, 0
5	-0.1, -0.1, 0	11	-0.2, -0.2, 0
6	-0.1, -0.1, -0.1	12	-0.2, -0.2, -0.2

Source: Author

The set of circuit equations is given by:

$$\dot{x} = \frac{1}{R1C1}y$$

$$\dot{y} = \frac{1}{R2C2}z$$

$$\dot{z} = -\frac{1}{R3C3}x - \frac{1}{R4C3}y - \frac{1}{R5C3}z - \frac{1}{10R6C3}x^2$$

The resistors R1 = 166.6k, R2 =R3 = 40k, R4 = R5 = 400k, R6 = 362.91k, component values are obtained after a rescaling time factor of 2500 is applied. The values of C1=C2=C3=1nF used with LM741 opamp and analog multiplier AD644. The new chaotic analog electronic circuit simulated in Pspice displayed the typical chaotic signals x, y and z are shown in Figure 65.6. And

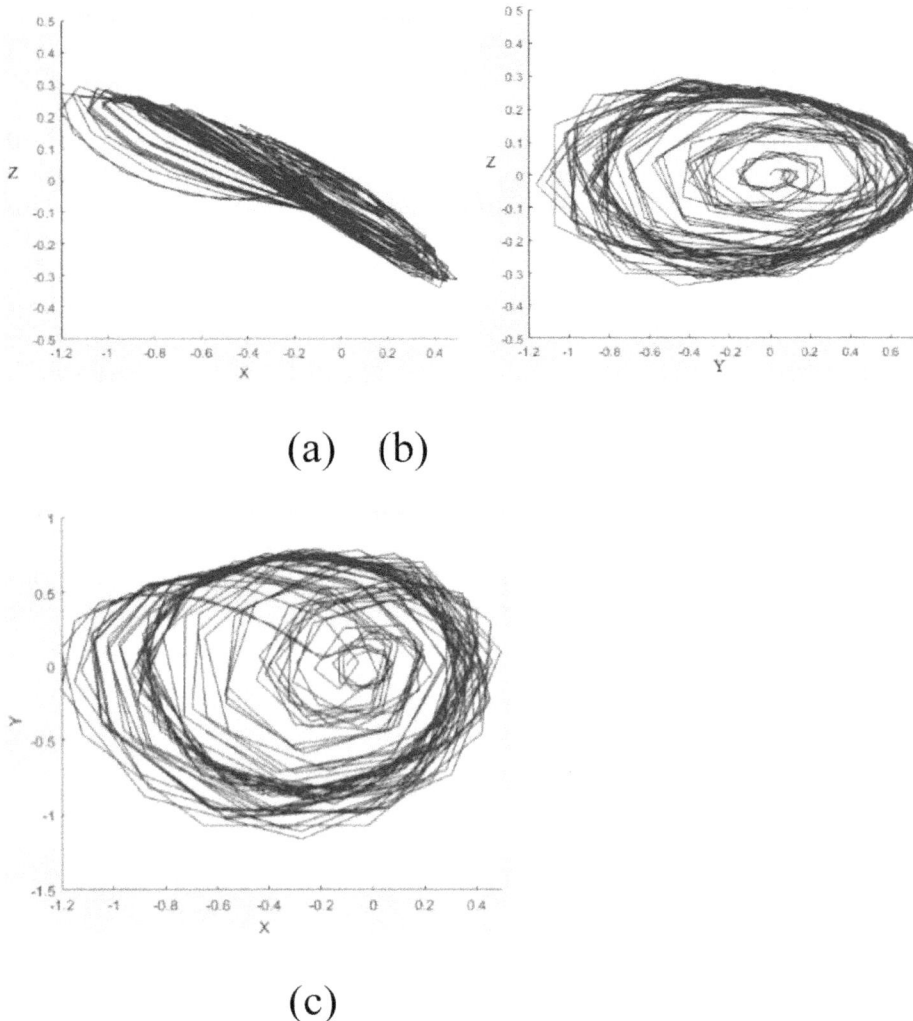

(a)   (b)

(c)

Figure 65.4 Illustrates the phase portraits of coexisting chaotic attractors in MATLAB-Simulink for conditions of (-0.1, 0, 0)

Source: Author

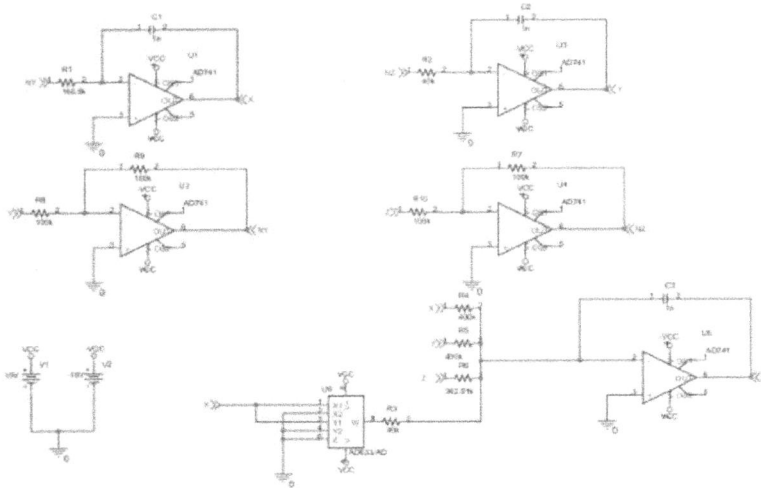

Figure 65.5 The proposed chaotic system of analog circuit schematic
Source: Author

the various phase portraits x-y, y-z, and x-z are shown in Figure 65.7. These results are in good agreement with our numerically analyzed results of MATLAB-Simulink. Furthermore, the same third dimensional chaotic system was simulated with various initial conditions i. e (-0.1,0,0) and the PSpice simulation of the various phase portraits indicated coexisting attractors as shown in Figure 65.8 which also was in concurrence with the numerically analyzed result indicated in Figure 65.4. This implies the proposed chaotic system has increased the encryption space for secure communication.

Secure Communication Application

In this work, schematic block diagram for simulating synchronized secure communication with

the proposed chaotic system along with other summing operation using op-amps and resistive components are shown in Figure 65.9.

Pspice simulation result of the proposed third order dimensional chaotic system for application in secure communication was simulated with unipolar and bipolar information signal with frequency of 1 Khz and amplitude of 1 V respectively. The results are shown in Figure 65.10(a) for the unipolar signal and Figure 65.10(b) shows for the bipolar signal. It can be observed from both the Figures 65.10(a) and (b) that the transmitted information signals I(t) were encrypted with chaotic signal C(t) and transmitted. Signal S(t) And the original message signal R(t) was successfully decrypted at the receiver side synchronously. Furthermore, according to our previous discussion the different initial condition of the

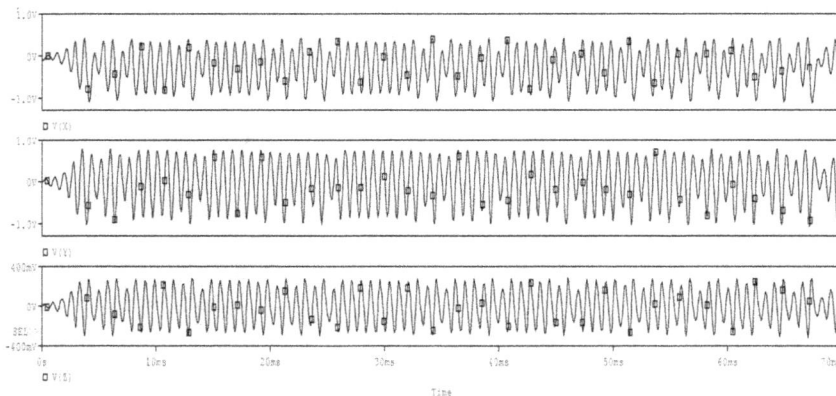

Figure 65.6 Presents the PSpice time series plot of the chaotic signals
Source: Author

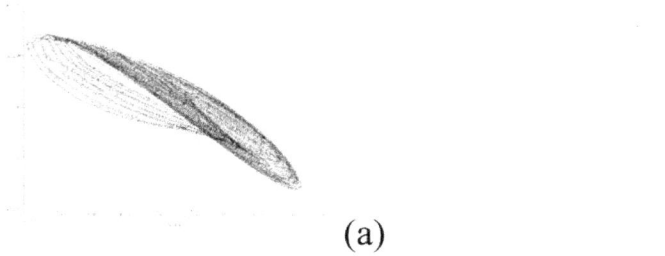

(a)

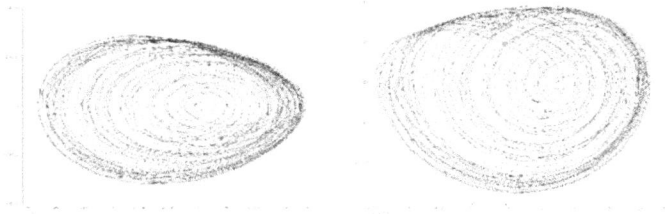

. (b) (c)

Figure 65.7 Shows the PSpice phase portraits of coexisting chaotic attractors for conditions of (0.1, 0, 0)
Source: Author

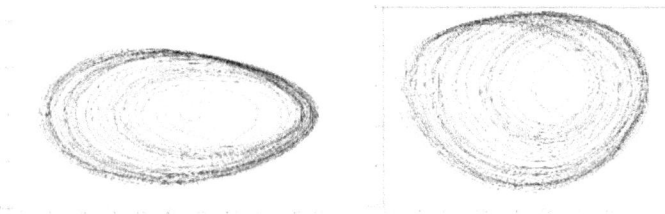

(b) (c)

Figure 65.8 Presents the PSpice phase portraits of coexisting chaotic attractors
Source: Author

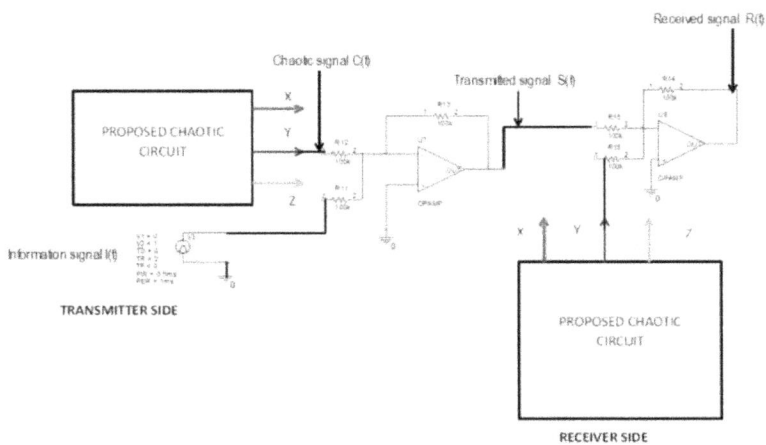

Figure 65.9 The schematic block diagram for synchronized chaotic masking for secure communication for the proposed chaotic coexisting attractor
Source: Author

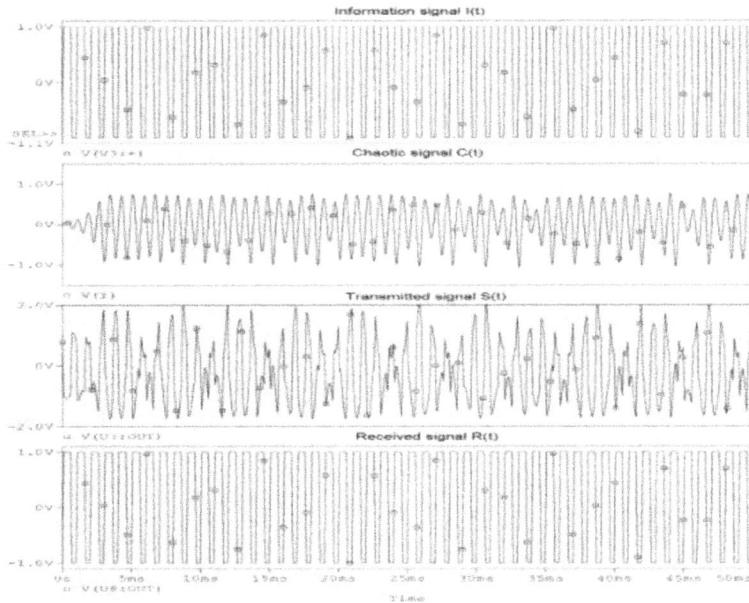

Figure 65.10a PSpice simulation results of chaotic masking method for the new system for the given information signal bipolar 1 V of 1 khz with chaotic signal time series 'y' waveform synchronized
Source: Author

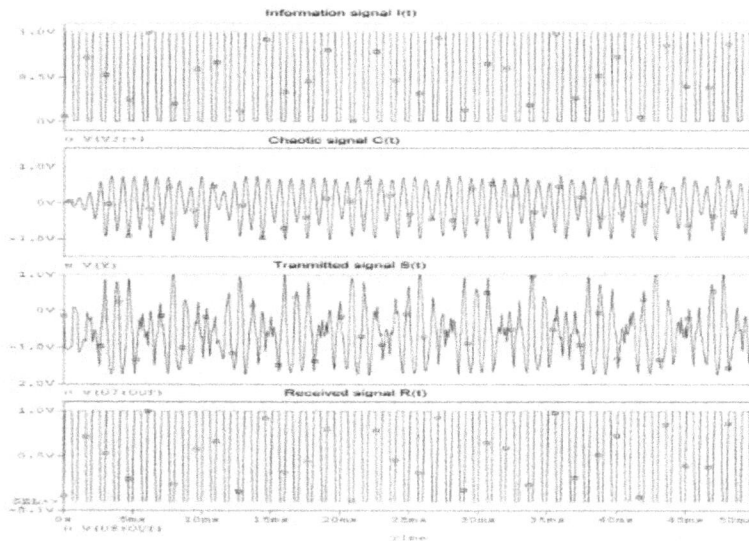

Figure 65. 10b PSpice simulation result of chaotic masking method for the new system for the given unipolar information signal of 1 V with 1 khz using ORCAD-PSpice with chaotic signal time series 'y' waveform synchronized
Source: Author

proposed chaotic system generating different chaotic attractors can increase the encryption space thus simulation results indicate for the different initial condition i.e (-0.1 0 0) in synchronized chaotic masking secure communication was found

that the original signal encrypted was decrypted at the receiver side successfully as shown in Figure 65.11. Figure 65.12 shown the chaotic masking method block diagram where the transmitter is modulated with chaotic y signal whereas the

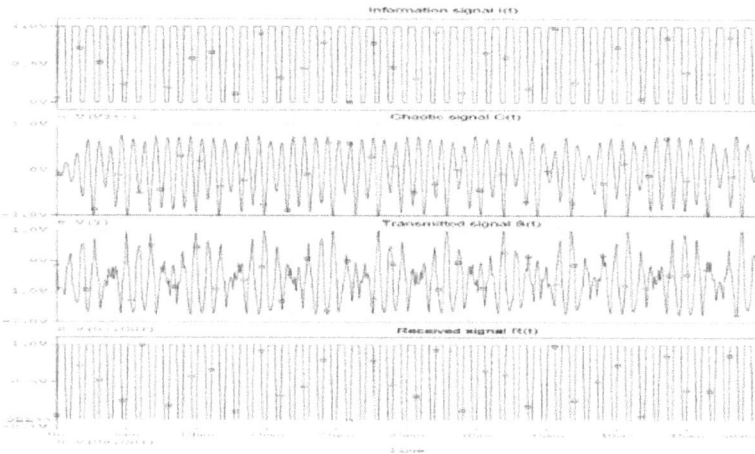

Figure 65.11 PSpice simulation results chaotic masking method for the proposed system for the given unipolar information signal of 1 V with 1 khz using ORCAD-PSpice decrypted successfully with different initial condition (-0.1 0 0)
Source: Author

receiver is decrypted with different chaotic signal to prove that the original message signal will not be decrypted at receiver side. Figure 65.13 shown the transmitted signal and at the receiver side the orginals messahe signal was not decrypted successfully.

Conclusion

A new third-order chaotic system with a single quadratic term was proposed and analyzed, revealing one fixed point and two equilibrium points. Simulations using MATLAB-Simulink demonstrated chaotic behavior and coexisting attractors, with Orcad-PSpice results aligning closely with these findings. Additionally, the proposed system was successfully applied to a synchronized secure communication system, where the receiver successfully decrypted the information signal. However, decryption failed when a different chaotic waveform was used instead of the original encrypted signal.

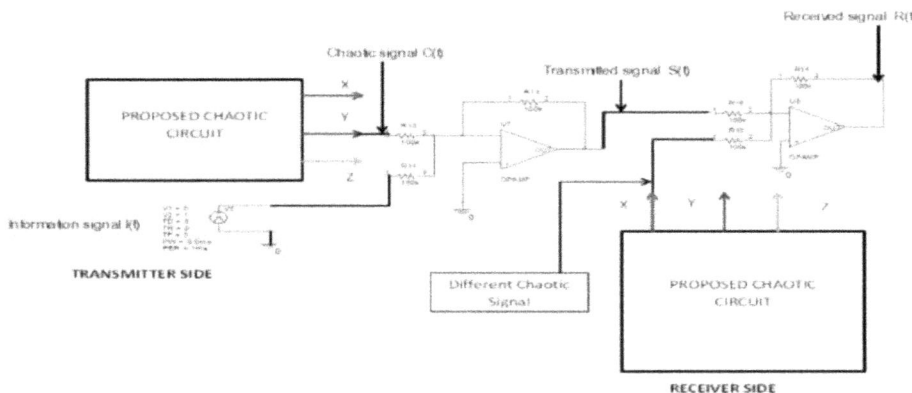

Figure 65.12 The schematic block diagram for synchronized chaotic masking for secure communication for the proposed chaotic coexisting attractor with different chaotic signals at the receiver side
Source: Author

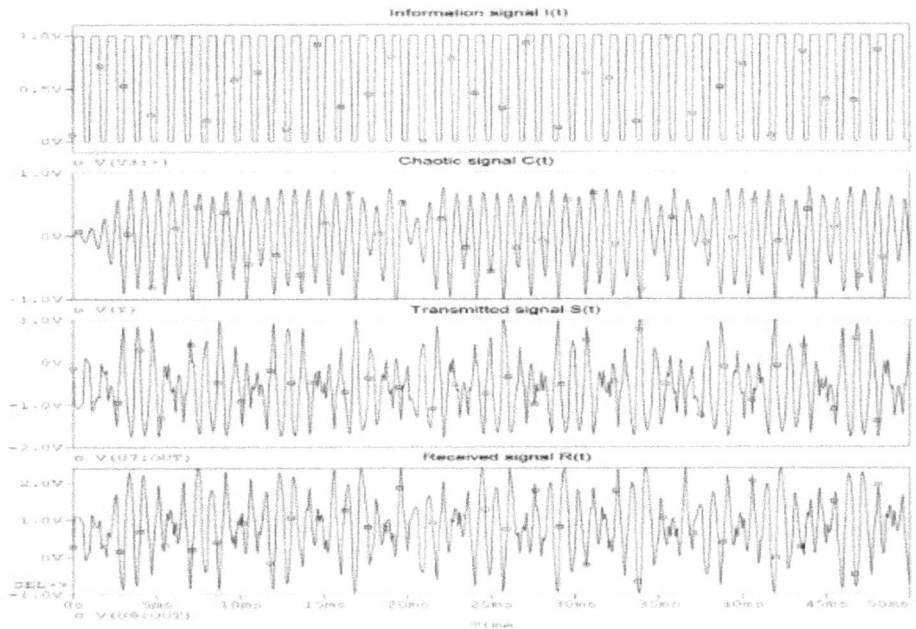

Figure 65.13 PSpice simulation result chaotic masking method for the proposed system for the given unipolar information signal of 1V with 1khz decrypted with different chaotic signal (time series 'x)' (i.e not synchronized)

Source: Author

References

[1] Senouci, A., Bouhedjeur, H., Tourche, K., and Boukabou, A. (2017). DPGA based hardware and device independent implementation of chaotic generation. *AEU - International Journal of Electronics and Communications*, 82, 211–220.

[2] Pham, V. T., Akgul, A., Volos, C., Jafari, S., and Kapitaniak, T. (2017). Dynamics and circuit realization of a non-equlibrium chaotic system with bootstable variable. *AEU - International Journal of Electronics and Communications*, 78, 134–140.

[3] Sprott J. C. (1994). Some simple chaotic flows. *American Journal of Physics*, 50(2), 647–650.

[4] Pandey, A., Baghei, R. K., and Singh, R. P. (2012). Analysis and circuit realization of a new autonomous chaotic system. *International Journal of Electronics and Communication Engineering*, 5(4), 487–495.

[5] Alsafasfeh, Q. H., and Al-Arni, M. S. (2011). A new chaotic behaviour form Lorenz and rossler systems and its electronic circuit realization implementation. *Circuits and Systems*, 2(2-5), 101–105.

[6] Karawanich, K., Kumngern, M., Chimnoy, J., and Prommee, P. (2022). A four scroll chaotic generator based on two non-linear functions and its telecommunication cryptography application. *AEUE- International Journal of Electronics and Communications*, 157(4), 154439.

[7] Emin, B., and Musayev, Z. (2023). Chaos-based Image encryption in embedded systems using lorenz-rossler system. *Chaos Theory and Applications*, 5(3), 133–140.

[8] Lozi, R. (2023). Are chaotic attractors just a mathematical curiosity or do they contribute to the advancement of science? *Chaos Theory and Applications*, 5(3), 133–140.

[9] Lorenz, N. (1963). Deterministic nonperiodic flow. *Journal of Atmospheric Sciences*, 20, 130–141.

[10] Yilmaz, P. (2010). A new chaotic attractor from general lorenz system family and its electronic experimental implementation. *Turkish Journal of Electrical Engineering and Computer Sciences*, 18(2) 171–183.

[11] Woods, D. D., and Hollnagel, E. (2012). Joint Cognitive Systems. Boca Raton: CRC Press/Taylor and Francis.

66 Optimizing fault coverage in VLSI circuits via balanced scan chain analysis

Vanithamani, P.[1,a], Sudhagar, G.[2,b] and Eswari, M.[3,c]

[1]Research Scholar, Dept. of ECE, Bharath Institute of Higher Education and Research, Chennai, India
[2]Associate Professor, Dept. of ECE, Bharath Institute of Higher Education and Research, Chennai, India
[3]Assistant Professor, Dept. of ECE Bharath Institute of Higher Education and Research, Chennai, India

Abstract

The built in-self test (BIST) is a particularly useful tool, where the problem of improving fault coverage in VLSI circuits through balanced scan chain analysis is highly relevant due to the increasing complexity of semiconductor designs. With circuits becoming more sophisticated, testability, especially in critical applications such as automotive and medical devices, faces challenges like test duration, defect detection, and optimization of scan chain length. Balancing these chains helps minimize test time and power consumption without compromising the fault coverage or increasing hardware overhead. The study focuses on optimizing the number and length of scan chains for ISCAS-89 benchmark circuits, which is important because balancing the scan chains improves the circuit's ability to self-test efficiently, enhancing reliability.

Keywords: Balanced scan chains, BIST, defect reach, scan chains, test duration

Introduction

A study focusing on test pattern generation using gray codes, which discusses newer approaches in test generation for fault detection [1]. The current techniques used for balancing scan chains while reducing power consumption during testing [2]. adaptive scan chains that dynamically adjust their length based on the test environment using machine learning algorithms. This approach reduces power consumption and test time while improving fault detection accuracy [4]. Design for testability (DFT) techniques can be employed to enhance chip testability and defect detection in a cost-effective and efficient manner [3]. Because it enables circuits to test themselves, the built in-self test (BIST) is very helpful in stand-alone and mission-critical applications. One important factor in determining how extensively a circuit may be evaluated for flaws is its testability. DFT's mainstay, scan design, improves a circuit's capacity to test flip-flops by granting external access. This approach has demonstrated to be a financially viable means of offering substantial test coverage, with clocking sections and scan components occupying about 40% of the chip area [5] multi-pattern BIST approach that enhances the fault detection capability of circuits under different testing conditions. The study focuses on balancing scan chain lengths to achieve improved test coverage and efficiency [6]. By reducing complex sequential tests to simpler combinational tests, and switching all or some of a design's memory elements to scan flip-flops or scan cells, streamlines the test-generating process [7].

By using distinct scan-in and scan-out inputs, these scan cells are linked to establish a framework known as a scan chain, which is comparable to a serial-in serial-out shift register [8,9]. Depending on the circuit's requirements for testability, multiple scan chains may be employed. Scanning chains operate in test mode to move test inputs through the chains during testing. They then switch back to normal mode, apply clocks and inputs, record test results, and shift those responses out via the scan-out pin [10,4]. Two forms of design for testability techniques that make use of scan chains are partial scan and full scan designs [11]. Adaptive scan chains that

[a]vanithamani.ece@bharathuniv.ac.in, [b]sudhagar.ece@bharathuniv.ac.in, [c]eswari.ece@bharathuniv.ac.in

DOI: 10.1201/9781003616399-66

dynamically adjust their length based on the test environment using machine learning algorithms. This approach reduces power consumption and test time while improving fault detection accuracy. Sequential test generation is made simpler using full scan designs, which reduce it to a combinational test problem [6].

Scan chains are useful for hardware security [12], BIST [13–15], and IC testing. However adding more flip-flops to a scan chain means using more clock cycles, which lengthens the test duration. Using numerous scan chains can reduce this, but doing so raises the pin count [18]. For systems on chip (SoCs), where test time and test storage are crucial concerns, using numerous scan chains can greatly reduce test time [18]. Making numerous scan chains the same length is a typical practice [19], which lowers the test time required for serial scan designs. Utilizing a chip's internal BIST capability is one way to tackle the analyzing issue at the chip level. While there are fewer test vectors in pseudo-exhaustive testing, there are more in exhaustive testing. One-pattern and two-pattern built-in self-test pattern generators are frequently distinguished from one another [20]. A circuit's scan chains are referred to as balanced scan chains when their lengths are equal. This article examines scenarios with lowest and highest amounts of scan chains in ISCAS'89 circuits to evaluate the trade-offs related to balanced scan chains. Chains and full scan design circuits are the subject of this study.

Scan Chains

Scan design improves the testability of circuits and was first proposed for system testing in the early 1970s [4]. In particular research, it was originally recommended for hardware testing [21]. Controllability and observability are two important factors that influence a circuit's testability. While observability is the capacity to keep an eye on the reactions at the output pins, controllability is the capacity to drive internal logic states from external pins [7]. The circuit being tested for scan design must only have D-type flip-flops, while it may also contain one or more clocks that are managed by primary inputs. This design is a highly effective DFT technique since it greatly increases controllability and observability [17].

Scan chains do have a disadvantage, though, in that the test application time is longer [21].

The fundamental principle of scan design is to increase the ability to regulate and visibility of each memory component throughout the circuit. There are three main methods for implementing scan routes: border scan, partial scan, and full scan. In a partial scan, only some of the flip-flops in the circuit are connected via scan chains, whereas a full scan links every flip-flop. Boundary scan, however, adds a boundary scan cell at each input/output (I/O) instead of altering the memory contents. In this study, equal-length scan chains are evaluated and circuits constructed with complete scans are the subject of analysis using ISCAS-89 benchmark circuits. Both greatest and lowest balanced scan chains are analyzed. Additional details regarding guidelines for scan design can be found in relevant literature [10].

Analyzing using scan circuits

There are two stages involved in testing scan-inserted circuits. To verify the scan chain, a shift test is run in the first step. The test-control (TC) pin's value determines whether the circuit operates in regular mode or test mode, which is also referred to as scan mode. Both single and dual clock designs can use this method. After a time period equal to the total number of gate lags in the scan chain path, the shift test detects outputs at scan-out. It applies 0 and 1 inputs at scan-in. This study focuses on the single-clock circuit benchmarks from ISCAS '89. The second stage's objective is to identify a single stuck-at fault in the logical combination process. On the presumption that every flip-flop input and output is completely adjustable and noticeable, test vectors are created using combinational ATPG.

Multiple scan chains

Placing flip-flops into numerous scan chains becomes useful when the sum of flip-flops rises. There are specific scan-in, and scan-out pins needed for each scan chain. Primary inputs can be multiplexed to give scan-in inputs when pin counts are low, as foremost and scan-in inputs are not used simultaneously. In a similar manner, the TC pin functions as a control signal to multiplex scan-out outputs with the principal output pins of the design. Generally, the lengths of several scan chains can differ, and the longest register determines how long the scan-in and scan-out sequences last. The longest scan register for NSFF is used to determine how long the scan test will be. This paper investigates the properties of circuits with several balanced scan chains. The lowest and largest amount of scan chains are used in evaluations to help better understand the features of benchmark circuits. Multiple scan chains of the same length are taken into consideration for the experiments.

Simulation Framework

Full scan design has been used in a great deal of research. Techniques including the incorporation of a single scan chain into the design are covered in one study [20]. In this study, we examine balanced multiple scan chains. Using the Tessent tool, the analysis entails constructing the lowest and highest balanced scan chains. The research makes use of the ISCAS-89 benchmark circuits, with feature flip-flop counts ranging between 3 to 48. To establish a foundation for the inquiry, only circuitry with an even quantity of flip-flops are considered. Every circuit contains a minimum of one multiple scan chain and one set of multiple flip-flops. The circuits that employ these scan chains are subsequently subjected to test patterns. For this study, a total of 16 ISCAS-89 benchmark circuits are examined.

Results and Discussions

This study is conducted in two stages: the first involves applying the fewest symmetrical scan chains to the ISCAS-89 benchmark circuits and the second stage involves applying the finest symmetrical scan chains. When the number of flip-flops exceeds five, neither step uses a single scan chain; instead, it only uses many scan chains with the same length involved. The behavior of numerous scan chains in relation to the number of flip-flops is evaluated by taking into account only circuits with an even number of flip-flops. Three subsections comprise this section: stage 1, stage 2 and an analysis based on the results of both stages. The ISCAS-89 benchmark circuits are shown in Table 66.1. Other circuit difficulties are not taken into consideration in this analysis

because this study is part of a bigger effort on security in scan chains connected with similar works [17]. To help determine the impact of a circuit's scan chain count and how it relates to the flip-flop count, Table 66.1 includes a list of all 16 circuits from the ISCAS-89 benchmarked circuits, as well as the number of I/O's.

Stage 1
In Table 66.1, the ISCAS-89 circuits are displayed. Full scan insertion is carried out during the stage 1. Each circui"s flip-flops are separated into as many equal-length scan chains as possible, but no more than that. The details of the scan chains that were added to every circuit in Table 66.1 are listed in Table 66.2.

Stage 2
In stage 2, all of the scan functionality for the circuits listed in Table 66.1 is integrated, using as many uniformly lengthened scan chains as is practical. Table 66.3 lists the circuits used in this step along with the amount of scan chains that correspond to them. Table 66.2 further demonstrates the rise in input/output needs related to the scan chains. The circuits are described in Tables 66.2 and 66.3, along with the amount of balance multiple scan chains. Test sequences are created and run through the circuits, and then their performance in stages 1 and 2 is analyzed. The entire set of experiment findings is shown in Tables 66.4 and 66.5. An in-depth analysis of the stage 1 and stage 2 experiments is given in the section that follows. It looks at how the circuit behaves as the number of multiple scan chains rises and whether there are any relationships with the flip-flop count.

Table 66.1 Benchmarked circuits for ISCAS-89

Circuits	PI	PO	FF
s-27	4	1	3
s-298	3	6	14
s-344	9	11	15
s-349	9	11	15
s-382	3	6	21
s-386	7	7	6
s-400	3	6	21

Circuits	PI	PO	FF
s-420	18	1	16
s-444	3	6	21
s-510	19	7	6
s-526	3	6	21
s-820	18	19	5
s-832	18	19	5
s-1196A	14	14	18
s-1238	14	14	18
s-1488	8	19	6

Source: Author

Table 66.2 The least quantity of scan chains

Circuits	PI	PO	FF	PI_{min}	PO_{min}	Scan chains
s-27	4	1	3	6	2	1
s-298	3	6	14	6	8	2
s-344	9	11	15	13	14	3
s-349	9	11	15	13	14	3
s-382	3	6	21	7	9	3
s-386	7	7	6	22	9	2
s-400	3	6	21	7	9	3
s-420	18	1	16	21	3	2
s-444	3	6	21	7	9	3
s-510	19	7	6	22	9	2
s-526	3	6	21	7	9	3
s-820	18	16	5	20	20	1
s-832	18	19	5	20	20	1
s-1196A	14	14	18	17	16	2
s-1238	14	14	18	17	16	2
s-1488	8	19	6	11	21	2

Source: Author

Table 66.3 The highest quantity of scan chains

Circuits	PI	PO	FF	PI_{max}	PO_{max}	Scan chains
s-27	4	1	3	8	4	3
s-298	3	6	14	11	15	7
s-344	9	11	15	15	16	5
s-349	9	11	15	15	16	5
s-382	3	6	21	11	13	7
s-386	7	7	6	11	10	3
s-400	3	6	21	11	13	7

Circuits	PI	PO	FF	PI_{max}	PO_{max}	Scan chains
s-420	18	1	16	27	9	8
s-444	3	6	21	11	13	7
s-510	19	7	6	23	10	3
s-526	3	6	21	11	13	7
s-820	18	19	5	24	24	5
s-832	18	19	5	24	24	5
s-1196A	14	14	18	24	23	9
s-1238	14	14	18	24	23	9
s-1488	8	19	6	12	22	3

Source: Author

PI/PO analysis

For every circuit, the PI/PO of the two stages are evaluated. Figure 66.1 demonstrates the impact of PI variations on the quantity of multiple scan chains needed for stages 1 and 2. The standard PI requirements are represented by the red lines, stage 1 experiments by the blue lines, and stage 2 experiments by the green lines. It is clear that as the number of scan chains rises, so does the requirement for PI. When the quantity of PI resources is limited, multiplexing strategies using the available PI resources must be taken into consideration [20].

PI/PO variations

The differences in PI between the stage 1 and stage 2 studies are shown in Figure 66.1. The PI and the PI of the original circuit show a linear relationship in the stage 1 studies. On the other hand, stage 2 studies show a linear trend at first, but as the number of flip-flops increases, so does the PI requirements. Figure 66.2 shows how PO requirements have changed. The normal POs of the circuit are represented by the red lines; Stage 1 and stage 2 tests are indicated by the blue and green lines, respectively. Whereas stage 2 studies demonstrate a consistent increase in PO until the flip-flop count surpasses 21, stage 1 PO has a linear behavior akin to the original PO. This demonstrates a direct correlation between the quantity of scan chains and the increase in PO. When it comes to the circuit's available PI/PO, the PI/PO fluctuations for the fewest scan chains are linear. However, as more scan chains are added, the more PI/PO the design requires.

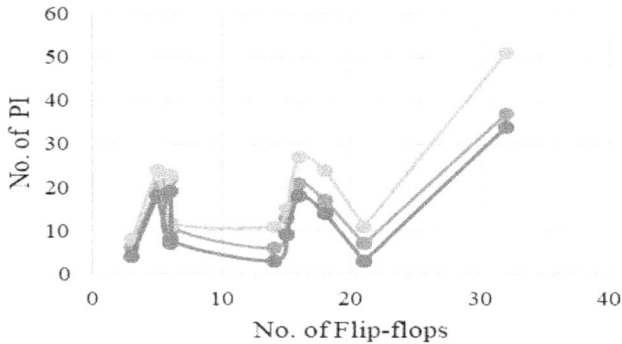

Figure 66.1 PI variations
Source: Author

Table 66.4 Stage 1 simulation results

Circuit	Total fault	Untestable faults	Test pattern	Simulated patterns	Fault coverage	Cpu Time
s-27	124	1	9	10	92.00	3.5
s-298	944	2	28	30	96.70	4.1
s-344	1128	3	22	25	96.80	3.7
s-349	1138	3	22	25	96.40	3.7
s-382	1596	3	34	37	96.00	3.7
s-386	1148	2	70	85	98.50	4.0
s-400	1288	3	32	36	94.80	3.7
s-420	1468	2	80	85	97.20	3.6
s-444	1386	3	30	36	94.80	3.6
s-510	1430	2	65	80	98.70	3.6
s-526	1248	3	70	75	97.00	3.7
s-820	2248	1	115	120	99.30	4.2
s-832	2268	1	110	115	98.60	3.7
s-1196A	3384	2	170	175	98.70	4.0
s-1238	3406	2	160	180	96.30	4.1
s-1488	4242	2	130	130	99.60	4.0

Source: Author

Number of faults

The number of faults for the stage 1 and stage 2 studies are shown in Figure 66.3. Stage 1 and stage 2 fault differences are negligible, with the exception of situations in which there are more than 21 flip-flops. This discrepancy can get worse as flip-flops become more and more common. Further studies using larger designs will provide additional light on how the overall defects in the two stages differ from one another.

Complete mistakes Figure 66.3 shows the total defects for both stage 1 and stage 2. Stage 2 faults do not significantly differ from stage 1 faults. There is only a noticeable change when there are more flip flops than 21. As the quantity of flip-flops is growing further, these modifications can also increase. The difference in total flaws in both stages will be further elaborated in future work with large designs. Figure 66.4 compares and plots the fault coverage of stages 1 and 2. The

Table 66.5 Stage 2 simulation results

Circuit	Total fault	Untestable faults	Test pattern	Simulated patterns	Fault coverage	Cpu Time
s-27	152	3	10	12	92.50	1.9
s-298	1014	7	30	31	96.70	1.9
s-344	1156	5	24	26	96.80	1.9
s-349	1166	5	24	24	96.40	1.9
s-382	1304	7	35	38	95.95	1.9
s-386	1162	3	77	88	98.40	1.9
s-400	1344	7	35	39	94.80	1.9
s-420	1552	8	82	90	97.20	1.9
s-444	1442	7	33	39	94.80	1.9
s-510	1444	3	70	85	98.70	2.0
s-526	1652	7	68	73	96.80	1.9
s-820	2304	5	118	124	99.30	2.0
s-832	2324	5	118	122	98.50	2.0
s-1196A	3482	9	170	180	98.70	2.2
s-1238	3504	9	162	185	96.30	2.2
s-1488	4256	3	130	136	99.60	2.1

Source: Author

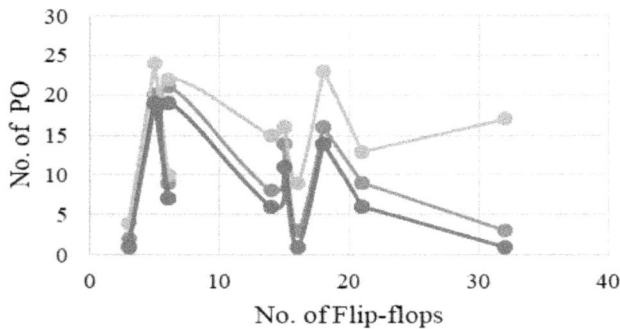

Figure 66.2 P0 variations
Source: Author

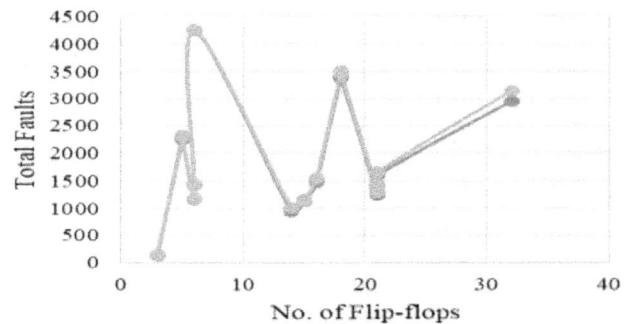

Figure 66.3 Total faults of stage 1 and stage 2
Source: Author

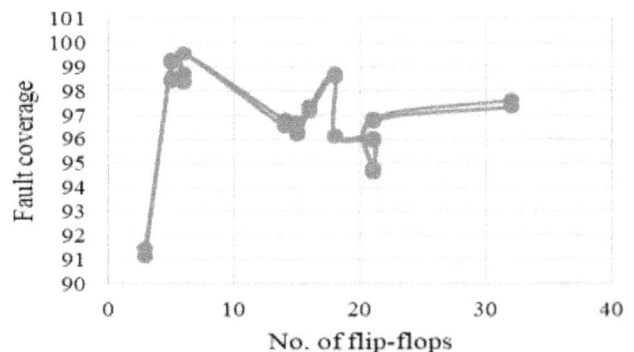

Figure 66.4 Fault coverage
Source: Author

fault coverage is represented by a blue line for the greatest number of scan chains and a green line for the minimum number. There is no discernible variation in fault coverage between circuits with fewer scan chains. There will only be a noticeable difference if there are more flip-flops. Figure 66.5's CPU time required for stage 1 and 2 shows a significant difference, suggesting that the time needed to apply the test patterns will decrease as the number of scan chains increases.

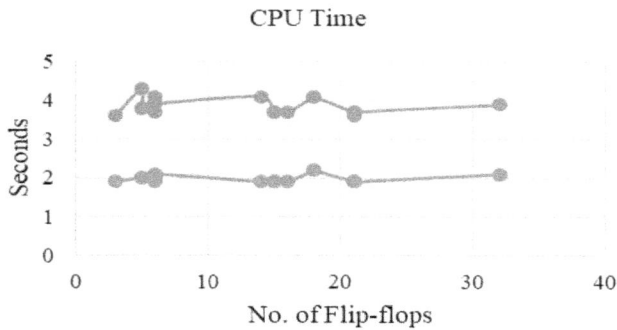

Figure 66.5 Time requirements for CPU
Source: Author

Conclusion and Future Work

The purpose of the paper is to analyze the performance trade-offs that result from increasing the number of flip-flops in balanced multiple scan chains. The findings suggest that there can be a significant variation in the different design performance metrics when the flip-flop count is increased. To assess these characteristics even further, the inquiry will be broadened to encompass instances of noteworthy industrial designs. This work lays the foundation for enhancing the circuits' fault coverage in crucial applications, like the automotive and medical sectors.

This article discusses strategies to optimize testing in VLSI systems, addressing challenges such as application time, data volume, and power consumption, making it highly relevant for secure [16].

References

[1] Dilip, P. S., Somanathan, G. R., and Bhakthavatchalu, R. (2020). Gray code for test pattern generation. In AIP Conference Proceedings. American Institute of Physics Inc. https://doi.org/10.1063/5.0004319.

[2] Anand, K., and Kundu, S. (2023). Design techniques for balanced and low-power scan chains in VLSI circuits.

[3] Chen, X., Aramoon, O., Qu, G., and Cui, A. (2018). Balancing testability and security by configurable partial scan design. In Proceedings - 2nd IEEE International Test Conference Asia, ITC-Asia 2018, (pp. 145–150). IEEE. https://doi.org/10.1109/ITC-Asia.2018.00035.

[4] Bhunia, S., Khatri, S., and Roy, K. (2022). Adaptive scan chain design using machine learning for power and test time optimization IEEE transactions on VLSI systems 2022.

[5] Wang, L. T., Wu, C. W., and Wen, X. (2006). VLSI Test Principles and Architectures. Morgan Kaufmann Publishers.

[6] Lai, T., Zhang, Y., and Yang, X. (2022). Enhancing fault detection in VLSI circuits using multi-pattern BIST techniques. *IEEE Transactions on Computers*.

[7] Kim, Y. C., and Saluja, K. K. (1998). Sequential test generators: past, present and future. *Integration, the VLSI Journal*, 26, 41–54. https://doi.org/10.1016/s0167-9260(98)00020-0.

[8] Shastry, N. (1992). Tutorial on design for testability. In Proceedings Fifth Annual IEEE International ASIC Conference and Exhibit, 1992, (pp. 139–142). https://doi.org/10.1109/ASIC.1992.270291.

[9] Xiang, D., Chen, M. J., Sun, J. G., and Fujiwara, H. (2003). Improving test quality of scan-based BIST by scan chain partitioning. In Proceedings, Asian Test Symposium. 2003-January, (pp. 916–927). https://doi.org/10.1109/ATS.2003.1250774.

[10] Nicolici, N., and Al-Hashimi, B. M. (2000). Scan latch partitioning into multiple scan chains for power minimization in full scan sequential circuits. In Proceedings of the Conference on Design, Automation and Test in Europe, 2000, (pp. 715–722). https://doi.org/10.1109/DATE.2000.840866.

[11] Lala, P. K. (2008). An Introduction to Logic Circuit Testing. Morgan and Claypool Publishers.

[12] Tehranipoor, M. (2012). Introduction to Hardware Security and Trust. Springer. https://doi.org/10.1007/978-1-4419-8080-9.

[13] Agrawal, V. D., Kime, C. R., and Saluja, K. K. (1993). A tutorial on built-in self-test. I. principles, test. *IEEE Design and Test of Computers*, 10, 73–82. https://doi.org/10.1109/54.199807.

[14] Agrawal, V. D., Kime, C. R., and Saluja, K. K. (1993). A tutorial on built-in self-test part 2: applications, design. *IEEE Design and Test of Computers*, 10, 69–77. https://doi.org/10.1109/54.211530.

[15] Dilip, P. S., Somanathan, G. R., and Bhakthavatchalu, R. (2019). Reseeding LFSR for test pattern generation. In Proceedings 2019 IEEE International Conference on Communication and Signal Processing, ICCSP 2019, (pp. 921–925). https://doi.org/10.1109/ICCSP.2019.8698025.

[16] Solana, J. M. (2009). Reducing test application time, test data volume and test power through virtual chain partition. *Integration, the VLSI Journal*, 42, 385–399. https://doi.org/10.1016/j.vlsi.2008.12.001.

[17] Narayanan, S., and Gupta, R. (1993). Optimal configuring of multiple scan chains. *IEEE Transactions on Computers*, 42, 1121–1131. https://doi.org/10.1109/12.241600.

[18] Angell, J. B. (1973). Enhancing testability of large-scale integrated circuits circuits via test points and additional logic. *IEEE Transactions on Computers*, C–22, 46–60. https://doi.org/10.1109/T- C.1973.223600.

[19] Thomas, K. P. P., and Williams, W. (1982). Design for testability- a survey. *IEEE Transactions on Computers,* c 2–15.

[20] Sudhagar, G., and Kumar, S. S. (2013). VLSI design of efficient architecture in recursive pseudo-exhaustive two-pattern generation. *Journal of Theoretical and Applied Information Technology*, 55(2), 232–239. ISSN: 1992-8645.

[21] Narayanan, S., and Breuer, M. A. (1995). reconfiguration techniques for a single scan chain. *IEEE Transactions on Computer-Aided Design of Integrated Circuits and Systems*, 14, 750–765. https://doi.org/10.1109/43.387735.

67 Robust test pattern generators for secure built-in self-test implementation

Vanithamani, P.[1,a], Sudhagar, G.[2,b] and Prathiba, T.[3,c]

[1]Research Scholar, Department of Electronics and Communication Engineering, Bharath Institute of Higher Education and Research, Chennai, India

[2]Associate Professor, Department of Electronics and Communication Engineering, Bharath Institute of Higher Education and Research, Chennai, India

[3]Assistant Professor, Department of Electronics and Communication Engineering, Bharath Institute of Higher Education and Research, Chennai, India

Abstract

Design testing is growing more and more difficult as integrated circuit technology advances. About 60–80% of the design time is devoted to process testing. In testing, data patterns are essentially fed into the device under test (DUT), outcomes are observed, and the outcome is compared to the golden answer, or the optimal response. Chip sub-circuit examination becomes more challenging as device density increases. Design testing is therefore growing more and more of an expensive and time-consuming procedure. When more logic is added, the circuit tests itself to determine what the problem is. built-in self-test (BIST) is a testability technique that is more commonly used to allow integrated circuits to be thoroughly tested. It is made up of the outcome analyzer, the circuit under evaluation, and the test design generator. BIST can guarantee rapid diagnosis and excellent fault coverage. Test pattern generators (TPGs), are compelled by the growing circuit complexity to produce test patterns that will cause the CUT to become more sensitive to errors. TPGs are susceptible to harmful actions like side-channel attacks that rely on scanning. An aggressor can recover private data from the chip by looking through the test comes about. Securing TPGs emerge as a result of these dangers. In addition to protecting TPG against harmful assaults such IP privacy breaches and scan-based side-channel assaults, this also offers integrated circuits (ICs) excess output protection. This method shows how to protect the TPG logic with a keyword or key produced by the key era circuit in order to offer a secure test design generator for BIST circuits.

Keywords: BIST, equipment security, figuring out, overproduction, rationale locking, TPG

Introduction

A significant part of the technological revolution was performed by very large scale integration (VLSI). In order to lower assembly costs, most design organizations would, on the one hand, seek other parties to assist in the manufacturing process as design complexity and chip design expenses rise [5]. Advanced fabrication technology is needed to assemble these complex semiconductors. The primary cause of small design firms' inability to afford a foundry is the high setup and operating costs of fabrication facilities; the price tag for establishing a foundry is about five billion dollars.

In any case, in the coordinates circuit industry, globalization has incited integrated circuits (ICs) originators to recover the handle of making their plans for toward the ocean foundries [1]. Whereas this plan on a very basic level brings down costs, it has too made a auxiliary passage point for a few security imperfections such as robbery of mental property (IP), invert designing, falsifying, Trojan horse addition, and overbuilding. The IP of a arrange was found after the plan record was made accessible to exterior foundry workers [2]. Reverse engineering the design and guaranteeing IP responsibility are two possibilities open to a dishonest client in the foundry. Another possible method of gaining control over

[a]vanithamani.ece@bharathuniv.ac.in, [b]sudhagar.ece@bharathuniv.ac.in, [c]prathi.deepa89.ece@bharathuniv.ac.in

DOI: 10.1201/9781003616399-67

a design is overproduction and selling the excess integrated circuits. Every year, the semiconductor industry loses several billions of dollars due to these kinds of design thefts. In order to combat these security threats, design-for-security (DFS), has emerged as an integrated aspect of integrated circuit design [7].

A common countermeasure against intellectual property theft and illegal foundry overproduction is logic encryption. An outside foundry can be tricked into thinking a circuit is not as valuable as it is by introducing a few repeating key-gates via logic encryption [13]. Applying the appropriate keys to the key-gates is necessary for an encrypted IC to be useful. By using the mystery keys, the produced IC is activated. In a thoughtfully crafted memory within the chip, these mysterious keys are stored [16]. If the appropriate keys are not available, an unauthorized client cannot access the design document and claim ownership of the design. Illegally manufactured overproduction integrated circuits are prohibited from sale in the market since they do not work properly until the correct keys are inserted [3]. The intention is to modify the behavior of ICs to prevent unexpected output unless the relevant keys are used to activate them. Moreover, the key must not be readily retrieved by an unauthorized user.

Equipment security work has been done to neutralize these concerns.

1. Combinatorial rationale confusion: This method stows away usefulness by adding additional entryways (xor, xnor) to the unique plan, known as key doors [9].
2. IC camouflaging: A format approach that presents fake contacts or structure cells utilized to build rationale doors in arrange to avoid aggressors from turning around building [14].

Literature Review

The handle of analyzing, confirming, and rating a system's useful behavior and plan is known as switch designing. It is the handle of making a high-level representation of a working framework in arrange to make it less demanding for somebody to get it. This algorithmic fabricating handle creates portrayals at the most elevated levels of deliberation. Each step in the prepare of making coordinates circuits (ICs) includes distinguishing the sets of components that make up a unique work and at that point recasting those components utilizing the assigned deliberations [7,9]. Switch designing is a common method utilized by creators to decide the determinations, other highlights, and yield capacities of a framework from an existing execution. Switch designing in the setting of the computer program industry proposes overhauling and reusing he misplaced program determinations.

Overproduction: Due to the high costs associated with semiconductor generation, many system-on-design firms were forced to offshore their fabrication to distant industrial sites. Chips can be beneficially created and sold by a questionable plant. The architect may lose cash as a result of this overproduction, and in certain cases, there may be security dangers. In order to anticipate unapproved overproduction of chips, analysts have advertised an assortment of plan confusion procedures over time [19].

Mentor design a source-level confirmation device called "demonstrate sim test system" is valuable for mimicking equipment depiction dialects like verilog, framework verilog, and VHDL [5]. It is competent of carrying out reenactments at each level, counting behavioral, basic, and back-annotated simulations [21]. Clients may effectively identify and investigate flaws with ModelSim's user-friendly client interface. The client can utilize the test system to alter, construct, and re-simulate after a botch is recognized. Also, smaller scale semi-FPGA libraries are bolstered [20].

Proposed Implementation Flow

The exertion, which incorporates planning TPGs and upgrading them in understanding with the security prerequisites, is summarized in the execution stream over. To begin with things to begin with, security requires DUS (plan beneath security) to be outlined. The DUS is assessing design generators in this ponder, which incorporate counter and straight criticism move registers (LFSR) with diverse bit arrangements. In arrange to protect built-in self-test (BIST) circuits against scan-based assaults, it is regularly required to secure TPGs. TPGs are vulnerable to assaults leveraging filter chains that target discernibleness and controllability. In this way, in planning the chips, guaranteeing security for TPGs is crucial.

The handle of executing the errand starts with the plan of TPGs. The circuit is portrayed in the show sim plan using Verilog, an HDL dialect. Following the plan, those have been tested and found to function with various inputs. In relation to the 12 security of these TPGs, these plans are altered so that, in the event that an exact key—001 in this case—is provided, the circuit generates test designs; if an inaccurate key is provided, it remains in the previously set state, which, in the case of a counter or a linear-feedback shift register, consists of all 0s.

In any case, why fair in these two states? Since shielding TPGs contrasts from ensuring the broader circuit in the taking after ways. When DUS produces irregular yields by giving the erroneous key, the comes about can too be utilized as test designs to look at a particular circuit, making it vulnerable to controllability and perceptibility assaults. In this manner, the yield

is limited to reset and preset states in arrange to avoid the creation of subjective test designs when the inaccurate key is input. Utilizing a 3-bit counter as the key era circuit, particular keys are delivered at foreordained interims of time (ns). When the circuit that produces the 001 state in the key producing circuit, TPGs provide the circuit test designs needed for the evaluation circuit. The DUS key encoder yield is still in the preset or reset condition for the remaining states. The show sim program is utilized to carry out the previously mentioned method. This is what we can allude to as case 1.

After the plan has been made secure, it needs to be synthesizable in arrange for the security to be fulfilled with negligible control utilization and without causing zone overhead amid worldly imperatives. The examination strategy yielded the taking after security. RTL investigation, blend, and usage come following, after which plan entry.v records are required for the Vivado program. Taking after recreation and confirmation of the plan passage, RTL (Enlist Exchange Level) examination creates a high-level representation of the plan that appears the information stream between different rationale components and their intercontinental in the frame of schematics. A utilization report enumerating the sum of LUTs, FFs, and IOs utilized out of the add up to number of accessible is delivered by run blend of the confirmed plan. Whether as well numerous consistent components are utilized, blend comes to a conclusion. It is in charge of optimizing rationale. Run Execution, which gives control reports and transient restrictions like WHS (most exceedingly bad hold slack) and WNS (most exceedingly bad negative slack), is the final step in the security investigation handle. This vvivado stage closes control utilization, covering both inactive and energetic control as well as worldly restrictions, which in turn wraps up circuit delay.

Results

It is clear from Tables 67.1 and 67.2 that the security advertised is viable and doesn't require any extra space. The overall amount of flip flops required for the TPG and the key interval circuit adds up to the overall amount of flip flops required for each DUS. The identification of this

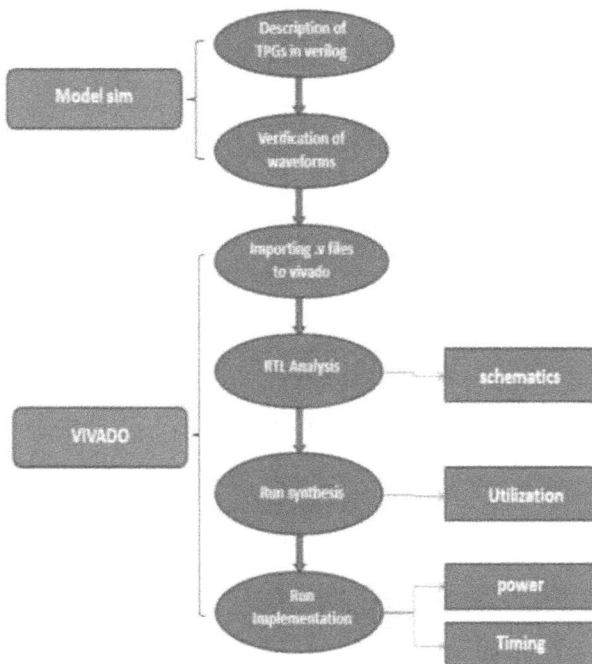

Figure 67.1 Implementation flow
Source: Author

area problem resulted from a table evaluation showing that the total flip flips in DUS fulfilled the flip flounder requirement

A comparison of the circuit's power consumption in working and standby modes can be done using the static and dynamic power values found in Tables 67.3 and 67.4. Three types of power constraints are presented in the dynamic power report: I/O, logic, and signaling. Because static power is less than dynamic power, it can be inferred from the tables that there is very little power leakage in the suggested TPG security. Power consumption by I/O increases as a result of interconnects growing as a result of variations in the total of bits of implemented TPGs. The dynamic power levels of the LFSR TPG are irregular because LFSRs have logic components

Table 67.3 LFSR energy analysis

No. of bits	Inert energy(mv)	Dynamic energy (mw)
5	0.07	0.4062
6	0.07	1.4097
7	0.07	1.4132
8	0.07	0.4205
9	0.07	0.4231

Source: Author

Table 67.4 Counter energy analysis

No. of bits	Inert energy(mv)	Dynamic energy (mw)
5	0.07	0.4003
6	0.07	0.4048
7	0.07	0.4059
8	0.07	0.4085
9	0.07	0.4111

Source: Author

Table 67.1 LFSR synthesis and simulation elements

Performance	5 Bit	6 Bit	7 Bit	8 Bit	9 Bit
State generated	31	63	127	255	512
Key bits	3	3	3	3	3
Required time	320-630ns	640-1270ns	1280-2550ns	2560-5200ns	5210-10480ns
Cycle time	13ns	13ns	13ns	13ns	13ns
Clock cycle Duration	320ns	640ns	1280ns	2560ns	5120ns
Flipflops	9	10	11	12	13
XOR gates	2	2	2	4	4
LUT	5	6	6	8	8

Source: Author

Table 67.2 Counter synthesis and simulation entries

Performance	5 Bit	6 Bit	7 Bit	8 Bit	9 Bit
State generated	31	63	127	255	512
Key bits	4	4	4	4	4
Required time	330-650ns	650-1290ns	1290-2570ns	2570-5130ns	5140-10260ns
Cycle time	15ns	15ns	15ns	15ns	15ns
Clock cycle duration	330ns	650ns	1290ns	2570ns	5140ns
Flip-flops	9	10	11	12	13
XOR gates	7	9	9	11	12
LUT	12	13	14	15	16

Source: Author

like XOR gates that increment and decrement depending on the duration of the LFSR's input. Regularity in the change of logic components leads to regularity in the dynamic power values when counters are taken into account.

The planning report gives a exhaustive examination of the plan taking after the run usage. This planning think about involves checking that each way in the plan fulfills the planning details, looking at setup and hold limitations, affirming that the working recurrence remains inside execution bounds, and affirming that no pivotal way remains unhindered. Negative most exceedingly bad case slack, or hold time, is spoken to by WHS and negative most exceedingly bad case slack, individually, as takes after: slack = information essential time - information arriving time. It is apparent from the arranged values of the LFSR and counter that the worst negative slack and worst hold slack are favourable, demonstrating that there is positive slack—that is, the information entry time surpasses the information

Table 67.5 LFSR timing analysis

No. of bits	Worst negative slack	Worst hold slack
5	5.637	0.115
6	5.795	0.04
7	5.430	0.114
8	5.435	0.080
9	5.470	0.056

Source: Author

Table 67.6 Counter timing analysis

No. of bits	Worst negative slack	Worst hold slack
5	7.115	0.159
6	7.187	0.16
7	6.550	0.154
8	6.336	0.136
9	6.026	0.115

Source: Author

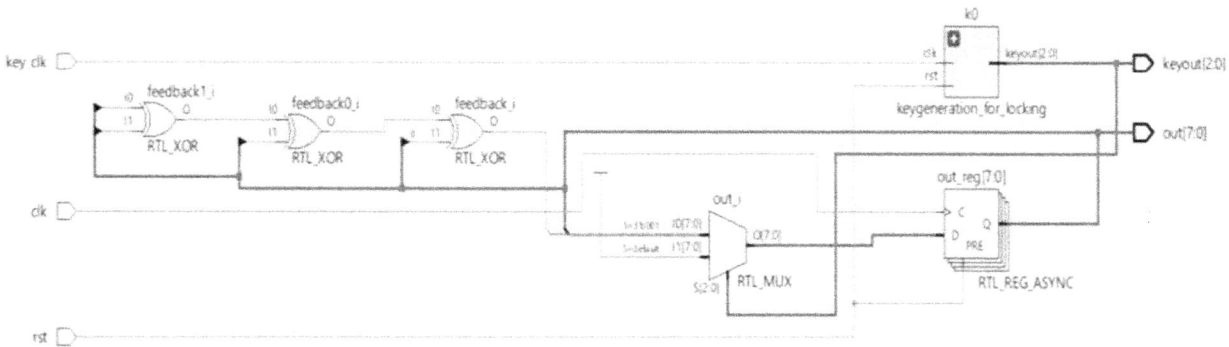

Figure 67.2 LFSR - 8-bit RTL designs
Source: Author

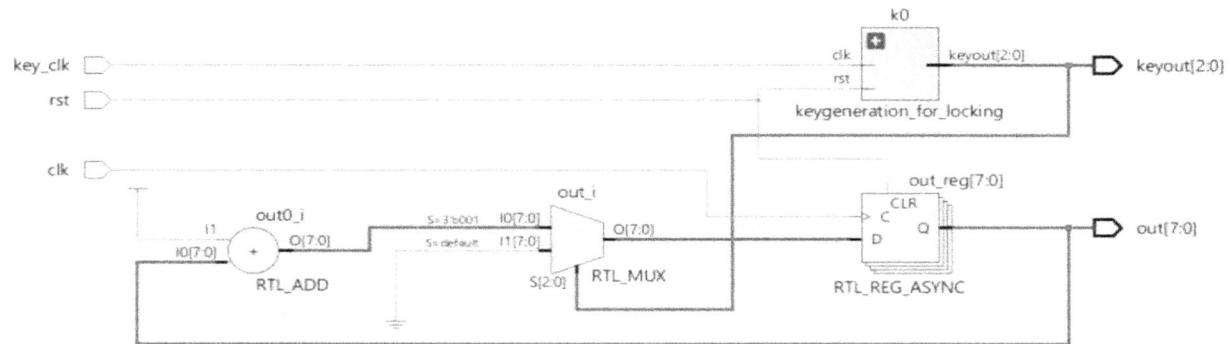

Figure 67.3 Counter 8-bit RTL designs
Source: Author

required time—forming a delay-free circuit. This kind of DUS plan is working without any slack, creating overhead-free secure TPGs. The circuit's timing pathways are completed by secure TPGs.

This paper proposes a security solution to protect hardware from scan-based attacks, which exploit the scan chains used in built-in self-test (BIST) for reverse engineering and malicious tampering. The authors present a method to mitigate such attacks by modifying the scan chain design and using secure encryption techniques to prevent unauthorized access during testing. This solution aims to enhance the security of hardware systems, particularly in environments vulnerable to scan-based vulnerabilities [4,6,8,10–12, 15, 17, 18, 22].

Conclusion

This work focused on designing secured test pattern generators (TPGs) for built-in self-test (BIST) systems, aiming to enhance the security of test patterns while maintaining system performance. The results demonstrated that, although higher bit-width configurations introduce complexity with increased hardware components and processing time, our approach effectively balanced security and efficiency. Secured TPGs improve fault detection without significant overhead, protecting the system from vulnerabilities like side-channel attacks during testing.

Future Work

Future research could explore scaling secured TPG designs for larger circuits, optimizing resource usage, reducing power consumption, and integrating adaptive security protocols. Additionally, investigating the application of secured TPGs with emerging technologies and improving hardware Trojan detection within built-in self-test systems will further enhance security and performance.

References

[1] Dilip, P. S., Somanathan, G. R., and Bhakthavatchalu, R. (2019). Reseeding LFSR for test pattern generation. In Proceedings [5] of the 2019 IEEE International Conference on Communication and Signal Processing, ICCSP, (pp. 921–925).

[2] Tsai, I. C., Liu, F., and Feng, J. (2019). A dominant gate insertion algorithm implementation for logic locking in IP protection. In 2019 IEEE International Conference on Electron Devices and Solid-State Circuits Circuits (EDSSC), Xi'an, China, (pp. 1–3). doi: 10.1109/EDSSC.2019.8754092.

[3] BUSHNELL M.L. (2005). Essentials of electronic testing for digital, memory and mixed-signal VLSI circuits . Springer.

[4] Mehta, A., Saif, D., and Rashidzadeh, R. (2016). A hardware security solution against scanbased attacks. In 2016 IEEE International Symposium on [8] Circuits and Systems (ISCAS), Montreal, QC, (pp. 1698–1701). doi: 10.1109/ISCAS.2016.7538894.

[5] Thangam, T., Gayathri, G., and Madhubala, T. (2017). A novel logic locking technique for hardware security. In 2017 IEEE International Conference [3] on Electrical, Instrumentation and Communication Engineering (ICEICE), Karur, (pp. 1–7). doi: 10.1109/ICEICE.2017.8192439.

[6] Rani, R. U., Jayanthi, D., Vignesh, N. A., and Kavitha, K. (2019). Key-based functional obfuscation of integrated circuits for a hardware security. In 2019 2nd International Conference on Intelligent Computing, Instrumentation and Control Technologies (ICICICT), Kannur, Kerala, India, (pp. 733–737). doi: 10.1109/ICICICT 46008.2019.8993122. 23.

[7] Liu, Y., Zuzak, M., Xie, Y., Chakraborty, A., and Srivastava, A. (2020). Strong anti-SAT: secure and effective logic locking. In 2020 21st International Symposium on Quality Electronic Design (ISQED), Santa Clara, CA, USA, (pp. 199–205). doi: 10.1109/ISQED48828.2020.9136983.

[8] Karmakar, R., Prasad, N., Chattopadhyay, S., Kapur, R., and Sengupta, I. (2017). A new logic encryption strategy ensuring key interdependency. In 2017 30th International Conference on VLSI Design and 2017 16th International Conference on Embedded Systems (VLSID), (pp. 429–434). IEEE.

[9] Trends in the global ic design service market. DIGITIMES Research. [Online]. Available from: http://www.digitimes.com/news/a20120313RS400. html?chid=2.

[10] Rostami, M., Koushanfar, F., and Karri, R. (2014). A primer on hardware security: models, methods, and metrics. *Proceedings of the IEEE*, 102(8), 1283–1295.

[11] Roy, J. A., Koushanfar, F., and Markov, I. L. (2008). Epic: ending piracy of integrated circuits. In Proceedings of the conference on Design, Automation and test in Europe, (pp. 1069–1074).

[12] Innovation is at risk: losses of up to $4 billion annually due to ip infringement. SEMI. [Online]. Available from: http://semi.org/en/ innovation-risk- losses4-billion-annually-due-ip-infringement.

[13] Chakraborty, R. S., and Bhunia, S. (2009). Harpoon: an obfuscation-based soc design methodology for hardware protection. *IEEE Transactions on CAD of Integrated Circuits and Systems*, 28(10), 1493–1502.

[14] Zhang, J. (2016). A practical logic obfuscation technique for hardware security. *IEEE Transactions on Very Large Scale Integration (VLSI) Systems*, 24(3), 1193–1197. doi: 10.1109/TVLSI.2015.2437996.

[15] Doulcier, M., Flottes, M. L., and Rouzeyre, B. (2008). AES-based BIST: self- test, test pattern generation and signature analysis. In 4th IEEE International Symposium on Electronic Design, Test and Applications (delta 2008), Hong Kong, (pp. 314–321). doi: 10.1109/DELTA.2008.86.

[16] Jin, Y. (2014). Design-for-security vs. design-for-testability: a case study on DFT chain in cryptographic circuits. In 2014 IEEE Computer Society Annual Symposium on VLSI, Tampa, FL, (pp. 19–24). doi: 10.1109/ISVLSI.2014.54.

[17] Tan, E., Qian, W., and Li, Y. (2009). An improved pattern generation for built-in selftest design based on boundary-scan reseeding. In 2009 International Conference on Communications, Circuits and Systems, Milpitas, CA, (pp. 1082–1086). doi: 10.1109/ICCCAS.2009.5250336.

[18] Rajendran, J., Pino, Y., Sinanoglu, O., and Karri, R. (2012). Security analysis of logic obfuscation. In DAC Design Automation Conference 2012, San Francisco, CA, (pp. 83–89). doi: 10.1145/2228360.2228377.

[19] Liu, Y., Zuzak, M., Xie, Y., Chakraborty, A., and Srivastava, A. (2020). Strong anti-SAT: secure and effective logic locking. In 2020 21st International Symposium on Quality Electronic Design (ISQED), Santa Clara, CA, USA, (pp. 199–205). doi: 10.1109/ISQED48828.2020.9136983.

[20] Seeram, S. S. S. G., Polireddi, S. N. N., Somanathan, G. R., and Bhakthavatchalu, R. (2020). Synthesis of synchronous gray code counters by combining mentor graphics HDL designer and xilinx VIVADO FPGA flow. In 2020 International Conference on Communication and Signal Processing (ICCSP), Chennai, India, (pp. 738–742). doi: 10.1109/ISQED48828.2020.9136983.

[21] Sumanth, B. N., Reddy, B. L., Somanathan, G. R., and Ramesh (2020). A proposal for synthesis of synchronous counters. In 2020 4th International Conference on Trends in Electronics and Informatics (ICOEI)(48184), Tirunelveli, India, (pp. 80–84). doi: 10.1109/ICOEI48184.2020.9142898.

[22] Dilip, P. S., Somanathan, G. R., and Bhakthavatchalu, R. (2019). Comparat ive study of test pattern generation systems to reduce test application time. In 2019 9th International Symposium on Embedded Computing and System Design (ISED), Kollam, India, (pp. 1–4). doi: 10.1109/ISED48680.2019.9096234.

68 Design and performance analysis of automated floor cleaning robot

Arunamary, S.[1,a]*, Kumutha, D.*[2,b]*, Thirilogasundari, V.*[3,c]*,*
Venkates Kanna, T.[4,d]*, Ohm Shankar, S.,*[1,e] *and Sudhagar, G.*[5,f]

[1]Research Scholar, Department of ECE, Bharath Institute of Higher Education and Research, Chennai, India

[2]Professor, Department of ECE, Jeppiaar Institute of Technology, Kunnam, Sriperumbudur, Chennai, India

[3]Assistant Professor, Department of ECE, Bharath Institute of Higher Education and Research, Chennai, India

[4]Assistant Professor, Department of ECE, VCET, Madurai, Tamil Nadu, India

[5]Associate Professor, Department of ECE, Bharath Institute of Higher Education and Research, Chennai, India

Abstract

Human free floor cleaning robot is a cost effective small robotics device which cleans floors in industries and home while reducing huge manpower. Essentially, like a robot, it reduces human error and enhances the cleaning process. The manual method of cleaning floor has chance of missing some areas to be unclean. Manual cleaning activities are time consuming and challenging task in workplace. Also, the floor area in large scale enterprises is enormous, and the employees responsible for cleaning it cannot clean it as efficiently as they could in smaller offices. That is where the robot proves to be helpful. In addition, the robot is small and compact. So we can carry it around the home and position it anywhere we like. In addition, when compared to manual labor, robots are more cost-effective in industries. The proposed human free floor cleaning model has been the right alternative for conventional models because of its versatility, time savings, and efficiency.

Keywords: Cost-effective, floor cleaning robot, time-saving, versatile

Introduction

Assisting people with floor-floor cleaning applications at homes, hotels, restaurants, enterprises, healthcare industries, workstations, and other locations is essential. Traditionally, a dry or wet mop is used to clean the floor, with a hand tool as an option. They scrape the surface vigorously. Cleaning is done on various characters, including cement floors, highly polished timber floors, and marble floors. A thick layer of dust covers the rough surface floors, namely cement floors, primarily found in semi-urban areas. Humans have become more reliant on machines since the dawn of civilization. Humans are attempting to reduce the amount of work they are required to do. We can also achieve a high level of efficiency with the help of machines because there is no risk of human error. Intelligence and robotics have advanced at a breakneck speed in the last 30 years. Every human uses at least two robots per day.

If we look back 30 years, we can observe how robotics has evolved from enormous structures to small and minuscule ones in the nano range. Sensors that are extremely complex have been built to assist the robot with a variety of tasks. Pneumatic and actuation systems that are complex have been devised. The cell phone is one of the best examples. When it comes to floor cleaning robots, iRobot is the industry leader with its 90 sq. cm robot that uses indoor navigation as its primary control system. Indoor navigation is also a significant difficulty for many in-house mobility

[a]arunamary.ece@bharathuniv.ac.in, [b]kumutha.d@jeppiaarinstitute.org, [c]thirilogas@gmail.com, [d]tvk@vcet@ac.in, [e]ohmshankar.ecee@gmail.com, [f]sudhagar.ece@bharathuniv.ac.in

DOI: 10.1201/9781003616399-68

robots. Indoor GPS is also evolving at the moment, with unsupervised learning and path determination in its maiden run. Since then, indoor navigation has been a challenge. Complicated artificial intelligence techniques such as unsupervised and supervised learning, swarm optimization, ANT classifier, and natural heuristic search are currently playing a crucial part in designing most mobile robot control systems.

Cleaning machines are essential in healthcare industries, home, halls, railway stations, and few more public places for cleaning floors and outside ground. Cleaning of inner and outer region of living place is essential, as in our daily life we visiting various places and entering the home can carry disease affecting microorganism. It may spread on the ground area and whenever we standing or walking on that place will prompt to attack the unhealthy person. We know that cleaning up after ourselves is highly important for our health and decreases the workforce required. There are multiple floor cleaning models in the market, but this proposed model is quite easy to construct and use. This machine is easy to run for everyone and it is more useful for healthcare industries and several other enterprises. It completes the task within a short amount of time and costs very little. The maintenance cost is said to be less. A variety of machines are used for this function. In this study, we designed the model to functioning mechanically with less number of electrical equipment's. It is made of basic materials and extremely simple to handle; without training anybody can runs safely.

This generation's need for cleaning is critical. In general, numerous approaches are utilized to clean different types of surfaces in colleges and hospitals regularly. The below facts explain why floor cleaning is must:

- Slips and falls on the floor are the major factor for accidental injuries and deaths.
- Lack of floor maintenance practices frequently cause accidents. To keep the floor dust-free and attractive, debris and impediments should be eliminated; allergens and fine particles must be destroyed; surfaces that should be avoided; keep the environment clean (kitchens); No slippage should occur if traction is maintained maximum level.

The operation of proposed model starts with a pair of brushes fixed at front of the vehicle scrubs away any dust or water on the floor. The vacuum cleaner collects the dust and water, and the detergent water is sprayed on the floor. The mop, located in the middle area of the chassis, cleans the fine particles on the floor by rotating action. The residual water on the floor is wiped away using the wiper at the cleaning machine's end.

Numerous industries are collaborating in the field of developing human free self-cleaning robots. Robotics is receiving a lot of attention these days as a way to reduce human labour. Cleaners with only one or two functions currently dominate the market. We are utilising Arduino because of its plenty of advantages and easy to access. The cleaner will be a step toward making living more comfortable by addressing issues with existing floor cleaning methods [1]. The design, development, and construction of a smart floor cleaning robot (CLEAR) using IEEE Standard 1621 are replicated in this study. The subject robot has the ability to function in both automated and manual modes, as well as including additional characteristics were scheduling for a certain time and a bag less dirt container with an auto-soil disposal mechanism. This study has the capability of improving human's life style. The controller is used to adjust the motors and suction unit, as well as a few sensors to avoid obstacles. This has the potential to enhance humanity's way of life [2,3]. Using a wireless robotic cleaning model, the cleaning process would be easier and less time consuming. This wireless system comprises of an android smartphone app that runs a transmitter application that allows the robot to respond to commands issued by the user through the transmitter app. The suggested robot comprises of an Arduino UNO controller with fourteen digital input/output pins, a robotic arm with a cleaning pad and a water sprayer for effective cleaning, and a robotic arm with a cleaning pad and a water sprayer. When the Arduino UNO receives commands via Bluetooth from an Android device, it decodes the commands and controls the motors to obtain the required course and direction [4–7]. The system contains a built-in battery power supply, which boosts the device's mobility. It's a straightforward, modern housekeeping appliance that even youngsters can use safely. It has suction and mopping capabilities, as well as obstacle detection and automated water spray [8–10].

In general, automatic cleaning models are distinguished by their cleaning capabilities, namely floor mopping and dry vacuuming. Robotic floor cleaners have various cleaning and operating mechanisms, each with its benefits and drawbacks. Robotics is receiving more research attention as technology advances to make humanity lives more comfortable. The design, circuit configuration, and fabrication of a prototype is presented in this study. This robot is self-contained and includes a dirt container with an air vacuum system and a pick-and-place mechanism. This model is highly beneficial to the advancement of humanity lifestyle.

Section 2 regards the process involved in the floor cleaning robot and its functioning. The circuit configuration of the proposed method is expressed in section 3. Section 4 of this study also includes a descriptive hardware analysis of the proposed method and its operation in conjunction with Bluetooth-controlled applications. Section 5 concluded with advantages and defined the necessity of cleanliness through the survey.

Method of Floor Cleaning

This study aims to create a small floor cleaner which can have the capability of cleaning the entire house. The process starts with the vacuum pump present at the front portion. It is utilized to clean up dried materials on the floor. This is particularly useful for pre-cleaning surfaces that have heavy fine particles. The debris that has been vacuumed must be kept in order to remove later. This is accomplished by fixing a debris chamber to a 12v vacuum pump. The next task is to wet the surface, which can be accomplished by sprinkling water on the floor. The model design is completely accomplished with the usage of a sprinkler system and a motor.

The model has a shower-like outlet and a chamber with a dc motor pump that controls the outlet. To clean the floor, the surface scrubber must move or scrape over it. The dirt has been removed, and the debris-laden water should flow back to the bot's rear. Clamps are utilized to secure the scrubber to the chassis. One side of the scrubber

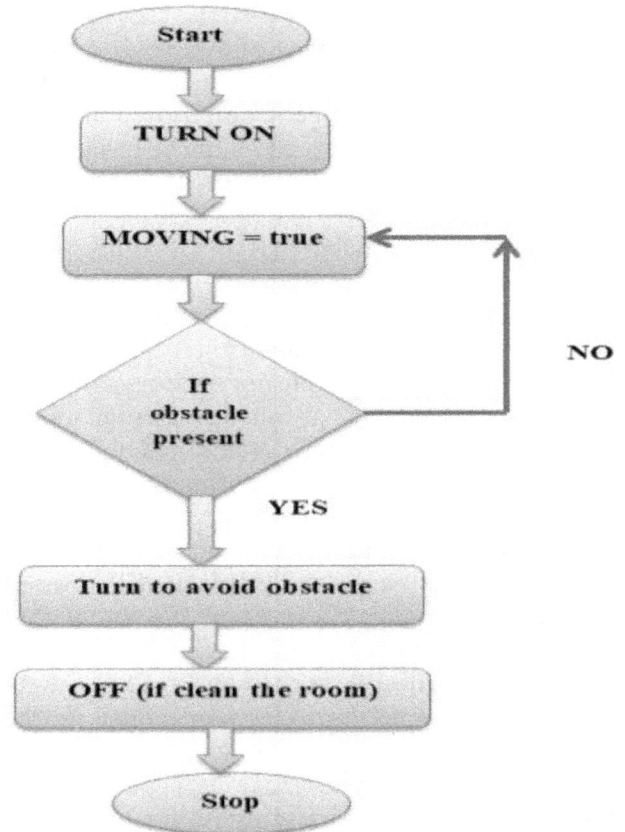

Figure 68.1 Process involved in-floor cleaning robot
Source: Author

is fixed to the motor, the other is attached to the ball bearing. The bearing is secured to the chassis by a clamp. A vacuum mechanism present at the back of the model to suck in the debris-laden filthy water. The entire system is controlled automatically from floor to floor in any room.

The control system's objective is to make the machine move automatically. Aside from that, it ensures that all of the components work correctly and at precise intervals. It should, for example, ensure that less liquid flows through the sprinkler system while turning. It must once again trace all of the components of a room. In another way, no area of the floor should be left undisturbed. This is accomplished through the employment of a 90 percent accurate spiral motion algorithm. An image sensing approach is utilized to avoid obstructions. Sensors are employed on the machine's front, left, and right sides. If the front sensor detects any obstacles, the following step is to use the suitable sensor to see them. If this sensor detects no impediment, the machine will travel to the right. However, if the suitable sensor encounters an obstruction, the motion will be to the left, based on the sensing data obtained by the left sensor.

If all of the sensors detect an obstruction, the machine goes back and forth in a spiral motion. The motion is also optimized using particle swarm optimization. It may move over a surface several times if only a spiral motion is used. This algorithm is used to reduce the number of repetitions, which boosts efficiency. Aurdino is used to automate the process.

Circuit Configuration

An autonomous dust cleaner with a pentagon shape has been proposed to avoid the misconception that robots can move in any direction. The submitted form can be used in the development of miniature robots to clean pentagon-shaped corners that are currently unclean able by existing round-shaped autonomous cleaning machines. Simple components such as a microcontroller, an LCD, dc motors, a dc centrifugal fan, line drivers, and ultrasonic and infrared sensors are used.

The Atmega89S52 microcontroller has four ports, each with eight pins, as illustrated in the circuit diagram. We used port one and port two for output connections such as LCDs, DC motors, and centrifugal fans, and port 2 for input connections such as ultrasonic and infrared sensors for obstacle detection.

The DC motor that rotates the mop has a higher torque than the motor that rotates the brushes. The other two DC motors with high RPMs could complete cleaning process of floor's front portion. The DC motor turns the brushes via a shaft attached to the motor shaft by a nut and bolt.

During the summer season, the front two brushes clean the uneven particles that collect on the floor's surface, and the dirt particles enter the vacuum cleaner from the suction pipe through the middle slots. The location of the mop can be varied in addition with the arc attached at the left-hand side of the chassis. The water supply is turned off during the dry cleaning process.

The operation of the model alters a bit during the rainy season, as water and dust or fine particles are drawn into the middle area of the chassis by moving brushes. The bushes rotate in opposing directions to gather additional water

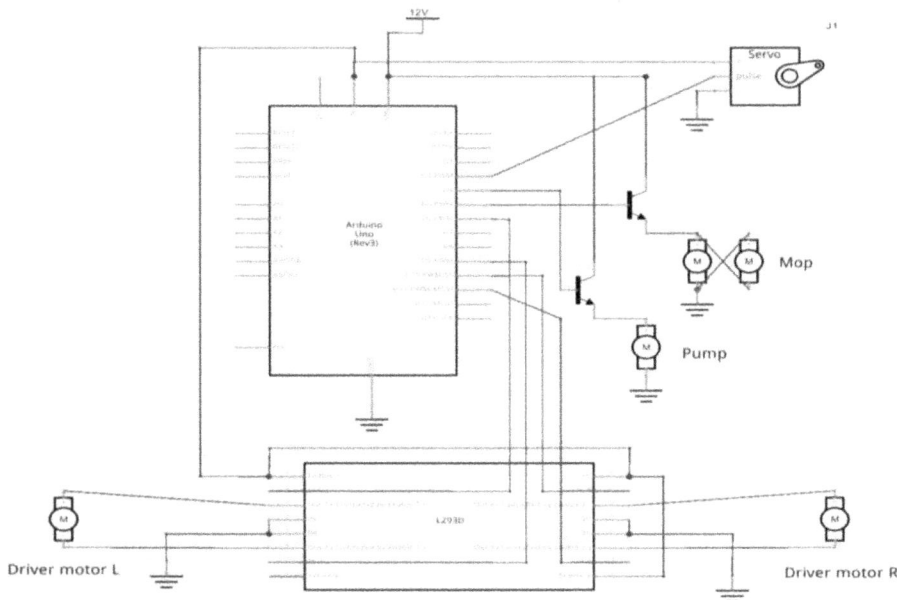

Figure 68.2 Showing the circuit of the proposed system
Source: Author

in the central portion. This mixture of water and debris is collected into the vacuum cleaner via the inlet line that runs among two brushes. The third motor rotates the mop to ensure thorough cleaning. The water spray pump is located at the bottom of the tank and supplies fresh water for efficient cleaning. The control valve controls the delivery of freshwater. Several holes are formed in the flowing water tube by an equivalent amount of water. Each floor cleaning machine's electrical supply is controlled by a different button on the electrical board.

Hardware Analysis

IRobot and Scooba are now essential players in the automatic floor cleaner sector. They control over 80% of the market. Their prices range from $25,000 to $35,000. Furthermore, the algorithms they employ are ineffective. They are employing algorithms that yield roughly 70% accuracy. To run their robot, they don't use any image processing methods. However, the robot we designed is cost-effective, costing approximately $15,000. Also, we can utilize a camera lens to identify small dust particles, which will result in a more efficient decision in governing the particle's motion, saving a significant amount of power and reducing the timing with improved efficiency and sensitivity. That will function similarly to a pheromone in an ant algorithm. When the pheromone density of ants in a specific route

Figure 68.3 Hardware analysis of proposed method
Source: Author

is higher, all other ants follow that direction in the ant algorithm. Similarly, if the robot detects a particular size of dust on the floor on one side but none on the other three, it will proceed to the dusty area if no obstruction is there. The primary possibility for marketing this consumer product is time redundancy and power savings at a reasonable cost.

Initially, connect the gear motor with driver board. Solder some wire to the motor terminals and then link it to the driver circuits screw terminals. The remaining pins must be connected in the following order: D6 on Arduino-Signal 1; D9 on Arduino-Signal 2; D10 on Arduino-Signal 3; D11 on Arduino-Signal 4; +5V-Arduino +5V; Gnd-Arduino Gnd; +12V (motors will run on this voltage)- to be linked to the battery later. After that, there is the Bluetooth module. The following are some connections: Arduino Vcc-+5V; Gnd-Arduino Gnd; Tx on Arduino-Rx; Arduino Tx-Rx.

If you're worried about the signal pins on your Arduino burning out, use a voltage divider. When seen from the front, the two mop motors in parallel so that the left one rotates anticlockwise and the right one rotates clockwise. To keep the connections safe, heat-shrink tubes are recommended. As shown in the schematic, solder the motor wires to the transistor circuit. Connect the water pump wires in the same way. The 12V will be sent straight from the battery to the transistor circuit and then to the Arduino's Vcc and the motor driver circuit. Connect the base of transistor two, which controls the mops, to D5 on the Arduino and the bottom of transistor one, which contains the pump, to D4. All of the motors' standard ground wires must be linked to the Arduino's GND pin. The servo motor is all that left now. The following are the links: Arduino Vcc-+5V; Gnd-Arduino Gnd; Arduino signal-D3.

The Bluetooth Serial Controller is used to connect the floor cleaning robot to the phone. Click settings and then 'visibility' after opening the app. Because we won't be using buttons 5, 9, or 12, turn off their visibility. After that, click the 'names' icon to customize the display names for each Button. Make them 3-4 letters long. Please take a look at the names I provided earlier. Set the following commands (without quotes) for each button under the 'commands' option

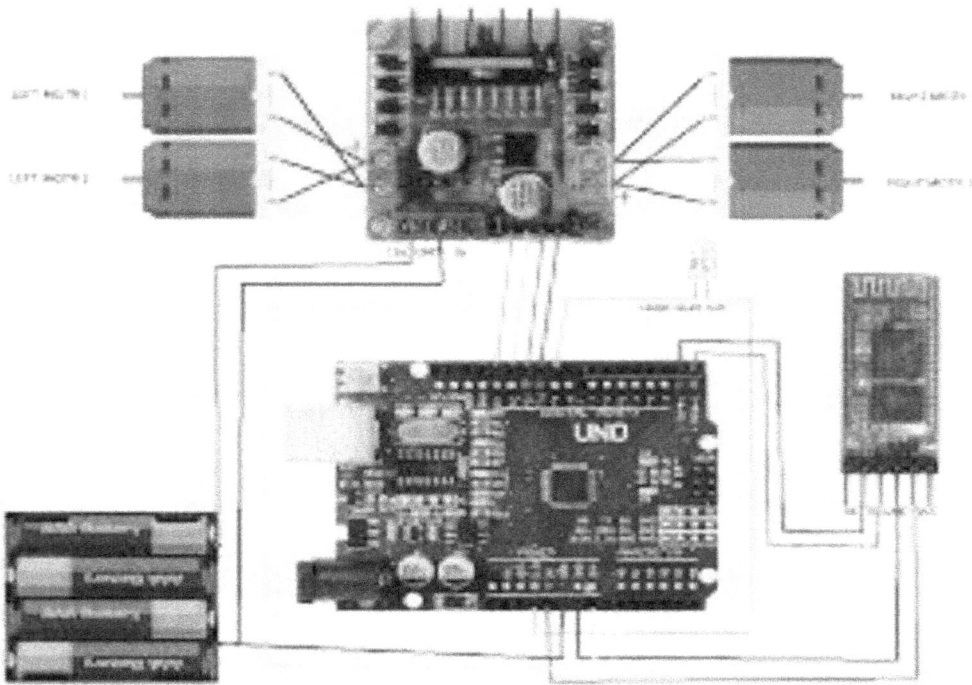

Figure 68.4 Configuration of Arduino with several components
Source: Author

(case sensitive): 'F' on Button 1 (FWD); Button 2 (BCK): The letter 'B'; LFT Button 3: 'L'; RGT Button 4: 'R'; 'M' on Button 6 (MPON); MPOF Button 7:m; 'P' on Button 8 (PMP); RUP Button 10: 'U'; RDWN Button 11: u; '1' on Button 13 (S1); '2' on Button 14 (S2); S3 Button 15: '3'; '4' on Button 16 (S4). You must specify the following stop commands ONLY for the buttons listed below in the stop commands' section of 'commands' itself: 1st Button: 'S'; 'S' on Button 2; 3rd Button: 'S';'S' is the fourth Button; p for Button 8. This would mean that if Button two isn't touched, the instruction 'S' will be delivered, causing the robot to halt. To link the robot, first, attach the 'HC-05' or other Bluetooth modules. '0000' or '1234' will be the password. Then, using the app, connect the linked module. One by one, press and inspect all of the app's buttons.

Conclusion

In this research, we introduced a mopping-capable floor cleaning robot. This study aims to address the issue of cleanliness in society. The various applications provide a wide range of functions, such as cleaning the pipe, scouring the

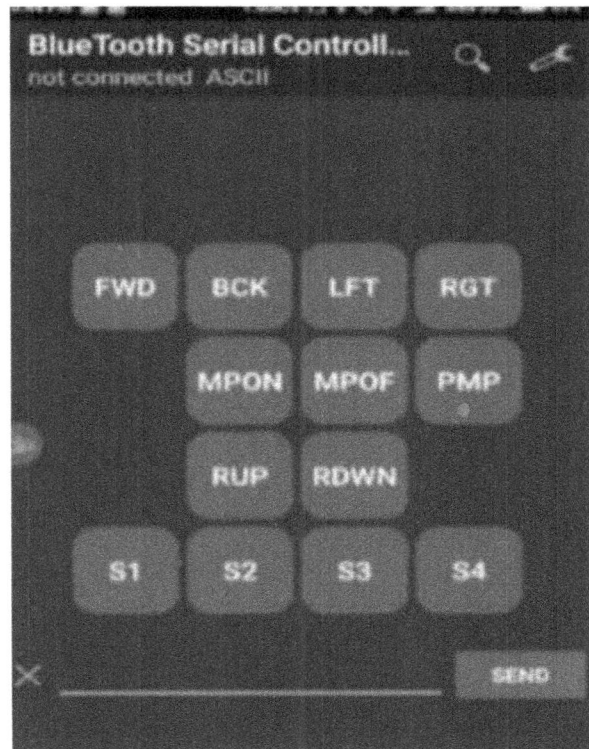

Figure 68.5 Representing Bluetooth controlled application
Source: Author

surface for good floor cleaning, removing dust and debris from the road, and providing a pick and place machine to remove impediments. This endeavor is highly beneficial to society and serves as an essential part in maintaining the countries cleanliness. The motor is not detachable, and the high rpm causes the entire model to vibrate. That will work nicely if these feature are changed. Overall, this is a successful product that may have helpful to today's Indian household. This type of automatic floor cleaning equipment can clean any remote location. Because the motors chosen can consume significantly less power, it will save both energy and money. DC motor and wiper mechanism are used to design and construct semi-automatic floor cleaning equipment. The manufactured machine is adaptable and simple to operate. Manual sweeping by hand may not be as successful as using a floor cleaner because it will not take up everything that is not visible. An alternative notion for avoiding such issues is to use a manually powered eco-friendly cleaner. Compared to conventional models, the human-free operating user-friendly cleaner may perform very efficiently in covering an area, time, and cost of cleaning.

Reference

[1] Khalid, U., Baloch, M. F., Haider, H., Sardar, M. U., Khan, M. F., Zia, A. B., et al. (2015). Smart floor cleaning robot (CLEAR).
[2] Jain, M., Rawat, P. S., and Morbale, J. (2017). Automatic floor cleaner. *International Research Journal of Engineering and Technology (IRJET)*, 04(04), 2395–0056.
[3] Monika, S., Manjusha, K. A., Prasad, S. V. S., and Naresh, B. (2019). Design and implementation of smart floor cleaning robot using android app. *International Journal of Innovative Technology and Exploring Engineering (IJITEE)*, 8(4S2), 250–252. ISSN: 2278-3075.
[4] Bangare, P., Chougule, A., and Shinde, S. (2018). Smart home cleaning robot. *IJSRD International Journal for Scientific Research and Development*, 6(02).
[5] Kaur, M., and Abrol, P. (2014). Design and development of floor cleaner robot (automatic and manual). *International Journal of Computer Applications*, 97(19). (0975 – 8887).
[6] Borkar, N. M., Mishra, P., Mishra, A., Bisen, A., and Tiwari, T. (2018). Autonomous vacuum cleaner with smartphone compatibility. *IJESC - International Journal of Engineering Science and Computing*, 8(4).
[7] Meghana, K., Harshitha, V., Mahima Padmanabha, B., Dikshit, N. N., and Kumar, B. R. S. (2019). Automatic and manual floor cleaning robot. *JETIR - Journal of Emerging Technologies and Innovative Research*, 6(5).
[8] Pandey, A., Kaushik, A., Jha, A. K., and Kapse, G. (2014). A technological survey on autonomous home cleaning robot. *International Journal of Scientific and Research Publications*, 4(4).
[9] Pardeshi, A., More, S., Kadam, D., and Patil, V. A. (2017). Automatic floor cleaner. *International Journal of Educational Communications and Technology (IJECT)*, 8(1).
[10] Gutmann, J. S., Culp, K., Munich, M. E., and Pirjanian, P. (2012). The social impact of a systematic floor cleaner. In IEEE International Workshop on Advanced Robotics and its Social Impacts, Technische University Munchen, Germany, May 21–23.

69 Designing and simulations of PCF-SPR based biosensor

Srikar, D.[a], T. Vasudeva Reddy[b], Santhosh Kumar, Siddivinayak, Veeramalla[c], M., Siddivinayak.[d], Lokesh, M.[e], and Sharath Chandra, M.[f]

B V Raju Institute of Technology, Vishnupur, Narsapur, Medak District – 502313. Greater Hyderabad, Telangana, India

Abstract

Designing a photonic crystal fiber-surface plasmon resonance-based optical sensor using COMSOL Multiphysics involves integrating advanced simulation techniques with practical sensor design principles [2]. This abstract outline the methodology and key components of such a design process. The biosensor's performance is optimized through rigorous simulation of the PCF structure's modal properties and its interaction with surface plasmon resonance phenomena [4]. COMSOL Multiphysics enables accurate modeling of electromagnetic fields within the PCF, considering material properties, geometric parameters, and environmental conditions. Key design considerations focus on improving sensitivity and specificity by optimizing the PCF geometry, including parameters such as core size, hole diameter, and periodicity. The abstract concludes by highlighting the potential of COMSOL Multiphysics in advancing PCF SPR biosensor design [8], offering a robust platform for integrating theoretical insights with experimental validation, thereby paving the way for enhanced sensing performance in biomedical and environmental applications.

Keywords: Photonic Crystal Fiber (PCF), Surface Plasmon Resonance (SPR), Optical Sensor, COMSOL Multiphysics, Biosensor, Performance Optimization, Electromagnetic Fields, Sensitivity, Specificity, Core Size, Biomedical Applications, Environmental Applications

Literature Survey

Gold: Gold is widely used in SPR applications for its stable optical properties and strong SPR responses in the visible and near-infrared spectrum, commonly employed in PCF-SPR biosensors to enhance sensitivity. Homola et al., [6] emphasize its effectiveness in achieving high sensitivity and stable performance [6].

Silver: Silver offers strong SPR responses but is prone to oxidation, affecting long-term stability. Liedberg et al., [10] explore its SPR characteristics and potential for enhancing sensitivity in optical biosensors [10].

Copper: Copper is gaining attention for its lower cost and good SPR sensitivity in specific wavelengths. Zhang et al., (2020) [9] discuss copper nanostructures' potential in cost-effective, sensitive PCF-SPR biosensors.

Bronze and tungsten: These materials offer unique SPR responses for specialized biosensing applications, though specific research in PCF-SPR biosensors is limited and requires further exploration.

Existing Model

The design and material selection for the existing model of PCF-SPR structure are based on parameters that influence loss and sensitivity. The setup for the experiment of the sensor is given in Figure 69.1. A LASER is used as the light source, and there is an entry-exit section to introduce the analyte. Various sensor parameters were adjusted, with pitch values ranging between p1(1–2) μm and p2(0.5–2 μm). The radius of the core (dc) is set between (0.10–0.2) μm, and the smaller hole radius (d1) matches the radius of the core. The radius of the larger hole (d2) varies from (0.1 to 0.35) μm, the gold layer thickness varies up to 0.06 um. A change in the resonance peak is detected with fluctuations in the analyte. The influence on confinement loss and peak definition is observed by modifying the gold layer thickness (30, 40,

[a]srikar.d@bvrit.ac.in, [b]vasu.tatiparti@bvrit.ac.in, [c]santhosh.v@bvrithyderabad.edu.in ,[d]22211a04f7@bvrit.ac.in, [e]22211a04d4@bvrit.

DOI: 10.1201/9781003616399-69

50, 60 nm) to avoid distortion. The mesh size is set to an extra-fine level, with a sweep in wavelength ranging from (0.6–0.9) μm conducted in COMSOL software. The mode analysis window controls the number of modes to be generated and simulations are run with mode counts of 20, 40, 60, 80, and 100. The refractive index of 1.45 is used to search for the modes. The materials used in the designing of the sensor include gold, fused silica, analyte (which varies upon user input), and air. The design evolved iteratively during simulations, and intermediate designs are illustrated in Figure 69.1, along with plots optimizing confinement loss. Analytical expressions for confinement loss, wavelength sensitivity, and sensor resolution are derived from previous research.

Limitations in Existing Model

Confinement loss in PCF SPR biosensors with a gold sensing layer can critically affect sensor performance. Gold's high absorption in visible and near-infrared regions leads to increased confinement loss, as light energy is absorbed rather than propagating through the fiber, reducing sensor sensitivity. It's essential to optimize the gold layer thickness; if it's too thick, absorption losses become significant, while if it's too thin, the SPR signals are weak, leading to inefficient excitation. Furthermore, successful Insufficient overlap resulting from elevated confinement losses can diminish the sensor's precision in detecting variations in the refractive index of the analyte. The photonic crystal fiber's design, mainly, the air holes size and the core material influence confinement losses, with intricate designs sometimes

exacerbating the problem. Additionally, environmental variables like temperature fluctuations can change the optical properties of both sensing layer and PCF, resulting in inconsistent sensor performance and higher confinement losses.

Proposed Design

The design and material selection for the proposed model of the PCF-SPR structure are based on parameters that influence loss and sensitivity. The setup for the sensor experiment is shown in Figure 69.1. A LASER is used as the light source, with an entry-exit section for introducing the analyte. Various sensor parameters were adjusted, with pitch values ranging between p1(1–2) μm and p2(0.5–2 μm). The radius of the core (dc) is set between (0.10–0.2) μm, and the smaller hole radius (d1) matches the radius of the core. The radius of the larger hole (d2) varies from (0.1 to 0.35) μm, while the thickness of the silver, tungsten, or bronze layer varies up to 0.06 μm. The width of the analyte layer is varied between (0.8–0.9) μm, and the width of the phase matched layer (PML) ranges from (3– 3.5) μm. A shift in the resonance peak is detected with variations in the analyte. The impact on confinement loss and peak sharpness is noted by altering the silver, tungsten, or bronze layer thickness (30, 40, 50, 60 nm) to prevent distortion.

The mesh size is set to an extra-fine level, with a wavelength sweep between (0.6–0.9) μm performed in COMSOL™ software. The mode analysis window controls the number of modes generated, and simulations are run with mode counts of 20, 40, 60, 80, and 100. A refractive index of 1.45 is used to search for the modes. The materials used in the design of the sensor include silver, tungsten, bronze, fused silica, the analyte (which varies upon user input), and air. The design evolved iteratively during simulations, and intermediate designs are illustrated in Figure 69.1, along with plots optimizing confinement loss. The dielectric constants of silver, tungsten, and bronze follow the Drude-Lorentz model. Analytical expressions for confinement loss, wavelength sensitivity, and sensor resolution are referenced from earlier studies.

Multiple designs emerged during iterative simulations, and intermediate designs were produced in [1].

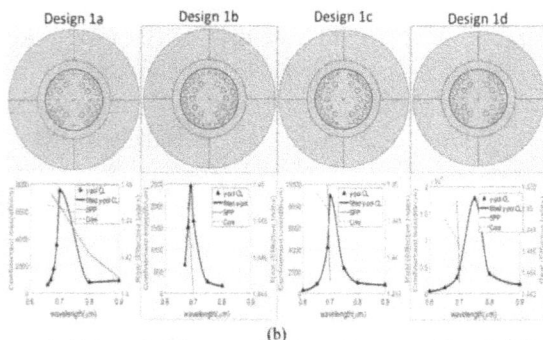

Figure + (a) Graphical illustration of Experimental Setup (b) Few of the successive designs of PCF-SPR sensor.

Figure 69.1 Design analysis of sensor
Source: Author

Table 69.1 [1] Design specifications of the sensor

Parameter Specification	Values (μm)
Radius of core (d_c)	0.15
Radius of large holes (d_1)	0.15
Radius of large holes (d_2)	0.30
Gold layer width	0.04
Pitch (p_1)	2.0
Pitch (p_2)	1.0
PML layer width	3.5
Analyte layer width	0.98

Source: Author

SENSOR DESIGN

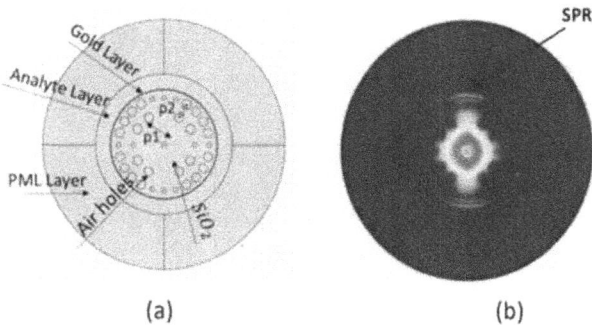

Figure 69.2 (a) Final design of the sensor. (b) spr of the sensor

Source: Author

FLOW CHART

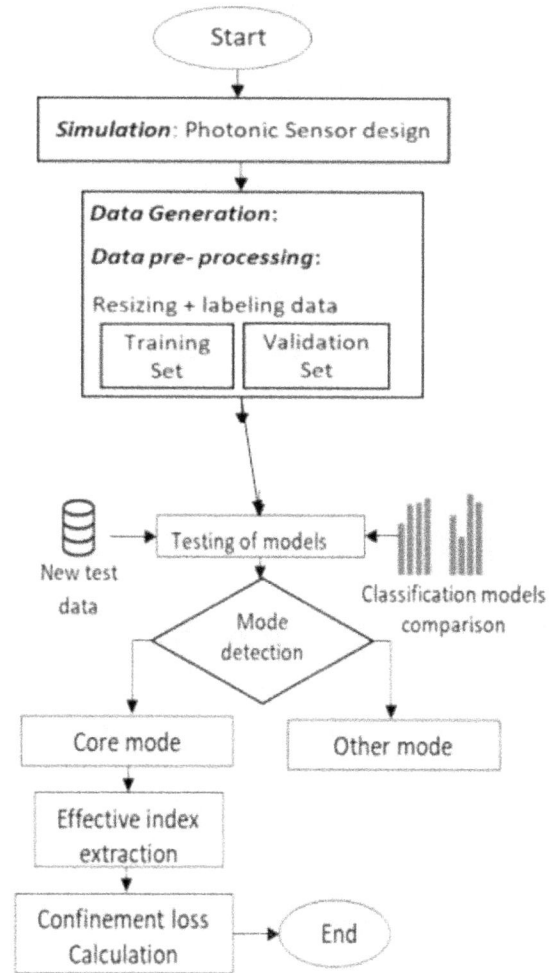

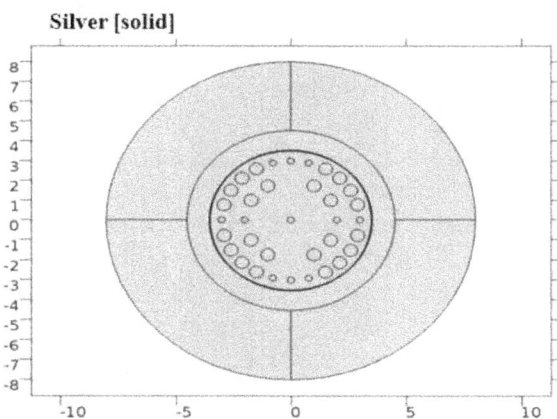

Figure 69.3 Silver sensing layer

Source: Author

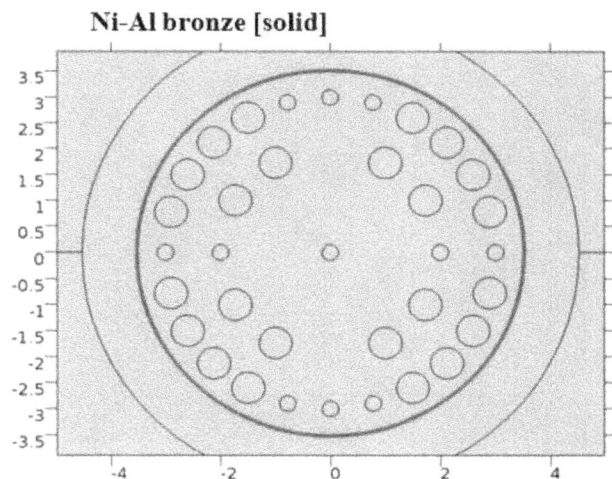

Figure 69.4 Bronze sensing layer

Source: Author

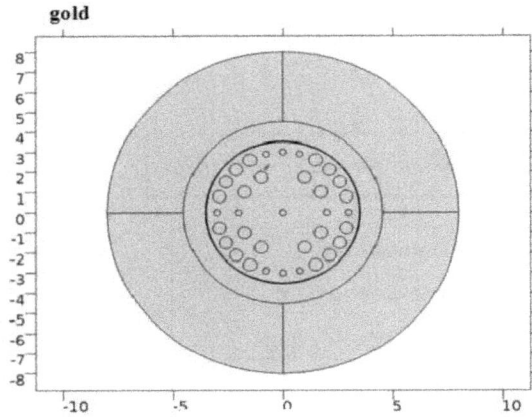

Figure 69.5 Gold sensing layer
Source: Author

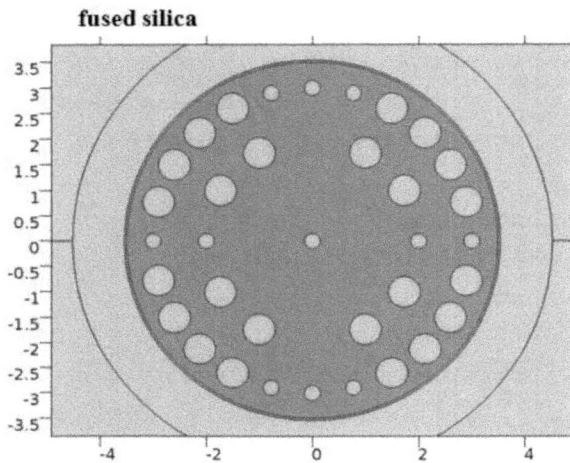

Figure 69.6 Fused silica as analyte layer
Source: Author

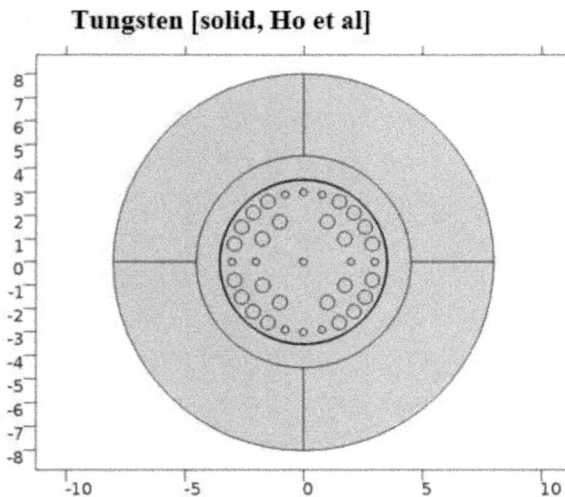

Figure 69.7 Tungsten as sensing layer
Source: Author

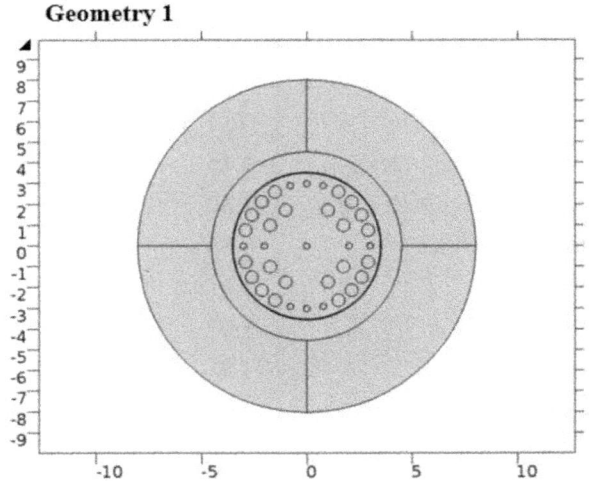

Figure 69.8 Final geometry of the sensor
Source: Author

Properties and Characteristics of Materials Used

1. Gold (Au)
   - Advantages: Gold is highly stable and provides a strong plasmonic response between visible to near infrared spectrum, ensuring a well-defined SPR signal ideal for biosensing.
   - Confinement loss: Exhibits moderate confinement loss, balancing sensitivity with signal stability.
   - Simulation results: FEM and FDTD methods confirm strong and stable SPR responses, making gold-coated PCFs suitable for high-sensitivity detection [7].
2. Silver (Ag)
   - Advantages: Silver offers stronger plasmonic responses than gold, leading to higher sensitivity and sharper resonance peaks in the visible spectrum.
   - Confinement Loss: Higher confinement loss compared gold; prone to oxidation, which affects reliability.
   - Simulation results: FEM simulations show higher sensitivity, though protective layers are needed to prevent oxidation.
3. Bronze(Cu-Sn Alloy)
   - Advantages: Bronze alloys can be tailored for specific plasmonic responses based on composition.

- Confinement loss: Generally higher than gold but can be optimized depending on the alloy composition.
- Simulation results: Limited studies suggest potential for reliable SPR responses with further research needed.
4. Tungsten (W)
   - Advantages: Provides SPR responses in the mid- infrared range and is highly durable and oxidation- resistant.
   - Confinement loss: Higher confinement loss compared to gold and silver; suitable for robust mid- infrared applications.
   - Simulation results: FEM and FDTD simulations show good sensitivity for mid-infrared applications, but less effective in the visible spectrum.

BLOCK DIAGRAM

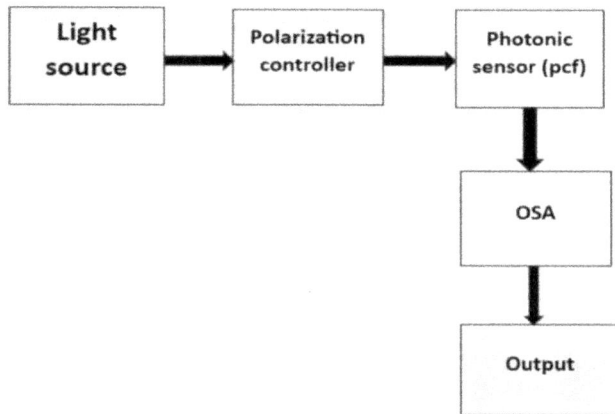

Comparative Analysis

Conclusion

Based on confinement loss, silver is generally considered the best material for PCF SPR-based biosensors among gold, silver, tungsten, and bronze.

1. Silver (Ag):
   - Low confinement loss: Silver exhibits the lowest confinement loss among the materials listed due to its superior plasmonic properties. It supports sharper and stronger plasmon resonance, which translates to lower losses and higher sensitivity.
   - Efficient light confinement: Silver's ability to confine light efficiently leads to enhanced SPR signals, making it the preferred material when minimizing confinement loss is critical.
2. Gold (Au):
   - Moderate confinement loss: Gold has a higher confinement loss compared to silver due to its slightly weaker plasmonic properties. However, it still offers a good balance between loss and stability, making it a common choice despite the higher loss.
3. Tungsten (W):
   - Higher confinement loss: Tungsten typically has higher confinement loss compared to gold and silver, making it less effective for applications requiring low loss and high sensitivity.
4. Bronze:
   - Highest confinement loss: Bronze has the poorest plasmonic properties among the materials listed, leading to the highest confinement loss. This makes it the least suitable for SPR-based biosensors.

Table 69.2 Comparison table of the results

S.No	SPR material	Minimum confinem ent loss (DB/CM)	Maximum confinem ent loss (DB/CM)
1	Gold (lam=0.6)	2.1479	2.21E+05
2	Gold (lam=0.7)	1.7231	1.22E+06
3	Gold (lam=0.8)	3.3396	2.13E+05
4	Silver (lam=0.6)	0.37298	1.41E+06
5	Silver (lam=0.7)	1.3623	1.16E+06
6	Silver (lam=0.8)	5.3677	9.08E+05
7	Bronze(lam=0.6)	2.9265	2.43E+05

S.No	SPR material	Minimum confinem ent loss (DB/CM)	Maximum confinem ent loss (DB/CM)
8	Bronze (lam=0.7)	1.7584	1.31E+06
9	Bronze: (lam=0.8)	3.7667	9.11E+05
10	Tungsten (lam=0.6)	0.73481	1.02E+06
11	Tungsten (lam=0.7)	9.3109	7.00E+0S
12	Tungsten (lam=0.8)	34.99	5.82E+05

Source: Author

Advantages

Here's a summary of the advantages of using silver, bronze, and tungsten as sensing layers in PCF SPR-based biosensors, compared to gold:

1. Silver (Ag):
   - Higher sensitivity: Silver provides a stronger plasmonic response and sharper SPR resonance peaks than gold, leading to higher sensitivity and improved detection limits.
   - Enhanced SPR signal: Silver's superior plasmonic properties result in a more intense SPR signal, which can enhance the signal-to-noise ratio and provide more accurate measurements.
   - Effective in visible spectrum: Silver is particularly effective in the visible wavelength range, making it suitable for applications that require high sensitivity in this spectrum.
2. Bronze (Cu-Sn Alloy):
   - Customizable plasmonic properties: Bronze alloys can be tailored by adjusting the tin content to achieve specific plasmonic responses, offering versatility for different sensing needs.
   - Cost-effective: Bronze can be more affordable compared to precious metals like gold and silver, making it a cost-effective option for various applications without significantly compromising performance.
   - Potential for Unique SPR characteristics: The composition of bronze allows for optimization of SPR properties, which can be advantageous for specialized biosensing applications.

3. Tungsten (W):
   - Mid-Infrared detection: Tungsten provides effective SPR responses in the mid-infrared range, which is beneficial for applications requiring detection in this wavelength range, such as certain biomedical and environmental sensing applications.
   - Durability and stability: Tungsten is highly durable and resistant to oxidation, which improves the sensor's longevity and performance in challenging environments.
   - Robustness: Tungsten's robustness makes it suitable for applications where physical durability and resistance to harsh conditions are critical, offering a reliable alternative for long- term use.

Applications

1. Silver (Ag):
   - Medical diagnostics: Silver's high sensitivity makes it ideal for detecting low concentrations of biomolecules or pathogens, improving diagnostic accuracy in medical testing.
   - Environmental monitoring: Silver's effectiveness in the visible spectrum is useful for detecting contaminants or pollutants in water and air.
   - Food safety: Enhanced sensitivity helps in identifying trace levels of contaminants or pathogens in food products, ensuring safety and quality.
2. Bronze (Cu-Sn Alloy):
   - Affordable biosensing: Bronze's cost- effectiveness allows for the development

of budget-friendly biosensors for applications in educational settings or for widespread use in resource-limited environments.

- Customized applications: By adjusting the tin content, bronze can be tailored for specific detection needs, such as detecting specific chemicals or biological agents in industrial or research applications.
- Industrial process monitoring: Cost-effective and customizable SPR sensors can be used for monitoring various chemical processes and quality control in manufacturing.

3. Tungsten (W):
- Mid-infrared sensing: Tungsten's effectiveness in the mid-infrared range makes it suitable for applications that require detection in this wavelength range, such as biomedical imaging and analysis of complex biological tissues.
- Harsh environment monitoring: Tungsten's durability and resistance to oxidation are beneficial for sensors used in extreme environments, such as high-temperature or corrosive conditions.
- Advanced materials research: In materials science, tungsten-coated PCFs can be used for studying and developing new materials with specific optical properties in the mid-infrared range.

References

[1] Kharel, P., and Goswami, M. AI algorithm for mode classification of PCF – SPR sensor design. Divyadrishti Laboratory, Department of Physics, IIT Roorkee, Roorkee, India Department of Physics, IIT Roorkee, India #mayank.goswami@ph.iitr.ac.in.

[2] Li, L., Huang, T., Zhao, X., Wu, X., and Cheng, Z. (2018). Highly sensitive SPR sensor based on hybrid coupling between plasmon and photonic mode. *IEEE Photonics Technology Letters*, 30(15), 1364–1367. Doi: 10.1109/LPT.2018.2847907.

[3] Jabin, M. A., Ahmed, K., Rana, M. J., Paul, B. K., Islam, M., Vigneswaran, D., et al. (2019). Surface plasmon resonance based titanium coated biosensor for cancer cell detection. *IEEE Photonics Journal*, 11(4), 1–10. Doi: 10.1109/JPHOT.2019.2924825.

[4] Kaur, V., and Singh, S. (2019). Design of titanium nitride coated PCF-SPR sensor for liquid sensing applications. *Optical Fiber Technology*, 48, 159–164.

[5] Singh, Y., Paswan, M. K., and Raghuvanshi, S. K. (2021). Sensitivity enhancement of SPR sensor with the black phosphorus and graphene with Bi-layer of gold for chemical sensing. *Plasmonic*, 1–10.

[6] Homola, J. (2008). Surface plasmon resonance sensors for detection of chemical and biological species. *Chemical Reviews*, 108(2), 462–493.

[7] Nooke, A., Beck, U., Hertwig, A., Krause, A., Krüger, H., Lohse, V., et al. (2010). On the application of gold based SPR sensors for the detection of hazardous gases. *Sensors and Actuators B Chemical*, 149(1), 194–198.

[8] Li, L., Liang, Y., Guang, J., Cui, W., Zhang, X., Masson, J. F., et al. (2017). Dual kretschmann and otto configuration fiber surface plasmon resonance biosensor. *Optics Express*, 25(22), 26950–26957. Doi: 10.1364/OE.25.026950.

[9] Yue Zhang, Na Li, Yangjun Xiang, Debo Wang, Peng Zhang, Yanyan Wang, Shan Lu, Rongqing Xu, Jiang Zhao, A flexible non-enzymatic glucose sensor based on copper nanoparticles anchored on lainduced graphene, Carbon, Volume 156, 2020.

[10] Liedberg, B., Nylander, C., and Lundstrom, I. (1983). Surface plasmon resonance for gas detection and biosensing. *Sensors and Actuators*, 4, 299–304.

70 Predicting energy consumption for smart buildings in a smart grid scenario using machine learning models

Sheri Ruthvikar Reddy[1,a], Tirumalaraju Sri Manoj Kumar[1,b], Yadam Srujan Kumar[1,c], Krishna Pavan Inala[1,d] and Nilotpal Chakraborty[2,e]

[1]Department of Electronics and Communication Engineering, B V Raju Institute of Technology, Narsapur, India

[2]Department of Computer Science and Engineering, Indian Institute of Information Technology, Guwahati, Assam, India

Abstract

Forecasting the consumption of energy in smart buildings within a smart grid scenario is crucial for optimizing energy use, reducing costs, and enhancing grid stability. Existing literature emphasizes the importance of accurate forecasting models, as energy consumption is determined by a variety of features like weather, occupancy, and appliance usage patterns. Traditional linear models often fail to capture the nonlinear interactions in this data, leading to a shift towards more advanced machine learning approaches. Recent studies have shown that ensemble methods like random forests (RF) and decision trees (DT) outperform simpler models in predicting complex energy patterns. These advancements are key to improving energy management in smart grids.

Keywords: Load prediction, machine learning, smart buildings, smart grid

Introduction

Smart grids (SG) have gained popularity as a modern solution to match the world's rising power requirements. These advanced grids enable two-way communication between utilities and consumers, incorporating sensing functions to prevent and address abnormal energy usage [1]. Key components of SG include sophisticated controls, computers, automation technologies, and renewable energy resources, all working together in a flexible and efficient energy system [2]. Buildings account for 40% of end-user energy consumption, so managing their energy use is crucial for reducing overall energy costs and improving efficiency [3–5]. SG, which facilitate the bi-directional flow of power and data between the data centers and end users, have emerged as a key solution for more accurate and effective energy resource management [6].

Smart buildings, integrated with SG, can dynamically manage their energy needs by using battery storage to charge or discharge power, a process enabled by smart meters. This capability is further enhanced when multiple smart buildings operate within a network as multi-agent systems, coordinating energy use and distribution [7–10]. Efficient energy management system (EMS) operation is central to SG, as it regulates power flow across the grid to minimize costs while improving quality. With rising demand for environmentally-friendly energy in business operations and buildings consuming 40% of global energy, optimizing energy use in buildings is crucial for reducing operational costs and mitigating the environmental impact of energy production and consumption [10–13]. The advent of SG has significantly advanced energy management by enabling bi-directional flows of energy and information between utility providers and users, allowing for real-time adjustments and more efficient distribution [14]. With the emergence of smart buildings, dynamic energy management is further enhanced through

[a]22211a04m9@bvrit.ac.in, [b]22211a04p5@bvrit.ac.in, [c]22211a04q7@bvrit.ac.in, [d]dr.kpinala@gmail.com, [e]nilotpal@iiitg.ac.in

DOI: 10.1201/9781003616399-70

key components like energy meters and batteries, which charge, or discharge energy based on current data and demand, leading to more effective energy management in buildings [15–17].

Smart buildings dynamically collaborate with the SG to optimize energy distribution and reduce consumption [18]. Leveraging advanced energy management technologies enabled by real-time data, SG will significantly enhance the sustainability of the energy ecosystem, reducing both operational costs and the environmental impact of energy use [19].

The integration of SG and smart buildings represents a significant leap forward in energy management [20]. By enabling real-time, bi-directional communication between utility providers and consumers, these technologies allow for dynamic energy distribution, optimized usage, and enhanced sustainability [21]. Smart buildings, equipped with advanced tools like smart meters and battery energy storage systems, further contribute to this efficiency by managing energy based on real-time demand. This not only reduces operational costs but also mitigates the environmental impact of energy consumption, underscoring the critical role of these innovations in shaping a more sustainable energy future [22].

Machine Learning Models for Load Prediction

Machine learning algorithms for load prediction are explained below and procedure is explained using flow chart as shown in Figure 70.1.

Linear regression

Linear regression is a widely used method for predicting load in smart grids, utilizing smart meter data [22]. It involves creating separate forecast models at the building level and aggregating these predictions to estimate total grid demand. Studies have applied linear regression in smart buildings, including multiple linear regression and time series models, demonstrating its effectiveness. The accuracy of these models can be enhanced by incorporating relevant variables such as weather data and historical load patterns [23].

Support vector machine (SVM)

SVMs are effective for load prediction in smart buildings within smart grids, capable of modeling

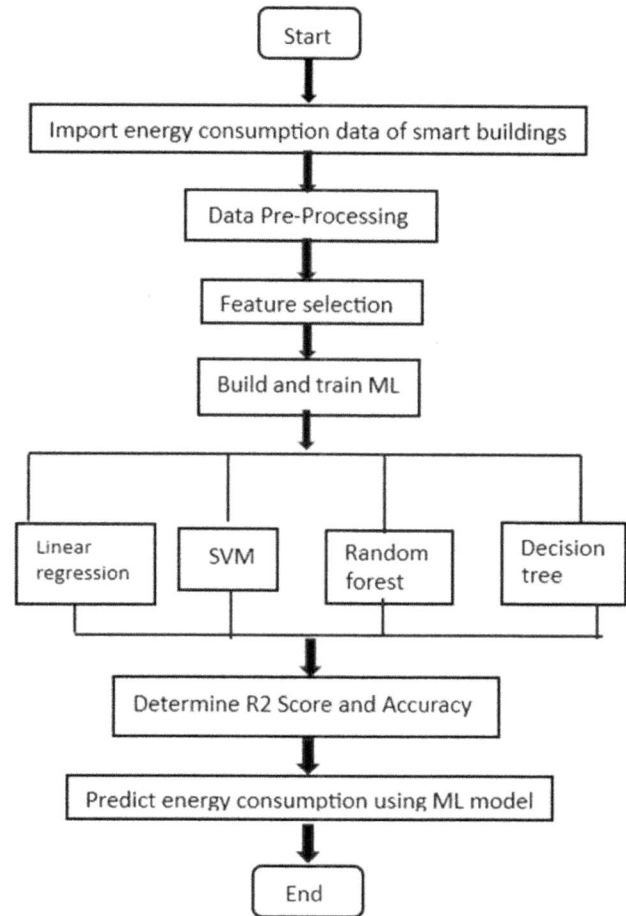

Figure 70.1 Flow chart for load forecasting in smart buildings using ML models
Source: Author

both linear and non-linear relationships in energy consumption data. SVM fits well for short-term and long-term electricity load prediction by leveraging historical consumption patterns and factors like weather and occupancy. Recent studies demonstrate that SVM can achieve high accuracy in load forecasting through feature selection and parameter optimization techniques [24].

Random forest regression

Random forest (RF) regression effectively handles complex energy consumption data by aggregating predictions from multiple decision trees. Studies highlight RF's high accuracy through feature selection and parameter optimization, with hybrid models further enhancing prediction performance across various building types. A study by Dudek [25] optimized RF by representing data and training in a focused manner for energy prediction. The scalability of RF makes it ideal for bottom-up approaches, where individual building forecasts are aggregated to estimate total grid demand.

Decision tree regression

DT regression is capable of modeling complex energy consumption patterns by recursively partitioning the input space and fitting simple models within each partition. Studies show that DT achieves high accuracy in load forecasting through feature selection and parameter optimization. DT's scalability makes it well-suited for bottom-up approaches, where individual building forecasts are aggregated to estimate total grid demand [26].

Results and Discussions

From Table 70.1, it is clear that using linear regression, the low R^2 score (0.294637) and accuracy (29.46%) indicate that the model doesn't capture the complexity of the data well, possibly because energy consumption in smart buildings is determined by various nonlinear terms such as occupancy, climate, and appliance usage, which a linear model can't fully represent. The actual vs predicted load using linear regression model is shown in Figure 70.2.

SVM regression tries to determine best hyperplane, but it may struggle with complex, noisy, or highly nonlinear data. The low R^2 score (0.217211) and accuracy suggest that SVM(21.7211%) may not be well-suited for this particular task, possibly because it is not

capturing the intricate relationships between features that drive energy consumption in smart buildings. The actual vs predicted load for SVM model is shown in Figure 70.3.

The high R^2 score (0.9591067) and accuracy (95.9106%) suggests that using random forest regression model captures the complex relationships in the data very well, likely due to its ability to model nonlinear interactions between features. This makes it highly effective for predicting energy consumption, where various factors interact in complex ways. The Actual vs predicted load for SVM model is shown in Figure 70.4.

Decision trees regression also performs well, with a high R^2 score (0.888241) and accuracy (88.8241%). This model is good at capturing nonlinear relationships but may lead to overfitting sometimes. The slightly lower performance compared to random forests indicates that while decision trees capture most of the important

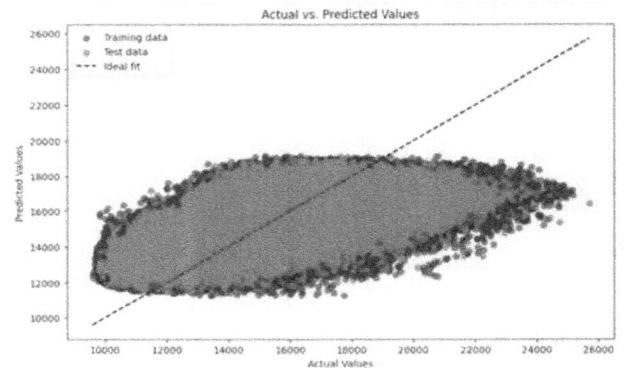

Figure 70.2 Actual vs predicted load using linear regression model
Source: Author

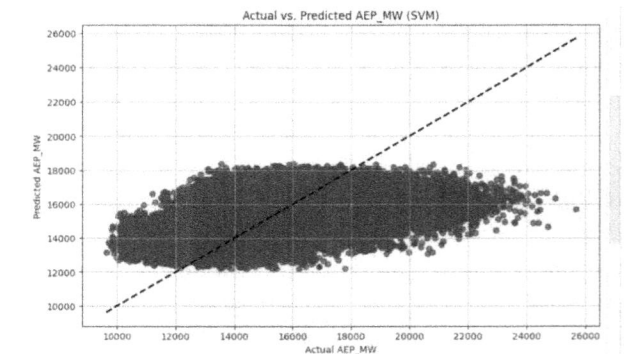

Figure 70.3 Actual vs predicted load for SVM model
Source: Author

Table 70.1 R^2 score of different algorithms

S. No	Algorithm	R^2 score	Accuracy
1	Linear regression	0.294637	29.46%
2	Random forest regression	0.9591067	95.9106%
3	Decision trees regression	0.888241	88.8241%
4	SVM	0.217211	21.7211%

Source: Author

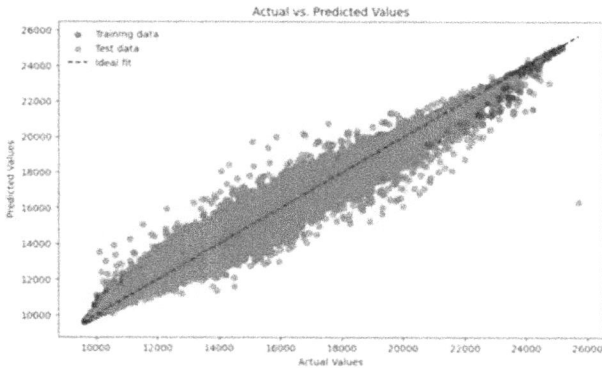

Figure 70.4 Actual vs predicted load using random forest regression
Source: Author

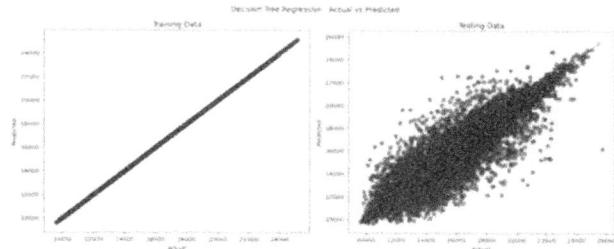

Figure 70.5 Shows the actual v/s predicted for decision tree
Source: Author

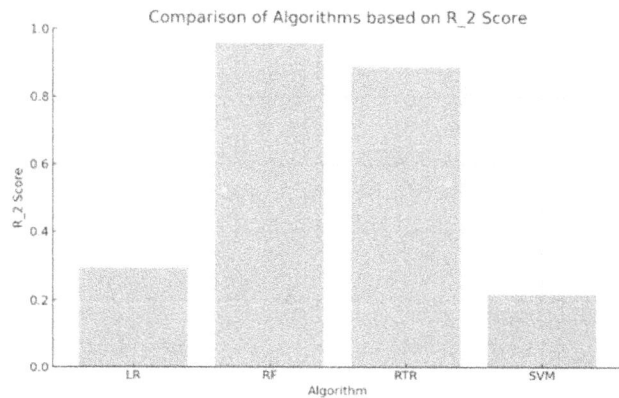

Figure 70.6 Comparison of R2 score for load prediction using different machine learning models
Source: Author

patterns, the ensemble approach in random forests adds robustness and generalization ability. The actual vs predicted load for SVM model is shown in Figure 70.5.

From the above results, it is clear that RF regression is the most effective, achieving the highest R² score of 0.9591 and an accuracy of 95.91%, indicating it captures the complex, nonlinear relationships in the data very well. DT regression also performs strongly with an R² score of 0.8882, though slightly less robust than the random forest approach. In contrast, linear regression and SVM regression exhibit poor performance, with low R² scores and accuracies as shown in Figure 70.6, suggesting they are not well-suited for this task due to their inability to effectively model the complex factors influencing energy consumption. The dataset in [27] which gives hourly energy consumption in United States is considered in this research.

Conclusion

The results of this study demonstrate that random forest regression is effective for predicting energy use at smart buildings within a smart grid (SG) framework. The findings suggest that methods such as random forest (RF) offer strong and precise forecasts which are important for effective energy management. Future research work would focus on the incorporation of more sophisticated techniques including deep learning with the aim of boosting accuracy further.

References

[1] Hernandez, L., Baladron, C., Aguiar, J. M., Carro, B., Sanchez-Esguevillas, A. J., Lloret, J., et al. (2014). A survey on electric power demand forecasting: future trends in smart grids, microgrids and smart buildings. *IEEE Communications Surveys and Tutorials*, 16(3), 1460–1495.

[2] Rahman, A., Srikumar, V., and Smith, A. D. (2018). Predicting electricity consumption for commercial and residential buildings using deep recurrent neural networks. *Applied energy*, 212, 372–385.

[3] Venayagamoorthy, G. K. (2011). Dynamic, stochastic, computational, and scalable technologies for smart grids. *IEEE Computational Intelligence Magazine*, 6(3), 22–35.

[4] Alquthami, T., Zulfiqar, M., Kamran, M., Milyani, A. H., and Rasheed, M. B. (2022). A performance comparison of machine learning algorithms for load forecasting in smart grid. *IEEE Access*, 10, 48419–48433.

[5] Raza, M. Q., and Khosravi, A. (2015). A review on artificial intelligence based load demand fore-

casting techniques for smart grid and buildings. *Renewable and Sustainable Energy Reviews*, 50, 1352–1372.

[6] Habbak, H., Mahmoud, M., Metwally, K., Fouda, M. M., and Ibrahem, M. I. (2023). Load forecasting techniques and their applications in smart grids. *Energies*, 16(3), 1480.

[7] Wang, J., Song, Y., Liu, F., and Hou, R. (2016). Analysis and application of forecasting models in wind power integration: a review of multistep-ahead wind speed forecasting models. *Renewable and Sustainable Energy Reviews*, 60, 960–981.

[8] Wang, S., Wang, X., Wang, S., and Wang, D. (2019). Bi-directional long short-term memory method based on attention mechanism and rolling update for short-term load forecasting. *International Journal of Electrical Power and Energy Systems*, 109, 470–479.

[9] Shihabudheen, K. and Sheik Mohammed, S. (2022). Review and Analysis of Machine Learning Based Techniques for Load Forecasting in Smart Grid System. In Hybrid Intelligent Approaches for Smart Energy (eds A. John, S.K. Mohan, S. Padmanaban and Y. Hamid). https://doi.org/10.1002/9781119821878.ch1

[10] Alquthami, T., Zulfiqar, M., Kamran, M., Milyani, A. H., and Rasheed, M. B. (2022). A performance comparison of machine learning algorithms for load forecasting in smart grid. *IEEE Access*, 10, 48419–48433.

[11] Aurangzeb, K. (2019). Short term power load forecasting using machine learning models for energy management in a smart community. In 2019 International Conference on Computer and Information Sciences (ICCIS), (pp. 1–6). IEEE.

[12] Rai, S., and De, M. (2021). Analysis of classical and machine learning based short-term and mid-term load forecasting for smart grid. *International Journal of Sustainable Energy*, 40(9), 821–839.

[13] Ungureanu, S., Topa, V., and Cziker, A. (2019). Industrial load forecasting using machine learning in the context of smart grid. In 2019 54th International Universities Power Engineering Conference (UPEC), (pp. 1–6). IEEE.

[14] Kim, B., and Lavrova, O. (2013). Optimal power flow and energy-sharing among multi-agent smart buildings in the smart grid. In 2013 IEEE Energytech, (pp. 1–5). IEEE.

[15] Alquthami, T., Zulfiqar, M., Kamran, M., Milyani, A. H., and Rasheed, M. B. (2022). A performance comparison of machine learning algorithms for load forecasting in smart grid. *IEEE Access*, 10, 48419–48433.

[16] Liu, D., Yang, Q., and Yang, F. (2020). Predicting building energy consumption by time series model based on machine learning and empirical mode decomposition. In 2020 5th IEEE International Conference on Big Data Analytics (ICBDA), (pp. 145–150). IEEE.

[17] Chou, J. S., and Tran, D. S. (2018). Forecasting energy consumption time series using machine learning techniques based on usage patterns of residential householders. *Energy*, 165, 709–726.

[18] Gonzalez-Briones, A., Hernandez, G., Corchado, J. M., Omatu, S., and Mohamad, M. S. (2019). Machine learning models for electricity consumption forecasting: a review. In 2019 2nd International Conference on Computer Applications and Information Security (ICCAIS), (pp. 1–6). IEEE.

[19] Dong, X., Deng, S., and Wang, D. (2022). A short-term power load forecasting method based on k-means and SVM. *Journal of Ambient Intelligence and Humanized Computing*, 13(11), 5253–5267.

[20] Zhang, L., Wen, J., Li, Y., Chen, J., Ye, Y., Fu, Y., et al. (2021). A review of machine learning in building load prediction. *Applied Energy*, 285, 116452.

[21] Yadav, P. K., Bhasker, R., Stonier, A. A., Peter, G., Vijayakumar, A., and Ganji, V. (2023). Machine learning based load prediction in smartgrid under different contract scenario. *IET Generation, Transmission and Distribution*, 17(8), 1918–1931.

[22] Anand, H., Nateghi, R., and Alemazkoor, N. (2023). Bottom-up forecasting: applications and limitations in load forecasting using smart-meter data. *Data-Centric Engineering*, 4, e14.

[23] Dewangan, F., Abdelaziz, A. Y., and Biswal, M. (2023). Load forecasting models in smart grid using smart meter information: a review. *Energies*, 16(3), 1404.

[24] Zhang, S., Liu, J., and Wang, J. (2023). High-resolution load forecasting on multiple time scales using long short-term memory and support vector machine. *Energies*, 16(4), 1806.

[25] Dudek, G. (2022). A comprehensive study of random forest for short-term load forecasting. *Energies*, 15(20), 7547.

[26] Koukaras, P., Mustapha, A., Mystakidis, A., and Tjortjis, C. (2024). Optimizing building short-term load forecasting: a comparative analysis of machine learning models. *Energies*, 17(6), 1450.

[27] https://www.kaggle.com/datasets/robikscube/hourly-energy-consumption .

71 A novel machine learning and deep learning feature for identification of cardiac arrhythmia from ECG – images

Bhagya Sree, G. V. N.[a] and Durga Prasad, Y.[b]

Department of Computer Science and Engineering, Aditya College of Engineering and Technology, Surampalem, Andhra Pradesh, India

Abstract

Early forecast is essential since cardiac arrhythmia problems, especially heart issues, are a main source of death around the world. By following cardiac arrhythmia movement, the painless, minimal expense electrocardiogram (ECG) aids the determination of different circumstances. Four significant cardiac arrhythmia peculiarities are distinguished utilizing deep learning procedures: strange heartbeat, myocardial dead tissue, history of myocardial localized necrosis, and typical occurrences. This further develops prediction accuracy. The undertaking mixes a modified convolutional neural network (CNN) engineering with transfer gaining from profound brain organizations like Squeeze Net and Alex Net. By extricating critical elements, this strategy can be joined with ordinary machine learning methods to improve expectations. The recommended model is novel in that it performs uncommonly well, significantly working on the capacity to conjecture ailments from photographs. It underscores how significant man-made brain power is to changing medical care methods. Utilizing ECG pictures, the coordinated Xception model further develops include extraction for the recognizable proof of heart irregularities. Machine learning (ML) models utilize removed qualities as information sources, which works on the models' ability to recognize complex examples and anomalies. The joining of complex component extraction strategies with strong ML calculations improves the undertaker's ability to convey exact clinical diagnostics. The framework's common sense is featured by the smoothed-out client corporations made conceivable by Flask with SQLite. It gives safe information exchange, sign in, and powerful testing for better medical services methodology. Found that the Xception transfer learning model yielded 100% recall, accuracy, precision, and F1-score.

Keywords: Cardiac arrhythmia, deep learning, electrocardiogram (ECG) images, feature extraction, machine learning, transfer learning

Introduction

As indicated by the World Health Organization, cardiac arrhythmia issues (heart diseases) are the main source of death universally. Consistently, they kill an expected 17.9 million individuals, making up around 32% of worldwide mortality. Heart attacks, or myocardial infarctions (MI), represent around 85% of all cardiac arrhythmia illness passings [1]. Many lives can be saved assuming that cardiac arrhythmia sickness is appropriately analyzed at the beginning phase [1]. The medical services framework utilizes various methods [15] to analyze cardiac arrhythmia illness, including electrocardiogram (ECG), echocardiogram (echo), cardiac arrhythmia attractive reverberation imaging, figured tomography, blood tests, etc [2,3]. The ECG is a typical, minimal expense, and painless technique for deciding the electrical action of the heart [4]. It is used to identify heart-related cardiac arrhythmia problems [4,5]. Cardiac arrhythmia illness can be distinguished by an exceptionally experienced clinician utilizing ECG waves. Be that as it may, this manual method can create wrong discoveries and is tedious [5].

In particular, the utilization of machine learning and deep learning procedures for independent expectation of heart issues [3, 6–10]. ML approaches require the utilization of a specialist element for highlight extraction and choice to

[a]bhagyasree2702@gmail.com, [b]durgaprasad12@gmail.com

DOI: 10.1201/9781003616399-71

find the reasonable elements before the order stage. Highlight extraction is the most common way of bringing down the quantity of elements in an information assortment by changing or extending the information into a new, lower-layered include space while holding the significant data from the information [11,12].

The thought of element extraction is engaged with building another arrangement of highlights (not the same as the information highlight) that joins the first highlights into a lower-layered space and concentrate the larger part, while perhaps not all, of the data in the information. Head part examination is the most generally utilized include extraction approach [13,14]. In any case, highlight determination is the demonstration of erasing unimportant and excess elements (aspects) from an information assortment during the preparation of ML calculations. There are two kinds of component determination techniques: unsupervised, which don't need a result name, and managed, which do. There are three different ways for supervised feature selection: filter, wrapper, and embedding [11,12].

We thought about ML strategies (DT, NB, K-NN, and NN) on the UCI Cleveland heart disease dataset. They inferred that DT had the most elevated precision (89%). Dissanayake and Md Johar [16] researched the effect of the element determination technique on ML classifiers for anticipating heart disease utilizing the UCI Cleveland heart disease data.

Literature Survey

Cardiac arrhythmia diseases (CAD) are normal and lethal. A new examination found that weight, cholesterol, hypertension, and tobacco use are expanding mortality. Because of these conditions, the condition is declining. Concentrating on these elements and their consequences for CAD is essential. Current techniques are expected to identify the early infection and lessen mortality [3]. Artificial intelligence and data mining offer tremendous exploration potential to gauge CAD convent and uncover standards of conduct in huge informational indexes. These figures will help clinicians in navigation and early determination, diminishing patient mortality [6,8,24,28]. This examination looks at and reports cardiac

arrhythmia disease prediction models using classification, data mining, machine learning, and deep learning [17]. The review has three sections: CAD, machine learning classification, and data mining.

This overview incorporates reports exactness estimations, expectation and characterization datasets, and apparatus for every class. ECG is the P-QRS-T wave showing heart action. Patient disease is shown by unassuming adjustments in electric possible examples of repolarization and depolarization. These clinical time space ECG attributes can analyze heart wellbeing. Commotion and moment morphological boundary values make it hard to perceive ECG classes by sight [5]. This study examines CACD frameworks, examination strategies, impediments, and cardiac arrhythmia illness screening's future. Time space, recurrence change area, and time-recurrence space examination strategies like the wavelet change can't precisely reflect fundamental separating characteristics [6,9,10,23]. Nonlinear methodologies that catch little ECG signal vacillations and increment precision in commotion tend to be long in this paper. A CACD framework utilizing these nonlinear properties can assist clinicians with diagnosing CAD all the more precisely.

Heart disease (HD) kills the vast majority around the world. Early and precise infection identification will save incalculable lives. Clinical trials, ECG signals, heart sounds, and CT pictures can uncover HD [6,9]. Of all HD identification strategies, ECG signals are vital. This article utilizes subject ECG tests as HD recognition model sources of info. Many articles have suggested ML and DL models for HD arrangement. Lopsided HD information decreases detection accuracy.

This work recognized possible DL and ML models and developed and assessed order models to further develop HD identification [6]. The generative adversarial network (GAN) model is utilized to find imbalanced information by creating and taking advantage of phony information. This paper fosters a gathering model utilizing LSTM and GAN that beats the singular DL model [9]. The recommended GAN-LSTM model has the most elevated precision, F1-score, and AUC of 0.992, 0.987, and 0.984 in customary MIT-BIH recreations. The GAN-LSTM model outperforms any remaining models on PTB-ECG dataset with accuracy, F1-score, and AUC of 0.994, 0.993, and 0.995. From the five models tried, the GAN model performs best while the NB model has the least location potential. Pick any remaining outfit models and utilize other datasets to analyze execution in later examinations. The best discovery approach can be utilized for different infections and medical services issues.

During an ordinary sinus beat, following supervised AI algorithms can distinguish left ventricular brokenness, round about atrial fibrillation, and other underlying and valvular illnesses. The survey [7] talks about the numerical foundation of these calculations. Huge informational indexes can be utilized to recognize non-heart problems like coronavirus without grasping the organic instrument, however information security issues emerge [6,10]. AI ECGs should be tried in clinical settings like any clinical assessments. Artificial intelligence might offer immense versatility to democratize medical services with portable structure factors that permit cell phones and wearables to procure clinical grade ECGs.

ECGs are utilized to analyze heart arrhythmias in clinical practice. This review [8] utilizes a DL engineering prepared on a general picture informational index to consequently analyze ECG arrhythmia by ordering patient ECGs into cardiac arrhythmia problems. Transferred deep convolutional neural network (Alex Net) separates highlights, which are taken care of into a basic back engendering brain network for characterization. The proposed engineering is tried utilizing three ECG waveform conditions from the MIT-BIH arrhythmia information base. This work centers around grouping three heart sicknesses utilizing a basic, solid, and essentially versatile DL procedure. Results showed deep learning classification transfer.

This work centers around grouping three heart sicknesses utilizing a straightforward, dependable, and basically versatile DL method. Results showed elite execution rates for the moved DL highlight extractor flowed with a norm back propagation neural network. The most noteworthy acknowledgment rate is 98.51% and it is 92% to test accuracy. In light of these outcomes, transferred deep learning was a powerful programmed

cardiac arrhythmia location strategy that killed the need to prepare a deep convolutional neural network.

Methodology

Proposed work

The proposed model includes picture handling and model development. Image data generator gets ready information for rescaling, shear change, zooming, flipping, and reshaping during picture handling. Deep learning models like Press Net, Alex Net, and CNN separate elements for the model structure stage, and exemplary machine learning algorithms like random forest, SVM, KNN, decision tree, and Naive Bayes evaluate them. This total strategy vows to estimate cardiac arrhythmia ailment precisely and dependably, helping medical services applications. ECG highlight extraction for cardiac arrhythmia anomaly finding improves with the coordinated Xception model. Extricated highlights assist with machining learning calculations to distinguish complex examples and irregularities. High level component extraction and strong ML strategies assist the task with diagnosing precisely. Cup with SQLite works on client collaborations for safe information exchange, sign in, and speedy testing to further develop medical care methodology.

System architecture

Patients' ECG pictures are utilized as information for the cycle. These photographs are the establishment for the prediction system. Deep learning models are utilized to extricate highlights from input information. Squeeze Net, Alex Net, CNN and a drawn out Xception model are instances of models that can naturally recognize significant examples and elements in ECG pictures.

ECG picture attributes are recovered and utilized for machine learning classification methods. ML models process separated qualities and produce forecasts or characterizations in light of what they realized during preparing. The last result shows ML arrangements demonstrating the presence or nonappearance of specific cardiac arrhythmia issues [19].

The system architecture as shown in Figure 71.1.

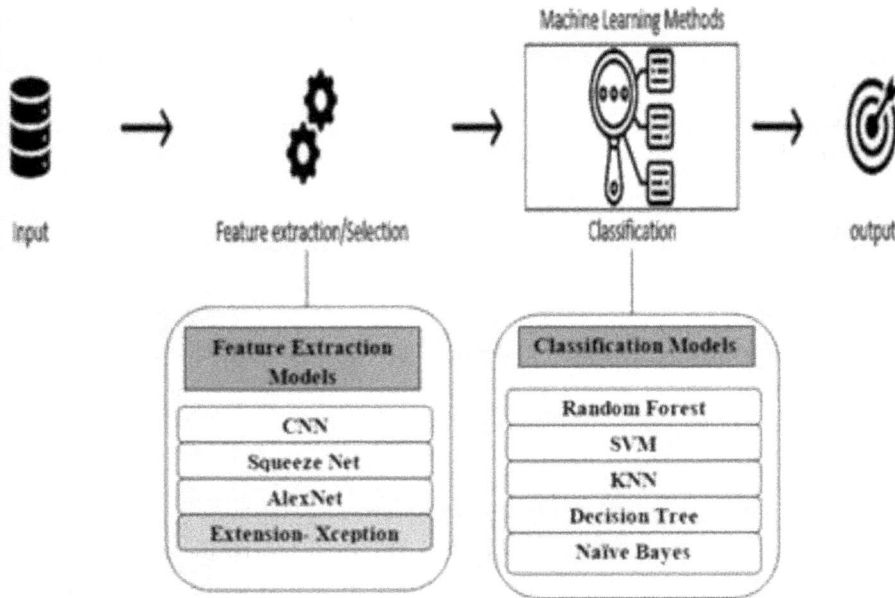

Figure 71.1 System architecture
Source: Author

Dataset collection

Envisioning the heart's electrical action with ECG picture information supports the distinguishing proof of heart issues and powers ML based robotized diagnostics. Visual portrayals of heart electrical movement are found in ECG picture information, which is helpful for study and finding. These photos assume a basic part in the recognition of heart issues and are used in AI to make computerized findings. As found in Figure 71.2, these are sample images.

Image processing

Autonomous driving systems use image processing to distinguish objects at different levels. Enhancing the information picture for examination and adjustment starts with mass item change. Following this, the calculation's objective classifications are determined by characterizing object classes. Bounding boxes are likewise pronounced to demonstrate where things ought to be in the picture. Changing over handled information into a NumPy exhibit fundamental for mathematical calculation and examination.

Stacking a pre-prepared model with huge datasets follows. This incorporates getting to the pre-prepared model's organization layers, which contain learnt elements and boundaries for exact

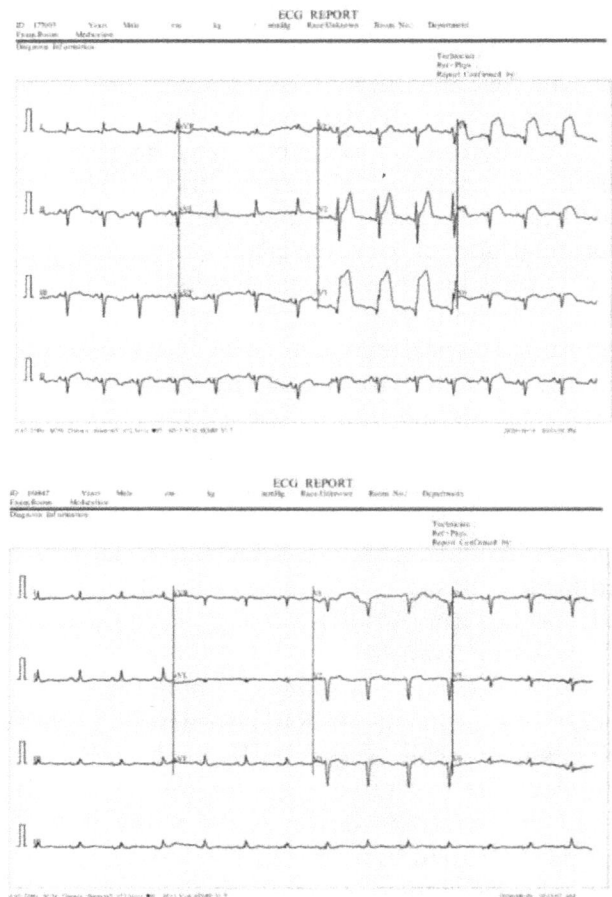

Figure 71.2 ECG image data
Source: Author

article discovery. Extraction of result layers gives last forecasts and helps object acknowledgment and characterization.

Annexing the image and explanation record in the picture handling pipeline guarantees total information for examination. Changing BGR over completely to RGB changes the variety space, and a veil features significant qualities. A last resize streamlines the picture for handling and examination. This total picture handling procedure lays the foundation for heart and exact item acknowledgment in independent driving frameworks' dynamic setting, further developing street wellbeing and direction [19].

Feature extraction

Separating mathematical elements from crude information while keeping its data is called include extraction [12]. It outflanks crude information-based ML.

Manual or automated feature extraction [11]:

- Manual feature extraction includes finding and portraying significant qualities for an issue, and executing an extraction technique. By and large, knowing the background or area could assist with picking valuable highlights. Through many years of exploration, architects and researchers have made picture, sign, and text feature extraction innovations. Signal window means straightforward usefulness.
- Automated feature extraction utilizes calculations or deep networks to separate elements from signs or pictures without human cooperation. This strategy assists you with rapidly developing ML calculations from crude information. Wavelet dispersing robotizes feature extraction [11,12].

The principal layers of deep networks have substituted feature extraction for picture information as DL has developed. For sign and time-series applications, include extraction is the main issue that requests ability prior to building prescient models.

Experimental Results

Precision: Precision estimates the level of accurately sorted examples or cases among the positive examples. Thus, coming up next is the recipe to decide the precision:

$$\text{Precision} = \frac{\text{True positives}}{(\text{True positives} + \text{False positives})}$$

The performance classification of precision is shown in Figure 71.3.

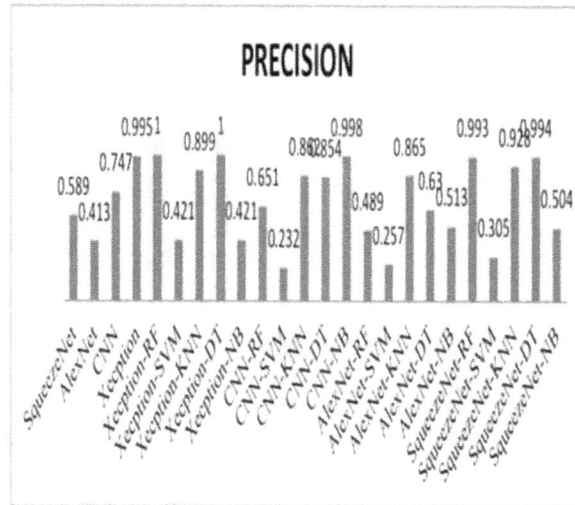

Figure 71.3 Precision comparison graph
Source: Author

Recall: Recall is a machine learning metric that evaluates a model's capacity to perceive all occurrences of a given class. It is the proportion of accurately anticipated positive perceptions to add up to real up-sides, which gives data on a model's culmination in gathering instances of a particular class. Figure 71.4 portrays the exhibition classification of recall.

$$\text{RECALL} = \frac{\text{TP}}{\text{TP} + \text{FN}}$$

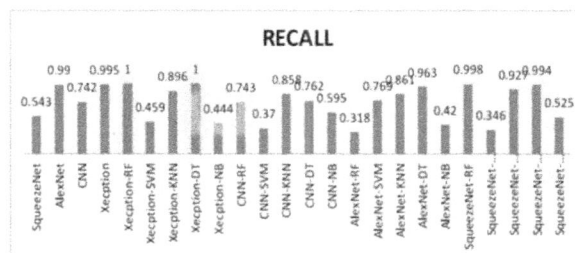

Figure 71.4 Recall comparison graph
Source: Author

Accuracy: Accuracy is characterized as the extent of right forecasts in an order work, which estimates a model's general accuracy. Figure 71.5 portrays the exhibition characterization of accuracy.

$$Accuracy = \frac{TP + TN}{TP + FP + TN + FN}$$

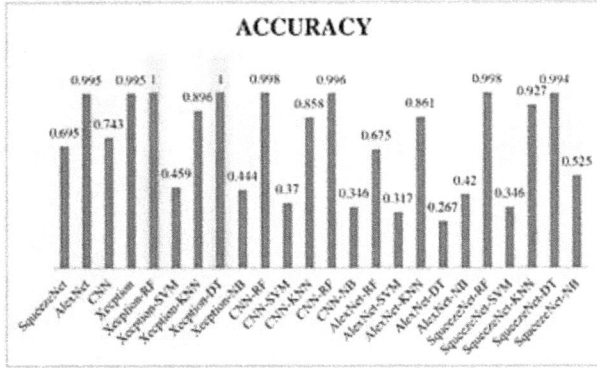

Figure 71.5 Accuracy graph
Source: Author

F1 Score: The F1-score is fitting for imbalanced datasets in light of the fact that it gives a reasonable metric that considers both false positives and false negatives. It is determined as the consonant mean of precision and recall. Figure 71.6 shows the exhibition classification of the F1-score.

$$F1\ Score\ = 2 * \frac{Recall * Precision}{Recall\ + Precision} * 100$$

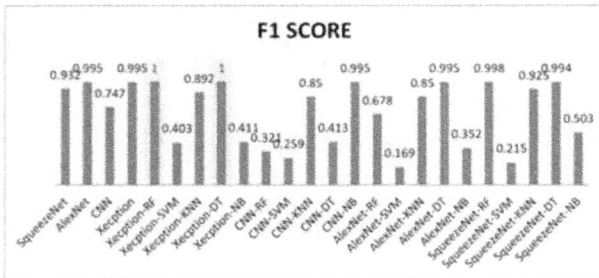

Figure 71.6 F1 score
Source: Author

The most extreme 100 percent accuracy, precision, recall, and F1-score are accomplished by means of the Xception approach. Decision tree calculations yield the best exhibition of 100 percent in ML calculations. Thus, the most ideal methodology that anyone could hope to find is Xception-DT.

Figure 71.7 shows the performance evaluation.

ML Model	Accuracy	Precision	Recall	F1_score
SqueezeNet	0.695	0.589	0.543	0.932
AlexNet	0.995	0.413	0.99	0.995
CNN	0.743	0.747	0.742	0.745
Xception	0.995	0.995	0.995	0.995
Xception-RF	1	1	1	1
Xception-SVM	0.459	0.421	0.459	0.403
Xception-KNN	0.896	0.899	0.896	0.892
Xception-DT	1	1	1	1
Xception-NB	0.444	0.421	0.444	0.411
CNN-RF	0.998	0.651	0.743	0.321
CNN-SVM	0.37	0.232	0.37	0.259
CNN-KNN	0.858	0.862	0.858	0.85
CNN-RF	0.996	0.854	0.762	0.413
CNN-NB	0.346	0.998	0.595	0.995
AlexNet-RF	0.675	0.489	0.318	0.678
AlexNet-SVM	0.317	0.257	0.317	0.169
AlexNet-KNN	0.861	0.865	0.861	0.85
AlexNet-DT	0.267	0.63	0.963	0.995
AlexNet-NB	0.42	0.513	0.42	0.352
SqueezeNet-RF	0.998	0.993	0.998	0.998
SqueezeNet-SVM	0.346	0.305	0.346	0.215
SqueezeNet-KNN	0.927	0.928	0.927	0.925
SqueezeNet-DT	0.994	0.994	0.994	0.994
SqueezeNet-NB	0.525	0.504	0.525	0.503

Figure 71.7 Performance evaluation
Source: Author

Conclusion

Deep learning was utilized to anticipate critical heart issues utilizing ECG pictures [32]. DL can anticipate precisely, as discussed in Squeeze Net and Alex Net's close wonderful arrangement. The augmentation, Xception, anticipated heart issues well. This shows that strong DL models further develop diagnostics past customary strategies. Traditional machine learning didn't function admirably with DL-based feature extraction; however, models did. This shows that DL succeeds at separating complex ECG designs [32, 33]. Jar with SQLite gave a protected and consistent client testing front-end. This is easy to understand and get interface works on model testing and client experience. The fruitful examination features the commitment of AI, especially DL, for early conclusion of cardiac arrhythmia issues. This permits convenient intercessions, further developing medical services results. The examination infers that AI is vital for early disease detection. It advances research in this basic medical services region since further developed advancements change demonstrative abilities and patient results. At long last, Xception model Decision Tree scores 100% accuracy, precision, recall, and F1.

Future Scope

Future review could refine the CNN model's hyperparameters to further develop execution. Deliberately adjusting learning rates, cluster sizes, and dropout rates works on model precision and proficiency. CNN model combination into IIoT offers new potential. The model can be utilized for IIoT order undertakings like modern hardware peculiarity location and assembling quality control notwithstanding cardiac arrhythmia infection expectation. Adding layers or changing organization plans can help execution. Specialists might add convolutional or repetitive layers or concentrate new organization geographies to work on the [31,33,36] CNN model's cardiac arrhythmia illness discovery. The framework can be worked on by supporting bigger and more expanded datasets. To make the model generalizable across different cardiac arrhythmia circumstances and patient qualities, this extension ought to incorporate information from a few sources and populaces.

References

[1] Abubaker, M. B., and Babayigit, B. (2022). Detection of cardiovascular diseases in ECG images using machine learning and deep learning methods. *IEEE Transactions on Artificial Intelligence*, 4(2), 373–382. April 2023. [Online]. Available from: https://doi.org/10.1109/TAI.2022.3159505.

[2] Government of Western Australia, Department of Health (2021). Common medical tests to diagnose heart conditions. Accessed: Dec. 29, 2021. Available from: https://www.healthywa.wa.gov.au/Articles/A_ E/Common-medical-tests-to-diagnose-heart- conditions.

[3] Swathy, M., and Saruladha, K. (2021). A comparative study of classification and prediction of cardio- vascular diseases (CVD) using machine learning and deep learning techniques. *ICT Express*, to be published, 2021. Available from: https://doi.org/10.1016/j.icte.2021.08.021.

[4] Rath, A., Mishra, D., Panda, G., and Satapathy, S. C. (2021). Heart disease detection using deep learning methods from imbalanced ECG samples. *Biomedical Signal Processing and Control*, 68(2021), 102820. [Online]. Available from: https://doi.org/10.1038/s41519-018-0306-1.

[5] Isin, A., and Ozdalili, S. (2017). Cardiac arrhythmia detection using deep learning. *Procedia Computer Science*, 120, 268–275. [Online] Avalible from: https://doi.org/10.1016/j.procs.2017.11.238.

[6] Bleijendaal, H., Ramos, L. A., Lopes, R. R., Verstraelen, T. E., Baalman, S. W., Pool, M. D. O., et al. (2020). Computer versus cardiologist: is a machine learning algorithm able to outperform an expert in diagnosing phospholamban (PLN) p.Arg14delmutation on ECG? *Heart Rhythm*, 18(1), 79–87. [Online] Available from: https://doi.org/10.1016/j.hrthm.2020.08.021.

[7] Aljohani, M. S. (2022). Competency in ECG interpretation and arrhythmias management among critical care nurses in Saudi arabia: a cross sectional study. *Healthcare*, 10, 2576. 10.3390/healthcare10122576. [PMC free article] [PubMed] [CrossRef] [Google Scholar].

[8] Andreotti, F., Carr, O., Pimentel, M. A., Mahdi A., and De Vos, M. (2017). Comparing feature-based classifiers and convolutional neural networks to detect arrhythmia from short segments of ECG. In 2017 Computing in Cardiology (CinC), France, 24-27 September 2017. [Google Scholar].

[9] Antzelevitch, C., and Burashnikov, A. (2011). Overview of basic mechanisms of cardiac arrhythmia. *Cardiac Electrophysiology Clinics,* 3, 23–45. 10.1016/j.ccep.2010.10.012. [PMC free article] [PubMed] [CrossRef] [Google Scholar].

[10] Attia, Z. I., Kapa, S., Lopez-Jimenez, F., McKie, P. M., Ladewig, D. J., Satam, G., et al. (2019). Screening for cardiac contractile dysfunction using an artificial intelligence–enabled electrocardiogram. *Nature Medicine*, 25, 70–74. 10.1038/s41591-018-0240-2. [PubMed] [CrossRef] [Google Scholar].

[11] Chen, C., Hua, Z., Zhang, R., Liu, G., and Wen, W. (2020). Automated arrhythmia classification based on a combination network of CNN and LSTM. *Biomedical Signal Processing and Control*, 57, 101819. 10.1016/j.bspc.2019.101819. [CrossRef] [Google Scholar].

[12] Chu, M., Wu, P., Li, G., Yang, W., Gutiérrez-Chico, J. L., and Tu, S. (2023). Advances in diagnosis, therapy, and prognosis of coronary artery disease powered by deep learning algorithms. *JACC Asia*, 3, 1–14. 10.1016/j.jacasi.2022.12.005. [PMC free article] [PubMed] [CrossRef] [Google Scholar].

[13] Dinakarrao, S. M. P., Jantsch, A., and Shafique, M. (2019). Computer-aided arrhythmia diagnosis with bio-signal processing: a survey of trends and techniques. *ACM Computing Surveys*

(CSUR), 52, 1–37. 10.1145/3297711. [Cross-Ref] [Google Scholar].

[14] Ebrahimi, Z., Loni, M., Daneshtalab, M., and Gharehbaghi, A. (2020). A review on deep learning methods for ECG arrhythmia classification. *Expert Systems with Applications: X*, 7, 100033. 10.1016/j.eswax.2020.100033. [CrossRef] [Google Scholar].

[15] Esteban, C., Staeck, O., Baier, S., Yang, Y., and Tresp, V. (2016). Predicting clinical events by combining static and dynamic information using recurrent neural networks. In 2016 IEEE International Conference on Healthcare Informatics (ICHI) (IEEE), Chicago, 04-07 October 2016, (pp. 93–101). [Google Scholar].

[16] Flores, N., Avitia, R. L., Reyna, M. A., and García, C. (2018). Readily available ECG databases. *Journal of Electrocardiology*, 51, 1095–1097. 10.1016/j.jelectrocard.2018.09.012. [PubMed] [CrossRef] [Google Scholar].

[17] Fu, L., Lu, B., Nie, B., Peng, Z., Liu, H., and Pi, X. (2020). Hybrid network with attention mechanism for detection and location of myocardial infarction based on 12-lead electrocardiogram signals. *Sensors*, 20, 1020. 10.3390/s20041020. [PMC free article] [PubMed] [CrossRef] [Google Scholar].

[18] Hammad, M., Iliyasu, A. M., Subasi, A., Ho, E. S., and Abd El-Latif, A. A. (2020). A multitier deep learning model for arrhythmia detection. *IEEE Transactions on Instrumentation and Measurement*, 70, 1–9. 10.1109/tim.2020.3033072. [CrossRef] [Google Scholar].

[19] Hammad, M., Kandala, R. N., Abdelatey, A., Abdar, M., Zomorodi-Moghadam, M., San Tan, R., et al. (2021). Automated detection of shockable ECG signals: a review. *Information Science*, 571, 580–604. 10.1016/j.ins.2021.05.035. [CrossRef] [Google Scholar].

[20] He, Z., Yuan, S., Zhao, J., Du, B., Yuan, Z., Alhudhaif, A., et al. (2022). A novel myocardial infarction localization method using multibranch densenet and spatial matching-based active semi-supervised learning. *Information Science*, 606, 649–668. 10.1016/j.ins.2022.05.070. [CrossRef] [Google Scholar].

72 Low power single phase clock flip-flop design with redundancy elimination and power gating technique

Anusha Pillemula[1,a], John Alex Edward[2,b] and Niranjan Reddy Kallem[2,c]

[1]Research Scholar, Dept. of ECE, CMRIT, Hyderabad, Telangana, India

[2]Associate professor, Dept. of ECE, CMRIT, Hyderabad, Telangana, India

Abstract

Flip-flops play an essential part in digital systems. This work presents an innovative single-phase clocked flip-flop (SPCFFs) design that eliminates redundancies and operates with low power consumption by incorporating a power gating module (PGM) to tackle significant power consumption issues in digital circuits. By integrating redundancy elimination techniques and power gating mechanisms, the proposed flip-flop architecture achieves remarkable improvements in power efficiency. Careful optimization of the flip-flop structure results in the removal of redundant transistors, thereby reducing dynamic power dissipation without affecting functionality. Furthermore, the Power Gating Module effectively prevents power wastage. SPCFF marks a major advancement in low-power design, offers a solution to the power efficiency challenges in contemporary digital circuits. The proposed flip-flop displays a 12–15% lowering of leakage power and a 11–16% reduction in dynamic power. Overall, the total power consumption is reduced by 17–23% due to the combined decrease in leakage and dynamic power of the flip-flop.

Keywords: Leakage-power, power-efficiency, redundancy, RTSP, single-phase clocked flip-flops

Introduction

As digital electronics continue to advance at a rapid pace and more complicated, quicker, and smaller devices are required, power efficiency has become a key problem. The entire power consumption of integrated circuits is greatly influenced by flip-flops, which are essential components of digital systems. It is imperative to develop novel flip-flop designs that can satisfy the strict demands of contemporary applications, which call for ever-lower power consumption without sacrificing functionality. Because of duplicated transistors, conventional flip- flop designs frequently have inefficiencies that result in needless power dissipation. Leakage currents and dynamic power consumption, two significant factors in the overall amount of power used of digital circuits, aggravate this problem even further. To meet these problems, a design strategy that integrates cutting- edge power-saving methods together with minimal redundancy is required. This work presents a revolutionary design for single-phase clocked flip-flops (SPCFFs) that integrates a power gating module (PGM) and removes redundancy, therefore greatly improving power efficiency. The flip- flop topology is carefully optimized in the suggested design to eliminate extraneous transistors and lower dynamic power dissipation. Furthermore, the PGM's incorporation successfully reduces leakage power, which increases the total power savings. This work's advances mark a significant development in the field of low-power digital design. Power efficiency problems may be effectively solved by the SPCFF design, which reduces dynamic power by 13–16% and leakage power by 12–15%. When these enhancements are added together, the overall power reduction is between 17% and 23%, indicating that the suggested method is successful in resolving the power consumption problems that are common in modern digital circuits. With the increasing need for designs that are power-efficient, the suggested

[a]anushapillamulla045@gmail.com, [b]john.alex@cmritonlince.ac.in, [c]nianreddy@gmail.com

DOI: 10.1201/9781003616399-72

SPCFF offers a viable route to the development of high-performing, low-power digital systems.

Literature Survey

Digital integrated circuits (ICs) are not complete without flip-flops, which often make up the majority of the system's size and power. According to Shin et al., [1], 2.6 million flip-flops of the SPARC T4 processor account for more than 20% of the CPU's total core a flip-flop (SAFF) with a sensing amplifier with low power consumption and high-speed operation. Furthermore, notable is the flip-flop's power and latency power systems-on-a-chip (SoC) flip-flops are notorious for their high dynamic power consumption, This, even in the absence of data changes, is mostly brought on by the quick transitions between several internal timed nodes. One of the main conditions for Internet-of-Things (IoT) applications to extend battery life is energy-optimal operation. Based on application demands, a set operating frequency is chosen to accomplish the energy-optimal functioning [2].

Power budgets are starting to restrict how many more transistors designers can include into typical CMOS designs. Moore's law is still producing an increasing number of transistors per chip [3]. Utilizing just 18, the fewest transistors yet documented for this type of totally static contention-free single-phase clocked (SPC) FF in a unique architecture. In 65-nm CMOS, it provides a 20% reduction in cell area over the conventional transmission gate FF (TGFF) for ultra-low power applications. The proposed CSFF uses an internal change-sensing unit to eliminate needless transitions of internal timed nodes when there is no change in the flip-flop content. Comparatively speaking, no extra transistors are needed in contrast to the traditional transmission-gate flip-flop (TGFF) [4–6].

Conditional precharge and conditional capture technologies are two categories into which high-performance flip-flops are categorized after analysis. The categorization is predicated on methods for mitigating or eliminating superfluous internal switching operations. The conditional discharge flip-flop (CDFF) is a brand-new flip-flop, capture flip-flops that are conditional (CCFFs). By removing unnecessary transitions between internal nodes, they reduce statistical power [7–11].

The development of low-power solutions has been stressed in recent research on flip flop design, particularly for activities in the low-voltage zone. A 28-nm version of the proposed FF was created for ultra low-voltage operation in fully-depleted silicon-on-insulator (FDSOI) CMOS technology. When compared to reference designs, the suggested FF's performance derived from clock divider measurements is Using footed differential latches instead of redundant internal clock toggling, Similar to a conventional transmission-gate flip-flop (TGFF), the SCDFF offers completely static and contention-free operation in the same region [12] through [15] decreased by using a new sense-amplifier stage and a new single-ended latch stage. In order to notify the completion of the sense- amplifier stage transition, the SAFF-TCD uses the internally generated detection signal. The operational yield deterioration, current contention, and glitches of earlier SAFFs are eliminated by the detection signal, which gates the pull-down route of the sense-amplifier stage and the slave latch [16,17].

Another method was figuring out the best approach to generate internally inverted clocks in order to minimize dynamic power usage. This allowed redundant internal clock transitions to be removed without compromising dependability. Then, in order to maintain everything completely static and free of conflict, superfluous transistors are found and removed using a topological and logical technique. Change-sensing FF (CSFF) is a very low-voltage, low-power, single-phase clocking, redundant-transition-free flip-flop (FF). Through the use of a local change-sensing technique to remove internal clocked nodes' unnecessary transitions [18–20].

Low Power Existing Flip Flops

The digital systems that use flip flops include TGFF, ACFF, TCFF, and S^2 CFF. Because of its stability, resistance to voltage scaling, and immunity to contention, the TGFF (Figure 72. 1) is the most widely used kind of flip-flop. However, since it has several internal timed nodes that constantly toggle, it uses excessive power. These repeated transitions occur even when the input

D does not modify the flip-flop's content. There have been numerous suggestions for low-power flip-flops to address this primary issue.

The adaptive-coupling FF (ACFF) replaces the traditional double-channel transmission-gate with multiple single-channel transmission-gates. The ACFF is a dynamic circuit, the process variance influences the ACFF. The ACFF is impacted by contemporary conflicts Therefore, in situations of insufficient supply, ACFF cannot operate as intended. In [3], the topologically compressed FF (TCFF) is proposed; Figure 72.3 illustrates this concept. The strain on the clock signal and the needed area are decreased by TCFF's topologically compressed method. TCFF uses 21 transistors in the design and compared to TGFF, its fully compressed architecture enhances power efficiency for whole circuit. However, the huge number of shared transistors causes considerable voltage drops in internal nodes and reduces resilience at low voltages. Hence TCFF is can't work properly under low voltage operation. The S^2CFF is the retentive TSPC flip flop. Which is supported by the low voltage operations. This flip flop uses single phase clock operation. which support for the near threshold voltage (NTV) operation. The S^2CFF is having some benefits like low area requirement, single phase clock, low power requirement.

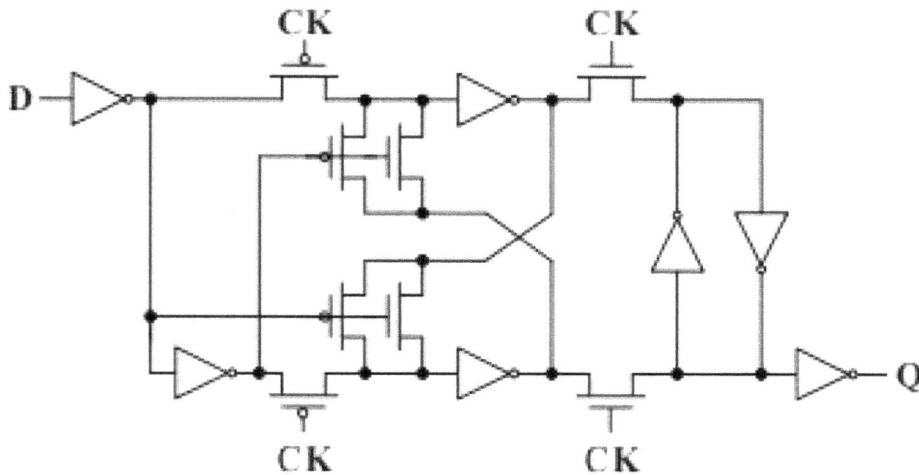

Figure 72.1 TGFF
Source: Author

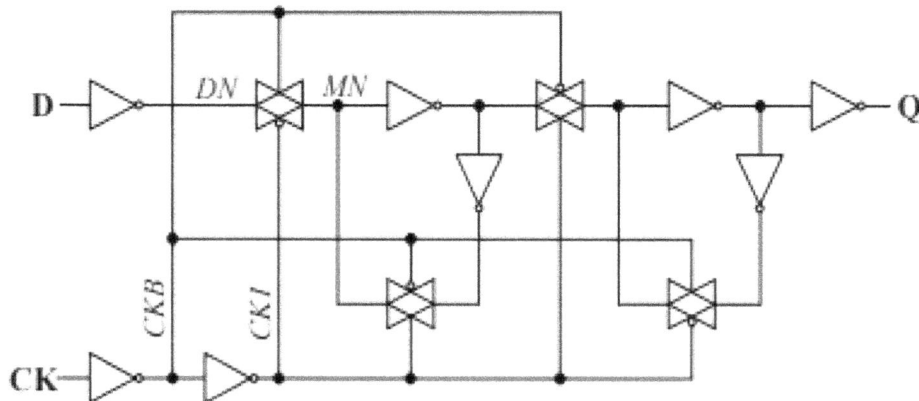

Figure 72.2 ACFF
Source: Author

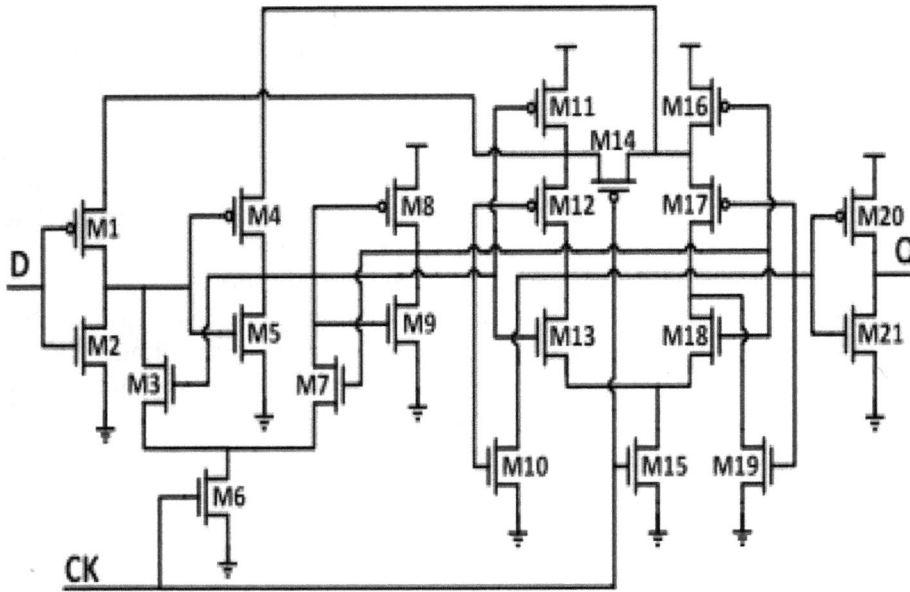

Figure 72.3 TCFF
Source: Author

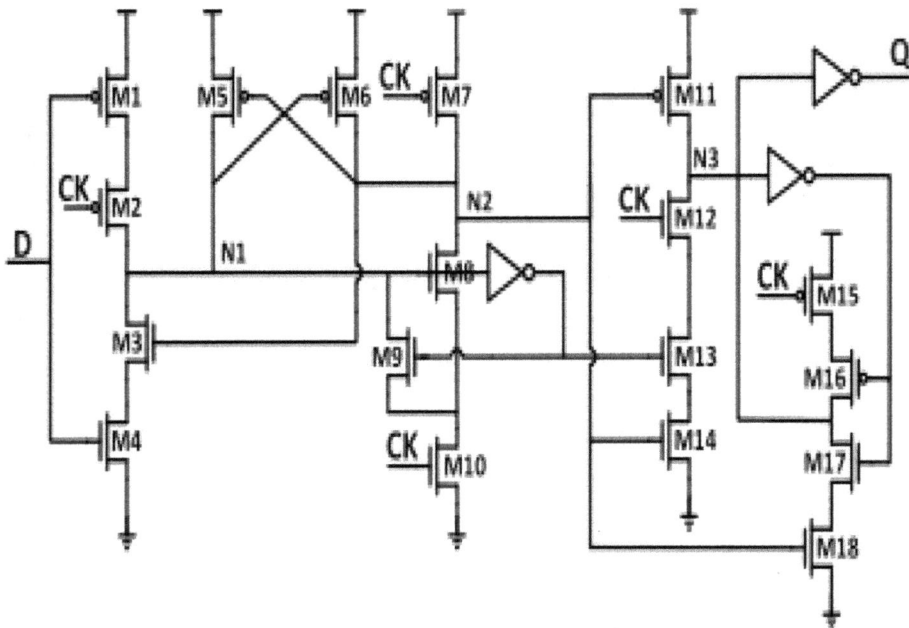

Figure 72.4 S²CFF
Source: Author

Proposed Flip Flops

In this paper all the existing flip flops are the TGFF, ACFF and TCFF are having drawn backs like high power consumption, low speed, low performance. Hence a flip flop is proposed to overcome the drawbacks of all flip flops. The S²CFF is proposed the basic principle for this flip flop is it uses single phase clock operation like all the exsisted flip flops This flip flop is proposed with three new methods one is retentive TSPC flip-flop, power gating and redundancy elimination techniques.

The *S²CFF* flip-flop, designed for single-phase clock operation suitable for NTV operation, introduces three novel methods. These include RTSPC, aimed at reducing dynamic power consumption, minimizing unwanted transitions, and preventing short circuits between transistor paths. Additionally, the Retentive TSPC flip flop employs a precharge operation approach to decrease dynamic power consumption. Furthermore, two additional techniques are incorporated to enhance the suggested flip flop design: power gating, which diminishes leakage power, and the redundancy transistor elimination idea, which removes the flip flop's redundancy and reduces the area of the flip-flop.

Proposed retentive TSPC structure
The single phase clocked flip flop with retention is a flip-flop that operates on a single clock, similar to the *S²CFF* flip-flop that is currently in use [2]. This flip-flop mostly has three shortcomings. those are examination of floating nodes, precharge operation and optimization at the transistor level. This flip flop operation can be explained by using the node based analysis using nodes only we can analyze the flip flop conditions and operations. The flip-flop goes through repeated precharge and discharge operations, wasting a lot of energy. A PMOS M1 is turned on and the

required precharge procedure proceeds according to schedule when the input value is 1. The input data remains at 0, but the additional transistor disables the precharge path and turns off the PMOS M1. This eliminates the unnecessary precharge process completely.

The "examination of floating nodes" technique is utilized to mitigate short circuit paths. When CK is low and the input data is 0, N2's voltage remains stable without excessive charging. This is achieved by ensuring only M3 is ON, preventing any short circuit path. When the next piece of input data is zero, a transistor M2 is included to maintain the voltage of N2. The charge on node N2 can be efficiently regulated by adding an input-aware transistor M2, especially during the negative half cycle. Since N2 is isolated from its pull-down path (M4 and M5) via M4 (CK = 0) when N3 = 1, CK = 0, and D = 0, the voltage of N2 has no effect on N3. N2's voltage has no effect on N1, and through M14 (D = 0), N1 is also separated from its pull-down path (M13 and M14).

The ultimate goal of transistor-level optimization is to minimize internal node transitions of the clock. To achieve this, one method is integrating PMOS M11_1 into M11 for input data inversion. Connecting transistors M14 and M15 directly would disrupt the functionality of the

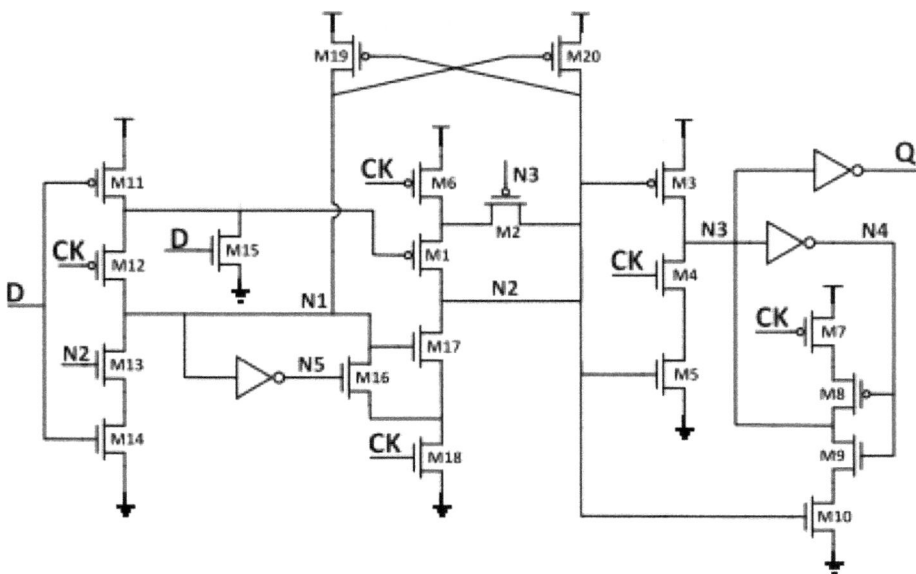

Figure 72.5 Proposed RTSPC flip flop
Source: Author

flip flop. Hence, we opt to directly link the drain of M11 to M14 instead. Consequently, transistor M13 in S^2CFF becomes redundant for the desired structure and is consequently removed. This elimination doesn't introduce any discernible errors in the output.

Proposed power gating S^2CFF

A method for lowering the flip flop's leaking power is called power gating. Here the flip flop circuit is completed with the addition of header and footer transistors. That implies the footer transistor can ground the flip flop's power if it uses too much power. Additionally, the supply voltage is stored in the header transistor, which means it retains the supply within and supplies as needed. Power gating's primary objective is this. Figure 72.2 below shows the suggested flip-flop with power gating module. The module is made up of three inverters and eighteen transistors. We added two transistors, designated M1 and M12, to the exsisting circuit, connecting them as the design's header and footer. M1 serves as the design's header, and M12 serves as its footer.

The merged state of transistors M2 and M5 indicates a connection between their two gates to form the input 'D' of the flip flop. Efforts to reduce power consumption in the flip-flop circuit encompass a range of methods, with a focus on dynamic and total power. However, the implementation of power gating is particularly directed at addressing leakage power. By employing low-leakage PMOS transistors, this approach effectively interrupts power delivery to components during periods of standby or sleep. NMOS footer switches serve as sleep transistors in this setup. Essentially, power gating is a strategic measure aimed at deactivating power to inactive components, thereby minimizing wasteful power usage. In the proposed power gating circuit the M1 is the header and M12 is the footer. The M12 transistor which acts as a sleep transistor blocks the leakage power of the flip flop. And the M1 transistor which is connected to the Vdd.

Redundancy eliminated S^2CFF

The technique designed to eliminate redundancy in the flip flops is called redundancy transistor removal. We can eliminate the redundancy of the flip flop by implementing two methods: a logical method and a topological method. By applying logical approach in our design, redundancy transistors are eliminated. In the given circuit all the transistor elements have some particular operation. Transistors are utilized to obtain the output, while some are utilized for clock operations, the remainder for input data transfer. In doing so, the flip-flop circuit makes use of the three are connected circuit, two transistors are included in each. The output part of one inverter is linked

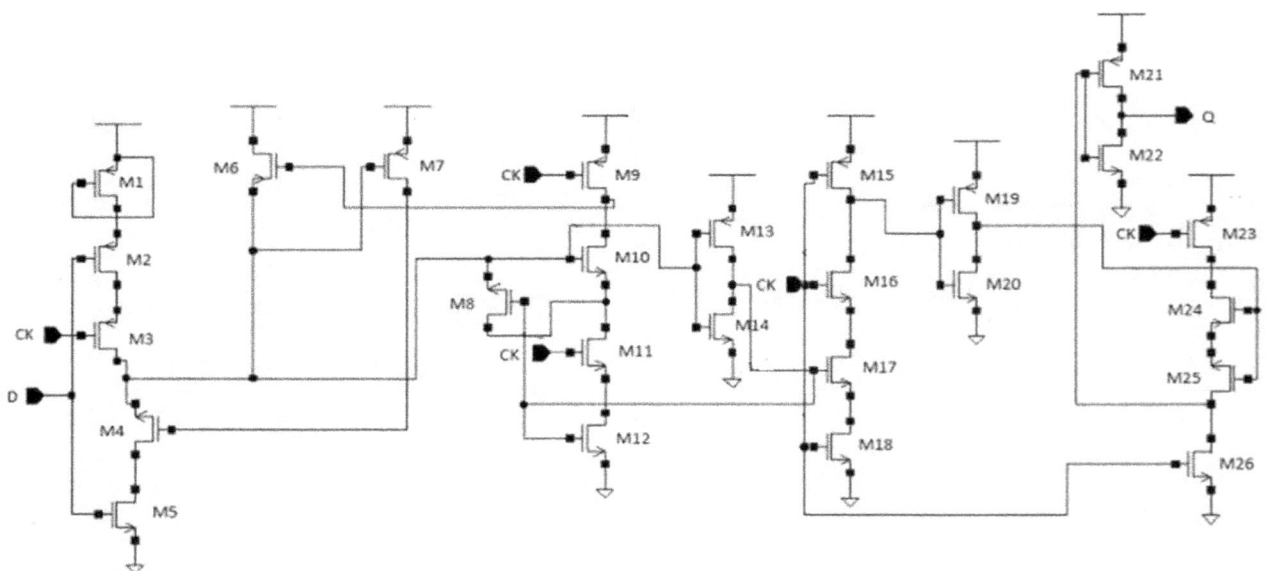

Figure 72.6 Proposed power gating flip flop
Source: Author

to it at the same location as every other inverter. Figure 72.3 below depicts the circuit layout for the recommended flip flop with redundancy transistor elimination, which is used to provide redundancy to the flip flop.

The S^2CFF circuit uses transistors M13 and M14, which are employed as sleeping transistors but also draw power. This results in increased power usage. in the flip flop circuit. To overcome this problem, we are now using redundancy transistor elimination. By using logical redundancy elimination technique is now being used to remove transistors by removing the transistors from the flip flop and therefore eliminating its redundancy.

In the Figure 72.7. shows that after removing or eliminating the two transistors how the proposed circuit has changed eliminating the connection from transistor M12 we can remove the transistors and this can eliminate the redundancy of the flip flop and this will helps to increase the performance of the proposed S^2CFF circuit. We are able to achieve dynamic power reduction and reduced space consumption by implementing the redundancy elimination technique in the proposed flip flop.

Measurement Results

The performance variation of all the suggested and exsisting flip flops is displayed in the below figures. The proposed flip-flop aims to reduce both the operational leakage power and dynamic power consumption associated with its operation. The Power consumption of the suggested flip-flop in real time 1.2V and 1.2V is depicted in Figures 72.8 and 72.9, respectively. And the leakage power of the PG S^2CFF is shown in below Figure 72.10. In contrast to the S^2CFF, ACFF, and TCFF, the power gating circuitry implemented in the proposed flip-flop significantly decreases leakage power consumption, providing energy-efficient performance particularly during periods of low activity. Compared to TGFF, ACFF, and TCFF, the proposed flip-flop is estimated to achieve a substantial reduction in leakage power consumption, varying between 12% and 15%. In the same manner the remaining flip flops' dynamic power consumption is more it means that ACFF, S^2CFF Consumes excessive power so that the proposed flip flop RE S^2CFF reduces the dynamic power consumption by eliminating redundancy of the flip flop.

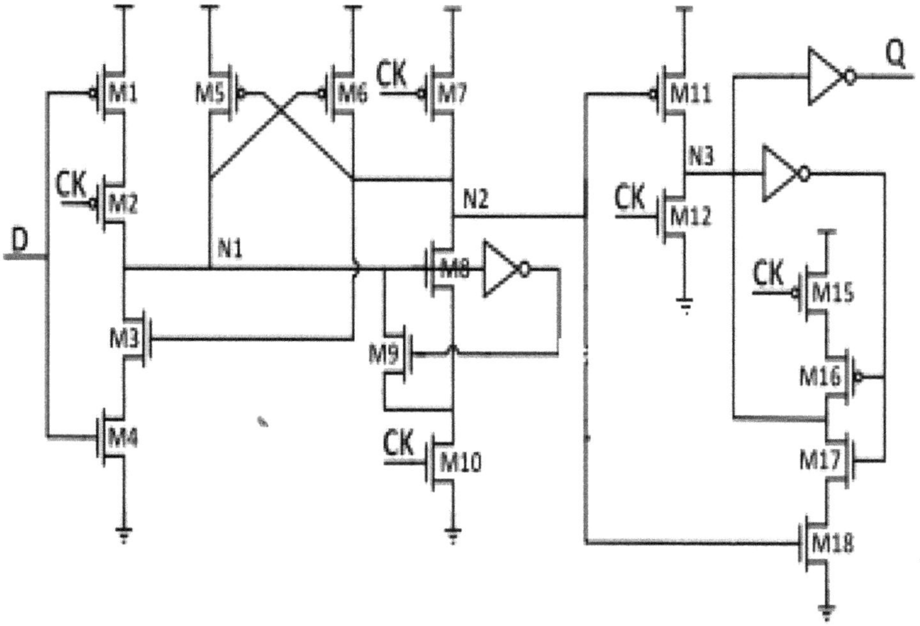

Figure 72.7 Redundancy transistor elimination
Source: Author

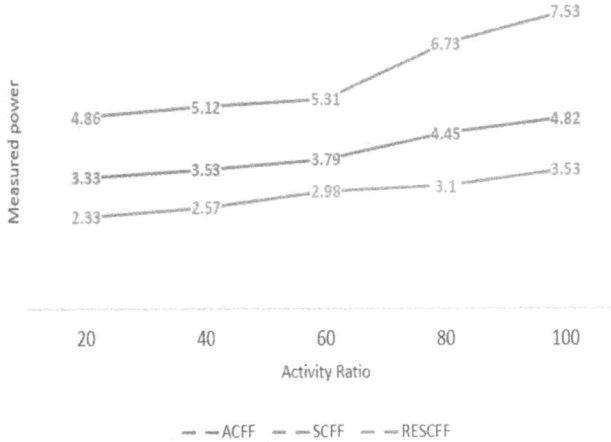

Figure 72.8 Dynamic power at 1.2V@10%
Source: Author

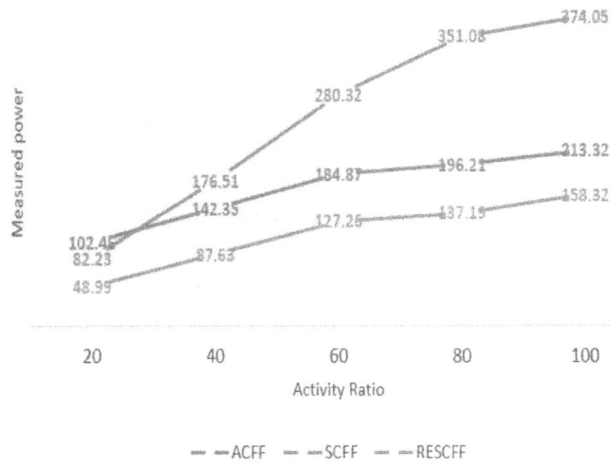

Figure 72.9 Dynamic power at 1.2V@90%
Source: Author

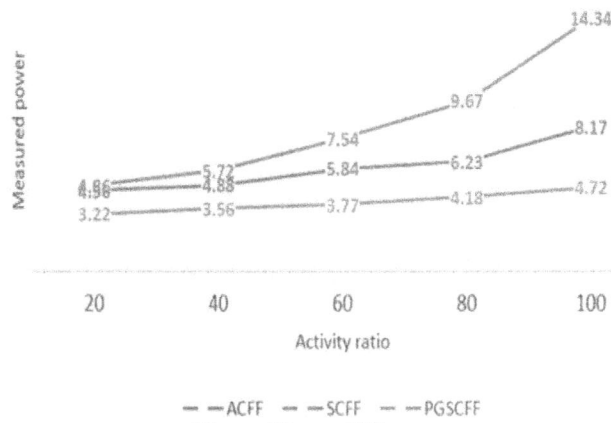

Figure 72.10 Leakage power consumption at 1.2V
Source: Author

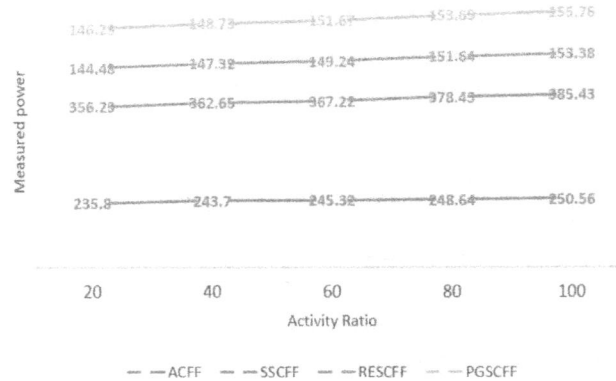

Figure 72.11 Total power consumption at 1.2V
Source: Author

Figure 72.10. shows the proposed power gating flip flops in addition to the observed overall power consumption of the current flip flops, such as ACFF and S^2 CFF. Every flip flop that is still in use has its power assessed at 10% and 90% data activity at 1.2 V and 1.2V of power supply. All the current flip flops use more power than the two that are suggested, one uses power gating, and the other uses redundancy transistor elimination techniques, which use less power. Each flip-flop's power measurement is done in accordance with the various power and activity ratios that are provided.

However, when compared to other flip-flops, the suggested flip-flop is the only one that uses minimal power at both 10% and 90% data activity. Conversely, the leakage power is also detected at 90% data activity, at 1.2V. The power gating approach was employed to lower the flip-flop's leaky power usage. Through careful observation of each flip-flop's leakage power, the suggested flip-flop lowers the leakage power. The suggested flip flop leakage powers and the ACFF, SSCFF flip-flops measured at various power and activity ratios respectively.

Comparison Table

The comparison Table 72.1 shows all currently available and suggested flip-flops. The table includes all the data, including transistor count, power consumption, and technology utilized in the creation of the specified flip-flops. Additionally, the table provides details about how much space each flip-flop takes up and whether or not all flip-flops are free from contention.

Using this table, we can analyze which flip-flops are better choice for the low voltage operation. And also it gives information about which flip flop uses output inverter network. This table is the major part in the measurement results of all the exsisted and proposed flip flops to check the all the requirements of the proposed methods of the flip -flops.

The above figure illustrates how the highly advanced technology in the proposed flipflops 45 nm for the PGS^2CFF and 45 nm for the RES^2CFF was used in their design.In terms of area, the ACFF and RES^2CFF are the flip flops that occupy less space than all other exsisting flip flops, and when comparing the flip flops based on leakage power consumption, the suggested PGS^2CFF is the best option for the application. The dynamic power of the flip flops which are exsisted consumes more power so the RES^2CFF is the flip-flop which consumes the less dynamic power. The flip-flop's performance is affected by redundancy, which is another observational parameter. Redundancy can be caused by an undesired clock or unwanted circuit components; hence, the RES^2CFF is the optimum option for redundancy-free operation. The proposed flip flops all

are used at the low voltage operations. Which are also having contention free operations.

Conclusion

This paper introduces a single-phase clock flip-flop with redundancy eliminated operates at low power consumption. with a power gating module (PGM). The test chip is fabricated to the 45nm technology which provides low power consumption of the fli-flop. We eliminated the undesired recharge and discharge operations of the Retentive single phase clocked flip flop by putting the input aware precharge strategy into practice. Furthermore, the redundancy of the proposed RESCFF is minimized using redundancy transistor elimination technique resulting in a reduction of the dynamic power. The suggested flip flop's leakage power is decreased by using the power gating technique. simulation results show that the proposed flip flops leakage power reduction between 13–16% and the dynamic power also reduced between the 12% to 15% Reducing the flip flop's leakage power and dynamic power allows us to lower the overall power from 17–23%. Hence the proposed three

Table 72.1 Calculation table of flip-flops

Parameter	TGFF	ACFF	TCFF	S^2CFF	RTSPC	PGS^2CFF	RES^{2}CFF
Technology	65 nm	6 5 nm	45 nm	65nm	45 nm	45 nm	45 nm
No. of transistors	24	22	21	24	26	24	22
Dynamic power(nW) @1.2V, 90% data activity	438.95	213.32	240.18	370.80	162.35	158.32	157.24
Dynamic Power(nW) @1.2V, 10%Data Activity	27.8	4.82	6.15	8.97	4.15	3.96	3.53
Area (µm^2)	5.88	5.88	6.16	5.83	6.16	5.88	5.73
Redundancy	Yes	Yes	No	Yes	No	Yes	No
Leakage(nW)@1.2V	12.52	14.34	8.89	6.45	5.86	4.22	4.25
Contention-free	No	Yes	Yes	No	No	Yes	No
Total power(nW)@1.2V	562.78	250.56	284.73	385.43	157.21	155.76	153.38
Low-voltage operation	No	No	No	Yes	Yes	Yes	Yes
Output inverter	Yes	Yes	No	Yes	Yes	Yes	Yes

Source: Author

methods achieves the power reduction of the flip flop.

References

[1] Shin, J. L., Golla, R., Li, H., Dash, S., Choi, Y., Smith, A., et al. (2013). The next generation 64b SPARC core in a T4 SOC processor. *IEEE Journal of Solid-State Circuits*, 48(1), 82–90.

[2] You, H., Yuan, J., Yu, Z., and Qiao, S. (2021). Low-power retentive true single-phase clocked flip-flop with redundant-precharge-free operation. (pp. 1063 –8210). IEEE.

[3] Lee, J., Zhang, Y., Dong, Q., Lim, W., Saligane, M., Kim, Y., et al. (2020). A self-tuning IoT processor using leakage-ratio measurement for energy-optimal operation. *IEEE Journal of Solid-State Circuits*, 55(1), 87–97.

[4] Dreslinski, R. G., Wieckowski, M., Blaauw, D., Sylvester, D., and Mudge, T. (2010). Near-threshold computing: reclaiming moore's law through energy efficient integrated circuits. *Proceedings, of the IEEE*, 98(2), 253–266.

[5] Cai, Y., Savanth, A., Prabhat, P., Myers, J., Weddell, A. S., and Kazmierski, T. J. (2019). Ultra-low power 18-transistor fully static contention-free single-phase clocked flip-flop in 65-nm CMOS. *IEEE Journal of Solid-State Circuits*, 54(2), 550–559.

[6] Alghareb, F. S., Zand, R., and Demara, R. F. (2019). Non-volatile spintronic flipflop design for energy-efficient SEU and DNU resilience. *IEEE Transactions on Magnetics*, 55(3), 1–11.

[7] Van Loi, L., Li, J., and Chang, A. (2017). An 82% energy-saving change-sensing flip-flop in 40nm CMOS for ultra-low power applications. In IEEE Asian Solid-State Circuits Conference, November 6-8.

[8] Zaho, P., Darvish, T. K., and Bayuomi, M. A. (2004). High performance and conditonal discharge flip flop. *IEEE Transactions on Very Large Scale Integration (VLSI) Systems*, 12(5), 477–484. doi:10.1109/tvlsi.2004.826132.

[9] Kong, B. S., Kim, S.-S., and Jum, Y.-H. (2001). Conditional capture flip flop for statistical power reduction. *IEEE Journal of Solid-State Circuits*, 36(8), 1263–1271. doi:10.1109/4.938376.

[10] Tech, C. K., Hamada, M., Fujita, T., Hara, H., Hikumi, N., and Oowaki, Y. (2006). Conditional data mapping flip flops for low power and high performance systems. *IEEE Transactions on Very Large Scale Integration (VLSI) Systems*, 14(12), 1379–1383. doi:10.1109/tvlsi.2006.887833.

[11] Consoli, E., Palumbo, G., Rabaey, J. M., and Alioto, M. (2014). Novel class of energy efficient very high speed push-pull pulsed latches. *IEEE Transactions on Very Large Scale Integration (VLSI) Systems*, 22(7), 1593–1605. doi:10.1109/2013.2276100.

[12] Stas, F., and Bol, D. (2018). A 0.4-V 0.66-fJ/cycle retentive true-single-phase-clock 18 T flip-flop in 28-nm fully-depleted SOI CMOS. *IEEE Transactions on Circuits and Systems I: Regular Papers*, 65(3), 935–945.

[13] Kawai, N., Takayama, S., Masumi, J., Kikuchi, N., Itoh, Y., Ogawa, K., et al. (2014). A fully static topologically-compressed 21-transistor flip-flop with 75% power saving. *IEEE Journal of Solid-State Circuits*, 49(11), 2526–2533.

[14] Shin, G., Lee, J., and Lee, Y. (2020). A static contention-free differential flip-flop in 28nm for low-voltage, low-power applications. In 2020 IEEE Custom Integrated Circuits Conference (CICC), (pp. 1–4). 978-1-7281-6031-3/20/$31.00. IEEE.

[15] Yang, B. D. (2015). Low-power and area-efficient shift register using pulsed latches. *IEEE Transactions on Circuits and Systems—I: Regular Papers*, 62(6), 1564–1571.

[16] You, H., Tang, W., and Yu, Z. (2020). A low-power high-speed sense-amplifier-based flip-flop in 55 nm MTCMOS . doi:10.3390/electronics9050802.

[17] Jeong, H., Oh, T. W., Song, S. C., and Jung, S.-O. (2018). Sense-amplifier-based flip-flop with transition completion detection for low-voltage operation. *IEEE Transactions on Very Large Scale Integration (VLSI) Systems*, 26, 609–620.

[18] Pan, D., Ma, L., Cheng, H., and Min, H. (2020). A highly efficient conditional feedthrough pulsed flip-flop for high-speed applications. *IEEE Transactions on Very Large Scale Integration (VLSI) Systems*, 28, 243–251.

[19] Shin, G., Lee, J., and Lee, Y. (2021). An ultra-low-power fully-static contention-free flip-flop with complete redundant clock transition and transistor elimination. *IEEE Journal of Solid-State Circuits*. 0018 -9200.

[20] Shin, G., Lee, E., Lee, J., Lee, Y., and Lee, Y. (2020). A redundancy eliminated flip-flop in 28 nm for low-voltage low-power applications. *IEEE Solid-State Circuits Letters*, 3, 446–449.

73 Variations in total electron content (TEC) and earth's magnetic field at some stage in quiet and disturbed days

Kiran, S. S.[a], Gurucharan, K.[b], Anil Kumar, P.[c], Aswini, A.[d], Bhavani, A.[e] and Tanmai, B.[f]

Department of Electronics and Communication Engineering, Lendi Institute of Engineering and Technology, Andhra Pradesh, India

Abstract

This research examines the interrelationships between seismic events, 'total electron content' (TEC), and the Earth's magnetic field to gain insights into earthquake phenomena. The study focuses on measuring TEC values in regions with higher seismic activity. The Earth's geomagnetic field serves as a vital protective function, shielding our planet from solar wind and cosmic radiation. This field exhibits both spatial and temporal variability. TEC, a metric quantifying the aggregate of free electrons within the Earth's ionosphere above a given point, is subject to influences from solar and geomagnetic activities, as well as ionospheric conditions. During periods of low solar activity, both the Earth's magnetic field and ionosphere maintain relative stability, resulting in lower and more consistent TEC measurements. In contrast, periods of heightened solar activity and geomagnetic disturbances lead to pronounced fluctuations in these systems, causing irregular and elevated TEC values. This investigation aims to elucidate the behavior of TEC and the Earth's magnetic field within specific geographic contexts under varying solar and geomagnetic conditions. Comprehending these fluctuations is essential for enhancing space weather prediction capabilities and improving communication systems that rely on ionospheric propagation. The research methodology incorporates the Dobrovolsky equation and statistical analysis of TEC data to forecast seismic events. By exploring the relationships between TEC, the Earth's Magnetic field, and earthquake occurrences, this study contributes to the advancement of early warning systems for seismic activity. Ultimately, this research endeavors to develop our acceptance of the difficult interplay between ionospheric phenomena and seismic activity, potentially leading to improved earthquake prediction capabilities.

Keywords: Earth's magnetic field, ionosphere, radial basis function, total electron content (TEC)

Introduction

Seismic events, commonly known as earthquakes, are natural geological occurrences characterized by the unexpected discharge of energy within the Earth's coating. This sudden release results in ground vibrations and can potentially lead to structural damage and environmental alterations. The primary cause of these events is the progress of tectonic plates, which are an enormous segment of the Earth's on the outside layer. These tectonic plates are in perpetual motion, driven by convection currents in the underlying semi-fluid mantle. The interactions between these plates, whether through convergence, divergence, or lateral movement, can trigger seismic activity. The origin point of an earthquake within the Earth is termed the focus or hypocenter, while the position directly above this point on the plane is designated as the epicenter. During a seismic event, the released energy manifests as seismic waves that propagate outward from the focus. These waves induce ground motion, which can result in surface deformation and displacement, potentially causing extensive devastation. Total electron content (TEC) is an important metric in the field of space weather research and ionospheric physics. It is a

[a]sskiranece@gmail.com, [b]charan.lendi@gmail.com, [c]anil135483@gmail.com, [d]aswiniraju6328@gmail.com, [e]bhavanianumalasettyab9@gmail.com, [f]tanmaisreenivas@gmail.com

DOI: 10.1201/9781003616399-73

way to quantify the overall number of unbound electrons in a unit-cross-sectional-area vertical column that stretches from the surface of the Earth to the topmost border of the ionosphere. Atoms and molecules that have been ionized by solar radiation make up the ionosphere, a part of Earth's upper atmosphere. This process creates a stratum of free electrons capable of affecting radio wave transmission. Understanding TEC is essential for comprehending ionospheric behavior and its impact on various technological systems. TEC is typically expressed in TEC units, where 1 TECU represent 10^{16} electrons per m^2. TEC values vary with altitude, latitude, longitude, time of day, and solar activity. Solar activity, particularly solar flares and geomagnetic storms can significantly influence TEC by increasing the ionization rate in the ionosphere.

Methodology

Earth's magnetic field records

Earth's atmosphere's ionospheric layer runs around 50–1,000 kilometers above the surface of the planet. Free electrons and ions, produced when solar ultraviolet (UV) light interacts with and ionizes atmospheric gases, define this zone. Total electron content (TEC) is a fundamental measurement in the field of ionospheric research as it shows the total amount of electrons integrated along a path between the surface of Earth and a satellite or receiver. Solar flares and coronal mass ejections (CMEs) are two examples of solar occurrences that significantly alter the ionosphere by increasing ionization levels and, therefore, TEC. Solar storms and other times of higher solar activity cause the ionosphere to become more ionized, which increases TEC readings.

TEC changes are also linked to geomagnetic activity, often resulting from the interaction between solar wind and Earth's magnetic field. Geomagnetic storms occur due to an increased inflow of charged particles from the Sun colliding with Earth's magnetosphere. These interactions can induce notable changes in TEC, typically manifesting as initial increases during the storm's onset, followed by decreases as the storm progresses and the ionosphere begins to recover. In contrast, during periods of geomagnetic quiescence, the ionosphere maintains relative stability. Under these conditions, TEC variations are primarily influenced by diurnal (daily) and seasonal shifts in solar radiation. Generally, TEC values are lower during nighttime hours due to the absence of solar ionization, while daytime measurements tend to be higher.

The Figure 73.1 represents the visualizations of GPS data, plotting latitude against longitude to trace the path of movement, illustrating positioning trends.

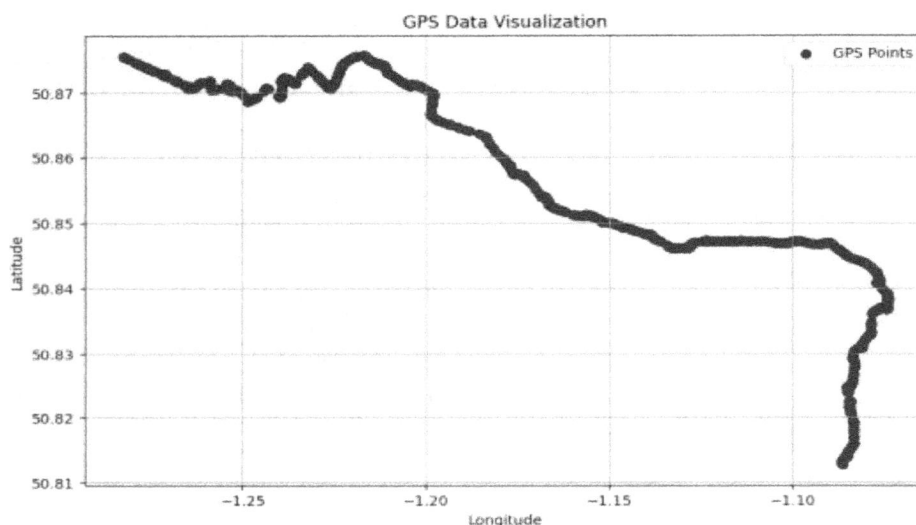

Figure 73.1 GPS Data visualization is based on GPS data which consists of longitude and latitude points
Source: Author

During periods of geomagnetic disturbance, such as storms or sub storms, TEC can exhibit significant fluctuations. The initial phases of geomagnetic storms often result in TEC enhancements, primarily due to increased solar wind pressure and particle influx, which intensify ionization within the ionosphere. However, as these storms progress, TEC may decrease owing to complex interactions between the ionosphere and magnetosphere, including the redistribution of ionospheric plasma and increased atmospheric drag. Researchers utilize both theoretical models and observational studies to gain insight into these processes. Notable models such as the International Reference Ionosphere (IRI) and the Global Ionosphere-Thermosphere Model (GITM) are employed to simulate ionospheric behavior under varying solar and geomagnetic conditions. These models aid in understanding TEC variations during both quiet and disturbed periods and can predict how TEC changes in response to geomagnetic activity.

In our study [1–10], we acquired Earth's magnetic field measurements from multiple geological stations, which provided data on the temporal variations of the geomagnetic field. We implemented initial quality control measures on this data, including the removal of outliers and corrections for sensor noise. For TEC data, we utilized information from GNSS receivers. This data illustrated spatiotemporal variations in electron content along the paths between satellites and receivers.

We applied screening procedures to the TEC data to minimize ionospheric turbulence effects. Additionally, we performed coordinate transformations to ensure compatibility between the TEC and magnetic field datasets. Combining observational data with theoretical models in an all-encompassing method lets one grasp the intricate interactions among geomagnetic activity, ionospheric conditions, and TEC fluctuations. Such insights are crucial for advancing our knowledge of space weather phenomena and their potential impacts on technological systems.

In our analysis [11–23], we applied various mathematical techniques to the magnetic field time series data. We extracted statistical moments, frequency domain functions, and wavelet transform coefficients. These methods allowed us to capture both short-term fluctuations and long-term trends in the magnetic field readings.

For the TEC data, we calculated geographical gradients and temporal derivatives to characterize the spatial and temporal variations in electron density. We also employed spatial autocorrelation techniques and principal component analysis to identify patterns in TEC changes across different regions. Melted iron and nickel's migration in the planet's outer core produces a complicated and dynamic phenomenon known as the Earth's magnetic field. This field extends into space and

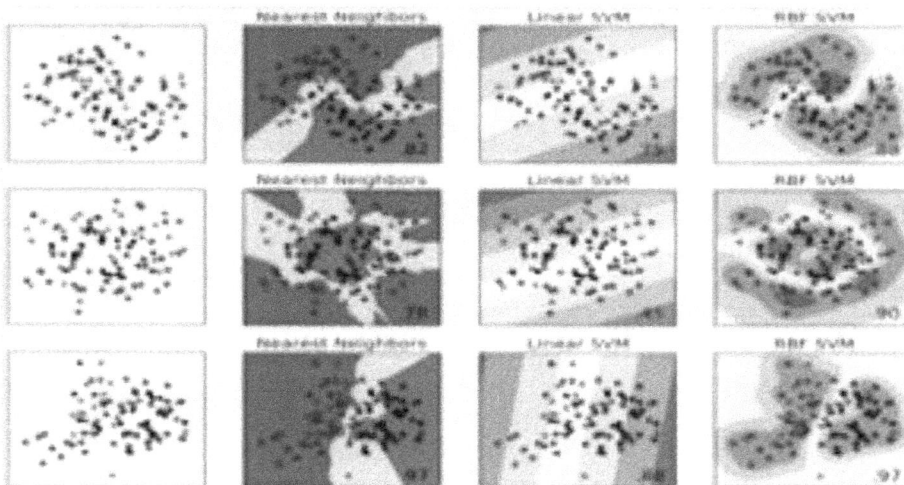

Figure 73.2 Comparison of earth's magnetic field for different computational methods
Source: Author

influences numerous natural processes. The study of Earth's magnetic field as shown in Figure 73.2, known as geomagnetism, is a sub discipline of geophysics that encompasses various research areas aimed at understanding the geomagnetic field and its effects.

Globally distributed magnetic observatories, equipped with sensitive magnetometers, continuously measure the strength and direction of the magnetic field. These observations contribute to our understanding of magnetic anomalies on the Earth's surface, providing insights into underlying geological structures. Paleomagnetism, another aspect of geomagnetic research, focuses on studying ancient magnetic fields preserved in rock formations. To investigate the relationships between the extracted features and seismic events, with a radial basis function (RBF) kernel, we used a support vector machine (SVM) classifier as shown in Figure 73.3 and 73.4. This machine learning approach allowed us to explore potential connections between geomagnetic and ionospheric parameters and earthquake occurrences. This multifaceted approach, combining time series analysis, spatial statistics, and machine learning techniques, enables a comprehensive examination of the complex interplay between Earth's magnetic field, ionospheric conditions, and seismic activity. Such integrative methods are essential for advancing our understanding of these intricate geophysical phenomena and their potential interconnections.

We used a grid search to find the great hyper parameters, which include the regularization parameter (C) and the kernel coefficient (gamma).

To further enhance our analysis, we implemented a Gradient Boosting framework. This approach involved training an ensemble of decision trees to capture complex interactions between magnetic field and TEC features.

We used k-fold cross-valuation for model validation to evaluate the generalizability of Gradient boosting and SVM models. Under this method, the data was split into k subsets, each of which was a testing set while the other data was utilized for training. We assess model presentation using accuracy, precision, recall, and F1-score thereby enabling a thorough comparison between the SVM and Gradient boosting methods. Additionally, we generated confusion

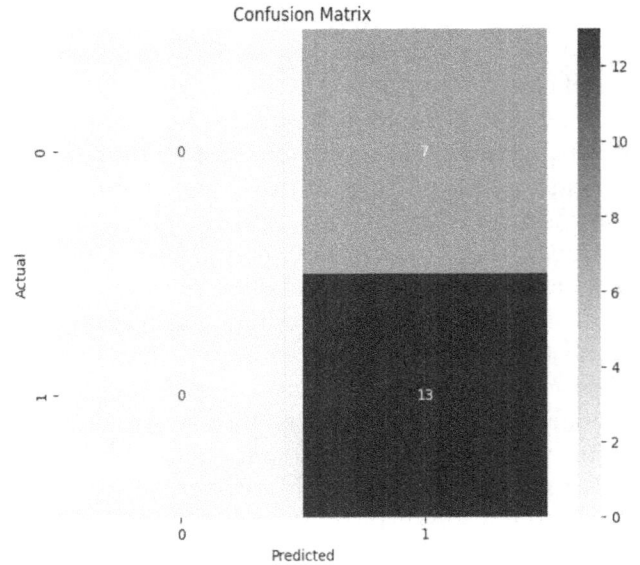

Figure 73.3 The figure represents confusion matrix of SVM with a RBF kernel to enhance accurateness for earthquake prediction using TEC data
Source: Author

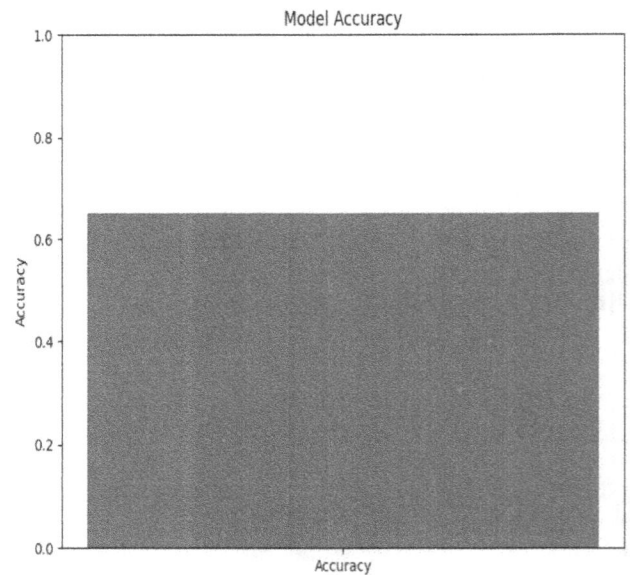

Figure 73.4 The figure represents model accuracy of SVM with RBF kernel to enhance accuracy for earthquake prediction using TEC data
Source: Author

matrices to visualize classification outcomes and assess model performance across different earthquake categories.

The process of evaluating and validating systems, models, or hypotheses is a critical aspect of scientific and technological advancement. This comprehensive approach typically integrates empirical evidence, statistical analysis, and logical reasoning. Whether in scientific research, technological development, or practical applications, rigorous validation is essential for establishing the reliability and utility of theories or systems.

Importance equation with assistance of anomalies

$$M = A * 0.1 + R * 0.002 + 4.288$$

M is the value; A is the ambiguity's amplitude; R is the station's distance from the center of shade.

$$R = \sqrt{(X - X0)^2} + \sqrt{(Y - Y0)^2}$$

M = A*0.1+ R*0.002 + 4.288 [12]

Dobrovolsky equation

The Dobrovolsky equation is a relationship that describes the spatial distribution of aftershocks around the epicenter of a mainshock, or a large earthquake. It is named after the Russian seismologist Vladimir Dobrovolsky, who first proposed the equation in 1965.

The Dobrovolsky equation states that the radius of the area around the epicenter of a mainshock, within which aftershocks are expected to occur, is proportional to the cube root of the magnitude of the mainshock. Mathematically, the equation is represented as:

$$R = 10^{(M/3)}$$

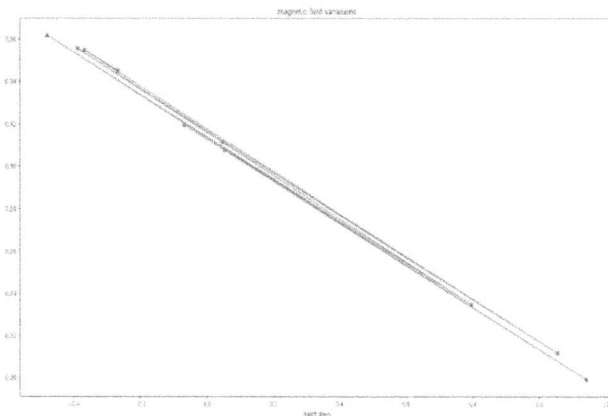

Figure 73.5 This shows that magnetic field is quite stable during quiet days, and it will strengthen and unstable during the disturbed days due to additional geomagnetic storm
Source: Author

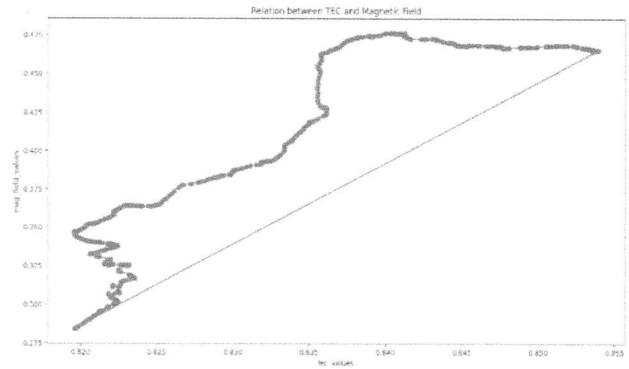

Figure 73.6 This shows the relation between TEC and magnetic field, and if they are indirectly dependent on each other, these values will be helpful in predicting the earthquake in early hours
Source: Author

where R is the radius of the aftershock zone, in kilometers, and M is the magnitude of the mainshock.

The Dobrovolsky equation is used in earthquake prediction to estimate the size of the area around the epicenter of a mainshock that is at risk of experiencing aftershocks.

In scientific research, the evaluation of hypotheses and theories typically involves the design and execution of experiments. These experiments aim to gather empirical data that can either support or challenge the proposed ideas. Rigorous experimentation, with controlled variables and statistical analyses, helps researchers draw meaningful conclusions about the validity of their hypotheses. Results are shown in the Figure 73.5 and 73.6.

Accuracy comparison table of different methods

From the above table, we can say that Gradient boosting, k-NN, RBF are the computational processes which gave us high accuracy results compared to the remaining computational methods. From the tables below (Table 73.1 and 73.2), we can say SVM is the computational process which gave us the high accuracy results compared to the remaining computational methods. With the help of these results, i.e. 0.8 accuracy, we can predict earthquake occurrence in some cases. We also have better accuracy by computing with the remaining methods also.

Table 73.1 For Earth's Magnetic Field

S. No	Different Methods	Accuracy
1	Logistic Regression	0.6
2	Random Forest Classifier	0 .55
3	Support Vector Machine	0 .4
4	Gradient Boosting	0 .6
5	k-NearestNeighbors (k-NN) Classifier	0.6
6	Voting Classifier	0.55
7	Radial Basis Function (RBF) Kernel	0 .6

Source: Author

Table 73.2 For Total Electron Content

S. No	Different Methods	Accuracy
1	Random Forest Classifier	0.4
2	Support Vector Machine	0.8
3	Radial Basis Function (RBF) Kernel	0.65
4	Gradient Boosting	0.5

Source: Author

Conclusion

Our aim in this work was to investigate if adding total electron content (TEC) measurements to Earth's magnetic field data may improve the accuracy of earthquake forecasts. The primary aim was to leverage the sensitivity of these geophysical factors to subtle underground changes, thereby improving seismic forecasting methods.

Demonstrated the potential of an integrated analytical approach, encompassing data collection, preprocessing, feature extraction, and advanced machine learning techniques. Our research indicates that the synergy between magnetic field data and TEC can contribute to more reliable seismic event predictions. By merging geophysical insights with machine learning, we can deepen our understanding of the interplay between geophysical phenomena and seismic activity. Our study advances knowledge of the underlying processes that trigger earthquakes, providing a foundation for more effective disaster prevention and response. The complex and dynamic nature of seismic events necessitates ongoing research, testing, and collaboration across various geographic contexts. We encourage the scientific community to build on the momentum generated by our work and further refine and extend our integrated analysis approach. Ultimately, our study highlights the potential of combining geophysical data with cutting-edge machine learning techniques. We envision a future where this integration significantly enhances earthquake prediction, fostering more resilient communities and better disaster preparedness globally.

Acknowledgement

The authors gratefully acknowledge the students, staff, and authority of our Electronics and Communication Engineering for their cooperation in the research.

References

[1] Space weather prediction center, national oceanic and atmospheric administration . https://www.swpc.noaa.gov/phenomena/total-electron-content.

[2] Nishioka, M., Saito, S., Tao, C., Shiota, D., Tsugawa, T., and Ishii, M. (2021). Statistical analysis of ionospheric total electron content (TEC): long-term estimation of extreme TEC in

Japan. *Earth Planets Space*, 73, 52. https://doi.org/10.1186/s40623-021-01374-8.

[3] Arikan, F., Nayir, H., Sezen, U., and Arikan, O. (2008). Estimation of single station inter-frequency receiver bias using GPS-TEC. *Radio Science*, 43, RS4004.

[4] Astafyeva, E., Yasyukevich, Y., Maksikov, A., and Zhivetiev, I. (2014). Geomagnetic storms, super-storms, and their impacts on GPS-based navigation systems. *Space Weather*, 12(7), 508–525. https://doi.org/10.1002/2014SW001072.

[5] Astafyeva, E., Zakharenkova, I., and Forster, M. (2015). Ionospheric response to the 2015 St. Patrick's Day storm: a global multi-instrumental overview. *Journal of Geophysical Research: Space Physics*, 120(10), 9023–9037. https://doi.org/10.1002/2015JA021629.

[6] Astafyeva, E., Zakharenkova, I., Hozumi, K., Alken, P., Coïsson, P., Hairston, M., et al. (2018). Study of the equatorial and lowlatitude electrodynamic and ionospheric disturbances during the 22–23 June 2015 geomagnetic storm using ground-based and spaceborne techniques. *Journal of Geophysical Research: Space Physics*, 123(3), 2424–2440. https://doi.org/10.1002/2017JA024981.

[7] Basu, S., Makela, J. J., MacKenzie, E., Doherty, P., Wright, J., Rich, F., et al. (2008). Large magnetic storm-induced nighttime ionospheric flows at midlatitudes and their impacts on GPS-based navigation systems. *Journal of Geophysical Research: Space Physics*, 113, A00A06. https://doi.org/10.1029/2008JA013076.

[8] Kumar, S., and Kumar, V. V. (2019). Ionospheric Response to the St. Patrick's Day space weather events in March 2012, 2013, and 2015 at southern low and middle latitudes. *Journal of Geophysical Research: Space Physics*, 124(1), 584–602. https://doi.org/10.1029/2018JA025674.

[9] Kalita, B. R., Hazarika, R., Kakoti, G., Bhuyan, P. K., Chakrabarty, D., Seemala, G. K., et al. (2016). Conjugate hemisphere ionospheric response to the St. Patrick's Day storms of 2013 and 2015 in the 100 E longitude sector. *Journal of Geophysical Research: Space Physics*, 121(11), 11–364. https://doi.org/10.1002/2016JA023119,11,364–311,390.

[10] Hernández-Pajares, M. (2022). GNSS Ionosphere. In: Sideris, M. G. (Eds.), Encyclopedia of Geodesy. Encyclopedia of Earth Sciences Series. Cham: Springer. https://doi.org/10.1007/978-3-319-02370-0_172-1.

[11] Schonlau, M., and Zou, R. Y. (2020). The random forest algorithm for statistical learning.

The *Stata Journal*, 20(1), 3–29. https://doi.org/10.1177/1536867X20909688.

[12] Tehseen, R., Farooq, M. S., and Abid, A. (2020). Earthquake prediction using expert systems: a systematic mapping study. *Sustainability*, 12(6), 2420. https://doi.org/10.3390/su12062420.

[13] Beroza, G. C., Segou, M., and Mostafa Mousavi, S. (2021). Machine learning and earthquake forecasting—next steps. *Nature Communications*, 12, 4761. https://doi.org/10.1038/s41467-021-24952-6. https://rdcu.be/djqCI.

[14] https://www.researchgate.net/publication/353343231_Analysis_and_Prediction_of_Earthquakes_using_different_Machine_Learning_techniques.

[15] Maharana, K., Mondal, S., and Nemade, B. K. (2021). Analysis and Prediction of Earthquakes using different Machine Learning techniques, 10.13140/RG.2.215085.10727.

[16] Xing, H., Junyi, S., and Jin, H. (2020). The casualty prediction of earthquake disaster based on extreme learning machine method. *Natural Hazards*, 102, 873–886. https://doi.org/10.1007/s11069-020-03937-6.

[17] Furukawa, A., Spence, R., Ohta, Y., and So, E. (2010). Analytical study on vulnerability functions for casualty estimation in the collapse of adobe buildings induced by earthquake. *Bulletin of Earthquake Engineering*, 8, 451–479. https://doi.org/10.1007/s10518-009-9156-z.

[18] Heelis, R., Sojka, J. J., David, M., and Schunk, R. (2009). Storm time density enhancements in the middle-latitude dayside ionosphere. *Journal of Geophysical Research: Space Physics*, 114(A3), A03315. https://doi.org/10.1029/2008JA013690.

[19] Elias, A. G., and de Adler, N. O. (2006). Earth magnetic field and geomagnetic activity effects on long-term trends in the F2 layer at mid-high latitudes. *Journal of Atmospheric and Solar-Terrestrial Physics*, 68(17), 1871–1878. Enders, W. (2008). Applied Econometric Time Series. New York: John Wiley & Sons. https://doi.org/10.1016/j.jastp.2006.02.008.

[20] De Michelis, P., Consolini, G., Tozzi, R., and Marcucci, M. F. (2016). Observations of high-latitude geomagnetic field fluctuations during St. Patrick's Day storm: swarm and Super DARN measurements. *Earth, Planets and Space*, 68(1), 105. https://doi.org/10.1186/s40623-016-0476-3.

[21] Kiran, S. S., Revathi, R., and Ramesh, K. S. (2023). Analysis of ionosphere day to day variability using parametric methods on GPS TEC. In Re-

cent Advances in Wireless Communications and Emerging Technologies - RAWCET-2022, IOP Publishing, Journal of Physics: Conference Series, (Vol. 2471, pp. 012004). doi:10.1088/1742-6596/2471/1/012004.

[22] Kiran, S. S., Revathi, R., and Ramesh, K. S. (2023). Evaluation and comparison of power spectral density for GPS signals using UTC and NMC parameters. In Recent Advances in Wireless Communications and Emerging Technologies - RAWCET-2022, IOP Publishing, Journal of Physics: Conference Series, (Vol. 2471, pp. 012019). doi:10.1088/1742-6596/2471/1/012019.

[23] Kiran, S. S., Vagdevi, N., Devarao, M. V., Babu, M. K., and Swamy, K. S. V. L. N. (2022). Predicting earthquake by using GPS seismology and GNSS based system. In 2022 International Conference on Computing, Communication and Power Technology (IC3P), (pp. 199–203). doi: 10.1109/IC3P52835.2022.00049.

74 Embedded AI for agriculture: the Agro onion bo Agro Onion Bot for efficient onion cultivation

Sai Prasanna, K.[1,a], Anirudh Reddy, R.[1,b], Yempally Sangeetha[2,c], Sathwik Reddy Kademgari[3,d], Sale Sowmya[3,e] and Police Srilekha[3,f]

[1]Assistant Professor, Department of Electronics and Communication, B.V Raju Institute of Technology, Narsapur, Medak, Telangana, India

[2]Associate Professor, Department of Electronics and Communication, B.V Raju Institute of Technology, Narsapur, Medak, Telangana, India

[3]Research scholar, Department of Electronics and Communication, B.V Raju Institute of Technology, Narsapur, Medak, Telangana, India

Abstract

Onion farming plays a crucial role in agriculture, but it faces challenges such as labor shortages and inefficiencies in traditional farming methods. To address these issues, we present the Agro Onion Bot, a robotic system designed to improve onion cultivation practices. The Agro Onion Bot is equipped with high-precision sensors that monitor and optimize soil moisture levels, ensuring optimal growing conditions for onions. Its movement is controlled by an advanced microcontroller, which enables smooth and precise navigation across the field. This bot is also equipped with specialized mechanisms for cutting, picking, and trimming onions. These features help in automating the harvesting process, reducing the need for manual labor and minimizing damage to the produce. Built to withstand harsh agricultural environments, the Agro Onion Bot combines durability with maneuverability, making it an efficient tool for modern onion farming. By automating labor-intensive tasks, this bot not only increases productivity but also supports sustainable farming practices.

Keywords: Cutting mechanisms, motor control system, stm32f401re, sustainable farming

Introduction

India's agriculture sector is crucial for its economic and social fabric, as nearly 70% of the poor are found in rural areas. To meet the growing population's demands, a productive, competitive, diversified, and sustainable sector is needed. India is a global agricultural powerhouse, producing milk, pulses, spices, cattle herd, wheat, rice, cotton, sugarcane, farmed fish, fish, vegetables, and tea. With 195 million hectares under cultivation, 63% are rained, 37% irrigated, and 65 million hectares of forests.

The Agro Onion Bot is a groundbreaking innovation in the field of onion cultivation, designed to streamline agricultural processes by incorporating cutting-edge technologies. This sophisticated robotic system addresses several major problems facing contemporary agriculture, include a lack of labor, inefficient resource use, and the need for sustainable farming practices. By focusing on the assessment and management of soil moisture levels, the Agro Onion Bot ensures optimal conditions for onion growth, thus enhancing both crop yield and quality.

Central to the Agro Onion Bot's functionality is its capability to accurately measure soil moisture content. Equipped with high-precision sensors, the bot continuously monitors soil moisture levels, providing real-time data that informs irrigation decisions. This capability allows farmers to optimize water usage, reducing waste and conserving a vital resource. The bot's ability to adjust its movements based on soil conditions

[a]K.saiprasanna.k@bvrit.ac.in, [b]anirudhreddy.r@bvrit.ac.in, [c]sangeetha.b@bvrit.ac.in, [d]21211a04n1@bvrit.ac.in, [e]21211a04m7@bvrit.ac.in, [f]21211a04k9@bvrit.ac.in

DOI: 10.1201/9781003616399-74

further enhances irrigation efficiency, ensuring that water is delivered precisely where and when it is needed.

The Agro Onion Bot's sophisticated motor control systems are a testament to its advanced design. Powered by four DC motors, the bot navigates through the soil with remarkable accuracy and stability. This precise navigation minimizes crop damage during field operations, which is crucial for maintaining high productivity and ensuring the health of the plants. The bot's robust construction, coupled with its agile movement, allows it to operate effectively even in challenging field conditions.

One of the standout features of the Agro Onion Bot is its specialized mechanisms for onion harvesting. The bot is equipped with a servo motor that enables gentle and efficient harvesting, ensuring that the onions are not damaged during the process. Additionally, a dedicated DC motor is responsible for trimming the top leaves of the onions, a critical step in post-harvest processing. These specialized mechanisms ensure that the harvesting process is both efficient and effective, Both the quantity of labor needed, and the rate of operation are raised.

The design of the Agro Onion Bot emphasizes both functionality and sustainability. Constructed primarily from wooden sticks, the bot is lightweight yet durable, offering an eco-friendly solution that reduces the environmental impact of manufacturing. This sustainable approach not only lowers production costs but also aligns with the growing emphasis on environmentally responsible farming practices. By promoting the use of renewable materials and minimizing waste, the Agro Onion Bot contributes to a more sustainable agricultural ecosystem.

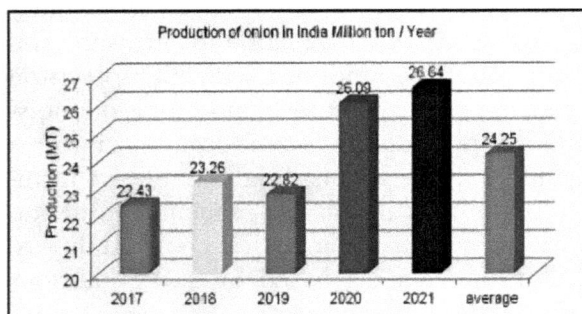

Figure 74.1 Production of onion in India
Source: Author

In addition to its practical benefits, the Agro Onion Bot represents a significant leap forward in the application of robotics in agriculture. By leveraging state-of-the-art technologies, this project demonstrates the potential of automation to transform traditional farming practices. The integration of sensors, actuators, and advanced motor control systems showcases the capabilities of modern robotics to enhance precision, efficiency, and sustainability in agriculture.

The Agro Onion Bot's comprehensive approach to soil moisture management and onion harvesting sets a new standard for agricultural automation. By providing farmers with a reliable and efficient tool, the bot improves productivity and supports the adoption of sustainable farming practices. This innovative system is poised to make a substantial impact on the agricultural industry, clearing the path for further developments in robotic agricultural technologies.

An important development in the field of farming technology is the Agro Onion Bot. This robotic system offers a transformative solution for onion cultivation through the integration of advanced sensing, precise motor control, and sustainable design principles. By addressing key challenges and enhancing efficiency, the Agro Onion Bot has the potential to revolutionize the way onions are grown and harvested, contributing to a more sustainable and productive future for agriculture.

Literature Survey

The microcontroller, as detailed by STMicroelectronics, is a critical component in the Agro Onion Bot's design, offering high processing power and low energy consumption, which are essential for precise motor control and reliable operation in agricultural environments [1].

Soil moisture monitoring: Soil moisture is a crucial parameter in crop management, and the Agro Onion Bot utilizes high-precision soil moisture sensors to optimize growing conditions. Khan et al. [2] provide an extensive review of soil moisture sensors, outlining their applications in agriculture to maintain optimal soil conditions and improve crop yields [2].

Robotic harvesting technologies: The concept of robotic harvesting, particularly for onions, has been explored in various studies. Bontsema et al. [3] developed a robotic onion harvester that addresses the challenges of harvesting, such as precise cutting and picking mechanisms [3].

Patel and Mehta [4] discuss the importance of motor control systems in agricultural robots, emphasizing how advanced microcontrollers can significantly enhance the accuracy and efficiency of robotic movements, particularly in field operations such as cutting and picking onions [4].

Big data and IOT in agriculture: The application of IOT and big data in agriculture has been transformative, as highlighted by Wolfert et al. [5]. Their review discusses how the integration of IOT systems into farming practices allows for better data collection and decision-making, which is essential for the Agro Onion Bot's operation [5].

The bot's ability to collect and process large amounts of data in real-time is enhanced by edge analytics, as explored by Nano Edge AI [6, 7]. These technologies enable the bot to make immediate adjustments to farming practices, such as irrigation and harvesting, improving overall efficiency.

The Agro Onion Bot builds on this research by integrating advanced mechanisms for efficient and clean harvesting. studies by Khan et al. [8] and Dalsgaard et al. [9] also contribute to the understanding of automated harvesting systems, highlighting the technological advancements necessary for the effective harvesting of onions [8, 9]. These works provide a foundation for the Agro Onion Bot's design, ensuring it meets the practical requirements of onion farming.

Robotics and automation in agriculture: The broader context of robotics and automation in agriculture is explored by several studies. Loi and Low [10] discuss the concepts and application of agricultural robots, highlighting their potential to increase productivity and reduce the reliance on manual labor [10].

Gonçalves et al. [11] provide a review of robotics and automation in agriculture, emphasizing the benefits of these technologies in improving farming efficiency and sustainability [11]. These insights support the development of the Agro Onion Bot as a solution to labor shortages and inefficiencies in traditional onion farming practices.

AI and sensing technologies: Artificial intelligence plays a significant role in the functionality of the Agro Onion Bot, allowing it to perform complex tasks autonomously. Silva et al. [12] discuss the role of AI in agriculture, particularly in enhancing the decision-making capabilities of robotic systems like the Agro Onion Bot [12].

Proposed Model

The Agro Onion Bot is a sophisticated robotic system designed to revolutionize onion cultivation by automating soil moisture monitoring and onion harvesting. This system addresses key agricultural challenges such as labor shortages and inefficient farming practices, promoting sustainable farming. The proposed model integrates high- precision soil moisture sensors, a robust motor control system powered by the microcontroller, and specialized harvesting mechanisms.

The agricultural sector faces significant challenges, including labor shortages and the need for sustainable farming practices. Robotic solutions, such as the Agro Onion Bot, offer potential benefits by automating critical farming processes. This paper presents the design and implementation of the Agro Onion Bot, focusing on soil moisture monitoring, motor control, and harvesting mechanisms.

System architecture

Soil moisture monitoring system

1. High-precision soil moisture sensors: The Agro Onion Bot employs capacitive soil moisture sensors to provide accurate and real-time soil moisture data. These sensors are strategically placed across the field to create comprehensive soil moisture profiles.
2. IOT integration: The soil moisture sensors are connected to an IOT platform, allowing for remote monitoring and data analysis. This integration facilitates informed decision-making regarding irrigation and soil management.

Motor control system

1. Microcontroller: The motor control system is powered by the STM32F401RE microcon-

troller, known for its high performance and low power consumption. This microcontroller manages the bot's movement and operation of its harvesting mechanisms.

2. DC motors and encoders: The bot is equipped with DC motors and encoders to ensure precise movement and positioning. The motors provide the necessary torque for field navigation, while the encoders offer feedback for accurate control.

Onion harvesting mechanisms

1. Cutting and picking mechanism: specialized cutting tools are integrated into the bot for harvesting onions. These tools are designed to cut onions at optimal points, minimizing damage and ensuring a clean harvest.
2. Leaf trimming mechanism: An additional mechanism trims the top leaves of the onions, preparing them for storage and transport.
3. Collection system: Harvested onions are collected and stored in an onboard bin, which can be periodically emptied, reducing the need for continuous manual intervention.

Frame and maneuverability

1. Durable frame: The Agro Onion Bot is built on a durable and lightweight frame, ensuring robustness and ease of movement across the field. The frame design enhances stability and minimizes the risk of damage during operation.
2. Navigation system: Equipped with GPS and obstacle detection sensors, the bot navigates the field efficiently, avoiding obstacles and ensuring thorough coverage of the cultivation area.

Operational workflow

Soil moisture monitoring
The bot continuously monitors soil moisture levels, sending real-time data to the IOT platform. Alerts are generated if soil moisture falls below optimal levels, prompting irrigation.

Harvesting operation
The bot navigates the field, identifying onions ready for harvest. Using its cutting and picking mechanisms, it harvests the onions and trims the top leaves. Harvested onions are collected in the onboard bin for later collection.

Data collection and analysis
Soil moisture and harvesting data are collected and analyzed to optimize future farming practices. This data-driven approach enhances productivity and sustainability.

Benefits

A. Labor efficiency: By automating soil monitoring and harvesting, the Agro Onion Bot improves manual labor reliability and addresses labor shortages in agriculture.
B. Precision agriculture: High-precision sensors and advanced control systems ensure optimal growing conditions and efficient harvesting, improving crop yields and quality.
C. Sustainability: Automated soil moisture monitoring and data-driven irrigation practices reduce water usage and minimize environmental impact.
D. Productivity: The bot's continuous operation and efficient harvesting mechanisms increase productivity, enabling farmers to manage larger fields with fewer resources.

Methodology

The methodology for developing the Agro Onion Bot involved a structured approach, beginning with requirements analysis to identify the needs for soil moisture monitoring, motor control, and onion harvesting. Key components, including capacitive soil moisture sensors, the microcontroller, DC motors, and specialized harvesting mechanisms, were selected based on performance and compatibility. The system architecture was designed to integrate these components, featuring a control unit for processing data, a sensor network for real-time soil moisture monitoring, and an IOT platform for remote data access. The hardware integration phase involved setting up the sensor network, calibrating the motor control system, and assembling the harvesting mechanisms onto a durable frame. The final step included rigorous testing in field conditions to ensure the bot's efficiency, accuracy, and reliability in automating onion cultivation tasks.

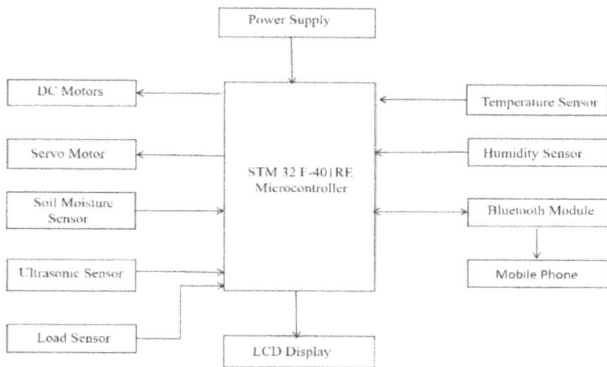

Figure 74.2 Block diagram
Source: Author

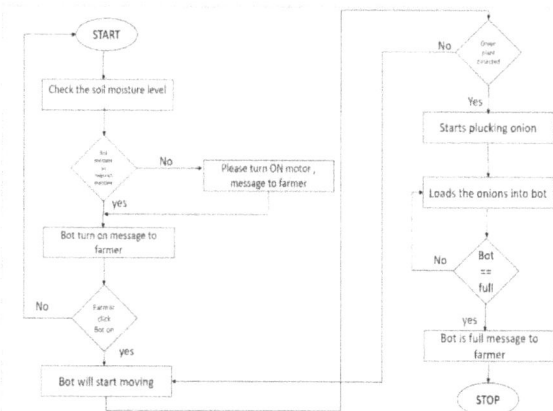

Figure 74.3 Flow chart
Source: Author

Figure 74.4 Agro onion bot
Source: Author

The hardware integration phase involved the strategic placement of soil moisture sensors across the field to ensure comprehensive coverage and accurate data collection. The motor control system, powered by the microcontroller, was calibrated to achieve precise movement and positioning of the bot, ensuring efficient navigation and operation in varying field conditions. Specialized cutting and leaf trimming tools were designed and integrated into the bot to handle onions efficiently, ensuring minimal damage during the harvesting process.

A durable and lightweight frame was constructed to enhance the bot's maneuverability and stability, equipped with GPS and obstacle detection sensors for effective navigation and obstacle avoidance. The IOT integration allowed for real-time monitoring and data analysis, facilitating informed decision-making regarding irrigation and soil management.

Finally, the bot underwent rigorous testing in simulated and actual field conditions to validate its performance, accuracy, and reliability. This testing phase included verifying the precision of soil moisture measurements, the efficiency of the motor control system, and the effectiveness of the harvesting mechanisms. The collected data was analyzed to optimize the bot's operations and ensure its suitability for sustainable and efficient onion cultivation. Data collection for the Agro Onion Bot was comprehensive and focused on evaluating key performance metrics. Soil moisture levels were continuously monitored using capacitive sensors, with data collected every 15 minutes and transmitted to a central IOT platform for real- time analysis, ensuring optimal irrigation. Motor control data, including positional accuracy, speed consistency, and response times, was logged continuously to assess the bot's navigation and obstacle avoidance efficiency. Harvesting data was collected in real-time, recording the number of onions harvested, the time taken for each cycle, and the condition of the harvested onions to evaluate the effectiveness of the harvesting mechanisms. Overall system performance metrics, such as the total area covered, number of irrigation cycles triggered, total water used, and cumulative onions harvested, were aggregated daily. Additionally, environmental data, including temperature, humidity, and weather conditions, was recorded hourly to contextualize the bot's performance under varying conditions. This thorough data collection approach provided a detailed understanding of the Agro Onion Bot's operational efficiency and its impact on farming productivity and sustainability.

Result

The development of the Agro Onion Bot leveraged a diverse set of tools and integrations, each contributing distinct advantages to the project. STM IDE and Cube MX played pivotal roles in configuring the microcontroller and generating efficient initialization code, ensuring seamless integration of hardware components such as sensors and actuators. This setup not only streamlined the development process but also optimized the bot's performance in field conditions. VS code provided a versatile platform for coding, debugging and executing the firmware, enabling rapid iteration and refinement of the operational logic. Its compatibility with the GCC toolchain facilitated cross-platform development, enhancing code efficiency and reliability. Furthermore, the integration of AI-linked graph plotting tools allowed for real-time data analysis of environmental variables, motor performance indicators, and soil moisture levels. This capability enabled the generation of actionable insights through visual data representation, empowering farmers with informed decision-making capabilities in onion cultivation practices.

The integration of Nano Edge AI with the Agro Onion Bot significantly enhanced its data processing and analytics capabilities. Using STM IDE and Cube MX, we configured the microcontroller, enabling precise sensor data collection and real-time monitoring. In VS Code, the firmware was developed and optimized, allowing seamless execution and debugging of the bot's operations. Nano Edge AI was then employed to analyze the collected data, implementing advanced anomaly detection and predictive analytics. This integration facilitated the generation of real-time insights into soil moisture levels, motor performance, and environmental conditions. Graphs and visualizations produced through this AI integration provided clear, actionable data, enhancing decision-making processes in onion cultivation and

Table 74.1 Data sheet

Day	Height (cm)	Temperature (°C)	Soil moisture
1	0	24.9	553.1
2	0.2	24.6	583.6
3	0.6	24.4	534.3
4	1	24.1	543.7
5	1.3	25	567.1
6	1.5	23.7	579.3
7	1.7	23.5	582.6
8	1.9	23	543.7
9	2	25	523.2
10	2.4	24.2	547.1
11	2.5	23.9	432.2
12	4	23.6	475.8
13	4.2	24.7	49.7
14	4.6	27.3	540.6
15	5.3	24.7	533.9
16	6.1	24.8	524.3
17	7	27.2	498.3
18	9.6	26.4	495.7
19	12.8	25.9	512.8
20	16.7	25.2	532.7
21	21.3	24.8	527.7
22	24.8	23.9	565.4
23	27.4	23.7	475.8
24	29.1	24.1	49.7
25	31.2	25.8	540.6
26	31.9	23	533.9
27	33.4	24.8	524.3
28	34.1	24.2	543.7
29	34.8	22.1	567.1
30	35.2	22.3	579.3

Source: Author

demonstrating a significant advancement in the bot's capability to support sustainable and efficient farming practices.

The dataset represents a collection of measurements taken over a 30-day period, specifically tracking the height, soil moisture, and temperature levels of onion plants. Each day, data is recorded for the plant's growth in centimeters, the moisture content of the soil in percentage, and the ambient temperature in degrees Celsius. The height of the onion starts from a small value and steadily increases over time, reflecting the plant's growth. Soil moisture levels fluctuate slightly, depending on factors like irrigation or rainfall, indicating how much water is available for the plant's development. Temperature levels also vary daily, which could be due to natural environmental changes. By analyzing this dataset, one can explore the relationship between environmental factors, such as soil moisture and temperature, and how they impact the growth of onions over time. This dataset can be useful for studying optimal growth conditions or improving agricultural practices for onion farming.

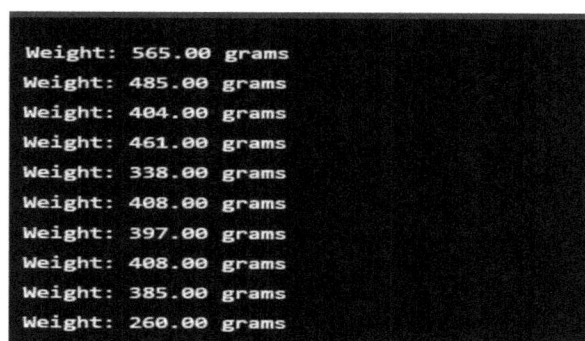

Figure 74.5 Load result in nano edge
Source: Author

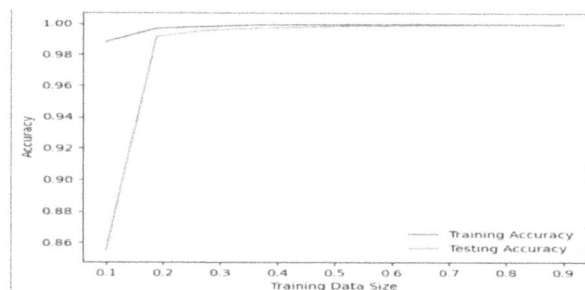

Figure 74.6 Training and testing accuracy
Source: Author

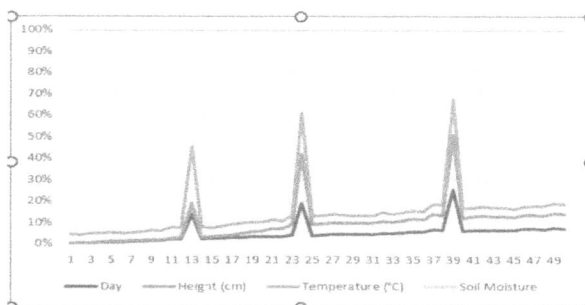

Figure 74.7 Soil moisture, temperature, day and crop height graph
Source: Author

Conclusion

The Agro Onion Bot is a significant advancement in agricultural technology, addressing key challenges in onion farming with precision and efficiency. By integrating advanced soil moisture sensors, robust motor control systems, and specialized harvesting mechanisms, the bot optimizes crop yield and quality while promoting sustainable practices. Its eco-friendly design and real-time monitoring capabilities ensure optimal growing conditions and efficient resource use.

This innovative system reduces the need for manual labor, enhances productivity, and sets a new standard for precision agriculture. The Agro Onion Bot paves the way for future advancements in sustainable and efficient farming, making a lasting impact on the agricultural industry.

Future Scope

The Agro Onion Bot has the potential to be expanded beyond onion farming to accommodate a variety of crops, integrating advanced AI and machine learning algorithms to further enhance its adaptability and efficiency across diverse agricultural practices.

The Agro Onion Bot can be enhanced with real-time data analytics and IOT connectivity, enabling remote monitoring and control, predictive maintenance, and integration with smart farming ecosystems to further optimize agricultural productivity and sustainability.

References

[1] STMicroelectronics. CITE: https://www.st.com/en/microcontrollers-microprocessors/stm-32f401re.html.
[2] Khan, M. S., Ahmad, I., and Ahmad, S. (2018). Soil moisture sensors and their applications in agriculture. In Husain, A. (Ed.), Sustainable Agriculture Reviews, (Vol. 30, pp. 177–198). Cham: Springer.

[3] Bontsema, J., van Tuijl, B., and Hemming, J. (2016). Development of a robotic onion harvester. *Biosystems Engineering*, 144, 95–106.

[4] Patel, R., and Mehta, P. (2018). Motor control systems in agricultural robots: a review. *Agricultural Engineering Today*, 42(1), 15–22.

[5] Wolfert, S., Ge, L., Verdouw, C., and Bogaardt, M. (2017). Big data in smart farming – a review. *Agricultural Systems*, 153, 69–80.

[6] NanoEdge AI (n.d.). Edge Analytics for IoT and industrial applications. Retrieved from https://ieeexplore.ieee.org/document/9328189.

[7] Schneider Electric (n.d.). NanoEdge AI - edge analytics with schneider electric. Retrieved from https://www.se.com/ww/en/work/solutions/for-business/nanoedge-ai.jsp.

[8] Khan, M. R., Hassan, S., and Khan, M. K. (2019). A review of automated harvesting systems for onions. *Journal of Agricultural Engineering and Biotechnology*, 2(1), 1–10.

[9] Dalsgaard, A., Jørgensen, R. N., and Larsen, R. (2016). Innovative technologies for harvesting onions: a review. *Journal of Agricultural Machinery Science*, 25(3), 31–42.

[10] Loi, L., and Low, T. (2018). Agricultural robots for field operations: concepts and applications. *International Journal of Agricultural and Biological Engineering*, 11(4), 1–14.

[11] Goncalves, J., Lemos, M., and Oliveira, R. (2019). Robotics and automation in agriculture: a review. *Agricultural Engineering International: CIGR Journal*, 21(3), 1–14.

[12] Silva, V., Melo, T., and Faria, D. (2018). Artificial intelligence in agriculture: a review. *Computers and Electronics in Agriculture*, 161, 280–293.

[13] Iqbal, L. B., Rahman, M. M., Mamun, S., Nabi, N., and Ahamed, M. S. (2022). OnionBangla: a supervised machine learning approach for predicting onion yield using Bangladeshi climate data. In 2022 32nd International Conference on Computer Theory and Applications (ICCTA), Alexandria, Egypt, (pp. 110–115).

[14] Ronquillo, D. N. T., Selda, J. M. S., and Caya, M. V. C. (2023). Classification of onion species in the Philippines using a convolutional neural network (Cnn). In 2023 IEEE 15th International Conference on Humanoid, Nanotechnology, Information Technology, Communication and Control, Environment, and Management (HNI-CEM), Coron, Palawan, Philippines, (pp. 1–6).

[15] Gbadebo, G. O., Alhassan, J. K., and Ojerinde, O. A. (2022). Detection of onion leaf disease using hybridized feature extraction and feature selection approach. In 2022 5th Information Technology for Education and Development (ITED), Abuja, Nigeria, (pp. 1–6).

[16] Iqbal, L. B. (2022). Onion Bangla: a supervised machine learning approach for predicting onion yield using Bangladeshi climate data. https://doi.org/10.1109/ICCTA58027.2022.10206199.

[17] Ronquillo, D. N. T. (2023). Classification of onion species in the Philippines using a convolution neural networks (CNN). https://ieeexplore.ieee.org/document/10589121t

[18] Gbadebo, G. O. (2022). Detection of onion leaf disease using hybridized feature extraction and feature selection approach. doi: 10.1109/ITED56637.2022.10051500.

75 Design and development of egg incubator to reduce pre-mature hatching

Sai Prasanna, K.[1,a], Anirudh Reddy, R.[1,b], Vasudev Reddy, T.[2,c], Tarun Rajesh, P.[3,d], Revanth, T.[3,e] and Sree Raga Priya Reddi[3]

[1]Assistant Professor, Department of Electronics and Communication, B V Raju Institute of Technology, Narsapur, Medak, Telangana, India

[2]Associate Professor, Department of Electronics and Communication, B V Raju Institute of Technology, Narsapur, Medak, Telangana, India

[3]Research Scholar, Department of Electronics and Communication, B V Raju Institute of Technology, Narsapur, Medak, Telangana, India

Abstract

Egg incubation is a crucial process in modern poultry farming, impacting hatch rates, chick quality, and profitability. This paper presents an innovative approach to egg incubation using a fully automated system. The system employs "cutting-edge" technology to establish and sustain an optimal incubation environment, utilizing advanced sensors for temperature, humidity, and gas composition. This data-driven approach allows for precise control of environmental parameters, ensuring they remain within the required ranges for successful egg incubation. The incubator features an intuitive graphical user interface (GUI) that provides hatchery personnel comprehensive insights into the incubation process, displaying key metrics such as temperature curves, humidity trends, and turning intervals. Users can input desired settings, track progress, and receive alerts in case of deviations, enabling timely interventions and adjustments. Integrating into the design is an automated egg-turning mechanism, which simulates the natural nesting process, creating a nurturing environment that maximizes the likelihood of healthy chick development. Experimental results show that the developed incubator system consistently achieves and sustains the optimal conditions for successful egg incubation, resulting in marked improvements in hatch rates compared to traditional methods and a significant reduction in developmental issues.

In conclusion, the novel egg incubator system addresses critical challenges faced by the poultry industry in achieving optimal hatchery conditions. By leveraging advanced technology, real- time monitoring, and user-friendly interfaces, this innovation not only improves hatch rates and chick quality but also contributes to the overall sustainability and profitability of poultry farming enterprises. As the poultry industry continues to evolve, this advancement is poised to shape the future of egg incubation practices.

Keywords: Arduino IDE, Arduino uno board, egg incubator, exhaust fan, heat bulb, MQ-2 gas sensor, stepper motor, W1209 temperature driver

Introduction

Overview

The global population is expected to reach 10 billion by 2050, and an increment in this population leads to demand for protein-rich food consumption and production. Commonly consumed protein-rich food is EGG.835M is the current poultry population in India and keeps rising year by year. With the rising demand for egg consumption, quality and the maximum hatch rate of eggs are important. Main aim is to design and develop an artificial incubator for various egg hatching. Incubators are well-known as contemporary technologies for hatching eggs without involving the brooding parent. The process of natural incubation involves the birds sitting. On the egg to maintain the necessary conditions until the hatchings emerge. An insulated box is utilized in artificial incubation where climate variables including humidity, ventilation, and temperature.

[a]Saiprasanna.k@bvrit.ac.in, [b]Anirudhreddy.r@bvrit.ac.in, [c]21211a04p8@bvrit.ac.in, [d]21211a04p5@bvrit.ac.in, [e]21211a04p1@bvrit.ac.in

DOI: 10.1201/9781003616399-75

The environment is adjusted to facilitate hatching. During artificial incubation, a sizable proportion of egg hatching took place all year long. Egg incubation is a long-standing practice, however the act of. day by day, artificial incubation is becoming more common day. Making an effective incubator at a reasonable price is difficult. As egg embryos can be fractured, even egg incubation is a crucial process in modern agriculture and poultry farming, affecting productivity and efficiency. An advanced egg incubator system is being developed to revolutionize the way eggs are hatched. Historically, natural incubation methods were used, but they often lacked consistency and precision, leading to varying hatching rates and reduced efficiency. As demand for poultry products increase globally, innovative solutions are needed to enhance hatchery operations, improve hatching success rates, and promote sustainable egg production. Technology-driven solutions, such as intelligent egg incubators, address these challenges by providing a tightly controlled environment throughout the incubation period. These incubators use advanced sensors, automation systems, and data analysis techniques to replicate the conditions required for successful egg hatching. The comprehensive design and development process includes temperature and humidity control mechanisms, automatic turning systems, real-time monitoring interfaces, and predictive analytics algorithms. Real-time monitoring allows farmers to oversee and adjust incubation parameters from a distance, improving operational efficiency and allowing timely intervention in case of deviations from optimal conditions. This innovative solution contributes to the sustainability and scalability of poultry farming while ensuring consistent hatching success.

Objectives

The main aim of an egg incubator is to maintain consistent temperature, regulate humidity, provide fresh oxygen, and have a turner mechanism for better hatching outcomes.

- They also serve as bio secure environments, protecting embryos from pathogens and contaminants.
- Modern incubators have built-in sensors for continuous monitoring, ensuring better hatch rates.
- They also play a role in conservation efforts, efficiency, and support for scientific research.

Literature Survey

Vick et al., [1], state an experiment that investigated the effects of various eggshell temperatures (EST) during incubation on embryo mortality, hatchability, and development, as well as post-hatch growth and rectal temperature under diverse housing temperatures. The eggs were incubated at 36.7 or 37.8°C in week one, 37.8°C in week two, and 37.8 or 38.9°C in week three. The high EST in week 3 minimized the disparity between machine temperature and EST (DT) in batch 2. Embryo growth was most slowed at 36.7°C EST during week 1. The highest hatchability and development occurred at a constant temperature of 37.8°C EST. Chicks from low EST eggs exhibited lower post-hatch rectal temperatures, particularly in colder living conditions. Rearing and incubation circumstances impact early post-hatch rectal temperature.

Lourens et al., [2], states how incubation humidity affects hatchability and embryonic development in flocks of varying ages. In Experiment 1, eggs from broiler breeders aged 28 to 64 weeks were incubated at wet bulb temperatures of 28.3°C or 30.0°C, while the dry bulb temperature remained constant at 37.5°C. Hatchability improved, and early embryonic mortality decreased at 28.3°C, particularly in younger flocks. Experiment 2, which involved 34- and 66-week-old flocks, found that reduced embryonic mortality at 28.3°C was caused by higher water loss and oxygen influx in younger flocks. However, in older flocks, lower wet bulb temperatures affected the hatchability of larger eggs. A lower wet bulb temperature promotes water loss and gas diffusion in tiny eggs from young flocks.

Dutta and Anjum [3] state that the inference system optimizes temperature and relative humidity in an automated egg incubator. The closed-loop feedback system compares temperature and humidity inputs to previously recorded ideal values and operates the heater and humidifier fan based on the output. The model regulates an egg incubator's heater and humidifier fan to ensure steady output levels. The model can be adapted to examine egg incubation in various bird species by adjusting input parameters.

Lestari et al., [4] state the implementation of a temperature control model for chicken egg incubators. The work aims to optimize chicken egg hatching efficiency with fuzzy logic temperature regulation. The report provides information on fuzzy system testing, implementation success, and overall system performance. However, the appropriate temperature range for hatching chicken eggs, the role of the DFT11 sensor in the fuzzy logic control system, and its application to various animal incubators are not fully explored.

Gutierrez et al., [5]. states that the creation of an Internet of Things-based intelligent system for hatching hen eggs. The device is intended to assist farmers automatically controlling temperature, humidity, and egg rotation, as well as remotely monitoring the incubator. It was created using MIT App inventor, LabVIEW, google firebase, and Arduino. The suggested incubator is depicted in block diagram form in the article, along with a description of its essential parts, such as the Arduino board, DHT11 sensor, and SG90 servo motor. It has been demonstrated that the technique increases the success rate at which hen eggs hatch.

Tangsuknirundorn and Sooraksa [6], state that the design and installation of a low-cost, effective forced air egg incubator powered by a microcontroller are shown. The setter and hatcher are combined in the incubator, which has three basic components: casing, forced air, and an automated egg tray rotating mechanism. Temperature, humidity, ventilation, and egg flipping are just a few of the incubation characteristics that are monitored and controlled by the microcontroller-based control unit. When using eggs from the same breeder and carefully controlling the temperature and humidity, the success rate for hen and duck eggs was 100.

Kabir and Abedin [7], state that the use of ozone in agrotechnical processes. This paper discusses the advantages and disadvantages of ozonation as a means of disinfection and deodorization in the agricultural industry. In addition, research on the impact of electro filtration systems on the air quality of incubators by increasing ozone production and the rate of performance of healthy chickens is presented. This paper highlights that the use of ozone is promising and offers many advantages over conventional disinfection and deodorization methods in the agricultural industry. In conclusion, this file contains a table with data on the use of ozone in industrial processes of agricultural complexes.

Vozmilov et al., [8] explain how STEM education may be used to teach students about developing and implementing a cyber-physical system for an incubator for chicken eggs. The document includes graphs and tables that display the experiment's findings along with references to several similar investigations. Overall, the method was deemed effective since the students were able to properly manage and hatch a healthy chicken. In the satisfaction poll, there were certain questions, nevertheless, where there was little agreement.

Almeida, et al., [9], states the impact of physical incubation factors, such as temperature, humidity, O2 and CO2 levels, and egg turning, on hatchability, chick quality, and overall poultry performance. It emphasizes the influence of pre-incubation factors on embryonated eggs and the significant advancements in incubation technology. The paper also questions the effectiveness of current incubation conditions in enhancing hatchability and chick quality under various field conditions and explores future prospects for optimizing the incubation process as a critical link between egg development and poultry production.

Radhakrishnan et al., [10], states the creation of an egg incubator system based on an ATmega16 microcontroller that automatically maintains an optimal environment for embryo development. A temperature sensor monitors the incubator's internal and external temperatures and sends data to the microcontroller. The microprocessor uses relays to operate a light bulb and a fan, regulating the temperature between 37°C and 38.5°C. A user-programmed timer controls a gear motor that tilts the egg holder, while an LCD displays the temperature.

This project models, designs, and develops an egg incubator system capable of maintaining temperatures between 35–40°C [11]. The system uses sensors to monitor temperature and humidity, automatically adjusting conditions for optimal incubation. Electric bulbs, water, and fans control temperature, humidity, and ventilation, while a DC motor rotates eggs for even heating. An AT89C52 microcontroller with a PID controller manages the system, tuned using the Zeigler-Nichol method. MATLAB Simulink was used for simulation and optimization, resulting in improved overshoot, rise time, peak time, and system stability.

This focuses on integrating IoT technology into a smart egg incubator system, featuring temperature and humidity sensors that monitor conditions and send data to a microcontroller [12]. The microcontroller, programmed with fuzzy logic, controls actuators to maintain optimal conditions, which vary based on egg type. A servo motor tilts the eggs 45° every 4 hours to prevent embryo adhesion to the shell. An LCD screen displays the incubator's status. The next step involves developing an IoT system to enable remote control of the incubator from anywhere in the world.

Implementation

The main goal of an egg incubator is to provide a controlled environment that mimics the conditions necessary for the successful development of eggs. The primary purpose of using an incubator is to hatch eggs artificially, outside of the natural nesting environment. The key goals of an egg incubator include temperature control, humidity regulation, ventilation, ventilation, candling, protection, and efficiency. Premature egg hatching is our stated issue. According to previous surveys, it is observed that there is nearly 30.

Working
The Arduino UNO microcontroller was chosen for this project because of its low power requirements for all sensors. This model utilizes a W1209 temperature driver, a gas sensor, and a step motor. A thermostat (W1209) monitors the incubator's temperature and adjusts heating elements accordingly. The W1209 temperature controller is used to monitor temperatures ranging from -50–110°C. The second sensor we used was a gas sensor. We employ a variety of gas sensors, including MQ-135, MQ-2, and MQ-3. MQ-2 is the best suited to our project. The MQ2 gas sensor runs on 5V DC and consumes about 800 mW. It can detect amounts of LPG, smoke, alcohol, propane, hydrogen, methane, and carbon monoxide from 200 to 100,000 ppm. Next, we employ a stepper motor with a voltage-current of 12V at 400 mA. Stepper motors move in discrete stages,

known as the step angle. The step angle typically ranges from 90° (four steps per rotation) to 0.75° (500 steps per revolution). For a fertile egg to hatch, it must be kept in an egg incubator for 21 days. The first 18 days are referred to as settler. The latter three days are referred to as Hatcher.

For the first 18 days, the temperature should be 99 to 100 f and for the last 3 days the temperature should be 98 f for the first 18 days humidity should be 55–60, and for the last 3 days humidity should be 65 to 70 Next comes to the turning which is done by a stepper motor. It should be done for every 3 hours a day. By this mechanism, the embryo does not stick to the shell which reduces chances of premature hatching.

Software used.

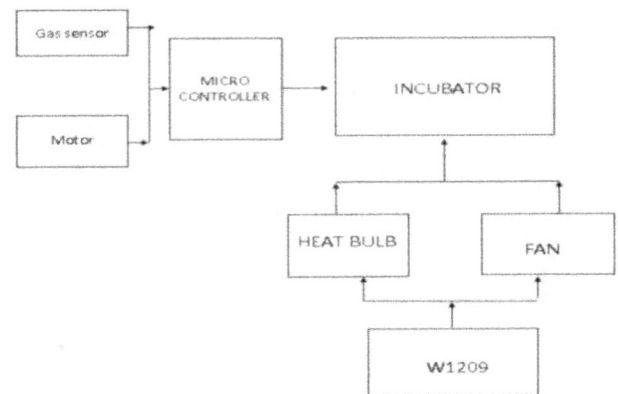

Figure 75.1 Block diagram
Source: Author

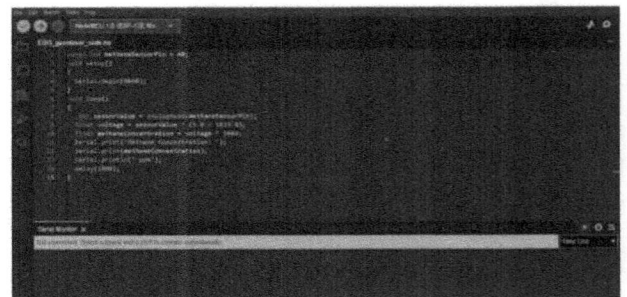

Figure 75.2 Code
Source: Author

Result

The egg incubator project achieved a 15% increase in hatch rates by implementing precise temperature control and automated egg-turning mechanisms. control and automated egg-turning mechanisms. These improvements ensured optimal conditions for embryo development and reduced manual intervention. As a result, more eggs successfully hatched into healthy chicks. This advancement showcases the potential of technology-driven enhancements in poultry farming for improved efficiency and productivity.

Day	Temperature (°C)	Humidity (%)
Day 1	36.1	57
Day 2	36.5	55.4
Day 3	36.3	58
Day 4	36.8	57.1
Day 5	37	50
Day 6	36.9	55.7
Day 7	37.1	57
Day 8	36.5	58.2
Day 9	36.4	58.3
Day 10	36.6	56
Day 11	36.4	56.5
Day 12	36.7	57.6
Day 13	37	55
Day 14	36.5	54
Day 15	36.8	56
Day 16	37.1	57
Day 17	37	59
Day 18	36.9	55.2
Day 19	38.1	67
Day20	38.2	67.5
Day 21	38.1	68

Figure 75.3 Observation values
Source: Author

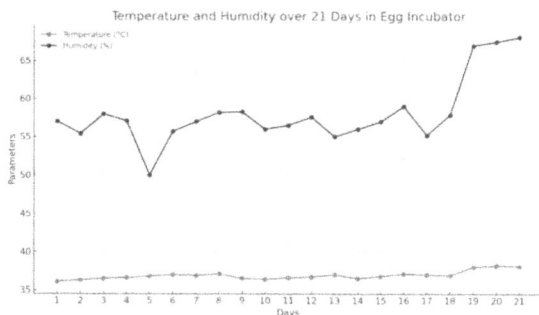

Figure 75.4 Graph
Source: Author

Day	LPG	Methane	Propane	Hydrogen	CO$_2$
Day 1	0.1	0.05	0.02	0.5	0.5
Day 2	0.1	0.04	0.01	0.4	0.6
Day 3	0.1	0.05	0.03	0.6	0.4
Day 4	0.1	0.04	0.02	0.5	0.6
Day 5	0.1	0.03	0.02	0.7	0.5
Day 6	0.1	0.05	0.02	0.6	0.7
Day 7	0.1	0.04	0.02	0.5	0.6
Day 8	0.1	0.05	0.02	0.5	0.5
Day 9	0.1	0.05	0.02	0.6	0.5
Day 10	0.1	0.04	0.02	0.5	0.6
Day 11	0.1	0.04	0.02	0.5	0.5
Day 12	0.1	0.05	0.02	0.4	0.4
Day 13	0.1	0.05	0.02	0.5	0.5
Day 14	0.1	0.04	0.02	0.6	0.6
Day 15	0.1	0.05	0.02	0.4	0.4
Day 16	0.1	0.04	0.01	0.5	0.5
Day 17	0.1	0.05	0.01	0.5	0.5
Day 18	0.1	0.05	0.02	0.6	0.6
Day 19	0.1	0.04	0.02	0.4	0.4
Day 20	0.1	0.05	0.02	0.5	0.5
Day 21	0.1	0.04	0.01	0.6	0.6

Figure 75.5 Observation table
Source: Author

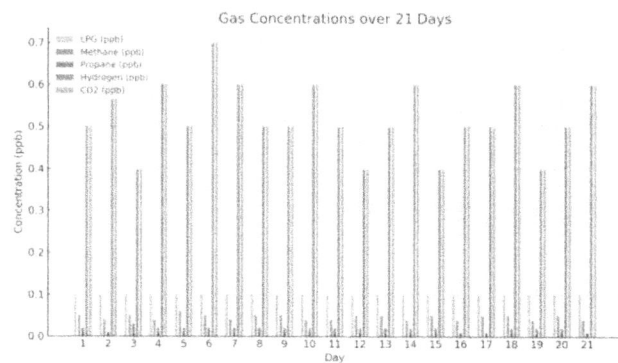

Figure 75.6 Graph
Source: Author

Conclusion

The egg incubator project is a significant advancement in poultry farming, conservation, and education. It offers a controlled and optimized environment for successful egg hatching, revolutionizing the way eggs are hatched across

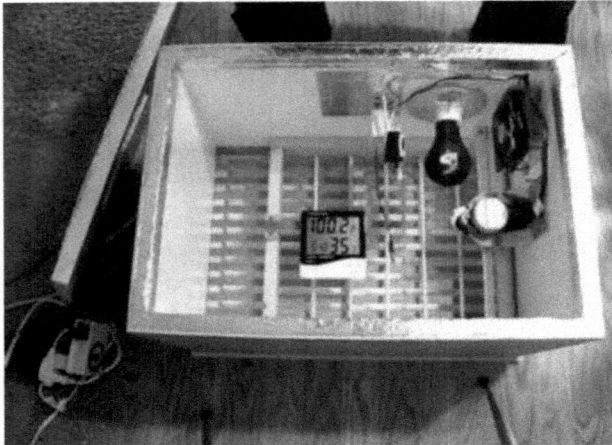

Figure 75.7 Prototype
Source: Author

various sectors, including small-scale breeders, hobbyists, and commercial hatcheries. The project also serves as an educational tool, allowing students, researchers, and enthusiasts to explore embryology, avian biology, and environmental science. By providing insight into the critical role of temperature, humidity, and other factors in life development, the project stimulates curiosity and fosters a deeper understanding of the natural world. The egg incubator's versatility extends to supporting endangered species, providing sustenance for poultry farms, and gamebird breeding. Its integration into conservation efforts, zoos, educational institutions, and aquaria highlights its importance in maintaining biodiversity and raising awareness about the delicate balance of ecosystems. The egg incubator project contributes to sustainable agricultural practices, wildlife preservation, and engaging individuals of all ages in meaningful scientific exploration, ensuring increased productivity and economic growth in the poultry industry.

Future scope
The egg incubator project has immense potential for future development and expansion across various domains. Smart and IoT-enabled incubators can be developed through the integration of IoT technology, allowing remote monitoring and control of environmental parameters. Automated environmental regulation could be achieved through advanced algorithms and control systems, ensuring optimal conditions for egg

hatching. Future iterations could focus on energy efficiency and sustainability, incorporating renewable energy sources and optimizing insulation. Multi-species compatibility could broaden the incubator's applications in fields like herpetology, entomology, and wildlife conservation. Data analytics and predictive models could help identify patterns in environmental data and egg development, optimizing hatching success rates. Integration with genetic research could lead to insights into genetic traits, disease resistance, and overall health. Improved gas sensing and analysis can lead to more accurate monitoring and analysis of gas concentrations within the incubator. Biosecurity and disease prevention can be achieved through advanced biosecurity measures in hatcheries and 17 breeding facilities, contributing to improved animal health and welfare. The future scope of egg incubator technology is boundless, as it combines cutting-edge technology with a deep understanding of biology and ecology, revolutionizing various sectors, including agriculture, education, conservation, and scientific research. As innovations continue to shape our world, the egg incubator symbolizes our capacity to nurture and safeguard life in its various forms.

References

[1] Vick, S. V., Brake, J., and Walsh, T. J. (1992). Relationship of incubation humidity and flock age to hatchability of broiler hatching eggs . doi:10.3382/ps.0720251.
[2] Lourens, A., van den Brand, H., Meijerhof, R., and Kemp, B. (2005). Effect of eggshell temperature during incubation on embryo development, hatchability, and posthatch development. *Poultry Science*, 84(6), 914–920. doi:10.1093/ps/84.6.914.
[3] Dutta, P., and Anjum, N. (2021). Optimization of temperature and relative humidity in an automatic egg incubator using mamdani fuzzy inference system. In 2021 2nd International Conference on Robotics, Electrical and Signal Processing Techniques (ICREST), Jan. 2021. doi: 10.1109/icrest51555.2021.9331155.
[4] Lestari, I. N., Mulyana, E., and Mardi, R. (2020). The implementation of mamdani's fuzzy model for controlling the temperature of chicken egg incubator. In 2020 6th International Conference on Wireless and Telematics (ICWT), Sep. 2020. doi: 10.1109/icwt50448.2020.9243647.

[5] Gutierrez, S., Contreras, G., Ponce, H., Cardona, M., Amadi, H., and Enriquez-Zarate, J. (2019). Development of hen eggs smart incubator for hatching system based on internet of things. In 2019 IEEE 39th Central America and Panama Convention (CONCAPAN XXXIX), Nov. 2019. doi: 10.1109/concapanxxx-ix47272.2019.8976987.

[6] Tangsuknirundorn, P., and Sooraksa, P. (2019). Design of a cyber-physical system using STEM: chicken egg incubator. In 2019 5th International Conference on Engineering, Applied Sciences and Technology (ICEAST), Jul. 2019. doi: 10.1109/iceast.2019.8802564.

[7] Kabir, M. A., and Abedin, M. A. (2018). Design and implementation of a microcontroller based forced air egg incubator. In 2018 International Conference on Advancement in Electrical and Electronic Engineering (ICAEEE), Gazipur, Bangladesh, 2018, (pp. 1–4). doi:10.1109/ICAEEE.2018.8642976.

[8] Vozmilov, A. G., Ilimbetov, R. Y., and Astafev, D. V. (2016). The usage of ozone in agriculture technological processes. In 2016 2nd International Conference on Industrial Engineering, Applications and Manufacturing (ICIEAM), Chelyabinsk, Russia, 2016, (pp. 1–4). doi: 10.1109/ICIEAM.2016.7911012.

[9] Boleli, I., Morita, V., Matos Jr, J., Thimotheo, M., and Almeida, V. (2016). Poultry egg incubation: integrating and optimizing production efficiency. *Brazilian Journal of Poultry Science*, 18(spe2), 1–16. https://doi.org/10.1590/1806-9061-2016-0292K.

[10] Radhakrishnan, K., Jose, N., Sanjay, S. G., Cherian, T., and Vishnu, K. R. (2014). Design and implementation of a fully automated egg incubator. *International Journal of Advanced Research in Electrical, Electronics and Instrumentation Engineering*, 3(2), 2056–5860.

[11] Okpagu, P. E., and Nwosu, A. W. (2016). Development and temperature control of smart egg incubator system for various types of egg. *European Journal of Engineering and Technology*, 4(2).

[12] Aldair, A. A., Rashid, A. T., and Mokayef, M. (2018). Design and implementation of intelligent control system for egg incubator based on IoT technology. In 2018 4th International Conference on Electrical, Electronics and System Engineering (ICEESE), Kuala Lumpur, Malaysia, 2018, (pp. 49–54). doi: 10.1109/ICEESE.2018.8703539

76 Lung sounds classification using parallel pooling structure with CNN model

Ohmshankar, S.[1,a], Sudhagar, G.[1,b] and Hema, M.[2,c]

[1]Electronics and communication Engineering, Bharath Institute of Higher Education and Research, Chennai, India

[2]Electronics and communication Engineering, Information Technology, Easwari Engineering College, Chennai, India

Abstract

The role played by electronic stethoscopes in identifying different types of lung sounds is significant in many aspects, especially in early diagnoses of respiratory ailments. Machine learning (ML) techniques are extensively employed in the field of diagnosis for the past three decades with a purpose i.e., to enhance the diagnostic accuracy of the healthcare professionals. In order to extract deep features, the present reading suggests a unique pre-skilled convolution neural network (CNN) model. In the projected CNN architecture, the classification performance is enhanced by connecting the average-pooling layer and the max-pooling layer in parallel. Further, the parameters are also key in as input in the linear discriminant analysis (LDA) classifier by following the random subspace ensembles (RSE) method. The performance of the proposed method was evaluated with the help of ICBHI 2018, a challenge dataset. Both deep features with RSE method yielded the optimal accuracy levels than the rest of the methods while a 5.75% increase was found in the classification accuracy of the proposed method.

Keywords: Convolution neural network model, HHT, LDA, lung sound, parallel pooling, RSE method, SVM

Introduction

Globally, lung diseases remain the third most common cause behind death, according to the World Health Organization (WHO). The WHO reported every year, more than 3 million deaths are recorded due to respiratory ailments [1]. In the domain of pulmonary pathology, the attributes of the lung's sounds and its diagnosis play a critical role. In general, the sounds of the lungs can be segregated as two types such as normal and abnormal. In the absence of any pulmonary disease, the normal lung sounds are heard while it happens vice versa, in other situations [2,3]. When an additional breathing noise is heard parallel to the typical lung sound, then it is termed as an abnormal lung sound. Such sounds are identified as continuous in it possess wheezes while discontinuous in case of crackles. The existence of a lung disease can be confirmed, when such sounds are heard [4].

In general, physicians assess a patient's symptoms and diagnose lung diseases with the help of stethoscope and the method is known as auscultation. being an affordable, easy and reliable diagnostic method, it requires only a minimal amount of time for diagnosis [5]. The procedure can help in understanding the patient's lung diseases and the associated symptoms [6]. In spite of its benefits, the hearing sensitivity remains a challenge to be addressed in conventional auscultation process. It is challenging to determine the lung sounds and differentiate it using traditional auscultation techniques, owing to the inclusion of non-stationary signals. So, the application of electronic stethoscope in combination with artificial intelligence (AI) system remains a highly reliable, cost-effective and comfortable method that can overcome the challenges encountered in traditional auscultation process. Further, it provides real-time and reliable outcome through automated diagnostics [7].

[a]ohmshankar.ece@gmail.com, [b]Sudhagar344@gmail.com, [c]hemsit82@gmail.com

DOI: 10.1201/9781003616399-76

Traditional methods have been used in literature and it encompasses classifiers as well as hand-crafted features to categorize the lung sounds. In literature [6], the extraction of the features was executed using the frequency ratio of power spectral density (PSD) values by following the Hilbert-Huang transform (HHT) method. Then, the authors made use of support vector machine (SVM) algorithm. In the study conducted earlier [8], the authors used the features that were extracted from time-frequency and time-cale analysis methods in order to distinguish normal lung sounds from crackles. In this study, k-Nearest neighbors (kNN), multilayer perceptron (MLP) and SVM were used for the purpose of classification amongst which the SVM achieved the optimal accuracy.

For the purpose of classifying the normal lung sounds from abnormal ones, the authors [9] used a feature set constituted by instant kurtosis, discriminating function and entropy. In general, the abnormal lung sounds include stridor, rhonchi and wheezes. Amongst the classifiers used, the SVM classifier achieved the optimal classification accuracy. In literature [10], the features were extracted from the respiratory signals using Mel frequency cepstral coefficients (MFCCs) while Gaussian mixture model (GMM) was utilized for the evaluation of the proposed approach. The higher order statistics (HSO) was utilized in the study conducted earlier [7] for the purpose of feature extraction. In this study, the authors used genetic algorithms as well as Fisher's discriminant ratio upon the feature set in order to reduce the number of features. In literature, the authors created the feature set with a few crackle parameters, wavelet coefficients and autoregressive model coefficients. In this study, both k-NN and artificial neural network (ANN) deployed for the purpose of classification. In recent times [12], extensive application of deep learning-based models can be observed, owing to their supreme performance in comparison with the traditional methods.

The CNNs were utilized in the study conducted earlier [13] for the classification of environmental sounds with the help of spectrogram images. These pictures were key into CNN. On the other hand, the authors [14] made use of a CNN model to categorize the respiratory sounds in which the

CNN exhibited a superior performance. In this background, the current study proposes a hybrid model so as to enhance the classification performance as well as determination of the lung sounds. As mentioned earlier, various types of lung sounds have been established such as normal, crackles, wheezes and crackles plus wheezes. In this study, the authors used a pre-trained CNN model and fed it with spectrogram images for the purpose of deep-feature extraction. During the classification stage, the authors used linear discriminant analysis (LDA) classifier in addition to random subspace ensembles (RSE) method.

The current research paper is organized under various sections as briefed herewith; section 2 deals with methodology while section 3 details about the experimental works while section 4 concludes the research work. The methodology section provides a bird's eye view LDA, RSE and the CNN model along with the spectrogram image. Under section 3, i.e., experimental works, the method proposed in this study is investigated with the help of a robust dataset. The experimental outcomes are tabulated in this section. Finally, the conclusion section interprets the study findings in line with performance criteria and compare with the existing methods using the same dataset.

Methodology

Figure 76.1 shows the framework for the proposed method. During the pre-processing stage, the lung sounds are used to generate the spectrogram images. Since. Afterwards, Viridis Color Map is used for the transformation of the spectrogram data into images. Thus, the spectrogram images are generated and stored in the folders. The pretrained CNN model, generated by training a specific section of the spectrogram images. The extraction of the deep features is performed from the fully-connected (FC) layer of the pretrained CNN model.

For the purpose of enhancing the classification performance, the average pooling process of the characteristic information is planned at the time of performing the down-sampling process with the help of pooling layers. In general, the max-pooling process outperforms the average pooling process. This results in a scenario

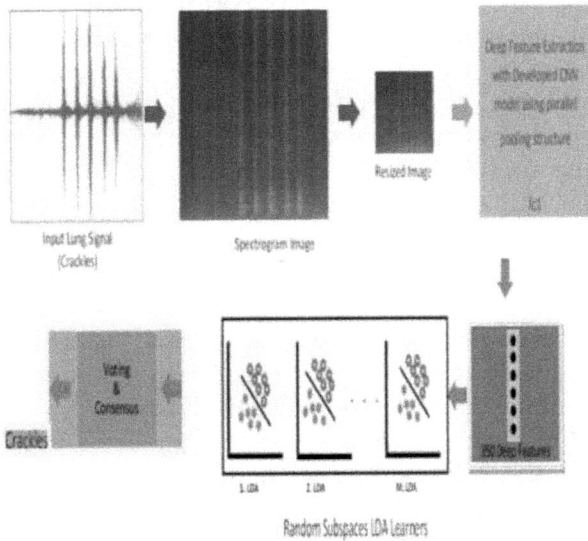

Figure 76.1 Proposed framework
Source: Author

where the pooling structure that is utilized in the pre-trained CNN model is connected with the max-pooling layer and the average pooling layer in parallel. The deep features are then sent across the LDA classifier so that the proposed method can be verified for its classification performance. The LDA classifier is made to follow the RSE method so as to enhance the classification performance further.

Spectrogram

Spectrogram can be defined as a visual process that can portray the loudness or power of a signal over a specific period of time at varying frequencies in a certain waveform. The spectrogram has the potential to display the changes in energy levels over a period. Equation 1 shows the short-time Fourier transform (STFT) formula.

$$F(n, \omega) = \sum_{i=-\infty}^{\infty} x(i) \omega(n - i) e^{-jwn} \qquad (1)$$

Here, the input is denoted by x(i) while ω(i) corresponds to the window function (for instance, rectangular window and hamming window), which is usually focused on time n. It is possible to exhibit the spectrogram as STFT's squared magnitude. Viridis Color Map is utilized to construct the spectrogram images while the map is a homogenous mapping tool and it makes use of colors that change [16,17].

CNNs

There exist two primary steps in the CNN process such as forward-propagation and back-propagation. In line with the backpropagation techniques, the optimization of the forward-propagation's learning parameters is accomplished [18]. In forward-propagation step, various convolutional layers exist in addition to one or more than one FC layers. The extraction of the apparent attributes out of the input signal remains the primary goal of the convolutional layer. This primary aim is conveyed through the layers. Generally, the first convolutional layer extracts the low-level features whereas the next set of convolutional layers proceed with the extraction of highly-complicated features. The CNNs are trained as briefed herewith. In forward-propagation stage, there exists multiple layers such as convolutional, activation, batch normalization (BN), pooling and SoftMax. The convolution stage has a key goal to achieve. Equation 2 shows the convolution operation of the 2D data.

$$y_i^n = \sum_i y_i^{n-1} * \omega_{ij}^n + b_i^n \qquad (2)$$

The preparation of the data is executed in such a way that it does not show any abnormal distribution of the BN layer. This phenomenon ensures that the gradient vanishing does not occur at the time of training. In this manner, the optimization of the learning parameters is executed so as to fasten the convergence by giving protection to a state of higher gradient across the timeline. On the other hand, the level of noise is heavily reduced by deploying the BN layer [19]. Here, the input is denoted by xi whereas mb corresponds to the mini batch mean. Further, the mini-batch variance is denoted by vb while the input size is denoted by k. Finally corresponds to the small constant. Here, c represents the scale factors whereas d corresponds to the shift factors. These factors are nothing but parameters with learning capability and are adjusted to the most convenient values at the time of training. The value y n,

In CNN method, the predominantly used activation layer is rectified linear unit (ReLU) as it ensures the non-occurrence of gradient explosion and gradient disappearance problems within the sigmoid activation function. The following equation shows the ReLU activation function in

$$r_i^n = \mathbf{max}\left(0, y_i^n\right) \tag{3}$$

Which rn denotes the ith output of the nth ReLU layer. The pooling layer performs the down-sampling operation so as to reduce the matrix size. This scenario mitigates the cost incurred upon the computation and also avoids over-fitting issues [20]. Average and maximum pooling layers are the most commonly used pooling layers in CNN.

In the initial FC layer, the flattening of the matrices that are conveyed from the earlier layers is performed and then connected to the rest of the FC layers. The structure of the CNN from the FC layer to the classification layer remains the same as found in MLP. The SoftMax layer is fed with values from the earlier FC layers as input. This SoftMax operation is defined as a learning method in order to tally the classification scores. Here, SoftMax remains the single operation that involves in the transformation of the neutral network's output with the help of probability distribution. Thus, SoftMax helps in achieving different classes.

Random subspace ensembles
For the purpose of enhancing the performance of the classifiers, the RSE method is used. The underlying mechanism of this method lies on a stochastic operation that selects the components for the training model in a random manner so as to create each classifier [22]. The training data is segregated into random number of subspaces in this RSE method. The most suitable, appropriate and convenient subspace class membership is allocated with the influence of learner algorithm of the classifiers. Afterwards, the class memberships that are transferred from each and every subspace learner, are brought together in the class vector. The predicted scores are presented on the basis of the highest average score of the class vector. The following RSE method is applied upon the LDA classifier.

- Step 1: Choose random data of K size without modifying it from training data. (K < N).
- Step 2: Use only the predictors to train an LDA learner

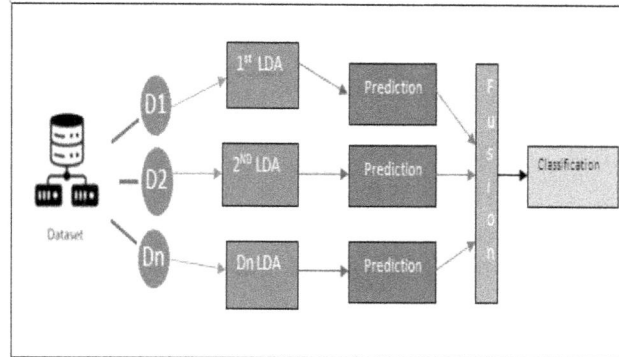

Figure 76.2 Representation of random space ensemble with LDA
Source: Author

- Step 3: Use step 1 and 2 up till M LDA students are present.
- Step 4: Put the LDA learners' prediction values together.
- Step 5: Sort the test dataset based on its greatest average value.

IT shows how RSE is represented in which the LDA classifier is deployed. Here, K corresponds to the dimensions of the subspace, M denotes the number of LDA learners and d corresponds to the randomly-chosen training samples.

Experimental Works

Dataset
The method proposed in this study was investigated for its performance using the ICBHI 2018 challenge dataset, containing more than 900 lung sounds. These lung sounds were recorded with the help of three varying types of stethoscopes at the following sampling frequencies. The ICBHI 2018 challenge dataset has different classes such as crackles, normal, wheezes, and wheezes plus crackles. As the sound files have been separated into different cycles, a 20-second sound file may contain one or more than one class tags too. Table 76.1 shows how a typical sound file's cycle breakdown looks like.

As shown in the table, there would be columns such as cycle index, start time, end time, and values for crackles as well as wheezes. The respective

Table 76.1 Cycle details of Sound file

Cycle	Start time	End time	Cracle value	Wheeze value
1	0.704	3.156	0	0
2	3.156	5.466	0	0
3	5.466	7.751	0	1
4	7.751	9.054	0	1
5	9.054	11.054	1	0
6	11.054	14.373	1	0
7	14.373	16.596	1	1

Source: Author

wheeze and crackle values for various elements such as crackles, wheezes, normal, and wheezes plus crackles tags.

Evaluation method and criteria

Majority of the data in the ICBHI 2018 challenge dataset i.e., 90% was separated to train the proposed CNN model followed by its validation. The rest of the dataset i.e., 10%, was utilized for the LDA classifier in combination with RSE method during the classification stage. In this study, the authors followed 10-fold cross-validation method to determine the classification performance. Accuracy, precision, specificity, sensitivity and F-score were chosen as the performance criteria for this study. Equations 18-22 show the formula for calculating these measures along with the confusion matrix.

$$Accuracy = \frac{TP + TN}{TP + FP + TN + FN}$$

$$Specificity = \frac{TN}{FP + TN}$$

$$Precision = \frac{TP}{FP + TP}$$

$$F - Score = 2 \times \frac{precision \times sensivity}{precision + sensivity}$$

Experimental Setup and Results

The model was simulated in MATLAB software (R2019a) installed in a PC configured with the

specifications. The lung sound data was fed into the spectrogram operation in the proposed model. Both of the window size and partly cover were fine-tuned according to the sampling frequencies. Based on the sampling frequencies such as 5 KHz, 15KHz, and 55.1 KHz, the window size and overlap were selected as given herewith; 64-8, 128-16, and 524-64, correspondingly. The resolution of the spectrogram images remains the crucial factor in this selection process since those images are fed into the proposed CNN method for training purpose.

The training parameters were fixed as follows; initial learning – 0.005, max-epochs – 12 and validation frequency – 30. For the purpose. Once the 419 iterations got concluded, the model achieved 60% training accuracy while the validation accuracy stood at 59.78%.

The figures infers that 83.2% i.e., best accuracy score was accomplished using normal class whereas the wheezes class achieved the least accuracy score of 40.4%. On average, the model achieved 71.15%. It shows the outcomes of other performance criteria such as F-score, precision, sensitivity and specificity while the best score for each criterion has been highlighted in the table. The categorization outcomes of different classifiers are portrayed from which it can be inferred that the LDA classifier accomplished the best accuracy achieved with the help of RSE method. It compares and contrasts the cla performance of the proposed model with the rest of the popular pre-trained models. The classifiers were used upon the deep features, extracted from the CNN models, with the purpose of achieving the optimal performance.

The VGG16 was the top performer in terms of accuracy i.e., 65.4%, in comparison with the rest of the popular pre-training CNN models. The proposed model achieved the following accuracy values i.e., 67.2% and 68.6%. On the other hand, the optimal accuracy value i.e., 71.15% was achieved. In literature [23], MFCC was utilized to extract the features after which the Hidden Markov Model classifier was utilized in the study, which in turn achieved an accuracy of 49.56%. Then, the features were fed into the decision tree classifier while the latter achieved an accuracy of 49.62% for lung sound classification of lung sound.

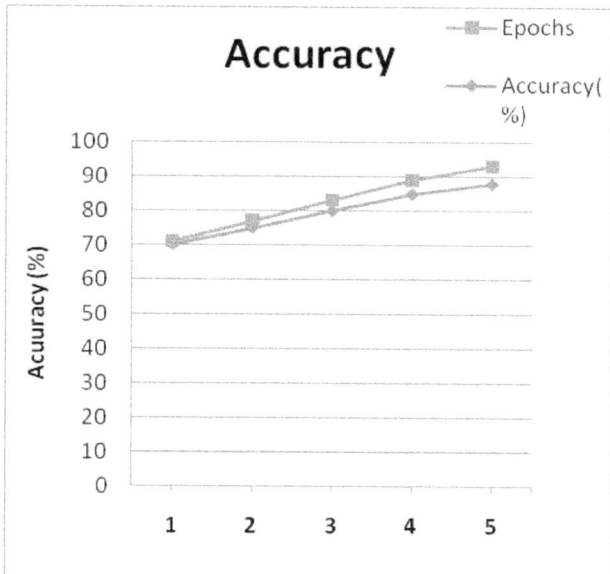

Accuracy

In literature [25], the authors made use features of wavelet disintegration and STFT accordingly, it was used for comparison in this study which achieved 57.88% accuracy using the SVM classifier. In the study conducted earlier [26], two methods were utilized for the classification of lung sounds. At first, the classification of the lung sounds was performed using the transfer learning technique. Here, the technique was made to undergo training by fine-tuning the pre-training VGG16. This study achieved an optimal accuracy of 63.09%. In the next method, the FC layers of the pretraining VGG16 model were extracted to retrieve the deep features in which the study achieved 65.50% accuracy with the SVM classifier.

Conclusion

In the current study, the classification of the lung sounds was investigated so as to diagnose pulmonary disorders. In the studies conducted earlier, conventional ML techniques were utilized for the purpose of classifying the lung sounds whereas deep learning has become the most sought-after technique in recent times to accomplish supreme classification results. Some of the popular pretraining CNN models like AlexNet, VGG16 etc., provide excellent outcomes for image identification purpose and also in sound classification applications, in a few cases. In spite of this, there is a lack of comprehensive representation of

the sound characteristics since the CNN models have not been exposed to training using the sound datasets. In this background, the current study proposed a CNN model, trained it with spectrogram images constructed based on lung sounds and analyzed its performance. The proposed CNN model was supplemented with parallel-pooling structure to enhance the classification performance. The first FC layer in the proposed CNN was used to extract the deep features while the retrieved features were employed in different classification algorithms. The LDA-RSE classifier achieved the optimal result i.e., 71.15% accuracy. In addition to this, the proposed model was also compared with the rest of the pretrained CNN models in terms of accuracy. The comparative analysis outcomes infer that the proposed CNN model achieved the best classification accuracy. Further, the proposed method achieved an increase in accuracy up to 5.75% than the existing optimal outcomes, using the same dataset.

References

[1] Wanasinghe, T., Bandara, S., Madusanka, S., Meedeniya, D., Bandara, M., and De La Torre Díez, I. (2024). Lung sound classification for respiratory disease identification using deep learning: a survey. *International Journal of Online and Biomedical Engineering*, 20(9).

[2] Arar, M. E., and Sedef, H. (2023). An efficient lung sound classification technique based on MFCC and HDMR. *Signal, Image and Video Processing,* 17(8), 4385–4394.

[3] Wang, Z., and Sun, Z. (2024). Performance evaluation of lung sounds classification using deep learning under variable parameters. *EURASIP Journal on Advances in Signal Processing*, 2024(1), 51.

[4] Koppad, D., Kumar, P., Kantikar, N. A., and Ramesh, S. (2024). Multi-task learning for lung sound and Lung disease classification. arXiv e-prints, arXiv-2404.

[5] Saldanha, J., Chakraborty, S., Patil, S., Kotecha, K., Kumar, S., and Nayyar, A. (2022). Data augmentation using variational autoencoders for improvement of respiratory disease classification. *Plos One*, 17(8), e0266467.

[6] Cozzatti, M., Simonetta, F., and Ntalampiras, S. (2022). Variational autoencoders for anomaly detection in respiratory sounds. In International Conference on Artificial Neural Networks, (pp. 333–345). Cham: Springer Nature Switzerland.

[7] Ketfi, M., Belahcene, M., and Bourennane, S. (2024). Transfer learning fusion and stacked auto-encoders for viral lung disease classification. *New Generation Computing*, 42, 1–34 .

[8] Zhou, Q., Wang, S., Zhang, X., and Zhang, Y. D. (2022). WVALE: weak variational autoencoder for localisation and enhancement of COVID-19 lung infections. *Computer Methods and Programs in Biomedicine*, 221, 106883.

[9] Jin, F., Sattar, F., and Goh, D. Y. T. (2014). New approaches for spectrotemporal feature extraction with applications to respiratory sound classification. *Neurocomputing*, 123, 362–371. doi: 10.1016/j. neucom.2013.07.033.

[10] Hema, M., and Raja, S. K. S. (2023). A quantitative approach to minimize energy consumption in cloud data centres using VM consolidation algorithm. *KSII Transactions on Internet and Information Systems*, 17(2), 312–334.

[11] Jayalakshmy, S., and Sudha, G. F. (2020). Scalogram based prediction model for respiratory disorders using optimized convolutional neural networks. *Artificial Intelligence in Medicine*, 103, 101809. doi: 10.1016/ j.artmed.2020. 101809.

[12] Fraiwan, M., Fraiwan, L., Alkhodari, M., and Hassanin, O. (2021). Recognition of pulmonary diseases from lung sounds using convolutional neural networks and long short-term memory. *Journal of Ambient Intelligence and Humanized Computing*, 13, 4759–4771.

[13] Aykanat, M., Kılıc, O., Kurt, B., and Saryal, S. (2017). Classification of lung sounds using convolutional neural networks. *EURASIP Journal on Image and Video Processing*, 2017(1), 1–9.

[14] Yanai, K., and Kawano, Y. (2015). Food image recognition using deep convolutional network with pre-training and fine-tuning. In Proceedings IEEE International Conference on Multimedia Expo Workshops (ICMEW), Jun. 2015, (pp. 1–6). doi: 10. 1109/ICMEW.2015.7169816.

[15] Zhou, Y., Nejati, H., Do, T. T., Cheung, N. M., and Cheah, L. (2016). Image-based vehicle analysis using deep neural network: a systematic study. In Proceedings IEEE International Conference on Digital Signal Processing (DSP), Oct. 2016, (pp. 276–280). doi: 10.1109/ICDSP.2016.7868561.

[16] Dong, S., Wu, W., He, K., and Mou, X. (2020). Rolling bearing performance degradation assessment based on improved convolutional neural network with anti-interference. *Measurement*, 151, 107219. doi: 10.1016/j.measurement.2019.107219.

[17] Ioffe, S., and Szegedy, C. (2015). Batch normalization: accelerating deep network training by reducing internal covariate shift. In Proceedings 32nd International Conference on International Conference on Machine Learning (ICML), (Vol. 1, pp. 448–456).

[18] Wang, S. H., Phillips, P., Sui, Y., Liu, B., Yang, M., and Cheng, H. (2018). Classification of alzheimer's disease based on eight-layer convolutional neural network with leaky rectified linear unit and max pooling. *Journal of Medical Systems*, 42(5), 85. doi: 10.1007/s10916-018-0932-7.

[19] Ho, T. K. (1998). Nearest neighbors in random subspaces. In Advances in Pattern Recognition (Lecture Notes in Computer Science, Lecture Notes in Artificial Intelligence, and Lecture Notes in Bioinformatics). 1998, (pp. 640–648). doi: 10.1007/bfb0033288.

[20] Jakovljević, N., and Lončar-Turukalo, T. (2018). Hidden markov model based respiratory sound classification. In Proceedings International Conference on Biomedical and Health Informatics, Springer, (Vol. 66, pp. 39–43).

[21] Serbes, G., Ulukaya, S., and Kahya, Y. P. (2018). An automated lung sound preprocessing and classification system based onspectral analysis methods. In Proceedings International Conference on Biomedical and Health Informatics Springer, 2018, (pp. 45–49).

[22] Demir, F., Sengur, A., and Bajaj, V. (2020). Convolutional neural networks based efficient approach for classification of lung diseases. *Health Information Science, and Systems*, 8(1), 1–8.

77 Design of peripheral component interconnect express physical layer

U. Ganeshwara Chary[1,a], G.R.L.V.N. Srinivasa Raju[2,b], Nrusimhadri Vyshnavi[1,c], Akathota Bhavana[1,d], Sravya kovvuri[1,e], Asral Bahari Jambek[3,f]

[1]Department of ECE, B V Raju Institute of Technology, Narsapur, Telangana, India

[2]Department of ECE, Shri Vishnu Engineering College for Women, Bhimavaram, India

[3]Faculty of Electronic Engineering Technology, Universiti Malaysia Perlis (UniMAP), Perlis, Malaysia

Abstract

Peripheral component interconnect express (PCIe), a contemporary and high-performance communication protocol, streamlines the incorporation of hard drives, solid-state-drives, ethernet, Wi-Fi connections, and graphic cards into the framework of computing systems, ensuring a cohesive integration experience. Its widespread adoption as a standard motherboard interface is fueled by its superior bandwidth, making it the preferred choice across various applications. It comprises three key layers, facilitating packet-based data transfer within its architecture for efficient communication. This paper aims to enhance data transfer speeds within the PCIe physical layer, accelerating communication in diverse applications. Simultaneously, it endeavors to reduce spatial requirements, optimizing overall system efficiency. By addressing challenges associated with both speed and spatial constraints in PCIe technology, this research contributes to advancing the capabilities of data transmission while ensuring an efficient use of resources in modern computing systems. This paper introduces the utilization of LCG scrambler as an alternative to LSFR for data randomization, with the primary objectives of minimizing randomization timing and reducing overall area requirements. The study entails the development of a 128b/130b encoder, decoder, and related components using Verilog HDL. Subsequent to the implementation, synthesis reports were generated, and a comprehensive analysis of the results was conducted.

Keywords: 128b/130b decoder, 128b/130b encoder, Cadence, LCG Scrambler, PHY

Introduction

In an era marked by rapid technological progress, the need for efficient and swift data transfer has taken center stage. A pivotal player in modern computing, the peripheral component interconnect express (PCIe) standard serves as the linchpin, facilitating seamless communication among various system components. Known for its adaptability and scalability, the PCIe architecture has undergone multiple revisions, continually pushing the boundaries of data transfer rates. At its core, the physical layer plays a foundational role in the PCIe standard, overseeing the transmission of data between devices and upholding signal integrity. With an escalating demand for increased bandwidth and reduced latency, the meticulous design and optimization of the PCIe physical layer emerge as crucial factors directly influencing overall system performance. Recognized for its ability to handle faster data transfers, PCIe represents an evolution beyond the PCI protocol, employing a lane-based design. This design involves the transfer and reception of data across multiple lanes, each comprised of two differential pairs—one for transmitting data (TX) and the other for receiving data (RX).

The PCIe protocol stack comprises multiple layers, each assigned specific duties and responsibilities. These layers include the physical layer (PHY), data link layer (DLL), and transport layer (TLL).

Physical layer: The functionality of the PCIe PHY is centered on the tangible transmission of data across the communication medium.

[a]gnaneshwara.chary@bvrit.ac.in, [b]grln@svew.edu.in, [c]nrusimhadri.vyshnavi@gmail.com, [d]akuthotabhavana@gmail.com, [e]kovvurusravya97@gmail.com, [f]asral@unimap.edu.my

DOI: 10.1201/9781003616399-77

Employing a point-to-point topology, PCIe establishes dedicated lanes connecting pairs of devices. These lanes, comprising differential pairs for the transmission and reception of data signals, form the backbone of the inter-device communication. The specifications of the physical layer meticulously outline the electrical characteristics, signaling rates, and connector types, laying the foundation for a robust and dependable communication framework between connected devices.

Datalink layer: Within PCIe, the DLL manages flow control, error detection, and link negotiation. Comprising the logical link layer and transaction layer, it establishes and sustains a reliable connection between devices, ensuring efficient data transmission through meticulous error handling and flow control mechanisms.

Transaction layer: The TLL in PCIe intricately handles data assembly and disassembly, ensuring error-free transfers. While PCIe doesn't explicitly define a transport layer in the OSI model, the transaction layer within the data link layer serves analogous functions. It adeptly manages segmentation and reassembly of data packets, enabling the efficient transmission of sizable datasets over the PCIe link, showcasing its critical role in optimizing data integrity and transfer efficiency within the architecture.

This research outlines the development of the Physical layer, where we integrated key components including multiplexers, LCG scramblers, and 128b/130b encoders and decoders. Additionally, parallel-to-serial and serial-to-parallel converters were designed using Verilog Hardware Description Language (HDL). Our approach aims to enhance the functionality and efficiency of the Physical layer through the implementation of these components, contributing to advancements in signal processing and communication technologies.

Related Work

Within this framework, scholars [1–4] have engaged in a study focusing on the technology of the PCIe PHY. One study focuses on the verification of the MAC-PHY layer for PCIe Gen5.0, demonstrating impressive performance and backward compatibility through the utilization of SystemVerilog and UVM. Another paper delves into the design and simulation of PCIe's physical layer, employing Verilog in Quartus Intel and ModelSim. To tackle power consumption concerns, a separate paper explores low-power design in PCIe switch PHY, emphasizing adherence to protocol standards and achieving significant reductions in power usage. Lastly, another contribution involves the development of Verification IP for the PCIe PHY, utilizing UVM and SystemVerilog to showcase efficient data transfer and validate the protocol's implementation through a variety of test cases and simulations. Collectively, these works offer valuable insights into PCIe verification methodologies, addressing aspects such as performance, power consumption, and design considerations within this essential communication protocol.

In the literature survey, two research papers [5,6] address advancements in data transmission technologies. In the first paper, "design and implementation of a high-speed encryption and decryption system based on PCIe bus," the focus is on modernizing cryptographic systems by substituting the conventional PCI BUS with PCIe, enhancing high-speed communication between FPGA and PC. The second paper, "FPGA-based Train Onboard PCIe Board Design and Implementation," explores the evolution of PCI interfaces and introduces FPGA-based solutions for PCIe board design, aiming to boost performance and adaptability in comparison to traditional PCI interfaces. Both studies highlight the significance of utilizing PCIe for more efficient data transmission.

The literature survey encompasses three research papers [7–9] that address advanced technologies in data transmission. The first paper focuses on an optimal implementation of an 8b/10b encoder for Xilinx FPGAs, introducing a structurally efficient design tailored to minimize look-up tables and prioritize resource utilization, logic delay, and power consumption. Comparative assessments against contemporary solutions demonstrate superior performance. The second paper explores USB 3.0 optimization using FPGA for 8b/10b encoding and decoding, emphasizing the increased transmission speed and practical implementation details. The third paper proposes a novel 128b/130b line coding algorithm for high-speed data transfer, doubling payload compared to conventional techniques, and achieving superior data rates with Verilog implementation using Quartus II 9.0v and cadence encounter 14.26. The literature review highlights the importance of these papers in advancing efficient encoding and decoding solutions for various data transmission scenarios.

The literature survey of the research papers [10–12] highlights two pivotal contributions in circuit testing and design for testability. "A programmable and parameterizable reseeding linear feedback shift register" focuses on enhancing LBIST capabilities, providing adaptable bit vector generation and a reseeding technique. In "low power linear feedback shift register," emphasis shifts to BIST, introducing an efficient, low-power pattern generation method tailored for VLSI circuit testing, optimizing multipliers, and minimizing switching activity between test patterns.

The literature survey cites research papers [13–15] highlighting the need to enhance data security in cryptographic transmission. "Performance analysis of pseudo random bit generator using modified dual-coupled linear congruential generator" introduces the modified dual coupled linear congruential generator (MDCLCG) as a secure alternative to existing pseudo random bit generators (PRBGs). The study evaluates MDCLCG's performance in terms of area, power, and speed, examining the impact of various adder topologies. Practical results highlight the efficiency of ripple carry adders and 3-operand modulo carry save adder configurations. The research emphasizes optimizing resource utilization and improving performance metrics in secure pseudo-random bit generation. In this context, the study integrates MDCLCG into the data encryption standard (DES) algorithm to boost key generation efficiency and security. The implementation is conducted using Verilog-HDL, with the prototype developed on an FPGA Spartan3E XC3S500E. Overall, the MD-CLCG offers improved area usage and enhanced security compared to traditional algorithms.

Architecture

The PHY within PCIe, also known as peripheral component interconnect express, plays a vital role in managing the electrical and mechanical facets of transmitting data. PCIe serves as a high-speed serial standard for expanding computer buses, facilitating connections between the mother-board of a computer and diverse hardware components like graphics cards, storage devices, and network adapters.

The architecture of the PCIe-PHY, illustrated in Figure 77.1, comprises two main segments: logical and electrical blocks. These segments are crucial for encoding, decoding, and overseeing electrical signaling to guarantee dependable communication within PCIe systems.

Logical sub-block: The logical sub-blocks in PCIe are crucial components that ensure efficient encoding and decoding of data. The physical coding sublayer (PCS) plays a pivotal role in this process, employing sophisticated methods like 128b/130b encoding and scrambling. The 128b/130b encoding is particularly essential for maintaining DC balance, which is vital for reliable communication and preventing signal integrity issues. The scrambling process further enhances data security and integrity during transmission. In addition, the PCS is responsible for clock

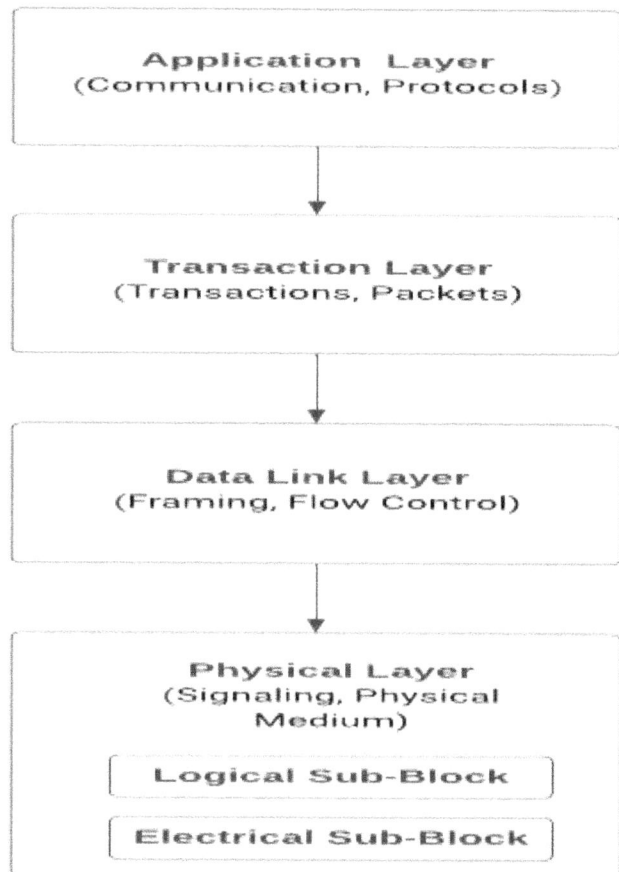

Figure 77.1 Layers of PCIe
Source: Author

recovery, ensuring synchronization between the sender and receiver for seamless communication.

The DLL operates within the logical sub-block and is responsible for overseeing critical link-related functions. This includes the training and initialization processes that are imperative for establishing a robust communication link. The DLL optimizes the link by synchronizing both ends and fine-tuning parameters for optimal performance. It plays a key role in managing flow control, error detection, and retransmission of data packets, contributing to the overall reliability and efficiency of the PCIe communication link

Electrical sub-block: The electrical sub-blocks of PCIe are equally integral to the overall architecture, consisting of the physical media attachment (PMA) and physical medium dependent (PMD). The PMA focuses on the electrical signaling aspect of PCIe communication. It employs techniques such as pre-emphasis and equalization to counteract issues like attenuation, ensuring that the transmitted signals maintain their integrity over the physical medium. Pre-emphasis helps in boosting high-frequency components of the signal, compensating for losses incurred during transmission, while equalization adjusts for frequency-dependent attenuation, ensuring a robust and clear signal.

Simultaneously, the PMD interfaces directly with the physical medium, employing serializers and deserializers to adeptly adapt data between parallel and serial formats. This capability is crucial for ensuring compatibility across diverse physical mediums, allowing PCIe to operate seamlessly in various environments. The serializers and deserializers play a key role in efficiently converting data between different transmission formats, contributing to the flexibility and adaptability of PCIe technology. Together, the PMA and PMD within the electrical subblocks ensure the reliable and high-performance transmission of data in PCIe architectures.

Methodology

The depicted data flow in Figure 77.2, within the PCIe physical layer, is managed through a sequence of crucial components. Throughout the transmission of data, information follows a route involving buffers, multiplexers (mux), LCG scramblers,

128b/130b encoders, and parallel-to-serial converters. Conversely, in the receiver phase, the data follows a reverse path, encountering elements like serial-to- parallel converters, 128b/130b decoders, LCG de-scramblers, and receiver buffers.

The process unfolds as data from the transmitter buffer is directed through the mux, facilitated by a control signal. From the mux, the data proceeds to the scrambler, where it undergoes randomization. The randomized data is subsequently routed to the encoder to ensure security, and then enters the parallel-to-serial converter before embarking on transmission. On the receiver end, the serialized data undergoes reconversion to parallel form through a serial-to-parallel converter. The parallel data is then subject to decoding and routed through the de-scrambler. Finally, the receiver buffer captures the trans- mitted data, thereby completing the intricate data flow within the PCIe physical layer. This meticulously designed process not only ensures the security of the transmitted data but also facilitates an efficient and seamless transfer mechanism within the PCIe architecture.

Implementation

The transmit and receive buffer handles TLPs and DLLPs acquired from the data link layer in the PCIe physical layer. Using a control signal, the physical layer encapsulates the packet by adding start and end characters. Subsequently, the byte stream is placed into the receiver buffer and

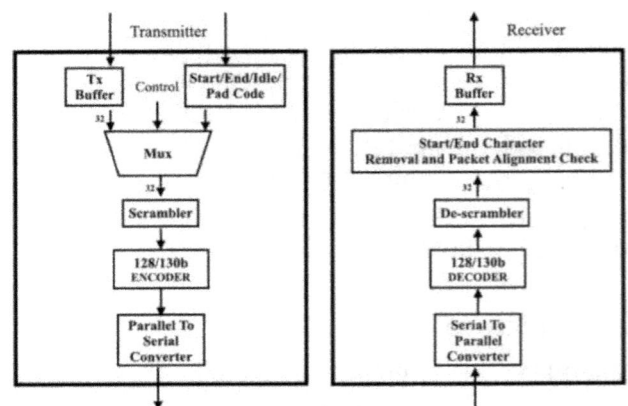

Figure 77.2 Workflow of proposed PCIe physical layer
Source: Author

forwarded to the data link layer. Playing a crucial role in the physical layer of the PCIe protocol, the Multiplexer oversees data flow. The Tx-buffer at this layer accepts incoming bits from the data connection layer. The received data undergoes processing and preparation for transmission over the physical layer. Simultaneously, a control signal is employed by the physical layer to frame the packet with pad code.

The PCIe specification mandates a scrambling/descrambling method, utilizing a linear congruential generator for implementation. PCIe employs a serial XOR operation on the data using the seed output from a linear congruential generator (LCG). Upon reception, the descrambler reverses the scrambling process, recovering the original data. The descrambler utilizes the identical pseudorandom bit sequence generated by the LCG to execute the XOR operation and successfully de-scramble the received data.

The 128b/130b encoder accepts a 128-bit input and pro- duces a 130-bit encoded output. Its operation is dependent on the usage of the special code K28.5 for alignment. Initially, the encoder checks the final five bits of input data to see if they are all ones. If this condition is satisfied, the output data is allocated to the 10-bit code (10'b0011111100). The remaining bits of the data supplied are rearranged. If the input's last five bits are not all ones, the data is simply rearranged. This encoding technique assures alignment with the supplied code. In contrast, the decoder accepts a 130-bit input and returns a decoded 128-bit output. It works by checking the final ten bits of incoming data to see if they match the format 10'b0011111100. If the condition is met, these bits are replaced with all 5'b11111. If the criterion is not satisfied, the decoder uses the same rearrangement technique as the encoder. This reciprocal encoding and decoding process guarantees that data is accurately transformed.

The transmit buffer within the electrical sub-block plays a pivotal role in converting encoded/packetized data from the logical sub-block into a serial format. Following serialization, the data is directed to the appropriate lane for transmission across the connection. On the receiving end, the data is deserialized, and subsequently returned to the logical sub- block for further processing, completing the cycle of data transmission and reception.

Simulation Results

Simulation involves component design in Verilog HDL, implemented and tested using the Cadence tool. This comprehensive process ensures accurate performance evaluation and verification of the designed components within the specified framework.

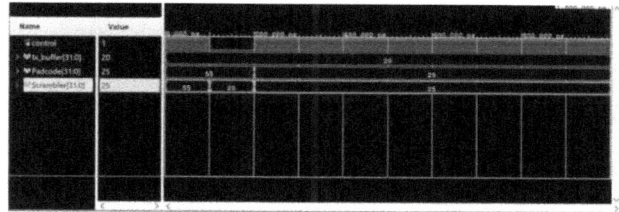

Figure 77.3 Multiplexer
Source: Author

Operating with an input Tx buffer and a 32-bit start and finish pad code, the multiplexer, illustrated in Figure 77.3, operates seamlessly under the guidance of a specialized controller. This control mechanism oversees the selection of input signals, enabling the conveyance of data to the scrambling process for subsequent processing.

Figure 77.4 Scrambler
Source: Author

The Scrambler transforms a 32-bit input data into a 32-bit scrambled output. Illustrated in Figure 77.4, the waveform depicts the transformation of input (5)10 into the scrambled value (4)10, considering the lcgstate as (1)10. The alteration of the scrambled data is influenced by the specific lcgstate in use.

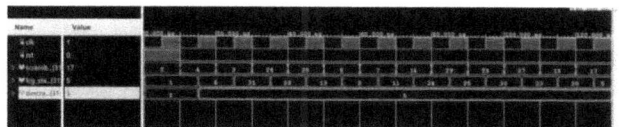

Figure 77.5 Descrambler
Source: Author

Descrambler converts 32-bit scrambled data into a 32-bit descrambled output. Figure 77.5 shows the waveform with scrambled input (4)10 and descrambled value (5)10 for lcgstate (1)10. The descrambled data is altered based on the lcgstate and scrambled data.

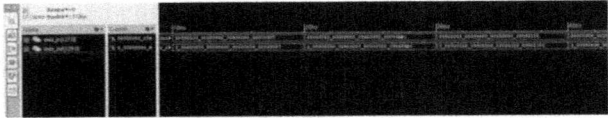

Figure 77.6 Encoder
Source: Author

In the depicted illustration, it is evident that the encoder processes a 128-bit data input, executing the operations specified in the 128b/130b encoder segment. The outcome of this process is presented as shown in Figure 77.6 as the 130-bit data output, referred to as "data-out."

Figure 77.7 Decoder
Source: Author

Much like the encoder, the decoder operates by receiving a 130-bit input, denoted as "data-in." It executes the operations outlined in the 128b/130b decoder section, ultimately producing a 128-bit output referred to as "data-out" as seen in Figure 77.7.

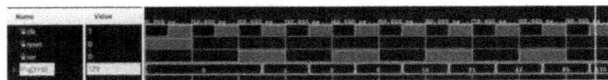

Figure 77.8 Serial to parallel
Source: Author

Serial to parallel converts the input data (170)10 which is sent bit by bit and obtained as parallel data (170)10 as shown in the Figure 77.8.

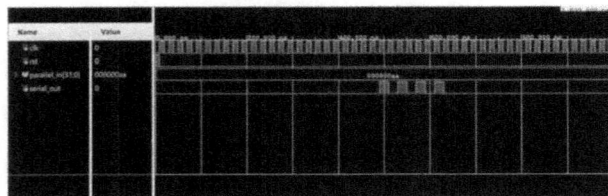

Figure 77.9 Parallel to serial
Source: Author

Parallel to serial converts the input data (170)10 that is transmitted into bit by bit data (serial data), as seen in Figure 77.9.

Synthesis Results

The images below depict the synthesis reports for the scrambler, de-scrambler, and LSFR. These reports generated using the Prime Time tool by Synopsys, provide valuable insights into area, power, and timing metrics.

LSFR reports: The synthesis reports for the linear feedback shift register (LSFR) are depicted in Figures 77.10, 77.11, and 77.12, covering area, power, and timing aspects. The reported values are 4495.039816 for area, 13.8468 mW for power consumption, and 0.75 for timing parameters. These figures provide a comprehensive assessment of LSFR's performance characteristics, crucial for evaluating its efficiency in a given context. Analyzing each metric individually aids in understanding the design's strengths and potential areas for improvement. The reported area value signifies the physical footprint of LSFR, power indicates its energy consumption, and timing reflects the speed at which it operates. Such detailed reports facilitate informed decision-making during the design and optimization phases.

LCG Scrambler: The Figures, specifically 77.13, 77.14 and 77.15, illustrate the area, power, and timing reports for the LCG Scrambler, with corresponding values mentioned as 1598.000013 for area, 91.7271 uW for power, and 0.35 for timing, providing a comprehensive overview of its performance characteristics.

Analysis

Figure 77.16 displays a comparative analysis of LSFR and LCG_Scrambler in terms of area,

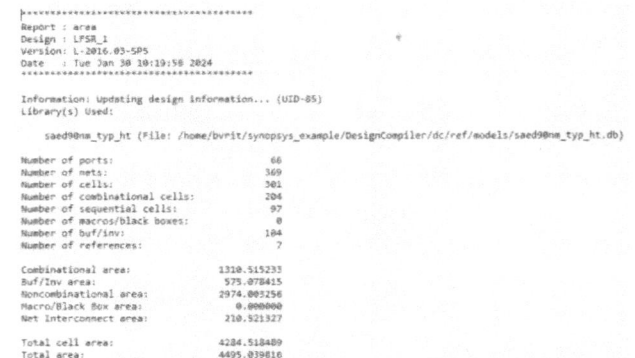

Figure 77.10 LSFR area report
Source: Author

```
********************************
Report : power
        -analysis_effort low
Design : LFSR_1
Version: L-2016.03-SP5
Date   : Tue Jan 30 10:20:58 2024
********************************

Library(s) Used:

    saed90nm_typ_ht (File: /home/bvrit/synopsys_example/DesignCompiler/dc/ref/models/saed90nm_typ_ht.db)

Operating Conditions: TYPICAL   Library: saed90nm_typ_ht
Wire Load Model Mode: enclosed

Design     Wire Load Model      Library
-------------------------------------------
LFSR_1        8000             saed90nm_typ_ht

Global Operating Voltage = 1.2
Power-specific unit information :
    Voltage Units = 1V
    Capacitance Units = 1.000000ff
    Time Units = 1ns
    Dynamic Power Units = 1uw   (derived from V,C,T units)
    Leakage Power Units = 1pw

  Cell Internal Power  =   9.7970 mw  (71%)
  Net Switching Power  =   4.0498 mw  (29%)
  ---------
Total Dynamic Power   =  13.8468 mw  (100%)

Cell Leakage Power    =  61.5505 uw
```

Power Group	Internal Power	Switching Power	Leakage Power	Total Power	(%) Attrs
io_pad	0.0000	0.0000	0.0000	0.0000 (0.00%)	
memory	0.0000	0.0000	0.0000	0.0000 (0.00%)	
black_box	0.0000	0.0000	0.0000	0.0000 (0.00%)	
clock_network	0.0000	0.0000	0.0000	0.0000 (0.00%)	
register	2.2102e+03	1.6483e+03	4.2980e+03	3.9014e+03 (28.05%)	
sequential	0.0000	0.0000	0.0000	0.0000 (0.00%)	
combinational	7.5868e+03	2.4014e+05	1.0651e+07	1.0007e+04 (71.95%)	
Total	9.7970e+03 uw	4.0498e+03 uw	6.1551e+07 pw	1.3800e+04 uw	

Figure 77.11 LSFR power report
Source: Author

```
********************************
Report : timing
        -path full
        -delay max
        -max_paths 1
        -sort_by group
Design : LFSR_1
Version: L-2016.03-SP5
Date   : Tue Jan 30 10:21:16 2024
********************************

Operating Conditions: TYPICAL   Library: saed90nm_typ_ht
Wire Load Model Mode: enclosed

  Startpoint: rand_data_reg[0]
              (rising edge-triggered flip-flop clocked by clk)
  Endpoint: newbit_reg (rising edge-triggered flip-flop clocked by clk)
  Path Group: clk
  Path Type: max

  Des/Clust/Port   Wire Load Model      Library
  -------------------------------------------------
  LFSR_1              8000             saed90nm_typ_ht

  Point                                    Incr      Path
  ----------------------------------------------------------
  clock clk (rise edge)                    0.00      0.00
  clock network delay (ideal)              0.00      0.00
  rand_data_reg[0]/CLK (DFFASRX1)          0.00      0.00 r
  rand_data_reg[0]/QN (DFFASRX1)           0.27      0.27 f
  U201/ZN (INVX0)                          0.10      0.37 r
  U207/QN (NAND3X0)                        0.10      0.47 f
  U209/QN (NAND3X0)                        0.14      0.61 r
  newbit_reg/D (DFFX1)                     0.04      0.64 r
  data arrival time                                  0.64

  clock clk (rise edge)                    0.03      0.03
  clock network delay (ideal)              0.00      0.03
  newbit_reg/CLK (DFFX1)                   0.00      0.03 r
  library setup time                      -0.14     -0.10
  data required time                                -0.10
  ----------------------------------------------------------
  data required time                                -0.10
  data arrival time                                 -0.64
  ----------------------------------------------------------
  slack (VIOLATED)                                  -0.75
```

Figure 77.12 LSFR timing report
Source: Author

```
********************************
Report : area
Design : LCG_Scrambler_1
Version: L-2016.03-SP5
Date   : Wed Jan 24 14:10:19 2024
********************************

Information: Updating design information... (UID-85)
Library(s) Used:

    saed90nm_typ_ht (File: /home/bvrit/synopsys_example/DesignCompiler/dc/ref/models/saed90nm_typ_ht.db)

Number of ports:                    98
Number of nets:                    152
Number of cells:                   113
Number of combinational cells:      49
Number of sequential cells:         64
Number of macros/black boxes:        0
Number of buf/inv:                   1
Number of references:               12

Combinational area:            567.705614
Buf/Inv area:                    5.529600
Noncombinational area:         956.620792
Macro/Black Box area:            0.000000
Net Interconnect area:          73.673606

Total cell area:              1524.326406
Total area:                   1598.000013
```

Figure 77.13 LCG_Scrambler area report
Source: Author

```
********************************
Report : power
        -analysis_effort low
Design : LCG_Scrambler_1
Version: L-2016.03-SP5
Date   : Wed Jan 24 14:14:38 2024
********************************

Library(s) Used:

    saed90nm_typ_ht (File: /home/bvrit/synopsys_example/DesignCompiler/dc/ref/models/saed90nm_typ_ht.db)

Operating Conditions: TYPICAL   Library: saed90nm_typ_ht
Wire Load Model Mode: enclosed

Design     Wire Load Model      Library
-------------------------------------------
LCG_Scrambler_1  8000          saed90nm_typ_ht

Global Operating Voltage = 1.2
Power-specific unit information :
    Voltage Units = 1V
    Capacitance Units = 1.000000ff
    Time Units = 1ns
    Dynamic Power Units = 1uw   (derived from V,C,T units)
    Leakage Power Units = 1pw

  Cell Internal Power  =  83.5950 uw  (91%)
  Net Switching Power  =   8.1321 uw  (9%)
  ---------
Total Dynamic Power   =  91.7271 uw  (100%)

Cell Leakage Power    =  26.8337 uw

Information: report_power power group summary does not include estimated clock tree power. (PWR-789)
```

Power Group	Internal Power	Switching Power	Leakage Power	Total Power	(%) Attrs
io_pad	0.0000	0.0000	0.0000	0.0000 (0.00%)	
memory	0.0000	0.0000	0.0000	0.0000 (0.00%)	
black_box	0.0000	0.0000	0.0000	0.0000 (0.00%)	
clock_network	0.0000	0.0000	0.0000	0.0000 (0.00%)	
register	0.0000	0.0000	0.0000	0.0000 (0.00%)	
sequential	23.1057	2.0182	1.5639e+07	40.7625 (34.30%)	
combinational	60.4894	6.1139	1.1195e+07	77.7982 (65.62%)	
Total	83.5950 uw	8.1321 uw	2.6834e+07 pw	118.5608 uw	

Figure 77.14 LCG_Scrambler power report
Source: Author

power, and timing. The results indicate that the LCG_Scrambler shows a noticeable reduction in both timing and area compared to LSFR, high-lighting its potential efficiency in these aspects.

Conclusion

To sum up, optimizing time and area in the PCIe physical layer can be achieved through various methods, with randomization proving particularly effective. The randomization process, facilitated by the LCG_scrambler, is showcased in the

```
*****************************************
Report : timing
        -path full
        -delay max
        -max_paths 1
        -sort_by group
Design : LCG_Scrambler_1
Version: L-2016.03-SP5
Date   : Wed Jan 24 14:07:36 2024
*****************************************

Operating Conditions: TYPICAL    Library: saed90nm_typ_ht
Wire Load Model Mode: enclosed

 Startpoint: lcg_state_reg[0]
            (rising edge-triggered flip-flop)
 Endpoint: lcg_state[0]
            (output port)
 Path Group: (none)
 Path Type: max

 Des/Clust/Port   Wire Load Model    Library
 -------------------------------------------------------
 LCG_Scrambler_1    8000             saed90nm_typ_ht

 Point                              Incr      Path
 -------------------------------------------------------
 lcg_state_reg[0]/CLK (DFFASX1)     0.00      0.00 r
 lcg_state_reg[0]/Q (DFFASX1)       0.35      0.35 f
 lcg_state[0] (out)                 0.00      0.35 f
 data arrival time                            0.35
 -------------------------------------------------------

 (Path is unconstrained)
```

Figure 77.15 LCG scrambler timing report
Source: Author

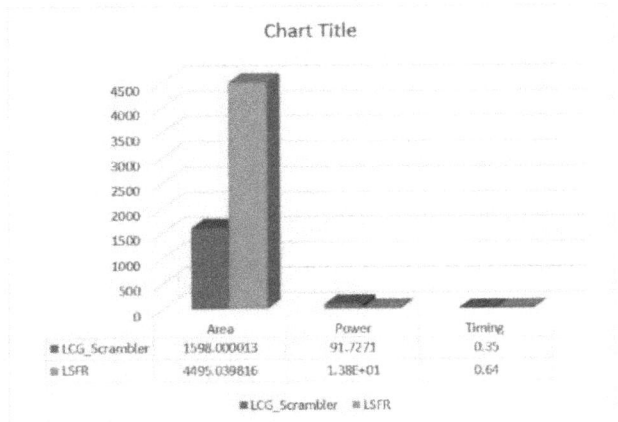

Chart Title

	Area	Power	Timing
LCG_Scrambler	1598.000013	91.7271	0.35
LSFR	4495.039816	1.38E+01	0.64

■ LCG_Scrambler ■ LSFR

Figure 77.16 LCG vs LSFR
Source: Author

paper to significantly reduce area to 1598.000013 and timing to 0.35. This reduction is notably superior compared to alternative randomization techniques like LSFR or scrambler. Additionally, adjusting or modifying other components within the PCIe physical layer flow also offers avenues for minimizing timing and area. The paper underscores the effectiveness of this particular randomization method, contributing valuable insights into the optimization of the PCIe Physical layer and emphasizing the role of randomization for enhanced efficiency. The findings highlight the potential for broader applications of randomization processes in the design and improvement of communication protocols. Overall, these outcomes underscore the importance of exploring various avenues to enhance the performance metrics of the PCIe physical layer in a comprehensive and efficient manner.

References

[1] Vaidya, V. N., Ingale, V., and Gokhale, A. (2022). Development of verification IP of physical layer of PCIe. In 2022 IEEE 3rd Global Conference for Advancement in Technology (GCAT). IEEE.

[2] Hukare, S., Vyas, V., and Agrawal, V. (2023). Design and simulation of physical layer of peripheral component interconnect express (PCIe) protocol. In 2023 4th International Conference for Emerging Technology (INCET). (2023), (pp. 1–4). IEEE.

[3] Rohilla, G., Mathur, D., and Ghanekar, U. (2020). Functional verification of MAC-PHY layer of PCI express Gen5. 0 with PIPE interface using UVM. In 2020 International Conference for Emerging Technology (INCET), Belgaum, India, 2020, (pp. 1–5). doi: 10.1109/INCET49848.2020.9154176. IEEE.

[4] Zhang, H., Zhu, H., Zhu, X., and Gao, C. (2022). Low-power design in PCIe switch PHY. In 2022 3rd International Conference on Electronics, Communications and Information Technology (CECIT). IEEE.

[5] Tao, Y., Fu, Q., Liu, J., Cui, Y., Liang, Z., Nie, R., et al. (2020). Design and implementation of high speed encryption and decryption system based on PCIE bus. In 2020 IEEE 2nd International Conference on Civil Aviation Safety and Information Technology (ICCASIT). Weihai, China, 2020, (pp. 369–372). IEEE. doi: 10.1109/ICCASIT50869.2020.9368599.

[6] Chen, X. Q., Zhang, L. Y., and Li, C. X. (2023). FPGA-based train onboard PCIe board design and implementation. In 2023 3rd International Conference on Electrical Engineering and Mechatronics Technology (ICEEMT). IEEE.

[7] Mhaboobkhan, F., Fathimaparveen, M., Gokila, K., and Logapriya, P. (2019). Implementation of high speed data transfer serialized 128/130bit encoding algorithm using 90nm technology. In 2019 5th International Conference on Advanced Computing and Communication Systems (ICACCS). 2019, (pp. 732–736). IEEE.

[8] Popa, Ş., Coliban, R. M., and Ivanovici, M. (2022). An optimal implementation of an 8b/10b encoder for xilinx FPGAs. In 2022 International Symposium on Electronics and Telecommunications (ISETC). Timisoara, Romania, 2022, (pp. 1–4). doi: 10.1109/ISETC56213.2022.10010077. IEEE.

[9] Su, C. Y., Chen, C. A., Chen, S. L., and Lai, J. Y. (2021). USB 3.0 using FPGA optimization for 8b/10b Encoder/Decoder. In 2021 International Symposium on Intelligent Signal Processing and Communication Systems (ISPACS). IEEE.

[10] Saleem, H. I., Geethu, R., and Bhakthavatchalu, R. (2022). A programmable and parameterisable reseeding linear feedback shift register. In 2022 Second International Conference on Artificial Intelligence and Smart Energy (ICAIS). 2022, (pp. 1629–1633). IEEE.

[11] Jayasanthi, M., and Kowsalyadevi, A. K. (2019). Low power implementation of linear feedback shift registers. *International Journal of Recent Technology and Engineering (IJRTE)*, 8(2), 1957–1965.

[12] Madhulatha, K., Jyothika, K., Harini, S. V. B., Somanathan, G. R., and Bhakthavathchalu, R. (2022). Reconfigurable linear feedback shift register. In 2022 4th International Conference on Smart Systems and Inventive Technology (ICSSIT). IEEE.

[13] Sujitha, A., Lakshmi, L., Mathan, N., and Narmadha, R. (2023). Analysis of an efficient linear congruential generator architecture for digital applications. In 2023 Fifth International Conference on Electrical, Computer and Communication Technologies (ICECCT). (pp. 1–4). IEEE.

[14] Akhila, N., Kumari, C. U., Swathi, K., Padma, T., and Rao, N. M. (2021). Performance analysis of pseudo random bit generator using modified dual-coupled linear congruential generator. In 2021 International Conference on Intelligent Technologies (CONIT). Hubli, India, 2021, (pp. 1–5). doi: 10.1109/CONIT51480.2021.9498354. IEEE.

[15] Akhila, N., Kumari, C. U., Swathi, K., Padma, T., and Kora, P. (2021). Implementation of modified dual-coupled linear congruential generator in data encryption standard algorithm. In 2021 Third International Conference on Inventive Research in Computing Applications (ICIRCA). IEEE.

78 Design and development of multilevel security system in automated teller machine

Yempally Sangeetha[a], Anirudh Reddy, R.[b], Vasudeva Reddy, T.[c], Katike Madhukar[d], Madduri Karthik[e] and Ganti Lasya Preethi[f]

Department of ECE, B V Raju Institute of Technology, Narsapur, Medak(dist), Telangana, India

Abstract

The existing automated teller machines (ATM) security system based primarily on personal identification numbers (PINs) is facing challenges in terms of security threats like PIN skimming and shoulder-surfing, thereby the unauthorized accesses causing financial loss. We tackle these concerns through our ATM security system by combining the use of radio frequency (RF) technology and facial recognition at transaction level. Users present an RF tag for identification, which causes a picture of the user to be taken and compared against a database of authenticated users. When a successful match happens, transactions are carried out in one shot while an OTP and the image of who is trying to go into the bank account can be sent to another number for user confirmation. Through this multi-layered solution, unauthorized access is effectively thwarted, and monies are protected from being accessed by any entity other than the account owner even in a case where another person fraudulently gained knowledge of the user's PIN delivering an unyielding defines against security threats at all costs to further secure accounts use safety first.

Keywords: Automated teller machines security, facial recognition, multi-layered authentication, RF technology, unauthorized access

Introduction

In the past few years, the necessity of more advanced security measures for automated teller machines (ATM) has been highlighted by increasing cyber threat activity and unauthorized access to financial accounts.

Conventional ATM security mechanisms that are mostly reliant on personal identification numbers (PINs) have become progressively vulnerable to sophisticated attacks like PIN skimming, shoulder surfing and cloning. This has led to considerable financial loss and decreased confidence in the safety of ATM transactions.

Innovation is crucial as the finance sector evolves so as to implement stronger security protocols that can safeguard users' data and their finances effectively. Our study presents an advanced automated teller machine security system that combines two powerful forms of verification; radio frequency technology and face recognition.

RF technology offers secure means for authenticating users through unique RF tags thereby giving additional layer of protection beyond traditional pin-based systems. Moreover, facial recognition enhances security further by ensuring only authorized individuals have access to ATMs. In order to match with a pre-registered user database, captured images are processed using complex image processing algorithms. Therefore, this creates dual-layer authentication system whereby no one can gain access without being approved first through both means at once.

Existing Systems

In this research article ATM privacy security system for enhanced pilot Encrypted monitoring, other and exclusive types of authentication, and continuous vibration sensor to secure the transaction and provide a quick response to the suspicious activities. This system offers adequate

[a]sangeetha.b@bvrit.ac.in, [b]anirudhreddy.r@bvrit.ac.in, [c]vasu.tatiparthi@bvrit.ac.in, [d]22215a0411@bvrit.ac.in, [e]22215a0408@bvrit.ac.in, [f]21211a0486@bvrit.ac.in

DOI: 10.1201/9781003616399-78

security to the users of ATM and management of the business [1].

In this research article puts forward a new protection method implementing two-factor authentication, namely the combination of ATM cards and dynamic PINs. A proof of concept of the proposed ATM and mbanking application was implemented and user feedback for the generated PINs were collected using questionnaires while the randomness was analyzed mathematically and systematic observation for quality of service of the system was done [2].

In this research article recommend improved security measures that can be taken by ATM, like using fingers and RFID gadgets instead of normal ATM cards that are at risk of being compromize. The system locks the panel for a specific period after three attempts in a day for enhanced secure of the ATM transactions [3].

In this research article presents a synthesis of the ATM card whereby the account holder is able to have all his/her accounts with the different banks under one single card to make the operations more secure and convenient. The elements of the system are based on the state-of-the-art technology, including biometric scanner, GSM module, RFID based two factor security and are specifically suited to prevent identity theft that is a major problem for the current ATM system [4].

In this research article different methods that help in the improvement of ATMs security and the problems like card cloning and PIN theft that are still obscured, in spite of having CCTV cameras. It looks at integrating physical security mechanisms with electronic security mechanisms with a view of enhancing on the security on ATM machines against physical and electronic theft [5].

In this research article focuses on RFID cards, IR sensors, GSM for alarms and for tracking GPS, and finally fingerprint authentication for the personnel. The proposed system will create a highly secured ATM environment with the help of an embedded system as well as some state-of-art technologies [6].

In this research article addresses ATM fraud in Indonesia, Fingershield ATM as a solution that includes finger scan identification that works hand in hand with smart cards and a database server. Based on the analysis of the experimental descriptive method, it can be stated that the introduction of this system leads to greatly enhanced ATM security even if the time taken to authenticate a user is slightly higher [7].

In this research article proposes a novel security system for the protection of ATM from bodily up-closing and hacking through the use of sensors such as Reed's Switch, Ultrasonic switch and Surveillance Camera. Intruder definitely surfaces when unauthorized attempts are made, and disseminates pictures of the intruder by sending an IP address in addition to sending an alarm through a text message as compared to use of PIN only for security unlock [8].

In this research article presents an ATM security solution that employs an embedded system that incorporates sundry sensors and a node MCU board with ESP8266 microcontroller to respond to physical threats. The system have the provision latching off the ATM door during anomalous activities and employs RFID for maintenance purpose with the monitoring being constant and alerts sent to the authorities through the IoT [9].

In this research article aims to enhance ATM security by adding face-ID authentication to the existing static PIN method. Utilizing machine learning and imaging algorithms such as Eigenface design, the system uses unique facial features to provide greater security and user access control [10].

Proposed System

To cope with the vulnerabilities inherent in conventional ATM security structures, we propose a complicated ATM Security System that integrates radio frequency (RF) generation with facial popularity to provide a robust, multi-layered authentication mechanism. This gadget is designed using readily available components and open-source software, making sure fee-effectiveness and simplicity of implementation. The primary processing unit of the device is the Raspberry Pi, which controls all other additives and manages the authentication method. A Pi camera is used to seize the consumer's facial image for the facial reputation procedure. Each user is issued an RF card, serving as a completely unique identifier, and the RF reader detects the card to initiate the authentication method.

Figure 78.1 Proposed prototype
Source: Author

A keyboard is supplied for customers to go into their PIN as an extra layer of protection, whilst an LCD gives commands and remarks during the authentication method. OpenCV, an open-supply pc imaginative and prescient library, is utilized for implementing facial reputation. For brought safety, SMTP is used to ship an e mail containing a one-time password (OTP) and the captured photo to the registered person for verification in case of a mismatch. Additionally, Twilio is employed to send SMS messages to the consumer's cellular cellphone for in addition verification and notifications. This multi-faceted technique guarantees an excessive level of protection, extensively lowering the risk of unauthorized get entry to and enhancing the reliability of ATM transactions.

Our proposed ATM security system utilizes numerous key additives, every playing a important role in ensuring robust and secure authentication. Here, we offer an in depth explanation of every factor and the way they characteristic within the project.

Raspberry Pi

The Raspberry Pi serves because the central processing unit of the device, orchestrating the operations of all different additives. It runs the software program that controls the RF reader, Pi camera, keyboard, and LCD, and strategies statistics from these inputs to manage the authentication technique. The Raspberry Pi also handles verbal exchange with external offerings like SMTP and Twilio to ship OTPs and notifications. It is selected for its versatility, affordability, and simplicity of use, making it perfect for integrating diverse hardware and software additives.

Pi camera

The Pi camera is used to capture the person's facial picture in the course of the authentication process. When a person provides their RF card, the Raspberry Pi triggers the Pi Camera to take a photo of the user's face. This picture is then processed the use of the OpenCV library to examine it with saved pix inside the database. The digicam's high-decision talents make certain clean and accurate pix for dependable facial popularity.

RF reader and cards

Each user is issued an RF card, which acts as a unique identifier. The RF reader, connected to the Raspberry Pi, detects the presence of an RF card whilst it's miles introduced close to the reader. This detection initiates the authentication manner by way of signaling the Raspberry Pi to capture the consumer's facial photograph. The RF generation guarantees a stable and quick manner to discover users earlier than intending with similarly verification steps.

Keyboard

The keyboard is utilized by users to go into their PIN as an extra layer of security. After the RF card is detected and the facial photo is captured, the gadget prompts the person to enter their PIN the use of the keyboard. The entered PIN is in comparison with the stored PIN for that precise person. This step guarantees that even if an unauthorized man or woman possesses the RF card, they could still want the perfect PIN to continue.

LCD

The LCD presents instructions and remarks to the user during the authentication technique. It displays prompts for providing the RF card, coming into the PIN, and any other important steps.

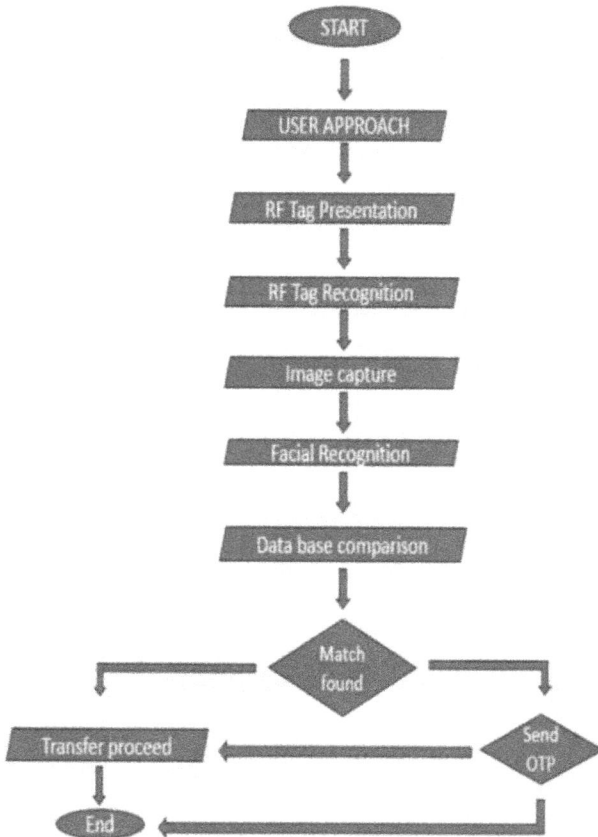

Figure 78.2 Flow chart of proposed system
Source: Author

In case of a mismatch or failure in any a part of the authentication system, the LCD also shows applicable errors messages and instructions for further movement, ensuring a consumer-pleasant level in.

Open CV

OpenCV, an open-supply laptop vision library, is hired for implementing facial reputation. Once the Pi camera captures the user's photo, OpenCV strategies the photograph to extract facial capabilities and evaluate them with the stored pix inside the database. This contrast is accomplished using superior algorithms to ensure high accuracy and reliability in identifying legal customers.

Simple mail transfer protocol

Simple mail transfer protocol (SMTP) is used to send an e mail containing a OTP and the captured photograph to the registered person for verification in case of a mismatch at some stage

in the facial reputation manner. If the facial popularity fails or there's any doubt approximately the user's identification, an electronic mail is dispatched to the user's registered e-mail cope with an OTP and the picture of the individual trying get entry to. The consumer ought to then enter the OTP on the ATM to verify their identification and authorize the transaction.

Twilio

Twilio is a provider used to ship SMS messages to the person's cell phone for added verification and notifications. In scenarios wherein the facial reputation is no longer healthy the registered consumer, an SMS containing an OTP is sent to the person's mobile phone. The user has to input this OTP to verify their identity and proceed with the transaction. Twilio ensures that users are promptly notified and can take on the spot action if an unauthorized access strive is detected

Results

The implementation of our advanced ATM Security System has confirmed vast enhancements in transaction protection and user authentication. By integrating RF era and facial popularity, the device has efficaciously mitigated the risks related to conventional PIN-based totally ATM safety. The multi-layered authentication mechanism, combining RF card detection, facial reputation, and PIN entry, has furnished strong security towards unauthorized get admission too. Even if an attacker obtains the user's PIN, they can't get admission to the account without additionally passing the facial reputation step.

Using OpenCV, the device performed excessive accuracy in facial recognition, reliably distinguishing among legal users and ability impostors. The advanced photograph processing algorithms ensured that handiest legitimate customers ought to complete transactions. In cases in which facial reputation did not now shape the registered consumer, the machine efficaciously applied OTP verification. The integration of SMTP and Twilio allowed for immediate conversation with the consumer, sending an OTP through email and SMS. This additional layer of security ensured that the rightful account holder could authorize the transaction best.

atmmachine427@gmail.com
to me ▾

•••

Image captured from ATM. Use the OTP for verification which was sent to your mobile number

One attachment • Scanned by Gmail ⓘ

Figure 78.3 Mail from ATM to registered Email
Source: Author

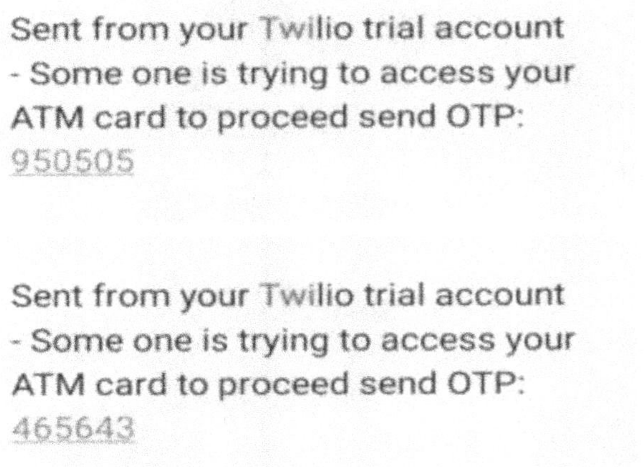

Sent from your Twilio trial account - Some one is trying to access your ATM card to proceed send OTP: 950505

Sent from your Twilio trial account - Some one is trying to access your ATM card to proceed send OTP: 465643

Figure 78.4 OTP to register mobile number to give access to unknown person
Source: Author

The gadget successfully notified customers of any get admission to try through email and SMS. The email included a connected picture of the character trying to get entry to the account, providing the user with clean evidence of the get right of entry to strive. This characteristic better consumer awareness and protection, allowing customers to take spark off movement if unauthorized get admission to turned into detected. The LCD provided clear instructions and feedback all through the authentication method, making it person pleasant. The activates for offering the RF card, entering the PIN, and coming into the OTP have been intuitive and clean to follow, ensuring a smooth user enjoyment.

The use of Raspberry Pi because the important processing unit ensured the device's reliability and responsiveness. The integration of hardware and software additives functioned seamlessly, supplying regular overall performance all through the authentication and transaction processes. The effects of our task display that the proposed ATM Security System notably enhances transaction security via incorporating a couple of layers of authentication. The aggregate of RF technology, facial recognition, and OTP verification gives robust safety towards unauthorized get admission to, ensuring that person finances stay stable. A hit implementation of this machine highlights its potential for huge adoption, offering a reliable and person-pleasant approach to the vulnerabilities of traditional ATM safety systems.

Conclusion

The development and implementation of our advanced ATM security system have correctly addressed the vulnerabilities of conventional PIN-based protection mechanisms. By integrating RF era, facial reputation, and OTP verification, we have created a strong, multilayered authentication system that notably complements transaction security. The system's ability to reliably distinguish between legal users and capability impostors via excessive-accuracy facial recognition ensures that unauthorized get admission to is successfully prevented, even supposing a user's PIN is compromised.

The use of without problems to be had additives and open-supply software program, which includes the

Raspberry Pi, Pi camera, RF reader, keyboard, LCD, OpenCV, SMTP, and Twilio, underscores the assignment's value-effectiveness and simplicity of implementation. The integration of those technologies supplied a unbroken user level in even as retaining stringent protection requirements.

The gadget's fulfillment in notifying customers of any get entry to try through electronic mail and SMS, consisting of sending an OTP and the photograph of the man or woman attempting access, similarly complements person consciousness and safety. This characteristic ensures that users are at once alerted to any unauthorized tries, taking into account set off motion and extra verification.

In end, our proposed ATM Security System gives a dependable and user-friendly option to the constraints of conventional ATM protection structures. By combining a couple of layers of authentication, it offers robust protection against unauthorized get admission to and guarantees that finances continue to be steady. The assignment's results spotlight its potential for substantial adoption, promising to noticeably decorate the safety and reliability of ATM transactions across the banking enterprise.

References

[1] Vikram, N., and Sivaprakasam, S. (2023). ATM security and privacy preserving system. In 2023 2nd International Conference on Applied Artificial Intelligence and Computing (ICAAIC), Salem, India, (pp. 1295–1300). doi:10.1109/ICAAIC56838.2023.10141508.

[2] Munadi, R., Irawan, A. I., and Romiadi, Y. F. (2019). Security system ATM machine with one-time passcode on M-banking application. In 2019 International Conference on Mechatronics, Robotics and Systems Engineering (MoRSE), Bali, Indonesia, (pp. 92–96). doi:10.1109/MoRSE48060.2019.8998716.

[3] Saranraj, B., Dharshini, N. S. P., Suvetha, R., and Bharathi, K. U. (2020). ATM security system using arduino. In 2020 6th International Conference on Advanced Computing and Communication Systems (ICACCS), Coimbatore, India, (pp. 940–944). doi:10.1109/ICACCS48705.2020.9074429.

[4] Sricharan, B., Sanjana, J. U., Vani, T. V., and Sujatha, C. N. (2022). RFID based ATM security system using IOT. In 2022 International Conference on Intelligent Controller and Computing for Smart Power (ICICCSP), Hyderabad, India, (pp. 1–6). doi: 10.1109/ICICCSP53532.2022.9862486.

[5] Jacintha, V. M. E., Rani, S. J., Beula, J. G., and Johnsly, J. J. (2017). An extensive resolution of ATM security systems. In 2017 Third International Conference on Science Technology Engineering and Management (ICONSTEM), Chennai, India, (pp. 934–938). doi: 10.1109/ICONSTEM.2017.8261340.

[6] Nelligani, B. M., Reddy, N. V. U., and Awasti, N. (2016). Smart ATM security system using FPR, GSM, GPS. In 2016 International Conference on Inventive Computation Technologies (ICICT), Coimbatore, India, (pp. 1–5). doi:10.1109/INVENTIVE.2016.7830093.

[7] Christiawan, B. A. S., Rahardian, A. F., and Muchtar, E. (2018). Fingershield ATM – ATM Security system using fingerprint authentication. In 2018 International Symposium on Electronics and Smart Devices (ISESD), Bandung, Indonesia, (pp. 1–6). doi: 10.1109/ISESD.2018.8605473.

[8] Takkar, S., Rakhra, M., Ratnani, A., Protyay, D. S., Pandey, P., and Arora, M. (2021). Advanced ATM security system using arduino uno. In 2021 9th International Conference on Reliability, Infocom Technologies and Optimization (Trends and Future Directions) (ICRITO), Noida, India, (pp. 1–5). doi: 10.1109/ICRITO51393.2021.9596341.

[9] Abhijith, S., Sreehari, K. N., and Chalil, A. (2022). An IOT based system for securing ATM machine. In 2022 8th International Conference on Advanced Computing and Communication Systems (ICACCS), Coimbatore, India, (pp. 1764–1768). doi:10.1109/ICACCS54159.2022.9785243.

[10] Soundari, D. V., Aravindh, R., and Abishek, S. (2021). Enhanced security feature of ATM's through facial recognition. In 2021 5th International Conference on Intelligent Computing and Control Systems (ICICCS), Madurai, India, (pp. 1252–1256). doi:10.1109/ICICCS51141.2021.9432327.

79 Full-custom design-based efficient 2D-FIR filter architecture using approximate multipliers and high speed adders

Srilatha Reddy, V.[1,2,a], A. Vimala Juliet[3,b], Esther Rani Thuraka[4,c] and Venkata Krishna Odugu[4,d]

[1]Research Scholar, Department of EIE, SRMIST, Chennai, Tamil Nadu, India

[2]CVR College of Engineering, Hyderabad, Telangana, India

[3]Department of EIE, SRMIST, Chennai, Tamil Nadu, India

[4]Department of ECE, CVR College of Engineering, Hyderabad, Telangana, India

Abstract

Image processing applications use two-dimensional finite impulse response (FIR) Filters, which are standard, modular, linear, and easier to construct in very large-scale integration (VLSI) than IIR filters. The digital platform offers many FIR filter architectures using HDL programming and semi-custom design. This research introduces an innovative architecture for a two-dimensional FIR filter design and implemented in a full-custom platform, where all transistor-level blocks are optimized and integrated. All registers, multipliers, and adders for the 2-D FIR filter design are transistor-level created utilizing full-custom design-based tools. To simplify multiplier construction, upgraded and optimized approximate 4:2 compressor adders are used in arithmetic block design. To approximate compressors at the transistor level, transistor-level implementation is the key reason. All hardware blocks are integrated and designed in cadence full custom virtuoso 45 nm CMOS tools. The suggested filter architecture is compared to existing filter architectures in size, delay, and power.

Keywords: 2-D FIR filter, 4:2 compressors, approximate multipliers, CMOS, low power, mixed logic, TGL gates, transistor-level, tree multiplier

Introduction

The two-dimensional (2-D) digital filter processes two-dimensional signals by propagating information in two directions. Many theoretical and real-time image processing applications use 2-D digital filters [1].

Any architecture's very large-scale integration (VLSI) design can optimize from transistor to system levels. Optimization can include some inexactness, which is acceptable [2–4]. Minor inaccuracies can reduce area, delay, and power usage. Approximated circuits are used for optimizing VLSI designs for multimedia, image, and video processing. Low-area, power-efficient, and high-performance 2-D FIR filters are recommended for these applications. In the filter architecture multipliers are approximated in this work.

Mohanty et al. [5–8] developed memory-efficient generic and unified filter bank topologies employing separable and non-separable 2-D-FIR filters using memory sharing and reuse are used to optimize memory in this study.

In the existing works, many optimized multipliers are used such as pipelined DA [9], canonical signed digit (CSD) [10]. Some other 2-D FIR filters using various techniques of adders and multipliers [11,12] and parallel processing works [13,14]. Edavoor et al. [15] proposed two approximated 4:2 compressors and eight and 24 transistor-based 4:2 compressors are designed [16]. Approximate multipliers employing 4:2 and 5:2 compressor circuits are given in [17,18].

[a]srilathareddy.cvr@gmail.com, [b]vimala@gmail.com, [c]estherlawrenc@gmail.com, [d]venkatakrishna.odugu@gmail.com

DOI: 10.1201/9781003616399-79

This study develops and implements complete filter architecture using a full custom VLSI design approach. To optimize size and power, each transistor-level block of the 2D FIR filter architecture is constructed here. This work designs transistor-level approximation multipliers and 4:2 compressors utilizing mixed logic design to provide an area-power-delay efficient 2-D FIR filter architecture. This work replaces power-consumed multipliers with pipelined DA and regular adders with carry-save adders. Chen et al. [9] presented symmetric filter coefficients for power-efficient 2D FIR filter topologies. The filter architecture needs fewer multipliers due to symmetry. To decrease multiplication adders, Odugu et al. [10] suggested optimized 2-D FIR filter topologies using the CSD number format. Additionally, CSE reduces the number of adders. By rearranging the systolic structuring process, Van et al. [11,12] established 2-D FIR and IIR filter architectures without global broadcast and offered a thorough survey study on the various symmetry principles. To optimize the filter architecture, a multimode filter architecture is created with shared hardware modules and memory parts.

The contributions of the work are as follows:

- Transistor-level flip-flops, registers, and shift register blocks (SRB) are developed for the memory modules, employing a reduced transistor count.
- A mixed logic design is used to implement the proposed Approximate 4:2 compressor (A42C) adders.
- The area and power-efficient approximated tree multipliers (ATM) are implemented using the proposed A42C circuits.
- A fully customized FD 2-D FIR filter architecture is implemented at the transistor level using CADENCE design tools.

Block Diagram of the Proposed 2-D FIR Filter Architecture

This section presents a two-dimensional FIR filter architecture in the form of FD is described. The transfer function of the 2-D FIR filter is, with coefficient impulse matrix is given by Eq. (1).

$$H(z_1, z_2) = \sum_i^{N-1} \sum_j^{N-1} h(i,j) z_1^{-i} z_2^{-j} \qquad (1)$$

The aforementioned 2-D filter equation can be realized using four types of filter architecture styles: Fully Direct, Fully Transposed (FT), Mixed-1 (Direct-Then-Transposed), and Mixed-2 (Transposed-Then-Direct) configurations.

In this study, the chosen structure for the suggested design is the FD transistor-level architecture design, due to less memory. The FD form structure of a 2-D-FIR filter requires fewer memory elements than the other form of 2-D filter structures. In the FD structures, all storage components are located on the input side, their size depends on the number of input sample bits and coefficient bits. In contrast, other structures place memory elements on the output side. After the filter coefficients and input samples are multiplied, the output bit width becomes larger than the input bit width, resulting in larger memory requirements for the output side.

Due to less memory, the FD structure is selected for the proposed transistor-level architecture design. The FD form structure of a 2-D-FIR filter requires fewer memory elements than the other form of 2-D filter structures. In the FD form, all storage elements are positioned exclusively on the input side. So, the size is dependent on input sample bits and coefficient bits. In contrast, other architectures position storage elements on the output side, where multiplying the filter coefficients with the input samples results in an output bit width larger than the width of the input bits. As a result, the dimension of the memory element on the output side increases.

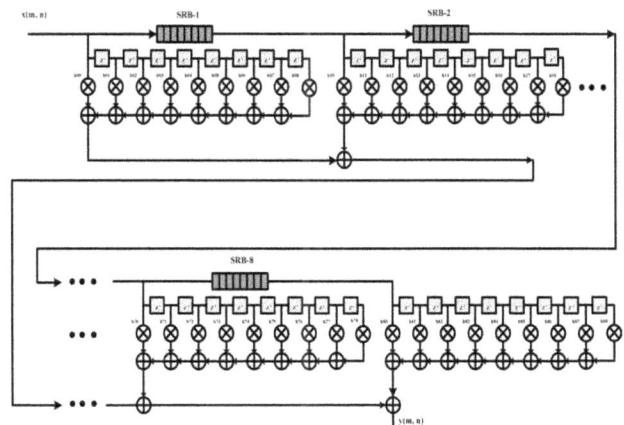

Figure 79.1 Design of the FD 2-D filter for N = 9
Source: Author

The overall 2-D FIR architecture needs SRBs, each row filter needs registers, -multipliers, adders, and extra adders to add the sub-filter or row filter outputs. In the suggested two-dimensional FIR filter, each block is realized at the transistor level, and optimization is performed to minimize the transistor count and power utilization of the design.

The transistor level diagram of delay elements D-FFs using a very small number of transistors is presented in Figure 79.2. These registers are arranged properly to construct an SRB. The SRB transistor level diagram is shown in Figure 79.3. A total of 40 transistors are needed to realize one 8-bit register. These registers are arranged properly to construct an SRB. The SRB transistor level diagram is shown in Figure 79.4.

In the 2-D FIR filter structure, the multiplier is the complex block where the approximation will be inserted to optimize filter architecture design. Approximate 4:2 compressors are employed to construct the custom-designed approximate multiplier. The precise 4:2 compressors collect the tree multiplier's MSB partial products to improve multiplier accuracy. The suggested approximate 4:2 compressors incorporate residual product terms such as intermediate partial products and LSB partial products.

Proposed approximate multiplier
In the 2-D FIR filter structure, the multiplier is the complex block where the approximation will

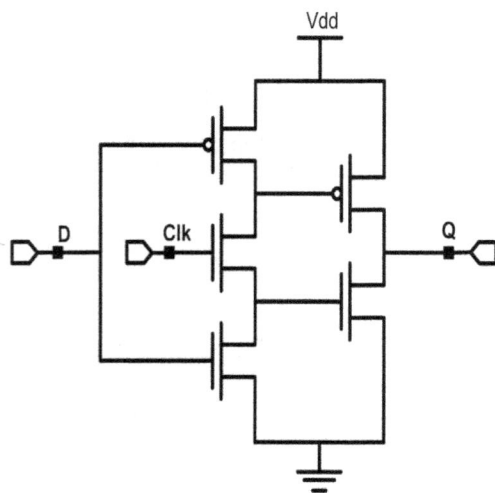

Figure 79.3 8-bit register block using D-FFs
Source: Author

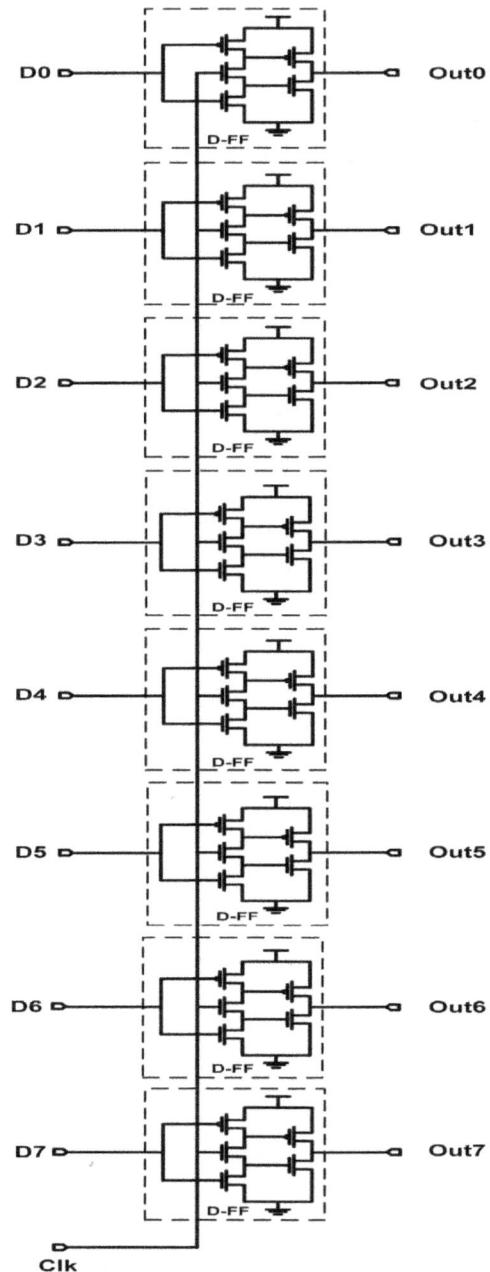

Figure 79.2 The five transistor-based D-FF
Source: Author

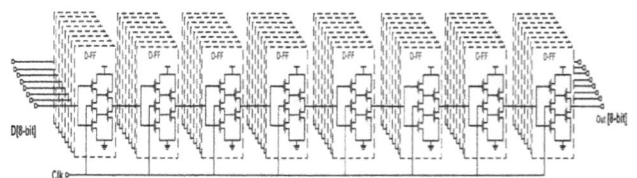

Figure 79.4 Shift register block with the size of M = 8
Source: Author

be inserted to optimize filter architecture design. We use 4:2 compressors with reduced precision to implement the custom-designed approximate multiplier. The precise 4:2 compressors collect the tree multiplier's MSB partial products to improve multiplier accuracy. The suggested approximate 4:2 compressors incorporate residual product terms such as intermediate partial products and LSB partial products.

The suggested tree multiplier approximates the LSB product terms by truncating them to zero. Small and negligible is the LSB product term error. Approximation in the tree multiplier and 4:2 compressors minimize multiplier structure area, latency, and power consumption.

This study uses the 8 × 8 tree multiplier structure to multiply filter coefficients and input data. Figure 79.4 shows the planned ATM dot diagram. The suggested tree multiplier approximates the LSB product terms by truncating them to zero. Small and negligible is the LSB product term error. Approximation in the tree multiplier and 4:2 compressors minimizes multiplier structure area, latency, and power consumption.

This study uses the 8 × 8 tree multiplier structure to multiply filter coefficients and input data. Figure 79.4 shows the planned ATM dot diagram.

Proposed 4:2 compressor with reduced precision (A42C)

The early 4:2 compressors used a small approximation to reduce transistor count. The 4:2 compressor's key advantage over the single FA is the

decrease of adder blocks for multiplier partial product summation. The actual sum and carry equations of the 4:2 compressor can be approximated to lower this transistor count. Figure 79.7 depicts the anticipated 4:2 compressor (A42C).

The Sum and Carry expressions are modified to reduce the transistor count and expressed in Eqs. (2) and (3). In this case, the sum is obtained through basic binary addition of four bits, while the carry is determined using a straightforward AND operation followed by binary addition of the inputs.

$$\text{Sum} = (X_1 + X_2) + (X_3 + X_4) \quad (2)$$
$$\text{Carry} = (X_1 + X_2) \cdot (X_3 + X_4) \quad (3)$$

The above equations are designed by 3 TGL-OR gates and one TGL-AND gate, which needs a total of 18 transistors only. The transistor level diagram is shown in Figure 79.10. The A42C needs 18 transistors instead of 24 transistors because of the mixed logic design.

The proposed A42C uses mixed logic, mixing TGL and CMOS gates. CMOS designs inverters, while TGL builds other gates. Alternative CMOS

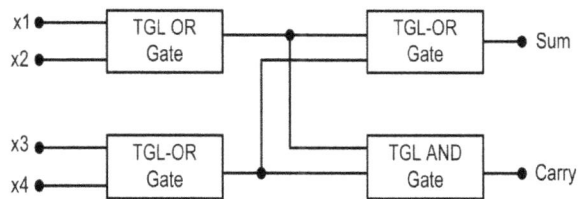

Figure 79.6 Gate level diagram of 4:2 approximate compressor
Source: Author

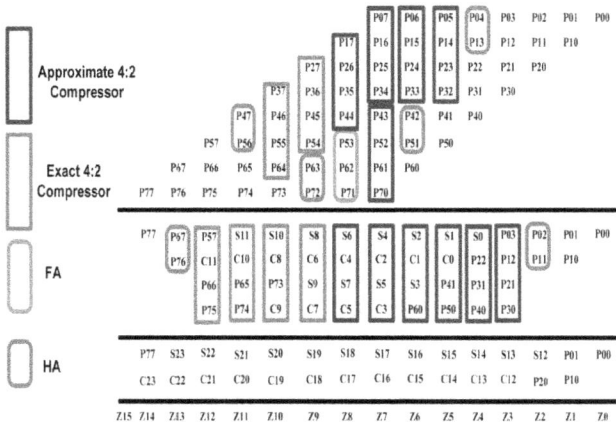

Figure 79.5 Proposed approximate tree multiplier arrangement
Source: Author

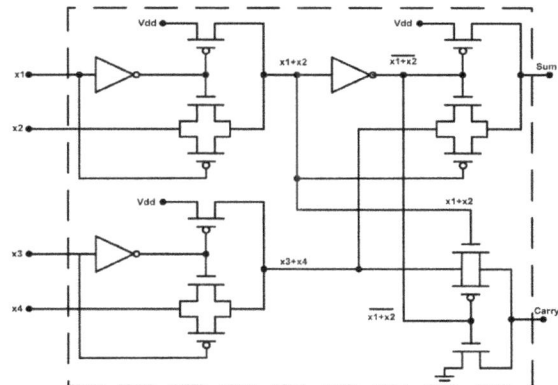

Figure 79.7 Transistor level diagram of proposed A42C
Source: Author

designs like this mixed logic design optimize area and power.

Implementation Results

The cadence virtuoso full-custom-based design tools are employed to develop the suggested 2-D FIR filter architecture in the form of FD for N = 9 filters in 45nm CMOS technology with Vdd = 1 volt. Simulate it with test-bench inputs and estimate power at 20 M Hz. The power and delay characteristics were also compared to filter topologies built upon VLSI design.

The proposed filter consists of (N-1) SRBs, Nx(N-1) registers, NxN approximate multipliers Nx(N-1) adders. Each proposed multiplier is constructed by 11 proposed approximate compressors, six exact compressors, 7 HAs, one FA and one ripple carry adder (RCA). The proposed approximate compressor is realized by18 transistors. Each DFF is constructed by five transistors and each register is constructed by 40 transistors and each SRB is constructed by 320 transistors. The total transistor count needed for the proposed multiplier and 2-D FIR filter is provided in equations Eq. (4) and Eq. (5).

Transistor count of approximate multipliers =
$A42C(11 \times 18) + Exact\ C\ (6 \times 34) + FA\ (1 \times 28) + HA\ (7 \times 12) + RCA\ (180) = 198 + 204 + 28 + 84 + 180 = 694$ (4)

Transistor count of 2D FIR
$= SRB\ (8 \times 320) + Reg\ (72 \times 40)$
$+ Mul\ (81 \times 694) + add\ (72 \times 180)$
$= 2560 + 2880 + 56214 + 12960 = 74614$ (5)

In the suggested design for the two-dimensional FIR filter, the critical path consists of one multiplier and two sets of (N-1) number of adders. The critical path delay of the 2-D FIR is given by Eq. (6)

$Dealy = T_{Mul} + 2\ (N - 1)T_{addr}$ (6)

Where, T_{Mul} is delay of the multiplier and is the delay of adders.

Table 79.1 compares the proposed custom-designed two-dimensional FIR filter architecture with semi-custom-based architecture regarding the area, delay, total power, area-delay metric (ADM) and power-delay metric. Several filter lengths, such as 4 and 8, are considered in existing works. In these cases, both area and power surpass those of the proposed design. Additionally, the proposed architecture demonstrates improved efficiency in several key performance metrics.

The proposed work's ADP is 16.9, 2.83, and 2.74 times lower than Alawad et al [18]. Odugu et al [10], and Odugu et al [16]. The PDP of the proposed work is 3.08, 16.18, 11.59, 16.74, and 1.67 times lower than the above-existing works.

Table 79.1 An evaluation of performance metrics between VLSI design-based two-dimensional FIR filter architectures and the proposed filter architecture

Filters	N	Area (µm¹)	Delay (ns)	Total Power (mW)	ADP (µm² . ms)	PDP (mW . ns)
Alawad et al. [18]	8	153325	11.47	2.016	1.758	23.123
Mohanty et al. [5]	4	472219	22.22	4.556	10.49	121.224
Odugu et al. [10]	9	17809	16.56	5.243	0.2949	86.827
Khoo et al. [17]	4	1009878	14.17	8.854	14.30	125.472
Odugu et al. [16]	9	27599	10.348	1.211	0.2855	12.541
Proposed Custom 2D-FIR Filter	9	12496	8.365	0.895	0.104	7.492

Source: Author

Figures 79.8 to 79.10 present a comparative analysis of delay, area, power, ADP, and PDP using bar graphs.

Conclusion

The FD-type 2-D FIR filter with minimal memory complexity is considered for Full-Custom VLSI implementation with a length of 9. To optimize

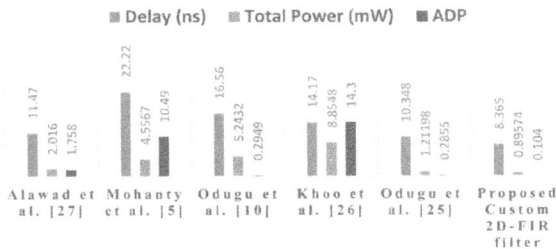

Figure 79.8 Delay, power, and ADP of the proposed work with existing works
Source: Author

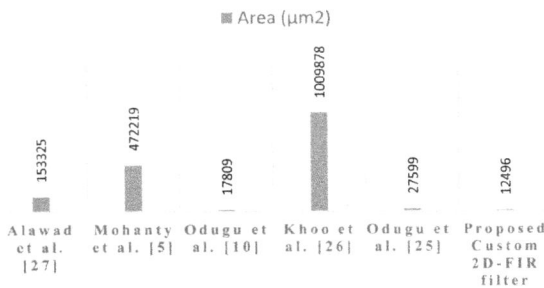

Figure 79.9 Comparison of the area between the proposed two-dimensional FIR filter and existing filter structures
Source: Author

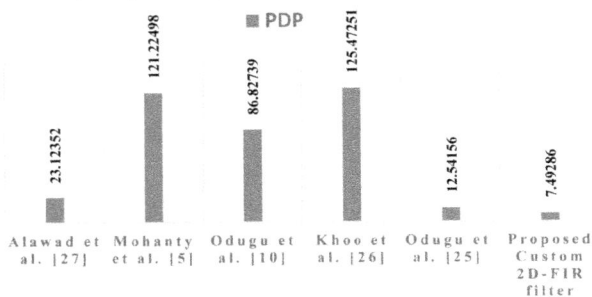

Figure 79.10 PDP For the suggested filter architectures with existing architectures
Source: Author

this 2-D FIR filter architecture, Registers, Shift Register Blocks (SRB), multipliers, and adders are transistor-level hardware blocks. To minimize power, area, and latency, an Approximate Tree Multiplier (ATM) is proposed using Approximate 4:2 Compressors (A42C). The design and simulation of the two-dimensional FIR filter architecture are carried out using Cadence Virtuoso tools within a 45nm CMOS technology library.

References

[1] Mersereau, R., Mecklenbrauker, W., and Quatieri, T. (1976). McClellan transformations for two-dimensional digital filtering-part I: design. *IEEE Transactions on Circuits and Systems*, 23(7), 405–414.

[2] Khaleqi Qaleh Jooq, M., Ahmadinejad, M., and Moaiyeri, M. H. (2021). Ultraefficient imprecise multipliers based on innovative 4: 2 approximate compressors. *International Journal of Circuit Theory and Applications*, 49(1), 169–184.

[3] Priyadharshni, M., and Kumaravel, S. (2020). Low power and area efficient error tolerant adder for image processing application. *International Journal of Circuit Theory and Applications*, 48(5), 696–708.

[4] Cilardo, A., De Caro, D., Petra, N., Caserta, F., Mazzocca, N., Napoli, E., et al. (2014). High-speed speculative multipliers based on speculative carry-save tree. *IEEE Transactions on Circuits and Systems I: Regular Papers*, 61(12), 3426–3435.

[5] Mohanty, B. K., Meher, P. K., and Amira, A. (2014). Memory footprint reduction for power-efficient realization of 2-D finite impulse response filters. *IEEE Transactions on Circuits and Systems I: Regular Papers*, 61(1), 120–133.

[6] Mohanty, B. K., and Meher, P. K. (2020). An efficient parallel DA-based fixed-width design for approximate inner-product computation. *IEEE Transactions on Very Large-Scale Integration (VLSI) Systems*, 28(5), 1221–1229.

[7] Mohanty, B. K., and Meher, P. K. (2008). New scan method and pipeline architecture for VLSI implementation of separable 2-D FIR filters without using transposition. In Proceedings IEEE Region 10 TENCON2008 Conference, Hyderabad, India, 2008.

[8] Mohanty, B. K., Meher, P. K., Singhal, S. K., and Swamy, M. N. S. (2016). A high-performance VLSI architecture for reconfigurable FIR using distributed arithmetic. *Integration*, 54, 37–46.

[9] Chen, P. Y., Van, L. D., Khoo, I. H., Reddy, H. C., and Lin, C. T. (2010). Power-efficient and cost-effective 2-D symmetry filter architectures. *IEEE Transactions on Circuits and Systems I: Regular Papers*, 58(1), 112–125.

[10] Odugu, V. K., Venkata Narasimhulu, C., and Satya Prasad, K. (2020). esign and implementation of low complexity circularly symmetric 2D FIR filter architectures. *Multidimensional Systems and Signal Processing*, 31(4), 1385–1410.

[11] Van, L.-D. (2002). A new 2-D systolic digital filter architecture without global broadcast. *IEEE Transactions on Very Large Scale Integration (VLSI) Systems*, 10(4), 477–486.

[12] Van, L. D., Khoo, I. H., Chen, P. Y., and Reddy, H. H. C. (2019). Symmetry incorporated cost-effective architectures for two-dimensional digital filters. *IEEE Circuits and Systems Magazine*, 19(1), 33–54.

[13] Odugu, V. K., Narasimhulu, C. V., and Prasad, K. S. (2021). Implementation of low power generic 2D FIR filter bank architecture using memory-based Multipliers. *Journal of Mobile Multimedia*, 18(3), 583–602.

[14] Odugu, V. K., Narasimhulu, C. V., and Prasad, K. S. (2022). A novel filter-bank architecture of 2D-FIR symmetry filters using LUT based multipliers. *Integration, the VLSI Journal*, 84, 12–25.

[15] Edavoor, P. J., Raveendran, S., and Rahulkar, A. D. (2020). Approximate multiplier design using novel dual-stage 4: 2 compressors. *IEEE Access*, 8, 48337–48337.

[16] Odugu, V. K., Narasimhulu, C. V., and Prasad, K. S. (2021). An efficient VLSI architecture of 2D FIR filter using enhanced approximate compressor circuits. *International Journal of Circuit Theory and Applications*, 49(11), 3653–3668.

[17] Khoo, I. H., Reddy, H. C., Van, L. D., and Lin, C. T. (2010). Generalized formulation of 2-D filter structures without global broadcast for VLSI implementation. In Proceedings, IEEE MWSCAS, Seattle, WA, USA, (pp. 426–529).

[18] Alawad, M., and Lin, M. (2021). Memory-efficient probabilistic 2-d finite impulse response (FIR) filter. *IEEE Transactions on Multi-Scale Computing Systems*, 4(1), 69–82. 2017.3668.

For Product Safety Concerns and Information please contact our EU
representative GPSR@taylorandfrancis.com
Taylor & Francis Verlag GmbH, Kaufingerstraße 24, 80331 München, Germany

www.ingramcontent.com/pod-product-compliance
Lightning Source LLC
Chambersburg PA
CBHW081211220326
41598CB00037B/6744